wwnorton.com/nawr

The StudySpace site that accompanies *The Norton Anthology of World Religions* is FREE, but you will need the code below to register for a password that will allow you to access the copyrighted materials on the site.

WRLD–RLGN

Contents

Maps and Illustrations

Preface

Welcome to *The Norton Anthology of World Religions.* The work offered to you here is large and complex, but it responds to a simple desire—namely, the desire that six major, living, international world religions should be allowed to speak to you in their own words rather than only through the words of others about them. Virtually all of the religious texts assembled here are primary texts. Practitioners of Hinduism, Buddhism, Daoism, Judaism, Christianity, and Islam have written and preserved these texts over the centuries for their own use and their own purposes. What is it like to read them, gathered as they are here like works of religious art in a secular museum?

For practitioners of any of these six religions, who number in the hundreds of millions, this anthology is likely to provide some of the surprise and fascination of a very large family album: some of one's religious ancestors trigger an immediate flash of recognition, while others look very distant and perhaps even comical. For an army of outsiders—those whose religion is not anthologized here, those who practice no religion, those who are "spiritual but not religious," and those who count themselves critics or antagonists of religion—the experience will be rewarding in different ways. No propaganda intrudes here on behalf either of any given religion or of religion in general. The goal at every point is not conversion, but exploration. The only assumptions made are that the most populous and influential of the world's religions are here to stay, that they reward study best when speaking to you in their own words, and that their contemporary words make best sense when heard against the panoramic background of the words they have remembered and preserved from their storied pasts.

Many of the texts gathered here have been translated from foreign languages, for the religions of the world have spoken many different languages over the course of their long histories. A few of the works—the *Bhagavad Gita,* the *Daode jing,* the Bible, the Qur'an—are readily available. Many more are available only in the libraries of a few major research universities or, though physically available, have not been intellectually available without detailed guidance that was impossible for the lay reader to come by. Bibliographic information is always provided for previously published translations, and a number of translations have been made especially for this anthology. A central concern throughout has been that the anthologized texts should be not just translated but also framed by enough editorial explanation to make them audible and intelligible across the barriers of time and space even if you are coming to them for the first time. When those explanations require the use of words in a foreign language with a non-Roman writing system, standard academic modes of transliteration have sometimes been simplified to enhance user-friendliness.

Globalization, including international migration in all its forms, has brought about a large-scale and largely involuntary mingling of once-separate religious communities, and this historic change has created an urgent occasion for a deeply grounded effort at interreligious understanding. Yes, most of the world's Hindus still live in India, yet the Hindu Diaspora is enormous and influential. Yes, many Jews have migrated to Israel, but half of the world's Jews still live in deeply rooted Diaspora communities around the world. Conventionally, Islam is thought of as a Middle Eastern religion, yet the largest Muslim populations are in South and Southeast Asia, while the Muslim minority in Europe is growing rapidly. By the same token, Christianity is not thought of as an African religion, yet the Christian population of sub-Saharan Africa is growing even more rapidly than the Muslim population of Europe. In a bygone era, the six religions treated here might have been divided geographically into an "Eastern" and a "Western" trio, but we do not so divide them, for in our era they are all everywhere, and none is a majority. Religiously, we live and in all likelihood will continue to live in a world of large and mingling minorities.

This involuntary mingling has created a state of affairs that can be violently disruptive. Terrorism in the name of religion, more often within national borders than across them, has turned many minds against religion in all forms. And yet, paradoxically, religious violence during the twenty-first century has persuaded many that, contrary to innumerable past predictions, religion is by no means fading from modern life. And though the threat of religious violence is a dark challenge of one sort, the bright new opportunities for cross-cultural and interreligious learning present an unprecedented challenge of a different and, in the end, a more consequential sort. On the one hand, whatever some of us might have wished, religious violence has made religion a subject that cannot be avoided. On the other, for those who engage the subject in depth, the study of religion across cultural and political borders builds a uniquely deep and subtle form of cosmopolitan sophistication.

In all its formal features—the format of its tables of contents; its use of maps and illustrations; its handling of headnotes, footnotes, glossaries, and bibliographies; its forty-eight pages of color illustration in six inserts—*The Norton Anthology of World Religions* announces its membership in the venerable family of Norton anthologies. As was true of *The Norton Anthology of English Literature* upon its first publication more than half a century ago, this anthology is both larger and more rigorously realized than any prior anthology published in English for use by the general reader or the college undergraduate. It opens with a generous introduction addressing a set of basic questions not linked to any single tradition but affecting all of them. Each of the six religious traditions is then presented chronologically from its origins to the present (the Buddhism volume also uses a geographical organizing principle). Each presentation begins with a substantial overview of the tradition being anthologized. Each is also punctuated by period introductions tracing the history of the tradition in question. And yet this work is not a history merely enlivened by the inclusion of original texts. No, history here is simply the stage. The texts themselves are the performance, displaying as only they can the perennial and subversive power of religious literature. The difference might be compared to the difference between English history with a bit of Shakespeare and Shakespeare with a bit of English history. The histories come and go, but Shakespeare is irreplaceable. Shakespeare is, to use a term that originated in the church, *canonical.*

Derived from the Greek word for a ruler or measuring rod, *canon* came to mean a rule or criterion of any kind. By extension, the same word came to mean the church rule or "canon" law governing the contents of the Bible: which books were to be included and which excluded. And by yet a further extension, canon came to refer to the understood list of acknowledged masterpieces in English or some other literature. So, the Bible has a canon. English literature has a canon (however endlessly contested). But what works of religious literature constitute the world religious canon?

Aye, dear reader, there was the rub as plans were laid for this anthology. In 2006, when the editorial team began work in earnest, no canons existed for the literatures of the world's major religions. There were limited canons within that vast expanse of written material, the Bible itself being the paradigmatic example. But the literature of Christianity is larger than the Bible, and the situation grows only more complicated as one ranges farther afield into traditions whose concentric canons are more implicit than explicit. Even though more than one canon of the Bible exists, Bible scholars can easily handle that limited variety and still quite literally *know what they are talking about*: they can deal with a clearly delimited body of material within which evidence-based historical interpretation can go forward. But what canon of religious texts exists to help define the entire field of religious studies for religion scholars? The field has never had an agreed-upon answer to that question, and some of the most sweeping theoretical statements about religion turn out, as a result, to rest on an astonishingly small and vague empirical base.

Granted that no master canon in the original religious sense of that term can ever be devised for the religions of the world, the lack of a limited but large and serious study collection of texts is one major indication that the study of religion remains at an early stage of its development as a discipline. For the religions of Asia, especially, it has been as if the Elizabethan theater were being studied without ready access by students to the plays of Shakespeare or with, at most, access to *Hamlet* alone. This lack has been particularly glaring in the United States for reasons that deserve a brief review. Until the early 1960s, the study of religion was largely confined to private colleges and universities, where, thanks to the country's Protestant intellectual heritage, it consisted overwhelmingly of biblical studies and Christian theology. Often, the department of religion was a department of philosophy and religion. Often, too, there was a close relationship between such departments and the college chaplaincy. In public colleges and universities, meanwhile, the situation was quite different. There, the traditional constitutional separation of church and state was understood to preclude the formal study of religion, perhaps especially of the very religions that the student body and the faculty might turn out to be practicing.

But then several events, occurring at nearly the same moment in both the public and the private spheres, created a new climate for the study of religion, and "religious studies" emerged as a new academic discipline distinct from philosophy or theology, on the one hand, and even more distinct from the chaplaincy, on the other. We are still reckoning with the consequences of this shift.

In 1963, Associate Justice Arthur Goldberg wrote for the Supreme Court of the United States in a concurring opinion in *Abington v. Schempp* (374 U.S. 203, 306): "It seems clear to me . . . that the Court would recognize the propriety of . . . the teaching *about* religion, as distinguished from the teaching *of* religion, in the public schools," language that seemed to clear a path for the study of religion in tax-supported schools. Significantly, Goldberg was a Jew; just three years earlier, Americans had elected John F. Kennedy as their first Roman Catholic president. American religious pluralism was becoming increasingly inescapable at the highest levels in American public life; and as it came to be understood that university-level religious studies was to be the study of various religions at once, including but by no means confined to the religions of the United States, the Founding Fathers' fear of an imposed, national religion began to recede from the national consciousness. American pluralism was now as powerful a factor in American religious life as the Constitution itself.

This anthology is published on the fiftieth anniversary of an event little noticed in the cultural ferment of the 1960s but of great importance for the study of religion—namely, the 1964 reincorporation of the National Association of Biblical Instructors (NABI), the principal association of college professors teaching these subjects, as the American Academy of Religion (AAR), whose current mission statement focuses pointedly on "the understanding of religious traditions, issues, questions, and values"—all in the plural. The formal incorporation of the AAR was intended first as a quiet but magnanimous gesture of invitation by a Protestant academic establishment toward the scholars of America's Catholic and Jewish communities, but this was just the beginning. Others would soon be drawn into a conversation whose animating academic conviction is well captured in a dictum of the great nineteenth-century scholar Max Müller: "He who knows one religion knows none."

Catholics and Jews had had their own seminaries and their own institutions of higher learning, but scholarship produced in them tended to remain in them—partly, to be sure, because of Protestant indifference but also because of defensive or reactively triumphalist habits of mind among the residually embattled minorities themselves. But this was already changing. Optimism and openness in the Roman Catholic community had been much assisted in the earlier 1960s by the Second Vatican Council, whose byword was the Italian *aggiornamento*—roughly, "updating"—as employed by the benignly bold Pope John XXIII. American Jews, meanwhile, profoundly traumatized as they had been during and after World War II by the Shoah, or Holocaust, Nazi Germany's attempted genocide, breathed a collective (if premature) sigh of relief in 1967 after Israel's stunning victory over its Arab opponents in the Six-Day War. During the same period, the Reverend Dr. Martin Luther King, Jr., had spearheaded a revolution in American race relations, as segregation ended and the social integration began that would lead to the election of a black president, Barack Obama, in 2008. In short, the mood in the early 1960s was in every way one of barred doors swung open, locked windows flung up, and common cause undertaken in moral enterprises like the interfaith campaign to end the war in Vietnam.

One influential scholar saw the shift occurring in the study of religion as cause for academic jubilation. Writing in 1971 in the *Journal of the American Academy of Religion* (which had been, until 1966, *The Journal of Bible and*

Religion), Wilfred Cantwell Smith clearly welcomed the change that was taking place:

> Perhaps what is happening can be summed up most pithily by saying that the transition has been from the teaching of religion to the study of religion. Where men used to instruct, they now inquire. They once attempted to impart what they themselves knew, and what they hoped (of late, with decreasing expectation) to make interesting; now, on the contrary, they inquire, into something that both for them and for their students is incontrovertibly interesting, but is something that they do not quite understand.

And yet there was a shadow across this scene. The newborn American Academy of Religion had bitten off rather more than it could chew. The spread of religious studies to the state university campuses that were proliferating in the late 1960s and the 1970s was vigorously pluralist. Jewish studies experienced an enormous growth spurt, and so did Hindu studies, Buddhist studies, Islamic studies, and so forth. Smith, a scholar of comparative religion who had made his first mark as a specialist in Islam, could only welcome this in principle. But others, writing later, would be troubled by growth that seemed to have spun out of control.

Recall that in 1971, *globalization* was not the byword that it has since become. The Hindu Diaspora in the United States was still tiny. Christian Pentecostalism, though well established, had not yet achieved critical mass in Africa. Europe's Muslim minority, if already substantial, was relatively dormant. Mainland China's population was still in Maoist lockdown. And in the United States, Americans had not yet begun to grasp the coming effects of the passage of the Immigration and Nationality Act of 1965, which removed quotas that had been in place since the 1920s; the resulting explosive growth in Hispanic and Asian immigration would by 1990 make non-Hispanic Caucasians a minority in Los Angeles, America's second-largest city. Americans still saw themselves as a colonized people who had achieved independence, rather than as a colonizing people. The rhetoric of European postcolonialism had not yet been applied to the United States, a superpower whose world hegemony was quasi-imperial in its reach and neocolonialist in its effects. Worldwide, the transformative interrogation of religious traditions by women and about women had barely begun.

While all of these changes, as they have brought about the multiplication and intensification of religious encounters, have made the study of world religions more important than ever, they have not made it easier. They have not, in particular, lent it any internal intellectual coherence. They have not created for it a new study canon to replace the narrowly Protestant study canon, as the founding of the AAR seemed in principle to require. The creation of religious studies as a field had been an academic gamble on a barely perceived religious future. Had the bet paid off? An eminent senior scholar, Jonathan Z. Smith, wrote in 1995 of the change that had taken place: "The field made a decision to give up a (limited) coherence for a (limitless) incoherence."

That limitless incoherence was the context in which we took up the challenge to produce *The Norton Anthology of World Religions*. How ever were we to begin?

There came first the recognition that we would be creating for the field of religious studies a first draft of the very canon that it lacked—a canon covering nearly four thousand years of history in a score of different languages, aspiring not to be authoritative regarding belief or practice but to be plausibly foundational for the study of the subject.

There came second the recognition that though canons, once achieved, are anonymous, they do not begin anonymously. They begin with somebody who declares this in and that out and defends his or her choice. This realization shifted the decision to be made from *What?* to *Who?*

There came third the question of whether the answer to the question *Who?* would come in the singular or in the plural and if in the plural, how multitudinously plural. For each of the traditions to be anthologized, would a large board of specialist advisers be assembled to determine what would be included? Would the selections be formally approved by some kind of plebiscite, as in the verse-by-verse ratification by translators of the language included in the King James Version of the Bible? Would the work of annotating the resulting selections be divided among committees and subcommittees and so forth? Would some governing board formulate a set of topics that each editor or team of editors would be required to address so as to confer a sturdy structure upon the whole? Would there be, for example, a different board of consultants for each period in the long history of Judaism or each language across the geographic breadth of Buddhism?

Our decision was to reject that kind of elaboration and gamble instead on six brilliant and creative individuals, each with a distinct literary style and a record of bold publication, and then to impose no common matrix of obligatory topics or categories on them, nor even a common set of chronological divisions. (Does China have its own Middle Ages? When does modernity begin in Turkey?) It was understood, however, playing to an institutional strength at W. W. Norton & Company, that the prose of these editors, formidable though they were, would be edited very heavily for explanatory clarity even as we second-guessed very lightly indeed their actual anthological choices. To what end this blend of laxity and severity? Our aim has been simply to enhance the intelligent delight of students in religious literature both as literature and as religion. "Intelligent" delight does not mean the delight of intelligent people. The reference is rather to the delight that a strange and baffling ancient text can provide when a great scholar, speaking in his or her own voice, renders it intelligible for you and you recognize, behind it, a human intelligence finally not all that unlike your own.

If that has been our aim for students, our aim for professors has been rather different. Professors of religious studies often find themselves called upon to teach insanely far beyond their area of trained academic competence. For them, we hope to have provided both an invaluable reference tool and a rich reservoir of curricular possibilities. For their graduate students, we hope to have provided breadth to complement the depth of doctoral study at its best. A student studying in depth and probably in the original language some particular religious text can discover here what *else* was being written in the same tradition at the same time. What preceded that text in the life of the religious tradition? What followed it? Who celebrated it? Who attacked it? The fine art of page flipping, crucial to the unique operating system of an ink-on-paper anthology, enables just this kind of exploratory learning. Over time, by repeated forays backward and forward in the evolution of a religious tradition, a serious student can come to know its literature like the interior of a large residence. But this is just the beginning. Comparable forays into the development of other traditions can by degrees situate the target religious tradition in the global religious context. Finally, to further aid all users, the companion website to *The Norton Anthology of World Religions* will provide, over time, both supplementary substantive content—other religious traditions, to begin with—not included in the print anthology and an array of aids for the use of teachers and students.

Beyond these conventional services, however, lies something riskier. We acknowledge that we have provided the professoriate a target to shoot at: "How could you *possibly* omit X?" some will exclaim. And others: "Why on *earth* did you ever bother with Y?" We welcome all such objections. They betray nothing more than the real, existential condition of a field still in many ways struggling to be born. Disciplines do not spring into existence overnight. They are negotiated into existence over time through trial and error. The more vigorously our colleagues find fault with this first draft of a canon for their field, the more productive will be the ensuing negotiation.

Intuition based on deep scholarship and teaching experience has surely played a role in the choices made by the six associate editors responsible, respectively, for anthologizing the six religious literatures covered: Wendy Doniger (Hinduism), Donald S. Lopez, Jr. (Buddhism), James Robson (Daoism), David Biale (Judaism), Lawrence S. Cunningham (Christianity), and Jane Dammen McAuliffe (Islam). They have all sought to include those incipiently canonical texts that few of their colleagues would dare exclude. More intuitively, they have sought to include neglected works of beauty and power whose very appearance here might help them become canonical. The editors have even included occasional attacks on the religious traditions anthologized—for example, excerpts from Kancha Ilaiah, "Why I Am Not a Hindu," in the Hinduism anthology and from Bertrand Russell, "Why I Am Not a Christian," in the Christianity anthology. As these two contrarian entries nicely demonstrate, the canon of texts regarded as permanent and irreplaceable in a religious tradition does not coincide exactly with the canon of texts arguably crucial for the study of the tradition. Coping with all these complications, the editors have coped in every case as well with the painful space limitations that we have had to impose on them even after allowing the anthology to grow to nearly twice its originally envisioned size.

One large question remains to be addressed in this brief preface: *By what criteria did you choose to anthologize these and only these six religions?* This question has a theoretical as well as a practical dimension. How, to begin with, do we distinguish that which is religious from that which is not? Is atheism a religion, or at least a "religious option"? Whatever atheism is, it is certainly no modern novelty. *The Cambridge Companion to Atheism* (2007) begins with a substantial chapter, "Atheism in Antiquity," by the distinguished Dutch classicist Jan Bremmer. Whether atheism in a given ancient or modern form should be considered a strictly religious option may depend on how a given atheist "plays" it. The novelist Alain de Botton, nothing if not playful, dreams or artfully feigns dreaming of a floridly religious enactment of atheism in his *Religion for Atheists: A Non-believer's Guide to the Uses of Religion* (2012). Meanwhile, a 2010 survey by the Pew Forum suggests that the religiously unaffiliated might actually be both more interested in and better informed about religion than the affiliated. But back to the question at hand: If we cannot clearly distinguish religion from irreligion or the "strictly" from the "casually" religious, how can we be sure that we are choosing six versions of the same thing? Arcane and obscure as this question may sound, it did bear rather directly on one of our six key choices, as will be explained below.

In the end, in making our choices, we fell back to an infra-theoretical, practical, or "working" criterion for inclusion: we required that the religions anthologized should be the six most important *major, living, international* religions, a rubric in which each of the three italicized words counted.

Because we anthologize only *living* religions, we do not anthologize the religions of ancient Mesopotamia, Greece, and Rome, despite the fact that these religious traditions loom large in the history of the study of religion in the West, thanks to the dominance of the Bible and of the Greco-Roman classics in Western higher education.

Because we anthologize only *international* religions, we do not anthologize folkloric or indigenous religions, which are typically and symbiotically confined to a single locale, despite the fascination that these religions have had for the sociological or anthropological study of religion, from Johann Gottfried Herder and Émile Durkheim in the late eighteenth and nineteenth century to Clifford Geertz in the twentieth.

Geography, except as the difference between national and international, is not the principle of organization in this anthology. One consequence, however, of our anthologizing only literary religions and then applying a mostly demographic criterion in choosing among them has been the omission of indigenous African religion. While it is true that Yoruba religion is now international and that some texts for it are now available, no such text has become canonical even for practitioners themselves. Rather than saying anything about the limitations of African or other indigenous religious traditions, notably the rich array of Amerindian religions, our decision says something about the inherent limitations of any text-based approach to the study of religion. Texts can indeed teach much, but they cannot teach everything about everybody.

As for the key criterion *major*, we apply it demographically with one glaring exception. Religious demography tends to overstate or understate the size of a religion depending on whether and how that religion counts heads. Roman Catholicism, which counts every baptized baby as a member, probably ends up with somewhat overstated numbers. Daoism, by contrast, probably ends up with its adherents undercounted because formal affiliation is not a recognized criterion for basic participation in it.

Yet even after these difficulties have been acknowledged, there can be no quarrel that Christianity and Islam are demographically major as well as living and international. The same goes at almost equal strength for Hinduism and Buddhism. The obvious exception is Judaism, whose numbers worldwide, though far from trivial, are small even when the question "Who is a Jew?" is given its most broadly inclusive answer. Too small to be reckoned major by a head count, Judaism is too important on other counts to be reckoned less than major. It is the exception that breaks the rule. Its categories, its legends, and many of its practices have been decisive not only for Christianity and Islam but also, arguably, for Western secularism.

As many readers will have noticed by now, this grid of six does not stray very far from the textbook areas of religious studies, as is only right and proper in a reference work, yet this claim of relative "normality" calls for qualification in two final regards if only to provide the occasion for a pair of disclaimers.

First, this anthology does not deal with several religious traditions that, though fully literary and indeed of great intrinsic interest, do not meet its stated criteria. Three that might be named among these are Sikhism, Jainism, and Shinto, but several other traditions commonly enough included in textbooks might easily be added to the list. No judgment of intrinsic worth or importance should be inferred from their exclusion, just as none should be inferred from the omission of indigenous African or Amerindian religion. A less ample presentation of a larger number of religious traditions would always have been possible. Our choice, and all such choices come at a cost, has been to produce ampler presentations of plausibly canonical texts for those most populous religions traditions that the world citizen is likeliest to encounter in the new religious environment that we all inhabit.

To name a second perhaps surprising choice, our grid of six, though generally familiar, has "Daoism" where most textbooks have "Chinese religion." The usual textbook grid resorts to geography or ethnicity as a naming criterion in and only in the Chinese case. Why so? Though, as noted, the designations "Eastern" and "Western" do still have some textbook currency, no one speaks of Christianity as "European religion" or of Islam as "Afro-Asiatic religion." Why proceed otherwise in the Chinese case alone?

Our decision, breaking with this practice, has been, in the first place, to anthologize Chinese Buddhism within the Buddhism anthology, allowing that sub-anthology to become, by the inclusion of its Chinese material, the longest of the six. Our decision, in the second place, has been not to anthologize Chinese Confucianism at all. We have a secondary and a primary reason for this second decision.

The secondary reason not to anthologize Confucianism is that the People's Republic of China does not regard it as a religion at all. The government recognizes only five religions: Buddhism, Daoism, and Islam plus (as separate religions) Catholicism and Protestantism. Confucianism it simply defines as altogether out of the category *religion*.

Properly so? Is Confucianism a religion, or not? This question is notoriously one that "the West has never been able to answer and China never able to ask," and we do not presume to give a definitive answer here. It is true, on the one hand, that at many points during its long history, Confucianism has seemed to be neither a religion nor quite a philosophy either but rather a code of wisdom and conduct for the Chinese gentleman scholar—or, perhaps better, the aspiring Chinese statesman. Yet at other points in Confucian history, it must be noted, Confucius has been accorded the honor of a virtual god. We choose to leave that question in abeyance.

Our primary reason, in any case, to set Confucianism aside and dedicate our limited space to Daoism is that while the Confucian canon has been widely translated and, as ancient religious texts go, is relatively accessible, the Daoist canon has only recently been rescued from near death and has never before been presented for the use of nonspecialists in an overview of any historical completeness.

While two pre-Daoist classics—the gnomic *Daode jing* of Laozi and the tart wisdom of Zhuangzi—have been endlessly translated and are in no danger of disappearance, their relationship to the Daoist canon as a whole is, to borrow from an observation quoted in James Robson's introduction to the Daoism anthology, like the real but distant relationship of Plato and Aristotle to the Christian canon. What would we know of Christianity if Paul, Augustine,

Dante, Luther, Milton, and so on down the hallowed list had all been lost and only Plato and Aristotle survived?

Such a fate did indeed very nearly befall Daoism. In the nineteenth century, leading up to the establishment of the first Republic of China in 1912, Qing dynasty authorities systematically confiscated Daoist temples and turned them into schools and factories. Having begun as an underground movement in the second century, Daoism—long out of official favor—was largely forced underground only again and more deeply so after the establishment of the Republic, which condemned it as superstition.

For the Daoist canon, the cost of this persecution was nearly outright extinction. By the early twentieth century, few copies of Daoism's canon of eleven hundred religious texts survived in all of China. But then, remarkably, circumstances eased enough to permit the reprint in 1926 of a rare surviving copy of the full 1445 Ming dynasty canon. This had been the last great effort at canon formation in Daoist history before Daoism's long decline commenced. As this reprint reached the West, scholarship on the history of Daoism and the interpretation of its texts slowly began. Nonetheless, particularly after the establishment of the Communist People's Republic of China in 1949, with its aggressive early persecution of all religions, many in the West believed that the actual practice of Daoism had finally died out in its birthplace.

They were mistaken. Over the past few decades, reliable reports have made it clear that Daoism is still alive and indeed is growing steadily stronger, having survived as if by taking Mao Zedong's advice to his guerrillas that they "move among the people as a fish swims in the sea." Just as the fish in the sea are not easily counted, so the Daoists of China escape the usual forms of Western quantification and Communist surveillance alike. But the Daoist fish are numerous, even if they have reason to swim deep.

Meanwhile, the work of translating and contextualizing the recovered texts has attracted a growing corps of Western scholars—initially in France and more recently in other Western countries, including the United States. As their work has gone forward, the world has begun to hear of Daoist messiahs and utopian dreams of peace; Daoist confession rituals and community liturgies; Daoist alchemy and proto-scientific experimentation; Daoist medicine, bodily cultivation (as distinct from asceticism), and sexual practices; Daoist prayer, including Daoist letter-writing to the gods; and Daoist pageantry, costume, magic, and music. In short, a lost religious world—the central, popular, indigenous, full-throated religious world of China—has been brought back to textual life. Our decision was to bring our readers a major sampling from this remarkable recovery.

The major religions of the world are probably better grasped, many scholars now insist, as a set of alternative customs and practices in loose organization—worship liturgies, pilgrimages, dietary restrictions, birth and burial practices, art, music, drama, dance, and so forth—than as a set of contending ideologies. Millions of men and women, even when they practice religions that we rightly regard as literary, are themselves illiterate. Yet when writing remade the world, it did remake religion as well. The major religious traditions of the world would not be major today had they not become literary traditions as well.

Because it is *written*, religious literature can be and has been shared, preserved through wars and persecutions, transmitted over time and space, and, most important of all, *taught* with ease and delight. When all else perishes, the written word often survives. The work before you is a self-contained, portable library of religious literature. You may read it on a plane, in the park, or in a waiting room and trust that every foreign or otherwise strange term will be explained on or near the page where it occurs. No foreign alphabets are used. Transliterations have been simplified to serve pedagogical utility rather than philological perfection. Diacritical marks have been kept to the absolute minimum. Though, as noted, a few of the large theoretical considerations that religion raises as a subject for human inquiry will be addressed in the general introduction, the emphasis in this work is overwhelmingly pragmatic rather than theoretical. For in this domain, more perhaps than in any other, outsiders have historically been as important as insiders, and beginners as welcome as veterans. So, to conclude where we began, whether you are an outsider or an insider, a beginner or a veteran, we welcome you to the pages of *The Norton Anthology of World Religions.*

JACK MILES
IRVINE, CALIFORNIA

Acknowledgments

The Norton Anthology of World Religions would not have been possible without the help of many generous and able friends. We are grateful for the help of those named below as well as of others too numerous to list.

From W. W. Norton & Company, we wish to thank Roby Harrington, head of the college division, who conceived this volume; Pete Simon, its first editor, who contributed its title; Carly Fraser Doria, who has managed the assembly of illustrations and ancillary materials with intelligence and taste; developmental editors Alice Falk, Carol Flechner, and Kurt Wildermuth, who have tamed its prose to the demanding Norton standard; Adrian Kitzinger, who created the beautiful maps; Megan Jackson and Nancy Rodwan, permissions experts; art directors Debra Morton Hoyt and Ingsu Liu, designer Chin-Yee Lai, and artist Rosamond Purcell; production managers Sean Mintus and Julia Druskin; managing editor Marian Johnson, whose project-editorial wisdom is quietly evident on every page; and, most of all, Julia Reidhead, editorial director, whose taste and managerial finesse have preserved and advanced this work sagaciously for fully seven years.

Wendy Doniger wishes to thank Velcheru Narayana Rao for finding "Sita Lost in Thought" for her, and for finding and translating "Kausalya in Fury"; Vasudha Naranayan and Richard Fox for the Southeast Asian materials; Eleanor Zelliot, Gail Omvedt, and Dilip Chitre for the Dalit materials; her student assistants, Jeremy Morse and Charles Preston, for assembling all the texts; and Anne Mocko for help with the pronouncing glossaries.

James Robson wishes to thank Stephen R. Bokenkamp, for helping to get this project started; Alice Falk, for helping to get it completed; and Billy Brewster, for help with the pronouncing glossaries.

David Biale wishes to thank Ariel Evan Mayse and Sarah Shectman for research assistance beyond the call of duty.

Lawrence S. Cunningham wishes to thank his beloved wife, Cecilia, and their two daughters, Sarah and Julia.

Jane Dammen McAuliffe wishes to thank her splendid research associates, Carolyn Baugh, Sayeed Rahman, Robert Tappan, and Clare Wilde, and to recognize with appreciation both Georgetown University and Bryn Mawr College for their support of this work.

For generous financial support of this project, Jack Miles wishes to thank the John T. and Catherine D. MacArthur Foundation, the Getty Research Institute, and the University of California, Irvine. He thanks, in addition, for early editorial consultation, his publishing colleague John Loudon; for generous technical assistance, Steve Franklin and Stan Woo-Sam of UCI's information technology office; for invaluable assistance with the initial enormous delivery of texts, his former student Matthew Shedd; for helpful counsel on Asian Christianity, his colleague Tae Sung; for brilliant assistance in editorial rescue and rewrite, his irreverent friend and colleague Peter Heinegg; and for her sustaining and indomitable spirit, his irreplaceable Catherine Montgomery Crary.

This work is dedicated—in gratitude for all that they have preserved for our instruction—to the scribes of the world's great religions.

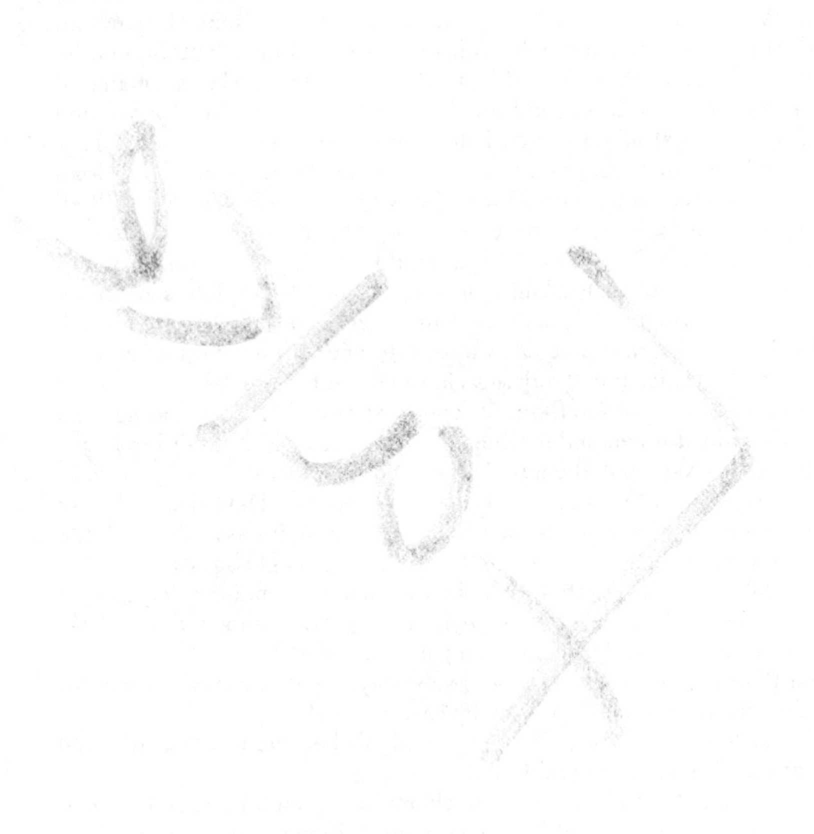

THE NORTON ANTHOLOGY OF

WORLD RELIGIONS

HINDUISM

The relation of the various peoples of the earth to the supreme interests of life, to God, virtue, and immortality, may be investigated up to a certain point, but can never be compared to one another with absolute strictness and certainty. The more plainly in these matters our evidence seems to speak, the more carefully must we refrain from unqualified assumptions and rash generalizations.

—Jacob Burckhardt,
*The Civilization of
the Renaissance in Italy* (1860)

GENERAL INTRODUCTION

How the West Learned to Compare Religions

BY JACK MILES

How to Read This Book: A Poetic Prelude

The Norton Anthology of World Religions is designed to be read in either of two ways. You may read it from start to finish, or you may pick and choose from the table of contents as in a museum you might choose to view one gallery rather than another or one painting rather than another.

Imagine yourself at the entrance to a large museum containing a great many strange works of religious art. If you enter, what will you do? Will you devote equal time or equal intensity of attention to every work in the huge museum? Or will you skip some works, linger over others, and shape as you go a kind of museum within the museum? In the latter case, what will be your criteria? Those, too, you may well shape as you go. You may not entirely know even your own mind as you begin. You may not know exactly what you're after. You may be detached, and yet—disinterested? No, you are not exactly disinterested. You're looking around, waiting for something to reach you, some click, some insemination, a start. Entering is sometimes enough. You do not need a briefing by the curator to begin your visit.

So it is with this anthology. Take the works assembled here as lightly as you wish. You will still be taking them properly: you will be taking them for what they are. A new path begins to open into the consideration of religion when it is regarded as unserious, un-adult—but only in the way that art, poetry, and fiction in all its forms (including the theatrical and the cinematic) are so regarded. They all deal with made-up stuff. And yet will we ever be so adult as to outgrow them?

The Western cast of mind has undeniably had an intrusive and distorting effect in many parts of the world as Western culture has become a world culture, and yet that cast of mind has also had a liberating and fertilizing effect. It has opened a space in which the once incomparable has become comparable. Looking at the religions of others even from the outside but with a measure of openness, empathy, and good will can enable those of any religious tradition or none to see themselves from the outside as well, and that capacity is the very foundation of human sympathy and cultural wisdom.

In church one morning in the eighteenth century, the poet Robert Burns spotted a louse on a proper lady's bonnet and started thinking: If only she could see herself as he saw her! He went home and wrote his wonderfully earthy and witty "To a Louse, On Seeing One on a Lady's Bonnet, at Church 1786." The fun of the poem is that it is addressed to the louse in a mock "How dare you!" tone almost all the way to the end. At that point, however, it becomes suddenly reflective, even wistful, and Burns concludes, in his Scots English:

> O wad some Pow'r the giftie gie us
> To see oursels as ithers see us!
> It wad frae monie a blunder free us,
> An' foolish notion:
> What airs in dress an' gait wad lea'e us,
> An' ev'n Devotion!

Burns dreams, or half-prays, that some power would "the giftie gie us" (give us the gift) to see "oursels" (ourselves) as others see us—to see, as it were, the lice on our bonnets. Our fine and flouncing airs then "wad lea'e us" (would leave us). But it might not be simply vanity that would depart. The last words in the poem are "an' ev'n Devotion!" (and even devotion). Even our religious devotions might be affected if we could see ourselves at that moment just as others see us. So many of the cruelest mistakes in religion are made not out of malice but out of simple ignorance, blunders we would willingly avoid could we but see ourselves as others see us. Looking at other traditions, you need to see the bonnet and not just the louse. Looking at your own, however you define it, you need to see the louse as well as the bonnet.

Can Religion Be Defined?

What is religion? The word exists in the English language, and people have some commonsense notion of what it refers to. Most understand it as one kind of human activity standing alongside other kinds, such as business, politics, warfare, art, law, sport, or science. Religion is available in a variety of forms, but what is it, really? What makes it itself?

Simple but searching questions like these may seem to be the starting point for the study of religion. Within the study of religion, they are more precisely the starting point for the *theory* of religion. And readers will not be surprised to learn that academic theoreticians of religion have not been content with the commonsense understanding of the subject.

The theoretical difficulties that attend any basic element of human thought or experience are undeniable. What is mathematics? What is art? What is law? What is music? Books have been written debating number theory, aesthetic theory, legal theory, and music theory. It should come as no surprise then that the theory of religion is no less actively debated than are those other theories. Some definitions of religion are so loose as to allow almost anything to qualify as a religion. Others are so strict as to exclude almost everything ordinarily taken to be a religion (prompting one recent contributor to the *Journal of the American Academy of Religion* to give his article the wry or rueful title "Religions: Are There Any?").[1]

The inconvenient truth is that no definition of religion now enjoys general acceptance. In *The Bonobo and the Atheist* (2013), the primatologist Frans de Waal writes:

> To delineate religion to everyone's satisfaction is hopeless. I was once part of a forum at the American Academy of Religion, when

> someone proposed we start off with a definition of religion. However much sense this made, the idea was promptly shot down by another participant, who reminded everyone that last time they tried to define religion half the audience had angrily stomped out of the room. And this in an academy named after the topic![2]

A survey of competing theories, if we were to attempt one here, could quickly jump to twenty-three entries if we simply combined the contents of two recent handbooks—the eight in Daniel L. Pals's *Eight Theories of Religion* (2006) and the fifteen in Michael Stausberg's *Contemporary Theories of Religion: A Critical Companion* (2009).[3]

Though no one writing on religion can entirely escape theoretical commitments, *The Norton Anthology of World Religions* is foremost an anthology of primary texts. By the term *primary* we understand texts produced by the practitioners of each of the anthologized religions for their fellow practitioners. Such an anthology does not collect theories of religion, for the simple reason that such theories are secondary texts. They belong not to the creation and practice of religion but, retrospectively, to its study and analysis. Accordingly, they have rarely been of much interest to religious practitioners themselves.

Religious practitioners are far from unique in this regard. "Philosophy of science is about as useful to scientists as ornithology is to birds," Richard Feynman (1918–1988), a Caltech physicist, famously quipped.[4] The philosophy (or theory) of religion is of as little use to, say, the Buddhist as philosophy of science is to the scientist. Just as the scientist is interested in her experiment rather than in the philosophy of science and the painter in his painting rather than in the philosophy of art, so the Buddhist is interested in the Buddha rather than in the philosophy of religion. The term *religion* itself, as an academic term comprising—as indeed it does in this work—many different religious traditions, may not be of much practical utility to the practitioner of any one of the traditions.

And yet we who have assembled this work may not excuse ourselves altogether from addressing the question "What is religion?" simply on the grounds that our pages are filled with primary texts, for introducing, framing, and contextualizing these texts are the words of our six anthologizing editors as well as the general editor. The seven of us speak in these pages not as practitioners of the religions anthologized here but as scholars writing *about* those religions. Scholarship at its most empirical cannot escape theory, because, to quote a dictum from the philosophy of science, all data are theory-laden. A theory of some sort will be found operative even when no explicit theoretical commitment has been made.

If, then, some tacit theory or theories of religion must necessarily have informed the choices made by our associate editors, given the general editor's decision to impose no single theory, has any silent theoretical convergence occurred? Now that the results are in and the editors' choices have actually been made, do they reflect a working answer to the question "What is religion?"

As general editor, I believe that they do, though it would take some rather elaborate spelling out to explain just *how* they do. Something more modest but more readily discernible must suffice for this introduction—namely, the claim that the choices made by the respective associate editors reflect a common method or, more modestly still, a common approach to the task of presenting a major religious literature with some coherence. In brief, the six associate editors have approached the six religions whose texts they anthologize as six kinds of practice rather than as six kinds of belief. In common usage, religious and unreligious people are divided into "believers" and "unbelievers." The editors have departed from this common usage, proceeding instead on the silent and admittedly modest premise that religion is as religion *does*. Even when speaking of belief, as they do only occasionally, they generally treat it as embedded in practice and inseparable from practice. Monotheism in the abstract is a belief. "Hear, O Israel, the Lord is our God, the Lord alone" as sung by a cantor in a synagogue is a practice.

When religion is approached as practice, what follows? Clearly, Daoist practice, Muslim practice, Christian practice, and so on are not identical, but the substantial differences *within* each of them can loom as large as the differences from one to another among them. *The goal of this anthology is to present through texts how this variety has developed and how the past continues to shape the present.* Thus, the body of material put on exhibit here serves less to answer the question "What is religion?" in any theoretically elaborate or definitive way than to question the answers others have given to that question—answers such as those offered by, for example, the twenty-three theories alluded to above. Whatever fascinating questions a given theory of religion may have posed and answered to its own satisfaction, it must also, we submit, be able to account for the complexity of the data that these primary texts exhibit. Rather than serving to illustrate some fully developed new theory of religion, in other words, the texts gathered here constitute the empirical evidence that any such theory must cope with. In the meantime, the working focus is squarely on practice.

Each of the religions anthologized here has contained multiple versions of itself both over time and at any given time, and the anthology does not attempt to drive past the multiplicity to the singular essence of the thing. Practitioners, of course, have not always been so neutral. Many have been or still are prepared to deny the legitimacy of others as Hindu, Muslim, Christian, Jewish, and so on. But for the purposes of this anthology, those denials themselves simply become a part of the broader story.

Syncretism, moreover—namely, the introduction of a feature from one religion into the life of another—is in itself an argument that the borrower and the lender are, or can be, related even when they are not, and never will be, identical. Multiple religious belonging—double or triple affiliation—sometimes takes syncretism a step further. And while borrowings across major borders are an additive process, adjustments within borders can often be a subtractive process, as seen in many statements that take the form "I am a Buddhist, but . . . ," "I am a Catholic, but . . . ," "I am a Muslim, but . . . ," and so forth. In such statements, the speaker takes the broad term as a starting point and then qualifies it until it fits properly.

Yet we do not claim anything more than practical utility for this default approach to the subject, knowing as we do that a great many scholars of religion decline to define the essence of religion itself but do not find themselves inhibited by that abstention from saying a great deal of interest about one religious tradition or another. Rather than name at the outset the one feature that establishes the category *religion* before discussing the particular religion that interests them, they make the usually silent assumption that the full range of beliefs and practices that have been conventionally thought of as religious is vast and that each religion must be allowed to do as it does, assembling its subsets from the vast, never-to-be-fully-enumerated roster of world religious practices. Having made that assumption, the scholars take a deep breath and go on to talk about what they want to talk about.

Twenty-first-century religion scholars are prepared to acknowledge coherence when they find it but determined never to impose it. They are aware that the entries made under the heading *religion* may not all be versions of just the same thing, but they are equally aware that the overlaps, the innumerable ad hoc points of contact, are also there and also real—and so they find the continued use of the collective term *religion* justified for the enriching and enlightening comparisons that it facilitates. All knowledge begins with comparison.

In telling the life stories of six major, living, international religions through their respective primary texts, the editors of *The Norton Anthology of World Religions* have neither suppressed variability over time in service to any supposedly timeless essence of the thing nor, even when using the word *classical*, dignified any one age as truly golden. Each of the stories ends with modernity, but modernity in each case is neither the climax nor the denouement of the story. It is not the last chapter, only the latest.

How Christian Europe Learned to Compare Religions

Most people, we said earlier, understand religion as "one kind of human activity standing alongside other kinds, such as business, politics, warfare, art, law, sport, or science." Another way to say this is that they understand religion to be one domain among many, each separate from the others. Broadly compatible with this popular understanding is a widely influential definition of religion formulated by the anthropologist Clifford Geertz (1926–2006).

In "Religion as a Cultural System," first published in 1966, Geertz defined religion as

> *(1) a system of symbols which acts to (2) establish powerful, pervasive, and long-lasting moods and motivations in men by (3) formulating conceptions of a general order of existence and (4) clothing these conceptions with such an aura of factuality that (5) the moods and motivations seem uniquely realistic.*[5]

Geertz does not claim that all cultures are equally religious. In fact, toward the end of his essay he observes that "the degree of religious articulateness is not a constant even as between societies of similar complexity."[6] However, he does tacitly assume that religion is if not universal then at least extremely widespread and that it is a domain separate from others, such as—to name two that he explores—science and ideology.[7]

But just how widespread is religion, and is it truly a domain separable from the rest of culture? Can religion really be distinguished from ideology? In Geertz's terms, wouldn't Marxism qualify as a religion? In recent decades, some have argued that even a thoroughly secular anthropologist like Geertz, in whose definition of religion neither God nor Christ is mentioned, can be seen as carrying forward an ideological understanding of religion that originated in the Christian West and has lived on in Western academic life as a set of inadequately examined assumptions. That religion is a domain separate from either ethnicity or culture is one of two key, historically Christian assumptions. That religion is a universal phenomenon—in some form, a part of every human society and even every human mind—is the other key assumption.

Perhaps the most widely cited historical critique of these assumptions is Tomoko Masuzawa's revealing *The Invention of World Religions, Or, How European Universalism Was Preserved in the Language of Pluralism* (2005). Masuzawa's book is not about the invention of the world's religions themselves but about the invention of *world religions* as a phrase used in the West to talk about them, postulating their parallel existence as separable and separate realities, available as an indefinitely expandable group for academic discussion.[8]

When and how, she asks, did this omnibus-phrase *world religions* come into the general usage that it now enjoys? She concludes her influential investigation with the candid confession that the invention and, especially, the very widespread adoption of the phrase remain something of a puzzle—but her analysis traces the usage back only to the nineteenth century. Our claim below is that though the phrase *world religions* may be recent, its roots run much deeper than the nineteenth century, as deep in fact as early Christianity's peculiar and unprecedented self-definition.

To say this is not to undercut the strength of the criticism. Christian explorers, traders, missionaries, and colonists encountering non-Western societies, especially after the discovery of the Americas and the colonial expansion of the West into Asia, have often isolated and labeled as "religions" behaviors that they took to be the local equivalents of what they knew in the West as Christianity. This process of isolating and labeling was a mistake when and if the societies themselves did not understand the behaviors in question as constituting either a separate domain or merely one instance of a more general phenomenon called religion. Moreover, when those purporting to understand non-Western societies in these historically Christian terms were invaders and imperialists, a perhaps unavoidable theoretical mistake could have grievous practical consequences. And when, in turn, ostensibly neutral, secular theories of religion—not imposed by conquerors or missionaries but merely proffered by Western academics—are alleged to make the same historically Christian assumptions, the entire project of comparative religious study may be faulted as Christian imperialism.

Because the viability and indeed the enormous value of such study are premises of this anthology, the challenge calls for a significant response, one that necessarily includes substantial attention to just how Christianity influenced the study of what the West has defined as world religions. The intention in what follows, however, is by no means to make a case for Christianity as inherently central or supreme among the world's religions. We intend rather, and only, to trace how, in point of fact, Christianity began as central to the Western *study* of religions and then, by degrees, yielded its position as more polycentric forms of study emerged.

Let us begin by stipulating that Christians did indeed acquire very early and thereafter never entirely lost the habit of thinking of their religion as a separate domain. Once this is conceded, it should come as no great surprise that as a corollary of this habit, they should have adopted early and never entirely lost the habit of thinking of other religions, rightly or wrongly, as similarly separate domains. This would be simply one more instance of the human habit of beginning with the known and with the self and working outward to the unknown and to the others.

But we must stipulate further that Christians made a second assumption—namely, that theirs should become humankind's first-ever programmatically "world" religion. The idea of universally valid religious truth was not new in itself. Ancient Israel had long since been told that its vocation was to be the light of the world. In the book of Isaiah, God says to his people through the prophet (49:6):

> It is too light a thing that you should be my servant to raise up the tribes of Jacob and to restore the preserved of Israel; I will give you as a light to the nations, that my salvation may reach to the end of the earth.[9]

In the Gospel of Matthew, Jesus turns this latent potential into a radically intrusive program for action. His final words to his apostles are

> Go therefore, and make disciplines of *all nations*, baptizing them in the name of the Father and of the Son and of the Holy Spirit, teaching them to observe all that I have commanded you; and, lo, I am with you always, even to the close of the age. (Matthew 28:19–20; emphasis added)

How ever did this instruction, as the first Christians put it into practice, lead to the secular study of "world religions" as we know it today?

The Social Oddity of the Early Church

In the earliest centuries of its long history, the Christian church defined its belief as different from the official polytheism of the Roman Empire, on the one hand, and from the monotheism of Rabbinic Judaism, on the other, inasmuch as the rabbinic Jews did not recognize Jesus as God incarnate. But if the church was thus, to borrow a convenient phrase from contemporary American life, a faith-based organization, it was not just a school of thought: it was also an *organization*. As faith-based, it undeniably placed unique and unprecedented stress on belief (and indeed set the pattern by which today all those religiously active in any way are routinely called *believers*, even when not all regard belief as central to their practice). Yet as an organization, the church depended not just on a distinct set of beliefs but also on a social identity separate, on the one hand, from that of the Roman Empire (or any other empire) and equally separate, on the other, from that of the Jewish nation (or any other nation). As a faith-based, voluntary, nonprofit, multiethnic, egalitarian, nongovernmental organization, the Christian church was a social novelty: nothing quite like it had ever been seen before. And as Christians, growing steadily in number, projected their novel collective self-understanding upon Roman and Jewish social reality alike, the effect was profoundly disruptive. Though many others would follow, these were the first two instances of Christian projection, and an analysis of how they worked is especially instructive.

By encouraging Roman polytheists to *convert* to Christianity while maintaining that they did not thereby cease to be Romans, the Christians implicitly invented religious conversion itself as an existential possibility. The term *religion* did not exist then in Greek, Latin, or Aramaic as a fully developed universal category containing both Roman polytheism and Christianity, but in the very action of conversion the future category was already implicit. By seeking to convert Roman polytheists to Christianity, the early Christians implied that Roman religiosity was a domain both separate from the rest of Roman life and replaceable. You could exchange your Roman religiosity for this modified Jewish religiosity, as the very act of conversion demonstrated, while bringing the rest of your Roman identity with you.

In the first century, conversion thus defined was an unprecedented and socially disruptive novelty. Until the destabilizing intrusion of Christianity, respect for the Roman gods had always been inseparable from simply being Roman: religious identity and civic identity had always constituted an unbroken whole. Christianity encouraged Romans to split that single identity into a double identity: religion, on the one hand; culture and ethnicity, on the other. In this sequestration of the religiously meaningful from the religiously neutral or meaningless was born the very possibility of secular culture, as well as religion as Western modernity has come to understand it—religion as involving some semblance of faith and some form of collective identity separable from ethnicity or culture.

In by far the most important instance of this division of social identity, the original Christian Jews, having adopted a minority understanding of Jewish tradition, denied that they were any less Jewish for that reason. Writing of his Jewish critics, St. Paul fumed (2 Corinthians 11:22): "Are they Israelites? So am I!" Much of first-century Jewry would not have disagreed with him had the matter stopped there, for there were many peacefully coexisting Jewish views about Jewish belief and practice. As no more than the latest variation on the old themes, the Christian Jews would not have created anything structurally new. But they did create something new by taking the further step of bringing themselves, with their recognizably Jewish religious views (views indeed unrecognizable as anything except Jewish), into an unprecedented social relationship with non-Jews—namely, into the Christian church. By linking themselves to non-Jews in this way, without renouncing their Jewish identity, the Christian Jews—enjoying particular success in the Roman Diaspora—demonstrated that as they conceived their own Jewish religiosity to be distinguishable from the rest of what was then the Jewish way of life, so they conceived the same two components of identity to be likewise distinguishable for all other Jews.

Rabbinic Judaism, dominant in Palestine and the Mesopotamian Diaspora, would eventually repudiate this Christian projection and reassert that Jewish religiosity and Jewish identity are one and indistinguishable. In the rabbinic view that became and has remained dominant in world Judaism, there are no "Judaists," only Jews. But this reassertion did not happen overnight: it took generations, even centuries. Neither the Romans nor the Jews nor the Christians themselves immediately understood the full novelty of what was coming into existence.

Through most of world history, in most parts of the world, what we are accustomed to call religion, ethnicity, culture, and way of life have been inextricable parts of a single whole. How did Christianity begin to become an exception to this general rule? On the one hand, it appropriated a set of Jewish religious ideas—including monotheism, revelation, covenant, scripture, sin, repentance, forgiveness, salvation, prophecy, messianism, and apocalypticism—without adopting the rest of the highly developed and richly nuanced Jewish way of life. On the other hand, it universalized these Jewish religious ideas, creating a new social entity, the church, through which non-Jews could be initiated into an enlarged version of the ancestral Jewish covenant with God. The Jews had believed for centuries God's declaration, "I am the LORD your God, who have separated you from the peoples" (Leviticus 20:24) and "you are a people holy to the LORD your God" (Deuteronomy 7:6). In effect, the Christian Jews split the idea of covenanted separateness and holiness from what consequently became the relatively secularized idea of nationality. The Jews were still a people, they maintained, but God had now revised and universalized the terms of his covenant. In the words of Jesus' apostle Peter, "Truly I perceive that God shows no partiality, but in every nation any one who fears him and does what is right is acceptable to him" (Acts 10:34–35).

The original Greek word for church, *ekklēsia*, suggests a collective understanding of church members as "called out" from other kinds of religious, ethnic, or political membership into this new—and now, in principle, universal—"people set apart as holy." The *ekklēsia* offered its members a sense of sacred peoplehood, but it tellingly lacked much else that ordinarily maintains a national identity. It had no ancestral land, no capital city, no language of its own, no literature at the start other than what it had inherited from the Jews, no distinct cuisine, no standard dress, and no political or governmental support beyond the organizational management of the church itself. Moreover, this ethnically mixed and socially unpromising group was atheist in its attitude toward all gods except the God of Israel as they had come to understand him—God as incarnate in Jesus the Messiah. Within the political culture of the Roman Empire, this rejection of the empire's gods was a seditious and rebellious rejection of Roman sovereignty itself. When, unsurprisingly, the empire recognized it as such and began intermittently to persecute the church, the Christian sense of separateness only grew.

In this form, and despite intermittent persecution, the church grew quietly but steadily for more than three centuries. At that point, with perhaps a fifth of the population of the Roman Empire enrolled in separate local Christian churches under relatively autonomous elected supervisors (bishops), the emperor Constantine (r. 312–37) first legalized Christianity and then stabilized its doctrine by requiring the Christian bishops—ordered to convene for the first time as a council at Nicaea, near his eventual capital city of Constantinople—to define it. In 381, the emperor Theodosius (r. 379–95) made this newly defined Christianity the official religion of the Roman Empire, and the new religion—no longer persecuted but now operating under a large measure of imperial control—began a fateful reversal of course. It began to fuse with the political governance and the Hellenistic culture of imperial Rome, compromising the character of the *ekklēsia* as a domain separate from nationality or culture. In a word, it began to normalize.

The establishment of Christianity as the state religion of the Roman Empire ushered in a period of rapid growth, pushed by the government, within the borders of the empire. Beyond them, however, most notably in the Persian Empire just to the east, its new status had the opposite effect.

Once relatively unhindered as a social movement taken to be as compatible with Persian rule as with Roman, Christianity now became suspect as the official religion of the enemy.

Meanwhile, in Rome itself—the "First Rome," as historically prior to the Eastern Empire's capital, Constantinople—and in the western European territories that it administered, a partial but significant return to the original separation of domains occurred just a century later. In 476, Odoacer, king of an invading Germanic tribe, deposed the last Roman emperor, Romulus Augustulus, without effectively assuming authority over the Christian church. Instead, the power of the bishop of Rome—the highest surviving official of the old imperial order—over the church in western Europe began to grow, while the power of kings and feudal lords over all that was not the church steadily grew as well. The nominally unified imperial authority over the empire and its established religion thus split apart. To be sure, for centuries the pope claimed the authority to anoint kings to their royal offices, and at certain moments this was a claim that could be sustained. But gradually, a sense that civilian and religious authority were different and separate began to set in. At the same time, the identity of the church as, once again, detached or disembedded from the state and from culture alike—the church as a potentially universal separate domain, a holy world unto itself—began to consolidate.

The Four-Cornered Medieval Map of Religion

Wealth, power, and population in the world west of India were concentrated during the sixth century in the Persian Empire and in the Eastern Roman or Byzantine Empire. Western Europe during the same century—all that had once been the Western Roman Empire—was far poorer, weaker, more sparsely populated, and culturally more isolated than the empires to its east. Then, during the seventh and eighth centuries, a third major power arose. Arabia had long provided mercenary soldiers to both of the then-dominant empires; but religiously inspired by the Islam newly preached by Muhammad (ca. 570–632) and militarily unified under his successors, it became a major world power in its own right with stunning speed. Arab armies conquered the entirety of the Persian Empire within a generation. Within a century, they had taken from the Eastern Roman Empire its Middle Eastern and North African possessions (half of its total territory) as well as the major Mediterranean islands. From what had been the Western Roman Empire, they had subtracted three-quarters of Spain and penetrated deep into France until driven back across the Pyrenees by the unprecedented European alliance that defeated them in the 732 Battle of Poitiers.

The political map of the world had been redrawn from India to the Atlantic, but what of the religious map? How did western European Christians now understand themselves among the religions of the world? The symbolic birth date of Europe as Christendom has long been taken to be Christmas Day of the year 800. On that date, Pope Leo III crowned Charles the Great, better known as Charlemagne—the grandson of Charles Martel, who had unified the European forces at Poitiers—as the first "Holy Roman Emperor." The Muslim invasion from distant Arabia had shocked an isolated and fragmented region into an early assertion of common religious and geographical identity. As a result, there was a readiness to give political expression to a dawning collective self-understanding. The lost Western Roman Empire was by no means reconstituted: Charlemagne was an emperor without much of an empire, his coronation expressing a vision more than a reality. But the vision itself mattered decisively in another way, for what came into existence at about this time was an understood quadripartite map of the world of religion that would remain standard in Europe for centuries.

There was, first and foremost for Christians, Christianity itself: the Christian church understood to be the same single, separate domain wherever it was found, with the same distinct relationship to national and cultural identity. To the extent that it rested on common faith, the church could be divided by heresy; but even heretical Christians, of whom there would be fewer in the early ninth century than there had been in earlier Christian centuries, were still understood to be Christians. They were practicing the right religion in a wrong way, but they were not practicing another religion altogether.

There was, second, Judaism: the Jews of Europe, a population living among Christians, disparaged but well known, whose relationship to Christianity was well remembered and whose religious authenticity rested on a recognized if more or less resented prior relationship with the same God that the Christians worshipped. Christian understanding of Jewish religious life as the Jews actually lived it was slender, and Christian knowledge of the vast rabbinic literature that had come into existence between the second and the ninth century, much of it in far-off Mesopotamia, was virtually nonexistent. Knowledge of Greek had been lost in Latin Europe, and knowledge of the Hebrew and Aramaic that the Jews of Europe had managed to preserve (despite recurrent persecution) was confined to them alone. Yet, this ignorance notwithstanding, Christian Europe was well aware that the Jews practiced a religion different from their own. And the implicit Christian understanding of religion as a separate domain of potentially universal extent was reinforced by the fact that from the outside, Jewish religious practice appeared to be at least as deeply divorced from national and cultural practices as was Christian religious practice: the Jews, who had lost their land and were dispersed around the world, lived in Europe much as Europe's Christians lived.

The third corner of Europe's four-cornered understanding of world religion was Islam, though the terms *Islam* and *Muslim* would not come into European usage until centuries later. Even the term *Arab* was not standard. The multinational religious commonwealth that we now call world Islam has been traditionally referred to by the Muslims themselves with the Arabic expression *dar al-islam*, the "House of Islam" or the "House of Submission" (because *islam* means "submission"—that is, submission to God). Whether it was *Saracen, Moor, Turk, or Arab,* the ethnic terms used by Christians to refer to the Muslims who faced them in the south and the east depended on time and place. Christendom as the Holy Roman Empire had become a domain geographically separate from the House of Islam. Similarly, Christianity as distinct from Christendom was evidently a domain of belief and practice separate from that of Islam. But among Christians, the further inference was that as Christian identity was separate from Bavarian or Florentine identity, so Muslim identity must be separate from Arab or Turkish identity. To some extent, this was a false inference, for obligatory Arabic in the Qur'an and obligatory pilgrimage to Mecca did much to preserve the originally Arab identity of Islam. Yet the tricontinental distribution and ethnic variability of the House of Islam fostered among Europeans an understanding of Islam as, like Christianity, a potentially universal religion separable from the ethnicity of any one of its component parts.

As Christian anxiety mounted that the year 1000 might mark the end of the world (an outcome that some Christians saw predicted in the New Testament book of Revelation), Muhammad came to be seen by some as the Antichrist, a destructive figure whose appearance during the last apocalyptic period before the end had been foretold (again in the book of Revelation). Yet gradually, albeit as "Mohammedanism," Islam came to be differentiated from Christianity in theological rather than in such floridly mythological terms. The Qur'an was translated into Latin in 1142. The High Middle Ages began to witness various forms of religious and cultural encounter—some as an unintended consequence of the Crusades; others through the influence of large Christian minorities living under Muslim rule and, over time, substantial Muslim minorities living under Christian rule, notably in Spain and Sicily. Finally, there was the mediating influence of a cross-culturally significant Jewish population residing on either side of the Muslim–Christian border and communicating across it. One result of these minglings was a gradually growing overlap in the techniques in use in all three communities for the exegesis of the sacred scriptures that for each mattered so much.

As Muslim monotheism came gradually into clearer focus, medieval Christianity came to recognize Muslims as worshippers of the same God that Jews and Christians worshipped. Meanwhile, Islam was, like Christianity, a religion that actively sought converts who were then made part of a separate quasi-national, quasi-familial, yet potentially universal social entity. The genesis of the Western understanding of religion as such—religion as a separate but expandable social category—was thus significantly advanced by Christianity's encounter with another social entity so like itself in its universalism and its relative independence from ethnic or cultural identity.

The fourth corner of the world religion square was occupied by a ghost—namely, the memory of long-dead Greco-Roman polytheism. Christianity was born among the urban Jews of the Roman Empire and spread gradually into the countryside. Even in largely rural Europe, monasteries functioned as surrogate cities and Christianity spread outward from these centers of structure and literacy. *Pagus* is the Latin word for "countryside," and in the countryside the old polytheisms lingered long after they had died out in the cities. Thus, a rural polytheist was a *paganus*, and *paganismus* (paganism) became synonymous with polytheism. In England, pre-Christian polytheism lingered in the inhospitable heath, and so *heathenism* became an English synonym for *paganism*. Though polytheism is not necessarily idolatrous (one may believe in many gods without making a single idol), polytheistic belief and idolatrous practice were generally conflated. More important for the centuries that lay ahead, the increasingly jumbled memory of what Greco-Roman polytheism—remembered as "paganism"—had been in the Christian past was projected upon the enormous and almost entirely unknown world beyond the realms occupied by Christians, Muslims, and Jews.

The quadripartite typology just sketched was only one long-lived stage in the development of the comparative study of religion in Christian Europe. We may pause to note, however, that as of the year 800 Judaism and Islam were operating under similar typologies. The Qur'an, definitive for all Islamic thought, takes frequent and explicit note of Judaism and Christianity, while the place occupied by the memory of Greco-Roman polytheism in Christianity is occupied in the Qur'an by the memory of polytheism as it existed in Arabia at the time when Muhammad began to receive his revelations. World Jewry, as a minority maintaining its identity and its religious practice in both Christendom and the House of Islam, had a richer experience of both Christians and Muslims than either of those two had of the other. Yet what functioned for Jews in the way that the memory of Greco-Roman polytheism functioned for Christians and the memory of Arabian polytheism functioned for Muslims was the memory of ancient Canaanite, Philistine, and Babylonian polytheism as recorded in the Bible and used thereafter as a template for understanding all those who were the enemies of God and the persecutors of his Chosen People.

Now, the comparison of two religions on terms set by one of them is like the similarly biased comparison of two nationalities: the outcome is a predictable victory for the side conducting the comparison. In fact, when religion and ethnicity are fused, religious comparison is commonly stated in ethnic terms rather than in what we would consider religious terms. Thus, in the Hebrew Bible, apostasy from the religion of Israel is called "*foreign* worship" (*'avodah zarah*) rather than simply false worship, though falsehood or worse is unmistakably implied. To the extent that ethnicity is taken to be a matter of brute fact, and therefore beyond negotiation, religion bound to ethnicity has seemed a nonnegotiable matter of fact as well.

In this regard, however, the condition of medieval Christian Europe was interestingly unstable. Demographically, the two largest religious realities it knew—Islam and Christianity itself—were consciously and ideologically multinational in character, and both actively sought converts from all nations. Judaism was not evangelistic in this way, but world Jewry was uniquely the world's first global nation: the bulk of its population was distributed internationally in such a way that Jews were accustomed in every place to distinguish their ethnicity from the ethnicity of the locale and their religion from its religion. Christian prejudice often prevented Jewish acculturation (not to suppose that Jews always wished to acculturate), but it did not always do so. And so during extended periods of Christian toleration, even the generally firm Jewish sense that religion, ethnicity, and culture were a seamless whole may have become more difficult to sustain. This three-sided—Christian, Muslim, and Jewish—embrace of the notion that religion was a separate domain set the stage in Europe for the comparison of the three on terms derived from a neutral fourth entity that was not to be equated with any one of them.

This fourth entity was Aristotelian philosophy as recovered in Europe during the eleventh and twelfth centuries. Of course, the philosophical discussions that began to be published—such as Abelard's mid-twelfth-century *Dialogue among a Philosopher, a Jew, and a Christian*, in which the philosopher of the title often appears to be a Muslim—always ended in victory for the imagined Christian. Yet Abelard (1079–1142) was eventually condemned by the church because his dialogue clearly recognized reason, mediated by philosophy, as independent of the religions being discussed and as capable of rendering judgments upon them all. Philosophy as that fourth, neutral party would be joined over time by psychology, sociology, anthropology, economics, evolutionary biology, cognitive science, and other analytical tools. But these enlargements lay centuries in the future. As the Middle Ages were succeeded by the Renaissance, philosophy had made a crucial start toward making neutral comparisons, even though Europe's quadripartite map of the world's religions was still quite firmly in place, with most comparisons still done on entirely Christian and theological terms.

The Renaissance Rehearsal of Comparative Religion

The Italian Renaissance—beginning in the fourteenth century and flourishing in the fifteenth and sixteenth—is commonly taken to be more important as a movement in art and literature than in philosophy or religion. To be sure, it did not attempt a transformation of European Christianity comparable to that of the Protestant Reformation of the sixteenth century. But the kind of religious comparison that began in the early eighteenth century, in the aftermath of Europe's devastating seventeenth-century Protestant–Catholic Wars of Religion, was foreshadowed during the Renaissance by the revival of classical Greek and Latin and by the recovery of masterpieces of world literature written in those languages.

First of all, perfected knowledge of Latin and the recovered knowledge of Greek enabled Italian scholars to publish critical editions of the texts of classical antiquity as well as philologically grounded historical criticism of such later Latin texts as the Donation of Constantine, exposed as a papal forgery by the Italian humanist Lorenzo Valla (1407–1457). It was in Renaissance Italy, too, that Christian Europe first recovered knowledge of biblical Hebrew. The earliest chair of Hebrew was established late in the fifteenth century at the University of Bologna. Despite repeated persecutions, ghettoizations, and expulsions, the Jewish population of Italy grew substantially during the Renaissance, enthusiastically embracing the then-new technology of printing with movable type. The first complete publication of the Hebrew Bible in the original, with Jewish commentaries, appeared in Venice in 1517 and proved highly instructive to Christian Europe; by the end of the following century, Italian scholars were even starting to read both the postbiblical rabbinic literature and the Kabbalah, writings in a later extra-rabbinic Jewish mystical tradition that fascinated some of them. Little by little, Christian Europe was beginning to learn from Europe's Jews.

As the Renaissance began to introduce Christian Europe by slow degrees to the critical examination of ancient texts as well as to the inner religious life of Judaism, it accomplished something similar in a more roundabout way for the lost religions of Greece and Rome. The humanists of the Renaissance did not believe in the gods and goddesses of Olympus as they believed in God the Almighty Father of Christianity, but even as they read the classical literature only as literature, they nonetheless were taken deep inside the creedal, ritual, imaginative, and literary life of another religion—namely, the lost Greco-Roman polytheism. During the Italian Renaissance, the term *humanist* (Italian *umanista*), we should recall, was not used polemically, as if in some sort of pointed contrast to *theist*. Rather, it was a declaration of allegiance to the humanizing, civilizing power of art and imaginative literature. Renaissance humanism's imaginative engagement with the religions of classical Greece and Rome thus constituted an unplanned rehearsal for the real-world, real-time imaginative engagements with non-Christian religions and cultures that lay immediately and explosively ahead for Europe. When the Spanish *conquistadores* encountered the living polytheism of Aztec Mexico, their first interpretive instinct was to translate the gods of Tenochtitlán into their nearest Greek and Roman equivalents. This was an intellectually clumsy move, to be sure, but less clumsy than interpreting them exclusively in monotheist Christian terms would have been. Moreover, because neither classical paganism nor Aztec polytheism was taken to be true, the two could be compared objectively or, if you will, humanistically—and from that early and fumbling act of comparison many others would follow.

In the study of philosophy, the Renaissance added Plato and various ancient Neoplatonists to the Aristotle of the medieval universities. More important, perhaps, it began to read late-classical moral philosophies—notably Stoicism and Epicureanism—whose frequent references to the gods made them in effect lost religions. Sometimes inspiring, sometimes scandalous, these recovered moral philosophies introduced personality and inner complexity into the inherited category of paganism. Philosophical recoveries of this sort could remain a purely academic exercise, but for that very reason their influence might be more subtly pervasive. Often, those who studied these texts professed to be seeking only their pro forma subordination to the truth of Roman Catholic Christianity. Nonetheless, the ideas found their way into circulation. To be sure, the few who took the further step of propagating pagan worldviews as actual alternatives to Christian faith or Aristotelian cosmology could pay a high price. The wildly speculative Neoplatonist Giordano Bruno (1548–1600) was burned at the stake as a heretic. But others, scarcely less speculative, spread their ideas with little official interference and in response to widespread popular curiosity.

Comparative Christianity in the Protestant Reformation

Important as the Renaissance was to the development in Europe of a capacity for religious comparison, the Protestant Reformation was surely even more important, for it forced Europeans in one region after another to compare forms of Christianity, accept one, and reject the others. Frequently, this lacerating but formative experience required those who had rejected Catholicism to reject one or more contending forms of Protestantism as well. This was clearly the case during the English Civil War (1642–51), which forced English Christians to side either with the Anglican king or with the Puritan rebels who beheaded him; but there were other such choices, some of them much more complicated.

Tentative moves toward tolerance during these struggles were far less frequent than fierce mutual persecution and, on either side, the celebration of victims as martyrs. The Catholics tried to dismiss and suppress the Protestants as merely the latest crop of Christian heretics. The Protestants commonly mythologized Rome as Babylon and compared Catholics to the ancient Babylonians, viewing them as pagans who had taken the New Israel, the Christian church, into exile and captivity. The century and a half of the reformations and the Wars of Religion certainly did not seem to promise a future of sympathetic, mutually respectful religious comparison. And yet within the religious game of impassioned mutual rejection then being played, each side did develop formidable knowledge of the practices, beliefs, and arguments of the other. To the extent that the broader religious comparison initiated during the Enlightenment of the late seventeenth and the eighteenth centuries called for close observation, firsthand testimony, logical analysis, and preparatory study of all kinds, its debt to both the Protestant Reformation and the Catholic Counter-Reformation is enormous.

Particularly important was the historical awareness that the Protestant Reformation introduced into Christian thought. Protestantism took the New Testament to be a historically reliable presentation of earliest Christianity and, using that presentation as a criterion, proceeded to reject the many aspects of Roman Catholic practice that appeared to deviate from it. To be sure, the Roman church had been reading, copying, and devotedly commenting on the Bible for centuries, but it had not been reading it as history. Here the Renaissance paved the way for the Reformation, for the Bible that Rome read was the Bible in a Latin translation; and the Renaissance, as it recovered the knowledge of Hebrew and Greek, had recovered the ability to read the original texts from which that Latin translation had been made. In 1516, the Dutch humanist Desiderius Erasmus published a bilingual, Greek-Latin edition of the New Testament, correcting the received Latin to bring it into conformity with the newly recovered Greek. Armed with this new tool, the many educated Europeans who knew Latin but not Greek could immediately see that the Latin on which the church had relied for a thousand years was at many points unreliable and in need of revision. In this way, Erasmus, a child of the Renaissance, took a first, fateful step toward historicizing the Bible.

The Reformation, launched just a year later with the publication by Martin Luther of "Ninety-Five Theses on the Power and Efficacy of Indulgences," would take the further, explosive step of historicizing the church itself. To quote a famous line from Reformation polemics, Erasmus "laid the egg that Luther hatched." Thus, two epoch-making historical tools of Protestantism as it would dynamically take shape became integral parts of the later comparative study of non-Christian religions as undertaken by Christian scholars: first, the reconstruction of the composition history of the original texts themselves by scholars who had mastered the original languages; and second, the comparison of later religious practice to earlier through the study of the recovered and historically framed original texts.

In one regard, finally, Protestantism may have indirectly contributed to the comparative study of religion by setting in motion a gradual subversion of the very understanding of religion as a domain separate from ethnicity and culture that had been constitutive of Christian self-understanding almost from its start. Mark C. Taylor argues brilliantly in *After God* (2007) that what is often termed the disappearance of God or the disappearance of the sacred in modernity is actually the integration of that aspect of human experience with the rest of modern experience—a process whose onset he traces to Martin Luther's and John Calvin's sanctification of all aspects of human life as against medieval Christianity's division of the religious life of monks and nuns from the worldly (secular) life of laypeople.[10]

This progressive modern fusion of once separate domains would explain the spread in the West of the experience of the holy in ostensibly secular contexts and of the aesthetic in ostensibly religious contexts. Clearly the earlier Christian sense of religion as a separate domain has lingered powerfully in the West. Yet if Taylor is right, then post-Protestant religious modernity in the West, though deeply marked by Protestantism, may be a paradoxical correction of Christianity to the world norm. Or, to put the matter more modestly, the diffuse post-Christian religiosity of the modern West may bear a provocative similarity to the much older but equally diffuse religiosity of South and East Asia or indeed of pre-Christian world Jewry.

Toleration, Science, Exploration, and the Need for a New Map

After decades of controversy climaxing in all-out war, it became clear to exhausted Protestants and Catholics alike that neither could dictate the religious future of Europe. The Wars of Religion came to a close in 1648 with the Peace of Westphalia, which, though it by no means established individual freedom of religion, did end international religious war in Europe. Its key principle—*Cuius regio, eius religio* (literally, "Whose the rule, his the religion")—allowed the king or the government of each nation to establish a national religion, but effectively banned any one nation from attempting to impose its religion upon another. At the international level, in other words, there was agreement to disagree. Christian religious fervor itself—at least of the sort that had burned heretics, launched crusades, and so recently plunged Europe into civil war—fell into relative disrepute. The latter half of the seventeenth century saw what Herbert Butterfield (1900–1979), a major historian of Christianity in European history, once called "the Great Secularization." [11]

The old religious allegiances remained, but by slow degrees they began to matter less, even as national allegiance and national devotion—patriotism, as it came to be called—began to take on the moral gravity and ceremonial solemnity of religious commitment and the fallen soldier began to supplant the martyr. In 1689, John Locke published *A Letter Concerning Toleration*, in which he advanced the idea that a state would better guarantee peace within its borders by allowing many religions to flourish than by imposing any one of them. Locke favored a division of the affairs of religion as essentially private from the affairs of state as essentially public, capturing an attitudinal shift that was already in the air during the Enlightenment and would significantly mark the comparative study of religion as it took lastingly influential shape in the following century.

More intensely than by nascent toleration, the mood of the late seventeenth century was marked by wonder at the discoveries of natural science, above all those of Isaac Newton, whose major work establishing the laws of motion and universal gravitation was published in 1687. The poet Alexander Pope captured the popular mood in a famous couplet, written as Newton's epitaph (1730): "Nature, and Nature's Laws lay hid in Night. / God said, *Let Newton be!* and All was *Light*." Light was the master image of the Enlightenment—light, light, and "more light" (the legendary last words of Johann Wolfgang von Goethe [1749–1832]). Though the notion of natural law did not begin with Newton, his vision of the vast, calm, orderly, and implicitly benign operation of the laws of motion and gravity was unprecedented and gave new impetus to the search for comparable natural laws governing many other phenomena, including religion. Was there such a thing as a natural religion? If so, how did Christianity or any other actual religion relate to it? This idea, too, was pregnant with the promise of a future comparative study of religion.

While northern European Christianity was fighting the Wars of Religion, southern European Christianity had been transforming both the demography of Christendom and its understanding of the physical geography of the planet. The globe-spanning Portuguese and Spanish empires came into existence with speed comparable only to the Arab conquests of the seventh and eighth centuries. In evangelizing the Americas, the Portuguese and the Spaniards may have made Christianity for the first time the world's largest religion. In any case, their success in establishing colonial trading outposts along the African, Indian, Japanese, and Chinese coasts as well as founding the major Spanish colony of the Philippine Islands (named for the king of Spain) meant that European trade with India and China, above all the lucrative spice trade, no longer needed to pass through Muslim Central Asia or the Muslim Middle East.

Catholic missionaries did not have the success in Asia that they enjoyed in the Americas, yet the highly educated and culturally sophisticated Jesuit missionaries to Asia and the Americas became a significant factor in the evolving religious self-understanding of Europe itself. As extensive reports on the religions of Mexico, Peru, and above all India, China, and Japan reached Europe, they were published and read by many others besides the religious superiors for whom they had been written. Portugal and Spain had opened Europe's doors to a vastly enlarged world. The centuries-old quadripartite European division of the world's religions—Christianity, Judaism, Islam, and Paganism—was still generally in place in European minds. But from that point forward, as the sophistication of the religions of Asia and the Americas as well as the material and social brilliance of their civilizations came into focus, the inadequacy of *paganism* as a catchall term became evident, as did the need for new ways to speak of the newly recognized reality.

A New Reference Book Defines a New Field of Study

If any occasion can be singled out as the juncture when all these factors coalesced and produced a powerful new engagement with *world religions* in a way that approached the modern understanding of that phrase, it is the publication in Amsterdam between 1723 and 1737 of an epochal reference work, one that should indeed be seen as a direct ancestor of *The Norton Anthology of World Religions*. Appearing in seven sumptuous volumes comprising more than 3,000 pages with 250 pages of engravings, this encyclopedic production was *Religious Ceremonies and Customs of All the Peoples of the World* (*Cérémonies et coutumes religieuses de tous les peuples du monde*) by Jean Frédéric Bernard and Bernard Picart. Here, for the first time, was a presentation in one large work of all the religions of the world then known to Europe. Here, for the first time, was an attempt to reckon with how Europe's religious self-understanding would have to change in light of the previous two centuries of exploration, far-flung evangelization, and colonization.

It is important to note that this work, which was an immediate success and went through many editions and translations (and plagiarizations and piracies) over the next two hundred years, did not begin in the academic world and spread outward to the general public. Its address was directly to the general literate public—to the French public first, but quickly to other publics reading other languages. Jean Frédéric Bernard, brilliant but far from famous, was not just its behind-the-scenes research director, editor, and author: he was also its entrepreneurial publisher. It was a masterstroke on his part to secure the collaboration of Bernard Picart, already famous as an engraver producing reproductions of masterpiece paintings in an era before public art museums and long before photography, when what the public knew about art was limited to what they saw in church or what they acquired as engravings. By enabling the European public to see Picart's depictions of Aztec and Asian temples, costumes, and ceremonies, reconstructed from missionaries' descriptions, Bernard and Picart introduced the stimulating possibility of visual comparison. Where visual comparison led, philosophical and other critical comparison were intended to follow—and did.

As noted above, in the latter decades of the seventeenth century and the first of the eighteenth John Locke and a few other thinkers began to argue forcefully for religious toleration. Like Locke, Bernard and Picart were radical Calvinists as well as early "freethinkers," and the Netherlands was unique in their lifetimes as a haven for refugee dissidents and minorities of various kinds. Locke himself took refuge in the Netherlands during a turbulent and threatening period in England. Bernard's Huguenot (French Calvinist) family had fled to the Netherlands when Jean Frédéric was a boy. Picart, having abandoned Catholicism, moved there permanently as an adult, joining a large émigré French or French-speaking population in Amsterdam. The Peace of Westphalia, though it had imposed mutual forbearance in religious matters at the international level, had not done so at the national level. Protestants were still severely persecuted in France, as were Catholics in England. In the Netherlands, by contrast, though Calvinists were overwhelmingly dominant in public life, the private practice of Catholicism was indulged, while Jews were allowed public worship, and even deists or atheists had little to fear from the government. So it happened that though their great work was written in French, Bernard and Picart had good reason to publish it in the Netherlands.

In their magisterial account of the making of this work, *The Book That Changed Europe: Picart and Bernard's "Religious Ceremonies of the World,"* the historians Lynn Hunt, Margaret C. Jacob, and Wijnand Mijnhardt speculate about another possible consequence of its publication in the Netherlands—namely, the relative oblivion that overtook it in the twentieth century. The most populous European nations have tended to understand the intellectual history of the West through the minds of their own most influential thinkers, then through those of their major rivals, and only then through authors, however important, whose works were written or published in the smaller nations. Be that as it may, "Picart," as the work was commonly called, had two lasting effects far beyond the borders of the Netherlands. First, by discussing and illustrating the religions of Asia and of the Americas at length, it ended forever the quadripartite division of the world's religions that had structured European thought for eight hundred years. Second, it further solidified the conception of religion as a domain separable from culture and ethnicity. To quote *The Book That Changed Europe*, "This global survey of religious practices effectively *disaggregated and delimited* the sacred, making it specific to time, place, and institutions."[12]

There was now a greatly enlarged universe of religions to reckon with, to be sure, and Christian "teach ye all nations" missionary universalism had already mobilized to engage it. But also now, more strongly than ever, there was "religion" as an incipiently secular category capable of growth: it had lately been expanded by several new members and conceivably could be expanded further as further reports came in. The universalism of this emergent understanding of religion explains in part why the French Revolution, at the end of the eighteenth century, could presume to declare the "Rights of Man" rather than merely "of the [French] Citizen."

Bernard's and Picart's personal libraries suggest two favorite areas of reading: the ancient classics and travel books. The three historians note that 456 travel books were published in Europe in the fifteenth century, 1,566 in the seventeenth, and 3,540 in the eighteenth.[13] The co-creators' reading in the classics put them in touch with that pluralism of the mind made possible by the Renaissance recovery of classical moral philosophy and by the humanists' imaginative participation in the beliefs that figure so largely in classical literature. Their avid reading of travel reports gave them the enlarged geographical awareness made possible by the age of exploration.

As an early theorist of religion in this transformed mise-en-scène, Bernard blended elements of deist "natural religion" with classic Protestantism. His discussion of the religious customs of the world was scholastically Protestant in its combination of meticulous footnotes and sometimes-strenuous argumentation. More important for its later influence, Bernard's discussion was structurally Protestant in that it cast contemporary religious practice, wherever it was observed around the world, as the corruption of an earlier purity. But where sixteenth-century Protestantism had seen the purity of primitive Christianity, Bernard, writing in the full flush of eighteenth-century enthusiasm for natural science, saw the purity of an early, universal, natural, and "true" religion corrupted by the variously scheming priests of the religions reviewed. Despite this structural Calvinism in their philosophy of religion, Bernard and Picard were indebted to John Locke as well as to John Calvin; and especially when the non-Christian religions were under discussion, their manner was more often expository than forensic.

There is no doubt that Bernard discusses and Picart illustrates the religious customs and ceremonies of the world on the assumption both that each religion is, like Christianity, a separate, practice-defined domain and that these domains are all comparable. For better and for worse, the two of them contributed massively to the establishment of "religion" as a category projecting elements of Christian identity upon the vast, newly discovered worlds that lay beyond Christendom. Discussing Bernard and Picart's treatment of indigenous American religion, Hunt, Jacobs, and Mijnhardt declare:

> In short, Picart's images, especially when read alongside Bernard's text, *essentially created the category "religion."* Whereas the text sometimes wandered off on tangents about the sources of particular ceremonies, the similarities between rituals across space (Jewish and Catholic) and time (Roman antiquity and American Indian), or the disputes between scholars on the origins of different peoples, the images kept the focus on the most commonly found religious ceremonies—birth, marriage, death rituals, and grand processions—or on the most strikingly different practices,

> which could range from the arcane procedures for the election of popes in Rome to human sacrifice in Mexico. Implicitly, the images transformed religion from a question of truth revealed to a select few of God's peoples (the Jews, the Catholics, and then the Protestants) to an issue of comparative social practices.[14]

The charge of Christian projection can plausibly be lodged against Picart and Bernard's interpretation of particular non-Christian rituals through their nearest equivalents in Christianity or Western antiquity. And yet if such habits of mind were limiting, they were scarcely crippling; and for Picart and Bernard themselves, they were evidently enabling and energizing. Is it true to say that between them, these two "essentially created the category 'religion'"? If they did so, we would claim, they did so largely through the convergence in their work and in themselves of the complex heritage that we have tried to sketch above.

Picart and Bernard carry forward the age-old, often suppressed, but never entirely forgotten understanding of the church as a thing in itself, not to be confounded with any nation or any set of cultural habits or practices. They carry forward the relatively subversive late medieval assumption that philosophy provides a neutral standpoint from which all religions may be compared. When considering religions remote from them in space rather than in time, they carry forward the Renaissance habit of drawing freely on classical paganism interpreted with textual sophistication and literary sympathy. They collate, as no one before them had yet done, the reports streaming into Europe about the religions of Asia and the Americas and, in their most brilliant stroke, they make these the basis for a major artistic effort to *see* what had been reported. They apply to their undertaking a distinct blend of moral seriousness, commercial enterprise, and erudite documentary attention to the particulars of religious practice that is their legacy from French Calvinist Protestantism. Finally, as sons of the Enlightenment, they bring a pioneering openness and breadth of vision to what they study.

Bernard can seem genuinely and intentionally prophetic when he writes:

> All religions resemble each other in something. It is this resemblance that encourages minds of a certain boldness to risk the establishment of a project of universal syncretism. How beautiful it would be to arrive at that point and to be able to make people with an overly opinionated character understand that with the help of charity one finds everywhere *brothers*.[15]

The place of good will—the sheer *novelty* of good will—in the study of religion has received far less attention than it deserves. Bernard's dream may seem commonplace now, when courteous interfaith dialogue is familiar enough in much of the West, but it was far from commonplace when he dreamed it.

Like *The Norton Anthology of World Religions*, Bernard and Picart's great work attended first and foremost to rituals and practices, considering beliefs only as expressed or embedded in these. Their work was path-breaking not just as a summary of what was then known about the religions of the world but also as an early demonstration of what sympathetic, participative imagination would later attain in the study of religion.

In painting their portraits of the religions of the world and in dreaming Bernard's dream ("How beautiful it would be . . . !"), Bernard and Picart were at the same time painting their own intellectual self-portrait as representative Europeans—neither clerics nor philosophers but thoughtful professionals—avid to engage in the comparison of the religions of the world on the widest possible scale. Religious comparison did not begin with them, nor had they personally created the intellectual climate in Europe that welcomed religious comparison once they so grandly attempted it. But it is not too much to say that in their day and to some significant degree because of them, Christian Europe finally learned how to compare religions.

Broadening the Foundation, Raising the Roof: 1737–1893

In 1737, when Picart and Bernard completed their work, Europe had barely discovered Australia. The peoples of the Arctic and of Oceania were living in nearly unbroken isolation. And even among peoples well-known to Europe, Japan was a forbidden kingdom, while China's first engagement with the West had only recently come to a xenophobic close. India was becoming relatively familiar, yet the doors of many smaller nations or regions remained barred. Europe had not yet lost its North and South American colonies to revolution; its later, nineteenth-century colonialist "scramble for Africa" had not yet begun. Russia had not yet expanded eastward to the Pacific. The English colonies in North America had not yet become the United States or expanded westward to the Pacific. The enlarged world that Bernard and Picart had sought to encapsulate in their illustrated reference work had many enlargements ahead, with corresponding consequences for the study of religion.

Though the intellectual framework for a global and comparative study of religion was essentially in place among an intellectual elite in Europe by the middle of the eighteenth century, much of even the known religious world remained culturally unexplored because the local languages were not understood. The accepted chronology within which Europeans situated new cultural and religious discoveries did not extend to any point earlier than the earliest events spoken of in the Old Testament. All this was to change during the century and a half that separates the publication of Picart from the convocation of the first World's Parliament of Religions at the 1893 Columbian Exposition in Chicago. That date may serve to mark the entrance of the United States of America into the story we have been telling and will bring us to the more immediate antecedents of *The Norton Anthology of World Religions.*

Broadening the Textual Base

Of special relevance for our work as anthologists is the enormous broadening of the textual foundation for religious studies that occurred during this long period. To review that transformation, we will consider the pivotal roles played by four European linguistic prodigies: F. Max Müller (1823–1900), James Legge (1815–1897), Sir William Jones (1746–1794), and Eugène Burnouf (1801–1852). One may grasp at a glance the scope of the documentary change that took place during the 150 years that followed the publication of Bernard and Picart's *Religious Ceremonies and Customs of All the Peoples of the World* by looking forward to the London publication between 1879 and 1910 of *The Sacred Books of the East* in no fewer than fifty volumes.

This enormous reference work, a superlative and in some regards still unsurpassed academic achievement, was produced under the general editorship of F. Max Müller, a German expatriate long resident in England. Müller's role in the nineteenth-century evolution of the disciplines of both comparative linguistics and comparative religious studies is large, but for the moment what concerns us is the sheer scope of the landmark reference work that he edited: two dozen volumes on Hinduism and Jainism translated into English from Sanskrit; nine on Buddhism alike from Sanskrit, from Pali (the canonical language of Indian Buddhism), and from other Asian languages; seven from Chinese on Confucianism, Daoism, and Chinese Buddhism; eight from Persian on Zoroastrianism; and two from Arabic on Islam. The range is astonishing, given that at the time when Bernard and Picart were writing and engraving, knowledge of *any* of these languages, even Arabic, was rare to nonexistent in Europe. How did Europeans learn them over the intervening century and a half? What motivated them to do so? The story blends missionary daring, commercial ambition, and sheer linguistic prowess in different proportions at different times.

Let us begin with Chinese. The first two modern Europeans known to have mastered Chinese were the Italian Jesuit missionaries Michele Ruggieri (1543–1607) and the preternaturally gifted Matteo Ricci (1552–1610), who entered China from the Portuguese island colony of Macao. Over time, as French Jesuits largely succeeded their Italian brethren in the Jesuit mission to China, the reports that they sent back to France about Qing dynasty (1644–1912) culture and the Confucian scholars they encountered stimulated French and broader European curiosity both about China itself and about the Chinese language. Though the Vatican terminated the Jesuits' Chinese mission on doctrinal grounds and though the Qing dynasty suppressed further Christian missionary work and expelled the missionaries themselves in 1724, a seed had been planted. In retirement on Macao, the French Jesuit Joseph Henri Marie de Prémare would compose the first-ever Chinese grammar in 1729. Later, during the nineteenth century, as Britain forced a weakening Qing dynasty to sign a treaty establishing coastal enclaves or "treaty ports" under British control, British Protestants commenced a new round of missionary activity in China, including the first attempt to translate the Bible into Chinese.

James Legge, originally a Scottish missionary to China, building on de Prémare's grammar and working with the help of Chinese Christians, undertook a major effort to translate the principal Confucian, Daoist, and Chinese Buddhist classics into English, always with the ultimate intention of promoting Christianity. Meanwhile, in 1814, Europe's first chair of Chinese and Manchu was established at the Collège de France. In 1822, Jean-Pierre Abel-Rémusat published in France a formal grammar of Chinese intended not for missionaries alone but for all interested European students. Legge himself became Oxford University's first professor of Chinese in 1876, and near the end of his life he was F. Max Müller's principal collaborator for Chinese texts in *The Sacred Books of the East.*

European penetration into China proceeded almost entirely from offshore islands or coastal enclaves under European colonial control; China as a whole never became a Western colony. India, by contrast, did indeed become a Western colony—specifically, a British colony—and the West's acquisition of the Indian languages and first encounter with the Indian religious classics is largely a British story. From the sixteenth through the early eighteenth century, Portuguese, Dutch, French, and British commercial interests vied for primacy in the lucrative Indian market. By late in the eighteenth century, however, Britain had overtaken all European rivals and established India, including what is now Pakistan, as its most important future colony—more lucrative at the time than the thirteen North American colonies that would become the United States of America. Britain's colonial motives were originally commercial rather than either evangelical or academic, but after British commercial and political control was firmly established in the Indian subcontinent, first cultural and linguistic explorations and then Christian missionary activity would follow.

In the launch of Sanskrit studies in the West, no figure looms larger than Sir William Jones, an Anglo-Welsh jurist in Calcutta who was at least as prodigiously gifted in language study as Matteo Ricci or James Legge. Fascinated by all things Indian, Jones founded an organization, the Asiatic Society, to foster Indian studies; and in 1786, on its third anniversary, he delivered a historic lecture on the history of language itself. In it, he expounded the thesis that Sanskrit, Greek, Latin, most of the European vernacular languages, and probably Persian were all descendants of a vanished common ancestor. Today, linguistic scholarship takes for granted the reality of "Proto-Indo-European" as a lost ancient language whose existence is the only conceivable explanation for the similarities that Jones may not have been the very first to chart but was certainly the first to bring to a large European public.

Jones's lecture detonated an explosion of European interest in studying Sanskrit and in tracing the family tree of the Indo-European, or "Aryan," languages, including all the languages mentioned in the previous paragraph but notably excluding Hebrew and Arabic—descendants of a different linguistic ancestor, later postulated as Proto-Semitic. (In the Bible, it is from Noah's son Shem—*Sēm* in Greek—that the peoples of the Middle East are descended—whence the term *Sem*-itic.) Now, the New Testament had been written in Greek rather than Hebrew or Aramaic, and Western Christianity had quickly left its Aramaic-speaking Palestinian antecedents behind and become a Greek-speaking Mediterranean religion. Did that mean that Christianity was actually Indo-European, or "Aryan," rather than Semitic, even though Jesus and Paul were Jews? This became one cultural strand within the European enthusiasm for Sanskrit studies, as further discussed below. Suffice it to say for now that it was during this period that *Semitic* and *Semitism* were coined as linguistic terms and the anti-Jewish *anti-Semitic* and *anti-Semitism* were coined as prejudicial, pseudo-anthropological counterterms.

Of greater immediate importance for the broadening of the study of religion was the window that Sanskrit opened on an almost unimaginably vast Indian literature whose most ancient and venerated texts, the Vedas, may be as old as, or even older than, the oldest strata of the Old Testament. Sanskrit is the classical language of India, no longer spoken and perhaps artificially perfected as a sacred language at some unrecoverable point in the past. But India has in addition a great many vernacular languages, more of them than Europe has, and in a number of these languages, other extensive Hindu literatures exist. These, too, gradually came to light in the nineteenth and the early twentieth century as knowledge of the relevant languages gradually spread to Europe.

India, for all its immense internal variety, did and does have a sense of itself as a single great place and of its gods as the gods of that place. Siddhartha Gautama, the Buddha, was born in India, and Indian Buddhism was the first Buddhism. Buddhist texts in Sanskrit are foundational for all students of Buddhism. But after some centuries had passed, Buddhism largely died out in India, living on in Sri Lanka, Southeast Asia, China, Korea, Japan, Mongolia, and Tibet. The linguistic and cultural variety of these countries was enormous. The Buddha was not called by the same name in all of them (in China, for example, he was called "Fo"). Western travelers, not knowing the languages of any of the countries where Buddhism was dominant, were slow to recognize even such basic facts as that the Buddha himself was a historical personage and not simply one among the many deities and demons whose statues they saw in their travels.

Donald S. Lopez, Jr., Buddhism editor for *The Norton Anthology of World Religions*, has written or edited several books telling the fascinating tale of how the puzzle of international Buddhism slowly yielded to the painstaking Western acquisition of several difficult languages and the related gradual recovery of a second, astoundingly large multilingual religious literature standing alongside that of Hinduism. In his *From Stone to Flesh: A Short History of the Buddha* (2013), Lopez allows what we might call the statue story—the gradual realization that sculptures of the Buddha represented a man, not a god—to become the human face on this much larger and less visible story of literary and historical recovery.[16]

In the story of how a broad textual foundation was laid for the study of Buddhism, a third linguistic genius stands between the Anglo-Welsh William Jones and the expatriate German F. Max Müller—namely, the French polymath Eugène Burnouf, the last of the four gifted linguists mentioned near the start of this section. Because of the enthusiasm for Sanskrit studies that Jones had touched off in Europe, copies of texts in Sanskrit began reaching European "orientalists" during the first decades of the nineteenth century. Those that arrived from India itself, as they were translated, would enable the assembly of the twenty-one volumes of Hindu texts that open Müller's *Sacred Books of the East.* Initially, however, no Sanskrit texts dealing with Buddhism were forthcoming from the Indian subcontinent. This situation would change, thanks to the fortuitous posting of an energetic and culturally alert English officer, Brian Houghton Hodgson (1801?–1894), to Nepal, where Buddhism thrived. Hodgson collected dozens of Nepalese Buddhist texts in Sanskrit, including the crucially important *Lotus Sutra*, and arranged for copies to be shipped to Europe.

Burnouf had been appointed to the Sanskrit chair at the Collège de France five years before the first shipment from Hodgson arrived. Thanks in part to earlier work he had done in the study of Pali, the Indian language in which the oldest Buddhist texts survive, Burnouf seems to have quickly grasped that what he had before him was the key to the historical roots of Buddhism in India. But this recognition was father to the further insight that Buddhism was the first true world religion (or, as he was inclined to think, the first internationally embraced moral philosophy) in human history. Burnouf was among the first, if not the very first, to see Buddhism whole. His 1844 *Introduction à l'histoire du Buddhisme indien* (*Introduction to the History of Indian Buddhism*) was the first of a projected four volumes that, had he lived to write them, would surely have been his greatest work. The one lengthy volume that he did bring to completion was already of epoch-making importance, particularly in light of his influence on his student F. Max Müller.

What the discovery and European importation of the classical religious literatures of India and China meant for the comparative study of religion in the West can be signaled concisely in the terms *Confucianism*, *Daoism* (earlier, *Taoism*), *Hinduism*, and *Buddhism*. They are all Western coinages, hybrids combining an Asian word at the front end and the Greek morpheme *–ism* at the back end, and each represents the abstraction of a separate domain of religious literature and religious practice from the cultural and ethnic contexts in which it originated. The coinage of these terms themselves may not coincide exactly with the recovery of the respective literatures; but to the extent that nineteenth-century Western scholarship viewed the texts as the East's equivalent of the Bible, it all but unavoidably engaged them on structurally Christian and even Protestant terms, thereby furthering the European conception of each related *–ism* as a religion in Europe's now consolidated and universalist sense of the word.

Structurally, Protestant influence was apparent again whenever, in the manner of Bernard and Picart, the great nineteenth-century linguist-historians judged the early texts to be superior to the later ones. Thus, in the interpretation of newly available Chinese texts, the earlier, more interior or "philosophical" versions of Daoism and Confucianism were often judged superior to the later, more ceremonial or "religious" versions, in which Laozi or Kongzi (Confucius) seemed to be deified or quasi-deified. Similarly, in the nineteenth-century interpretation of Hindu literature, India's British colonial rulers celebrated the supposed nobility and purity of the early Vedas and Upanishads while disparaging later Hindu religious texts and especially actual nineteenth-century Hindu practice. In the Buddhist instance, Eugène Burnouf set the early, human, historical Indian Buddha—whom he understood to have preached an ethics of simplicity and compassion—against the later, superhuman metaphysical Buddha. Consciously or unconsciously, Burnouf's contrast of the historical and the metaphysical Buddha coincided strikingly with the contrast then being drawn for a wide Christian audience between the historical Jesus of Nazareth and the divine God incarnate of Christian faith.

In short, as this new, broadened textual foundation was laid for the documentary study of Hinduism, Buddhism, and Daoism, a Christian theology of scripture and a post-Protestant philosophy of history were often projected upon it by the brilliant but Eurocentric scholars who were shaping the field. However, once primary texts are in hand, their intrinsic power can exert itself against any given school of interpretation. Thus, for example, late twentieth-century scholarship began to foreground and valorize the late and the popular over the early and the elite in several traditions, dignifying texts and practices once thought unworthy of serious scholarly attention.

Though nineteenth-century scholars might shudder at such a shift, it is essentially to them that we owe the availability of the key texts themselves. To be sure, the full recovery and the translation of these literatures are works in progress; nonetheless, knowledge of their great antiquity and their scope—barely even dreamed of by Picart and Bernard—was substantially complete by the end of the nineteenth century. The literary foundation had been put in place for an enormously enlarged effort at comparative study.

Enlarging the Chronological Frame

As already noted, Europeans as late as the early nineteenth century situated new cultural and religious discoveries, including all the texts whose recovery we have been discussing, in a chronology of religion understood to commence no earlier than the earliest events spoken of in the Old Testament. This framework led to efforts, comical in retrospect, to link newly discovered places and newly encountered legends or historical memories in Asia and the Americas to place-names in the book of Genesis, to the Noah story of Genesis 6–9, and to legends about the eastward travels of the apostles of Christ. All this would change with a discovery that might be described as blowing the roof off recorded history.

During Napoleon Bonaparte's occupation of Egypt in 1798–99, a French soldier stationed near the town of Rosetta in the Nile delta discovered a large stone bearing an inscription in three scripts: first, ancient Egyptian hieroglyphics, a script that no one then could read; second, another unknown script, which turned out to represent a later form of the Egyptian language; and finally, a third script, Greek. It took two decades of work, but in 1822, Jean-François Champollion deciphered this "Rosetta Stone." In the ensuing decades, his breakthrough enabled later scholars to translate hundreds of ancient Egyptian hieroglyphic inscriptions recovered from the ruins of ancient Egypt's immense tombs and temples and to discover, as they did so, that the Egyptians had maintained a remarkably complete chronology stretching back millennia before the oldest historical events recorded in the Bible. Decades of archaeological excavation in Egypt further enabled the construction of a chronological typology of Egyptian pottery. And then, since Egyptian pottery and pottery fragments are found all over the ancient Near East in mounds (tells) left by the repeated destruction and reconstruction of cities on the same sites, Egyptian pottery could be used to date sites far removed from Egypt. Over time, the Egyptian chronology would become the anchor for a chronological reconstruction of the entire lost history of the Near East, much of it written on thousands of archaeologically recovered clay tablets inscribed in the Mesopotamian cuneiform script that at the start of the eighteenth century was as undecipherable as Egyptian hieroglyphic.

The cuneiform (literally, "wedge-shaped") writing system was used as early as the late fourth millennium B.C.E. for the representation of Sumerian, a mysterious language without known antecedents or descendants. Sumeria, the oldest civilization of the ancient Near East—situated near the southern tip of Iraq, just north of the Persian Gulf—appears to have invented cuneiform writing. Most extant cuneiform texts, however, survive as small tablets representing several ancient Semitic languages rather than Sumerian. Starting in the mid-nineteenth century, hundreds of thousands of cuneiform tablets were recovered by archaeological excavations nearly as important as those in Egypt.

Cuneiform was deciphered thanks to the discovery in Persia in 1835 of a trilingual set of incised cuneiform wall inscriptions in Behistun (Bisitun, Iran) that, like the Rosetta Stone, included one already-known language—in this case ancient Persian—that scholars were eventually able to recognize behind the mysterious script. The challenge lay in going beyond the Persian of that inscription to decipher the language—now known to be the Mesopotamian Semitic language Akkadian—represented by one of the other two inscriptions. Though Eugène Burnouf played almost as important a role in this decipherment as he played in the recovery of Indian Buddhism, it is Henry Rawlinson, the British East India Company officer who first visited the Behistun inscriptions in 1835, whose name is usually linked to the recovery for European scholarship of the lost cuneiform literatures of Mesopotamia.

None of the now-extinct religions whose literatures survive in cuneiform is anthologized in *The Norton Anthology of World Religions*; we have chosen only major, living international religions. But the recovery of these lost literatures significantly affected the evolving historical context for all religious comparison. What these texts made clear was that recorded history had not dawned in Athens and Jerusalem. The religion of ancient Israel, in particular, was relocated from the dawn of history to a late morning hour, and thus could no longer be seen as in any sense the ancient ancestor of all the religions of the world. On the contrary, it now became possible to study the Bible itself comparatively, as a text contemporaneous with other texts, produced by a religion contemporaneous with and comparable to other ancient Semitic religions. And since the Bible is an anthology produced over a millennium, it became possible and even imperative to study each stratum within the Bible as contemporaneous with differing sets of non-Israelite religions and their respective texts.

European Protestantism, accustomed since the Reformation to employing the Bible as a historically reliable criterion for criticizing and revising the inherited practices of Christianity, was deeply affected by the discovery of both prebiblical and contemporaneous extrabiblical literatures, for they were clearly a way to deepen the historical understanding of the Bible. But the recovery of these literatures, set alongside related evidence from archaeological excavation, was a threat as well as an opportunity. It was an opportunity because it enabled illuminating comparisons of key motifs in Hebrew mythology with their counterparts in other ancient Near Eastern mythologies; it was a threat because though it corroborated the historicity of some biblical events, it undermined that of others.

Arguably, religious truth can be conveyed as well through fiction as through history. Patristic and medieval Christianity had been content for centuries to search the Bible for moral allegories rather than for historical evidence. Where history was not a central concern, comparative Semitic studies could and did enrich the linguistic and literary interpretation of the Bible without impugning its religious authority. But because Protestantism, rejecting allegorical interpretation, had consistently emphasized and valorized the historical content of the Bible, Protestant Christianity had particular trouble entertaining the notion that the Bible could be historically false in some regards and yet still religiously valid. A desire to defend the Old Testament as historically valid thus arose as a second motivation for Semitic studies. In the process, the prestige of the study of history itself as an intellectual discipline able to produce authoritative judgments about religion was significantly enhanced if not indeed somewhat inflated.

The discovery of the Rosetta Stone and the Behistun inscriptions affected the comparative study of Islam as well, though less directly. The recovery of lost Semitic languages and their lost literatures invited comparative linguistic study of the now-increased number of languages clearly related to Aramaic, Hebrew, and Arabic—the three principal languages of this family that were already known at the end of the eighteenth century. This study led to the postulated existence of a lost linguistic ancestor, Proto-Semitic, from which they were all plausibly descended. Proto-Semitic then began to play a role in the study of the religions practiced by the peoples who spoke these languages, somewhat like the role that Proto-Indo-European was playing in the study of the religions practiced by the peoples who spoke Sanskrit, Greek, Latin, German, and the other languages of that linguistic family.

As Proto-Semitic was reconstructed, moreover, it became clear to scholars that classical Arabic, the Arabic of the Qur'an, resembled it very closely and thus was an extremely ancient language that preserved almost the entire morphology of the lost ancestor of all the Semitic languages. Classical Hebrew, by contrast, was shown to be a much younger Semitic language. In an era of so much speculation about the relationship between ancient religions and ancient languages, the near-identity of classical Arabic and Proto-Semitic suggested to some that Islam might have preserved and carried forward ancient features of a Semitic proto-religion that was the lost ancestor of all the Semitic religions, just as Proto-Semitic was the lost ancestor of all the Semitic languages.

Orientalism, Neo-Hellenism, and the Quest for the Historical Jesus

The emergence of "Semitic languages" and "Semitic religions" as groups whose members were identifiable through comparison meant that biblical studies and Qur'anic studies—or more generally the study of ancient Israel and that of pre- and proto-Islamic Arabia—were more closely linked in the nineteenth century than they usually are in the twenty-first. Julius Wellhausen (1844–1918), a major German biblical scholar, reconstructed the formative stages of both. Historical linguists in Wellhausen's day who engaged in such comparative study of languages and history were called "orientalists." *Orientalism* is a term now associated with cultural condescension to the peoples of a region extending from Turkey through Persia to the borders of Afghanistan; but when first coined, it connoted primarily a stance of neutral comparison across that large cultural realm, a realm that the study of the languages, ancient and modern, had now thrown open for historical study as never before.

Interest in the language and history of classical Greece also grew enormously in nineteenth-century Europe, fed both by Hellenic revivalism and by Christian anxiety. The upper class generally celebrated Greek literature and thought as expressing a humane ideal distinct from and even superior to that of Christianity. In the late eighteenth century, in his *The History of the Decline and Fall of the Roman Empire* (1776–88), the English historian Edward Gibbon had already presented the emergence of Christianity as in itself the key factor in the decline of a superior classical civilization; Gibbon elevated the nobility and civic virtue of republican Rome above the faith, hope, and charity of Pauline Christianity as celebrated by classic Protestantism.

In the nineteenth century, it was Greece rather than Rome that defined the cultural beau ideal for an intellectual elite across western Europe. The German philosopher Friedrich Nietzsche (1844–1900), a classicist by training, was steeped in this philo-Hellenic tradition and drew heavily upon it for his well-known critique of Christianity. In its devout classicism, nineteenth-century European culture thus continued and intensified a celebration of an idealized and indeed a more or less mythologized Greece that had begun during the Renaissance and continued during the Enlightenment.

This European cultural identification with Greece, whether or not tinged with antipathy toward Christianity, sometimes worked symbiotically with a larger geographical/cultural identification already mentioned—namely, Europe's identification with the larger world of the Indo-European peoples as distinct from and superior to the disparaged Semitic peoples, most notably the Jews. Religiously motivated Christian prejudice against Jews had by no means disappeared, but it was now joined by a form of pseudo-scientific racism that made more of national than of religious difference. Because nationalist self-glorification linked to invidious anti-Semitism had a seriously distorting effect on the comparative study of religion in nineteenth-century Europe, the full enfranchisement of Europe's Jews as fellow scholars would have, as we will see, a comparably important corrective effect.

A second motivation for classical studies, especially in Lutheran Germany, was Christian: an urgently felt need to write the still-unwritten history of the New Testament in the context of first-century Hellenistic Judaism. The historical reliability of the New Testament had been the foundation of the Lutheran critique of sixteenth-century Catholicism. But nineteenth-century New Testament scholars now claimed to recognize adulterations by the church within the Gospels themselves. To exaggerate only slightly, the challenge that nineteenth-century Protestant scholars saw themselves facing was to recover the historical Jesus from the church-corrupted Gospels in the same way that they understood the sixteenth-century reformers to have recovered the historical practice of Christianity from the corrupted church practice of their day.

"Historical Jesus" scholarship of this sort grew enormously in scope and erudition during the first decades of the nineteenth century, fed by the growing prestige of history as a social science and climaxing with the publication in 1835–36 of David Friedrich Strauss's massive, learned, sensationally successful, but scandalously skeptical *Life of Jesus, Critically Examined*, a German work that appeared in English in 1846 in an anonymous translation by the aspiring English novelist George Eliot (Marian Evans). Decades of further scholarship followed, some of it indirectly stimulated once again by archaeology. As the excavations by Heinrich Schliemann (1822–1890) proved that there was a Troy and that a great war had occurred there, thus allegedly proving the historical reliability of the *Iliad*, so, it was hoped, further archaeological and historical research might yet demonstrate the historical reliability of the New Testament.

A denouement occurred in 1906 with the publication of the German first edition of Albert Schweitzer's epoch-making *The Quest of the Historical Jesus.*[17] Schweitzer believed that the quest for the historical Jesus had actually succeeded as history. Yet the recovered historical Jesus was more a problem for contemporary Christianity than a solution, the renowned scholar ruefully concluded. Schweitzer's work continues to haunt historical Jesus scholarship, even though fresh quests and fresh alleged recoveries of the lost historical Jesus, both learned and popular, have continued to appear.

In sum, narrowly Christian though the quest for the historical Jesus may seem, it did much to establish historical study as the default mode of religious study. Its shadow lies across studies of the historical Buddha, the historical Laozi, and the historical Muhammad, among others, stamping them all with the assumption that in the study of any religious tradition, historical truth will prove the indisputable form of truth.

The Haskalah and Its Impact on the Comparative Study of Religion

The character of the literature of religious studies is determined as much by who is writing as by what is written about. So far, we have concentrated on changes in what was available as subject matter to be written about, thanks to the recovery of religious literatures either lost in time or remote in place. We turn now to a new line of inquiry and a new question: Who was to be commissioned to conduct the study, to do the writing, to tell the story of the religions of the world? In the late eighteenth and the nineteenth centuries, above all in Germany, a Jewish religious, cultural, and intellectual movement called the *Haskalah* emerged, one of whose effects would be the historic enfranchisement of Jews as, for the first time, full participants in Europe's comparative study of religion. Before saying more about the impact of the Haskalah upon secular religious studies in Europe, we should briefly review its direct and complex impact upon the Jews of Europe themselves.

Religiously, thanks in good measure to the pathbreaking work of the Jewish-German philosopher Moses Mendelssohn (1729–1786), the Haskalah gave rise to Reform Judaism as a revised form of Jewish belief and practice more attentive to the Tanakh, or Hebrew Bible (Christianity's Old Testament), than to the Talmud. However uncontroversial it may seem in the twenty-first century for the reformers to honor the biblical prophets rather than the Talmudic sages as the ethical pinnacle of the Jewish tradition, the shift was highly disruptive in the late eighteenth and the nineteenth centuries, for the emphasis in Jewish religious practice until then had been squarely on the Talmud and on the rabbinical sages whose debates, preserved in the Talmud, had made the rabbinate the final authority in Jewish religious observance. In the rabbinic tradition, the Talmud is the heart of the "Oral Torah" that Moses, the original rabbi (teacher), received from God and conveyed in speech to his first (rabbinical) students, beginning a teacher-to-student chain that legitimated the rabbinate as authoritative. To undercut the Talmud, Rabbinic Judaism's foundational second scripture, was thus to undercut the rabbis themselves.

Reform Judaism was religiously unsettling in another way because by going back to the Bible, thereby setting aside centuries of venerable Jewish tradition and subverting established rabbinical religious authority, its founders, beginning with Moses Mendelssohn, delivered a critique that bore a striking structural resemblance to German Lutheranism's back-to-the-Bible critique of Roman Catholicism. The Jewish reformation looked rather like the Christian, to the exhilaration of many Jews at the time in Lutheran northern Germany but to the consternation of others.

Religiously disruptive in these ways, the Haskalah—often referred to as the Jewish Enlightenment—represented as well a major turning point in Jewish European cultural life, away from oppressive and once inescapable social restriction and confinement. The *Maskilim*, as the leaders of the Haskalah were called, recognized that the dawn of a culture of toleration in Christian Europe might just light the path to an escape for Jews who were willing to acculturate in certain manageable ways. Mendelssohn himself, for example, became an acknowledged master of literary German as written by the intellectual elite of Berlin. German culture was then entering its most brilliant century. In an earlier century, German Jews would have had to become Christians to exit the ghetto and take part. But absent the requirement to convert, perhaps German Jews could become Jewish Germans. Such was the tacit hope of the Haskalah.

As Reform Judaism grew in popularity, thousands of Jews gambled that the ghetto walls were indeed coming down, and ultimately they were not mistaken. Despite the murderous anti-Semitism that would rise in the later nineteenth century and the genocide that would so profoundly scar the twentieth, a page had been turned for good in Western academic life—not least in the comparative study of religion.

For this anthology, the Haskalah mattered in one further, only slightly narrower regard: while no longer deferring to the immense corpus of rabbinic literature as authoritative, the Maskilim did not ignore it. On the contrary, they began to apply to it the same techniques of critical scholarship that the Renaissance had pioneered and that Protestantism and the Enlightenment had further developed for the interpretation of the Bible and other classical texts. The process of critically editing and translating the rabbinic literature, which placed yet another major religious literature within the reach of secular study, began very slowly and approached completion only in the twentieth century. Yet were it not for the Maskilim, that great work would not have been undertaken.

Most important of all, however, was the inclusion of Christianity's original "other" in the corps of those attempting in the West to make comparative sense of the religions of the world. This inclusion was truly a watershed event, for it foreshadowed a long list of subsequent, cumulatively transformative inclusions of the previously excluded. Religious studies in the twenty-first century is open to all qualified participants, but such has not always been the case. Broadening the textual basis for religious studies and exploding the temporal frame around it were important nineteenth-century developments. Broadening the composition of the population that would engage in religious studies was even more important.

The gradual inclusion of non-Christian scholars in the Western discussion of world religions has not entailed retiring the historically Christian but now secularized concept of religion (or the related concept of world religions), but Christian or Western scholars have lost any presumptive right to serve as moderators or hosts of the discussion. The overcoming of insufferable condescension, not to speak of outright prejudice, has played a part, but so too, and more importantly, have matters of perception, perspective, and the "othering" of Christianity: the rest had long been accustomed to see themselves through the eyes of the West; now the West has begun to see itself through the eyes of the rest.

The dynamic entry of Europe's Jews not just into the European study of religion but also into many other areas of European life brought about a massive backlash in the late nineteenth century, then the Nazi genocide in the twentieth, the post–World War II triumph of Zionism, and belatedly, among other consequences, a distinct mood of remorse and repentance in late twentieth-century European Christianity.[18] Somewhat analogous emotions accompanied the end of European colonialism during the same late twentieth-century decades amid exposés of the exploitation and humiliation suffered by the colonized. The comparative study of religion has both influenced and been influenced by these ongoing revisionist shifts of mood and opinion, but, to repeat, the first steps down this long path were taken by and during the Haskalah.

Evolution and the Comparative Study of Religion

While the decipherment of Egyptian hieroglyphic and Mesopotamian cuneiform were still throwing new light on the earliest centuries of recorded history, Charles Darwin's *On the Origin of Species by Means of Natural Selection* in 1859 and *The Descent of Man, and Selection in Relation to Sex* in 1871 shone a beam into the deeper darkness of the unrecorded, biological prehistory of the human species. At the time, no one, including Darwin, knew just how old *Homo sapiens* was as a species; the technique of absolute dating by the measurement of radioactive decay would not be developed until the mid-twentieth century. What Darwin could already demonstrate from the fossil record, however, was that the human species had evolved from earlier species in a process that antedated recorded history. The implications of this discovery for all forms of scientific and historical investigation were enormous and are still being explored. For the study of religion, the discovery meant that behind the religions of recorded history, there now stood in principle all the religions of human prehistory. At what point in human evolution did religion first appear, or was that even the right question? Should the question rather be about precursors to religion—earlier behaviors that would evolve into what we now call religion? How, if at all, could the practitioners of these prehistoric proto-religions or precursors to religion be studied?

Answers to that question are still being devised, but none involves their texts, for they left none. Tempting as it would be to explore new work being done on the evolution of religion before the invention of writing, such work is not properly a part of the study of religion to which *The Norton Anthology of World Religions* contributes, for ours is, after all, a collection of texts. We know that the human species emerged some two hundred thousand years ago in southwest Africa and migrated from there eastward and then northward through the Great Rift Valley in what appear to be two noteworthy spikes. One spike proceeded by way of Lake Victoria up the Nile River to where its delta empties into the Mediterranean Sea. The other spike crossed from Africa to Arabia at the Strait of Bab el Mandeb and then proceeded along the southeast coast of Arabia to the Strait of Hormuz, where it crossed into Asia. From there, one stream of human migrants veered northward to the delta of the Tigris River at the upper end of the Persian Gulf, while the other moved southward to the delta of the Indus River. The Indus delta and the river system above it cradled the civilization that, as it moved south into the Indian subcontinent, would produce the Vedas, written in Sanskrit, the earliest scriptures of ancient India. The Nile and the Tigris deltas and the river systems that lay above them would together define the "Fertile Crescent" within which ancient Israel would produce the earliest Hebrew scriptures. The invention of writing in the Tigris delta (Sumer) and the Nile Valley (Egypt) does not antedate the late fourth millennium B.C.E. The oldest works honored as scripture by Hinduism or by Judaism may be a full millennium younger than that. As recoverable from surviving texts, the story of the world's major, living, international religions can reach no further back in time than this.

To concede this much is not to concede that the earlier evolution of religion cannot be reconstructed at all or indeed even reconstructed in a way that would link it to the story told here. It is to concede only that that reconstruction would call for another kind of book than this one, assembling very different kinds of evidence than are assembled here.

The First World's Parliament of Religions

We may close this review of the development of religious studies between 1737 and 1893 with a visit to the World's Parliament of Religions at the World's Columbian Exposition in Chicago in 1893. The vast exposition, which ran for six months and attracted millions of visitors, was a celebration of progress—scientific, political, and cultural—during the five hundred years since Columbus had discovered America. (The exposition missed its intended 1892 opening by a few months.) Though the organizers often seemed to tacitly assume that the latest and greatest chapter in world progress was the American chapter and that thriving, optimistic Chicago was the epitome of American progress, nonetheless an exuberant, generally benevolent and inclusive curiosity characterized much on display. And though there was condescension in the presentation of model villages from "primitive" societies as natural history exhibits, there was also an acknowledgment that many fascinating and once entirely unknown societies were now no longer unknown and could be presented for the instruction of the interested.

As for the World's Parliament of Religions, it seemed to reflect a contemporary, enlightened, Protestant American view that there existed—or there could come into existence—something like a generic religion whose truth all specific religions could acknowledge without renouncing their respective identities. This view may have owed something to the many translations and plagiarizations of *The Religious Ceremonies and Customs of All the Peoples of the World* that for a century and a half had been steadily propagating Bernard and Picart's confidence that a pure, "natural" religion underlay the variously corrupted historical religions of the world. It may have owed something as well to the 1890 publication of James Frazer's *The Golden Bough*, a romantic and enormously popular work that marshaled classical mythology and selected early anthropological studies of primitive tribes in a grand evolutionary march from magic to science.[19] It may have reflected in addition the gradual influence on American Protestants of the Enlightenment ideas underpinning the United States Constitution. Under the Constitution, since there was no "religious test" for public office, a Muslim or even an atheist could legally become president.[20] The legal leveling explicit in the Constitution implicitly encouraged a comparable leveling in American society, first among Protestants but later extended to Catholics and Jews, and gradually to the adherents of other religions. The process was slow, but its direction was unmistakable.

What is most remarkable about the Parliament, however, is the simple fact that when the organizers invited representatives of Hinduism, Buddhism, Daoism, Confucianism, Shinto, Jainism, Islam, and Zoroastrianism to come together and deliberate with Christians and Jews, everyone accepted the invitation. Swami Vivekananda (1863–1902) accepted both the invitation and the idea behind it—namely, that Hinduism was a world religion. He did not object that there was no such thing as "Hinduism," that the religious life of India was not a separate province within a postulated empire named "religion," that Indians who honored the Vedas did not see themselves as en route to any brighter collective religious future, and so forth and so on. Objections like this are legitimate, but Vivekananda agreed to attend anyway, gave a sensationally well-received speech, and went on to found the Vedanta Society as an American branch of Hinduism. Plainly enough, he had begun to construe Hinduism as potentially a global religion, separable from Indian ethnicity. The Sri Lankan Buddhist Anagarika Dharmapala (1864–1933) did something similar. In the real world of religious practice, these were important ratifying votes for a vision of world religious pluralism.

"How beautiful it would be," Jean Frédéric Bernard had written, "to arrive at that point and to be able to make people with an overly opinionated character understand that with the help of charity one finds everywhere *brothers*." If the organizers of the World's Parliament of Religions thought that they had arrived at that blessed point when Swami Vivekananda thrilled his American audience with the opening words of his oration, "Sisters and Brothers of America," they were mistaken. And yet something was happening. A change was taking place. In various related European and American venues, a subtle but distinct shift of attitude was under way.

Is it possible to contemplate beliefs that one does not share and practices in which one does not engage and to recognize in them the shaping of a life that one can recognize as human and even good? When attitudes shift on a question as basic as that one, novelists and poets are often the first to notice. The novelist Marcel Proust wrote as follows about the Hindu and Buddhist concepts of *samsara* and *karma*—though without ever using those words—in his early twentieth-century masterpiece *In Search of Lost Time* (1913–27):

> He was dead. Dead for ever? Who can say? . . . All that we can say is that everything is arranged in this life as though we entered it carrying a burden of obligations contracted in a former life; there is no reason inherent in the conditions of life on this earth that can make us consider ourselves obliged to do good, to be kind and thoughtful, even to be polite, nor for an atheist artist to consider himself obliged to begin over again a score of times a piece of work the admiration aroused by which will matter little to his worm-eaten body, like the patch of yellow wall painted with so much skill and refinement by an artist destined to be for ever unknown and barely identified under the name Vermeer. All these obligations, which have no sanction in our present life, seem to belong to a different world, a world based on kindness, scrupulousness, self-sacrifice, a world entirely different from this one and which we leave in order to be born on this earth, before perhaps returning there to live once again beneath the sway of those unknown laws which we obeyed because we bore their precepts in our hearts, not knowing whose hand had traced them there[.][21]

Marcel Proust was not a Hindu, he was a Frenchman of Jewish descent. Like not a few writers of his day, he may have been influenced by Frazer's *The Golden Bough*, but *In Search of Lost Time* is in any case a novel, not a work of science, philosophy, or theology. And yet we might say that in the words quoted, Proust is a Hindu by sympathetic, participative imagination and thus among the heirs of Jean Frédéric Bernard and Bernard Picart. This kind of imaginatively participant sympathy was taking hold in a new way.

In the United States, the World's Parliament of Religions reflected the same *Zeitgeist* and heralded, moreover, an organizational change that would occur in the latter third of the following century, building on all that had transpired since Bernard dreamed his dream. That change—the decision of the National Association of Biblical Instructors to reincorporate in 1964 as the American Academy of Religion—reflected the emergent conviction that some knowledge of the world's religions was properly a part of every American's education.[22]

If American intellectual culture is distinctive in any regard, it is distinctive in its penchant for popularization or for the democratization of knowledge. The intellectual leadership of the country has generally assumed that the work of intellectual discovery is not complete until everybody has heard the news. But judgment about what constitutes "news"—that is, what subjects constitute the core of education for all people—has changed over time, and knowledge of the world's religions has not always been on the list. It was during the twentieth century that it made the list, and so for the study of religion we may regard the World's Parliament of Religions as opening the twentieth century.

In the comparative study of religion, Europe was America's teacher until the end of World War II. The secular, neutral comparative study of religion was a European inspiration. The heavy lifting necessary to assemble linguistic and archaeological documentary materials for such study—the story we have been reviewing here—was almost entirely a European achievement as well. But a distinctive aspect of the American contribution to the story has been the impulse to share inspirations, achievements, and knowledge gained in the study of religion with the general public. A work like *The Norton Anthology of World Religions*, intended for the college undergraduate or the willing general reader, is a work entirely in the American grain. If you find the texts assembled in the collection that now follows surprising, if you find the editorial frame around them instructive, please know that you are cordially invited to explore the remaining five anthologies that with this one constitute the full *Norton Anthology of World Religions*.

Notes

The intellectual debts incurred in the foregoing introduction are far greater than could be registered even in a far longer list of footnotes than appears here. The subject matter touched upon could obviously command a far longer exposition than even so lengthy an introduction as this one has allowed. I beg the indulgence alike of the students I may have overburdened and of the scholars I have failed to acknowledge. JM

1. Kevin Schilback, "Religions: Are There Any?" *Journal of the American Academy of Religion* 78.4 (December 2010): 1112–38.
2. Frans de Waal, *The Bonobo and the Atheist: In Search of Humanism among the Primates* (New York: Norton, 2013), p. 210.
3. Daniel L. Pals, *Eight Theories of Religion*, 2nd ed. (New York: Oxford University Press, 2006); Michael Stausberg, ed., *Contemporary Theories of Religion: A Critical Companion* (London: Routledge, 2009). Strikingly, they do not overlap on a single entry.
4. Feynman is quoted in Dennis Overbye, "Laws of Nature, Source Unknown," *New York Times*, December 18, 2007.
5. Clifford Geertz, "Religion as a Cultural System," in *The Interpretation of Cultures: Selected Essays* (New York: Basic Books, 1973), p. 90 (emphasis his).
6. Ibid., p. 125.
7. Ibid., pp. 193–233.
8. Tomoko Masuzawa, *The Invention of World Religions, Or, How European Universalism Was Preserved in the Language of Pluralism* (Chicago: University of Chicago Press, 2005).
9. All Bible quotations in this introduction are from *The Holy Bible, Revised Standard Version* (New York: Thomas Nelson & Sons, 1952).
10. Mark C. Taylor, *After God* (Chicago: University of Chicago Press, 2007).
11. Herbert Butterfield, *The Englishman and His History* (Cambridge: The University Press, 1944), p. 119.
12. Lynn Hunt, Margaret C. Jacob, and Wijnand Mijnhardt, *The Book That Changed Europe: Picart and Bernard's "Religious Ceremonies of the World"* (Cambridge, Mass.: Belknap Press of Harvard University Press, 2010), p. 2 (emphasis added).
13. Ibid., p. 5.
14. Ibid., pp. 155–57 (emphasis added).
15. Jean Frédéric Bernard, quoted in ibid., p. 241 (emphasis in original).
16. Donald S. Lopez, Jr., *From Stone to Flesh: A Short History of the Buddha* (Chicago: University of Chicago Press, 2013).
17. *The Quest of the Historical Jesus* is the colorful title of the English translation first published in 1910; Schweitzer's sober German title was *Von Reimarus zu Wrede: Eine Geschichte der Leben-Jesu-Forschung* (From Reimarus to Wrede: A History of Research into the Life of Jesus). Hermann Reimarus and William Wrede were earlier scholars.
18. For the background in World War II and its aftermath, see John Connelly, *From Enemy to Brother: The Revolution in Catholic Teaching on the Jews, 1933–1965* (Cambridge, Mass.: Harvard University Press, 2012).
19. James Frazer, *The Golden Bough: A Study in Magic and Religion: A New Abridgment from the Second and Third Editions* (Oxford: Oxford University Press, 2009). Frazer's extravaganza eventually grew to twelve volumes, now out of print. For a more recent and more richly informed account of the evolution of religion, see Robert M. Bellah, *Religion in Human Evolution: From the Paleolithic to the Axial* Age (Cambridge, Mass.: Belknap Press of Harvard University Press, 2011).
20. See Denise A. Spellberg, *Thomas Jefferson's Qur'an: Islam and the Founders* (New York: Knopf, 2013).
21. Marcel Proust, *In Search of Lost Time*, vol. 5, *The Captive; The Fugitive*, trans. C. K. Scott Moncrieff and Terence Kilmartin, rev. D. J. Enright (New York: Random House, 1993), 5:245–46.
22. See Preface, p. xxii.

Poets have told it before, and are telling it now, and will tell it again. What is here is also found elsewhere, but what is not here is found nowhere else.

—Mahabharata

HINDUISM

EDITED BY

Wendy Doniger

INTRODUCTION
The Zen Diagram of Hinduism

The religion commonly known as Hinduism has existed from at least 1500 B.C.E. (if one begins with the earliest text, the *Rig Veda*) or even perhaps 2500 B.C.E. (if one includes the Indus Valley Civilization, from which we have rich archeological evidence but no deciphered texts) to the present. And it has thrived over a wide geographical area, enriched by many different language groups and types of cultures. So wide is this span of time and space, and so diverse the ideas and myths and rituals and images that it encompasses, that some scholars resist calling it a single religion. But the widespread scholarly convention of gathering together the many forms of these ideas and myths and rituals and calling them "Hinduism" is supported by the intertextual tradition of the Hindus themselves, who tie the earliest texts to the latest in an unbroken chain (what they call a *param-para*, "from one to the other") and distinguish themselves from other religions (Buddhism, Islam, Christianity) by various terms, including, for the past four hundred years, "Hinduism." In that spirit, the present anthology brings together texts from the widest reaches of time and space under the umbrella term "Hinduism."

Some scholars have tried to identify a cluster of beliefs and practices that are important but not essential to Hinduism; not every Hindu will believe in all the ideas or follow all the practices, but each Hindu will adhere to some combination of them, as a non-Hindu would not. Scholars differ as to the number and nature of the elements of this cluster, but they should combine aspects of both the literary tradition and popular Hinduism: belief in the ancient sacred texts called the Vedas (which excludes Buddhism and Jainism); karma (the doctrine of actions that determine one's reincarnation, which does not exclude Buddhism and Jainism); dharma (Hindu religion, law, and justice, different from Buddhist *dhamma*); a cosmology centered around Mount Meru; devotion (*bhakti*) to one or more members of an extensive pantheon; the ritual offering (*puja*) of fruit and flowers to a deity; sacrificial offerings of butter into a fire; vegetarianism as an ideal, if not necessarily a practice; nonviolence and blood sacrifice (which may or may not be mutually exclusive); pilgrimage; offerings to snakes; worship of local gods and goddesses; worship at shrines of Muslim saints; and so forth. This polythetic approach could be represented by a Venn diagram, a chart made of intersecting circles. It might be grouped into sectors of different colors, one for beliefs or practices that some Hindus shared with Buddhists and Jains, another largely confined to Hindu texts in Sanskrit (the ancient literary language of India), a third more characteristic of popular worship and practice, and so forth. But since there is no single central quality that all Hindus must have, the emptiness in the center suggests that the figure might better be named a Zen diagram, a Venn diagram that has no central ring.

Among the many advantages of the cluster approach is the fact that it does not endorse any single authoritative view of what Hinduism is; it allows them all. The diversity of the tradition, however, as well as the sheer mass of available texts, means that any anthology of Hinduism will involve a selection so drastic as to be inevitably subjective, though not necessarily arbitrary. The present selection aims to present as many variations as possible on the great religious themes, both those specific to Hinduism—such as dharma, karma, and *samsara* (the cycle of reincarnation)—and those that Hinduism shares with other religions—death, the origins of things, and the relation between humans and divine powers. It strives to include as wide a range as possible of historical periods, geographical areas, and the voices of all genders and social classes.

History

The texts in this anthology are presented in their historical order in order to show not only how each idea is a reaction to ideas that came before but also how the central themes changed over time. When we cannot date events precisely, we can often at least arrange them in a plausible chronological order. The periodization, however, must not be confused with causation. We cannot assume that the texts line up like elephants, each holding on to the tail of the elephant in front; that everything in the Upanishads, for example, was derived from the Brahmanas just because some Upanishads cite some Brahmanas. We must also ask, each time, how the new text or group of texts was at least in part inspired by the circumstances of its own time and the originality of its author.

Indian history is like a banyan tree, which, unlike the mighty oak, grows branches that return down to the earth again and again and become the roots and trunks of new trees with new branches so that, eventually, we have a forest of a banyan tree, and we no longer know which was the original trunk. The vertical line of time is intersected constantly by the horizontal line of space. And so we will have to keep doubling back in time to find out what has been going on in one place while we were looking somewhere else. Some of the banyan branches are older and thicker and have been growing for a long time; some are just saplings. But forward movement always involves looking in a rearview mirror.

The Indus Valley Civilization

As this is an anthology of texts, we begin with the Vedas, the earliest texts of ancient India. But that is not where the history of Hinduism begins. Texts are not the only source of our knowledge of a religion; there are also visual images, archeological remains, anthropological reports, the testimony of foreign witnesses, and so forth. (To compensate, at least in part, for the limitations of texts, we have added a number of images to suggest some of the lived aspects of nontextual Hinduism.) And the earliest period of what might be called proto-Hinduism has no verbal texts.

Passing over the early stone age cultures of India in 50,000 B.C.E. and the ancient village cultures of Baluchistan (located in what is now Pakistan), ca. 6,000 B.C.E., we must note that, from about 2300 B.C.E., great cities arose in the valley of the Indus River (150 miles south of Baluchistan, also in present-day Pakistan). This culture was the Indus Valley Civilization (IVC) or the Harappan Civilization, named after Harappa, one of the two most famous great cities on the Indus—the other being Mohenjo-Daro (though more recently several other important cities have been excavated). The material remains of this culture present a tantalizing treasure chest of often enigmatic images that hover just beyond our reach, taunting us with what might well be the keys to the roots of Hinduism.

The civilization of the Indus Valley extends over more than one thousand sites, stretching over more than half a million square miles (approximately five times the size of ancient Egypt); in Mohenjo-Daro alone, as many as forty thousand people once lived. Four hundred miles separate the two biggest cities, from Harappa in the north down to Mohenjo-Daro, and on down to the ports of the delta on the sea. Yet the Indus cities were stunningly uniform and remarkably stable over this wide range, changing little over a millennium, until they begin to crumble near the end. They had trade contacts with Sumer, Crete, and other Mesopotamian cultures, perhaps also Egypt and Central Asia.

Among the treasures that they left were carved stones—flat, rectangular sections of soapstone about the size of a postage stamp—which were used as stamps or seals, as well as sealings (impressions) made by such stamps. Most of the seals, which are found throughout the IVC, are engraved with a group of signs in the Indus script, or a drawing or design, or a combination of these. There are well over two thousand inscriptions, using about four hundred graphemes (recurring, clearly meaningful written signs). Many people have claimed to have deciphered them, but no one has definitively done so.

The ruins of Mohenjo-Daro, Pakistan. The remarkable uniformity of the bricks and the perfect geometry of the grid of streets extend over the full range of this great civilization.

An ancient seal, about 3 by 6 inches, and a modern impression of a unicorn (or, possibly, the side view of a two-horned bull), with a few graphemes, from the Indus Valley Civilization.

The fascination with the IVC comes in part from the intrinsic appeal of its artifacts but also from a perceived need to claim *non-Vedic*, indeed *pre-Vedic* antiquity for most of Hinduism—for Shiva and goddess worship and all the rest of Hinduism that is not attested in the Vedas. And the resemblances between some aspects of the IVC and later Hinduism are simply too stunning to ignore. As the Late Harappan culture declined, its survivors must have carried some of it into the Ganges-Yamuna basin. The two material cultures do not show continuities. The Harappan use of bricks of standard sizes, the geometrical grids, the seals, the sewers, the large urban plan—none of this is preserved in the Ganges-Yamuna basin. Above all, the technique of administration was lost; not for many centuries would anyone know how to govern such a large community in India. But someone succeeded in preserving on the journey south and east some of the cultural patterns nurtured in the Indus cities, for some of these forms lived on long after the cities themselves were gone. The Indus civilization may not have simply gone out like the flame of a candle—or, at least, not before lighting another candle.

We can see the possible survival, in transformation, of a number of phenomena. Some of the images on these seals, as well as terra-cotta and bronze figurines of women, may prefigure images that appear many centuries later as images of Hindu gods and goddesses. The Harappan motif of the fig (*pipal*)—as a leaf decoration on pottery and as a tree on seals—reappears in the imagery of some later religious sects. There is a conch shell, etched in vermilion, that may well have been used as a libation vessel, just as conch shells, etched in vermilion, are used in Hinduism today. Not only individual images, but also aspects of the art forms—especially the so-called animal style, stylized and rounded, with just a few meticulous and suggestive details—seem to have survived. Some of the depictions of the animals on the seals bear a striking resemblance to the depictions of the same animals two thousand years later (and magnified many hundredfold) on the capital plinths of the pillars of Ashoka. These patterns, and the rough outlines of other images, may have gradually merged with the culture of the people of the

Veda. But, in an anthology of texts such as this one, the rest is silence.

Bronze statue of a dancing girl, 4.3 inches high, from the Indus Valley Civilization.

Geography and Language

Oral and Written Texts, Sanskrit and Vernacular Texts

Our history begins with the texts, and within the broader outline of the historical framework we must consider many regional and linguistic variations—for example, the unique characteristics of Bengal Vaishnavism (the worship of Vishnu in Bengal and in texts in Bangla), Telugu Shaivism (the worship of Shiva in Andhra and in texts in Telugu), and so forth—through space as well as time.

Hinduism is composed of local as well as pan-Indian traditions, oral as well as written traditions, vernacular as well as Sanskrit traditions, and nontextual as well as textual sources. But the contrasting pairs did not translate neatly into polarized groups of people; a single person would often have both halves (as well as non-Hindu traditions) in his or her head; a Brahmin would know the folk traditions, just as, among Jews and Christians, many people study paleography and then go to church and read Genesis. It is not the case that only a puritanical Brahmin studied the dharma texts and only a libertine merchant read the *Kama-sutra* (the textbook of the science of erotics); no, the same man, of either class, might well read dharma with learned men (pandits) by day and the *Kama-sutra* with his mistress by night.

The elite tendencies of written traditions were exacerbated by the climate. The wet heat and the red ants destroyed any written text within a century or two, particularly since vellum was ruled out by the taboo against using animal substances and palm leaf was far more fragile than vellum. So these written texts by definition belonged to the privileged classes; the written texts that survived had to have been copied over and over again by a scribe patronized by someone with money to spare, and the scribe himself was invariably a male of high caste.

Yet oral and written traditions interact throughout Indian history, with oral recitations of written texts and written records of texts recited by people who may or may not have been technically illiterate. This interaction is exemplified by the relationship between writing and reciting in two of the defining texts of Hinduism, the *Rig Veda* and the *Mahabharata*. The *Rig Veda* was preserved orally, but it was frozen, every syllable preserved for centuries, through a process of rigorous memorization. There are no significant variant readings of the *Rig Veda*, no critical editions or textual apparatus. Just the *Rig Veda*. So much for the alleged fluidity of orally transmitted texts. By contrast, the *Mahabharata*, preserved both orally and in manuscript, changed constantly; it is so extremely fluid that there is no single *Mahabharata*; there are hundreds of *Mahabharatas*, hundreds of different manuscripts and innumerable oral versions.

The relationship between Sanskrit and the other languages of India (the vernaculars) further complicates this picture. Sanskrit is the model for most North Indian languages (such as Hindi, Bangla, Punjabi, Marathi, and Oriya) and the source of much of their grammar and some of their vocabulary, as Tamil is for the Dravidian languages of the South (such as Telugu, Kannada, and Malayalam). The Sanskrit/Tamil distinction therefore overlaps with the North/South distinction, but we certainly cannot simply equate Sanskrit with North and Tamil with South. Many South Indian ideas—like devotion (*bhakti*), to take a case at random—entered Sanskrit literature, not just Tamil literature, through South Indian Brahmins who wrote in Sanskrit in South India. Not only did southern ideas go north, and vice versa; and not only did Tamil flow into Sanskrit and Sanskrit into Tamil, but Tamil went north, and Sanskrit south.

Greater than the divide between Sanskrit and the vernaculars is the great divide between written and nonwritten, particularly as the Sanskrit corpus incorporated more and more popular elements and the vernaculars eventually became Sanskritized themselves, imitating Sanskrit values and conventions and sharing many of the habits of the Brahmin Sanskritists, such as grammars and lexicons. The bad news is that some of the vernacular literatures are marred by the misogynist and class-bound mental habits of Brahmins, while the good news is that even some Sanskrit texts, and certainly many vernacular texts, often break out of those strictures and incorporate the more open-minded attitudes of the oral vernaculars.

Diverse Voices

Because of this constant interaction between Sanskrit and vernacular sources, oral and written traditions, the groups that conventional wisdom says were oppressed and silenced and played no part in the development of the tradition—Pariahs (oppressed castes, sometimes called Untouchables) and women of all castes—actually contribute a great deal to Hinduism.

Women

Women are sometimes said to have been excluded from the ancient Indian texts and therefore to have left no trace, history having been written by the winners, the men. But in fact women made significant contributions to the texts, both as the (usually unacknowledged) sources of many ancient as well as contemporary narratives and as the inspiration for many more. Some Hindu women did read and write, forging the crucial links between vernacular languages and Sanskrit. Women were forbidden to study the most ancient sacred text, the Veda, but the wives, whose presence was required at Vedic rituals, both heard and spoke Vedic verses, and they may well have had wider access to other Sanskrit texts. Later, in the second or third century C.E., the *Kama-sutra* tells us not only that women had such access but even that they sometimes commissioned such texts to be written. Women in Sanskrit plays generally speak only dialects (Prakrits), while men speak only Sanskrit, but since the men and women converse together, generally without translators, the women must understand the men's Sanskrit, and the men the women's dialects. Moreover, some women in plays both speak and write Sanskrit, and some men speak in dialects, trampling on what is left of the convention. It is a basic principle of one school of Indian logic that something can be prohibited only if its occurrence is possible. The fact that the texts keep shouting that women should not read Vedic texts suggests that women were quite capable of doing so and probably did so whenever the scholars (pandits) weren't looking.

We can also look for the implied author and identify in men's texts the sorts of things that a woman might have said. Such texts at least keep women in the picture, however biased a picture that may be, until they do finally get to speak as named authors, much later. Even within the Sanskrit texts, women are quoted as expressing views of matters as basic as *karma* in terms quite different from those of men, and these views become even more prominent when women compose their own texts. Of course, excavating women's voices in male texts must always be qualified by the realization that there may be ventriloquism, misreporting of women, and false consciousness. But ventriloquism is a two-way street: there is also a ventriloquism of women's voices in male minds. For even when a male Brahmin hand actually held the pen, as was usually the case, women's ideas may have gotten into his head. We can never know for sure when we are hearing the voices of women in men's texts, but we can often ferret out traces, what the Hindus call "perfumes" (*vasanas*), that women have left in the literature.

A hermeneutic of gentle suspicion is therefore required. Are the stated motivations of the author the only motivations? Or can an attentive and sympathetic listener sometimes hear the texts talking about things that they do not officially say they are talking about but actually do? We can try to resurrect the women actors in Hinduism through a combination of references to them, both unsympathetic (which shows us what they had to put up with from some men) and sympathetic (which shows us that some men did treat them humanely), and moments when we can hear women's own voices getting into the texts and, more rarely, discover actual female authorship.

For example, we may sense a female voice behind a Vedic hymn (10.145) attributed to the wife of Indra, the king of the gods (who is, like his Indo-European counterparts—the Greek Zeus and the Norse Odin, German Wotan—a notorious philanderer), and transmitted by a male poet, but possibly "perfumed" by the input of a human woman. It says, in part:

> I dig up this plant with which one drives out the rival wife and wins the husband entirely for oneself. . . . Make the rival wife go far, far into the distance. [She addresses her husband:] Let your heart run after me like a cow after a calf, like water running in its own bed.

So, too, we may hear echoes of women's voices in the many poems and stories in which male authors imagine themselves as women in love with the god Krishna, or in the text that imagines the god Shiva taking the form of an older woman to help a young woman deliver her first child.

Lower Classes

Brahmins are members of the highest and purest class. (Every Vedic priest had to be a Brahmin, but not every Brahmin was a priest, and the lowest classes also had their own, non-Vedic priests.) Brahmins may have had a monopoly on liturgical Sanskrit for the performance of certain public rites, but even then the sacrificer uttered some of the ritual words and performed the domestic rites. And though the sacrificer had to belong to one of the three upper classes, he need not have been a Brahmin. The other two "twice-born" social classes—warriors/rulers (Kshatriyas) and, below them, merchants (Vaishyas)—were also initiated and therefore could be sacrificers. The three upper classes were called "twice-born" because of the ritual of initiation—by which a man was born (again) as a fully developed member of the community. The lowest of the four classes, the servants (Shudras), were excluded from these and many other aspects of religious life.

Sanskrit texts were almost always subject to a final filter in the hands of the male Brahmins who usually composed and preserved them. But we cannot equate "Sanskrit" and "Brahmin." First of all, not all Sanskrit texts were written by Brahmins. Woven into the Brahmin texts, as well as standing alongside them, is another great strand of narratives by that extraordinarily prolific writer Anonymous, who was usually *not* a Brahmin and who should be credited with a great deal of the ancient literature of South Asia. He—or, just as likely, she—often wrote under the nom de plume of the heavily mythologized authors to whom many of the ancient texts are attributed. Even texts primarily composed by Brahmins were constantly infused with the contributions of the lower classes and women; the diverse voices of brilliant and creative thinkers constantly slipped through the filter put in place by Brahmin Sanskritists. And the filter itself was quite diverse, for there were many different sorts of Brahmins; some whispered into the ears of kings, but others were dirt poor and begged for their food every day. Not all Brahmins were highly literate or elitist.

The Brahmins did produce a great literature, but they did not compose it in a vacuum. They did not have complete authority or control the minds of everyone in India. They drew upon, on the one hand, the literate people who ran the country, the political actors (generally Brahmins and kings, but also merchants), and, on the other hand, the nonliterate lower classes. Because of the presence of oral and folk traditions in Sanskrit texts, even Dalits (the people formerly known as Untouchables) do manage to speak, not always in voices recorded on a page but in signs that we can read if we try. As with women's voices, we can ferret out voices of many castes in the ancient texts, and once we have access to the oral and folk traditions, we can begin to write the alternative narrative with more confidence.

These texts tell us a great deal not only about the philosophical and intellectual traditions of Hinduism, but also about praxis, about the ritual actions and everyday individual religious acts that Hindus performed in order to influence the course of their lives. They also tell us about power; the authors of Hindu texts attempted to control many aspects of society (particularly with respect to gender and caste), and often succeeded. They tell us about the life of the mind, and also about the life of the body, in vivid detail and with profound insights strikingly different from those of other cultures.

Sanskrit Texts

The texts in this anthology range from the earliest known composition, the *Rig Veda,* ca. 1500 B.C.E., to the works of writers still alive and well in the twenty-first century. There is a preponderance of poetry, in part because short poems, unlike longer prose works, can be included in an anthology in their entirety, without having to suffer the indignity of being reduced to excerpts, but also because poetry is the atomic unit of religious expression; you can recite a short poem every day, indeed every minute, which you cannot do with the entire *Ramayana.* Moreover, poems, in Hinduism, carry a special religious power; the Vedic Sanskrit word *kavi* means both a poet and an inspired sage, inspired not by a muse but by a god. Bold in its metaphor, sensuous in its imagery, profound in its philosophical insights, the poetry of Hinduism—chanted, meditated upon, set to music, danced—has continued to express and inspire every mood from passionate devotion to cynical satire.

Each major section, and subsection, of the anthology is introduced by a detailed survey of the texts in that section, but here is a brief chronological survey of the texts as a whole.

The earliest texts are all in Sanskrit, beginning with the *Rig Veda,* probably composed in around 1500 B.C.E. by a nomadic people in what is now the Punjab, in northwest India and Pakistan. From about 1100 to 1000 B.C.E., Vedic texts begin to mention the Doab ("Two Waters"), the land between the Ganges and the Yamuna (Jumna), and in about 900 B.C.E., the Vedic people gradually moved down from the Punjab and built palaces and kingdoms in the western and middle Ganges Valley. Between 1000 and 500 B.C.E., Vedic rituals spawned more and more commentaries, and by the sixth century B.C.E. the different schools, or branches (*shakhas*), had been well established. Between 800 and 600 B.C.E. the Brahmanas were composed, as mythological, philosophical, and ritual glosses on the Vedas.

By the time the philosophical texts called the Upanishads were composed, from around the sixth century B.C.E., the Vedic people had moved to the Eastern Ganges, a place of kingdoms dominated by the great city of Kashi (Varanasi, Benares). At this time, too, there arose schools of yoga, and the first renouncers, who believed that release from the wheel of transmigration could be achieved by the concentration and discipline of the mind and the body. Among these renouncers were both Vardhamana Mahavira (also called the Jina), the founder of Jainism, and Gautama Siddhartha, the founder of Buddhism, both of whom were born into distinguished clans in one of the nonmonarchical state systems that flourished at this time. Buddhists grew powerful throughout India, often competing with Hindus for royal patronage but also engaging in serious philosophical conversations with Hindus. Eventually Buddhism spread to Sri Lanka and to Southeast and East Asia, never entirely dying out in India but greatly diminished in numbers and royal patronage after the twelfth century C.E. Jains never grew as numerous as Buddhists, nor proselytized as Buddhists did, but remained a small, prosperous community in India.

What followed was a time of invasions but also of cosmopolitanism and intellectual ferment, between the end of the Mauryan Empire in the second century B.C.E. and the rise of the Gupta Empire in the fourth century C.E. Buddhism thrived, and India was enriched by material and intellectual trade with cultures—Greek, Central Asian, Roman, Southeast Asian, Chinese—that arrived both by sea and by land, over the Central Asian silk route and down through the mountain passes in the Northwest. It was at this time that the two great Sanskrit epics called the *Mahabharata* and the *Ramayana* were composed. They mark the transition from the corpus of texts known as *shruti*, the unalterable Vedic canon, to those known as *smriti*, the human tradition, constantly revised. Near the end of this period, a time of invasions but also of cosmopolitanism and intellectual ferment, the Brahmins began to consolidate the texts known as Shastras, or sciences.

Then, from about the fourth century C.E., the great Gupta dynasty unified most of North India and much of South India as well, building roads and stone temples, patronizing Buddhism and Jainism as well as various sects of Hinduism. This is when the Sanskrit texts known as Puranas began to take shape. The Puranas taught people the way to live a pious life and to worship the gods and goddesses, through rituals (*pujas*) performed at home, in the temple, and on special festival days; places to visit on pilgrimage; prayers to recite; and stories to tell and to hear. At this same time, great dynasties arose in South India, enriched by sea trade from the great South Indian ports. From about the tenth century C.E., Sanskrit Puranas began to represent the religious sentiment of *bhakti*, a passionate, intimate devotion to a deity, which resulted from a synthesis between North Indian and South Indian cultural forms, active interaction between several religious movements, and powerful political patronage of religion. In tandem with the Puranas, the esoteric texts known as Tantras developed, with features that included the worship of the Goddess, initiation, group worship, secrecy, and antinomian behavior, particularly sexual rituals and the ingesting of bodily fluids. This was also the time when two great philosophers of Vedanta (the philosophy based on the Upanishads, the "end of the Vedas" or Veda-anta) lived in South India, Shankara (788–820) and Ramanuja (1056–1137). These philosophies were further developed in the magical realist philosophical narratives of the twelfth-century Kashmiri Sanskrit text, the *Yoga-vasishtha*.

Bhakti and the Vernaculars

From the sixth century C.E., there had been constant trade with Arabs in both South and North India. From the tenth century on, Muslims established dynasties in North India and eventually, under the great Mughal empire (1526–1719), in most of South India as well. Sufism, the mystical branch of Islam, took several new forms in India and had considerable influence on the development of Hinduism.

While the Sanskrit literary forms were developing, first in North India and then throughout the subcontinent, other religious movements were also finding expression in vernacular languages. The earliest sources we have for Hinduism in a language other than Sanskrit are poems in Tamil, a South Indian language from a linguistic family, Dravidian, entirely separate from the Indo-European family from which Sanskrit is descended. The *bhakti* movement began in South India, first among Tamil writers and soon after in the literatures of other Dravidian languages, such as Telugu in Andhra, Kannada in Mysore, and Malayalam in Kerala, and subsequently among nonliterate people. It swept over the subcontinent, fertilizing widespread traditions of pilgrimage and temple festivals. The spirit of *bhakti* disdained power and privilege, revering humility and the spirit of service; it therefore privileged women and low castes, at least in theory and often in practice, too. Women, in particular, played active roles in *bhakti* sects, being responsible for such tasks as gathering the flowers for the shrines, offering prayers on behalf of male members of their families, and cooking the food offered to the gods.

Beginning in about 600 C.E., the wandering poets and saints devoted to Shiva (the Nayanmars, traditionally said to number sixty-three) and to Krishna-Vishnu (the twelve Alvars) sang Tamil poems in the devotional mode of *bhakti*. Tamil had its epics, too, of which the older, the *Cilappatikaram,* or "lay of the anklet," probably composed in the fifth century C.E., is a major source for our understanding of the early stages of the worship of the goddess Pattini.

Kannada, the language of Mysore, is second to Tamil in antiquity, among the Dravidian languages. Early Kannada poetry was composed by the Virashaivas ("Shiva's Heroes") or Lingayats ("People of the Linga"), also called Charanas ("Wanderers") because they prided themselves on being moving temples, itinerant, never putting down roots. Worshippers of both Shiva and Vishnu thrived in Andhra, and the fifteenth-century Telugu poet Annamayya dedicated his poems to his "god on the hill" of Tirupati (a form of Vishnu), while the male poet Kshetrayya (1622–1673) composed poems (also to Vishnu) in the voices of courtesans. The literature in Malayalam, the language of Kerala, flowered later than that of the other Dravidian languages; the *Shivasurabhi* of Kumaran Asan (1873–1924) expresses the poet's personal interpretation of the philosophy of Shankara.

The ideas of the *bhakti* authors from South India inspired, and were in turn inspired by, writers who composed in the North Indian vernaculars derived from Sanskrit: Hindi, Bangla, Marathi, and so forth. The first great poet in any of the medieval dialects of Hindi was Kabir (1398–1448), who blended Hindu and Muslim themes in a poetry that celebrated a god without qualities (*nirguna*) whom he called Ram. He was closely followed by three Hindi poets who celebrated a god with qualities (*saguna*): Surdas (1483–1563), who sang of Krishna; the woman poet Mirabai (1498–1547), who also sang of Krishna; and Tulsi Das (1532–1623), whose Hindi version of the *Ramayana*, called the *Ramcharitmanas* ("The Holy Lake of the Acts of Rama"), became the best-known telling of that story. The most beloved and prolific poet in the early Marathi tradition (in Maharashtra) was the daring and free-spirited Tukaram (1608–1649).

Beginning at roughly the same time, the literature in Bangla, the language of Bengal, began to celebrate Krishna. The poets Vidyapati in the fourteenth century, Chandidas in the fifteenth, Govinda-das and Balarama-das in the sixteenth, and Ramprasad Sen in the eighteenth wrote passionate songs to Krishna. The poet-saint Chaitanya (1486–1533) left no writings of his own but inspired an enduring school of Vaishnava theology and poetry centered around Krishna's adventures during childhood and adolescence (his "sport" or *lila*) in the village of Vrindavan (near Mathura). Among the great theologians in the Chaitanya tradition were Rupa Goswamin (sixteenth century) and Narottama Das (seventeenth century). In the early seventeenth century, Krishnadas Kaviraj composed the most influential of the many hagiographies of Chaitanya, the *Chaitanya-charita* ("Acts of Chaitanya").

Alongside these Krishna traditions, the worship of goddesses grew steadily in Bengal. Several long Bangla poems, called *mangals*, celebrated the goddess Manasa, goddess of snakes; one of the most beautiful is the early seventeenth-century *Manasa Mangal* of Ketaka Das. During the period of the British colonial presence in India (1757–1947), Michael Madhusudan Datta published a new Bangla version of the *Ramayana* (1861), using it as an allegory for the oppression of India by the British, and the Bengali reformer Ram Mohun Roy (1774–1833) published a number of documents protesting the burning of living women on their dead husbands' funeral pyres. Another Bengali religious tradition, the Tantric tradition of the Bauls, gave us the poetry of Fakir Lalon Shah, in the late eighteenth century. There are still Bauls performing in Bengal today.

The Colonial Period

By this time, Hinduism was a world religion, thriving in many places outside India. Though it was not a proselytizing religion, Hinduism was carried by traders throughout the world, to such a degree that it can be said to have colonized (intellectually, and sometimes politically, too) major parts of Southeast Asia. But Hinduism was, in turn, colonized, first, briefly, by French, Dutch, and Portuguese forces, and then, more lastingingly and profoundly, by the British, who entered India first in the eighteenth century as traders (through the East India Company). Eventually, after a powerful but ultimately thwarted revolution in 1857, Queen Victoria officially annexed India to the British Empire. Thus began the British Raj (the British reign in India), a connection ended only by Indian Independence in 1947.

British attitudes toward Hinduism left marks that are still sharply visible in the contemporary period. British scholars picked up from certain Hindus, and then reinforced in other Hindus, the belief that there was one essence of Hinduism, eternal and unchanging, captured in Sanskrit (related, through Greek and Latin, to the revered classical tradition in which the British ruling class educated its colonial administrators). But the real damage was done by government administrators and by Christian evangelical missionaries (whom the British East Asia Company administrators managed to keep out of India until 1813, when evangelists in London, some in Parliament, successfully lobbied to be allowed in). The British administrators were determined to find a single essence of Hinduism in order to govern Hindus by it (an early antecedent of *Star Trek*'s prime directive: do not interfere with the value systems of people on other planets). They wanted a Bible—a single, canonical text—by which they could define and control all of Hinduism, and they decided that the *Bhagavad Gita* (a philosophical text in the form of a discourse by the incarnate god Krishna) was that Bible and gave it a prominence that it never had before but has had ever since.

The Hinduism that the British administrators and missionaries regarded as ancient and unchanging was the high-caste male tradition, the tradition of the Brahmins, the pure, vegetarian tradition; it was also the belief system of monistic Upanishads, the *Gita*, and certain other texts in Sanskrit. This aspect of Hinduism was also what attracted the American transcendentalists Emerson and Thoreau, as well as Voltaire and Nietzsche and Goethe and Yeats. But this Hinduism that the British cordoned off relegated all the rest of Hinduism to an inauthentic status, thereby dichotomizing the religion. In contrast with their reverence for ancient Hinduism, the British by and large despised the Hinduism that they actually found alive and well in the India that they governed, the Hinduism of local practice and lower castes, of oral texts in the languages that people actually spoke, of ritual and folklore, a Hinduism in which women played a far more important role than they did in the Hinduism that the British Raj preferred. This popular Hinduism was the earthy religion of Hindus who sacrifice goats and worship a goddess whose image wears a girdle made of the severed hands of children. The British (who were, after all, Victorians in every sense) regarded popular Hinduism as something late and false, an inferior, decadent, debased, pagan, idolatrous form of the religion, sexy, dangerous, dirty, and out of control—so many gods with so many arms! They alleged squalid incompetence, indeed immorality, in this sort of Hinduism as partial justification for their presence in India: to raise up the benighted heathens from the depths into which they had sunk from their glorious but vanished past.

Modern India

Upper-class Hindus, who learned English and hobnobbed with the British, often parroted the British view of Hinduism and set out to "reform" it. They still revered their philosophical traditions, and the *Gita*, and the ideal of nonviolence, but they became ashamed of the erotic carvings on their temples, the *Kama-sutra*, the many arms of the gods, the goat sacrifices. They regarded Hinduism as monotheistic (rather than monistic) and argued that the undeniable polytheism of myth and ritual was a superficial and meaningless local overlay. Ironically, the very Hindu nationalists who were determined to drive the British out of India bought into the British view, though for very different reasons: in order to paper over serious differences among the many sorts of Hindus so as to present a united front against both the British and the Muslims.

But against this elite current, Hinduism became ever more enriched by a spectacularly diverse range of semi-marginalized people. The narratives of groups on the fringes of Hinduism found their way into print through English translations by folklorists, such as A. K. Ramanujan, and anthropologists, such as Verrier Elwin. The tribal peoples (Adivasis, or "First Dwellers") form a kind of internal diaspora, a parallel to the more obvious diaspora groups in Southeast Asia, the United Kingdom, and North America: though some of them regard themselves as non-Hindus, and many are totally ostracized by (other) Hindus, Hindu concepts and Hindu gods pervade their stories, even as many of their ideas have, over the centuries, enriched Hindu texts. The twentieth century also witnessed the sudden emergence of a literature by Dalits, whose poems often mock Hinduism and Brahmins, and who form, like the Adivasis, a kind of internal diaspora Hinduism.

The great themes of Hinduism live on, always in transformation, in authors writing in contemporary Indian languages in the twentieth and twenty-first centuries. Rabindranath Tagore (1861–1941) wrote both in English and in Bangla and won the Nobel Prize in 1913. Mohandas K. Gandhi (1869–1948) is best known as a political leader, but he was also a religious leader and a prodigious writer of religious texts, in both English and Gujarati; his essay on the *Bhagavad Gita* attempts to reconcile it with his own crucial principle of nonviolence. Two of the most famous writers in Hindi and in Urdu (a closely related, more Persian-influenced language) are Prem Chand (1880–1936) and Nirala (1899–1961). A story by the Bangla writer Mahasveta Devi (b. 1926) uses the story of the stripping of Draupadi, in the *Mahabharata*, to speak out against police brutality toward tribal women in the present. The novel *Samskara*, by the Kannada writer Udupi Rajagopalacharya Anantha Murthy (b. 1932) raises still pressing issues of caste.

A number of Indian writers are producing original Hindu texts in English. Vilas Sarang (b. 1942) writes both in English and in Marathi, revisioning Vedic texts for the modern age. Salman Rushdie (b. 1947) understands Hinduism from the vantage point of a brilliant outsider who is also very much an insider. Kancha Ilaiah (b. 1952) writes as the Dalit outsider within. And, finally, A. K. Ramanujan (1929–1993) has transformed ancient Hindu myths into explorations of contemporary subjectivities.

The penultimate text in this anthology is an instance of a steadily growing faction of Hinduism in the twenty-first century, the nationalist movement known as Hindutva ("Hindu-ness"). Hindutvavadis (as its adherents are called) seek to purify their own tradition of what they regard as foreign and impure elements and to claim India for Hindus, at the expense of other religions in India. Many Hindutvavadis would deny the authenticity of the many texts in this anthology that cannot be squeezed into the rather narrow Hindutva definition of Hinduism. Hindutva texts, however, are also Hindu texts. The argument made by Purushottam Nagesh Oak (1917–2007) that the Taj Mahal is a Hindu palace or temple has met with general ridicule. Other Hindutva revisions of Hindu history are both more subtle and more deeply injurious, such as the claim that the great mosque of Babur in Ayodhya was built over a Hindu temple commemorating the birth of the god Rama, a claim that led to the destruction of that mosque and riots that left more than a thousand dead, both Hindu and Muslim. But these revisions, too, have met with powerful opposition from the many Hindus who still value their broader, more humanistic and pluralistic traditions.

Hindu writers in the modern period simultaneously expose the problems built into the Hindu construction of society and testify to the enduring social conscience of Hindus who have protested against that construction and raised their voices in an effort to change it. The writings of these authors are original works of art in the literature of India, worthy inheritors of the wisdom and brilliance of the very classical traditions whose assumptions about the givenness of the world they so boldly challenge.

A NOTE ON TRANSLITERATION

The *Norton Anthology of World Religions* rule for representing words from Indian languages and alphabets in the characters of the Roman (Latin) alphabet is to simplify as much as possible, since the text is designed for the general reader rather than the scholar. To enable consistent public pronunciation of key names and terms in the texts anthologized here, ś = sh, c = ch, and no macrons (markers of vowel length) or other diacritics are employed to modify the Roman characters. Thus, "Śiva" appears as "Shiva," "Caitanya" as "Chaitanya," and "Mahābhārata" as "Mahabharata" in all texts in Sanskrit, Telugu, Tamil, and so forth. In this way, besides enabling consistent classroom and other public pronunciation, we obviate the confusion that might otherwise arise from citing several texts in a given language, each from a scholar who uses a different system of transliteration.

Chronology

ANCIENT SANSKRIT ROOTS

ca. 1500–1000 B.C.E. *Rig Veda* composed

ca. 1300–1000 B.C.E. City of Kaushambi founded
City of Kashi (Varanasi, Benares) founded

ca. 1200–900 B.C.E. *Yajur Veda* and *Sama Veda* composed

ca. 1100–1000 B.C.E. Vedic texts mention the Doab, the land between the Ganges and Yamuna

ca. 950 B.C.E. Traditional date of the *Mahabharata* battle

ca. 800–600 B.C.E. Brahmanas composed

ca. 700 B.C.E. *Atharva Veda* composed

ca. 600–500 B.C.E. Aranyakas composed

ca. 600–400 B.C.E. Early Upanishads composed

ca. 500 B.C.E. *Shrauta Sutras* composed

486 B.C.E. Death of Siddhartha Gautama, the Buddha, according to the "long chronology"

ca. 468 B.C.E. Death of Vardhamana Mahavira, the Jina, founder of Jainism

ca. 400–100 B.C.E. Later Upanishads composed

ca. 400 B.C.E. Jaimini composes *Purva Mimamsa Sutras*
Badarayana composes *Vedanta Sutras* (*Brahma Sutras*)

327 B.C.E. Alexander the Great invades the northwestern part of the subcontinent

ca. 321–185 B.C.E. Mauryan dynasty (founded by Chandragupta, who rules until ca. 298 B.C.E.)

ca. 300 B.C.E. *Grihya Sutras* composed
Greeks and Ashoka mention the Pandyas, Cholas, and Cheras, dynasties of southern India

ca. 300–200 B.C.E. Kanada founds Vaisheshika school of Indian philosophy

ca. 300–100 B.C.E. *Dharma-sutras* composed

ca. 300 B.C.E.–300 C.E. *Mahabharata* composed

265–232 B.C.E. Reign of Ashoka, last major Mauryan emperor

ca. 250 B.C.E. Ashoka convenes Buddhist Council at Pataliputra

ca. 200–100 B.C.E. Gautama founds Nyaya school of Indian philosophy

ca. 200 B.C.E. –200 C.E. Valmiki composes his *Ramayana*

ca. 166 B.C.E. –78 C.E. Invasion of India by Greeks, Scythians, Bactrians, and Parthians

ca. 150 B.C.E. Patanjali composes *Yoga Sutras*

ca. 50 B.C.E. Diodorus Siculus, Greek historian, mentions widow-burning

ca. 50 B.C.E. –50 C.E. Peak of Roman trade with India

ca. 1 C.E. Manu composes his *Dharmashastra*

ca. 100 C.E. Hinduism spreads to Vietnam

Bhagavad Gita composed

ca. 100–300 C.E. *Cankam* poems begin to be composed in Tamil Nadu

ca. 300 Vatsyayana composes the *Kama-sutra*

ERA OF PURANIC HINDUISM AND THE RISE OF VERNACULARS

ca. 320–ca. 540 Gupta dynasty (founded by Chandragupta, r. ca. 320–35)

ca. 350–500 *Matsya Purana* composed
Markandeya Purana composed (*Devimahatmya* portion is later)

ca. 350–950 *Brahmanda Purana* composed

ca. 400 Hinduism spreads to Borneo and other parts of Southeast Asia

ca. 5th century Ilanko Atikal composes Tamil epic, *Cilappatikaram*

405–11 Faxian (Fa-Hsien), Chinese Buddhist monk, travels to India

ca. 450 *Harivamsha* composed

ca. 450–500 *Vishnu Purana* composed

ca. 450–550 Rock-cut Cave of Shiva constructed at Elephanta

ca. 450–750 *Vamana Purana* composed

ca. 455 Huns first attack North India

6th–8th centuries The *Tevaram* collection composed by Nayanmar Shaiva Tamil poets

ca. 500–900 Early Tantras

ca. 550–750 *Kurma Purana* composed
Padma Purana composed

ca. 600–900 Flourishing of Alvar Vaishnava Tamil poets

ca. 600–1000 *Linga Purana* composed

ca. 700–1100 *Skanda Purana* composed

711–13 Arabs conquer Sind and other parts of northwest India
736 Dhillika (Delhi) founded

ca. 750–1142 Pala dynasty of Bengal and Bihar

ca. 750–1350 *Shiva Purana* composed

765–73 Krishna I builds Kailasa temple to Shiva at Ellora

788–820 Life of Shankara, South Indian philosopher

9th or 10th century Life of Matsyendranatha, author of *Kaulajnananirnaya*
Brahmayamala Tantra composed

ca. 880–930 Life of Nammalvar, author of the *Tiruvaymoli*

ca. 950 *Bhagavata Purana* composed

1001–27 Conquest of northwest India by Mahmud of Ghazni (971–1030)

1014–47 Reign of Rajendra, "the Great," who expands Chola empire to Sri Lanka

1030 Al-Biruni (973–ca. 1052), great Muslim scientist and scholar, in India

1053 Sdok Kak Thom Inscription in Thailand (Khmer empire)

ca. 1056–1137 Life of Ramanuja, South Indian philosopher

12th century Life of Mahadeviyakka, Kannada woman poet
Jayadeva composes *Gita Govinda* in Bengal
Yoga-vasishtha composed

1106–1167/68 Life of Basava, founder of sect of Lingayats/Virashaivas

ERA OF MUSLIM DOMINANCE

1192–1206 Muhammad of Ghor establishes Ghorid capital at Delhi

ca. 1200 *Ramacharitam* (Malayalam version of *Ramayana*) composed
Early Sufis in North India

1206–1526 Delhi sultanate, established by Aibak (r. 1206–10)

ca. 1221 Forces of Genghis Khan invade Punjab

ca. 1238–1317 Life of Madhva, dualist philosopher, in Karnataka

ca. 1250 Palkuriki Somanatha composes the *Basava Purana*
Narasimhadeva I, Ganga king, builds temple of Konarak in Orissa

1292–93 Marco Polo visits South India

ca. 14th century *Sang Hyang Naishthika-Jnana* composed in Java

14th century Life of Annamayya, Telegu poet

ca. 1336–1565 City of Vijayanagar, first capital of Vijayanagar dynasty

ca. 1350 Sayana composes commentary on the *Rig Veda*

ca. 1352–1448 Life of Vidyapati, Bangla poet of Mithila

ca. 1375–1450 Life of Chandidas, Bangla poet

1398 Timur (1336–1405) sacks Delhi

1398–1448 Life of Kabir, North Indian Hindi poet
Krittibas Ojha composes a Bangla *Ramayana*

1451–1526 Lodi dynasty, final rulers of Delhi sultanate

1469–1539 Life of Guru Nanak, founder of Sikhism in the Punjab

1479–1531 Life of Vallabha, founder of a sect devoted to Krishna

ca. 1483–1563 Life of Surdas, Hindi poet

1486–1533 Life of Chaitanya, Bengali mystic and saint

1489–1505 Reign of Sikander in Agra, new capital of the Delhi sultanate

1498 Vasco da Gama arrives at Calicut

1498–1547 Life of Mirabai, woman Hindi poet

early 16th century Life of Balaramadas, Bangla poet

16th century Life of Rupa Gosvamin, theologian
Life of Krishnadas Kaviraja, hagiographer of Chaitanya

1502 Portuguese establish trading station at Kochi: first European colonial presence

1510 Portuguese occupy Goa
Chaitanya initiated as an ascetic

1526 Babur (1483–1530) founds Mughal Empire

1532–1623 Life of Tulsi Das, poet and devotee of Rama

1537–1612 Life of Govinda-das, Bangla poet

1556–1605 Reign of Akbar, Mughal emperor

1565 Vijayanagar destroyed by four Muslim sultans in the battle of Talikota

1580 Jesuit mission to Akbar

1582 Akbar launches the Din-I-Ilahi, a syncretic religion

17th century Life of Narottama Das, Bangla poet

1600 Queen Elizabeth I charters the East India Company (EIC)

ca. 1600 Kashirama Das composes a Bangla *Mahabharata*

1602 Dutch East India Company founded

1605–27 Reign of Jahangir, Mughal emperor

1608–1649 Life of Tukaram, Shudra Marathi poet

1614–18 First British ambassador to the Mughal court (Sir Thomas Roe)

1622–1673 Life of Kshetrayya, Telegu poet

1627/30–1680 Life of Shivaji, founder of Maratha kingdom

1632–53 Shah Jahan, Mughal emperor (r. 1627–58), constructs the Taj Mahal

1639 Trading post at Madras granted to EIC

ca. 1650 Floruit of Ketaka Das, Bangla poet

1651 First translation of Sanskrit (poems of Bhartrihari) into a modern European language (Dutch)

1658–1707 Reign of Aurangzeb, last of the great Mughal emperors

1664 French East India Company founded

1687 Bombay becomes the headquarters of the EIC

1699 Guru Gobind Singh (1666–1708), tenth and last Sikh Guru, founds the Khalsa (the military brotherhood of the Sikhs)

ca. 1700 *Mahanirvana Tantra* composed

18th century *Parthayana* composed, an Old Javanese retelling of the *Mahabharata*

Life of Fakir Lalon Shah, Bengali Baul singer

ca. 1720–1781 Life of Ramprasad Sen, Bangla poet

BRITISH RULE AND INDEPENDENCE

1757 Battle of Plassey: Robert Clive (1725–1774) leads EIC soldiers to victory over the Muslim ruler of Bengal and his French allies

1764 Battle of Baksar: British decisively gain control of Bengal and Bihar by defeating Mughals and the nawabs of Bengal and Oudh

1765 Robert Clive becomes governor of Bengal

1774–1833 Life of Rammohun Roy, Bengali Brahmin religious reformer

1782 Tipu Sultan (1750–1799) resists the British

1785 Lord Cornwallis defeats Tipu Sultan

1813 EIC loses its monopoly on trade

1817–18 Cholera epidemic throughout India

1818 Third British–Maratha war ends with British victory, cementing their supremacy in India

1824 Sepoys (Indian troops employed by the British) mutiny at Barrackpur

1824–1873 Life of Michael Madhusudan Datta, Bengali poet and dramatist

1824–1883 Life of Dayananda Sarasvati, Hindu reformer

1828 Rammohun Roy founds Brahmo Samaj, Hindu reform movement

1829 EIC bans "suttee" (widow-burning)

1833 East India Company ceases to trade

1836–1886 Life of Ramakrishna, Bengali Hindu mystic

1843 Debendranath Tagore (1817–1905) revives Brahmo Samaj

1843–49 British conquer and annex Sind and the Punjab

1853 First commercial passenger rail service

1856 EIC legalizes remarriage of Hindu widows

1857–58 The Rebellion (often called the "Indian Mutiny") of sepoys against British authorities

1858 British Raj (direct rule) begins, as the rule of the EIC is transferred to the Crown (a viceroy) and the last Mughal ruler is exiled

1861 Imperial Legislative Council (Indian members nominated by the viceroy) established

1861–1941 Life of Rabindranath Tagore, Bangla poet, dramatist, and writer of prose

1863–1902 Life of Vivekananda, proselytizing guru

1869–1948 Life of Mohandas Karamchand (Mahatma) Gandhi

1872–1950 Life of Aurobindo Ghose, Hindu reformer

1873–1924 Life of Mahakavi Kumaran Asan, Malayali poet

1875 Dayananda Sarasvati (1824–1883) founds Arya Samaj, Hindu reform movement
Helena Blavatsky (1831–1891) founds Theosophical Society

1877 "Empress of India" is added to the titles of Queen Victoria (r. 1837–1901)

1880–1936 Life of Prem Chand, writer of Hindi novels and short stories

1885 Indian National Congress Party founded

1891 Age of Consent Act raises the age of statutory rape from 10 to 12

1891–1956 Life of Bhimrao Ramji Ambedkar, Dalit leader

1892 Reform of legislative councils increases the number of Indian members

1893 Vivekananda attends the World's Parliament of Religions in Chicago
Hindu–Muslim violence breaks out at the height of the cow protection movement

1896–1977 Life of A. C. Bhaktivedanta, Swami Prabhupada (founder of the International Society for Krishna Consciousness)

1897 Vivekananda founds Ramakrishna Mission

1898 The radical Sikh Bhai Kahn Singh Nabha (1861–1938) writes *Ham Hindu Nahin* (*We Are Not Hindus*)

ca. 1899–1961 Life of Nirala, Hindi writer

1905 Bengal partitioned into largely Muslim (eastern) and Hindu (western) provinces
Swadeshi ("of our own country") movement promotes boycott of British goods

1906 Muslim League founded

1909 Morley–Minto reforms (the Indian Councils Act of 1909) reserve seats for Muslims

1912 New Delhi replaces Calcutta as the capital of British India

1913 Rabindranath Tagore wins Nobel Prize in Literature

1915 Gandhi returns to India from South Africa

1916 Lucknow Pact between the Indian National Congress Party and Muslim League

1918–2008 Life of Maharishi Mahesh Yogi, who introduced transcendental meditation to the West

1919 Amritsar Massacre: British troops fire on unarmed Indians

1920–22 Gandhi's noncooperation campaign, in pursuit of Indian self-government

1926 Birth of Mahasveta Devi, Bangla writer

1926–2011 Life of Sathya Sai Baba, Indian spiritual teacher

1927 Ambedkar leads a Dalit protest at Chavadar Lake

1929–1993 Life of A. K. Ramanujan, a founder of South Asian studies

1930 Gandhi leads the *satyagraha* against tax on salt

1931–1990 Life of Bhagwan Shree Rajneesh (Osho), Indian spiritual teacher and founder of a controversial commune in Oregon

1932 Birth of Anantha Murthy, Kannada writer
Gandhi–Ambedkar pact reserves seats for Dalits in Indian legislatures

1940 Mohammed Ali Jinnah (1876–1848), the head of the Muslim League, proposes separate Muslim state (Pakistan)

1942 Quit India Movement launched
Birth of Vilas Sarang, Marathi writer

1947 India officially gains independence from England; Partition creates modern India and Pakistan
Birth of Salman Rushdie, British Indian novelist

1948 Sri Lanka gains independence from Britain
Gandhi assassinated

1950 Indian Constitution established

1952 Birth of Kancha Ilaiah, political scientist and activist on behalf of Dalits

1956 Ambedkar and many fellow Dalits convert to Buddhism
India reorganizes internal administrative boundaries to align with major regional languages

1959 Fourteenth Dalai Lama (b. 1935) flees Tibet for India

1960s Sharp rise in Western interest in Hinduism and yoga

1961 Indian troops liberate Goa and other Portuguese possessions in the subcontinent
Dowry Prohibition Act bans asking for or accepting dowry as a precondition for marriage

1970 Diaspora Hindus come to the United States and Europe and build temples

1971 Tamil Nadu government declares Sanskrit no longer the sole language of liturgy in that state
Bangladesh (formerly East Pakistan) gains independence

1975 Indira Gandhi (prime minister, 1966–77, 1980–84) declares state of emergency and assumes extraordinary powers

1980 Mandal Commission report addresses caste discrimination

1984 Government soldiers attack the Golden Temple at Amritsar to remove armed Sikh militants

1992 Destruction of the Babri Masjid in Ayodhya by Hindus contending that the builders of the 16th-century mosque had destroyed a temple; thousands die in ensuing riots

2000 India's population reaches 1 billion

2002 Deadly Hindu–Muslim riots in Gujarat

2007 Hindutva groups sue to halt construction of a shipping canal through a chain of shoals they believe created by Rama

2010 Allahabad High Court rules that the disputed Ayodhya site should be split among two Hindu groups and one Muslim group

2011 Indian Supreme Court stays Allahabad High Court ruling on Ayodhya

HINDUISM IN SANSKRIT
1500 B.C.E.–1200 C.E.

TEXTS HEARD AND TEXTS READ

Sanskrit is the literary language of ancient India, the language in which the earliest text (the *Rig Veda*, ca. 1500 B.C.E.) was composed and in which both religious and secular texts continue to be composed to the present day. Sanskrit is an Indo-European language closely related to ancient Greek and Latin, and ultimately to French, German, English, and so forth. Sanskrit texts were almost always subject to a final filter in the hands of the male Brahmins (the highest of the four social classes, the class from which priests were drawn) who composed and preserved them. The written texts were preserved in libraries; but since the Indian climate and Indian insects tend to destroy manuscripts, the texts have to be recopied every two hundred years or so if they are to survive; someone has to choose them and go to the trouble and expense of having them copied, generating merit for the patrons and income for the scribes. Sanskrit, the language of power, emerged in India from a minority, and at first its power came precisely from its non-intelligibility and unavailability, which made it the instrument of an elite group. Many English-speakers mispronounce it "Sanscript," implying that it is a language without (*sans*) an (intelligible) script, or "Sand-script," with overtones of ruined cities in the desert or a lost language written in sand.

But most people who knew Sanskrit must have been bilingual; the third-century C.E. *Kama-sutra* remarks that a well-cultivated man should be able to tell stories "neither too much in Sanskrit, nor too much in the local dialect" (1.4.37). The etymology of Sanskrit ("perfected, artificial") is based upon an implicit comparison with Prakrit ("primordial, natural"), the ancient language that was actually spoken. Sanskrit texts from the earliest period assimilated texts that were largely oral and composed in vernacular languages. Even in the earliest period, Sanskrit was not what has been called a kitchen language, not the language in which you said, "Pass the butter." (Actually, Brahmins probably did say, "Pass the butter" in Sanskrit when they put butter as an oblation, or offering, into the fire in the course of the sacrifice, but those same Brahmins would have to have known how to say it in another language at home.) At the very least, male Sanskritists had to be bilingual in order to talk to their wives and servants and children. It was through those interactions that oral traditions got their foot in the Sanskrit door.

Sanskrit and oral traditions flow back and forth, producing a constant infusion of lower-class words and ideas into the Brahmin world, and vice versa. It must have been the case that Prakrit and the other vernaculars came first, while Sanskrit, the refined, artificial language, came later. But Sanskrit was the first to be written down and preserved, and we only

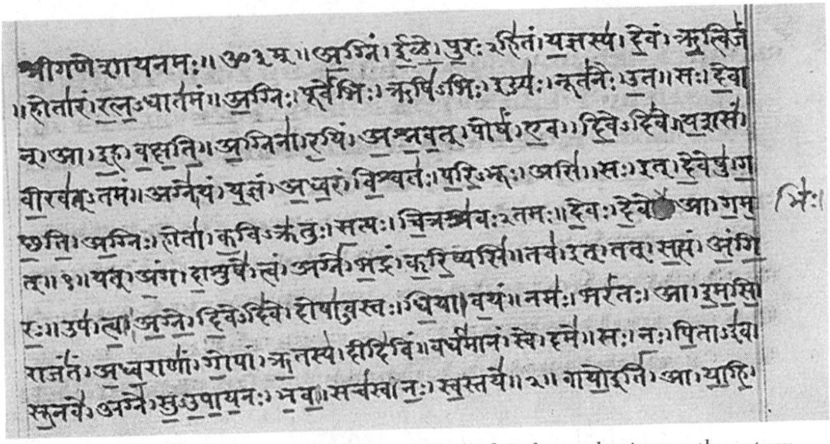

A manuscript of the *Rig Veda* in Sanskrit on palm leaf, India, early nineteenth century. The *Rig Veda* was transmitted only orally for many centuries but was eventually preserved in manuscripts.

encounter vernaculars in written form much later. Scholars therefore often regard Prakrit and the vernaculars as derived from Sanskrit, through some process of decay, which is less likely to be the case.

The Indian sociologist M. N. Srinivas, in 1952, coined the useful term "Sanskritization" to describe the way that Vedic social values, Vedic ritual forms, and Sanskrit learning seep into local popular traditions of ritual and ideology (in part through people who hope to be upwardly mobile, to rise by imitating the manners and habits, particularly food taboos, of Brahmins). But the opposite of "Sanskritization," the process by which the Sanskritic tradition simultaneously absorbs those same popular traditions, is equally important, and that process might be called oralization (or popularization). "Cross-fertilization" might be a good, equalizing term for the combination of the two processes. "Written" does not necessarily mean "written in Sanskrit," nor are oral texts always in the vernacular (the *Rig Veda* was preserved orally in Sanskrit for many centuries before it was consigned to writing). We cannot equate vernacular with oral, for people both write and speak both Sanskrit and the vernacular languages of India, though Sanskrit is written more often than spoken. The distinction between Sanskrit and the vernacular languages is basically social as well as geographical: though there are regional Sanskrits, the vernaculars are defined and named by their place of origin (Bangla from Bengal, Oriya from Orissa, and so forth), while the script in which Sanskrit is most often written nowadays is defined as having no particular earthly place of origin (it is called "the [script of the] city of the gods").

Many ideas, and in particular many narratives, seem to enter Sanskrit literature either from parts of the Sanskrit canon that have fallen away or from non-Sanskrit sources. It's an old joke among linguists that a language is a dialect with an army, and this is sometimes used to explain the dominance of Sanskrit texts, since, as usual, the victors wrote the history, and in ancient India, they usually wrote it in Sanskrit. (The earliest inscriptions—royal edicts on stone or metal—were in Prakrit, not Sanskrit, but from about 150 C.E., Sanskrit dominated the inscriptions too.) Sanskrit is perched on top of the vernacular literatures of India like a mahout (elephant driver) on an elephant.

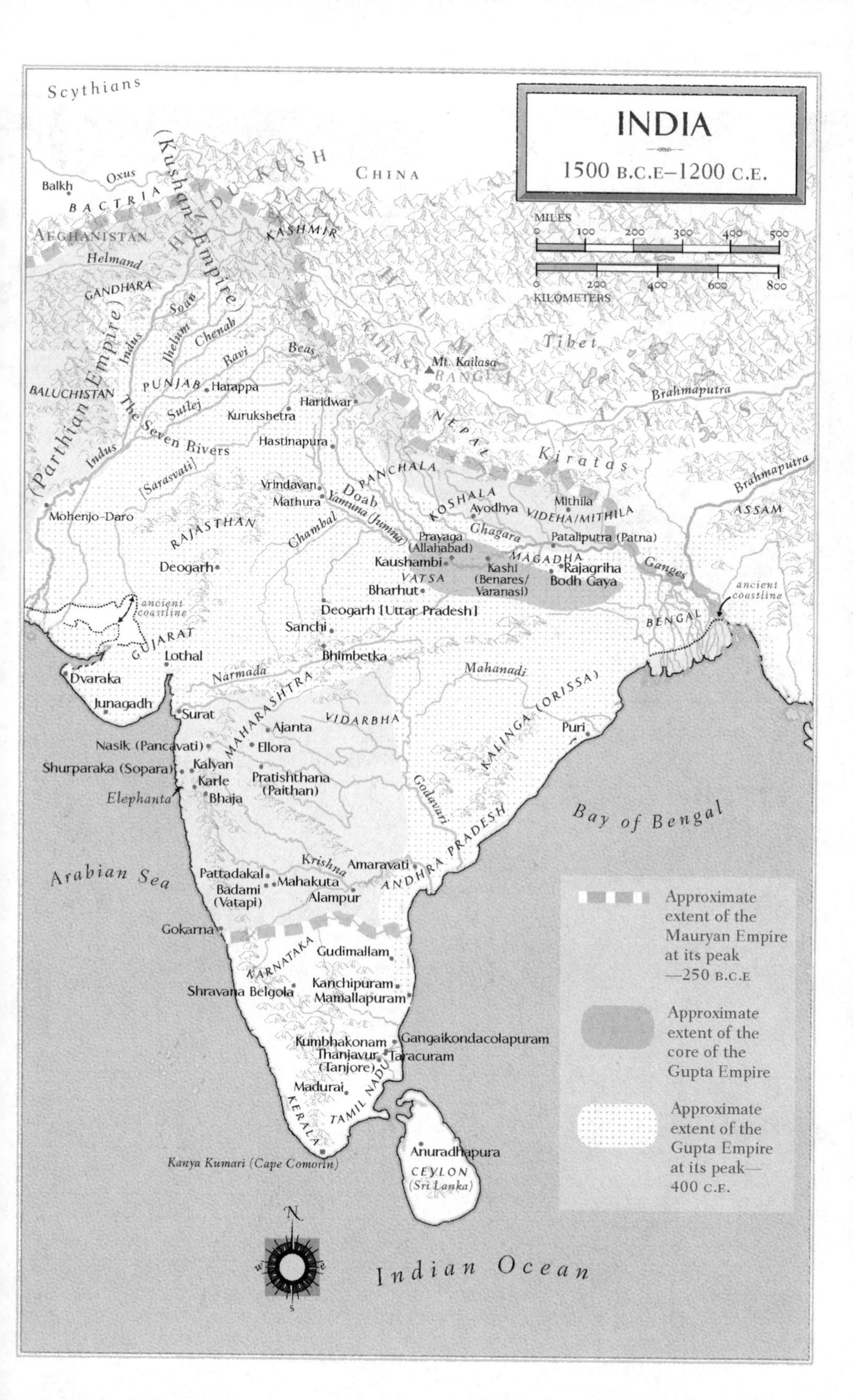
INDIA
1500 B.C.E–1200 C.E.
MILES
0 100 200 300 400 500
0 200 400 600 800
KILOMETERS
Scythians
CHINA
Balkh
Oxus
BACTRIA
HINDU KUSH
(Kushan Empire)
AFGHANISTAN
KASHMIR
Helmand
GANDHARA
Soan
Jhelum
Chenab
Indus
(Parthian Empire)
HIMALAYAS
KAILASA RANGE
Tibet
Beas
Ravi
Mt. Kailasa
PUNJAB
Harappa
BALUCHISTAN
The Seven Rivers
Sutlej
Kurukshetra
Haridwar
Brahmaputra
NEPAL
Hastinapura
Indus
[Sarasvati]
Kiratas
PANCHALA
Vrindavan
Doab
Mathura
Yamuna (Jumna)
KOSHALA
Ayodhya
Mithila
VIDEHA/MITHILA
ASSAM
Mohenjo-Daro
RAJASTHAN
Chambal
Ghagara
Prayaga (Allahabad)
Pataliputra (Patna)
MAGADHA
Kaushambi
Kashi (Benares/ Varanasi)
Rajagriha
Bodh Gaya
Ganges
VATSA
Deogarh
Bharhut
ancient coastline
Deogarh [Uttar Pradesh]
BENGAL
Sanchi
GUJARAT
Lothal
Bhimbetka
Dvaraka
Narmada
Mahanadi
MAHARASHTRA
Junagadh
Surat
VIDARBHA
KALINGA (ORISSA)
Ajanta
Puri
Nasik (Pancavati)
Ellora
Shurparaka (Sopara)
Kalyan
Karle
Pratishthana (Paithan)
Elephanta
Bhaja
Godavari
Bay of Bengal
ANDHRA PRADESH
Krishna
Amaravati
Arabian Sea
Pattadakal
Badami (Vatapi)
Mahakuta
Alampur
Gokarna
Gudimallam
KARNATAKA
Kanchipuram
Shravana Belgola
Mamallapuram
Gangaikondacolapuram
Kumbhakonam
Thanjavur (Tanjore)
Taracuram
Madurai
TAMIL NADU
KERALA
Anuradhapura
Kanya Kumari (Cape Comorin)
CEYLON (Sri Lanka)
N
S
W
E
Indian Ocean
Approximate extent of the Mauryan Empire at its peak —250 B.C.E
Approximate extent of the core of the Gupta Empire
Approximate extent of the Gupta Empire at its peak— 400 C.E.

Ancient Texts
1500–200 B.C.E.

Sanskrit texts begin with the *Rig Veda* ("Knowledge of Verses"), composed, probably ca. 1500 B.C.E., by a nomadic people in what is now the Punjab, in northwest India and Pakistan. They lived in the area of the Seven Rivers, the five tributaries of the Indus plus the Indus itself and the Sarasvati. By around 900 B.C.E., the verses were rearranged for chanting as the *Sama Veda* ("Knowledge of Songs") and, with additional prose passages, for ritual use as the *Yajur Veda* ("Knowledge of Sacrifice"); together with the *Rig Veda*, they are known as the three Vedas. A fourth, the *Atharva Veda* ("Knowledge of the Fire Priest"), devoted primarily to practical, worldly matters and spells to deal with them, was composed a few centuries later, sharing some poems with the latest parts of the *Rig Veda*.

In about 900 B.C.E., the Vedic people gradually moved down from the Punjab and built palaces and kingdoms in the western and middle Ganges Valley. Between 1000 and 500 B.C.E., Vedic rituals spawned more and more commentaries, and by the sixth century B.C.E. the different schools had been well established. Between 800 and 600 B.C.E., the Brahmanas were composed, as mythological, philosophical, and ritual glosses on the Vedas.

By the time the philosophical texts called the Upanishads were composed, from around the sixth century B.C.E., the Vedic people had moved to the eastern Ganges, a place of kingdoms dominated by the great city of Kashi (also called Varanasi,

A Vedic fire sacrifice. The patron is on the right, the priests on the left. Each priest played a different role: one recited verses, one performed the ritual, and one watched in silence to make sure nothing was done improperly.

or Benares). Here, both Vardhamana Mahavira (also called the Jina), the founder of Jainism, and Gautama Siddhartha, the founder of Buddhism, were born into distinguished clans in the nonmonarchical state systems that flourished at this time. The Upanishads laid the foundation for all of subsequent Indian philosophy, with their basic concept of the identity of the individual soul (the *atman*) with the world-soul (*brahman* or *atman*). These texts also began to proselytize for the renunciation (*sannyasa*) of world and family life and the seeking of release (*moksha*) from the wheel of rebirth (*samsara*). Coming as they did at the end of the Vedas, the Upanishads were known as the "end of the Vedas," or "Vedanta," a name later applied to schools of philosophy that further developed the doctrine of the identity of the individual soul and the world-soul.

HUMANS, ANIMALS, AND GODS IN THE *RIG VEDA* 1500–1000 B.C.E.

> tat savitur varenyam bhargo devasya dhimahi
> dhiyo yo nah prachodayat.
>
> Let us meditate on this beloved light of the god who enlivens.
> May he inspire our thoughts.

This verse, called the Gayatri Mantra ("an incantation in the Gayatri meter") or the Savitri Mantra ("an incantation to the sun god in his aspect of Savitri"), verse 3.62.10 of the *Rig Veda*, is recited by pious Hindus every day as they greet the rising sun; it is often introduced by the sacred syllable "Om" and the words "bhur bhuvah svah" ("earth, atmosphere, heaven"). The *Rig Veda* is the oldest religious text of India, composed, in Sanskrit, by people who lived in what is now the Punjab, in northwest India and Pakistan, around 1500 B.C.E.. The Vedic people were nomads and pastoralists who grazed their cows and horses, sheep and goats, in the hills. The *Rig Veda* (which means "Knowledge of Verses") consists of 1,028 poems, often called *mantras* (incantations, words with powers to affect reality), grouped into ten "circles" (*mandalas*). (It is generally agreed that the first and last books are later additions.)

The *Rig Veda* was preserved orally for centuries, even when the Indians had long come to use writing for everyday matters. It was a powerful text, whose power must not fall into the wrong hands. Unbelievers and infidels, as well as Dalits and women, were forbidden to learn the Veda, because they might defile or injure the power of the words. Its exclusively oral preservation ensured that the *Rig Veda* could not be misused even in the right hands: you couldn't take the *Rig Veda* down off the shelf in a library, for you had to learn it in the company of a wise teacher or guru, who would make sure that you understood its application to your life. Thus the Veda was usually passed down from father to son, and the lineages of the schools or "branches" that passed down particular commentaries "from one to another" were often also family lineages, patriarchal lineages. Those who taught and learned the *Rig Veda* in this early period were therefore invariably male Brahmins, though later other classes, too, may have supplied teachers; and from the start those who composed the poems may well have been more varied, even perhaps including women, to whom some poems are attributed.

The oral nature of the *Rig Veda* (and of the other Vedas, too) was expressed in the term often applied to it: it was called *shruti* ("what is heard"), both because it was originally "heard" (*shruta*) by the human seers to whom the gods dictated it and because it continued to be transmitted not by being read or seen but by being *heard* by the worshipers when the priests chanted it. The oral metaphor is not the only one—ancient sages also "saw" the Vedic verses—but it does reflect the dominant mode of transmission. It made no more sense only to "read" the Veda than it would only to read the score of a Brahms symphony.

One might suppose that a text preserved orally in this way would be subject to steadily encroaching inaccuracy and unreliability, that the message would become increasingly garbled like the message in a game of telephone; but one would be wrong. For the very same sacredness that made it necessary to preserve the *Rig*

A teacher with his students at a school in Thrissur, one of the few schools that still teach according to ancient Vedic methods.

Veda orally rather than in writing also demanded that it be preserved with meticulous accuracy. People regarded the *Rig Veda* as a text revealed to human poets by the gods, and one does not tinker with revelation. The *Rig Veda* was memorized in a number of mutually reinforcing ways, including matching physical movements (such as nodding the head) with particular sounds and chanting in a group, which does much to prevent individual slippage. There are no significant variant readings in any of the numerous copies of the *Rig Veda*; people preserved it intact orally long before they preserved it intact in manuscripts.

RITUAL

All the poems of the *Rig Veda* are ritual hymns in some sense, since all were sung as part of the Vedic ceremony, but only some are self-consciously devoted to the meaning of the ritual. Although detailed instructions on the performance of the rituals were spelt out only in later texts, the *Rig Veda* presupposes the existence of some proto-version of those texts. As far as we can reconstruct the rituals from what is, after all, a hymnal, the Vedic people made offerings to various gods by throwing various substances, primarily butter, into a fire that flared up dramatically in response and consumed the offering (the oblation). The Vedic ritual of sacrifice established bonds between the human world (particularly the components of the ritual) and corresponding parts of the universe. Ritual was thought to have effects on the visible and invisible worlds because of such connections. The verses served as *mantras* to be pronounced during rituals of various sorts: solemn or semi-public rituals such as royal consecrations, life-cycle rituals (weddings, funerals, and even such tiny concerns as a baby's first tooth), healing rituals, and both black and white magic spells. The personal concerns of the priests interest the authors of the poems (most of whom were priests themselves): the priest whose patron is the king laments the loss of his royal friend and praises faith and generosity, while other priests, whose tenure is more secure, express their happiness and gratitude. There were animal sacrifices (usually of a goat, occasionally of a horse) and simple offerings of butter into the consecrated fire. The more violent sacrifices have been seen as a kind of life insurance, giving the gods what they need to live (butter, animal sacrifices, etc.) in order that they will give us what we need to live.

The great gods of later Hinduism, Shiva (here called Rudra) and Vishnu, make only cameo appearances in the Veda ("Have Mercy on Us, Rudra" and "The Three Strides of Vishnu"). By contrast, the most important gods of the Veda, such as Agni, Soma, Indra, and Varuna, all closely tied to the Vedic sacrifice, become far less important in later Hinduism, though they survive as symbolic figures of natural forces: fire, the moon, rain, and the waters, respectively.

Agni, god of fire, sitting on his vehicle, the sacrificial ram, with the beard and paunch of a human Brahmin. Bhubaneshwar, in Orissa, eleventh century.

Agni, the god of fire (whose name is cognate with the English "ignite"), is invoked at the very beginning of the *Rig Veda* ("I Pray to Agni"). Agni is the divine model for the sacrificial priest, the messenger who carries the oblation from humans to the gods, brings all the gods to the sacrifice, and intercedes between gods and humans. When Agni is pleased, the gods become generous. The building of the fire-altar is a literally foundational Vedic ceremony, and the kindling and maintaining of three fires—the household fire, the ceremonial fire, and the sacrificial fire—were a basic responsibility of every householder.

An important ritual was devoted to Soma, a plant with hallucinogenic properties, which was pressed to release its fluid, consumed by the priests, and offered to the gods in the course of the sacrifice. Indra, the king of the gods, the paradigmatic warrior, is also the god of rain (a cousin of Zeus and Wotan). As the great Soma drinker, he appears often in the Soma poems, and he is the one who brings Agni back when the anti-gods (Asuras) steal him. The poets also praise Indra for freeing the cows that have been stolen and hidden in a cave, but his greatest deed is the killing of the dragon Vritra, who is called a Dasa, an "alien" or "slave." By killing Vritra, Indra simultaneously releases the waters or rains that Vritra has held back and conquers the enemies of the Vedic people, getting back the waters that are likened to cows trapped in the cave. Other Vedic gods, too, are personifications of natural forces, particularly solar gods. There are exquisite poems to the goddesses Dawn and Night, and to the god Surya, the Sun.

But most of the gods, even those representing natural forces, are vividly anthropomorphized. The gods are like us, only more so. They want what we want, things like marriage (and adultery), and fame, and praise. And most of the gods are closely associated with particular social classes: Agni is the Brahmin priest, Varuna the Brahminical sovereign ("Varuna Provoked to Anger," p. 88), Indra the warrior king.

We can also reconstruct a great deal of the belief system preserved in the *Rig Veda*, according to which the enemies of the Vedic gods are the anti-gods (Asuras), who live in the sky with the gods, and the ogres (Rakshasas), lower-class demons on earth that harass humans rather than gods. The anti-gods are the older brothers of the gods, the "dark, olden gods," like the Titans of Greek mythology, in contrast with "the mortal gods of heaven." The gods and anti-gods have the same moral substance (indeed, the gods lie and cheat far more than the anti-gods do—power corrupts, and divine power corrupts divinely); the anti-gods are simply the other team. The players on each side are not intrinsically differentiated by their morals, which shift back and forth from one category to another during the course of history and even from one text to another in any single period: As there are good humans and evil humans, so there are good gods and evil gods, good anti-gods and evil anti-gods. In the absence of ethical character, what the gods and anti-gods have is power, which they can exercise at their pleasure. The gods and anti-gods compete for the goods of the sacrifice, and since humans sacrifice to the gods, humans are against the anti-gods, who always, obligingly, lose to the gods in the end. It is therefore important for humans to keep the gods on their side. Moreover, since the gods live on sacrificial offerings provided by devout humans, the gods wish humans to be virtuous, for then they will continue to offer sacrifices.

The Vedic gods were light eaters; they consumed only a polite taste of the butter, or the animal offerings, or the expressed juice of the Soma plant, and the humans got to eat the leftovers. What was fed to the fire was fed to the gods. Not only did the gods live upon the sacrificial foods, but the energy generated in the sacrifice kept the universe going. The offerings that the priest made into the fire kept the fire in the sun from going out; if no one sacrificed, the sun would not rise each morning. Moreover, the heat that the priest generated in the sacrifice was a powerful weapon for gods or humans to use against their enemies. Heat is life, in contrast with the coldness of death; and Hindus believe that there is a fire in the belly (called "the fire that belongs to all men"), which digests all the food people eat, by cooking it (again). When that fire goes out, it's all over physically for the person in question, as it is ritually if the sacrificial fires go out; you must keep the sacrificial fire in your home burning, and carefully preserve an ember to carry to the new home if you move.

What the Vedic people asked the gods for most often in the prayers that accompanied sacrifice was life, health, victory in battle, and material prosperity, primarily in the form of horses and cows. As nomadic tribes, the Vedic people sought pastureland for their horses and their cattle, not only cows but other livestock kept for meat or milk, such as sheep and goats. As pastoralists and, later, herders and farmers, they lived in rural communities. They sacrificed cattle to the gods and ate them themselves, and they counted their wealth in cattle. They ate the beef from steers (the castrated bulls), both ritually and in secular feasts; they sacrificed the bulls and kept most of the cows for milk. One verse states that cows were "not to be killed," but another says that a cow should be slaughtered on the occasion of marriage, and another lists among animals to be sacrificed a cow that has been bred but has not calved, while still others include cows among animals whose meat was offered to the gods and then consumed by the people at the sacrifice. The usual meal of milk, ghee (liquid butter that has been heated and clarified until it is transparent), vegetables, fruit, wheat, and barley would be supplemented by the flesh of cattle, goats, and sheep on special occasions, washed down with *sura* (wine) or *madhu* (a kind of mead).

WOMEN

In the *Rig Veda*, a book dominated by men in a world dominated by men, women appear as objects. Every Vedic man valued equally his two most precious possessions: his cattle and his wife. A man needed a wife to be present when he performed any Vedic sacrifice, though she had to stay behind a screen. Women were expected to live on after the deaths of their husbands, as we learn from "The Funeral Fire" and the "Burial Hymn." Women also appear occasionally as subjects, even as possible authors, of Vedic poems. And women may have had a voice in poems that treat women's interests sympathetically, such as magic spells to incapacitate rival wives and to protect unborn children in the womb and the Vedic ritual that an unmarried virgin performs to get a husband. Some spells are directed against evil powers but addressed to human women, warning them to be careful.

Several poems explore the relationships between men and women, mortal and immortal. These poems present narratives centering on courtship, marriage, adultery, and estrangement, often in the form of conversations, such as the one between Agastya and Lopamudra. One long poem celebrates the marriage of the moon and the daughter of the Sun, and another alludes to the marriage of the Sun to the equine goddess Saranyu. But these are not simple hierogamies (sacred marriages), for the celestial gods also share our sexual frailties. To say that a marriage is made in heaven is not necessarily a blessing; in the Vedic world, adultery, too, is made in heaven.

Not all the females in the *Rig Veda* are anthropomorphic. Abstract nouns (usually feminine) are sometimes personified as female divinities, such as Destruction (Nirriti) and Speech (Vach). There are also natural entities with feminine names, such as the Waters, and terrestrial goddesses, such as the nymphs (Apsarases) and the Forest. But there are also divine wives, named after their husbands (Mrs. Surya, Mrs. Varuna, etc.) and at least one divine husband, named after his rather abstract wife: Indra is called "The Lord of Shachi" (*shachi-pati*), *pati* meaning "husband" or "master" (literally, "protector") and *shachi* meaning "power" (from the verb *shak* or *shach*). Together, they suggest that Indra is the master of power or married to a goddess named "Shachi," which became another name for Indrani, Mrs. Indra. So, too, later goddesses played the role of the *shakti* (another form derived from the same verb) that empowered the male gods. But no goddesses (except Vach, Speech) have any part in the sacrifice that was the heart of Vedic religion. Most Vedic creator gods (like most Vedic gods in general) are male, as in the "Creation Hymn" and "The Hymn of the Primeval Man," but one Vedic poem ("Aditi and the Birth of the Gods") imagines cosmic creation through the down-to-earth image of a female giving birth.

Prithivi ("broad"), with the connotation of something very much like "wide open spaces," is a name of the Earth, a goddess who was the natural consort of any king. The opposite of the word *prithu* is the word for a tight spot, in both the physical and the psychological sense; that word is *amhas*, signifying a kind of claustrophobia, the uneasiness of being constrained in a small space. (*Amhas* is cognate with the English word "anxiety" and the German *Angst*.) In this context, *amhas* might well be translated, "Don't fence me in," since it occurs in a number of Vedic poems in which the poet imagines himself trapped in a deep well or a cave, from which he prays to the gods to extricate him. (Sometimes it is the cows who are trapped in the cave, or the waters, or the sun.) Many of the poems take this form; the poet thanks the god for his help in the past ("Remember the time I was in that tight spot, and you got me out?"), reminds him of his gratitude ("And didn't I offer you great vats of Soma after that?"), flatters him ("No one but you can do this; you are the greatest"), and asks for a return engagement ("Well, I'm in even worse trouble now; come and help me, I beg you"). It is often the Ashvins who rescue people from such tight spots and bring them back into the good, broad places; they are twin horse-headed gods (whose name means "equine"), like the Gemini or Dioskuroi of Roman and Greek mythology. The other Vedic gods generally snub the Ashvins, in part because they are animal herders and physicians (the latter a low trade in ancient India, involving as it does polluting contacts with human bodies) and in part because they persist in slumming, helping out mortals in trouble. They are associated with the social class of workers (Vaishyas).

POLYTHEISM AND MONISM

The *Rig Veda* has a kind of polytheism that contains the seeds of what will later flower into monism (which assumes that all living things are elements of a single, universal substance). A much-quoted line proclaims this singular multiplicity, in a context that is theological rather than philosophical: "They call it Indra, Mitra, Varuna, Agni, and it is the heavenly bird that flies. The wise speak of what is One in many ways" (1.164.46). This is a tolerant, hierarchical sort of polytheism: the worshiper acknowledges the existence, and goodness, of gods other than the god that he or she is addressing at the moment.

The polytheism of Vedic religion is actually a kind of serial monotheism that Friedrich Max Müller (1823–1900) named "henotheism" or "kathenotheism," the worship of a number of gods, one at a time, regarding each as the supreme, or even the only, god while you are talking to that god. Thus, one Vedic poem will praise a god and give him credit for separating heaven and earth, propping them apart with a pillar, but another Vedic poem will use exactly the same words to praise another god. (In addition, each god has characteristics and deeds that are his alone; no one but Indra kills Vritra.) Vedic kathenotheism made possible a quasi-hierarchical pantheon; the attitude to each god was hierarchical, but the various competing practical monotheisms canceled one another out, so that the total picture was one of equality: each of several was the best.

This time-sharing property of the Vedic gods is an example of individual pluralism: each individual worshiper would know, and might use, several different poems to different gods. And the text is intolerant of intolerance: one Rig Vedic verse curses people who accuse others of worshiping false gods or considering the gods useless (7.104.14). When the double negatives in this statement cross one another out, we are left with a record of heretics and atheists. But the broader intellectual pluralism of the Vedas regards the world, or the deity, or truth itself as plural; the Vedas tackle the problem of ontology, of being, from several different angles, branching off from an ancient and still ongoing argument about the way the world *is*, about whether it is basically uniform or basically multiform.

PRONOUNCING GLOSSARY

Aditi: *uh-di-tee´*
Agastya: *uh-gus´-tyuh*
Agni: *ug´-nee*
Angiras: *un´-gi-rus´*
Apsaras: *up´-suh-ruhs´*
Atharva Veda: *uh-tahr´-vuh vay´-duh*
Daksha: *duk´-shuh*
Kiyamba: *ki-yahm´-buh*
Lopamudra: *loh-pah´-moo-drah´*
Manu: *muh´-noo*
Martanda: *mahr´-tahn´-duh*
Marut: *muh-root´*
Mitra: *mi´-truh*
Pakadurva: *pah´-kuh-door´-vah´*
Purusha: *poo´-roo-sha*
Rig Veda: *rig vay´-duh*
Rudra: *roo´-druh*
Sadhya: *sah´-dyuh*
Sama Veda: *sah´-muh vay´-duh*
Sindhu: *sind´-hoo*
Soma: *soh´-muh*
Tvashtri: *tvuh´-shtree*
Varuna: *vuh-roo´-nuh*
Vasishtha: *vuh-sish´-tuh*
Viraj: *vee-rahj´*
Vishnu: *vish´-noo*
Vyalkasha: *vyul-kuh-shah´*
Yajur Veda: *yuh´-joor vay´-duh*
Yama: *yuh´-muh*

I PRAY TO AGNI

Appropriately placed at the very beginning of the *Rig Veda*, this hymn invites Agni, the divine priest, to come to the sacrifice.

Rig Veda 1.1.1

I pray to Agni, the household priest who is the god of the sacrifice, the one who chants and invokes and brings most treasure.

Agni earned the prayers of the ancient sages, and of those of the present, too; he will bring the gods here.

Through Agni one may win wealth, and growth from day to day, glorious and most abounding in heroic sons.

Agni, the sacrificial ritual that you encompass on all sides—only that one goes to the gods.

Agni, the priest with the sharp sight of a poet, the true and most brilliant, the god will come with the gods.

Whatever good you wish to do for the one who worships you, Agni, through you, O Angiras,[1] that comes true.

To you, Agni, who shine upon darkness, we come day after day, bringing our thoughts and homage

to you, the king over sacrifices, the shining guardian of Order, growing in your own house.

Be easy for us to reach, like a father to his son. Abide with us, Agni, for our happiness.

TRANSLATED BY Wendy Doniger O'Flaherty.

1. The Angirases were an ancient family of priests, often identified with Vedic gods such as Agni and Indra.

CREATION HYMN

The *Rig Veda* imagines several quite different creation scenarios, most of which occur in the first and tenth books, the last to be composed, which already show the seeds of the philosophical speculation that was to emerge fully in the Brahmanas and Upanishads within a few centuries. The most basic form of Vedic cosmogony, or theory about the origins of the universe, is implicit in several hymns, though never spelled out: it is the formation of distinct elements out of the primeval cosmic flux, the evolution of order out of chaos. Other hymns describe creation as a result of the incest of the primeval father with his daughter, the dismemberment of a cosmic giant ("The Hymn of the Primeval Man"), or the first oblation offered into the fire.

This short hymn, though linguistically simple (with the exception of one or two puzzling nouns), is conceptually extremely provocative and has provoked hundreds of complex commentaries among Indian theologians and both Hindu and non-Hindu scholars. Called the "Nasadiya" from its opening words ("There was neither"), in many ways it is meant to puzzle and challenge, to raise unanswerable questions, to pile up paradoxes. It has an extraordinary humility and open-mindedness, a tolerance, a celebration of plurality, even in asking unanswerable questions about the beginnings of all things. For in the end it clearly implies that the gods cannot be the source of creation since they came after it.

Rig Veda 10.129

There was neither non-existence nor existence then; there was neither the realm of space nor the sky which is beyond. What stirred?[1] Where? In whose protection? Was there water, bottomlessly deep?

There was neither death nor immortality then. There was no distinguishing sign[2] of night nor of day. That one breathed, windless, by its own impulse. Other than that there was nothing beyond.

Darkness was hidden by darkness in the beginning; with no distinguishing sign, all this was water. The life force that was covered with emptiness, that one arose through the power of heat.[3]

Desire came upon that one in the beginning; that was the first seed of mind. Poets[4] seeking in their heart with wisdom found the bond of existence in non-existence.

Their cord[5] was extended across. Was there below? Was there above? There were seed-placers; there were powers.[6] There was impulse beneath; there was giving-forth above.

Who really knows? Who will here proclaim it? Whence was it produced? Whence is this creation? The gods came afterwards, with the creation of this universe. Who then knows whence it has arisen?

Whence this creation has arisen—perhaps it formed itself, or perhaps it did not—the one who looks down on it, in the highest heaven, only he knows—or perhaps he does not know.

TRANSLATED BY Wendy Doniger O'Flaherty.

1. The verb "stir" is often used to describe the motion of breath. The verse implies that the action precedes the actor.
2. That is, the difference between night and day, light and darkness, or possibly sun and moon.
3. "Heat" here refers to *tapas*, in particular the heat generated by ritual activity and by physical discipline of the body.
4. The Sanskrit term used here designates poets or inspired sages.
5. Possibly a reference to the "bond" mentioned in verse 4, or a kind of measuring cord by which the poets delimit—and hence create—the elements.
6. The verse contrasts male seed-placers, giving-forth, above, with female powers, impulse, below.

ADITI AND THE BIRTH OF THE GODS

This creation hymn poses several different and paradoxical answers to the riddle of origins. It is evident from the tone of the very first verse that the poet regards creation as a mysterious subject, and a desperate series of eclectic hypotheses (perhaps quoted from various sources) tumbles out right away: the craftsman (the priest, Brahmanaspati or Brihaspati, lord of inspired speech); the philosophical paradox of nonexistence (which we have just encountered in the "Creation Hymn"); contradiction (the earth born from the crouching divinity and then said to be born from the quarters of the sky); and mutual creation (Aditi and Daksha, the female principle of creation or infinity and the male principle of virile efficacy, creating one another). A Vedic commentator on this verse (Sayana, who probably lived in the fourteenth century C.E.) takes pains to explain that for the gods, two births can mutually produce one another.

The dominant visual image of this poem is the goddess of infinity, who crouches with knees drawn up and legs spread wide, a position designated by a term primarily associated with a woman giving birth but later associated with yoga, and one which is also depicted on seals from the Indus Valley. The poem then moves on to the myth of Aditi and Daksha, with vaguely incestuous overtones, and then to the creation of gods and humans. When the poet speaks of "seeing" the births of the gods (v. 1), he may refer not to being actually present at that early time but rather to the poet's gift of "seeing" mythic events by means of his inspired vision. The creation of the universe out of water (vv. 6–7) and the rescuing of the sun from the ocean (v. 7) move the hymn back to the cosmic level, from which it then returns to the anthropomorphism of the story of Martanda, whose name originally meant "born of an egg" (i.e., a bird) and is an epithet of the sun-bird. The verb describing what his mother did to him (in v. 8) may mean either to throw aside or to miscarry, and a later etymology of Martanda is "dead in the egg" (i.e., miscarried). Later Hindu texts tell how Aditi bore seven healthy sons, the Adityas, but the eighth was unformed, until the Adityas made him into the sun. On another level, Martanda is an epithet of the human being, born from the "dead egg" that is the embryo: he is thus an ancestor of humankind, born to die.

Rig Veda 10.72

Let us now speak with wonder of the births of the gods—so that some one may see them when the hymns are chanted in this later age.

The lord of sacred speech, like a smith, fanned them[1] together. In the earliest age of the gods, existence was born from nonexistence.

In the first age of the gods, existence was born from nonexistence. After this the quarters of the sky were born from her who crouched with legs spread.

The earth was born from her who crouched with legs spread, and from the earth the quarters of the sky were born. From Aditi, Daksha was born, and from Daksha Aditi was born.

For Aditi was born as your daughter, O Daksha, and after her were born the blessed gods, the kinsmen of immortality.

When you gods took your places there in the water with your hands joined together, a thick cloud of mist[2] arose from you like dust from dancers.

When you gods like magicians[3] caused the worlds to swell,[4] you drew forth the sun that was hidden in the ocean.

Eight sons are there of Aditi, who were born of her body. With seven she went forth among the gods, but she threw Martanda, the sun, aside.

With seven sons Aditi went forth into the earliest age. But she bore Martanda so that he would in turn beget offspring and then soon die.

TRANSLATED BY Wendy Doniger O'Flaherty.

1. "Them" must refer to the two worlds, heaven and earth, rather than to the gods.
2. "Mist" or "dust" refers to the atomic particles of water, half water and half air, mediating between matter and spirit.
3. These are Yatis, who may be a class of sages or ascetics or, most likely, magicians, among whose traditional bag of tricks in ancient India was the ability to make plants suddenly grow. They may be linked with the dancers in verse 6, another aspect of creative shamanism.
4. "Swell" implies filling up with milk from the breast.

THE HYMN OF THE PRIMEVAL MAN

In this hymn, the gods create the world by dismembering the cosmic giant, the Man, the primeval male, Purusha; *purusha* later comes to designate any male creature, indeed the male gender. He is both the victim that the gods sacrificed and the divinity to whom the sacrifice was dedicated; that is, he is both the subject and the object of a Vedic sacrifice that creates the whole universe, when the gods "spread" (v. 6) the sacrifice, stretching it out like the earth spread out on the cosmic waters. The sacrifice creates not only living creatures but the verses (of the *Rig Veda*), chants (of the *Sama Veda*), meters and formulas (of the *Yajur Veda*) (v. 9)—that is, the elements of the Vedic sacrifice! It also creates (v. 16) the first ritual laws, that is, the dharmas, a protean word that here designates the patterns of behavior established during this first sacrifice to serve as the model for all future sacrifices.

Moreover, the "sacrifice" means both the ritual and the victim killed in the ritual. The Vedic chicken-or-egg paradox is repeated in a more general pattern, in which the gods sacrifice to the gods, and a more specific pattern, in which one particular god, Indra, king of the gods, sacrifices (as a king) to himself (as a god). This tautological thinking is also reflected (v. 5) in the mutual creation of the Man and Viraj (the active female creative principle, who is later replaced, as the mate of Purusha, by Prakriti or material nature). Though the theme of the cosmic sacrifice is a widespread mythological motif, this hymn is part of a particularly Indo-European corpus of myths of the dismemberment of a cosmic giant. The underlying concept is, therefore, quite ancient; yet the fact that this is one of the latest hymns in the *Rig Veda* is evident from its reference to the four social classes or *varnas* (v. 12), the first time that this concept appears in an Indian text.

The fourth social class, the servants (or Shudras), may have consisted of the people new to the early Vedic system, perhaps the people already in India when the Vedic people entered, people from a system already in place in India, or simply the sorts of people who were always outside the system. That the Shudras were an afterthought is evident from the fact that the third class, the people (Vaishyas), is sometimes said to be derived from the word for "all" and therefore to mean "everyone," leaving no room for anyone below them—until someone added a class below them. In support of this supposition is the fact that the final combination often functioned not as a quartet but as a dualism: all of us (in the first three classes) versus all of them (in the fourth class, the non-us, the Others).

This text ranks the kings below the priests. The supremacy of Brahmins was much contested throughout later Hindu literature and may have been nothing but a Brahmin fantasy. Many texts argue, or assume, that Kshatriyas (the class of kings and warriors) never were as high as Brahmins, and others assume that they always were, and still are, higher than Brahmins. Buddhist literature puts the kings at the top, the Brahmins second, and many characters in Hindu texts also defend this viewpoint.

The French sociologist Georges Dumézil (1898–1986) argued that the Indo-European speakers—that is, the hypothetical people from whose hypothetical language, Proto-Indo-European, all Indo-European languages such as Sanskrit were derived—had been divided into three social classes or functions. At the top were kings who were also priests, then warriors who were also policemen, and then the rest of the people. But by the end of the period in which the *Rig Veda* was composed, a fourfold social system that deviates in two major regards from the Dumézilian model was in place: this new system adds a fourth class at the bottom, and it detaches the status of kings from that of priests, demoting kings to the second, warrior-policeman function. The kings have come down one rung from their former alleged status by no longer sharing first place with the Brahmins. This, then, would have been one of the earliest documented theocratic takeovers, a silent, totally mental palace coup—the Brahmins forcing the Kshatriyas into second rank by dissociating them from the exercise of priesthood. Thus, even in this hymn that supposedly assumes a social charter that was created at the very dawn of time and is to remain in place forever, we can see, in the positioning of the kings in the second rank, movement, change, slippage, progress, or decay, depending upon one's point of view.

Rig Veda 10.90

The Man has a thousand heads, a thousand eyes, a thousand feet. He pervaded the earth on all sides and extended beyond it as far as ten fingers.

It is the Man who is all this, whatever has been and whatever is to be. He is the ruler of immortality, when he grows beyond everything through food.

Such is his greatness, and the Man is yet more than this. All creatures are a quarter of him; three quarters are what is immortal in heaven.

With three quarters the Man rose upwards, and one quarter of him still remains here. From this[1] he spread out in all directions, into that which eats and that which does not eat.

From him Viraj was born, and from Viraj came the Man. When he was born, he ranged beyond the earth behind and before.

When the gods spread the sacrifice with the Man as the offering, spring was the clarified butter, summer the fuel, autumn the oblation.

They anointed[2] the Man, the sacrifice born at the beginning, upon the sacred grass.[3] With him the gods, Sadhyas,[4] and sages sacrificed.

From that sacrifice in which everything was offered, the melted fat[5] was collected, and he[6] made it into those beasts who live in the air, in the forest, and in villages.

From that sacrifice in which everything was offered, the verses and chants were born, the meters were born from it, and from it the formulas were born.

Horses were born from it, and those other animals that have two rows of teeth;[7] cows were born from it, and from it goats and sheep were born.

When they divided the Man, into how many parts did they apportion him? What do they call his mouth, his two arms and thighs and feet?

His mouth became the Brahmin; his arms were made into the King, his thighs the People, and from his feet the Servants were born.

The moon was born from his mind; from his eye the sun was born. Indra and Agni came from his mouth, and from his vital breath the Wind was born.

From his navel the middle realm of space arose; from his head the sky evolved. From his two feet came the earth, and the quarters of the sky from his ear. Thus they[8] set the worlds in order.

TRANSLATED BY Wendy Doniger O'Flaherty.

1. That is, from the quarter still remaining on earth, or perhaps from the condition in which he had already spread out from the earth with three quarters of his form.
2. The word actually means "sprinkle" with consecrated water, but it indicates the consecration of an initiate or a king.
3. A mixture of special grasses was strewn on the ground for the gods to sit upon.
4. A class of demigods or saints, whose name literally means "Those who are yet to be fulfilled."
5. Literally, a mixture of butter and sour milk used in the sacrifice; figuratively, the fat that drained from the sacrificial victim.
6. Probably the Creator, though possibly the Man himself.
7. Incisors above and below, such as dogs and cats have.
8. The gods.

There were seven enclosing-sticks[9] for him, and thrice seven fuel-sticks, when the gods, spreading the sacrifice, bound the Man as the sacrificial beast.

With the sacrifice the gods sacrificed to the sacrifice. These were the first ritual laws. These very powers reached the dome of the sky where dwell the Sadhyas, the ancient gods.

9. Green twigs that keep the fire from spreading; the fuel sticks are seasoned wood used for kindling.

THE FUNERAL FIRE

Just as the Vedic poets speculate in various contrasting, even conflicting ways about the process of creation, so do they vary in their speculations about death and in the questions they ask about death. The poets view death and sleep as a part of chaos, in contrast with the ordering of life in the hierarchy of social classes. (Later, some forms of Hinduism stood this value system on its head and viewed life as a terrifying chaos and death as the liberating peace of perfect order.) Surprisingly for a document so devoted to war and sacrifice, both of which involve killing, the *Rig Veda* actually says relatively little about death. What it does say, however, is comforting: for the virtuous, the world of death is a hazy but pleasant place.

The poet prays, "Deliver me from death, not from immortality" (7.59.12). By "immortality" the ancient sages meant not an actual eternity of life—even the gods do not live forever, though they live much longer than we do, and they never age—but rather a full life span (usually conceived of as seventy or a hundred years). Death in the Vedas is something to be avoided as long as possible; one hopes only to escape premature death, never to live forever; the prayer is that people should die in the right order, that children should not die before their parents. When it comes to the inevitable end of the life span, the *Rig Veda* offers varied but not necessarily contradictory images of a rather muted version of life on earth—shade (remember how hot India is), lots of good-looking women (this heaven is imagined by men), and good things to eat and drink. There is also some talk about a deep pit into which evil spirits and ogres are to be committed forever, but no evidence that human sinners would be sent there.

The poems also propose many different nonsolutions to the insoluble problem of death, many different ways that the square peg of the fact of death cannot be fitted into the round hole of human rationality. These approaches are often aware of one another; they react against one another and incorporate one another, through the process of intertextuality. And there is general agreement on some points, such as that the dead person would go to the House of Clay, to be punished, or to the World of the Fathers (that is, dead male ancestors), to be rewarded. Sometimes, as in this hymn, the corpse was burned; sometimes either the ashes of the cremated corpse were buried (as in the "Burial Hymn") or the corpse was.

The poet in another hymn addresses the corpse: "Leaving behind all imperfections, go back home again; merge with a glorious body" (10.14.8). Despite this "glorious body" with which the dead person merges, the poet of "The Funeral Fire" expresses concern that the old body be preserved, and confidence that it will be. Not only is the fire not to destroy the body, but it is to preserve it. Yet, when this poem addresses the dead man, it speaks of the ultimate cosmic dispersal of the old body, the eye to the sun, in a reversal of the dismemberment in "The Hymn of the Primeval Man."

There are even some vague intimations of transmigration—the passage of souls at death to another state of existence. There is a rather suggestive, if cryptic, allusion to rebirth: "Let him reach his own descendants, dressing himself in a life span" (10.16.5). This verse can be interpreted to mean that Agni should let the dead person come back to his former home and to his offspring. The dead in the Upanishads come back to the earth in the form of rain, and that idea may be encoded here, too. "Take root in the plants with your limbs" (10.16.3) might also be a hint of the sort of rebirth in plants that the Upanishads will describe in detail. The plants in verses 13 and 14, some called by obscure names, others by descriptive epithets ("cool one"), are water plants. These verses accompany the ritual of dousing the fire with water so thoroughly that it produces a marsh where water plants and frogs may thrive. The female frog, in particular, is a symbol of rain and fertility. Thus new life sprouts at the end of the funeral.

When the poet says, "Go to the sky or to earth, as is your nature" (10.16.3), he may mean that the dead man will be reborn according to the record of his good works, his karma. A line in another poem also hints at the importance of good karma: "Unite with the fathers, with Yama [king of the dead], with the rewards of your sacrifices and good deeds, in the highest heaven" (10.14.7). Still, these are, at best, the early, murky stirrings of a doctrine that will become clear only in the Brahmanas and Upanishads.

Rig Veda 10.16

Do not burn him entirely, Agni, or engulf him in your flames. Do not consume his skin or his flesh. When you have cooked him perfectly, O knower of creatures, only then send him forth to the fathers.

When you cook him perfectly, O knower of creatures, then give him over to the fathers. When he goes on the path that leads away the breath of life, then he will be led by the will of the gods.

[*To the dead man:*] May your eye go to the sun, your life's breath to the wind. Go to the sky or to earth, as is your nature; or go to the waters, if that is your fate. Take root in the plants with your limbs.

[*To Agni:*] The goat is your share; burn him with your heat.[1] Let your brilliant light and flame burn him. With your gentle forms, O knower of creatures, carry this man to the world of those who have done good deeds.

Set him free again to go to the fathers, Agni, when he has been offered as an oblation in you and wanders with the sacrificial drink.[2] Let him reach his own descendants, dressing himself in a life span. O knower of creatures, let him join with a body.

[*To the dead man:*] Whatever the black bird has pecked out of you, or the ant, the snake, or even a beast of prey, may Agni who eats all things make it whole, and Soma[3] who has entered the Brahmins.

Gird yourself with the limbs of the cow as an armor[4] against Agni, and cover yourself with fat and suet, so that he will not embrace you with his impetuous heat in his passionate desire to burn you up.

TRANSLATED BY Wendy Doniger O'Flaherty.

1. This refers to the practice of placing the limbs of a goat over the dead man, so that Agni would consume them and not the corpse with his violent flames.
2. The libation offered to the gods at the funeral.
3. Soma appears here in his capacity of god or plant (compare the cooling plants in the final verses), or simply as the Soma juice inside the priests.
4. This refers to the limbs and caul (inner membrane of the embryo) or skin of a dead cow that would be used in addition to or in place of the scapegoat, while the corpse would be anointed with fat and suet.

[*To Agni:*] O Agni, do not overturn this cup[5] that is dear to the gods and to those who love Soma, fit for the gods to drink from, a cup in which the immortal gods carouse.

I send the flesh-eating fire far away. Let him go to those whose king is Yama,[6] carrying away all impurities. But let that other, the knower of creatures, come here and carry the oblation to the gods, since he knows the way in advance.

The flesh-eating fire has entered your house, though he sees there the other, the knower of creatures; I take that god away to the sacrifice of the fathers.[7] Let him carry the heated drink to the farthest dwelling-place.

Agni who carries away the corpse, who gives sacrifice to the fathers who are strengthened by truth—let him proclaim the oblation to the gods and to the fathers.

[*To the new fire:*] Joyously would we put you in place, joyously would we kindle you. Joyously carry the joyous fathers here to eat the oblation.

Now, Agni, quench and revive the very one you have burnt up. Let Kiyamba, Pakadurva and Vyalkasha plants grow in this place.

O cool one, bringer of coolness; O fresh one, bringer of freshness; unite with the female frog. Delight and inspire this Agni.

5. A wooden cup that the dead man had used in life to make Soma offerings to the gods and to "those who love the Soma" (i.e., the fathers) was filled with melted butter and placed at the corpse's head.

6. Yama is the king of the dead, therefore king of the fathers.

7. The hot oblation for the fathers, who either come to the sacrifice (brought by the non-flesh-eating Agni) or have Agni bring them the drink.

BURIAL HYMN

The *Rig Veda* is more concerned with the living than with the dead, as is clear from the way this burial hymn, which begins by addressing Death and occasionally the dead man, addresses the mourners. The poet urges the widow to go on living. Certainly she is not expected to die with her husband, though "lying beside a dead man" may have been a survival from an earlier period when the wife was actually buried with her husband; the *Atharva Veda* (18.3.1) regards the practice of the wife lying down beside her dead husband (but perhaps then getting up again) as an ancient custom. On the other hand, women in the Vedic period may have performed a purely *symbolic* suicide on their husbands' graves, which was later cited as scriptural support for the *actual* self-immolation of women on their husbands' pyres, which the British, much later, called "suttee."

Rig Veda 10.18

Go away, death, by another path that is your own, different from the road of the gods. I say to you who have eyes, who have ears: do not injure our children or our men.

Translated by Wendy Doniger O'Flaherty.

When you have gone, wiping away the footprint of death, stretching farther your own lengthening span of life, become pure and clean and worthy of sacrifice, swollen with offspring and wealth.

These who are alive have now parted from those who are dead. Our invitation to the gods has become auspicious today. We have gone forward to dance and laugh, stretching farther our own lengthening span of life.

I set up this wall[1] for the living, so that no one else among them will reach this point. Let them live a hundred full autumns and bury death in this hill.

As days follow days in regular succession, as seasons come after seasons in proper order, in the same way order their life spans, O Arranger, so that the young do not abandon the old.

Climb on to old age, choosing a long life span, and follow in regular succession, as many as you are. May Tvashtri[2] who presides over good births be persuaded to give you a long life span to live.

These women who are not widows, who have good husbands—let them take their places, using butter[3] to anoint their eyes. Without tears, without sickness, well dressed let them first climb into the marriage bed.

Rise up, woman, into the world of the living. Come here; you are lying beside a man whose life's breath has gone. You were the wife of this man who took your hand and desired to have you.

I take the bow[4] from the hand of the dead man, to be our supremacy and glory and power, and I say, 'You are there; we are here. Let us as great heroes conquer all envious attacks.'

Creep away to this broad, vast earth, the mother that is kind and gentle. She is a young girl, soft as wool to anyone who makes offerings; let her guard you from the lap of Destruction.[5]

Open up, earth; do not crush him. Be easy for him to enter and to burrow in. Earth, wrap him up as a mother wraps a son in the edge of her skirt.

Let the earth as she opens up stay firm, for a thousand pillars[6] must be set up. Let them be houses dripping with butter for him, and let them be a refuge for him here for all his days.

I shore up the earth all around you; let me not injure you as I lay down this clod of earth. Let the fathers hold up this pillar for you; let Yama build a house for you here.

On a day that will come, they will lay me in the earth, like the feather of an arrow.[7] I hold back speech that goes against the grain,[8] as one would restrain a horse with a bridle.

1. The wall may have been a stone to mark the boundary of the world of death, while the hill was the mound over the grave.
2. The artisan and smith of the gods.
3. Ritually purified butter would be used instead of mascara or eye shadow to protect the women among the mourners.
4. Probably done only when the dead man was a warrior.
5. Destruction (Nirriti) is the female personification of disorder and disintegration, in contrast with the orderly and peaceful aspects of death.
6. Yama, the king of the dead, built a house, with pillars, for the dead man, perhaps symbolized by the urn containing his bones (or his cremated ashes) placed in the earth.
7. An elliptic metaphor, perhaps referring to the way the feather is stuck into the cleft made for it in the arrow, or as a feather floats gently down to earth when it is freed from the arrow.
8. Most likely, a command to remain silent lest one say something ill-omened, but also perhaps a reference to the poet's satisfaction in having made a good hymn, or his pleasure in returning to more auspicious subjects, or a statement that the rest is silence.

VARUNA PROVOKED TO ANGER

Varuna combines aspects of the roles of priest and king. His original function was that of a sky god, in particular the god of the waters in the heavenly vault (like Ouranos, a sky god who is Varuna's Greek counterpart). But by the time of the *Rig Veda* Varuna had developed into a god whose primary role was watching over human behavior (as a sky god was well situated to do) and punishing those who violated the sacred law, of which Varuna was the most important custodian. He would snare miscreants in his bonds, which often revealed their presence through disease (particularly edema, the retention of water) or misfortune.

This hymn to Varuna has an extraordinarily introspective tone, a sense of personal unworthiness and uncertainty ("What did I do?"). The poem assumes that, on the one hand, one may not be blamed, or perhaps not entirely blamed, for errors committed under the influence of passionate emotions, and, on the other hand, one may be punished not only for conscious errors but also for errors committed unconsciously (in sleep, or under the sway of wine) or even by other people (both one's parents and one's children). "The evil that sleep does not avert" may be a bad dream or a deed committed during sleep. The implication of someone else in one's own evil deed tends to negate the sense of remorse; one can regret the results of an unknown act (visible in Varuna's punishment) even if someone else is responsible for it, but not repent for intending to do it. The worshiper, like the sage Vasishtha, said to be the author of this hymn, wishes to serve Varuna in order to become free from the effects of his misdeeds. This idea becomes much more important in later Hinduism, in texts that characterize the Vedic transaction as one in which the ritual transfers to the sponsor the good karma that the priest generates. Eventually, the idea of the transfer of good karma in a ritual act with effects in this life develops into the idea of the moral consequences of any act, not only in this life but also in future lives.

Rig Veda 7.86

The generations have become wise by the power of him who has propped apart the two world-halves even though they are so vast.[1] He has pushed away the dome of the sky to make it high and wide; he has set the sun on its double journey[2] and spread out the earth.

And I ask my own heart, 'When shall I be close to Varuna? Will he enjoy my offering and not be provoked to anger? When shall I see his mercy and rejoice?'

I ask myself what that transgression was, Varuna, for I wish to understand. I turn to the wise to ask them. The poets have told me the very same thing: 'Varuna has been provoked to anger against you.'

O Varuna, what was the terrible crime for which you wish to destroy your friend who praises you? Proclaim it to me so that I may hasten to prostrate myself before you and be free from sin, for you are hard to deceive and are ruled by yourself alone.

TRANSLATED BY Wendy Doniger O'Flaherty.

1. Creation consists in the act (here attributed to Varuna, elsewhere to other gods) of propping apart heaven and earth and releasing the sun.

2. Either by day in the sky and under the earth by night, or, less likely, the sun's daily and annual revolutions.

Free us from the harmful deeds of our fathers, and from those that we have committed with our own bodies. O king, free Vasishtha like a thief who has stolen cattle, like a calf set free from a rope.

The mischief was not done by my own free will, Varuna; wine, anger, dice, or carelessness led me astray. The older shares in the mistake of the younger.[3] Even sleep does not avert evil.

As a slave serves a generous master, so would I serve the furious god and be free from sin. The noble god gave understanding to those who did not understand;[4] being yet wiser, he speeds the clever man to wealth.

O Varuna, you who are ruled by yourself alone, let this praise lodge in your very heart. Let it go well for us always with your blessings.

3. The elder brother may be implicated in his younger brother's lapse, or he may be the cause of it. "Older" may also refer to an older generation, the ancestral sin mentioned in the previous verse.
4. The wisdom that Varuna gives to the generations is his own truth. Varuna himself is "yet wiser" either than those to whom he gave understanding or than the clever man that he helps. Varuna is wise in a pious and mystical sense; the clever man is merely worldly-wise.

AGASTYA AND LOPAMUDRA

The conversation poems of the *Rig Veda* often involve goddesses and heavenly nymphs, are particularly associated with fertility, and may have been part of a special ritual performance involving actors and dancers. The dialogues with women present situations in which one member of the pair attempts to persuade the other to engage in some sort of sexual activity; sometimes, as in "Agastya and Lopamudra," it is the woman who takes the role of persuader, sometimes the man. In general, the mortal women and immortal men are successful in their persuasion, while the quasi-immortal women and mortal men fail. Often, as here, the poem zeroes in on a story that is already well under way, taking it up at a crucial turning point in a plot that we are presumed to know (and that the later commentaries spell out for us).

In this conversation, Lopamudra seeks to turn her husband, Agastya, who has taken a vow of chastity, away from his asceticism so that he will beget a child upon her. Agastya implies that he will ultimately give in to her desires, and she overpowers him (v. 4). Afterward, he wishes to atone for his lapse by drinking Soma. Finally, the poet affirms that the two of them, by uniting after each had perfected a power (she eroticism, he asceticism), achieved both forms of immortality, spiritual and corporeal (through children). This story was retold often and is perhaps best known from the *Mahabharata* (3.94–97).

Rig Veda 1.179

[*Lopamudra:*] 'For many autumns past I have toiled,[1] night and day, and each dawn has brought old age closer, age that distorts the glory of bodies. Virile[2] men should go to their wives.

TRANSLATED BY Wendy Doniger O'Flaherty.

1. This word often refers to the exertion of religious activity. When Lopamudra uses it, she may refer to her work as Agastya's wife or to her own asceticism (the commentator suggests that both of them practice asceticism), and when he uses it (v. 3) he refers to his asceticism.
2. The basic meaning of this word (*vrishan*), which recurs throughout this hymn (and elsewhere in the *Rig Veda*), is one who sheds rain or seed; it comes to mean a potent male animal, particularly a bull or a stallion.

'For even the men of the past, who acted according to the Law and talked about the Law with the gods, broke off when they did not find the end.[3] Women should unite with virile men.'

[*Agastya:*] 'Not in vain is all this toil, which the gods encourage. We two must always strive against each other, and by this we will win the race that is won by a hundred means, when we merge together as a couple.'

[*Lopamudra:*] 'Desire has come upon me for the bull who roars and is held back,[4] desire engulfing me from this side, that side, all sides.

[*The poet:*] Lopamudra draws out the virile bull: the foolish woman sucks dry the panting[5] wise man.

[*Agastya:*] 'By this Soma which I have drunk, in my innermost heart I say: Let him forgive us if we have sinned, for a mortal is full of many desires.'

Agastya, digging with spades,[6] wishing for children, progeny, and strength, nourished both ways, for he was a powerful sage. He found fulfilment of his real hopes among the gods.

3. The end of their asceticism: that is, they died childless and unsuccessful.
4. He holds back his seed. If this verse is spoken by Agastya, it would mean: "The desire of my swelling reed, which is held back, overwhelms me . . ."
5. He pants either with desire (before) or with exhaustion (after); "panting" merely indicates heavy breathing. This verse may follow an episode of mimed sexual intercourse.
6. A fairly obvious sexual metaphor.

HAVE MERCY ON US, RUDRA

Though only three entire hymns in the *Rig Veda* are addressed to the storm god Rudra, the rich ambivalence of his character is the basis of an important line of theology that culminates in the Hindu god Shiva, who inherits several of Rudra's characteristics, including his name. Rudra is fierce and destructive like a terrible beast, like a wild storm; but he is also a healer. He is invoked with Vedic hymns but not invited to partake in the regular Vedic sacrifice; as the embodiment of wildness and unpredictable danger, he is addressed more with the hope of keeping him at bay than with the wish to bring him near.

Rig Veda 1.114

We bring these thoughts to the mighty Rudra, the god with braided hair,[1] who rules over heroes, so that it will be well with our two-footed and four-footed creatures, and in this village all will flourish unharmed.

Have mercy on us, Rudra, and give us life-force. We wish to bow low in service to you who rule over heroes. Whatever happiness and health Manu[2] the father won by sacrifice, we wish to gain that with you to lead us forth.

We wish to gain your kindness, Rudra, through sacrifice to the gods, for you are generous. O ruler over heroes, come to our families with kindness. Let us offer the oblation to you with our heroes free from injury.

TRANSLATED BY Wendy Doniger O'Flaherty.

1. Rudra's long hair is braided in dreadlocks or matted on top of his head.
2. As the primeval ancestor of humankind, Manu (p. 202) performed the first sacrifice by mortals for immortals.

We call down for help the dreaded Rudra who completes the sacrifice, the sage who flies. Let him repel far from us the anger of the gods; it is his kindness that we choose to have.

Tawny boar of the sky, dreaded form with braided hair, we call you down and we bow low. Holding in his hand the healing medicines that we long for, let him grant us protection, shelter, refuge.

These words are spoken for Rudra, the father of the Maruts,[3] words sweeter than sweet, to strengthen him. And grant us, O immortal, the food for mortals. Have mercy on us, and on our children and grandchildren.

Do not slaughter the great one among us or the small one among us, nor the growing or the grown. Rudra, do not kill our father or our mother, nor harm the bodies dear to us.[4]

Do not harm us in our children or grandchildren, nor in our life span, nor in our cows or in our horses. Rudra, do not in fury slaughter our heroes. With oblations we call you here for ever.

I have driven these praises to you as the herdsman drives his cattle. Grant us kindness, father of the Maruts, for your kindness brings blessings most merciful, and so it is your help that we choose to have.

Keep far away from us your cow-killing and man-killing power, O ruler of heroes. Have mercy on us and speak for us, O god, and grant us double protection.[5]

Seeking help, we have spoken in homage to him. Let Rudra with the Maruts hear our call. Let Mitra, Varuna, Aditi, Sindhu,[6] Earth and Sky grant this to us.

3. Gods of wind and storm.
4. This phrase means both our own bodies and the bodies of people we love.
5. Probably protection from Rudra's own wrath as well as that of the other gods (before whom he is here asked to speak on behalf of the worshiper), or from the killing of men and the killing of cattle.
6. A river goddess. "Sindhu" means "river" and is the basis of both the name of the Indus River and the words "Hindu" and "India."

THE THREE STRIDES OF VISHNU

Vishnu is, like Rudra, invoked alone in only a few Vedic hymns, but he is a more typically Vedic god, solar, benevolent, and procreative. This hymn is the basis of the myth of Vishnu's dwarf avatar (developed in later Sanskrit texts), who expands into a giant form and takes three steps to win the world from the anti-gods. Here, Vishnu is a giant, whose three space-creating steps prop apart and thereby make the earthly regions and the "upper dwelling-place" (v. 1) or "highest footstep" (vv. 5–6), the seat of the immortal gods; the resulting space in between, covered by the second step, makes the universe threefold. His three steps are dawn, noon, and sunset, or the three phases of the year that Vishnu "measures apart" (vv. 1 and 3). The word *pada* (cognate with the Latin *pes, pedis*, and the English *foot*) recurs with several meanings: "foot," "step," "footprint," and "base" (in the sense of dwelling place); in the final verse it refers both to the actual place where humans and gods dwell and to the footstep made by a cow's hoof.

Rig Veda 1.154

Let me now sing the heroic deeds of Vishnu, who has measured apart the realms of earth, who propped up the upper dwelling-place, striding far as he stepped forth three times.

They praise for his heroic deeds Vishnu who lurks in the mountains, wandering like a ferocious wild beast, in whose three wide strides all creatures dwell.

Let this song of inspiration go forth to Vishnu, the wide-striding bull who lives in the mountains, who alone with but three steps measured apart this long, far-reaching dwelling-place.

His three footprints, inexhaustibly full of honey, rejoice in the sacrificial drink. Alone, he supports threefold the earth and the sky—all creatures.

Would that I might reach his dear place of refuge, where men who love the gods rejoice. For there one draws close to the wide-striding Vishnu; there, in his highest footstep, is the fountain of honey.[1]

We wish to go to your dwelling-places, where there are untiring, many-horned cattle.[2] There the highest footstep of the wide-stepping bull shines brightly down.

Translated by Wendy Doniger O'Flaherty.

1. The honey in the footprints acts like Soma, intoxicating the creatures who dwell there—the "men who love the gods"—and making them rejoice. Though the honey is in all three of Vishnu's footsteps (v. 4), the highest footstep is the fountain of the nectar of immortality.

2. The cattle may simply stand for cattle (and, by extension, the riches of life) or for something more. They may be rays of light (coming from Vishnu as the sun); they may be stars. As cattle, they are untiring; as rays, unfading; "many-horned" would mean something like "twinkling" (for stars) or "widely diffused" (for sunbeams).

SACRIFICE IN THE BRAHMANAS 800–500 B.C.E.

Where the *Rig Veda* expressed uncertainty and begged the gods for help, the Brahmanas (mythological, philosophical, and ritual glosses on the Vedas) express confidence that the Vedic verses (*mantras*) can deal with all dangers.

What accounts for this dramatic shift in tone, from questions to answers? In part, it was caused by a major change in the living conditions of the authors of these texts. For the Brahmanas were composed during a time of social and intellectual transformation so extreme that it could well be called revolutionary. From about 1100 to 1000 B.C.E., Vedic texts begin to mention the Doab ("Two Waters"), the land between the Ganges and the Yamuna (later called the Jumna). Then, in about 800 B.C.E., we find references to an area farther down in the western and middle Ganges Valley, where people built palaces and kingdoms. The move to the Ganges took place incrementally over several centuries, and the political changes were correspondingly gradual. Among the first cities were Kashi, later known as Varanasi (or Benares, the capital of Koshala/Videha), and, west of Kashi, Kaushambi (in Vatsa, now Uttar Pradesh), probably founded between 1300 and 1000 B.C.E. The Brahmanas must have been composed a few centuries after the founding of these cities, for considerable time must have passed since the composition of the *Rig Veda* (even of the first and last books, which are already noticeably later than the other eight). The language of the Brahmanas is significantly different, somewhat like the shift from *Beowulf* to Chaucer in early English. The Brahmanas cite Vedic verses and explain them, describing the circumstances under which those verses were first created. Not only the language but the nature of the texts changed: between 1000 and 500 B.C.E., Vedic rituals spawned more and more commentaries, and by the sixth century B.C.E. the different schools, or branches, were well established.

PRONOUNCING GLOSSARY

Agni/agni: *ug´-nee*
Agnihotra: *ug´-nee-hoh´-truh*
agri: *uh´-gree*
aha: *ah´-huh*
Bhrigu: *bri´-goo*
charati: *chuh´-ruh-tee*
charu: *chuh´-roo*
Indra: *in´-druh*
Jaiminiya Brahmana: *jai´-muh-nee´-yuh brah´-muh-nuh*
jhasha: *juh´-shuh*
Manu: *muh´-noo*
nishkriti: *nish-kri´-tee*
oshadhayas: *oh´-shuh-dah´-yuhs*
Prajapati: *pruh-jah´-puh-tee´*
purusha: *poo-roo´-sha*
Pushan: *poo´-shun*
Shatapatha Brahmana: *shuh´-tuh-puh´-tuh brah´-muh-nuh*
Surya: *soor´-yuh*
sva: *svuh*
Svaha: *svah-hah´*
Ugradeva Rajani: *oo´-gruh-day´-vuh rah´-juh-nee*
Varuna: *vuh´-roo-nuh*
Vayu: *vah´-yoo*

SHATAPATHA BRAHMANA

Each of the Brahmanas developed within a separate school of one of the three Vedas; the *Shatapatha Brahmana* ("The Brahmana of a Hundred Paths") is attached to the *Yajur Veda*, the Veda dealing with sacrificial ritual. Every part of the *Shatapatha* is linked in some way to the ritual, particularly to the sacred fire ("Prajapati Creates Fire"), and although there is little information about actual ritual procedure (which is taken up by the later texts called the Prayogas), the text does go into considerable detail about the horse sacrifice ("Killing the Sacrificial Horse" and "Restoring the Horse"). It also contains a number of myths, some of which were reworked in later texts ("The Fish Saves Manu from the Flood").

PRAJAPATI CREATES FIRE

The principal gods in this, as in most Brahmana rituals and myths, are Prajapati, "lord of progeny" or "lord of creatures," the Vedic god of creation, and Speech (Vach), a feminine noun in Sanskrit, a goddess in the *Rig Veda*. This passage is typical in its interest in Speech as a creative force; in its concern with food and death, and the relationship between them; and in its use of verbal etymologies, many of them different from what philologists believe to be the derivations of the words. Like most of the Brahmanas, it strives to determine a way not to die. In this episode, the author puns on the idea that Prajapati loses his power of speech (as he will lose other powers in the course of creation) because he becomes literally speechless with terror. The eater versus the noneater (or the eaten) and the appeasing of a dangerous, hungry creature are scenarios that recur in the Brahmanas. Here, Prajapati spills his seed into the fire, and the seed takes the form of milk that is milked out of him or butter that is churned from him, the verb "rubbed" implying either or both of these acts.

Shatapatha Brahmana 2.2.4.1–8

Truly, Prajapati alone existed here in the beginning. He thought, 'How can I bring forth creatures?' He exhausted himself and produced heat. He gave birth to Agni, fire, from his mouth. Since he created him from his mouth, therefore Agni is an eater of food. And whoever knows that Agni is an eater of food in this way, he himself becomes an eater of food. Thus he gave birth to him first of the gods; since *'agni'* is the same as *'agri'* ('first'), he is called Agni. As soon as he was born, he went in front; and people say of anyone who goes in front, 'He goes first.' This is why Agni is called Agni.

Then Prajapati thought, 'I have given birth to this Agni, this eater of food, from my own self. But there is no food here but me, whom he would surely not eat.' Now, at that time the earth was quite bald; there were no plants or trees. This was what was on his mind.

Then Agni turned toward Prajapati with a wide-open mouth, and as Prajapati became frightened, the female who was his greatness went away from

Translated by Wendy Doniger O'Flaherty.

him. For Speech is his own greatness, and Speech left him. He wished to make an offering into his own self. He rubbed[1] (his hands), and because he rubbed them, they have no hair on them. And there he found the offering of clarified butter or the offering of milk—both of them are essentially milk.

But this offering did not satisfy Prajapati, for it had become mixed with hairs. He poured it out (into the fire, Agni) and said, 'Suck this and burn it' (*osha dhaya*). The plants arose from it, and therefore they are called plants (*oshadhayas*). He rubbed (his hands) a second time, and there he found another offering of clarified butter or of milk—both of them are essentially milk.

This offering satisfied him. But he was in doubt, wondering, 'Shall I offer it or not?' His own greatness (i.e., Speech) said to him, 'Offer it!' Prajapati realized, 'What is my own (*sva*) has spoken (*aha*),' and he made the offering. And therefore one says 'Svaha!'[2] when making an offering. From that there arose the (sun) who heats and the (wind) who blows.[3] And Agni turned away from him.

Thus, by making an offering, Prajapati gave birth to himself and saved himself from Agni, from Death, who was about to eat him. And whoever knows about this and offers the Agnihotra oblation,[4] he gives birth to himself in his progeny, just as Prajapati gave birth to himself. And in this very same way, he saves himself from Agni, from Death, when he is about to eat him.

For when he dies, and they place him on the fire, then he is born out of the fire, and then the fire consumes only his body. And just as he is born from his father or from his mother, in that very way he is born from the fire. But whoever does not offer the Agnihotra oblation, he *never* comes to life again. And that is why the Agnihotra *must* be offered.

1. By rubbing or churning with his hands he produces sacrificial butter. The Vedic fire was produced using a fire-drill, which consists of a bottom slab with a central depression (often compared to a vagina) on which a long stick (often compared to a penis) is twirled either with the hands or using a string wrapped around it. The friction ignited the tinder, and blowing on it made the fire blaze.

2. "Svaha," the exclamation made when an oblation is offered to the gods, is the name of the oblation and of the wife of Agni.

3. Another possible translation would be: "Then Agni arose and grew hot and became mighty and purified."

4. The offering, usually butter, made into the sacrificial fire.

THE FISH SAVES MANU FROM THE FLOOD

The myth of the fish and the flood is ancient and widespread in the Indo-European and Semitic worlds. In this, its earliest extant Indian manifestation, it is Manu, the ancestor of humankind (p. 202), who saves the fish; in later Hinduism, the fish becomes an avatar of the god Vishnu. "Fish swallows fish" was the basis of the Indian term for anarchy (*matsya-nyaya*), the equivalent of our "dog eat dog."

Shatapatha Brahmana 1.8.1.1–6

In the morning they brought Manu water for ablutions, just as they bring it for washing the hands. As he was washing, a fish came into his hands and said, 'Care for me and I will save you.' 'From what will you save me?' 'A flood will carry away all these creatures; I will save you from it.' 'How should you be cared for?' 'As long as we are tiny,' said the fish, 'our destruction is great, for fish swallows fish. Care for me at first in a pot, and when I outgrow it, dig a trench and care for me in it. And when I outgrow that, then take me down to the ocean, for then I will be beyond destruction.'

The fish grew steadily into a *jhasha*,[1] for that grows largest. It said, 'In a certain year, the flood will come. Then you will build a ship and come to me, and when the flood has risen you will enter the ship and I will save you from the flood.' Manu cared for it in this way and carried it down to the ocean. And in the very year which the fish had indicated, he built a ship and came to him, and when the flood had risen he entered the ship. The fish swam up to him, and he fastened the rope of the ship to the horn of the fish, and with it he sailed through to the northern mountain. 'I have saved you,' said the fish. 'Fasten the ship to a tree, but do not let the water cut you off when you are on the mountain; as the water subsides, keep following it down.' And he kept following it down, in this way, and so that slope of the northern mountain is known as Manu's Descent. The flood swept away all other creatures, and Manu alone remained here.

TRANSLATED BY Wendy Doniger O'Flaherty.

1. The *jhasha*, a large fish of indefinite species, is the constellation Pisces.

KILLING THE SACRIFICIAL HORSE

One of the few great public ceremonies alluded to in the Vedas is the sacrifice of a horse, by suffocation rather than beheading but followed by dismemberment. There are inscriptional records of (as well as literary satires on) horse sacrifices throughout Indian history. The original political symbolism of the Vedic horse sacrifice is blatant: the consecrated white stallion was "set free" to wander for a year before he was brought back home and killed, a ritual enactment of the actual equine wandering typical of Vedic culture. During that year, the horse was guarded by an army that followed him and claimed for the king any land on which he grazed. By the late Vedic period, when the Vedic people had begun to grow fodder crops, the stallion would have been stabled, and a stabled stallion behaves quite differently from one in the wild; he tends to return to the stable where he has been fed. The idea that he will wander away in the Ganges Valley, as he used to do up in the Punjab, was by this time an anachronism, a conscious archaism. The king's army therefore drove the horse onward and guided him into the neighboring lands that the king intended to take over. Thus the ritual that presented itself as a casual equine stroll over the king's lands was in fact an orchestrated annexation of the lands on a king's border; a ritual about grazing became a ritual about increasing political power. No wonder the Sanskrit texts insist that a king had to be very powerful indeed before he could undertake a horse sacrifice, and very few kings did in fact perform this ritual.

One Vedic poem (1.162) describes the horse sacrifice in strikingly concrete, rather gruesome detail, beginning with the ceremonial procession of the horse accompanied by a dappled goat, who was killed with the horse but offered to a different, less important god. The poet in that hymn intermittently consoles the horse (and himself) with the assertion that all will be restored in heaven, words in which we may see the stirrings of ambivalence about the killing of an animal, even in a religious ceremony, an ambivalence that will become much more explicit in the next few centuries. We may see even here a kind of ritual nonviolence that is expressed in a concern that the victim should not bleed or suffer or cry out (one reason the animal was strangled). The euphemism for the killing of the horse, "pacifying" or "quieting," further muted the growing uneasiness associated with killing an animal. Moreover, unlike cows, goats, and other animals that were sacrificed, some in the horse sacrifice, the horse was not actually eaten (though it was cooked and served to the gods). Certain parts of the horse's carcass (such as the marrow, or the fat from the chest, the caul, pericardium, or omentum containing the internal organs) were offered to Agni, the god of the fire, and the consecrated king and the priests would inhale the cooking fumes (regarded as "half-eating-by-smelling"). The gods and priests, as well as guests at the sacrificial feast, ate the male livestock (rams, billy goats, and steers); only the gods and priests drank the Soma; no one ate the horse. Perhaps the horse was not eaten because of the close relationship between the Vedic people and their horses.

The Brahmanas tell us more about the way in which the horse sacrifice, which began as a relatively simple ritual at the time of the *Rig Veda*, developed into a far more complex and expensive ceremony in this later period, 800 to 500 B.C.E. The horse was identified both with the king and with Indra, the Vedic king of the gods and god of fertility, the divine alter ego of the king. The ceremony was intended, in part, to assure the fertility of both the king and the land, and obscene terminology alternates with fairly blatant sexual euphemisms. Polite words for "mother" or "lady" are also used to designate the various queens who participate in the ritual, in which the king's wives pantomime copulation with the dead horse, to the accompaniment of obscene verses. Euphemisms also obscure the speech made by one queen to another, perhaps complaining that she is not being brought to the stallion. These verses were already a source of embarrassment to the author of this text, who prescribes a restoration of clean, "perfumed" speech at the end, to purify the vital breath that may have been driven out by the dirty talk that has gone before.

Shatapatha Brahmana 13.2.8.1–4

When the gods went upwards, they did not know the world of heaven, but the horse knew it; they go upwards with a horse in order to know the world of heaven. A cloth, an upper cloth, and gold is what they spread out for the horse, as they do for no other sacrificial animal, and on that they 'quiet' him. Thus they set him apart from all other sacrificial animals.

They kill this sacrificial animal when they 'quiet' him. As the priest 'quiets' him he says, 'Svaha to the breath! Svaha to the outward breath! Svaha to the inward breath!' and he offers the oblations. Thus he places the vital breaths within him, and thus the sacrifice is made with him as if he were a living sacrificial beast.

He leads up the (king's) wives, saying, 'Mother, Little Mother, Dear Little Mother!' 'No one is leading me!' (says one woman). Thus he summons them, and thus he makes them fit for the sacrifice. Saying, 'We call on you, (Indra), leader of the hosts of the hosts,' the wives walk around (the horse) and thus make amends to him; and they also make amends to him by fanning him.

TRANSLATED BY Wendy Doniger O'Flaherty.

They walk around him three times, for there are three worlds; and they fan him with these worlds. They walk around him three times more, which makes six; for there are six seasons; and they fan him with the seasons.

But the vital breaths go out of those who perform the fanning in the sacrifice. Nine times they walk about him, for there are nine vital breaths; thus they place the vital breaths in themselves, and the vital breaths do not go out of them. (They say,) 'I will urge the one who places the embryo'; 'You urge the one who places the embryo.' Now, the embryo means progeny and animals; thus she places progeny and animals in herself.

RESTORING THE HORSE

In addition to its political purposes, the horse sacrifice, like most, was designed to restore things that had gone wrong, in this case to restore the king who had been sullied by the bloodshed necessitated by his office. But new things could go wrong during the period when the horse was said to wander freely. So restorations were prescribed if the horse met with any of an imagined series of possible disasters, and at the end of the ceremony there is even a restoration for the obscene language that is a part of the ritual. The text invokes Vayu, god of the wind, the god who transforms the seed within the womb and who breathes life into the embryo. It also invokes Agni as the digestive fire within the bellies of all creatures; Pushan ("the nourisher"), a solar deity, keeper of herds and bringer of prosperity; Surya, the sun; and Varuna, god of the waters. The penultimate part of this ritual may also be performed not as part of the horse sacrifice but merely by itself, to find lost objects.

Shatapatha Brahmana 13.3.8.1–6

Now for the restorations. If the horse should mount a mare, (the priest) should make an oblation of milk to the wind (Vayu); for the wind is the one who transforms the seed; the wind is the vital breath, and the vital breath is what transforms the seed. Thus he puts seed (back) into (the horse) by means of seed.

And if the horse should become lame, he should make an offering of rice and milk to Pushan, for Pushan rules over domestic animals; thus he satisfies the one who owns domestic animals, who rules over domestic animals, and so the horse becomes healthy.

And if the horse should be sick but not lame, he should make an offering to the fire within-all-men, the offering of a cake on twelve bricks, on earth-bricks; for this (earth) is the fire within-all-men; thus he satisfies this earth, and so the horse becomes healthy.

And if the horse's eye should become injured or diseased, he should make an offering of rice and milk to the sun, Surya; for the sun is the eye of creatures; when he rises, everything here moves; thus he puts an eye (back) into (the horse) by means of an eye. And he uses an offering of rice and milk (*charu*) because it is by means of the eye that the self moves (*charati*).

Translated by Wendy Doniger O'Flaherty.

And if the horse should die in water, he should make an offering of rice and milk with barley to Varuna, for Varuna seizes the one who dies in water; thus he satisfies the god who seizes (the horse). And when that god is satisfied with him, he allows him to slaughter another (horse), and so he slaughters one that has been approved by that god. And he uses an offering made of barley because barley is of the nature of Varuna.

And if the horse should get lost, he should make a sacrificial offering of three oblations: an offering of a cake on one brick for heaven and earth, an offering of milk for the wind, and an offering of rice and milk for the sun. For whatever is lost is lost between heaven and earth; and the wind blows upon it, and the sun warms it; nothing is ever lost beyond the realm of these gods. And even by itself, this ritual finds what has been lost; whatever other thing of his is lost, let him sacrifice with this ritual, and he will surely find it.

And if enemies should get the horse, or if the horse should die other than in water, they should bring another horse and consecrate it by sprinkling it with water; this is the restoration for that.

JAIMINIYA BRAHMANA

The *Jaiminiya Brahmana* is (along with the *Panchavimsha* and the *Sadvimsha Brahmanas*) attached to the *Sama Veda*, the "Veda of Chants." Everything in the *Sama Veda* is longer than its counterparts in the two other Vedas, drawn out, repeated, sung with variations. And the stories in the *Jaiminiya* are longer (as well as livelier and funnier) than those in any other Brahmanas. The *Jaiminiya* is famous for its stories; the first parts of it that were published in Europe (in 1878) were the stories.

Like all Brahmanas, the *Jaiminiya* tells us how someone "saw" a particular chant and thereby got what he wanted, which other people who know the story can also do (as in "Bhrigu's Journey in the Other World"). Many of the stories were told to restore details omitted in the version of a story in the *Rig Veda* or to explain an allusion. The old gory, chaotic, heroic world of Vedic sacrifice bred these stories in its violent, passionate way; but then they had to be simultaneously fleshed out and flattened to bring them into the ordered world of the sacrifice in the Brahmanas. Often the stories break out of the rigid priestly mold and sprout new images of great emotional power before lapsing back into the cooler tone of the genre. Ultimately, however, the *Jaiminiya* tends to turn Vedic tragedies into stories with happy endings; this is particularly apparent in the usual formulaic punch line: "He saw this chant and praised with it and found success."

Some of the stories are myths, dealing with cosmic problems, in a sacred context and with supernatural actors ("The Gods Make Men Evil"); but others are folktales, dealing with human problems ("How Men Changed Skins with Animals"). We can see in the folktales patterns that are shared by folktales in other cultures, even while we place them in their own specific cultural and sacrificial context. These folktales are stories about families and about the problems that the human body often poses for us, stories closely tied to folk traditions. When the *Jaiminiya* supplies a long folktale, self-contained and consistent in its details, to gloss a short phrase, it is almost certainly telling a story that had been in the air in India for a long time. Often the Brahmins who retold the folktale had to tamper with it in order to fit it into the sacrificial world. Yet they did not filter out the psychological profundity of these stories, their insights into the fears that underlie dreams, myths, and rituals (such as the sacrifice). The stories retain their power to trigger the full emotional range that is built into the ritual.

HOW MEN CHANGED SKINS WITH ANIMALS

This passage is best read as a reply to a widespread assumption in the Brahmanas that animals take revenge on those who have eaten them. Thus other Brahmanas say: "Just as in this world men eat cattle and devour them, so in the other world cattle eat men and devour them," or, "Whatever food a man eats in this world, that [food] eats him in the other world" (*Kaushitaki Brahmana* 11.3; *Shatapatha Brahmana* 12.9.1.1). According to the *Jaiminiya Brahmana,* this consequence may be avoided if one performs the appropriate offerings (as in "Bhrigu's Journey in the Other World") or sacrifice, but apparently this reassurance did not fully satisfy later Hindus; the *Lawbook of Manu* (5.55) offers a pun on this subject: flesh is called *mamsa* because he (*sa*) eats me (*mam*) in the other world if I eat him now, or, "He whose *meat* in this world I eat, will in the other world *me eat*" ("To Eat or Not to Eat Meat," p. 203). The *Jaiminiya* takes a narrative tack, in a passage explaining why the sacrificer should wear a red cowhide.

The transaction in the other world is here interpreted as the reversal of a reversal: men and cattle traded places long ago, and, as a result, cattle *willingly* supplied men with food and clothing but also, apparently, won the boon of eating men (and, perhaps, flaying them) in the other world. To avoid this, the sacrificer pretends to restore things to the way they were in the mythical past: by putting on the cow's skin, he prevents her from eating him.

The text leaves out terms that the ancient priests would have assumed, but that we have inserted, in brackets, for the contemporary reader.

Jaiminiya Brahmana 2.182–83

In the beginning, the skin of cattle was the skin of a man, and the skin of a man was the skin of cattle [i.e., cattle then had the skin that men now have, and the reverse]. Cattle could not bear the heat, rain, flies, and mosquitoes. They went to man and said, 'Man, let this skin [of ours] be yours, and that skin [of yours] be ours.' 'What would be the result of that?' [man asked]. 'We could be eaten by you,' [the animals said], 'and this [skin of ours] would be your clothing.' So saying they gave [man] his clothing. Therefore, when [the sacrificer] puts on a red hide, he flourishes in that form. Then cattle do not eat him in the other world [if he wears the skin, they think he is one of them]; for cattle do eat a man in the other world [otherwise]. Therefore, one should not stand naked near a cow, for it is liable to run away from one, thinking, 'I am bearing his skin [and he may try to get it back from me].' And this skin has got a tail, which makes it complete.

TRANSLATED BY Wendy Doniger O'Flaherty.

BHRIGU'S JOURNEY IN THE OTHER WORLD

The tale of Bhrigu in the otherworld is much retold in India. It is long and encompasses several major themes, including fathers and sons, the struggle with death, the symbolism of dreams, and the ethics of eating. Bhrigu is a mortal sage, but he is the son of the god Varuna; he moves back and forth between the world of mortals and the world of immortals. The hell that Bhrigu visits is a Vedic otherworld, perhaps above the earth, perhaps below it, perhaps even on the same level. It is a hell from which one can return during this life, but one that might also be interpreted as a vision of the next life in *this* world, once the idea of reincarnation takes root. This otherworld is the inverse of this world, an upside-down, looking-glass world, reversing the roles of subject and object.

Each of the three final worlds—above, below, and here—has positive as well as negative elements, so that they form a kind of transition from all the negative hells to the entirely positive final world, which is a heaven. The hells are depicted far more vividly than the heavens: the hells come first, there are more of them, and they are described in far greater detail than the heavens.

The central scene deals with the dangers that arise from incorrect, profane eating and are warded off by correct, sacred eating. The two types of eating are inextricably linked by the ancient Indian belief that it is wrong to take food without offering some, at least mentally, to the gods; in the broadest sense, all human food consists of divine leftovers. The fact that the trees eat the men in the otherworld, whereas in this world men do not eat trees, makes sense if one defines the things that are "eaten" not as literal food but as the things that humans consume. The text is not saying, "Do not consume things, for then they will consume you," but, rather, "Be sure to consume things in the right way, or they will consume you."

Bhrigu's immediate reaction to the first scene is to ask, "Has this happened?"—i.e., is it real or is it a dream, a nightmare? The images in his adventure recur in dreams: images of dismemberment, forbidden foods, sexual temptation, and cannibalism. But this is not the report of a dream; it is a highly stylized recasting of a dream in the form of a story with a happy ending: the son emerges stronger than before, for he has learned how to protect himself from the dangers he has seen. The other world turns out to be not a place from which one cannot escape but a nightmare from which one can awaken.

Jaiminiya Brahmana 1.42–44

Bhrigu, the son of Varuna, was devoted to learning. He thought that he was better than his father, better than the gods, better than the other Brahmins who were devoted to learning. Varuna thought to himself, 'My son does not know anything at all. Come, let us teach him to know something.' He took away his life's breaths, and Bhrigu fainted and went beyond this world.[1]

Bhrigu arrived in the world beyond. There he saw a man cut another man to pieces and eat him. He said, 'Has this really happened? What is this?' They said to him, 'Ask Varuna, your father. He will tell you about this.' He came to a second world, where a man was eating another man, who was screaming. He said, 'Has this really happened? What is this?' They said to

TRANSLATED BY Wendy Doniger O'Flaherty.

1. The father's violence against his son takes other forms in other versions, such as *Rig Veda* 10.135; *Shatapatha Brahmana* 11.6.1–13; *Katha Upanishad* 1.6; and *Mahabharata* 1.3.146–75.

him, 'Ask Varuna, your father. He will tell you about this.' He went on to another world, where he saw a man eating another man, who was soundlessly screaming; then to another, where two women were guarding a great treasure; then to a fifth, where there were two streams flowing on an even level, one filled with blood and one filled with butter. A naked black man[2] with a club guarded the stream filled with blood; out of the stream filled with butter, men made of gold were drawing up all desires with bowls of gold. In the sixth world there were five rivers with blue lotuses and white lotuses, flowing with honey like water. In them there were dancing and singing, the sound of the lute, crowds of celestial nymphs, a fragrant smell, and a great sound.

Bhrigu returned from that world and came to Varuna, who said, 'Did you arrive, my son?' 'I arrived, father.' 'Did you see, my son?' 'I saw, father.' 'What, my son?' 'A man cut another man to pieces and ate him.' 'Yes,' said Varuna; 'when people in this world offer no oblation and lack true knowledge, but cut down trees and lay them on the fire, those trees take the form of men in the other world and eat [those people] in return.' 'How can one avoid that?'[3] 'When you put fuel on the sacred fire, that is how you avoid it and are free of it.

'What [did you see] second?' 'A man was eating another man, who was screaming.' 'Yes,' he said; 'when people in this world offer no oblation and lack true knowledge, but cook for themselves animals that cry out, those animals take the form of men in the other world and eat in return.' 'How can one avoid that?' 'When you offer the first oblation with the voice, that is how you avoid it and are free of it.

'What third?' 'A man ate another man, who was soundlessly screaming.' 'Yes,' he said; 'when people in this world offer no oblation and lack true knowledge, but cook for themselves rice and barley, which scream soundlessly, that rice and barley take the form of men in the other world and eat in return.' 'How can one avoid that?' 'When you offer the last oblation with the mind, that is how you avoid it and are free of it.

'What fourth?' 'Two women were guarding a great treasure.' 'Yes,' said he, 'they were Faith and Nonfaith. When people in this world offer no oblation and lack true knowledge, but sacrifice without faith, that [sacrifice] goes to Nonfaith; what [they sacrifice] with faith goes to Faith.' 'How can one avoid that?' 'When you eat with your thumb, you avoid it and are free of it.

'What fifth?' 'Two streams were flowing on an even level, one filled with blood and one filled with butter. A naked black man with a club guarded the stream filled with blood; men made of gold were drawing up all desires with bowls of gold out of the stream filled with butter.' 'Yes,' said he; 'when people in this world offer no oblation and lack true knowledge, but squeeze out the blood of a Brahmin, that is the river of blood; and the naked black man who guarded it with a club is Anger, whose food is that [blood].' 'How can one avoid that?' 'When you eat with a sacrificial spoon, you avoid it and are free of it. And when you wash out the spoon and pour the water out toward the north, that is the river of butter; and out of that [butter] the men made of gold draw up all desires with bowls of gold.

2. Probably a form of Yama, the god of the dead (who is often described as a black man with a golden club); blood would then naturally be his food, while gold is symbolic of immortality; the golden men seem to represent the benefit of good deeds in the other world.

3. The term for "avoid" (*nishkriti*) describes not an attempt to suffer in order to pay for a sin but a plan to avoid making a mistake that will bring unwanted consequences.

'What sixth?' 'Five rivers, with blue lotuses and white lotuses, flowed with honey like water; in them there were dancing and singing, the sound of the lute, crowds of celestial nymphs, a fragrant smell, and a great sound.' 'Yes,' said he; 'those were my own worlds.' 'How can one get that?' 'By dipping in[4] five times and drawing out five times.' Then he added, 'There is no chance of getting worlds except by the oblation. Today I am fasting before building the sacrificial fire.' And they made it for him in that way. Whoever offers the oblation with this true knowledge, he is not eaten in return by trees who take the form of men in the other world, nor by animals, nor by rice and barley; nor do his good deeds and sacrifices go to Faith and Non-faith. He wards off the streams of blood and wins the streams of butter.

4. That is, dipping in and out with the sacrificial spoon that is the subject of the previous explanation.

THE GODS MAKE MEN EVIL

Although the majority of the Brahmanas depict the relationship between gods and humans as one of mutual nourishment, some passages reveal a deep-seated jealousy and even hostility of the gods toward humans, a conflict that will re-emerge in later texts. In the following passage, the gods of the three worlds unite to keep humans out of heaven; they take away from humans the Vedic hymns that are the source of their divine strength, hymns that the gods use in their battles against their fraternal enemies, the anti-gods (Asuras). When the human pawn outlives its usefulness in the fraternal battle, the battle between divine fathers and human sons takes precedence over the battle between brothers. The thunderbolt-man is dismembered in order to destroy him and to protect the gods. The concept of sacrifice as a force that joins together the powers of gods and humans has been transformed into the concept of sacrifice as a force that has the potential to drive humans and gods apart, by making humans so good, and hence so powerful, that they rouse the jealousy of the gods.

Jaiminiya Brahmana 1.97–98

The gods and demons[1] were striving against each other. The gods created a thunderbolt, sharp as a razor, that was man [*purusha*].[2] They hurled this at the demons, and it scattered the demons, but then it turned back to the gods. The gods were afraid of it, and so they took it and broke it into three pieces. Then they saw that the divinities had entered into this man in the form of hymns. They said, 'When this man has lived in the world with merit, he will follow us by means of sacrifices and good deeds and asceticism. Let us therefore act so that he will not follow us. Let us put evil in him.' They put evil in him: sleep, laziness, anger, hunger, love of dice, desire for women. These are the evils that assail a man in this world.

Translated by Wendy Doniger O'Flaherty.

1. The anti-gods (Asuras).
2. This is the paradigmatic male that we encountered in the Vedic "Hymn of the Primeval Man," p. 82.

Then they enjoined Agni [fire] in this world: 'Agni, if anyone escapes evil and aspires to do good things in this world, try to ruin him.' And they enjoined Vayu [wind] in the intermediate air in the same way, and the sun in the sky. But Ugradeva Rajani[3] said, 'I will not harm mankind, though I have heard that these three high gods are inclined to harm mankind.' And the gods do not harm the man who knows this, though they do try to destroy the man who tries to harm the man who knows this.

3. In the *Rig Veda* (1.36.18) Ugradeva Rajani is a powerful protector; in the *Panchavimsha Brahmana* and the *Taittiriya Aranyaka* he is a leper. Here he seems to be saying that a human like himself cannot be blamed for injuring human beings, since he is acting as an instrument of the gods. He may be referring to his own situation—as a leper he may have been regarded as dangerous and as personally responsible for the danger he was producing.

RENUNCIATION IN THE UPANISHADS 600–200 B.C.E.

The Upanishads (meaning "sitting beside," which may refer to the method of placing one thing next to another, to making connections, or to pupils sitting beside their teacher) are often referred to as "the end of the Veda" (Vedanta), for they are the final texts in the body of literature called *shruti* ("what is heard"), unalterable divine revelation, in contrast with the rest of Hindu literature, called *smriti* ("what is remembered"), the tradition attributed to human authors, which is therefore fallible and can be changed. Just as the Brahmanas are, among other things, footnotes to the Vedas, so the Upanishads began as notes to the Brahmanas and as explanatory meditations on the meaning of the Vedic rituals and myths. The different Upanishads belong to different branches of the Vedic traditions, but they share so many stories and ideas that they are clearly in conversation with one another. The early Upanishads probably were composed in the sixth and fifth centuries B.C.E. Again we find a major shift in language, between the Sanskrit of the Brahmanas and that of the Upanishads, not merely in the grammar and vocabulary but also in the style, which is far more accessible, conversational, reader-friendly.

In the kingdoms of the eastern Ganges at this time, trade flourished, and the towns were connected by trade routes: all roads led to Kashi. The development of the idea of action (karma) whose merit (also karma), once earned, can be accumulated, occasionally transferred, and eventually cashed in, owes much to the post-Vedic moneyed economy. More generally, where there's trade, people leave home; new commercial classes emerge; and, above all, new ideas spread quickly and circulate freely. They certainly did so at this time in India, and there was little to stop them: the Vedas did not constitute a closed canon, and there was never any religious authority to enforce a canon had there been one.

A vast transformation of society was taking place in response to the social, economic, and political reorganization of northern South Asia, as small-scale, pastoral chiefdoms gave way to hierarchically ordered settlements organized into states. Students and thinkers moved over a wide geographical area in search of philosophical and theological debate, encountering not merely royal assemblies of South Asian thinkers but new peoples and ideas from outside of South Asia.

Like other great religious innovations, such as those inspired by Jesus, Muhammad, and Luther, the Upanishads did not replace but merely supplemented and reinterpreted the earlier religion, so that, just as Catholicism continued to exist alongside Protestantism within Christianity, Vedic Hinduism (sacrificial, worldly) continued to exist alongside Vedantic Hinduism (philosophical, renunciant). But in Hinduism, unlike Christianity, there was no official schism. Certain words from earlier periods—karma (now in the sense of merit as well as action), *tapas* (as ascetically generated inner heat as well as the heat of sacrificial action)—took on new meanings at this point, though their original meanings never disappeared, resulting in a layering that served as one of the major sources of multiplicity within Hinduism.

The early *dharma-sutras* (ca. 300–100 B.C.E.) speak of four *ashramas* or ways of life (also, confusingly, the word for a hermitage) as four options for lifestyles that could be undertaken during any period in a person's life: the chaste student (*brahmacharin*), the householder or family man (*grihastha*), the forest dweller (*vanaprastha*),

An older sage instructing a younger sage.

and the renouncer (*sannyasin*). The system was an attempt, on the part of Brahmins who inclined to renunciation, to integrate that way of life with the other major path, that of the householder. Hinduism came up with various solutions to the potential conflicts between renunciation and the householder life. First, it was said that the goals of family life and renunciation were to be followed not simultaneously but in sequence, first one then another. The four *ashramas* came to be known no longer as simultaneous options (ways of life) but as four stages of life. The first *ashrama*, the chaste student, always retained its primary meaning of a vow of chastity undertaken *at any time of life*. But by the second century C.E., the four *ashramas* had become serial, rather than choices that one could make at any time.

The Upanishads speak of the self or soul (*atman*), the individual self that is also the universal Self, identified with the world-soul (*brahman*), the divine substance of which the universe is composed. *Brahman*, which in the *Rig Veda* designates sacred speech, is the root of a number of words in later Sanskrit distinguished by just one or two sounds (or letters, in English): *brahman* (the divine substance of the universe); Brahma (the creator god); Brahmin or Brahman (a member of the first or priestly class); Brahmana (one of a class of texts that follow the Vedas and precede the Upanishads); and Brahma-charin ("moving in *brahman*," designating a chaste student).

The world of *brahman* is a world of monism (which assumes that all living things are elements of a single, universal being). This is the central teaching of the Upanishads, a doctrine of pantheism (in which God is everything and everything is God). This philosophy views the very substance of the universe as divine, and views that substance and that divinity as unitary. The pluralistic world has a secondary, illusory status in comparison with the enduring, real status of the underlying monistic being.

PRONOUNCING GLOSSARY

Aditi: *uh´-di-tee´*
archatas: *ar-chah´-tus*
arka: *ar´-kuh*
Aruna: *uh-roo´-nuh*
ashva: *uh´-shvuh*
Ashva-medha: *uh´-shvuh-may´-duh*
ashvat: *ush-vut´*
atman: *aht´-mun*
atti: *uh´-tee*
Bhan: *bhun*
Brihadaranyaka Upanishad: *bree´-hud-ah´-run-yuh-kuh oo-puh´-ni-shud*
Chandogya Upanishad: *chun-dohg´-yuh oo-puh´-ni-shud*
Gandharva: *gun-dar´-vuh*
Gautama: *gow´-tuh-muh*
Janashruti Pautrayana: *juh-nuh-shroo´-tee pow-truh´-yuh-nuh*
kam: *kum*
Kshatriya: *kuh-shah´-tri-yuh*
medhyam: *may´-dyum*
Panchala: *pun-chah´-luh*
pat: *puht*
pati: *puh´-tee*
patni: *puht´nee*
Prajapati: *pruh-jah´-puh-tee´*
Pravahana Jaibali: *pruh-vah´-huh-nuh jai´-buh-li*
Purusha: *poo-roo´-shuh*
purva: *poor´-vuh*
Raikva: *raik´-vuh*
Shudra: *shoo´-druh*
Shvetaketu: *shvay´-tuh-kay´-too*
Shvetashvatara Upanishad: *shvay´-tash-vuh-tuh-ruh oo-puh´-ni-shud*
Soma: *soh´-muh*
Vaishya: *vaish´-yuh*
Yajnavalkya: *yuj´-nuh-val´-kyuh*

BRIHADARANYAKA UPANISHAD

Bridging the Brahmanas and the Upanishads are the Aranyakas ("Jungle Books"), so called presumably because they were composed in the wilderness, or jungle, outside the village; they dealt both with ritual, like the Brahmanas, and with cosmology and metaphysics, like the Upanishads. The Upanishads seem to have been composed by people who left the settled towns for rustic settings where master and student could sit under a tree, the ancient Indian equivalent of the bucolic liberal arts college; the renouncers are said to live in the wilderness, in contrast with the conventional Vedic sacrificers, who live in villages (or cities). No individuals in the Ganges Valley could have remembered the old days up in the Punjab, but there was certainly a group memory, or at least a literary memory, of an idealized time when people lived under the trees and slept under the stars, a cultural memory of wide open spaces. The movements to renounce the fleshpots of the Ganges Valley may have been inspired in part by a longing to return to the lost world preserved in the texts, when life was both simpler and freer, more heroic. Such a longing is reflected in the name of the Aranyakas, in the village settings of so much of the Upanishads, and in the forest imagery that abounds in the writings of the early Indian sects, both inside and outside of Hinduism.

The earliest of the Upanishads, the *Brihadaranyaka* ("Great Jungle Book"), is the final section of the massive *Shatapatha Brahmana*, and its name indicates that it is both an Aranyaka and an Upanishad. It is, like the Aranyakas and the early Upanishads, mostly in prose.

THE CREATOR CREATES DEATH

This Upanishad begins with a brief meditation on the horse sacrifice ("Killing the Sacrificial Horse," p. 96) before it goes back to the beginning of creation. A number of etymologies establish connections among the sounds of the names of things, the origins of their names, and their cosmic meaning. Death here functions both as death and as the creator, Prajapati (an earlier form of the god Brahma), who exerts himself simultaneously ritually and sexually. As in the Brahmanas, food and eating is a central theme; the rich and powerful eat the poor and weak, by the "law of the fish." To eat the world is to have complete power over the world.

Bridhadaranyaka Upanishad 1.1.1–2, 1.2.1–7

Om! The dawn is the head of the sacrificial horse. The sun is his eye, the wind his breath, the fire within-all-men his open mouth. The year is the body of the sacrificial horse. The sky is his back, the middle realm of space his stomach, the earth his underbelly; the quarters of the sky are his sides, the intermediate quarters his ribs; the seasons are his limbs, the junctures between the months and the fortnights his joints; day and night are his feet, the stars are his bones, and the clouds are his flesh. The food in his stomach is the sands, and the rivers are his entrails; his liver and lungs are the mountains, and the plants and trees are the hairs on his body. The east is his forehand, and the setting sun is his hindquarters. When he yawns, then there is lightning; when he shakes himself, it thunders; and when he urinates, it rains. Speech is his whinny.

The day is the golden bowl in front of the horse; its womb is in the eastern ocean. The night is the golden bowl behind the horse; its womb is in the western ocean. These two bowls arose on both sides of the horse. He becomes a charger and carries the gods; he becomes a racehorse and carries the Gandharvas; he becomes a running horse and carries the demons; he becomes a stallion and carries men. The sea is his kinsman; the sea is his womb.

In the beginning, there was nothing at all here. This world was enveloped by death, by hunger, for truly hunger is death. Then (death) thought to himself: 'I wish I had a body.' He moved about, praising, and water[1] came out of him as he was praising. 'Water (*kam*) came out of me while I was praising (*archatas*),' he thought; and this is why brightness is called brightness (*arka*). Whoever knows this reason why brightness is called brightness always has water. For the waters are brightness.

The froth of the waters became solid; it became the earth. He became exhausted on this (earth); and from him, exhausted and heated, came out a heat[2] that became fire. He divided himself into three parts. (Fire was one third); the sun was one third; and air was one third. Thus the vital breath is divided into three parts. The eastern quarter is his head; the north-east and south-east are his shoulders; the western quarter is his tail; the north-west

Translated by Wendy Doniger O'Flaherty.

1. The cosmic ocean.
2. Heat is said to be the essence of the god, which can also mean his semen, with which he impregnates the earth.

and south-west are his thighs; the south and north are his flanks; the sky is his back; the middle realm of space is his stomach. This (earth) is his chest. He stands firm in the waters; whoever knows this stands firm wherever he goes.

He desired, 'I wish that a second body were produced for me.' He, who was hunger, death, caused speech to copulate with mind. The seed that was there became the year; for there had not been a year before that. (Death) bore (the year) for as long a time as a year, and after that he emitted him. As soon as (the year) was born, (death) opened his mouth wide to eat him. (The year) made the sound, 'Bhan!',[3] and that became speech.

(Death) thought to himself, 'If I kill him, I will make just a little food for myself, less (than if I let him live and grow).' With that speech, with that body, he emitted this whole world, whatever exists—the hymns, the formulas, the chants, the meters, the sacrifices, the creatures, the animals. And whatever he emitted, he started to eat. Indeed, he eats (*atti*) everything; that is why Aditi (the infinite) is called Aditi. And whoever knows why Aditi is called Aditi becomes an eater of everything; everything becomes his food.

He desired, 'Let me sacrifice more, with a greater sacrifice.' He exhausted himself, and he generated heat in himself, and out of him as he was exhausted and heated came glory and virility. Now, glory and virility are the vital breaths; and so when the vital breaths had gone out of him, his body began to swell. His mind was in his body.

He desired, 'I wish this body were fit for sacrifice: I wish that I could have it for my own body.' And it became a horse (*ashva*) because it had swelled (*ashvat*). 'It has become fit for sacrifice (*medhyam*),' he thought, and that is why the horse sacrifice is called the Ashva-medha. Whoever knows him in this way really knows the horse sacrifice.

He thought about him but did not confine him.[4] After a year, he sacrificed him to himself, and assigned (other) sacrificial animals to the (other) gods. Therefore when men sacrifice to Prajapati they call it a sacrifice to all the gods.

The (sun) who heats is really the horse sacrifice, and the year is its body. This (earthly) fire is brightness, and the worlds are its body. They are two, the (solar) brightness and the (earthly fire of the) horse sacrifice; but they are also a single god, death.

He (who knows this) conquers repeated death;[5] death does not get him; he becomes one of these gods.

3. A double meaning: it is the cry that the baby makes, and it is a verbal root meaning "to speak."
4. Because the sacrificial horse is said to wander freely for a year ("Killing the Sacrificial Horse," p. 96).
5. This may mean either that after the natural death on earth a person would die a second or third time, or, more likely, that a person would keep on being born and dying.

CREATION

Like the *Rig Veda*, the Upanishads offer several different models for the origins of the universe. This passage in the *Brihadaranyaka* concentrates on a quasi-incestuous myth of androgyny. It combines all three of the major methods of creation in the Vedas and Brahmanas—incest, oblation, and dismemberment—together with a concern for the relationship between the names of things and the nature of those things. The distinction between mortal and immortal is further developed, but now a ritual etymology for the name for a human being is derived from the androgynous primeval Man, the Purusha ("The Hymn of the Primeval Man," p. 82), here regarded as a mortal but also identified with Brahma, the Creator, the god who supersedes the Prajapati of the earlier Brahmanas.

Brihadaranyaka Upanishad 1.4.1–6

In the beginning this world was just a single body (*atman*) shaped like a man.

He looked around and saw nothing but himself. The first thing he said was, 'Here I am!' and from that the name 'I' came into being. Therefore, even today when you call someone, he first says, 'It's I,' and then states whatever other name he may have. That first being received the name 'man' (*purusha*), because ahead (*purva*) of all this he burnt up (*ush*) all evils. When someone knows this, he burns up anyone who may try to get ahead of him.

That first being became afraid; therefore, one becomes afraid when one is alone. Then he thought to himself: 'Of what should I be afraid, when there is no one but me?' So his fear left him, for what was he going to be afraid of? One is, after all, afraid of another.

He found no pleasure at all; so one finds no pleasure when one is alone. He wanted to have a companion. Now he was as large as a man and a woman in close embrace. So he split (*pat*) his body into two, giving rise to husband (*pati*) and wife (*patni*). Surely this is why Yajnavalkya used to say: 'The two of us are like two halves of a block.' The space here, therefore, is completely filled by the woman.

He copulated with her, and from their union human beings were born. She then thought to herself: 'After begetting me from his own body (*atman*), how could he copulate with me? I know—I'll hide myself.' So she became a cow. But he became a bull and again copulated with her. From their union cattle were born. Then she became a mare, and he a stallion; she became a female donkey, and he, a male donkey. And again he copulated with her, and from their union one-hoofed animals were born. Then she became a female goat, and he, a male goat; she became a ewe, and he, a ram. And again he copulated with her, and from their union goats and sheep were born. In this way he created every male and female pair that exists, down to the very ants.

It then occurred to him: 'I alone am the creation, for I created all this.' From this 'creation' came into being. Anyone who knows this prospers in this creation of his.

Translated by Patrick Olivelle.

Then he churned[1] like this and, using his hands, produced fire from his mouth as from a vagina. As a result the inner sides of both these—the hands and the mouth—are without hair, for the inside of the vagina is without hair. 'Sacrifice to this god. Sacrifice to that god'—people do say these things, but in reality each of these gods is his own creation, for he himself is all these gods. From his semen, then, he created all that is moist here, which is really Soma.[2] Food and eater—that is the extent of this whole world. Food is simply Soma, and the eater is fire.

This is *brahman*'s supercreation. It is a supercreation because he created the gods, who are superior to him, and, being a mortal himself, he created the immortals. Anyone who knows this stands within this supercreation of his.

1. Or "rubbed." That is, he twirled the fire sticks, his two hands, as in the Brahmana myth "Prajapati Creates Fire," p. 94. The sexual symbolism of the churning of the fire stick within the concave base of the bottom slab, a symbolism always implicit, here becomes explicit in the concern for semen and the references to human anatomy.
2. The ambrosia that the gods drink to make them immortal; Soma is an elixir, unlike the solid ambrosia that the Greek gods eat.

DREAMING

The Upanishads have a lot to say about altered states of consciousness, beginning with ordinary dreaming. Some Upanishads (such as *Mandukya Upanishad* 3–7) speak of four levels of consciousness: waking, dreaming, sleeping without dreaming, and deep meditation; each of these is progressively closer to the correct perception of reality, waking life being furthest from it. The passage below speaks only of the first three states and of the imaginative power of dreaming.

Brihadaranyaka Upanishad 4.3.9–14, 18

The individual person has two states: the state in this world, and the state in the other world; and there is a third, liminal state, the state of dreaming. When one remains in this liminal state he sees both states—this world and the other world. Now, whatever approach there is to the state in the other world, by taking that approach one sees both the evils (of this world) and the ecstasies (of that world). When he dreams, he takes the elementary matter of this all-encompassing world, and he himself takes it apart, and he himself builds it up, and by his own brightness, by his own light, he dreams. For the individual person becomes his own light in this state.

There are no chariots there, no harnessings, no roads; but he emits chariots, harnessings, and roads. There are no ecstasies, joys, or delights there; but he emits ecstasies, joys, and delights. There are no ponds, lotus pools, or flowing streams there, but he emits ponds, lotus pools, and flowing streams. For he is the maker.

And there are verses about this:

Striking down with sleep what belongs to the body, he who does not dream looks down upon those that dream. Taking up the bright seed, he goes back

TRANSLATED BY Wendy Doniger O'Flaherty.

to his place; he is the golden person,[1] the one swan.[2] Guarding the low nest with his breath, the immortal one wanders about outside the nest. The immortal one goes wherever he wishes; he is the golden person, the one swan. Moving up and down inside the dream, he makes many forms, for he is a god. Now he seems to take pleasure in women, now he laughs, or sees terrifying things. People see his pleasure, but no one at all sees him. And that is why people say, 'Don't wake him up suddenly.' For it is hard to find a cure for the one who does not come back.

Now, some people say, 'This (dream state) is just his waking state, for whatever things he sees when he is awake, he sees them too when he dreams.' (But this is not so, for) here (in his dream) the person himself becomes his own source of light. . . .

As a big fish moves along both banks of a river, the eastern side and the western side, even so this person moves along both of these states, the state of dreaming and the state of being awake.

1. A common Upanishadic image for the world-soul, the indescribable *brahman* (see "The Origins of the Self," below).
2. This wild swan, or wild goose, is a common metaphor for the soul, perhaps suggested by the migratory habits that the wild birds share with the soul.

THE ORIGINS OF THE SELF

This passage, which follows the general cosmogony in the passage about creation, speaks of the creation of the individual self.

Brihadaranyaka Upanishad 1.4.7

At that time, all of this (world) was undifferentiated. By means of name and form[1] it became differentiated—'This has this name; this has this form.' And even now people say, 'This is his name; this is his form,' distinguishing by means of name and form. He entered in here, right up to the tips of his fingernails, as a razor is hidden in a razor sheath, or as fire is inside firewood.[2] People do not see him, for (whatever they see) is incomplete. Whenever one breathes, he becomes breath; whenever one speaks, he is speech; seeing, he is the eye; hearing, the ear; thinking, the mind. These are just the names for his acts. Whoever worships one (aspect) or another does not understand, for he is incomplete in any one or another. Rather, one should worship with the thought, 'This is the Self,' for all of these become one in that. That by which one can follow the footprints of this All, that is the Self, through which this All is known, just as one might track down and find something by a footprint. Whoever knows this finds fame and praise.

TRANSLATED BY Wendy Doniger O'Flaherty.

1. *Rupa* (here "form") is often translated as "visible appearance" but probably means something more like "hue."
2. Another reading of this verse is "as a termite (or 'ant' or 'insect' in general) is inside a termite-hill (or ant-hill)."

CHANDOGYA UPANISHAD

Although the *Chandogya Upanishad* ("Upanishad of the Singers of the *Sama Veda*") belongs to the *Sama Veda*, it has a number of close parallels with the *Brihadaranyaka*, and parts of it are even older than the *Brihadaranyaka*. Predictably, its central concern is the cosmic significance of the chants of the *Sama Veda*.

THE SELF

The passages below are part of a long instruction that the sage Uddalaka Aruni gives to his son Shvetaketu. After discussing the nature of sleep (somewhat differently from the parallel discussion in the *Brihadaranyaka*), Uddalaka says, "The finest essence here—that constitutes the self of this whole world; that is the truth; that is the self (*atman*). And that's how you are (or, that is what you are: *tat tvam asi*), Shvetaketu." When Shvetaketu replies, "Sir, teach me more," Uddalaka begins with the analogy of bees gathering honey, and then goes on to rivers and salt (in the passage here) as well as trees, a banyan fruit, a dying man, and a thief in chains. For the soul can never be described, merely analogized; whatever you say it is *like*, it is not really that: "Not thus, not thus" (*neti, neti*).

Chandogya Upanishad 6.10.1–4, 6.13.1–3

'Now, take these rivers,[1] son. The easterly ones flow towards the east, and the westerly ones flow towards the west. From the ocean, they merge into the very ocean;[2] they become just the ocean. In that state they are not aware that "I am that river," and "I am this river." In exactly the same way, son, when all these creatures reach the existent, they are not aware that "We are reaching the existent." No matter what they are in this world—whether it is a tiger, a lion, a wolf, a boar, a worm, a moth, a gnat, or a mosquito—they all merge into that.

'The finest essence here—that constitutes the self of this whole world; that is the truth; that is the self (*atman*). And that's how you are, Shvetaketu.'

'Sir, teach me more.'

'Very well, son.'

* * *

'Put this chunk of salt in a container of water and come back tomorrow.' The son did as he was told, and the father said to him: 'The chunk of salt you put in the water last evening—bring it here.' He groped for it but could not find it, as it had dissolved completely.

'Now, take a sip from this corner,' said the father. 'How does it taste?'

TRANSLATED BY Patrick Olivelle.

1. These may be terrestrial rivers that flow down from the Himalayas, or the celestial rivers in the Milky Way, which flow down to earth eventually as the Indus and Ganges.
2. The two oceans may be the heavenly and earthly (Indian) oceans.

'Salty.'

'Take a sip from the center.—How does it taste?'

'Salty.'

'Take a sip from that corner.—How does it taste?'

'Salty.'

'Throw it out and come back later.' He did as he was told and found that the salt was always there. The father told him: 'You, of course, did not see it there, son; yet it was always right there.[3]

'The finest essence here—that constitutes the self of this whole world; that is the truth; that is the self (*atman*). And that's how you are, Shvetaketu.'

'Sir, teach me more.'

'Very well, son.'

3. The meaning seems to be that even when the son throws the water on the ground, the salt, though invisible, is still present in the ground and would become visible when the water evaporated.

TRANSMIGRATION

Where did the potentially revolutionary ideas of transmigration and karma come from? In the Upanishads, as in the *Rig Veda*, the body of the dead man returns to the elements—his eyes to the sun, the hair of his body to plants, the hair of his head into trees, his blood and semen into water—but the Upanishadic sages regard this as the beginning, not the end, of the explanation of death. In the *Brihadaranyaka Upanishad* (3.2.13), the sage Yajnavalkya lists the correspondences between the parts of the body and the cosmos, whereupon his pupil asks, "What happens to the person then?" In answer to his pupil's question, Yajnavalkya takes him aside: "And what did they talk about? Nothing but karma. They praised nothing but karma. Yajnavalkya told him: 'A man becomes something good by good karma and something bad by bad karma.'"

The first and most basic meaning of karma is action. The noun *karma* comes from the verb *kri*, cognate with the Latin *creo*, to make or do, to make a baby or a table or to perform a ritual. Karma in the sense of "action" is often contrasted with mind and speech: one can think, say, or do [*kri*] something. The second meaning of karma is ritual action, particularly Vedic ritual action; this is its primary connotation in the *Rig Veda*. Its third meaning, which begins to be operative in the Upanishads, is morally charged action, good or bad, a meter that is always running, that is constantly charging something to one's account. And its fourth meaning, which follows closely on the heels of the third, is morally charged action that has consequences for the soul in the future, both within one's life and across the barrier of re-death: you become a sheep that people eat if you have eaten a sheep. (We saw the germ of this theory in the Brahmana descriptions of people soundlessly screaming in the other world in "Bhrigu's Journey," p. 101; it also recurs in statements that sacrifice generates merit that guarantees an afterlife in the other world.) In this sense, karma determines the nature of your future rebirths. Consequences have consequences, and first thing you know, you're born as a sheep.

Turned on its head, this link led to a fifth meaning of karma, not as the cause of future lives but as the result of past lives and the agenda for this life, the inescapable role in life that one was born to play, one's work, or innate activity. Many people besides Hindus believe that we often cannot remember the past causes of present circumstances, and that the present will influence the future; but the Hindu view differs from this in extending the past and future beyond the boundaries of this life span. The last (sixth) meaning of karma is the implication that good and bad karma maybe transferred from one person to another under certain circumstances, not merely between parents and children (as we saw in the Vedic poem "Varuna Provoked to Anger," p. 88) and between sacrificial priest and patron, but between any people who meet. This transfer may take place either intentionally or unintentionally: if someone lets a guest depart unfed, the guest will take away the host's good karma and leave behind his own bad karma. It is not always clear which of these meanings of *karma* is intended in any particular passage in the Upanishads (or in other texts).

Moreover, the idea of karma was certainly not accepted by everyone as the final solution to the problem of death (or the problem of evil); many other, conflicting ideas were proposed and widely accepted, alongside the karma theory. The Upanishads continue to speak of "recurrent death" (BU 3.2.10, 3.3.2) and describe the process in cruel detail (BU 4.3.36, 4.4.2). For heaven is no longer the end of the line, as it was in some of the Brahmanas; it is simply another place that, eventually, everyone leaves. The Upanishads spell out the assumption, sketched in the Brahmanas, that we are all on the wheel of re-death, transmigration (*samsara*, literally, "flowing around"). From the very start, the idea of transmigration was qualified by two other ideas: that some people wanted to get out of it, and that there was a way to do this—a restoration not merely for any one of life's mistakes but for life itself, a way to put the fix in on death.

The theory of reincarnation, the recycling of souls, may reflect an anxiety of overcrowding, the claustrophobia of a culture fenced in, a kind of urban *angst*. The spread of paddy rice cultivation into the Ganges Valley, producing a surplus that could support cities, and the emergence of societies along the Ganges created an unprecedented proximity of people. Population densities significantly increased, the result of the incorporation of indigenous peoples, a soaring birthrate, and agricultural surpluses. The Upanishadic discussion of the doctrine of transmigration begins when a teacher asks his pupil (the young sage Shvetaketu), "Do you know why the world beyond is not filled up, even when more and more people continuously go there?" and it ends with the statement, "As a result, that world up there is not filled up" (CU 5.10.8; BU 5.1.1 and 6.2.2). Reincarnation addressed this social problem and formulated it in terms of individual salvation. The Upanishads emphasize a more personal religious experience than the one addressed by the Brahmanas. In this way, at least, these movements were individualistic—"Look to your own house"—rather than socially oriented, as nonrenunciant Hinduism was—"Your identity is meaningful only as one member of a diverse social body." This was a tremendous innovation.

The Upanishads assume, like the Vedas and Brahmanas, that people pass into heaven or hell when they die, but they are far more concerned with the fate of the dead beyond heaven or hell. The *Brihadaranyaka Upanishad* (6.2) tells us that people within the Vedic fold at this time had two ways to be religious. The people who reach *brahman* have lived in the forest, the jungle, either permanently as forest ascetics or merely on the occasions when they held religious rituals there. By contrast, the sacrificers, who follow the Vedic path of generosity (to gods and priests, or to people more generally) or engage in the ritual practices that generate internal heat (*tapas*), go to heaven but do not stay there; they die again and are reborn. This text does not tell us where these people have lived, but the *Chandogya Upanishad* (5.10.1–8) tells us that the people who devote themselves to giving gifts to gods and to priests live in villages. *Tapas*, internal heat, can belong to either group, for it is a transitional power: for sacrificers, it is the heat that the priest generates in the sacrifice, while for people of the forest, *tapas* becomes detached from the sacrifice and internalized as the heat that an individual ascetic generates within himself. The only criterion that marks the sacrificers in both texts is their generosity, and the only criterion that marks the people of the forest is their life in the forest.

The people who reach the moon in the *Brihadaranyaka* are eaten by the gods (as they were eaten by animals in the other world in the Brahmanas), but the gods in the *Chandogya* merely eat the moon, a more direct way to account for its waning. The *Chandogya* also has a slightly different ending for the second group, the sacrificers who pass through the smoke. It is clear from the *Chandogya*, and implicit in the *Brihadaranyaka*, that one does not want to end up in the company of the worms and other tiny creatures in the third state, the place from which no traveler returns. It's better to be a dog.

But it is not so clear from these texts that the path of Vedic gift-giving is undesirable, that *everyone* wants to get off the wheel and onto the path of flame. For renouncers, the very idea of good karma is an oxymoron: any karma is bad, because it binds you to the wheel of rebirth. But the *Chandogya* spells out the belief that, for sacrificers, some rebirths are quite pleasant, the reward for good behavior. Their fate corresponds to Yajnavalkya's statement "A man becomes something good by good karma and something bad by bad karma." The *Brihadaranyaka* says much the same thing: "What a man turns out to be depends on how he acts. If his actions (karma) are good, he will turn into something good. If his actions are bad, he will turn into something bad." But then it adds that this applies only to the man who has desires; the man who is freed from desires, whose desires are fulfilled, does not die at all; he goes to *brahman* (BU 4.4.5–6). So, too, the funeral ceremonies include instructions that ensure that the dead person will not remain in limbo but will move forward, either to a new life or to final Release (*moksha*) from the cycle of transmigration, further evidence of a deeply embedded tension between the desire to assure a good rebirth and the desire to prevent rebirth altogether. The fear of re-death led to the desire for Release (including release from the values of Vedic Hinduism); but then the ideal of Release was reabsorbed into Vedic Hinduism and reshaped into the desire to be reborn better, in worldly terms: richer, with more sons, and so forth. These two tracks—one for people who want to get off the wheel of re-death, and one for those who don't want to get off the wheel of rebirth—continue as options for South Asians to this day.

Chandogya Upanishad 5.3–10

Shvetaketu the descendant of Aruna went to the assembly[1] of the Panchala (kings). Pravahana Jaibali said to him, 'Young man, has your father taught you?' 'Yes, sir, he has.' 'Do you know where created beings go from here?' 'No, sir.' 'Do you know how they come back again?' 'No, sir.' 'Do you know about the separation between the two paths, the path of the gods and the path of the fathers?' 'No, sir.' 'Do you know how the world (of heaven) over there does not get filled up?' 'No, sir.' 'Do you know how, in the fifth oblation, water comes to have a human voice?' 'No, sir.' 'Then why did you say that you had been taught? How could someone who didn't know these things say that he had been taught?'

Quite upset, he went to his father's place and said to him, 'Sir, you said, "I have taught you," but in fact you *didn't* teach me. Some man of the ruling class[2] asked me five questions, and I wasn't able to answer a single one of them.' (His father) said, 'As you have told them to me, I don't know a single one of them. If I had known them, how would I not have told you?'

Then Gautama (the father of Shvetaketu) went to the king's place, and when he arrived he was received with honor. The next morning, he went to

TRANSLATED BY Wendy Doniger O'Flaherty.

1. The king's audience hall, where privileged people gathered to speak about religious and political issues.

2. The term (*rajanya bandhu*) is quite pejorative, perhaps better rendered as "second-rate prince."

the assembly hall and (the king) said to him, 'Gautama, sir, choose anything you want of human wealth.' 'Your majesty,' answered (Gautama), 'human wealth is for you. But tell me just what you said to the young man.' (The king) was troubled and commanded him, 'Wait a while.' Then (the king) said to (Gautama), 'What you are asking me, Gautama, is knowledge that has never gone to Brahmins before you.[3] And that is why, among all people, only the Kshatriyas have had the power to rule.' But then he told him:

'The world (of heaven) over there, Gautama, is a sacrificial fire. The sun is its fuel, the rays of the sun are its smoke, the day is its flame, the moon its coals, the stars its sparks. Into this fire the gods make an offering of faith, and from that oblation king Soma is born.

'The rain cloud, Gautama, is a sacrificial fire. The wind is its fuel, the mist its smoke, lightning its flame, the thunderbolt its coals, and the roar of the thunder its sparks. Into this fire the gods make an offering of king Soma, and from that oblation rain is born.

'The earth, Gautama, is a sacrificial fire. The year is its fuel, space its smoke, night its flame, the four directions its coals, the four intermediate directions its sparks. Into this fire the gods make an offering of rain, and from that oblation food is born.

'Man, Gautama, is a sacrificial fire. Speech is his fuel, breath his smoke, the tongue his flame, the eye his coals, the ear his sparks. Into this fire the gods make an offering of food, and from that oblation semen is born.

'Woman, Gautama, is a sacrificial fire. The vagina is her fuel, foreplay her smoke, the womb her flame, the penetration her coals, and the orgasm her sparks.[4] Into this fire the gods make an offering of semen, and from that oblation the embryo is born.

'Thus in the fifth oblation, water comes to have a human voice. When the embryo has lain inside there for ten months or nine months, or however long, covered with the membrane, then he is born. When he is born, he lives as long as his allotted life-span. When he has died, they carry him to the appointed place and put him in the fire, for that is where he came from, what he was born from.

'Those who know this, and those who worship in the forest, concentrating on faith and asceticism,[5] they are born into the flame, and from the flame into the day, and from the day into the fortnight of the waxing moon,[6] and from the fortnight of the waxing moon into the six months during which the sun moves north; from these months, into the year; from the year into the sun; from the sun into the moon; from the moon into lightning. There a Person who is not human leads them to the ultimate reality. This is the path that the gods go on.

'But those who worship in the village, concentrating on sacrifices and good works and charity, they are born into the smoke, and from the smoke

3. In the *Brihadaranyaka* the king says, "This knowledge has never before been in the possession of a Brahmin. But I will reveal it to you, to keep you or an ancestor of yours from doing harm to me" (BU 6.3.8). In the *Chandogya*, the king adds, "That is why, among all people, only the Kshatriyas have had the power to rule." These are among a number of hints in the Upanishads that the new ideas about karma and rebirth may not have developed entirely within the Brahmin community.

4. The idea that the sacrifice is a sexual act is developed in great detail at *Brihadaranyaka* 6.4.3.

5. The meaning seems to be that the forest people accept the equality of the two concepts. "Faith" here is associated with giving gifts, while "asceticism" as usual translates the more complicated concept of generating inner heat (*tapas*).

6. The moon's waxing and waning were believed to be caused by dead people arriving there to become the food of the gods. It was also believed that the immortal drink of the gods, Soma, was stored in the moon.

into the night, and from the night into the other fortnight, and from the other fortnight into the six months when the sun moves south. They do not reach the year. From these months they go to the world of the fathers, and from the world of the fathers to space, and from space to the moon. That is king Soma. That is the food of the gods. The gods eat that.

'When they have dwelt there for as long as there is a remnant (of their merit), then they return along that very same road that they came along, back into space; but from space they go to wind, and when one has become wind he becomes smoke, and when he has become smoke he becomes mist; when he has become mist, he becomes a cloud, and when he has become a cloud, he rains. These are then born here as rice, barley, plants, trees, sesame plants, and beans. It is difficult to move forth out of this condition; for only if someone eats him as food and then emits him as semen, he becomes that creature's semen and is born.

'And so those who behave nicely here will, in general, find a nice womb, the womb of a Brahmin or the womb of a Kshatriya or the womb of a Vaishya. But those whose behavior here is stinking will, in general, find a stinking womb, the womb of a dog or the womb of a pig or the womb of an Untouchable. Then they become those tiny creatures who go by neither one of these two paths but are constantly returning. "Be born and die"—that is the third condition. And because of that, the world (of heaven) over there is not filled up. And one should try to protect oneself from that. There is a verse about this: "One who steals gold, or drinks wine, or sleeps with his teacher's wife, or kills a Brahmin—these four fall, along with the fifth, (any person who is) their companion." But whoever knows these five fires is not smeared with evil, not even if he is the companion of these people. He becomes pure, purified, and wins a world of merit, if he knows this, if he really knows this.'

JANASHRUTI AND RAIKVA

Kshatriyas were not the only non-Brahmins who contributed new ideas to the Upanishads. Even homeless people could have unique religious knowledge. In the following passage, Janashruti is a rich king. Raikva is, by contrast, evidently a street person. At first the steward presumably searches for a Brahmin, for he has to be specifically instructed to search elsewhere; and elsewhere is where he finds Raikva. Raikva despises cows and gold (two things that Brahmins like best) and likes women. It is extremely bold of him to call Janashruti a Shudra, a member of the lowest of the four social classes. Raikva is said to be a gatherer, which may refer to his knack of gathering up everyone else's good karma, as a successful gambler gathers up the dice of the losers—another early example of the transfer of karma from one person to another. (This Upanishad goes on to say that the two gatherers are the wind and the breath.) But "gathering" may also refer to Raikva's poverty, for he may have been a gleaner (like Ruth in the Hebrew Bible), gathering up the dregs of the harvest after everyone else has taken the real crop, or even, like so many homeless people, gathering up other peoples' garbage for his own use. The two meanings work well together: the man who lives on richer peoples' garbage also lives off their good deeds. (Much later, in the *Mahabharata* [14.90], several people—including a mongoose—sing the virtues of "the way of gleaning.")

That Janashruti can understand the talking animals (wild geese, who often carry messages in Hindu mythology) is evidence of his high spiritual achievement, but the non-Brahmin Raikva is higher still; his secret knowledge (about the wind and breath as gatherers) trumps Janashruti's Vedic generosity.

Chandogya Upanishad 4.1–2

There was one Janashruti Pautrayana, a man who was totally devoted to giving and used to give a lot, a man who gave a lot of cooked food. He had hospices built everywhere, thinking: 'People will eat food from me everywhere.'

Now, it so happened that some wild geese were flying overhead at night, and one of them said to another: 'Hey, Bright-Eyes! Look out, Bright-Eyes! Look, a light like that of Janashruti Pautrayana has spread out through the sky. Don't touch it, it you don't want to be burnt.'

The other replied: 'Come now! Given who he is, why do you speak of him as if he were Raikva, the gatherer?'

'That man—how is he Raikva, the gatherer?'

'As the lower throws all go to the one who wins with the highest throw of the dice, so whatever good things people may do, all that goes to him. I say the same of anyone who knows what Raikva knows.'

Now, Janashruti Pautrayana overheard this conversation, and, as soon as he got up in the morning, he said to his steward: 'Look, my man! [This is what I heard:]

> '"Why do you speak of him as if he were Raikva, the gatherer?" "That man—how is he Raikva, the gatherer?"
>
> "As the lower throws all go to the one who wins with the highest throw of the dice, so whatever good things people may do, all that goes to him. I say the same of anyone who knows what Raikva knows."'

The steward searched for Raikva and returned, saying: 'I didn't find him.' Janashruti told him: 'Look for him, my man, in a place where one would search for a non-Brahmin.'

The steward respectfully approached a man under a cart scratching his sores and asked: 'Sir, are you Raikva, the gatherer?' The man replied: 'Yes, I am.' The steward then returned, saying: 'I did find him.'

Taking with him six hundred cows, a gold necklace, and a carriage drawn by a she-mule, Janashruti Pautrayana went back to Raikva and said to him: 'Raikva, here are six hundred cows, a gold necklace, and a carriage drawn by a she-mule. Please, sir, teach me the deity that you venerate.' But Raikva replied: 'Hey, you! Drive them back to your place, Shudra! Keep your goods and your cows!'

Then, taking with him a thousand cows, a gold necklace, a carriage drawn by a she-mule, and his daughter, Janashruti Pautrayana went back to him once again and said: 'Raikva, here are a thousand cows, a gold necklace, and a carriage drawn by a she-mule, here is a wife, and here is the village where you live. Sir, please teach me.'

Lifting up her face, Raikva said: 'Hey you! Drive them to my place, Shudra! With just this face you would have swindled me!'

Translated by Patrick Olivelle.

SHVETASHVATARA UPANISHAD

The *Shvetashvatara Upanishad* ("Upanishad of the Man with a White Mule"), traditionally ascribed to the *Yajur Veda*, is much later than the *Brihadaranyaka* and the *Chandogya* and is in verse. It shares many of the words and ideas of the *Gita* (*Bhagavad Gita*, p. 166), though its deity is Rudra (analogized in many ways to Agni) rather than Krishna. It incorporates a number of rather disparate cosmologies and theologies.

THE TWO BIRDS

This passage represents another attempt to describe, in metaphor, the relationship between the individual soul and the world-soul. It also begins to endow that world-soul with specific characteristics that are more theistic than pantheistic, to identify it with the god Rudra, and to address him. The unborn Person to whom the passage refers is Purusha ("The Hymn of the Primeval Man," p. 82), the male, spirit; the female is Prakriti, nature. Each soul is an unborn spirit that becomes involved with Prakriti during each incarnation and leaves her at each death. The passage quotes *Rig Veda* 1.164.20, a famous verse about two birds, which tells us that the one who does not eat is the world-soul; the other, the one who does eat, is the individual soul.

Shvetashvatara Upanishad 4.1–10

The One who has no color himself but distributes many colors in his secret purpose, by the various uses of his power (*shakti*), the One into whom the whole world dissolves, as he is its end and its beginning—he is god. Let him give us clear minds! It is he who is fire, he who is the sun; he who is the wind, and he who is the moon. He is what is pure; he is Brahma. He is the waters; he is Prajapati.

You are woman; you are man. You are the boy and also the girl. You are an old man stumbling with his cane. As soon as you are born, you face in every direction. You are the dark blue bird and the green bird with red eyes. The lightning is your child. You are the seasons and the seas. You have no beginning, but you exist with power, from which all creatures are born.

The one unborn[1] Person takes his pleasure in lying with the one unborn female, who is red, white, and black,[2] and produces many creatures like herself. Another unborn person takes his pleasure from her and then leaves her.[3]

'Two birds, friends joined together, clutch the same tree. One of them eats the sweet fruit; the other looks on but does not eat.' On that one tree one person grieves for his impotence; he is deluded and depressed. But when he

TRANSLATED BY Wendy Doniger O'Flaherty.

1. This verse plays on the double meaning of the word *aja* ("unborn"), which also means "goat." So the unborn male is both the soul and a billy goat, and the unborn female is both Nature (Prakriti) and a nanny goat. The sexual and metaphysical meanings overlap.

2. The three colors are associated with the three strands (*gunas*) of Nature or matter, according to Sankhya philosophy: goodness (*sattva*, white), energy (*rajas*, red), and darkness (*tamas*, black).

3. The unborn male who leaves his partner is the soul that has achieved Release (*moksha*).

sees the other, the Lord who takes pleasure in his own greatness, (the first) becomes free from sorrow.

The undying syllable[4] of the hymn [the *Rig Veda*] is the final abode where all gods have taken their seat. What can one who does not know this do with the hymn? Only those who know it sit together here. The sacred chants,[5] the sacrifices, the ceremonies, the laws, the past, the future, and what the Vedas declare—the one who uses Illusion[6] projects the whole world out of this (ultimate reality) and confines the other one in it by means of Illusion. So you should realise that Nature is Illusion, and that the great lord is the one who uses Illusion. This whole universe is pervaded by creatures that are parts of him.

4. The word *akshara* means both "syllable" and "undying"; as "syllable" it refers particularly to the sacred syllable "Om."
5. A reference to the Vedic hymns.
6. This may be an early reference to Illusion as a cosmic category or simply an example of the Rig Vedic usage of the word to denote a trick or magic. On the cosmic level, "the one who uses Illusion" is the cosmic magician, the Lord, who creates the illusory world that traps "the other one" (i.e., the individual soul).

THE DISCIPLINE OF MIND AND BODY IN THE *YOGA-SUTRA* OF PATANJALI

150 B.C.E.

The basic meaning of the word *yoga* is "to yoke" or "connect" (as in "to yoke horses to a chariot")—and then to harness and control (the body and the senses) through meditation, breath control, and spiritual exercises. The word *sutra* designates a scientific treatise, generally in prose, consisting of lines "sewn together" (*sutra* being cognate with the English "suture"); the Sutras are the antecedents of the Shastras, which are generally in verse ("Shastras," p. 200). The *Yoga-sutra* of the philosopher Patanjali was composed a few centuries after the Upanishads, a foundational text for the philosophical school of Yoga that emphasized exercises of the mind and the body, primarily breath control, culminating in the difficult exercise of not exercising them *at all*. This philosophy held that *moksha* (Release) came not from knowledge but from the concentration and discipline of body and mind. Yoga assumes a personal god, Ishvara ("the Lord"), who controls the process of periodic creation and dissolution and is omniscient and omnipotent, but is also a kind of eternal, archetypal practitioner of yoga, or a yogi. "Ishvara" is a frequent epithet of the god Shiva, a master yogi, but it is also applied to other gods, including Krishna in the *Gita* (*Bhagavad Gita*, p. 166).

PRONOUNCING GLOSSARY

AUM / om: *ohm*
moksha: *mohk´-shuh*
Patanjali: *puh-tun´-juh-lee*
Yoga-sutra: *yoh´-guh soo´–truh*

QUIETING THE MIND

The *Yoga-sutra* attributed to Patanjali is a work of uncertain date, though most scholars believe it was composed in about the third century C.E. It distills into 195 dense Sanskrit prose aphorisms the essence of the philosophy of yoga that had been developing in India for several centuries, perhaps from the time of the *Rig Veda* or even earlier, and it remained the basis of the major systems of yoga from that time forth. Patanjali's name is said to have resulted from his birth: he fell in the form of a newborn serpent into the hands of his mother as she was offering water in the worship of the sun. She called him Patanjali, from *pata* (meaning both "serpent" and "fallen") and *anjali* (the hands cupped in worship).

Part One, reproduced here, lays out the basic principles of yoga. The first four aphorisms define the nature of yoga as a state of mental tranquillity and spiritual freedom and outline the means to achieve this state. The next seven aphorisms list and then define five modes of thought and warn that each of them may be corrupted. Then (1.12–40), Patanjali describes the ways in which one can make thought become still. The final verses describe the sorts of contemplation that do and do not bear "seed"; thought that depends on an object leaves traces, which are seeds for additional thoughts, and the object of yoga is to stop this. Later sections detail other powers that result from the mastery of the mind, which include flying, becoming invisible, walking on water, having foreknowledge of death, having knowledge of past and future, entering the minds of others, and understanding the languages of animals (3.16–34).

This is the teaching of yoga.
Yoga is the cessation of the turnings of thought.
When thought ceases, the spirit stands in its true identity as observer to the world.
Otherwise, the observer identifies with the turnings of thought.

The turnings of thought, whether corrupted or immune to the forces of corruption, are of five kinds.
They are valid judgment, error, conceptualization, sleep, and memory.
The valid means of judgment are direct perception, inference, and verbal testimony.[1]
Error is false knowledge with no objective basis.
Conceptualization comes from words devoid of substance.
Sleep[2] is the turning of thought abstracted from existence.
Memory is the recollection of objects one has experienced.[3]

Cessation of the turnings of thought comes through practice and dispassion.
Practice is the effort to maintain the cessation of thought.
This practice is firmly grounded when it is performed for a long time without interruption and with zeal.
Dispassion is the sign of mastery over the craving for sensuous objects.
Higher dispassion is a total absence of craving for anything material, which comes by discriminating between spirit and material nature.

Conscious cessation of thought can arise from various forms of conjecture, reflection, enjoyment, and egoism.[4]
Beyond this is a state where only subliminal impressions[5] remain from the practice of stopping thought.
For gods and men unencumbered by physical bodies, but still enmeshed in material nature, the cessation of thought is limited by reliance on the phenomenal world.

TRANSLATED BY Barbara Stoler Miller.

1. These valid means of judgment are the so-called authorities (*pramanas*), the basis of all later systems of Indian logic and argument. See also "Ramanuja Dreams," p. 289.
2. Sleep includes both dreaming and dreamless states.
3. According to Patanjali, all thoughts are preserved as subliminal impressions or memory traces, which allow us to recall past events and perceptions.
4. At the first level, ordinary conscious processes can be used to cause thought to be stilled.
5. The residues left on the mind by past thoughts and actions; they remain subconscious.

Cessation of thought may also come from dedication to the Lord of Yoga.
The Lord of Yoga is a distinct form of spirit[6] unaffected by the forces of corruption, by actions, by the fruits of action, or by subliminal intentions.
In the Lord of Yoga is the incomparable seed of omniscience.
Being unconditioned by time, he is the teacher of even the ancient teachers.
His sound is the reverberating syllable *AUM*.[7]
Repetition of this syllable reveals its meaning.

When *AUM* reveals itself, introspection is attained and obstacles fall away.
The obstacles that distract thought are disease, apathy, doubt, carelessness, indolence, dissipation, false vision, failure to attain a firm basis in yoga, and restlessness.
These distractions are accompanied by suffering, frustration, trembling of the body, and irregular breathing.
The practice of focusing on the single truth is the means to prevent these distractions.

Tranquillity of thought comes through the cultivation of friendship, compassion, joy, and impartiality in spheres of pleasure or pain, virtue or vice.
Or through the measured exhalation and retention of breath.[8]
Or when the mind's activity, arisen in the sense world, is held still.
Or when thought is luminous, free from sorrow.
Or when thought is without passion in the sphere of the senses.
Or when its foundation is knowledge from dreams and sleep.
Or through meditation on a suitable object.
For one whose thought is tranquil, mastery extends from the most minute particle to the vast expanse.

When the turnings of thought stop, a contemplative poise occurs, in which thought, like a polished crystal, is colored by what is nearby—whether perceiver, process of perception, or object of perception.
When concepts formed from knowledge based on words and their meanings taint it, contemplative poise is broken by conjecture.
When memory is purified, then contemplative poise is free of conjecture, empty of its own identity, with the object alone shining forth.
Contemplative poise that is both reflective and intuitive, with subtle elements[9] as its objects, is explained by this.
The subtlety of objects results in their being free of defining marks.
These modes of contemplative poise are the contemplation that bears seeds.

The profound clarity of intuitive cognition brings inner tranquillity.
Here wisdom is the vehicle of truth.

6. The word here translated as "spirit" is *purusha*, a term from Sankhya philosophy, which is dualistic, dividing the universe into a primeval male and spiritual principle of *purusha* (spirit, self, or person) and a female *prakriti* (matter, nature). Sankhya as a philosophy has roots from the time of the Upanishads and is important in the *Mahabharata* (especially in the *Gita*) but was first formally codified around the 3rd century C.E.

7. Also spelled "Om," this is the primordial sound, the cosmic vibration.

8. The control of breathing (*prana*) was the basis of ancient Indian meditative practice from the time of the *Rig Veda* and the Upanishads.

9. A term from Sankhya philosophy; these elements have no recognizable name and form, no "defining marks," and thus give thought nothing to fix on.

It has a different scope than scriptural or inferential knowledge because its object is singular.
A subliminal impression generated by wisdom stops the formation of other impressions.
When the turnings of thought cease completely, even wisdom ceases, and contemplation bears no seeds.

THE AGE OF FERMENT

300 B.C.E.–400 C.E.

The Mauryas (324–185 B.C.E.) ruled an empire that extended throughout North India and much of South India. Ashoka Maurya (265–232 B.C.E.) published, on the earliest stone edicts in India, an ethic that spanned both Hindu and Buddhist ideals and that is reflected in the two great Sanskrit epics, the *Mahabharata* and the *Ramayana*. For, during roughly the same period in which Hindu sages had composed the Upanishads, Gautama Shakyamuni, the Buddha, had inspired the new religion of Buddhism in India, and Mahavira, the Jina, had founded the religion of Jainism. Though all three of these movements shared a number of important philosophical doctrines, such as karma and rebirth, and developed many ideas in conversation and friendly competition, they differed on other essential points and on matters of ritual and social organization, and sometimes they competed for royal patronage.

This period was also marked by important alliances with the Greeks, beginning with Alexander the Great in 327 B.C.E. After the collapse of the Mauryan Empire, India was both threatened and enriched by a series of invasions from the north, by more Greeks as well as Central Asians such as Scythians and Kushanas, and by a dramatic increase in trade with Greece, Central Asia, West Asia, the ports of the Red Sea, and Southeast Asia. Trade flowed along the mountainous northern routes through Central Asia and by sea to the great ports of South India.

Narrative bas-relief frieze depicting a battle scene from the *Mahabharata*. From Cave 16 at Ellora, in Aurangabad, eighth century.

The foreign flux on the one hand loosened up and broadened the concept of knowledge, making it more cosmopolitan—more things to eat, to wear, to think about—and at the same time posed a threat that drove the Brahmins to tighten up some aspects of social control. These two forces, working in tandem, inspired the creation and preservation of the many texts of scientific literature, the Shastras, particularly the science of dharma, Hindu religious and moral law, as well as the *Mahabharata* and the *Ramayana*.

Dharma had already been somewhat codified from between the third and first centuries B.C.E., when the *dharma-sutras* (the antecedents of the *dharma-shastras*) set forth, in prose, the rules of social life and religious observance. Now the Brahmins were circling the wagons against the multiple challenges of Buddhism, Upanishadic *moksha*, yoga, and the diverse growth of Hindu sects. Buddhists presented their own ideas about what they called (in Pali) *dhamma*, ideas that overlapped with but were certainly not the same as Hindu ideas about dharma. Before Buddhism became an issue, there had been no need to define dharma in great detail. But now there was such a need, for the Buddha called his own religion the *dhamma*, and eventually dharma came to mean, among other things, one's religion (so that Hindus would later speak of Christianity as the Christian dharma).

The earliest image of the Shiva-linga, just under 5 feet high, from Gudimallam, Andhra Pradesh, ca. third to first century B.C.E.

Despite (or because of) the rise of Buddhism in this period, both Vedic sacrificers and members of the evolving Hindu sects of Vaishnavas and Shaivas (worshipers of the gods Vishnu and Shiva) found new sponsors among the ruling families and court circles. Kings still performed Vedic sacrifices to legitimize their kingship, but the sectarian worship of non-Vedic deities (that is, the formation of sects devoted to particular gods) began partially to replace Vedic sacrifice. As the gods of the Vedic pantheon (Indra, Soma, Agni) faded into the background, Vishnu and Rudra/Shiva, who had played small roles in the Vedas, attracted more and more worshipers. This was the time of the beginning of the Bhagavata sects, the worship of Bhagavan, the Lord, a name of Vishnu or Shiva.

Pilgrimage and *puja* were the main forms of worship at this time. Sacred fords (*tirthas*) were shrines where one could cross over (which is what *tirtha* means) simultaneously a river and the perils of the world of rebirth. The "conquest of the four corners of the earth," originally a martial image, was now applied to a grand tour of pilgrimage to many shrines, circling the world (India), always to the right. *Puja* (from the Dravidian *pu*, "flower") consisted of making an offering to an image of a god (flowers, fruits, sometimes rice), and/or moving a lamp through the air in a circular pattern, walking around the god, and reciting prayers, such as a litany of the names of the god. Krishna in the *Bhagavad Gita* (9.26) says that pious people offer him a leaf or flower or fruit or water.

Now, too, a new social system was taking shape, the system of castes, which could not be neatly and automatically subsumed as subcategories of classes; class (*varna*) and caste (*jati*) began to form a single, though not yet unified, social system. New communities were beginning to coalesce, their identities defined by a shared occupation and caste status, or by religious sectarian affiliation, or by the use of a particular language. Most of the castes probably derived from clans or guilds, in which, increasingly, families specialized in professions. (The Sanskrit word for caste, *jati*, means "birth.") But other castes might have consisted of foreign sects, tribes, and professions, of people of various geographical, sectarian, and economic factions. Invaders like the West Asian Scythians or the Central Asian Kushanas, and tribal forest-dwellers, as well as other groups on the margins of settled society (Introduction: "The Zen Diagram of Hinduism," p. 45), could also be absorbed into a specific caste, often of uncertain class, or sometimes into a class, mainly Kshatriya (kings and warriors, the second of the four classes) for rulers, occasionally Brahmins or even Shudras.

The division of society into castes facilitated the inclusion of new cultures and groups of people who could eventually be classified in the open shelving of the caste system. This was an effective way to harness the energies and loyalties of skilled indigenous people who were conquered, subordinated, or encroached upon by a society that observed class distinctions. The system of castes was rationalized through an ideology of purity and pollution that was applied to the subgroups, both ethnic and professional, within the four classes. As some professions were defined as purer than others, the hierarchy took over. Like the Buddhists and Jains, many of the new sects disavowed caste, or at least questioned its assumptions. At the same time, there was an increasing tendency to define a dharma that could be all things to all people, a dharma/*dhamma* so general (*sadharana*, "held in common"), so perpetual (*sanatana*), that it applied to all right-thinking people always, transcending the differences between various sects.

This evolving Hindu dharma is at the core of both the Shastras and the two great epic poems, which use compelling narratives to pose unanswerable questions about the ways in which human beings should live.

DUTY AND DISASTER IN THE *MAHABHARATA* OF VYASA 300 B.C.E.–300 C.E.

Over the period of half a millennium, from about 300 B.C.E. to 300 C.E., the two great Sanskrit epics called the *Mahabharata* and the *Ramayana* were composed. They mark the transition from the corpus of texts known as *shruti*, the unalterable Vedic canon of texts "heard" from the words of the gods, to those known as *smriti*, the human tradition, constantly revised, the "remembered texts" of human authorship, texts that could be altered. The texts of the two epics, originally composed orally, have been preserved both orally and in manuscript form for more than two thousand years. Their oral origins made it possible both for a great deal of folklore and other popular material to find its way into these Sanskrit texts and for the texts to get into the people. This popularization also means that we find more input from non-Brahmin authors and that new issues arise regarding the status of the lower classes and women. The *Mahabharata* ("The Great [Story] of the Descendants of Bharata," or "The Great [War] of the Bharatas") is a Sanskrit text of about 75,000 verses (or 100,000, depending on which of several different editions you use) or 3 million words, some fifteen times the combined length of the Hebrew Bible and the New Testament, or seven times the *Iliad* and the *Odyssey* combined. It resembles the Homeric epics in many ways (such as the theme of the great war, the style of its poetry, and its heroic characters, several of them fathered by gods), but, unlike the Homeric gods, many of the *Mahabharata* gods were then, and still are, worshiped and revered in holy texts, including parts of the *Mahabharata* itself. The story is narrated by a bard to a king descended from the original Bharata.

The bare bones of the central story (and there are hundreds of peripheral stories, too) can be summarized like this:

> King Pandu had been cursed to die if he tried to beget children; therefore his wife Kunti saw to it that five gods gave her five sons, called the Pandavas: Yudhishthira (son of Dharma), Arjuna (son of Indra, king of the gods), Bhima (son of Vayu, the wind), and the twins Sahadeva and Nakula (sons of the twin equine gods, the Ashvins). The first three are the sons of Kunti, the twins the sons of Madri. All five of them married the same woman: Draupadi. When the eldest, Yudhishthira, lost the kingdom to his cousins in a game of dice ("The Stripping of Draupadi"), the Pandavas and Draupadi went into exile for twelve years, at the end of which they regained their kingdom through a cataclysmic battle in which almost everyone on both sides was killed. They all went to heaven and died happily ever after.

This story may have been told in some form as early as 900 B.C.E.; its resemblance to Persian, Scandinavian, Greek, and other Indo-European epic traditions suggests that the core of the tale may reach back to the time when these cultures had not yet dispersed, well before 2000 B.C.E. But although stories about the heroes of the two epics circulated from a much earlier period, the *Mahabharata* did not reach something like its present form until between 300 B.C.E. and 300 C.E.—it takes a long time to compose 3 million words. The *Mahabharata* calls itself "The Fifth Veda" (as do several other texts) and dresses its story in Vedic trappings (such as ostentatious Vedic sacrifices). It looks back to the Vedic age and may well preserve many memories of that period, and that place, up in the Punjab. The Painted Gray Ware artifacts discovered at sites identified with locations in the *Mahabharata* may be evidence of the reality of the great *Mahabharata* war, which is usually supposed to have occurred around 950 B.C.E. But the text is very much the product of its times, the centuries before and after the turn of the first millennium.

COMPOSITION AND PERFORMANCE

The story of the Bharata war was probably composed and performed first in the intervals between engagements on a battleground, to an audience that consisted largely of warriors and miscellaneous camp followers. The first bards who recited it were a caste called "Charioteers" (Sutas). Each Charioteer would have gone into battle with one warrior as a combination chauffeur and bodyguard. And then at night, when all the warriors retired from the field and took off their armor, the bards would tell the stories of their exploits as everyone sat around the campfire. Later, traveling bards no longer participated in battle, or drove chariots at all, but still recited the great poems in villages and at festivals; scenarios in the texts may have been recreated in dramatic performance in towns and villages.

In addition, priestly singers praised the king in the course of the sacrifice, while the royal bard would sing poems praising the king's accomplishments in war and battle. Now the Charioteers told their stories during the intervals of a great sacrifice, and the audience in this later period would have been on the one hand more Brahminical—for the Brahmins (the class of priests, highest of the four classes) were in charge of both the sacrifice and the literature of sacrifice—and on the other hand more diverse, as the camp followers would now be replaced by men and women of high as well as low class, who would have been present at the public ceremonies where the tales were recited. At this point, the texts were probably circulated orally, as is suggested by their formulaic, repetitious, and relatively simple language.

Later still, the reciters and improvisers were probably the Brahmins who were officiating at the sacrifice and recited the *Mahabharata* in the intervals between rituals on the sacrificial ground and probably also at shrines along pilgrimage routes. These Brahmins eventually committed the text to writing and wrote commentaries on written versions of it. But the bards continued to memorize the *Mahabharata*, and the literate, too, knew the texts by heart. It was retold very differently by all of its many authors in the long line of literary descent. It is so extremely fluid that there is no single *Mahabharata*; there are hundreds of *Mahabharatas*, hundreds of different manuscripts and innumerable oral versions (one reason why it is impossible to make an accurate calculation of the number of its verses). Among its most recent incarnations are the retellings in Indian classic comics ("Amar Chitra Katha"), a televised series (108 episodes—a holy number—from 1988 to 1990, on Sunday mornings), and Peter Brook's international stage and video versions. To this day, India is called the land of Bharata, and the *Mahabharata* functions much like a national epic.

The *Mahabharata* is not contained in a text; the story is there to be picked up and found, salvaged as anonymous treasure from the ocean of story. It has been called "a work in progress," a literature that "does not belong in a book," and "a library." Yet a single author may have edited the final massive work, unifying the various pieces that had been added over the centuries. Hindu tradition attributes the work to a single author named Vyasa, but Vyasa is also the author (that is, the father) of the two fathers of the warring heroes, Pandu and his brother, Dhritarashtra.

MYTH AND RITUAL

The *Mahabharata* is not just a story. It is a religious text, foundational for Hinduism. Onto the central plot were grafted, over the centuries, hundreds of myths and folktales ("The Churning of the Ocean"), philosophical discourses and religious parables. It is thus "great," as its name claims, not only in size but in scope. Hindus from the time of the composition of the *Mahabharata* to the present know the characters in the texts just as Christians and Jews and Muslims, even if they are not religious, know Adam and Eve. The *Mahabharata* functions as a religious text; many passages end with the "fruits of hearing" them ("Anyone who hears this story [about snakes] will never die of snakebite," etc.). At moments scattered through the text, the Pandavas' cousin, the incarnate god Krishna, intervenes, most famously in his counsel to the hero Arjuna on the battlefield of Kurukshetra, which many Hindus revere as the *Bhagavad Gita*, "the song of god" (*Bhagavad Gita*, p. 166).

Many chapters are devoted to formal discussions of the nature of spiritual peace (*shanti*) and liberation (*moksha*) from the wheel of transmigration (*samsara*). And the text not only describes several great sacrifices—a triumphal horse sacrifice after the great war at the end of the story, and a grotesque sacrifice of snakes at the beginning—but often imagines the battle itself as a great sacrifice, with the warriors offering themselves as victims. The great battle on the field called Kurukshetra—a name as familiar to Hindus as Armageddon to the Abrahamic religions—is also an eschatological conflict at the moment when the universe is about to self-destruct. For the end of that battle marks the beginning of the Kali Age, the fourth of the four degenerating Ages or Yugas ("The Four Ages," p. 228). Even within this moment of degeneration, Krishna is said to descend to earth (as an avatar of the god Vishnu) to restore dharma (the moral law) when it has declined in the course of the cycle.

Hindu tradition regards the *Mahabharata* as both a history and a textbook of the moral law (*dharma-shastra*). The text debates the clash between, on the one hand, the growing doctrine of nonviolence toward all creatures (*ahimsa*) ("The Pandavas Go to Heaven, with a Dog"; "King Shibi Saves the Dove from the Hawk"), and, on the other, both the justice of war and the still dominant tradition of animal sacrifice. The *Mahabharata* both challenges and justifies the entire class structure ("Ekalavya Cuts Off His Thumb"; "The Dog Who Would Be Lion"). Many other deep philosophical questions, too, grow out of the dilemmas that tangle the protagonists in their coils. Dharma continued to denote the sort of human activity that leads to human prosperity, glory, and victory ("Where there is dharma, there is victory," the text famously proclaims), but now it had much more to do. For now the text was often forced to acknowledge the impossibility of maintaining any sort of dharma at all in a world where every rule seemed to be canceled out by another. Time and again when a character finds that every available moral choice is the wrong choice, or when one of the good guys does something obviously very wrong, he will mutter, or be told, "Dharma is subtle" (*sukshma*), thin and slippery as a fine silk sari, elusive as a will o' the wisp, internally inconsistent as well as disguised, hidden, masked. People try again and again to do the right thing, inevitably failing, until they no longer know what the right thing is. The *Mahabharata* deconstructs dharma, exposing the inevitable chaos of the moral life. The narrators kept painting themselves into a corner with the brush of dharma. Their backs to the wall, they could only reach for another story.

The gods, too, were sometimes tripped up by the subtlety of dharma ("The Karma of Dharma"). Krishna straddles the line between a human prince and an incarnation of Vishnu. Other gods, however, appear in unambiguous full divinity. Throughout the *Mahabharata*, we encounter people who say they worship a particular god, the start of sects and therefore of sectarianism. The epic includes a "Hymn of the Thousand Names of Shiva" (13.17) and tells a story about the circumstances under which Shiva came to be worshiped ("Daksha's Sacrifice"). Shiva appears to Arjuna in the form of a naked tribal hunter, in a pivotal episode, and occasionally goes in human disguise among mortals. Pilgrimage is described at length, particularly but not only in the "Tour of the Sacred Fords" (3.80–140).

WOMEN

The *Mahabharata* also depicts women with powers and privileges that they would seldom have again in Sanskrit literature. Polyandry (multiple husbands) is rampant in the epic, and the text offers us, in four consecutive generations, positive images of women who had several sexual partners (sometimes premarital). The prize goes to Draupadi, who has five legitimate husbands—the five Pandavas. Her polyandrous pentad is truly extraordinary, for though polygyny (multiple wives) was the rule, and men could have several spouses throughout most of Hindu history, women could not. It is always possible that the *Mahabharata* was recording a time when polyandry was the custom (as it is nowadays in parts of the Himalayas), but there is no evidence to support this. Since there is no reliable testimony that women at this time actually had multiple husbands, these stories can only be suggestive, evidence either of women's greater sexual freedom or, perhaps, of men's fears of what might happen were women to have that freedom, of the male redactors' nightmare vision of where all that autonomy might lead. Draupadi's hypersexuality may simply have validated an ideal that was understood to be out of reach for ordinary women—imagined precisely in order to be disqualified as a viable option. King Pandu tells his wife Kunti a story explicitly remarking upon an archaic promiscuity that is no longer in effect, pointedly reminding her, and any women who may have heard (or read) the text, that female promiscuity was an ancient option no longer available to them ("The End of Female Promiscuity"). The persistent polyandry in the lineage of the heroines is therefore a remarkably positive fantasy of female equality, which is to say a major resistance to patriarchy, and the polyandrous *Mahabharata* women are a feminist's dream (or a sexist's nightmare): smart, aggressive, steadfast, eloquent, tough as nails, and resilient. Other queens in the *Mahabharata* show remarkable courage and intelligence, too, but their courage is often used in subservience to their husbands. Gandhari, the wife of the blind king Dhritarashtra, kept her eyes blindfolded from the day of her marriage to him, in order to share his blindness. Pandu's two widows vied for the privilege of dying on his pyre.

A partial explanation for the *Mahabharata*'s open-minded attitude toward polyandrous women may come from a consideration of the historical context. The text took shape during a cosmopolitan era that encouraged the loosening of constraints on women in both court and village. The king used women archers for his bodyguards in the palace, and Greek women (Yavanis, "Ionians") carried the king's bows and arrows on hunts. Women served as spies. Female ascetics moved around freely. Prostitutes paid taxes. The state provided supervised work, such as spinning yarn, for upper-class women who had become impoverished, widowed, or deserted, and for aging prostitutes. If a slave woman gave birth to her master's child, both she and the child were immediately released from slavery. Thus women were major players during this period, and the *Mahabharata* may reflect this greater autonomy.

Only two of our selections from the *Mahabharata* (the stripping of Draupadi and Yudhishthira's entry into heaven) are from the central story of the Pandavas; the rest are relatively short myths complete in themselves, sometimes loosely involving the Pandavas. The reasons for this selection are twofold: most of the passages describing the great events are too long to be included in an anthology; and many stories peripheral to the Pandava saga are central to later Hinduism ("The Churning of the Ocean"; "Daksha's Sacrifice"; "King Shibi"), particularly to the submerged strains of marginalized Hinduism ("Ekalavya"; "The Karma of Dharma"; "The End of Female Promiscuity"). For stories from the *Mahabharata* continue to be told in India today, and, as the great scholar A. K. Ramanujan famously remarked, no Indian ever hears the *Mahabharata* for the first time.

THE STRIPPING OF DRAUPADI

Gambling is one of the four great addictive vices that Hindu texts constantly warn us against (the other three being wine, women, and hunting). (One of the men present at the stripping of Draupadi points this out: "They say that kings are subject to four vices: hunting, drinking, dicing and addiction to sex" [2.61.20]). But gambling is an inescapable part of Hinduism. The four Ages of time, or Yugas, form a series named after the four throws of the die ("The Four Ages," p. 228). The first Age, the Krita Yuga ("Winning Age") or the Satya Yuga ("Age of Truth"), is the winning throw of four, a time of happiness, when humans are virtuous and live for a long time. The second Age, the Treta Yuga ("Age of the Trey"), is the throw of three, the trey; things are not quite so perfect. In the third Age, the Dvapara Yuga (the "Age of the Deuce"), the throw of two, things fall apart. And the Kali Age is the dice throw of one, the Present Age, the Iron Age, the Losing Age, the time when people are no good and die young, and barbarians invade India, the time when all bets are off. This fourth Age was always, from the start, entirely different from the first three in one essential respect: unlike the other Ages, it is now, it is real. The end of the *Mahabharata* ushers in the Kali Age, and the main action begins with a disastrous game of dice.

As part of his royal consecration ceremonies, Yudhishthira agrees to play a game of dice with Duryodhana, his cousin and enemy; Duryodhana gets his uncle, Shakuni, to play in his place. Shakuni is a skilled gambler and plays with rigged dice; Yudhishthira, a compulsive but incompetent gambler, loses everything he has, including his wife, who is dragged into the court and humiliated. The words spoken in anger on this occasion become curses that are fulfilled throughout the long course of the subsequent battle, and the stripping of Draupadi is often cited to justify various forms of violent revenge.

Present at this ceremony are several members of the two families, including, on Duryodhana's side, besides Duryodhana himself, Dhritarashtra (Duryodhana's father), Vikarna and Duhshasana (Duryodhana's brothers), Drona, Karna, and Kripa; and on Yudhishthira's side, the other four Pandavas and Vidura ("The Karma of Dharma"). Bhishma, the grandfather of both branches, tries to remain neutral but generally favors Duryodhana's side. Draupadi is sometimes called the Panchala princess, as she comes from the land of Panchala, or Krishnā ("the Dark One"; in Sanskrit, the long final "a" distinguishes her name from that of the incarnate god Krishna).

We join the story as Yudhishthira has already lost heavily.

PRONOUNCING GLOSSARY

Arjuna: *ar´-joo-nuh*
Bharata (the person): *buh´-ruh-tuh*
Bharatas (plural people): *bah´-ruh-tuhz*
Bharadvaja: *buh-rud-vah´-juh*
Bhima: *bee´-muh*
Bhishma: *beesh´-muh*
dharma: *dahr´-muh*
Dhritarashtra: *dri´-tuh-rahsh´-truh*
Draupadi: *drow´-puh-dee*
Drona: *droh´-nuh*
Drupada: *droo´-puh-duh*
Duhshasana: *dooh-shah´-suh-nuh*
Duryodhana: *door-yoh´-duh-nuh*
Gandhara: *gahn-dah´-ruh*
Indra: *in´-druh*
Karna: *kar´-nuh*
Kashi: *kah´-shee*
Kaurava: *kow´-ruh-vuh*
Kripa: *kri´-puh*
Krishna: *krish´-nuh*
Krishna (i.e., Draupadi): *krish-nah´*
Kshatriya: *kuh-shah´-tri-yuh*
Kunti: *koon´-tee*
Kuru: *koo´-roo*
Madri: *mah´-dree*
Mahabharata: *muh-hah´-bah´-ruh-tuh*
Nakula: *nuh´-koo-luh*
Nara: *nuh-ruh*
Narayana: *nah´-rah´-yuh-nuh*
Panchala: *pahn´-chah´-luh*
Pandava: *pahn´-duh-vuh*
Pandu: *pahn´-doo*
Radha: *rah-dah*
Sahadeva: *suh-huh-day´-vuh*
Shakuni: *shuh´-koo-nee´*
Shri: *shree*
Subala: *soo´-buh-luh*
Suta: *soo'-tuh*
Vidura: *vi-doo'-ruh*
Vikarna: *vi-kar'-nuh*
Yama: *yuh'-muh*
Yudhishthira: *yoo-dish'-tee-ruh*

Mahabharata 2.58–60, 2.61.1–51

Now Shakuni addressed Yudhishthira once more. 'You have already lost much of the Pandavas' wealth, son of Kunti; declare what wealth you stake now, if any remains unlost!'

'I know that I have incalculable wealth, Shakuni son of Subala,' answered Yudhishthira; 'why do you question me about my wealth? Let the wager be ten thousand, a million, ten billion and one billion more, a hundred million, a thousand billion, a thousand million, a hundred thousand billion! This is my stake, king; I wager it against you!'

Hearing this, Shakuni resolved and performed his deceit; and 'I have won!' said Shakuni to Yudhishthira.

'I have horses and cows, including many milkers,' said Yudhishthira; 'I have numberless sheep and goats; and I have all the livestock of every kind to the east of the Sindhu,[1] son of Subala. This is my stake, king; I wager it against you!'

Hearing this, Shakuni resolved and performed his deceit; and 'I have won!' said Shakuni to Yudhishthira.

'My remaining wealth is my city, my country, my land,' said Yudhishthira, 'together with all the wealth belonging to non-Brahmins, and the non-Brahmin populace itself. This is my stake, king; I wager it against you!'

TRANSLATED BY John D. Smith.

1. The Indus River.

Hearing this, Shakuni resolved and performed his deceit; and 'I have won!' said Shakuni to Yudhishthira.

'The earrings and neck-chains,' said Yudhishthira, 'and all the bodily adornments that lend luster to these princes—this is my stake, king; I wager it against you!'

Hearing this, Shakuni resolved and performed his deceit; and 'I have won!' said Shakuni to Yudhishthira.

'My wager is this dark young man Nakula,' said Yudhishthira, 'with red eyes, lion-like shoulders and strong arms, together with whatever wealth he owns.'

'King Yudhishthira,' said Shakuni, 'Prince Nakula, so dear to you, has been added to our treasure! What will you wager next?' With these words he took up the dice; and 'I have won!' said Shakuni to Yudhishthira.

'Sahadeva here expounds the different dharmas,' said Yudhishthira, 'and has acquired a worldwide reputation as a scholar. I love the prince, and he does not deserve this, but I wager him against you as though I loved him not.'

Hearing this, Shakuni resolved and performed his deceit; and 'I have won!' said Shakuni to Yudhishthira. 'Madri's twin sons are dear to you, O king; now you have lost them to me. But I think that Bhima and wealth-winner Arjuna mean even more to you!'

'Be sure that you are breaching dharma, fool,' said Yudhishthira, 'in disregarding propriety and seeking to sow dissension among those who wish each other well!'

'The drunk man may fall in a ditch,' replied Shakuni, 'and the absent-minded man may bump into a post; but you are the eldest and best, O king! I pay honor to you, bull-like heir of Bharata! When these cheating gamesters gamble like crazy men, they rave about things never seen, asleep or awake!'

'Prince Arjuna is the world's most spirited hero,' said Yudhishthira; 'like a boat he rescues us in battle and defeats our enemies. He does not deserve this, but I wager him against you, Shakuni.'

Hearing this, Shakuni resolved and performed his deceit; and 'I have won!' said Shakuni to Yudhishthira. 'I have won from you the bowman of the Pandavas, the ambidextrous warrior, the son of Pandu! Now, king, wager your beloved Bhima, for he is all the stake that you have left!'

'Prince Bhima is our leader and the leader of our warriors,' said Yudhishthira, 'like Indra himself, the god of the thunderbolt and enemy of the demons; noble Bhima with his lion-like shoulders, glaring with knitted brows, ever unforbearing, foe-crusher and foremost of club-wielders, is unmatched in strength by any other man. He does not deserve this, but I wager him against you, O king.'

Hearing this, Shakuni resolved and performed his deceit; and 'I have won!' said Shakuni to Yudhishthira. 'You have lost much wealth; you have lost your brothers, your horses and elephants, son of Kunti; declare what wealth you stake now, if any remains unlost!'

'I myself remain,' said Yudhishthira, 'seniormost of all the brothers, and loved by them. If you win me I shall work for you, for I shall be my own downfall.'

Hearing this, Shakuni resolved and performed his deceit; and 'I have won!' said Shakuni to Yudhishthira. 'This is a most sinful thing that you have done, to lose your own self; if other wealth remains, O king, loss of oneself is a sin!'

Thus Shakuni, who knew the ways of the dice, won every one of those world-heroes by wagering, throw after throw. Now he spoke again: 'One stake is left to you unlost, your own beloved queen. Wager Draupadi, the Panchala princess; win yourself back with her!'

'I wager her against you,' said Yudhishthira. 'She is neither short nor tall, neither swarthy nor florid, and her silken garments are dyed red; her eyes are like petals of autumn lotuses, her scent is the scent of autumn lotuses, she decks herself with autumn lotuses, and she is equal in beauty to Shri.[2] She is a woman such as any man might want who wished for gentleness, who wished for perfect beauty, who wished for perfect disposition. Last to retire to bed and first to rise, she knows everything that has been done or left undone by everybody, even the cowherds and shepherds. Her sweat-flecked face is lovely as a lotus or jasmine flower, her waist slender as a sacrificial altar; her hair is long, her eyes the color of copper, her body not marred by too much hair. Such is the Panchala princess Draupadi, O king, with her slender waist and her lovely limbs; alas, I wager her against you, son of Subala.'

When Yudhishthira lord of dharma spoke these words, O heir of Bharata, all the elder courtiers were heard to cry, 'Woe! Woe!' The hall was in turmoil; all the kings fell to talking, while Bhishma, Drona, Kripa and the other senior Kurus broke into a sweat. Vidura sat plunged in thought, head in hands, looking like a dead man; staring at the ground, he hissed like a snake. But Dhritarashtra was elated, and asked over and over again, 'Has he won? Has he won?,' making no attempt to maintain his dignity. Karna was overwhelmed with joy, and so were Duhshasana and the other Kauravas, while others in the hall wept. As for Subala's crazed son Shakuni, he did not hesitate; and 'I have won!' he said triumphantly as he took up the dice yet again.

Now Duryodhana spoke. 'Come, chamberlain,' he said, 'and fetch here Draupadi of great renown, the Pandavas' beloved wife! She shall sweep the house, and then hurry away to enjoy her life with our other slave-girls!'

'The unthinkable is happening, thanks to you and your kind,' answered Vidura. 'Fool! You do not see that you are caught in a trap; you do not realize that you are hanging over a precipice; you are like a deer that stupidly provokes tigers to fury! You are carrying on your head snakes of deadly venom, their poison-sacs full; do not enrage them, fool! Do not set out for Yama's[3] realm! In my judgement Draupadi Krishna has not fallen into servitude, heir of Bharata, for King Yudhishthira was not his own master when he wagered her.

'This prince, Dhritarashtra's son, is like the bamboo that dies in putting forth fruit: he is ripe, and this is the time for his death, yet he does not understand that gambling leads to the most dangerous of feuds. A man should not act to wound; he should not speak cruelly; he should not snatch the final possession from one who has lost all; he should not utter that hurtful, infernal word which causes another man distress. When bad words leave a

2. Goddess of Fortune.

3. King of the dead.

person's mouth to bring grief night and day to those they hurt, they never fail to strike the weakest spots; therefore no learned man will direct them at others.

'It is said that once, when men had lost a knife, their goat tore at the ground with its hooves till it dug up another: its throat was cut most horribly. Do not do likewise! Do not dig up a feud with the Pandavas! Men do not speak ill of a praiseworthy man, whether pious householder, forest-dwelling sage, or learned ascetic; but curs forever bay like you. Son of Dhritarashtra, you do not realize that this is the dreadful, crooked gate to hell: many of the Kurus will follow you and Duhshasana through it, thanks to your success at gambling! Bottle-gourds may sink and stones may float, boats may forever sail the wrong way on the water, but this foolish prince, Dhritarashtra's son, will never listen to my beneficial words. Without doubt he will be the end of the Kurus, a terrible destruction sweeping all away, for the prophetic, beneficial words of his friends are ignored, and only greed flourishes!'

'Curse you, chamberlain!' said the son of Dhritarashtra, and in his mad pride he caught the eye of his page and addressed him in the midst of all the nobles in the hall. 'Fetch Draupadi, my page! You have no fear of the Pandavas, even if the chamberlain here is scared and disputes my order! But, after all, he has never wanted us to prosper!'

The page, a Suta,[4] received his orders. He set off as soon as he learnt King Duryodhana's command, entered the dwelling as a dog might enter the den of a lion, and approached the Pandavas' queen. 'Yudhishthira is overcome by the intoxication of gambling,' he said, 'and so, Draupadi you have been won by Duryodhana. You must therefore now enter Dhritarashtra's household: I shall conduct you to your duties, daughter of Drupada!'

'How can you speak so, page?' replied Draupadi. 'What prince would ever wager his own wife? The foolish king may be overcome by the intoxication of gambling, but had he nothing else to stake?'

'It was when he had nothing else to stake that Pandu's son Yudhishthira wagered you,' answered the page. 'First the king staked his brothers and, indeed, himself; then, princess, he staked you.'

'Go, son of a Suta,' said Draupadi; 'go and ask that gambler in the hall: "Heir of Bharata, did you first lose yourself, or me?" Return when you have learnt this, son of a Suta; then you may conduct me there.'

So he went back to the hall and announced what Draupadi had said. 'These were Draupadi's words to you: "When you lost me, of whom were you master? Did you first lose yourself, or me?"' But Yudhishthira remained motionless, like a dead man, and made no answer to the Suta, whether for good or ill.

Now Duryodhana spoke. 'Let the Panchala princess, Draupadi Krishna, come here in person to pose this question! Here in this hall let everyone hear what she and this man have to say!'

The Suta page, obedient to Duryodhana's will, returned to the royal quarters and spoke to Draupadi in evident distress. 'Princess, the courtiers there summon you! I think that the destruction of the Kauravas must be at hand, for if you are to come to the hall, princess, it is clear that Duryodhana, basest of men, cares nothing for our welfare.'

4. A low caste of charioteers and bardic poets.

Draupadi answered, 'This, for sure, is what the ordainer ordained. The wise and the foolish are touched alike by both good and ill, but a single dharma has been declared paramount in this world which will, if protected, maintain us in peace.'

Now when Yudhishthira realized what Duryodhana intended to do, he sent to Draupadi a messenger whom she trusted, O bull-like heir of Bharata; and the Panchala princess came to the hall and stood before her father-in-law Dhritarashtra, weeping and wearing a single unbelted garment, for she was in the midst of her period. King Duryodhana looked at the faces before him and exultantly addressed the Suta: 'Bring her right here, page! Let the Kurus speak to her face to face!'

Then the Suta, who was obedient to his will but fearful of the anger of Drupada's daughter, put aside pride, and appealed once more to the courtiers: 'What should I say to Draupadi Krishna?'

'Look, Duhshasana,' said Duryodhana, 'this idiot son of a Suta of mine is frightened of wolf-belly Bhima! Lay hold of Drupada's daughter yourself, and bring her here. Our rivals are powerless: what can they do?'

Prince Duhshasana listened to his brother, then arose, his eyes red with anger. He entered the quarters of the mighty chariot-fighters, and spoke to Princess Draupadi. 'Come, Panchala girl, come! You have been won. Put aside modesty, Draupadi, and look upon Duryodhana with your long lotus-eyes! Now you must transfer your affections to the Kurus, for they have won you fairly. Come to the hall!'

Then she arose, her heart full of grief, and she wiped her pale face with her hand. In her distress she ran to the womenfolk of old King Dhritarashtra, the bull-like Kuru; but Duhshasana rushed at her, roaring in fury, and grabbed the wife of the lord of men by her long, dark, flowing hair. Her hair, which had been sprinkled with water purified by *mantras*[5] during the ritual bath concluding the great rite of the royal consecration, was now handled roughly by Dhritarashtra's son to slight the Pandavas' manhood. Duhshasana laid hold of Draupadi Krishna with her deep black hair and led her towards the hall, unprotected in the midst of her protectors, dragging her as the wind drags at a battered plantain tree. As she was dragged along, she bowed her slender body low and spoke softly: 'Today I am in the midst of my period, dull-witted prince, and I am wearing a single garment! You ignoble man, you should not take me to the hall!'

But he held Draupadi Krishna firm by her black hair, and he said to her, 'Call for aid to Arjuna and Krishna, to Nara and Narayana;[6] I am taking you! You may be in the midst of your period, daughter of Drupada, and you may be wearing a single garment or, indeed, none at all; you have been won at gambling and you have been made our slave! Enjoy your pleasures now amongst our other slave-girls!'

Her hair was dishevelled and her garment fallen half off through Duhshasana's manhandling. But, modest and burning with anger, Draupadi Krishna softly spoke these words: 'The men here in this hall expound learned texts and perform the rituals; all of them are warriors like Indra; all of them

5. Vedic verses.
6. Nara and Narayana are names of Arjuna and Krishna regarded as gods, aspects of Vishnu.

are my elders or as good as my elders. I cannot stand before them like this! You are acting cruelly and ignobly. Do not strip my clothes from me! Do not drag me! The princes could never forgive what you are doing, even if the very gods with Indra were to take your side!

'King Yudhishthira is the son of Dharma and abides by dharma, and dharma is subtle, requiring skill to understand it. I would not wish even a word of mine to deviate from virtue and bring my lord the least atom of blame. But for you to drag me into the midst of the Kuru heroes in the midst of my period is ignoble; and nobody here shows me any respect! Clearly they all approve your way of thinking. A curse upon you! The dharma of the Bharatas is destroyed, and so is adherence to the Kshatriya way, for every one of the Kurus in this hall is watching whilst the limits of Kuru dharma are breached. Drona has no mettle, nor Bhishma, nor, for sure, noble King Dhritarashtra here, for they, the seniormost of the Kurus, take no notice of this savage violation of dharma!'

Thus the slender-waisted lady lamented, and she gazed at her furious husbands, inflaming the Pandavas with her glances till they were ready to burst with anger. Neither the loss of their kingship, nor that of their wealth or their finest jewels, caused them to grieve as did the angry gaze that Draupadi Krishna directed at them in her distress.

As for Duhshasana, when he saw her looking at her wretched husbands, he shook her roughly till she nearly fainted, and 'Slave!' he said with a savage laugh. And Karna praised his words, laughing aloud in great glee; and Subala's son, Shakuni king of Gandhara, likewise applauded Duhshasana. But apart from these two, and from Duryodhana son of Dhritarashtra, the other courtiers who were present were greatly grieved to see Draupadi Krishna dragged into the hall.

'Good lady,' said Bhishma, 'it is true that dharma is subtle, so that I cannot properly decide this question of yours; for I recognize that whilst a man without property cannot wager the property of another, a woman is always subservient to her husband. Pandu's son Yudhishthira would give up the world and all its wealth, but he would never abandon truth, and he stated that he had been won; this is why I cannot judge this question of yours. Shakuni is unequaled among men at gambling, but he allowed Yudhishthira son of Kunti free choice, and that noble man did not consider that what took place was deceit; this is why I cannot address this question of yours.'

'The king was challenged in this hall by skilled gamblers,' replied Draupadi, 'by wicked, ignoble deceivers, men who love gambling, while he had had little practice. How can you say that he was allowed free choice? Foremost among the Kurus and the Pandavas, he is pure by nature and does not understand the ways of deceit; that is why, even though he had been won by all of them conspiring together, he agreed to wager me afterwards. Let all the Kurus present in this hall, men with sons and daughters-in-law under their authority, consider what I have said, and properly decide this question of mine!'

Thus she lamented and wept, gazing over and over again at her husbands, while Duhshasana spoke to her words that were harsh and hateful and bitter. Dragged along in the midst of her period, with her garment slipping from her, though she least deserved such treatment—wolf-belly Bhima looked at her, and then at Yudhishthira, and in his unbearable distress he gave vent to his fury.

'The gamblers in this land have their whores, Yudhishthira,' he said, 'but they do not wager them; indeed, they show them kindness! The offerings of wealth and other fine goods that the king of Kashi brought, the jewels that other kings presented to us, our steeds, our riches, our armor, our weapons, our kingdom, we ourselves and you yourself, have all been wagered and won by others, and this has not angered me, for you are master of all we own. But it seems to me that in staking Draupadi you went too far. The girl does not deserve this; she has joined herself to the Pandavas, yet, thanks to you, she is tormented by base, cruel, deceitful Kauravas! It is for her sake that I turn my fury on you, king. I shall burn these arms of yours! Fetch fire, Sahadeva!'

'Bhima!' said Arjuna. 'Never before have you spoken such words! Our cruel enemies must have destroyed your respect for dharma. You should not give those enemies what they desire. Practice highest dharma, and do not rebel against your righteous elder brother; for if a king is challenged by others, he should recall his Kshatriya dharma and gamble at their wish: this brings us great glory!'

'Wealth-winner Arjuna,' answered Bhima, 'if I believed that he had acted out of self-indulgence, I would overpower him and burn his two arms in a blazing fire!'

Now when Dhritarashtra's son Vikarna saw the Pandavas so distressed, and Draupadi in such torment, he spoke these words: 'Princes, you must decide the matter put to you by Drupada's daughter; if we fail to judge this matter we shall go straight to hell! Bhishma and Dhritarashtra, the two seniormost of the Kurus, both say nothing, and so does sagacious Vidura; Bharadvaja's son Drona, the Teacher of us all, and Kripa too, the two truest of Brahmins, do not address this question. But the other lords of the earth who are assembled here from every quarter should put aside personal anger and desire, and speak as they judge. Fair Draupadi has raised this matter repeatedly; consider it, princes, and give your answer: which of you takes which side?'

Many times Vikarna addressed all those courtiers thus, but the lords of the earth did not reply to him, whether for good or ill. Then, after speaking so several times to them all, he wrung his hands, exhaled deeply, and said, 'Decide the matter, or decide it not, lords of the earth! Either way, O Kauravas, I shall tell you what I think proper in this case. It is said, O best of men, that kings are subject to four vices: hunting, drinking, dicing and excessive sexual indulgence. The man who is addicted to these lives his life shunning dharma, and the world holds the deeds of such an unfit person to be of no account.

'Pandu's son entered upon the wager of Draupadi when he was utterly given over to one such vice, having been challenged by cheating gamesters; further, this blameless girl is the common wife of all of the Pandavas, and the wager was made by Yudhishthira after he himself had been lost; what is more, it was Subala's son Shakuni himself who first named Draupadi Krishna when he was seeking a stake. Bearing all this in mind, I consider that she has not been won.'

At these words, there arose in the hall a great uproar of voices praising Vikarna and condemning Shakuni. When the noise was stilled, Radha's son

Karna, nearly swooning with rage, brandished a handsome arm and spoke: 'Many perversities are to be seen in Vikarna, which, though they spring from him, will destroy him as fire burns the firestick that kindles it. These princes have said not a word, for all the pleading of Draupadi Krishna: I think they think Drupada's daughter fairly won! Son of Dhritarashtra, it is your own childish folly that tears you apart, so that you, a boy, speak an old man's words in the midst of the assembly. Nor do you truly understand dharma, dull-witted younger brother of Duryodhana, if you claim that Draupadi has not been won, when won she was! How can you think Krishna not won, son of Dhritarashtra, when Pandu's eldest son staked all his possessions in this hall, and Draupadi was one of those possessions? How can you think Krishna not won, bull-like heir of Bharata, when she was fairly won? Draupadi was named aloud, and the Pandavas assented; so for what reason do you think her not won?

'Or perhaps you think it was not right that she was brought to this hall wearing a single garment; well, hear my superior view of this issue too. The gods ordain one husband for a woman, heir of Kuru, yet she submits to several: thus she is clearly a whore, and in my judgement it is not remarkable that she should be brought to the hall, or that she should be wearing a single garment, or, indeed, none at all! Subala's son Shakuni fairly won all the Pandavas' wealth: whatever riches they possessed, and this woman, and themselves.

'Duhshasana, this Vikarna with his wise talk is just a foolish boy. Strip off the Pandavas' garments, and those of Draupadi too!'

When the Pandavas heard this, heir of Bharata, they all removed their upper garments and sat down in the hall. Then Duhshasana forcibly grabbed Draupadi's garment in the middle of the hall, O king, and began to pull it from her. But, lord of the peoples, as he pulled at Draupadi's garment, another garment just like it appeared,[7] and this happened over and over again. At this, all the lords of the earth gave a dreadful cry as they saw this most wonderful sight in the world.

But Bhima, wringing his hands, his lower lip throbbing in anger, loudly pronounced a curse in the midst of the kings: 'Kshatriyas of the world, hear these words of mine that no other man ever spoke before, nor will ever speak again! Lords of the earth, may I not attain the realm of all my ancestors if, having said this, I do not carry it out; if in battle I do not rip open the breast of this wicked sinner, this bastard Bharata, and drink his blood!'

His words made the hair rise on everyone's body. Those who heard them did him great honor, and reviled Dhritarashtra's son. As for Duhshasana, having amassed a pile of garments in the middle of the hall, he sat down, wearied and ashamed. The princes of men present in the hall uttered many a hair-raising cry of 'Alas! Alas!' when they saw the sons of Kunti; people called out, 'The Kauravas will not decide Draupadi's question!' and they censured Dhritarashtra.[8]

7. In later retellings of this episode, Draupadi cries out to Krishna for help, and it is he who works the miracle of the inexhaustible garments. But here Draupadi does it all by herself.

8. Eventually, Draupadi successfully argues a point of dharma—that since Yudhishthira had already lost himself, he no longer owned her when he wagered her—and so moves Dhritarashtra that he sets all of the Pandavas free, though Duryodhana keeps their kingdom and their wealth.

EKALAVYA CUTS OFF HIS THUMB

Ekalavya, the son of a chief of the Nishada tribe, a person outside the Hindu class system, becomes a great archer. Drona, the teacher of martial arts, has to punish him, both to prevent him from excelling in this skill reserved for the class of warriors (Kshatriya), and to protect both dharma and the reputation of Arjuna, his own world-class archery student. Drona claims his retroactive tuition, the gift that one gives to the guru upon the completion of one's education (called the *guru-dakshina*): he demands that Ekalavya cut off his thumb, which Ekalavya does. To add insult to injury, Drona really didn't teach Ekalavya at all and hardly deserves any tuition fees, let alone such a grotesque payment. But where is the author's sympathy? It is hard to be sure. The text assumes that it is arrogant of Ekalavya to push in where he does not belong; he cannot be a royal archer, for he was born into the wrong family for that. But Ekalavya does not act arrogant. His outward appearance invokes all the conventional tropes for tribals: he is literally dirt, made of the wrong stuff (or, as we would say, has the wrong genes). But his inner soul, reflected in his behavior, is pious and respectful; he does what the teacher tells him to do; not only is he a brilliant archer, but he is honest and humble. To this extent, at least, the *Mahabharata* likes him and, presumably, pities him; it refers to Drona's command as "terrible" (*daruna*).

Yet the act by which Ekalavya proves his mettle as an archer is one of gratuitous and grotesque cruelty to a dog, the unclean, carrion-eating animal that is in many ways the animal counterpart, even the totem, of a Nishada ("The Dog Who Would Be Lion"). The dog barks at him; he doesn't like the way Ekalavya looks and smells. Does Ekalavya's unsympathetic treatment of this dog cancel our sympathy for Ekalavya as the victim of interhuman violence? Does it justify Drona's cruel treatment of him—what goes around, comes around, travels down the line—or, at least, remind us of the cruelty inherent in the particular caste dharma of a hunter? But the text shows no sympathy for the dog, and therefore no condemnation of Ekalavya for his treatment of the dog.

This is a brutal story, even for the *Mahabharata*. How are we to understand it? First of all, who is Ekalavya? He is a prince among his own people, but that wins him no points with Drona or the Pandava princes. The Nishadas here embrace Hindu dharma and Hindu forms of worship but are still beneath the contempt of the caste system. For such a person to stand beside the Pandava princes in archery classes was unthinkable; that is what Drona, who "knew dharma," realized. But the author subtly challenges this view.

The text assumes that this is the way things must be, but it does not like the way things must be. It paints Ekalavya sympathetically despite itself. Ekalavya's physical repulsiveness is contrasted with his high moral qualities. In the face of his defense of the class system, the author of this story saw the humanity in Ekalavya, saw that tribals were human beings of dignity and honor. It doesn't necessarily mean that tribals tried to break into the professions of Kshatriyas. Nor does it mean that Kshatriyas went around cutting off the thumbs of tribals. It means that the author of this text imagined the situation and was troubled by it. So were the people who heard and, eventually, read the text; during the long history of this story, different people read it differently, and even today many Dalits (formerly known as Untouchables) have made Ekalavya (or Eklavya) their hero ("Eklavya," p. 616).

The story is narrated to a king, descended from Bharata, whom the narrator occasionally addresses parenthetically.

PRONOUNCING GLOSSARY

Arjuna: *ar´-joo-nuh*
Bharata: *bah´-ruh-tuh*
Drona: *droh´-nuh*
Ekalavya: *ay´-kuh-luv-yuh*
Hiranyadhanus: *hee-run´-yuh-duh´-noos*
Kaunteya: *kown-tay´-yuh*
Kaurava: *kow´-ruh-vuh*
Nishada: *ni-shah´-duh*
Pandava: *pahn´-duh-vuh*

Mahabharata 1.123.1–39

Arjuna did his best to honor his teacher and made the greatest effort at mastering arms. He became Drona's favorite. Drona summoned the cook and told him in secret, "Never give Arjuna anything to eat when it is dark." Then, one day when Arjuna was eating, a breeze rose and blew out the lamp by which light he was eating. Arjuna went on eating, nor did his hand fail to find his mouth, so accustomed was it to the motions of handling food. Realizing now what practice could accomplish, the Pandava started practicing at night. Drona heard the twang of his bowstring, and he rose and came and embraced him, and said, "I shall do anything to see that no archer on earth shall ever be your equal, I promise you!"

Thereafter Drona taught Arjuna the arts of fighting from chariots, on elephants, horseback, and on the ground. He instructed the Pandava in combat with clubs, in swordsmanship, in hand-thrown weapons like spears, javelins, and lances, and in battles with mixed weapons. Seeing his skill at them, kings and princes came by the thousands to master the science of weaponry.

So, great king, a certain Ekalavya came, the son of Hiranyadhanus, the chief of the Nishadas. But Drona, who knew the Law, declined to accept him for archery, out of consideration for the others, reflecting that he was a son of a Nishada. Ekalavya, enemy-burner, touched Drona's feet with his head and went into the forest. There he fashioned a likeness of Drona out of clay. This image he treated religiously as his teacher, while he spent all his efforts on archery, observing the proper disciplines. And so great was his faith, and so sublime his discipline, that he acquired a superb deftness at fixing arrow to bowstring, aiming it, and releasing it.

Upon a day Drona allowed the Kauravas and Pandavas leisure, and the warlike princes all went out hunting in their chariots. As it happened, sire, the Pandavas had one man who followed them with their gear and a dog. While they all roamed about, each bent on his own design, the dog wandered off in the woods, got lost, and came upon the Nishada. When the dog smelled that black Nishada in the woods, wrapped in black deerskin, his body caked with dirt, it kept about him, barking away. When the cur kept on barking, the Nishada, displaying his deft skill, shot almost simultaneously seven arrows into its mouth. Its mouth full of arrows, the dog went back to the Pandavas, and on seeing the animal the heroes were greatly surprised. As they looked and noticed this supreme feat of fast, blind shooting, they became

Translated by J. A. B. van Buitenen.

humble and praised its author in every way. The Pandavas then went out into the woods to look for the forest-dweller and found him, king, ceaselessly shooting arrows. They did not recognize the man with his wild aspect and questioned him, "Who are you and whose?"

Ekalavya said:

"Know me for the son of Hiranyadhanus, chieftain of the Nishadas, and also for a pupil of Drona, who toils on mastering archery."

The Pandavas now in fact recognized him, and when they returned they told Drona the whole miraculous story as it had happened. But Arjuna Kaunteya kept thinking of Ekalavya, king: and when he met alone with Drona, he said to him affectionately, "Didn't you once embrace me when I was alone and tell me fondly that no pupil of yours would ever excel me? Then how is it that you have another powerful pupil who excels me, who excels all the world—the son of the Nishada chief?"

Drona thought for a moment, then came to a decision, and, taking the left-handed archer with him, repaired to the Nishada. He found Ekalavya, his body caked with dirt, hair braided, dressed in tatters, bow in hand, ceaselessly shooting arrows. When Ekalavya saw Drona approaching, he went up to him, embraced his feet, and touched the ground with his head. After honoring Drona duly, the Nishada-born boy declared himself to be his pupil and stood before him with folded hands. Thereupon, sire, Drona said to Ekalavya, "If you are my pupil, then give me at once my fee!" Hearing this, Ekalavya said happily, "What can I offer you, sir? Let my guru command me! For, great scholar of the Brahman, there is nothing I shall withhold from my guru!"

Drona replied, "Give me your right thumb!" And hearing Drona's harsh command, Ekalavya kept his promise; forever devoted to the truth, with a happy face and unburdened mind, he cut off his thumb without a moment's hesitation and gave it to Drona. When thereafter the Nishada shot with his fingers, he was no longer as fast as he had been before, O king of men. Arjuna's fever was gone and his heart was happy; and Drona's word was proved true: no one bested Arjuna.

THE PANDAVAS GO TO HEAVEN, WITH A DOG

Dharma sometimes becomes incarnate as a human being (Vidura, in "The Karma of Dharma"). He is also the father of Yudhishthira, the oldest of the Pandavas, known as "the Dharma King" because of both his lineage and his constant concern for justice. Dharma fathers Yudhishthira upon Kunti, the wife of Pandu, when Pandu, because of a curse, is unable to produce children himself. In the course of the *Mahabharata*, Dharma reveals himself in a variety of forms. When he appears at the very end, he reminds Yudhishthira of one of those incidents: once, Dharma disguised himself as a forest spirit to test the virtue of the brothers when they were in search of water; all but Yudhishthira failed and were killed, but he survived and revived them all. (When asked whom he would revive first, ever concerned for equality, he chose one of his half-brothers, son of another mother, so that each of the two wives of Pandu would have one surviving son.) The final encounter between Dharma and the Pandavas takes place when, after most of their relatives, male and female, have been killed, the five Pandava brothers—Yudhishthira, Arjuna, Bhima, and the twins Sahadeva and Nakula—with their joint wife, Draupadi, go north toward the sacred mountain Meru. They are followed by a dog, an animal that Hindus regard as unclean and whose touch is polluting.

Yudhishthira refuses to go to heaven without the stray dog who has attached itself to him. Dharma uses the dog to make a powerful ethical point; this is surely a way of arguing about the sorts of humans who should or should not go to heaven or even, perhaps, by extension, about the castes who should or should not be allowed into temples. All good Hindus go to heaven, but they do so after dying and being given different, heavenly bodies ("The Funeral Fire," p. 84); Yudhishthira is unique in being given the gift of going to heaven in his own body.

The issue of noncruelty to animals is a variant on the heavier problem of nonviolence (*ahimsa*, "the absence of the desire to kill or harm") toward both animals and humans, in a culture that views violence—toward humans, as well as toward animals—as inevitable. Elsewhere, Yudhishthira says that noncruelty is the highest dharma (3.297.72). Here, he refuses to abandon a dog who is "devoted" (*bhakta*) to him. The dog, the loyal dog, is, after all, the natural *bhakta* of the animal kingdom. But *bhakti* at this period meant little more than belonging to someone, being dedicated to someone as a servant or loyal friend (or, occasionally, a lover, as the term is sometimes also used for carnal love); it did not yet have the specific overtone of passionate love between a god and his devotee that was to become characteristic of a branch of medieval Hinduism ("The Flowering of Bhakti," p. 295). Yet as the word expanded its meaning, the story of Yudhishthira and his dog was often read as a model for that later sort of devotion. In the end, the dog never does go to heaven, never violates (or reforms) Hindu law, because there was no dog; it was all an illusion. The story shows just how problematic the caste system is, but does not change it. No dogs get into heaven.

PRONOUNCING GLOSSARY

Arjuna: *ar´-joo-nuh*
Ashvin: *ush´-vin*
Bhima: *bee´-muh*
Dharma: *dahr´-muh*
Dvaita: *dvai´-tuh*
Indra: *in´-druh*
Kuru: *koo´-roo*
Marut: *muh´-root*
Meru: *may´-roo*
Narada: *nah´-ruh-duh*
Pandava: *pahn´-duh-vuh*
Sahadeva: *suh-huh-day´-vuh*
Yudhishthira: *yoo-dish´-tee-ruh*

Mahabharata 17.2–3

They gathered together their inner forces and entered into a yogic state[1] and set out for the north. They saw the great Himalayan mountain and went beyond it until they saw the ocean of sand, and they gazed down upon mount Meru,[2] the ultimate mountain. As they were all moving along quickly, absorbed in their yoga, Draupadi lost her yogic concentration and fell to the ground. When the mighty Bhima saw that she had fallen, he spoke to Yudhishthira, the king of dharma, about her, saying, 'The princess Draupadi

TRANSLATED BY Wendy Doniger O'Flaherty.

1. A state of deep meditation and fasting.
2. The Himalayan mountain at the center of the world.

never did anything against dharma; then what has caused her to fall to the ground?' Yudhishthira replied, 'Draupadi was greatly partial to Arjuna (among us, her five husbands); and now she has experienced the fruit of that partiality.' When Yudhishthira the son of Dharma had said this, he went on, never glancing at her, for he concentrated his mind; he was the very soul of dharma, a bull among men.

Then the wise Sahadeva fell to the ground, and when Bhima saw that he had fallen he said to the king (Yudhishthira), 'This man was always eager to serve us all, with no thought for himself; why has he fallen to the ground?' Yudhishthira said, 'He did not think that anyone was as wise as he was. This flaw in his character has caused the prince to fall.' And when he had said this, Yudhishthira left Sahadeva behind and went on with his brothers, and with the dog.

When the warrior Nakula saw that Draupadi and Sahadeva had fallen, he was tormented, for he loved his family, and he himself fell to the ground. And when the handsome hero Nakula had fallen, Bhima spoke to the king again, saying, 'This man, my brother, Nakula, never violated dharma, and always did what he said he would do; and he was the handsomest man in the world. But now he has fallen to the ground!' When Bhima had said this about Nakula, Yudhishthira, the soul of dharma, the most intelligent of all men, replied: 'His philosophy was, "There is no one as handsome as me; I am the best, the only one." This thought stuck in his mind, and so Nakula has fallen. Come along, Bhima, Wolf-belly. Whatever is fated for anyone, that is what he must, inevitably, experience.'

But when Arjuna, the Pandava who rode on a white horse, the killer of enemy heroes, saw that they had fallen, he himself fell to the ground after them, overcome by grief. And when that tiger among men, the seed of Indra, hard to withstand, had fallen and was dying, Bhima said to the king, 'I cannot recall anything that this noble man ever did wrong, particularly on purpose. To whom, then, did he do some harm that has caused him to fall to the ground?' Yudhishthira replied, 'Arjuna said, "I will burn up my enemies in a single day." But, though he was proud of his heroism, he did not do this; and so he has fallen. He despised all (the other) archers; but a man who wishes for greatness must do what he says he will do.'

Having said this, the king went forth; and Bhima fell. As he fell, Bhima said to Yudhishthira, the king of dharma, 'Your highness! Look! I, whom you love, have fallen! What has caused me to fall? Tell me, if you know.' And Yudhishthira replied, 'You ate too much, and boasted about your vital energy, and despised your enemy. That is why you have fallen to the ground.' And when he had said this, the great-armed Yudhishthira went on, never looking down. Only the dog followed him—the dog that I have already told you about quite a lot.[3]

Then Indra came to Yudhishthira in his chariot, making heaven and earth reverberate everywhere, and he said to him, 'Get in.' But Yudhishthira, the king of dharma, had seen all his brothers fallen, and burning with grief he said to Indra, the thousand-eyed, 'My brothers have all fallen here; let them come with me. I do not want to go to heaven without my brothers.

3. It is highly unusual for the narrator to mention himself like this. It seems to be a way of reminding the listener/reader that the story is about to end, or even that it is all just a story.

And the delicate princess (Draupadi), who deserves to be happy—let her come with us. Give your permission, O lord of the gods.'

'You will see all your brothers and your sons, who have reached heaven before you, together with Draupadi' said Indra. 'Don't be sad. They have cast off their human bodies and gone; but you will go to heaven with this body; this is certain.' Then Yudhishthira said, 'O lord of all that has been and is to be, this dog has been devoted to me constantly. Let him come with me; for my heart is incapable of cruelty.' 'Today, great king, you have become immortal, like me,' said Indra, 'and you have won complete glory and great fame, and all the joys of heaven. Abandon this dog; there is no cruelty in this.' 'Noble god, god of a thousand eyes,' said Yudhishthira, 'it is hard for one who is noble to commit an ignoble act like this. I do not want to achieve glory if I must do it by abandoning someone who has been devoted to me.'

'But there is no place for dog-owners in heaven,' said Indra, 'for the evil spirits called Overpowered-by-anger carry off their sacrificial merit (that would earn them a place in heaven). And so, king of dharma, you should think before you act; abandon this dog; there is no cruelty in this.' Yudhishthira said, 'People say that to abandon one who is devoted to you is a bottomless evil equal to murdering a Brahmin. Therefore, great Indra, I will never, in any way, abandon him now in order to achieve my own happiness.' Indra said, 'The evil spirits called Overpowered-by-anger carry off what has been offered, sacrificed, and given as an oblation into the fire, if it is left uncovered and a dog has looked at it. Therefore you must abandon this dog, and by abandoning the dog you will win the world of the gods. By abandoning your brothers, and even your darling Draupadi, you reached this world by your own heroic action; how is it then that you will not abandon this dog? Perhaps, having abandoned everything, you have now lost your mind.'

Yudhishthira said, 'There is no such thing as either union or separation for mortals when they are dead; this is common knowledge. I could not keep them alive, and so I abandoned them—but (I would not abandon) those who are alive. Handing over someone who has come to you for refuge; killing a woman; confiscating the property of a Brahmin; and betraying a friend; these four acts, Indra, are equaled by the act of abandoning someone who is devoted to you; this is what I think.'

When he heard these words spoken by the king of dharma, the god (who had been there in the form of the dog) took his own form, Dharma. He was satisfied with king Yudhishthira, and spoke to him with smooth words of praise: 'Great king, you are well born, with the good conduct and intelligence of your father,[4] and with compassion for all creatures. Once upon a time, my son, in the Dvaita forest, I tested you, that time when your brothers were all killed as they went too far in their search for water, and you abandoned Bhima and Arjuna, your two brothers, and chose to save the life of Nakula, because you wanted to deal equally with the two mothers (yours and Nakula's). And now you abandoned the celestial chariot, for you insisted, "This dog is devoted to me." Because of this, great king, there is

4. Dharma is here referring to himself.

no one your equal in heaven. And because of this, you have won the undying worlds, won the supreme way of heaven, and won them with your own body.'

Then Dharma and Indra and the Maruts[5] and the two Ashvins and all the other gods and celestial sages made Yudhishthira mount the chariot, and along with them, in their own chariots, went the perfected beings that go wherever they wish to go, all of the dustless gods with their great virtue and with their virtuous speech, thoughts, and actions. The perpetuator of the Kuru[6] family (Yudhishthira) flew swiftly upwards in that chariot, encompassing heaven and earth with his blazing glory. Then Narada,[7] who knew all about everyone and lived among the gods, and who was a great ascetic and a great talker, said, out loud, 'This Kuru king has eclipsed the fame of all the royal sages who are here. For I have never heard of anyone but this Pandava who has won all the worlds with his own body, encompassing them with his glory and splendor and noble behavior.'

But when king Yudhishthira heard what Narada said, he who was the very soul of dharma bade farewell to the gods and the kings of his own family, saying, 'Whether my brothers are right now in a good place or a bad place, that is where I want to be; I don't want any other worlds.' When Indra, the king of the gods, heard the words of king Yudhishthira, a speech utterly devoid of cruelty, he replied, 'Great king, live in this place, that you have won by your own good actions. Why do you still drag human affection about, even now? You have achieved supreme success, such as no other man has ever achieved; your brothers have not attained a place like this. Yet even now human emotion touches you. Look, this is heaven; look at the gods and perfected beings who inhabit this triple paradise.'

But the wise Yudhishthira answered the king of the gods with a speech full of meaning: 'O conqueror of demons, I cannot bear to live here without them. I want to go where my brothers have gone,[8] and where Draupadi has gone, big, dark, wise, virtuous, incomparable Draupadi, the woman I love.'

5. Vedic gods of wind and storm, the entourage of Indra.
6. An ancestor of the Pandavas.
7. A meddlesome, gossipy sage.
8. In the next episode, Yudhishthira seeks his brothers in hell and is eventually reunited with them in heaven.

THE CHURNING OF THE OCEAN

The churning of the ocean creates the world by generating chaos, disrupting the serene primeval waters so that all the oppositional pairs may emerge and meet in creative conflict. The Hindu cosmos is reborn over and over again, as each cycle disintegrates into the evil Kali Age ("The Four Ages," p. 228) and ends in a doomsday fire and flood that destroys the cosmos. But the flood is then transformed into the primeval ocean out of which the cosmos is re-created, undergoing a sea change in a new cosmogony. In this version of the story, the universe is churned back into existence.

We have encountered creative churning in myths from the Brahmanas in which the churning of the fire sticks functions simultaneously as a sexual and ritual image ("Creation," p. 110). Here what is churned is not fire but liquid, more precisely salt-water that is churned into milk that is churned into butter. In the course of this process, the agents of the churning (the gods and anti-gods) become differentiated, for at first they are united in their task, but then they are opposed. The basic symbolic dialectic is that of liquids, the neutral water that is transmuted into various elixirs—human (milk), ritual (butter), and divine (ambrosia, or Soma—the drink that makes the gods immortal)—as well as into the counterpart of all elixirs: poison. According to Hindu cosmology, the earth is ringed by several concentric oceans—first the salt ocean, then oceans of sugarcane juice, wine, clarified butter, milk, whey, and fresh water. The gods here churn the first, the salt ocean, and produce from it first milk, then butter, then wine, then poison, and finally Soma. The ambrosia is trapped in the neck of a beheaded anti-god, while the poison is kept in the neck of the god Shiva. Almost every essential element of the myth is duplicated: the ambrosia itself is obtained twice, and there are two snakes, two mountains (both in the Himalayas: Meru, the great mountain at the center of the world, and Mandara, whose name means "the churn"), two eclipses, and two rains (one creative and one destructive).

The extensive cast of characters includes a number of gods (Narayana and Hari, names of Vishnu; Brahma, the creator; Shri, goddess of prosperity, also called Lakshmi; Dhanvantari, the physician of the gods); anti-gods or demons (including Rahu, the demon that causes eclipses); demi-gods (Gandharvas, associated with fertility and music, husbands of the celestial nymphs called Apsarases); Kinnaras, "What?-men" (horse-headed creatures); Pishachas (flesh-eating ghouls); and animals (the great cobra named Ananta ["Infinite"]; another serpent king named Vasuki; Ucchaihshravas, the white horse of the sun; Airavata, the elephant that the god Indra rides on). Even the poison has a name: Kalakuta, "Black Peak."

PRONOUNCING GLOSSARY

Airavata: *ai-rah´-vuh-tuh*
Ananta: *uh-nun´-tuh*
Brahma: *bruh-mah´*
Dhanvantari: *dun-vun´-tuh-ree*
Gandharva: *gun-dar´-vuh*
Hari: *huh´-ree*
Indra: *in´-druh*
Kalakuta: *kah´-luh-koo´-tuh*
Kaustubha: *kow´-stoo-buh*
Kinnara: *kin´-nuh-ruh*
Mandara: *mun´-duh-ruh*
Meru: *may´-roo*
Mohini: *moh´-hee-nee´*
Nara: *nuh-ruh*
Narayana: *nah´-rah´-yuh-nuh*
Pishacha: *pi-shah´-chuh*
Rahu: *rah´-hoo*
Shiva: *shi´-vuh*
Shri: *shree*
Soma: *soh´-muh*
Sudarshana: *su-dar´-shuh-nuh*
Ucchaihshravas: *ooch-chai´-shruh-vus*
Vasuki: *vah´-soo-kee´*
Vishnu: *vish´-noo*

Mahabharata 1.15–17

There is a shining mountain named Meru, an unsurpassed mass of energy; its blazing golden peaks outshine even the light of the sun. The gods and Gandharvas frequent its glittering, gold-adorned slopes, but men who

TRANSLATED BY Wendy Doniger O'Flaherty.

abound in *adharma*[1] cannot approach that immeasurable mountain. Dreadful beasts of prey wander over it and divine herbs[2] illuminate it. The great mountain stands piercing the firmament with its peak, and it is graced by trees and streams. It resounds with the charming songs of various flocks of birds, but others cannot approach it even in thought. Its magnificent slopes are studded with many gems, and an infinity of magic wishing-trees grow there. The gods, who dwell in heaven and are of great vigor, rich in ascetic powers, came together, mounted its plateau, and sat there to take counsel in order to obtain the ambrosia. While the gods were thinking and conferring together, the god Narayana said to Brahma, 'Let the gods and demons churn the ocean which is like a churning pot, and when the great ocean is churned there will be ambrosia, and you will also obtain all the herbs and gems. Churn the ocean, O gods, and you will find ambrosia in it.'

The tremendous mountain named Mandara is adorned with mountain peaks like pointed clouds; it is covered with a net of vines, it rings with the song of many birds, and it is crowded with tusked animals. Celestial nymphs and gods and Kinnaras frequent it, and it extends for eleven thousand leagues above the earth and as many leagues below. All the bands of gods were unable to uproot it, and so they came to Vishnu and Brahma and said, 'Think of some perfect and effective plan to uproot Mount Mandara for our welfare.' Vishnu and Brahma agreed, and the potent serpent Ananta arose at Brahma's behest and was instructed by Narayana in the task. Then the mighty Ananta forcibly uprooted that king of mountains with all its forests and forest-dwellers, and the gods went with the mountain to the ocean and said to him, 'We will churn your water to obtain ambrosia.' The lord of waters said, 'Let me also have a share of it. I will bear the intense agitation from the whirling of Mandara.' The gods and demons then said to the king of tortoises, the supreme tortoise, 'You are the one suited to be the resting-place for this mountain.' The tortoise agreed, and Indra placed the tip of the mountain on his back, fastening it tightly. They made Mandara the churning-stick and the serpent Vasuki the cord, and they began to churn the ocean, the treasure of waters, for ambrosia. The gods acted together with the demons, for they all wished for the ambrosia.

The great demons grasped one end of the king of serpents, and all the gods held him by the tail. Ananta and the blessed god Narayana would lift the head of the serpent first from one side and then from the other and throw it down again and again. As the gods vigorously hurled the snake Vasuki about, winds full of smoke and flame came out of his mouth repeatedly, and these masses of smoke became clusters of clouds with lightning, and they rained down upon the bands of gods who were exhausted and over-heated from their exertions. Showers of flowers fell down from the tip of the mountain peak, strewing garlands everywhere on the gods and demons. Then a great roar, like the thunder of a great cloud, came forth from the ocean as it was churned by the gods and demons with Mount Mandara; for various water creatures, crushed by the great mountain, were dying by the hundreds in the salt water, and the mountain destroyed many kinds of aquatic beings living in the subterranean levels of hell. The mountain whirled about so that great trees filled with birds spun off and fell from

1. The opposite of dharma, moral chaos.
2. Magic herbs on great mountains shine in the dark.

the mountain peak. As the trees were crushed against one another, a fire born of their friction blazed forth into flames and enveloped Mount Mandara, which looked like a dark cloud charged with lightning. The fire burnt the elephants and lions who were driven out, and all the various creatures there lost their life's breath. Then Indra, the best of immortals, put out that burning fire everywhere with water from his clouds. But the various saps exuded from the great trees and the juices from many herbs flowed into the water of the ocean. And from these juices, which had the essence of ambrosia, and from the exudation of liquid gold mixed with the water, the gods obtained immortality. Then the water of the ocean turned to milk as it became mixed with those supreme juices, and from that milk there arose clarified butter.

The gods then said to Brahma, the giver of boons, 'We are terribly tired, O Brahma, all of us, and all the demons and supreme snakes, all except for the god Narayana, but no ambrosia has come forth. We have been churning this ocean for a long time.' Then Brahma said to the god Narayana, 'Give them the strength, Vishnu. You are our last resort.' Vishnu replied, 'I grant strength to all who are engaged in this action. Churn the ocean-pot all together; twirl Mount Mandara.' When they heard the words of Narayana they became strong, and all together violently stirred the milk of the great ocean once more. Then from the ocean there arose Soma, the calm moon, with its cool rays, and the sun of a hundred thousand rays. And immediately after this the goddess Shri, dressed in white, appeared from the clarified butter; then the goddess of wine; then Ucchaihshravas, the white horse of the sun; and then came the divine, shining Kaustubha gem[3] for the chest of the blessed Narayana, blooming with rays, born of the ambrosia. And the great elephant Airavata, with his enormous body and his four white tusks, came forth and was taken by the Wielder of the Thunderbolt.[4]

But as they continued to churn excessively, the terrible Kalakuta poison came forth and immediately enveloped the universe, blazing like a smoky fire; the poison paralyzed the triple world with the smell of its fumes. The lord Shiva took the form of a sacred chant and held that poison in his throat, and from that time forth he has been known as Blue-throated; thus it is traditionally told. At the request of Brahma and for the sake of protecting all people, Shiva swallowed the poison, and from it there arose the Eldest,[5] her dark form adorned with every kind of gem.

When, Shri, Wine, the moon, and the horse swift as thought had come forth, the gods went on the path of the sun, the path that leads to immortality. And then the magic tree and magic cow that grant the fruits of all desires were born. At last, the god Dhanvantari came forth incarnate, holding a white pot in which the ambrosia was contained. When the demons saw this marvel they let out a great roar for the ambrosia, each crying, 'It is mine!' Then the lord Narayana took the form of Mohini,[6] a magic illusion of the marvellous body of a woman, and he went to the demons. As their minds were bewitched, they gave the ambrosia to him in his female form, for all the demons had their hearts set on her. The goddess who was made of the

3. A magical gem that Vishnu wears on his chest.
4. Indra, king of the gods.
5. Jyeshtha, the goddess of misfortune.
6. "The Enchantress," the name of Vishnu in the form of an Apsaras (celestial nymph).

illusion wrought by Narayana held the bowl and gave it to the gods to drink, but although the demons were seated in a row she did not give it to them to drink.

Then the demons began to scream and, arming themselves with superb armor and various weapons, they attacked all the gods together; it was then that the mighty Vishnu, accompanied by Nara,[7] took the ambrosia from the demon chiefs. When all the bands of the gods had obtained the ambrosia from Vishnu, they drank it amid great excitement and tumult. As the gods were drinking the ambrosia which they so desired, a demon named Rahu took the form of a god and began to drink, but when the ambrosia had reached his throat, the moon and the sun reported it, for they wished to help the gods, and the lord Vishnu, took his discus and cut off the well-adorned head of that demon who was drinking the ambrosia he had obtained by force. The great head of the demon, which was like the peak of a mountain, fell to the earth as it was cut off by the discus, and it shook the earth. The severed head rose up to the sky, roaring terribly, but the headless torso of the demon fell and split open the surface of the earth, causing a tremor throughout the earth with its mountains, forests, and islands. Since then there has been a deadly enmity between the head of Rahu and the moon and sun, and the immortal head swallows them up even today.

The lord Hari then gave up his incomparable female form and routed the demons with various frightening weapons. Then a great battle began on the shore of the salt ocean, the most terrible of all battles between gods and demons. Sturdy, sharp darts, sharp-pointed javelins, and various weapons fell by the thousands. Demons pierced by the discus vomited forth quantities of blood; those wounded by knives, spears, and maces fell to the ground. Heads adorned with burnished gold were cut off by swords in the terrible battle and fell ceaselessly; great demons were struck down, their bodies smeared with blood, and they lay like mountain peaks crimson with mineral ores. Everywhere thousands of cries of distress were heard, and the sun grew red with the blood of those who were hacking at each other. As they struck at one another in the battle with clubs of iron or gold, or fought at close quarters with their fists, the noise seemed to touch the very heavens: 'Cut!' 'Break!' 'Attack!' 'Put them to flight!' 'Advance!' These terrible sounds were heard everywhere.

As the fierce, tumultuous battle raged, the two gods Nara and Narayana entered the field. The lord Vishnu looked at the divine bow of Nara and thought of the discus that subdues demons. As soon as it was remembered, the shining discus called Sudarshana ('Beautiful') came from the sky; its glory was immeasurable; it shone like the sun; its curved edge was unblunted; it was terrifying, invincible, supreme, blazing like a fire devouring the oblation, frightening, nimble, glorious, a destroyer of hostile cities. The unfallen Vishnu, whose arms were like elephant trunks, threw it abruptly with great force; blazing like the fire of doomsday, it fell swiftly again and again, hurled from the hand of the best of men, piercing the demons by the thousands in battle. Sometimes it blazed like fire, licking the demon armies with its tongues; sometimes it cut them up violently as it was hurled through the sky; then it would fall on the battleground and drink their blood as if it were a

7. "The Man," the primeval Man associated with the form of Vishnu known as Narayana.

flesh-eating Pishacha.[8] But the mighty demons, still undaunted, continued to harass the bands of the gods again and again by hurling mountains, mounting to the sky by the thousands like clouds whose rain has dispersed. And from the sky would fall terrifying great mountains like clouds of various shapes, still bearing trees, the tips of their peaks having broken off, roaring as they struck with great force against one another. The earth with all its forests trembled as it was struck on all sides by the fall of the great mountains, and on the battlefield the warriors roared loudly and incessantly at one another.

Then Nara took his celestial bow and covered the heavens with his great, gold-tipped, feathered arrows, shattering the mountain peaks among the terrible bands of demons. The great demons, hard pressed by the gods, entered the earth and the salt ocean, for they saw Sudarshana raging angrily through the sky like a blazing fire devouring oblations. Then the gods, who were victorious, honored Mount Mandara and placed it in its proper place, and they returned home like water-bearing clouds, making the air and the heavens resound on all sides with their thunderous shouts as they rejoiced greatly and loudly. Then Indra the Shatterer of Armies and the immortals gave the treasure of ambrosia to the diademed Vishnu to guard and keep very safe.

8. A ghoul.

THE END OF FEMALE PROMISCUITY

One of the arguments made to justify the public humiliation of Draupadi, the wife of the Pandavas, is that she has five husbands and is therefore, according to the classical dharma that limits each woman to one husband (though a man could have several wives), not a chaste woman in the first place and deserves what she gets. But Kunti, the mother of the Pandavas, also has several sexual partners, without any slur on her character, perhaps because all her partners are gods. Pandu tells Kunti the story of the end of female promiscuity in order to persuade her that it *is* legal for her to give him children by sleeping with an appointed Brahmin (since he himself cannot father children); he is thus carefully distinguishing the Brahmin that he advocates for her from the loose-cannon Brahmin in the story that he tells. He explicitly remarks upon an archaic promiscuity that is no longer in effect, pointedly reminding her, and any women who may have heard (or read) the text, that female promiscuity was an ancient option no longer available to them.

Pandu's suggestion prompts Kunti to tell him about the Vedic *mantra* by which she can summon gods to father her children; eventually she gives birth to Yudhishthira, Bhima, and Arjuna, impregnated by a different god each time. Even before her marriage, she had used her *mantra* to summon another god, the Sun, who forced himself upon her when she resisted him and fathered on her a child she abandoned (Karna). The story that Pandu tells Kunti also begins with an attempted rape but concludes with a law (dharma, here called "the Law") against willing female adultery, as uncontrollable male sexuality is projected onto the control of allegedly oversexed women. The *Mahabharata* keeps insisting that all this is hearsay, as if to make us doubt it; it invokes a vivid, quasi-Freudian primal scene to explain a kind of sexual revulsion.

The ability of Brahmins, kings, and other men in power to demand the sexual services of any woman they fancied evoked violent protest in ancient Indian texts. Draupadi herself is subjected to such sexual harassment on one notorious occasion when she is in disguise as a servant and not recognized as the princess Draupadi (4.21.1–67).

Shvetaketu, the son who here witnesses his mother's abduction, is a hero of the Upanishads, the boy whose father teaches him the doctrine of transmigration ("Transmigration," p. 114); here, his father defends promiscuity, using cows as paradigms not, as is usual, of motherly purity, but of bovine primeval female promiscuity. (Perhaps because they are so pure that nothing they do is wrong?) We may read the story of Shvetaketu in part as an anti-Brahmin (and anti-cow-purity) tract—depicting, as it does, a Brahmin as sexually out of control, and cows as naturally promiscuous animals—as well as an explicit rejection of archaic polyandry. The *Kama-sutra* (1.1.9) names Shvetaketu as one of its original redactors, and the commentary on that passage cites this *Mahabharata* story to explain how a chaste sage became simultaneously an enemy of male adultery and an authority on sex.

PRONOUNCING GLOSSARY

Kunti: *koon´-tee*
Kuru: *koo´-roo*
Pandu: *pahn´-doo*
Uddalaka: *ood-dah´-luh-kuh*
Shvetaketu: *shvay´-tuh-kay´-too*

Mahabharata 1.113.9–20

Now I shall tell you the Law, listen to me, the ancient Law that the great-spirited, law-minded seers saw.

"In the olden days, so we hear, the women went uncloistered, my lovely wife of the beautiful eyes; they were their own mistresses who took their pleasure where it pleased them. From childhood on they were faithless to their husbands, but yet not lawless, for such was the Law in the olden days. Even today the animal creatures still follow this hoary Law, without any passion or hatred. This anciently witnessed Law was honored by the great seers, and it still prevails among the Northern Kurus, Kunti of the softly tapering thighs, for this is the eternal Law that favors women. But in the present world the present rule was laid down soon after—I shall tell you fully by whom and why, sweet-smiling wife!

"There was, so we hear, a great seer by the name of Uddalaka, and he had a hermit son who was called Shvetaketu. It was he, so we hear, who laid down this rule among humankind, in a fit of anger, lotus-eyed Kunti—now hear why. Once, in full view of Shvetaketu and his father, a Brahmin took Shvetaketu's mother by the hand and said, 'Let us go.' At this, the seer's son became indignant and infuriated, when he saw how his mother, as if by force, was being led away. But his father, on seeing him angered, said to Shvetaketu, 'Do not be angry, son. This is the eternal Law. The women of all classes are uncloistered on earth. Just as the cows do, so do the creatures each in its class.' Shvetaketu, the seer's son, did not condone the Law, and laid down the present rule for men and women on earth, for humans

TRANSLATED BY J. A. B. van Buitenen.

but not for other creatures, good lady. Ever since, we hear, this rule has stood. 'From this day on,' he ruled, 'a woman's faithlessness to her husband shall be a sin equal to aborticide, an evil that shall bring on misery. Seducing a chaste and constant wife who is avowed to her husband shall also be a sin on earth. And a wife who is enjoined by her husband to conceive a child and refuses shall incur the same evil.' Thus did Uddalaka's son Shvetaketu forcibly lay down this rule of the Law in the olden days, my bashful wife.

THE KARMA OF DHARMA

The frame of the *Mahabharata* is a conversation between the narrator of the story and a king named Janamejaya, who is a descendant of the Pandavas. One chapter narrates the birth of Vidura, regarded as a brother of Pandu (father of the Pandavas): like Pandu, he was begotten by the sage Vyasa (as an official proxy for Pandu's father) but he was born to a slave woman (as an unofficial proxy for one of the wives of Pandu's father). The narrator casually remarks that "The god Dharma himself, through a curse from the noble Mandavya, was born as Vidura." In response to this, Janamejaya asks, "What deed had Dharma done that made him incur a curse? And by whose curse was he born in the womb of a Shudra (i.e., a woman of the lowest of the four classes, a servant)?" The narrator replies with the following story.

PRONOUNCING GLOSSARY

Dharma: *dahr´-muh*

Mandavya: *mahn´-duhv-yuh*

Mahabharata 1.101

There was once a certain Brahmin known as Mandavya; he was steadfast, an expert on all dharma, firm in truth and asceticism. The great ascetic and great yogi would stand at the entrance to his hermitage at the foot of a tree with his arms above his head, and keep a vow of silence. He had stood there in this asceticism for a long time when there came to his hermitage robbers carrying plunder, closely followed by many policemen. They stashed their plunder in his house and hid there in fear as the police force approached. While they were hiding there, the police force soon arrived in pursuit, and they saw the seer. Then they asked the ascetic, who was still under his vow of silence, 'Great Brahmin, which way did the robbers go? We want to go the same way, to catch up with them.' But the ascetic did not say anything at all, good or bad, in reply to the question of the police. The king's men searched the hermitage and saw the thieves hiding there, and the loot, too. Then the police began to have doubts about the sage; they tied him up and reported him and the robbers to the king. The king passed judgement on him along with the thieves: 'Kill him.' The executioners did not know

Translated by Wendy Doniger O'Flaherty.

who he was, and so they impaled the great ascetic on a stake. And when the police had had the sage impaled on the stake, they went back to the king with the recovered wealth.

The Brahmin seer, who was the very soul of dharma, remained on the stake for a long time. Though he had no food, he did not die. He held fast to his vital breaths and summoned together the seers. The sages suffered terribly when they saw the noble ascetic suffering ascetically on the tip of the stake. In the night, they became birds and came back to him from all around, demonstrating their powers; and then they questioned that excellent Brahmin: 'We want to hear what evil deed you committed, Brahmin.' Then the tiger among sages said to the ascetics, 'Whom can I blame? For no one but me is guilty.'

The king heard the sage and came out with his counsellors; then he tried to appease the great seer who was still on the stake. He said, 'Greatest of seers, please forgive me for the mistake that I made in my delusion and ignorance; you shouldn't be angry at me.' When the king said that, the sage forgave him; and when he was forgiven, the king had him taken down from the stake. But when he had taken him down from the tip of the stake and started to pull the stake out of him, he was unable to pull it out, and so he cut off the stake at its base. And so the sage went about with the stake still inside him. As he moved around with the stake in his neck, ribs, and entrails, he started to think, '(The stake) could be used as (a pole) to carry flower baskets.' By means of this asceticism he conquered worlds that were hard for other people to conquer; and people used to call him, 'Tip-of-the-stake Mandavya.'

Then the Brahmin, who knew the highest meaning, went to the house of Dharma; when the powerful sage saw Dharma seated there, he scolded him, saying 'What *was* the bad deed that I did, without knowing what I had done, a deed which has earned me such a fruit of retribution? Tell me the truth at once; see the power of my asceticism.' Dharma said, 'You stuck blades of grass up the tails of little butterflies, and this is the fruit that you have obtained from that karma, ascetic.' Tip-of-the-Stake Mandavya said, '*When* did I do this? Tell me the truth.' To this question the king of dharma replied, 'You did it when you were a child.'

Then Tip-of-the-Stake Mandavya said, 'For a rather small offence you have given me an enormous punishment. Because of that, Dharma, you will be born as a man, in the womb of a Shudra. And I will establish a moral boundary for the fruition of dharma in the world: no sin will be counted against anyone until the age of fourteen, but it will be regarded as a fault for those who do it after that age.' And so, because he was cursed by the noble sage for the offence that he had committed, Dharma was born in the form of Vidura, in the womb of a Shudra.

THE DOG WHO WOULD BE LION

The dog in this story has a human heart, but he must not be allowed to reach above his canine station. The phrase "his own proper form by birth" (*jati*) can also be translated "his own proper form by caste," for *jati* means both birth and caste. Both the dog and the sage are wrong; the dog violates dog dharma by being a vegetarian, where he should be a carnivore (or omnivore), and the sage is wrong, too, to change the dog into carnivores of entirely different natures from that of a dog. This story affirms the immutable categories of the Hindu caste system.

Mahabharata 12.117.2–45, 118.1

In some great forest where no other human beings lived, there was a seer who observed many strict restraints: He lived upon roots and fruits, his senses were strictly restrained, and he was dedicated to self-control as part of his consecration; he had become calm within, was dedicated to his daily recitation of the Vedas, and was untainted; his body had been cleaned out by fasting, and he was committed to staying always upon the path of the strictly observant. All the forest creatures became thoroughly familiar with the exalted goodness of that wise one who sat there, and they would approach him—lions, tigers, *sharabhas,*[1] rutting elephants, leopards, rhinos, bears, and other frightful-looking animals. These carnivorous beasts would simply greet the seer with polite inquiries about his well-being. They would humble themselves before him and do him favors as if they were his pupils.

Normally they would go as they had come after making their inquiries, but there was one animal there, a village dog, who never left the great seer. Devoted to the seer, and attached to him affectionately, the dog was emaciated and weak from constant fasting. Eating only roots, fruits, and garbage, having become completely calm within, he had something of the look of a wise man. The creature was intensely bound by affection, and when the seer was seated, it would go to the soles of the great hermit's feet, but in a human way.[2]

Once a tremendously powerful, carnivorous leopard came there because of the dog; it was an absolutely wicked, cruel beast, like end-making Time—famished, licking its lips, whipping its tail back and forth; wracked with hunger, its mouth was open, and it was stalking that dog as its prey. O king, when he saw that cruel beast approaching, the dog, in fear of its life, spoke to the hermit. Highly intelligent man, hear what he said. "Blessed one, a leopard, an enemy of dogs, wants to kill me. Great sage, may I have no fear of it, by your grace!"

The hermit said:

"Have no fear at all of death from the leopard. You are losing your dog form, son, and becoming a leopard!"

TRANSLATED BY James Fitzgerald.

1. Mythical beasts, said to have eight legs and famous for killing lions; pronounced *shuh'-ruh-buhs.*

2. Presumably prostrating itself before the sage, rather than curling up at his feet like a dog.

Then the dog became a leopard with a golden form. Delighted, his beautiful body flashing, he lived in the forest without any fear. Then a terribly ferocious, blood-thirsty tiger approached the leopard; its mouth was gaping with hunger, and its tongue was licking at the corners of its mouth. When he saw that hunger-wracked tiger, that fanged beast of the forest, the leopard went to the hermit for protection to save its life. Expressing, as always, the affection that grew from their life together, the seer turned the leopard into a tiger more powerful than his enemy. When the tiger saw him then, it did not attack, O lord of peoples.

But having become a powerful tiger with meat for its food, the dog now had no taste at all for its former fare of roots and fruits. As the king of beasts regularly stalks the denizens of the forest, so did this tiger, great king. Once, the tiger had gorged himself upon his prey and was asleep near the hermit's hut. A rutting elephant came to that spot; it was as if a cloud had moved across the sky. Its temples secreting fluid, the elephant was large—it had a wide head, long tusks, and a massive body—and it rumbled deeply like a thunder-head. When he saw that rutting elephant coming at him with the surliness of rut, the tiger was terrified with fear of the elephant and went to the seer for protection. That most excellent of seers then turned the tiger into an elephant, and the attacking elephant was afraid when he saw the other looking like an immense thunder-head. Then he wandered about, joyously plunging into lotus-clusters and frankincense thickets, and he was decorated with the pollen dust of lotuses. Time went by, night by night, with the elephant cheerfully enjoying himself near the seer's hut.

One time a tawny-maned lion came to that place. Born in a mountain valley, that terrifying lion had spelled the end of whole herds of elephants. When the elephant saw the lion coming, he was beside himself with fear of it. Terrified and trembling, he went to the seer for protection. The hermit then turned that lord of elephants into a lion, and that one then took no notice of the wild lion, because he belonged to the same species. But the wild lion disappeared when he saw the other, his roar suppressed from fear. That lion then dwelled happily in the hermitage in the forest. But the smaller animals that lived in the ascetic grove were too scared ever to be seen there, as they wished to stay alive.

Then, at some point later in the working of Time, a powerful, carnivorous denizen of the forest, an eight-legged *sharabha* (with some of its feet directed upwards) that frightened every kind of creature, came to the seer's dwelling to kill the lion. O tamer of your enemies, the hermit made the lion into a *sharabha* of even more ferocious might. Then the wild *sharabha* saw the hermit's *sharabha* before him, and when he saw that that one was even more powerful and ferocious than himself, he ran off swiftly in terror.

After the hermit had in this way put him in the situation of being a *sharabha*, he was always at the hermit's side, and regularly he enjoyed the pleasures of being a *sharabha*. The herds of the animals, terrified of the *sharabha*, fled the forest in every direction, trying to save their lives. The absolutely wicked *sharabha* regularly engaged in killing creatures and eating their flesh, though he had no desire to eat the tranquil sage who ate roots and fruits. Then, overcome with a mighty thirst for blood, the ungrateful *sharabha*, born of a dog's womb, wanted to kill the hermit. But, by virtue of his asceticism, the hermit saw this with the eye of knowledge. Having understood the matter, the wise hermit said to the dog,

"You were a dog who became a leopard, and as a leopard you became a tiger, as a tiger you became an elephant raging in rut, as an elephant you became a lion, as a lion of tremendous power you next became a *sharabha*. But I, filled with affection, did not take into account your affiliation with your race. Since you, wicked beast, wish to harm me who am not wicked, you have thus come back to your own nature and so you shall be a dog again."

Then that stupid one of the dog species, corrupted to the point of being hostile toward the seer, was cursed by the seer, and that *sharabha* acquired his proper form once again.

That dog, having returned to its original nature, became very depressed. The seer buzzed *hum*[3] at the evil beast and expelled him from his ascetic grove.

3. Kept saying "Hum!" to shoo the dog away.

KING SHIBI SAVES THE DOVE FROM THE HAWK

Even nonviolence could be violent in India; the urge to refrain from killing animals for food, for instance, or to control addiction, often erupts in violence against the self. The Shylockian pound of flesh and the use of hawks and doves to symbolize military aggression and peacefulness in the following story are themes that Americans and Europeans can recognize from their own world. In a Buddhist version of the story, King Shibi vows to give his living heart, his flesh, his blood, or his eyes to anyone who asks for them; Indra, king of the gods, disguised as a blind Brahmin, asks him for his eyes, which Shibi has his court physician cut out, causing him excruciating pain, and gives to Indra; eventually, Indra restores Shibi's eyes (Jataka 499). The king's indifference to physical pain is both a macho Kshatriya virtue and a badge of the ascetic conquest of the body.

The logical *reductio ad absurdum* of the vegetarian agenda—letting animals and even plants eat one's own body (as in "Bhrigu's Journey in the Other World," p. 101)—also results from the tension between the bitter realism of the *Mahabharata* and the challenge of nonviolence. The story of Shibi resolves the conflict by reducing the entire episode to an illusion: there was no dove, no hawk; it was just a test. But in a world where there are, after all, hawks that eat doves, a human may avoid personally taking animal life by eating vegetables. Extending *ahimsa* into a universal law, however, including plants as well as animals, an "eternal dharma for everyone" (*sanatana dharma*), would make most creatures starve to death.

PRONOUNCING GLOSSARY

Indra: *in´-druh*
Lomasha: *loh-muh´-shuh*
Shibi: *shee-bee*

Mahabharata 3.131.1–30

Desirous to try the great-spirited [Shibi], and willing to grant a boon, Indra became a hawk and the Fire a dove; and they went to his sacrifice. From fear of the hawk the dove settled on the king's thigh, and, seeking shelter, O king, the timid bird nestled there.

The hawk said:

All the kings name you as one who is Law-minded: so why do you want to do a deed that runs counter to Law? Do not out of greed for Law begrudge me who am starving the food that has been ordained for me, king, or you will throw away the Law!

The king said:

Trembling and looking for shelter, and frightened of you, great fowl, this bird has sought me out, praying for its life. Do you not see, hawk, that if I did not give this refuge-seeking, safety-craving dove its safety, it would be a heinous Unlaw?[1] The dove looks ashiver and much upset, hawk. It has come to me seeking life; abandoning it is condemned.

The hawk said:

Great lord, it is through food that all creatures find their being, by food that they thrive, by food that they live. Even after losing possessions that are hard to give up, a man can live for many a long night; but he could not abide long were he to give up eating. If I am deprived of my portion, lord of your people, my spirits will desert my body and go the way of no return. When I predecease them, Law-spirited king, son and wife will perish: so by protecting this dove you will kill many lives. A Law that spoils the Law is no Law but a bad Law; no, that Law is Law that runs counter to nothing, O king whose might is your truth! When matters are in conflict, guardian of earth, you should decide what is better and what is worse and observe that Law that does not oppress. After ascertaining the weightier and the less weighty in a decision on Law and Unlaw, you should decide on the Law where it does most good, king!

The king said:

Best of birds, your speech sounds very beautiful. Are you the Fair-winged Bird, king of the fowl? You are doubtless wise in the Law, for thus do you speak, lengthily and wondrously, concerning the Law. I see that nothing is obscure to you. Then how do you think it right to abandon a refugee? All this enterprise of yours, bird, is to get some food. But you can get your food in another, even better, way: I shall have a steer, a boar, a deer, or even a buffalo cooked for you, or whatever you want!

The hawk said:

I don't feed on boar or bullocks or any kind of deer, great king, so what use is their meat to me? Bull of the barons, let go of the staple that fate has ordained for me! Guardian of the earth, let that dove loose for me. Hawks eat doves, that is the everlasting rule. If you know the way, king, do not climb up a banana tree!

The king said:

TRANSLATED BY J. A. B. van Buitenen.

1. *Adharma*, the violation of dharma (here translated as "Law").

You that are adored by the hosts of birds, reign over this rich kingdom of the Shibis. Or I shall give you whatever you want, hawk, but not, hawk, this bird that has sought shelter with me! Tell me what I should do, best of birds, so that you may desist, for I shall not give up this little dove.

The hawk said:

If you love this dove, overlord of kings, cut off a piece of your flesh and weigh it against the dove. When your flesh balances the dove's, king, you will give it to me, and I shall be satisfied.

The king said:

Your request I deem a favor, hawk, so I shall give you at once as much of my flesh as balances the dove.

Lomasha [the narrator] *said:*

Then the king, who knew the highest Law, cut his flesh and weighed it against the dove. But on balance the dove was the heavier. Once more King Shibi cut from his flesh and gave it; and when there was no more left of his flesh to balance the dove, he himself, all cut up, mounted the scale.

The hawk said:

I am Indra, Law-knowing king, and this dove is the sacrifice-carrying fire. We have come to you in your offering grove to test you in the Law. This shall be your shining glory, to master the worlds, lord of the people, that you cut the flesh from your limbs! As long as people in this world shall tell of you, king, so long shall your fame and your worlds last, eternally!

DAKSHA'S SACRIFICE

This important myth, retold in various transformations several times in the *Mahabharata* and in other Hindu texts, is, in part, a historical narrative of what did happen in the history of Hinduism: Shiva was not part of the Vedic sacrifice and then he became part of the Hindu sacrifice. The gods, particularly Daksha (a Creator, mentioned in the *Rig Veda*, in "Aditi and the Birth of the Gods," p. 80), exclude Shiva from their sacrifice because Shiva, called Rudra in the Vedas, is the outsider, the other, the god to whom Vedic sacrifice is not offered; he is not a member of the club of gods who sacrifice to the gods ("The Hymn of the Primeval Man," p. 82). The myth of Daksha's sacrifice verifies Shiva's otherness but modifies it so that Shiva is, in fact, given a share in some sacrifices, still not part of the Vedic world but the supreme god of the post-Vedic world, at least in the eyes of those who tell this myth. Shiva interrupts the gods' sacrifice and makes, instead, a sacrifice of his own, which destroys the sacrifice (and the world). Eventually, placated, he puts it back together again, but this time with himself as one of the gods who receive the offerings.

The story is set at the end of the "age of the gods," probably the end of the first of the four Ages, the Winning Age ("The Four Ages," p. 228). The "world sacrifice" is probably Shiva's sacrifice of the world at doomsday. The gods attempt to maintain the world with a Vedic sacrifice, of which the myth mentions many details: the sacrifice of rites is the public sacrifice, in contrast with the domestic sacrifice; the fivefold sacrifice may be the sacrifices to the world-soul (*brahman*), the ancestors, the gods, the spirits, and human guests; the four parts of the sacrifice may be the four types of sacrifice: obligatory, occasional, optional, and expiatory. "Vashat!"

is what the priest exclaims at the end of a verse, as he casts the oblation into the fire.

Another cyclical cosmogony is embedded in the statement that Shiva throws his rage into the ocean, where, "becoming fire, it incessantly evaporates the sea." This is a reference to the belief that a mare roams at the bottom of the ocean; the flames that shoot out of her mouth are simultaneously bridled by and bridling the waters of the ocean. This delicate balance, this hair-trigger suspension, is disturbed at the end of the Kali Age, the moment of Doomsday, when the mare gallops out of the ocean and sets the world on fire, and the newly unchecked ocean leaves its bed and floods the ashes of the universe, which then lie dormant until the next period of creation, when the ashes of the entire universe are revived as it is reborn.

Rudra/Shiva is here called Sthanu, "the Pillar" (probably a reference to his form as the *linga*, an elongated stone icon) and Kapardin ("with matted hair," i.e., dreadlocks, the mark of an ascetic). He has three eyes; the third, in his forehead, channels the heat from his asceticism and generates the power with which he burns the universe to ashes. He also has a blue throat, from swallowing poison ("The Churning of the Ocean"). He wears a deerskin (the mark of a celibate Vedic student) but carries a powerful bow (as an ordinary Vedic student certainly would not). Present at the sacrifice are Bhaga, Savitri, and Pushan, three Vedic solar deities. Krishna tells the story to Yudhishthira (whom the bard occasionally addresses: "O king").

PRONOUNCING GLOSSARY

Bhaga: *buh-guh*
Kapardin: *kuh-par´-din*
Mahadeva: *muh-hah´-day´-vuh*
Pushan: *poo´-shun*
Rudra: *roo´-druh*
Savitri: *suh-vih´-tree´*
Shiva: *shi´-vuh*
Sthanu: *sthah´-noo*

Mahabharata 10.18.1–24

After their age had elapsed, the gods prepared
To make a sacrifice, wanting to give an
Offering in line with Vedic injunction.
Insouciantly, they assigned the shares proper to
The sacrifice, the gods entitled to a share,
And the material worthy of sacrifice.
But ignorant of the reality of
Rudra, the gods failed to assign a share to the
Divine Sthanu, O king.
With no share assigned to him by the celestials,
Rudra-Shiva, covered in a deer skin,
Desiring his portion, to that end swiftly
Created a bow.

There is the world-sacrifice, the sacrifice
Of rites, the eternal domestic sacrifice,
And the fivefold sacrifice, whose fifth part
Is the sacrifice to be offered to men.
Kapardin, desiring his sacrificial share,

TRANSLATED BY W. J. Johnson.

Produced, through a world-sacrifice, a bow
With a hundred and twenty thumb-breadth span.
That bow's string was the *vashat mantra*, and
The four parts of the sacrifice were in its strength.

Enraged, Mahadeva grasped that weapon,
And came to the place where the gods had assembled.
Seeing the imperishable celibate armed
With his bow, goddess Earth quaked, and the mountains shook.
The wind dropped, fire though fed did not burn, in heaven
Terrified clusters of stars spun from their orbits.
The sun was eclipsed, the moon's halo went out;
From point to point the sky brimmed with darkness.
Stupefied, the gods were thrown from their purpose—
The sacrifice would not manifest for them,
The Vedas tottered.[1]

Then with an arrow Rudra pierced that sacrifice
Through the heart—at which, turning into a deer,
The sacrifice fled, together with the fire.[2]
Pursued in that form to the firmament
By Rudra, the sacrifice, on reaching
High heaven, flared up.

And after the sacrifice had fled away,
The gods had no idea what was happening,
And once the gods had lost their understanding
Everything toppled into confusion.
Then, with the curved end of his bow, three-eyed
Shiva, in a fury, broke Savitri's arms,
Blinded Bhaga, and knocked out Pushan's teeth.
At this, the gods and the limbs of the sacrifice
Fled away together, some shaking as though
In the throes of death.

But blue-throated Rudra, who had put all the gods
To flight, laughed, and with the curved end of his bow
Stopped them in their tracks.
Then the gods cried out, the bowstring broke, and the bow
Immediately lost tension and straightened out.
Then the gods, together with the sacrifice,
Sought the protection of the bowless god of gods.

And the god was kind.

Soothed, the lord cast his rage into the ocean,
Where, becoming fire, it incessantly
Evaporates the sea.
Then he restored Bhaga's eyes, Savitri's arms,

1. This is the culminating moment of the eschatological imagery; the world is coming to an end.

2. Probably the fire incarnate as the god Agni.

And Pushan's teeth, together with the sacrifice,
So the world returned to its natural state; and as
His share, the gods gave Shiva all the oblations.

When he was angry everything was out of joint;
But when he was pleased all became sound again.

OBLIGATION, LIBERATION, AND DEVOTION IN THE *BHAGAVAD GITA*

CA. 100 C.E.

The *Bhagavad Gita* ("The Song of God," often simply called the *Gita*, "The Song") is now probably the most famous part of the *Mahabharata*. Always a popular text in India, but originally just one among many types of sacred texts, it became canonical for a particular branch of reformed Hinduism in the nineteenth century, partly in response to the popularity of the *Gita* among the British in India and among Americans such as Ralph Waldo Emerson and Henry David Thoreau.

On the brink of the great battle, the warrior Arjuna is suddenly assailed by many doubts; his mouth gets dry, his legs tremble, and he does not want to fight ("Arjuna Questions Krishna"). The *Gita* records the conversation that takes place at that moment between Arjuna and the god Krishna, who is serving as Arjuna's charioteer. (Krishna had graciously offered to take this inferior position, a combination bodyguard and biographer, with its bardic dimension appropriate to Krishna's role of counselor.) Arjuna asks Krishna many difficult, indeed unanswerable, age-old questions about violence and nonviolence, questioning the necessity of violence for warriors. The sheer number of different reasons that Krishna gives to Arjuna—including the argument that, since you cannot kill the soul, killing the body in war (like killing an animal in sacrifice) is not really killing ("The Soul Does Not Die")—is evidence of the author's deep disquiet about killing and the need to justify it. The moral impasse is not so much resolved as blasted away when, after Krishna has given a series of complex and rather abstract answers, Arjuna asks him to *show* him his true cosmic nature. Krishna shows him the form with which he consumes the universe at Doomsday, and Arjuna cries out in terror and awe. And right in the middle of the terrifying epiphany, Arjuna apologizes to Krishna for all the times that he had rashly and casually called out to him, "Hey, Krishna! Hey, pal!" He begs the god to turn back into his pal Krishna, which the god consents to do.

Arjuna is comforted when Krishna returns to his usual human form; yet as a warrior with ethical misgivings, Arjuna has now been persuaded to kill just as Krishna must kill. Analogously, the Hindu worshiper—represented in the text by Arjuna—has been persuaded, outside the text in the real political life of the day, to accept the political necessity of war on the grounds that it cannot be evil because it is not real. This political message is made palatable by the god's resumption of his role as an intimate human companion. Yet the *Mahabharata* as a whole is passionately against war, vividly aware of the tragedy of war, despite the many statements about the inevitability of violence. Nor, despite the way that Krishna persuades Arjuna to fight, is the *Gita* used in India to justify war; it is generally taken out of the context of the narrative of battle and used only for its philosophy, which can be used to support arguments for peace—as, notably, in the hands of Mahatma Gandhi ("The Gospel of Selfless Action," p. 630).

Krishna's broader teaching in the *Gita* resolves the tension between dharma (moral obligation) and *moksha* ("Release" or "freedom," spiritual liberation from material life) by forming a triad with *bhakti* (worship, love, devotion) as the mediating term ("The Two Paths"; "The Path of Devotion"). Dharma as a blueprint for the organization and maintenance of society had to respond to the appeal of the Buddhist goal of release from transmigration (*nirvana*) but also to the potentially even more disruptive appeal of the similar Hindu goal of *moksha*, which had made major social headway since the time of the early Upanishads. Ideas about both dharma (and the closely related karma) and *moksha* had been in the air for centuries, but now they were brought into direct confrontation with one another, in the *Bhagavad Gita*.

Arjuna faces a dilemma. He can choose neither dharma (he doesn't want to kill his relatives, but warfare is his own particular dharma as a member of a warrior caste) nor *moksha* (he is a Kshatriya, of the class of kings for whom "dropping out" is desertion). Krishna offers him a third alternative—devotion, *bhakti*—that bridges the conflicting claims of the two. This third alternative, in effect, is Krishna in person. *Bhakti* introduces into the abstract Upanishadic formula that self and world-soul are one ("The Soul Does Not Die"), a mediating option that does not deny the truth of the formula but reconciles it with the demands of society. Krishna is a god with qualities (*sa-guna*), whom Arjuna can love and through whom he can achieve union with the god without qualities (*nir-guna*), the world-soul (*brahman*), otherwise so difficult for ordinary people to reach ("The Path of Devotion"). By acting with personal devotion to Krishna, Arjuna is freed from the hellish consequences of his actions ("The True Nature of Action"; "Salvation and Damnation").

The *Gita* employs some Buddhist terminology (*nirvana*, for instance, the blowing out of a flame, which is a more Buddhist way of saying *moksha*), and Arjuna starts out with what might appear to be a quasi-Buddhist attitude (which Krishna proceeds to demolish). But *nirvana* is a word and concept in the Upanishads as well as in Buddhist texts. The *Gita* addresses a tension within Hinduism itself, the challenge of assimilating the ascetic ideal into the socially anchoring ideology of an upper-class householder.

PRONOUNCING GLOSSARY

Arjuna: *ar´-joo-nuh*
Bhagavad Gita: *buh´-guh-vud gee´-tah*
Bharata: *bhuh´-ruh-tuh*
Bhishma: *beesh´-muh*
Dhritarashtra: *dri´-tuh-rahsh´-truh*
Drona: *droh´-nuh*
guna: *goo´-nuh*
Krishna: *kreesh´-nuh*
Kunti: *koon´-tee*
Madhu: *muh´-doo*
pandit: *pun´-dit*
Pandu: *pahn´-doo*
Pritha: *pree´-tuh*
Sankhya: *sanh´-kyuh*
Shastra: *shah´-struh*
Vrishni: *vrish´-nee*

ARJUNA QUESTIONS KRISHNA

The sage Sanjaya narrates the *Gita* to the blind king Dhritarashtra, father of Duryodhana ("The Stripping of Draupadi," p. 134); sometimes he addresses him as "Scorcher of the Enemy," dragging the narrative frame for a moment out of the inner conversation (between Krishna and Arjuna) to the outer one (between Sanjaya and Dhritarashtra). He describes the marshaling of the great heroes on both sides of the family, and then Arjuna's reaction to it: Arjuna does not want to fight against his own people, his cousins, his teachers, his friends, and he worries that such a fight would violate dharma. In response, Krishna tells him to stop behaving like a eunuch (not literally a castrated person, but someone effeminate, unmanly), to which Arjuna repeats his objections, adding new reasons for them, in a passionate indictment of war.

Bhagavad Gita 1.20–47, 2.1–10

When he saw
the sons of Dhritarashtra
drawn up in battle array
in the emerging
clash of weapons,
the Son of Pandu,
with his monkey banner,[1]
raised his bow.

Then straight-haired Arjuna
spoke these words
to bristling-haired Krishna:
'Lord of the Earth,
Unchanging One,
make my chariot stand
in the middle of
the two armies,

until I see fully
these men drawn up
in a hunger
for battle.
With whom
must I fight
in beginning
this battle?

I see those
who are about to fight—
those who have
gathered here,
wishing to do
loving service in battle
for the hard-souled son
of Dhritarashtra.'

Son of Bharata:
in this way,
bristling-haired Krishna
was spoken to
by thick-haired Arjuna,
while Krishna made
the great chariot
stand between both armies.

TRANSLATED BY Laurie L. Patton.

1. Arjuna, who has a monkey on his war banner.

Facing Bhishma
and Drona[2]
and all the rulers
of the world,
Arjuna,
son of Pritha,[3] said,
'Look at the Kurus,
gathered in this way!'

Arjuna, son of Pritha,
saw fathers,
and then grandfathers
standing there—
teachers, mothers' brothers,
brothers, sons,
grandsons,
and friends, too;

fathers-in-law,
and companions
of strong heart.
Looking at all
his relatives
come together
in both armies,
the son of Kunti

broke down
with deep compassion
and said,
'Krishna, now that
I have seen
my own people here,
coming near and
longing to fight,

my legs
collapse,
my mouth
is parched,
my body
trembles,
and my hair
bristles;[4]

2. Bhishma, the grandfather, and Drona ("Ekalavya Cuts Off His Thumb," p. 143) fight on the side of Duryodhana.
3. Pritha is another name of Kunti, mother of Yudhishthira, Bhima, and Arjuna.
4. Hair bristles either with happy excitement (as in Krishna's epithet "bristling-haired") or, as in this case, with agitation or even fear.

the Gandiva bow[5]
drops from my hand,
my skin
is burned,
and I find
no rest;
my mind
seems to wander;

I see
perverse omens;
and before me
I see no good
in killing
my people
in battle,
Lovely-Haired Krishna!

Krishna, I long
neither for victory,
nor kingship
nor pleasures.
Lord of the Cows,[6]
what is kingship to us,
what are delights,
or life itself?

The ones
on whose behalf
we long for kingship,
delights, and pleasures—
these are the very ones
drawn up in battle,
giving up
life-breath and wealth!

Teachers,
fathers and sons
and grandfathers, too,
mothers' brothers,
fathers-in-law
grandsons,
brothers-in-law—
also other family—

Killer of Madhu,[7]
even though they
are ready to kill,
I don't want to kill them—

5. Arjuna's bow is named Gandiva.
6. In his youth, Krishna was raised incognito among cowherds.
7. There are two Madhus: This one is a demon whom Krishna kills; the one in Krishna's epithet "Son of Madhu" is, like Vrishni, a human ancestor of Krishna's family.

even for the kingship
of the three worlds,
and certainly not
for the earth.

Mover of Men,
what joy would it be
for us to kill
the sons of Dhritarashtra?
Evil would still cling to us
when we'd killed
these men here,
with their bows drawn.

Therefore we are not
entitled to kill
the sons of Dhritarashtra,
our own kinsmen.
After we had killed
our own people,
how would we take pleasure,
Son of Madhu?

Even if those whose thoughts
are overwhelmed by greed
do not see the wrong done
by the destruction
of family,
and the fault
of meanness
and injury to friends,

Mover of Men,
how would we not know
through clear vision
to turn away
from this evil—
the wrong done
by the destruction
of family?

In the destruction
of family,
the eternal dharma
of family perishes;
when dharma perishes,
its absence
also conquers
the whole family.

Son of Vrishni,
when the absence
of dharma has conquered,

the women of the family
are defiled,[8]
and caste-confusion is born
in the corruption
of women;

the caste-blending
of the family
and the family-destroyers
indeed brings them hell:
bereft of offerings
of rice and water,[9]
their ancestors
will surely fall.

The dharma of caste,
and the eternal dharma
of family,
are uprooted
by these wrongful acts
of family-destroyers,
since they create
a blending of caste.

Mover of Men,
those humans
whose dharma
has vanished
will live
for ever in hell;
we have heard this
over and over again.

Oh! we are set
upon doing
a great harm;
we are eager to kill
our own people,
all for the sake
of pleasure
and a kingdom.

If the sons
of Dhritarashtra,
weapons in hand,
should strike me
unarmed in battle,
this would be

8. The corruption of women leads to the birth of illegitimate children and hence to both the confusion of castes and the blending of castes.
9. In ancient India, and in parts of India to this day, rice balls and water were offered to the ancestors as food, to maintain them in the world of the ancestors; if this was not done, the ancestors would fall to either a hell or a limbo from which they could never be reborn.

greater peace
for me!'

After he spoke,
Arjuna sat down
on the chariot seat,
in the midst of battle,
and let go of
both his bow and arrow,
his whole being
recoiling in grief.

Sanjaya said:

Krishna,
Killer of Madhu,
spoke these words
to the despairing one
whose eyes were
filled with tears,
and who was overcome
with pity.

The Blessed One said:

How does
this faint heart
come to you
in time of difficulty?
This is not suitable
for a noble one;
it is not heavenly,
and brings on disgrace.

Do not become
a cowardly eunuch,
Son of Pritha;
this is not fitting for you.
Let go of this
lowly weakness of the heart
and stand up,
Scorcher of the Enemy!

Arjuna said:

Killer of Madhu,
how will I fight
Drona and Bhishma
with arrows
in battle?
How will I fight

these honorable men,
Killer of the Enemy?

Better to eat beggar's food
than to kill these great-souled
teachers here on earth;
for if I killed these teachers,
Striving after their goals
here on earth,
I would eat food
covered in blood.

Facing the sons
of Dhritarashtra,
we do not know
which has more weight for us:
should we conquer them,
or should they conquer us?
Even after we've killed them,
we would not want to live!

My own nature is struck
by pity, and a sense of wrong,
and my mind is clouded
as to dharma:
I ask you which is best—
tell me! I am your student!
Correct me, who lies
fallen before your feet.

I don't ever see
what would take away
my grief—that grief
which dries up the senses,
even though I might gain
opulent and unrivalled
kingship here on earth,
or even lordship of the gods.

Sanjaya said:

Scorcher of the Enemy,
after speaking
to bristling-haired Krishna,
thick-haired Arjuna
said: 'I will not fight!'
He spoke this way
to Krishna, the cow finder,
and then became quiet.

Son of Bharata,
bristling-haired Krishna

seemed to
begin to laugh,
and in between
both armies,
spoke these words
to the despairing one.

THE SOUL DOES NOT DIE

Now Krishna begins a penetrating philosophical response to Arjuna's refusal to fight. He draws upon the Upanishadic idea of the embodied self (*atman*), identical with the world-soul (*brahman*) ("The Self," p. 113), which is unborn, in the sense that the soul is not touched by birth or death as it transmigrates from body to body. Krishna addresses Arjuna as "son of Bharata" (an epithet that could also apply to Dhritarashtra, on the outer frame of the story) and "Strong-Armed One."

Bhagavad Gita 2.11–27

The Blessed One said:

You speak as if
with words of wisdom,
[but] you have mourned
that which is
not to be mourned.
Wise men mourn neither
those whose life-breath is gone,
nor those whose breath remains.

I have never
not existed;
nor have you, nor have
these lords of men.
Nor will we
cease to exist,
all of us,
from now onwards.

Just as childhood,
youth and age
exist in the body
of the embodied self,
in this way, one takes on
another body.
Those who see clearly
are not confused by this.

Translated by Laurie L. Patton.

Son of Kunti,
the touches of the senses,
bringing pain and pleasure,
heat and cold:
they come and go,
and they don't last for ever.
You must try to endure them,
son of Bharata.

Bull among Men,
the one whom
these touches
do not make tremble,
the one for whom
pain and pleasure are alike,
that one is ready
for immortality.

Being is not found
in that which does not exist.
Non-being is not found
in that which exists.
The limit of both
being and non-being
is perceived by those
who see the truth.

Know this:
that with which
all this world is woven
is not to be destroyed.
No one is able
to effect
the destruction
of the imperishable.

These bodies
have an end;
but they are said
to belong to the eternal
embodied self—
that which is never lost
and cannot be measured.
So fight, Son of Bharata!

The one who perceives
the self as a killer,
and the one who perceives
the self as killed:
neither of them know
that this self
does not kill,
nor is it killed.

The self is not born
nor does it ever die.
Once it has been, this self will
never cease to be again.
Unborn, eternal,
continuing from the old,
the self is not killed
when the body is killed.

The one who
knows the eternal
and the indestructible,
that which is unborn,
and imperishable,
how does he cause to die,
Son of Pritha, and whom?
How does he kill, and whom?

Just as one
throws out old clothes
and then takes on
other, new ones;
so the embodied self
casts out old bodies
as it gets
other, new ones.

Weapons do not
cut the self,
nor does fire
burn it,
nor do waters
drench it,
nor does wind
dry it.

The self
is not to be pierced,
nor burned,
nor drenched,
nor dried;
it is eternal,
all-pervading and fixed—
unmoving from the beginning.

The self
is not readily seen;
by sight or mind;
it is said to be formless
and unchanging;
so, when you
have known this,
you should not mourn.

And even
if you think
the self *is*
eternally born,
or eternally dead—
still, you should not
mourn it,
Strong-Armed One.

Death is fixed
for those
who are born,
and birth is fixed
for those who die;
since such an end
is certain,
you should not grieve.

THE TWO PATHS

Krishna speaks here of two paths, which he calls two *yogas*, loosely based on the two paths described in the Upanishads ("Transmigration," p. 114), one concerned with ritual (karma, also translated as "action"), and one with meditation (*jnana*, also translated as "knowledge"). Karma contains within it the worldly Vedic path of rebirth, the world of dharma, in contrast with *jnana*, which represents the meditational, transcendent Vedantic path of release, the world of *moksha*; we may see a parallel here with what Martin Luther would have called works (karma) and faith (*jnana*). The state "beyond action" is not the same as nonaction, which Krishna deplores; it means a state in which one does not need to act. *Bhakti* still bridges the conflicting claims of the original opposition between dharma and *moksha*, but now there is a new triad, with contemplation or wisdom (*jnana*) taking the place of *moksha*, and action (karma, both action in general and ritual action in particular) standing in for dharma. Each member of the triad of *jnana*, karma, and *bhakti* was regarded by its adherents as the best, if not the only, path to salvation.

Krishna also draws upon Sankhya philosophy ("Quieting the Mind," p. 122), beginning with its basic idea of the male spirit (*purusha*, self or person) and female matter (*prakriti*, or Nature), the latter constituted by the three *gunas* (qualities) of lucidity (*sattva*), energy (*rajas*), and entropy or darkness (*tamas*). Early Sankhya philosophers argued that there are an infinite number of similar but separate *purushas*, no one superior to another, and that god may or may not exist but is not needed to explain the universe; later Sankhya philosophers assumed that god does exist. Sankhya as a philosophy has roots that date from the time of the Upanishads but were first formally codified by about the third century C.E.

Bhagavad Gita 3.3–9

The Blessed One said:

Blameless One,
in this world,
a double foundation
was taught by me in ancient times:
the *yoga* of knowledge
for those who follow *sankhya*,
and the *yoga* of action
for those who practice *yoga*.

One does not reach
the state
beyond action
by abstaining
from actions;
nor does one
reach fulfilment
only by renunciation.

No one, not even
for one moment,
ever stands without acting;
by virtue of the *gunas*
born in nature,
without willing it,
everyone is made
to perform action.

The person who sits
and subdues
the active senses,
while remembering and mindful
of the objects of the senses:
it is said that such a one
is a confused self—
who proceeds falsely.

But, Arjuna,
the one who begins
to rein in the senses
through the mind
and who, without clinging,
begins the *yoga* of action
through the active senses,
is unique.

So perform action
which is restrained,

Translated by Laurie L. Patton.

for this action is better
than non-action;
and even the working
of your body
would not succeed
without action.

Except for action
whose end is sacrifice,
this world is bound by action;
without clinging,
perform action
towards this end
of sacrifice,
Son of Kunti.

THE TRUE NATURE OF ACTION

The *Gita*'s brilliant solution to the tension between renunciation and family life is to urge Arjuna (and the reader/hearer of the *Gita*) to renounce not his actions but their fruits, to live with "karma without *kama*," actions without desires, a way of acting, well or badly, without amassing any of the effects or fruits of action that cling to the reincarnating soul and keep it from finding freedom in *moksha*. This is a way to reconcile a renouncer's state of mind with the duties of his class and stage of life (his *varna-ashrama-dharma*). Maintaining this spiritual state of mind, in the midst of his material life, will provide Arjuna with a kind of moral Teflon that will block the consequences of his actions for his transmigrating soul. It will make him a pandit (a wise, learned man).

"Karma without *kama*" means not that one should not desire certain results from one's actions, but merely that one should not expect the results (for so much is out of our control) or, more important, regard the results as the point; it's the journey that counts, not where you end up. Karma without *kama* means that each of us must perform our own dharma—in Arjuna's case, to kill his kinsmen in battle—with the attitude of a renouncer. In the film *The Legend of Bagger Vance* (2000), loosely based on the *Gita*, with golf taking the place of war (though the hero has been traumatized by World War I), the Krishna figure (played by Will Smith) describes to [Ar]Junuh (Matt Damon), for whom he is the caddy (charioteer), the feeling of karma without *kama* as playing in the zone; this is a brilliant analogy for our times.

Bhagavad Gita 4.17–23

One should have watchful insight
into action,
watchful insight
into wrong action,
and watchful insight

Translated by Laurie L. Patton.

into non-action.
The way of action
is hard to fathom.

Among humans,
the person who sees
non-action in action,
and action in non-action,
has insight;
that one undertakes
all actions,
steady in *yoga*.

Insightful ones
call that one a pandit
who has winnowed
all aims and desires
from all endeavors
and whose action is burned
in the fire
of wisdom.

When one has let go
of clinging
to the fruits of action,
always content
and independent,
even when turning
towards action,
that one does nothing at all.

One who is without desire,
but with a self
whose thought is restrained,
and who has left off
all grasping,
undertaking action
with the body alone,
that one does no evil.

Content with
accidental gifts,
moving beyond dualities,
free from malice,
the same in fulfilment
and frustration,
even after acting,
that one is not bound.

For the one who is free,
whose clinging is gone,
and whose thought
stands firm
in wisdom,

action performed
for sacrifice
dissolves altogether.

THE PATH OF DEVOTION

Here Krishna describes the third path or *yoga*, the path of devotion (*bhakti*), and contrasts it not with the other two paths (the *yogas* of action and knowledge) but with the worship of the ineffable form of god without form, without qualities (*nir-guna*).

Bhagavad Gita 12.1–7

Arjuna said:

Between the ones who are
always joined to *yoga*,
and honor you with devotion,
and the ones who honor
the imperishable one,
the one without form,
who is the wisest
about *yoga?*

The Blessed One said:

Those who are
eternally joined to *yoga*,
and who honor me
with the mind fixed on me,
and gifted with
the highest trust,
I think of them
as the most joined to *yoga*.

But those who honor
the imperishable one,
who is undefinable,
and without form,
who pervades all
and is beyond thought,
unmoving, steady,
as if fixed on a mountaintop,

and those whose many senses
are reined in together,
with equal insight

TRANSLATED BY Laurie L. Patton.

in all places,
and who exult
in the good
of all beings,
also reach me.

The pain of those
whose thought focuses on
the one without form
is greater.
The goal of the
one without form
is hard to reach
for those with bodies.

But those
who give up
all actions to me,
who hold me as highest,
and with *yoga*
where the goal is clear,
in pure concentration,
they honor me.

Son of Pritha,
for those whose thoughts
have entered
into me,
I will very soon become
their uplifter
from the ocean
of death and rebirth.

SALVATION AND DAMNATION

Most of the *Gita* encourages good people to do the right thing. But the text is both a philosophical tract and a *dharma-shastra* (a textbook on correct behavior), and like all *dharma-shastras* it tells you also about what *not* to do. The statement that some people are born with the nature of a god and some with the nature of a demon or anti-god (Asura), together with the statement that the anti-god people "never ever reach" Krishna, qualifies earlier statements that anyone can reach Krishna through *bhakti*. The hell into which these bad people fall may well be a physical place (as was imagined by several texts by this time, and earlier ["Bhrigu's Journey," p. 101]), or a metaphorical hell like that of Christopher Marlowe in *Doctor Faustus* ("For this is hell, nor am I out of it") or Jean-Paul Sartre in *No Exit* ("Hell is other people").

Bhagavad Gita 16.1–24

The Lord said, 'Fearless and pure in nature, steadfast in the practice of wisdom,[1] generous and self-controlled, performing sacrifice, devoted to the study of scripture, ascetic, sincere, injuring no one, truthful, without anger, renouncing (everything), peaceful, never slanderous, compassionate to (all) beings, never greedy, gentle, modest, never fickle, ardent, patient, enduring, pure, never malicious, never arrogant—these are the qualities of a man who is born to have the fate of a god. But a hypocrite, proud and arrogant, angry, harsh, and ignorant—these are the qualities of a man who is born to have the fate of a demon.

'The fate of a god is Release; the fate of a demon is bondage—that is what is generally believed. But do not worry, Arjuna; you were born to have the fate of a god. There are two classes of beings in this world—the godlike and the demonic. I have told you about the godlike at some length; now listen to the demonic.

'The demonic do not understand activity nor the cessation of activity; there is no purity in them, no morality, no truth.[2] They say, "The universe has no reality, no firm basis, no lord; it has not come into existence through mutual causation; desire is its only cause—what else?" Since they insist upon this doctrine, their souls are lost and their wits are feeble; and so they commit horrible actions in their wish to harm and destroy the universe. Immersing themselves in insatiable desire, possessed by hypocrisy, pride, and madness, in their delusion they grasp at false conceptions and undertake impure enterprises. They are afflicted by countless worries that end only at doomsday, for their only aim is to enjoy what they desire, since they are convinced that this is all there is. Bound by the fetters of hope, by the hundreds, obsessed by desire and anger, they long to amass great wealth, by whatever foul means, to satisfy their desires.

"I got this today! I'll satisfy this whim. This is my money, and this, and this will be mine soon. I killed that man—he was my enemy; and I will kill the others, too. I'm master, here; I'm the one who enjoys this; I'm successful and powerful and happy. I'm rich and superior; who else is there the likes of me? I'll sacrifice, and I'll give to charities, and I will have *fun*." This is what people say when they are deluded by ignorance.[3]

'They are led astray by their many notions; they are caught up in the net of delusion; they are addicted to the satisfaction of their desires—and so they fall into a filthy hell. Full of themselves, rigid, maddened by their pride in their wealth, in their hypocrisy they offer sacrifices that are sacrifices in name only, not performed in the proper manner at all.[4] They rely on their egotism, brute force, pride, desire, and anger; and they hate me and are unable to stand me—though I dwell in their own bodies, as in the bodies of all others. I always throw these hateful, cruel, vile, bad men into the wombs of demons in the course of their rebirths; and when they have fallen into a

TRANSLATED BY Wendy Doniger O'Flaherty.

1. That is, the *yoga* of knowledge.
2. These are the people known as atheists, literally "Naysayers," people who say there is no heaven, no god.
3. These may be the people known as Materialists (Lokayatas), also called Charvakas, after their founder (Charvaka).
4. This may imply people who sacrifice to gods other than Krishna, or simply those who ignore the Vedic rules.

demonic womb, they are deluded in birth after birth, and they never ever reach me; and so they go the lowest way.

'The door to hell, that destroys the soul, is three-fold: desire, anger, and greed; that is why you should abandon these three. For when a man is released from these three doors of darkness, he acts for the good of his soul; and then he goes the highest way. Whoever discards the laws of the Shastras, and acts to accomplish his desires, never achieves fulfilment, nor happiness, nor the highest way. Therefore let the Shastras be your authority, determining what you should do and what you should not do. When you know what the Shastras say about something, you should do what they tell you to do.'

LOST LOVES AND TRAGIC MISTAKES IN THE *RAMAYANA* OF VALMIKI 200 B.C.E.–200 C.E.

The *Ramayana* may have circulated as a story as early as 750 B.C.E., but it did not reach its present form until between 200 B.C.E. and 200 C.E.. Its world therefore begins in the North Indian world of the Upanishads and continues through the world of the Shastras (ca. 200 C.E.) ("Shastras," p. 200). Valmiki's Sanskrit *Ramayana*, the oldest surviving version of the tale, a text of some 20,000 verses, establishes the basic plot:

> Ravana, the ogre (Rakshasa) king of Lanka, was a Brahmin and a devotee of the god Shiva. He had obtained, from the god Brahma, a boon that he could not be killed by gods or anti-gods or ogres or any other creatures—though he neglected to mention human beings, as beneath contempt. The god Vishnu therefore became incarnate as a human being, the prince Rama, in order to kill Ravana. Sita, born of the goddess Earth, became Rama's wife. When Rama's father, Dasharatha, put Rama's younger brother Bharata (not the same person as the Bharata of the *Mahabharata*) on the throne instead of Rama, Rama went into exile in the jungle with Sita and another brother, Lakshmana. Ravana stole Sita and kept her captive on the island of Lanka for many years. With the help of an army of monkeys and bears, and in particular the monkey Hanuman, who leaped across to Lanka and then built a causeway for the armies to cross over, Rama killed Ravana and brought Sita back home with him. But when he began to worry about talk that her reputation, if not her chastity, had been sullied by her long sojourn in the house of another man, he forced her to submit to an ordeal by fire. Later he banished her, but she bore him twin sons who came to him when they were grown. Sita, too, returned briefly but then disappeared forever back into the earth, her mother. Rama ruled for many years, a time of peace and justice.

Rama breaks the bow of Shiva at the court of Janaka, Sita's father. Mid nineteenth-century painting.

The *Ramayana*, composed at a time when kingdoms were becoming powerful, legitimates monarchy through the vision of the golden age of Ram-raj, Rama's Rule: "There were no widows in distress, nor any danger from snakes or disease; people lived for a thousand years." This vision of a time of peace and prosperity became the template for an ideal of theocracy that haunted Indian politics for centuries. But the actual historical scene of the time, with its parricides and usurpations, also produced a royal paranoia that is revealed in the underside of Ram-raj, surfacing in the palace coups and armed conflicts in the realms of monkeys and ogres.

Bronze statue of Rama from the Chola dynasty in South India

Valmiki's Rama usually forgets that he is an incarnate god, an avatar (a "crossing-down," from heaven to earth) of Vishnu. He genuinely suffers and despairs when he's separated from Sita. Sometimes Valmiki treats Rama as a god, sometimes not. For the *Ramayana* is situated on the cusp between the periods in which Rama changed from a minor god to a major god. Hindus in later periods often took the devotion to Rama expressed by Hanuman and Lakshmana as a paradigm for human devotion (*bhakti*) to a god. Yet in the *Ramayana* these relationships lack the passionate, often violent qualities that characterize the fully developed *bhakti* of the Tamil texts and the Puranas beginning in the tenth century C.E.

The double nature of incarnation—simultaneously human and not human—can be traced back to the Upanishadic belief that our souls are all incarnations of the immortal *brahman* though our bodies are subject to the cycle of reincarnation. But why do the two great human avatars of Vishnu, Krishna and Rama, appear at this moment in Indian history? Perhaps because an avatar was a way to attach already extant divinities to the growing sect of Vishnu, a way to synthesize previous strands and appropriate other peoples' stories. The avatar was also an answer to the challenge that Buddhism and Jainism posed for Hinduism, for by this time the Buddha and the Jina had successfully established the paradigm of a religious movement centered upon a human being. But Rama and Krishna beat the Buddhists and Jains at their own game of making the human form a locus of superhuman wisdom and power, for Rama and Krishna are humans with a direct line to divinity, drawing their power from a god (Vishnu) far greater than any Vedic god and at the same time, through the incarnations, grounded in humanity.

Buddhism and Jainism were forces to be reckoned with at this time, and they influenced doctrines, narratives, and characters in both the *Mahabharata* and the *Ramayana*. The karma theory may have developed many of its crucial details within Jainism, and moved from there to Buddhism and Hinduism. All three religions remained in conversation, their rivalry often spurring them to borrow from one another in a positive way. One of the ideas that they debated together was the treatment of animals, with a great deal of soul-searching about the meaning of *ahimsa*, nonviolence to all living creatures ("The Dog Who Would Be Lion," p. 158; "The Pandavas Go to Heaven," p. 145).

Yet Buddhists and Jains differed from Hindus in significant ways, even in the degree of their engagement with *ahimsa*. The Jains took vegetarianism to the greatest extremes, taking pains to avoid injuring even tiny insects. (This stricter *ahimsa* prevented the Jains from farming, which killed the tiny creatures caught under the plow; they were therefore forced to become bankers and get rich.) Yet, though *ahimsa* was often cited as the reason that Jains and Buddhists abhorred animal sacrifice, there were other reasons, too. They may also have wanted to make a clean break with Hinduism by eliminating the element by which most Hindus defined themselves: Vedic sacrifice. It was factors such as these, as much as compassion for furry creatures, that made Buddhists and Jains abjure animal sacrifice.

But Hindus, Buddhists, and Jains often became rivals for political patronage as well as for the hearts of men and women. It was advantageous for the Buddhists to promote a religion that did not need priests to intercede for individual humans with gods, indeed that denied the effectiveness of gods altogether, scorning them as insignificant and/or ridiculous, and this was the final move that distinguished Buddhists and Jains from Hindus, many of whom may not have employed Brahmins themselves but did not deny their authority for others. Jains and Buddhists also rejected the Veda as revelation, which, with their disregard for Brahminical teachings and Brahminical claims to divine authority, distinguished them even from those Hindus who were beginning to take up some of the new doctrines and practices. The Buddhists also denied the existence of an individual soul and, like the authors of some of the Upanishads, argued that conduct rather than birth determined the true Brahmin—all significant departures from most Hindu doctrines. They differed even in their practice of renunciation: Buddhist monks lived together in monasteries, at first only during the rainy season but later at other times as well, while the Hindu renouncers during this period renounced human companionship and wandered alone.

The Buddhists thrived, as their sources of income shifted to a wider base. Buddhist monuments depict many scenes of popular devotion and were often financed not by dynastic patronage but by individual benefactors, both monks and nuns within the institutions and, outside, merchants increasingly interested in the security and patronage that religious centers offered in an age of political uncertainty. Often the whole community—landowners, merchants, high officials, common artisans—funded major Buddhist projects. Women, including women from marginal social positions (such as courtesans), also patronized Buddhists and Jains. The widespread public recognition of such women both as donors and as renouncers also had an impact on the role of women within Hinduism and on the development of Hindu religious rituals, performed by women, that came to replace the Vedic sacrifice, performed by men.

This was the context in which the *Ramayana* developed the concept of the human avatar and endowed that avatar, Rama, with gentle virtues, many of which owed as much to Buddhism as to Hinduism.

PRONOUNCING GLOSSARY

Agni: *ug´-nee*
Brahma: *bruh-mah´*
Daitya: *dait´-yuh*
Daksha: *duk´-shuh*
Dasharatha: *duh´-shuh-ruh´-tuh*
Devarata: *day´-vuh-ruh-tuh*
Dhundhumara: *doon´-doo-mah´-ruh*
Dilipa: *dih-lee´-puh*
Gandharva: *gun-dar´-vuh*
Indra: *in´-druh*
Janaka: *juh´-nuh-kuh*
Janamejaya: *juh-nuh-may´-jah´-yuh*
Jatarupa: *jah´-tuh-roo´-puh*
Kakutstha: *kah´-koot´-stuh*
Kausalya: *kow´-sul-yah´*
Krittika: *krih´-ti-kuh*
Kshatriya: *kuh-shah´-tree-yuh*
Kumara: *koo-mah´-ruh*
Lakshmana: *luk´-shmuh-nuh*
Marut: *muh´-root*
Menaka: *may´-nuh-kah´*
Mithila: *mee´-tee-lah´*
Naga: *nah´-guh*
Nahusha: *nuh-hoo´-shuh*
Nimi: *nee´-mee*
Raghava: *rah´-guh-vuh*

Raghu: *ruh´-goo*
Rama: *rah´-muh*
Ramayana: *rah-mah´-yuh-nuh*
Rudra: *roo´-druh*
Sagara: *suh´-guh-ruh*
Sarayu: *suh-ruh-yoo´*
Shaibya: *shaib´-yuh*
Shastra: *shah´-struh*
Shiva: *shih´-vuh*
Shudra: *shoo´-druh*
Shukra: *shoo´-kruh*
Sita: *see´-tah*
Skanda: *skun´-duh*
Uma: *oo-mah´*
Vaishya: *vai´-shyuh*
Vaivasvata: *vai´-vus-vuh´-tuh*
Varuna: *vuh´-roo-nuh*
Vasava: *vah´-suh-vuh*
Vayu: *vah´-yoo*
Vishvamitra: *vish´-vuh-mit´-ruh*
Yama: *yuh´-muh*

THE BIRTH OF SITA AND THE BENDING OF THE BOW

Rama and Lakshmana, two sons of King Dasharatha, accompanied by their family priest, the sage Vishvamitra, have journeyed from their capital city of Ayodhya to Mithila, the capital city of King Janaka; Janaka is ruler of the kingdom of Videha and father of the princess Sita. They have come to try to win Sita's hand by winning the contest set for all suitors, which consists in bending a certain bow. This bow came into existence when the god Rudra destroyed Daksha's sacrifice ("Daksha's Sacrifice," p. 162); it cannot be bent by anyone among anti-gods (demons, Asuras), spirits (Yakshas), ogres (Rakshasas), horse-headed What?-men (Kinnaras), demigods (Gandharvas), or Nagas (great serpents, sometimes cobras, sometimes snake from the waist down and anthropomorphic from the waist up). Significantly, as in the boon granted to Ravana, human beings are not mentioned. Rama alone is able to bend the bow and win the princess.

In the course of the contest, the heroes hear the story of Sita's birth, which took place when Janaka was plowing the sacrificial arena, in preparation for the ceremony of royal consecration. Years later, Sita is scorned and insulted until she goes back down into the earth during Rama's horse sacrifice; thus both her birth and her death are framed by sacrifices. Her life follows the pattern of swan maidens and other animal goddesses: she comes from another world to a mortal king, bears him children (twins), is mistreated by him, and leaves him forever, with only the children to console him. The fact that Rama does not merely string the bow that will win Sita but breaks it foreshadows the way that he will, in a sense, injure her and ultimately lose her.

Ramayana 1.65–66

In the clear light of dawn, King Janaka performed his rituals and then summoned the noble Vishvamitra and Rama and Lakshmana. The king, who was the very soul of dharma, honored the sage and the two Raghu princes, honored them with the ritual set down in the Shastras, and then he said, 'Welcome to you, sir. What can I do for you, sinless one? Command me, for

TRANSLATED BY Wendy Doniger O'Flaherty.

I am yours to command.' When the sage, who was the very soul of dharma, and also clever with words, heard the speech of the noble hero, Janaka, he answered him with this speech: 'These two Kshatriyas are the two sons of King Dasharatha, and are famous throughout the world. They wish to see that special bow that you have. Do please show it to them, and when they have satisfied their desire by seeing the bow, the two princes will go back home as they please.'

When he heard this, Janaka replied to the great sage, 'Let me tell you the purpose for which that bow is here. The king called Devarata, sixth in descent from Nimi, received this bow in trust from the noble god Rudra, who placed it in his hands. For, once upon a time, when Daksha's sacrifice was destroyed, the mighty Rudra bent this bow and said to the gods, in mock fury, "Since you gods did not set aside any share in the sacrifice for me, and I want a share, I am going to knock your precious heads off with this bow." Then the gods trembled with fear, and they bowed low to Rudra and begged him to forgive them, and he was satisfied by them. In his satisfaction, he restored to their former condition all their limbs that the noble god of gods had lopped off or mutilated or shattered with his bow. That celestial bow remains even today in our family, where it is highly valued.

'Now, one day when I was in the sacrificial grounds, I saw the ultimate celestial nymph, Menaka, flying through the sky, and this thought came to me: "If I should have a child in her, what a child that would be!" As I was thinking in this way, my semen fell on the ground. And afterwards, as I was ploughing that field, there arose out of the earth, as first fruits, my daughter, who has celestial beauty and qualities, and can only be won by one whose bride price is his manliness. Since she arose from the surface of the earth, and was born from no womb, she is called Sita, the furrow.

'In the past, kings kept coming here and coming here, wooing her, and I told those kings, "She will be given to the man whose bride-price is his manliness." Then all the kings who sought my daughter came to my city to prove their manliness. I showed them the bow, to test their manliness, but they could not even lift up that bow. And when I saw how little manliness they had, I refused to let any of them have my daughter. Then all those kings became angry, and they surrounded the city of Mithila on all sides and laid siege to it. For those kings, each individually thinking that he had been insulted, were filled with great anger, and so they oppressed Mithila. For a full year they besieged Mithila, with firm determination, and when, as a result of that siege, all my resources were exhausted, I asked help from the god of gods, (Rudra) the husband of Uma. The lord was satisfied by my propitiation and gave me an army, complete with all four divisions (infantry, cavalry, chariots, and the armored division [elephants]). Then the power of the kings was broken and they went away, for they had little manliness in the courage of their army, and they were too proud of the little manliness that they had. This, then, is the incomparable celestial bow, that I will show to Rama and Lakshmana. And if Rama can string this bow, I will give him Sita, who was born of no womb, to be the daughter-in-law of Dasharatha.'

When the great sage Vishvamitra heard king Janaka's words, he said to him, 'Show the bow to Rama.' Then king Janaka commanded his ministers: 'Adorn the celestial bow with perfume and garlands and bring it here.' At Janaka's command, the ministers entered the city, placed the bow in front of them, and went back out, as the king had commanded. Five thousand tall, noble men put the chest (containing the bow) on (a carriage with) eight wheels and dragged it, with considerable difficulty. And when they had brought the iron chest that contained the bow, the king's counsellors said to the godlike Janaka, 'Here, king, is the incomparable bow that all the kings revere; if you wish, great king of Mithila, it can be seen.' At their words, the king cupped his hands in reverence and spoke to the noble Vishvamitra, and to Rama and Lakshmana: 'Here is the incomparable bow that the Janakas revere, O Brahmin, and that all those kings with their great manliness were unable to draw. None of the hosts of gods, none of the demons or ogres, or the foremost Gandharvas or spirits, none of the What?-men or great Nagas can bend this bow or string it or fit an arrow to it or pluck the string or even lift it. What chance is there then for men? This bow is the very best; bull of sages, show it to these two sons of the king.'

When the sage Vishvamitra heard what the king said, he said to Rama, 'Rama, my little calf, look at the bow.' And Rama did as the sage said; he opened the chest in which the bow lay and looked at the bow and said, 'I touch this great bow with my hand; now I will make a great effort to lift it, and even to string it.' 'Very well,' said the king and the sage, and as the sage had told him to do, he grasped the bow in the middle, playfully. And then, as many thousands of kings watched him, Rama strung the bow as if he were playing. With his manliness, Rama strung the bowstring and then drew the bow; and that incomparable man of great fame broke that bow right in the middle. It made a loud noise, loud as a thunderclap, and a great earthquake, as if a mountain had been shattered. The noise so stunned all the men that they fell down—all except the great sage, the king, and the two princes descended from the great king Raghu.

When the people revived again, the king—whose worries were over—cupped his hands in reverence and spoke to the bull among sages, for he knew how to make speeches: 'Sir, now I have seen the manliness of Rama the son of Dasharatha; it is surpassingly marvelous, inconceivable; I had no idea what it was like. My daughter Sita will bring great fame to the family of the Janakas when she takes Rama, the son of Dasharatha, as her husband. And so I have kept my promise, that her only bride-price would be manliness; I will give Rama my daughter Sita, who is as precious as life itself. With your permission, please, Brahmin, my counsellors will go quickly to Ayodhya, hastening in chariots. With courteous words they will bring the king to my city and tell him all about the betrothal of the girl whose only bride-price was manliness. And they will tell the king that his two sons are under the protection of the sage; this will satisfy the king, and then they can bring him here right away.' 'Yes,' said Vishvamitra, and the king spoke to his counsellors and gave them orders and sent them to Ayodhya; for he was the very soul of dharma.

DASHARATHA KILLS A BOY HE MISTAKES FOR AN ELEPHANT

When Rama, the eldest son of Dasharatha, and the son of the oldest queen, Kausalya, was about to ascend the throne, a younger queen, Kaikeyi, forced Dasharatha to put her son, Bharata, on the throne instead and send Rama into exile. She achieved her purpose in part by reminding Dasharatha of a promise he had made to her years ago and in part by sexual blackmail (she locked herself into her "anger room," put on filthy clothes, lay down on the ground, and refused to look at the king or speak to him). The besotted Dasharatha was powerless to resist her beauty (2.9.16–19) and complied, though he was deeply unhappy about exiling Rama. Five days after Rama's departure, "there suddenly flashed upon [Dasharatha's] mind an evil deed he had once done, unintentionally, long ago, when he was shooting arrows by the sound of the target alone" (2.56.2). That night, Dasharatha went to sleep with Kausalya and remembered, in a dream, the details of this evil deed.

The connection between blindness (aiming by sound alone at the child of sightless parents) and desire (hunting as the equivalent of taking a cold shower to control premarital desire) suggests that desire was Dasharatha's blind spot long before Kaikeyi manipulated him by locking him out of her bedroom. By the end of this episode, Dasharatha can no longer see Kausalya at all and is, like the father in the story, blind, weak, and grieving for his lost son.

There are strong parallels between Dasharatha's mistaking a boy for an elephant and Pandu's act of killing, while hunting, a sage who had taken the form of a stag and was coupling with a doe (*Mahabharata* 1.90.64; 1.109.5–30). For interrupting this mating couple, Pandu was cursed to be childless ("The End of Female Promiscuity," p. 154). So, too, when "The Gods Interrupt Shiva and Parvati," the goddesses are cursed to be childless. Hunting errors and fatal interruptions are not limited to the sexual arena. Krishna, in the *Mahabharata*, dies when a hunter mistakes him for a deer. And at the end of the *Ramayana*, Lakshmana is forced to break in on Rama and Death when they are closeted together, under strict instructions not to be interrupted, on pain of death. This is the ultimate fatal interruption: interrupting Death himself. All of these themes resonate in this story about Dasharatha.

Ramayana 2.57–58

A short time later, his heart crushed by grief, King Dasharatha awoke, and began to brood once more. Heartache over the exile of Rama and Lakshmana once more swept over him, the equal of Vasava,[1] as the demon's darkness sweeps over the sun. It was at midnight, on that sixth night since Rama's banishment to the forest, when King Dasharatha fully remembered the evil deed he had once done. He then addressed Kausalya, who lay anguished with grief for her son.

"Whatever a person does, be it good or evil, my dear and precious wife, he receives in like measure, the direct result of the deeds he has done himself. One deserves to be called a fool who sets about a deed without understanding the gravity of its consequences, what he stands to gain or lose. A

TRANSLATED BY Sheldon I. Pollock.

1. Vasava is a name of Indra, king of the gods; the demon of eclipse is Rahu ("The Churning of the Ocean," p. 149).

person who cuts down a mango grove and instead waters flame trees—made greedy for their fruit by the sight of their flowers—would be sorry when that fruit appears. I cut down a mango grove and watered flame trees instead. When the fruit appeared I had to give up Rama, and now, too late, I see my folly and grieve.

"When I was a young man, Kausalya, I earned a reputation as a bowman. It was said, 'The prince can shoot by the sound of the target alone.' But I did an evil deed, my lady, and it has now come home to me, this sorrow that I have brought upon myself. But just as a child might eat something poisonous out of ignorance, so I, too, was unaware of the fruits my shooting by sound would bear. We were not yet married, my lady, and I was still prince regent. The rains had come, the season that quickens lust and desire. After having drawn up the moisture of the earth and scorched the world with its rays, the sun had entered the awful region the dead inhabit. All at once the heat vanished, dark rain clouds appeared, and all creatures began to rejoice—frogs, cuckoos, peacocks. Engulfed by the rain that had fallen and continued to fall incessantly, the mountain with its wild white cuckoos looked like one vast body of water.

"At this most pleasant of seasons I decided to take some exercise, and with bow and arrows and chariot I set out along the Sarayu River. I was an intemperate youth, eager to kill a buffalo at the waterhole in the nighttime, an elephant coming down to the river, or some other wild animal. Now, in the darkness I heard a noise, beyond the range of vision, of a pitcher being filled in the water, but just like the sound an elephant[2] makes. I drew out a shaft that glared like a poisonous snake. I shot the keen-edged arrow, and it darted like a poisonous snake. And there, as day was breaking, the voice of a forest dweller rang out clearly, 'Ah! Ah!'—the voice of a young man crying there as he fell into the water: 'Why should someone shoot a weapon at a person like me, an ascetic?

"'I came to the deserted river at night only to fetch water. Who has struck me with an arrow? What have I done to anyone? I am a seer who has renounced violence, who lives in the wilderness on things of the wild. Why should someone take up a weapon to kill a person like me? The one burden I carry is my matted hair, my garments are nothing but barkcloth and hides. What could anyone stand to gain by killing me? What wrong could I have done him? No, he cannot have had any purpose at all in what he did; pure malice must have prompted it. No one shall ever forgive him, like the man who violates his guru's bed. But it is not for the loss of my own life that I am grieving so. It is for two others I grieve that am slain, my mother and father. For they are an aged couple and have long been dependent on me. When I am dead what sort of existence are they to lead? My aged mother and father and I all slain by a single arrow! Who can have been so reckless, so malicious as to strike us down all at once?'

"When I heard that piteous voice, I who had always striven to do right, I shuddered and the bow and arrow dropped from my hands to the ground. Desolate to my innermost being, in the depths of misery I went to the place and saw on the bank of the Sarayu an ascetic struck down by my arrow. He fixed me with his eyes—I was beside myself with terror—and he spoke these

2. It is in any case against dharma to kill a wild elephant.

harrowing words as though ready to burn me up with his ascetic power: 'What harm have I, living here in the forest, ever done to you, your Majesty, that you should attack me when all I wanted was to fetch some water for my elders? The very same arrow that has pierced me to the quick has also struck down two blind old people, my mother and my father. The two of them are frail and blind; they are thirsty and waiting for me. And now they will have to bear their parching thirst, as long as they can, on the strength of hope alone. I now see there is no reward for austerity or learning, since my father does not know that I lie fallen upon the ground. And even if he knew, what could he do? He is helpless and unable even to move about, as helpless as one tree to save another that is being felled. You yourself, Raghava, must go at once to my father and tell him, lest in his wrath he consume you as a raging fire consumes a forest. There is the footpath, your Majesty, leading to my father's ashram. Go and beg his forgiveness, lest he curse you in his rage. Draw out the arrow from me, your Majesty, the keen-edged shaft is tearing me apart at the quick, as a rushing water current tears a soft riverbank apart. I am not a Brahmin, your Majesty, set your mind at ease. For I was born of a Vaishya father and a Shudra[3] mother, lord of the country.'

"So he spoke, in pain, and as he lay doubled over, I pulled out the arrow from where it pierced him to the quick. I stared at him lying there by the Sarayu, his body drenched in water, as he painfully lamented, all the while gasping from his mortal wound; and as I stared, my dear wife, I grew utterly sick at heart.

"It was a great sin I had committed, however unintentionally. I hardly had my wits about me as all alone I put my mind to the question of how might it be righted. At last I took the pot filled with pure water and went along the path he had told me of, until I reached the ashram. There I saw his parents, a frail, blind old couple with no one to guide them, like a pair of birds whose wings have been clipped. They could not move about and were sitting there listless and helpless, talking about him, their one hope that I robbed them of. Hearing the sound of my footsteps the sage spoke: 'Why did you take so long, my son? Bring the water at once. Your mother here was worried, my child, and all because you were playing in the water. Come into the ashram at once. If perhaps your mother or I have offended you in some way, my son, you should not take it to heart. For you are an ascetic, my child. You are the recourse for us who have no other, the eyes for us whose sight is gone. Our very lives are in your hands. Won't you say something to us?'

"The longer I looked at the sage, the more frightened I became, and in a choked voice, stammering and slurring the syllables, I spoke to him. With effort I managed to collect my thoughts and recover the power of speech. Then I began to tell him the frightful story of his son's calamity. 'I am Dasharatha, a Kshatriya, not the great one's son. A sorrowful thing, which all good men would condemn, has happened by my own doing. Holy one, I came to the bank of the Sarayu, bow in hand, eager to kill some animal, an elephant perhaps, coming down to the water hole. There I heard the sound of a pitcher being filled in the water and, thinking it an elephant, I shot an arrow at it. I went to the riverbank and there I saw an ascetic lying on the ground

3. The boy tells Dasharatha that he is of mixed class (his father of the third, merchant class and his mother of the fourth, servant class), to reassure Dasharatha lest he hesitate to pull out the arrow for fear of killing a Brahmin.

with an arrow piercing his heart and his life ebbing away. Holy one, I was aiming at a sound, meaning to kill an elephant. I released the iron shaft toward the water, and it struck your son. When the arrow was pulled out he went to heaven, then and there, grieving for both of you holy ones, lamenting your blindness. It was unintentional, holy one, it was an accident that I struck down your son. Whatever awaits me now may the sage forgive me!'

"The mighty sage gasped when he heard these harrowing words, and broken with grief he spoke to me as I stood before him, hands cupped in reverence. 'If you had not told me yourself of this impious deed, your Majesty, your head would have instantly burst into a myriad fragments. If a Kshatriya intentionally commits a murder—and the murder of a forest hermit at that—it topples him from his place, be he Indra himself, the wielder of the thunderbolt. But since this act was unintentional, and for that reason alone, you shall live. Were it not so, the entire House of the Raghavas, not just you, would cease at once to be. Take us, your Majesty, to the place,' he said to me. 'We want to see our son now, to have one last sight of him, his body spattered with blood and his hide garments in disarray, lying on the ground unconscious, under the sway of the King of Righteousness.'[4]

"So all alone I led the sage and his wife to that place, and brought the deeply grieving parents near to where they could touch their son. The wretched couple drew close, they touched their son and collapsed upon his body. And his father cried out: 'My son, don't you love me any more? At least have regard for your mother then, righteous child. Why don't you embrace me, my son? Speak to me, my tender child. Whom shall I hear late at night—how it used to touch my heart—so sweetly reciting the sacred texts or other works? And after the twilight worship, the ritual bath, and offerings to the sacred fire, who will sit down beside me, my son, to allay the grief and fear that anguish me? Who will bring me tubers and fruit and roots, and feed me like a welcome guest—me an invalid, without leader or guide? And how, my son, shall I support your poor mother, blind and aged as she is, wretched and yearning for her son?

"'Stay! Don't, oh don't go, my son, to the abode of Yama. You may go tomorrow, with your mother and me to lend you strength. For we too shall soon be going to the house of Yama, bereft of you and left helpless in the forest, wretched and anguished with grief. And then, when I see Vaivasvata,[5] I will make this speech: "May the King of Righteousness forgive me, but this boy is needed to support his parents." You were free of evil, my son, and were struck down by a man of evil deeds. By the power of this truth may you go straight to the worlds they win who fight under arms. Proceed to the supreme state those heroes reach, my son, who do not turn their backs in battle but die facing the foe. Go, my dear son, to the state attained by Sagara, by Shaibya, Dilipa, Janamejaya, Nahusha, and Dhundhumara.[6] Go, my dear son, to the state awarded to all holy men for their Vedic study and austerities, to one who donates land, who keeps the sacred fires, who is faithful to his one wife; to those who make a gift of a thousand cows, who support their gurus, who lay their bodies down. For no child of this family ever goes to the state of the accursed.'

4. Yama, king of the dead, the king of dharma because he judges the dead.
5. Another name of Yama.
6. Heroes from the family of Raghu, the ancestor of Rama (who is therefore called Raghava, descended from Raghu).

"So he mourned there, wretchedly and without pause, and then with his wife he set about making the funeral libation for his child. But just then the sage's son appeared in a heavenly form procured by his own good deeds, and for one brief moment he addressed these words of solace to his parents: 'I have attained a high station because I took care of you. And both of you shall soon come into my presence.' With this, the sage's disciplined son ascended straightway to heaven upon a heavenly chariot of wonderful construction. The ascetic and his wife hurriedly made the libation, and as I stood before him, my hands cupped in reverence, the mighty sage said to me: 'Slay me this very moment, your Majesty; dying holds no terror for me. For I had but one son and you have taken him from me with your arrow. Since it was unintentionally that you struck down my pure son, I will only lay a curse on you, though it is a grievous and very dreadful one: Just as I now sorrow over my son's calamity, so you, too, your majesty, shall end your days grieving for a son.'

"The words of the noble sage have thus come home to me, dear wife, for now I am to lose my life grieving for my son. If only Rama could touch me or speak to me now just once. How unlike me it was, my lady, to do what I did to Raghava. I cannot see you with my eyes, Kausalya, my mind is failing. Here, the messengers of Vaivasvata are here, hastening me on! What greater sorrow than this, that in the final moments of my life I cannot rest my eyes on righteous, truthful Rama. They are not men, they are gods who in the fifteenth year will see Rama's face again, that lovely face with flashing earrings. His eyes like lotus petals, his perfect brows, his perfect teeth and lovely nose: how fortunate the men who will see Rama's face, so like the lord of stars, the moon. Like the autumn moon or a full-blown lotus, and so fragrant: how fortunate the men who will see the face of my defender. When Rama has ended his stay in the forest and returns to Ayodhya, what happiness for those who will see him, like the planet Shukra[7] moving forward on its course. The grief arising here in my very soul has left me helpless and insensible. In its wild rush it is sweeping me away, as a raging river sweeps away its bank. O great-armed Raghava, the one relief of my agony!"

With this last cry of grief King Dasharatha reached the end of his life. And so it came about, just after midnight, when he had finished his mournful tale, that the lord of men, a man of noble vision, anguished by the exile of his beloved son and afflicted with the most profound sorrow, breathed his last.

7. The planet Venus, moving forward auspiciously.

THE GODS INTERRUPT SHIVA AND PARVATI

Like the *Mahabharata*, the *Ramayana* weaves into its central tale a number of myths. The sage Vishvamitra, Rama's family priest, tells the following story to Rama and his brother Lakshmana in answer to their question about the river Ganges. In the course of the myth, Shiva places his seed in Fire (Agni), rather than in his wife Parvati, as an anthropomorphization of the Vedic ritual act of throwing butter into the consecrated fire that carries the oblation to the gods, acting out the

Upanishadic equation of the sexual act and the oblation. The curse of childlessness that the frustrated Parvati gives to the wives of the gods explains why so many children of the gods are born to mortal women or from male gods or sages who create children unilaterally merely at the thought, or sight, of a woman, ejaculating into some womb substitute—a flower, a female animal, a river, a furrow—to produce a motherless child "born of no womb" (*a-yoni-ja*). Sita is born of a furrow, and so of the goddess Earth, in this way ("The Birth of Sita").

The *Ramayana* tells the story of Shiva and Parvati twice, first to explain why the wives of the gods were cursed and then to explain why one goddess, the Ganges, was exempt from the curse. The story of the birth of the god Skanda (also called Kartikeya ["son of the Krittikas"] and Kumara ["the Prince"]) to Shiva (also called Rudra) and Parvati (also called Uma) is told in many texts, including the *Mahabharata* (3.213–16). But the *Ramayana* version is unique in having Parvati curse not merely the wives of the gods in general but the Earth in particular, and to curse her not merely to have no son but to have too many husbands—like Draupadi and Kunti, the heroines of the *Mahabharata* ("The End of Female Promiscuity," p. 154).

The sage Vishvamitra tells this story to Rama.

Ramayana 1.35.6–26, 1.36.1–31

Long ago, Rama, when the great ascetic, black-throated Shiva, had gotten married, he looked with desire upon the goddess and began to make love to her. Thus engaged, the black-throated god passed a hundred years of the gods.[1] But even so, foe-consuming Rama, the goddess conceived no child. By that time the gods, led by Grandfather Brahma, had become alarmed and thought, 'Who will be able to withstand the being who will be born from this union?' Drawing near, all the gods prostrated themselves and spoke: 'Great god, god of gods, you are devoted to the welfare of this world. Please be gracious to the gods who have fallen at your feet. Best of gods, the worlds cannot contain your semen. You should, instead, perform with the goddess the austerities prescribed in the Vedas. For the sake of the three worlds, you must retain your semen in your body. You should protect all these worlds, not destroy them.'

When the great lord of all the worlds heard the words of the gods, he said, 'Very well.' Then he spoke to them further: 'With the help of Uma, I shall retain the semen in my body. Let the thirty gods and the earth rest easy. But tell me this, great gods: who will contain such of my incomparable semen as has already been dislodged from its place?' Addressed in this fashion, the gods replied to Shiva, whose standard is the bull, 'The Earth will bear the semen that has been dislodged.' And so, when they had addressed him in this fashion, the lord of gods released his semen upon the Earth, thereby filling it together with its mountains and forests.

Then the gods spoke to Agni, the eater of oblations, 'You and Vayu[2] must enter Rudra's abundant semen.' Permeated by Agni, it was transformed into a white mountain on which there was a celestial thicket of white reeds that looked like the sun surrounded by fire. It was there that Kartikeya came into being, born from fire. Then the gods and the hosts of seers were

TRANSLATED BY Robert P. Goldman.

1. A year of the gods equals 360 human years.

2. The god of the wind.

delighted at heart and worshiped Uma and Shiva. But the daughter of the mountain was enraged, Rama. Her eyes red with anger, she spoke to the gods, cursing them: 'Since I have been thwarted while making love in the hope of begetting a son, you shall be unable to father children upon your own wives. From this day forward, your wives shall remain childless.'

After addressing all the gods in this fashion, she cursed the Earth as well. 'O Earth, you shall be manifold in form; and the wife of many.[3] Moreover, since you did not want my son, you evil-minded creature, you shall never experience a mother's love for a son, defiled as you are by my anger.' When the lord of gods had seen all the gods thus put to shame, he set out for the west, the direction guarded by Varuna.[4] There the great lord and the goddess undertook austerities on the northern slope of a mountain peak in the Himalayas. I have told you the story of the mountain's daughter in detail, Rama. Now, you and Lakshmana shall hear from me the tale of the origin of the Ganges.

Long ago, while the god Shiva was engaged in austerities, the gods and hosts of seers, wishing to find a leader for their army, approached Grandfather Brahma. Indra and all the gods made Agni, the god of fire, their spokesman, and prostrating themselves, they spoke these eloquent words to the Grandfather, their lord. 'Lord, he whom you long ago gave us to lead our army has taken to extreme asceticism and is now engaged in austerities with Uma. You know how to arrange things. Arrange something for us to do next in our desire for the welfare of the worlds. You are our last recourse.' Hearing the gods' words, the grandfather of all the worlds comforted them with soothing words, saying: 'What the mountain's daughter said, that you will never father children on your wives, is inviolable truth. Let there be no doubt about this. But here is the Ganges who moves through the sky. Agni, the eater of oblations, will father on her a son who will be a foe-conquering commander for the army of the gods. The eldest daughter of the mountain lord will acknowledge that son. There can be no doubt that Uma will accept this.'

The gods heard Grandfather Brahma's words, and having accomplished their purpose, delight of the Raghus, they all bowed low and worshiped him. Then, all the gods proceeded to Mount Kailasa,[5] adorned with metallic ores, and charged Agni, the god of fire, with the task of begetting a son. 'You are a god, eater of oblations, and should carry out this task of the gods. Great is your splendor. You must release the semen into the Ganges, the daughter of the mountain.' Agni, the purifier, promised the gods he would do this and so, approaching the Ganges, he said, 'Bear this embryo, goddess, as a favor to the gods.' Hearing these words, she assumed her divine form, and he, seeing her extraordinary beauty, scattered the semen all over. Agni, the purifier, showered it all over the goddess, so that all the channels of the Ganges were filled with it, delight of the Raghus.

Then the Ganges spoke to him, the priest of all the gods. 'O god, I cannot bear your powerful semen. A fire is burning me, and my mind is confused.' The eater of all the gods' oblations replied to the Ganges, 'Let the embryo be placed at the foot of the Himalayas.' When the mighty Ganges heard

3. That is, the Earth gives birth to various soils and crops; and since every king is regarded as the husband of the Earth, she has many husbands, a promiscuity that is regarded as degrading for a woman ("The Stripping of Draupadi," p. 134; "The End of Female Promiscuity," p. 154).
4. God of the waters.
5. The mountain on which Shiva lives.

Agni's words, blameless man, she released the unbearably brilliant embryo from her channels. Since it had emerged from her, it had the luster of molten gold, and as it touched the earth, it turned to gold and silver, pure and beautiful. From its acrid quality, copper and iron were produced, while its impurities became tin and lead. Thus, when it touched the earth, it turned into the various elements. The moment the embryo was set down, the whole mountain forest was pervaded by its splendor and turned to gold. And ever since that time, Raghava, tiger among men, gold, lustrous as Agni, eater of oblations, has been known as Jatarupa, formed-at-birth.

As soon as the boy was born, Indra and all the Marut hosts[6] engaged the Krittikas[7] to provide sufficient milk for him. They offered him milk as soon as he was born, and came to an excellent arrangement, saying, 'He shall be the son of all of us.' It was for this reason that all the gods called him Kartikeya, saying, 'There can be no doubt but that this child will be famous throughout the three worlds.' When the Krittikas heard those words, they bathed the child who had come forth from that outpouring of the embryonic waters shining with the greatest splendor, like fire. And, Kakutstha, since that illustrious and fiery Kartikeya had come forth from that outpouring of embryonic waters, the gods called him 'Skanda.'[8]

Then all six Krittikas put forth wonderful milk, and he grew six heads to take it as it sprang from their breasts. After that lord had drunk their milk for but a single day, he conquered the hosts of Daitya[9] warriors through his own might, though his form was that of a tender boy. Therefore the hosts of the gods assembled and making Agni, the god of fire, their spokesman, consecrated him whose radiance was unblemished, as commander of the hosts of the gods. Now, Rama, I have told you the detailed history of the Ganges and also of the auspicious and holy birth of Kumara.

6. Storm gods, the entourage of Indra.
7. The six Krittikas (Pleaides) nurse Kartikeya, who gets that name, and his six heads, from them; the seventh Pleiade, often invisible in ancient India, is said to have refrained from nursing the child.
8. The verb *skand* means "to leap."
9. Anti-gods, cousins of the Asuras.

THE BRAHMINS EXPLAIN EVERYTHING IN THE SHASTRAS 100–600 C.E.

In the first centuries of the first millennium of the Common Era, Sanskrit still dominated the literary scene as "the language of the gods," as it had long claimed to be. But now it also became a cosmopolitan language, patronized by a sophisticated community of literati and royalty. It was no longer used only, or primarily, for sacred texts but also as a vehicle for literary and political expression throughout South Asia and parts of Southeast Asia. It was now the language of science and art as well as religion and literature—the language, in short, of the Shastras.

Shastra means a text, or a teaching, or a science; *ashva-shastra* in general is the science of horses, while the *Ashva-shastra* is a particular text about the science of horses. The word *shastra* comes from the verb *shas*, meaning to teach or to punish or discipline, but it also means "discipline" in the sense of an area of study, such as the discipline of anthropology. It comes from the verb *shams*, which is related to our own "chasten," "chastise," and "chastity," through the Latin *castigare*.

Like dharma, which describes both the way things are and the way they should be, the Shastras are simultaneously descriptive and proscriptive. And like the class and caste system itself, the Shastric structures were formulated to accommodate diversity. Yet many Brahmins perceived this diversity as a threat and therefore set out to hierarchize, to put everything in its proper place, to form, to mold, to repress, to systematize—in a word, to discipline (*shas*) the chaos that they saw looming before them. They herded all the new ideas, like so many strange animals, into their intellectual corrals, and they branded them according to their places in the scheme of things. Attitudes toward women and the lower classes hardened in the texts formulated in this period, even while those same texts give evidence, almost against the will of their authors, of an increasingly wide range of human options. The Shastras spelled out the dominant paradigm with regard to women, animals, and castes, the mark at which all subsequent movements of resistance or protest within Hinduism aimed.

Foundational to the Shastras is the paradigm of the Aims of Life or Goals of a Person (the *purusha-arthas*). Originally, they were a triad: dharma, *artha*, and *kama*, known collectively as the Trio (*trivarga*). Dharma includes duty, religion, religious merit, morality, social and ritual obligations, the law, and justice; dharma is both the way things are and the way they *should* be. *Artha* is money, political power, and success; it can also be translated as goal or aim (as in the three aims of human life), gain (versus loss), money, the meaning of a word, and the purpose of something. *Kama* represents pleasure and desire, not merely sexual but more broadly sensual—music, good food, perfume, silk sheets. Every human being was said to have a right, indeed a duty, to all these aims, in order to have a full life.

Most texts regard the aims of life as triple, but sometimes, from the time of the Upanishads, the aims of life are listed as a Quartet (*chatur-varga*), in which the fourth aim is *moksha*, Release from the cycle of transmigration, the banner of a shift away from the worldly goals to a life of renunciation.

The persistent open-endedness, and even open-mindedness, of many of the Shastras can be seen in the ways in which they consider variant opinions and offer escape

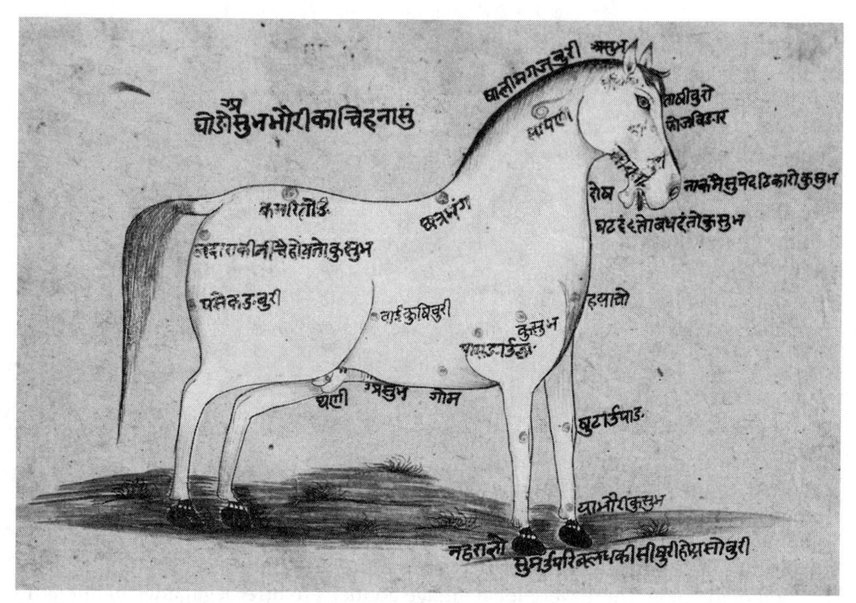

An illustration from an *Ashva-Shastra*, a textbook about horses. Twentieth century.

clauses. Each Shastra quotes its predecessors and shows why it is better than they are; the dissenting opinions are cited in the course of what Indian logic called the "other side" (the "former wing," *purva-paksha*), the arguments that opponents might raise. These arguments are rebutted one by one, until the author finally gives his own opinion, the right opinion. But along the way, we get a strong sense of a loyal opposition and the flourishing of a healthy debate. The Shastras are therefore, above all, dialogical or argumentative.

PRONOUNCING GLOSSARY

Agni: *ug´-nee*
Agnivesha: *ug´-nee-vay´-shuh*
Angiras: *un-gee´-rus*
Arhat: *ar´-hut*
Asura: *uh´-soo-ruh*
Avanti: *uh-vahn´-tee*
Bhadrakapya: *buh´-druh-kahp´-yuh*
Bharadvaja: *buh´-rud-vuh´-juh*
Bhikshu Atreya: *bik´-shoo uh-tray´-yuh*
bhrama: *bruh´-muh*
bija: *bee´-juh*
Brahma: *bruh-mah´*
Charaka Samhita: *chuh´-ruh-kuh sum-hih-tah´*
Daitya: *dait´-yuh*
darbha: *dar´-buh*
Grihya Sutra: *grih´-yuh soo´-truh*
Hiranyaksha: *hee-rahn´-yahk´-shuh*
jaya: *jah´-yah*
jayate: *jah´-yuh-tay*
Kankayana: *kahn-kah´-yuh-nuh*
karma: *kar´-muh*
Kashi: *kah´-shee*
Kaushika: *kow´-shih-kuh*
krishnapaksha: *krish´-nuh-puk´-shuh*
Lanka: *lahn´-kah*
Manavadharmashastra: *mah´-nuh-vuh-dhar´-muh-sha´-stra*
Manu: *muh´-noo*
Manusmriti: *muh´-noo-smree´-tee*
Meru: *may´-roo*
Mudgala: *mood´-guh-luh*
nakshatra: *nuk´-shuh-truh*
paksha: *puk´-shuh*
Panchasiddhantika: *pahn´-chuh-sih-dahn´-tih-kuh*

Parikshi: *puh-rik´-shee*
pinda: *pin´-duh*
Prajapati: *pruh-jah´-puh-tee*
pravaha: *pruh-vah´-huh*
Punarvasu: *poo´-nar-vuh-soo*
rajas: *rah´-jus*
saman: *sah´-mun*
Sankhya: *sahn´-kyuh*
sattva: *sut-vuh*
Sharaloman: *shuh-ruh-loh´-mun*
shuklapaksha: *shook´-luh-puk´-shuh*
Soma: *soh´-muh*
Sumeru: *soo-may´-roo*
sutra: *soo´-truh*
Svadha: *svuh-dah'*
tamas: *tuh´-mus*
tantra: *tun´-truh*
Vamaka: *vah´-muh-kuh*
Varyovida: *vahr-yo´-vih-duh*
Vasishtha: *vuh-sish´-tuh*
Vayu: *vah´-yoo*
Yama: *yuh´-muh*

MANU

There are many dharma texts (*dharma-shastras*), but the one that was most prominent in ancient India was by the author called Manu. This text was made even more prominent by the British when they ruled India and disastrously attempted to establish their legal codes on the basis of Manu. For Hindus cited Manu's text not as a practical guide (there were local village councils to offer legal advice) but as an ideal system, a philosophy of law. Manu himself was a mythological character said to be the first human being, like Adam (human beings are called *manavas* in derivation from his name). Indeed, the Puranas insist that there is a long chain of Manus, since a new Manu is born every time the world is re-created after the doomsday at the end of the Kali Age ("Puranas," p. 221; "The Four Ages," p. 228). The text that we have was the product of many hands, refining the verses over many centuries, but attributed to Manu.

The *Laws of Manu* (in Sanskrit, the *Manavadharmashastra* or *Manusmriti*, informally known as *Manu*) consists of 2,685 verses on topics as varied—but actually intimately interrelated in Hindu thought—as the social obligations and duties of the various castes and of individuals in different stages of life; the proper way for a just king to rule and to punish transgressors in his kingdom; the appropriate social relations between men and women of different castes, and between husbands and wives in the privacy of the home; birth, death, and taxes; cosmogony, karma, and rebirth; ritual practices; error and restoration or redemption; and such details of everyday life as settling traffic accidents, adjudicating disputes with boatmen, and atoning for sexual improprieties with one's teacher's wife.

The text is, in sum, an encompassing representation of life in the world—how it is, and how it should be lived. Probably composed sometime around the beginning of the Common Era or slightly earlier, *Manu* is a pivotal text of the dominant form of Hinduism as it emerged historically and at least in part in reaction to its religious and ideological predecessors and competitors. More compendiously than any other text, it provides a direct line to the most influential construction of the Hindu religion and Indian society as a whole. No modern study of Hindu family life, psychology, concepts of the body, sex, relationships between humans and animals, attitudes toward money and material possessions, politics, law, caste, purification and pollution, ritual, social practice and ideals, and world renunciation and worldly goals can ignore *Manu*.

TO EAT OR NOT TO EAT MEAT

Among many other subjects, the *dharma-shastras*, like the texts that precede them, wrestle with the question of vegetarianism. At first, Manu reflects the Vedic view of limited retribution for meat eaters in the Other World ("Bhrigu's Journey," p. 101), but then he switches to the Upanishadic view of transmigration ("Transmigration," p. 114) and to vegetarianism, including an expression of sympathy for the suffering of slaughtered animals. In one verse, he seems actually to punish a person for *not* eating meat at the proper time and to encourage people to eat meat—if they follow the rules; but elsewhere he describes meat eating as an addiction that some people cannot give up entirely. Clearly Manu has sympathy for the vegetarian, with his veggie cutlets, though also for the addicted carnivore. But since it is traditional to give the opponent's view first, and then one's own; and since Manu sanctions meat eating in only the first three verses and devotes the rest of his text to vegetarianism, we can assume that his own sympathies are with the vegetarians.

The commentators explain that a person should merely refrain from eating the meat specifically prohibited by the teachings. One verse implies that it is better to eat all sorts of foods except meat (or except certain meats) than to subsist on hermit food alone, and another verse implies that certain worldly activities are permitted under specified circumstances, but that, even then, it is better to refrain from them. Indeed, Manu suggests that it is, perhaps, better to refrain from engagement in life in general (*pravrtti*), which is here, as often, explicitly contrasted with a word that means disengagement (*nivrtti*) from life in general. The acts of engagement, which include all rituals and both moral and immoral acts, prolong worldly existence, either in heaven or in a good rebirth. The acts of disengagement, which include the pursuit of knowledge, meditation, and renunciation, curtail worldly existence and lead to *moksha*. Manu cares deeply for both of these goals.

Laws of Manu 5.27–56

Now I will tell the rule for eating and not eating meat.

You may eat meat that has been consecrated by the sprinkling of water, or when priests[1] want to have it, or when you are properly engaged in a ritual, or when your breath of life is in danger. The Lord of Creatures[2] fashioned all this (universe) to feed the breath of life, and everything moving and stationary is the food of the breath of life. Those that do not move are food for those that move, and those that have no fangs are food for those with fangs; those that have no hands are food for those with hands; and cowards are the food of the brave. The eater who eats creatures with the breath of life who are to be eaten does nothing bad, even if he does it day after day; for the Ordainer himself created creatures with the breath of life, some to be eaten and some to be eaters. 'Eating meat is (right) for the sacrifice': this is traditionally known as a rule of the gods. But doing it on

TRANSLATED BY Wendy Doniger O'Flaherty and Brian K. Smith.

1. That is, Brahmins.
2. A name of the Creator, Prajapati, also called the Ordainer and the Self-existent One. Here, he seems to sanction meat eating in general, while elsewhere he seems to limit it to sacrifices.

occasions other than this is said to be the rule of ogres.[3] Someone who eats meat, after honoring the gods and ancestors, when he has bought it, or killed it himself, or has been given it by someone else, does nothing bad.

A twice-born person[4] who knows the rules should not eat meat against the rules, even in extremity;[5] for if he eats meat against the rules, after his death he will be helplessly eaten by them (that he ate). The guilt of someone who kills wild animals to sell them for money is not so great, after his death, as that of someone who eats meat for no (religious) purpose. But when a man who is properly engaged in a ritual does not eat meat, after his death he will become a sacrificial animal during twenty-one rebirths. A priest should never eat sacrificial animals that have not been transformed by Vedic verses; but with the support of the obligatory rule, he may eat them when they have been transformed by Vedic verses. If he has an addiction (to meat), let him make a sacrificial animal out of clarified butter or let him make a sacrificial animal out of flour; but he should never wish to kill a sacrificial animal for no (religious) purpose.

As many hairs as there are on the body of the sacrificial animal that he kills for no (religious) purpose here on earth, so many times will he, after his death, suffer a violent death in birth after birth. The Self-existent one himself created sacrificial animals for sacrifice; sacrifice is for the good of this whole (universe); and therefore killing in a sacrifice is not killing. Herbs, sacrificial animals, trees, animals (other than sacrificial animals), and birds who have been killed for sacrifice win higher births again. On the occasion of offering the honey-mixture (to a guest), at a sacrifice, and in rituals in which the ancestors are the deities, and only in these circumstances, should sacrificial animals suffer violence, but not on any other occasion; this is what Manu has said.

A twice-born person who knows the true meaning of the Vedas and injures sacrificial animals for these (correct) purposes causes both himself and the animal to go to the highest level of existence.[6] A twice-born person who is self-possessed should never commit violence that is not sanctioned by the Veda, whether he is living in (his own) home, or with a guru, or in the wilderness, not even in extremity. The violence to those that move and those that do not move which is sanctioned by the Veda and regulated by the official restraints—that is known as non-violence,[7] for the law comes from the Veda.

Whoever does violence to harmless creatures out of a wish for his own happiness does not increase his happiness anywhere, neither when he is alive nor when he is dead. But if someone does not desire to inflict on creatures with the breath of life the sufferings of being tied up and slaughtered, but wishes to do what is best for everyone, he experiences pleasure without end. A man who does no violence to anything obtains, effortlessly, what he thinks about, what he does, and what he takes delight in. You can never get

3. The text may be echoing the *Gita*'s division of people into well-behaving godlike people and evil people who are like demons (Asuras, or here, ogres, *rakshasas*) ("Salvation and Damnation," p. 183). But it also may be saying that gods eat meat only during sacrifices, while ogres (*rakshasas*) eat flesh all the time.

4. The first three of the four classes or *varnas*—the Brahmins, Kshatriyas, and Vaishyas—are called twice-born because they are reborn during their initiation, a ritual denied to the fourth class, the Shudras. But Manu often uses the term "twice-born" to refer to Brahmins alone; context suggests the best reading in each case.

5. Extremity (*apad*) is the escape clause of the Shastras, a time of famine or war when *all* the rules are suspended and even cannibalism is allowed.

6. This may be *moksha* or the highest heaven.

7. *Ahimsa*, in contrast with violence, *himsa*.

meat without violence to creatures with the breath of life, and the killing of creatures with the breath of life does not get you to heaven; therefore you should not eat meat. Anyone who looks carefully at the source of meat, and at the tying up and slaughter of embodied creatures, should turn back from eating any meat.

A man who does not behave like the flesh-eating ghouls[8] and does not eat meat becomes dear to people and is not tortured by diseases. The one who gives permission, the one who butchers, the one who slaughters, and the one who buys and sells, the one who prepares it, the one who serves it, and the eater—they are killers. No one is a greater wrong-doer than the person who, without reverence to the gods and the ancestors, wishes to make his flesh grow by the flesh of others. The man who offers a horse-sacrifice every year for a hundred years, and the man who does not eat meat, the two of them reap the same fruit of good deeds. A man who eats pure fruits and roots, or who eats what hermits eat, does not reap fruit (as great as that) of refraining from eating meat. 'He whose *meat* in this world do I eat will in the other world *me eat*.'[9] Wise men say that this is why meat is called meat. There is nothing wrong in eating meat, nor in drinking wine, nor in sexual union, for this is how living beings engage in life, but disengagement yields great fruit.

8. Pishachas, low-ranking demons.
9. Meat is called *mamsa* because he (*sa*) eats me (*mam*) in the other world if I eat him now. A similar pun is made in Vedantic texts on a metaphor for the soul, the swan (*hamsa*), said to express the identity of the individual soul (*atman*) and the world-soul (*brahman*): "I am he" (*aham sa*).

THE DEPENDENCE OF WOMEN

Manu's misogyny is notorious. He is not alone in ancient India in this view, but he takes pains to justify wide-ranging repressive practices against women.

Laws of Manu 9.1–18

I will tell the eternal duties of a man and wife who stay on the path of duty both in union and in separation. Men must make their women dependent day and night, and keep under their own control those who are attached to sensory objects. Her father guards her in childhood, her husband guards her in youth, and her sons guard her in old age. A woman is not fit for independence.[1] A father who does not give her away at the proper time[2] should be blamed, and a husband who does not have sex with her at the proper time should be blamed; and the son who does not guard his mother when her husband is dead should be blamed.

Translated by Wendy Doniger O'Flaherty and Brian K. Smith.

1. This idea evidently appeals to Manu; he expresses it, in slightly different words, at 5.148 as well.
2. The "proper time" to have intercourse is during a woman's fertile season, the days immediately after she has finished menstruating and taken a ritual bath to purify herself.

Women should especially be guarded against addictions, even trifling ones, for unguarded (women) would bring sorrow upon both families. Regarding this as the supreme duty of all the classes, husbands, even weak ones, try to guard their wives. For by zealously guarding his wife he guards his own descendants, practices, family, and himself, as well as his own duty. The husband enters the wife, becomes an embryo, and is born here on earth. That is why a wife is called a wife (*jaya*), because he is born (*jayate*) again in her.[3] The wife brings forth a son who is just like the man she makes love with;[4] that is why he should guard his wife zealously, in order to keep his progeny clean.

No man is able to guard women entirely by force, but they can be entirely guarded by using these means: he should keep her busy amassing and spending money, engaging in purification, attending to her duty, cooking food, and looking after the furniture. Women are not guarded when they are confined in a house by men who can be trusted to do their jobs well; but women who guard themselves by themselves are well guarded. Drinking, associating with bad people, being separated from their husbands, wandering about, sleeping,[5] and living in other people's houses are the six things that corrupt women. Good looks do not matter to them, nor do they care about youth; 'A man!' they say, and enjoy sex with him, whether he is good-looking or ugly. By running after men like whores, by their fickle minds, and by their natural lack of affection these women are unfaithful to their husbands even when they are zealously guarded here. Knowing that their very own nature is like this, as it was born at the creation by the Lord of Creatures, a man should make the utmost effort to guard them. The bed and the seat, jewellery, lust, anger, crookedness, a malicious nature, and bad conduct are what Manu assigned to women.[6] There is no ritual with Vedic verses for women; this is a firmly established point of law.[7] For women, who have no virile strength and no Vedic verses, are falsehood; this is well established.

3. This is an old saying, that can be traced back to the Brahmanas (*Aitareya Brahmana* 7.13.6).
4. Some commentaries interpret the verb "make love" (*bhaj*) as a reference to the physical act of sexual intercourse; some take it as an indication that the woman's heart must be given to the man at the moment of union for the child to resemble him.
5. By "sleeping," the commentaries specify sleeping at the wrong time, too much, or in the day; one might also add, in the wrong place.
6. Manu is not merely the primeval lawgiver but also the son of the Lord of Creatures, and hence a creator himself. He thus "assigns" these qualities to women in both capacities: making them originally, and recognizing them in his laws.
7. This means that this opinion is sanctioned by a Vedic source, such as *Taittiriya Samhita* 6.5.8.2, which closely resembles this verse.

RETRIBUTION IN REBIRTH

Manu interweaves the problem of killing and eating with the theme of rebirth in various classes of creatures, and the animals that are the problem are also the solution: various crimes, some having nothing to do with animals, are punished by animals. Thus an adulterous women is to be paraded on a donkey and reborn as a jackal, and thieves are to be trampled to death by elephants, while cow killing and various other misdemeanors may be atoned for by keeping cows company and refraining from reporting them when they pilfer food and water (8.370–71, 9.30,

8.34, 11.109–15). The distinction between good and bad people is further interwoven into the discussion of rebirth as animals.

Along the route of transmigration, we encounter various sorts of creatures: gnomes (Guhyakas), the servants of Kubera, the god of wealth; anti-gods, Daityas, the sons of Diti; the Amenables (Sadhyas), auspicious inhabitants of heaven; ghosts (Pretas), also designating dead spirits or dead bodies; and priest-ogres (Brahma-Rakshasas), a particular kind of ogre—for ogres have castes and classes just like everyone else.

The human body undergoes various transformations in death: first it dissolves into the five elements of which it is constituted (earth, water, air, fire, and ether) (12.21)—indeed, a common euphemism for death is "to dissolve back into the five elements"—in order for the transmigrating soul to take on a special, indestructible body to be tortured when the dead person goes to Hell, where Yama rules. But then another body is made of the five elements, this time a body to enjoy heaven. And after that the dying person may enter any one of a number of human or animal bodies, depending on how s/he has lived.

Laws of Manu 12.16–81

After the death of men who have done bad deeds, another solid body, designed to be tortured, is born out of the five elements. When (the living souls) here have suffered with that body the tortures given by Yama, (the bodies) dissolve, each part distributed into its own basic element. And after he has suffered for the faults that are born of attachment to the sensory objects and that result in unhappiness, his stains are erased and he approaches the two who have great energy.[1] Those two together tirelessly watch his religious merit and his evil, for it is through being thoroughly intermingled with that pair[2] that he attains happiness or unhappiness here on earth and after death. If he mostly does right and only a little wrong, he is enveloped in those very elements and experiences happiness in heaven. But if he mostly indulges in wrong and only a little in right,[3] he is abandoned by those elements and experiences the tortures given by Yama. And after the living soul has suffered the tortures given by Yama and his stains are erased, he enters those same five elements again, each part distributed (into its own element). Seeing with his very own intellect these levels of existence of the living soul that result from right and from wrong, a man should always set his mind-and-heart on what is right.

Know that lucidity, energy, and darkness[4] are the three qualities of the self, through which the great one pervades and endures in all these existences, without exception. Whenever one of these qualities entirely prevails in a body, it makes the particular quality predominant in the embodied (soul). Lucidity is traditionally regarded as knowledge, darkness as ignorance, and energy as passion and hate; this is their form, that enters and pervades all living beings. Among these (three), a person should recognize

TRANSLATED BY Wendy Doniger O'Flaherty and Brian K. Smith.

1. "He" is the individual soul. The "two who have great energy" are probably the highest consciousness and the world-soul (*brahman*) or the individual soul (*atman*) and the world-soul.
2. The pair are almost certainly the dead man's religious merit (dharma) and evil.
3. "Right" and "wrong" here translate dharma and *adharma*.
4. Lucidity or goodness (*sattva*), energy or passion (*rajas*), and darkness or torpor (*tamas*), the three qualities (*gunas*) of matter, according to Sankhya philosophy, are here also regarded as the qualities of the self ("The Two Paths," p. 178).

as lucidity whatever he perceives in his self as full of joy, something of pure light which seems to be entirely at peace. But he should recognize as energy whatever is full of unhappiness and gives his self no joy, something which is hard to oppose and constantly seduces embodied creatures. And he should recognize as darkness whatever is full of confusion, undifferentiated, whatever is sensual and cannot be understood through reason or intelligence.

Now I will also explain, leaving nothing out, the highest, middle, and hindmost fruits that result from these three qualities.

The recitation of the Veda, inner heat, knowledge, purification, suppression of the sensory powers, the rites of duty, and meditation on the soul are the mark of the quality of goodness. Delight in enterprises, instability, persistence in doing what should not be done, and continual indulgence in the sensory objects are the mark of the quality of energy. Greed, sleep, incontinence, cruelty, atheism, losing jobs, habitually asking for hand-outs, and carelessness are the mark of the quality of darkness.

The following should be regarded as the marks of the qualities in a nutshell, in order, as each of these three qualities occurs in the three (time periods).

When someone who has done, or is doing, or is going to do an act feels ashamed, a learned man should realize that that whole act has the mark of the quality of darkness. When someone hopes to achieve great fame in this world by a certain act, but does not feel sorry if it fails, that should be known as (an act with the quality of) energy. But when he longs with his all to know something and is not ashamed when he does it, and his self is satisfied by it, that (act) has the mark of the quality of lucidity. Pleasure is the mark of darkness, profit is said to be the mark of energy, and religion the mark of lucidity, and each is better than the one before it.[5]

Now I will tell you, in a nutshell and in order, the transmigrations in this whole (universe) that one achieves by each of these qualities: people of lucidity become gods, people of energy become humans, and people of darkness always become animals; this is the three-fold level of existence. But it should be realized that this three-fold level of existence, which is dependent on the qualities, is itself three-fold: lowest, middle, and highest, according to the specific act and learning (of the actor).

Stationary objects, worms and bugs, fish, snakes, turtles, livestock, and wild animals are the hindmost level of existence to which darkness leads. Elephants, horses, servants, despised barbarians, lions, tigers, and boars are the middle level of existence to which darkness leads. Strolling actors, birds, deceiving men, ogres, and ghouls are the highest level of existence to which darkness leads.

Pugilists, wrestlers, dancers, arms-dealers, and addicted gamblers and drunks are the lowest level of existence to which energy leads. Kings, rulers, the personal priests of kings, and those obsessed with the battle of words are the middle level of existence to which energy leads. Centaurs, gnomes, genies, servants of the gods, and celestial nymphs are the whole of the highest level of existence to which energy leads.

5. The three human goals (*purusarthas*: pleasure [*kama*], profit [*artha*], and religion [dharma]) ("The Brahmins Explain Everything in the Shastras," p. 200) are thus correlated with the three qualities.

Ascetics, renouncers, priests, the hosts of gods who fly about on celestial chariots, the constellations, and the anti-gods are the first level of existence to which lucidity leads. Sacrificers, sages, gods, the Vedas, the celestial lights, the years, the ancestors, and the Amenables are the second level of existence to which lucidity leads. Wise men say that Brahma, the creators of the whole universe, religion, the great one, and the unmanifest are the highest level of existence to which lucidity leads.

All that results from the three sorts of action has thus been explained, the entire system of transmigration for all living beings, which is divided into three types, each of which is further subdivided into three. Because of their addiction to their sensory powers and their failure to uphold religion, the worst of men, who have learned nothing, undergo evil transmigrations. Learn, now, in full and in order, what particular womb this living soul enters in this world as a result of each particular action here.

Those who commit major crimes spend a great many years in terrible hells, and when that is over they experience the following transmigrations:

A priest-killer gets the womb of a dog, a pig, a donkey, a camel, a cow, a goat, a sheep, a wild animal, a bird, a 'Fierce' Untouchable, or a 'Tribal.' A priest who drinks liquor enters (the womb) of a worm, bug, or moth, of birds who eat excrement, and of violent creatures. A priest who is a thief (is reborn) thousands of times in spiders, snakes, and lizards, aquatic animals, and violent ghouls. A man who violates his guru's marriage-bed (is reborn) hundreds of times in grasses, shrubs, and vines, in (beasts) that are carnivorous or that have fangs, and (in people) who engage in cruel actions. Violent men become carnivorous (beasts); people who eat impure things become worms; thieves (become animals that) devour one another; and men who have sex with women of the lowest castes become ghosts. A man who has associated with fallen men or has had sex with the wife of another man or has stolen the property of a priest becomes a priest-ogre. A man who out of greed has stolen jewels, pearls, or coral, or the various gems, is born among goldsmiths.

For stealing grain, a man becomes a rat; for brass, a goose; for water, an aquatic bird; for honey, a stinging insect; for milk, a crow; for spices, a dog; for clarified butter, a mongoose; for meat, a vulture; for marrow, a cormorant; for sesame oil, an 'oil-drinker';[6] for salt, a cricket; and for yogurt, a crane; for stealing silk, a partridge; for linen, a frog; for cotton cloth, a curlew; for a cow, an iguana; for molasses, a bat; for fine perfumes, a muskrat; for leafy vegetables, a peacock; for various kinds of cooked foods, a porcupine, and for uncooked food, a hedgehog. For stealing fire he becomes a heron; for household articles, a house-builder wasp; for stealing dyed clothes, he becomes a pheasant; for a deer or an elephant, a wolf; for a horse, a tiger; for fruit and roots, a monkey; for a woman, a bear; for water, a sparrow; for vehicles, a camel; for livestock, a goat.

Whenever a man has forcibly taken away another man's property, or has eaten an oblation when it has not been offered into the fire, he inevitably becomes an animal. Women, too, who steal in this way incur guilt; they become the wives of those very same creatures. But those classes who slip from their own innate activites when they are not in extremity pass through evil transmigrations and then became the menial servants of aliens.[7] A priest

6. The "oil-drinker" may be a cockroach.
7. These are the Dasyus, who may be a particular ethnic group, or barbarians, or bandits.

who has slipped from his own duty becomes a 'comet-mouth' ghost who eats vomit; a ruler becomes a 'false-stinking' ghost who eats impure things and corpses. A commoner who has slipped from his own duty becomes a ghost 'who sees by an eye in his anus,' eating pus; a servant becomes a 'moth-eater' (ghost).

The more that sensual men indulge in the sensory objects, the more their weakness for them grows. Through the repetition of their evil actions, men of little intelligence experience miseries in womb after womb in this world: they are rolled about in dreaded hells like the hell of 'Darkness,' and are tied up and chopped up in hells like the 'Forest of Sword Leaves'; they suffer various tortures; they are eaten by crows and owls, burnt by scorching sand, and boiled in pots, which is horrible; they are reborn in bad wombs, which causes constant and overwhelming unhappiness, and are assailed with cold and heat and various terrors; over and over they dwell in wombs and undergo birth, which is horrible; wretched chains are theirs, and they are the menial servants of other men; they are separated from their relatives and dear ones and live with bad people; they make money and lose it, and they make friends and enemies; then comes old age, that cannot be held back, and the suffering brought by diseases, and various troubles; and finally death, that cannot be conquered. But a man reaps the appropriate fruit of any act in a body that has the qualities of the frame of mind in which he committed that act.[8]

8. That is, if he commits an act when his disposition is predominantly characterized by lucidity, he will be reborn in the body of a god, and so forth.

CHARAKA, HIRANYAKESHIN, AND VARAHAMIHIRA

The Shastras aim not at innovation but at consolidation. The spirit of the Shastras is totalizing and cosmopolitan, an attempt to bring together in one place, from all points in India and all levels of society, a complete knowledge of the subject in question. Totality was the goal of the encyclopedic range both of the subject covered in each text (everything you ever wanted to know about *x*) and of the span of subjects, including grammar, architecture, medicine, dancing and acting, aesthetics in fine art, music, astronomy and astrology, training horses and elephants, various aspects of natural science, and in particular mathematics. The following selections deal with medicine, funeral rituals, and astronomy/astrology.

THE ETIOLOGY OF DISEASES

Medicine is known in India as the science of long life (*ayur-veda*). Since the goal of many Hindu texts was to prolong and perfect the human life span (a goal not inconsistent with the ultimate goal of renouncing the rebirth of the body altogether), and since the moral and physical aspects of life were regarded as inextricably intertwined, medicine is a sacred science, a part of religion. The oldest medical text is that of Charaka, who may have lived in the first century C.E., though his text, the *Charaka Samhita*, may have been re-edited and supplemented as late as 800 C.E.

This passage from Charaka is typical of the way that all of the shastras strive to be open-minded and inclusive. Despite the equal time that this passage gives to various approaches, several of which represent major philosophical as well as medical traditions, there is, as always, hierarchy: not only is the final sage right, and the others presumably wrong, but he even has a retort ready in case they still do not grant that he is right ("It is hard to get to the truth when people take sides"). Yet since they do still refuse to give in to him, the subject remains open after all.

Charaka Samhita 1.1.15.3–34

Once upon a time, when all the great sages had assembled before lord Punarvasu, who was dharma incarnate, this dispute arose in order to determine the primordial origin both of this creature called the person—who is a mass of soul, senses, mind, and sense objects—and of his diseases. Then Vamaka, the king of Kashi,[1] who understood the subject, approached the assembly of sages, greeted them, and uttered this speech: 'Good sirs, is the origin of the person also thought to be the origin of diseases, or not?' When the king had said this, Punarvasu said to the sages, 'Every one of you has dispelled all doubts through your unlimited knowledge and understanding. You should dispel the doubt of the king of Kashi.'

Parikshi, the son of Mudgala, thought about this and said, 'The individual person is born from the Soul, and so the diseases are also born from the Soul; this is their cause. (The Soul) collects and enjoys karma and the fruits of karma. Happiness (health) and unhappiness (disease) cannot function without this seat of all consciousness.'

But Sharaloman said, 'No. The soul never by itself yokes the soul with diseases or other unhappinesses, for it hates unhappiness. But when the mind that is conscious of goodness (*sattva*) is overwhelmed by energy and darkness (*rajas* and *tamas*), then it causes the origin both of the body itself and of pathological changes in the body.'

Varyovida, however, said, 'No. The mind alone cannot be the cause. Neither the diseases of the body nor one's state of mind can exist without the body. But all creatures are born from *rasa* (the fluid essence of digested food), and so the various diseases are also born from *rasa*. And since the waters abound in *rasa*, they are said to be the causes of origins.'

But Hiranyaksha said, 'No. The soul is not regarded as born from *rasa*, nor is the mind, that is beyond perception by the senses. But there are diseases caused by sound and so forth. Indeed, the individual person is born of the six elements of matter (earth, water, fire, wind, space and mind or soul), and so diseases are also born from the six elements. That the person is a mass of the six elements is well known from the Sankhya school of philosophers, among others.'

But as he said this, Kaushika said, 'No. How could someone be born out of the six elements, without a mother and a father? A person is born from a person; a cow from a cow, and a horse from a horse. Diseases such as urinary disorders are known to be hereditary. So the two parents are the cause.'

Translated by Wendy Doniger O'Flaherty.

1. Varanasi (Benares).

'No,' said Bhadrakapya. 'For a blind person is not born from a blind person. And how could you explain the primordial origin of the first mother and father? But a creature is known to be born of his karma, and so diseases are also born from karma. Neither a person nor diseases are born without karma.'

But Bharadvaja said, 'No. An agent must always precede an action (karma). And no person can be the result of an action that has not been done; this is clear enough. No, nature is the cause, one's own nature, the cause of both diseases and the person, just as it is the nature of earth to be rough, water to be fluid, wind to move, and fire to be hot.'

But Kankayana said, 'No. If this were so, there would be no fruits of individual efforts. Success or failure would simply result from the very nature of creatures. Prajapati, the child of Brahma, had an unlimited imagination, and it was he who created the happiness and unhappiness of this universe, sentient and insentient.'

'No,' said Bhikshu Atreya. 'Prajapati constantly wished for the welfare of his offspring, and so he would never yoke them with miseries as if he were not a good man. No, the individual person is born of time, and diseases are born of time. The whole universe is in the power of time; time is the cause of everything.'

Now, as the sages were arguing in this way, Punarvasu said, 'Don't talk like this. It is hard to get to the truth when people take sides. People who utter arguments and counter-arguments as if they were established facts never get to the end of their own side, as if they were going round and round on an oil press. Get rid of this collision of opinions and think about the heart of the matter. Not until you shake off the darkness of factionalism from what you want to know will true knowledge emerge. The same factors that give birth to man when they are working in harmony give rise to the various diseases when they are in disharmony.'

When he heard Punarvasu say this, Vamaka the king of Kashi asked him again, 'Sir, what *is* the cause of the growth of a person who is born of harmonious causes and of the diseases that are born from disharmonious causes?' Punarvasu said to him, 'The use of good food is one cause of the growth of a person, and the use of bad food is a cause of diseases.' As Punarvasu said this, Agnivesha said to him, 'Good sir, how can we recognise, without fear of contradiction, the signs that distinguish the sorts of food that are good and bad? For we find that contrary effects result from the foods regarded as good and the foods regarded as bad, as a result of variations in the amount, time, method of use, geographical area, constitution of the body, condition of the humors, and age of the individual.'

Punarvasu said to him, 'Agnivesha, the foods that maintain the elements of the body in balance according to nature, and that even out their disequilibrum—consider these to be good foods. The opposite kind are bad foods. This is an irrefutable way to distinguish between good and bad foods.' When he said this, Agnivesha replied, 'Sir, physicians have an abundance of different opinions. Not all of them will understand this sort of teaching . . .'

HOW TO PERFORM A FUNERAL

The *Grihya Sutras*, or "Household Aphorisms" (a *sutra*, literally "thread," is a pithy aphorism that states a principle or rule), are the texts of the household (*griha*). Some of them may have been composed as early as 300 B.C.E., though the one here, attributed to Hiranyakeshin, one of the ancient sages and law-makers, is not one of the oldest. These texts laid down the rules for domestic rituals or sacrifices ("daily rites" such as kindling the domestic fire); life-cycle rituals ("occasional rites" at birth, initiation, marriage, and death); and codes of acceptable behavior and ritual purity. They regulated and normalized domestic life, bringing about the penetration of ritual regulation into the daily life of the household on a scale not seen before. On the one hand, this brought greater power to householders who now had many rituals that they could perform without the help of a Brahmin; on the other hand, it extended Brahmin power, through the codification of texts about householders' rituals that had not previously been regulated by Brahmins, and some of the Vedic rituals that had previously been performed by all of the twice-born classes now could be performed only by Brahmins. The earlier *Shrauta Sutras* ("Aphorisms of the Veda [*shruti*]") had made mandatory large-scale ritual performances, in some of which (such as the horse sacrifice) the sacrificer's wife had to be present, and even to speak—though not to speak Vedic mantras. But the *Grihya Sutra*s that regulated daily practices in the home required the more active participation of the sacrificer's wife and other members of the household. Much of this new literature on religious and social law may have been designed to incorporate newcomers or social groups into a ranking system, or to accommodate local power relations.

The funeral ritual, or *shraddha*, is performed not only at the time of death but every month, and then every year, to continue to nourish the spirit of the departed ancestor; balls of rice (*pindas*) and water are offered to them ("Arjuna Questions Krishna," p. 167). The belief is that without this food, the ancestors would be bogged down in the world of the ancestors, as a species of ghost, and never be able to progress either to rebirth or to final liberation. This text cites several Rig Vedic funeral verses (from "The Funeral Fire," p. 84, "Burial Hymn," p. 86, and others) that address several different people: the mourners, the dead man, and the god of fire. The verses also invoke several Vedic gods, obliquely: Soma, god of the Soma plant and Soma drink; Agni, god of fire; Yama, god of the dead; and Vayu, the wind. Hiranyakeshin, however, addresses only the descendants who are to perform the ritual. His text closes with a statement that many texts include: if you cannot get a particular ingredient of the ritual, use a substitute. In this case, the substitution is particularly significant: vegetables in place of meat, killing plants instead of animals.

Hiranyakeshin-Grihya-Sutra 20.4.1–26

(Perform) the monthly (funeral ritual) on the day of the new moon, in the afternoon, or on the odd-numbered days of the dark fortnight. Prepare food for the ancestors and make seats by arranging blades of *darbha* grass[1] pointing south; then invite an odd number of Brahmins who are pure, who know the (Rig Vedic) mantras, who have all their limbs intact, and who are not related to you by their mother, by their male ancestral line, or by having

TRANSLATED BY Wendy Doniger O'Flaherty.

1. Also called Kusha or Munja, or panic grass, it belongs to the genus *Borage*. It is found in damp, marshy, low-lying areas, grows to a height of about two feet, and is pointed at the top, sharp enough to cut through skin. Brahmins use it for purification in all Vedic ceremonies.

learnt the Vedas with you. Feed them without any regard for your own advantage.

Put fuel on the fire and scatter all around it blades of *darbha* grass pointing south and east; then prepare the clarified butter in a special pot for clarifying butter, a pot in which there is a single filter. Sprinkle water around the fire from right to left, and put a piece of fig-tree wood on it for kindling; then offer the oblation with a special spoon made of fig-tree wood. Perform the ritual that ends with the offering of the clarified butter; place your sacred thread over your right shoulder; then summon your ancestors with this verse: 'Come here, fathers, fond of Soma, on your hidden, ancient paths; bring us progeny, wealth, and a long life-span, one that lasts for a hundred autumns.'

Then sprinkle water in the same (southern) direction, while reciting this verse: 'Divine waters, send Agni forth. Let our ancestors take pleasure in this sacrifice. Let them enjoy their monthly nourishment and refreshment and give us wealth and (sons who are) all heroic.' Then put your sacred thread over the left shoulder and perform the ritual that ends with the utterance of the names of the seven worlds; put your sacred thread back on your right shoulder and offer the oblation while reciting these verses: 'Svadha! This drink and all honor to Soma with the ancestors! This drink and all honor to Yama with the Angiras sages[2] and the ancestors! The waters that arise in the east, and those that arise in the north—by means of these waters, that support the entire universe, I place someone else between (myself and my) father. This drink and all honor! I place someone else between (myself and) my grandfather by means of the mountains; by means of the great earth; by means of the sky and the quarters of space; by means of infinite nourishments. This drink and all honor! I place someone else between (myself and) my great-grandfather by means of the seasons; by means of days and nights with beautiful twilights; by means of the half-months and the months. This drink and all honor!'

Then offer the oblation with their names: 'This drink and all honor to so-and-so! This drink and all honor to so-and-so! Whatever sexual misdeameanor my mother has committed, lustfully violating her vows of chastity—let my father take that semen as his own; let the other man who is present go away. This drink and all honor!' And in the same way, make a second and third oblation, altering the verse to say, 'Whatever my grandmother . . . ,' 'Whatever my great-grandmother . . .'

(Recite the Rig Vedic verses), 'The ancestors that are here, and those that are not here, those that we know and those that we do not know: Agni, you know them, if you are the knower of all creatures; let them rejoice in what is eaten with this sacrificial drink. This drink and all honor! Whatever limb of yours (addressing the dead man) the flesh-eating fire, the knower of all creatures, has burnt up while leading you to the worlds (of the ancestors)—I restore that limb to you again. Arise, uninjured, with all your limbs, O ancestors! This drink and all honor! Carry the clarified butter, Agni, knower of creatures, to the fathers where you know they are resting, far away. Let streams of butter flow to them; let all their wishes come true, and all their desires be fulfilled. This drink and all honor!'

And in the same way, make a second and third oblation, altering the verse to say, 'Carry the butter to the grandfathers . . . ,' '. . . to the great-

2. A family of famous Vedic sages.

grandfathers . . .' And in the same way, make an oblation of food, altering the verse to say, 'Carry the food . . .'

Then offer the oblation of the 'successful sacrifice,' saying, 'This drink and all honor to Agni who carries the oblation of food and makes a successful sacrifice!' Then touch the food and say, 'The earth is your pot; the sky is its lid. I offer you as an oblation into the mouth of the Brahmin. I offer you as an oblation into the upward breath and outward breath of the Brahmins. You are unperishing; do not perish for the fathers over there, in the world beyond. The earth is just right; Agni watches over it so that there will be no careless errors in what is given.

'The earth is your pot; the sky is its lid. I offer you as an oblation into the mouth of the Brahmin. I offer you as an oblation into the upward breath and outward breath of the Brahmins. You are unperishing; do not perish for the grandfathers over there, in the world beyond. The middle realm of space is just right; Vayu, the wind, watches over it so that there will be no careless errors in what is given.

'The earth is your pot; the sky is its lid. I offer you as an oblation into the mouth of the Brahmin. I offer you as an oblation into the upward breath and outward breath of the Brahmins. You are unperishing; do not perish for the great-grandfathers over there, in the world beyond. The sky is just right; the sun watches over it so that there will be no careless errors in what is given.'

Then have the Brahmins touch the food while you say, 'I enter into the vital breath as I offer the oblation of ambrosial Soma.' Watch over them while they are eating, and say, 'My soul is in ultimate reality for the sake of immortality.' When they have eaten (and are leaving), follow after them and ask their permission for (you to make use of) their leftovers. Then take a water-pot and a fistful of *darbha* grass and go to a place midway between the south and the east; spread the *darbha* grass out with points to the south, hold your hands palms down, and pour out three handfuls of water, ending towards the south, while saying, 'Let the fathers, fond of Soma, wipe themselves! Let the grandfathers, fond of Soma, wipe themselves! Let the great-grandfathers, fond of Soma, wipe themselves!' And then, 'So-and-so, wash yourself!' 'So-and-so, wash yourself!'

Then turn your hands palms down and put down on those grasses three balls of rice (*pindas*), ending in the south; give the ball to your father, saying, 'This is for you, father'; give the ball to your grandfather, saying, 'This is for you, grandfather'; give the ball to your great-grandfather, saying, 'This is for you, great-grandfather.' You may give a fourth ball, in silence; but this is optional.

Now, if you don't know the names (of your ancestors), just give the ball to your father and say, 'This drink to the ancestors who dwell on the earth'; give the ball to your grandfather and say, 'This drink to the ancestors who dwell in the middle realm of space'; and give the ball to your great-grandfather and say, 'This drink to the ancestors who dwell in the sky.' And give, with each respective ball, collyrium, some other ointment, and a garment. When you give the collyrium, say, three times, 'So-and-so, anoint your eyes!' 'So-and-so, anoint your eyes!' When you give the other ointment, say three times, 'So-and-so, anoint yourself!' 'So-and-so, anoint yourself!' (When you give the garments, say,) 'These garments are for you, O ancestors. Do not grab anything else of ours.' Then tear off a piece of cloth or a wisp of wool and put that down, if you are in the first half of your life; tear out some of the hair on your own body if you are in the last half of your life.

Wash the pot and sprinkle that water all around, from right to left, while saying this verse: 'These honeyed waters, that refresh sons and grandsons, that milk themselves of the sacrificial drink and Soma for the ancestors, these divine waters that refresh both (the living and the dead), these rivers full of water, full of semen, with good places to cross over—let them flow up to you in that world beyond!' Then turn the pot upside down, and cross your hands so that the right hand is the left hand and the left hand is the right hand, and honor (your ancestors) with the words of greeting: 'I bow to you, my ancestors, for the sap.'

Then go to the brink of some body of water and pour out three handfuls of water and say, 'This is for you, father, this flowing wave of honey. As great as Agni is, and as great as the earth is, so great is its measure, so great is its power. I give this, that has become so great. And as Agni is unperishing and inexhaustible, may this drink be unperishing and inexhaustible for my father. So-and-so, live on that unperishing drink together with those (other ancestors). The verses (*rig*) are your power.

'This is for you, grandfather, this flowing wave of honey. As great as Vayu, the wind, is, and as great as the middle realm of space is, so great is its measure, so great is its power. I give this, that has become so great. And as Vayu is unperishing and inexhaustible, may this drink be unperishing and inexhaustible for my grandfather. So-and-so, live on that unperishing drink together with those (other ancestors). The formulas (*yajur*) are your power.

'This is for you, great-grandfather, this flowing wave of honey. As great as the sun is, and as great as heaven is, so great is its measure, so great is its power. I give this, that has become so great. And as the sun is unperishing and inexhaustible, may this drink be unperishing and inexhaustible for my great-grandfather. So-and-so, live on that unperishing drink together with those (other ancestors). The chants (*saman*) are your power.'

Then come back and pour out whatever is left in the water-pot, saying, 'Go away, my ancestors, fond of Soma, on your hidden, ancient paths. After a month, come back again to our house to eat our offerings—come back with good progeny, good heroic sons.'

That is the description of the funeral sacrifice that is performed in the middle of the rainy season. In that ritual, offerings of flesh are prescribed; but if there is no flesh, you can use vegetables.

HOW TO READ THE STARS

Astronomy was an important science in India, needed to set the calendars and times for both practical and religious tasks. Great attention was paid to the movements of the sun and the moon, as well as the constellations (*nakshatras*) and planets, and accurate mathematical calculations were made, using the fixed stars as background.

Varahamihira was a Maga Brahmin, which is to say a descendant of one of the Persian Zoroastrians who entered India toward the beginning of the Common Era. Born in Ujjain, an ancient city in western Malwa, in Central India, he lived from

505 to 587 C.E. He was a philosopher, an astronomer, and a mathematician, and his *Panchasiddhantika* ("Five Treatises") is a compendium of Greek, Egyptian, Roman, and Indian astronomy and astrology. This monumental work progresses through Indian and Western astronomy, uses calculations based on Greek and Alexandrian science, and gives complete Ptolemaic mathematical charts and tables.

Varahamihira's *Panchasiddhantika 1.1–2, 5–7; 13.1–12; 13.37–42*

Revering in the beginning with devotion the various leaders of the sages, beginning with the Sun and Vasishtha,[1] and my father and teacher by whom I was instructed in this science; whatever is the best, easy, accurate correction (*bija*) according to the opinions of the former teachers, that secret in its entirety I shall attempt to tell here.

* * *

Whatever is the highest secret where the minds of the authors of tantras[2] are perplexed, that—the eclipse of the Sun—I will explain in this (work), putting aside envy.

In it (in this work) are (the rules for computing) the direction, duration, totality, hypotenuse, magnitudes, and times (of solar eclipses), the occurrence or non-occurrence of lunar eclipses, the conjunctions of stars and planets, and the computation of longitudinal differences.

* * *

The sphere of the earth, which consists of the five elements, stands in the cage of the constellations in the sky like a round piece of iron standing at the end of a loadstone.

It is all covered by trees, mountains, towns, parks, rivers, oceans, and so on. In the middle of it is Sumeru,[3] the abode of the wise (gods); the Daityas[4] stand below.

As the reflection of those who sit on the shore of (a body of) water is seen to be facing downwards, so the motion of the Asuras (appears to the gods); and they (the Asuras) think that the wise (gods) are below.

As here among men the flame of a fire ascends to the sky and something heavy when thrown descends to the earth, so (does it happen) below among the Asuras.

Directly above Meru in the sky is (one) fixed pole, below in the sky is another; bound to these the constellations are turned around by the *pravaha*[5] wind.

Others say: "The earth, as if situated on a potter's wheel (*bhrama*), revolves, not the constellations." If that were so, hawks and so on would not come back again to their abodes from the sky.

TRANSLATED BY Otto Edward Neugebauer and David Pingree.

1. Not the Vedic sage of that name, but the author of a famous astronomical treatise that Varahamihira says is the most accurate of the five Indian treatises on which he based his own.
2. Esoteric Sanskrit texts ("Sects and Sex in the Tantras," p. 275).
3. Another name for Meru, the mountain at the center of the earth.
4. Like Asuras, Daityas are anti-gods or demons, the sons of the goddess Diti ("Limit"), said to live below the earth.
5. One of seven winds said to cause the motion of the planets.

Another thing: if there were (a revolution) of the earth (every) day, bees, geese, flags, and so on would always be driven to the west; if it were moving slowly, how would it revolve (once a day)?

According to what is said by the Arhats,[6] there are two Suns and two Moons which rise one after the other; if this were so, why does a fixed mark from the *sutra* (measuring line) of the Sun revolve in a day?

For the gods, the rising Sun at the beginning of Aries, moving on the terrestrial equator, revolves to the right; (for those) at Lanka[7] it revolves overhead; and for the foes of the gods in the opposite direction.

At the end of Gemini the Sun revolves, going up 24° from the terrestrial equator for the gods, (while) it is directly overhead (for those) at Avanti.[8]

Thus the (noon) shadow is destroyed (there); the (noon) shadow is to the north for those dwelling in the north of that (place); for those places which are to the south of it the shadow at noon is southern.

Reverence be to those who say: "For the wise (gods) who dwell on Meru it is day when the Sun is in Aries, Taurus, and Gemini, night when it is in Cancer and so on."

* * *

Every day, because of the change in its position from the Sun (since conjunction), there is an increase in the illuminated portion of the Moon just as there is on the western part of the pot in the afternoon;

(this is) from after the *krishnapaksha*,[9] but the dark (portion increases) from after the *shuklapaksha*. Those who dwell on the Moon see the Sun for half a *paksha* on either side of the disappearance of the Moon; otherwise there is no light.

Above the Moon are Mercury, Venus, the Sun, Mars, Jupiter, Saturn, and then the *nakshatras*. All the planets, moving in their own orbits, travel to the east with the same velocity.

As the interstices of the spokes of the wheel of an oil-press are small at the hub but large at the rim, so are the interstices of the zodiacal signs (as one goes) higher.

The Moon, which is (furthest) below the orbit of the *nakshatras*, revolves fast about its small (orbit); Saturn, which is high(est), travels with an equal velocity around its large (orbit).

(Ascending) up from the Moon (each successive planet) is lord of the month, (descending) down from Saturn lord of the hour. (Ascending) up in order (every) fifth (planet) is lord of the day; the lords of the year are clear.

6. Jain sages and saints.
7. Lanka may be, at this time, the island now known as Sri Lanka, i.e., a place in the South, though earlier it was known by other names.
8. A kingdom originally part of Malwa, the home of Varahamihira; it is now part of Madhya Pradesh.
9. The *shuklapaksha* ("bright wing") is the waxing half of the month; the *krishnapaksha* ("dark wing") the waning half.

The Synthesis of Hinduism
400–1200 C.E.

Beginning in the fourth century C.E., the Sanskrit texts known as Puranas began to be composed. The Puranas cover everything from the duration of almost infinite cosmic ages to the most trivial concerns of daily life; often they disguise innovations as traditions. From about the tenth century C.E., Sanskrit Puranas began to present the religious sentiment of *bhakti*, a passionate, intimate devotion to a deity, which resulted from a synthesis of North Indian and South Indian cultural forms, active interaction between several religious movements, and powerful political patronage of religion. Well into the early modern period, Puranas continued to be composed, both in Sanskrit and, eventually, in vernacular languages.

In tandem with the Puranas, the esoteric texts known as Tantras developed. Several Puranas contain what might be considered proto-Tantric myths and rituals, not yet part of the formal Tantric system but containing tell-tale Tantric elements, such as the worship of the Goddess, initiation, group worship, secrecy, and transgressive behavior, particularly sexual rituals and the ingesting of bodily fluids. Buddhism and Hinduism once again, as in the Upanishadic period, share a number of features, in this case certain rituals and images. Tantra probably began in the northern fringes of India, Kashmir, Nepal, Bengal, and Assam (places where

The temple, carved down from ground level, representing Mount Kailasa, the home of the god Shiva, at Ellora, mid eighth century.

Buddhism, too, flourished), but it soon took hold in central and South India. Something in the social conditions of the time inspired the Tantric innovations, a combination of the growing anti-Brahmin sentiment of some *bhakti* sects and the impulse, present from the days of the Upanishadic renouncers, to find new religious ways to alter consciousness. In both yoga and Tantra the transformation was controlled by meditation.

The Upanishadic texts were a far more direct inspiration for the philosophical writings of two great Vedantic philosophers who lived in South India, Shankara (788–820) and Ramanuja (1056–1137), as well as for the magical realist philosophical narratives of the twelfth-century Kashmiri Sanskrit text, the *Yoga-vasishtha*.

The Sanskrit texts of this period drew into the earlier conversations of the Vedas and Shastras whole new worlds of ideas, from South India as well as North, from vernacular and folk traditions that had not yet begun to write down their texts, and from other religions that were beginning to thrive in India, including new forms of Buddhism and early forms of Islam. The texts of this rich synthesis also reflect the influence, sometimes only an indirect one, of classes of society (including women, foreigners, and lower castes) that did not yet have an official voice in Sanskrit texts.

THE GODS—AND A GODDESS—IN THE PURANAS 400–1200 C.E.

The Puranas are Sanskrit collections of myth, ritual, and history. Scholars of Sanskrit poetry poke fun at the bad Sanskrit of the Puranas, which they view as the pulp fiction of ancient India, in comparison with court poetry that has the cachet of Shakespeare. But historians of religion value the Puranas all the more for their connection with popular elements of Hinduism, and for their earthy imagination.

There are often said to be eighteen Puranas, and innumerable "Sub-Puranas" (Upa-puranas), but the lists vary greatly, as do their dates and their contents. The early Puranas (which include the *Brahmanda, Kurma, Markandeya, Matsya, Padma, Shiva, Skanda, Vamana*, and *Varaha*) were composed between approximately 350 and 750 C.E., and the later Puranas (*Agni, Bhagavata, Bhavishya, Brahma, Brahmavaivarta, Devibhagavata, Garuda, Kalika, Linga, Mahabhagavata*, and *Saura*) between approximately 600 and 1000 C.E.

The Puranas are not about what they say they are about. They *say* they are about the "Five Signs," which are listed at the start of most Puranas: creation (*sarga*, "emission"), secondary creation (*pratisarga*), the genealogy of gods and kings, the reigns of the Manus (a different mythical Manu was born in each age, to help create the world) ("Manu," p. 202), and the history of the solar and lunar dynasties. But the genealogies of gods, Manus, and kings form an open-ended armature; into the rather vague categories of this armature (which some Puranas ignore entirely) individual authors fit what they really want to talk about: the way to live a pious life and to worship the gods and goddesses. This includes the rituals (*pujas*) that one should perform at home, in the temple, and on special festival days; places to visit on pilgrimage; prayers to recite; and stories to tell and to hear. Some Puranas are devoted to Shiva, some to Vishnu, some to a goddess, while even a Purana officially devoted to a particular god will often give considerable space to other gods. The eclectic variety of the Puranas gives them both their fascinating detail and their amazing range of subjects.

"Purana" means "ancient," and these texts look to the past, a conservative stance; they position themselves as age-old, anonymous. They also strike an imperial stance: the improved communications across the empire, and the sense that it was all part of a single cultural whole, inspired a kind of literary cosmopolitanism. But the Puranas also provided a Sanskrit medium for popular material transmitted through all classes and places in India, fusing the cosmopolitan, translocal vision that prevailed in India under the Gupta Empire (fourth to sixth centuries C.E.) with new local traditions, the praise of the particular shrine (*tirtha*) in our village, this temple, our river, and instructions on how to worship right here. What set the Puranas apart from one another was primarily the sectarian focus; all the stories (as well as rituals and doctrines) were about *our* god, *our* pilgrimage place. Their sectarian view says not "This is the whole world," but "This is *our* whole world."

The authors of the early Puranas appropriated popular beliefs and ideas from people of various castes. The excluded people (rural storytellers, lower classes, women) who had had only episodic success in breaking into Sanskrit literature managed now to get major speaking roles. Nurtured first by the patronage of the Guptas

During the chariot festival, Hindu men pull on enormous hawsers to drag the giant wooden chariot of Shiva and Parvati through the crowded streets of Madurai, Tamil Nadu, to gain merit.

and then by the less structured political systems that followed, the nonhegemonic, non-Vedic traditions supply the major substance of the Puranas.

The growth of temples, from about the sixth century C.E., also led to the greater use of ritual texts, both the Puranas and the texts called Agamas, which instructed worshippers in the way to make offerings to the gods. One of the great innovations of the rise of temple worship is that it made it possible for people who could not read Sanskrit texts to have access to Sanskrit myths and rituals. The images carved on temples brought the mythology of the Puranas into the public sphere. For iconography transcends illiteracy; people can see images even if they can't read texts, and somebody—possibly but not necessarily the priest in the temple—knows the story and tells it. Often someone sitting beside the person reciting the Purana would explain it to those innocent of Sanskrit; these public recitals were open to everyone, regardless of caste or gender. Moreover, once the images are on the *outsides* of temples, people can see them even if they are Pariahs (the lowest castes, sometimes called Untouchables or Dalits) and not allowed inside the temples. And, in turn, the temples were part of a system by which folk deities and local religious traditions entered the Brahmin world.

The Puranas mediate between the Sanskrit of court poetry and the oral or vernacular traditions. Sometimes, there was a social and/or economic distance between the classes that produced the vernacular texts, Puranas, and court poetry, but we cannot assume that the Puranas come from the poor. The Puranas cut across class lines and included wealthy merchants among their patrons. One reason the Puranas were able to assimilate an astonishingly wide range of beliefs, and Hindus were able to tolerate that range not only within their scriptures and communities but also within their own families, was the Puranas' lack of strict orthodoxy. Storytellers smuggled new ideas into the Puranas under the Brahmin radar, stashing them in older categories, often categories to which the new ideas did not really belong. Significantly, most of the rituals described in the Puranas do not require the mediation of a Brahmin priest. Moreover, the folk materials made their way into the Sanskrit corpus because the Brahmins were no longer able to ignore them—they were part of widespread religious movements—and also because the Brahmins, like the privileged in all periods, knew a good thing when they saw it, and the Puranas were terrific stories—indeed, in many cases they were the Brahmins' own household stories, told to them by nurses or cooks from local families.

THE PURANIC WORLD

Though most of the Puranas are sectarian, which is to say devoted to the worship of a particular god, they all share certain basic assumptions. These include belief in the power of the Puranas; the cosmogonic structure of the Four Ages; heaven and hell, as well as transmigration; and the transfer of karma. The sins that send you to hell and the virtues that send you to heaven are often described in detail that rivals that of the *shastras*, as the texts seem to vie with one another in imagining gruesome and appropriate punishments to fit various crimes. After hearing the spine-chilling descriptions of the tortures of hell, the interlocutor (who is, as in the *Mahabharata*, built into the frame) often asks: "Isn't there anything that I can do to avoid having that happen to me?" And yes, there is: just as there was a Vedic ritual to protect the worshiper, now there is a Puranic ritual, or a Puranic mantra, or a Puranic shrine, or a Puranic pilgrimage, that the text mercifully teaches right then and there.

THE FRUITS OF HEARING A PURANA: DEVARAJA THE SINNER

The Puranas, like many Hindu sacred texts, contain advertisements for themselves, discussions explaining and stories exemplifying the benefits that one gains by listening to or reading any particular text. These benefits are called the "fruits of hearing" (*phala-shruti*). Many Puranic myths also acted as pamphlets for a particular shrine, magnifying its powers of salvation, presumably to drum up business by boasting that anyone—even women and people of low castes—could go straight to heaven after any contact with the shrine. But this sort of argument often ran head-on into the hierarchical structures of Hinduism, according to which some were saved and some were not ("Salvation and Damnation," p. 183).

The basic structures of Hindu cosmology, constantly reinterpreted, served as an armature on which authors in each generation sculpted their musings on the structure of human society. In the *Rig Veda*, the Hindu universe was an egg, the two halves of the eggshell forming heaven and earth, with the sun as the yolk in the middle; it was a sealed, perfectly enclosed space with a given amount of good and evil and a given number of souls. This is why the sage in the Upanishads asks why heaven does not get filled up, with all the dead souls going into it ("Transmigration," p. 114). Ethically, this is a world of limited good, or a zero-sum game: if someone is saved, someone else has to be damned. For Brahmins to be pure, Pariahs have to be impure; if you win, I lose. Since evil is a substance, space is a problem.

But this structure was challenged by the emergence of the concept of *bhakti*, the passionate mutual love between the devotee (the *bhakta*) and the god. The *bhakti* Puranas cracked open the egg of the closed universe, so that the world of limited good gave way to a world of infinitely expandable good karma and *bhakti*. When the shape of the universe seemed to constrain the ethical possibilities, and when those possibilities grew intense, the cosmos changed its shape. The payoff is generally still in the next life: most of the *bhakti* Puranas are not saying that a Pariah can act like a Brahmin in this life, merely that a Pariah, too, can be freed from this life. But some seem to imply that people of all castes can change their forms of worship in *this* life and thus gain a better rebirth. And these stories are not only about Pariahs, but also about the relationship between all humans and their salvation.

Moreover, some of these texts say that even with no *bhakti* within you, you can be saved from your sins; the god has enough *bhakti* for both of you. There are stories about people who are neither good nor (consciously) *bhaktas*, but are nevertheless saved. The god to whom the unrepentant sinner is devoted comes to him and announces that he is to be taken forever to the heaven of the god, which can accommodate not only all reformed sinners but even *unreformed* sinners too, as well as people of all classes. Indeed, this heaven is *particularly* partial to unreformed sinners. None of the sinners in these stories reforms as a result of the accidental encounter with the god; all go on sinning until they die, presumably of syphilis, cirrhosis, or execution. But the mere encounter is enough to save them. This is a world of not only unlimited good but also undeserved good, of what might be called accidental grace. Whether or not the *bhakta* is conscious that his body is going through the actions of *bhakti*, the god loves the person who has performed these acts of devotional worship, and so everyone goes to heaven. These narratives seem counterintuitive and were perceived as perverse by some subsequent Hindu commentators, who demanded a conscious reformation for salvation.

The story of Devaraja is by no means the most extreme example. The hero (if one may call him that) is a Brahmin, referred to as a "god upon the earth," a term normally used for a Brahmin, though here it seems somewhat sarcastic. It may also be significant that Devaraja's name, "King of the Gods," is the name of Indra, the greatest sinner (an inveterate womanizer, drinker, and killer) among the Hindu gods.

PRONOUNCING GLOSSARY

Amba: *um´-bah*
Devaraja: *day´-vuh-rah´-juh*
Kailasa: *kai-lah´-suh*
Kirata: *kee´-rah´-tuh*
Kshatriya: *kuh-shah´-tree-yuh*
Pratisthanam: *pruh-teesh-tah´-num*
Rudra: *rood´-ruh*
Shiva Purana: *shih´-vuh poo-rah´-nuh*
Shudra: *shoo´-druh*
Vaishya: *vaish´-yuh*
Yama: *yuh´-muh*

Shiva Purana 1.2.15–40

Once upon a time, in the city of the Kiratas,[1] there was a Brahmin who was not at all strong when it came to sacred knowledge. He was a poor man, a seller of liquors, and he turned away from the gods and from dharma. He had ceased to perform the ritual of bathing at twilight and he devoted himself instead to making a living like a Vaishya; he was called Devaraja ('King of the Gods'), and he used to deceive people who trusted him. He took as his prey various sorts of people—Brahmins, Kshatriyas, Vaishyas, Shudras, and even people lower than that—and he would kill them and take their money. Through this violation of dharma he eventually accumulated great wealth, but he was such an evil man that he didn't use even a small part of his money for dharma.

One day, that god upon the earth went to a pond to bathe, and there he saw a whore named 'Gorgeous' who excited him wildly. The beautiful woman

TRANSLATED BY Wendy Doniger O'Flaherty.

1. A tribal people, on the borders of Hinduism. For Devaraja to live among such polluting, low-caste people in the first place would be sufficient to seal his doom, under normal conditions.

was delighted when she realized that a rich Brahmin was in her power; and she satisfied his mind with her professional banter. He decided to make her his wife, and she to make him her husband; thus overpowered by lust, they made love for a long time. Sitting, lying, drinking, eating, and playing, the two of them constantly seduced one another, like newlyweds. Though his mother and father and (first) wife kept trying to stop him, he paid no attention to their words, so intent was he on his evil ways.

Stone carving of a celestial courtesan (Apsaras) or perhaps just a seductive human woman. From the Lakshmana Temple of Khajuraho, in Madhya Pradesh, tenth century.

One day he became so impatient that he completely lost control, and in the night he killed his mother, father, and wife as they slept; and then that wretch took their money. He was so out of his mind with lust that he gave that whore all his own money as well as the money that he had taken from his father and the others. Then that sinner, the lowest of Brahmins, took to eating what should not be eaten, and he became addicted to drinking wine; he always ate out of the same plate as his whore.

Now, as fate would have it, one day he came to the town of Pratisthanam, and there he saw a Shiva temple filled with good people. While he stayed there, constantly hearing the *Shiva Purana* recited from the mouths of the Brahmins, that Brahmin was laid low by a fever. At the end of a month, Devaraja was dead of that fever; the minions of Yama (god of the dead) bound him with nooses and led him by force to the city of Yama. At the same time, the hosts of Shiva, shining with their tridents in their hands, smeared with white ashes all over their bodies, wearing the rosaries of Shiva, set out from the world of Shiva and came in fury to the city of Yama. They beat up the messengers of Yama and reviled them over and over; they set Devaraja free, put him up on their marvelous celestial chariot, and got ready to go to Kailasa (the mountain of Shiva).

Then a great tumult arose in the middle of the city of Yama, and (Yama) the King of Dharma heard it and came out of his palace. There he saw the four messengers like four more Rudras before his eyes, and as he knew dharma, the King of Dharma honored them with the proper ritual. Then, through his eye of knowledge, Yama realized all that had happened, but he was too frightened to ask a single question of the noble messengers of Shiva. When they had been honored and asked for their blessings, they went to Kailasa and gave (Devaraja) to Shiva, the ocean of compassion, and to Amba (the wife of Shiva).

Precious is the reciting of the *Shiva Purana*, the highest purification, by the mere hearing of which even a very evil person attains Release. It is the great place of the eternal Shiva, the highest dwelling, the high spot; those who know the Vedas say that it stands above all worlds. That evil man who, in his greed for money, injured many Brahmins, Kshatriyas, Vaishyas, Shudras, and even other creatures that breathe, the man who killed his mother and father and wife, who slept with a whore and drank wine, the Brahmin Devaraja went there and in a moment became released.

THE FOUR AGES

Time in India is named after throws of the dice ("The Stripping of Draupadi," p. 134) and always gets worse and worse. At first, there is no need for the basic social system, the *varna-ashrama-dharma*, that consists of the dharma of the four *varnas* or classes of society (Brahmin, Kshatriya, Vaishya, and Shudra) and the four *ashramas* or stages of life (*brahmacharin*, chaste student; *grihastha*, householder; *vanaprastha*, forest-dweller; and *sannyasin*, renouncer). But as time decays, the need for such a system arises; and as time further decays, it is no longer possible to maintain such a system. Human life subsides back into the wilderness, and the next cycle of civilization is born again. This text is one of many that describe this inevitable, cyclical process. In some (such as "How Rudra Destroys the Universe"), there is a cataclysmic doomsday at the end of the Fourth Age.

PRONOUNCING GLOSSARY

Agni: *ug´-nee*
Angiras: *uhn-gee´-rus*
Apastamba: *ah´-puh-stum´-buh*
Atri: *uh´-tree*
Bhagavata: *buh´-guh-vuh´-tuh*
Bhavishya: *buh-vish´-yuh*
Brahma: *bruh´-mah*
Brahmana: *brah´-muh-nuh*
Brahmanda: *bruh-mahn´-duh*
Brahmavaivarta: *bruh´-muh-vai-var´-tuh*
Brihaspati: *bree-hus´-puh-tee*
Daksha: *duhk´-shuh*
Garuda: *guh-roo´-duh*
Gautama: *gau´-tuh-muh*
Harita: *huh´-ree-tuh*
Kalpasutra: *kuhl´-puh-soo´-truh*
Katyayana: *kuht-yah´-yuh-nuh*
kshatat-tratum: *kuh-shuh´-tut trah´–tum*
Kurma: *koor´-muh*
Likhita: *lih´-kee-tuh*
Linga: *ling´-guh*
mantra: *mun´-truh*
Manu: *muh´-noo*
Markandeya: *mar´-kun-day´-yuh*
Matsya: *maht´-syuh*
Narada: *nuh´-ruh-duh*
Padma: *pud´-muh*
Parashara: *puh-rah´-shuh-ruh*
rajas: *rah´-jus*
Rig Veda: *rig vay´-duh*
Sama Veda: *sah´-muh vay´-duh*
Samvarta: *sum-var´-tuh*
sattva: *sut´-vuh*
Shankha: *shahn´-kuh*
Shastra: *shah´-struh*
Shatapata: *shuh´-tuh-puh´-tuh*
Skanda: *skun´-duh*
tamas: *tuh´-mus*
Ushanas: *oo´-shuh-nuhs*
Vamana: *vah´-muh-nuh*
Varaha: *vuh-rah´-huh*
Vasishtha: *vuh-shish´-tuh*
Vyasa: *vyah´-suh*
Yajnavalkya: *yaj´-nyuh-vuhl´-kyuh*
Yajur Veda: *yuh´-joor vay´-duh*
Yama: *yuh´-muh*

Linga Purana 1.39–40

First, you should know, comes the Golden Age, and then the Age of the Trey; and the Age of the Deuce and the Fourth Age[1] come next: these are the four Ages, in brief. The Golden Age is the age of goodness (*sattva*); the Age of the Trey is the age of energy (*rajas*); the Age of the Deuce is a mixture of energy and darkness (*tamas*); and the Dark Age is the age of darkness; each age has its characteristic ways of behaving. Meditation is the main thing in the Golden Age; sacrifice in the Age of the Trey; worship in the Age of Deuce; purity and charity in the Dark Age. The Golden Age lasts for four thousand years, and is followed by a twilight of four hundred years. And the lifespan of living creatures lasts for four thousand human years in the Golden Age.

After the twilight of the Golden Age has passed, one of the four feet[2] of the dharma of the Ages is gone in all of its aspects. The excellent Age of the Trey is one fourth less than the Golden Age; the Age of the Deuce lasts for half the time of the Golden Age, and the Dark Age lasts for one half the time of the Age of the Deuce. The last three twilights last for three hundred, two hundred, and one hundred years; this happens in aeon after aeon, Age after Age. In the first Age, the Golden Age, the eternal dharma walks on four feet; in the Age of Trey, on three feet; in the Age of Deuce, on two feet. In the fourth Age it lacks three feet and is devoid of the element of goodness.

In (every) Golden Age, people are born in pairs; their livelihood consists in revelling in the taste of what exists right before one's eyes. All creatures are satisfied, always, and take delight in all enjoyments. There is no distinction between the lowest and the highest among them; they are all good, all equal in their life-span, happiness, and form, in the Golden Age. They have no preferences, nor do they experience the opposing pairs of emotions; they do not hate or get tired. They have no homes or dwelling-places, but live in the mountains and oceans; they have no sorrow, but consist mostly of goodness and generally live alone. They go wherever they wish, constantly rejoicing in their minds; in the Golden Age, people do not engage in any actions, good or bad.

At that time there was no system of separate classes and stages of life, and no mixture (of classes or castes). But in the course of time, in the Age of the Trey, they no longer revelled in the taste (of existence). When that fulfilment was lost, another sort of fulfilment was born. When water reaches its subtle state, it is transformed into clouds; from thundering clouds, rain is emitted. As soon as the surface of the earth was touched by that rain, trees appeared on it, and they became houses for the people, who used those trees for their livelihood and all their enjoyments. People lived off those trees at the beginning of the Age of the Trey.

But then, after a long time, people began to change; the emotions of passion and greed arose, for no apparent cause, as a result of a change in the people that arose out of time. Then all the trees that they regarded as their houses vanished, and when they had vanished, the people who were born in pairs became confused. They began to think about their fulfilment, considering the matter truthfully, and then the trees that they regarded as their

TRANSLATED BY Wendy Doniger O'Flaherty.

1. The first can also be translated the Winning Age and the last, the Losing Age (or Kali Age).

2. Dharma is imagined in the form of a cow.

houses appeared again. These trees brought forth clothing and fruits and jewelry; and on the very same trees there would grow, in bud after bud, honey made by no bees, powerful honey of superb aroma, color, and taste. People lived on that honey, lived happily all their life long, finding their delight and their nourishment in that perfection, always free from fever.

But then, as another time came, they became greedy. They lopped off the limbs of the trees and took by force the honey that no bees had made. As a result of that crime that they committed in their greed, the magic trees, together with their honey, vanished, first here, then there, and as time exerted its power, very little of that fulfilment was left. As the Age of the Trey came on, the opposing pairs of emotions arose, and people became quite miserable as a result of the sharp cold and rain and heat. Tortured by these opposing pairs, they began to cover themselves; and then they made houses on the mountain to ward off the opposing pairs. Formerly, they had gone wherever they wished, living without fixed dwellings; now they began to live in fixed dwellings according to their need and their pleasure. . . .

Then, by the force of that Age, all the people were so crazy with rage that they seized one another and took their sons, wives, wealth, and so forth, by force. When he realized all this, the lotus-born (Brahma) created the Kshatriyas to protect people from getting wounded (*kshatat-tratum*), in order to establish a firm support for the moral boundaries. Then by means of his own brilliance, the god who is the soul of all established the system of the classes and stages of life, and he himself established the livelihood for each profession to live on. Gradually, the institution of sacrifice evolved in the Age of the Trey, but even then some good people did not perform animal sacrifices. For eventually Vishnu, who sees everything, performed a sacrifice by force, and then as a result of that the Brahmins prescribed the nonviolent sacrifice.

But then, in the Age of the Deuce, men began to have differences of opinion, to differ in mind, action, and speech, and to have difficulty making a living. Then, gradually, as a result of the exhaustion of their bodies, all creatures became subject to greed, working for wages, working as merchants, fighting, indecision about basic principles, lack of interest in the schools of the Vedas, confounding of dharmas, destruction of the system of the classes and stages of life, and, finally, lust and hatred. For in the Age of the Deuce, passion, greed, and drunkenness arise.

And in (every) Age of the Deuce, a sage named Vyasa[3] divides the Veda into four. For it is known that there was a single Veda, in four parts, in the Ages of the Trey; but as a result of the shrinking of the life-span, it was divided up in the Ages of the Deuce. And these divisions were further divided by the sons of the (Rig Vedic) seers, according to their deviant opinions; they transposed the order of the (Rig Vedic) mantras and the Brahmanas, and they changed the accents and the syllables. Wise men compiled the collections of the *Rig Veda, Yajur Veda*, and *Sama Veda;* though they were composed in common, they have been (subsequently) separated by people of various opinions, divided into Brahmanas, Kalpasutras, and explications of the mantras. Now, some of these works still follow the line of (the Vedas), and others depart from them.

3. Vyasa, whose name means "The Divider," is known as the author of the *Mahabharata* (in which he also plays a part, fathering several key figures) and as the one who divided the Vedas.

The Epics and Puranas are distinguished according to the weight of their age; thus the (eighteen) Puranas are divided as follows (beginning with the oldest): the Brahma, Padma, Vishnu, Bhagavata, Bhavishya, Narada, Markandeya, Agni, Brahmavaivarta, Linga, Varaha, Vamana, Kurma, Matsya, Garuda, Skanda, Shiva, and Brahmanda. The *Linga Purana*, the eleventh, was established in the Age of the Deuce. There are thousands of sages, including Manu, Atri, Vishnu, Harita, Yajnavalkya, Ushanas, Angiras, Yama, Apastamba, Samvarta, Katyayana, Brihaspati, Parashara, Vyasa, Shankha, Likhita, Daksha, Gautama, Shatatapas, and Vasishtha.

Drought, death, disease, and other plagues cause sufferings born of speech, mind, and action, and as a result one becomes numb. From this numbness people begin to think about release from suffering. From this thinking there arises detachment, and from detachment they begin to see their faults. As a result of seeing their faults, knowledge arises in the Age of the Deuce. Now, it will be recalled that the behavior characteristic of the Age of the Deuce was a mixture of energy and darkness. But there was dharma in the first age, the Golden Age, and that dharma still functions in the Age of the Trey; in the Age of the Deuce, however, it becomes disturbed, and in the Dark Age it vanishes.

In the fourth Age, men's senses are disturbed by darkness and they fall prey to illusion and jealousy; they even kill ascetics. In the Dark Age, there is always carelessness, passion, hunger, and fear; the terrible fear of drought pits one country against another. Scripture has no authority, and men take to the violation of dharma; they act without dharma, without morality; they are very angry and not very smart. . . . When scripture is destroyed, and the dharma that is known from the Shastras, then people will kill one another, for they will have no moral boundaries, no check to their violence, no affection, and no shame. When dharma is destroyed, and people attack one another, they will become stunted and live only twenty-five years; their senses will become confused with arguing, and they will abandon their sons and wives. When they are struck by drought, they will abandon agriculture; they will leave their own countries and go to lands beyond their borders, seeking water in rivers, oceans, wells, and mountains.

Suffering greatly, they will live on honey, raw meat, roots, and fruits; they will wear garments of bark, leaves, and antelope skins; they will perform no rituals and have no possessions. They will fall away from the system of classes and stages of life and fall prey to the terrible mingling of classes. Then there will be very few people left, caught up in this calamity. Afflicted by old age, disease, and hunger, their minds will be numbed by suffering. But from this numbness there will arise thought, and thought makes the mind balanced. Understanding comes from a balanced mind, and from understanding comes a dedication to dharma. The people who are left at the end of the Dark Age will have a kind of formless mental peace.

Then, in a day and a night, the age will be transformed for them, deluding their wits as if they were dreaming or insane. And then, by the power of the goal of the future, the Golden Age will begin. And when the Golden Age has begun again, the people left over from the Dark Age become the people born in the Golden Age. . . .

THE TRANSFER OF KARMA IN HELL

At the end of the *Mahabharata* (18.1–5), Yudhishthira visits hell. Unable to abide the heat and the stench of corpses, he turns to go, but then he hears the voices of his brothers and his wife Draupadi crying, "Stay here, as a favor to us, just for a little while. A sweet breeze from your body wafts over us and brings us relief." He determines to stay there, to help them, but suddenly Dharma incarnate, together with other gods, appears and everything else disappears—the darkness, the tortures, everything. It had all been an illusion sent to test Yudhishthira, like the illusion of the dog ("The Pandavas Go to Heaven," p. 145).

Yudhishthira's ability to ease his brothers' and wife's torments takes the form of a cool, sweet breeze that counteracts the hot, putrid air of hell through a kind of transfer of merit. He therefore wants to stay with his brothers and wife in hell, even though he himself does not belong there, just as he wanted to stay with the dog outside heaven, where the dog did not belong. A sure sign of a moral impasse in any narrative is the invocation of the "it was just a dream" motif at the end, erasing the impasse entirely. Another is the *deus ex machina* (the god who suddenly appears out of nowhere). The *Mahabharata* invokes both here, a double red flag.

But the illusory excuse—it wasn't really a dog, it wasn't really hell—is challenged by the Hindu belief that people atone for their sins in a real hell. The Puranas return to the moral impasses of the *Mahabharata*, some of which were resolved only by illusion *ex machina*, and offer solutions that were not available to the authors of that text. The idea of transfer of merit, merely sketched in the *Mahabharata*, is more fully developed a few centuries later in the *Markandeya Purana* story of King Vipashchit's visit to hell, which is clearly based on the *Mahabharata* and uses some of the same phrases. Both texts assume that everyone, after death, must visit both heaven and hell, to work off both good and bad karma.

Significantly, the people in hell now are not related to the king in any way; his compassion extends to all creatures. And now the text begins to speak of Buddhist/Hindu concepts like *nirvana* and the transfer of karma, making it possible for the real, heavenbound king to release real sinners from a real hell. Karma and rebirth have the last word, though: in the end, having passed through heaven and hell, the sinners are reborn according to their just deserts—a theory that the *Mahabharata* had not invoked.

We join the story as King Vipashchit has just asked the servant of Yama, king of the dead, why he is in hell when he had led a life of virtue.

PRONOUNCING GLOSSARY

Brahma: *bruh´-mah*
Dharma: *dar´-muh*
Indra: *in´-druh*
Kaikeyi: *kai-kay´-yee*
nirvana: *neer-vah´-nuh*
Pivari: *pee´-vuh-ree´*
Prajapati: *pruh-jah´-puh-tee*
Vidarbha: *vih-dar´-buh*
Yama: *yuh´-muh*

Markandeya Purana 14–15

When the servant of Yama had been questioned by the king, he replied politely, fierce though he was, 'Great king, what you said is true, without any

Translated by Wendy Doniger O'Flaherty.

doubt. However, you did commit one small sin; let me remind you about it. Your wife, a princess from Vidarbha,[1] named Fatso (Pivari), came into her fertile season on one occasion in the past, but you left her barren, for you were infatuated with your other wife, the very beautiful Kaikeyi.[2] And because you transgressed the rule that requires a man to have intercourse with his wife during her fertile season, you have come to this terrible hell. Just as the fire expects the purified butter to fall into it at the time of the oblation, even so Prajapati[3] expects the seed to fall at the fertile season. If a man who cares for dharma overlooks that duty because he is distracted by lust, he commits a sin because he neglects the debt (of a son) that he owes to his ancestors, and so he falls to hell. But this is the full extent of your evil; no other sin is found in you. Therefore come and enjoy the fruits of your many meritorious deeds. . . . Let us go somewhere else. You have seen everything now; and you have seen hell. So let us go somewhere else.'

At that, the king prepared to go, letting the servant precede him. But then all the men who were being so hideously tortured there cried out, 'Have mercy on us, your majesty! Stay here just a little moment more! For the wind that comes from contact with your body refreshes our hearts and dispels the pain that we feel when our limbs are burnt and crushed and beaten all over. Tiger among kings, have pity on us.'

When he heard what they said, the king asked Yama's man, 'How can I have the power to refresh these people? Have I committed some great meritorious karma in the mortal world of which this gift of refreshment is the reward? Tell me.' (The servant replied,) 'Your body has been nourished by the food that remained after the ancestors, gods, guests, and ghosts (were fed); and since your heart went out to (these people in hell), therefore the wind that comes from contact with your limbs grants them refreshment, and these people who have committed evil deeds are not tormented by their torture. Since you sacrificed properly with the horse sacrifice and other sacrifices, therefore by the mere sight of you Yama's torture machines, knives, fires, and birds, that are the causes of great suffering from crushing, cutting, burning, and so forth, become gentle, for they are counteracted by your splendor.'

The king said, 'Men cannot obtain in heaven or in the world of Brahma such happiness as arises from giving peace (*nirvana*) to suffering creatures; this is what I think. If their torture does not hurt these people in my presence, then I will be one of those people whose faces confer prosperity on those who see them, and I will stay here, like an immovable pillar.' Yama's man said, 'Come, your majesty, let's go. Enjoy the pleasures that you have won by your own merit, and let these men of evil karma enjoy their torture.'

The king said, 'For that very reason, I *won't* go, as long as these people suffer. The people who live in hell are happy in my presence. What use is the life of that man who does not show favor to a man in trouble, even a confirmed enemy who comes to him for help? Sacrifice, charity, and asceticism do no good to a man in the world beyond if he has no heart to help people in trouble. A man who is hard-hearted toward children and people who suffer

1. An important ancient kingdom, in what is now the eastern part of Maharashtra, in Western India.
2. This text gives the sexually preferred second wife the name of the sexually preferred second wife in the *Ramayana*, Kaikeyi ("Dasharatha Kills a Boy," p. 192).
3. Lord of Creatures, the Creator.

and old people and so forth, I do not regard as human; he is an ogre. The torture of hell that these people experience from being heated by fire or smelling revolting smells or from hunger or thirst that make them faint—that torment is destroyed as a result of my presence; and I regard that, good sir, as a happiness greater than heaven. If many people become happy while I suffer, what can there be that I have not attained? Tell me that, right away.'

Yama's servant said, 'Here is Dharma[4] and here is Indra; they have come to take you away. You can't help going away from here; so go, your majesty.' Dharma said, 'I myself will lead you to heaven, for you have served me properly. Mount this celestial chariot; do not delay; come.' But the king said, 'Dharma, men are being tortured in hell by the thousands. "Save us!" they cry out to me; and so I will not go away from here.' Indra said, 'These people reached hell as a result of their own most evil karma; but you, on the other hand, are supposed to go to heaven as a result of your good karma.'

The king replied, 'Dharma, if you know—or you, Indra, who have performed a hundred horse sacrifices—just how far my authority extends, you should tell me that right away.' 'Like the drops of water in the ocean, or like the stars in the sky, or like the streams of water in the rain or the grains of sand in the Ganges, or like all the creatures in the various wombs—as these cannot be counted, great king, so too it is impossible to count your merits. And by evincing this compassion right now, here in hell, you brought the count to hundreds of thousands. Therefore, go, matchless king, and enjoy all those merits in the home of the immortals; but let these wear away here in hell the evil born of their own karma.' 'How,' replied the king, 'will men ever take pleasure in associating with me if these people are not uplifted in my presence? Therefore, let whatever good deeds I have done be used to release these people of evil karma from their torments in hell.'

Then Indra said, 'By this, great king, you have reached an even higher place; and see how these people of evil karma are released from hell.' Then a rain of flowers fell on to the king, and Indra had him mount the celestial chariot and led him to heaven. And all who were there were released from their tortures—though they all went from there immediately to another womb that was determined by the fruits of their own karma.

4. Dharma is the incarnation of the moral law (dharma), and Indra is king of the gods. Both play a central role in the *Mahabharata* story of Yudhishthira in hell.

SHIVA

Shiva is one of the great gods of Hinduism and is even named "The Great God" (Mahadeva). Aspects of his worship (and one of his names) can be traced back to the Vedic figure of Rudra ("Have Mercy on Us, Rudra," p. 90), though he also assimilates aspects of the mythology of the gods Prajapati, Indra, and Agni. He became a great Hindu god at the time of the *Mahabharata* ("The Churning of the Ocean," p. 149; "Daksha's Sacrifice," p. 162) and the *Ramayana* ("The Gods Interrupt Shiva and Parvati," p. 196). His mythology comes into its full scope in the Puranas ("The Fruits of Hearing a Purana"). He is responsible for cosmic destruction ("How Rudra Destroys the Universe"), though he is as much a creator as he is destroyer. He is also both ascetic ("Mankanaka Dances for Shiva") and erotic ("The Gods Interrupt Shiva and Parvati") and is widely worshipped in the form of the *linga* ("The Origin of *Linga* Worship").

THE ORIGIN OF *LINGA* WORSHIP

Numerous Sanskrit texts and ancient sculptures (such as the Gudimallam *linga* from the third century B.C.E.) define the *linga* as an iconic representation of the erect male sexual organ, in particular as the erect phallus of the god Shiva. And many Hindus have, like Freud, seen *lingas* in every naturally occurring elongated object, the so-called self-created (*svayambhu*) *lingas*, including "found objects" such as stalagmites. The *linga* in this physical sense is well known throughout India and is understood across barriers of caste and language. But some texts treat the *linga* as a pillar of light or an abstract symbol of god (the word means simply a "sign," as smoke is the sign of fire), with no sexual reference. To some, *lingas* convey an ascetic purity, while others see in them an obvious sexual symbolism.

Some myths of the origin of *linga* worship emphasize its sexual associations. Typical of these are the myths in which Shiva appears to the sages in the Pine Forest naked and with an erect penis and seduces their wives; in their fury, they curse his *linga* to fall from his body to the ground. But then the world is immediately plunged into darkness, nor is any new life born, since Shiva's *linga* is the source of all heat and life in the world. Realizing their mistake, the sages eventually restore the *linga* to Shiva and promise to worship it forever.

Another group of myths, exemplified in the following text, emphasize the purely abstract power of the *linga*. Here Shiva is opposed not by human sages but by two other male gods, Vishnu and Brahma. The tensions between the worshippers of Vishnu and Shiva were relatively mild but important enough to be explicitly addressed in narratives. The concept of a trinity, a triumvirate of Brahma, Vishnu, and Shiva (the Trimurti or "Triple Form"), is misleading. (The triumvirate may have been sustained, though not invented, in response to the Christian trinity.) The idea that Brahma is responsible for creation, Vishnu for preservation or maintenance, and Shiva for destruction does not correspond to the mythology, in which both Vishnu and Shiva are responsible for both creation and destruction and Brahma was not worshipped as the other two were. If one wanted to find a trinity of important deities in Hinduism, it would be more accurate to speak of Vishnu, Shiva, and Devi, but since there are so many different Vishnus, Shivas, and Devis, even that trinity makes little sense. The relationship between the two major male gods is better viewed as an aspect of Hinduism's penchant for fusing, with Vishnu and Shiva frequently functioning as a pair, often merged as Hari-Hara (Vishnu-Shiva).

The relative status of the three members of this trinity is explicitly discussed in a variant of the myth of the origin of the *linga* that begins with an argument between Brahma and Vishnu and then segues into another popular myth, the tale of Shiva's first appearance out of the *linga*, in the form of a pillar of fire. In some versions of this variant, each of this pair says to the other, "You were born from me," and both of them are right. Each god sees all the worlds and their inhabitants (including both himself and the other god) inside the belly of the other god. Each claims to be the creator of the universe, yet each contains the other creator. Sometimes each one calls the other *tata*, a two-way word that a young man can use to call an older man "Grandpa," while an older man can use it to call a younger man "Sonny boy"; the word actually designates the relationship between young and old. Sometimes Brahma falsely claims that he has measured the end of the *linga*, and in punishment for this lie he is cursed never again to be worshipped. And this is in fact the case: though Brahma remains an important mythological figure, responsible for various forms of creation, there are few Brahma temples or Brahma-*bhaktas*.

The following version of the myth of the origin of the *linga* is set at the in-between moment when the universe has been reduced to a cosmic ocean (dissolution) and is about to undergo a new creation, which will be followed by another dissolution, then another creation, and so on *ad infinitum*—another series of mutual creations. Shiva appears first as a blaze of light with no distinct form ("unmanifest") and then reveals his anthropomorphic form ("manifest"). Vishnu narrates the story in the first person.

PRONOUNCING GLOSSARY

Aditya: *uh-dit´-yuh*
Ashvin: *ush´-vin*
Brahma: *bruh´-mah*
dundubhi: *doon´-doo´-bee*
Gayatri: *gah´-yuh-tree*
Kama: *kah´-mah*
Kuhu: *koo´-hoo*
Lakshmi: *luk´-shmee*
Marut: *muh´-root*
Pinaka: *pih-nah´-kuh*
Rudra: *roo´-druh*
Shankara: *shahn´-kuh-ruh*
Sinivali: *see´-nee-vah´-lee*
Sita: *see´-tah*
Soma: *soh´-muh*
Svadha: *svuh-dah´*
Svaha: *svah-hah´*
Uma: *oo-mah´*
Valakhilya: *vah´-luh-keel´-yuh*
Varuna: *vuh´-roo-nuh*
Vashat: *vuh´-shuht*
Vasu: *vuh´-soo*

Brahmanda Purana 1.2.26.10–61

Once upon a time, when the whole triple world was unmanifest, in darkness, swallowed up by me, I lay there alone, with all the creatures in my belly. I had a thousand heads and a thousand eyes, and a thousand feet; I held in my hands the conch shell, discus, and mace, as I lay in the immaculate water. Then, all of a sudden, I saw from afar the four-headed (Brahma), the great yogi, the Person with golden luminosity, infinitely luminous, as bright as a hundred suns, blazing with his own brilliance. The god was wearing a black antelope skin and carrying a water-pot; and in the space of the blinking of an eye, that supreme Person[1] arrived. Then Brahma, to whom all people bow, said to me, 'Who are you? And where do you come from? And why are you staying here? Tell me, sir. I am the maker of the worlds, self-created, facing in all directions.' When Brahma had spoken like that to me, I said to him: '*I* am the maker of the worlds, and also the one who destroys them, again and again.' As the two of us were talking together in this way, each wishing to surpass the other, we saw a flame arising in the northern quarter. As we looked at that flame we were amazed, and its brilliance and power made us cup our hands in reverence and bow to that light from Shiva. The flame grew, a surpassing marvel, and Brahma and I hastened to run up to it. It broke through heaven and earth with its halo of flame, and in the middle of the flame we saw a *linga* of great luster, measuring just a handsbreadth, unmanifest and full of supreme light. In the middle, it was neither gold nor stone or silver; it was indescribable, unimaginable, visible and invisible again and again. It had a thousand garlands of flames, amazing, miraculous; it had great brilliance, and kept getting much bigger. It was covered with a halo of flame, terrifying all creatures with its monstrous form, excessive, bursting through heaven and earth.

TRANSLATED BY Wendy Doniger O'Flaherty.

1. Here Brahma is identified with the Primeval Man (*purusha*) ("The Hymn of the Primeval Man," p. 82).

Then Brahma said to me, 'Quickly, go down and find out the (bottom) end of this noble *linga*. I will go up until I see its (top) end.' We agreed to do this, and went up and down. I kept going down for a thousand years, but I did not reach the end of the *linga*; and then I became afraid. In the very same way, Brahma did not find its end above, and came back to join me right there in the expanse of water. Then we were amazed and frightened of the noble one; deluded by his power of illusion, we lost our wits and became confused. But then we meditated on the lord who faces in all directions, the origin and resting place of the worlds, the unchanging lord. Cupping our hands in reverence, we paid homage to Shiva, the trident-bearer, who makes the great, terrifying sound, who has a frightening form, and fangs, who is manifest, and great:

'We bow to you, O lord of the gods and people; we bow to you god, noble lord of all creatures. We bow to you, the eternally successful yogi, the support of all the universe, the highest ruler, the highest ultimate reality, the undying, the highest place. You are the eldest, the lovely god, the ruddy one, the jumper, the lord Shiva; you are the sacrifice; you are the utterance of "Vashat!"[2] and the utterance of "Om!" the heater of enemies; the utterance of "Svaha!"; you are obeisance and the perfection of all holy rituals; you are the utterance of the sweet drink, "Svadha!"; you are the sacrifice, the vows, and the observances; the Vedas, the worlds, the gods, the true god everywhere. You are the quality of sound in space; you are the origin and dissolution of creatures. You are the perfume in the earth, the fluidity of the waters, the brightness of fire, great lord. You are the touch of the wind, lord of gods, and the form of the moon. You are the knowledge in intelligence, lord of gods, and the seed in nature. You destroy all the worlds; you are Time, the Ender, made of death. You alone maintain the three worlds, and you alone create them, o lord. With your eastern face you act as Indra, and with your southern face you withdraw the worlds again. With your western face you act as Varuna;[3] this is certain. With your northern face you are Soma, o best of gods. In one way or in many ways, you create the worlds and destroy them, O god. You are the Adityas, the Vasus, the Rudras, the Maruts, and the Ashvins. You are the Perfected Beings, the magicians, the Nagas, the sorcerers, the ascetics; the noble Valakhilya sages,[4] and those who have achieved success in their asceticism, and who have kept their vows. O lord of gods, from you all of these goddesses, firm in their vows, and others, have been born: Uma, Sita, Sinivali, Kuhu, Gayatri, and Lakshmi; and the goddesses Fame, Fortitude, Wisdom, Modesty, Loveliness, Form, Sweetness, Contentment, Growth, and Activity; and Sarasvati, the goddess of speech; and, O lord of gods, from you have sprung Twilight and Night. We bow to you who have the power of a million million suns, who are as white as a thousand moons; we bow to you who hold the thunderbolt and the bow called Pinaka; we bow to you who hold the bow and arrows in your hand. We bow to you whose body is adorned with ashes; we bow to you who destroyed the body of Kama,[5] we bow to you, god of the golden embryo, the golden robe, the golden womb, the

2. These are all utterances that the priest makes as he throws the oblation into the Vedic fire.
3. Varuna, Soma, and the others in this first list are Vedic gods. After that come various creatures, and various goddesses, as well as abstract virtues, all identified with the great god.
4. Tiny sages the size of a thumb.
5. In a well-known myth, Shiva burned Kama, the god of erotic love, to ashes when Kama tried to inspire him with desire for Parvati; later, when Shiva married Parvati, he restored Kama's power, but not his body.

golden navel, the golden semen, variegated with a thousand eyes; we bow to you, god of the golden color and the golden hair, you the golden hero and the giver of gold; we bow to you, god, master of gold with the sound of gold. We bow to you with the Pinaka bow in your hand, Shankara, the blue-necked.'

When he had been praised like that, he became manifest, the one of great intellect, the god of gods, womb of the universe, shining as bright as a million suns; and filled with pity, the great god, the great light, spoke to us, as if he would swallow up the sky with his thousands of millions of mouths. His neck was shaped like a conch shell; his belly was lovely; he was adorned with various kinds of jewels; his body was variegated with all sorts of gems, and he wore various kinds of garlands and unguents. The lord had the Pinaka bow in his hand and he held the trident; he was fit to be worshipped by the gods. He wore a great serpent for his sacred thread, but he did not frighten the gods.

He sent forth a great laugh, with the noise of the sound of *dundubhi* drum,[6] like the roar of thunder, a laugh that filled the entire universe. The two of us were terrified by that great sound, but then the great god said, 'I am satisfied with you two, best of the gods. See my great yoga, and lose all your fear. Both of you, eternal, were born from my limbs in the past; Brahma here, the grandfather of all people, is my right arm, and Vishnu is my left arm, always unconquered in battles. I am satisfied with the two of you, and so I will give you a boon, whatever you ask.'

Then the two of us were ecstatic, and we bowed to the feet of the lord, and we said to the great god, who was standing there inclined to favor us, 'If you are really satisfied, and if you are going to give us a boon, then let the two of us always have devotion for you, O god, lord of the gods.' The god of gods said, 'So be it, fortunate ones. Create masses of progeny.' And when he had said this, the lord god vanished.

6. A large kettledrum.

HOW RUDRA DESTROYS THE UNIVERSE

The Puranas tell of several different sorts of doomsday, on different levels; the one described here is the occasional dissolution, which occurs when Brahma sleeps, as distinguished from the elemental dissolution, which occurs at the end of Brahma's life. It is the particular task of Rudra to destroy the universe (as it is Brahma's task to create it); but as the following text was composed by a worshipper of Vishnu, and therefore regards Vishnu as responsible for everything that happens in the universe, it says that Vishnu takes the form of Rudra. (Later in the story, Vishnu takes the form of Brahma to re-create the universe.)

The text describes several different levels of worlds within the universe. Within the encompassing ocean of eternity and infinity, Vishnu sleeps on the great serpent of Infinity, Ananta, also called Shesha ("What is left," i.e., what remains when all else is destroyed). Above the triple world (hell, earth, heaven) inhabited by humans and gods is the fourth world, the Maharloka ("World of Greatness"), which remains intact during doomsday and is inhabited at that time by certain perfected beings. Though it is not destroyed, it is uncomfortably hot, and some of its denizens move out to another world. The Janaloka ("World of People") is the fifth world, where the sons of Brahma and other perfected beings live; in some cosmologies, the world of Brahma is beyond the Janaloka; in others, it is equated with it. Above this world, in the sky, live the Seven Sages, mind-born sons of Prajapati, the seven stars of the Plough, in Ursa Major (the Big Dipper).

PRONOUNCING GLOSSARY

Brahma: *bruh´-mah*
Hari: *huh´-ree*
Janaloka: *juh´-nah-loh´-kuh*
kalpa: *kuhl´-puh*
Maharloka: *muh-har´-loh-kuh*
Manu: *muh´-noo*
naimittika: *nai-mee´-tee-kuh*
nimittam: *nih-mih´-tum*
Rudra: *rood´-ruh*
Sanaka: *suh´-nuh-kuh*
Shesha: *shay´-shuh*
Vasudeva: *vuh´-soo-day´-vuh*

Vishnu Purana 6.3–4

Twelve thousand divine years constitute a period of the four Ages, and a thousand of the four Ages is called a day of Brahma, or an aeon (*kalpa*), in which there are fourteen Manus. At the end of the aeon there occurs the occasional dissolution brought about by Brahma. It is very terrible; I will tell you about it. Listen. Later on, I will tell you about the elemental dissolution.

At the end of a thousand cycles of the four Ages, when the surface of the earth is mostly exhausted, a very fierce drought occurs and lasts for a hundred years. As a result, the creatures who live on earth lose most of their vital essence, and then they are so afflicted that they perish; none are left. Then the unchanging lord Vishnu takes the form of Rudra and sets to work to destroy all those creatures that dwell in him. The lord Vishnu enters into the seven rays of the sun and drinks up all the waters, leaving none. When he has drunk up all the waters that are inside living creatures that breathe, he dries up the entire surface of the earth. Whatever water there is in rivers and oceans and mountain streams, or in the subterranean watery hells—he absorbs it all.

All the water that he has taken away goes directly, by his authority, to the seven rays of the sun, which, enlarged by those waters, become seven suns. These seven suns blaze above and below, burning the entire triple world, including the subterranean watery hells. When it is burnt by these blazing fires, the triple world with its mountains, rivers, and oceans becomes entirely devoid of moisture; the moisture of its trees is burnt up, and the earth becomes like the back of a tortoise. When Vishnu has become Rudra of the doomsday fire, the one who withdraws everything, he becomes the hot breath of the serpent of Infinity and burns down the subterranean watery hells. And when it has burnt all the hells, the great fire goes to the earth and burns up the whole surface of the earth. Then a most terrible whirlwind haloed in flames envelops the middle realm of space and the world of heaven, and now the entire triple world, enveloped by this flame whirlwind that destroys all creatures, moving and still, looks like a frying pan. When the creatures that

TRANSLATED BY Wendy Doniger O'Flaherty.

live in these upper two worlds are enveloped by heat, those who have discharged their duties go up to the great world above heaven (Maharloka). But since they are still heated by that great heat, those creatures go from there to the world beyond, the World of People (Janaloka), turning away from their present condition of life in their wish to go beyond.

When Vishnu in the form of Rudra has thus burnt the entire universe, he creates clouds that are born out of the breath from his mouth. These are the terrible, thick clouds called whirlwinds, that look like herds of elephants as they roar and send bolts of lightning through the sky. Some are as dark as blue lotuses; some are as pale as water lilies; some are thick, the color of smoke; some are yellow; some are dun, like donkeys; some as red as lac; some the color of lapis lazuli; some the color of a sapphire. Some are as white as a conch shell or jasmine; some are as black as collyrium. Some are as red as cochineal; some are red as red arsenic; some are like the wings of the blue jay. Thus the thick masses of clouds arise. In shape, some of these fat clouds are like big cities; some are like mountains; some are like huts or houses.

Roaring loudly, they fill the sky with their huge bodies. Sending down their rain in great torrents, they extinguish the terrible fire that has penetrated everywhere inside the triple world. When the fire has gone out, they continue to rain ceaselessly for a thousand years, flooding the entire universe. Inundating the whole earth with drops the size of dice, they flood the middle realm of space in the same way, and heaven above, too. And when the whole world, moving and still, has been destroyed in blind darkness, the great clouds go on raining for a hundred years more.

When the water reaches the dwelling-place of the Seven Sages, the entire triple world becomes nothing but a single ocean. Then a wind comes out of the breath from the mouth of Vishnu, that blows for more than a hundred years and destroys those waters. Then the Lord, the Unthinkable, the existence of all beings, the one of whom all beings are made, who has no beginning, who is the beginning of everything, drinks up that wind, leaving nothing. Then the lord lies down in that single ocean, using the serpent Shesha as his bed; and the lord Hari (Vishnu), who creates the beginning, takes the form of Brahma. Praised by all those perfected creatures who had gone to the World of People, the sage Sanaka and the others, and contemplated by all those creatures desirous of Release who had gone to the world of Brahma, the supreme lord partakes of the celestial yogic sleep that is made of his own divine illusion; and he contemplates his own self in the form known as (Krishna), the son of Vasudeva.

This is the dissolution that is called occasional (*naimittika*), because it takes place on the occasion (*nimittam*, occasion or cause) when Vishnu takes the form of Brahma and sleeps.

MANKANAKA DANCES FOR SHIVA

Shiva is the lord of the dance (Nataraja); he dances the dance of death (the Tandava) and he dances erotically in the Pine Forest ("The Origin of *Linga* Worship"). In the myth of Mankanaka, these two dances confront one another; the mortal ascetic uses his magic to transmute blood to plant sap, and he dances in erotic joy, disturbing the world just as Shiva does when he "dances" (or makes love) with Parvati. But then Shiva uses his own far greater ascetic power to change blood to ashes, which are the symbol of the seed of life transfixed in death.

PRONOUNCING GLOSSARY

Bhava: *buh´-vuh*
Brahma: *bruh´-mah*
Kashyapa: *kush´-yuh-puh*
kusha: *koo´-shuh*
Mankanaka: *muhn-kuh´-nuh-kuh*
Marut: *muh´-root*
Rambha: *rum-bah´*
Saptasarasvata: *sup´-tuh-sah´-ruhs-vuh-tuh*
Sarasvata: *sah´-ruhs-vuh-tuh*
Shiva: *Shih´-vuh*
Siddha: *sid´-duh*

Vamana Purana Saromahatmya 17.2–23

The twice-born sage Mankanaka, the mind-born son of Kashyapa,[1] set out to bathe in his bark garment, and the celestial nymphs, Rambha and the others, who were pleasing to look upon, shining, affectionate, and flawless, bathed there with him. Then the sage, whose ascetic power was great, became excited and shed his seed in the water; he collected that seed in a pot, where it became divided into seven parts, from which were born seven sages who are known as the bands of the Maruts:[2] Wind-speed, Wind-force, Wind-destroyer, Wind-circle, Wind-flame, Wind-seed, and Wind-disc, whose heroic power is great. These seven sons of the seer support the universe, moving and still.

Once, long ago, the Siddha[3] Mankanaka was wounded in the hand by the tip of a blade of (*kusha*) grass,[4] and plant sap flowed from that wound—so I have heard. When he saw the plant sap, he was filled with joy, and he started to dance; and then everything that was moving or still started to dance; the universe started to dance, for it was bewitched by his energy. When Brahma and the other gods and the sages rich in ascetic power saw this, they reported to the great god Shiva about the sage: 'You should do something so that he does not dance, O god.' When the Great God saw that the sage was filled with joy to excess, he spoke to him for the sake of the welfare of the gods, saying, 'Best of twice-born sages, what is the reason that has occasioned this joy in you who are an ascetic stationed on the path of dharma?' 'Why, brahmin,' said the sage, 'do you not see the plant sap flowing from my hand? When I saw it I began to dance with joy.'

The god laughed at the sage who was deluded by passion, and he said to him, 'I am not amazed, priest. Look at this,' and when Bhava,[5] the god of gods, of great luster, had said this to the eminent sage, he struck his own thumb with the tip of his finger, and from that wound ashes shining like snow came forth. When the priest saw this he was ashamed, and he fell at Shiva's feet and said, 'I think that you are none other than the noble god who holds the trident in his hand, the best in the universe moving and still, the Trident-bearer. Brahma and the other gods appear to be dependent upon

TRANSLATED BY Wendy Doniger O'Flaherty.

1. A powerful ascetic sage.
2. Storm gods of Indra's entourage.
3. A Perfected Being, with magic powers.
4. A sharp-edged grass (also called *darbha*) used in Vedic ceremonies.
5. "Existence" or "Becoming," a name of Shiva.

you, faultless one. You are the first of the gods, the great one who acts and causes others to act. By your grace all the gods rejoice and fear nothing.' When the sage had thus praised the great god, he bowed and said, 'O lord, by your favor let my ascetic power not be destroyed.' Then the god was pleased, and he answered the sage, 'Your ascetic power will increase a thousand-fold by my favor, O priest, and I will dwell in this hermitage with you for ever. Any man who bathes in the Saptasarasvata[6] and worships me will find nothing impossible to obtain in this world and in the other world, but he will certainly go to the Sarasvata world and, by the grace of Shiva, he will obtain the highest place.'

6. The region of the seven branches of the Sarasvati River, here visualized as a special heaven.

VISHNU

Vishnu is generally more benevolent, human, and conventional than Shiva. He is often said to have ten avatars, or "descents" from heavenly to earthly form, sometimes associated with the progression of the Ages (Yugas) through time ("The Four Ages"): first the fish, the tortoise, the boar, and the Man-lion (aquatic animals or part-animals, all in the Krita Yuga, the first Age); then Parashurama, Rama, and the dwarf (humans, in the second Age); Krishna and the Buddha (humans in the third Age); and finally Kalki in the last age, the Kali Yuga ("The Ten Avatars," p. 480). The texts often describe the avatars as various functions of the god that emanate out of him and express his many manifestations. But historically, various gods already in existence were attracted to Vishnu and attached themselves to him like iron filings to a magnet.

We have already encountered two human avatars, Krishna and Rama, in the *Mahabharata* and *Ramayana*; the *Mahabharata* also mentions the tortoise, Parashurama, and Kalki. The authors of the Puranas then created other avatars out of figures from earlier texts, such as the dwarf who becomes a giant, which they developed out of the Vedic figure of the wide-striding giant ("The Three Strides of Vishnu," p. 91), and the fish and the boar, adopted from forms of Prajapati in the Brahmanas ("The Fish Saves Manu from the Flood," p. 95). Other avatars, such as the Man-lion, are mentioned in the *Vishnu Purana*, ca. 400–500 C.E, and probably came from newer regional and popular figures.

All of the avatars are said ultimately to bring about our well-being, though two—the Buddha ("Vishnu as the Buddha") and Kalki ("Vishnu as Kalki")—do cause some moral and physical destruction to humankind in the course of achieving their beneficial goal.

VISHNU AS THE BUDDHA

The Buddha avatar was originally not, as it might seem at first (and as it later became), a genuine attempt to assimilate the teachings of the Buddha into Hinduism (though this was certainly done in many other ways). On the contrary, although Vishnu in this myth expresses the anti-Vedic sentiments that Hindus sometimes attributed to Buddhists, Jains, Materialists, and other dissident groups, he does this in order to destroy the demons by means of an *evil* doctrine—Buddhism—on the principle that one cannot destroy a virtuous person unless one first corrupts him.

The anti-gods are destroyed because they abandon their own, anti-god dharma in order to join the new religious movement. The great deluder, whose defense of non-violence (*ahimsa*) is here regarded as part of the great lie, is both a Jain (with peacock feathers) and a Buddhist (in ochre robes). His argument about one man eating for another is a standard Hindu satire on the Materialist satire on the Hindu rite of feeding the dead ancestors; and the remark about the sacrificer killing his own father correctly quotes a real argument in a Buddhist text. But the conversion of humankind to Buddhism (or Jainism, or Materialism, or any other heresy) is merely an unfortunate side effect of Vishnu's attack on the anti-gods, a kind of theological fallout; and the fact that the doctrine is directed against the anti-gods indicates the degree of anti-Buddhist sentiment that motivated the author of this myth.

Yet the narrative is more like a playful satire on Buddhism and Jainism than a serious attack. And some of the later Puranas, and other Sanskrit texts of this period, put a positive spin on the Buddha avatar. The *Bhagavata Purana* (6.8.19) says that Vishnu became the Buddha in order to protect us from lack of enlightenment and from fatal blunders. Jayadeva's twelfth-century *Gita Govinda* says that Vishnu became the Buddha out of compassion for animals, to end bloody sacrifices ("The Ten Avatars," p. 480). These texts may express a Hindu desire to absorb Buddhism peacefully, both to win Buddhists to the worship of Vishnu and to account for the fact that such a significant heresy could prosper in India. They may also reflect the rising sentiment against animal sacrifice *within Hinduism.* Hindus spoke in many voices about the Buddha: some positive, some negative, and some indifferent or ambivalent.

PRONOUNCING GLOSSARY

The following list uses common English syllables and stress accents to provide rough equivalents of selected words whose pronunciation may be unfamiliar to the general reader.

Arhata: *ahr´-huh-tuh*
Brahma: *bruh´-mah*
Garuda: *guh-roo´-duh*
Hari: *huh´-ree*
Hrada: *huh-rah´-duh*
Narmada: *nar´-muh-dah´*
Nirvana: *neer-vah´-nuh*
shami: *shuh´-mee*
Vishnu: *vish´-noo*

Vishnu Purana 3.17–18

There was once a battle between the gods and the demons that lasted for a hundred celestial years, in which the gods were conquered by the demons. The gods went to the northern shore of the ocean of milk and practiced asceticism in order to propitiate Vishnu, and they sang a hymn of praise to him . . . When they had finished praising him, the gods saw the supreme lord Hari mounted on the Garuda bird,[1] with his conch and discus and mace in his hands. All the gods prostrated themselves before him and said, 'Have mercy, lord; protect us from the demons, as we have come for refuge. The demons under the command of Hrada have stolen away our portions of the sacrifices in the triple world, but they have not violated the command of Brahma, O supreme lord. Even though we and they are both born of portions

TRANSLATED BY Wendy Doniger O'Flaherty.

1. A mythical eagle on which Vishnu flies.

of you, who are the essence of all creatures, nevertheless we see the universe as divided, a distinction caused by ignorance. They take pleasure in the duties of their own class, and they follow the path of the Vedas and are full of ascetic powers. Therefore we cannot kill them, although they are our enemies, and so you should devise some means by which we will be able to kill the demons, O lord, soul of everything without exception.'

When the lord Vishnu heard their request, he emitted from his body a deluding form of his magic power of illusion, and he gave it to the supreme gods and said, 'This magic deluder will bewitch all the demons so that they will be excluded from the path of the Vedas, and thus they will be susceptible to slaughter. For no matter how many gods, demons, or others obstruct the way of the authority of Brahma, I will slaughter them all in order to establish order. Therefore go away and do not fear; this magic deluder will go before you today and assist you, gods.' When the gods heard this they prostrated themselves before him and went back whence they had come, and the magic deluder went with the great gods to the place where the great demons were.

When the magic deluder, naked, bald, carrying a bunch of peacock feathers,[2] saw that the great demons had gone to the banks of the Narmada river[3] and were practicing asceticism, he spoke to the demons with smooth words, saying, 'Lord of demons! Tell me why you are practicing asceticism—do you wish for the fruits of asceticism in this world or in the world beyond?' The demons replied, 'Noble one, we have undertaken this practice of asceticism in order to obtain the fruits of the world beyond. What is there here for you to dispute?' He said, 'Do as I say, if you wish for release, for you are worthy of this dharma which is the open door to release. This is the dharma worthy of release, and there is none better than this; by following it you will obtain heaven or release. All of you, mighty ones, are worthy of this dharma.' With many deductions, examples, and arguments of this sort, the magic deluder led the demons from the path of the Vedas: 'This would be dharma, but it would not be dharma; this is, but it is not; this would give release, but it would not give release; this is the supreme object, but it is also not the supreme object; this is effect, but it is not effect; this is not crystal clear. This is the dharma of those who are naked; this is the dharma of those who wear many clothes.' Thus the magic deluder taught a varying doctrine of more than one conclusion to the demons, who abandoned their own dharma. And they who took refuge in this dharma became Arhatas,[4] because the magic deluder said to them, 'You are worthy [*arhata*] of this great dharma.'

When the magic deluder had caused the demons to abandon the dharma of the triple Vedas, they themselves became his disciples and persuaded others; and yet others were persuaded by these, and still others by those, and so in a few days most of the demons abandoned the three Vedas. Then the magic deluder, who had subdued his senses, put on a red garment and went and spoke to other demons in soft, short, and honeyed words: 'If you demons wish for heaven or for Nirvana, then realize that you must stop these evil rites such as killing animals. Comprehend that all this universe is perceived

2. Jains went about naked and carried small brooms of peacock feathers with which they brushed their paths so that they would not tread on insects or other small living creatures.

3. The Narmada ("Jester"), the great river that divides the North from the South, has inspired an extensive mythology that mirrors that of the Ganges in the North.

4. "Arhatas" here clearly designates Jains, in contrast with the Buddhists who are about to appear; but "Arhata" in general could also designate a Buddhist monk.

only by means of knowledge; understand my speech properly, for it has been said by wise men. All this universe is without support and is intent upon achieving what it mistakenly believes to be knowledge; it wanders in the straits of existence, corrupted by passion and the other emotions.' As he said to them over and over, 'Understand! [*budhyata*],' the magic deluder caused the demons to abandon their own dharma, and with various speeches employing logic he made them gradually abandon the dharma of the triple Vedas. Then they spoke in this way to others, who addressed yet others in this way, so that they abandoned the highest dharma which is taught in the Vedas and lawbooks.

Then the magic deluder, capable of producing total delusion, corrupted other demons with many other sorts of heresy, and in a very short time the demons were corrupted by the magic deluder and abandoned the entire teaching of the triple path of the Vedas. Some reviled the Vedas; others the gods; and others the collection of sacrificial rituals and the twice-born. 'This speech is not logical, that "injury is conducive to dharma."' 'It is the babbling of a child, to say that butter burnt as an oblation in the fire is productive of reward.' 'If the *shami* fire-sticks and other wood are consumed by Indra, who has become a god by means of many sacrifices, then a beast who eats leaves is better than Indra.' 'If an animal slaughtered in the sacrifice is thus promised entry into heaven, why does not the sacrificer kill his own father?' 'If the oblation to the ancestors which is eaten by one man satisfies another, then people travelling abroad need not take the trouble to carry food.'[5] 'When you have understood what contemptible people will believe in, then the words I have uttered will please you. The words of authority do not fall from the sky, great demons; only the speech based upon logic should be accepted by men and by others like you.'

When the magic deluder had made the demons freethinkers with many speeches like this, not one of them took pleasure in the triple Vedas. And when the demons were thus set upon the wrong path, the immortals made the supreme effort and prepared for battle. Then the battle between the gods and demons was resumed, and the gods slew the demons, who now stood in opposition to the right path. The armor of their own dharma which had at first been theirs had formerly protected them, and when it was destroyed, they were destroyed.

5. The Materialists argued that their sons and others could eat food for them at home in the village, just as the living son nourishes his dead and absent ancestors—so the commentator explains.

VISHNU AS KALKI

Kalki (or Kalkin) is Vishnu's final avatar, the only one yet to come in the future, the messiah who will appear at the end of the present age, the Kali Age. This idea may have entered India with the invading Scythians and Parthians (the people whose empire occupied all of what is now Iran, Iraq, and Armenia) in the first centuries C.E., a time when millennial ideas were rampant in that part of the world, as well as the Mediterranean and Central Asia. Kalkin himself takes the form of an invader: he comes riding on a white horse. But his purpose is to destroy the invaders, to raze the wicked cities of the plain that have been polluted by invading foreign horsemen, as well as to exterminate all heretics, including the Buddhists that he himself (in his overarching form of Vishnu) had just produced in his penultimate incarnation (Vishnu as the Buddha).

In reversing the Kali Age in this manner, Vishnu challenges the force of time itself, for the Kali Age was *meant* to be evil. Yet the dice of fate are not loaded, for the tide of evil civilization seems to turn even before Vishnu appears: people leave the wicked cities and eat roots and wear bark garments, just like virtuous sages; the seeds of a new Winning Age, the golden age, are already sown in the Kali Age, and Vishnu merely acts as a catalyst, a cog in the wheel of time.

PRONOUNCING GLOSSARY

Brahma: *bruh´-mah*
Dasyu: *duhs´-yoo*
Kalkin: *kuhl´-kin*
Vasudeva: *vuh´-soo-day´-vuh*
Vishnuyashas: *vish´-noo-yuh´-shus*

Vishnu Purana 4.24.25–29

Unable to support their avaricious kings, the people of the Kali Age will take refuge in the chasms between mountains, and they will eat honey, vegetables, roots, fruits, leaves, and flowers. They will wear ragged garments made of leaves and the bark of trees, and they will have too many children, and they will be forced to bear cold, wind, sun, and rain. No one's age-span will reach twenty-three years, and thus without respite the entire race will become destroyed in this Kali Age.

When Vedic religion and the dharma of the lawbooks have undergone total confusion and reversal and the Kali Age is almost exhausted, then a part of the creator of the entire universe, of the guru of all that moves and is still, without beginning, middle, or end, who is made of Brahma and has the form of the soul, the blessed lord Vasudeva[1]—he will become incarnate here in the universe in the form of Kalkin, endowed with the eight supernatural powers, in the house of Vishnuyashas,[2] the chief brahmin of the village of Shambala.[3] His power and glory will be unlimited, and he will destroy all the barbarians and Dasyus[4] and men of evil acts and thoughts, and he will reestablish everything, each in its own dharma. Immediately at the conclusion of the exhausted Kali Age,[5] the minds of the people will become pure as flawless crystal, and they will be as if awakened at the conclusion of a night. And these men, the residue of mankind, will thus be transformed, and they will be the seeds of creatures and will give birth to offspring conceived at that very time. And these offspring will follow the ways of the Winning Age.

Translated by Wendy Doniger O'Flaherty.

1. Krishna.
2. "Fame of Vishnu." In the *Mahabharata*, the only indication that Kalkin is an avatar of Vishnu is the statement that Kalkin himself is "Vishnuyashas."
3. An early reference to the city that was to become the hub of a widespread myth about a mysterious lost civilization in the Himalayas.
4. Slaves or aliens, here probably denoting any non-Hindus.
5. The transition to the Winning Age happens because of the very nature of time itself, the commentator explains.

KRISHNA

The Puranas record major changes in the worship of Krishna at this time. When we meet Krishna in the *Mahabharata*, he is already an adult; the *Harivamsha*, the appendix to the *Mahabharata*, composed a century or two after it (ca. 450 C.E.), gives Krishna a childhood. This childhood may have been derived, in the early centuries C.E., from popular, vernacular, non-Brahminical stories about a village boy who lived among the cowherd people, a far cry from the powerful prince Krishna of the *Mahabharata*. In a stroke of genius, the *Harivamsha* put the two mythologies together, the *Mahabharata* story of the prince and the folk/vernacular stories of a cowherd child, by bridging them with a third story, a variant of the one that Freud called the family romance, the myth of a noble boy who is raised by animals, or by the herders of animals, until he grows up and finds his real parents. (The pattern applies to Karna in the *Mahabharata* as well as to Oedipus, Moses, Cyrus, and Jesus. The animals are more prominent in the myths of Tarzan and Kipling's Mowgli.) The family romance is a ready-made story available to be used when there is a need to construct a childhood for a god who has appeared only as an adult in earlier texts.

Once the two mythologies were joined, the *Harivamsha* quickly absorbed the cowherd mythology and developed it in its own ways. Krishna in the *Mahabharata* was already a double figure, a god pretending to be a prince, but now he was doubly doubled: a god pretending to be a prince (the son of Vasudeva and Devaki) pretending to be a cowherd (the son of Nanda and Yashoda) in the village of Vrindavan (in present-day Uttar Pradesh). This opened up the way to the worship of the child Krishna, and to a theology brilliantly developed in the *Bhagavata Purana*, a Sanskrit text composed in South India in the tenth century reflecting the influence of the *bhakti* movement that had begun there. This text explores the theology of the hidden god, revealed through a series of charming miracles ("Krishna Kills the Ogress Putana") that puzzle everyone in the cowherd world, including Krishna's mother (Krishna's Mother Looks Inside His Mouth) but not the reader or hearer.

KRISHNA KILLS THE OGRESS PUTANA

The mythology of the baby Krishna, like the myth of Vishnu the giant dwarf ("The Three Strides of Vishnu," p. 91), plays constantly upon the contrast between appearance and reality: the apparently tiny mortal (the dwarf, the infant, the individual soul) occasionally reveals its true nature as the infinite immortal (the giant, the god, the universal godhead). Images of concealment abound in descriptions of Krishna in the story of the ogress (Rakshasa) Putana: the sword in the sheath, the spark in ashes. A parallel masquerade takes place in the forces of evil, in the hideous, putrid ogress disguised as a charming woman, and the virulent poison that appears to be nourishing milk. The double edge of milk/poison is a persistent motif in Hindu mythology ("The Churning of the Ocean," p. 149). The poison that substitutes for Putana's milk undergoes another reversal when the infant uses the act of suckling to kill *her* as she intended to kill him. But in the end this reversal is reversed yet again, for by killing her he purifies her and makes her sweet-smelling, which is to say that he makes real the virtue that she had falsely assumed.

As the present episode begins, Nanda, the cowherd who is Krishna's foster father, has been to see Vasudeva, the nobleman who is Krishna's birth father; and Vasudeva has warned Nanda that Krishna might be in danger.

PRONOUNCING GLOSSARY

Anakadundubhi: *uh´-nuh-kuh-doon-doo´-bee*
Devaki: *day´-vuh-kee´*
Govinda: *goh-vin´-duh*
Hari: *huh´-ree*
Indra: *in´-druh*
Kamsa: *kanh´-suh*
Krishna: *krish´-nuh*
Mathura: *muh-too-rah´*
Nanda: *nun´-duh*
Putana: *poo´-tuh-nah´*
Rakshasa: *rahk´-shuh-suh*
Rohini: *roh´-hee-nee´*
Satvata: *saht´-vuh-tuh*
Shri: *shree*
Vasudeva: *vah´-soo-day-vuh*
Vishnu: *vish´-noo*
Vritra: *vrih´-truh*
Yashoda: *yuh-shoh´-dah´*

Bhagavata Purana 10.6

When Nanda heard the speech of Vasudeva he thought, as he went on the road homewards, that this could not be false, and he sought refuge with Hari,[1] for he feared some misfortune.

The horrible Putana ('Stinking'), a devourer of children, was sent by Kamsa.[2] She wandered through cities, villages, and pastures, killing infants. Wherever men do not recite the deeds of Krishna the Lord of the Satvatas, a recitation which destroys Rakshasas, there evil demons work their sorcery. One day Putana came to Nanda's village, wandering at will, flying through the sky, and by her magic powers she assumed the form of a beautiful woman. Jasmine was bound into her hair; her hips and breasts were full, her waist slender. She wore fine garments, and her face was framed by hair that shone with the luster from her shimmering, quivering earrings. She cast sidelong glances and smiled sweetly, and she carried a lotus in her hand. When the wives of the cow-herds saw the woman, who stole their hearts, they thought that she must be Shri[3] incarnate, come to see her husband. The infant-swallower, searching for children, happened to come to the house of Nanda, and she saw there on the bed the infant Krishna, whose true energy was concealed, like a fire covered with ashes. Though he kept his eyes closed, he who is the very soul of all that moves and all that is still knew her to be an ogress who killed children, and she took the infinite one onto her lap, as one might pick up a sleeping deadly viper, mistaking it for a rope. Seeing her, whose wicked heart was concealed by sweet actions like a sharp sword encased in a scabbard, his mother was overcome by her splendor, and, thinking her to be a good woman, stood looking on.

Then the horrible one, taking him on her lap, gave the baby her breast, which had been smeared with a virulent poison. But the lord, pressing her breast hard with his hands, angrily drank out her life's breath with the milk. She cried out, 'Let go! Let go! Enough!' as she was squeezed in all her vital parts. She rolled her eyes and thrashed her arms and legs and screamed again and again, and all her limbs were bathed in sweat. At the sound of her

TRANSLATED BY Wendy Doniger O'Flaherty.

1. A name of Vishnu.
2. The wicked uncle who wants to kill Krishna and whose plots against the baby made it necessary to remove Krishna from the palace and conceal him among cowherds.
3. "Prosperity," another name for Lakshmi, the wife of Vishnu and therefore by extension the wife of Krishna. She always carries a lotus, as Putana does here.

deep roar, the earth with its mountains and the sky with its planets shook; the subterranean waters and the regions of the sky resounded, and people fell to the ground fearing that lightning had struck. The night-wandering ogress, with agonizing pain in her breasts, opened her mouth, stretched out her arms and legs, tore her hair, and fell lifeless on the ground in the cow-pen, like the serpent Vritra[4] struck down by Indra's thunderbolt. Then she resumed her true form, and as her body fell it crushed all the trees for twelve miles around; this was a great marvel. Her mouth was full of terrible teeth as large as plough-shafts; her nostrils were like mountain caves; her breasts were like boulders, and her hideous red hair was strewn about. Her eyes were like deep, dark wells; her buttocks were terrifying, large as beaches; her stomach was like a great dry lake emptied of water, her arms like dams. When the cow-herds and their wives saw her corpse they were terrified, and their hearts, ears, and skulls had already been split by her terrible roar.

The infant Krishna killing the ogress Putana. Wood carving with traces of red and blue pigments. Kerala, seventeenth century.

When they saw the little boy playing on her breast fearlessly, the wives of the cow-herds were frightened and quickly took him away, and Yashoda and Rohini[5] and the others protected the boy by waving a cow's tail on him and performing similar rites. They bathed the baby in cow's urine and cow-dust, and with cow-dung they wrote the names of Vishnu on his twelve limbs, to protect him . . . [6] Thus the loving wives of the cow-herds protected him, and then his mother gave her son her breast to suck and put him to bed.

Meanwhile, Nanda and the other cow-herds returned to the village from Mathura,[7] and when they saw the body of Putana they were astonished. 'Indeed, Anakadundubhi[8] has become a seer or a master of yoga,' they said, 'for he foresaw and foretold this whole calamity.' Then the villagers cut up the corpse with axes and threw the limbs far away, and they surrounded them with wood and burnt them. The smoke that arose from Putana's body as it burnt was as sweet-smelling as aloe-wood, for her sins had been destroyed when she fed Krishna. Putana, a slayer of people and infants, a female Rakshasa, a drinker of blood, reached the heaven of good people because

4. The serpent/dragon that Indra, king of the gods, kills, in the *Rig Veda*.
5. Yashoda is the foster mother of Krishna, and Rohini is another wife of Vasudeva (Krishna's birth father) and the mother of Krishna's older brother Balarama.
6. Here they chant a series of spells to protect the baby from various ogresses and diseases.
7. A town near the cowherds' village, in Uttar Pradesh.
8. A name of Vasudeva, so called because at birth the gods, foreseeing the birth of Krishna, caused two sorts of drums (*anaka* and *dundubhi*) to resound in heaven.

she had given her breast to Vishnu—even though she did it because she wished to kill him. How much greater, then, is the reward of those who offer what is dearest to the highest Soul, Krishna, with faith and devotion, like his doting mothers? She gave her breast to Krishna to suck, and he touched her body with his two feet which remain in the hearts of his devotees and which are adored by those who are adored by the world, and so, though an evil sorceress, she obtained the heaven which is the reward of mothers. What then is the reward of those cows and mothers whose breasts' milk Krishna drank? The lord, son of Devaki, giver of beatitude and all else, drank their milk as their breasts flowed because of their love for their son. Since they always looked upon Krishna as their son, they will never again be doomed to rebirth that arises from ignorance.

When the inhabitants of the village smelled the sweet smoke from the pyre they asked, 'What is this? What has caused it?', and they returned to the village. There they heard the cow-herds describe the arrival of Putana and the subsequent events, and when they learned of the death of Putana and the safety of the baby, they were amazed. The noble Nanda lovingly took his son on his lap like one who had returned from the dead, and kissed his head and rejoiced. Whatever mortal faithfully hears this tale of the marvellous deed of the baby Krishna, the liberation of Putana, he finds his joy in Govinda.[9]

9. "Cow-finder," a name of Krishna.

KRISHNA'S MOTHER LOOKS INSIDE HIS MOUTH

The motif of concealment, of the big inside the little, of banal detail obscuring/revealing sacred majesty, is also part of the myth of looking into the mouth of god. The myth appears first in the *Mahabharata*, where the sage Markandeya, floating in the cosmic ocean after the dissolution of the universe, comes upon a young boy sleeping under a banyan tree, He enters the mouth of the boy (who is Vishnu) and sees the entire universe within him. In book 11 of the *Bhagavad Gita*, Krishna reveals to Arjuna the unbearable image of Doomsday inside his mouth. The *Bhagavata Purana* domesticates this myth: Yashoda looks into the mouth of her toddler Krishna and sees in it the universe and herself, a vision that she finds unbearable, just as Arjuna did. In both cases, Krishna grants, in his infinite love, the boon that Arjuna and Yashoda will forget the vision.

In the selection here, we also see the theme of Krishna's mischief, a domesticated form of the cosmic mischief that Vishnu wreaks in other avatars ("Vishnu as the Buddha" and "Vishnu as Kalki").

PRONOUNCING GLOSSARY

Hari: *huh´-ree*
Keshava: *kay´shuh-vuh*
Krishna: *krish´-nuh*
Rama: *rah´-muh*
Sankhya: *sahnh´-kyuh*
Satvata: *saht´-vuh-tuh*
Upanishad: *oo-puh´-nuh´-shud*
Yashoda: *yuh-shoh-dah´*

Bhagavata Purana 10.8

After a little while, Rama[1] and Keshava began to play in the village, crawling on their hands and knees. They slithered about quickly, dragging their feet in the muddy pastures, delighting in the tinkling sound.[2] They would follow someone and then, suddenly bewildered and frightened, they would hasten back to their mothers. Their mothers' breasts would flow with milk out of tenderness for their own sons, whose bodies were beautifully covered with mud, and they would embrace them in their arms and give them their breasts to suck, and as they gazed at the faces with their innocent smiles and tiny teeth they would rejoice. Then the children began to play in the village at those boyish games that women love to see. They would grab hold of the tails of calves and be dragged back and forth in the pasture, and the women would look at them and forget their housework and laugh merrily. But the mothers, trying to keep the two very active and playful little boys from horned animals, fire, animals with teeth and tusks, and knives, water, birds, and thorns, were unable to do their housework, and they were rather uneasy.

After a little while, Rama and Krishna stopped crawling on their hands and knees and began to walk about the pastures quickly on their feet. Then the lord Krishna began to play with Rama and with the village boys of their age, giving great pleasure to the village women. When the wives of the cow-herds saw the charming boyish pranks of Krishna, they would go in a group to tell his mother, saying, 'Krishna unties the calves when it is not the proper time, and he laughs at everyone's angry shouts. He devises ways to steal and eat curds and milk and thinks food sweet only if he steals it. He distributes the food among the monkeys; if he doesn't eat the food, he breaks the pot. If he cannot find anything, he becomes angry at the house and makes the children cry before he runs away. If something is beyond his reach, he fashions some expedient by piling up pillows, mortars, and so on; or if he knows that the milk and curds have been placed in pots suspended in netting, he makes holes in the pots. When the wives of the cow-herds are busy with household duties, he will steal things in a dark room, making his own body with its masses of jewels serve as a lamp. This is the sort of impudent act which he commits; and he pees and so forth in clean houses. These are the thieving tricks that he contrives, but he behaves in the opposite way and is good when you are near.' When his mother heard this report from the women who were looking at Krishna's frightened eyes and beautiful face, she laughed and did not wish to scold him.

One day when Rama and the other little sons of the cow-herds were playing, they reported to his mother, 'Krishna has eaten dirt.' Yashoda took Krishna by the hand and scolded him, for his own good, and she said to him, seeing that his eyes were bewildered with fear, 'Naughty boy, why have you secretly eaten dirt? These boys, your friends, and your elder brother say so.'

TRANSLATED BY Wendy Doniger O'Flaherty.

1. In Puranic stories about Krishna, "Rama" always refers to Balarama, Krishna's brother, and has nothing to do with the Rama of the *Ramayana* ("The Birth of Sita," p. 189). Keshava is a name of Krishna.

2. The commentator says that this is the sound of their own anklets and bangles.

Krishna said, 'Mother, I have not eaten. They are all lying. If you think they speak the truth, look at my mouth yourself.' 'If that is the case, then open your mouth,' she said to the lord Hari,[3] the god of unchallenged sovereignty who had in sport taken the form of a human child, and he opened his mouth.

She then saw in his mouth the whole eternal universe, and heaven, and the regions of the sky, and the orb of the earth with its mountains, islands, and oceans; she saw the wind, and lightning, and the moon and stars, and the zodiac; and water and fire and air and space itself; she saw the vacillating senses, the mind, the elements, and the three strands of matter. She saw within the body of her son, in his gaping mouth, the whole universe in all its variety, with all the forms of life and time and nature and action and hopes, and her own village, and herself. Then she became afraid and confused, thinking, 'Is this a dream or an illusion wrought by a god? Or is it a delusion of my own perception? Or is it some portent of the natural powers of this little boy, my son? I bow down to the feet of the god, whose nature cannot be imagined or grasped by mind, heart, acts, or speech; he in whom all of this universe is inherent, impossible to fathom. The god is my refuge, he through whose power of delusion there arise in me such false beliefs as "I," "This is my husband," "This is my son," "I am the wife of the village chieftain and all his wealth is mine, including these cow-herds and their wives and their wealth of cattle."'

When the cow-herd's wife had come to understand the true essence in this way, the lord spread his magic illusion in the form of maternal affection. Instantly the cow-herd's wife lost her memory of what had occurred and took her son on her lap. She was as she had been before, her heart flooded with even greater love. She considered Hari—whose greatness is extolled by the three Vedas and the Upanishads and the philosophies of Sankhya[4] and yoga and all the Satvata[5] texts—she considered him to be her son.

3. A name of Vishnu.
4. The philosophy of *purusha* and *prakriti* and the three *gunas* (qualities) ("The Two Paths," p. 178).
5. The family into which Krishna was born.

DEVI, THE GODDESS

The Puranas begin to tell stories about goddesses. We will never know for how many centuries a goddess was worshipped in India by people who had no access to Sanskrit texts and whose voices we therefore cannot identify. Though there are a few goddesses in the *Rig Veda* ("Aditi and the Birth of the Gods," p. 80), they are generally personifications of abstract nouns or little more than wives, such as Indrani, "Mrs. Indra," the wife of the god Indra. The births of Draupadi ("The Stripping of Draupadi," p. 134) and Sita ("The Birth of Sita," p. 189) reveal that both Draupadi and Sita began as goddesses (and Draupadi went on to become a goddess with a sect of her own), though the *Mahabharata* and *Ramayana* treat them by and large as mortal women. There are other, more substantial hints of the worship of a goddess in the *Mahabharata:* tantalizingly brief references to the seven or eight "Little Mothers" (Matrikas), dark, peripheral, and harmful, especially for children, and to the Great Kali (Maha-Kali), and to the goddess of Death and Night who appears in a vision in the *Book of the Night Raid*, right before the massacre of sleeping warriors begins (10.8.64). But these females do not kill the anti-gods; it remained for the Puranas to tell of a goddess who did this and to offer a vibrant mythology of independent goddesses.

Such a goddess, first called Chandika ("the Fierce"), later often called Durga ("Hard to Get [To]") or Kali ("Death" or "Doomsday," a black goddess who wears a necklace of human skulls and a girdle made of the fingers of children [Ramprasad Sen, p. 526]), bursts onto the Sanskrit scene full grown in a complex myth that includes a hymn of a thousand names. Many of the names allude to entire mythological episodes that must have grown onto the goddess, like barnacles on a great ship, gradually for centuries. The stories may have come from villages or tribal cultures where the goddess had been worshipped; early in her history she may have been associated with tribal or low-caste peoples who worshipped her in wild places. This was a time when devotional texts of all sorts flourished; and since people worshipped Devi ("the Goddess"), she, too, needed texts. What may have started as a local sect began to spread under royal patronage inspired by *bhakti*. At some moment, the critical mass of Devi worship forced the Brahmin custodians of Sanskrit narratives to acknowledge it. And that is what the Puranas did.

THE BIRTH OF THE GODDESS

The slaughter of the buffalo demon (Mahisha) is the most famous accomplishment of the Goddess and is therefore the usual occasion for the narration of her birth. There are many different versions of this myth. The relatively late *Skanda Purana* (700–1100 C.E.) describes the births of both the buffalo and the Goddess. The buffalo is born from an unnamed daughter of Diti ("Limit," mother of the anti-gods called Daityas) and a sage named Suparshva ("Having Beautiful Sides") and fights for an anti-god named Vidyunmalin ("Garlanded with Lightning"), the son of Viprachitti ("Sagacious"), against the gods led by Indra, king of the gods, also called Shatterer of Cities and the husband of Shaci ("Power"). The Goddess is born through a reversal of the Vedic myth of creation by dismemberment ("The Hymn of the Primeval Man," p. 82), in a process of re-memberment: parts of all the Vedic gods (Yama, god of the dead; the Vasus, solar gods; Varuna, god of the waters; Kubera, god of wealth; Prajapatis, creator gods; the Oblation-bearer, fire; and several forces of nature) combine to form a deity more powerful than all of them, the whole that is greater than the sum of its parts.

PRONOUNCING GLOSSARY

Agni: *ug´-nee*
Amaravati: *uh-muh-rah´-vuh-tee´*
Brahma: *bruh´-mah*
Diti: *dih´-tee*
Durga: *door´-gah*
Indra: *in´-druh*
Krishna: *krish´-nuh*
Kubera: *koo-bay´-ruh*
Lakshmi: *luk´-shmee*
Mahisha: *muh-hee´-shuh*
Narayana: *nah-rah´-yuh-nuh*
Prajapati: *pruh-jah´-puh-tee*
Shaci: *shuh-chee*
Shambhu: *shum´-boo*
Shiva: *shih´-vuh*
Suparshva: *soo-parsh´-vuh*
Varuna: *vuh´-roo-nuh*
Vasu: *vuh´-soo*
Vidyunmalin: *vid-yoon´-mah´-lin*
Viprachitti: *vih´-pruh-chit´-tee*
Vishnu: *vish´-noo*
Yama: *yuh´-muh*

Skanda Purana 3.1.6.8–42

In times past, in the battle between gods and demons, the sons of Diti were destroyed by the gods. Then Diti was distraught by grief, and she said to her daughter, 'Go, my daughter, and practice asceticism in a grove of asceticism for the sake of a son, so that because of that son Indra and the other gods, who have restrained their senses and are self-controlled, will no longer remain, O fair-hipped one.' When the daughter heard her mother's words, she bowed to her and took the form of a buffalo; she went to the forest and sat between five fires.[1] She practiced asceticism so dreadful that the worlds trembled and the triple world was agitated by fear of her asceticism, and Indra and the other bands of gods and the supreme twice-born ones were stupefied. The sage Suparshva was shaken by her asceticism and said to her, 'Fair-hipped one, I am satisfied. You will have a son with the head of a buffalo and the body of a man, and your son's name will be Mahisha ["Buffalo"]. He will have heroic energy in excess, and he will oppress heaven and Indra and his army.' When Suparshva had thus spoken to her to cause her to desist from her asceticism, he went back to his own world, taking the ascetic woman with him. Then the buffalo was born as Brahma had formerly predicted, and he grew up and increased in heroic power as the great ocean grows during a lunar fortnight.

Then Vidyunmalin, the general of the demons, the son of Viprachitti, and other demon chiefs who live on the surface of the earth all heard of the boon that had been given to the buffalo, and they assembled joyously and said to the buffalo demon, 'Formerly we were kings in heaven, O clever one, but our kingdom was forcibly stolen by the gods when they sought refuge with Vishnu.[2] Bring that kingdom back to us by force; display your heroic power and your majesty today, buffalo demon. Your strength and heroism are unparalleled, and you have been elevated by the boon given by Brahma. Conquer the husband of Shachi and the hosts of the gods in battle.' When the buffalo of great heroic power heard what the demons said, he began to wish to fight with the immortals, and he set out for Amaravati, the city of the gods.

A fierce, hair-raising battle between the gods and demons then took place for a hundred years, and at first the multitude of gods was put to flight in all directions; placing the Shatterer of Cities before them, they went to Brahma in terror. Then Brahma took all the immortals back to Narayana[3] and Shiva, the protectors of everything, and he arrived and bowed and praised them with many hymns of praise, and he reported to the two gods, Shambhu[4] and Krishna, what the buffalo demon had done and how the demons had oppressed the gods: 'He has thrown Indra, Agni, Yama, the sun, the moon, Kubera, Varuna and the others out of their positions of authority and assumed these positions himself; and he has usurped the positions of others among the multitude of gods as well. The gods have been thrown out of the world of heaven down to the surface of the earth and are wandering like men, hard

TRANSLATED BY Wendy Doniger O'Flaherty.

1. That is, she built four fires, one on each side of her, and sat beneath the sun as the fifth.
2. Vishnu, incarnate as the dwarf, stole heaven (back) from the anti-god Bali ("The Ten Avatars," p. 480).
3. A name of Vishnu.
4. A name of Shiva.

The goddess Durga killing the buffalo demon, Mahisha. Relief in the Mahishamardini temple at Mamallapuram, seventh century.

pressed by the buffalo demon. I have come here with the bands of gods to report this to you two gods; protect those who have come here.'

When Vishnu, the husband of Lakshmi, and the great lord Shiva heard the speech of Brahma, their angry faces became so monstrous that one could not look upon them. From Vishnu's mouth, that blazed with extreme anger, his great energy came forth, and similarly from Shambhu and from the Creator, and from the bodies of Indra and all the other gods the cruel energies came forth and they all became one. The great mass of their united energies seemed to all the multitudes of gods like a blazing mountain that pervaded all the regions of the sky with flames. Then from the combination of these energies a certain woman appeared: her head appeared from the energy of Shiva, her two arms from the energy of Vishnu, her two feet from the energy of Brahma, and her waist from the energy of Indra; her hair was made from Yama's energy, her two breasts from the moon's energy, her thighs from the energy of Varuna, her hips from the earth's energy, her toes from the sun's energy; her fingers were formed by the energy of the Vasus, her nose by Kubera's energy, her rows of teeth from the energy of the nine Prajapatis; her two eyes arose from the energy of the Oblation-bearer; the two twilights became her two brows, and her ears were made from the energy of the wind; and from the incredibly fierce energies of the other gods other limbs were made for the woman who was the supremely radiant Durga, more dangerous than all the gods and demons.

THE DEATH OF THE BUFFALO DEMON

The founding text for the worship of the Goddess is "The Glorification of the Goddess" (*Devi-mahatmya*), a long poem probably woven into the *Markandeya Purana* (which also tells other stories about powerful women and goddesses) between the fifth and seventh centuries C.E. It is clear from the complexity of "The Glorification of the Goddess" that it must be a compilation of many earlier texts about the Goddess, either from lost Sanskrit texts or from lost or never-preserved vernacular sources. The Purana goes out of its way to tell us that merchants and kings worshipped the Goddess; in the outer frame, a sage tells the story of the Goddess of Great Illusion (Maha-maya) to a king who has lost his kingdom and a Vaishya (a merchant, a man of the third class) who has lost his wealth and family; at the end of the story, the Goddess grants each of them what he asks for: the king gets his kingdom (and the downfall of his enemies) while the Vaishya gets—not wealth, which he no longer covets, but the knowledge of what he is and what he has (and the conquest of his worldly addictions). Clearly the Vaishya is the man this text prefers.

In this, the earliest version of the killing of the buffalo demon, the Goddess's orgiastic drinking of wine and blood may reflect the darker side of her erotic nature. The "supreme wine" that she drinks is the blood of victims sacrificed to her.

Markandeya Purana 80.21–33

When his own army was totally destroyed, the buffalo demon assumed his own buffalo form and terrified the troops of the Goddess. Some he struck with his muzzle; others he trampled with his hooves. Some he lashed with his tail and pierced with his two horns; others he rushed at and roared at and whirled around; and still others he hurled down upon the surface of the earth by means of the hurricane of his breath. When he had thus felled the vanguard of the Goddess's army, the great demon attacked her lion in order to kill him, and then the Mother became angry. The great hero was angry too, and he pounded the surface of the earth with his hooves and tossed the mountains high with his two horns, and he roared. The earth was shattered by the poundings of his swift turns; the ocean, lashed by his tail, overflowed on all sides; the clouds, pierced by his swaying horns, were broken into fragments; and mountains fell from the sky by the hundreds, cast down by the blast of his breath.

When the fierce Goddess saw the great demon attacking, swollen thus with anger, she became frantic to slay him. She hurled her noose over him and bound the great demon; but when he was thus bound in the great struggle he abandoned his buffalo form and became a lion. When the Mother cut off his head, he appeared as a man with a sword in his hand and a shield made of hide, but the Goddess took her arrows and quickly pierced the man. Then he became a great elephant, who pulled at the great lion with his trunk and trumpeted, but the Goddess took her sword and cut off his trunk as he pulled. Then the great demon once more assumed his buffalo shape and shook the triple world, moving and still. Enraged by this, the furious

TRANSLATED BY Wendy Doniger O'Flaherty.

mother of the universe drank the supreme wine again and again; her eyes became red, and she laughed. The demon roared, puffed up and intoxicated with his own strength and courage, and with his two horns he hurled mountains at the furious Goddess, but she pulverized his missiles with a hail of arrows.

Then she spoke to him, her syllables confused with passion as they tumbled from her mouth which was loosened by intoxication. The Goddess said, 'Roar and roar for a moment, you fool, while I drink this honeyed wine. The gods will soon roar when I have slain you here.' Then she leaped up and mounted that great demon and kicked him in the neck with her foot and pierced him with her trident. When he was struck by her foot he came halfway out of his own mouth, for he was enveloped in the Goddess's heroic power. And as the great demon came halfway out, fighting, the Goddess cut off his head with his great sword, and he fell. Thus the demon named Buffalo was destroyed by the Goddess, together with his army and his band of friends, when he had bewitched the triple world. And when the buffalo had fallen, all creatures in the triple world, along with all the gods and demons and men, shouted, 'Victory!' A cry of lamentation arose from the entire demon army as it was destroyed, and all the bands of gods rejoiced. Then the gods and the heavenly great sages praised the Goddess, the Gandharva leaders[1] sang, and the bands of celestial nymphs danced.

1. Gandharvas are celestial musicians and demigods of fertility, the husbands of the celestial dancers and courtesans called Apsarases.

SHRINES AND PILGRIMAGES

The word for a shrine in Sanskrit is *tirtha*, a ford, a place where one "crosses over" a river; once, all shrines were on rivers, and even now they usually have some sort of water, if only a human-made pool in which the worshippers can bathe. The word *tirtha* comes from the verb *tri*, which is also the basis of ava-*tara*, "crossing down" from heaven to earth. And indeed, shrines are where one can cross simultaneously over the river and over the perils of the world of rebirth, or cross from earth to heaven. In addition to shrines on rivers, there are also shrines at the hermitages of famous sages.

The Emperor Ashoka, in the third century B.C.E., inaugurated the tradition of royal pilgrimages to Buddhist shrines in place of touring the kingdom in a series of royal hunts (itself a substitute for touring kingdoms in a series of royal battles). The Hindus soon established shrines of their own; the *Mahabharata* describes pilgrimages to Hindu shrines at length, particularly but not only in the "Tour of the Sacred Fords" (3.80–140). The *Mahabharata* applied the idea of the "conquest of the four corners of the earth" (*dig-vijaya*), originally a martial image, to a grand tour of many shrines, circling the world (India), always to the right, in a "journey to the shrines" (*tirtha-yatra*), which is the Sanskrit term for a pilgrimage. Many pilgrimage sites are described in the *Mahabharata*, but each Purana promotes one special place, a single shrine, often presenting a pilgrimage to that shrine as the most effective form of worship, better even than sacrifice or meditation, a way to achieve one's highest goal—which might be *moksha* or, more often, rebirth in the heaven of the chosen god.

THE DESCENT OF THE GANGES

The story of the birth of the Ganges is told in the *Ramayana* ("The Gods Interrupt Shiva and Parvati," p. 196), the *Mahabharata*, and many Puranas. The sacred river Ganges is also called the Jahnavi (after the sage Jahnu, through whose hermitage the river once flowed) and the Alakananda ("Delighting in Curls"). The following version of the story covers a lot of ground, beginning among mountains (the "Snowy Mountain," Himalaya, literally the "abode of snow," and Kailasa, the home of Shiva), then going down to the watery hell named Patala and up to the heaven called Vaikuntha (Vishnu's heaven). Several deities are involved: Shiva (called Mahadeva and Sharva), Vishnu (also called Hari), and Krishna (Keshava). The story extols both the Ganges and Vishnu, depicting even the god Shiva as a Vishnu-*bhakta* who, on occasion, takes the form of Vishnu.

PRONOUNCING GLOSSARY

Alakananda: *uh-luh-kuh-nun-dah´*
Bhagiratha: *buh-gee´-ruh-tuh*
Hari: *huh´-ree*
Haridvara: *huh´-rid-vah´-rah*
Jahnavi: *jah´-nuh-vee´*
Kailasa: *kai-lah´-suh*
Keshava: *kay´-shuh-vuh*
Narada: *nah´-ruh-duh*
Patala: *pah´-tah´-luh*
Sharva: *shar´-vuh*
tapas: *tuh´-puhs*
Vaikuntha: *vai-koon´-tuh*

Padma Purana 6.22.9–28

Narada[1] asked, "How was the Ganges brought down? What great *tapas*[2] did Bhagiratha[3] perform to ensure that his ancestors would have the proper obsequies? Tell me all, you are true to your vows, O ocean of compassion!"

Mahadeva replied, "The seer Bhagiratha went to the Snowy Mountain to rescue his ancestors, and having gone there did *tapas* for ten thousand years. The primeval god who is without taint became graciously disposed and gave him the Ganges, which came from the sky. God Sharva saw the Jahnavi coming where he, the lord of the universe, always resides, and he caught her in his twisted hair-tuft and held her there for ten thousand years; because of the power of the lord the Ganges did not come out. Bhagiratha wondered where his little mother had gone, and through meditation discerned that she had been caught by the lord. The powerful man thereupon betook himself to Kailasa, O best of hermits, and having gone there he practiced abundant *tapas*.

"Placated by him I gave him the river; relinquishing one hair I released the stream of the three courses. He took the Ganges and went to the netherworld Patala, where his ancestors lay. The first name of the Ganges is known

TRANSLATED BY Cornelia Dimmitt and J. A. B. van Buitenen.

1. A gossipy and meddlesome sage, here simply playing the role of the interlocutor.
2. Inner ascetic heat, generated by physical mortifications and meditation.
3. A king whose ancestors had been burned to ashes; he needs to bathe their ashes in the Ganges so that he can perform the proper funeral ceremonies.

as Alakananda. When it descends to Haridvara[4] it becomes the Water of Vishnu's Foot which is a preeminent ford hard to attain even for the gods. When a man bathes there and visits Hari (in particular), and performs the circumambulation, he will not know suffering. Multitudes of evil deeds including brahmin murders, however many, all vanish from a mere visit to Hari.

"Once I myself went to Haridvara, which is the sanctuary of Keshava, and because of the power of that ford I took on the form of Vishnu. The good people who go there find good health—men, women, the four-cornered worlds themselves. From merely visiting Hari they all go to the heaven Vaikuntha. Beautiful Haridvara is also a grand pilgrimage place of mine. This best of all fords bestows the four goals of life[5] in the Kali Age; it gives Dharma to people, and release and success as well, there where the lovely and pure Ganges flows perennially."

This little tale, called Haridvara, is holy and fine. They who listen to the great fame of the place obtain the same fruit as offering up a Horse Sacrifice or giving away a thousand cows. Such blessing does the wise man receive from just visiting Hari, be he a cow killer, a brahmin murderer, or a parricide; even such sins, however numerous, O Brahmin, all disappear from seeing Hari.

4. "The Doorway of Vishnu," a town where the Ganges descends from the Himalayas to the plains of India.

5. These are dharma, release (*moksha*), success (*artha*), and pleasure (*kama*) (Shastras, p. 200). For some reason this text specifies four but mentions only three, omitting *kama*.

THE RIVER YAMUNA

The Yamuna (or Jumna) River joins the Ganges at Prayaga (Allahabad), one of the holiest places in India. Every twelve years there is a great pilgrimage to Prayaga, called the Kumbha Mela, which attracts millions of pilgrims. In 2001 some 60 million people attended the Great Kumbha Mela, which is celebrated every 144 years.

This story is about both the Yamuna and Baladeva (also called Balarama and Balabhadra). In the *Mahabharata*, Balarama is the half-brother of Krishna, renowned for his physical power and his prowess with the mace and the plough. In the Vaishnava Puranas, Balarama becomes far more important and is sometimes regarded as one of the avatars of Vishnu; sometimes Balarama and Krishna are alternative incarnations, and sometimes partial incarnations, born of one white hair (Balarama) and one black hair (Krishna) of Vishnu. Balarama is also a notorious drinker, addicted to wine just as his brother Krishna is noted for his attachment to women, and the Puranas tell stories about this. This story is being told to a sage named Maitreya.

PRONOUNCING GLOSSARY

Ananta: *uh-nun´-tuh*
Balabhadra: *buh´-luh-bud´-ruh*
Baladeva: *buh-luh-day´-vuh*
kadamba: *kuh-dum´-buh*
Lakshmi: *luk´-shmee*
Madira: *muh´-dee-rah´*
Maitreya: *mai-tray´-yuh*
Rama: *rah´-muh*

Shesha: *shay´-shuh*
Varuna: *vuh-roo´-nuh*
Varuni: *vah´-roo-nee´*
Vrindavana: *vrin-dah´-vuh-nuh*
Yamuna: *yuh-moo-nah´*

Vishnu Purana 5.25.1–17

Once the great-souled upholder of the earth, the serpent Shesha,[1] after accomplishing some great task, was roaming around the forest with the cowherds in the guise of the man Baladeva. In order to reward him with great pleasure, Varuna[2] said to his wife, "O Madira (Wine), that mighty hero Ananta will find you desirable and beneficent. Go in joy, pure woman, and make him happy!" At his words, Varuni materialized in the hollow of a *kadamba* tree[3] that grew in Vrindavana.[4]

The handsome Baladeva, wandering around in the forest, smelled the exquisite aroma of Madira and conceived a thirst for the wine. When the plough-bearer saw a stream of wine flowing from the tree, Maitreya, he was delighted. And filled with joy, he drank it up, in the company of the cowherd men and women who, skilled in the ways of singing and music-making, sang sweetly to him.

When he was drunk and disoriented, covered with drops of perspiration that shone like pearls, he shouted to the river Yamuna, "Come over here! I want to take a bath!" Ignoring the words of the drunken man, the river refused to come, at which the furious plough-bearer snatched up his plough. Crazed with drink, he grabbed her and dragged her after him with the edge of his plough, exclaiming, "You refused to come to me, wicked woman. Now escape if you can!"

Hauled around by him, the river left her course at once and flooded the forest where Balabhadra was. Then she approached Rama in human form, eyes rolling in terror, and said to him, "Have mercy on me, club-wielder! Let me go!" The plough-weaponed hero answered her sweet words, "You would not respect my bravery and strength, O river, so I shall pull you in a thousand different directions with the thrust of my plough!" But after the Yamuna had flooded that part of the earth, Baladeva was moved by the words of that river, who was so afraid, and set her free.

After the great-souled Baladeva had bathed, the goddess Lakshmi[5] appeared and gave him a lovely lotus-blossom earring, a never-fading garland of lotus flowers sent by Varuna, and two garments deep blue like the sea. Thus adorned with a beautiful earring, dark blue robes, and a lovely garland, he shone forth in radiant beauty.

Translated by Cornelia Dimmitt and J. A. B. van Buitenen.

1. "What Is Left," also called Ananta ("Infinite"), the great serpent on which the earth rests. Balarama is regarded as an incarnation of Shesha.
2. Vedic god of the waters. His wife, Varuni, is a kind of wine.
3. A tree, *Nauclea cadamba,* said to put forth its fragrant buds at the roaring of thunderclouds.
4. Krishna's village, in present-day Uttar Pradesh.
5. Goddess of good fortune, the wife of Vishnu.

THE VIRTUES OF VARANASI

Varanasi (Benares, Kashi), on the Ganges, is said to derive its name from two tributaries of the Ganges that flow through it, the Varana and the Asi. Founded between 1300 and 1000 B.C.E., the city was already a great cultural center by the sixth century B.C.E. and remains the holiest city in India today. Hindus hope to die in Varanasi, and the river's banks are crowded with corpses waiting to be consigned to its waters. The shrine of Avimukta ("Unforsaken") is particularly sacred to worshippers of Shiva, who are said to take on the form of Shiva himself there, for it is Shiva who has the crescent moon on his head, three eyes, and a bull for his mount. The shrine is said to save people of all four classes (Brahmins, Kshatriyas [rulers and warriors], Vaishyas [merchants], and Shudras [servants]), even terrible sinners ("The Fruits of Hearing a Purana"). Shiva narrates this story to his wife.

PRONOUNCING GLOSSARY

Asi: *uh´-see*
Avimukta: *uh´-vee-mook´-tuh*
Chandala: *chun-dah´-luh*
Gandharva: *gun-dar´-vuh*
Mahadeva: *muh-hah´-day´-vuh*
Maya: *mah-yah´*
Narayana: *nah-rah´-yuh-nuh*
Rakshasa: *rahk´-shuh-suh*
Shiva: *shih´-vuh*
shraddha: *shrah´-duh*
tapas: *tuh´-puhs*
Varana: *vuh´-ruh-nuh*
Varanasi: *vah-rah´-nuh-see´*
Yaksha: *yuk´-shuh*
yogin: *yoh´-gin*

Kurma Purana 1.29.22–54

The city of Varanasi is my place of utmost mystery, said Shiva, which conveys all creatures across the ocean of existence. There dwell great-souled devotees of mine, keeping their vows to me, great goddess, observing supreme self-control. Pre-eminent among all sacred fords, the best of places, superior to all knowledge, is this my place, the supreme Avimukta.

Within this area are to be found sanctuaries, purifying fords, and shrines in cremation grounds surpassing those in other divine spots in earth. This abode of mine floats in the sky, unattached to the earth. Those without Yoga cannot see it, but *yogins* witness it with their minds. This is the famous burning ground known as Avimukta.

Becoming Time, there I destroy the world, O lovely woman. This is my most favored place among all mysteries, O goddess. My devotees who go there enter into me. There gifts, prayers, offerings, oblations, *tapas*[1] and all other acts, meditation, Vedic study and knowledge become indestructible. All the evil accumulated in a thousand previous lives is destroyed for one who enters Avimukta.

Brahmins, kshatriyas, vaishyas and shudras, people of mixed caste, women, foreigners and others born from impure wombs, all these together, as well as worms and ants, game and fowl, after dying in Avimukta, O lovely-faced

TRANSLATED BY Cornelia Dimmitt and J. A. B. van Buitenen.

1. Inner ascetic heat.

woman, are reborn as men in my auspicious city, O goddess, with a crescent moon on their heads, three eyes, and mounted on great bulls.

If a sinner dies in Avimukta, he does not go to hell because everyone favored by the lord gains the highest goal. Recognizing that release is most difficult to attain, and that rebirth is most horrible, a man should crush his own feet with a stone in order to remain in Varanasi. That goal, supreme mistress, is hard to attain even by *tapas* for a pure man who dies anywhere else. This benefit springs from my kindness, O delight of the king of the mountains; those who remain unenlightened, still deluded by my Maya,[2] do not see it. Those fools, wrapped in ignorance, who do not visit Avimukta, are reborn again and again into semen, urine and excrement.

A wise man, even if beset by a hundred obstacles, gains that supreme goal which ends suffering if he should live here, and goes to the supreme abode of Shiva where there is no birth, old age or death. For those who seek release, this is the only place to go to escape rebirth. Having reached it, one's task is done, so think the wise. Not by gifts, nor by *tapas*, nor even by sacrifices or knowledge is the marvelous goal attained which can be found in Avimukta. People of various castes, outcastes, disgusting Chandalas[3] and others, those whose bodies are filled with impurities, and those who are covered with crimes, for these the only remedy is Avimukta. This the wise know.

Avimukta is supreme wisdom! Avimukta is the final goal! Avimukta is ultimate reality! Avimukta is matchless well-being! To those who live in Avimukta, who dedicate themselves to me, I grant supreme knowledge and, in the end, the highest goal.

The river Ganges which flows through heaven, earth and the netherworld, enters Varanasi in particular, and there she destroys the evil accumulated in a hundred life-times. Anywhere else but in Varanasi it is most difficult to find easy access to the Ganges, or to perform shraddha,[4] gifts, *tapas*, prayer and vows. A man who lives in Varanasi should continually make sacrifices, give gifts and worship the gods, while living on air. Whether one be a sinner, a crook or a wicked person, one is wholly purified by a visit to Varanasi. . . .

One can acquire the ultimate truth called Avimukta, O goddess, in a single life-time in Varanasi. This Avimukta lies between the eyebrows in the center of the navel, in the heart, in the head, in the sun, and also in Varanasi. This city lies between the Varana and the Asi rivers; here dwells the true and eternal Avimukta. There is not now nor shall there ever be a place superior to Varanasi where both Narayana and Mahadeva,[5] lord of the heaven, are to be found. There gods and Gandharvas, Yakshas, Snakes and Rakshasas[6] always honor me, as the Grandfather, god of gods. Those who have committed a major crime, and men even more wicked than they, gain the supreme goal by going to Varanasi.

2. God's power of illusion; it makes the world seem real when it is not.
3. People who inhabit the cremation grounds and handle the corpses.
4. The funeral ceremony for dead ancestors.
5. Vishnu and Shiva.
6. Equine demigods, forest spirits, half-cobra demigods, and ogres.

THE PILGRIMAGE OF SHIVA TO VARANASI

According to a much-told myth, Shiva once cut off Brahma's fifth head (leaving him with four, as he is often depicted), making Shiva guilty of Brahminicide. The skull stuck to Shiva's hand until he reached Varanasi, where the skull fell away and the god himself found salvation. This version of the story primarily reveres not Shiva (also called Rudra, Sharva, Shankara, Shambhu, Maheshvara, and the destroyer of Tripura [the triple city of the anti-gods]) but Krishna (also called Madhava [an epithet derived from *madhu*, which means both "honey" and "springtime"]), Keshava, Hrishikesha, the discus-bearer, and the one whose banner bears the bird).

PRONOUNCING GLOSSARY

Asi: *uh´-see*
Brahmahatya: *bruh´-muh-huh-tyah´*
Dasashvamedha: *duhs-ahsh´-vuh-may´-duh*
Gandharva: *gun-dar´-vuh*
Hari: *huh´-ree*
Hrishikesha: *hrih´-shee-kay´-shuh*
Kapalamochana: *kuh-pah´-luh-moh´-chuh-nuh*
Kapalin: *kuh-pah´-lin*
Keshava: *kay´-shuh´-vuh*
Kurukshetra: *koo´-rook-shay´-truh*
Lola Ravi: *loh´-luh ruh´-vee*
Madhava: *mah´-duh-vuh*
Maheshvara: *muh-haysh´-vuh-ruh*
Prayaga: *pruh-yah´-guh*
Rudra: *roo´-druh*
Shambhu: *shum´-boo*
Shankara: *shun´-kuh-ruh*
Sharva: *shar´-vuh*
Tripura: *tree-poo´-ruh*
Varana: *vuh´-run-nuh*
Yogashayin: *yoh´-guh-shah-yin*

Vamana Purana 3.1–5, 11–13, 23–36, 40–51

When that ghastly skull remained stuck to the palm of his hand, Rudra grew disturbed, O brahmin, his mind upset at the thought. Then that dreadful, terrifying female called Brahmahatya, or Brahmin-Murder, black as a heap of collyrium, with flaming red hair, approached Hari.[1] When he saw that ghastly apparition coming, he said to her, "Who are you, gruesome woman? Why have you come?"

The horrible Brahmahatya answered that skull-carrying god, "I am Brahmin-Murder. Accept me, three-eyed one!" And so speaking, Brahmahatya entered the trident-bearer Rudra, setting his body afire. . . .

That cloud-bannered god Sharva, although yoked to Yoga, was weighed down by Brahmahatya wherever he went. Not at ponds, fords or hermitages, nor at the Holy shrines of the gods could he find release from the burden of his crime. Finally the desperate Shankara went to Kurukshetra[2] where he found the god whose banner bears the bird, discus in hand. . . .

TRANSLATED BY: Cornelia Dimmitt and J. A. B. van Buitenen.

1. Hari normally refers to Vishnu, while Shiva is called Hara. Here, however, Hari clearly designates Shiva.

2. "The Field of the Kurus," where the great battle of the *Mahabharata* took place.

"Praise be to you, immortal god who bears the discus! Glory be to you, Madhava, in the form of a fish! I know you have compassion for the world, so set me free, Keshava, from the bondage of this sin! Destroy the evil which has lodged in my body and which overpowers me because of brahmin murder!

"I am on fire! I shall perish! I have acted heedlessly! Purify me! You yourself are a sacred shrine. Praise be to you!"

So honored by the great-souled Shankara, the blessed discus-bearer answered this, in order to destroy Brahmahatya, "Listen to my sweet speech, Maheshvara; it shall annihilate Brahmin-Murder, confer purity and increase merit. There is a certain one who lives in the holy east, born of a portion of myself, who is known as Yogashayin. He inhabits Prayaga, and from his right foot flows the beautiful, pure and sin-destroying river famed as the Varana. From his left foot streams another river renowned as the Asi. Both these fine rivers have been venerated in the world.

"The area which lies between these two rivers is the field of Yogashayin, the ultimate sacred ford in the three worlds, which gives release from all evil. It has no equal anywhere in heaven, on earth or in the netherworld. Here there is a pure and holy city celebrated as Varanasi, in which even people devoted to pleasure gain absorption in you, O lord, and where the elders, hearing the jingling belts of playful women mingled with the sound of the Veda chanted by the bulls of brahmins, commend them both with good humor, over and over again. In this city, when the moon sees lac-reddened[3] footprints at the crossroads where women have strayed, it wonders if a pond of rosy lotuses has just passed by. At night in Varanasi, lofty temples hide the moon, and they conceal the sun by day, with their fine long pennants waving in the breeze.

"Here black bees ignore their flower-cups, lured instead by the shining faces of painted women which are reflected in the moonstone walls. Here men grow fatigued, worn out by bewitching play, O Shambhu, no one enters the fine houses by force, except for dice, and no one attacks women violently, except in the play of love.

"O lord of gods, in this great shrine of Varanasi, such as I have just described, dwells the blessed Lola Ravi[4] who removes all sins. If you go to the place called Dashashvamedha[5] where Keshava, a portion of myself, resides, O excellent god, you shall gain release from your crime."

Thus addressed by the eagle-bannered Vishnu, the bull-bannered Shiva bowed with bent head, and sped swift as an eagle to Varanasi to rid himself of evil. When he reached that holy city full of shrines, he visited Lola and Dashashvamedha, bathed in the sacred fords, and with his sins cleansed, he sought out Keshava.

When he found Keshava, Shankara prostrated himself before him and said, "By your grace, O Hrishikesha, Brahmahatya has been destroyed. But this skull still sticks to my hand, O lord of gods. Please tell me why, for I don't know!"

3. Indian women redden the palms of their hands and the soles of their feet with a red dye called lac, made from insects.

4. A form of the sun.

5. "The Place of the Ten Horse Sacrifices."

At Mahadeva's words, Keshava replied, "There is a reason, Rudra, which I shall tell you. This holy pool full of lotuses in front of me is the best of the sacred fords, revered by gods and Gandharvas.[6] As soon as you have taken a ritual bath in this supreme ford, O Shambhu, the skull shall fall off. Thereafter you shall be called Kapalin, or Skull-Bearer in the world, O Rudra, and this sacred ford shall be known as Kapalamochana, or Skull-Releaser."

Thus addressed by Keshava, lord of the gods, Maheshvara duly bathed at Kapalamochana, by the Vedic rule, O seer. And after the destroyer of Tripura had taken a ritual bath at that ford, the skull fell from the palm of his hand. And so, by the grace of the lord, that choicest of fords was named Skull-Releaser.

6. Demigods associated with music, fertility, horses, and the celestial nymphs (Apsarases).

YUDHISHTHIRA AT PRAYAGA

King Yudhishthira's dilemma in hell, in the *Mahabharata*, was caused by a kind of transfer of merit: Yudhishthira sent a cool breeze to ease the torment of his brothers and Draupadi, as well as a few other relatives. That concept, merely sketched there, was more fully developed a few centuries later in the *Markandeya Purana* ("The Transfer of Karma in Hell"). But Yudhishthira is also haunted by the same problem that troubled Arjuna centuries earlier in the *Gita*, even though what Arjuna did was in keeping with the dharma of the Kshatriyas (the class of warriors and kings): "Many men who had committed no offense were killed in the battle." In the *Mahabharata*, Yudhishthira performed a horse sacrifice to restore himself and the kingdom; in the Puranas, he makes a pilgrimage to Prayaga. This myth—with its statement of a sin ("the mess I got myself into"), followed by the promise of a restoration, a solution—is a set piece, new Puranic wine poured into old Brahmana bottles.

The *Mahabharata* cast of characters is still in place: the Pandavas, five sons of Pandu, the three born to Kunti (Yudhishthira, the eldest, then Bhima and Arjuna), two to Madri (Nakula and Sahadeva), and their wife, Draupadi; their enemies (King Dhritarashtra, Duryodhana, Bhishma, Drona, and Karna); the great snakes (Vasuki, Kambala, Ashvatara, and Bahumulaka); various demigods (Danavas [anti-gods], Gandharvas [fertility spirits], Siddhas [perfected beings], Charanas [celestial musicians]); the gods Shiva (Maheshvara) and Vishnu (Hari); and, as always, Krishna (Vasudeva, Govinda).

PRONOUNCING GLOSSARY

Ashvatara: *ush´-vuh-tuh-ruh*
Bharata: *bhah´-ruh-tuh*
Bhishma: *beesh´-muh*
brahmacharin: *bruh´-muh-chah´-rin*
Charana: *chah´-ruh-nuh*
Danava: *dah´-nuh-vuh*
Dhritarashtra: *dri´-tuh-rahsh´-truh*
Draupadi: *drow´-puh-dee*
Drona: *droh´-nuh*
Duryodhana: *door-yoh´-duh-nuh*
Gandharva: *gun-dar´-vuh*
Hastinapura: *huh´-stee-nuh-poo´-rah*
Kambala: *kuhm´-buh-luh*
Karna: *kar´-nuh*

Kshatriya: *kuh-shah´-tri-yuh*
Kunti: *koon´-tee*
Markandeya: *mar´-kun-day´-yuh*
Pandava: *pahn´-duh-vuh*
Prajapati: *pruh-jah´-puh-tee*
Pratishthana: *pruh´-tish-tah´-nuh*
Prayaga: *pruh-yah´-guh*
Pritha-Kunti: *pree´-tuh koon´-tee*
Siddha: *sid´-duh*
Vasudeva: *vah´-soo-day´-vuh*
Vasuki: *vah´-soo-kee´*
Yamuna: *yuh-moo-nah´*
Yudhishthira: *yoo-dish´-tee-ruh*

Matsya Purana 102–103

After the Bharata war, King Yudhishthira, son of Pritha-Kunti, won the kingdom. Overcome with grief at the death of his kinsmen, he thought over and over again, "King Duryodhana was the general of eleven armies. After causing us much pain, they are all dead, and only we five Pandavas remain, because we turned for help to Vasudeva.

"We have slain Bhishma, Drona and the mighty Karna, King Duryodhana and all their sons and brothers. All these kings who considered themselves brave have been killed. O Govinda, what is the use of having a kingdom now? How can we be happy? What is the point of living?" Thinking, "This is shameful and wicked," the king grew despondent. He stood there listless without moving, with his face downcast.

When the king recovered, he asked himself over and over again, "Is there some ritual duty, some vow or pilgrimage which will remove the stain of this great crime—one which will conduct a man to Vishnu's matchless heaven? How can I ask Krishna what to do; he is the one who made me do all this in the first place! And how can I ask Dhritarashtra after I have killed his hundred sons?" And so Yudhishthira, king of Dharma, fell into despair. And all the great-souled men known as the Pandavas, overcome by their brother's grief, wept too. And others who had gathered there, along with Kunti and Draupadi, all fell crying to the ground.

Meanwhile in Varanasi, the sage Markandeya[1] knew that Yudhishthira was sorrowful and crying, overwhelmed by grief. Shortly thereafter that great ascetic arrived at Hastinapura[2] and stood at the king's gate. "Markandeya the seer is standing at the door, anxious to see you," announced the gate-keeper, at which the son of Dharma went at once to the door.

"Welcome, great seer! Welcome, illustrious one! Now my life bears fruit and my family is saved! At the sight of you my Fathers are gratified, great seer, and my body is purified by your presence!" Seating that seer on his lion throne, the great-souled Yudhishthira worshipped him with water for his feet and other offerings. Pleased and honored, Markandeya said to the king, "Tell me at once, O king, why you are weeping! What has made you so despondent? What troubles you? What causes you such distress?"

"Remembering everything we have done in order to win this kingdom, great seer, causes me continual anguish!" he replied.

TRANSLATED BY Cornelia Dimmitt and J. A. B. van Buitenen.

1. A great sage.

2. "The city of the elephant," the Pandava capital.

Amar Chitra Katha comics retell many of the classic stories of Hinduism; here is a scene from the story of Karna in the *Mahabharata*.

"Hear, mighty king, the established Dharma of the Kshatriyas. There should be no guilt for a wise man who must fight in battle, especially for a Kshatriya under the law of kingship. Take this to heart, and stop feeling guilty!"

At his words King Yudhishthira bowed his head to the seer and asked his visitor to remove all his crimes, saying, "I beg you, most wise one, you who understand the triple world[3] at all times, tell me how a person is released from his sins!"

"Hear, mighty king," said the seer, "for people who do meritorious acts, the most effective way to annihilate sins is to go to Prayaga."

Yudhishthira then said, "I want to hear the story of the last Eon, blessed seer, as related by the mouth of god Brahma! I want to know how and why man should go to Prayaga, where people go when they die in Prayaga, and what is the benefit of living in Prayaga. Tell me all this!"

"I shall tell you, my son" replied Markandeya, "the supreme benefit as I heard it long ago from Brahma. The area that extends from Pratishthana to Prayaga and from the pool of Vasuki to that city, which includes the sanctuaries of the Snakes Kambala, Ashvatara and Bahumulaka, is known in the three worlds as the field of Prajapati. Those who bathe there go to heaven; those who die there are not reborn. There Brahma and the other gods all together give protection. And there are also many other holy shrines that remove all sins, O king, so many that I could not describe them in many hundreds of years. Now I shall relate in brief the glory of Prayaga.

3. Heaven, earth, and the underworld.

"Sixty thousand bows there are that guard the river Ganges. And the sun with its seven horses continually protects the Yamuna. Indra watches over Prayaga in particular, at all times. And Hari guards its boundaries, along with the celestials. The trident-bearing lord Shiva protects the banyan tree, and the gods guard the holy shrine that removes all evil.

"One who is immersed in wickedness does not go there at all; but when one's crime is small, or rather small, O lord of mankind, it is destroyed by just the thought of Prayaga. A man is released from evil just by visiting the shrine, by saying its name, or by getting some clay from it, O king! At Prayaga there are beautiful lakes through which flows the Ganges river. Evil is instantly destroyed at the entrance of the city.

"An evil-doer who only thinks of the Ganges, even from a distance of a thousand miles, gains the supreme goal. By reciting its name, one is released from evil. By visiting it, one finds riches. Bathing in it, drinking it, or washing in it, one purifies one's family to the seventh generation.

"One who bathes at the confluence of the Ganges and Yamuna rivers, who speaks the truth, controls his anger, practices non-injury, follows Dharma, knows the elements of existence and is bent upon the well-being of cows and brahmins, is released from stains. With his mind concentrated, he gains his desires. One who goes to Prayaga, which is guarded by all the deities, and lives there as a celibate *brahmacharin*[4] for a month, satisfying the Fathers[5] and the gods, gets all his wishes and desires wherever he is born again.

"Famed in the three worlds as the divine daughter of the sun, the illustrious river Yamuna meets with the Ganges at Prayaga where the god Maheshvara is always present in person. After going to holy Prayaga, most difficult to attain by humans, O Yudhishthira, the gods, Danavas and Gandharvas, the seers, Siddhas and Charanas, after touching water here, O chief among kings, gained heaven."

4. A chaste student of the Vedas.

5. Ancestors.

MEDICINE AND ETHICS

Medicine is treated in detail in the medical Shastras ("The Etiology of Diseases," p. 210), and ethics in the *dharma-shastras* ("To Eat or Not to Eat Meat," p. 203; "The Dependence of Women," p. 205; "Retribution in Rebirth," p. 206), but these are also fitting subjects for the Puranas, which generally explain them through more extensive narratives.

EMBRYOLOGY

Embryology, the study of the development of the human from conception to birth, is a particularly religious aspect of Hindu medicine, due to the importance of the doctrine of rebirth. As rebirth is a wheel, any discussion of birth also involves a discussion of death, and Hindus usually begin the cycle with death, though here we will break into the circle with birth. Embryology is implicit in the Upanishadic discussions of karma ("Transmigration," p. 114), but the Puranas go into far more detail. They contain several different explanations of conception and birth, including one that assumes that both men and women have seed which they contribute equally to conception. The explanation offered by the following text, however, assumes that menstrual blood (*rajas*, also the term for the quality of energy) is the woman's seed.

PRONOUNCING GLOSSARY

Jada: *juh´-duh*

Jaimini: *jai´-mih-nee*

Markandeya Purana 10.1–7, 11.1–21

(The sage Jaimini asks the birds,)

O tigers of twice-born ones, dispel my doubts when I ask you about the appearing and vanishing of creatures. How is a living creature born? How does it grow? How does it exist when it stays in the middle of the stomach, squeezed in all its limbs? When it comes out of the stomach, how does it grow? And how does it become separated from its feelings at the moment when it departs? A person who has died consumes both his good deeds and his bad deeds; how, then, do they cause his fruits to arise? How is the fetus not digested like a lump of food there in the stomach? For even very heavy foods are digested there in the woman's stomach; so how is the little creature not digested? And how will it experience all of the karma of its good deeds? Tell me all this, without any ambiguity; for it is a very great secret, about which men are quite confused.

(The birds answer by repeating a conversation that took place between a young boy and his father; the boy, nicknamed Jada ['Impotent'] because he was regarded as an idiot, in fact remembers his former lives and deaths, and tells his father about them:)

The impregnation of human women is the emitting of the seed in the menstrual blood. As soon as (the soul) is released from hell, or from heaven, it arrives (in the womb). Overpowered by that (soul), the two-fold seed becomes solid, father. It becomes a speck of life, and then a bubble, and then flesh. And just as a shoot of a plant is born from a seed, so from the flesh the five limbs (two arms, two legs, and the head) are born, with all their parts. The subsidiary limbs, too—fingers, eyes, nose, mouth and ears—grow out of the (five) limbs; and out of the subsidiary limbs, in the same way, grow the nails and so forth. The hair on the body grows in the skin, and the hair of the head grows after that.

The birth-sheath grows larger as it takes on flesh. Just as a coconut grows big along with its shell, so the sheath of the embryo, that opens out on the bottom, grows bigger. The embryo grows up in the bottom of the womb, placing its two hands beside its knees, with its two thumbs on top of its knees, the fingers in front; behind the two knees are the two eyes, and in between the

TRANSLATED BY Wendy Doniger O'Flaherty.

knees is the nose; the buttocks rest on the two heels, and the arms and shanks are outside. In this way, the living (human) creature gradually grows up inside the woman's womb; other living creatures position themselves in the stomach according to their shapes.

The fire inside the stomach makes the embryo hard, and it lives on what is eaten and drunk (by the mother). The sojourn of the living creature inside the stomach is meritorious and is made of retained merit. A channel called the 'Strengthener and Nourisher' is attached to the inside of the embryo's navel and to the channel from the woman's entrails, and the embryo stays alive by that means. For what the woman eats and drinks goes into the embryo's womb, and the living creature's body is strengthened and nourished by that so that it grows.

Then it begins to remember its many previous existences in the wheel of rebirth, and that depresses it, and it tosses from side to side, thinking, 'I won't ever do *that* again, as soon as I get out of this womb. I will do everything I can, so that I won't become an embryo again.' It thinks in this way as it remembers the hundreds of miseries of birth that it experienced before, in the power of fate.

Then, as time goes by, the embryo turns around, head down, and in the ninth or tenth month it is born. As it comes out, it is hurt by the wind of procreation; it comes out crying, because it is pained by the misery in its heart. When it has come out of the womb, it falls into an unbearable swoon, but it regains consciousness when it is touched by the air. Then Vishnu's deluding power of illusion assails him, and when his soul has been deluded by it, he loses his knowledge. As soon as the living creature has lost his knowledge, he becomes a baby.

After that he becomes a young boy, then an adolescent, and then an old man. And then he dies and then he is born again as a human. Thus he wanders on the wheel of rebirth like the bucket on the wheel of a well . . .

SUFFERING

Another text goes into more physiological detail of both embryology and old age in order to underscore, as an ethical point, the evils of human life on earth.

Vishnu Purana 6.5.9–35

Suffering takes thousands of different forms, as it arises from conception, birth, old age, disease, death, and hell. The living creature that has a very delicate body becomes encased in abundant filth inside the embryo, where he is enveloped by the membrane and his back, neck, and bones are all twisted out of shape. As he grows, he suffers greatly from the excessively

TRANSLATED BY Wendy Doniger O'Flaherty.

acrid, bitter, spicy, salty, and burning hot food (that his mother has eaten). He can't stretch out his own limbs or contract them or anything else, and he is squashed on all sides, lying there in the feces and urine and slime. Though he is unable to breathe, he is conscious, and he remembers his hundreds of former births. Thus he sits there in the womb bound by his own karma, and very miserable.

As he is born, his face is smeared with feces, blood, urine, and semen, and his bones and sinews are hurt by the wind of procreation. He is turned head downwards by the powerful winds of childbirth, and he comes out from his mother's stomach bewildered by pain. He faints, and when he is touched by the outside air he loses his understanding, and is born. His body is hurt as if pierced by thorns, as if split open by saws; he falls from his pustulent wound like a worm upon the ground. Incapable of even scratching himself, or of turning over, totally without any control, he obtains his food, such as the milk he drinks at the breast, by the will of another person. Lying asleep on a bed, unclean, he is bitten by insects' stings and other things, and can do nothing to ward them off.

There are many sufferings in birth, and many that come right after birth; and there are many that he encounters in childhood, inflicted by elemental factors and so forth. Covered over by the darkness of ignorance, a man's heart becomes stupefied; he does not know, 'Where have I come from? Who am I? Where am I going? What am I made of? What bond is it that binds me? What is the cause, and what is not the cause? What is to be done, and what is not to be done? What is to be said, and what is not to be said? What is dharma, and what is against dharma? What does it consist in, and how? What is right to do, and what is not right to do? What is virtue and vice?'

Thus, confused like an animal, a man stumbles into the great misery that arises from ignorance, for he is primarily intent upon his penis and stomach. Ignorance is the source of inertia (*tamas*), and so the undertakings of ignorant men are deficient in good karma. But the seers say that hell is the reward for a deficiency in good karma, and so ignorant men suffer the most, both here and in the other world.

When old age shatters the body, gradually the limbs become loose; the old person's teeth decay and fall out; he becomes covered with wrinkles and sinews and veins; he can't see far, and the pupils of his eyes are fixed in space; tufts of hair appear in his nostrils, and his body trembles. All his bones become prominent; his back and joints are bent; and since his digestive fire has gone out, he eats little and moves little. It is only with pain and difficulty that he walks, rises, lies down, sits, and moves, and his hearing and sight become sluggish; his mouth is smeared with oozing saliva. As he looks toward death, all of his senses are no longer controlled; and he cannot remember even important things that he had experienced even at that very moment. Speaking takes a great effort, and he repeats himself; he is wakeful and very tired because of his heavy breathing and coughing. An old man is lifted up by someone else, and dressed by someone else; to his servants, his own sons, and his wife he is an object of contempt. He has lost all his cleanliness, though he still has his desire for amusement and food; his dependents laugh at him and all his relatives are disgusted with him. Remembering the things that he did in his youth as if he had experienced them in another birth, he sighs deeply and becomes very sad.

HELL

The dharma texts, sources of religious law, list the sorts of rebirths that people will experience as a result of their sins in this life ("Retribution in Rebirth"). But before going on to the next life, individuals are rewarded in heaven and punished in hell. Both King Yudhishthira and King Vipashchit, sojourning in hell, find ways to transfer some of their good karma to the sinners there ("The Transfer of Karma in Hell"). While still in hell, Vipashchit questions a servant of Yama, king of the dead, about the particular torments that result from particular sins. This is a part of the servant's reply.

Markandeya Purana 14.39–96

Those base men who have gazed covetously with a sinful eye at the wives of other men, or who have had sinful, covetous thoughts about other men's possessions—birds with adamantine beaks tear out their eyes; and their eyes grow back again and again. And as many times as these evil men blinked their eyes, for that many thousands of years do they undergo the eye-torture. People who have taught false Shastras or advised that they be taught, with the purpose of destroying the proper vision even of their enemies, and people who have recited the Shastras improperly, or who have uttered false speech, or who have reviled the Vedas, the gods, and the twice-born, or their guru—cruel birds with adamantine beaks tear out their tongues, which are renewed again and again, for the same number of years.

And those base men who cause dissension between friends, between a father and a son or people of the same family, between a sacrificer and his priest, between a mother and the son who is her companion, between a wife and husband—they are torn apart with a saw. People who annoy others, and interfere with their fun, who take away their fans, breezy places, sandalwood paste, or bamboo screens; and base men who trouble dying people who have done no harm—these people who have parceled out evil are stuck into gruel and sand. If a man has eaten the funeral offering of another man, when that man has invited him to a ritual for the gods or for the ancestors, he is torn in half by birds. A man who cuts at the vital spot of good men by speaking lies about them—these birds peck away at him ceaselessly. A man who slanders another, who dissembles in speech or thought—his tongue is split in half with sharp razors.

A proud person who looks down upon his mother, father, or guru—he hangs head-down in a pit full of pus, feces, and urine. A man who eats when the gods, guests, other creatures, dependants or visitors still have not been fed, or when the ancestors, the fire, or the birds have not been fed, this bad person takes the form of a creature with a mouth as tiny as a needle and a stomach as big as a mountain, and in this form he eats pus and exudations. But a man who feeds different food to a Brahmin, or a man of another class, when he is in the same group as other men, this man eats feces (in hell). And if a man has been in the company of a poor man who is involved in the same

Translated by Wendy Doniger O'Flaherty.

enterprise as he is, seeking money, and has eaten his own food after spurning the poor man—such a man eats phlegm (in hell).

A man who touches a cow, Brahmin, or fire before he has washed after eating—his hands are put into blazing fire pots. A man who looks at the sun, moon, or stars with desire, without washing his hands after eating—the servants of Yama place a fire in his eye and stoke it up. A man who allows his feet to touch cows, fire, his mother, a Brahmin, his eldest brother, father, or sister, or his daughter-in-law, gurus, or old people—his feet are bound with iron chains that have been heated in a fire, and he stands in the midst of a pile of hot coals that burn him up to his knees.

A man who has eaten milk, a dish of sesame seeds and grain, goat's flesh, or the food for the gods, without the proper ceremony—this evil man is thrown down on the ground, and as he stares with wide-open eyes, the servants of Yama tear his eyes out of his head with pincers. A base man who listens to blasphemy against gurus, gods, Brahmins, or the Vedas, taking pleasure in it—the servants of Yama thrust red-hot iron wedges again and again deep in the ears of such an evil man, ignoring his moans. A man who, under the power of anger or greed, breaks up and destroys a roadside reservoir or the home of a god or a Brahmin, or an auspicious assembly in a temple—the cruellest servants of Yama flay the skin from his body, using sharp instruments, over and over, as he screams.

If a man has urinated in the path of a cow, Brahmin, or the sun—crows drag his entrails out of his body through his rectum. If someone promises his daughter to one man but then gives her to a second man, he is chopped into many pieces and swept away in a river of acid. A man who is intent upon his own nourishment and abandons his son, servant, wife, or any other relatives, whoever they may be, in a time of famine or disturbance—the servants of Yama slice off pieces of his own flesh and put them in his own mouth, and he eats them hungrily. A man who through greed abandons those who come to him for protection, or a man who lives on bribes—the servants of Yama torment him by squeezing him in great vices. A man who has tried to prevent good deeds all his life long—he is ground up by grinding rocks, as are all men of evil karma.

A man who steals a deposit is bound with ropes on all his limbs and is bitten, day and night, by worms, scorpions, and ravens, while he grows thin from hunger, his tongue hangs out with thirst, and the back of his throat throbs with pain. An evil man who has sexual intercourse during the day, or with the wife of another man—he is made to mount a prickly silk-cotton tree; his limbs are pierced by its sharp, iron thorns and fouled by the streams of his blood as it flows out of him. Or a man who defiles the wives of other men may be put in a crucible called a 'female mouse'[1] which the servants of Yama fan with bellows.

A man who in his stubborn pride puts down his teacher and goes on with his studies or his craft—he carries on his head a big rock that causes him anguish and he walks down the main street in pain, emaciated with hunger day and night, his skull throbbing with the pressure of his burden. A man who has emitted his urine, phlegm, or feces in water—he goes to a foul-smelling hell of phlegm, feces, and urine. People who did not feed their guests, with

1. A euphemism for the female sexual organ.

the proper ceremony, before they fed one another—these people now, starving, eat one another's flesh. A man who has discarded the Vedas and the sacred fire, once he has been given the sacred fire—he falls down from the tip of a high mountain, again and again. A man who marries a woman who was widowed as a virgin when he is already an old man—he becomes a worm and is eaten by ants.

A man who accepts favors from someone low, or who sacrifices for him or constantly serves him—he becomes a worm living in rocks. A man who eats sweets while he is watched by the group of his dependants, or his friend, or a guest—he eats piles of hot coals. A man who used to be a backbiter of people—the flesh of his back is constantly eaten by terrifying wolves. The lowest of all men, the man who is ungrateful to those who have done favors for him—he wanders around blind, deaf, and dumb, starving. A man who harms his friends and returns evil for good falls screaming into the Hot-pot hell and is burnt up; then into gruel and sand; then he is squeezed by the vice; then he goes to the Sword-leaf-forest and is cut up by the razor-sharp leaves; then he is cut by the thread of Time, and suffers many different torments. And I simply do not know how he will ever find a way to make restorations and get out of that place.

Wicked Brahmins who assemble at a funeral celebration and then argue with one another—they drink the froth that is exuded from (each other's) every limb. A man who steals gold, a man who kills a Brahmin, a man who drinks wine, and a man who sleeps with his guru's wife—these are burnt in a blazing fire, above them and below them and on all sides of them; they stay there for many thousands of years. Then they are born again as men marked by leprosy, consumption, diseases and other afflictions; they die again and go again to hells such as these. And they suffer from this sickness until the very end of the aeon. A man who kills a cow goes to hell for a shorter time, just for three births, and so does one who has committed one of the minor sins; this is a fixed rule.

When men who have committed major sins get out of hell, they go forth to be born in various different wombs.

SECTS AND SEX IN THE TANTRAS

Tantra is a religious movement or sect involving secret and sometimes transgressive rituals. How you define Hindu Tantra is largely determined by what you want to say about it; some scholars define it in terms of its theology (connected with goddesses, and usually with Shiva, though this is not unique to Tantrism), some its social attitudes (which are often unorthodox, also not unique to Tantrism), and some its rituals (such as the ingesting of bodily fluids, particularly sexual fluids such as semen and menstrual blood, which is indeed a Tantric specialty). Tantric rituals generally involve initiation, group worship, secrecy, sexual rituals, and antinomian behavior. There are Tantric texts (called Tantras), Tantric rituals, Tantric myths, Tantric art forms, and, above all, Tantric worshippers. There are Tantric mantras (repeated formulas), Tantric yantras (mystical designs), and Tantric gods and their consorts. Within Hinduism, there are Shaiva, Vaishnava, and Shakta Tantras (the latter dedicated to Shiva's Shakti or Power, the Goddess) as well as Tantras devoted to other gods; there are, in addition, Buddhist Tantras and some Jain Tantras.

Tantra originated in north India sometime between the sixth and eighth centuries C.E., and flourished from the tenth century, having changed significantly in the course of those centuries. In particular, from the tenth century on many Tantras were infused with the spirit of *bhakti*. The Tantric "path of mantras," open to both ascetics and householders, promised to grant not only Release (which the Tantras often call *nirvana*) from the world of transmigration but magical powers (*siddhis*) and pleasures (*bhogas*), on the way to Release. Tantra thus offered the best of both worlds, or, as the Tantric mantra has it, "enjoyment-Release" (*bhukti-mukti, bhoksha-moksha*, or *bhoga-yoga*).

Much of Tantric ritual took place during secret initiations in relatively remote areas, but these rites were not a particularly well-guarded secret. Tantra and Tantric practices were well-publicized, esoteric but not necessarily marginal or even subversive; much Tantric worship was public, even royal. Tantra is often divided into its "left-hand" (*vama*) or transgressive traditions (those that violated caste laws of purity—trafficking in blood, death, skulls, sex) and its "right-hand" or conservative traditions. But most non-Tantric Hindus regard *all* Tantrics as following a "left-hand," i.e., sinister, path. Another significant division may be made between those people (among both practicing Hindus and secular scholars) who believe that the left-hand Tantras are to be taken literally, that when they say they drink blood they mean it; and those (again, in both camps) who believe that the left-hand Tantras were meant to be interpreted symbolically, that prescriptions for such actions as drinking blood really designate various levels of meditation—that, in a word, the rituals described in the texts were never actually performed.

But it is also possible that there were two levels of myth and ritual from the start, that some people would meditate on the ritual *and* perform the ritual, which also allows for the possibility that others would merely meditate, and still others would merely perform the ritual without meditating. In this view, the two paths of Tantra, meditation and action, *jnana* and karma, lived side by side, like the two paths in the Upanishads, and sometimes even coexisted in a single worshipper. What is significant is not whether these acts were imagined or performed, but that the discourse in which the debate about them took place was of central concern not only to the Tantrics but to mainstream Indian religion.

PRONOUNCING GLOSSARY

akarshya: *ah´-karsh-yuh*
ashtapattram: *ahsh´-tuh-puht-rum*
chakra: chuh´-kruh
divyakanyaka: *div´-yuh-kun-yah´-kuh*
granthi: *gruhn´-tee*
Kshatriya: *kuh-shah´-tree-yuh*
Kula: *koo´-luh*
kundala kritim: *koon´-duh-lah´ krih-teem*
Kundalini: *koon´-duh-lee´-nee*
mahavighnani: *muh-hah´-vig-nah´-nee*
Mandhuka: *mahn´-doo-kuh*
mantra: *muhn´-truh*
mundasandhi: *moon´-duh-sun´-dee*
padma: *puhd´-muh*
pancharum: *pun-chah´-rum*
Pathina: *pah´-tee-nuh*
pristamadhye: *prish´-tuh-mud-yay´*
Rohita: *roh´-hih-tuh*
samirastobhakam: *suh-mee´-rus-toh´-buh-kum*
Shakti/shakti: *shuk´-tee*
Shala: *shah´-luh*
Shali: *shah´-lee*
shuddhi: *shuh´-dee*
Shudra: *shoo´-druh*
tantra: *tuhn´-truh*
Tara: *tah´-rah*
tridandakam: *tree-dun´-duh-kum*
Vaishya: *vaish´-yuh*
Vama: *vah-mah´*
yoni: *yoh´-nee*

TANTRIC POINTS IN THE BODY

A great Tantric master named Matsyendranatha is said to have incorporated the teachings and practices of a group called the Yogini Kaula ("The Family of the Yoginis") into his work, called the *Kaulajnananirnaya.* These Yoginis are not merely female yogis but divine maidens, magical women who help the Tantric adept to achieve his special powers (*siddhis*). A foundational text for this branch of Tantra, the *Kaulajnananirnaya* presents detailed information about the mythical origins, specific doctrines and practices, and principal actors of the Kaula. It may have been composed in the ninth or tenth century C.E. and is thus one of the oldest Hindu Tantras.

The passages here discuss the *chakras*, circles or wheels of subtle energy located within the yogic body, sometimes imagined as wheels with spokes, sometimes as lotuses with petals. They are arranged vertically along the spine from the genitals to the top of the head, and the Tantric adept must raise his energy from the lowest *chakra* to the highest in the course of the ritual. (Some Tantric rituals interpret this process sexually: engaged in intercourse, the male adept does not ejaculate but causes his semen to rise up through his spine to the highest *chakra*, at the top of the head; the "End of the Twelve" refers to this *chakra*.) The second passage elaborates on the phrase "they are of eleven sorts" in the first passage, adding five more sites to the original six. Like most Tantras, this one is addressed to the Goddess.

Kaulajnananirnaya Tantra 5.25–27, 17.2b-4b

The various spokes [of the wheels] of divine maidens (*divyakanyaka*) are worshipped by the immortal host in (1) the secret place (genitals), (2) navel, (3) heart, (4) throat, (5) mouth, (6) forehead, and (7) crown of the head. [These maidens] are arrayed along the spine (*prishtamadhye*) [up] to the trident (*tridandakam*) [located at the level of] the fontanel (*mundasandhi*).

TRANSLATED BY David Gordon White.

These chakras are of eleven sorts and comprised of thousands [of maidens?], O Goddess! [They are] five-spoked (*pancharam*) and eight-leaved (*ashtapattram*), [as well as] ten- and twelve-leaved, sixteen- and one hundred-leaved, as well as one hundred thousand-leaved.

The (1) rectum, (2) secret place (genitals), along with the (3) navel [and] (4) the downturned lotus (*padma*) in the heart, (5) the chakra of breath and utterances (*samirastobhakam*) [i.e., the throat], (6) the cooling knot (*granthi*) of the uvula, (7) the root (or tip) of the nose, and the (8) End of the Twelve; the (9) [site] located between the eyebrows; (10) the forehead; and the brilliant (11) cleft of brahman, located at the crown of the head: it is the stated doctrine that [this] elevenfold [system] is located in the midst of the body.

THE TANTRIC GANDER

A goddess named Kundalini ("She who wears earrings") is said to live at the base of the spine. When the Tantric yogi awakens her through his yogic postures or breath control, she pierces the lower door to the channel of *chakras* and rises to the place of Shiva in the cranial vault. Usually the Kundalini takes the form of a serpent coiled around the base of the spine, but here she is imagined as a (male) gander or wild goose or swan (*hamsa*), an ancient symbol of the transmigrating soul, who flies up through the *chakras*. She is also called the goddess Vama ("Left-hand," but also "Beautiful"), representing the sinister and erotic aspect of Tantra.

Kaulajnananirnaya Tantra 17.18b–20a, 21a–24a

From below to above the gander sports, until it is absorbed at the End of the Twelve. Seated in the heart it remains motionless, like water inside a pot. Having the appearance of a lotus fiber, it partakes neither of being nor of nonbeing. Neither supporting nor supported, it is omniscient, rising in every direction. Spontaneously, it moves upward, and spontaneously it returns downward. . . . Knowing its essence, one [is freed] from the bonds of existence. . . . In the ear [orally] and in the heart, the description of the gander is to be made known. [Its] call becomes manifest in the throat, [audible] near and far. From the base of the feet to the highest height, the [goddess] named Vama has the form of a ring (*kundala kritim*). It is she who, seated in the anus, rises upward until she is absorbed at the End of the Twelve. Thus indeed the gander sports in the midst of a body that is both auspicious and inauspicious.

Translated by David Gordon White.

TERRIFYING TANTRIC VISIONS

The *Brahmayamala* is roughly contemporary with the *Kaulajnananirnaya*, which is to say, ninth or tenth century C.E. The passage here describes a series of ritually induced dreams or visions that practitioners are taught to cultivate in order to achieve the eight supernatural powers (*siddhis*): the ability to fly; to make the body very small (the size of an atom), very large, very heavy, or very light; to go wherever one wants; to get whatever one desires; and to gain to complete lordship. (Secondary powers include the ability to enter someone else's body and to obtain immunity to hunger or thirst or seasonal weather.) In Tantra, as in yoga (from which the Tantras took a great deal of theory and practice), both mental and physical transformations are effected by meditation and breath control.

The goddess Kali dancing on the corpse of the god Shiva. Nineteenth-century color lithograph.

In order to know his own past lives, the adept begins by meditating on the wombs or vulvas (*yonis*) of a circle of ritual consorts who represent the Shaktis, the incarnate Powers of the Goddess. As he is enclosed by a circle of four to eight women, he begins to experience visions as part of his initiation. If he stands firm and remains calm despite these terrifying visions, he becomes a Virile Hero, a fully initiated and empowered Tantric. This passage describes what he sees.

Brahmayamala Tantra 45.260b–265b

[T]he great obstructors (*mahavighnani*) [arise], all of them very terrifying. . . . He should not be frightened either by these creatures . . . or when he sees a fearsome serpent that seems to be devouring [him]. He sees a she-cat with sharp teeth and a deformed body. Even seeing her, he ought not to be frightened, nor should he halt the ritual. He sees a very terrifying she-rat, with the body of an obstructor. Drawing toward (*akarshya*) herself the person who abandons his worship [out of fear], that Shakti . . . kills [him]. [A demoness] will say the words: "Stand up! I devour [you]!" . . . He is not to be frightened. . . . Voices will come from outside [the underground chamber]. [He will hear] the words "Kill! kill! Throw out food! Draw in [this] sinner!" . . . [and] "Get up, get up, you witless one! You are taken by the order of the king!" See-

TRANSLATED BY David Gordon White.

ing [these demonesses], he is not to fear, and his mind should not depart from its meditation. The practitioner [will see] dreadful gape-mouthed forms. [There will be] buck-toothed Shaktis licking [him] with their tongues. Seeing them, he should not fear. . . . Without a doubt, they lick the essence [that is] inside the practitioner for the sake of knowledge. While this is taking place, supernatural experiences [will] arise, one at a time. . . . His supernatural power, pervading the triple-world, will manifest itself. When the full six months [have passed], there is the visible manifestation of the [great] Goddess. . . . [Even when she appears] with her gape-mouthed form, she should not be feared by the possessor of mantras. . . . [The] completion [of the practice] is to be carried out by the practitioner in [the midst of the circle of] the eight [women]. In the [circle of] seven, nothing more than the viewing of the yoni occurs. In the group of eight, there is, without a doubt, the daily arising of [supermundane] wisdom. Having attracted the bodies of every one of these beings, he thereby obtains that [wisdom]. He becomes a Virile Hero, surrounded by yonis.

THE FIVE ELEMENTS OF TANTRIC RITUAL

The *Mahanirvana* is a very late Tantra, perhaps as late as the eighteenth century, and it may incorporate a response—at times an apologetic one—to the British presence in India. Yet both its subject matter and its rhetoric reflect classic Tantric concerns, and it spells out in detail many matters that are merely alluded to cryptically by older texts such as the *Kaulajnananirnaya* and the *Brahmayamala*. In this passage, it elaborates upon each of the five ingredients in the central Tantric ritual.

The Tantras speak of the Five M's, or the Five M-Words (since all five of the terms begin with an "m" in Sanskrit), which might be called, in English, the Five F-Words: *madya* (fermented grapes, wine), *mamsa* (flesh, meat), *matsya* (fish), *mudra* (farina), and *maithuna* (fornication). Like so much of Tantra, the Five M's are an inversion, in this case an inversion of other pentads in more conventional forms of Hinduism. Hindus often speak of the "five elements"—earth, fire, water, wind, and space. More specifically relevant is the Hindus' practice of ingesting the "five products of the cow" (*pancha-gavya*) to purify themselves of pollution: clarified butter, milk, and yogurt, plus bovine urine and feces. Tantrism has, in addition to the Five M-Words, the Five Jewels (semen, urine, feces, menstrual blood, and phlegm) or Five Nectars (with marrow in place of phlegm). By deliberately subverting orthodox categories of purity, the Tantras forced participants to look beyond the dualities of purity and impurity and the conventions of food and sex that drive so much of Hinduism.

Wine, flesh, and fish were prohibited for high-caste Hindus, and there is little debate about the basic connotation or denotation of these terms in the context of Tantric ritual, though there is much debate about whether they are to be taken literally. *Mudra*, here interpreted as a material article, farina, or parched grain (sometimes kidney beans, or other, allegedly aphrodisiac, cereals), also means "signal" or "hand gesture." *Maithuna* is usually translated as sexual intercourse, more literally "pairing," but may also designate sexual fluids or menstrual blood. Menstrual blood, like sexual intercourse, plays a central role in the Tantras and is connected to the polluting but life-giving blood of the menstruating Goddess, which flows to the earth each year, and the blood of her animal victims, decapitated and offered in sacrifice. Yet this text also allows for a substitute that is not impure: red sandalwood paste.

The *Mahanirvana Tantra* mentions several sorts of women. Officially, it states that there may be problems if any woman other than one's own wife is used as a partner for the Tantric ritual of fornication. It distinguishes between one's own wife, who is permitted, and both another man's wife and a woman used in common by the entire Kula, or "family," the Tantric group. The latter two types of women are permitted as partners by Tantric texts from which the present author takes pains to distinguish himself. The ritual contact with one's own wife involves the use of her "flower," the ordinary euphemism for menstrual blood.

The other women present in the ritual are referred to as Shaktis, a term that may designate the women who are the partners of the other men participating in the ritual or, as in other Tantric texts, the female powers of the male worshippers (which is to say their partners in the ritual, their wives) and of the god Shiva. The Shaktis are said to be "beaten," and the commentator on this text says that "beating" refers to sexual intercourse. An alternative reading of the text says that the women are to be worshipped, but are *not* to be used in the ceremony of "beating." And yet another interpretation is that the women are to be divided into two groups, those who are to be "enjoyed" (the practitioners' own wives) and those to be "worshipped" (other men's wives). Even in this late text, the precise meanings of crucial terms are still open to debate.

As usual, the text is spoken by Shiva to the Goddess.

Mahanirvana Tantra 6.1–20

(The Goddess said to Shiva, 'My lord, if you have compassion for me, tell me more about the five elements used in rituals such as worship, that you have mentioned.' Shiva said:)

There are three sorts of very good wine: made from sugar (or molasses), made from rice, and made from honey (or from the Mandhuka flower or grapes). There are also various sorts made from palm tree juice or from date palms, and these are further subdivided according to the locality and the various substances in them. All the various sorts are recommended for the worship of the deity. There is no distinction of caste with regard to whoever makes it, or whoever brings it; all of it is purified and bestows all powers.

Meat is also said to be of three sorts: from animals that come from the water, the land, or the sky. Wherever it comes from, and whoever kills it, all of it gives pleasure to the deity; this is certain. The wish of the worshipper is what has the power to determine what thing is to be given to the deity; whatever he likes, that substance should be made into a sacrificial offering. The male sacrificial animal is the one prescribed for the ritual of offering to the minor deities, O goddess; for Shiva has commanded that female animals of the species fit to be sacrificed are not to be killed.

There are three sorts of the best kind of fish: Shala, Pathina, and Rohita.[1] The middling sort are the ones without bones, and the worst are the ones that have lots of bones—though these, too, may be offered to the Goddess if they are very well roasted or fried.

There are three sorts of parched grain: best, middle, and lowest. The kind made from Shali rice, white as a moonbeam, is very good, or the kind made from barley or 'cow-smoke' wheat, that is especially nice when fried in butter. This is the best parched grain. The middle variety is made from

TRANSLATED BY Wendy Doniger O'Flaherty.

1. Delicious fish—the rough Indian equivalent of salmon, trout, and sole.

broken wheat and so forth. When other sorts of seeds are roasted, they are regarded as of inferior quality.

Meat, fish, parched grain, fruits and roots offered to the divinity when wine is offered are known as the purification (*shuddhi*). Without such purification, any offering for a particular purpose, or any puja[2] or libation of water, will bear no fruit, O goddess; the divinity will take no pleasure in it. The drinking of wine without this purification, by itself, is like swallowing poison; the person who uses such a mantra becomes chronically ill and soon dies, after living only a short life-span.

O goddess, now that the destructive Dark Age[3] has become impotent, seedless, a mere remnant, only one's own wife is ever to be regarded as a flawless partner. Beloved of my very life's breath, for this ritual, the (menstrual) flower that comes from the woman herself is prescribed, but one may use red sandalwood paste as a substitute for it. If the five elements of the ritual of the leaves, flowers, and fruits are not purified, they should not be given to the Great Goddess; if a man gives them (unpurified), he goes to hell. The worshipper should set the sacred goblet in place in company with his own good woman; then he should sprinkle her with the purified wine or the communal water. To begin, he should pronounce the mantras over the girl, and salute the Goddess of the Triple City; and when this mantra is over, he should utter the mantra, 'Hail! Drive this *shakti* upward! Purify her! Make her my *shakti*!' If the woman has not been initiated, he should speak the mantra of illusion ('Hrim!') into her ear. The other *shaktis* are to be worshipped with the ritual of 'beating.'

2. An offering to a deity, usually fruit or flowers.
3. The last of the four Ages, the Kali Age, the present age ("The Four Ages," p. 228). The argument, somewhat paradoxical, is that in earlier ages, when people were virtuous, moral rules could be more lax; but now that human nature is at its lowest ebb, people must be more, not less, careful about their moral conduct.

TANTRIC SINS OF EXCESS

The passage in the *Mahanirvana Tantra* glossing the Five M's ("The Five Elements of Tantric Ritual") includes strong caveats. (This constitutes an argument for the original physical reality of the Tantric substances—why warn people about these dangerous substances, if they don't exist?) Continuing in this vein, the passage below, well aware of the fact that intoxicating liquors are one of the addictive vices, closely observes the social symptoms of alcoholism ("every step he takes results in something that he does not want and that other people do not want"). It takes pains to distinguish the ritual use of wine (which it regards as a goddess—though it warns that even wine that has been purified by the ritual is dangerous if taken in excess) from casual drinking, which it abhors. This distinction mirrors the dharma texts' distinction between the ritual and nonritual uses of meat ("To Eat or Not to Eat Meat," p. 203). Indeed, the general tone of the end of this passage is strongly reminiscent of the dharma texts' conflicted attitude to nonviolence (*ahimsa*) toward all creatures.

In a parallel with the three qualities of matter (lucidity, energy, and torpor) ("The Two Paths," p. 178), the Tantras recognize three grades of humans: those who are like beasts, capable only of conventional worship, such as image worship; the heroic, or

"Virile Heroes" (Terrifying Tantric Visions), who practice Tantric ritual; and the god-like, who practice Tantric meditation, having transcended and internalized Tantric ritual. The first two grades are in danger of committing certain excesses in the course of the Tantric ritual as well as in the rest of their lives.

Mahanirvana Tantra 11.104–43

Even the Kula[1] dharma leads only to evil rather than to Release and prosperity, if it is not followed according to the rules, and honestly. Wine is the liquid form of the Goddess Tara,[2] who is the savior of all living creatures, the mother of all enjoyment and Release, the destroyer of dangers and disease, who burns up all sins and purifies the worlds, O Beloved, who grants all success and increases knowledge, understanding, and learning. Those who have attained final Release, who strive for Release, who have mastered the techniques, who are engaged in using the techniques, kings, and gods always use wine to obtain success in whatever they want. Mortals who drink wine with the proper rituals and with a well-controlled mind are virtually immortals on earth. By partaking of any one of the five ritual elements at a time, with the proper ritual, a man becomes Shiva; who can know what fruit will arise from the use of all five elements?

But if this Goddess wine is drunk without the proper rituals, she destroys a man's entire intellect, life-span, reputation, and wealth. By excessive drinking of wine, people whose minds are intoxicated lose their intelligence, which is the means by which they achieve the four goals of a human life (release, dharma, profit, and pleasure). A man whose intelligence has been broken does not know what to do or what not to do; every step he takes results in something that he does not want and that other people do not want.

Therefore, the king or the lord of the wheel (the leader of the Tantric circle—*chakra*, wheel—or, possibly, a Buddhist king, in contrast with the [Hindu] king designated by the first term) should purify people who are excessively addicted to wine or to intoxicating substances, purify them by physical punishment or by fining them. The degree of destruction of the intellect of men who drink varies according to the type of wine, the nature of the individual, the quantity that is taken, and the time and place where it is used. Therefore, the degree of intoxication should be judged not by the amount of wine that has been drunk, but by the signs that reveal excessive drinking: slurred speech and unsteady hands, feet, and gaze. A man who is not in control of his senses because his mind is distracted by intoxication transgresses the moral bounds of gods and gurus and is terrible to see; he becomes involved in all sorts of unprofitable things, does bad deeds and opposes Shiva. The king should burn his tongue, confiscate his property, and beat him; the king should torture and confiscate the property of a man whom drink has made grotesque, with unsteady speech, feet, or hands, wandering in his wits and out of his mind. A king who wants to please his subjects should heavily fine a man whom drink has made foul-mouthed, crazy, or devoid of shame or fear.

TRANSLATED BY Wendy Doniger O'Flaherty.

1. "The family," the name of the Tantric group.
2. "The Star," a Tantric goddess, particularly popular in Tibet.

Even if a man of the Kula sect has been initiated a hundred times, O empress of the Kula, if he drinks too much he should be regarded as a beast and expelled from the Kula. A man who drinks too much wine, whether or not it has been purified, should be abandoned by the members of the Kula and punished by the king, too. If a twice-born man gets drunk and makes his wife get drunk with him, a wife that he has married by the Brahma wedding,[3] he should purify himself, together with her, by eating nothing but crumbs for five days. A man who has drunk unsanctified wine should purify himself by fasting for three days; if he eats unpurified meat, he should fast for two days. If he eats unsanctified fish or parched grain, he should fast for a day; but if he makes use of the fifth element (sex) without the proper ritual, he should be purified by being punished by the king.

Anyone who knowingly eats human flesh or the flesh of a cow, O gracious goddess, will be purified if he fasts for a fortnight; this is the prescribed restoration. My dear, a man who has eaten the flesh of an animal that has the form of a man, or a man who eats the flesh of an animal that eats flesh, may purify himself of this evil by a three-day fast. A man who has eaten food cooked by foreigners, Untouchables, men who are like beasts, or enemies of the Kula—he may become pure by fasting for a fortnight. If he should knowingly eat the leftovers of these people, O empress of the Kula, he should fast for a month to become pure; if he does it unknowingly, he should fast for a fortnight. If he eats food prepared by lower castes, even once, he should fast for three days to purify himself; this is my command.

But if food prepared by a beast-man or an Untouchable or a foreigner is placed within the circle (of Tantric worshippers) or in the hand of a (Tantric) adept, one can eat it without incurring any evil. Anyone who eats forbidden food to save his life in time of death or famine, in an emergency, or when it is a matter of life and death does not incur evil. No sins of improper eating count when food is eaten on the back of an elephant, on stones or logs so big that they can only be carried by several men, or where there is no one to notice anything reprehensible. My dear, one should not kill animals whose flesh is not to be eaten, or diseased animals, not even for the sake of a divinity; anyone who does this commits an evil act.

A man who knowingly kills a cow should perform the (following) 'difficult penance,' according to Shiva's command; and he should not shave or cut his nails or wash his clothes until he has completed his vow. This is the 'difficult penance': he should fast for a month and then eat nothing but crumbs for a month; then for a (third) month he should eat only food that he has begged for, O gracious goddess. At the end of the penance, he should shave his head; and then, if he has knowingly killed a cow, he may free himself from that crime by feeding members of the Kula, distant relatives, and close relatives. If a cow is killed as a result of lack of care, (a Brahmin) is

3. The finest and purest of the eight forms of Hindu marriages. They are (according to Manu 3.20.21–36; other texts rank them slightly differently) marriages sanctioned by (1) Brahma: a man gives his daughter to a good man he has summoned; (2) gods: he gives her, in the course of a sacrifice, to the officiating priest; (3) sages: he gives her after receiving from the bridegroom a cow and a bull; (4) the Lord of Creatures: he gives her by saying, "May the two of you fulfill your dharma together"; (5) anti-gods: a man takes the girl because he wants her and gives as much wealth as he can to her relatives and to the girl herself; (6) centaurs (Gandharvas): the girl and her lover join in sexual union, out of desire; (7) ogres (Rakshasas): a man forcibly carries a girl out of her house, screaming and weeping, after he has killed and wounded people and destroyed property; (8) ghouls (Pishachas): the lowest and most evil of marriages takes place when a man secretly has sex with a girl who is asleep, drunk, or insane.

purified by fasting for eight days, a Kshatriya by six days, a Vaishya by four, and a Shudra[4] by two, O gracious goddess.

O goddess of the Kula, if anyone willingly kills an elephant, camel, buffalo, or horse, he should fast for three days and then he is free of evil. If he kills a deer, ram, goat, or cat, he should fast for a day; for a peacock, parrot, or goose, he should fast as long as there is daylight (on the day of the killing). If he kills (any other) animals that have bones, he should eat no flesh for one night. If he kills living creatures that have no bones, he is purified merely by feeling sorry. Kings who, when they are hunting, kill beasts, fish, or birds do not commit evil, O goddess, for this is the eternal dharma of kings. But, my lady, one should always avoid injuring creatures except for the sake of the gods; a man who injures creatures according to the sacred rules is not smeared by evil.

4. The four classes of Hindu society: priests, warrior/rulers, merchants, servants ("Hymn of the Primeval Man," p. 82).

THEOLOGY AND/OR PHILOSOPHY IN THE VEDANTA

There are six major schools of Hindu philosophy, six Darshanas or "Points of View." These schools took root in earlier centuries but became more fully developed from the twelfth century on, in conversation with one another. Following is a brief summary of five of the schools, with slightly longer coverage of the last one, Vedanta.

Mimamsa ("Critical Inquiry") began with Jaimini (ca. 400 B.C.E) and was devoted to the interpretation of the Vedas, taking the Vedas as the authority for dharma and *karma*. Jaimini guaranteed the sacrificer life in heaven after death and decreed that women could sacrifice but Shudras could not.

Vaisheshika began with Kanada (ca. third century B.C.E.), who presented a cosmology according to which all material objects are made of atoms of the nine elements: the four material elements—earth, water, fire, and air—plus five more abstract elements—space, time, ether, mind, and soul. In this view, god created the world, but not out of nothing; he simply imposed order on preexisting atoms.

Nyaya (logic and reasoning) began with Gautama (ca. second century B.C.E.; no relation to the Buddhist Gautama) and was an analytical philosophy basic not only to all later Hindu philosophy but to the scientific literature of the *shastras*.

Patanjali's ***Yoga-Sutras*** (ca. 150 B.C.E.) codified yogic practices that had been in place for centuries ("The Discipline of Mind and Body," p. 122).

Sankhya as a philosophy has roots that date from the time of the Upanishads and are important in the *Mahabharata* (especially in the *Gita* ["The Two Paths," p. 178]) but were first formally codified by Ishvarakrishna (ca. third century C.E.). Sankhya is dualistic, dividing the universe into a male *purusha* (spirit, self, or person) and a female *prakriti* (matter, nature). There are an infinite number of similar but separate *purushas*, no one superior to another. Early Sankhya philosophers argued that god may or may not exist but is not needed to explain the universe; later Sankhya philosophers assumed that god does exist.

And then comes **Vedanta,** the philosophical school that reads the Upanishads through the lens of the unity of the individual soul (*atman*) and the world-soul (*brahman*). The Upanishads are often referred to as Vedanta ("The End of the Vedas"), because they are the final part of the texts called the Vedas, but the term is also used for this philosophy based upon the Upanishads. Often expressing their ideas in the form of commentaries on the Upanishads, on the *Gita*, and on Badarayana's *Vedanta Sutras* (ca. 400 B.C.E.), different branches of Vedanta relegate the phenomenal world to the status of an epistemological error (*avidya*), a psychological imposition (*adhyasa*), or a metaphysical illusion (*maya*). Evil, too, which the myths struggle to deal with, and, especially, death turn out to be nothing but illusions.

The major phase of Vedanta (in this second philosophical sense) began with three great South Indian philosophers, all of whom were Brahmins: Shankara (ca. 788–820), Ramanuja (ca. 1056–1137), and Madhva (ca. 1238–1317). A basic schism separated the Dualists, who argued that god and the universe (including the worshipper) were of two distinct substances, and the Non-dualists, who argued that they were of the same substance. Madhva, also known as Madhvacharya ("Madhva the teacher"), from Kalyan (in Karnataka), was the founder of the Dualist (*Dvaita*) school of Vedanta. Shankara, from Kerala, was an exponent of pure Non-dualism (*Advaita*) and idealism, and a worshipper of Shiva. Ramanuja, from Kanchipuram (Kanjeevaram), in Tamil country, was an exponent of Qualified Non-dualism (*Vishishta Advaita*) and of the religion of the Shri Vaishnavas (Tamil worshippers of Vishnu). These three philosophical schools were not limited to intellectuals but deeply affected devotional Hinduism, for Indian philosophers are also saints.

The philosophical side of Hinduism has been well represented, anthologized, and discussed in the American and European scholarly world. But it is merely one part of the larger story of Hinduism as represented in this anthology, which focuses on religion more in terms of narrative, belief, and practice than in theory, and so contrasting excerpts from the two great Non-dualists must serve here as placeholders for all the rest.

PRONOUNCING GLOSSARY

Bharata: *bah´-ruh-tuh*
Brihadaranyaka Upanishad: *bree´-hud-ah´-run-yuh-kuh oo-puh´-ni-shud*
Chandogya Upanishad: *chun-dohg´-yuh oo-puh´-ni-shud*
jiva: *jee´-vuh*
Katha Upanishad: *kuh´-tuh oo-puh´-ni-shud*
Kuru: *koo´-roo*
Nivara: *nih-vah´-ruh*
Panchala: *puhn-chah´-luh*
Putika: *poo´-tee´-kuh*
samsara: *suhm-sah´-ruh*
Shastra: *shah´-struh*
Soma: *soh´-muh*
tathyarupa: *tuht´-yuh-roo´-puh*
Vedanta Sutra: *vay-dahn´-tuh soo´-truh*

SHANKARA DREAMS

The hagiographies of Shankara arise at a time when *bhakti* is rampant, spreading so fast that it even gets into philosophy, while Buddhists and Muslims, as well as Christians in Kerala (Shankara's home territory), are gaining ground. Born into a high-caste Brahmin family near the end of the eighth century C.E., Shankara (a worshipper of Shiva, who is often called "Shankara," the bringer of peace) taught and debated with many other philosophers. In his travels throughout India, his biographies claim, he vehemently confronted Buddhists and tried to persuade kings and other influential people to withdraw their support from Buddhist monasteries. And so, just as the human avatars were, in part, a response to the human dimension of Buddhism in an earlier age ("Vishnu," p. 242), Shankara was the answer now, someone who was, like the Buddha (and Muhammad and Jesus), both a human being and the founder of a religion. He is said to have started a reform movement, proposing a moral agenda that could compete with the Buddhists and a philosophy that may have been developed, in part, to respond to the monotheist philosophies of Islam. Regarded as a guru and proselytizer as well as a philosopher, Shankara is known as the founder of the centers of learning (*matts*) that still thrive in his name in India today; his argument that the phenomenal world of everyday experience and its biological round of birth and death (*samsara*) was ultimately unreal, and the source of our bondage, was taken as the basis for a monastic or ascetic life of renunciation (*sannyasa*).

We can get some idea of the ways in which the approaches of Shankara and Ramanuja are both related and distinct by comparing their interpretations of the problem of the self in sleep, in their commentaries on a classic Upanishadic passage ("Dreaming," p. 111). Their arguments also incorporate interpretations of other Vedic texts, particularly the Vedanta Sutras or Brahma Sutras attributed to Badarayana (ca. 200 B.C.E.).

Commentary on Vedanta Sutras 3.2.2–4

(An opponent) might argue thus: It is agreed that the world created in our waking state, that is created by the highest consciousness, is the form of the real (*tathyarupa*), and so the world created in our dreaming state must also be real. There is a passage of scripture about this: 'Now, some people say, "This (dream state) is just (the same as) his waking state," for whatever things he sees when he is awake, he sees them too when he dreams' (*Brihadaranyaka Upanishad* 4.3.14). Thus the text tells us that the same logic applies to the state of dreaming and the state of waking. And so the world created in the liminal state (of dreaming) is real.

To this argument (the author of the *Vedanta Sutras*) says: 'But (the world created in dreams) is mere illusion, because its own form is not revealed with any totality' (3.2.3).

The word 'but' indicates that he rejects the opponent's argument. What the opponent says—that the world created in the liminal state (of dreaming) partakes of the highest reality—is not true. The world created in the liminal state is pure illusion, and there is not so much as a smell of reality in it.

'Why?' (an opponent might ask).

'Because its own form is not revealed with any totality' (says the author of the *Vedanta Sutras*). That is, because a dream does not reveal its form with the totality that is characteristic of things that partake of the highest reality.

Now, what is meant by 'totality' here?

It is the agreement of place, time, and cause, and the fact that no contradiction or falsification can be brought against it.

Is it not the case that all of these characteristics of real things—place, time, cause, and absence of contradiction—occur in a dream?

No. First, as regards place: There is no place in a dream for anything like a chariot. For a thing like a chariot could find no space within the constricted place of the human body.

Granted. But (the dreamer) will see the dream from a vantage point outside of his body. For one does perceive (in a dream) that things are separated from oneself by space. Scripture demonstrates that the dream is seen from outside the body: 'The immortal one wanders about outside the nest; the immortal one goes wherever he wishes' (*Brihadaranyaka Upanishad* 4.3.12). And this distinction between standing still and moving about would not be relevant if the (dreaming) creature did not actually go out.

No, is the reply. It is not possible for the dreaming creature to travel the distance of a hundred leagues and return again in a mere moment. And sometimes someone tells about a dream in which he didn't come back at all: 'Lying in bed last night in the land of the Kurus, I fell asleep, and in my

TRANSLATED BY Wendy Doniger O'Flaherty.

dream I went to the land of the Panchalas,[1] and then, while I was still there, I woke up.' Now, if he had really gone out of his own country, he would have awakened in the land of the Panchalas; but in fact he awakened in the land of the Kurus; from this one realizes, 'He did not really go there.' And the body by means of which he thinks he has gone to another place—other people standing beside him see that body lying right there in his bed. And he does not see the places that he sees in his dream as they really are; but if he actually ran around seeing them, he would perceive them as they really are when he sees them when he is awake. Indeed, scripture shows us that the dream is inside the body, in the passage that begins, 'When he moves about in his dream' and ends, 'he moves about wherever he wishes, in his own body' (*Brihadaranyaka Upanishad* 2.1.18). And so, lest there be a contradiction both of scripture and of reason, the scriptural passage about going outside the nest must be taken in a metaphorical sense: 'The immortal one wanders about *as if* he were outside the nest.' For someone who, even while he is dwelling inside his body, makes no use of it could be said to be outside of his body, as it were. This being so, the distinction between standing still and moving about must be understood as merely deceptive.

Now, when it comes to the question of time: there is a contradiction of time in a dream. A person dreaming in the land of Bharata (India) at night thinks that it is daytime; or sometimes a person experiences many masses of years in a dream that lasts only for a moment.

And as for causation: There are neither the usual causes for thought nor the usual causes for action in a dream. For, since the organs of perception are withdrawn in sleep, the dreamer does not have the eyes and so forth to perceive something like a chariot. And where could he get, in a mere blink of the eye, the ability—let alone the wood—to make something like a chariot?

And, finally, when it comes to noncontradiction: the chariots and so forth that are seen in a dream are contradicted by the waking state. And even in the dream itself such contradictions are easy to find, as can be demonstrated by the discrepancies between the beginning and end of a dream: 'This is a chariot,' you may sometimes decide in a dream; but then in a moment it becomes a man, and so you decide, 'This is a man'; but in a moment it is a tree. And scripture itself clearly states that the chariots and so forth in a dream do not exist: 'There are no chariots there, no harnessings, no roads' (*Brihadaranyaka Upanishad* 4.3.10). Therefore what is seen in a dream is mere illusion.

Then, since it is mere illusion, is there no smell of reality at all in a dream?

No, is the reply. (For then the author of the *Vedanta Sutras* goes on to say:)

'But scripture also says that a dream is a sign (of the future; a pointer, shower, manifester), and those who know say this too' (3.2.4).

For a dream is a sign of good and bad things that will happen. So scripture says, 'When a man engaged in actions for the sake of something he desires sees a woman in his dreams, then he may know from that vision in his dream that he will achieve success' (*Chandogya Upanishad* 5.2.9). And, 'If he sees a black man with black teeth, that man will kill him'—from dreams such as these, he may learn that he is not going to live long; this is what scripture says. And the people who know how to study dreams say, 'Riding on an ele-

1. Ancestors of heroes in the *Mahabharata* (p. 130).

HINDUISM

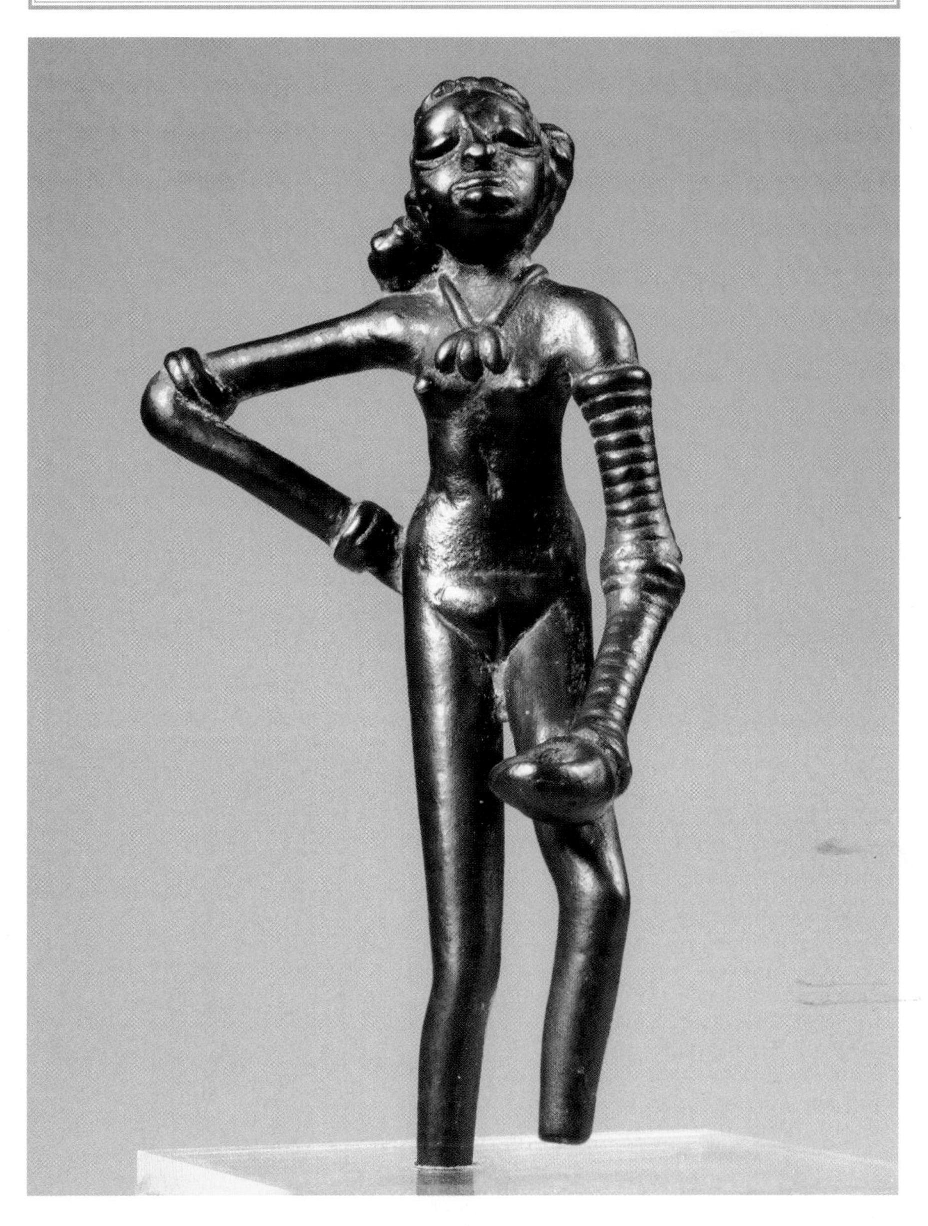

Dancing girl of Mohenjo-Daro, Indus Valley, Sindh, Pakistan (ca. 3000–1500 B.C.E.)

This bronze figure, only 4.3 inches high, was sculpted, using a lost wax method, sometime between 3000 and 1500 B.C.E. and excavated in 1926. The young girl wears nothing but massed bangles on her left arm, two on her right arm, and a necklace; her jewelry accentuates her nakedness, her flat belly, small, high breasts, and prominent pudenda. She has large eyes, a flat nose, curly hair, and a broad forehead. One British archaeologist, John Marshall, found her "half-impudent," and another, Mortimer Wheeler, thought her "pouting," "insolent," and "about fifteen years old." Scholars have suggested that she is a dancer, though she may just be a particularly bold young woman, challenging the male gaze. HARAPPAN/NATIONAL MUSEUM OF INDIA, NEW DELHI, INDIA/THE BRIDGEMAN ART LIBRARY

Krishna Killing the Horse Demon Keshi, Gupta period (ca. 321–500 C.E.)

One of the most popular of Vishnu's many "descents" (avatars) on earth is Krishna, the cowherd boy who grows up to be a warrior prince, killing many demons along the way. In this terra-cotta relief from Uttar Pradesh, Krishna combats the ferocious Keshi, a demon in the guise of a horse, whose name means "long-haired," i.e., "with a long mane and tail." He pushes Keshi back with his foot while thrusting his elbow down his throat. Below them, depicting a later moment, are the dead horse and balls of dung emitted at the moment of death. © THE METROPOLITAN MUSEUM OF ART. IMAGE SOURCE: ART RESOURCE, NY

The Goddess Durga Killing the Buffalo Demon, Mahisha, Pala period (ca. 700–1200 C.E.), Bangladesh or India

Five inches high. Carved in argillite (a fine-grained yellow-beige stone), this sixteen-armed goddess Durga is slaying a buffalo inhabited by the fierce but amorous demon Mahisha. A missing right hand held the spear with which she is about to stab Mahisha, having just severed his head. In her other right hands she holds an arrow, sword, chisel, hammer, thunderbolt, elephant goad, and discus; in her left hands are a shield, bow, bell, mirror, and noose. Mahisha, a tiny, chubby man, haloed by snake heads, emerges from the buffalo's decapitated body and looks up adoringly at the warlike but beautiful Durga, while her lion bites his toes. Smiling serenely, Durga hoists Mahisha by his hair and treads gracefully on the buffalo's body. © THE METROPOLITAN MUSEUM OF ART. IMAGE SOURCE: ART RESOURCE, NY

A scene from the second book of the *Ramayana,* in a Mewar manuscript illustrated by Sahib Din, at the court of Jagat Singh (1618–1646)

King Dasharatha here appears three times and Queen Kaikeyi four times. Kaikeyi is first seen at left lying on the ground, disheveled, angry, and not wearing her ornaments. In the scene to the right she rises to demand that her son be given the throne; King Dasharatha, to appease her, promises to do anything she wants. On the top right Dasharatha is first seen seated, listening to Kaikeyi's demands, and then, below, kneeling at her feet beseeching her to change her mind. In the center, the chief minister Sumantra waits to prepare what he thinks will be the consecration of Rama.

Meenakshi Sundareswarar Temple, Madurai, Tamil Nadu, India (built 1623–55)

The Meenakshi Sundareswarar Temple is located on the southern bank of the Vaikai River in the temple city of Madurai, Tamil Nadu. It is dedicated to the goddess Meenakshi ("With eyes shaped like fish"), a form of Parvati, and her consort Sundareswarar ("The beautiful lord"), a name of Shiva. There are fourteen gateway towers (called *gopurams*), of which the southern tower, 170 feet high, is the tallest. The temple attracts fifteen thousand visitors a day. © OCEAN/CORBIS

Bathing *ghats* at Varanasi, India (2004)

Varanasi (known in ancient times as Kashi, and in British times as Benares) is one of the oldest continuously inhabited cities in the world; it was already a famous center of learning and religion by 2000 B.C.E. It is the most sacred Indian city, not only to Hindus but also to Buddhists (for the Buddha first preached here). Situated on the left bank of the Ganges at the confluence of the Varuna and Asi rivers (which give the city its name), its miles of river frontage are banked by tiers of *ghats* (steps) for bathing. Every devout Hindu hopes to visit the city at least once and, if possible, to die there in old age, so that the cremated ashes may merge into the holy river. WARREN S. APEL, WWW.WARRENAPEL.COM

Kathkali dancers, Patna, Bihar, India (2004)

Kathkali ("Narrative Art") is a seventeenth-century form of classical dance-drama indigenous to southwestern India, particularly the state of Kerala. The performances take place outdoors, all night, and generally enact stories from the *Ramayana*, the *Mahabharata*, or the mythology of the god Shiva, often sung in Malayalam. Traditionally, men and young boys play the parts of both males and females, their faces made up to look like painted masks. The dancers wear heavy jackets and skirts, many garlands, and towering headdresses. This image depicts the Kathkali dancers Amaljeet and Rewati Aiyyer playing the *Mahabharata* characters of Krishna and Draupadi during a performance in Patna on December 1, 2004.

Elements of the Kohbar by Pinki Kumari, painting, Orissa, India (2004)

This painting was made in 2004 by Pinki Kumari, one of the first students at the Mithila Art Institute, in Orissa, where low-income village women formerly accustomed to throwing away their paintings are now encouraged to sell them. The Kohbar is the traditional image painted on the wall of the marriage chamber. Here, fish, parrots, snakes, lovebirds, and bugs generally appear in loving pairs, while the tortoise and elephant remain single. In the lower right corner, the bride, with the groom behind her, offers thanks to the goddess Gauri for finding her a (presumably good) husband. The sun and moon are on the upper left; on the lower left, bans (bamboo) represent either the extended and future male family line, or the capacity to grow tall, straight, and fast. PAINTING BY PINKI KUMARI, PHOTO COURTESY OF THE ETHNIC ARTS FOUNDATION

Hindu wedding, Kolkata, India

Hindu weddings vary widely, but generally, after the father gives away his daughter, the groom takes the bride's right hand with his left, ties his scarf to her sari, and leads her around the fire with seven steps; at every step each makes a vow to the other. They put food into the fire—the fire-deity, Agni, is the primary witness of a Hindu marriage—and into one another's mouths. Pre-wedding celebrations can last for one day or many and may include the arrival of the groom (on a white horse) and his party at the bride's residence, often in a formal procession with dancing and music; there may be post-wedding ceremonies to welcome the bride to her husband's home. © YUSEF TUVI

Hindu devotees immerse a statue of the Durga in the Hooghly River at the close of Durga Puja ("the Worship of the Goddess Durga"), Kolkata, India (2009)

The Durga Puja festival is celebrated for a week in autumn throughout the Hindu world. In Kolkata, thousands of elaborate stages (called *pandals*) are crafted, depicting Durga's triumph over the Buffalo (Mahisha). Colored lights and music fill the streets. Families offer flowers to the images of Durga. Bengalis view this as the period when Durga, having married Shiva, returns to Kolkata to visit her natal family. At the end of the week, the statues of Durga are carried to the river and thrown in, sending Durga back to her husband in the Himalayas. STEVE RAYMER/NATIONAL GEOGRAPHIC SOCIETY

Thillai Natarajah Temple, Chidambaram, Tamil Nadu, India (2009)

A woman performing ablutions at twilight in a sacred pool in the great temple to Nataraja ("Lord of the Dance," a form of Shiva) at Chidambaram, in Tamil Nadu. (It is also called the Thillai—"Mangrove"—temple, after the trees that once surrounded it.) The temple complex, which covers forty acres in the heart of the city, was begun by the Chola king Parantaka I (907–950 C.E.) but largely built during the twelfth and thirteenth centuries, and further enlarged and enriched by several subsequent rulers. There are a number of pools in which worshippers may perform their devotions at the particularly sacred moments of dawn and sunset, and from which they may bring home holy water.

phant and so forth in a dream is lucky, but riding on a donkey is unlucky.' And they also believe that certain dreams that are caused by spells or gods or drugs also have the smell of reality. Here, too, the thing of which the dream is a sign may be real, but the sign itself, the sight of the woman and so forth, is false, since it is contradicted (by the waking state); this is my opinion. Therefore the statement that the dream is merely illusion is upheld. . . .

When scripture says, 'The dreamer emits from himself chariots and so forth, for he is the maker,' it is said merely because he is the cause (of their creation), but not because the dreamer actually emits the chariots and so forth right before one's eyes. He is said to be the cause in the sense that he is the one who makes the good and bad deeds that become the cause of the visions of bliss and terror that are the cause of the images of the chariots and so forth. . . .

Thus the world of the liminal (dream) state is not truly real in the same sense that the world of the creation that consists of the sky and so forth is real; this is what has been established.

However. There is no transcendent reality even in the creation that consists of the sky and so forth. For as it was established above (*Vedanta Sutras* 2.1.14), the entire expanse of the phenomenal world is mere illusion. The phenomenal world consisting of the sky and so forth has a distinct and stable form only until one sees that its very self is the ultimate reality. But the phenomenal world that arises out of the liminal state (of dreams) is contradicted every day. Therefore the sense in which the liminal world is a mere illusion must be understood as different (from the sense in which the waking world is a mere illusion).

RAMANUJA DREAMS

Ramanuja (ca. 1056–1137 C.E.) was a worshipper of Vishnu. ("Ramanuja," meaning "Younger brother of [Bala-]Rama," is an epithet of Krishna ["The River Yamuna," p. 259].) Like Shankara, he was one of the founders of a movement, in this case the Shri Vaishnava movement in South India. Many stories are told about Ramanuja's clash not with disciples of Shankara but with other Shaivas like them, as well as with Muslims and Jains. This was primarily a competition for patronage, for many of the kings of that era supported Shaiva, Vaishnava, Jain, and Buddhist institutions. Yet we can see Shankara as the unnamed "opponent" who advances many of the positions against which Ramanuja argues in this passage.

Ramanuja invokes some of the classical tropes of the philosophy of illusion (*maya*), such as the rope that one mistakes for a serpent or the shell that one mistakes for silver, as well as standard metaphors for logical impossibility, such as the son of a barren woman (or of "no mother"). He also mentions darkness, energy, and goodness, the three strands or *gunas* of Sankhya philosophy ("Quieting the Mind," p. 122; "The Two Paths," p. 178), and the three basic authorities for knowledge: one's own eyes, inference, and scripture ("The Discipline of Mind and Body," p. 122). He refers to the practice of allowing substitutions to be made during Vedic rituals if the original substance is unavailable ("How to Perform a Funeral," p. 213). The Soma plant ("Humans, Animals, and Gods in the *Rig Veda*," p. 73), in particular, became impossible to get once the Vedic people had moved down from the mountains to the Gangetic plain, where it did not grow. The Putika plant, probably a kind of sarcostemma, is a common substitute for Soma.

Shribhashya 1.1.1

The opponent may falsely argue thus:

Perceptions of an elephant and so forth in a dream are not real, but they are the cause of the knowledge of real things, auspicious and inauspicious (that are portended by the dream). In the same way, scripture is unreal, because it is based upon ignorance, but it is the cause of the knowledge of the real thing that is its object, namely, ultimate reality. Is there any reason why this can be contradicted?

Yes. For it is not true that the perceptions in a dream are unreal. It is only the objects that are contradicted (by the perceptions of the waking state), not the perceptions. For no one ever decides, 'The perception that I experienced when I was dreaming does not actually exist here.' But one does decide that there is a contradiction, which one understands thus: 'The vision exists, but the objects of the vision do not exist.' And the illusory perception that arises out of a magician's spells, drugs, and so forth, is also real, as it is the cause of pleasure and fear. In this case, too, there is no contradiction of the perception. And the misperception of something like a serpent in something like a rope, arising out of something like a flaw in the senses or in the object of the senses, this, too, is real, the cause of things like fear. Real, too, is the belief that a man has been bitten, arising out of the proximity of a snake, even when he has not been bitten. Real, too, is the belief in the poison of apprehension, which may actually cause death. So, too, the reflected image of something like a face in something like water becomes a real thing, the cause of a definite opinion about the face, that is a real thing. Because all of these states of consciousness have a definite origin and are the causes of actual effects, they are real.

If you say, 'But in the absence of any elephant or such a thing, how could the ideas about them be real?', I say, No (the ideas about them *are* real). For it is a rule that the mere connection between the object of the senses and the sensation that it causes is a sufficient basis for ideas about it. The reflection of the object is thus precisely a sufficient basis for its perception. And there is in fact such a reflection in this case, as the result of some flaw (in the object or in the senses). As the object is contradicted, it is regarded as unreal; but the *belief* in the object is not contradicted, and so it is said to be real. . . .

Those who know the Veda believe that all perception has as its object what is real; it is known from scripture and Shastras that everything is the very nature of everything else. The creator began his work by thinking, 'Let me become many,' and each single element was divided into three parts (the three qualities of matter—darkness, energy, and goodness). This is what the scripture says; and so each thing is perceived before one's eyes as having a triple cause. The red color in fire is from elemental fire, the white from the waters, and the black from the earth; this is the triple form of fire. Thus scripture demonstrates that everything is combined with everything else. In

Translated by Wendy Doniger O'Flaherty.

the *Vishnu Purana* the beginning of creation is described thus: 'The separate elements, possessing various powers, could not create progeny without combining together, without mingling entirely. Having come together in union with one another, mixing with each other, all of them, beginning with the great element and ending with the essentially differentiated atomic particles, formed an egg' (*Vishnu Purana* 1.2.50–2). The author of this (*Vedanta*) *Sutra* also declares that the elements have three forms (*Vedanta Sutra* 3.1.3).

And scripture says that when there is no Soma available, one may use the Putika plant; for those who understand logic know that there are some qualities of the Soma plant (in the Putika plant). And when there is no rice available, one can use Nivara grains, because they have the quality of rice. One thing is similar to another when one thing contains one part of the substance of the other thing. And the scripture says that the quality of something like silver exists in something like a shell. The distinction between such things as silver and shells is simply the result of the preponderance (of silver in one and shell in the other). It is evident that things like shells resemble things like silver; therefore the existence of one in the other is established simply because it is self-evident.

Sometimes, if there is a defect in the eye or something of that sort, the part that is silver is apprehended, but without the part that is shell; then a man who wants silver will react to it. But when the defect (in the eye) is removed, and the part that is shell is apprehended, he turns back from it. Hence the perception of silver in a shell is true. So, too, the relationship between a perception that contradicts another, and the perception that is contradicted by it, becomes apparent as the result of the preponderance (of one quality over another): the preponderance of shell is grasped either in part or in its totality. The discriminations that are made in practical everyday life do not, therefore, depend upon a distinction between an object of perception that is false and one that is true, but merely upon the fact that everything is a part of the nature of everything else.

And in a dream, the Lord emits objects of the senses of such a sort that are perceived only by each individual person, according to the good or evil qualities of living creatures, and that last only for a particular time. This is what scripture says about dreams: 'There are no chariots there, no harnessing, . . . for he is the maker' (*Brihadaranyaka Upanishad* 4.3.10). Even if these things do not exist now in such a way that they may be experienced by another person in their totality, nevertheless the Lord emits objects of the senses of such a sort that they may be perceived only by that particular person. 'For *He* is the maker': the meaning is that such a sort of making comes from Him who has such a marvellous power that what he imagines is real.

The *Katha Upanishad* (2.5.8) says, 'He who is awake in those who dream, the Person who fashions desire after desire, he is the bright seed, he is the ultimate reality, he is what is called immortal. All worlds are contained in That, and no one goes beyond That.' And the author of this (*Vedanta*) *Sutra*, too, speaks of the world created in the liminal state (3.2.1) and of sons and so forth when there is no mother (3.2.2); then he suggests that the individual soul (*jiva*) emits the objects seen in dreams, but that the world created in dreams is mere illusion, because its own form is not revealed in any totality (3.2.3). But he says, finally, that the creation of the dream world does not come merely from the imagination of the individual soul. For, though the soul has the power to make what it imagines real, a power which is part of its own nature, nevertheless, as long as it is in the state of the world of rebirth (*samsara*), its own form—including that power—is not manifest in its totality. And so this creation (of the objects in the dream world) is a marvel that arises as a result of the Lord's power to create objects that are to be experienced by each individual person.

When the *Katha Upanishad* (5.8) says, 'All worlds are contained in That, and no one goes beyond That,' it is clear that the highest Self, the Creator, is to be understood. The person lying on his bed in his own bedroom sees in his dreams things such as going in his very own body to another country and being anointed king and having his head cut off and so forth, experiences that arise as the fruits of his merits and demerits, and this happens through the creation of another body that exactly resembles the body lying on the bed. . . .

Thus it has been proven that all perception is true. The flaws in other opinions have been discussed at length by various other philosophers; knowing this, no trouble has been taken here in that regard. And indeed, what need is there for a long proof? The authorities are one's own eyes, inference, and scripture. For those who acknowledge the highest ultimate reality who has the power to make what he imagines real, who is known from scripture, who is omniscient, free from even the merest smell of any flaw, and who is a mass of good qualities that cannot be counted—for them, what cannot be achieved? What cannot be proven? The Lord, the highest ultimate reality, created the entire universe to be enjoyed according to the qualities of virtue or vice of the individual souls; he made certain objects to be perceived in common by everyone, bringing the experience of happiness or unhappiness to all without regard for the fruits of their actions; and he made other objects to be experienced only by this or that individual person, and lasting only for a limited period of time. Thus the distinction between experiences that are contradicted (like dreams) and those that are contradicting (like waking life) is a distinction between objects of the senses that are experienced by everyone and those that are not. Thus everything is consistent.

THE MAN WHO BUILT A HOUSE OF AIR

The philosophy of illusion was developed in a particularly imaginative and brilliant way in the eleventh and twelfth centuries in Kashmir. Located on the northern border of India, Kashmir is close to the Central Asian strongholds of Buddhism, whose philosophers developed their own complex doctrines of illusion. Shaiva philosophers in Kashmir combined these Buddhist elements with the Non-dualist ideas of Shankara and fused them into a philosophy of their own, known as Kashmir Shaivism, also called the "Recognition" (Pratijna) school. Central Asia was also the home of a number of Muslim (Turkish and Arabic) cultures with highly developed storytelling traditions that rivaled those of ancient India, and the Hindu and Muslim traditions constantly interacted, each enriching the other. Eventually, a brand of idealist philosophy that was already a mix of Buddhism and Hinduism married a brand of storytelling that was already a mix of Hinduism and Islam.

And so it was here, and at this time, that the great Indian traditions of storytelling and illusion blossomed in the *Yoga-vasishtha* (in full, the *Yoga-Vasishtha-Maha-Ramayana* or "The Great Story of Rama in Which Vasishtha Teaches His Yoga"). This text deals with the traditional topics of creation, doomsday, and the nature of the universe, and it is a popular source of Hindu self-understanding. That Kashmir Shaivism was called the "Recognition" school is not irrelevant to the main theme of the *Yoga-vasishtha* narratives, which turn on individuals' recognition of their own identities and deepest essences. But the glory of the *Yoga-vasishtha* is that it transforms a rather difficult theoretical, philosophical discussion into a series of engaging, rather surreal narratives.

For Vedantic thinkers like Shankara, following the path of Release meant awakening from the dream of the material world to the reality of *brahman*. The twist that the *Yoga-vasishtha* adds is that you cannot wake from the dream, because it may be someone else's dream. For householders on the path of rebirth, Release means staying asleep but being aware that you are dreaming. This is a variant of the final advice that Krishna gives to Arjuna in the *Gita* (though the *Yoga-vasishtha* arrives at that point after a very different journey): continue to act, though with a newly transformed understanding of the unreality of actions, and therefore without the desire for the fruits of actions ("The True Nature of Action," p. 180).

The frame story of the *Yoga-vasishtha* presents the text as an episode that Valmiki left out of his version of the *Ramayana* (p. 186). It claims to fill in the supposed gaps in the older text, just as many folk versions of the *Ramayana* do. It frames the story in terms of the ancient tension between the householder life and the truth claims of renunciation. The *Yoga-vasishtha* takes the form of a long conversation between Rama and the sage Vasishtha, at a moment when Rama has returned from a pilgrimage in a state of depression and insanity (or so his father and the courtiers describe it). Rama says that anyone who says "Act like a king" is out of his mind, that everything is unreal, that it is false to believe in the reality of the world, that everything is just the imagination of the mind. Rama's father consults two great sages, Vishvamitra and Vasishtha, who assure him that Rama is perfectly right in his understanding of the world, that he has become enlightened—and then offer to cure him. That is, they promise to remove his depression and make him socially functional, while leaving his (correct) metaphysical apprehensions unimpaired. To do this, they tell him a number of stories, many of them very long and very complicated. This is a relatively short and straightforward one.

Yogavasishtha 6.1.112.16–35

Once upon a time there was a husky man made by a machine of illusion. He was a fool, with the feeble wits of a child, and he was exclusively concealed within his own idiocy. He was born one day, alone, and he remained right there, in an empty place. He was like the net-pattern that you see in space when your eyes are closed, or like a mirage that you see in a desert. There was no one there other than him; he was all that there was there. Whatever else there appeared to be there was a reflection of him, but that fool could not see it.

Then he got the idea of expanding his wealth, and he firmly resolved, 'I belong to empty space; I am empty space; empty space is mine. I will protect space; I will establish space firmly; and I myself will assiduously protect my cherished possession.' When he had made this decision, he made a house to

TRANSLATED BY Wendy Doniger O'Flaherty.

protect empty space. Inside this house, he marked out an area and said, 'Now I have protected this empty space.' And he took pleasure in that space in the house.

But in the course of time, that house of his was destroyed, as a little wave in the water is destroyed by a wind in the season of autumn. 'Oh my! My little house-space, you have been destroyed! Oh my! Where did you go in just a moment? Oh, oh! You have been shattered!'—this is how he mourned for that space. And when he had mourned a hundred times in this way, that fool built a well to protect his empty space, and he became obsessed with his well-space. But then, in time, the well, too, was destroyed, and when the well-space was gone he sank into grief; and when he had finished lamenting his well-space, immediately he made a pot, and he became obsessed with the pot-space through the illusion of his pleasure in it. But in time the pot, too, was destroyed; whatever part of the sky that unfortunate creature took, that too was destroyed. When he finished lamenting his pot-space, he made a bowl to protect his empty space, and he became obsessed with the bowl-space. In time, the bowl, too, was destroyed, as darkness is destroyed by blazing light; and he grieved for that bowl-space.

When he finished grieving for the bowl-space, he built a great palace with four halls, all made of space, in order to protect his empty space. Time swallowed it up, too, and destroyed it as a wind destroys a withered leaf; and he became obsessed with mourning for it, too. And when he had finished mourning for his palace with four halls, he built a great granary in the form of a cloud, to protect his empty space, and he became obsessed with the space in that. But time quickly carried it away, too, as if it had been a cloud, and he was tortured by his grief for his lost granary.

Thus time, whose essence never changes, outstripped his house, four-halled palace, pot, bowl, and granary. And thus he remained, powerless in his cave in a corner of the sky, coming and going in his own mind from one impenetrable house to another, from one misery, one cloud, to another cloud that had become a source of misery, deluded by the confusion between what had gone and what had never come.

VERNACULAR HINDUISM IN SOUTH INDIA, 800–1800 C.E.

THE FLOWERING OF BHAKTI

While the Sanskrit literary forms were developing, first in North India and then throughout the subcontinent, new religious movements were finding expression in vernacular languages. The constant, gradual, unofficial mutual exchange and cross-fertilization between Sanskrit (the "father tongue," the second language of many cultivated Hindus) and the vernacular languages (the "mother tongues") underwent a dramatic transformation toward the middle of the second millennium: local languages were now promoted officially, politically, and artistically, replacing the previously fashionable cosmopolitan and translocal language, Sanskrit. Instead of nourishing and supplementing Sanskrit, as they had done until now, the vernacular languages began to compete with Sanskrit as the language of literary production. This process has been called, in imitation of Srinivas's "Sanskritization" ("Texts Heard and Texts Read," p. 67), vernacularization, the deliberate creation of a written literature in local languages.

The great divide is between written and nonwritten, not between Sanskrit and the vernaculars, particularly as the Sanskrit corpus is constantly colored by contributions from the vernaculars while the vernaculars eventually became Sanskritized themselves, imitating Sanskrit values and conventions, sharing Sanskrit grammars and lexicons. Some of the vernacular literatures display the misogyny and class consciousness of some Brahmins, though some Sanskrit texts, and certainly many vernacular ones, break out of those strictures and incorporate the more open-minded attitudes of the oral vernaculars.

The earliest written sources we have for Hinduism in a language other than Sanskrit are poems in Tamil, a South Indian language from a linguistic family, Dravidian, that is entirely separate from the Indo-European family from which Sanskrit is descended. There was constant contact and trade between North and South India at least by Mauryan times, in the fourth century B.C.E. South India was already known to the Hebrew Bible as a land of riches, perhaps the place to which King Solomon sent his ships every three years to bring back gold, silver, ivory, monkeys, and peacocks. The southern trade route brought pearls, shells, and the fine cottons of Madurai to western lands. There was bustling contact with Rome, China, and Indianized cultures in Southeast Asia.

Islam, too, was established on the Malabar coast of Kerala during this early period. Arabs came to India long before the birth of Muhammad

(632 C.E.), trading across the Arabian Sea to India's southwest coast. Shortly after the Prophet's death, a group of Arabs, whom the Indians called Mapillai ("newlywed grooms" or "sons-in-law"), settled on the northern Malabar coast; when Arab merchants, newly converted to Islam, arrived there later, they converted many of the Mapillai to Islam, and Muslims have remained there to this day. These first Muslims interacted with Hindus on both the individual and the communal level, inspiring some to convert to Islam and provoking opposition from others.

The *bhakti* (devotional) movement began in South India, first among Tamil writers and soon after in the literatures of other Dravidian languages, such as Telugu in Andhra, Kannada in Mysore, and Malayalam in Kerala, and subsequently among nonliterate people. It swept over the subcontinent, fertilizing widespread traditions of pilgrimage and temple festivals. It moved into Sanskrit through works such as the tenth-century *Bhagavata Purana*, composed in Sanskrit in South India ("Krishna," p. 247). Always it kept its South Indian character and thus transported South Indian qualities to the North, transforming northern *bhakti* into a mix of northern and southern, Sanskrit and Dravidian forms.

The concept of *bhakti* was already developing in the *Bhagavad Gita* (which established devotion as a third alternative to ritual action and knowledge) ("The Path of Devotion," p. 182). But South Indian *bhakti* heightens the emotion, so that even a direct quotation from the *Gita* takes on an entirely different meaning in the new context, as basic words like karma and *bhakti* shift their connotations. The Tamils had words for *bhakti* (such as *anpu* and *parru*), though eventually they also came to use the Sanskrit term (which became *patti* in Tamil). But the Tamil poets transformed the concept of *bhakti* not only by applying it to the regional traditions of the miraculous exploits of local saints but also by infusing it with a more personal confrontation, an insistence on actual physical and visual presence, a passionate transference and countertransference. The emotional involvement, the pity, desire, and compassion of the *bhakti* gods cause them to forget that they are above it all—as metaphysics demands—and reduces them to the human level—as mythology demands. Despite its royal and literary roots, *bhakti* is also a folk, and oral, phenomenon. Many of the *bhakti* poems were based on oral compositions, some probably even by illiterate saints. Both Shaiva and Vaishnava *bhakti* movements incorporated folk religion and folk song into what was already a rich mix of Vedic and Upanishadic concepts, local mythologies, Buddhism, Jainism, conventions of Tamil and Sanskrit poetry, and early Tamil conceptions of love, service, women, and kings, to which, after a while, they added elements of Islam. This cultural mixture is the rule rather than the exception in India, but the South Indian use of it is particularly pronounced.

Unlike most Sanskrit authors, the *bhakti* poets revealed details of their own lives and personalities in their texts, so that the voice of the saint is heard in the poems. The older myths take on new dimensions in *bhakti* poetry; what happens to someone else in a mythic scenario happens to the speaker in the poem. And so we now encounter the use of the first person, a new literary register. It is not entirely unprecedented; we heard some voices, even women's voices, in direct speech in the *Rig Veda* ("Agastya and Lopamudra," p. 89) and a moment in the *Mahabharata* when the narrator breaks through and reminds the reader "I have already told you" ("The Pandavas

Go to Heaven," p. 145). But the first person comes into its own in South Indian *bhakti*. Similarly, the names of local rivers and hills and shrines anchor each poem, each story, in a particular place.

An essential component of Tamil *bhakti*, known throughout North and South India, from the time of the first *bhakti* poets to the present, was *darshan*, "seeing," the means by which favor passed from one to the other of the parties linked by the gaze. To see the deity, and to have him or her see you, was to make possible a transfer of power not unlike the transfer of karma or merit ("The Transfer of Karma in Hell," p. 232). This was the intimate transference that South Indian *bhakti* imagined for the god and the worshipper.

Darshan is a concept that comes to the world of the temple from the world of the royal court. One takes *darshan* of a king or a god, up close and personal. A feudal king, subject to a superior ruler, had to appear in person in the court of his overlord, publicly affirming his obedient service through a public demonstration of submission, so that he could see and be seen. So, too, the temple was both the god's private dwelling and a palace, a public site where people could not only make offerings but look at the deity and be looked at by him. Many temples have annual processions in which the central image of the god is taken out and carried around the town in a wooden chariot (*rath*), in clear imitation of a royal procession. *Darshan* may also have been inspired, in part, by the Buddhist practice of viewing the relics in *stupas*. But it was also surely a response to the new *bhakti* emphasis on the aspect of god in the flesh ("right before your eyes" [*sakshat*]), with flesh-and-blood qualities (*sa-guna*), in contrast with the aspect of god "without qualities" (*nir-guna*) that the philosophers spoke of. Indeed, *darshan* is a reversal of one of the basic metaphors of Indian philosophy, which takes the errors that we make in seeing (such as mistaking a rope for a snake) as a sign of the larger error that we make in mistaking the phenomenal world for reality ("Ramanuja Dreams," p. 289). Where philosophers could not trust their eyes, *bhaktas* (devotees) trusted mainly their eyes.

Artists, both Hindu and Buddhist, have always painted the eyes on a statue last, for that is the moment when the image comes to life, when it can *see* you, and you can no longer work on it; that is when the power begins. The Vedic gods Varuna and Indra were said to be "thousand-eyed," because as kings they had a thousand spies, overseeing justice, and as sky gods they had the stars for their eyes, and human eyes are analogized to the sun ("The Funeral Fire," p. 84). Varuna in the *Rig Veda* (2.27.9) is unblinking, a characteristic that later becomes one of the marks that distinguish gods from mortals. (The others are that the gods do not sweat, cast shadows, or get dirty; nor do their garlands wither or their feet quite touch the ground.) South Indian *bhakti* picks up these ancient concepts and moves them in entirely new directions.

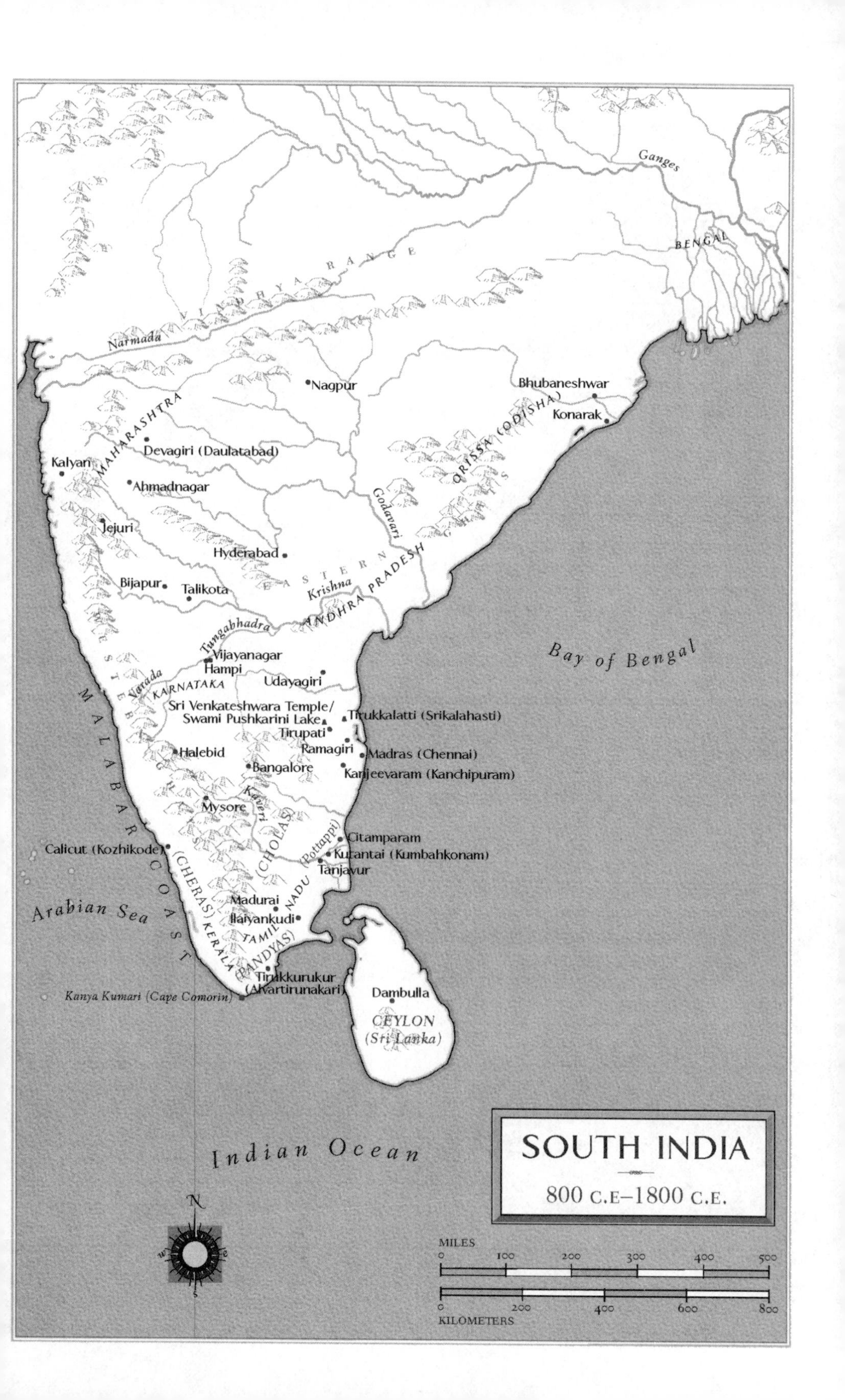
SOUTH INDIA
800 C.E–1800 C.E.
Ganges
BENGAL
VINDHYA RANGE
Narmada
Nagpur
Bhubaneshwar
Konarak
ORISSA (ODISHA)
MAHARASHTRA
Devagiri (Daulatabad)
Kalyan
Ahmadnagar
Godavari
Jejuri
Hyderabad
EASTERN GHATS
ANDHRA PRADESH
Krishna
Bijapur
Talikota
Tungabhadra
Vijayanagar
Hampi
Bay of Bengal
Udayagiri
Varada
KARNATAKA
WESTERN GHATS
Sri Venkateshwara Temple/
Swami Pushkarini Lake
Tirukkalatti (Srikalahasti)
Tirupati
Ramagiri
Madras (Chennai)
Halebid
Bangalore
Kanjeevaram (Kanchipuram)
Kaveri
Mysore
(CHOLAS)
Citamparam
Calicut (Kozhikode)
MALABAR COAST
Kutantai (Kumbahkonam)
Pottappi
Tanjavur
(CHERAS)
Madurai
TAMIL NADU
Arabian Sea
Ilaiyankudi
KERALA
(PANDYAS)
Tirukkurukur
(Alvartirunakari)
Kanya Kumari (Cape Comorin)
Dambulla
CEYLON
(Sri Lanka)
Indian Ocean
N
MILES
0 100 200 300 400 500
0 200 400 600 800
KILOMETERS

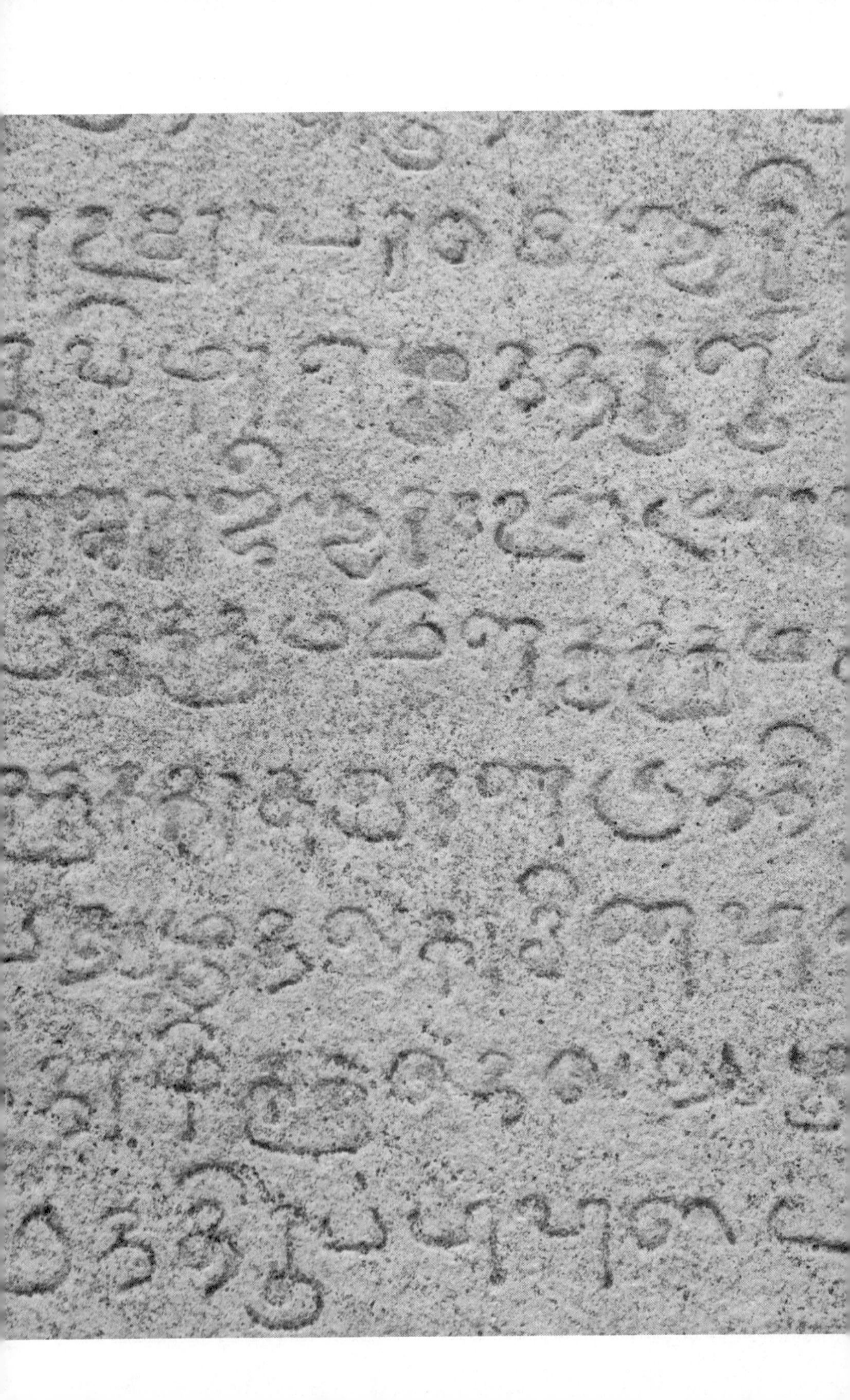

Tamil Finds Its Many Voices

800–1300 C.E.

The North Indian vernaculars (such as Hindi in much of North India, Bangla in Bengal, and Marathi in Maharashtra) derive from Sanskrit, while the South Indian vernaculars (such as Telugu in Andhra, Kannada in Mysore, and Malayalam in Kerala) derive from Tamil. Tamil was the language of royal decrees and poetry for many centuries before texts in Telugu, Kannada, and Malayalam began to be preserved. Tamil is spoken throughout much of South India and Sri Lanka, particularly in Tamil Nadu, at the southern tip of India. Tamil as a literary language appears to have developed from traditions separate from those of Sanskrit. Although we have no surviving literature in Tamil until the sixth century C.E., other forms of evidence tell us a great deal about a thriving culture in South India, much of it carried on in Tamil, from at least the third century B.C.E. Far from the Sanskritic culture that arose in the foothills of the Himalayas, ancient Tamil Nadu was a land where elephants and water buffalo thrived but horses did not, and its religious imagery was grounded in a landscape of lush paddy fields and ocean beaches.

The earliest extant Tamil texts are anthologies of roughly 2,300 short poems probably composed by the early centuries of the Common Era, but anthologized much later. The poems are known in their totality as *Cankam* ("assembly") poetry

An eleventh-century Tamil inscription on stone from the Brihadishvara temple in Thanjavur (Tanjore).

(Sanskrit *sangham*), named after a series of three legendary assemblies said to have lasted for 9,990 years, long, long ago. Brahmins who settled in the South when kingdoms were first established there gradually introduced Sanskrit (which had had Dravidian loan words from the time of the *Rig Veda*) into the local language and in return learned not only Tamil words but Tamil deities and rituals, and much else. The Tamil "local Puranas" (*sthala puranas*) both echoed Sanskritic forms and contributed new elements to works such as the *Bhagavata Purana*, composed in South India in the tenth century C.E.

A few of the *Cankam* poems are already devoted to religious subjects, singing the praise of Tirumal (Vishnu) and the river goddess Vaikai, or of Murukan, the Tamil god who had by now coalesced with the northern god Skanda, son of Shiva and Parvati ("The Gods Interrupt Shiva and Parvati," p. 196). But beginning in about 600 C.E., the wandering poets and saints devoted to Shiva (the Nayanmars, traditionally said to number sixty-three) and to Krishna-Vishnu (the twelve Alvars) sang poems in the devotional mode of *bhakti*. The group of Nayanmars known as "the first three" (Appar, Campantar, and Cuntarar, sixth to eighth centuries) speaks in the collection called the *Tevaram*. Nammalvar ("Our Alvar"), the last of the great Alvars, lived in the ninth century. Tamil had its epics, too, of which the older, the *Cilappatikaram* or "lay of the anklet," probably composed in the fifth century C.E., is a major source for understanding the early worship of the goddess Pattini, as Cekkilar's twelfth-century *Periya Puranam* is for the worship of Shiva.

Tamil literature also expresses the dark side of *darshan* in the martyrdom of blinding. The hagiography of the eighth-century Shaiva saint Cuntarar tells us that Shiva blinded him (*darshan* in its negative form) after he deserted his second wife but restored his vision (*darshan* in its positive form) when he returned home to her ("The Tevaram of Cuntarar"). Kannappar blinds himself in the service of his god ("Kannappar Gives His Eye to Shiva"). The gentler aspects of *darshan* are also expressed in the passionate, often erotic, visions of the Alvars and Nayanmars.

THE *TIRUVAYMOLI* ("SACRED SPOKEN WORD") OF NAMMALVAR

The Alvars (whose name means "immersed in god") were poets and saints devoted to Vishnu, particularly in his incarnation as Krishna. There were said to be twelve Alvars at first, wandering over the Tamil-speaking regions of South India between the sixth and the ninth century. They changed and revitalized Hinduism, simultaneously absorbing elements of Buddhism and Jainism and obstructing the spread of those rival religions.

Nammalvar ("Our Alvar"), the last of the great Alvars, who lived from approximately 880 to 930 C.E., is said to have been born into a Shudra caste, a peasant caste (Vellala) in Tirukkurukur (the present-day Alvartirunakari, in Tamilnadu). He lived only thirty-five years, but soon after his death images of him were installed in South Indian Vishnu temples, where they are worshipped to this day; his poems were chanted in temple services, and singers of his hymns often led the temple processions, walking before the god, with people chanting the Vedas following them.

Nammalvar composed four works, of which the *Tiruvaymoli*, often called "The Tamil Veda," a work of 1,102 verses, is the most important. The very title of the work—"the sacred spoken word" or "holy word of mouth" or "word of holy mouth"—suggests that it was meant to be performed orally, recited, and since the tenth century it has been performed, both in homes and in temples. Nammalvar's theology contributed much to the qualified nondualism of Ramanuja and to the tradition of the Shri Vaishnavas ("Ramanuja Dreams," p. 289), devotees of the Lord Vishnu (Shri Vishnu), who call their tradition the dual Vedanta because it combines the Sanskrit of the Veda with the Tamil of the Alvars. The earliest commentary on this work was composed between 1100 and 1150 C.E. by Tirukkurukai Piran Pillan, the cousin and disciple of the philosopher Ramanuja; his comments introduce several of the poems here.

The poems on pages 303–09, through "Our Masters," are translated by A. K. Ramanujan. The poems on pages 309–14, starting with "Who Is He Possessing . . . ," are translated by John Carman and Vasudha Narayanan.

PRONOUNCING GLOSSARY

Kali: *kah´-lee*
Kanna: *kun´-nah*
kayal: *kah´-yul*
Kutantai: *koo´-tun-tai´*
Jain: *jain*
Linga Purana: *ling´-guh poo-rah´-nuh*
Nammalvar: *num-mahl´-vahr´*
Tirukkurukur: *tih-rook´-koo´-roo-koor´*
Tiruvayamoli: *tih´-roo-vah´-yuh-moh´-lee*
Vinnakar: *vin´-nuh-kar*

HE IS BOTH THE CROOKED AND THE STRAIGHT

The god is here called "crooked" or "contrary" in that, though he is altogether auspicious, or favorable, he informs both good and evil. He pervades the universe, yet he is particularly present in Vinnakar, "sky-city," one of 108 holy shrines (*tirthas*) in Tamil Nadu, the Tamil-speaking region.

He is both the crooked
and the straight

the black
the white
the truths
the lies

youth and age
the ancient and the new:

our lord lives
in Vinnakar
strong-walled well-made city

and his grove there
is the triple world
of the gods

WORKER OF MIRACLES

This poem explores the god's play (*lila*), what the Tamils call his divine games. One of these games is his entrance into incarnations, such as the giant dwarf ("The Three Strides of Vishnu," p. 91). Another is his killing of demons, such as "Honey" ("Madhu") ("Arjuna Questions Krishna," p. 167), who was born from the ear of Vishnu as he slept at the end of an eon. Perhaps his most basic pastime is spinning the web of illusion (*maya*) that generates the material world, with its five elements (fire, water, earth, sky, and wind).

Worker of miracles,
magical dwarf,
and killer of the demon
named Honey,

only you can tell us:

becoming fire, water, earth,
  sky, and wind,

becoming father, mother,
  and the children too
  and all others
  and all things unnamed,

the way you stand there,
  being yourself—

what's it all about?

YOU DO STUNTS

The first reference in this poem is to Vishnu as Krishna, driver of Arjuna's chariot, in the *Mahabharata* ("Arjuna Questions Krishna," p. 167), and to Krishna's weapon, the discus (called "Sudarshana," "beautiful to look at"), accessories signaling attributes of Krishna on the intensely human level. This discus has cosmic aspects too, for it also stands for the wheel of time, its twelve spokes representing the months, its six hubs the seasons, and so forth. The focus then shifts entirely to the cosmic level, and to the god's presence in each of the four ages ("The Four Ages," p. 228).

You do stunts
  with your chariots

the discus your weapon:

tell us how

  managing every one of the four ages
  becoming every little thing in them

    harmonious now
      now quite contrary

you stand there

a marvel
  of contradictions!

LOOK HERE

This is a love poem to Vishnu in the form of Krishna, as he teases the young cowherd women (the *gopis*) in the village. The poet assumes the voice of the *gopis*, "this plain crowd," who tease Krishna in return, not realizing that as Vishnu he does, in fact, have complete access to the "queens of the three worlds."

Look here:

being naughty,
grabbing our dolls
and doing wild things

won't get you anywhere;

we know you
from old times,
how can we stand your pranks,
your airs?

There are any number
of lovely women,
queens of the three worlds;

so don't torment
this plain crowd.

Such stuff is childish,
even for you.

IT'S TRUE

This poem takes the doctrine of the identity of the individual soul and god ("Upanishads," p. 105; "Theology and/or Philosophy in the *Vedanta*," p. 285) from the philosophical and theological plane to the human psychological realm, and mocks it. It argues that, even though it is true that both paradise and hell (here identified with this world rather than an underworld) are made of god, as is the worshipper (the poet), still the worshipper fears hell and longs for the god's paradise.

It's true
even I am you

even the unbearable hell
of this world
is you:

this being so
what's the difference?

One may go to paradise
and reach perfect joy
or go the other way
and fall into hell

yet I being I
even when I remember
I am you
I still fear hell:

lord in perpetual paradise
let me be at your feet.

TALKING OF MONISM

This poem, like the previous one, satirizes Shankara and his followers, adherents of the monist doctrine of the identity of the human soul and the world-soul (*brahman*) ("Shankara Dreams," p. 286). Assuming the contrasting position of Ramanuja ("Ramanuja Dreams," p. 289), the poet assumes that individual souls do not merge with god but, rather, serve, love, and experience god forever. This god is a god with details and attributes, a god who is the Dark One (Krishna or Mayon), the herdsman god of the pastoral region, and who has a bird on his banner (the sacred Garuda eagle that Vishnu rides on). The poet even suggests that the most serious delusion (*maya*), the "fantasy," of the monist is his belief in monism.

If they should merge,
that's really good:

if the two that'll never meet
should meet,
then this human thing
will become our lord,
the Dark One
with the sacred bird
on his banner—
as if that's possible.

It will always be itself.

There are yogis
who mistake fantasy
for true release

and run around
in circles
in the world
of what is and what was
and what will be.

It takes all kinds.

KINGS WHO RULE THE EARTH ALL ALONE

This poem scorns the patronage of kings and imagines them reduced to the status of pariahs (Dalits), the lowest castes, who are allowed to eat and drink only from broken pottery and who are associated with dogs.

Kings
who rule the earth all alone
for long years

will one day hobble
on legs bitten by black dogs

and beg from a broken pot
here
in this very life
with the whole world watching:

don't tarry then

think of the lord's feet
and live

OUR MASTERS

This poem mocks the four classes or general castes (the *varnas*: Brahmin, Kshatriya, Vaishya, and Shudra) ("Hymn of the Primeval Man," p. 82) and warns that Vishnu, with his wheel (his discus) and his dark body, belongs to the very lowest castes, if they serve him.

The four castes
uphold all clans;
go down, far down
to the lowliest outcastes
of outcastes:

if they are the intimate henchmen
of our lord
with the wheel in his right hand,
his body dark as blue sapphire,

then even the slaves of their slaves
are our masters.

WHO IS HE POSSESSING THE HIGHEST GOOD?

Pillan's commentary on this verse says that the Alvar is addressing his holy soul, and that the flowerlike feet of the Lord dispel all the sorrows of his worshippers. The rhetoric of this verse recalls that of the refrain of a hymn of the *Rig Veda* (10.121) that asks, "Who is the god whom we should worship with the oblation?" ("Creation Hymn," p. 79).

Who is he possessing the highest good?
Who is he, who slashes ignorance,
by graciously bestowing wisdom and love?
Who is he, the commander of the never-tiring immortals?
O my mind!
Worship his radiant feet
that destroy all sorrow,
and rise.

BEYOND THE RANGE

This verse attributes to Vishnu the act of creation (often attributed to Brahma) and the act of destroying the triple city of the demons (usually attributed to Shiva). Pillan's commentary on this verse states that Vishnu, being within Brahma, instructed the immortals and, being within Shiva, destroyed the triple city: "Even they do not know that it is the Lord within them who is responsible for this." And so we know that Vishnu rules both Brahma and Shiva. This supremacy is expressed by the statement that Vishnu "ate them all," echoing the identification of eating and power in the Brahmanas ("Prajapati Creates Fire," p. 94).

Beyond the range of the divine ones' intelligence,
He, the first one of the skies and everything thereon,
Cause of the creator, most Supreme One, ate them all!
He indwells; as Shiva and as Brahma,
He burnt the triple cities, he enlightened the immortals,
He destroys, and then creates the worlds.

IF YOU SAY HE EXISTS

Pillan says that this verse refutes the Buddhists who say that everything is empty (*shunya*), that there is no Veda, no god, and no universe. On the contrary, Pillan argues, words for existence and nonexistence are themselves the very form of god, and whether you say he exists or does not exist, he still exists. Even where he does not seem to be, he is the inner soul of everything and therefore he exists.

If you say he exists, he does;
his forms are these forms.
If you say he does not,
his formlessness
is of these non-forms.
If he has the qualities
of existence and nonexistence,
he is in two states.
He who pervades is without end.

HE IS DIFFUSED IN EVERY DROP

The god is said to have eaten the universe that he pervades. This concept goes back to the Brahmanas and Upanishads ("The Creator Creates Death," p. 108).

He is diffused in every drop of the cool expansive sea,
and over this expansive earth,
all the lands and all of space, not missing a spot.
He the steady one, who ate all this,
is hidden, in every shining place.
He pervades everything, everywhere.

PEOPLE OF THIS WORLD

Tirukkurukur is where Nammalvar is said to have been born. Again the metaphor of eating expresses the power of the lord; Pillan says that "swallowing, spitting" are among the lord's divine acts. He adds that in this poem the Alvar is saying, if there is another god, prove it by even one authoritative source of knowledge: direct perception, scripture, or inference ("Ramanuja Dreams," p. 289).

People of this world!
Say there is none but the Lord!
Speak only of his excellence.
The Supreme One of Tirukkurukur, who the other day
created the many divine ones,
the sprawling worlds, and then
swallowed, hid, and spat them out.
He then strode over and bored through them.
The divine ones bow their heads to him.

LORD OF SHIVA

Some Vaishnavas claim that Vishnu freed Shiva from the skull that stuck to his hand after he killed Brahma ("The Pilgrimage of Shiva to Varanasi," p. 263). This poem refers to, and denies, a version of the story, in the *Linga Purana*, in which Shiva accomplishes his salvation without the help of Vishnu and even goes so far as to denounce him.

Lord of Shiva, Lord of Brahma, he is the Lord of all.
Look: He freed Shiva from the skull stuck on his hand.
This Lord stands in Tirukkurukur,
Surrounded by splendid, majestic towers.
Why should the followers of the Linga
Speak ill of him?

HE BECAME AND EXISTS

This poem argues that Vishnu is actually the substance of all his opponents and detractors, as he is the soul of everything. There is therefore no cause for debate—yet the poem does debate Vishnu's opponents.

He became and exists [as]
  you, the devotees of the Linga Purana,
  you, the Jains, Buddhists, you crafty debaters,
  and your various gods.
This is no falsehood.
This Lord flourishes in Tirukkurukur,
[city] filled with swaying fields of paddy.
  Praise him!

THE WHIRLING AGE OF KALI ENDS

This poem seems to say that at the end of the Kali Age (the last and worst of the four ages, the present age), the followers of Vishnu will either survive or be created anew in the Golden Age, the Winning Age ("The Four Ages," p. 228). But Pillan interprets it to mean that Vishnu will stop the Kali Age for all time, so that only the Golden Age will exist.

The whirling age of Kali ends;
the divine ones also enter [the earth].
The golden age dawns
and floods of great joy sweep [over the land].
The followers of
  him who is dark as a cloud,
  my Lord, the sea-colored one,
Fill this earth, singing with melody.
They are all over this land.

MONARCH OF LIONS

Kutantai is a name of Kumbhakonam, a place of pilgrimage on the Kaveri River, near Tanjavur. The god has four shoulders because he has four arms.

Monarch of lions, my golden flame,
dark as a cloud, eyes red,
[form that glows]
  like a coral mountain ablaze,
Lord with four shoulders!
Through your grace you took me,
  as your inseparable slave,

sacred, entrancing Lord of Kutantai!
[Without you] I cannot survive.
Give me your feet
and destroy my [cycle] of births.

PERHAPS YOU WILL DESTROY MY SORROW

Pillan says that the poet is asking the god to rescue him before his soul falters, before it ceases to exist.

Perhaps you will destroy my sorrow, perhaps not,
but I have no support other [than you].
O Lord who hold as your weapon
the discus with a whirling mouth,
When it is time for me to pass on,
my body will be limp, my soul will falter;
you then must will that I should not be weak
but clasp only [the splendor] of your feet.

YOU DO NOT COME

The god without form is the god without qualities (*nir-guna*), the abstract form of the godhead that never satiates the heart. But the poet longs for the god with qualities (*sa-guna*), the god who lives not in the entire universe but right here in Kutantai (Kumbhakonam). Paradoxically, this unsatisfied longing is what makes the poet wander, out of Kutantai or "astray," away from the god.

You do not come,
and then you come without form [in my heart],
my Lord of entrancing form!
Nectar that never satiates,
you taste so sweet within my soul!
You ruled me so my endless sins came to an end,
Lord who dwells in Kutantai!
Having become your servant,
why do I still wander astray?

I SHALL DIE IF YOU GO TO GRAZE THE COWS

Here the poet assumes the voice of one of the cowherd girls (*gopis*) who long for Krishna when he goes away to distant pastures, grazing the cows. Pillan says that the fire that scorches her is the fire of separation, that she has no companion because she still hopes that Krishna will be her lover, and that when one suffers such pangs of unrequited love, it is not bad to die.

I shall die if you go to graze the cows,
for my soul is ablaze with the fire of my breath.
I have no companion:
I shall not live to see your dark body move.
When you leave me, the day never ends,
my twin eyes, shaped like kayal fish,
swim in tears that never end.
Born in this humble state,
cowherd girls in a herder clan,
our loneliness [seems] death.

YOU WERE GONE THE WHOLE DAY

Again the cowherd girl pleads with Kanna (Krishna). Pillan says that she begs him to end the sorrow of their separation by making love to her. But, he adds, she immediately begs him to make her live by his sacred words, which are like nectar and give life to the dead.

You were gone the whole day,
grazing cows, Kanna!
Your humble words burn my soul.
Evening tramples like a rogue [elephant],
and the fragrance of the jasmine buds,
unleashing my desires, blows upon me.
Embrace my beautiful breasts
with the fragrance of the wild jasmine
upon your radiant chest.
Give me the nectar of your mouth,
and adorn my lowly head
with your jeweled lotus hands.

THE *TEVARAM* ("GARLAND OF GOD") OF CUNTARAR

We turn now from the Alvars, saints in the service of Vishnu, to the Nayanmars, saints in the service of Shiva. The Nayanmars are traditionally said to number sixty-three; the group known as "the first three" (Appar, Campantar, and Cuntarar, sixth to eighth centuries) are the authors of the collection called the *Tevaram* ("garland of god"), which forms the basis of the Tamil Shaiva canon.

Cuntaramurttinayanar, or Cuntarar, or Nampi Aruran (as he calls himself), the third and last of the Tamil poets of the *Tevaram*, was known for the angry tone of his poems. Sometimes he called himself "the harsh devotee," though the Tamil tradition called him "the friend of god." The hagiography of Cuntarar, told primarily in the *Periya Puranam* (p. 322), tells us that Shiva blinded him after he deserted his second wife but restored his vision when he returned home to her. Many of Cuntarar's bitterest poems, in which he quarrels with the god he loves, are ascribed to the period of his blindness. Some are in the genre of "blame-praise" or "worship through insult" that also became important (as "hate-devotion") in the Sanskrit tradition. Sometimes he threatens to abandon the god in revenge for the god's maddening silence and withdrawal, and sometimes he even hurls ironic curses at him, though he also blames himself for his forgetfulness, stubbornness, and sensuality. His poems, which range from humorous teasing to tragic jeremiads, combine an intimate ridicule of the god with self-denigration.

Cuntarar's *Tevaram* is a set of poems, called *patikams*, each *patikam* consisting of ten or more stanzas ending in a repeated refrain in praise of a particular shrine.

The poems from the *Tevaram* are translated by David Shulman.

PRONOUNCING GLOSSARY

Ancaikkalam: *un-chaik´-kuh-lum*
Arutturai: *uh-root´-too-rai*
Cuntarar: *choon´-tuh-ruhr*
Etirkolpati: *eh´-teer-koh´-pah´-tee*
Kama: *kah´-muh*
Makotai: *muh-koh´-tai'*
Onakantantali: *oh´-nuh-kahn´-tun-tuh´-lee*
Paccilacciramam: *pah´-chih-lah´-chih-rah´-mum*
Pennai: *pen´-nai*
Tevaram: *tay´-vuh-rum*
Uma: *oo-mah´*
Venneynallur: *ven-nay´-nuh-loor´*

A DOG AM I

This is a stanza from a *patikam* traditionally said to be Cuntarar's first, and dedicated to the shrine, or bathing ghat (a place of access to a body of water), of Arutturai, "Bathing ghat of mercy." Shiva appears to Cuntarar in a number of forms, including that of a cowherd, more usually associated with Krishna. The refrain—"how could I ever say / that I am not your slave?"—may have inspired the legend (narrated in the *Periya Puranam*) that on Cuntarar's wedding day an old Brahmin appeared and claimed him as his slave; he led Cuntarar away to a Shiva temple where the old man disappeared and became one, again, with the god that he was. At that moment, Cuntarar realized that he was, in fact, enslaved to the god. He abandoned his wife and began to serve Shiva.

A dog
am I:
for many days
I had no thought
of you.

Like a demon,
I wandered,
exhausted.

Impossible grace
was my gain.

Cowherd in Arutturai of Venneynallur
  to the south of the Pennai thick with bamboo—
how could I ever say
that I am not your slave?

YOU WON'T REMOVE THE FIERCE KARMA

This and the following poem are stanzas from a *patikam* said to have been sung in the presence of the Pandyan and Chola kings (who ruled over the eastern and southern parts of ancient Tamil Nadu), giving a double meaning to the frightened servants in the refrain, servants of both the god and the king. The first poem is an example of "blame-praise" (*ninda-stuti*), ironic praise through blame, though there is little irony in the fear that pervades the stanza and is openly admitted in the refrain. And Shiva is indeed terrifying, surrounded by demons, particularly one great demon (perhaps the demon that he tramples underfoot in his dance), and uncanny, with white ashes covering his own ruddy skin as well as his blue neck. Cuntarar nevertheless has the audacity to blame the god for refusing to use his power to remove Cuntarar's bad karma ("The Transfer of Karma in Hell," p. 232), apparently preferring to leave Cuntarar to work out his karma himself.

You won't remove the fierce karma
that afflicts us.
Together with your great demon,
you abide in the wilderness.
You wear skins
  over your tattered clothes;
a snake coils itself about you.

Smeared with dusty ashes,
you have one color over your
  color of sapphire—
lord of many hues and colors,
ever beautiful,

great lord and master! We are afraid
to serve you.

YOU SLEW A MURDEROUS ELEPHANT

Shiva killed an elephant demon (Gajasura) and wears the bloody skin draped around his body. When Uma (Parvati) wanted to marry Shiva, Kama, the god of erotic love, aimed his arrows at Shiva, who burned Kama to ashes with the fiery glance from the third eye in the middle of his forehead. Seemingly in spite of but actually because of these deeds of violence, Uma is madly in love with Shiva and is part of him in the form of the androgyne.

You slew a murderous elephant.
You have no shrine
  except the summit of a mountain.
With your glance
you burnt Kama, who aroused
  your desire.
For all that, you have Uma,
  arms supple as bamboo,
within you.

You can't enslave us
by giving us clothes to wear
or rice—
what you *can* do
is to rule over your slaves.

Master! We are afraid
to serve you.

WHAT IS THE USE OF RELEASE?

This poem is sung to the god of Ancaikkalam, the ancient Shaiva shrine in Kotunkolur that is said to be the last earthly shrine that Cuntarar visited. (Kannaki/Pattini, the heroine of a great Tamil poem [*The Tale of an Anklet*, p. 336], is worshipped here, too.) Though the poet questions the value of release (*moksha*), he immediately

The great frieze at Mamallapuram, Tamil Nadu, likely dates from the seventh century and depicts the descent of the river Ganges. Water originally cascaded through the image of the stream.

reverses direction and questions the value of being born in the first place; similarly, he holds in suspended balance the god's two animals and two women, one of whom, the Mountain Woman, is Parvati, daughter of the mountain Himalaya, while the other is the river Ganga (Ganges) that flows through Shiva's hair ("The Descent of the Ganges," p. 258). Finally he questions the meaning of meaning itself.

What is the use of release?
What is the point
of being born?

With a rutting elephant at your call,
why ride the bull?

With the one Mountain Woman already
  joined to you,
why crown your hair with Ganga?

What is the meaning
you grant to poets,

Father in Ancaikkalam graced by rich groves,
  in Makotai on the shore of the dancing sea
  where ships come and go, laden
  with their rich cargoes?

YOU KILL TIME TELLING LIES

The story goes that when Cuntarar came to this shrine of Onakantantali, in Kanjeevaram, Shiva hid in a tamarind tree and turned the fruit to gold. The tone of this poem, however, is not grateful but complaining. The god is accused of killing time, a pun on his notorious idleness (his failure to act) and the occasion when he did indeed act, when he literally killed time by conquering Kala—Time or Death—in order to save the life of a devotee ("When I Hear Death Has Come," below). Yet the poet complains bitterly about the imbalance of power between god and devotee.

You kill time telling lies.
You are neither outside
nor in.
You won't tell the truth, and
   enslave us.
You'll never be able to give us
   a thing.

Even when you take us,
you need nothing,
   give nothing,
   think of nothing
but yourself,

great lord
      in Onakantantali.

WHEN I HEAR DEATH HAS COME

In this poem, from the same *patikam* as the preceding one, the worshipper hopes that Shiva will rescue him from Death as he saved other devotees in the past. But the worshipper is still caught in the flame of the five passions (according to the traditional Hindu list), wrapped up in the sixth—the guise, or art, of Illusion (*maya*).

When I hear Death has come
to drag me away
with his noose,
that he is standing right here,
then, with my stony thoughts,
I worship your feet
to save my life.

Except in this way, I can't be whole
with you—

for my life is a fiery forge
fed by passion and rancor,
 anger, greed,
 intoxication,
all welded into a single guise,

O you who are in Onakantantali.

CAN'T YOU SEE HOW FALSE THEY ARE

According to the *Periya Puranam*, Cuntarar composed this *patikam* on his way to the shrine of Etirkolpati. It is an attack on the bourgeois life of the householder, particularly the wealthy householder, and on the sensuality that that life is thought to entail.

Can't you see how false they are,
those paragons of the good life?
To cover up for them,
you let yourselves be deceived.

Still there's no need to be hurt
any more—
joined with us, your hearts
grow soft.

Come: let us go
to the shrine of the lord
  whom we praise in this life

  and who will have mercy on us
  in the next

  at Etirkolpati.

I PLACED BEFORE HIM

This poem and the one that follows are from a *patikam* dedicated to Shiva at the shrine of Paccilacciramam. Cuntarar complains of his forced separation from the god, what Sanskrit poets would call *viraha*—love in separation. All he can do to express his grief and anger is to turn the tables and threaten to reject the god, but the power of the presence of Shiva, who ties his loincloth with a serpent, demonstrates the depth of Cuntarar's love for the god, whom he will never abandon.

I placed before him
  my head
  and my tongue;
I even offered him
  my heart.
I didn't try to cheat him.

But whenever I talk of being
the servant of his feet,
I'm just a man of metaphors
to him,

our supreme lord of Paccilacciramam,
that madman
  who ties his loincloth
  with a hooded serpent:

if *he* doesn't want us,
can't we find some other god?

I DON'T CALL TO HIM AS MY MOTHER

The image of god as a parent, particularly as a mother, leads to the image of god as an abandoning parent, an intimate, humanized version of the abandoning god who is central to the spirit of *bhakti*.

I don't call to him as my mother.
I don't call to him as my father.
I thought it would be enough
  to call him my lord—

but he pretends I don't exist,
doesn't show a trace of mercy.

If that lord who dwells in Paccilacciramam,
  surrounded by pools filled with geese,
postpones the mercies
  meant for his devotees—

can't we find some other god?

THE *PERIYA PURANAM* ("GREAT PURANA") OF CEKKILAR

The *Periya Puranam* of Cekkilar, dated to the reign of the Chola king Kulottunka II (1133–50 C.E.), is a long poem about the lives of the Tamil Shaiva saints known as the Nayanmars. Cekkilar was born near Chennai (Madras) and served as a minister of Kulottunka, whose kingdom was centered on the Kaveri River basin south of Chennai. Epic in its proportions, and indebted in many ways to the great Tamil epic (*The Tale of an Anklet*, p. 336) and to its sequel, the *Manimekhalai* ("The Dancer with the Magic Bowl"), the *Periya Puranam* is less like an epic and more like what it proclaims itself to be, a Purana, with separate stories loosely linked by the unifying theme of sainthood. The lives of the three principal Nayanmars (Appar, Campantar, and Cuntarar), the authors of the *Tevaram* hymns (p. 315), occupy more than half of the *Periya Puranam*.

The violence inherent in great passion is evident in even the most superficial summary of the acts committed by the Nayanmars in the *Periya Puranam*: one or another engages in violent conflicts with Jains, attempts or commits suicide (in various ways), chops off his father's feet or his wife's hand or a queen's nose or someone else's tongue, slashes his own throat, massacres his relatives, grinds up his own elbow, sets his hair on fire, or kills and/or cooks his/her son. *Bhakti*, like the ascetic movements, was strong on nonviolence to animals, generally (though not always) opposing animal sacrifice, but it was not as strong on nonviolence to humans. The ability to demonstrate indifference to physical pain was an intrinsic part of the narrative traditions of both ascetics (who mortified their flesh in various ways) and warriors. The Tamil martyrs often turn their violence against themselves ("Kannappar Gives His Eye to Shiva"). But the violence of *bhakti* was not always directed against the self. Sometimes the violence was for the god and, though usually directed against Hindus who refused to worship the god, occasionally arose in conflict with people of other religions. The shedding of blood in sacrifice—whether in self-sacrifice or the offering of a substitute—is both the supreme manifestation of *bhakti* toward the god and the ultimate way to atone for offenses against *bhakti*.

The selections from the *Periya Puranam* are translated by Alastair McGlashan.

PRONOUNCING GLOSSARY

Alakapuri: *uh-luh-kah´-poo´-ree*
Ayan: *uh´-yun*
Cekkilar: *check´-kih-lahr´*
Ilaiyankuti: *ih-lai´-yahn-koo´-tee*
Kalatti: *kah´-lut´-tee*
Kannappar: *kun´-nup-puhr´*
Katan: *kah´-tun*
Kubera: *koo-bay´-ruh*
Maran: *mah´-run*
Maravar: *muh´-ruh-vuhr´*
Mukali: *moo´-kuh-lee*
Murukan: *moo´-roo-kun*
Nakan: *nah´-kun*
Nanan: *nah´-nun*
Periya Puranam: *pay´-ree-yuh poo-rah´-num*
Ponmukali: *pohn´-moo´-kuh-lee*
Pottappi: *poh´-tup´-pee*
Shakti: *shuck´-tee*
Shankaran: *shun´-kuh-run*
Shiva: *shih´-vuh*
Shudra: *shoo´-druh*
Tattai: *tut´-tai*
Tinnan: *tin´-nun*

Tinnanar: *tin´-nuh-nahr´*
Tirukkalatti: *tih-rook´-kah´-lut-tee*
Utuppur: *oo´-toop-poor´*

MARAN FEEDS A GUEST

The theme of the poor man who offers everything to his guest, not knowing that the guest is a god in disguise, a story common in folklore throughout the world, is here combined with another theme that is widespread in Hinduism and best known to American and European readers from the story of Job in the Hebrew Bible: the man whom god tests by inflicting undeserved suffering upon him.

10.440–66

There was once a man devoted to the feet of him who dances in the fair golden court. He came to adorn this world below as the result of the penances performed by an honest family of the Shudra caste,[1] and he enjoyed a high reputation for his service to the Lord.[2] He lived at Ilaiyankuti,[3] and his name was Maran.

The produce of his fertile land yielded incalculable wealth. At the same time his mind was firmly set on performing loving service for the servants of the Lord. He wanted the whole world to enjoy the benefits of such wealth and service, just as he did himself. Whenever any friends of the Lord came to his door, whoever they might be, with warm affection he would greet them as his fellow-devotees, and with palms together speak kindly words of welcome. Then he would take them indoors, wash their feet, sit them down on a comfortable seat, and after making obeisance before them, for their pleasure he would serve four different kinds of food with six different flavors. Thus day by day innumerable friends of the sovereign Lord came to his house and gratefully enjoyed his hospitality. All the while, as his wealth and prosperity increased, he lived like Kubera,[4] whom the Lord appointed ruler of Alakapuri.

Now the Lord resolved to demonstrate that Maran was capable of pursuing such a course not only while his prosperity lasted, but also if he were to fall on hard times. Accordingly he planned that Maran's wealth should gradually diminish until it had all evaporated and he had been reduced to poverty. However, although his circumstances were thus straitened, the generosity of the lord of Ilaiyankuti was not straitened in the slightest. On the contrary, he sold his possessions and took out crippling loans, which enabled him to persevere in his sacred service as before.

While all this was going on, the Lord who is beyond the ken of Tirumal and Ayan[5] left behind his bull and his consort, and for the salvation of the world approached Maran's house in the guise of an ascetic. It was one night in the rainy season. Maran had locked the door and lay awake, hungry and

1. The lowest of the four classes, the class of servants.
2. Shiva.
3. A town about 70 km from Madurai.
4. The god of wealth, who rules over the mythical Himalayan city of Alaka.
5. Vishnu and Brahma.

impoverished. Nevertheless, he got up to greet his guest. First he wiped him down, then gave him a seat. Desiring to satisfy his hunger, he consulted with his wife: "The ascetic is famished, but what are we to do? We have nothing to eat ourselves. Yet he is a friend of the Lord, and it is our duty to feed him. What can we possibly do?"

"I have no idea," his wife replied, "At this time of night no one will give us anything, so there is nowhere else to turn. This must be the result of my past misdeeds, so there is nothing I can do about it." Then, after a moment's thought, she continued, "If you were to go and gather up the paddy seedlings that you planted out this morning in the field, I could perhaps make a meal. To get us out of this difficulty, that is the only course that I can see."

When he heard his wife's suggestion, Maran was as pleased as if he had regained all his previous wealth. He eagerly accepted her proposal, and set off at once for the paddy field. The rain was pouring down. It was so dark that you could not see your hand in front of your face. It was as though the inky darkness was itself dissolving and pouring like liquid over the whole earth. The night was pitch black, like an inky soup. Anyone, however bold, would think twice before going out on such a night. Nevertheless, driven on by the love in his heart, Maran set out on his accustomed path to the field where all the birds were still sound asleep, holding a large basket over his head. He felt his way step by step, and gathered in his hands the paddy seedlings from the water. When he had filled his basket, he placed it on his head and hurried home.

His wife was waiting at the door. She took the basket from him and briskly washed the mud from the paddy in a bowl of water. Then she exclaimed, "We have no wood to light a fire in the stove!"

At once the noble Maran cut down one of the rafters from the roof of the house, chopped it in pieces and put it on the stove. His chaste wife then dried out the grain, milled it, and put it in a pan to cook. Next, she asked her husband, "What shall we do for a curry?"

"Our guest must be exhausted by his journey, and perishing with hunger," Maran thought to himself. So, moved by compassion, he set out once more and felt with his hands for the unripened vegetables planted out in pits in the garden. He pulled them up as though pulling up by the root the bond of attachment from human hearts, and gave them to his wife to cook. She inspected the vegetables he had brought, washed them in water, and put them in a pan. As with a practiced hand she prepared a variety of dishes, the painful memory of their recent indigence was eased. Then, showing her husband the food she had prepared, she said, "Now we can serve our distinguished guest his meal."

So Maran approached the Lord who is beyond all comprehension, and standing by his side, made as though to wake him from his sleep. "Sir," he said, "By honoring me with a visit, you have rescued me from the deep trouble that beset me. Please come now, your meal is served."

At these words, as Maran and his good wife stood by in awe, the Lord unknown to Tirumal and Ayan arose in heavenly light. To their amazement, Shankaran[6] himself was pleased to appear in radiant form riding on his bull,[7] accompanied by his consort. "My friend," he said, addressing the devotee

6. An epithet of Shiva, "giver of peace."

7. The bull Nandi, on which Shiva rides.

who had performed such signal service. "For the service that you have offered to my friends, come with your wife to my world above. There you may enjoy eternal bliss, with Kubera to bring you untold riches and to fulfil your least command."

So the Lord blessed them with the felicity which they deserved, and then departed from their sight.

KANNAPPAR GIVES HIS EYE TO SHIVA

One of the great *bhakti* legends is the story of the Nayanar saint first named Tinnan or Tinnanar ("The Mighty One") but renamed Kannappar ("One Who Attaches His Eye [*kan*]") as a result of his encounter with Shiva. Kannappar is a hunter, a tribal on the margins of Hinduism. Tamil tradition regards him as the reincarnation of the warrior Arjuna, who (according to the *Mahabharata* [3.40–41]) fought against Shiva when the god appeared to him in the form of a hunter. Kannappar's mother was from the warrior caste of Maravars and his parents had worshipped Murukan, but Kannappar does not seem to know the rules of Brahmin dharma; he does not know that high caste Hindus—like the Brahmin for whose benefit Shiva stages the episode of the eyes—do not offer flesh to their gods. He does not know about the impurity of substances, like spit, that come from the body—the spit that he uses to clean the image as a mother would use her spit to scrub a bit of dirt off the face of her child. He reverses the proper order of head and foot by putting his foot on the head of the god, instead of his head on the god's foot, the usual gesture of respect.

Kannappar does not understand metaphor: the normal offering to a god is a flower, perhaps a lotus, and in fact he gives the god flowers (though ones that have been polluted, in high caste terms, by being worn on his own head). But Sanskrit poets often liken beautiful eyes to lotuses, and Kannappar offers the god the real thing, the eye, the wrong half of the metaphor. Kannappar's indifference to self-inflicted pain may have had conscious antecedents in similar acts committed by King Shibi ("King Shibi Saves the Dove," p. 160) and Ekalavya ("Ekalavya Cuts Off His Thumb," p. 143), in the *Mahabharata*.

Many texts retell this story, generally specifying that the form of Shiva that Kannappar found in the forest was a *linga*, the cylindrical stone iconic form of Shiva, and occasionally adding details designed to transform Kannappar from a cattle thief and hunter with dogs into a paradigm of *bhakti*: thus the animals that he kills are said to be ogres offering their bodies as sacrifice to Shiva. But in the *Periya Puranam* his "mistakes" are "happy faults" that make possible an unprecedentedly direct exchange of gazes: instead of trading mere glances, he and the god trade their very eyes. This is an inversion of *darshan*, "seeing," in its most direct, violent, passionate form ("The Flowering of Bhakti," p. 295). The vividness of this incarnation applies not only to the god, who participates so intimately in the life of Kannappar, but to the worshipper, to Kannappar himself, who reaches his god not through meditation or abstract philosophy but through his own body, and his instinctive, untutored love.

16.650–76, 733–830

Pottappi[1] is a land extolled by poets, a land of lakes and groves, rich in flowers and fertile fields. Also in that land, on the hill of Kalatti there stands a

1. An area in the Telugu country, present-day Andhra Pradesh.

shrine of the Lord, the keeper of the Vedas, who rides the bull and destroyed the cities of his enemies. This land was the home of Kannappar.

Kannappar lived in the ancient fortified town of Utuppur in Pottappi land. Its walls were like a line of ramparts raised by the tusks of bull elephants. All around stretch mountain ranges, their slopes gashed by pearl-strewn waterfalls. The people of that land were hunters. They used to tie up their sharpeared hounds in the groves of wood-apple trees, and hung up their nets on the branches. They spread their paddy to dry on the rocks before their houses, and kept captive boar and tiger, bear, buffalo and deer to use as decoys in the chase. Without benefit of schooling, the children of the hunter folk used to play with the tiger cubs and elephant calves. To the delight of the little girls, the does would fondly come to play as if they were tame. The warlike bands of hunters were armed to the teeth. The hubbub of their wild exultant cries of "Kill, shoot, stab!" mingled with the din of horns and drums, and all was drowned by the thunder of the surrounding waterfalls.

The hunters lived by robbery. Their villages were full of cattle of many different kinds, stolen from the lands of others; full too of bull elephants, whose trumpeting echoed the thunder of the clouds lowering in the sky above. The hunters were dark in countenance, violent in behavior. They knew neither fear nor favor. They wore skins and ate mountain honey, and rice cooked with meat. Their arrows were tipped with fiery poison. Their chieftain's name was Nakan.

Although in previous births Nakan had been naturally disposed to the practice of austerity, the circumstances of his present birth led him into a life of crime. In acts of violence he had no peer. He was expert in archery, ferocious as a lion. The wife who shared his life in the mountains was called Tattai. She came from an ancient family belonging to the renowned Maravar caste. She wore a necklace of tigers' teeth interlaced with cowry shells. Her hair was tied up on the crown of her head, with a garland of leaves and peacock feathers, which drew the beetles hovering around.

By common consent, for so unique a couple to have children would have been a very special blessing, and that was indeed their own deep desire. With that end in view, dutifully each day they used to go and worship in the temple of Murukan.[2] There they offered cockerels and peacocks, and hung up brightly colored bunting and branches of flowering trees, the beetles' favorites. They celebrated festivals with dancing and spirit possession in honor of the great Lord Murukan, who holds the mighty spear with which he cleft the mountain. So finally Nakan, chief of the battle-scarred hunters, received grace from the son of our father Shiva: to the glory of the hunter clan, Tattai became pregnant.

Marked by the offering of unblemished sacrifice and regular possession by the spirit, the months passed one by one. At last, as the fruit of long austerities, Tattai bore a son, just as the ocean gives birth to the beneficent full moon. The hunters showered upon the child pearls from the tusks of elephants, pearls from the streams among the bamboo thickets, and jewels from the mountains. To the thunder of the drums of mortals and immortals, flowers rained down from heaven, and set the striped beetles buzzing. Amid general rejoicing, all the hunter peoples of the mountain villages celebrated a festival. On that day the father picked up his son and set him on his massive

2. The South Indian form of Skanda, the god of war, son of Shiva.

shoulder, like a dark cloud resting on the black mountain top. The child was so beautiful that he seemed to emit a dark radiance. He grew in strength like a young tiger, and showed many signs of future greatness, which it was hard not only for the hunters themselves but for the entire world rightly to assess.

Because the child soon became too heavy for him to lift up in his arms, to the joy of the hunters his father commanded that he be called "Tinnan," the mighty one. In the eyes of the hunter folk, he was the reward of merit in previous births, the embodiment of all that is admirable. To enhance his beauty, they adorned him with many of their jewelled ornaments. The Maravar people, who lived under the protection of the mountain god, brought him up carefully observing all their ancient customs to the letter. With pleasing effect, they plaited margosa leaves and buds of fragrant flowers to make a garland, and tied a string of cowry shells around his waist. At each stage of his development, they showed their delight in the birth of a precious son by making splendid offerings to the gods and staging joyful celebrations, to the accompaniment of propitious music.

As the second year succeeded the first, the child became steadier on his feet. At this time, his parents placed an ornament made from a tiger's claw upon his forehead, and hung across his chest a plaited string of tigers' teeth interlaced with the quills of the ferocious red-eyed porcupine. The child wore glittering earrings of ivory set with jewels, and to protect him from evil, a string of coins threaded with green jewels and tinkling bells around his waist. Decked out in this array he went out to play in the village street. With his spittle, holier than Ganges water, running down his chin like nectar, his tender coral lips lisped out sweet childish words. All the while his delighted parents watched him grow.

One time the child stretched his tiny hand into the mouth of a tame tiger, thinking it was a cave. When his loving father saw it and picked him up in his arms, tears filled the child's pretty eyes, which would one day ease the suffering of the two heavenly lights, the very eyes of God. Then his mother wiped away his pearly tears with her kisses, themselves as rare as pearls. He played bowls with rounded blocks of wood and chased them down the street. He tangled up the leads of dogs, then let them go free. He kicked and trampled on the toy constructions of the little girls, and with the boys from round about played childish pranks among the village huts.

Such games occupied him until his sixth year. Then in company with the other children of the hunters, he began to play with snares and traps in the flower gardens, and to go outside the fence around the village through the gateway made of elephant tusks into the woods beyond. Running at full speed, he would chase the young of tiger, red dog, rabbit and wild boar, catch them and tie them up to the trees in the courtyard of his house. He succeeded in rearing innumerable wild animals in this way. In the evening after sunset, as smoke rose from the cooking mustard seed, an old woman of the hunter clan would give him food, and lay him down to sleep. Then at dawn she would feed him on meat and send him out to play. So the years passed.

* * *

Over the mountain slopes and throughout the forest, with its dense and leafy thickets, herds of elk and bear and buffalo wounded by arrows fled in agitation, until finally they collapsed like dark clouds dropping down to drink upon the surface of the sea. The wild beasts rushed in panic into the nets, then as they tried to break out and escape over the rocky paths, the hounds set upon them ferociously. Just as, when the soul lies trapped and helpless in the net of good and evil deeds, although it has the wisdom to find the way out, the senses block its path, so did the hounds block the animals' escape. Although the hunters were swift to pursue and dispatch their prey, some animals they left alone. They did not touch the elephant calves, with their broad ears and feet like kettle drums, nor did they harass the heavily pregnant females which could not get away.

While the hunters were engaged upon this slaughter, a boar rushed out at high speed like a dark rain cloud, its eyes flashing fire. Even the elephants were startled and the forest shook, as with a noise like thunder, it broke through the nets. As it ran, Tinnanar, lion of the fighting hunter folk, himself picked up its tracks and sped after it. Unbeknown to everyone else, except for two young men, both skilled archers who followed on behind, he alone gave chase. His two loyal friends, Nanan and Katan, quickly caught up with Tinnanar, guardian of the hill country. Meanwhile the boar, having avoided the hail of arrows and the ferocious hounds, sped on across the mountain slopes under the shade of the trees. Roaring like thunder and its eyes red like rowan berries, the great boar had strength enough to run for miles. At length it reached a spot among the foothills of the mountains, and there stopped exhausted near a row of trees.

When Tinnanar reached that wooded glade, well knowing the nature of the beast, he decided not to try to kill it with his bow and arrows. Instead he quickly advanced upon the boar to engage it more closely, then pierced it through the body and cleft it in two with his flashing sword.

When Nanan saw the boar thus cleft apart, he said to his companion, "Katan, we have chased this beast for many a league today, and now are quite worn out. Yet see, this youngster has felled it with a single stroke!" With that, the two of them fell at Tinnanar's feet in admiration.

Then together they addressed him: "We have come a long way today and now are hungry. When we have cooked this beast, you have some of it to eat and we shall too, then wash it down with water. Afterwards we can make our way back at leisure to that part of the forest from which we set out on this successful chase."

Hearing this, Tinnanar asked "Where can we find water in this forest?"

"Beyond that great teak tree over there," Nanan replied, "At the foot of that long ridge flows the river Ponmukali."

"Alright," said Tinnanar, "Let us go. You bring the carcass," and he set out in that direction. After they had gone about five miles, they saw a grove on the mountain side where there is a temple of the Lord. "Nanan!" Tinnanar exclaimed, "There is a hill over there, let us go and have a look."

"If you go over there," Nanan replied, "You will see a beautiful sight. That is the lofty hill of Tirukkalatti, the home of the Lord Shiva. Let us go and worship him."

"What can this be?" rejoined Tinnanar in amazement, "As we come in sight of this place, my burden seems to grow lighter. Longing wells up in my heart, and my mind races on ahead, filled with a new desire. Where is this dwelling of the god? Show me."

So he hurried on, and his two companions with him, until they reached the banks of the Ponmukali. On its sandy shore, the waves of the river had deposited pearls from the bamboo thickets along its banks, logs of dark eagle wood, gems from the mountains, sandal wood, gold and diamonds. There in a shady spot by the river bank, they put down the carcass of the boar. Tinnanar told Katan to light a fire, while he and Nanan went up the mountain. "When we have had a look, we shall rejoin you here," he said.

Along the river bank, the beetles swarmed among the groves of flowering trees. As Tinnanar entered the clear water of the stream, his mind too cleared and his heart was filled with joy. With his gaze fixed on Mount Kalatti, he waded through the cool waters and so reached the foot hills of the mountain. When the sun reached it zenith, on the summit of the mountain of God a fearful sound like the roar of the ocean thundered forth. "Nanan, what is that noise?" asked Tinnanar in amazement.

"On this mountain," Nanan explained, "the bees attracted by the nectar swarm around the scented flowers. Perhaps that is the noise you heard."

As a result of austerities performed in previous births, boundless ardor and devotion welled up within them, their bones melted and their hearts were filled with longing. So demonstrating their joyful love for the Lord, they made their way towards the sacred mountain, and together they began the ascent.

Just as the devotee climbs the path of the elements step by step and finally becomes one with Shiva, who in turn is one with his Shakti, so Tinnanar the embodiment of love climbed the lofty mountain of the Lord, turning neither to the right nor left. Before he could behold the Lord, Shiva in his grace looked with favor upon him. At once Tinnanar was freed from the entail of previous sins, and he was transformed into the image of matchless love, abiding in the shade of heavenly light. So he beheld Shiva, the only Lord, the flame of fire that burns on Mount Tirukkalatti. As his feelings of joy and love grew more intense, overcome with longing he ran forward in haste, embraced the Lord and kissed him. For some time he stood there to catch his breath. All the hair on his body stood on end, tears like flowers poured in torrents from his eyes, and his appearance was changed into the image of measureless love. "I am his servant, and I have found him here," he exclaimed. "What a miracle is this!"

"In this forest," he reflected, "elephant and tiger, bear and lion roam. Yet like a hunter of the fierce Maravar clan, here on the mountain side he is all alone, without anyone to look after him. Woe is me!" In his distress, his bow slipped from his hand and fell to the ground without him noticing. "But someone has brought flowers and leaves, and poured water over him. Who could have done that?" he wondered.

Nanan was standing close by. "I can tell you," he said. "A long time ago, when out hunting with your redoubtable father, we came to this mountain. On that day, a Brahmin bathed the Lord in cool water, decked him in a wreath of leaves and flowers, fed him and spoke with him. I expect it is the same man who has done it again today."

At this, Tinnanar's love welled up with even greater intensity. "This must give pleasure to the Lord of Tirukkalatti," he thought, and determined to do the same himself. But his devotion to the Lord did not allow him to leave the Great One on his own. "When I found him, he was all alone," he reflected, "but now if I do not leave him, there is no one else to bring him food to eat. Alas, what can I do?" At length he came to the conclusion that he himself must be the one to bring him food.

So he went a little way, but came straight back. He embraced the Lord, then set out again. He stood looking at him with love, like a cow separated from her calf. "My Lord," he said, "I shall choose some delicious tender meat, and bring it here for you to eat."

He was caught in a dilemma, unwilling to leave him there with no companion, and at the same time unable to stay while the Lord was hungry. At length, shedding copious tears he steeled himself to leave. He picked up his bow, joined his hands in reverence, and tore himself away from the presence of the Lord. With Nanan following behind, Tinnanar went down the mountain side, crossed the river Mukali, and entered the flowering woodland on the golden shore beyond. All other desire abandoned, it was love alone that drove him on.

There Katan came to meet them. He greeted them and said, "I have lit the fire, cut up the boar and laid out all the joints as you commanded. Come and see. But now it is getting late for us to be returning home. What kept you?"

Nanan replied, "There on the mountain Tinnanar saw the Lord, and having embraced him, he has become totally enthralled, like an iguana clinging for dear life to a hole in a tree trunk. Now he has come to fetch meat for him to eat. He has given up the leadership of our clan and become the servant of the Lord."

"Tinnanar, what have you done?" exclaimed Katan, "You must be out of your mind! Have you forgotten, you are our chief?"

Without looking at him, Tinnanar put the boar's flesh on the fire to roast. He separated out the choicest portions with an arrow, and threaded them on a stick. When the juiciest morsels were nicely done, he put them in his mouth to try them for taste. He chose out all the tastiest pieces, and gathered them in a basket of plaited leaves.

Meanwhile, Katan and Nanan stood by watching. "He has now gone completely mad," they said to one another. "First he cooked this boar we had such trouble in catching. Now he has tasted it and spat out each mouthful, although he is so hungry himself. He has not said a word to us, and seems to have forgotten the custom of giving us a share. He has caught some divine frenzy, and we have no idea how to cure him of it. We must bring the priestess here to see what she can do. Meanwhile, let us rejoin the servants on our own hunting ground."

Tinnanar did not notice that the two foresters had left. Instead he quickly arranged the meat in the basket, and took a mouthful of water from the river with which to bathe the god. He plucked a large bunch of fresh, fragrant flowers, and stuck them in his hair. Then with his bow and arrows in one hand and the basket of meat in the other, he hurried away towards the mountain of God, grieving that his sweet Lord would by now be faint with hunger. Full of concern, he reached the spot in haste and entered the presence of the Lord. At once, he brushed the flowers off the head of the holy one with the sandal on his foot, and spat out upon him the water from his mouth as if pouring out the love that welled up in his heart. With the flowers that he had brought in his hair, Tinnanar reverently adorned the head of the Lord of Mount Kalatti, and with his own hand practiced in the use of the bow, he set before him the meat which he had brought in the basket of plaited leaves.

Then he addressed the Lord: "I have chosen all the juiciest morsels, skewered them on a stick, and cooked them to a turn. I have tested them for tenderness with my own teeth, and for taste on my own discerning palate. Now Lord, I offer you this choice meat. Graciously eat your fill." With these words the hunter chief set the food before the Lord of Mount Kalatti.

The sun was now sinking over the hills, and drew in his rays as though joining his hands in worship. The sun himself could see the longing in Tinnanar's heart to provide yet more delicious food for the Lord. As evening drew on, Tinnanar was afraid that in the night wild beasts would prowl around. So with unwavering devotion in his heart and bow in hand, he sought no rest but stood beside the Lord, overshadowing him like a mountain crag.

Sages and heavenly beings reside among the forests and cloud-capped mountains, performing arduous austerities. Even for such as them to see the Lord is a rare privilege. Yet by virtue of deep love and longing, Tinnanar gained sight of him and stood there gazing directly upon him. On one side there glittered a mound of pearls fallen from the bamboo stands, and on the other a sparkling cluster of rubies disgorged by cave-dwelling snakes. Light illumined the scene as though the new moon and the radiant sun had both come together to worship at the mountain of the beloved Lord. While gems of many hues shed forth their rays, radiant emeralds and sapphires were locked in competition. It seemed as if the darkness of night withdrew in fear before the two celestial lights. The flame trees glowed like burning embers; the jewels hoarded by the monkeys in their caves glittered in the dark; the virtue of the ascetics who had conquered the five senses shone forth undimmed. In consequence, on Mount Kalatti where our Father dwells, night was turned to day.

At length, the birds knew that the watches of the night were passed, and sang to greet the dawn. Having stayed awake all night like the restless ocean, the hero heard their song and wanted to fetch food for the Lord to whose presence access is so hard to gain. It was time to put his skill to work, to hunt and kill the mountain boar, the deer and other kinds of game. So in the half light of dawn, with his mighty bow in hand he took leave of the Lord. Then riding in his chariot the sun arose and dispersed the remaining gloom. He drew back the curtain of darkness that concealed the quarry, and with his beams pointed out each target to the hunter as he bent his bow.

Meanwhile it was the task of Shivakocariar, sage and ascetic, to perform the worship of the dark-throated Lord.[3] Accordingly, deep in meditation, he now drew near, bringing flowers, water and other requirements for worship prescribed in the scriptures. As soon as he saw the cooked meat and bones before the sacred presence, he leapt back. "Woe is me!" he cried. "Who has done this horrible thing? It must be the act of some shameless hunter. O God of gods! How can he get away with such a thing? Is this the way you want people to come before you?" Thus weeping and wailing, he fell to the ground.

However, he determined that he could not allow what had happened to delay the worship of the Lord. So with his broom he swept away the flesh and bones, the leaves and the prints left by the hunter's sandals and the hounds' paws. Then he hurried away to bathe in the waters of the river Mukali. When he returned, he first performed the rituals of purification, then with the materials he had brought, prepared to offer the regular acts

3. Shiva swallowed poison to save the gods, and it stayed in his throat, which is therefore dark ("The Churning of the Ocean," p. 149).

of worship, beginning with the sacred bath. After faultlessly completing the whole sequence as prescribed, he bowed in worship before the feet of the Lord. Rising to his feet, the sage praised the Supreme Being who is the first cause of all things, and recited the many titles given him in scripture. Finally he took leave of the Lord, and with peace of mind restored, departed to his hermitage in the forest.

Now I will tell of the skill in the chase, which all on his own the hunter chief displayed in the forest, with his black hair tied in a knot and his great bow in his hand, and by the telling I will cancel the effect of evil deeds. After leaving the sacred hill, Tinnanar killed some of the great boars which had come to graze among the rocks on the mountain slopes. Hiding in ambush, he slew deer of various kinds as they left the forest by their accustomed path. He enticed the spotted deer by imitating their call, then shot them with his sharp arrows. The elk he tracked to the clearings where they slept, and killed them there. Others he pursued on foot and shot. Not until noon when the heat of the sun was at its fiercest did he give up this solitary chase.

Then he gathered together all the game that he had felled, and placed it in a clearing in the forest. With his gleaming sword he cut himself a kindling stick, broke down the boughs bearing the honey combs, and fashioned capacious round baskets out of teak leaves. He collected fire wood and laid a fire, then lit it with the kindling stick and fanned it to a blaze. He jointed the carcases with the sharp edge of an arrow, cut off the fat, and prepared to roast the remaining pieces on the fire. He sorted out the meat with an arrow, discarding the unwanted portions. After cutting up the joints he heaped up the pieces in one of the baskets. Then he skewered them on a long stick and put them on the fire to cook. To make sure that they were well done, he tasted them himself.

In sacrifice, food is placed in the mouth of the flaming god of fire, so that he may take and distribute it to countless other gods. So Tinnanar put the meat in his own mouth to see if it was done, before feeding it to the great Lord of Mount Kalatti. When he had thus confirmed that it was cooked, he put the meat in a basket, squeezed the honey from the comb and stirred it in. Then he took the food he had prepared together with water for the sacred bath and a garland of flowers, and hurried on his way. Having climbed the holy mount, the chief of the hunters reached the presence of the chief of the heavenly ones. There as before he removed the traces of Shivakocariar's worship, then made his own offering. He put down his basket of meat and said, "This food is better than last time. Your servant prepared it from joints of boar, deer and elk. I have flavored it with honey, and tasted it myself. It is good and sweet."

So day by day, Tinnanar made his offering of food and worship to the Lord. Inspired by ever-deepening love, by night he kept vigil before the Lord of Kalatti, and the daytime he spent in hunting. The hermit too came each day with increasing despondency, and removed as sacrilegious the offering of the hunter king. Then he would make his own offering according to the rules laid down in scripture.

As for Nanan and Katan, they went and told Nakan what had happened. Then without stopping for food or rest, they fetched the soothsayer and returned to Tinnanar, now exclusively engaged in caring for the Lord. They used every argument to make him change his mind. But when he would not come round to their way of thinking, they came away and left him.

The creator of all, the Lord of Mount Tirukkalatti, had looked on him in grace. Tinnanar had been changed by that experience of bliss, as if iron had been turned into gold. He was no longer bound to this mortal body, to good and evil deeds, and to the three impurities. He had become the embodiment of love. Can one so changed be judged by the standards of this world? So Tinnanar, lover of the Lord, continued to offer worship in the only way he knew, and the hermit also offered worship in the way prescribed in the eternal scriptures.

Then one day the hermit prayed, "My Lord, I do not know who is doing this. But in your grace, I beseech you to stop him doing it."

That very night, the Lord appeared to the hermit in a dream. "Do not think that this is the work of some violent, uncouth hunter," he said, "What he is doing is right and good. Listen, and I will tell you:

> His whole being is filled with love for me;
> His whole mind is set on me alone;
> All he does is pleasing in my sight;
> You have to understand, that is the way he is.

If you want me to show you what he does, tomorrow come and hide nearby. Then you will see how much he loves me. Do not be afraid." With these words the Lord graciously admonished the hermit, then departed.

At this, the dream left him and the hermit awoke from sleep. Until dawn, he spent the rest of the night wide awake, filled with wonder and with fear. When, riding on his swift horse-drawn chariot, the sun first cast his beams abroad, the hermit went out as on previous days and bathed in the waters of the Ponmukali. Turning over in his mind all that the Lord had said to him, he climbed the holy hill of Kalatti. There as before he offered worship to the Lord, then hid himself nearby.

On the sixth night, the archer chief took his stand once more like a dark cloud and did not so much as close his eyes. At dawn, before the hermit arrived, Tinnanar departed to hunt for food as before. Returning later with food and water, and with a garland of fresh flowers of various kinds, he drew near to the Lord of Tirukkalatti, rich in grace, the nectar of those who have attained clarity of mind. "I am very late," he thought as he hurried back. And seeing many omens all presaging ill, he said to himself, "So many evil omens point to some bloody deed. Alas, what can have happened to my Father?"

The great Lord of Tirukkalatti, wanting to show the hermit Tinnanar's great love, suddenly caused blood to flow from one of his eyes. The fierce hunter saw it from a distance and came running to the spot. When he saw the blood, his head spun; the water spilled from his mouth; his bow slipped from his hand; the food fell scattered on the ground; and the garland of clustered buds drooped wilting from his head. With his wreath of green leaves about his chest, Tinnanar fell to the earth in horror. At length he rose, and wiped the bleeding eye. But the flow of blood did not abate. Not knowing what to do, he breathed a great sigh and again fell down in a faint.

When his senses returned, he got to his feet. "Who can have done this?" he asked himself. He picked up his bow, chose an arrow from his quiver and searched around on every side. "In these mountains is there some warrior chief who is my enemy?" he wondered. "Or else some wild beast, a lion perhaps, has perpetrated this." Finding no answer, he searched the length and breadth of the mountains.

Shiva grabs Kannappar as he is about to dig out his second eye. Ca. 1820.

But there was no hunter to be found, and no wild animal at hand. So finding nothing, Tinnanar returned to the Lord's presence. There in deep grief he embraced his flower-feet, clasping them to his breast, and wept aloud. "Woe is me!" he groaned. "What has happened to the Lord most high before my very eyes? What has happened to my Father, who is sweeter to me than life itself? What has happened to the holy one, who never forsakes those who come to him? What am I to do? I have no idea how to cure this wound, nor can I find the one who did this to my Lord. But the hunter folk always find some herbs to use, which without fail will cure the wounds inflicted by their long bright arrows. On these gold-bearing mountain slopes, perhaps I can find some herbs like that."

With such anxious thoughts, like a red-eyed bull separated from its herd, he roamed through forests far and near. Having found the herbs, quicker than thought he returned to the presence of the Lord. He squeezed out the medicinal juice and poured it on the bleeding eye. However, in spite of the medicine the flow of blood from the eye of the king of Tirukkalatti showed no sign of abating. "What more can I do to staunch this flow?" Tinnanar exclaimed in anguish.

At that moment he remembered the proverb, to cure an illness apply like to like. "Let me dig out my eye with an arrow," he thought, "and apply it to my Father's eye, as like to like. Then perhaps it will act as a medicine and staunch the flow of blood." So as he stood before the Lord, joy rose in his heart. Then taking an arrow, he gouged out his whole eye and applied it to the eye of the First Cause of all. At once the flow of blood stopped. When Tinnanar saw that, he hugged himself and danced like a madman, beside himself for very joy. "That was a good scheme of mine!" he laughed.

The Lord now wanted to demonstrate further the virtue and compassion of his servant. So he caused blood to flow in a continuous stream from the other eye also. Tinnanar who came into this world by reason of the austerities performed by the hunter clan and surpassed even the gods in loving kindness, now saw the fresh flow of blood. "Alas!" he exclaimed. "One eye of the Lord of Kalatti has stopped bleeding. Now the other has started to bleed profusely! But there is no need to worry, because I have already found the remedy. I still have one eye. I can pluck that out too and apply it to the bleeding eye to staunch the flow."

Tinnanar was aware of the handicap that he would suffer if he plucked out his remaining eye and applied it to the eye of the Lord. Nevertheless, he placed his left foot on the Lord's eye to guide his hand, then with single-minded determination he took an arrow and was about to drive it into his eye. This the God of gods did not allow. The wonder-working Lord of Tirukkalatti who had already made Tinnanar his own, now stretched out his hand to check the hand of his devotee, before he could dig out his remaining eye. Then three times a heavenly voice called out, "Kannappar, stop!"

The wise hermit had been watching as the great hunter chief dug out his eye and placed it on the Lord's; and he saw how the Lord had gladly accepted the offering of flesh, and now firmly grasped the hunter's hand. At that moment the sound of chanting of the Vedas filled the air, and Ayan and the other gods rained down a shower of fresh flowers. When the eye of the Lord was injured, the hunter recoiled at the sight. But with his own hand he plucked out his eye and laid it on the wound. Now the Lord with his own hand grasped the hand that had done the deed. "Peerless one," he said in boundless grace, "take your place at my right hand."

So the chieftain succeeded in staunching with his own eye the blood that flowed from the eye of the king of Tirukkalatti, who dwells among the clouds. In honor of him, I place my head beneath his feet.

THE *CILAPPATIKARAM* ("THE TALE OF AN ANKLET") OF ILANKO ATIKAL

The Tale of an Anklet is traditionally believed to have been composed in the fifth century C.E. by Ilanko Atikal, a Tamil prince. It is an epic, a love story, and an important episode in the history of the goddess Pattini; it thus weaves together heroic, erotic, and mythic themes. It takes place at a time when Tamil Nadu, the Tamil-speaking southernmost tip of India, was divided into three great kingdoms: the Pandyas (or Pantiyans) in the East, the Cholas (or Colas) in the South, and the Cheras (or Cerals) on the western coast. As an epic, it is to Tamil what the Valmiki *Ramayana* and the *Mahabharata* are to Sanskrit: a tale of heroism and royal power.

As a love story, *The Tale of an Anklet* tells the tale of Kovalan and his wife, Kannaki, who live together happily for some years until Kovalan leaves Kannaki to live with the courtesan Matavi, on whom he squanders all of their money. Eventually he leaves Matavi and returns to Kannaki, but Matavi bears him a daughter, Manimekhalai (who later becomes the heroine of a second Tamil epic named after her). Traveling to Madurai, the capital of the Pandyan kingdom, Kovalan tries to sell one of Kannaki's gold anklets but is falsely accused of having stolen the Pandyan queen's anklet, for which crime he is executed. When Kannaki learns of his death, she rushes to the palace in a fury, accuses the king of murder, and proves that the anklet was hers by breaking it open and revealing jewels inside it, where the queen's anklet contained nothing but pearls. The king acknowledges his guilt and dies; the queen follows him.

Kannaki curses the city of Madurai, tears off her left breast, and hurls it over the city. Agni, the god of fire, appears before her and says, "Long ago I was told to burn this city on the day that you are wronged. Who shall live in it now?" And she asks him to spare Brahmins, good men, cows, chaste women, the old, and children, but to burn the wicked (21.59–70). He burns down the city. The poet then remarks:

> The goddess of Madurai appeared before her
> Who had wrenched off her fierce, youthful breast,
> Whose triumph equaled that of Lakshmi, Sarasvati,
> And Kali who slew the Buffalo Demon. (22.101–4)

The goddess of Madurai puts out the fire, and Kannaki, reassured by the goddess that she will join Kovalan in heaven, travels west to the kingdom of the Cheras, where she ascends to heaven in Indra's chariot, to become the goddess Pattini.

As a story about human life, *The Tale of an Anklet* argues for better treatment of women. Kannaki, a woman alone, is powerless in a patriarchy: she loses her father and husband and has no son; the king, the ultimate patriarch, betrays her. When she breaks her anklet she foreshadows the moment when she will tear off her breast, for both symbolize her womanhood; in addition, the anklet is symbolic of her virtue as a chaste wife. Breaking it breaks her ties to her marriage, just as tearing off her breast breaks her ties to motherhood. And the fact that she breaks the anklet in the temple of Korravai, the goddess of war and victory, is a further step in both her masculinization and her deification.

As a myth, *The Tale of an Anklet* is the foundational text for the worship of the goddess Pattini, the deified form of Kannaki. Pattini goes on to become one of the great goddesses of South India, a goddess of fertility and health, particularly invoked to ward off smallpox. Her worshippers say that she became incarnate as Kannaki in order to destroy the wicked king of Madurai.

The selection is translated by R. Parthasarathy.

PRONOUNCING GLOSSARY

Ceral: *seh´-rul*
Cilappatikaram: *sih´-lup-puh´-tee-kah´-rum*
Cola: *choh´-luh*
Ilanko Atikal: *ih-lahn´-koh uh-tee-kahl´*
kino: *kee´-noh*
Madurai: *muh´-doo-rai*
Pantiyan: *pahn´-tee-yun*
Pattini: *puht´-tee-nee´*
Villavan Kotai: *vih´-luh-vun koh´-tai*

PATTINI IS WORSHIPPED

After Kannaki ascended to heaven, the Chera king Cenkuttuvan, camping nearby, heard about what had happened to her. He marched north, defeating the northern rulers who had spoken contemptuously about the Tamil kings; there he had the image of Kannaki as the goddess Pattini engraved on a stone brought from the Himalayas and bathed in the Ganges. Returning to Vanchi (the Chera capital), he installed the stone in a temple and established the worship of Pattini. The political implications of this view of Pattini's origin are strong and clear: the martial victory of the king is the religious victory of the goddess.

We take up the story just as the king has released from prison all the northern kings he had conquered.

28.200–239

They were informed they could return
To their cities at the end of the sacrifice. He rejoiced
In saying:
"Villavan Kotai![1] Look to their comfort
As befits princes."
Orders were sent
To Alumpilvel[2] and to revenue officers to proclaim
In distant towns with fields brimming
With water:
"Throw open all prisons. Remit
All taxes due from the citizens of our state."

The Cola king, who wears a wreath
Of fig leaves, shone as an example.
Pattini whom the whole world now worships
Had proved the truth of the Tamil saying:
"The virtue of women is useless if the king
Rules unjustly." She made the Cola realize it.
She made the Pantiyan, lord of the south,
Realize, "The king cannot survive if his scepter

1. The mother of King Cenkuttuvan.
2. A chieftain under King Cenkuttuvan.

Is crooked." She made the Ceral,
Lord of the west, realize, "The wrath
Of kings will not be appeased till their vows
Are fulfilled, and made known to the kings
Of the north."

In her rage, Pattini lit
A fire from one of her breasts and burned down
The ancient city of Madurai, entered
Our country, and stood in the golden shade
Of the cool branches of the kino.[3] With the help
Of brahmans, royal priests, astrologers,
And expert sculptors, a shrine was dedicated
To that revered woman and built
According to established rules so that wise men
May approve it. The image of Pattini was installed
In it, engraved by skilled hands on the stone
Brought from the slopes of the Himalaya, the home
Of the gods, after prayers to Shiva who resides there.
She was adorned with precious ornaments
Exquisitely crafted and worshipped with flowers.
Images of the guardian deities stood
At the entrance to the temple. The lion among kings,
Who had extended his rule over the northern countries,
Performed the dedication and ordered:

"Worship
The goddess every day with offerings and festivities."

3. A tree valued for its medicinal properties.

SHIVA'S WARRIORS AND WIVES IN KANNADA

800–1700 C.E.

Kannada is a Dravidian language, spoken today in the South Indian state of Karnataka, whose cultural hub is in Mysore, and written in a script of its own. Kannada speakers, called Kannadigas, number approximately 38 million. Second only to Tamil, among the Dravidian languages, in the antiquity of its literary tradition, Kannada appears in epigraphs from the sixth century C.E. and flourished as a literary language from the ninth century. The earliest literature in Kannada is Jain, but from the twelfth century, poetry in Kannada was composed by the Shaiva poet-saints who belonged to the Virashaiva movement. By choosing to compose their poetry in colloquial Kannada rather than Sanskrit, the poet-saints of Karnataka gained access to the innovations and spontaneity of free verse, indeed to poetry that was often not recognizably in verse at all.

The first set of Kannada poems selected here is attributed to Basava, and the second set to Mahadeviyakka, a woman poet who was a contemporary of Basava.

Young Yakshagana dancers in Bangalore. Yakshagana ("Song of a Demigod") is a performance style that combines dance, music, dialogue, costume, and makeup to enact scenes from the Hindu epics and Puranas.

BASAVA AND THE VIRASHAIVAS

Sects of renouncers had always followed a religious path that led them away from houses to wilderness. But by the end of the first millennium C.E., when so many great temples were being built and the temple rather than the palace was the center of communal Hinduism, the pride and joy of South Indian rulers, and the bastion of the social, economic, and religious order of South India, one large and influential South Indian Hindu sect differed from earlier renouncers in spurning not houses but stone temples. These were the Lingayats ("People of the Linga," who wore the *linga*, the stone emblem of Shiva, in a silver casket around their necks) or Virashaivas ("Shiva's Heroes"), also called Charanas ("Wanderers") or Jangamas ("Movers"), because they prided themselves on being moving temples, itinerant, never putting down roots. The trinity of their faith consisted of guru (spiritual teacher), *linga*, and Jangamas (the human representatives of Shiva). They believed that the only temple one can trust is one's own body ("The rich will make temples").

Their founder was Basava (also called Basavanna and Basaveshvara) (1106–1167 C.E.), a Brahmin who served at the court of King Bijjala of Kalyana (*The Basava Purana*, p. 354) and preached a simplified devotion: no worship but that of a small *linga* worn around the neck, and no goal but to be united, at death, with Shiva. A number of Kannada poems to Shiva are attributed to him.

The Virashaivas were militants who rejected the normative social and cultural order of the medieval South; some people regarded them as heretics, and many classified them as "left-hand" castes (like artisans, merchants, servants) in contrast with "right-hand" castes (like agricultural workers). Legends about the early Virashaivas say that the son of a Pariah married the daughter of a Brahmin; the king condemned both their fathers to death; the Virashaivas rioted against the king and assassinated him; the government attempted to suppress the Virashaivas, but they survived.

The oral nature of the Virashaivas' poetry is indicated by the fact that the poems are called "speakings" (*vachanas*). The frequent epithet given to Shiva, "lord of the meeting rivers," resonates, among other things, with the meetings of the community of devotees from every caste and class and even outcastes, women as well as men, literate as well as illiterate.

The source for the poems is the S. S. Basavanal edition (Dharwar, 1962). The translations are by A. K. Ramanujan.

PRONOUNCING GLOSSARY

Basava: *buh´-suh-vuh*

Virashaiva: *vee´-ruh-shai´-vuh*

SHIVA, YOU HAVE NO MERCY

This is a poem in the genre of complaining to the god, known from the Tamil poems of Cuntarar ("The *Tevaram*," p. 315).

Shiva, you have no mercy.
Shiva, you have no heart.

Why why did you bring me to birth,
wretch in this world,
exile from the other?

Tell me, lord,
don't you have one more
little tree or plant
made just for me?

AS A MOTHER RUNS

The androgynous god Shiva (who is worshipped as Arddhanarishvara, "The Lord Who Is Half Woman") sometimes becomes a human woman in Kannada *bhakti* myth and poetry. This poem, quite straightforward, needs no gloss. But a Kannada listener/reader would hear echoes of a story told in Tamil temples:

> A devotee's daughter was about to give birth to her first child. Her mother could not cross the flooding Kaveri River and come in time to help her waiting daughter. So Shiva took the form of the old mother—"back bent like the crescent moon, hair white as moonlight, a bamboo staff in hand"—and came to her house. Parvati, Shiva's wife, and the river Ganges (often said to be a wife of Shiva) had been sent ahead with bundles. When labor began, Shiva played midwife; a boy was born and Mother Shiva cradled and cared for him as if he were Murukan (the son of Shiva). Soon the floods abated, and the baby's real grandmother appeared on the doorstep. Shiva began to slip away. Seeing the two women, the young couple were amazed. "Which is my mother?" cried the girl. Before her eyes, Shiva disappeared into the sky like lightning.[1]

"As if he were Murukan" is one of those switchbacks that the mythology of doubling and impersonation, so dear to Shaiva literature, delights in: a human woman might indeed treat her grandson like a god (in this case, Murukan, the son of Shiva), but in this story the god pretends that the child is his own son, pretends that he himself is a woman (the mother of the woman who has just had the baby) imagining that she is Shiva (the father of Murukan)—a double gender switch, too, by the way. Careful, down-to-earth details, such as Shiva sending "bundles" on ahead with his two wives, strongly suggest that this is a story about women's concerns, and therefore a place to hear women's voices. Shiva clearly enjoys being a woman—or else why did he not just stop the river from flooding so that the real grandmother of the baby could get to her daughter? He wanted to be there himself, to be intimately involved with this most basic of women's experiences.

1. David Dean Shulman, *Tamil Temple Myths: Sacrifice and Divine Marriage in the South Indian Saiva Tradition* (Princeton, N.J.: Princeton University Press, 1980), pp. 314–15.

As a mother runs
close behind her child
with his hand on a cobra
or a fire,

the lord of the meeting rivers
stays with me
every step of the way
and looks after me.

THE MASTER OF THE HOUSE

The repetitions and syntactical rhythms of this poem produce a parallelism—threshold : house :: body : heart—to which is added a second parallelism—grass : dirt :: lies : lust. The epithet in the last line applies primarily to the god, but it also refers, syntactically, to the master of the house, suggesting that all of the second set of parallels (grass, dirt, lies, lust) arise because the master is not at home, the god is not in the heart of the worshipper.

The master of the house, is he at home, or isn't he?
Grass on the threshold,
dirt in the house:
The master of the house, is he at home, or isn't he?

Lies in the body,
lust in the heart:
no, the master of the house is not at home,
our Lord of the Meeting Rivers.

DOES IT MATTER HOW LONG

Ghosts are believed to stand guard over hidden treasure, though they cannot touch it. There is a parallel in this poem between the relationship of rock and water and of ghost and gold: the rock is not affected by water, and the ghost cannot affect the gold, which symbolizes the untouched spirit of the person engaged in the world.

Does it matter how long
a rock soaks in the water:
will it ever grow soft?

Does it matter how long
I've spent in worship,
when the heart is fickle?

Futile as a ghost
I stand guard over hidden gold,

O lord of the meeting rivers.

WHEN A WHORE WITH A CHILD

Parables and metaphors about prostitutes are not uncommon in South Indian poetry ("A Courtesan to a Young Customer," p. 363).

When a whore with a child
takes on a customer for money,

neither child nor lecher
will get enough of her.

She'll go pat the child once,
then go lie with the man once,

neither here nor there.
Love of money is relentless,

my lord of the meeting rivers.

I WENT TO FORNICATE

Like the previous poem, this one can be read both literally and metaphorically.

I went to fornicate,
but all I got was counterfeit.

I went behind a ruined wall,
but scorpions stung me.

The watchman who heard my screams
just peeled off my clothes.

I went home in shame,
my husband raised weals on my back.

All the rest, O lord of the meeting rivers,
the king took for his fines.

DON'T YOU TAKE ON

The two metaphors in this poem are staples of *bhakti* poetry. "Walking the razor's edge" (an image that the British writer W. Somerset Maugham used for the title of his novel about an Englishman finding salvation in India) is the traditional Indian metaphor for "Keeping to the difficult path of salvation." Here the image is reversed, as the saw moves on the *bhakta*, the devotee, instead of the *bhakta* walking on the saw. The cobra in the pitcher is one of many ordeals or truth-tests (such as walking on fire or drinking poison) that a person might be subjected to in order to prove trustworthiness, chastity, or the truth of any statement.

Don't you take on
this thing called bhakti:

like a saw
it cuts when it goes

and it cuts again
when it comes.

If you risk your hand
with a cobra in a pitcher
will it let you
pass?

THE POT IS A GOD

This poem may be read as a satire on Hindu polytheism, which often deifies material objects (such as cylindrical stones, or pots), or on Hindu monism, which sees the material world as a manifestation (or illusion) of the world-soul (*brahman*). Or both.

The pot is a god. The winnowing
fan is a god. The stone in the
street is a god. The comb is a
god. The bowstring is also a
god. The bushel is a god and the
spouted cup is a god.

Gods, gods, there are so many
there's no place left
for a foot.

There is only
one god. He is our Lord
of the Meeting Rivers.

THE RICH WILL MAKE TEMPLES

This poem goes to the heart of the Virashaivas' refusal to worship in temples. Indian temples are traditionally built in the image of the human body—the two sides are the hands or wings, a pillar is called a foot, the top of the temple is the head, and the innermost sanctum is the womb-house (*garbha-griha*). But the Virashaivas turn the symbolism on its head: the parts of the human body are the true form of the temple.

The rich certainly did make temples, in Basava's time as in ours. Against this tradition of the privileged, Basava uplifted the poor, the outcaste, the illiterate, and gave them (back) the temples of their bodies. The structural oppositions are clear: rich/poor, temple/body, standing/moving, making/being. "Things standing" (*sthavara*) speaks of the great static temples, and "things moving" (*jangama*) speaks of the worshippers, the "Wanderers" (Charanas), the living representatives of the god on earth, for Jangama is another word for the Virashaiva saint.

The rich
will make temples for Shiva.
What shall I,
a poor man,
do?

My legs are pillars,
the body the shrine,
the head a cupola
of gold.

Listen, O lord of the meeting rivers,
things standing shall fall,
but the moving ever shall stay.

MAHADEVIYAKKA: A VIRASHAIVA WOMAN POET-SAINT

In the twelfth century, a Virashaiva poet-saint named Mahadeviyakka (or Mahadevi or Mahadevyyakka, *akka* being an honorific for "sister") composed poems in Kannada that simultaneously addressed the metaphysics of salvation and the banal problem of dealing with in-laws. The hagiographies tell us that she wandered naked, clothed only in her hair, until she died, still in her twenties.

The source for the poems is L. Basavaraju, *Akkana Vacanagalu* (Mysore, 1966). The translations are by A. K. Ramanujan.

PRONOUNCING GLOSSARY

Mahadeviyakka: *muh-hah´-day´-vee-yuk´-kuh*

MY BODY IS DIRT

Mahadeviyakka's attitude toward her body is ambivalent: it is the only temple she has, and the instrument through which she will reach her god, but she despises it when she exalts the immaterial spirit.

My body is dirt,
my spirit is space:
which
shall I grab, O lord? How,
and what,
shall I think of you?
Cut through
my illusions,
lord white as jasmine.

HUSBAND INSIDE

Mahadeviyakka regarded herself as married to Shiva and tried in vain to avoid marrying a human husband. Eventually she left her husband and wandered freely as a Virashaiva saint.

Husband inside,
lover outside.
I can't manage them both.

This world
and that other,
cannot manage them both.

O lord white as jasmine

I cannot hold in one hand
both the round nut[1]
and the long bow.

1. The *belavalada*, a large unripe hard-shelled nut.

WHO CARES

This poem displays many of the characteristics that distinguish the Virashaiva *vachanas* from other devotional poetry: it expresses the real internal conflicts of a real person; it is spoken in the voice of that person, unmediated by literary conventions; it is about basic human relationships—here, a woman and her lover(s); it describes the devotee rather than the god, the subject rather than the object of worship. It also challenges conventions of purity, both in the image of a woman used by several men and in the image of a dog feeding upon the body.

Who cares
who strips a tree of leaf
once the fruit is plucked?

Who cares
who lies with the woman
you have left?

Who cares
who ploughs the land
you have abandoned?

After this body has known my lord
who cares if it feeds
a dog
or soaks up water?

IF ONE COULD

This poem is often cited as Mahadeviyakka's answer to the challenge of another Virashaiva poet, Allama Prabhu, sometimes said to be her guru. Allama was a temple drummer who went mad with grief when his young wife died but then founded one of the great Virashaiva centers, in Kalyana. Allama is said to have said to Mahadeviyakka: "As long as you carry the pollutions of the body and the five senses, you cannot even touch the Lord." The following poem is her reply.

If one could
draw the fangs of a snake
and charm the snake to play,
it's great to have snakes.

If one can single out
the body's ways
it's great to have bodies.
The body's wrong
is like mother turning vampire.

Don't say they have bodies
who have Your love,
O lord
white as jasmine.

PEOPLE, MALE AND FEMALE

This poem reflects Mahadeviyakka's notorious lack of modesty, her reputation for going naked, and her assumption that gender does not matter when it comes to seeking god.

People,
male and female,
blush when a cloth covering their shame
comes loose.
When the lord of lives
lives drowned without a face
in the world, how can you be modest?

When all the world is the eye of the lord,
onlooking everywhere, what can you
cover and conceal?

PASSION FOR GOD IN TELUGU

1100–1300 C.E.

Telugu is a Dravidian language, the official language of Andhra Pradesh, also spoken in parts of Karnataka, Tamil Nadu, Orissa, and Maharashtra. Telugu was used in inscriptions from the sixth century C.E., and Telugu literature began to be preserved shortly thereafter. Its structures and vocabulary are very different from those of Sanskrit, but literary Telugu has assimilated many Sanskrit forms (meters, genres) as well as a great deal of Sanskrit vocabulary since the eleventh century, when the Sanskritic tradition of Telugu developed out of the indigenous tradition.

The great biography of Basava, the *Basava Purana*, composed by Palkuriki Somanatha probably in the thirteenth century, is not in Kannada but in Telugu. Vaishnavas, too, thrived in Andhra, and the fifteenth-century Telugu poet Annamayya dedicated his poems to his "god on the hill" (a form of Vishnu) in the town of Tirupati, in Andhra, while the male poet Kshetrayya (1622–1673) composed poems (also to Vishnu) in the voices of courtesans.

The huge granite statue of Shiva's bull Nandi at the Virabhadra Temple at Lepakshi, in Andhra Pradesh.

THE *BASAVA PURANA* ("THE ANCIENT STORY OF BASAVA") OF PALKURIKI SOMANATHA

The early poems of the Virashaivas were composed in Kannada, but the earliest extant full narrative of the Virashaivas, the thirteenth-century *Basava Purana* of Palkuriki Somanatha, is in Telugu. It is largely a hagiography of Basava (also called Basvanna and Basaveshvara), the founder of the Virashaivas. A Brahmin who lived from 1106 to 1167 and served at the court of King Bijjala of Kalyana, Basava was against caste and against Brahmins, though he always claimed that he was a scholar of the four Vedas. Muslim social customs, unrestricted by caste, influenced him deeply, and the Virashaivas' rejection of conventional Hinduism may be beholden to the influence of Muslim missionaries who were active on India's west coast just when the Virashaiva doctrine was developed there. On the other hand, the threat of destruction of Hindu temples and icons by Muslim rulers may have been one reason for the widespread use of portable temple images (or portable *lingas*). Eventually, Basava reacted against the Virashaivas' violence and lived his life away from the community he had founded.

The Virashaivas thrived in the political vacuum that existed in twelfth-century Kalyana. Much of the aggression in the *Basava Purana* is directed against bourgeois Hinduism: the god in the temple icon is so humiliated that he sneaks out the back door; washermen, thieves, and Pariahs win out over the political and religious power mongers; a devotee's dog (actually Shiva disguised in a dog's skin) recites the Veda, shaming the caste-obsessed Brahmins. Several stories also describe victories over Jains.

Palkuriki Somanatha chose to write in the more vernacular, indigenous style of Telugu—in a meter popular in oral tradition and closely related to the meters of folk songs—rather than in the Sanskritized style that had become popular in court literature by his day. He drew his material, too, from the *bhaktas* that he knew and from local traditions rather than from Sanskrit literature.

The stories in this section are translated by Velcheru Narayana Rao.

PRONOUNCING GLOSSARY

Basava: *buh´-suh-vuh*
Basava Purana: *buh´-suh-vuh poo-rah´-nuh*
Basavayya: *buh´-suh-vuh´-yuh*
Bijjala: *bij´-juh-luh*
Cokka Nayanaru: *chok´-kuh nah´-yuh-nah´-roo*
Ishvara: *eesh´-vuh-ruh*
jangama: *jung´-guh-muh*
Kalavva: *kah´-luv-vuh*
Kapileshvaram: *kuh-pih-laysh´-vuh-rum*
linga: *ling´-guh*
Madhura: *muh´-doo-ruh*
Palkuriki Somanatha: *pul-koo-ree´-kee soh´-muh-nah´-tuh*
Pandya: *pahn´-dyuh*
prana: *prah´-nuh*
Tripurari: *trih´-poo-rah´-ree*

THE STORY OF THE EGGPLANTS THAT BECAME *LINGAS*

The most popular variety of eggplant in South India has an oval shape rather than the bell shape more common in North America, or the long fingers of the so-called oriental variety. The shape of South Indian eggplants is thus very close to the shape of many *lingas*. There is a complex typology of *lingas* in Virashaivism. The *prana linga* ("*linga* of the vital breath") is a manifestation of the consciousness of Shiva (Ishvara, "the Lord") within the body of the worshipper. In the story here, the thieves' mastery of this *linga* means that they had become true Virashaiva *bhaktas* (here called *jangamas*, "movers") and their fake *lingas* had become real.

One day, while the commander-in-chief was devotedly serving the jangamas, some thieves decided to rob his house. They knew that anyone without a linga would never be allowed into the house, so they tied eggplants around their necks under their clothing. They then entered just as if they were wearing the linga. But when they saw Basava, the commander-in-chief, they were struck with fear.

As they bowed before him, he looked at them with smiling eyes and said, "People who do not wear the linga cannot enter our house. But since you are devotees, go worship Ishvara without any fear."

They looked at each other. Their minds were agitated, and their hearts were chilled with fear. They said to themselves, "We are trapped here. If only the linga were here, we would escape death. There is no way that we can get away."

But they had already taken their seats. And when they reached forth their hands as if they had lingas, with the blessing of Basava, the eggplants became prana lingas.

THE HERDSWOMAN'S BUTTERMILK POT

This is the story of a very small, very banal, working-class, literally earthy sort of miracle, all the more impressive for its intimate focus. It takes place in the kingdom of Bijjala, the king whom Basava served.

And one day when Basava, the sinless, the respectable, the commander-in-chief, the virtuous, the well-born, was sitting in Bijjala's court, he suddenly said, "Don't worry!" And he lifted up his hands as if to catch an earthen pot.

The king chuckled and said, "They say that if a man puts just a particle of ash on his forehead, it will produce a mountain of craziness! And it seems to be true. What is going on, Basavayya? Are you dizzy with Shiva? Has the nectar of devotion gone to your head and made you crazy? What do you mean by saying, 'Don't worry! Don't worry!' and raising up your hands like that in the middle of the court?"

"I really shouldn't sing my own praises," said Basava, "but if I don't, the court might take it wrong."

So he said, "A short distance east of the Tripurari Temple, in a place called Kapileshvaram, there lives an ascetic. Every day he bathes the linga with six measures of milk. The milk turns into rivulets and spreads all over the area, and under the elephant's feet, the whole place turns into a quagmire. A woman named Kalavva was walking along that path selling buttermilk. When she tried to get a footing, her feet slipped. As the buttermilk pot was about to fall, the milkmaid called, 'O Basava!' So I simply stretched out my hands and kept the pot from falling."

Then Basava proceeded to describe what the milkmaid looked like, what her house was like, and the particulars of the spot where she was. At once the king sent for the girl and asked her. She confirmed everything Basava had said. She even showed the mire on the hand with which she had reached out to catch herself, and the dirt she had gotten on her feet when she slipped.

"Don't you know this greatness? Is this a big thing for him to have done?" she asked.

THE FOXES THAT BECAME HORSES

This story became popular in South India and was often retold, in Tamil and Sanskrit. In later tellings, the foxes (or, sometimes, jackals) are turned into horses *before* the saint (usually not Basava but Tiruvatavurar) gets back to the Pandyan king who rules from Madurai ("Tamil Finds Its Many Voices," p. 301). The king is thrilled by the quality of the horses—until, during the night, they turn back into foxes and devour the king's horses in the stable. Shiva is called "the mountain slayer" and Cokka Nayanaru ("the beautiful saint") in the temple at Maturai. The story was celebrated until recent times in a festival that honors an image of Shiva mounted on a leaping horse and known as Pariviran ("the horse hero") or Parimel Alakan ("the beautiful one on a horse").

"The Pandya of Madhura gave his minister a large amount of money and asked him to buy horses with it. Because of his excessive devotion, the minister spent all of the money on worshipping jangamas. When the money was gone, there was nothing left with which to buy horses. Then, without the slightest hesitation, the minister rounded up all the foxes in the fields, brought them, and showed them to the Pandya king. On account of Cokka Nayanaru's great compassion, all the foxes turned into fine steeds. When you consider the might of Mountain Slayer's devotees, is it any wonder that such a thing could happen?" said all of the pure-hearted devotees, delighted. Bijjala was completely amazed. "This Basava is none other than Ishvara himself! How can he be anyone else?" he said. Then the king gave fine clothing and precious ornaments to Basava. Very lovingly and devotedly, while everyone listened, he said, "If anyone slanders my treasurer again, I'll have that person's tongue cut out; I'll have lime smeared on the wound; I'll have hot sand poured into his mouth." With that he took leave of the lionlike Basava. And he went to his palace while the people sang his praises.

TEMPLE POEMS FROM TIRUPATI BY ANNAMAYYA

Annamayya (also called Annamacharya and Tallapaka Annamayya) lived at the great hilltop shrine of Tirupati in Andhra Pradesh, in the fifteenth century. He composed, in Telugu, many songs to the god of this temple, a form of Vishnu called Venkateshvara. Thirteen thousand of these poems, in the genre called *padam*, were inscribed on copper plates shortly before or after his death; preserved over the centuries, they are important texts for the Shri Vaishnava tradition. The copper plates divide the poems into two groups: three-quarters of them are erotic (*sringara*), often couched in the female voice, and the rest are metaphysical (*adhyatma*), sung in the poet's own voice. Sometimes the two genres meet in a single poem.

The poems in this section are translated by Velcheru Narayana Rao and David Shulman.

PRONOUNCING GLOSSARY

Alamelumanga: *uh´-luh-may´-loo-mung´-guh*
Annamayya: *un´-nuh-mah´-yuh*
Tirupati: *tih´-roo-puh´-tee*

WHY CROSS THE BOUNDARY

This seems to be a love poem, in praise of dangerous, perhaps adulterous love, tormented love, love that is full of questions. Only in the last line do we see that it was also about the love of god, all along.

Why cross the boundary
when there is no village?
It's like living without a name,
like words without love.

What use is ecstasy
without the agony of separation?
Shade is nothing without the burning sun.
What is patience without fury of passion?
Why make anything—love or poetry—if two can't be one?

Why cross the boundary?

What good is profit without praise?
Why speak tender words when there is no closeness?

What use is love if you can't let go?
Beauty is empty without desire.

Why cross the boundary?

Why have a lover you don't need to hide?
Intimacy is dull without doubt.
What fun is there in just making love,
no extras, no questions?
Bring in our god on the hill.

Why cross the boundary?

SEEING IS ONE THING

"Seeing" is *darshan* ("The Flowering of Bhakti," p. 295), the passionate gaze that connects the god and the worshipper. "Looking" is the complementary force of active seeking, longing, desiring, and, ultimately, imagining the god.

Seeing is one thing;
looking is another.
If both come together,
that is god.

If you look for an elephant,
he comes as an elephant.
If you look for a tree,
he's a tree.
If you look for a mountain,
he'll be a mountain.
God is what you have in your mind.

If you look for empty space,
he appears as space.
If you look for an ocean,
he'll be an ocean.
If you look for a city,
he will come as a city.
God is what you have in your mind.

If you think of the god on the hill,
married to the goddess,
that's who you'll see.
What you look for
is the god in you.
What you see

is the god out there.
God is what you have in your mind.

I'LL SERVE YOU AS BEST I CAN

Here the double entendre is on "serve," whose sexual meaning dominates the poem until the last line, when once again the lover turns out to be the god.

I'll serve you as best I can,
but some things I just can't do.

I can melt your heart just like that,
but I can't stop you breaking out in sweat.
I can sink my teeth deep into your lips,
but I can't help it if they leave marks.

Some things I just can't do.

I can touch you where you are shy,
but can I stop you from feeling the thrill?
I can look you straight in the eyes,
but hey, can I keep you
from smiling?

Some things I just can't do.

I can wear you out with hugs and kisses,
but I can't stop your sigh.
Now that you've made love to me,
god on the hill,
can I keep you from wanting more?

Some things I just can't do.

LORD, I GIVE UP

Every boast that the worshipper makes is checkmated by his realization of the complete power of the god. Surrender is the only possible theological position.

Lord, I give up.
There's nothing like you in this world.

I can say I'm not frightened by anything,
but the courage must come from you.
I can boast of my strength, any time,
but inside me, all awareness is you.

I give up.

I can claim to be fully awake,
but you have to give me wisdom.
I'd like to think I'm free from fantasy.
Fantasy comes from you.

I give up.

Suppose I say I've conquered birth.
Only you can make me free.
I'd bring you some gift,
god on the hill,
but you already own the world.

I give up.

YOU THINK I'M SOMEONE SPECIAL

Again the poem seems to be about an ordinary human woman in love with a human man, until the final lines reveal not only that her lover is the god but also that she herself is his goddess, Alamelumanga, the goddess of Tirupati and the wife of the god Venkateshvara, worshipped in her temple at Mangapuram.

You think I'm someone special,
but I'm just your woman. Nothing more.

I get excited when we talk—and it's not enough.
I keep staring at you—but it's not enough.
We keep making love—and it's not enough.
How did you make me fall for you?

I'm your woman.

I serve you plenty—but I want more.
I bow to you—but I want more.
I think of you all the time—and I want more.
It's all your doing, not mine.

I'm your woman.

I embrace your feet.
I kiss you.
It's not enough. I want more.
God on the hill: I'm Alamelumanga.
I'm the one you chose.
That's all I know.

I'm your woman.

IT'S NO SMALL THING

The idea that the gods themselves have karma ("The Karma of Dharma," p. 156), that they too are punished for their mistakes, underlies this poem of complaint and irony. The gods in question here include the goddess Lakshmi, Vishnu's wife, who is said to dwell on his chest, and the form of Vishnu known as Venkateshvara, whose shrine is on the banks of the Svami-pushkarini Lake.

It's no small thing, this load you carry from the past.
It catches up with you.

You bind everyone in the world in the round of life and death.
For this sin, someone has bound that woman
to your chest, not sparing you even though
you're god.

It catches up with you.

Just for fun, you drown living beings
in the ocean of life, and then you dredge them up.
For this flaw, they make you sleep
on the ocean, even if
you're god.

It catches up with you.

You drive us through forests and over mountains.
You never let us rest.
That's why you have to live up on that hill
as the Lord of the Lake, whether you like it
or not.

It catches up with you.

I WAS BETTER OFF THEN

This poem can be read as a satire on the conventional Hindu view of reincarnation, where rebirth as an animal is regarded as a step down from the human condition ("Retribution in Rebirth," p. 206). Here, hell is other people, and the poet blames god for letting him fall into this sort of hell.

I was better off then.
Better off in my past lives
than in this misery.

When I was born as a worm,
at home in the mud,
I never had these worries.
It's much worse to be human.
I was better off then.

Born as a lowly beast,
subject to so much pain,
I didn't know poverty from riches.
Now I know.
I was better off then.

Committing so many wrongs,
I've fallen into hell.
You were there for me.
I was better off then.

POEMS BY KSHETRAYYA

Women's voices, produced by men, played a central role in the work of devotional poets who wrote in Telugu from the fifteenth to the eighteenth centuries in southern Andhra and the Tamil region. We have seen this in some of the poems of Annamayya ("I'll serve you as best I can"; "You think I'm someone special"), and we also find it in another Telugu poet, Kshetrayya, who may have lived in the mid-seventeenth century, under the Nayaka dynasty that ruled in the city of Vijayanagara. Kshetrayya worshipped a form of Krishna that he called Muvva Gopala, "Cowherd from the village of Muvva."

Kshetrayya's poems imagine a courtesan speaking to her customer who is also her god. Money forms a link between them; god is a customer of the worshipper, just as the worshipper may be the customer of a courtesan. A courtesan was not a prostitute; courtesans in ancient and medieval India were, unlike almost all other women in India, able to own property, to read and write, and to move about freely in society. Most of them had only a few, or even just one, patron, whom they would receive in their homes. They were like hetairas in ancient Greece or geishas in Japan. They may well have composed poems of their own in Telugu, though all we have are the poems that men composed for them.

The customer in these poems is not only the courtesan's lover and god but also her king. In early *bhakti*, the god was treated as a king, but Kshetrayya wrote at a time when the distinction between the king in his palace and the god in his temple had blurred to the point of disappearance. The poems thus function on three levels, uniting themes of ancient South Indian secular love poetry with *bhakti* poetry that was already simultaneously theological and royal; sex was a metaphor for religion and politics, and religion a metaphor for sex and politics. We can hear the triple registers in the poems.

Kshetrayya's songs survived among courtesans and were performed by male Brahmin dancers who played female roles.

The poems in this section are translated by A. K. Ramanujan, Velcheru Narayana Rao, and David Shulman. The source is *Kshetrayya Padamulu*.

PRONOUNCING GLOSSARY

Adivaraha: *ah´-dee-vuh-rah´-huh*
Kshetrayya: *kuh-sheht´-rah´-yuh*
Muvva Gopala: *moo´-vuh goh-pah´-luh*

A COURTESAN TO A YOUNG CUSTOMER

The poet, speaking as usual with the voice of a courtesan, addresses the god Vishnu by one of his epithets, Adivaraha, alluding to his incarnation as the Primeval Boar. Only at the end does the courtesan address the customer ("Young man") and accuse him of imitating not Vishnu in his grandiose avatar but Krishna as Muvva Gopala.

You are handsome, aren't you,
Adivaraha,
and quite skilled at it, too.

Stop these foolish games.
You think there are no other men
in these parts?
Asking for me on credit,
Adivaraha?
I told you even then
I won't stand for your lies.

Handsome, aren't you?

Prince of playboys you may be,
but is it fair
to ask me to forget the money?
I earned it, after all,
by spending time with you.
Stop this trickery at once.
Put up the gold you owe me
and then you can talk,
Adivaraha.

Handsome, aren't you?

Young man:
why are you trying to talk big,
as if you were Muvva Gopala?

A COURTESAN TO HER LOVER

Here the poet imagines that he is a woman (a courtesan) who imagines that there is a woman in the bed with her and Muvva Gopala. (In yet another poem, the poet imagines that he is a woman who thinks she is in bed with another woman and is tricked into pretending to be a man—only to discover that the "woman" is in fact a man, none other than Muvva Gopala.) The androgynous lover is the god who assumes all forms; the lover's tricks are clues to the god's cosmic magic.

Who was that woman sleeping
in the space between you and me?
Muvva Gopala, you sly one:
I heard her bangles jingle.

As I would kiss you now and then,
I took her lips into mine,
the lips of that woman fragrant as camphor.
You must have kissed her long.

But when I tasted them,
they were insipid
as the chewed-out fiber
of sugarcane.

Who was that woman?

Thinking it was you, I reached out for a hug.
Those big breasts collided with mine.
That seemed a little strange,
but I didn't make a fuss
lest I hurt you, lord,
and I turned aside.

Who was that woman?

You made love to me first,
and then was it her turn?
Does she come here every day?

A COURTESAN TO HER FRIEND

This poem is an example of a major theme in the worship of Krishna, in North Indian *bhakti* as well as in the South: the abandoning, absent god, imagined as an unfaithful lover. The mood is that of "love in separation" (*viraha*), the intense longing for the unfaithful lover/god who abandons and wounds his faithful beloved/worshipper.

It's so late.
He's not coming,
no way.
No use worrying about him.

Just because you've the misfortune
to be my friend,
you needn't wait up till dawn.
You can throw away
the sandal and the musk
and go to sleep.
Who knows where
he is spending the night,

and with what woman?
The whole village is fast asleep.

It's so late

Listen: every bird
has gone home to his mate.
It's rare we get what we desire.
Still, what was my special sin?

It's so late

All excited,
I made the bedroom ready,
waiting for my man.
What's the point now

A MARRIED WOMAN TO HER LOVER

This poem treats a woman's concern to find a drug or magic potion (both of which were traditionally made out of roots in India) to abort the child that she conceived from her lover—the king, the god, and her customer. Abortion is one of the defining mortal sins in the dharma texts. Here, however, abortion is called for because the god has raped the worshipper, with overtones of the king's power to possess, sexually, any woman in his realm. The mythological possibilities encapsulated in the last two lines—"so, in your image, / I'll bear you a son"—are staggering; the whole mythology of gods fathering human sons (as in the divine lineages of the *Mahabharata* heroes; p. 130) is cast in a different light, for, in the end, the woman intends to bear the child, not to have an abortion after all. Sex, religion, and politics mirror one another through a man's imagination of a woman's imagination of god as customer and the poet's vision of the love of god not as a lofty, abstract sentiment but as caught up in the most intimate, even sordid, of human concerns.

Go find a root or something.
I have no girlfriends here I can trust.

When I swore at you, you didn't listen.
You said all my curses were blessings.
You grabbed me, you bastard,
and had me by force.
I've now missed my period,
and my husband is not in town.

Go find a root or something

I have set myself up for blame.
What's the use of blaming you?
I've even lost my taste for food.
What can I do now?
Go to the midwives and get me a drug
before the women begin to talk.

Go find a root or something

As if he fell from the ceiling,
my husband is suddenly home.
He made love to me last night.
Now I fear no scandal.
All my wishes, Muvva Gopala,
have reached their end,
so, in your image,
I'll bear you a son.

Go find a root or something

Falling at Shiva's Feet and Rama's Feet in Malayalam

1850–1950

Malayalam is a Dravidian language spoken by more than 35 million people, mainly in the state of Kerala and among bilingual communities in parts of Karnataka and Tamil Nadu. The literature in Malayalam flowered later than that of the other Dravidian languages, and there is a sharp distinction between the formal, literary language and colloquial forms of speech. Malayalam evolved either from a western dialect of Tamil or from the source language from which modern Tamil also evolved. The script is derived from scripts used for Sanskrit, with letters to represent the entire corpus of sounds from both Dravidian and Sanskrit. Much of Malayalam literature developed in a style called *manipravalam* ("ruby coral"), a mixture of Malayalam and Sanskrit.

Mahakavi Kumaran Asan (1873–1924), the author of both of the selections here, was a poet from a low caste who grew up in Kerala amid the tension between tradition and modernity, facing the challenges generated by social reform movements during the British colonial rule in Kerala. His poems simultaneously express his love of god,

An eighteenth-century mural showing Shiva and Parvati. The Mattancherry Palace, Cochin.

in the *bhakti* mode, and address social issues associated with the caste system prevalent in the Kerala society of his time.

FEET LIKE LOTUS POWDER

Kumaran Asan's first publication was the *Stotrakritikal* (1901–03), a set of thirteen devotional hymns of praise to Shiva. These poems are deeply rooted in the philosophy of the Upanishads (p. 105; "Theology and/or Philosophy in the *Vedanta*," p. 285), particularly in the interpretation of the philosopher Shankara ("Shankara Dreams," p. 286). *Shivasurabhi*, one of the thirteen poems in this collection, sings of god and for god. The title refers simultaneously to the fragrance (*surabhi*) of Shiva and to the magic wishing cow whom you can milk of whatever you wish for; the cow is named Surabhi. The soul is called "the supreme swan," because swans and geese, like souls, (trans-)migrate. Shiva's "lotus feet" signify *prapatti*, surrendering completely at Shiva's feet, a traditional goal among south Indian *bhakti* saints. The poem expresses the love of god in the details of human life and activity in the modern world.

PRONOUNCING GLOSSARY

Kama: *kah´-muh*

Sarasvati: *suh´-rus´-vuh´-tee*

O feet like lotus powder,[1] even the slightest
thought of leaving you is painful.
Your mercy flows soothing to my ear.
I bow with love, Sarasvati.[2]

The Vedas are unable to explain
what expands beyond a physical state,[3]
the divine light that dispels darkness and shines eternally.
Shiva's feet are like that.

To the wandering ascetics who renounce the world,
you are the sole refuge and essence of the universe.
Inside, outside, you are everything.
Is this not the place of conscious bliss?

"I am the one who in the form of love makes joy.
I am the one that flows like a river of honey."
Your eternal glory cannot be described as something
separate from these qualities, standing apart from them.

The mind awakens from its silence and melts.
The body quivers with fear and trembling.

TRANSLATED BY George Pati.

1. The pollen that falls from lotus flowers, precious and delicate.
2. Goddess of literature, art, and music.
3. That is, without qualities, or *nir-guna* (*Bhagavad Gita*, p. 166).

Take me beyond the source of my being.
Isn't the body said to be destined to perish from birth?

Without attributes, without sign, and formless,
it doesn't have anything, not even a name sweet as ambrosia.
Isn't it said that realization comes through meditation,
the font of knowledge?

You are concerned entirely with the lowly,
as the supreme swan is caught up in fortunate experience,
as the beautiful, cold camphor[4] of the moon melts the heart—
Isn't it said that your silent state is the sweetest?

Wandering among your subjects, without the knowledge that stupefies,
mercifully, in the beautiful ocean of camphor,
my heart, exhausted in grief,
unites with purity, leaving its previous state.

I am sitting in joy, totally unaware of my state.
Why is this a mistake?
My thought flies like a ball or a top.
But aren't you even a little unhappy?

Everywhere sorrow abounds.
The Lord of the universe has no form or name.
How will he remove my suffering and come close to me?
Do not be concerned about this, O my heart.

What I speak of has peace for all and salvation from misery.
It is commonly called the way of refuge for all.
It is a final remedy: Shiva,
the only name for my contemplative mind.

Like a sprig nurtured with water,
or like a withered offshoot that does not decay,
the Ganges[5] rises from the long hair knot of the sovereign Lord.
The comforting moon is also present, my heart!

The sight of your loving lotus feet
removes the misery that arises out of our desires,
burning Kama.[6] The ashes on my forehead,
smeared in smoke, are dear to my heart!

Like Kama on this earth, the wayward enchantress[7]
(before dawn, as everything arises)
arrives, ignorantly showing off,
but my eyes see everything, O my heart!

4. A pale, strong-smelling, slippery substance that Indians apply to the body to cool it; the moon, too, is said to having cooling properties.
5. The Ganges flows through Shiva's hair ("The Descent of the Ganges," p. 258), and the crescent moon rests on his head.
6. The god of erotic desire and pleasure, whom Shiva burned to ashes ("The Origin of *Linga* Worship," p. 235); worshippers of Shiva place ashes on their foreheads, ashes that the poet identifies with the ashes of Kama burned by Shiva.
7. Kama here is like an enchantress who, in her ignorance, shows off his/her beauty, but the eyes of Shiva see Kama, and Shiva's third eye burns Kama to ashes.

You are my sole friend, the reason for everything,
you who protect me compassionately, eternally.
Beloved! So that people can find realization through knowledge,
the flowers of divine words drip the nectar of the Vedas.

SITA LOST IN THOUGHT

Malayalam literature, beginning with the earliest Malayalam work, the epic *Ramacharitam*, from the late twelfth or early thirteenth century, began to rethink the *Ramayana* (p. 186). The theme of Rama's treatment of Sita continues to inspire new thoughts, as in this poem by Kumaran Asan, which refers to two key episodes in Valmiki's version of the story: Rama's father had killed a boy he mistook for an elephant ("Dasharatha Kills a Boy," p. 192), and after Rama abandoned Sita, he created a golden image of her to take her place after she had gone into exile. Sita begins by recalling the loving idyll on the Godavari river but soon falls into sharp, if indirect, recriminations against Rama (his false pride, self-importance, imprudence, and so forth). Then she recoils from such bitterness and justifies Rama's harsh treatment of her, blaming herself for the war in which so many died. Finally, she turns to thoughts of suicide, and Kumaran Asan describes the return of the Rishi (Valmiki) with Rama's summons, and Sita's final flight into the Earth, her mother.

PRONOUNCING GLOSSARY

Godavari: *goh-dah´-vuh-ree*
Kumaran Asan: *koo´-muh-run uh´-sun*
maharshi: *muh-har´-shee*
Rishi: *ree´-shee*

I call to mind how, routine observances over,
I spent my time every day with my beloved
on the banks of the charming Godavari
as his dear mate and dear pupil.

In secret dalliance undreamt of by
any other couple on this earth,
unconscious of our separate selves,
we lived like one being with two bodies.

Swimming about and gathering lotuses,
diving down into the cool depths,
racing with me on the sand-beds,
my beloved then used to frolic like a boy!

Why dilate?—Like animals
endowed with intelligence,
like birds without wings,
we found our happiness in the woods.

TRANSLATED BY Kainikkara M. Kumara Pillai.

O love inborn, unsullied, you are
the brightest gem of the mind's mine;
you are the precious jewel
that the spirit proudly wears on its bosom.

You are the motive force of man's supreme quest,
you are the sum of womanly virtues;
in fact, you turn the arid desert
into a delightful flower garden!

For the righteous your light will rise
like a lamp to lead them up to heaven;
your perversion invariably leads
the unrighteous to perdition.

Even death will not harm you,
O Love, you prevail;
in memory, where the dead abide,
there is daily libation of tears for you!

Not honest anger is your enemy, O Love;
it is false pride that destroys you
by blocking within the heart
the passage of tender communion.

The feeling of equality, the sense of common good
forbearance, esteem for each other's virtues,—
these the rat of inner pride may
steadily, easily eat away.

Affluence, power, fame,
triumphs one after another, sovereignty,—
any man might, on account of these,
develop a sense of self-importance.

With the lamp of love blown out
by the blast of self-conceit,
the mind, misled by the voice of flattery,
might slip into the pitfalls of imprudence.

Otherwise would the king abandon in the woods
his faithful wife, while she was pregnant,
and continue to rule the country
quietly putting up with this calumny?

Hasn't the king valiant brothers
competent to rule the land?
And isn't there room enough in the forest
for him to live along with his life's partner?

Hasn't the king personal experience
of the sinless forest life?

Is not the king well versed
in the lofty ways of spiritual contemplation?

It is hard to say it—Even a scamp
would resent anyone slandering his wife.
How then did the noble king heed as gospel truth
the aspersions made against me?

* * *

Or, maybe, the king gathered reports
through spies in the course of governance;
and treasuring most his high reputation as he does,
he was deeply hurt by this malicious rumor.

He would then have carried out the clear mandate
of the moral valor surging up from the fire
which suddenly burst into flame within:
The man of honor heeds no hazard.

Mindful of a ruler's duty
the king must have felt constrained to do so:
The wise would bear the severance of a limb
to prevent the possible spreading of a poison.

Terrific indeed is the pent-up emotion
of a man of strength:
The whirlpool of the deep
is more frightful than its billows.

One who is self-less will undertake to perform
what at the moment occurs to him as his duty;
and Rama who is truthful will not rest
until he has performed what he promised.

* * *

Thinking that he was aiming at an elephant,
his father summarily arrowed to death the rishi's son;
and after having himself granted the boon
to his favorite wife, died of deep regret.

These were extremely imprudent acts—
Looked at dispassionately,
similar acts are excusable in the son:
the qualities of the source will pass down to the issue.

* * *

There's not the least doubt
the king still loves me and only me;
even if the loneliness of separation afflicts him,
he will not bestow his love on another.

My lord went mad during our first separation,
the passionate lover that he was;

and returning victorious, again gave evidence
day by day of his deep regard for me.

That being the fact, how much more would
he be sorrowing now in this new separation!
Would that remorseful soul be able to brook
this indignity my proud self is suffering?

Alas! by his secret wish, it appears a golden Sita
is to be his partner in the hall of sacrifice!
Inscrutable are the ways of the virtuous,
when you come to think of it.

The course of Justice is terribly painful;
alas! Kings are not their own masters:
my lord exiled me, and in consequence
he has become the worshipper of my statue!

* * *

Under the fierce pressure of convention
the free will of a king might perish:
a bird encaged for long
might forget the power of its wings.

* * *

One might throw away one's crown and go a-begging;
one might give up one's life for another;
it is not easy for one to keep living in order that
one might, without demur, rule the country as others wish!

Even the ascetics admire the great Rama for his
unparallelled self-control and discipline;
he excels the entire kingly order
in his strict observance of a monarch's duties.

* * *

Though endowed with superhuman powers,
Rama is more self-controlled than an ascetic;
that great soul is a radiant moral beacon:
to me an object of esteem in every way.

* * *

Lord, have mercy on your vain-glorious mate!—
pardon me for the blemishes
that in a state of mental disturbance
I discovered just now in you!

Though I am unblemished, my record,
viewed properly, is unworthy:
many a time have I consigned my lord
to great sorrows one after another.

Nay, how many women have, on account of me,
lost their husbands and grieved!
Even so, how many children have suffered,
robbed of their fathers and made destitute!

* * *

Perhaps, after all, I have not to part with
this most delightful world about me;
my body will join the earth,
my spirit will merge into these beauties.

Holy mother Earth, I can see you
going into your glorious chamber
bearing me in your arms
with exceeding parental affection.

I will lie in that bower there, listening
to the paean of peace of the mountain stream;
and the nearby trees and shrubs
will shower on me daily the wealth of their flowers.

High up, flocks of sweet-throated birds
will fly about and sing;
herds of deer will gambol on the meadow
spreading like a shimmering cloud.

Besides, the hoards of fresh gems
and the mineral wealth of the mountainside
will ever give me pleasure—
Nay, all that generally will become mine!

Mother Earth, thus will I luxuriate
in sound slumber on the bed of your lap,—
No, mother, no! I will pay my obeisance to you,
rise and soar aloft.

Like a star that through its reflection in the river
pays homage to the Earth,
I, merged in thy feet, O holy one,
am a light that has risen to the heavens.

Beloved Rama, salutations to you!—
I rise leaving the bough of your arm:
I will fly off into the sky
by myself, undaunted, unaided.

* * *

Forbear!—What?—Does the King intend
that I should again appear before him,
prove my innocence and live as his consort?—
Well, does he take me for a puppet?

O saintly Sage, pardon me!
don't you misunderstand me!—

Alas! neither mind nor spirit will yield;
the body, used to submission, might come.

(Like a girl with her clothes on fire
and body burning in the encircling flames,
she thus struggled with the scorching thoughts
that were fast over-spreading her mind.

* * *

It was near day-break when the maharshi
returned from Kosala with Rama's message.

Head bent and eyes fixed on the lotus feet of the
Rishi who was saying,
"Give up your grief, my daughter; come with me,"
she reached the royal hall, went up to Rama in silence,
and in one glance saw her lord
amidst his people, his face sad with self-reproach;—
and even so she left this world!)

DIASPORA INTERLUDE: HINDUISM IN CAMBODIA, JAVA, AND BALI

By the end of the first millennium C.E., Hinduism was a world religion, thriving in many places outside of India. After the early influence of India on the civilizations of Greece (from long before the time when Alexander the Great dipped his toe into Northwest India and fled back to Greece), Hinduism was carried to Southeast Asia by Indian merchants, then to Central Asia by Turks and Arabs who had established footholds in India, and eventually by the British, who carried Hindu culture with them to all those places where the sun never set on the Empire. To survey this aspect of Hinduism comprehensively, therefore, would mean considering Hinduism in the Caribbean and South Africa, not to mention Edinburgh and Atlanta. Though this anthology cannot do justice to Hinduism as it has been exported throughout the world, we can cast a brief glimpse at one of the first and most enduringly imprinted of the territories to which Hinduism was brought, Southeast Asia.

About the beginning of the Common Era, Indian merchants brought with them to Southeast Asia first the ideas of Brahmins and Buddhist monks and eventually the people themselves. A number of Southeast Asian rulers converted to Hinduism or Buddhism. Chinese chronicles attest to an Indianized kingdom in Vietnam by the second century C.E., and Sanskrit inscriptions testify to the performance of Vedic sacrifices by Brahmins on behalf of local rulers in Borneo by the late fourth century C.E. Hindu texts, theologies, rituals, architectural styles, and forms of social organization were taken up and transformed to fit the Southeast Asian context; Shiva was the Hindu god worshipped most widely, and Vishnu was also a major deity. There was traffic in both directions, as Hindus continued to settle in Southeast Asia and Southeast Asians began to visit India and to bring back elements of Hindu culture, while also leaving their imprint on Hinduism in India. Parts of the *Laws of Manu* (p. 202), brought to Southeast Asia, were transformed into indigenous documents with very different content. Stories from the *Ramayana* and the *Mahabharata* became widely known there and are still popular in local versions.

The Khmer rulers erected enormous temples to Shiva and Vishnu, most famously Angkor Wat, built in the twelfth century in what is now Cambodia; originally consecrated to Vishnu, it was soon converted to (and is still in use as) a Buddhist temple. One of the largest Hindu temples ever built, it contains an enormous bas-relief depicting the churning of the ocean of milk ("The Churning of the Ocean," p. 149).

Three examples from the Southeast Asian diaspora will have to stand for so many more: the Sdok Kak Thom Inscription from 1053, with its references to Hindu gods; the old Javanese "Perfect Knowledge" or *Sang Hyang Naishthika-Jnana*, portions of which probably date to the fourteenth century C.E. or so; and a passage from "The Romance of Arjuna and Ulupi," from eighteenth-century Bali.

THE SDOK KAK THOM INSCRIPTION[1]

Sdok Kak Thom (which can be translated as "Great Lake of Reeds/Herons") is the name of the eleventh-century Khmer temple to Shiva where this inscription was found, near the (present) border between Thailand and Cambodia. The 340-line inscription, from 1053, is in alternating verses of Sanskrit and ancient Khmer, praising twelve Khmer kings from the past two and a half centuries, together with their gurus. We include here a translation of the first forty-eight lines.

The inscription begins with an invocation to Shiva, the three-eyed god, husband of Himalaya's daughter Parvati, and then to Vishnu, the husband of Lakshmi (goddess of fortune). It then tells of King Udayaditya(varman), whose name means "Rising Sun" and who ruled during the eleventh century.

PRONOUNCING GLOSSARY

Bharati: *bah´-ruh-tee´*
Hara: *huh´-ruh*
Hiranyagarbha: *hee-run´-yuh-gar´-buh*
Jayendravarman: *jah-yen´-druh-var´-mun*
Kala: *kah´-luh*
Kali: *kah´-lee*
Kaustubha: *kow´-stoo-buh*
Manava: *mah´-nuh-vuh*
mandara: *mun-dah´-ruh*
Sdok Kak Thom: *suh-dohk´ kahk tohm*
Smara: *smuh´-ruh*
Udayaditya: *oo-duh-yah´-dit-yuh*

Praise be to Shiva! whose nature is proclaimed wordlessly yet thunderously by the subtle soul-life of his body—which reaches throughout the world and quickens the senses of all living beings.

May the benefactor protect the universe, he who through three eyes[2] has a pure and perfect perception of the true nature of the unveiled Atman.[3]

May the creator preserve you—he who bears a vessel of ambrosia, a crystal vessel shining as the moon, the deep source of that nectar-ocean which is his compassion for the worlds.

May Lakshmi's lord preserve you—he on whose breast seated Lakshmi seems to say, "As even those of stable nature need support, so I, of unstable nature, rest here on the Kaustubha[4] jewel."

There was once a sovereign of the world whose feet were clasped by all kings, whose part it was to cause the hearts of men to unfold as lotuses, who dispelled all gloom, and who by reason of his splendor was named Udayaditya.

"Love, whom I brought into being with the wisdom of my supreme briliancy, has become fuel for the fire in Hara's[5] eye." So saying, Brahma[6] (I fancy) with his ambrosia beams made manifest a Smara, whom he raised to sovereign power.

TRANSLATED BY Chhany Sak-Humphrey and Philip N. Jenner.

1. My colleague Professor Vasudha Narayanan brought this inscription to my attention.
2. The three eyes are moon, sun, and fire.
3. The world-soul, *brahman* ("Upanishads," p. 105).
4. A marvelous gem that Vishnu wears on his chest.
5. A name of Shiva, who destroyed Kama ("The Origin of *Linga* Worship," p. 235); Kama is also called Smara ("Remembrance" or "Recollection").
6. The Creator.

"Who am I who like Himalaya's daughter embrace half my gentle lord's body?" So wonders Lakshmi, as if outside herself, as she closely clasps his body, fair as that of love.[7]

Intent to hear from his very mouths this four-mouthed Brahma (whose self, for the world's good, is graced with charity and like royal virtues), the devoted Bharati[8] clings to his side and, taking him for the creator, with him fixes her abode.

His mind was trained in all accomplishments, the arts as well as others. Indeed, it is to count his excellences that the delighted creator still today employs a rosary, the telling of which is but a pretense.

Quick to recognize forbidden women, he would look upon another's wife unlustfully or as poison. Yet did he enjoy in other ways the ever sensual pleasures of those wives of duty: glory, faith, compassion, and steadfastness.

The earth (prey to suffering, exhausted, bewildered, miserable) sought refuge in his royal vigor of gentle brilliance, whereby with peerless activity he restored it to perfect felicity.

The *mandara*[9] of his glory (vast, shading the Three Worlds, covered with praises as with blossoms) sank its roots into the hearts of men as if in fear of cracking the egg of Hiranyagarbha.[1]

As a teacher exhorts his disciples, or a father his children, even so (with eyes fixed on his duty) he strove tirelessly for the protection and prosperity of his subjects.

In battle he bore a glaive[2] red with the blood of enemy kings it had slain, which cast a dazzling light in all directions, like a ravishing red lotus issued from its calyx which by sheer strength of arm he had ripped from the hair of the goddess of war.

In this war-sacrifice his majesty's roaring fire, fed by the fuel of hostile troops, fanned by the wind of his mighty arm, must surely have scorched the earth to such degree that it was compelled to take refuge in the moon's disk in the form of a gazelle.

His lotus-feet proclaimed his affection for his friends, for the host of kings bowing down before him were reflected in the gems of his nails, causing them to enter into him by force of his good-will for their devotion.

Miraculous was this king's potency: his magic power, beyond the range of others, may be judged by a sacrifice he once celebrated which bound Indra and the other gods forevermore.

Vishnu's body was engulfed in the rush of smoke spewing from the fire of his relentlessly celebrated sacrifices, which constantly invaded that god's abode—whence it happens that Vishnu is black to this day.

Having no fear of them, he spared hundreds of proud but distant foes, which kept him not from dispatching lesser pursuers close at hand: the Six Enemies.[3]

7. The king's wife wonders if she is sharing the body of Love (Kama, Smara), just as Parvati occupies half of Shiva's body when he is the androgyne.
8. A name of Sarasvati, the goddess of wisdom and eloquence, wife of Brahma.
9. The coral tree, one of the trees of paradise.
1. "Golden Womb" or "Golden Egg," a name of the god Brahma who produces the world-egg, the cosmos.
2. A three-bladed disk, a weapon.
3. Desire, greed, anger, intoxication, confusion, and jealousy.

How could Vishnu, had he been alert as protector, have slept at ease on the surface of the sea? This king sought to protect men by binding our wounds with the elixir of the wisdom of the Manavas.[4]

He gladdened his realm by his accomplishments. He emitted beams of light marked by mercy. He made lotuses to open. Ravishing, he was rightly hailed with the title of moon.

His glory at sea, ever bright with Kali's[5] burning, cooled his subjects amidst the heat of conflagration. Kala's[6] fire, fearful of having its ardor quenched by his, went into hiding in the deep of the creator's egg.

He had a guru commanding high respect for his understanding: the celebrated *deva*[7] Jayendravarman, born of a high-ranking family of irreproachable name.

His maternal line—the sundry achievements of which had earlier been won by the Sun's descendants without being thereby diminished—was as an earthly embodiment of the Moon for the world's good.

4. Descendants of Manu, the Indian Adam (p. 202); human beings.
5. Strife, or the losing throw of the dice, sometimes personified as the son of Anger and Injury.
6. Time or Death, a name of Shiva.
7. A god, in Sanskrit, but here merely a very high court official.

THE PERFECT KNOWLEDGE[1]

The *Sang Hyang Naishthika-Jnana* ("The Perfect[2] Knowledge") is a short prose text in which Sanskrit verses are explicated in Old Javanese. It is excerpted from a composite text called the *Jnanasiddhanta*, portions of which probably date to about the 14th century C.E.

"The Perfect Knowledge" is a theological discourse on the true nature of the god Shiva, who is given a number of names and epithets: Gauripati (the husband of Gauri, Parvati), Ishvara (the lord), Pashupati (Lord of Beasts), Shivasada (Shiva the Eternal), Sadashiva (the eternal Shiva), and Gayatri (the name of the most sacred hymn of the *Rig Veda* [p. 73]). The text itself glosses other epithets.

PRONOUNCING GLOSSARY

akashavat: *ah´-kah´-shuh-vut*
citta-maya: *chit´-tuh–muh´-yuh*
citta-rahitantya: *chih´-tuh–ruh-hih-tant´-yuh*
citta-virahita: *chit´-tuh–vih-ruh´-hee-tuh*
Gauripati: *gow´-ree-puh´-tee*
Gayatri: *gah´-yuh-tree´*
Ishvara: *eesh´-vuh-ruh*
Mahanatha: *muh-hah´-nah´-tuh*
nirakara: *nih-rah´-kah´-ruh*
Paramarahasya: *puh´-ruh-muh´-ruh-hus´-yuh*
Paramopadesa: *puh´-ruh-moh´-puh-day´-shuh*
Pasupati-Shiva: *puh´-shoo-puh´-tee–shih´-vuh*
Sadashiva: *suh-dah´-shih´-vuh*
Sang Hyang Naishthika-Jnana: *sahng hyahng naish´-tee-ku–nyah´-nuh*
shabda-maya: *shub´-duh–muh´-yuh*

TRANSLATED BY Haryati Soebadio.

1. My colleague Dr. Richard Fox brought this passage to my attention.
2. The term means "complete," but here it also designates a person who passes into the state of Renouncer without passing through the intermediate stage of Householder ("Upanishads," p. 105).

shantyatita: *shahnt´-yuh-tee´-tuh*
Shiva-jnana: *shih´-vuh–nyah´-nuh*
Shiva-karana: *shih´-vuh–kah´-ruh-nuh*
Shiva-tattva: *shih´-vuh–tut´-vuh*
Shivasada: *shih´-vuh sah´-duh*
shubha-shubham: *shoo´-bah–shoo´-bum*
Turya-pada: *toor´-yuh–puh-duh*

Let there be no hindrance.

> The true nature of Shiva[3] (*Shiva-tattva*) is a supreme secret, and the knowledge of Shiva (*Shiva-jnana*) is without compare;
> It is very difficult to comprehend (and) it is certainly the cause of liberation.

The meaning is:
The sacred teacher without equal teaches the divine true nature of Shiva (*San Hyan Shiva-tattva*) in brief in order that the slow may (also) know Lord Shiva. For the true nature of Shiva and the knowledge of Shiva are extremely difficult to comprehend. It is a secret within a secret, impossible to understand for the stupid. It is a difficulty upon a difficulty. That means: the importance of what is called the knowledge of Shiva is unsurpassed. There is nothing equal to it. For it is the cause of Release, for it means the finding of the true nature of Shiva, followed by the attainment of the knowledge of Shiva, (which again) is followed by the oneness of the Lord. In brief: unsurpassed is he who knows that the Lord Shiva is one. Oneness means:

> He, the Holy Shiva is one, the cause of Shiva as the primary cause;
> Shiva is (also) considered as more than one, because his activities are fourfold.

The meaning is:
The Lord's characteristics are oneness and plurality. Oneness means that he is conceived of as being characterized by the true nature of Shiva (*Shiva-tattva*). And he is considered as being one only, not two or three. He has also the cause of Shiva (*Shiva-karana*) as his one characteristic only, without any difference. Plurality means that the Lord is conceived of as having four characteristics. Four (characteristics) means: his characteristics are gross, subtle, supreme and void.

> Gross is said to consist of speech, subtle is said to consist of mind;
> Supreme is emptiness of mind, (and) extreme void is complete emptiness of mind.

The meaning is:
Gross means that the Lord is thought of as manifest in *shabda-maya*. *Shabda-maya* means that he is pronounced in the form of a mystic formula. He is *Gauripati*, he is *Ishvara*. (Then) he penetrates downwards, becoming *Pashupati-Shiva*. He is pronounced, (with) OM as his mystic syllable.

Subtle means that the Lord is thought of as embodied in *citta-maya*. *Citta-maya* means that he is the contents of thought, embodied in knowledge. He is *Shivasada*, he is Gayatri. He penetrates upwards, embodying himself in the Brahma-body. He is the Shiva-body. OM is his mystic syllable.

3. This often designates the final goal of yoga and liberation.

Supreme means that the Lord is thought of as embodied in *citta-virahita*. *Citta-virahita* means: abandoned by mind. Abandoned by mind means giving no hold to thought, (being) silent only. He is Paramasiva, he is exhalation, he is called the Fourth Stage[4] (*Turya-pada*), OM is his mystic syllable.

Void means that the Lord is considered to be *citta-rahitantya*. *Citta-rahitantya* means that the Lord is what is called not having (any) characteristics. Not having characteristics means that thought is empty, the intelligence empty, the teaching empty, the intentions empty. Its idea is isolation, characterized by void(ness). He is *shantyatita*.[5] He surpasses the best verbal expression of reality. He is called the Great King (*Mahanatha*). He is called Lord Shiva.

The teaching concerning him is very comprehensive. Various are the auxiliary texts (used in) teaching the true nature of the Lord Shiva. For numerous are his characteristics, all of them referring to different attributes. But the numerous sacred texts are useless. For what is called a sacred text serves no purpose. And in connection with the Supreme Secret (*Paramarahasya*) the auxiliary teachings are of little use for him who knows it; only one thing, the highest reality is known. What, then, is the reason that it is like that?

> It is not far, it is not near, and it is not in the beginning, the end or the center;
> When leaving the Manifest-Unmanifest, it is seen with the eye of knowledge.

The meaning is:

The Lord's whereabouts is indeed not demonstrable. His place is nonsubstantial. For it is neither far nor near, it has no dwelling in any place in all the quarters of the sky. And further, there is no beginning, center or end of it, it does not belong to the Manifest-Unmanifest (World). Nevertheless, he is visible for him who knows reality through the knowledge which is called the eye.

> It is imperishable and perfect, it is bodiless, it is empty of thought;
> It is invisible, incomparable, it is like the spotless(ness) of the sky.

He is also imperishable and perfect. He is bodiless and has no perception. He cannot be comprehended by the perception valid in this world. He cannot be perceived, indeed, for his appearance causes delusion only, (he is) *akashavat*, like the clear sky that is cloudless, (such) is his metaphor.

> It is endlessly small, difficult to grasp, and therefore insubstantial (?);
> It is supremely limitless, it is the (supreme) authority, the Lord.

And further, the characteristics of the Lord cannot be grasped. For it is subtle, limitlessly small, the end of its smallness is hidden, (for) it has no substance at all. That, then, is its own nature, which therefore is supremely excellent and utterly important. There is nothing which surpasses it. For he is *Sadashiva*, the most powerful in the Manifest-Unmanifest. I know, indeed, that such is his reality. Therefore you should do this:

4. The fourth and highest stage of realization, simply called "the fourth." The other three stages of consciousness, in ascending order, are waking, sleeping with dreaming, and dreamless sleep.

5. The stage that is "past peace," the final stage in the sequence of withdrawal from activity, engagement in activity, knowledge, peace, and the stage past peace.

Having left the Manifest-Unmanifest, one should ward off the eternal and transistory (noneternal);
(Also), the perceptible and imperceptible should be left behind. (That) is called the (sacred) teaching.

That means:
The reality of the Manifest-Unmanifest, leave it. Also the eternal and transistory in the nature of substance, leave it. (What) is perceptible and imperceptible, leave that also. When finally everything is left behind, then you will find what is called the Supreme Instruction (*Paramopadesa*). Thus spoke the Lord.

The formless void should be left behind, (and) the power which is the (consequence of) good and bad (deeds);
The lawful and the unlawful should be left behind, (and also) the darkness of mind.

And do this also: the void without external form, which is called formless (*nirakara*), leave that. The power (acquired) from *shubha-shubham,* evil and good deeds, leave that. The lawful and the unlawful, leave that. The darkness of mind, leave that.

THE ROMANCE OF ARJUNA AND ULUPI[1]

This passage is a narrative interlude from the *kakawin* (epic poem) called *Partha-yana* ("Arjuna's Journey"), which was composed in Bali in the eighteenth century C.E., in Old Javanese, retelling parts of the Sanskrit *Mahabharata* (p. 130). The selection here (cantos 4–7) narrates the episode in which Prince Arjuna (called Phalguna, Dhananjaya, and Partha, the latter a matronymic from Pritha, a name of his mother, Kunti) falls in love with Ulupuy (Sanskrit: Ulupi), a Nagini, a creature that is part cobra (usually from the waist down), part woman (from the waist up), and part demigod. Naginis are beautiful and dangerous, capable of granting love and fabulous jewels to a man they fancy, but also capable of killing. In this story, Ulupi bears Arjuna a son and later saves Arjuna's life on two occasions, once when he is killed by the son of another wife, and Ulupi revives him, and once when he is cursed by the brothers of a man he has slain in battle, and Ulupi redeems him from the curse.

PRONOUNCING GLOSSARY

Arjuna: *ar´-joo-nuh*
ashoka: *ah-shoh´-kuh*
brahmacarya: *brah´-muh-char´-yuh*
Dhananjaya: *duh-nun´-juh-yuh*
Dropadi: *droh´-puh-dee´*
gadung: *guh´-doong*
handul: *hun´-dool*
Hima: *hee´-muh*
Irawan: *ee´-ruh-wun*
Jahnawi: *jah´-nuh-wee´*
jangga: *jung´-guh*
kalpawrksa: *kul´-puh-wuh-rik´-suh*
katirah: *kuh´-tee-ruh*
Korawya: *kor-uh´-wuh-yuh*
madana: *muh´-duh-nun*
Manasija: *muh´-nuh-see´-juh*

TRANSLATED BY Helen Creese.

1. My colleague Dr. Richard Fox gave me this passage and the information about its provenance.

manguneng: *mun´-goo-neng´*
Narada: *nah´-ruh-duh*
Parijata: *puh-ree-jah´-tuh*
Partha: *par´-tuh*
Parthayana: *par´-tuh-yah´-nuh*
Phalguna: *fuhl´-goo-nuh*
priyaka: *pree´-yuh-kuh*
Rati: *ruh´-tee*
shridanta: *shree-dun´-tuh*
Siwa: *sih´-wuh*
Smara: *smuh´-ruh*
Ulupuy: *oo´-loo-poo´-yuh*

Canto 4

Thus Partha came to those sacred waters.
As he immersed himself in the waters of the source of that river, possessed of sanctifying power.
Its full-flowing waters truly cleansed his mind,
As he recited incantations and performed his devotions.

He concentrated his mind on the immaterial presence of Siwa,[2]
Arising from the eight-petaled lotus, and firmly established in the river.
The essence of the sun was invoked into the firmament,
As, absorbed in meditation, he became one in union with the sacred symbol.

A beautiful woman appeared in the presence of the prince.
Her perfection was such that she seemed to be the younger sister of Beauty itself, bringing love.
She was indeed the month of spring, the embodiment of all that is lovely.
Her sweetness held the longed-for charms of the moon.

Clearly she would arouse the bemused poet, wandering in pursuit of beauty, from his reverie.
Like the fall of a fine misty rain, her enchanting hair-knot diffused its fragrance.
Her earrings shone all the while, revealing sudden flashes of lightning,
And the glow of her shining face ever enhanced her radiance.

Partha had now finished his dawn worship,
And his heart seemed to stop as he saw her appear as if from nowhere.
None other than the Goddess of the Hima mountain[3] and the River Jahnawi[4] was she,
And now he became more convinced that she was a vision.

'Where are you bound, little sister? gently he asked,
'In journeying to this mountain, where I travel on pilgrimage to the sacred waters,
I had not thought it would also be the destination of those who wish to abandon themselves to the pursuit of Beauty.
Yet you are a jewel, Beauty itself, my wondrous one.

'How foolish I am, making bold to presume that you could only be properly
Depicted as the riches of a garden offering its beauty:
Your teeth gleam with the allure of *shridanta* flowers,
And [red] *handul* flowers are always as one with your gums.

2. Shiva.
3. Himalaya, father of the goddess Parvati, the wife of Shiva.
4. The Ganges.

'The striking beauty of the *katirah* flower finds refuge in your lips,
And in your eyes rests the dark beauty of the blue lotus.
In your neck is the slenderness of the fresh *jangga* vine, its shoots unfurling,
And I cannot but think, my lady, that the *manguneng* has taken on the form of your lovely hair-band.

'Your slender body is a blossoming *priyaka*.
Your arms put to shame the tendrils of the delightful *ashoka*,
Your calves disturb the fragrant pandanus,
While your full breasts imitate the rounded, ivory coconuts.'

Thus did Partha sing her praises with sweet words.
Understanding his allusion, the maiden said:
'O my Lord! Your perfection indeed exceeds that of mortal men.
For you have come here to this place, where I have never before seen a soul.

'Your mighty deed is great, even incomparable,
You have succeeded in penetrating the inaccessible Hima mountain.
It is the highest degree of excellence, and
You are fitting to be the refuge of those who seek the prosperity of the world.'

Thus she said, soothingly addressing kind and friendly words to him.
And Phalguna, with gentle words respectfully replied:
'Dear maiden, who are you, O beautiful one, who comes here?
Tell me truthfully, great is my concern [for you]!

'Dear maiden, are you, little sister, a goddess in immaterial form?
Because all that is charming waits upon you,
The flowers all seek refuge with you.
Clearly they lie in wait here to scratch you, that you might see how they long to attend upon you.

'Truly the incarnation of the entrancing beauty of the fourth month, are you,
The ethereal deity of the sea of honey in bodily form.
It is as if to seek to express the marvels of the ocean in poetry
Or to ascribe beauty to the mountains, would cause confusion.

'Further, my dear, is it not fruitless for you to stay so pitifully
In this inaccessible, remote place, all alone?
Though you seem undaunted, are you not fearful to stay in these wooded hills,
Where lions, elephants, snakes and tigers lie in wait?'

In this way the prince questioned her closely.
The one addressed so sweetly, answered him truthfully:
'My lord, listen to me, your servant,
I am a woman, called Ulupuy, beset by love.

'I will tell you why I have taken on the form of a woman.
There is a king, His Majesty, Korawya,[5] a renowned and illustrious mighty serpent,
Who alone is so awesome in his power
That his irresistible valor is without equal in the three worlds.

'His kingdom too is of extraordinary, outstanding splendor
Because of the luster of its countless gems and jewels.
Like Indra's heaven, its beauty is without flaw,
And by dint of its very nature, *parijata* and *kalpawrksa* trees grow there.

'Moreover, even heaven is inferior to it, its beauty rivalled
By the unique fashioning of the underworld.
Truly, it is a creation of Lord Brahma himself,
Unparalleled, for he has given his full attention to its creation.

'This then is where the foremost king of the snakes dwells in contentment.
All vassal snakes are loyal to him,
And as for me, I am the daughter of the snake king,
And from time immemorial, I have never known the least sorrow.

Canto 5

'My father has so lavished upon me the quintessence of supreme happiness,
That I found myself unable to take any pleasure in anything, so sated was I by such infinite bliss.
I could not resist searching out the peace of this lonely, secluded place,
But upon reaching here, suddenly I came upon you, seeking union with the god in the River Jahnawi.

'And thus I was smitten by violent passions, wounded by Smara's[6] fiery arrow.
It is only by tasting the flow of your sweetness that my desire and longing can find respite.
For the goddess Rati, Goddess of Love, has so enflamed the feelings of this yearning, lovesick woman,
Who hopes for the excellent ambrosia of your love, for you are the embodiment of the God of Love himself.

'Moreover, could it possibly be fitting for you to live in the forest, staying in the undergrowth in such a pitiable condition,
Eager to conceal yourself, seeking shelter under overhanging rocks, emaciated, unkempt and lackluster?
How can you find enjoyment, resting on a bed of dry, withered, fallen leaves?
Words cannot describe how your body has wasted away, and has lost its strength and become wrinkled from long contact with them.

'In short, my lord, please come with me now to the kingdom of the serpent king and seek

5. Sanskrit Kauravya, a great serpent king.
6. Kama ("The Origin of *Linga* Worship," p. 235), the god of erotic love, is also called Smara ("Memory") and Manasija ("Born in the heart"), and Rati, the goddess of pleasure, is his wife.

To enjoy the happiness that my great devotion will afford you. I beg of you, please accept my offer.
There is no doubt you will be accorded the devotion of all the snakes. Their only wish will be to serve you
With food and refreshments, caring for your every wish, joining with you in sexual union.'

Thus implored Ulupuy, overcome by passion. Partha answered lovingly and sweetly:
'O most excellent jewel among women! My dear! By stealth you have captivated my very heart.
Alas, though the charm of your seductive words cuts me to the quick, cruelly breaking my heart into little pieces,
My dear, I must ask you to accept that I must refuse your love, O little sister.

'For I am now bound by the agreement that Narada[7] has ordained,
To live as a *brahmacarya*,[8] holding to chastity. That is the reason I wander here in the Himalaya, seeking solitude.
Only after twelve years will it end and I must wait until that time has elapsed.
But how it casts me down, now that I, too, am filled with the desire to enjoy sexual union anew.'

Thus Arjuna gave her answer, and again the girl spoke:
'O my lord, you are mistaken in taking so much to heart the words of the seer.
I understand what he meant in urging you to comply with his instruction.
But surely your solemn and abiding vow was intended only to apply to the Lady Dropadi?[9]

'With another, how could it be wrong for you to devote yourself to love-making?
It would not be adultery if you were to accept my words that speak of seeking sensual pleasure.
The purpose of assiduously performing the yoga of love is the prosperity of your lineage,
So that in practicing it and becoming steadfastly absorbed in it, you may achieve the Absolute.'

Canto 6

How could the prince do other than accept her words, seeking to woo him?
He tried to curb his doubts then, for her words, asking to be accepted, rang true.
And so he sanctioned them, receiving them favorably, for they were so meet.
Moreover, their sweetness was without flaw. 'No harm can come of this,' he thought.

7. A meddlesome sage ("The Pandavas Go to Heaven," p. 145).
8. One who has taken a vow of celibacy.
9. Sanskrit Draupadi, Arjuna's wife (*Mahabharata*, p. 130).

And so he decided to follow his desires, as is the nature of hearts that share love.
The prince stood up, made ready, and followed the snake girl.
Through a split in the earth's surface, they took the road to the underworld.
But even as they walked on together, without stopping to rest, he took pleasure in the features of the path that she pointed out to him.

They came to her home, a place where the buildings were of incomparable splendor.
The houses were made of gold and all the gateways and fences were of gold and jewels.
With its adornments radiating a shimmering glow, it looked like an orb of light,
And its dazzling beauty seemed to emanate from heaven.

The world of the gods is made radiant by the sun, that most excellent of brilliant jewels.
It is impossible for it to grow dim there, even when daylight passes and night falls.
As for the underworld, when night comes there, the darkness is diminished,
For there is constant light from the ever-gleaming crystal and jewels.

The snake girl led the prince within,
And presented to him the beauty of the place: its golden encircling walls were indeed perfect.
Beautiful women sat there, like scattered jewels loosened from a string. Sweet were their charms,
Their sideways glances arousing desire, their supple bodies the very embodiment of young boughs.

There were some who drew near, ready to receive him, eager to provide all that is due to a guest,
Sweetly displaying the fire of their natures in their subtle gestures.
Delightfully bespattered with a dusting of flower-pollen, fragrantly perfumed with musk,
Their loveliness was enough to render him speechless, as they seemed to offer their sweetness to his gaze.

There was a pavilion of crystal, its roof a *madana*-lotus of chased gold,
With a wonderful arrangement of flower-shaped adornments, formed of brilliant jewels.
There was, as well, a couch awaiting there, the visible manifestation of a hymn to love.
Its painted cloths were decorated with clusters of rays, so that it seemed to be the moon's secret hide-away.

And so the beautiful girl and the prince mounted the curtained bedstead.
Under the ineluctable force of their love, they found harmony at once, their feelings as one.
Their union there on that lovely couch was full of joy, the essence of sweet delight,

And they seemed the incarnation of the beautiful jasmine, intertwined
with the *gadung*.[1]

Or their union was perhaps that of flower buds seeking to draw near to the
beauty of the river.
Clearly the two on the couch were Rati and Manasija, goddess and god of
Love.
The entwining of their souls in sexual congress formed a temple for the
innermost expression of the art of love.
Suddenly they could no longer resist tasting the welcome delights of love-
making.

Later, when they had been united together in the raptures of love there on
the bed,
Their sudden delight knew no bounds, their very hearts were touched in
their newfound mastery.
Together they came out and sat side by side outside the pavilion,
Where their waiting retinue approached them to wait upon them and offer
them all that had been prepared.

As they sat outside the crystal pavilion it was as if they had descended
from Smara's heaven.
Again and again they partook of the many delicacies of exquisite flavor
that stood ready.
After they had eaten they again withdrew and together climbed onto the
couch,
Tirelessly seeking union there on the bed, never wearying of love-making.

Blissfully, these enamored lovers dallied together there on the couch.
Then, they wandered together out into the garden, wanting to be alone.
Inseparable, they again sought bliss there in the moonlight,
Even resting together on a bed of flowers and leaves.

The joyful harbinger of the fourth month, the thunder, brought the promise
of soft rain.
They wandered here and there, happily stopping from time to time at a
hermitage.
Moreover on the bank of the river that descended into the ravines near the
most inaccessible gullies,
There was a spring where they disported together, constant companions,
taking with them as provisions only their love and desire.

For a long time they lived together in love, delighting in their passion and
love-making,
Adept at devoting themselves to love, ever-willing to surrender to pleasure,
Joyfully tasting the doctrine of love perfected by Dhananjaya,
Striving after union with the deity of love in immaterial form, abandoning
themselves to the delights of bliss.

1. The name of a flower.

Canto 7

For a long time he stayed in the underworld,
And before long an excellent and perfect child was born,
Who was later acknowledged as a hero in battle,
And was called Irawan, the renowned.

The prince had not forgotten
His mission, bearing it constantly in mind,
And so he prepared to set off again,
Gently explaining to his beloved.

He went on his way to other places,
And came finally to the Hima mountain.
Traveling easily wherever he wished, he made his way
Through the many hills and valleys.

VERNACULAR HINDUISM IN NORTH INDIA

800–1900

THE PARADOX OF RELIGIOUS COMPLAINT AND DISSENT

The ideas of the *bhakti* authors from South India inspired, and were in turn inspired by, writers who composed in the North Indian vernaculars derived from Sanskrit: Hindi, Bangla, Marathi, and so forth. Here, too, Islam had become a major force from the time of the Delhi Sultanate in the eleventh century C.E.; later, Turks from Central Asia had established the Mughal Empire (1526–1719), and the presence of Islam in India had a profound effect upon writers in both the North and the South. The first great poet in any of the medieval North Indian dialects was Kabir (1398–1448), who blended Hindu and Muslim themes in a poetry that celebrated a god without qualities (*nir-guna*) whom he called Ram. Kabir was closely followed by three Hindi poets who celebrated a god with qualities (*sa-guna*): Surdas (1483–1563), who sang of Krishna; the woman poet Mirabai (ca. 1498–1547), who also sang of Krishna; and Tulsi Das (1532–1623), whose Hindi version of the *Ramayana*, called the *Ramcharitmanas* ("The Holy Lake of the Acts of Rama"), became the best-known telling of that story.

The most beloved and prolific poet in the early Marathi tradition (in Maharashtra, on the west coast of India) was the daring and free-spirited Tukaram (1608–1649).

Beginning at roughly the same time as early Hindi, the literature in Bangla, the language of Bengal, began to celebrate Krishna. The poets Vidyapati in the fourteenth century, Chandidas in the fifteenth, Govinda-dasa and Balarama-dasa in the sixteenth, and Ramprasad Sen in the eighteenth wrote passionate songs to Krishna. The poet saint Chaitanya (1486–1533) left no writings of his own but inspired an enduring school of Vaishnava theology and poetry centered around Krishna's adventures during childhood and adolescence (his "sport" or *lila*) in the village of Vrindavan (near Mathura). Among the great theologians in the Chaitanya tradition were Rupa Gosvamin (sixteenth century) and Narottama Dasa (seventeenth century). In the early seventeenth century, Krishnadasa Kaviraj composed the most influential of the many hagiographies of Chaitanya, the *Chaitanya-charita* ("Acts of Chaitanya").

Alongside these Krishna traditions, the worship of goddesses grew steadily in Bengal. Several long Bangla poems, called *mangals*, celebrated the goddess Manasa, goddess of snakes; one of the most beautiful is the early seventeenth-century *Manasa Mangal* of Ketaka Dasa. During the period of the British colonial presence in India (1757–1947), Michael Madhusudan Datta published a Bengali version of the *Ramayana* (1861), using it as an allegory for the oppression of India by the British, and the Bengali reformer Ram Mohun Roy published a number of documents on suttee (often called widow-burning) between 1787 and 1818. Another Bengali religious tradition, the Tantric tradition of the Bauls, gave us the poetry of Fakir Lalon

Shah, in the late eighteenth century. There are still Bauls performing in Bengal today.

The Hindu religious literature of this broad period was feisty and defiant, sometimes rebelling against the Brahmins, sometimes against people of other religions (no longer Buddhists and Jains, but now Muslims and eventually Christians), often against the British, and most often against their own gods. Yet this is also a period of rich synthesis of all of these traditions as well as a time of highly original responses to the massive changes brought about by early modern political and economic developments.

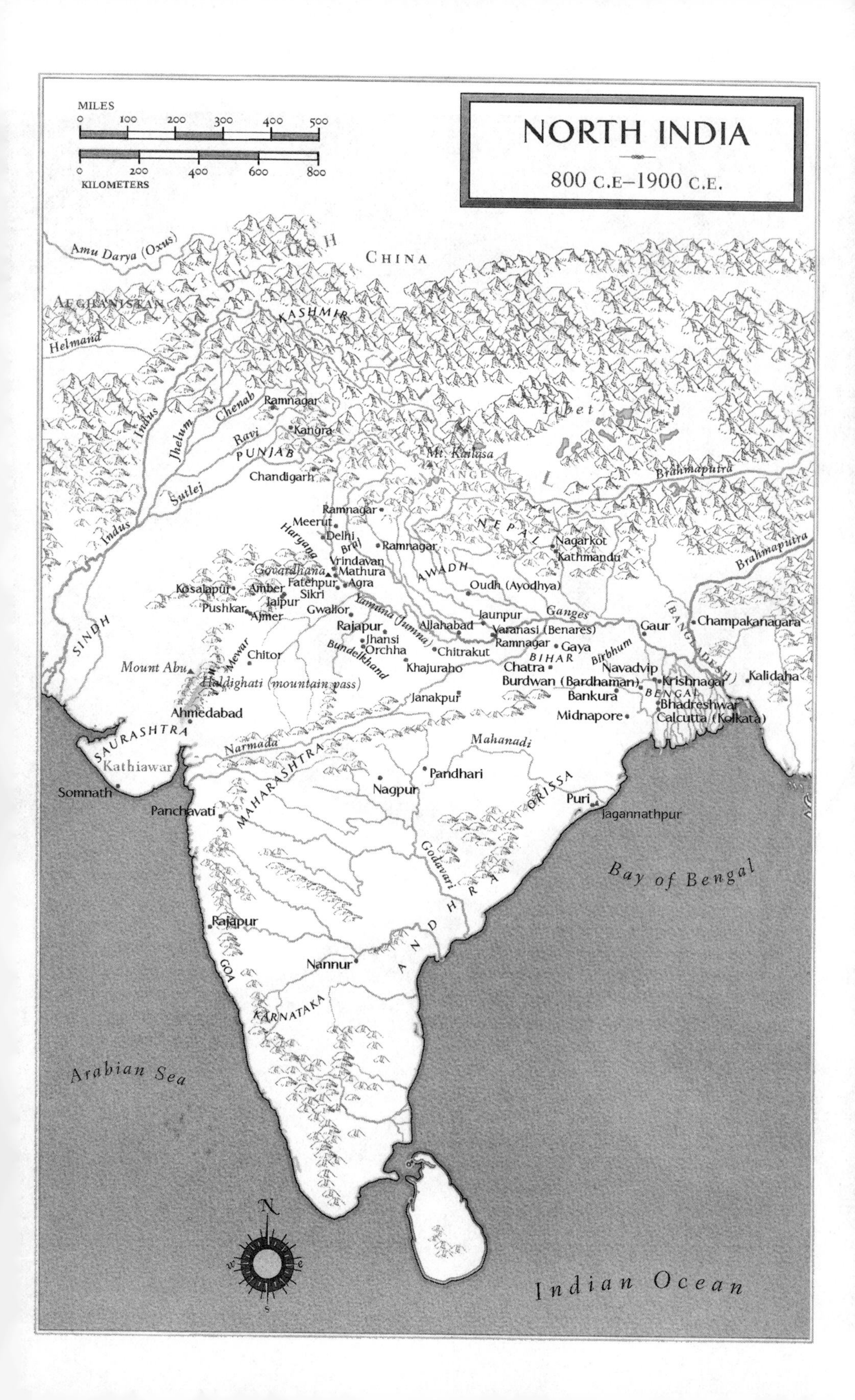

NORTH INDIA
800 C.E–1900 C.E.
MILES
0
100
200
300
400
500
KILOMETERS
0
200
400
600
800
CHINA
Amu Darya (Oxus)
AFGHANISTAN
Helmand
KASHMIR
Indus
Jhelum
Chenab
Ravi
Sutlej
PUNJAB
Ramnagar
Kangra
Chandigarh
Mt. Kailasa
Tibet
Brahmaputra
NEPAL
Nagarkot
Kathmandu
Ramnagar
Meerut
Delhi
Haryana
Braj
Ramnagar
Vrindavan
Govardhana
Mathura
Fatehpur
Agra
Sikri
AWADH
Oudh (Ayodhya)
Kosalapur
Amber
Jaipur
Pushkar
Ajmer
Gwalior
Yamuna (Jumna)
Jaunpur
Ganges
Allahabad
Varanasi (Benares)
Rajapur
Jhansi
Orchha
Bundelkhand
Chitrakut
Ramnagar
Gaya
BIHAR
Birbhum
Gaur
Champakanagara
SINDH
Mewar
Chitor
Mount Abu
Haldighati (mountain pass)
Khajuraho
Chatra
Navadvip
Burdwan (Bardhaman)
Krishnagar
Kalidaha
Bankura
BENGAL
Bhadreshwar
Calcutta (Kolkata)
Midnapore
Janakpur
Ahmedabad
SAURASHTRA
Kathiawar
Narmada
MAHARASHTRA
Mahanadi
Pandhari
Nagpur
ORISSA
Puri
Jagannathpur
Somnath
Panchavati
Godavari
Bay of Bengal
ANDHRA
Rajapur
GOA
Nannur
KARNATAKA
Arabian Sea
Indian Ocean
N
W
E
S

The Emergence of Hindi

Two early forms of Hindi, called Braj Bhasa ("The Language of Braj" [Krishna's town]) and Khari Boli ("Standing Dialect"), began to appear in the seventh century C.E.; Braj was the source of the literary language and Khari Boli the basis for modern standard Hindi and Urdu. Braj persisted as a medium for poetry until the late nineteenth century, while Khari Boli began to be widely used as a literary language after the seventeenth century and has now displaced Braj.

The North Indian *bhakti* Sants (saints) composed their songs in these Hindi dialects. Many of the Sants straddled Hinduism and Islam. Some, notably Kabir, emphasized the abstract aspect of god "without qualities" (*nir-guna*); others, notably Surdas, Mirabai, and Tulsi Das, sang to the god "with qualities" (*sa-guna*) (*Bhagavad Gita*, p. 166). But at all times, any poet who emphasized one aspect was well aware of the other; the interface was where the religious experience took place. *Sa-guna* verse uses detailed, often mundane specifics to convey the immediate personal presence of the god, while *nir-guna* verse also often begins with mundane images—catching fish or bartering with a merchant—but uses them to express more abstract messages of spiritual awareness, yoga, and devotion to the formless form of the god. Surdas and Mirabai were primarily devotees of

The mystic Kabir, born into the low caste of weavers, is portrayed weaving at his loom with two attendants, in this Mughal-style painting from the eighteenth century.

Krishna, while Tulsi Das is devoted to Ram, but each poet also paid homage to the other avatar of Vishnu, and sometimes also to Shiva. Each of them, in a different way, spoke up for women and for the lower castes.

Sanskrit's daughter languages, too, as they came of age, often blended quite casually with their parent, so that, for instance, final short "a"s—preserved in Sanskrit but not usually pronounced in Hindi—appear and disappear to fit the rhythm of the poetry. The verses themselves often refer to the contrast between mother tongues and daughter tongues.

THE *BIJAK* ("SEEDLING") OF KABIR

Kabir, the first of the great Hindi Sants, was born in Varanasi around the beginning of the fifteenth century. His theology, a mixture of Hindu and Muslim concepts as well as a repudiation of both, gave rise to many different stories of his mixed birth, some of which say that he was born into a class of low-caste weavers who had recently converted from Hinduism to Islam, while others insist that he was born a Hindu (sometimes said to be the child of a Brahmin widow) and adopted by Muslims, or that he was born a Muslim and adopted by low-caste weavers who had themselves once been Brahmins. He called his god by many names but particularly by the name of Ram; this Ram is not Sita's Rama, however (*Ramayana*, p. 186), but a god without qualities, whose name, evoking no story, is complete in itself, a *mantra*.

Kabir is widely believed (on scant evidence) to have become one of the disciples of the Hindu saint Ramananda (ca. 1370–1440), who was said to have been a disciple of the philosopher Ramanuja ("Ramanuja Dreams," p. 289) and who preached in Hindi and had many low-caste disciples. Kabir himself preached in the vernacular, insisting that Sanskrit was like water in a well and the language of the people a flowing stream. With the social identity of a Muslim and both the earlier family background and the belief system of a Hindu, he integrated Islam, particularly in the form of Sufi mysticism, into a religion of his own that emphatically distanced itself from both Hinduism and Islam. He once described the two religions, disparagingly, in terms of the animals that Hindus offered to the goddess Kali and Muslims killed at the end of a pilgrimage ("Brother, Where Did Your Two Gods Come From?"). Not surprisingly, both groups attacked him during his life; more surprisingly, both claimed him after his death. Religious affiliation was just window-dressing, as far as Kabir was concerned ("It's a Heavy Confusion").

Kabir challenged the authenticity of the amorphous word "Hindu" in part because it was beginning to assume a more solid shape at this time, precisely in contrast with "Turk" (which stood for Turks, Arabs, and other non-Hindus). He regarded caste as irrelevant to liberation ("Pandit, Look in Your Heart for Knowledge"). Yet Kabir was not a revolutionary in any political or even social sense. Iconoclastic, yes; anti-institutional, to be sure; poor and low in status, definitely—but not concerned about ending poverty. His goal was spiritual rather than economic or political liberation.

Not surprisingly, given Kabir's participation in so many different strands of Indian religion, several religious sects have made important collections of Kabir's works, of which the best known is the *Kabir Granthavali*. But the *Bijak* ("Seedling" or "Map for Hidden Treasure") is the sacred work of the Kabir Panth, the Hindu sect devoted to Kabir, probably formed in the early seventeenth century, several centuries after Kabir's death. Our selections are from this text. All are from the section called "Shabda." The poems are translated by Linda Hess and Shukdeo Singh.

PRONOUNCING GLOSSARY

Bijak: *bee´-juk*
Brahma: *bruh´-muh*
Brahmin: *brah´-min*
Garuda: *guh-roo´-duh*
Hanuman: *huh´-noo-mun*
Hari: *huh´-ree*
Hazrat: *huz´-rut*
Kabir: *kuh-beer´*
Kaliyug: *kah´-lee-yoog´*
Karim: *kuh-reem´*
Keshav: *kay´-shuv*
Khuda: *koo-dah´*
Mahadev: *muh-hah´-dayv*
namaz: *nuh-mahz´*
pandit: *pun´-dit*
puja: *poo´-juh*
Qazi: *kah´-zee*
rajas: *ruh´-jus*
Ram: *rahm*
sattva: *sut´-vuh*
Shiva: *shih´-vuh*
Shudra: *shoo´-druh*
tamas: *tuh´-mus*
Vishnu: *vish´-noo*
Yadav: *yah´-duv*

SAINTS, I'VE SEEN BOTH WAYS

Compassion for animals here underlies a critique, never explicit but always strongly implied, of the ways that Hindus and Muslims treat animals—both in their religious rituals and in their daily diets.

Saints, I've seen both ways.
Hindus and Muslims don't want discipline,
they want tasty food.
The Hindu keeps the eleventh-day fast
eating chestnuts and milk.[1]
He curbs his grain but not his brain
and breaks his fast with meat.
The Turk prays daily, fasts once a year,
and crows "God! God!" like a cock.
What heaven is reserved for people
who kill chickens in the dark?
For kindness and compassion
they've cast out all desire.
One kills with a chop, one lets the blood drop,[2]
in both houses burns the same fire.
Turks and Hindus have one way,
the guru's made it clear.
Don't say Ram, don't say Khuda.[3]
So says Kabir.

1. On the eleventh day of each lunar fortnight, Hindus are supposed to abstain from eating rice, wheat, and other grains.
2. Hindus cut off the sacrificial animal's head quickly; Muslims let the animal bleed to death slowly.
3. Ram is the Hindu god, Khuda a name for the Muslim god.

BROTHER, WHERE DID YOUR TWO GODS COME FROM?

Hinduism and Islam are again, in the end, contrasted in their treatment of animals, but now also in many other ways, particularly in the Babel of names. The various forms of *namaz* (or *namas*, bowing to the god) and *puja* (offering flowers or other small gifts) are arbitrarily sorted into two piles, as are the two forms of gold—not true gold and fool's gold, but the one true gold and the infinite number of ornaments that are made of gold.

Brother, where did your two gods come from?
Tell me, who made you mad?
Ram, Allah, Keshav, Karim, Hari, Hazrat—
so many names.
So many ornaments, all one gold,
it has no double nature.
For conversation we make two—
this *namaz*, that *puja*,
this Mahadev, that Muhammed,
this Brahma, that Adam,
this a Hindu, that a Turk,
but all belong to earth.
Vedas, Korans, all those books,
those Mullas and those Brahmins—
so many names, so many names,
but the pots are all one clay.
Kabir says, nobody can find Ram,
both sides are lost in schisms.
One slaughters goats, one slaughters cows,
they squander their birth in isms.

THAT CON MAN HARI

Kabir uses many names for his god; here he calls him Hari, a common name for Vishnu. He berates the god, as we have seen the South Indian poets do (*The Tevaram of Cuntarar*, p. 315; *Temple Poems from Tirupati*, p. 357), and calls him a "con man." The word *thaga*, in both Hindi and Marathi, found its way into English as "thug," but in India it means a highway robber, trickster, or conjurer, often a worshipper of the goddess Kali, roles impossible to capture in a single English word, though "rogue" comes close. On the metaphysical level, Vishnu's larcenous "conjuring" is nothing less than *maya*, the grand Illusion wrought by god. This conjuring often employs roots, which are used for Indian magic (as mandrakes are in European magic), and the reference also hints at the miraculous magic root that brings the dead back to life. But the Hindi word for "root," *mula* (which gets into Anglo-Indian British slang as "moola," meaning cash—the "root" of all evil), here also means "capital" in the sense of filthy lucre.

That con man Hari has conned the world,
but brother, who can live without him?
Who's whose husband? Who's whose wife?
Death's gaze spreads—untellable story.
Who's whose father? Who's whose son?
Who suffers? Who dies?
With his conjuring he snatches away
your roots. No one can see
Ram's trickery.
Kabir's heart accepts the thief.
Cheating disappears
when you recognize the cheat.

HERE'S HOW THE WORLD FIGHTS AGAINST GOD

This poem uses a kind of upside-down language (*ulat-bamsi*), which can be traced back to the riddles and paradoxes of the *Rig Veda* ("Aditi and the Birth of the Gods," p. 80) and remains popular in *bhakti* poetry, Tantric songs, and folklore. Upside-down language is provocative and impenetrable; it laughs in the face of reason and thumbs its nose at the natural and social order; it is designed to make the listener/reader feel like a fool: no matter what you say, you're wrong. Some of the images, such as the son born of a barren woman, are used in Indian logic; Vedantic philosophy ("The Man Who Built a House of Air," p. 292) uses them to express the paradoxes of *maya* (Illusion).

Here's how the world fights against God:
as a snake grabs Garuda,[1]
a mouse loves a cat,
or jackals strike lions.
What a wonderful world,
where dogs conquer elephants!
Kabir says, listen seekers, brothers:
a rare person
makes the connection.

1. The eagle, said to kill snakes, on which Vishnu rides.

THE PANDITS' PEDANTRIES ARE LIES

Elsewhere, Kabir praises the use of names, particularly the name of Ram, as a path to god, but here he uses words to demonstrate how useless words are in the face of the search for god. The mockery of banishing hunger by saying words also resonates with the much-cited Materialist satire on Vedic religion, which mocks the ceremony in which male descendants "feed" the ancestors at the funeral ceremony ("How to Perform a Funeral," p. 213); the Materialists argued that if you could do this, no one need take food along on a journey; the people at home could just eat for them as they did for the ancestors. "Pandit" in Sanskrit or Hindi means a learned man, or Sanskrit scholar, more respectful than its English form ("pundit").

The pandits' pedantries are lies.

If saying Ram gave liberation
saying candy made your mouth sweet
saying fire burned your feet,[1]
saying water quenched your thirst,
saying food banished hunger,
the whole world would be free.

The parrot gabbles "God" like a man
but doesn't know God's glory.
When he flies off to the jungle,
he'll forget God.
If you don't see, if you don't touch,
what's the use of the name?

If saying money made you rich,
nobody would be poor.

Lovers of lust and delusion
laugh at the lovers of God.

Kabir says, worship the one Ram,
or you'll go, trussed up, to Death City.

1. This line seems to follow a different logic than the others and may refer to the practice of walking on coals as a religious vow or to affirm a statement of truth.

PANDIT, LOOK IN YOUR HEART FOR KNOWLEDGE

The word *ghat* stands both for the body and for a clay pot. Both are porous and therefore impure; clay food pots are thrown away after a single use, as is, of course, the body, made of red flesh and blood and white bone and sinew. Potters, too, are regarded as impure, and the poem mocks the caste law that makes them literally un-touch-able. The challenge is to the pandits, who normally look to their texts for answers, to find new answers—or, in this case, new questions—in their hearts.

Pandit, look in your heart for knowledge.
Tell me where untouchability
came from, since you believe in it.
Mix red juice, white juice and air—
a body bakes in a body.
As soon as the eight lotuses[1]
are ready, it comes
into the world. Then what's
untouchable?
Eighty-four hundred thousand vessels
decay into dust, while the potter
keeps slapping clay
on the wheel, and with a touch
cuts each one off.[2]
We eat by touching, we wash
by touching, from a touch
the world was born.
So who's untouched? asks Kabir.
Only she
who's free from delusion.

1. The eight chakras or discs that are the basis of spiritual energy ("Tantric Points in the Body," p. 276).

2. The potter metaphorically beheads the cups; "neck-cutters" is a term of abuse for potters.

THINK, PANDIT, FIGURE IT OUT

The deconstruction of gender sets off a chain of further deconstructions, beginning with class, caste, and religion. Now the metaphor of a son of a barren woman becomes a social rather than logical paradox: an unmarried mother defies her in-laws and refuses to sleep with her husband, just as Mahadeviyakka was said to do ("Husband Inside," p. 348). The Kali Age ("The Whirling Age of Kali Ends," p. 312) is invoked more to epitomize than to justify this topsy-turvy behavior, which here characterizes the person with true understanding in any age.

Think, pandit, figure it out:
male or female?
In a Brahmin's house she's Mrs. Brahmin,
in a yogi's she's a disciple.
Reading the Koran she's a Turkish lady.

In Kaliyug she lives alone.
She doesn't choose a husband,
doesn't get married,
but has sons.
Not a single black-haired fellow escapes her,
but she's a permanent virgin.
She stays with her mother,
doesn't join her in-laws,
won't sleep with her husband.
Kabir says, he lives from age to age
who drops his family, caste and race.

HEY PANDITS, WHO DIDN'T DIE?

The Hindu gods live a very long time—different texts give different estimates—but not forever. Hanuman, the monkey ally of Rama, who built the causeway to Lanka for Rama's armies to cross over, is said to live as long as people recite the *Ramayana*.

Hey pandits, who didn't die?
If you find out, tell me.

Brahma, Vishnu and Shiva died,
Parvati's son Ganesha died,
so many suns and moons died,
Hanuman the bridgebuilder died,
Krishna died, the maker died.
One, the Original, didn't die.

No fall, no rise.
Kabir says, that one never dies.

PANDIT, THINK BEFORE YOU DRINK

The following comment on this poem by the translator, Linda Hess, says all that needs to be said:

> Water is the central image in this poem, which, like [the poem, "Pandit, look in your heart for knowledge"], attacks the delusion of untouchability. In the largest sense the water is the stream of life or world-ocean in which all are immersed. There are also references to an actual river, perhaps the Ganga [Ganges] at Varanasi where Kabir lived. Hindus drink Ganga water in the conviction that it is holy and incorruptible, despite the fact that many dead bodies are thrown into

the river, sewage is dumped there, and it is generally seething with the materials of life and death. Cow milk is also considered holy and pure. Nowhere are these beliefs ascribed to more generally than in Varanasi, the ancient pilgrimage center and bastion of orthodox Hinduism. The "house of clay" near the beginning of the poem is the pandit's body. The clay near the end can refer either to the impure clay cup or to the bodies of so-called untouchables.

Pandit, think
before you drink
that water.
That house of clay you're sitting in—
all creation is pouring through it.
Fifty-five million Yadavs[1] soaked there,
and eighty-eight thousand sages.
At every step a prophet is buried.
All their clay has rotted.
Fish, turtles and crocodiles
hatched there. The water is thick
with blood. Hell flows
along that river, with
rotten men and beasts.
Trickling through bones, melting through flesh—
where does milk come from?
That's what you drink after lunch, pandit.
And you call clay untouchable?
Throw out your holy scriptures, pandit,
those fantasies of your mind.
Kabir says, listen, Brahmin:
All this
is your own doing.

1. The Yadavs are a large North Indian caste, originally kings, then cowherds, and now generally classified as members of the lowest of the four classes.

SHE WENT WITH HER HUSBAND

On one level, this poem is the story of a human tragedy: a young girl is widowed on her wedding day, before the "real marriage," the consummation, takes place. On another level, Kabir reminds us that all marriages end in death and the only "real marriage" is with god.

She went with her husband to the in-laws' house
but didn't sleep with him,
didn't enjoy him.
Her youth slipped away like a dream.

Four met and fixed the marriage date,
five came and fixed the canopy,
girlfriends sang the wedding songs
and rubbed on her brow the yellow paste[1]
of joy and sorrow.
Through many forms her mind turned
as she circled the fire.
The knot was tied, the pledge was made,
the married women poured the water.
Yet with her husband on the wedding square[2]
she became a widow.
She left her marriage without the groom.
On the road the father-in-law explained.
Kabir says, I'm off to my real marriage now.
I'll play the trumpet
when I cross with my lord.

1. Turmeric is traditionally rubbed on the bodies of the bride and groom.

2. An area on the ground marked out with rice powder for a religious ritual.

BEAST-MEAT AND MAN-MEAT

Folk songs appear throughout the Kabir corpus, marked, as this poem is, by strong rhythm and rhyme. There are also echoes of the ancient Hindu belief that the animals that you eat in this world eat you in the other world ("Bhrigu's Journey in the Other World," p. 101) or in another life ("To Eat or Not to Eat Meat," p. 203; "Retribution in Rebirth," p. 206). The statement that jackals will not eat human flesh may be an instance of upside-down language, since throughout Indian literature jackals inhabit the cremation grounds and feast on corpses.

Beast-meat and man-meat are the same,
    both have blood that's red, sir.
Men eat beasts, but even jackals
    shun a man that's dead, sir.
The potter Brahma shaped the earth;
    death, birth—where do things pass, sir?
But you eat animals and fish
    as if they grew like grass, sir.
For gods and goddesses of clay
    you slaughter a living beast, sir.
If your god's real, why can't he go
    to the field and have his feast, sir?
Kabir says, saint, say Ram, Ram,
    and Ram and Ram again, sir.
The things men eat to please their tongues
    come back to eat the men, sir.

IT'S A HEAVY CONFUSION

The usual dichotomies of gender, caste, class, and religion are challenged here, now supplemented by an ingenious equation of the Hindu trinity ("The Origin of *Linga* Worship," p. 235) with the three elements of matter ("The Two Paths," p. 178): *sattva* (lucidity) for Vishnu, *rajas* (passion) for Brahma, and *tamas* (darkness) for Shiva.

It's a heavy confusion.
Veda, Koran, holiness, hell, woman, man,
a clay pot shot with air and sperm . . .
When the pot falls apart, what do you call it?
Numskull! You've missed the point.
It's all one skin and bone, one piss and shit,
one blood, one meat.
From one drop, a universe.
Who's Brahmin? Who's Shudra?
Brahma *rajas*, Shiva *tamas*, Vishnu *sattva* . . .
Kabir says, plunge into Ram!
There: No Hindu. No Turk.

THE SELF FORGETS ITSELF

The monkey is trapped when the trapper puts food into a narrow-mouthed container; the monkey cannot withdraw his fist with the food in it but will not let go. Parrots think they are safe when they are on a high branch or pole; the trapper simply carries off the entire pole.

The self forgets itself
as a frantic dog in a glass temple
barks himself to death;
as a lion, seeing a form in the well,
leaps on the image;
as a rutting elephant sticks his tusk
in a crystal boulder.
The monkey has his fistful of sweets
and won't let go. So
from house to house
he gibbers.
Kabir says, parrot-on-a-pole:
who has caught you?

QAZI, WHAT BOOK ARE YOU LECTURING ON?

The Qazi is a Muslim official who preaches and presides over ceremonies. Circumcision is the ceremony that marks the entrance of a Muslim male into the community. Under the rule of certain Muslims, some Hindus were forced to convert to Islam and undergo circumcision. The Hindu equivalent is the initiation ceremony, a ritual of second birth that makes the male within the first three of the four Hindu classes or *varnas*—the Brahmins, Kshatriyas, and Vaishyas—"twice-born" ("Hymn of the Primeval Man," p. 82). Since this ritual is denied to the fourth class, the Shudras, a Shudra's touch would pollute the food of the other three classes.

Qazi, what book are you lecturing on?
Yak yak yak, day and night.
You never had an original thought.
Feeling your power, you circumcise—
I can't go along with that, brother.
If your God favored circumcision,
why didn't you come out cut?
If circumcision makes you a Muslim,
what do you call your women?
Since women are called man's other half,
you might as well be Hindus.
If putting on the thread makes you Brahmin,
what does the wife put on?
That Shudra's touching your food, pandit!
How can you eat it?
Hindu, Muslim—where did they come from?
Who started this road?
Look hard in your heart, send out scouts:
where is heaven?
Now you get your way by force,
but when it's time for dying,
without Ram's refuge, says Kabir,
brother, you'll go out crying.

SURDAS

The life history of Surdas (or Sur) is clouded by the mists of hagiography. He lived in North India, probably sometime between 1483 and 1563. One tradition insists that he was blind from birth, another that he became blind later in life; his "inner eye" is sometimes said to have been opened when he met the sixteenth-century theologian Vallabha (or Vallabhacharya, 1479–1531), though scholars regard this meeting as unlikely. What we do know is that his great work, "Sur's Ocean" (*Sur Sagar*), became foundational for the community that traces its lineage back to Vallabha. Sur's devotion to Krishna is exclusive and intense, contrasting the sweetness of Krishna's *lila* (his "play" on earth, which we mistake for reality)—particularly the *lila* of the child Krishna—with the meditation of yogis, whom Kabir and Mirabai admired but Sur rejected.

The poems in this section are translated by John Stratton Hawley and Mark Juergensmeyer.

PRONOUNCING GLOSSARY

Braj: *bruj*
cakor: *chuh´-kor*
Gopal: *goh´-pahl*
Hari: *huh´-ree*
Jumna: *joom´-nah*
kadamb: *kuh´-dum*
Kama: *kah´-muh*
Kanh: *kahn*
Kans: *kuhns*
Kesi: *kay´-shee*
Madhav: *mah´-duv*
Nandanandan: *nun-dah´-nun-dun*
Narad: *nah´-rud*
Purana: *poo-rah´-nuh*
Radha: *rah´-dah*
Sanak: *suh´-nuk*
sravan: *shrah´-vun*
Suk: *sook*
Sur: *soor*
Surdas: *soor´-dahs*
Sur Sagar: *soor´ sah´-gur*
Syam: *shyahm*
Udho: *oo´-doh*
Yadu: *yuh´-doo*
Yashoda: *yuh´-sho-dah´*

IF YOU DRINK THE MILK

The speaker here is Yashoda, the foster mother of Krishna ("Krishna's Mother Looks Inside His Mouth," p. 250); Krishna here is called Gopal ("cowherd"). Trying to get Krishna to drink his milk, Yashoda argues that the milk of the black cow will give him more black hair and more strength. And she warns him that he will need that strength to fight the enemies that he will meet when he grows up: Kamsa (the wicked uncle who keeps trying to kill him), Keshin (a demonic horse), and a monstrous crane.

"If you drink the milk of the black cow, Gopal,
you'll see your black braid grow.
Little son, listen, among all the little boys
you'll be the finest, most splendid one.
Look at the other lads in Braj and see:
it's milk that brought them their strength.
So drink: the fires daily burn in the bellies
of your foes—Kans and Kesi and the crane."
He takes a little bit and tugs his hair a little bit
to see if his mother's telling lies.
Sur says, Yashoda looks at his face and laughs
when he tries to coax his curls beyond his ear.

FAR OFF AND FURTIVE

Here the speaker is a *gopi* (cowherd woman), who calls another *gopi*'s attention to Krishna (called Syam, "the dark one"), playing with butter, as he often, naughtily, does. His hands are like lotuses and his face like the moon, though the moon is usually the enemy of lotuses, which bloom only by day. He feeds butter to his friends—throwing butter balls sometimes to the other cowherd boys, sometimes to the monkeys.

"Far off and furtive, Gopal's in the butter.
Look, my friend, what a bright shimmer streams
from the dusk-toned body of Syam,
With drop after drop that was churned from curd
trickling down his face to his chest
As if the far ambrosial moon
rained beams on loves below.
His hand lends grace to the face beside it
and flashes forth as if
The lotus had dropped its feud with the moon
and come forth bearing gifts.
Look how he's risen to peer from his lair,
to look around on every side;
With wary eye he scans the scene and then
he cheerfully feeds his friends."
Seeing Sur's Lord in his boyish fun,
the maidens start, love-struck and weakened,
Until their hearts are lost to speech
in thought after thought after thought.

LOOK, MY FRIEND

Again one cowherd girl speaks to another, describing Krishna as Hari, "the Remover," who takes away the worshipper's troubles but also steals the hearts of women. The deer who pull the chariot of the moon here become Krishna's eyes, harnessed by his eyebrows to his moon face.

Look, my friend, look at Hari's nimble eyes.
How could the shimmer of lotuses and fish,
 even of darting wagtails,
  compare in charm with this?
When for a brilliant blink of time his hands
 and face and eyes bow down to the flute—
  they all become as one—
It seems the lotus no longer wars with the moon:
 together they sound a note to soothe
  those lunar steeds, the deer.
Look at that beauty: slender, mind-entrancing curls,
 how they ramble uncontrolled
  over eyebrows just below
And startle the deer, it seems: they flee their chariot
 till the moon with a tremor of worry
  moves to tighten its reins, the brows.
Hari is a mirroring, the image of all desire;
 for him the women of Braj are offering
  their wealth—that is, their life.
They look with loss and longing at the face of Sur's Dark Lord.
 With him to fill their thoughts, their minds
  have nowhere else to roam.

SHE'S FOUND HIM

Radha is Krishna's particular beloved among the cowherd women. Her doubt—about whether she is awake or dreaming, and whether Krishna loves her or someone else—is both theological and erotic.

She's found him, she has, but Radha disbelieves
That it's true, what she sees when her eyes behold
 her master's moonlike face.
Her gaze is fixed, but her mind is glazed;
 her eyes refuse to close;
And her intellect wages a raging debate:
 Is it a dream? Or is this her true Lord?

Her eyes fill and fill with beauty's high pleasure,
then hide it away in her breast:
Like bees driven wild by any distance from honey
they dart back and forth from the hoard to the source.
Sometimes she musters her thoughts; she wonders:
"Who does he love? Who can this Hari be?"
For love, says Sur, is an awkward thing.
It ripples the mind with waves.

RADHA IS LOST

As Radha searches for Krishna (here called "the Joy of the Yadus," a reference to his descent from King Yadu, ancestor of the Yadavs), the creatures of the forest mistake parts of her body for natural elements: her braid a snake, her feet lotuses, her voice the call of the cuckoo, her fingers young sprouts, her tears moonbeams (on which the *cakor* bird is said to feed), and her love a newborn child.

Radha is lost to the onslaught of love.
She weeps from tree to tree and finally succumbs,
searching through the forests and groves.
Her braid—a peacock grasps it, thinking it a snake;
her lotus feet attract the bees;
The honey of her voice makes the crow in the *kadamb* tree
caw, caw to mimic its cuckoo;
Her hands—the tender leaves of blossom-bringing Spring:
the parrot, when he sees, comes near to taste;
And the full moon in her face inspires the *cakor* bird
to drink the water washing from her eyes.
Her despair, her desperation—the Joy of the Yadus sees it
and appears at her side just in time;
Surdas's Lord takes that seedbud of new birth
and cradles it, a newborn in his arms.

WITH LOVE THERE'S NEVER A THOUGHT

The animals die for love. The deer are attracted to music and so become prey for the hunter. The cuckoo, thirsting for love even in the season of rains, cries out all night, as does the woman who loves Krishna.

With love there's never a thought that one might die.
With love the moth can be drawn into the flame
and never flinch from the fire.

With love the turtle dove will mount the skies
and dive to earth with no care for its life.
With love the deer lusts for sound, and draws so near
it's doomed to the hunter's arrow.
The thirsty cuckoo, in the rainy month of *sravan*,[1]
coos love, coos love—she shouts it out,
For what, says Surdas, does she have to fear?
A lonely woman speaks for herself.

1. *Sravan*, from late July to late August, is a month of monsoon rains.

BLACK STORM CLOUDS

Radha, or another of the cowherd women, describes the monsoon storm, both a metaphor for human passions and the practical opportunity to indulge them, since the rainy season makes travel difficult, and people stay home and make love. Krishna is here called Kanh (a diminutive of Krishna) and Syam (the Dark One). Kama, the god of erotic love ("The Origin of *Linga* Worship," p. 235), wields a bow that is analogized to the rainbow weapon of Indra, god of rain.

Black storm clouds have risen in the sky
and herons in an eerie row.
Please, Kanh, look: a rainbow—such beauty!—
bearer of all colors,
bow for the arrows of the gods.
Lightning flashes forth and strikes here and there
like an eager, restless woman
Whose husband, the rogue, is at every other house:
now she has the chance to range about herself,
ignited by the God of Love.
Peacocks and cuckoos cry out in the woods
and trees dispatch their messenger girls—the vines—
To find their loves, but it seems love's longing
has so impassioned the vines and angered them
that they break their vows, what they promised to do,
And mate with every tree they meet
in a network of darkened groves.
Kama, the expert, awakens to the wish
of Sur's dark Syam: he lifts his own hand
to decorate a bower as a home.

GOPAL HAS SLIPPED IN

Krishna is older now, and he steals not butter but the reputation and character of the cowherd women who fall for him.

Gopal has slipped in and stolen my heart, friend.
He stole through my eyes and invaded my breast
  simply by looking—who knows how he did it?—
Even though parents and husband and all
  crowded the courtyard and filled my world.
The door was protected by all that was proper;
  not a corner, nothing, was left without a guard.
Decency, prudence, respect for the family—
  these three were locks and I hid the keys.
The sturdiest doors were my eyelid gates—
  to enter through them was a passage impossible—
And secure in my heart, a mountainous treasure:
  insight, intelligence, fortitude, wit.
And then, says Sur, he'd stolen it—
  with a thought and a laugh and a look—
    and my body was scorched with remorse.

THOUGHTS OF HIM STALK ME

Radha is the speaker, and Krishna here is called Nandanandan, "Delighter of Nanda" (Krishna's stepfather). This poem is in the genre of love in separation (*viraha*) ("I Placed Before Him," p. 320). A frequent player in this scenario is the sheldrake (*chakravaka* or *cakai*), a waterbird that is separated from its mate every evening and cries out to the absent beloved across the water all night long. The final water image is taken from Indian philosophy, where the mind at rest is a pool with no ripples, while the mind disturbed by emotion blurs the sharp image of the true self.

Thoughts of him stalk me, even in my dreams,
Now that he has gone; and oh, my friend, it hurts
  as hard as on the day that Nandanandan left.
Last night, in fact, that cowherd came to my house:
  he laughed his laugh and grasped me by the arm.
What am I to do? The night is now my foe.
  Will I ever know another wink of sleep?
I've become like a sheldrake who sees her own reflection,
  takes it as the gladdening image of her mate,
And then, says Sur, that menacing Creator
  masquerades as wind and brings ripples to the lake.

EVER SINCE YOUR NAME HAS ENTERED

A friend speaks on behalf of Krishna (Hari) to Radha, who is angry with Krishna, presumably because of one of his notorious episodes of infidelity. The friend paints a picture of Krishna as a lover suffering in separation, who goes through the motions of a yogi, fasting, chaste, and constantly meditating—on Radha.

Ever since your name has entered Hari's ear
It's been "Radha, oh Radha," an infinite mantra,
a formula chanted to a secret string of beads.
Nightly he sits by the Jumna,[1] in a grove
far from his friends and his happiness and home.
He yearns for you. He has turned into a yogi:
constantly wakeful, whatever the hour.
Sometimes he spreads himself a bed of tender leaves;
sometimes he recites your treasurehouse of fames;
Sometimes he pledges silence: he closes his eyes
and meditates on every pleasure of your frame—
His eyes the invocation, his heart the oblation,
his mutterings the food to feed
the priests who tend the fire.
So has Syam's whole body wasted away.
Says Sur, let him see you. Fulfill his desire.

1. The river Yamuna, which flows through Krishna's village.

HAVING SEEN HARI'S FACE

Here the metaphor of yoga is more fully developed and applied not to Krishna (Hari) but to the cowherd women, who complain to Krishna's friend Udho, and whose sufferings in Krishna's absence mimic the physical regimen of yogis, or of naked Jain monks (Digamabara, "clad with the sky"): their pupils are fixed, and they go through the yogis' rituals and motions of dying.

Having seen Hari's face, our eyes are opened wide.
Forgetting to blink, our pupils are naked
like those who are clad with the sky.
They've shaved their Brahmin braids—their in-laws' teachings,
burned up the sacred thread of decorum,
And left their veils—their homes—to mumble exposed
through the forests, day and night, down the roads
In simple concentration—their ascetic's death:
beauty makes them vow their eyes will never waver,
And anyone who tries to hinder them—husbands,

cousins, fathers—fails.
So Udho, though your words touch our hearts
and we understand them all, says Sur,
What are we to do? Our eyes are fixed.
They refuse to be moved by what we say.

MADHAV, PLEASE, CONTROL THAT COW

Madhav, a name of Krishna the cowherd, is sometimes said to mean "one who controls [*dhav*] Illusion [*maya*]." Illusion in this poem takes the form of a cow, an unusual assertion in light of the Hindu reverence for cows; more typically, dharma is represented as a cow who goes on four legs in the Winning Age (the first age), three in the second, two in the third, and finally, in this Losing Age (the Kali Yuga), one leg ("The Four Ages," p. 228). Here, however, the cow represents the sensuality of *maya* and indeed of life itself. She wreaks havoc on the Vedas (*Rig Veda*, p. 73), the eighteen Puranas ("Puranas," p. 223), and generally eats all the forbidden foods, with an omnivorous appetite that Hindus more often attribute to dogs ("The Dog Who Would Be Lion," p. 158), goats, or pigs than to cows. She ranges through the fourteen worlds—seven below the earth and seven above—and combines the three colors of matter: black (here, dark blue), red, and white ("The Two Paths," p. 178). She eludes divine sages like Narad, Sanak, and Suk. Sur cannot control this unruly creature, and the poet implies that even Madhav may not be able to manage her.

Madhav, please, control that cow.
Night and day she wanders over paths that aren't paths,
too elusive to be caught,
And hungry, so hungry—why can nothing fill her?
She's stripped the Veda-tree of all its leaves.
From the eighteen vases she's drunk Purana-water
and still there's no slaking her thirst.
Place the six kinds of taste before her
and she'll sniff around for more,
Eating what's unhealthy, food she shouldn't touch,
things the tongue can scarcely describe.
Oceans, mountains, forests, heaven and earth—
she forages through them all. They're not enough.
So every day she tramples down the fields of fourteen worlds
and even there she cannot be contained.
Her hoofs are dark blue; her belly, brilliant red;
her horns, a satisfying white;
So when she does battle with the three-colored world
this threefold beast has nothing to fear:
She subjugates the demons with the power of hooves and heart
and she tosses the gods off the top of her head,
Whose face and eyebrows are artfully shaped:
as she roams about she captivates the mind.

Narad and the rest, and Sanak, Suk, and so forth—
they've wearied themselves to no avail,
So tell me, says Sur, how a bumbling fool like me
can ever hope to herd someone like her?

MIRABAI

Many of the Hindi Sants, such as Kabir the weaver, were both low-caste and rural. But not all *bhaktas* were of low caste; Guru Nanak (who founded Sikhism) was a Kshatriya (a member of the second of the four classes, the ruling, warrior class), and Mirabai was a Kshatriya princess. Mirabai (or Mira) lived sometime between 1450/1498 and 1525/1547. According to the earliest version of her life story, she was forced to marry a king's son but preferred the company of wandering mendicants and devotees of Krishna; the king (either her husband or her father-in-law—it differs in different stories) tried, in vain, to kill her; she left her marriage to join the devotees of Krishna. In later tellings, however (including the Amar Chitra Katha comic book, India's version of Classic Comics), it is her husband's brother who tries to kill her; her husband conveniently dies soon after the marriage, yet Mirabai is depicted as "an ideal Hindu wife." Although her poems are the most quoted, her life story the best known, of all the North Indian saints, few of her poems were anthologized in her time. Perhaps this is because her poems mock both marriage and asceticism, leaving her few allies.

The poems in this section are translated by John Stratton Hawley and Mark Juergensmeyer. All are taken from the edition of Parashuram Chaturvedi, *Mirabai ka Pavavali* (Allahabad: Hindi Sahitya Sammelan, 1973).

PRONOUNCING GLOSSARY

Bhil: *beel*
Braj: *bruj*
Gokul: *goh´-kool*
Hari: *huh´-ree*
Mira: *mee´-rah*
Mirabai: *mee´-rah-bai´*
Ram: *rahm*
rana: *rah´-nuh*
Shiva: *shih´-vuh*

I'M COLORED WITH THE COLOR OF DUSK

The male *bhakti* sants often speak with the voices of women, as we have seen—the voices of Krishna's mother, his lover, the lover's friend. But Mirabai can speak in her own voice, simultaneously as herself and as one of the cowherd women. The *rana*, the ruler, the man of Mirabai's warrior class, her husband, is poison to her; while the god, Krishna, has so thoroughly pervaded her that he has dyed her with his own dark color. He is called the Mountain Lifter in recognition of the time when the god of rain sent a devastating monsoon but Krishna lifted up Mount Govardhana to form an umbrella for the cowherd village. The Maddening One (*madana*) refers both to Krishna and to Kama, the god of erotic love; together, they have intoxicated Mira and driven her mad.

I'm colored with the color of dusk, oh *rana*,
colored with the color of my Lord.
Drumming out the rhythm on the drums, I danced,
dancing in the presence of the saints,
colored with the color of my Lord.
They thought me mad for the Maddening One,
raw for my dear dark love,
colored with the color of my Lord.
The *rana* sent me a poison cup:
I didn't look, I drank it up,
colored with the color of my Lord.
The clever Mountain Lifter is the lord of Mira.
Life after life he's true—
colored with the color of my Lord.

LIFE WITHOUT HARI

The mother-in-law, a figure who also plagued another woman devotee, Mahadeviyakka (p. 348), is still around, though no longer analogized to Illusion (*maya*).

Life without Hari is no life, friend,
And though my mother-in-law fights,
my sister-in-law teases,
the *rana* is angered,
A guard is stationed on a stool outside,
and a lock is mounted on the door,
How can I abandon the love I have loved
in life after life?
Mira's Lord is the clever Mountain Lifter:
Why would I want anyone else?

THE BHIL WOMAN TASTED THEM

This poem is based on a story that Valmiki (*Ramayana*, p. 186) and Kabir (p. 399) told before Mira told it, and Tulsi (p. 424) would tell after her. When Prince Rama was exiled in the forest, a woman from the low-caste Bhil tribe offered him a piece of fruit (a large, slightly sour fruit from the *ber* tree, something like a plum). He accepted it despite her low caste. Mirabai adds a woman's touch that makes the fruit doubly untouchable: the tribal woman first tastes the fruit herself, to make sure that it is not too sour, not realizing that the fluids from her mouth are polluting (a mistake that the Tamil saint Kannappar also made ["Kannappar Gives His Eye to

Shiva," p. 325]). Though Mirabai notes that such a woman could never have learned the Veda, her love carries her straight to heaven.

The Bhil woman tasted them, plum after plum,
 and finally found one she could offer him.
What kind of genteel breeding was this?
 And hers was no ravishing beauty.
Her family was poor, her caste quite low,
 her clothes a matter of rags,
Yet Ram took that fruit—that touched, spoiled fruit—
 for he knew that it stood for her love.
This was a woman who loved the taste of love,
 and Ram knows no high, no low.
What sort of Veda could she ever have learned?
 But quick as a flash she mounted a chariot
And sped to heaven to swing on a swing,
 tied by love to God.
You are the Lord who cares for the fallen;
 rescue whoever loves as she did:
Let Mira, your servant, safely cross over,
 a cowherding Gokul[1] girl.

1. "Cow-pen," Krishna's village.

SISTER, I HAD A DREAM

Past lives, like unremembered dreams, here reward the dreamer with a vision of union with the Mountain Lifter (Krishna, who held up Mount Govardhana), also called "Lord of Braj" (Krishna's village). And as the Upanishads teach us (p. 105), in many ways dreams are more real than waking life.

Sister, I had a dream that I wed
 the Lord of those who live in need:
Five hundred sixty thousand people came
 and the Lord of Braj was the groom.
  In dream they set up a wedding arch;
  in dream he grasped my hand;
  in dream he led me around the wedding fire
  and I became unshakably his bride.
Mira's been granted her mountain-lifting Lord:
 from living past lives, a prize.

OH, THE YOGI

Mira sends a message, through a female friend, to a yogi, telling him that now, in the season of rains, when the monsoon makes travel almost impossible and lovers are reunited, it is time to stop wandering and settle down—or else, after the rains, to wander together, yogi with yogini (female yogi). Mira often depicts Krishna as a yogi, perhaps because he is so distant, wandering away from her, and she depicts herself as a yogini, leaving behind conventional marriage in order to take up her idealized marriage, the union of a yogi and a yogini. Such a union contradicts the conventional Hindu categories of marriage and the householder life but not the more esoteric mythology of the god Shiva, the erotic ascetic whose clothing and jewelry are made of snakes. Mira often invokes Shiva, sometimes, as here, together with the god Ram, not the Rama of the *Ramayana*, Sita's Rama, but Kabir's Rama (p. 399), a god without qualities (*nir-guna*).

Oh, the yogi—
  my friend, that clever one
  whose mind is on Shiva and the Snake,
  that all-knowing yogi—tell him this:

"I'm not staying here, not staying where
  the land's grown strange without you, my dear,
But coming home, coming to where your place is;
  take me, guard me with your guardian mercy,
    please.
I'll take up your yogic garb—
  your prayer beads,
    earrings,
      begging-bowl skull,
        tattered yogic cloth—
          I'll take them all
And search through the world as a yogi does
  with you—yogi and yogini, side by side.

"My loved one, the rains have come,
  and you promised that when they did, you'd come too.
And now the days are gone: I've counted them
  one by one on the folds of my fingers
    till the lines at the joints have blurred
And my love has left me pale,
  my youth grown yellow as with age.
Singing of Ram,
  your servant Mira
    has offered you an offering:
      her body and her mind."

LET US GO TO A REALM BEYOND GOING

In this vision of a land beyond all the heavens, giving form and expression to the formless and indescribable land of *moksha* (release), the royal geese or swans settle on the lake of the heart (*manasarovar*) at the foot of Mount Kailasa, where Shiva meditates. There the devotees of Krishna dance, as the cowherd women danced in his village on earth; and they are married to him. The sixteen signs of beauty are the traditional cosmetics and ornaments of a married woman, such as the mark on the forehead and along the part of the hair, a pearl in the nostril, the gold bangles on the arm.

Let us go to a realm beyond going,
Where death is afraid to go,
Where the high-flying birds alight and play,
Afloat in the full lake of love.
There they gather—the good, the true—
To strengthen an inner regimen,
To focus on the dark form of the Lord
And refine their minds like fire.
Garbed in goodness—their ankle bells—
They dance the dance of contentment
And deck themselves with the sixteen signs
Of beauty, and a golden crown—
There where the love of the Dark One comes first
And everything else is last.

TULSI DAS

Tulsi Das (or Tulsidas, or Tulsi) was born in 1532 or 1543 in Rajapur and died in 1623 in Varanasi, where he lived most of his life. His name ("Servant of Tulsi") is taken from the sacred Tulsi plant, a type of basil used in the worship of Vishnu. A passionate devotee of Rama, he also embraced both a monistic doctrine of nondualism ("Theology and/or Philosophy in the *Vedanta*," p. 285) and the broader mythology of Hinduism. Unlike Surdas, he admired yogis as well as devotees (*bhaktas*), and unlike Kabir, he was moderate in his attitude toward conventional Hindu deities, Shiva as well as Vishnu. His cosmopolitanism and eclecticism, as well as his popularity among influential people at the Mughal court, made it possible for him to draw a wide range of believers to the worship of Rama, replacing the worship of Krishna as the dominant form of Hinduism in much of North India. Although Tulsi was almost certainly a Brahmin himself, and although, by and large, he toes the Brahmin line and upholds caste, he was scarred by intense poverty in his youth, and his works contain moments of compassion for Pariahs and tribals that were very bold for their time and place.

POEMS

Tulsi's poetry reveals intriguing bits of information about his life and confirms the theological eclecticism that emerges from the *Ramcharitmanas*. There are poems to Shiva, to the Ganges River, and to the monkey Hanuman, all lit by the same personal devotion that permeates the poems to Ram, Tulsi's primary deity, who is both the impersonal Ram of Kabir and the more personal Rama of the *Ramayana*.

The poems in this section are translated by John Stratton Hawley and Mark Juergensmeyer. They are from Tulsi's *Kavitavali* ("Garland of Verses") and *Vinaya Patrika* ("Petition to Rama").

PRONOUNCING GLOSSARY

Kavitavali: *kuh-vee-tah´-vuh-lee*
Ram: *rahm*
Tulsi: *tool´-see*
Tulsidas: *tool´-see-dahs´*

THE FIRE OF MY STOMACH

Tulsi here speaks of himself and, in the last lines, to himself. The "great sage" to whom he refers may be Valmiki, author of the Sanskrit *Ramayana*, on which Tulsi based his own.

The fire of my stomach has forced me
To grasp at the scraps of any caste—

My caste, high caste, low caste—
   and this in full public display.

I have done evil as if it were truth,
In thought and word and action—
I know they call me "servant of Ram,"
   but I'm treacherous even so.

Yet the force of the name of Ram is such,
The splendor of his feet so fine,
That the world has counted this Tulsi
   as great as some great sage.

Such a surprise. Pathetic are those
Who see this and hear of this
And do not love the feet of Ram.
   Such fools!

IT IS SAID IN ANCIENT WRITINGS

The city of Varanasi, or Benares, is sacred to Shiva and to death; to die beside the Ganges in Varanasi is the goal of every pious Hindu, who believes that Shiva whispers in the ears of dying Hindus a prayer with the power to carry them over from life to liberation. To Tulsi, that prayer must be the name of Ram, whose reign (Ram-raj) became the paradigm for a time of peace and justice. Leather, made from a dead cow, is anathema to Hindus; yet Tulsi has such faith in the name of Ram that he believes it would make even leather into valuable currency. Traditional interpretation sees Tulsi as referring to himself as this transformed leather.

It is said in ancient writings—
And the evidence is seen in the world—
That whatever is good rejoices
   because of the name of Ram.

Those who die in Benares
Are taught this by Lord Shiva,
Who looked at countless ways of faith
   and rejected everything else.

Because of Ram's name, that gracious food,
Those who craved even the water
Left over from butter now spurn
   the cream of fragrant milk.

One hears that the reign of Ram
Is a time of proper rule

When, by your name, O Ram, the currency
  could be leather hides.

A BLIND, MEAN-MINDED

As leather to a Hindu, so a pig is to a Muslim. Encountering a pig, the Muslim in this poem cries out, "Haram! Haram!" which means "Unclean!" and also has the force of "O God!" But there is a pun embedded in this exclamation: alter just one vowel and it becomes "He Ram! He Ram!" ("O Ram! O Ram!"), which is what a Hindu would exclaim in a similar moment of shock or despair. Tulsi imagines that the name of his god, even when uttered inadvertently ("The Fruits of Hearing a Purana," p. 225) and by a mean man, is so powerful that it immediately translates the Muslim not to "the jaws of death," as he fears, but straight to Tulsi's heaven. The final phrase usually means "impossible to go *beyond*," but Tulsi here forces its other sense, "impossible to go *to*," twisting the meaning intended by ordinary people who refer to Ram's heaven in the first sense, just as he transforms the meanings of the Muslim's exclamation.

A blind, mean-minded,
  dull-witted, withered-up
Old Muslim on the road
Got knocked down
  by a son of a pig.

As he fell, fear filled his heart.
"Oh God, Oh God! Unclean, unclean!
An unclean thing has killed me," he moaned
  and groaned as he fell
  into the jaws of death.

Tulsi says, his sorrows vanished
And he went straightaway
To the land of the lord of all worlds.
As everyone knows, it is because
  of the power of the name.

That very name of God
Is what people say with love.
So how can they say its grandeur places it
  where it's impossible to go?

SAY RAM, SAY RAM, SAY RAM

The "sick age" is the Kali Age ("The Four Ages," p. 228), in which the religious practices of earlier ages are no longer within the limited scope of benighted human beings. And just as Tantra worked for both "right-hand" and "left-hand" people ("Tantras," p. 275), so the name of Ram is a raft on which all can float across the river of life. The sky garden and cloud towers are common Vedanta metaphors ("Vedanta," p. 285) for metaphysical delusion.

Say Ram, say Ram, say Ram,
you fool!
That name is your raft
on the awful sea of life.

It is the only way of gaining
true gain and wealth,
For this sick age has swallowed ways
that helped in ages past.

Whether good or bad,
right-handed or left,
In the end the name of Ram
works for everyone.

This world is a sky garden
of flowers and fruits,
Towers that are only clouds—
you should never forget.

Those who abandon Ram's name
for something else, Tulsi says,
Leave the table set at home
to beg for filthy scraps.

THE NAME OF KING RAM

King Ram is the Rama of the *Ramayana*, often called "Rescuer of the Fallen," rather than the more general Ram to whom Tulsi dedicates most of his poems.

The name of King Ram: think of it with love.
It is provisions for those who journey empty-handed,
and a friend for those who travel alone,
It is blessedness for the unblessed,
good character for those with none,

A patron to purchase goods from the poor,
  and a benefactor to the abandoned.
It is a good family for those without one,
  they say—and the scriptures agree—
It is, to the crippled, hands and feet,
  and to the blind it is sight.
It is parents to those who are destitute,
  solid ground to the ungrounded,
A bridge that spans the sea of existence
  and the cause of the essence of joy.
Ram's name has no equal—
  Rescuer of the Fallen:
The thought of it makes fertile earth
  from Tulsi's barren soil.

O SHIVA, GREAT GIVER

The "earthly trials" that are Shiva's servants may refer to the belief that Shiva is the source of both suffering and the relief of suffering, both diseases and the medicines that cure diseases. Or it may refer to the servants of Shiva in his aspect of ascetic yogi, servants who are orthodox Brahmins and the enemies of the unorthodox Tulsi. There is also a contrast implied between the tree from which Tulsi gets his name (the sweet, medicinal basil, sacred to Vishnu), the tree whose "few leaves" are offered to Shiva, and the "trees of thorns" that are Tulsi's enemies.

O Shiva, great giver,
  great god of great simplicity,
You have sent away the sadness
  of all who join their hands in prayer:
They serve and remember and worship you
  with a little rice, a few leaves,
But you have given the world horses and chariots,
  elephants—whatever pleases.
Oh left-handed god, while living in your town
  I haven't asked for a thing
But now your servants, these earthly trials,
  have come to block my path.
Quick, I beg you, speak:
  Restrain the evil actions
Of those scoundrels who'd surround
  this Tulsi tree with trees of thorns.

THIS DARKEST OF AGES

The darkest of ages is this final age, the Kali Age, whose characteristics—the mixture of castes, the shuffling of the stages of life ("The Four Ages," p. 228)—are a horror to orthodox Brahmins, though not to the antinomian Tulsi. Shiva, however, is angered by the abuses of the Kali Age and sends plagues and poverty, while the gods in general are said to have worked black magic—magic designed to kill its victim—on the human race. But this is the final poem in the collection, and it ends with a sudden upbeat turn, as indeed the Losing Age itself ultimately transmigrates into the beginning of another Winning Age. In Tulsi's view, this change is triggered by nothing more than a gesture from Ram.

This darkest of ages has destroyed
  the lines of caste, the stages of life:
All that is proper has been tossed aside
  like a bundle thrown to the ground.

Shiva is angry:
  his anger is seen in the plague.
The Master is angry:
  daily poverty doubles.

They cry out, destitute men
  and women. No one hears.
Who are the gods who conspired to strike us
  with this thick, black-magic curse?

And then merciful Ram, remembered
  as protector of the terrified by Tulsi,
Praised for his fine compassion,
  gestured
    —he waved it all away.

RAMCHARITMANAS ("THE HOLY LAKE OF THE ACTS OF RAMA")

Though his shorter poems soon became, and remained, popular throughout North India, it was Tulsi's retelling of the *Ramayana*, in "The Holy Lake of the Acts of Rama" (*Ramcharitmanas*, or *Ramacharitamanasa*, or *Manas*), composed between 1574 and 1577, that became virtually canonical for the worship of Rama in North India. Tulsi transformed the Sanskrit of Valmiki's *Ramayana* (p. 186) into the far more accessible eastern Hindi dialect of Avadhi, in which form it attracted a wide audience. He also infused his poem with the non-Dualist theology and philosophy of the fifteenth-century *Adhyatma Ramayana* ("The *Ramayana* of the Soul"). The Brahmins of Varanasi, where some think Tulsi composed the text, are said to have been shocked by the composition of such a text in a vernacular language. According to a well-known legend, they tested Tulsi's text by placing it in the Shiva temple for one night, with the Sanskrit Vedas and Puranas on top of it; in the morning, Tulsi's text was on top of them all, legitimizing its authority. The text also gained importance as a Hindu response to the Indo-Muslim Mughal culture that was taking shape at this time.

To this day, individuals read and sing the *Ramcharitmanas* in their homes, and crowds of over a hundred thousand also come to hear and see the text read and enacted each autumn, for a period of between seven and thirty-one successive nights, at the "Rama Play" (Ramlila), throughout North India, particularly at Ramnagar near Varanasi, where the entire town is transformed into a stage on which the action unfolds. The performance culminates in a great battle between Prince Rama and the ogre Ravana (and the brothers of both protagonists), represented by massive effigies, ending in the victory and coronation of Rama.

The first selection from the *Ramcharitmanas* is translated by Daniel Gold. Subsequent selections are translated by R. C. Prasad.

PRONOUNCING GLOSSARY

agama: *ah´-guh-muh*
Anasuya: *uh-nuh-soo´-yah*
Atri: *uh´-tree*
Ayodhya: *uh-yohd´-yuh*

Hindu temple with restored murals. Mandawa Shekhawati, Northern Rajasthan.

The Kavad, a mobile temple. Jaisalmer, Rajasthan.

Bhavani: *buh-vah´-nee*
bhringi: *brin´-gee*
Brahma: *brah´-muh*
brahman: *bruh´-mun*
Chitrakuta: *chih´-truh-koo´-tuh*
Daksha: *duk´-shuh*
Dasharath: *duh´-shuh-rut*
Dushana: *doo´-shuh-nuh*
Durvasa: *doo´-vah´-sah´*
Ganga: *gun´-gah*
Garuda: *guh-roo´-duh*
guna: *goo´-nuh*
Hari: *huh´-ree*
Janaka: *juh´-nuh-kuh*
Janaki: *jah´-nuh-kee´*
japa: *juh´-puh*
Jayanta: *juh-yun-tah´*
kaivalya-moksha: *kai-vuhl´-yuh–mohk´-shuh*
Khara: *kuh´-ruh*
Kosalapura: *koh´-shuh-luh-poo´-ruh*
Kshatriya: *kuh-shut´-ree-yuh*
Lakshman: *luksh´-mun*
Lakshmi: *luksh´-mee*
Lanka: *lun´-kuh*
Mandara: *mun-dah´-ruh*
Mandeha: *mun-day´-huh*
Maricha: *mah´-ree-chuh*
Maya, maya: *mah´-yah*
moksha: *mohk´-shuh*
naracha: *nah-rah´-chuh*
Narada: *nah´-ruh-duh*
nigama: *ni´-guh-muh*
Panchavati: *pun-chuh´-vuh-tee´*
purana: *poo-rah´-nuh*
Raghava: *rah´-guh-vuh*
Raghu: *ruh´-goo*
Raghubira: *ruh´-goo-bee´-ruh*
Raghunatha: *ruh´-goo-nah´-tuh*
Rahu: *rah´-hoo*
Ram: *rahm*
Rama: *rah´-muh*
Ramcharitmanas: *rahm´-chuh´-reet-mah´-nus*
Ravana: *rah´-vuh-nun*
rishi: *ree´-shee*
Sanaka: *suh-nuh-kah´*
Sati: *suh´-tee*
Shambhu: *shum´-boo*
Shankara: *shahn´-kuh-ruh*
Shiva: *shih´-vuh*
Shurpanakha: *shoor´-puh-nuh-kah´*
Sita: *see´-tah*
Subahu: *soo-bah´-hoo*
Tadaka: *tah´-duh-kah´*
Trishira: *tree´-shee-rah´*
tulasi: *too´-luh-see*
Tulsidas: *tool´-see-dahs´*
Uma: *oo-mah´*
Vaitarani: *vai´-tuh-ruh-nee´*
Yama: *yuh´-muh*

SATI TAKES THE FORM OF SITA

Tulsi took pains to reconcile deities who were rivals for patronage in India in his day. Though Rama is the central hero and deity of the *Ramcharitmanas*, Tulsi also reveres the other Hindu gods, particularly Shiva, whom he depicts as an omniscient, ascetic yogi. After a long opening invocation of Rama, the action of the poem begins when the sage Bharadvaja asks the sage Yajnavalkya about Rama: "The Rama to whom we all pray, whose name is our salvation, is he the same Rama whose grief was uncontrollable when he lost his wife, and who flew into a rage and slew Ravana in battle? In other words, is Rama divine or human, *nir-guna* or *saguna*?" Yajnavalkya says, "Shiva's wife once asked Shiva about Rama, just as you asked me just now." And he tells the following story.

Once upon a time, the sage Agastya told the whole story of Rama (presumably Tulsi's version, but perhaps Valmiki's) to Shiva when he was with his wife, Sati, inspiring in Shiva a great desire to see Rama. Rama descended to earth to act out the story, and while he was wandering with his brother Lakshmana in search of Sita ("The Abduction of Sita"), they met Shiva and Sati. After they parted, Sati was puzzled by the apparent disjuncture between Rama's behavior as a normal grieving human and Shiva's treatment of him as a great god. To teach her a lesson, Rama revealed multiple Ramas, Lakshmanas, Sitas, and Satis, just as Krishna multiplied himself with the cowherd women in the great circle dance. And then Rama taught Sati another lesson, the story cited here. Afterward, Shiva resolved never to touch Sati again, because she had assumed the form of Sita and was therefore, in a sense, no longer his own wife. Miserable because of this rejection, Sati wanted to die; eventually she committed suicide in the sacrificial fire of her father, Daksha ("Daksha's Sacrifice," p. 162).

Balakanda 1.50.1–1.55.5

When Shiva then saw Ram, intense, uncommon joy grew in his heart.
Gazing at this beauty-sea, his eyes were filled.
Yet he did not reveal himself:
he knew it wasn't time
'O truth, consciousness, and bliss, O world-redeemer – triumph'
—this was all that Shiva said, who once destroyed the god of love.
As he walked away with Sati, Shiva, the abode of grace,
kept shuddering with bliss.
When Sati saw her husband's state, uncommon doubt grew in her heart:
'The world should worship Shiva, he's the ruler of the world.
To him all gods, all men and sages
bow their heads.
But *he* salutes that king's son—"O truth, consciousness, and bliss," he says,
"O other world!" How he was struck with rapture when he saw that form.
And love that can't be checked
keeps growing in his heart.
The all-pervading *brahman*, with no birth, no parts, no passion;
no wants and no distinctions – which the Vedas do not know,
can it really take a body and become a man?
Sure, Vishnu took a human form to benefit the gods,
but like my Shiva, he knows everything.

A group of people reading Tulsi's *Ramcharitmanas* in Varanasi.

That home of knowledge, Lord of wealth, that one who kills the demons—
can he be searching for his wife just like a stupid man?
Yet Shambhu's[1] word cannot be false;
for everybody knows that he knows everything.'
This boundless doubt stayed in her mind;
her heart knew no enlightenment.
She said nothing of her state, but Shiva knew.
He knows all, who controls within: 'Listen, Sati, you've a woman's nature;
don't ever keep this doubt within your heart.
That's my Ram, my chosen deity,
the one of whom the jar-born[2] *rishi* sang;
in whom I have professed my faith, whom sages serve unceasingly,
the hero of the Raghavas.[3]

Whom sages ever contemplate with spotless mind
—stern yogis, too, accomplished masters;
the *nigamas*, the *agamas*,[4] *puranas* all have sung his praises,
saying, "He's not this, not that":[5] the indescribable;
Maya's Lord, the all-pervading *brahman* that rules all the worlds
—that's Ram. For the sake of his devotees he has manifest,
forever self-sufficient, the jewel of Raghu's race.'

This teaching did not sit within her heart, despite Lord Shiva's repetitions.
But deep within the great Lord knew the power of Hari's *maya*
and so he smiled and said:
'If so much doubt is in your mind,
then why not go and make a test?
I'll sit beneath this banyan's shade

1. An epithet of Shiva.
2. Agastya was born out of a jar into which two gods, excited by a celestial courtesan, had spilled their seed. He is a wandering bard.
3. Descendants of Raghu, the founder of Rama's dynasty.
4. The *nigamas* here refer to the Vedas, and the *agamas* to later sectarian texts.
5. *Neti, Neti*, the negative statement made in many of the Upanishads (p. 105).

till you come back to me.
Consider carefully, then do something to take away
this stupid, strong delusion.' Sati took Shiva's leave and went away;
'Oh, brother,' she was thinking,
'Just what am I to do?'
Shiva sitting there reflected:
'Nothing good will come to Daksha's daughter.
If, with all I said to her, her doubt did not depart,
then the fates are against her, her fortune is bad.
Still, everything will come through Ram's arrangements;
no need to sit and think how matters could be worse.'
He muttered this, then took up Hari's name.
Sati went to where Ram was in person, the Lord, abode of joy.
She thought and thought within her heart
and took the form of Ram's wife Sita,
then walked along the road on which that king of men was coming.
Lakshman saw her in the guise of Sita.
Startled, he became confused within.
So grim he looked—he couldn't say a word.
Still, wise, he knew the power of the Lord.
That master of the gods saw through her pose
—all-seeing Ram, controlling all within.
Remember him and ignorance will cease;
Lord Ram knows all!
Yet Sati wanted to deceive him . . .
Behold—the power of woman's nature!
Admiring to himself the force of his illusions,
Ram smiled to speak sweet words.
His palms together, the Lord bowed;
and only after giving out his own name and his father's,
inquired where Shiva was—whose standard bears a bull.
And why was Sati wandering in the forest by herself?
These words of Ram, so soft and deep, made her embarrassed.
Sati, awestruck, walked toward Great Lord Shiva,
heavy-hearted, thinking: 'I disobeyed what Shiva said,
taking my ignorance to Ram.
What can I say to Shiva now?'
An awful fire grew in her heart.
Ram knew the pain that Sati felt,
so let her know some of his glory.
Walking down the road, she saw a spectacle:
in front of her was Ram, with his brother and his wife;
She looked around: behind she saw the Lord,
his brother, too, and Sita—beautifully clothed.
Whichever way she looked, she saw the Lord enthroned;
wise sages, adepts served him.
She saw many Shivas, Brahmas, Vishnus—
their splendor boundless, one beyond the next.
All the gods she saw, in different dress,
giving service to the Lord and bowing to his feet.
Satis, too, she saw, and Brahmas' wives and Vishnus'
—all limitless, unequaled: their bodies fit to wear

the raiments of the gods.
All the gods there, with their wives,
wherever she saw Ram;
all living and all lifeless things in the created world
—she saw them there, all kinds.
In many diverse guises, the gods worshipped the Lord.
But she saw Ram in just one form.
However many Rams and Sitas she beheld,
they all looked just the same.
Ram, Sita, Lakshman—all the same!
Sati was struck by mighty awe.
With quivering heart and no awareness of her body,
she closed her eyes and sat down by the road.
Then opening her eyes she looked again,
but Daksha's daughter could see nothing there.
She bowed her head repeatedly down toward the feet of Ram,
and went off to where Shiva had remained.
When she approached him, Shiva smiled
and asked her how she was: 'I want to hear the truth now, dear.
How did you test the Lord?'

THE CROW AND ANASUYA

Book 3 of Tulsi's *Ramayana* begins with an invocation to Shankara (Shiva) and then to Rama. The story of Rama's compassion to a crow, whose attack upon Sita foreshadows the attack by Ravana that is the main event of this book, is followed by Anasuya's lecture to Sita on the virtues of an obedient wife, which also sets the stage for Sita's abduction.

Aranyakanda 3.1.1–3, 3.4.3, 3.5.1–3.11.6

I reverence Shankara, the very root of the tree of righteousness, the full moon that brings joy to the ocean of wisdom, the sun that opens the lotus of dispassion, who dispels the thick darkness of sin and relieves of every distress, the heaven-born wind to scatter the massed clouds of delusion, the progeny of Brahma and the destroyer of sin, the beloved of Lord Rama the king.

I worship him whose body is dark and beautiful like a rain-bearing cloud teeming with abundant delights; the yellow-apparelled and handsome; who carries a bow and arrows in his hands and has a beautiful, shining and well-equipped quiver fastened to his waist; with a pair of large lotus eyes and a tuft of matted locks on his head; the most glorious Rama, the delighter of all, traveling in the company of Sita and Lakshmana.

O Uma, Rama's perfections are profound; the learned and the sage develop dispassion (when they appreciate them), but fools, who are hostile to Hari and have no love for righteousness, reap only delusion.

* * *

Hear now the all-holy exploits of the Lord which he wrought in the forest, to the delight of gods and men and sages.

One day Rama plucked some lovely flowers and with his own hands wove them together into ornaments of several kinds, with which he reverently decked Sita, as he sat on a beautiful crystal rock.

The foolish son of the king of the gods[1] took the form of a crow and wickedly thought to test Raghunatha's might, like an ant so utterly dull-witted as to try to sound the depths of the ocean.

In its wretched stupidity the foolish crow (who was actuated by a certain motive) bit Sita in the foot with its beak and flew away. When the blood began to flow, Raghunatha[2] saw it and fitted a reed shaft to his bow.

Raghunatha is extremely compassionate and is ever fond of the meek; and it was on him that this fool, this abode of all vices, came and played this trick!

Winged with a spell, the shaft presided over by Brahma sped forth; the crow in terror took to flight and assuming his proper form, fled to his father, but he would not shelter him, for he was Rama's enemy.

He was in despair and as panic-stricken at heart as was Durvasa the seer by the terror of Vishnu's discus. Weary and frightened and remorseful, he traversed the realm of Brahma, the city of Lord Shiva and every other region.

But no one even asked him to rest awhile. Who can dare afford shelter to an enemy of Rama? Listen, Garuda;[3] a mother becomes as terrible as death and a father assumes the role of Yama (the king of hell), ambrosia turns into poison.

—and a friend becomes as hostile as a hundred foes, the celestial river (Ganga) is converted into the Vaitarani (river of hell), and—listen, brother—all the world burns hotter than fire when a man sets his face against Raghunatha.

When Narada[4] saw Jayanta (Indra's son) in distress, he took pity on him, for saints are indeed tender-hearted and good, and sent him straight to Rama. 'Save me,' he cried, 'O friend of the suppliant!'

Bewildered and terrified, he went and clasped his feet and cried, 'Protect me, O protect me, gracious Raghunatha! Being a fool, I did not recognize your immeasurable might, your matchless majesty!

'I have reaped the fated fruit of my own actions and have now sought refuge in you. Protect me, my Lord!' When the all-merciful Lord heard his most piteous plea, he let him go with the loss of one eye.

Although in his infatuation Jayanta had antagonized him and therefore deserved to die, the Lord had compassion upon him and set him free. Who is so merciful as Rama?

Raghunatha stayed on at Chitrakuta and performed exploits of many kinds grateful as nectar to the ear. Rama then thought to himself, 'People will throng here, now that they all know who I am.'

Taking leave of all the sages, therefore, the two brothers (Rama and Lakshmana) left the place with Sita. When the Lord came to Atri's[5] hermitage, the great sage rejoiced at the news.

1. Jayanta, the son of Indra.
2. Rama, lord of the family descended from Raghu.
3. This part of the story is told to Garuda, the eagle on which Vishnu rides.
4. A great sage.
5. A great sage, the husband of Anasuya.

Trembling with emotion, Atri sprang up and ran to meet him, and seeing him come, Rama too advanced hurriedly and was falling prostrate before him, but the sage (raised him and) clasped him to his bosom and bathed the two brothers in tears of affection.

His eyes were gladdened by the sight of Rama's beauty. Then he reverently escorted them to his own hermitage, where he worshipped them and addressed them in gracious terms and offered them such roots and fruit as the Lord's soul relished.

As the Lord took his seat, Atri (the chief of sages), supremely wise, feasted his eyes on his loveliness, and then folding his hands in supplication, he sang this hymn of praise:

'I reverence you, who are so fond of your faithful followers, compassionate and gentle of disposition. I worship your lotus feet, which bestow upon the desireless your own abode in heaven.

'I worship you, O Lord, dark and exquisitely beautiful, Mount Mandara[6] to churn the ocean of mundane existence, with eyes like the full-blown lotus, the dispeller of pride and every other vice.'

Having prayed thus, the sage with bowed head and folded hands spoke again: 'Never, Lord, may my mind abandon your lotus feet!'

Then Sita, who was so urbane and modest, met Anasuya (Atri's wife) and clasped her feet. The seer's wife felt extremely pleased at heart; she blessed her and seated her by her side.

Then she arrayed her in heavenly robes and jewels which remained ever new, unsullied and lustrous. In sweet and gentle accents the saintly woman then began to discourse on wifely duty, making her an occasion for such discourse:

'Listen, O princess: mother, father and brother are all friendly helpers in a limited degree; but a husband, Sita, is an unlimited blessing; and vile is the woman who refuses to serve him,

'Fortitude, piety, a friend and a wife—these four are tested only in time of adversity. Though her lord be old, sick, dull-headed, indigent, blind, deaf, bad-tempered or utterly wretched,

'—yet if his wife treats him with disrespect, she shall suffer all the torments of hell. To be devoted in thought and word and deed to her husband's feet is her only religious duty, her only vow and her only guiding rule (for behavior).

'There are in the world four grades of faithful wives, so declare the Vedas, the Puranas and all the saints. The best are firmly convinced in their hearts that no other man exists in this world even in a dream.

'The next in order regard another's husband as their own brother, father or son. She who is restrained by consideration of her duty or by the thought of her family's honor is said in the Vedas to be a woman of low character.

'And reckon that woman the very lowest of all in the world whom fear alone restrains and want of opportunity. The woman who deceives her husband and loves a paramour is cast for a hundred aeons into the depths of the lowest hell.

'Who is so vile as she who for the sake of a moment's pleasure considers not the torments that shall endure through a thousand million lives? The

6. When the gods churned the ocean to obtain the ambrosia, they used Mandara as the churn ("The Churning of the Ocean," p. 149).

wife who without guile takes a vow of fidelity to her husband attains to salvation with the greatest ease;

'—but she who is disloyal to her lord becomes a widow in her early youth wherever she be born.

Though woman is inherently impure, she wins to a happy state (hereafter) by serving, her lord. (It is due to her loyalty to her husband that) *tulasi* is beloved of Hari[7] even to this day and her glory is sung by all the four Vedas.

'Listen, Sita; women will maintain their vow of fidelity by invoking your name, for Rama is dear to you as your own life. It is for the good of the world that I have spoken these words.'

Janaki[8] was overjoyed when she heard her and reverently bowed her head before Anasuya's feet. Then the gracious Lord said to the sage, 'With your permission I would go to some other forest.

'Continue to be ever gracious to me and knowing me to be your servant, cease not to love me.' Hearing these words of the Lord, the champion of righteousness, the enlightened sage affectionately replied,

'You are that same Rama (the Supreme Deity), the beloved of the desireless and the friend of the lowly, whose grace is sought by Brahma, Shiva, Sanaka and all other knowers of the essence of things and yet you are addressing these gentle words to me.

'Now do I understand the wisdom of Lakshmi[9] who chose you (as her lord) to the exclusion of all other gods. Such indeed must be the modesty of one whom there is none to rival.

'How can I say, "Depart now, my lord?" Tell me, my master, knowing as you do the secrets of all hearts.' Having thus spoken, the steadfast sage gazed upon the Lord, thrilling all over with emotion and his eyes streaming with tears (of affection).

Trembling with emotion in every limb, the sage riveted his loving eyes on the Lord's lotus face. He thought to himself, 'What prayers did I say, what austerity did I perform, that I should behold with my own eyes the Lord who transcends all thought and knowledge, the senses and the three *gunas*?'[1] It is by *japa* (uttering quiet prayers), yoga (concentration of mind) and a host of religious observances that man attains to the incomparable virtue of devotion to Raghubira, whose all-holy exploits Tulasidasa sings day and night.

7. Vishnu.
8. Sita, daughter of King Janaka.
9. Goddess of good fortune, the wife of Vishnu.

1. The three qualities of matter (lucidity, energy, and darkness) ("The Two Paths," p. 178).

THE MUTILATION OF SHURPANAKHA

Cutting off the nose and ears is a traditional punishment that the dharma texts prescribe for a promiscuous woman, an adulteress. But the mutilation of Shurpanakha has serious consequences for Rama, because she is Ravana's sister (*Ramayana*, p. 186). When Rama rejects her overtures of love and Lakshmana mutilates her, Shurpanakha flees in agony and humiliation, triggering the war. (Unlike Valmiki, Tulsi says nothing about Ravana being inflamed with passion for Sita; though Shurpanakha mentions Sita's beauty, Ravana is galvanized far more by his desire to avenge the death of the three male ogres whom Rama has killed.)

But *bhakti* neutralizes the aggression of most of the other ogres in the story. The ogres who die crying, "Rama! Rama!" are saved because they meditated on Rama, albeit to kill him—a striking example of both "hate-love" (*Tevaram*, p. 315) and salvation through accidental grace ("The Fruits of Hearing a Purana," p. 225). The ogres are tricked into killing one another by an illusion of multiplication—Rama has each of the demons see each of his own friends as Rama, so that they kill one another, a trick that we recognize from the illusion of multiple Ramas (and Sitas and Lakshmanas) that Rama creates to enlighten Sati ("Sati Takes the Form of Sita"). Even Shurpanakha quotes a maxim that noble deeds that are not dedicated to Vishnu bear no fruit, though she does not know that Rama is Vishnu. Ravana himself suspects that Rama may be god, but since, as an ogre, he cannot worship him (though he worships Shiva), he decides to fight him, hoping to die at the hands of the god; and if Rama turns out to be just an ordinary human prince, he'll fight him anyway, and carry off the woman.

Aranyakanda 3.17.1–3.20.4

Now Ravana (the demon king of Lanka) had a sister named Shurpanakha (*lit.*, a woman having nails as big as a winnowing fan), who was foulhearted and cruel as a serpent. One day she came to Panchavati[1] and was smitten with pangs of love when she saw the two princes.

At the very sight of a handsome man, be he her own brother, father or son, O Garuda,[2] a (wanton) woman is excited and cannot check her passion, like the sunstone that melts at the sight of the sun.

Having assumed a beautiful form, she approached the Lord and with many a smile thus addressed him: 'There is no man like you, nor a woman like me. It is with great deliberation that God has planned this match.

'Though I have searched through the three spheres, I have found no suitable match for me in all the world. And for this reason I have till now remained a maiden; but now that I have seen you my mind is somewhat eased.'

The Lord glanced at Sita and said in reply, 'My younger brother is a bachelor.' Then she went to Lakshmana, who, knowing that she was their enemy's sister, looked at the Lord and spoke in gentle tones:

'Listen, fair lady; I am his servant and dependant; you would not be happy with me. My lord is the mighty king of Kosalapura (Ayodhya); whatever he does becomes him.

'A servant who aspires after happiness, a beggar who expects honor, a dissolute man who hopes for riches, a profligate who seeks salvation, an avaricious man who covets fame and a proud man who craves the four rewards of life—all these are like men who would expect milk by milking the sky.'

Again she turned and came to Rama, but the Lord sent her back once more to Lakshmana. Said Lakshmana, 'He will be a match for you who has flung all sense of shame to the winds!'

Then in a fury she returned to Rama, revealing her own dreadful demon form. Raghunatha, seeing that Sita was frightened, made a sign to his brother.

With great agility Lakshmana struck off her nose and ears, sending, as it were, a challenge to Ravana by her hand.

1. The place where Rama was camped in the forest, on the banks of the Godavari River.
2. This part of the story is part of a conversation between Garuda, the eagle on which Vishnu rides, and a crow named Bhushundi. The misogynist sentiment is widespread in Hindu dharma texts.

Robbed of her nose and ears, she wore a hideous aspect and looked like a mountain flowing with torrents of red ochre. She went sobbing to Khara and Dushana[3] and cried, 'A curse, a curse, brothers, on your manhood and might!'

When Khara and Dushana asked her what had happened, she told them all. On hearing her report, the demon chiefs gathered an army, and swarming multitudes of monsters of diverse shapes rushed forth like hosts of winged hills of soot,

—mounted on vehicles of various kinds and armed with every kind of weapon, formidable and innumerable. At the head went Shurpanakha, a hideous, ill-starred form, shorn of her ears and nose.

Countless fearful omens of evil occurred to them, but the host heeded them not, being all death-doomed. They roared, they challenged, they flew through the air; on seeing their army, the champions were transported with joy.

Cried one, 'Capture the two brothers alive, and having seized them, slay them and carry off the woman!' The vault of heaven was overstrewn with dust. Rama summoned his brother (Lakshmana) and said to him,

'Go, take Janaki[4] away to some mountain cave, for a formidable army of demons has come; remain on your guard.' Obedient to his Lord's command, he withdrew (to a safe retreat) with Sita, bow and arrows in hand.

When Rama saw that the hostile forces had drawn near, he smiled as he strung his dreadful bow.

As he strung his formidable bow and bound up his matted locks in a knot on his head, it looked as though a pair of snakes were contending with a myriad lightning flashes on a mountain of emerald. Having slung his quiver by his side and clasped the bow with his long arms and put his arrows in order, he fixed his gaze upon the foe as a lion glares at a herd of noble elephants.

On came the champions with a rush, shouting, 'Seize him, seize him!' and closed in upon Rama as the demons called Mandeha[5] close in upon the rising sun when they see it all alone.

But at the sight of the Lord (who was a perfect treasure of beauty), the demon host stood entranced, nor could they shoot their arrows. Then Khara and Dushana summoned their ministers and said, This prince, whoever he may be, is an ornament of the human race.

'Serpents, demons, gods, human beings and sages of all sorts have we seen and vanquished and slain; but listen, our brethren all, never have we seen such beauty!

'Though they have made our sister hideous to behold, even yet so incomparable a hero is not worthy of death. "Surrender to us at once the woman whom you have hidden, and you two brothers return home alive."

'Give him my message and return swiftly with his answer.' The heralds went to Rama and delivered the message to him, but Rama smilingly replied,

'We are Kshatriyas and are given to hunting in the woods, and it is wretches like you that we seek for our prey. We are never dismayed at the sight of a mighty foe and would give battle to Death himself if he ever appeared before us.

3. Khara, Dushana, and Trishira are three of the many brothers of Ravana; Shurpanakha is their sister.
4. A name of Sita, daughter of King Janaka of Videha.
5. Demons the size of mountains; the sun burns them at sunrise, causing them to fall into the ocean until evening, when they roam again.

'Though human beings, we are the destroyers of the demon race and, though youthful in appearance, we are the protectors of the hermits and the torment of the wicked. If you are not strong enough to fight, you had better return home; I never kill an enemy in retreat.

'To play wily pranks on the field of battle or to show compassion to the enemy is utter cowardice.' The heralds returned forthwith and repeated all that they had been told. The hearts of Khara and Dushana were on fire when they heard it.

Their hearts were on fire and they shouted, 'Seize him!' The fierce demon champions rushed forth, all armed with bows and arrows, steel clubs, pikes, spears, scimitars, maces and axes. First of all, the Lord gave his bow a twang—shrill, terrific and frightening—that deafened the ears of the demons and caused them great agitation and deprived them at that moment of all knowledge of what they were doing.

Having realized that they were confronting a redoubtable enemy, the demon warriors now ran on with caution and began to hurl on Rama all kinds of missiles and weapons.

But Raghubira tore their weapons into pieces as small as sesame seeds, and then drawing the bowstring to his ear, discharged his own arrows.

Then the terrible arrows sped forth, hissing like so many serpents. When Rama waxed wrathful in the strife, his arrows, of exceeding sharpness, flew forth.

When they saw his shafts so keen, the demon warriors turned to flee. The three brothers (Khara, Dushana and Trishira) now flew into a rage: 'Whoever flees from the battle-field,' they cried, 'him will we slay with our own hands!' At this the warriors turned back, fully resolved to die, and faced their foe with weapons of every description.

When the Lord saw that the enemy was exceedingly enraged, he fitted an arrow to his bow and let fly many an iron bolt of the *naracha*[6] type, and the frightful fiends began to be mowed down.

Their breasts and heads, arms, hands and feet began to drop to the ground here, there and everywhere. The shrill arrows struck; they yelled and their trunks, like mountains, fell.

Though the warriors' bodies were cut into a hundred pieces, yet by demonic magic they rose again. A multitude of arms and heads flew through the air and headless trunks rushed to and fro.

Fiercely and grimly did kites, crows and jackals gnash their teeth (and gnaw at the bones).

Jackals gnashed; ghosts, spirits and fiends collected skulls; more warlike devils beat time on the fleshless heads, and witches danced. Raghubira's fierce arrows tore to pieces the champions' breasts and arms and heads; their bodies fell on every side, but rose again to fight with terrible cries of 'Seize, capture!'

Vultures flew away with the end of entrails in their claws; goblins scampered off with the other end that their hands had seized; it was as though a large number of children from the town of Battle were flying kites. Many a champion lay dead or vanquished; many others, whose breasts were torn in two, lay groaning. Seeing their army in distress, Trishira and Khara and Dushana and other champions turned towards Rama.

6. An arrow made of iron.

Countless demons hurled furiously on Raghubira arrows and spears, iron clubs, axes, javelins and scimitars all at once. In the twinkling of an eye the Lord warded off the enemy's shafts and with a shout of defiance sent forth his own arrows, driving ten shafts into the breast of each demon captain.

Their warriors fell to the ground, but they rose again and joined in the fray; they would not die but played all their delusive tricks. The gods were afraid when they saw the demons fourteen thousand in number and Rama but one. Finding the gods and sages alarmed, the Lord, who is the controller of Maya (cosmic illusion), devised a merry spectacle, on account of which the enemy saw each of his own friends as Rama, and joining battle with one another perished fighting.

(The demons bid defiance to one another, shouting, 'Kill him! He is Rama!') Thus crying, 'Rama! Rama!,' they left their bodies and attained beatitude (*kaivalya-moksha* or final emancipation). By this means the compassionate Lord slew the enemy in an instant.

The gods in their exultation rained down flowers, and kettle-drums sounded in the heavens. Then hymning their praises of the Lord, they all departed, resplendent in their celestial cars.

THE ABDUCTION OF SITA

The abduction of Sita follows directly upon the mutilation of Shurpanakha.

In Valmiki's *Ramayana* (p. 186), after Rama has brought Sita back from the island fortress of the ogre Ravana, he subjects her to an ordeal by fire to silence rumors that her chastity was compromised during her captivity. Sita passes through the flames unscathed, and Rama accepts her—for a while; when the rumors flare up again, he banishes her, and she eventually leaves him forever, returning to the Earth, her mother ("The Birth of Sita," p. 189). During the many centuries between Valmiki and Tulsi, Rama had become one of the two great gods of Vaishnavism (Krishna being the other), and consequently Rama's unfair treatment of Sita had become ever more troubling to his devotees. Tulsi dealt with this problem by incorporating into his poem from earlier Sanskrit texts, particularly the fifteenth-century *Adhyatma Ramayana*, the tradition of the illusory or Shadow Sita, an artificial, identical image of the real woman. In Tulsi's telling, Rama creates a Shadow Sita before Ravana enters the scene; the Shadow Sita is carried off and brought back; she enters the fire at the ordeal and is consumed. The real Sita never suffers, but comes *out* of the fire at the end of the ordeal and then stays with Rama happily ever after, for Tulsi omits the episode in which Sita returns to her Earth mother. Thus the Vedantic concept of illusion (*maya*) allows Tulsi to argue that Rama never intended or needed to test Sita (since he knew she wasn't in Ravana's house at all) but goaded the Shadow Sita into undertaking the fire ordeal merely to get her into the fire so that he could bring the real Sita back from the fire. Shiva narrates this episoda to his wife, called Bhavani or Uma.

Aranyakanda 3.20.5–3.29.3

When Raghunatha had vanquished the foe in battle the gods, men and sages were all rid of fear. Then Lakshmana brought Sita back, and as he fell at his feet, the Lord rapturously took him to his heart.

Sita fixed her gaze on his dark-hued, delicate body with utmost affection, but her eyes knew no satiety. Staying at Panchavati, the blessed Raghunatha performed deeds that gladdened gods and sages.

Perceiving the destruction of Khara and Dushana, Shurpanakha went to incite Ravana. In a furious rage she cried, 'You have lost all thought of land and treasure;

'—day and night you drink and sleep and take no heed of the enemy, who is now at your very door. Sovereignty without statecraft, wealth divorced from virtue, noble deeds not dedicated to Hari (God), and learning that begets not discernment—these all bring no fruit but toil to the student, the doer or the possessor. A recluse is swiftly undone by attachment, a king by evil counsel, wisdom by conceit, modesty by drinking,

'—love by conceit and a man of merit by vanity; such is the maxim I have heard.

'An enemy, disease, fire, sin, a master and a serpent should never be treated with scorn.' So saying, and with bitter lamentation besides, she began to weep.

In her distress she threw herself down in Ravana's court and with many tears and cries said, 'Do you think, O Ten-headed, that I should be treated thus while yet you live?'

At these words, the courtiers arose in great bewilderment and grasped her arms and raised her to her feet and consoled her. 'Tell me what has happened to you,' said the king of Lanka; 'who has struck off your nose and ears?'

'The sons of Dasharath, the lord of Ayodhya, who are lions among men, have come to hunt in the woods. I understood what they were about: they would rid the earth of demons.

'Relying on the might of their arm, O Ravana, the hermits roam the woods without fear. Though quite young to look at, they are terrible as Death himself, the most unwavering of archers and most accomplished.

'Both brothers are unequalled in might and majesty, vowed to the extermination of the wicked and the relief of gods and sages. He who is the very perfection of beauty is named Rama, and with him is a teenage girl,

'—whom the Creator has fashioned the loveliest of women, a match for a thousand million Ratis (consorts of the god of love). It was his younger brother (Lakshmana) who chopped off my ears and nose and made a mock of me when he learnt that I was your sister.

'When Khara and Dushana heard my cry, they came to avenge the wrong done to me, but Rama slew the whole of their army in an instant!' When he heard of the destruction of Khara, Dushana and Trishira, the news burnt its way into Ravana's heart.

Having consoled Shurpanakha, he bragged and boasted of his might in whatever manner he could, but he retired to his palace in a state of great anxiety and could not sleep all night.

'Among gods and men and demons, serpents and birds,' he thought, 'there is none who can face my servants. As for Khara and Dushana, they were as mighty as myself; who else could have killed them, had it not been the Lord himself?

'If the Lord himself has become incarnate to gladden the gods and relieve the earth of its burdens, then must I go and stubbornly fight with him and cross the ocean of mundane existence by falling to his arrows.

'Worshipping the Lord is out of question in this fallen form made up of darkness and ignorance; this therefore is my firm resolve, which I shall carry through in thought and word and deed; and if they be some mortal princelings, I shall overpower them both in battle and carry off the bride.'

Having thus made up his mind, he mounted his chariot and drove off alone to where Maricha[1] lived on the seashore. Now listen, Uma,[2] to the delectable account of the scheme that Rama devised.

When Lakshmana had gone into the woods to gather roots and fruit and bulbs, Rama, the very incarnation of compassion and joy, spoke with a smile to Janaka's daughter:

'Listen, beloved wife, beautiful, faithful and amiable; I am about to act an alluring human part; let fire then be your dwelling-place till I have completed the extirpation of the demons.'

No sooner had Rama finished speaking than she impressed the image of the Lord's feet on her heart and entered into the fire, leaving only her image there, of exactly the same appearance and the same amiable and modest disposition.

Not even Lakshmana knew the secret of what the Lord had done. Ravana, the self-absorbed, vile wretch, approached Maricha and bowed his head to him.

When a groveling, mean creature bends, it is only to give more pain, like an elephant-goad, a bow, a snake, or a cat; and the ingratiating speech of a blackguard, Bhavani,[2] is as portentous as flowers that bloom out of season.

After doing him reverence, Maricha respectfully asked him why he had come: 'Why, sire, are you so disturbed in mind and why have you come all the way alone?'

The wretched Ravana boastfully repeated the whole story to him and added, 'Do you assume the deceptive form of a deer, so that I may (trick him and) carry off the princess.'

To this Maricha replied, 'Listen, O Ten-headed; though disguised as a man, he is the Lord of all animate and inanimate creation; be not at enmity with him, sire; we die when he would have us die and live only by his sufferance.

'It was this prince who, when he went to protect the sage's sacrifice, smote me with a headless arrow so that I was hurled a thousand miles in an instant. No good can come of showing hostility to him.

'Now I find myself reduced to the position of a grub caught by a *bhringi* (a large black bee) inasmuch as I see the two brothers wherever I look. Even if he be only a man, sire, he is a valiant hero, and opposition to him will do no good.

'Can such a mighty champion, who killed Tadaka and Subahu,[3] broke Shiva's bow,[4] and slew Khara, Dushana and Trishira, be just an ordinary man?

'Think therefore of the welfare of your family and go home.' When he heard this, he flared up and directed a volley of abuses at Maricha: 'You fool, do you presume to teach me like a *guru*? Tell me, which warrior in the world is a match for me?'

Then Maricha thought to himself: 'It does not do one good to make enemies of the following nine: an armed man, one who knows one's secrets, a powerful master, a dunce, a wealthy man, a physician, a panegyrist, a poet and a cook.'

1. An ogre, sometimes said to be Tataka's son.
2. The goddess, the wife of Shiva.
3. Subahu is an ogre, and Tadaka (or Tataka) his mother; Rama kills them both.
4. Rama broke Shiva's bow when he won Sita ("The Birth of Sita," p. 189).

Realizing that he was doomed to death in either event, he sought refuge in Raghunatha. 'If I argue further,' he thought, 'the wretch would slay me; why then should I not die by a stroke of Raghunatha's shaft?'

With these thoughts in mind, he accompanied Ravana, with unbroken devotion to Rama's feet and an exceeding gladness of heart that he would be able to behold his greatest friend (Rama). But he did not reveal his joy to Ravana.

'I shall reward my eyes,' he thought, 'with the sight of my best-beloved and be happy. I shall be devoted to the feet of the gracious Lord, together with Sita and Lakshmana. Hari, the ocean of bliss, whose very wrath confers *moksha* (liberation) and who, though free, gives himself up entirely to the will of his devotees, will with his own hands fit an arrow to his bow and slay me!

'As he runs after me to seize me, bearing his bow and arrows, I shall turn round again and again and look upon the Lord! There is none else so blessed as I.'

When Ravana drew near to the forest, Maricha, helped by his illusive power, assumed the false form of a deer, so marvellous as to defy description, with a body of gold artistically studded with gems.

When Sita glimpsed the exquisitely ravishing deer, most lovely in every limb, she said, 'Listen, Raghubira,[5] my gracious Lord; this deer has a most charming skin.

'Pray slay this animal, O Lord, ever as good as your word, and get me its hide.' Raghunatha knew all the circumstances (that had led Maricha to assume the semblance of a golden deer) and gladly rose to accomplish the purpose of the gods.

Having marked the deer, he girded up his loins with a piece of cloth, took the bow in his hand and fitted to it a shining shaft. The Lord cautioned Lakshmana: 'A host of demons, brother, roam the woods.

'Take care of Sita, using thought and judgement and with due regard to your own strength and the needs of the hour.' The deer, seeing the Lord, took to flight, but Rama pursued it with ready bow.

How strange that he whom the Vedas describe in negative terms, such as 'Not this, not this,' and whom Shiva is unable to grasp by contemplation, ran in pursuit of an illusory deer! Now close at hand, now far, it fled, at times in full view and at another into the invisible depths of the forest.

Thus alternately showing and concealing itself and practicing many a wile, it drew the Lord far away. Now Rama took a steady aim and let fly the fatal shaft; when with a fearful cry the deer fell to the ground.

First, it called aloud to Lakshmana, then mentally invoked Rama. As life ebbed away, it manifested its real form and lovingly remembered Rama.

The all-wise Lord, who recognized the love of its heart, conferred on it the state to which even sages hardly attain.

The gods showered down abundant flowers and hymned the Lord's perfections and said, 'Raghunatha is such a friend of the humble that he bestowed his own state (divinity) on a demon.'

As soon as he had slain the wretch, Raghubira at once turned back, radiant with the bow in his hand and the quiver at his side. When Sita heard the cry of distress, she was sorely alarmed and said to Lakshmana,

5. A name of Rama, descended from Raghu.

'Make haste and go; your brother is in great peril!' 'Listen, mother,' said Lakshmana with a smile: 'is it possible that he by the play of whose eyebrows the entire creation is annihilated should ever dream of being in danger?'

But when Sita urged him with cutting words, Lakshmana's resolve, under Hari's mystic influence, was shaken. Committing her to the care of all the sylvan gods and the deities presiding over the quarters, he went to find Rama, that Rahu[6] to the moonlike Ravana.

Meanwhile Ravana, seeing the hermitage deserted, drew near to Sita in the guise of a recluse. He who is so dreaded by gods and demons that they sleep not by night nor eat by day,

—even that Ravana went furtively on his mission of thieving, glancing this side and that like a dog. When a man sets his foot on the path of evil, all bodily vigor, reason and strength desert him.

He invented alluring stories of various sorts; he persuaded her with a show of political wisdom (tact or diplomacy); he had recourse to threats and blandishments. But Sita said, 'Listen, sir anchorite! You speak like an unholy swindler!'

Then Ravana revealed his proper form, and when he declared his name, Sita was terror-stricken. But summoning up all her courage, she said, 'Stay awhile, O wretch; my lord has come.

'Even as a tiny hare would woo a lioness, so O king of demons, would you woo your own destruction (by setting your heart on me).' On hearing these defiant words the Ten-headed flew into a rage, though in his heart he rejoiced and adored her feet.

Full of rage, Ravana now seated her in his chariot and in anxious haste drove through the air; he was so agitated with fear that he could scarcely drive the chariot.

'Ah, Raghunatha,' she wailed, 'peerless champion of the world! For what fault of mine have you forgotten to be kind to me? Ah, reliever of distress and delighter of the suppliant! Ah, the sun that gladdens the lotus race of Raghu!

'Ah, Lakshmana, it was no fault of yours! I have reaped the fruit of the temper I showed!' Many were the lamentations that Sita uttered. 'Though his mercies towards me have no limits, my affectionate and loving lord is far away.

'Who will tell my lord of my misfortune? That an ass should desire to devour the oblation offered to the gods!' When they heard Sita's grievous lament, all created beings, moving and unmoving, were distressed.

6. The planet of eclipse, that swallows up the moon and sun.

Tukaram of Maharashtra Says *No!*

1608–1649

Marathi, the official language of the state of Maharashtra, in southwestern India, evolved from Sanskrit through Prakrit and Apabhramsha (two early dialects) and was first attested in the early eighth century C.E. Today it is spoken by some 90 million people, in Maharashtra as well as parts of Goa, Karnataka, and Andhra in India, and worldwide throughout the Indian diaspora. There were a number of women saints in the Maharashtrian tradition, including Muktabai and Janabai, whose verses to the Maharashtrian god Vithoba (also called Vitthal) sometimes address him as a woman, Vithabai, and refer to him as a mother, though he is generally male. Yet despite this female presence, other poems about Vithoba project negative images of women as temptresses who distract men from the path of detachment. Vitthal is sometimes said to be an avatar of Vishnu, or a form of Krishna, or a form of Vishnu's avatar as the Buddha, and is also sometimes associated with Shiva. Truly a protean god.

Tukaram (or Tuka) was a Shudra, a member of the lowest of the four classes or *varnas*, who lived in Maharashtra from 1608 to 1649. He spoke in the idiom that the Marathi poets had fashioned out of the songs that housewives sang at home and that farmers, traders, craftsmen, and laborers sang at religious festivals. None of his poems were

The ascension of the poet Tukaram into heaven, riding on the divine Garuda bird.

written down in his lifetime; all that we have were later transcribed from oral traditions, along with legends about him. According to these legends, Tuka married, but since his wife was chronically ill, he took a second wife. When his parents, his first wife, and some of his children died in the great famine of 1629, he abandoned the householder's life, ignored his debts and the pleas of his (second) wife and his remaining children, and went off into the wilderness. He became a poet, devoted to Vitthal. Tuka's poems, which challenge caste and denounce Brahmins, also denounce ascetics. He often imagines the relationship between the god and his devotee as the relationship between an adulteress and her secret lover (as many *bhakti* poets do) or as something more confrontational.

GODS AND NOT SO HOLY MEN

The poems in this section describe various religious actors—holy men, wandering ascetics, Tantric gurus, and others—and several gods, most of whom are forms of Vishnu or Krishna. The gods reveal themselves in dreams and in real-life encounters that are often violent or tragic, provoking anger and sardonic humor in the poet. The holy men reveal their feet of clay. The strong, often obscene language of the Marathi poems is preserved in the English translations.

The poems in this section are translated by Dilip Chitre. "I Pretend to Laugh" is translated by Gail Omvedt and Bharat Patankar.

PRONOUNCING GLOSSARY

bhang: *bung*
Brahman: *bruh´-mun*
Hari: *huh´-ree*
Namdeo: *nahm´-day-oh*
Nanda: *nun´-duh*
Pandhari: *pun´-duh-ree´*
Pandurang: *pahn´-doo-rung*
Pundalik: *poon´-duh-leek´*
Shakta: *shuk´-tah*
Tuka: *too´-kah*
Tukaram: *too´-kah-rahm*
Thug: *tug*
Vaikunth: *vai-koont´*
Vitthal: *vit´-tuhl*
Vithu: *vih´-too*

I WAS ONLY DREAMING

This poem links the god Vitthal (or Vithoba) with Namdeo (or Namdev), a poet-saint who lived in the late thirteenth and early fourteenth centuries in Maharashtra.

I was only dreaming
Namdeo and Vitthal
Stepped into my dream

"Your job is to make poems,"
Said Namdeo,
"Stop fooling around."

Vitthal gave me the measure[1]
And slapped me gently
To arouse me
From my dream
Within a dream

1. The god inspires the poet with the measure, the meter, by slapping him, presumably rhythmically.

"The grand total
Of the poems Namdeo vowed to write
Was one billion,"
He said,
"All the unwritten ones, Tuka,
Are your dues."

INSECTS IN A FIG

The concept of universes within universes, and within something as small as a fig, reflects the cosmic philosophy of the *Yoga-vasishtha* ("The Man Who Built a House of Air," p. 292). The reference to Nanda, Krishna's father in the cowherd village, evokes another familiar and familial image of a universe within a small place ("Krishna's Mother Looks Inside His Mouth," p. 250).

Insects in a fig
Cannot imagine
Worlds other than the fig.

There are so many fig-trees
In these woods:
And so many more
Vast clusters of stars.

To each his own is
Brahman
—Absolute Being.

How many such astral eggs
Will there be?

The Vast One bristles
With hairs
Of infinity.

Then there's the One who contains
Trillions of vast ones.

That same One is
Nanda's loved little son—
Krishna
—The Infant Bliss Infinite.

When Tuka experiences
That bliss,
God's poetry enters
His small head.

I PRETEND TO LAUGH

The doctrine of illusion, translated into the terms of everyday life.

I pretend to laugh;
I pretend to weep;
I pretend to leap
At the Pretender.

Mine is a pretence;
Yours is a pretence;
Pretence bears the burden
Of pretending.

I pretend to sing;
I pretend to worship;
All pretence goes
Toward pretending.

The pretender savors;
The pretender renounces;
The ascetic pretends
The world is unreal.

Tuka, the pretender,
With pretended devotion,
Pretends his dialogue
With the Pretender.

WHEN MY FATHER DIED

The god Vithoba, here called by the affectionate diminutive Vithu, is simultaneously blamed and praised, in the familiar *bhakti* combination (*Tevaram*, p. 315), for using ordinary human tragedies to enlighten the poet.

When my father died
I was too young to understand;
I had not to worry
About the family then.

Vithu, this kingdom is Yours and mine.
It's not the business of anyone else.

My wife died:
May she rest in peace.

The Lord has removed
My attachment.

My children died:
So much the better.
The Lord has removed
The last illusion.

My mother died
In front of my eyes.
My worries are all over
Says Tuka.

I WAS HELD CAPTIVE

The ancient Indian belief that the gods reveal themselves to humans in dreams is here given a new twist, as is the idea that dreaming sleep reveals a deeper reality than waking life ("Dreaming," p. 111; "Shankara Dreams," p. 286): the dream in this poem, precisely because it reveals the truth of the question of identity, is a nightmare, from which the poet escapes with the help of the saints.

I was held captive
In a nightmare.
It was over
And I woke up.
It became unreal.

Why was I
Begging You
To reveal to me
My identity?
What's a king,
A nobleman,
Or a pauper
In a dream?

But the pain
Of the dream
Still lived
In me.
As I woke up,
I opened
My eyes
In pain.

I was awake
But stunned
By the pain
I dreamt.
It was so real
That I remained
Speechless.
Says Tuka,
Thank God,
The saints
Broke the spell.

THE THUG HAS ARRIVED

Kabir had called god a Thug ("That Con Man," p. 401), a robber or killer, and so does Tuka, who owes much to the spirit of Kabir. The Thugs were said to strangle their victims; here the god uses a cord made of love.

The Thug has arrived in Pandhari.[1]
He will garrotte His victim with the cord of love.

He's robbed the whole world before.
He takes His victims no one knows where.

He's raised His arms
To grab your attention.

He's decamped from Vaikunth[2]
To hunt in Pandhari.

It was Pundalik[3] who gave this Robber
A foothold in Pandhari.

Says Tuka, let's all go there
And put Him under arrest.

1. Another name for Pandharpur, a pilgrimage city, the holy place of Vithoba, on the Bhima River in Maharashtra.
2. Vishnu's heaven.
3. A devotee of Vitthal and a resident of Pandharpur who once threw a brick at the god and asked him to stand on it, which he did, remaining there, invisible, to this day, according to his devotees.

GOD'S OWN DOG

Here, as often, Tuka imagines himself as the dog of god, the unclean animal ("The Dog Who Would Be Lion," p. 158) who is nevertheless the paradigmatic *bhakta* ("The Pandavas Go to Heaven," p. 145), especially in the eyes of someone of low caste.

Once I chase someone
I chase him
Out of this world

Then I come back
To Your feet
And hide
Till You send me out
Again

The moment this dog
Smells a stranger
He scrambles
To attention

Says Tuka,
My Master's trained me hard
I am allowed to eat
Only out of his own
Hand

LORD, YOU COULD BECOME

That Krishna (here called Pandurang) has sixteen thousand wives is attested to by the *Mahabharata* and the Puranas. Tuka laments that he is not one of them.

Lord, You could become sixteen thousand lovers
To the sixteen thousand wives you are reputed to have had.
I am just one and you are not even one for me!

Maybe such discriminatory behavior befits you
Since, after all, you are Almighty.

Such is your wont! You would of course prefer
The possession of their maidenheads.

Says Tuka, O Pandurang, distinguish me
From the objects of your promiscuity.

WITH A BIZARRELY PAINTED FACE

This passionate attack on a Tantric guru ("Tantra," p. 275) can be read in the voice of an appalled Brahmin or in the voice of Tuka, who cares little for the Vedic forms but even less for Tantric ritual, though he still loves Hari (Vishnu).

With a bizarrely painted face, glowering,
He flashes lights to dazzle their sight.

Tells his disciples, "This is beatitude!"
And indeed they are bamboozled.

He smothers the flame of the light itself!
His teaching begins when the sun goes down.

Drawing mystic squares on the ground, decorating them too,
He worships occult designs.

Placing lamps in all four corners and behind curtains
He assumes a posture and demonstrates *tantric* gestures.

As an oblation, he wants to be offered sweets—
Nothing short of a divine feast!

His preaching over, time to start the feast!
Forget about sipping water from the palm of the hand at the end
of the meal.

Committing sacrilege is his means of livelihood:
He sends his followers into the bottomless pit.

He makes them break the vows of body, mind, and speech:
He teaches them to recite only the Guru's name.

He has corrupted the doctrine of the self-beyond-the self:
In the name of the Guru, he is only indulging himself!

Sacred precepts are wiped out; the Vedas are sunk;
The teachings of the scriptures are lost beyond a trace.

He has lost the control of his breath as taught in Yoga;
He cannot control his senses or follow observances.

Asceticism is destroyed; the worship of Hari is disturbed;
This maniac has spread only sin.

Says Tuka, may his Guruhood end up in a creek of shit!
He has condemned his ancestors to Hell!

THE GREAT MOTHER OF THE SHAKTA

Another poem mocking the Tantric worship of the Goddess. A Shakta, one who worships the Shakti, or the female Power, is a common term for a Tantric.

The Great Mother of the Shakta
Is a Sow wallowing in shit by the roadside:
He is so habituated to it
He would chase his own mother for the sake of shit

The Great Mother of the Shakta is a she-donkey
Who goes braying all the way to the village-entrance
Says Tuka, to describe the slut
Would be to foul up one's own mouth

THE ASCETIC

There were always some people in India who feared or despised ascetics, and satirical portraits of ascetics are scattered throughout the literatures of Hinduism. But few are so totally damning as this brief poem by Tuka. Here, Pandurang is a name of Vitthal or Krishna.

Growing long shags of hair
He walks haughtily clasping a hooked iron rod.

He must not miss a single meal;
He must compulsively curse all people;
What wisdom can such an ascetic have?

He must consume a lot of *bhang*,[1] and opium, and tobacco;
But his hallucinations are perpetual.

Says Tuka, such a man, who has forefeited everything,
Has lost Pandurang forever.

1. A form of marijuana, sometimes smoked and sometimes ingested in a liquid form, that wandering ascetics often used. (The god Shiva is also notorious for his use of *bhang*.)

ONCE THERE WAS A CELIBATE MAN

A short but devastating critique of celibacy.

Once there was a celibate man who tried to bugger a donkey.
The donkey kicked him in the balls and ran away.

Gone was the donkey. Gone was the celibacy.
The man lost face.

If you say, "Whatever is to happen, happens"
This is what will happen!
Says Tuka, you'll lose either way.

THE REAL REASON WHY YOU CREATED

This poem, addressed to the god, is a vivid representation of *maya*, the illusory power of god, the "one sense" of *brahman*, the single light that is refracted in many flames, many souls ("Upanishads," p. 105). The good news of the empty mirror is a sign that the individual self has been reabsorbed back into *brahman*, into *moksha*.

The real reason why you created this drama and its actors
Is simply your love of theatre.

Otherwise, even I have long since suspected
That the tiger and the cow are both wooden puppets.

The play as a whole makes only one sense
That nothing is divisible: one light is many flames.

There's more good news, says Tuka,
The mirror is empty.

CASTE AND THE VARKARIS

In the poems in this section, Tuka reveals his feelings about his suffering as the result of his low caste status. He also speaks of the religious community, rather than the caste or ethnic group, to which he belongs, the Varkaris, worshippers of Vithoba/Vitthal. Their name means "Pilgrims" in Marathi, for every year Varkaris walk hundreds of miles to the holy town of Pandarpur, arriving there by the eleventh day of the Hindu month of Ashada (in July). Varkaris pride themselves on their Dalit or Shudra status and on including Muslims among their members and even among the Sants (saints) whom they regard as their founders.

Some of these poems have refrains, for they were sung and performed by poet-singers whom the audience joined in singing the choruses. Some are based upon songs sung by women at work in their homes or by devotees performing in religious festivals. In some, the translators attempt to capture the spirit of song by the use of English rhymes.

The poems in this section are translated by Gail Omvedt and Bharat Patankar. "We Are Lucky! We Are Lucky!" is translated by Dilip Chitre.

PRONOUNCING GLOSSARY

Chandal: *chun-dahl´*
Kunbi: *koon´-bee*
Kshatriya: *kuh-shut´-ree-yuh*
Nama: *nah´-muh*
Narayan: *nah-rah´-yun*
Pandari: *pahn´-duh-ree*
pandit: *pun´-dit*
Pandurang: *pahn´-doo-rung*
Sant: *sunt*
Shudra: *shoo´-druh*
Tuka: *too´-kah*
Vaishya: *vaish´-yuh*
Vithoba: *vih-toh´-bah*

BY CASTE AND LINEAGE A SHUDRA

This poem presents a litany of woes and an affirmation of faith in a god Tuka calls Narayan or Pandurang (names of Vishnu). Tuka refers to himself as a Shudra, a member of the lowest of the four classes or *varnas* ("The Hymn of the Primeval Man," p. 82); he probably shares the opinion, common in his day, that there were no true Kshatriyas or Vaishyas in Maharashtra, and that the Vaishyas were almost as degraded as the Shudras. He addresses the Saints, the saints of North Indian *bhakti*.

By caste and lineage a Shudra, I took to business.
At first he was just the family god.

I shouldn't talk, but I'm honoring the pledge
to answer your question, O Sants. (refrain)

My worldly life turned into extreme pain
after my mother and father passed away.
Drought wiped me out, took away wealth and honor,
and one of my wives died crying for food.
I was ashamed, my soul tormented by pain,
and I saw my business fall into loss.
The temple of the god had fallen into ruin,
it came into my mind to repair it.
At first I would do songs and stories on the holy day.
My mind was not inclined to study.
I memorized some sayings of the Sants,
in reverence and faith repeating them.
After that I would sing refrains after them,
making my mind and emotions pure.
I served the Sants the water of their feet,
never letting shame enter my mind.
I helped others as much as I could,
making my body strong for toil.
I never followed the advice of friends.
I was nauseated by the whole worldly round.
I applied my mind to discern truth from untruth,
never heeding the opinion of the majority.
I respected the guru's advice of my dream,
held firmly to trust in the name (in Nama).[1]
After this I was inspired to poetry—
my mind held to the feet of Vithoba.
A blow of denunciation fell on me,
paining my mind for some time.
My manuscripts were drowned,[2] I sat in protest,
and Narayan gave me satisfaction.
If I told all the details
it would become late; enough.
Now my thought is what it seems.
God knows what will happen next.
Narayan never forsakes his devotees.
I have learned his compassion.
Tuka says, My only assets are
that Pandurang has made me speak.

1. The line is ambiguous: Tuka could be referring to the person named Nama or to the name (*nama*, in Marathi) of a guru (named Baba). The former is more likely, given Tuka's well-known tendency to reject gurus.
2. This may be a reference to the story that angry Brahmins forced Tuka to throw all his manuscripts into the river in his native village. Tuka fasted and prayed, and after thirteen days the sunken notebooks reappeared from the river, undamaged. The form of the story is familiar from similar tales told of the magical rearrangement of texts, such as one told of Tulsi (*Ramcharitmanas*, p. 430).

I'VE NOT A SINGLE FRAUD

This song both boasts and complains of the lack of institutional backing for the radical Sants, and of Tuka's scorn for the holy men of his time. The poet worships Vetal (yet another form of the name of Vitthal) and mocks the worshippers of Shiva who wear a rosary, the string of "Rudra-eye" (*rudraksha*) beads.

I've not a single fraud
to infatuate the world.

I sing hymns that please
and praise your qualities. (refrain)

I don't know how to show
herbs or instant miracles.
I've no followers to dispense
stories of my holiness.
I'm no lord of a hermitage,
no habit of holding on to land.
I don't keep a shop
for idol worshippers to stop.
I don't tell how to placate
Vetal with chants and spells.
I'm no Puranic storyteller
who says one thing and does another.
I'm no vile pandit to engage
in meaningless debates.
I burn no lamps to say,
"Hail, arise, what happiness!"
I don't wave a rosary
and gather fools to me.
I've no shastric sorcery
for exorcism's trickery.
Tuka knows them well,
he's no crazed citizen of hell.

GOOD YOU MADE ME A KUNBI

The very first word, "good" (*bara*), is used ironically, as it often is in Marathi, and the rest of the poem follows in the same tone. Kunbi is the name of the large peasant caste to which Tuka belonged.

Good you made me a Kunbi,
else I'd have died of hypocrisy.

You've done well, O God,
Tuka dances and falls at your feet. (refrain)

If I had any learning
I would have fallen into evil.
I would have missed serving the Sants,
with fruitless plundering.
Arrogance is stiff,
it goes on the road to death.
Tuka says, Pride
and greatness go to hell.

WE ARE LUCKY! WE ARE LUCKY!

A bitter, sardonic joke about poverty.

We are lucky! We are lucky!
For a copper vessel, we use a dried gourd.

Others take pride in owning cattle;
We are content with rats and mice.

People ride horses and elephants;
We walk in rawhide shoes.

Says Tuka, we are barely clothed.
To touch us, even death does not dare.

I FEEL SHAME WHEN PEOPLE HONOR ME

This poem is in a mood more typical of South Indian *bhakti* than of Marathi satire, expressing the worshipper's feeling of total inadequacy.

I feel shame when people honor me,
there's nothing worth it in my body.
I'm used up like a measure[1] worn out through use.
Oh burn up this profitless greatness!
I'm a tender thorn with a piercing point,
hollow inside and fragile.
I'm a plastered picture decorated,

1. A measuring cord.

lifeless form with only a shadow.
Tuka says, A day is wasted, O God,
which has no experience.

BORN OF SHUDRA FAMILY

Another ironic poem about poverty. Like so many of Tuka's poems, it speaks of Pandhari, the city of Pandharpur.

Born of Shudra family
And so, free from hypocrisy—

Oh, you are mine now,
Mother and father, Pandari's lord. (refrain)

I have no right
To read and write.
In all ways poor—
Tuka says, My caste is low.

WHAT WILL I GAIN BY REMAINING DEFERENT?

Dr. Ambedkar, the great twentieth-century leader of caste reform ("Dr. Ambedkar's Speech at Mahad," p. 597), used the first four lines of this song on the masthead of his first paper, named *Mooknayak*, "the leader of the nonspeaking."

What will I gain by remaining deferent?
I have roared fearlessly.
No one in the world heeds the mute.
No one gains by shame of their deeds.
Came the answer, I spoke with the lord,
becoming bold, straightforward, fiery.
Tuka says, When you have business with the powerful,
you must speak firmly with them.

OH LISTEN NOW TO ME

An unusually optimistic song for Tuka. He speaks of the Chandals or Chandalas, regarded as Untouchable because they live in the cremation grounds and handle corpses, and of their rights (*adhikaar*), using a word that is used nowadays to translate "human rights" (*manavadhikar*). Narayan is a name of Vishnu.

Oh listen now to me,
the sign that makes you free:
keep the lord of Pandhari
in your heart always.

Then how can we be bound
when we speak and sing Narayan?
Who understands the world
will reach this shore. (refrain)

He'll end darkness and slavery,
Illusion's bonds will broken be;
Everyone will be
powerful and prosperous.

Brahman, Kshatriya, Vaishya, Shudra,
and Chandals also have rights;
women, children, male and female,
and even prostitutes.

Says Tuka, Through experience
we have torn down every fence.
Many divine joys immense
are taken by the devotees.

CRITIQUE OF BRAHMINS

The poems in this section mock Brahmins in many ways, depicting them sometimes as wrongly scornful of the lower castes and sometimes themselves debased in their greed for money and their willingness to do anything to get it.

The poems in this section are translated by Gail Omvedt and Bharat Patankar.

PRONOUNCING GLOSSARY

ashrama: *ah´-shruh-muh*
Brahmachari: *brah´-muh-chah´-ree*
Chandal: *chun-dahl´*
Chandala: *chun-dah´-luh*
Mahar: *muh-hahr´*
pandit: *pun´-dit*
sannyasi: *sun-yah´-see*
Shudra: *shoo´-druh*
Tuka: *too´-kah*
Vaishya: *vaish´-yuh*
vanaprastha: *vuh´-nuh-pruh´-stuh*

HE'S NOT A BRAHMIN WHO ABHORS

Reversing the Brahmin argument, Tuka argues that it is the Brahmins who are defiled by their treatment of the lower castes. The Mahars are a large Dalit caste in Maharashtra who are said to have been warriors and to have given *Maha*rashtra its name.

He's not a Brahmin who abhors
the touch of a Mahar.
What retribution will suffice
except to sacrifice his life?
He won't touch a Chandal,
it's his heart that's defiled.
Tuka says, His caste's defined
by what fills his mind.

HE SELLS HIS DAUGHTER, COWS, AND STORIES

Continuing his condemnation of Brahmins, whom he again likens to Chandalas (low-caste people who live in the cremation grounds and handle corpses), Tuka accuses them of selling their daughters by way of the traditional bride price, a custom—the opposite of the more usual dowry—by which the groom pays the father of the bride.

The lawmakers, including Manu (p. 202), generally disapprove of the practice, but it persists. Tuka accuses the Brahmins of selling their texts as well as their daughters, and he sends them straight to hell.

He sells his daughter, cows, and stories,
He is the true Chandala.
Merits and faults are the real measure,
They're not a result of caste, O god.
Entangled in desire, they do what they should not,
Tuka says, They go to hell.

THE CUNNING GRAB FOR COINS

Again the Brahmins come under Tuka's lash, but this time for different, less typically Brahminical sins: they undertake degrading tasks, become "servants of the base," subservient to the lower classes. This is Tuka's version of the sins of the Kali Age ("The Four Ages," p. 228), in which Brahmins no longer behave like Brahmins. The other classes, too, are corrupted: the king (a Kshatriya) fails to rule justly, and the Vaishyas and Shudras, too, are "green inside," rotten and festering.

The cunning grab for coins and sell
their daughters as concubines.

Such is the dharma of our time,
the good is slave, the evil strong. (refrain)

Leaving righteousness,
Brahmins have become vile thieves.
They hide the caste mark on their face,
and dress in Muslim clothes.
They sit on thrones oppressing,
to keep the people starving.
They manage public kitchens,
living on oil and butter.
They're servants of the base;
get beatings for mistakes.
The king exploits the people,
holy places nourish evil.
The Vaishyas, Shudras, and all
are naturally so low.
These are all the outer colors,
the green inside is masked by sham.
Tuka says, O God,
don't sleep, but run to help!

IF YOU DON'T KEEP THE *ASHRAMAS*

Here Tuka mocks the basic laws of the dharma texts, beginning with the *ashramas*, the four stages of life ("Upanishads," p. 105; "The Four Ages," p. 228), and continuing to cut a wide swath through asceticism, Vedic chants, vows, dharma, *bhakti* (which he calls universal love and says is ruined by hierarchical thinking), and ritual laws. There's not a lot left of Hinduism after that—except the love of god.

If you don't keep the *ashramas*,
you are bound to karma's laws.

Such is not our simple faith,
It unites us in god's grace. (refrain)

Austerities will get a blow,
when the senses overflow.
Chants work a while,
if they do you become a fool.
You tell us to depend on vows,
one lapse, they're useless to our cause.
Dharma should lead to righteousness,
otherwise it's valueless.
Universal love gets shaken,
when hierarchy's pride awakens.
Besides, says Tuka, they weigh us down,
their ritual "dos and don'ts" abound.

BRAHMACHARI DHARMA IS RECITING THE VEDAS

In this poem, Tuka indicts each of the four stages of life or *ashramas* ("Upanishads," p. 105): the first stage of chaste student, the *brahmachari;* the second stage of householder; the third stage of forest-dweller (*vanaprastha*), an unsatisfactory compromise between the householder (for the forest-dweller may have his wife with him) and the renouncer (for he is supposed to remain celibate); and the fourth stage of renouncer (*sannyasi*). Tuka also challenges caste and even dharma. But he attributes to some unnamed scripture a rule that he does believe in: follow the way that you speak of, as he does.

Brahmachari dharma is reciting the Vedas,
the householder's thought is of the six duties;
the *vanaprastha* stage is both separation and union,
while in the *sannyasi* purpose is renounced.
The devotee knows the easy secret,

there is no caste, clan, or dharma there.
He who speaks of a way and doesn't follow it
is known as the fallen, so the scriptures say.
Tuka says, There is nothing without a rule,
it's all empty toil that ends in pain.

CALL HIM PANDIT, HE'S IN BLISS

A diatribe against Vedic pandits, scholars.

Call him pandit, he's in bliss,
yet everywhere he looks an ass.
What will you do by muttering
the Vedas, wasted sputtering?
He does not do what the Vedas say,
the evil fellow knows no righteousness.
Tuka sees the good in life,
this is his experience.

ILLUSION AND BHAKTI

These poems praise renunciation of the world that is nothing but a false appearance. Tuka rejects the philosophy of Non-Dualism (Advaita), which argues that there is no duality, no distinction, between the individual soul and the world-soul (*brahman* or *brahma*). Instead, he speaks of a more pervasive sort of illusion that pervades all philosophies and, indeed, everything except the god that he loves.

The poems in this section are translated by Gail Omvedt and Bharat Patankar.

PRONOUNCING GLOSSARY

Advaita: *ud-vai-tuh*
Bali: *buh´-lee*
Brahma: *bruh-mah´*
chakravarti: *chuh´-kruh-vahr´-tee*
Damayanti: *duh´-muh-yun-tee*
dharna: *dhar-nah´*
Dombs: *dohmb*
Harischandra: *huh´-rees-chun´-druh*
Kaliyuga: *kah´-lee-yoo´-guh*
Karna: *kar´-nuh*
Murari: *moo-rah´-ree*
Nala: *nuh´-luh*
Narayan: *nah-rah´-yun*
Narayana: *nah-rah´-yuh-nuh*
Purana: *poo-rah´-nuh*
Sant: *sunt*
Shibi: *shee´-bee*
Shriyala: *shree´-yuh-luh*
Tuka: *too´-kah*

IT IS FOR THIS I WANDER WILD

This remarkable poem simultaneously indicts the central doctrines of Advaita (Non-dual) Vedanta (p. 285) and affirms the value of renunciation.

It is for this I wander wild,
Leave my home, go to the wood.
My love will be illuminated
My understanding liberated.
I will not hear the preaching
Of Advaita's teaching.
Illusions like "I am Brahma"
Should not, says Tuka, come in my way.

A GOD WITHOUT A DEVOTEE

The essence of *bhakti* is here distilled into the essence of mutuality, epitomized by a reversed and expanded version of what the Bengali tradition regards as one of the four ways to love god—as a mother loves a child—but here also as a child loves a mother.

A god without a devotee—
how will there be form or service?
They make each other beautiful,
a diamond set in gold.
A devotee without a god,
who will give desirelessness?
Says Tuka, They're related like
a mother and a child.

HARI, YOU ARE CRUEL AND WITHOUT QUALITIES

This is another song blaming the god for his treatment of his devotees, this time punning on the word *nir-guna*, "without qualities," which generally refers to the aspect of god that is beyond all qualities ("We've Treated *Moksha* with Scorn Because," p. 473), but here means "without any *good* qualities." Tuka lists a number of devotees who have been mistreated by various gods, all here regarded as aspects of Krishna:

Harishchandra (in the *Puranas*) was a king who was transformed, by a curse, into a Dalit (a Domb or Dom), and who lost his wife and his son, though he was ultimately restored to his family.

Nala and Damayanti (in the *Mahabharata*) were a king and queen, happily married until the jealousy of the gods and the spirit of Kali, the losing throw of the dice, destroyed their kingdom and separated them; they, too, were ultimately restored to one another and to their kingdom.

Shibi was tricked by the gods into cutting off his flesh ("King Shibi," p. 160).

Karna (in the *Mahabharata*) was abandoned by his mother and lived in misery until he was killed because he was cursed to forget a crucial magical formula.

Bali ("The Ten Avatars of Vishnu," p. 480) was an anti-god tricked and cheated by Vishnu.

Shriyala (Tamil Siriyala) was, in South Indian mythology, the child of a man (Ciruttontur) whom Shiva tested by getting the parents to kill, cook, and serve their son—until he was ultimately restored to life. In this Marathi version, the father is named Murari, also a name of Krishna.

Hari, you are cruel and without qualities,
you've no compassion, you're very hard,
you do what is unimaginable—
what no one else has done.
You took away Harishchandra's glory,
his kingdom, horse, all his wealth,
made him sell wife, son, his whole life
to the house of the Dombs.
You ruined the union
of Nala and Damayanti,
so the world understands
and the Puranas tell.
The *chakravarti*[1] king Shibi,
compassionate to all beings,
you made him weigh his flesh
on the scales.
Karna was engaged in war,
his speech was engulfed on the battlefield,
you demanded that he
be forced into submission.
Bali was generous to all,
to any who raised his hand;
acting with rage,
he was sent under the earth.
In the house of Shriyala[2]
Murari sat in *dharna*;[3]
you forced him to kill
his own baby with his hands.
This is life you've given
to those who praise you with devotion.
I have no idea, says Tuka,
what you will do next.

1. A *chakravarti* is a king who "turns the wheel" of a great empire.
2. For Shriyala (Siriyala) and Ciruttontur, see David Dean Shulman, *The Hungry God*.
3. A method of obtaining justice, such as the payment of a debt, by sitting, fasting, at the door of the person from whom reparation is sought.

I GAVE BIRTH TO MYSELF

Identifying himself with the god who is "self-born" or "self-created" (*svayambhu*), Tuka takes responsibility for his own life.

I gave birth to myself,
I came into my own womb.

Enough now of vows,
My yearnings have died away.
It is good that I fell prey
And I died that day.
Looking both ways,
Tuka is what he is.

WE'VE TREATED *MOKSHA* WITH SCORN BECAUSE

Tuka rejects *moksha* (Release) because he never wants to stop worshipping his god, and because he prefers the god with form, with qualities (*sa-guna*), to the formless god, without qualities (*nir-guna*). He chooses the solid, everyday god who endures forever on something as solid and everyday as a brick ("The Thug Has Arrived," p. 455).

We've treated *moksha* with scorn because
from age to age we want to be born.
Devotion is not a joy that tarnishes,
again and again we'll serve him with hope.
God has taken form in hand,
we won't let him be formless again.
Tuka says, My mind remained at ease
meditating on the feet on the brick.

SILENCE IN SPEECH, LIFE IN DEATH

"Nonbeing while being" quotes the great Rig Vedic creation hymn that begins, "There was neither nonbeing nor being" ("Creation Hymn," p. 79), and "Enjoying while renouncing" is a common Tantric equation (*bhoksha* is *moksha*). Tuka draws his own moral from these and other traditional Hindu paradoxes.

Silence in speech, life in death,
nonbeing while being, so are we.
Enjoying is renouncing,
solitude in company.
We have broken
both following and connections.
Tuka says, I am not what I seem:
if you want to ask, ask Pandurang.

BRAHMA IS ILLUSION, SAY THE CROOKS OF RELIGION

A diatribe against religious hypocrites, particularly within the Vedic fold, who do not truly know Narayan (Vishnu).

Brahma is illusion, say the crooks of religion,
they have looted people for themselves.
Addicted to sex, he teaches evil knowledge,
wandering infatuated after this mentality.
If you prepare *suran*[1] properly you don't get troubled,
but if you do it in haste you'll get sorrow.
If medicine is to be given to a child,
he's shown sweets to distract him.
Before seeking salvation he searches the Vedas,
do away with this barren talk of his.
Tuka says, He who only fattens his body
will never encounter Narayan.

1. The Maharashtrian name for a kind of yam.

ACCUMULATING WEALTH BY A NOBLE BUSINESS

Here Tuka equates the fruits of the worldly life, properly lived, with the fruits of asceticism, in a trope of equivalence known from the Tantras, which equate *bhoksha*—enjoyment—and *moksha* ("Tantras," p. 275), and even from the *Gita*, with its doctrine of freedom from the negative results of actions performed in the proper state of mind ("The True Nature of Action," p. 180).

Accumulating wealth by a noble business,
spending with detached mind,
he will reach a great goal,
he will enjoy greatly a life of treasure.
He knows not debtedness to another or scorn of others,
he treats all women as sisters and mothers,
he cares for cows, animals, all beings,
and hungry animals in the forest.
Of peaceful form, he does bad to none,
and increases the renown of his forefathers.
Tuka says, This is the fruit of worldly life,
it is the great strength of austerities.

AVATAR OF BUDDHA, O MY INVISIBLE ONE

Tuka, like Jayadeva ("The Ten Avatars of Vishnu," p. 480), views the Buddha ("Vishnu as the Buddha," p. 242) as a positive figure. But now that the Kali Yuga has come (the Kali Age, the age of the next avatar, Kalki ["Vishnu as Kalki," p. 245]), Tuka can no longer see the Buddha and longs for the compassion for which the Buddha was noted.

Avatar of Buddha, O my invisible one,
with mute countenance, fixed attention.
Dark blue, four-armed for the people,
you speak in whispers to the Sants.
The Kaliyuga has come, this has fallen to my lot;
however I move my eyes I cannot see you thus.
What have you done to me, Narayana?
Why no compassion? says Tuka.

I'VE BUILT A HOUSE IN BOUNDLESS SPACE

The house made of formless space is strikingly reminiscent of the Vedantic parable in the *Yoga-vasistha* ("The Man Who Built a House of Air," p. 292). But here the illusory house takes on a positive resonance, as a place of peace and purity, with a metaphysical reality of its own.

I've built a house in boundless space,
I live in formless infinity.
I've become completely without illusions, serene,
I've reached unbroken unity.
Tuka says, Now there's no ego,
I've become suddenly continuously pure.

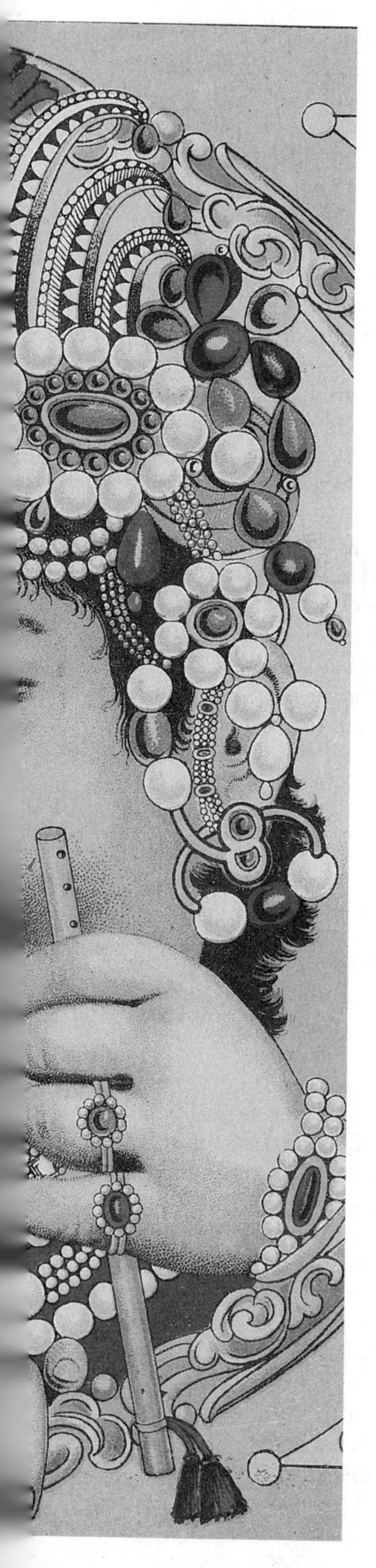

Love and Anger in Bengal

1500–1872

Bangla is a North Indian language spoken by about 230 million people in the region of Bengal, which now consists of West Bengal, Bangladesh, and parts of other states. Along with Hindi and other North Indian languages, Bangla evolved after 1000 C.E. from the Magadhi Prakrit, an early regional dialect.

The literature of Bengal was composed in both Sanskrit and Bangla (sometimes called Bengali); the two languages interacted thoroughly, citing one another's texts in a linguistic pas de deux. Of the many Bengalis who composed in Sanskrit, the twelfth-century poet Jayadeva, author of the *Gita Govinda* ("The Song of [Krishna] the Cowherd"), heavily influenced Bengali literature in Bangla when it developed, sometime before the fifteenth century. The disciples of the Bengali saint Chaitanya wrote in both Bangla and Sanskrit.

The earliest works in Bangla were in the genre of *mangal-kavya* ("poetry of an auspicious happening"), eulogies of gods and goddesses, composed and transmitted orally long before they were committed to writing; poems in this genre, such as the *Manasa-Mangal* of Ketaka Das, were composed well into the eighteenth century. Another Bangla genre was the *maha-kavya* (literally "great poem," or, more loosely, "epic"), such as the *Ramayana* of

"Radha-Krishna," in a late nineteenth-century chromolithograph from Kolkata. As always, Krishna is identified by his flute.

Krittibas Ojha (late fourteenth century) and the *Mahabharata* of Kashirama Das (seventeenth century), original works that often diverge significantly from the Sanskrit models on which they are based.

A third Bangla genre is the *pada-vali* ("string of verse"), consisting of songs inspired by *bhakti*. The earliest works in this distinctively Bengali style are the love poetry in praise of Krishna and his beloved Radha by Vidyapati, Chandidas, and Govinda-das, in the fourteenth and fifteenth centuries. These poems were heavily influenced by the movement called Sahaja or Sahajiya ("Inborn" or "Spontaneous" or "Naturalist"), which had begun to spread throughout Bengal as early as the twelfth century ("Mastering Sahaja Love"). Sahajiyas saw Krishna and Radha united in every man and every woman; their goal was not to worship or imitate Krishna or Radha, in a dualistic, *bhakti* sense, but to become them, in a monistic and Tantric sense, to realize both male and female powers within their own bodies. This was a quasi-Tantric form of Krishna-*bhakti* that praised erotic love as the easiest and quickest path (the natural, inborn path) to self-realization.

The Sahajiyas praised the ideal of a man's love for another man's wife or for a woman of unsuitably low caste, or an unmarried woman's love for a man (for even in texts in which Radha is not anyone else's wife, she is usually not Krishna's wife), because they admired the intensity of such love in the face of social disapproval. The adulterous love between Krishna and Radha or the cowherd women (Gopis) made adulterous passion, which had long been the benchmark of what religion was designed to prevent, a metaphor for the proper love of god. Yet these ideals were not meant to be taken as paradigms for ways of imitating god; they were theological parables, not licenses to commit adultery. They merely used adulterous love as a model for the love of god—more passionate, difficult, and dangerous than ordinary married love. Even a whiff of adultery was enough to evoke the scorn of most conventional Bengali Hindus, but the Sahajiyas inspired much of the Vaishnava poetry in praise of Krishna that was embraced by Bengali Hindus of all castes. The quasi-Tantric Bengal traditions debated for centuries whether Radha was Krishna's wife ("his own," *svakiya*) or his mistress ("someone else's," *parakiya*), and they decided, in 1717, that adulterous love was in fact orthodox.

The great Bengali mystic and saint Chaitanya (1486–1533) developed a theology of Krishna that heavily influenced the great flowering of Bengali literature in the sixteenth and seventeenth centuries. The most important work of this period was the long hagiography *Chaitanya-charitamrita* ("Elixir of the Life of Chaitanya"), by the sixteenth-century author Krishnadas Kaviraja. His followers, such as Rupa Goswamin and Narottama Das, took Chaitanya's theology into more complex realms.

The worship of goddesses, already robust in Bengal at the time of the *mangal* poems, stimulated and was in turn stimulated by the increasing importance, and divinity, of Radha in the worship of Krishna. But the less romantic and more terrible goddesses, such as Manasa, Kali, and Durga, also entered the literary scene at this time. By the eighteenth century, Ramprasad Sen took the tradition of *pada-valis* from an earlier time and dedicated it, with significant literary changes, to the goddess Kali. At the same time, the wandering Bauls (Fakir Lalon Shah), Tantrics and mystics, sang songs that combined the Sahajiya erotic tradition with the mysticism of the Tamil and Hindi Sants.

During the end of this period, by the eighteenth century, the British presence in India made its mark on the religious literature of Bengal, now written in both Bangla and English. Rammohun Roy used both languages in his writings in protest against *suttee* ("The Practice of Burning Widows Alive"), and Michael Madhusudan Datta's epic poem on the death of the son of Ravana ("The Funeral Rites of Meghanada") combines British and Indian sensibilities in a Bangla work that inverts many of the values of Valmiki's *Ramayana*.

JAYADEVA

Jayadeva's Sanskrit poem, the *Gita Govinda*, "The Song of [Krishna] the Cowherd," is a central text for Vaishnava worshippers throughout India. It was incorporated into the ritual and dance tradition of the Jagannatha temple in Puri, in Orissa; Chaitanya's love for it (p. 494) made it almost canonical for Bengal Vaishnavas, particularly among the Sahajiyas (p. 478), who claim Jayadeva as their "founding guru"; and it is a part of the classical South Indian music tradition.

Jayadeva is said to have been born into a Brahmin family (the place is debated: Bengal, Orissa, Mithila); it is more certain that he lived in the latter half of the twelfth century. Educated in the Sanskrit religious classics, he soon abandoned Sanskrit and became a wandering mendicant, an ascetic, until (according to legend) he met and married a dancing girl named Padmavati in the Jagannatha temple of Puri. He almost certainly enjoyed the patronage of the Bengali king Lakshmanasena (ca. 1179–1209).

The romance of Krishna and Radha in Jayadeva's great poem may owe something to the Persian romances that were becoming known in India through the Muslim presence at this time, particularly among some Sufi sects. But the power of Jayadeva's Radha is unprecedented; Krishna bends down before her and puts her feet on his head (10.8), and when they make love she gets on top of him in the "reverse position" (12.10). Though Jayadeva's lyrical eroticism occasionally inspired prudish criticism, it has generally been loved, appreciated, and imitated from his day to ours.

PRONOUNCING GLOSSARY

Balarama: *buh´-luh-rah´-muh*
Bali: *buh´-lee*
Gita Govinda: *gee´-tah-goh-vin´-duh*
Hari: *huh´-ree*
Hiranyakashipu: *hi-run´-yuh-kuh´-shee-poo*
Jayadeva: *jah´-yuh-day´-vuh*
Jumna: *jum´-nah*
Rama: *rah´-muh*
Ravana: *rah´-vuh-nuh*
Veda: *vay´-duh*

THE TEN AVATARS OF VISHNU

Jayadeva presents his own version of the ten avatars of Vishnu. Surprisingly, Krishna, who is almost always listed as one of the ten, is not mentioned at all here, though he is the hero of the rest of the poem. (Balarama takes Krishna's place as the eighth avatar in this list.) Jayadeva thus suggests that Krishna is actually Vishnu, and hence transcends the avatars. He also includes unusual details about some of the other avatars:

1. The fish is praised not for saving people from a flood ("The Fish Saves Manu," p. 95) but for recovering the Vedas, which a demon had stolen from Brahma;

Vishnu created a flood that killed the demon, then became a fish and rescued the Vedas from the bottom of the ocean.

2. The tortoise here supports the entire earth, always, not just Mount Mandara during the churning of the ocean ("The Churning of the Ocean," p. 149).

3. The boar rescues the earth when human overcrowding has made it sink into the ocean.

4. The Man-lion (Nara-simha) is the form in which Vishnu destroys the anti-god Hiranyakashipu, who had threatened to kill his son Prahlada, a Vishnu-*bhakta*. Hiranyakashipu had been given the boon that he could not be killed by day or night, by god, human, or beast, on earth or in the air; Vishnu appeared at twilight, in the form of the man-lion, held him on his lap and ripped him apart with his claws.

5. The dwarf avatar is based on a Vedic myth ("The Three Strides of Vishnu," p. 91); the Puranas expand the myth by saying that the anti-god Bali usurped the triple universe (earth, atmosphere, and heaven) until Vishnu, as a Brahmin dwarf, begged him for just as much earth as he could cover in three paces, and then assumed his cosmic form and stepped across all three worlds. Jayadeva adds the detail that Vishnu's toes are wet from the water that Bali poured on his feet in the ceremony of welcome, before he made his fateful promise.

6. Parashurama ("Rama with an Axe") murdered the entire class of Kshatriyas, twenty-one times over, in revenge for their killing of his father. Jayadeva shines a favorable light on this violence by saying that the Kshatriyas had been evil.

7. Rama (*Ramayana*, p. 186) here hurls Ravana's ten heads to the skies, which are guarded by the eight gods of the four directions (East, etc.) and the intermediate directions (Southeast, etc.), plus the directions up and down.

8. Balarama, Krishna's elder brother, is said to have drunkenly ordered the Yamuna (Jumna) River ("The River Yamuna," p. 259) to move; when she refused, he threw his weapon, the plow, into her and forced her to obey him.

9. The Puranas viewed the Buddha as a force of corruption ("Vishnu as the Buddha," p. 242); Jayadeva here interprets the Buddha's rejection of the Vedas positively, as a move toward compassion for animals (through the rejection of Vedic animal sacrifice). This change was facilitated by the change in the status of Buddhism in India, still powerful at the time of the early Puranas, no longer a threat by the time of Jayadeva.

10. Kalki is the avenging angel of the Kali Age ("Vishnu as Kalki," p. 245).

In seas that rage as the aeon of chaos collapses,
You keep the holy Veda like a ship straight on course.
  You take form as the Fish, Krishna.
  Triumph, Hari, Lord of the World!

Where the world rests on your vast back,
Thick scars show the weight of bearing earth.
  You take form as the Tortoise, Krishna.
  Triumph, Hari, Lord of the World!

The earth clings to the tip of your tusk
Like a speck of dust caught on the crescent moon.
  You take form as the Boar, Krishna.
  Triumph, Hari, Lord of the World!

TRANSLATED BY Barbara Stoler Miller.

Nails on your soft lotus hand are wondrous claws
Tearing the gold-robed body of black bee Hiranyakashipu.
  You take form as the Man-lion, Krishna.
  Triumph, Hari, Lord of the World!

Wondrous dwarf, when you cheat demon Bali with wide steps,
Water falls from your lotus toenails to purify creatures.
  You take form as the Dwarf, Krishna.
  Triumph, Hari, Lord of the World!

You wash evil from the world in a flood of warriors' blood,
And the pain of existence is eased.
  You take form as the axman Priest, Krishna.
  Triumph, Hari, Lord of the World!

Incited by gods who guard the directions in battle,
You hurl Ravana's ten demon heads to the skies.
  You take form as the prince Rama, Krishna.
  Triumph, Hari, Lord of the World!

The robe on your bright body is colored with rain clouds,
And Jumna waters roiling in fear of your plow's attack.
  You take form as the plowman Balarama, Krishna.
  Triumph, Hari, Lord of the World!

Moved by deep compassion, you condemn the Vedic way
That ordains animal slaughter in rites of sacrifice.
  You take form as the enlightened Buddha, Krishna.
  Triumph, Hari, Lord of the World!

You raise your sword like a fiery meteor
Slashing barbarian hordes to death.
  You take form as the avenger Kalki, Krishna.
  Triumph, Hari, Lord of the World!

Listen to the perfect invocation of poet Jayadeva,
Joyously evoking the essence of existence!
  You take the tenfold cosmic form, Krishna.
  Triumph, Hari, Lord of the World!

For upholding the Vedas,
For supporting the earth,
For raising the world,
For tearing the demon asunder,
For cheating Bali,
For destroying the warrior class,
For conquering Ravana,
For wielding the plow,
For spreading compassion,
For routing the barbarians,
Homage to you, Krishna,
In your ten incarnate forms!

1.5–16

VIDYAPATI

Vidyapati was born, probably around 1352, in Madhubani, Bihar, long known for its arts and in our day famous for paintings by the women of its villages. Vidyapati was a Brahmin scholar, courtier, and poet. He wrote several long poems in Sanskrit, one celebrating the dynasty of the Mithila king who employed him (Kirti Simha, r. 1370–80). But then he began to write love poetry in Maithili, the language of Mithila, which had never before been used as a literary language. His poems combined the traditions of Sanskrit court poetry and Mithila village songs, and he became the most famous poet of his time. He was a close friend of Shiva Simha, king of Mithila from 1402 to 1406, but when Shiva Simha was routed in battle and disappeared, Vidyapati went into retreat for many years, and his poems of longing for Krishna may be tinged with mourning for Shiva Simha. He continued to write and died around 1448, back in Madhubani.

PRONOUNCING GLOSSARY

Madhava: *mah´-duh-vuh*
tambul: *tahm´-bool*
Vidyapati: *vid-yah´-puh-tee*

THE NECKLACE-SNAKE

This is a fairly straightforward love poem, sung by a man to a woman, with no evidence that, like so many Indian love poems, it has a theological subtext. But it employs a central image redolent of Vedantic philosophy and Shaiva mythology: the snake that appears to be a rope (or vice versa) ("Vedanta," p. 285). The snake that serves the god Shiva as his necklace (as well as his bracelets and anklets and belt) ("Oh, the Yogi," p. 422) is now imagined as a necklace that turns (back?) into a snake.

This and the next three poems are translated by Deben Bhattacharya.

Listen, O lovely darling,
Cease your anger.
I promise by the golden pitchers of your breasts
And by your necklace-snake,
Which now I gather in my hands,
If ever I touch anyone but you
May your necklace bite me;
And if my words do not ring true,
Punish me as I deserve.
Bind me in your arms, bruise me with your thighs,
Choke my heart with your milk-swollen breasts,
Lock me day and night in the prison of your heart.

COUNTERFEIT

The deceitful lover is the micro-image of the god responsible for the cosmic deceit of making us believe that the whole world is real.

When you stay before my eyes
You make me feel your love is firm,
But out of sight how different you are!
How long does false gold shine?
Master of sweetness, I know your ways.
Your heart is counterfeit.
Your love is words.
Speech, love and humor
All are smooth
And only meant to tease.
When you shed a girl,
Do you laugh?
Are your arrows always
Poisoned with honey?

LET NO ONE BE A GIRL

The anguished, abandoned woman expresses a wish that may reflect the misogynist bias of Hinduism, in which the birth of a girl often means nothing but the need to provide a dowry that will cripple the family financially. The woman also begs to be free of her family, presumably free from their restrictions and their disapproval of her violation of them, and she begs for her beloved to be free of other girls, faithful to her alone. Realizing that none of this will happen, she asks that he at least be aware of her suffering and her love.

Let no one be born,
But if one must
Let no one be a girl.
If one must be a girl
Then may she never fall in love,
If she must fall in love,
Free her from her family.
Oh make me sure of him until I end.

Should I meet my lover
And his love flow strongly
Like currents of a river,
Let his darling heart
Be free of other girls.
If he yields to other loves,
Let him know his mind and heart. . . .

MY BODY HID MY BODY

The poet imagines himself as Radha, so stunned by the sight (*darshan*) ("The Flowering of Bhakti," p. 295) of Krishna (here called Madhava) that she turns away, her eyes (lotuses) avoiding the sun that they normally open to, and her hand (the night-lily) covering her face (the moon). Though her clothes have fallen off, she does not notice that she is naked; she sees nothing but Krishna.

My eyes encountered him
And left me.
The lotus snubbed the sun
And fled away.
The moon and the night-lily
Unite in love.
Madhava I saw today,
But with art I hid my passion.

Shyness dropped with my clothes.
My body hid my body.
My heart was another's.
Krishna I saw
Everywhere.

AS THE MIRROR TO MY HAND

Vidyapati here likens Krishna to a series of objects and substances both superficial and profound, both physical and emotional. The poem is inspired by the Bengal Vaishnava doctrines that Krishna and Radha are one soul in two bodies, and that Krishna became incarnate as both together (in Chaitanya) so that he could experience Radha's love for him and his for her, at the same time. And so Radha is inseparable from Krishna.

This and the following poem are translated by Edward C. Dimock and Denise Levertov.

As the mirror to my hand,
the flowers to my hair,
kohl[1] to my eyes,
tambul[2] to my mouth,
musk to my breast,
necklace to my throat,

1. Collyrium, applied around women's eyes as a cosmetic and around children's eyes as both a cosmetic and a medicinal ointment.

2. A mixture of nuts, lime, and spices, wrapped in a leaf of the betel tree, chewed for pleasure; nowadays it is called *pan*.

ecstasy to my flesh,
heart[3] to my home—

as wing to bird,
water to fish,
life to the living—
so you to me.
But tell me,
Madhava,[4] beloved,
who are you?
Who are you really?

Vidyapati says, they are one another.

CHILDREN, WIFE, FRIEND

A poem on the brink of death, a sudden vision of the unreality of family connections and all human ties, in comparison with the greatness of Krishna.

Children, wife, friend—
drops of water on heated sand.
I spent myself on them, forgetting you.
What are they to me now,
O Madhava, now that I am old and without hope,
apart from you. But you are the savior of the world
and full of mercy.
Half my life I passed in sleep—
my youth, now my old age,
how much time.
I spent my youth in lust and dissipation.
I had no time to worship you.
Ageless gods
have come and passed away.
Born from you, they enter you again
like waves into the sea.
For you have no beginning, and no end.
Now

at the end, I fear
the messengers of Death.
Apart from you, there is no way.
I call you Lord,
the infinite and finite,
my salvation.

3. That is, essence.

4. An epithet of Krishna.

CHANDIDAS

Chandidas probably lived between the end of the fourteenth century and the first half of the fifteenth, but little is known about him. He is said to have been born in one of two villages in West Bengal, Chatna (in Bankura) or, more likely, Nannur (in Birbhum); to have been connected with the Sahaja movement in Bengal, an antinomian and ecstatic worship of Krishna and Radha; to have been a village priest; and to have had a relationship with a low-caste washerwoman named Rami. His poems, in an early form of Bangla, say that he was a Brahmin and a village priest; legends say that he was dismissed as a priest and fasted to death as a protest but came to life again on the funeral pyre, or that the wife of the Nawab (ruler) of Gaur took such a fancy to him that her jealous husband had him whipped to death while tied to the back of an elephant.

PRONOUNCING GLOSSARY

Chandidas: *chun´-dee-dahs´*
kadamba: *kuh-dum´-buh*
Kala: *kah´-lah*
Sahaja: *suh´-huh-juh´*
Veda: *vay´-duh*

WHAT GOD IS THAT

This poem reflects the Sahajiya tradition in which the worshipper, male or female, imagines himself or herself as a married woman in love with Krishna.

This and the following four poems are translated by Deben Bhattacharya.

What god is that
Who molded me a woman?
I am always alone
Being married and watched.
Since falling in love
Is a disgrace for me,
I must then kill
My meaningless life.
I am not free
To open my mouth
But I am in rapture
With another man.

HE WAS BLACK

Krishna is often described as dark-skinned and beautiful, and male poets often imagine themselves as women in love with Krishna.

He was black,
He had poison-eyes.
A glance from him brought death to my side,
Life lay open to love's five arrows.[1]
Nothing else mattered—
Food or rest.
I disowned all decorative dress.
My heart raced for the *kadamba*[2] wood.
Having abandoned
Fear and shame,
Like a wild woman I begged for the jewel.[3]

1. Kama, the god of love, is said to shoot five arrows of increasing intensity into the hearts of people who fall in love.
2. A tree said to put forth its fragrant buds at the roaring of thunderclouds.
3. The jewel here stands for love.

IT'S NO USE TELLING ME

The poet imagines that he is a woman whose dark hair reminds him/her of the darkness of Krishna, also called Kala (Black). Letting one's hair down in Bengal (indeed, throughout India) means much of what it means in English—to abandon social formalities, release one's true feelings—but also, more culture-specifically, it means that the woman does not have her husband or lover with her and will not bind up her hair until he returns.

It's no use telling me what I should do,
The blackness of his skin fills my days and my dreams.
I can't even move my hand to fix my tousled tresses.
Taking them for Krishna I fill my lap with my hair.
As I call out for him, my dark darling Kala,
I cry and cry.
My black hair is left in a loose knot now.
When Kala my black one comes to my mind
I let my hair down and brood over it.
The blackness of his skin is forever present,
What can I do?

MASTERING *SAHAJA* LOVE

This prose poem reaches for several metaphors to describe the goals of the Sahaja ritual and praxis. The expansion of the body in space, an image that can be traced back to the Vedas, is a recurrent trope of trance and hallucination; the frog that dances in the mouth of the snake is a metaphor for *coitus reservatus* (sex without ejaculation) that is a part of some Tantric traditions ("Tantras," p. 275).

Mastering *Sahaja* love is a great art. It implies the ability to extend one's person to the very limits of space—east and west, north and south, all directions having an immediate and simultaneous meaning.

To extract happiness from *Sahaja* love, it must be treated as a deep secret yet the wishes must be fulfilled. It is as difficult as making a frog dance in the mouth of a snake which is not allowed to eat the frog. It is like dangling a mountain with a cotton thread, like imprisoning an elephant in a cobweb . . .

MY BODY CORRODES

This short poem vividly encapsulates the Sahajiya spirit that walks away from all that conventional Hindus value (beginning with the Vedas, the earliest Hindu texts [*Rig Veda*, p. 73]), as well as the price that the Sahaja worshipper pays for that freedom.

My body corrodes
And my heart grows heavy
Since I heard of *Sahaja* love.
I was so very young.

When the god wills
And I meet my love,
My honors and virtues
And my prides and patience,
The laws of the Vedas
Will totally erupt.

I have thrown in the river
The care of my caste,
Leaving my husband.
I have demolished
All religious rites,
My errors and guilts . . .

BELOVED, WHAT MORE SHALL I SAY?

The poet imagines a woman who speaks simultaneously to her human lover and to Krishna. He is absent, and she is in despair.

She speaks:

Beloved, what more shall I say to you?
In life and in death, in birth after birth
you are the lord of my life.
A noose of love binds
my heart to your feet.
My mind fixed on you alone, I have offered you everything;
in truth, I have become your slave.
In this family, in that house, who is really mine?
Whom can I call my own?
It was bitter cold, and I took refuge
at your lotus feet.
While my eyes blink, and I do not see you,
I feel the heart within me die.

A touchstone
I have threaded, and wear upon my throat,
says Chandidas.

TRANSLATED BY Edward C. Dimock and Denise Levertov.

GOVINDA-DAS

Govinda-das, who lived between 1537 and 1612, is regarded as one of the most lyrical of the poets in this *bhakti* genre in which divine love is symbolized by human love. He wrote in Bangla.

Both poems are translated by Edward C. Dimock and Denise Levertov.

PRONOUNCING GLOSSARY

Govinda-das: *goh-vin´-duh–dahs´*
Kan: *kahn*
Madhava: *mah´-duh-vuh*

O MADHAVA

This poem expresses the theme, beloved in miniature painting as well as in poetry, of the woman, usually married, who slips out in the night to meet her lover, braving the rain and the snakes and, often, demons and goblins. The terror and trouble testify to the intensity of the love that drives her and heighten the erotic mood. Here, the lover is Madhava, Krishna.

O Madhava, how shall I tell you of my terror?
I could not describe my coming here
if I had a million tongues.
When I left my room and saw the darkness
I trembled:
I could not see the path,
there were snakes that writhed round my ankles!

I was alone, a woman; the night was so dark,
the forest so dense and gloomy,
and I had so far to go.
The rain was pouring down—
which path should I take?
My feet were muddy
and burning where thorns had scratched them.
But I had the hope of seeing you, none of it mattered,
and now my terror seems far away . . .
When the sound of your flute reaches my ears
it compels me to leave my home, my friends,
it draws me into the dark toward you.

I no longer count the pain of coming here,
says Govinda-das.

THE MARKS OF FINGERNAILS

The unfaithful lover who comes back bearing the marks of his lovemaking with another woman—her fingernail marks on his body, her makeup on his lips, his eyes red from drinking and staying up all night—is a staple of Indian erotic poetry. In this poem, the lover is Krishna, called Kan, whose darkness is taken as a point of difference from his fair, and very angry, mistress.

The marks of fingernails are on your breast
and my heart burns.
Kohl of someone's eyes upon your lips
darkens my face.
I am awake all night;
your eyes are red.
So why do you entreat me, Kan,
saying that you and I have but one heart?
You come with choking voice
while I want to weep.
"Only our bodies are apart."
But mine is light,
and yours is dark.
Go home, then,

says Govinda-das.

BALARAMA-DAS

Balarama-das *(buh´-luh-rah´-muh–das´)* was a Brahmin who lived in the early sixteenth century, near Krishnagar, in Bengal. He wrote in Bangla.

A WICKED WOMAN

The first line expresses what all the people in the rest of the poem say about Radha, a married woman in love with Krishna. Her mother-in-law, so often a person of contention in *bhakti* literature ("Life without Hari," p. 420; Mirabai, p. 419), heads the list, followed by her husband and then by other, unnamed women. Still she persists in her love for Krishna, and the poet identifies himself with her.

To Krishna:

A wicked woman—fouler than the foulest poison.
So his mother's cruelty, like fire
burning in me.
My tyrant husband: the whetted
edge of a razor. And all around me,
reproachful dutiful women.
My love, what shall I tell you?
Whatever their calumnies, you
are my life itself.
                    My body
bears your brand—they know it.
For shame I cannot raise my head
                    before chaste women,
I cannot bear the cruelty, the knife-thrust
of seeing my fellow women make mocking signs to me.
I have weighed it all.
                    Yet I have chosen
to endure abuse for your sake.

So Balarama-das says.

Translated by Edward C. Dimock and Denise Levertov.

CHAITANYA AND KRISHNADAS KAVIRAJA

The Bengali saint Chaitanya (1486–1533) was born, as Vishvambara Mishra, into a Brahmin family in Navadvipa (in Bengal) and received a sound education in the Sanskrit sacred texts. After the death of his father when he was twenty-two, he made a pilgrimage to Gaya (in Bihar) to perform the funeral rituals, and there he had a religious experience that inspired him to renounce the world. The world, however, would not renounce him; people flocked to him and joined him in singing songs to Krishna and dancing in a kind of trance, as well as repeating the names of Krishna, worshipping temple icons or the Tulsi plant (a kind of basil sacred to Vishnu) (Tulsi Das, p. 424), and retelling Krishna's acts, particularly his love play with the cowherd women (Gopis).

In 1510 he received formal initiation as an ascetic and took the name Shri Krishna Chaitanya. He intended to live in Vrindavan, the area near Mathura that was regarded as the scene of Krishna's childhood and youth, and the place where Chaitanya had sent six of his disciples to establish a pilgrimage center, but, at his mother's urging, he settled in Orissa in the town of Puri, so that both she and his disciples could more easily keep in touch with him. Chaitanya was said to have reconverted to Hinduism the governor of Orissa, who had converted to Islam. He had frequent epileptic seizures (which he himself diagnosed) and may have died by drowning while in a state of religious ecstasy.

Chaitanya's intense religious life inspired the devotional movement known as Gaudiya (i.e., Bengali) Vaishnavism. The *Chaitanya-charita* tells us that Chaitanya was an incarnation of Krishna and Radha in the same body. In their previous incarnations, they were one soul in two bodies; Radha was Krishna's essential energy (*shakti*). Krishna decided to take on this incarnation both for his worshippers and for himself: for them, he established the form of religious devotion most suitable for the Kali Age ("The Four Ages," p. 228); for himself, he wanted to experience his love and Radha's love for him, simultaneously. In the passage included here, Krishna makes the decision to engage in the dual incarnation.

His followers included many groups, beginning with the antinomian Bengali Sahajiyas (p. 478) who were his contemporaries. His main disciples were the renouncers called Goswamins. One of them, Nityananda, continuing the paradigm of Chaitanya as Krishna and Radha, was said to be the incarnation of Balarama, Krishna's brother. In his efforts to convert the Bengali Tantrics, Nityananda is said to have consorted with prostitutes, drunkards, and others of dubious character, behavior that his followers justified by his association with Balarama, who was known for his excesses ("The River Yamuna," p. 259). Other Goswamins developed an erotic devotional theology that incorporated still more antinomian and ecstatic Tantric influences and took root among the people known as Bauls (Fakir Lalon Shah, p. 527).

At the same time, many worshippers in the Chaitanya tradition, recoiling from the antinomian Tantric variations on the theme of Krishna and Radha that had made them the target of social opprobrium, developed a different tradition and went back to the *Gita Govinda* (p. 480) for their central imagery, emphasizing not the union but the separation (*viraha*) of the two lovers and the suffering of longing for the absent god, the renunciation rather than the passion of love. Some Goswamins, anxious to prevent the story of Krishna and Radha from becoming a model for human behavior, hastened to sanitize the myth by reversing the locus of the real people and the shadows; where, in earlier texts, the Gopis (cowherd women) had left shadow images of themselves in bed with their husbands while they danced with Krishna, now some of the Goswamins specified that the *real* Gopis remained in bed with their husbands and sent their shadow doubles to dance with the god.

Chaitanya neither organized a sect nor wrote any works on theology, entrusting this work to his disciples, most of whom wrote in Sanskrit rather than Bangla. The hagiographical accounts of Chaitanya's life are many, but the Sanskrit *Chaitanya-charita* ("Deeds of Chaitanya," or, in full, the *Chaitanya-charitamrita*, "Elixir of the Life of Chaitanya") of Krishnadas Kaviraja is one of the best-known and best-loved. Composed around 1581, near the end of the author's life, it folds into the main episodes of Chaitanya's life citations from both the classical Sanskrit texts of the Krishna tradition, particularly the *Bhagavata Purana*, and the Bengali theologians of the Chaitanya tradition, particularly Rupa Goswamin (p. 497), who was Krishnadas Kaviraja's teacher. This text tells us that Chaitanya was particularly fond of the *Gita Govinda* (which he may have heard chanted in the temple of Jaganntha in Puri) and of the poetry of Vidyapati (p. 483) and Chandidas (p. 487).

PRONOUNCING GLOSSARY

Bhagavata Purana: *bah´-guh-vuh´-tuh poor-rah´-nuh*
Chaitanya: *chai-tun´-yuh*
Krishnadas: *krish´-nuh-dahs´*
Radha: *rah´-duh*
Ramananda Raya: *rah´-mah-nun´-duh rah´-yuh*
rasa: *ruh´-suh*

AN ENCOUNTER WITH THE DUAL FORM

Ramananda Raya, a minister to King Prataparudra, elsewhere in the text identifies himself as a Shudra, a member of the fourth and lowest class, a servant ("The Hymn of the Primeval Man," p. 82). This encounter of Ramananda Raya with Chaitanya in many ways mirrors Arjuna's encounter with Krishna in the *Bhagavad Gita* (p. 166). In both cases, the revelation is overwhelming. Here, Ramananda witnesses the only recorded revelation of Chaitanya's androgynous dual incarnation.

The devotee Ramananda Raya is speaking with Chaitanya: 'A confusion still remains within my heart; please be gracious and explain it to me with certainty. First I saw you in the form of a renouncer; now I see you in the form of the dark blue cowherd (Krishna). I see a golden image appearing before you, and its golden radiance is concealing your body. Within it I see a flute raised to your mouth and lotus eyes which are trembling with various emotions. Seeing you in this manner is astonishing. Tell me directly, O Lord, what is the cause of this?'

The Lord replied: 'You have an intense love for Krishna, and this is the nature of love; know this for certain! When a great devotee of the Lord looks at both animate and inanimate objects, Shri Krishna appears to him to be everywhere. He looks at animate and inanimate objects, but does not

TRANSLATED BY David Haberman.

see their form. Instead, his own cherished deity appears everywhere. As it says in the *Bhagavata Purana:*[1]

> The greatest devotee of the Lord is one who sees his own Lord in all beings and all beings in his own Lord. The trees and creepers of the forest, as if manifesting Vishnu in themselves, are richly laden with flowers and fruits and bow their branches under their burden; their bodies thrilled with love verily pour forth streams of honey.

You have a great love for Radha and Krishna; thus Radha and Krishna appear everywhere to you.'

Raya said: 'You are the Lord. Give up this pretence! Do not conceal your true form from me! Having assumed the complexion and emotional state of Radha you descended to taste your own *rasa.*[2] Your secret task is to taste your own love; simultaneously you infuse the three worlds with love. You came to rescue me, and now you trick me. What is the meaning of your behavior?'

The Lord smiled, and then revealed his true form: the Prince of Rasa (Krishna)–the Container of Profound Emotions (Radha), the two in one body. Seeing this, Ramanda became faint with ecstasy, was unable to control his body, and fell to the ground. The Lord touched him with his hand and thereby caused him to regain consciousness. Seeing the Lord once again in the guise of a renouncer, he was amazed. The Lord embraced him and consoled him: 'I have never showed this form to anyone except you. I have showed this form to you because of your knowledge of the essential truth of my love-play and *rasa.* Actually my body is not golden, but appears so because of the touch of Radha. She touches no one except the cowherd-king's son (Krishna). Having transferred my own heart into her emotional state, I taste my own sweetness.

'Now nothing concerning my activities is unknown to you. Even though I concealed it, you learned the inner truth of everything by the power of love. Guard it in secret! Do not reveal it to anyone! The world will only ridicule my mad activity. I am a madman; you also are a madman. Therefore, you and I are in the same position.'

1. A text devoted to Krishna. The verses cited here are 11.2.45 and 10.35.9.
2. Flavor, juice, or emotion.

RUPA GOSWAMIN

Rupa Goswamin, Chaitanya's most famous disciple, was one of the six that Chaitanya sent to Vrindavan to establish a pilgrimage center. Rupa wrote of "the devotion that follows from passion" (*raganuga bhakti*), in contrast to scriptural devotion (*vaidhi bhakti*). In the familiar pattern of Hindu pluralism, the texts teach that both paths lead to Krishna. *Bhakti* in general was regarded as better suited for women; in the Goswamins' theology, this meant that women could naturally be god's lovers and mothers, the most intimate roles, whereas male worshippers had to pretend to be women (some of them withdrawing to menstruate every month). This gave women a great measure of spiritual authority, though not necessarily practical authority. In Sanskrit plays composed by Rupa Goswamin, the love of Krishna and Radha is adulterous: Radha is married to Abhimanyu, the son of Krishna's friend Arjuna. In Rupa's theology, the worshipper is inspired to decide not which of the personae dramatis s/he would like to play, but who s/he *is*: the mother, lover, servant, or friend of Krishna.

PRONOUNCING GLOSSARY

Adi: *ah´-dee*
Ananta-Shesha: *uh-nun´-tuh-shay´-shuh*
Ashta-kaliya-lila-smarana-mangala-stotram: *ush´-tuh–kah´-lee-yuh–lee´-luh–smuh´-ruh-nuh–mun´guh-luh–stoh´-trum*
Bhagavata Purana: *bah´-guh-vuh´-tuh poo-rah´-nuh*
bhakti: *buk´-tee*
Bhaktirasamritasindhu: *buk´-tee-ruh-sahm´-rih-tuh-sin´-doo*
bhava: *bah´-vuh*
Bhavarthadipika: *bah´-var´-tuh-dee´-pee-kuh*
Chaitanya: *chai-tun´-yuh*
Govinda: *goh-vin´-duh*
Hari: *huh´-ree*
Haribhaktishudhodaya: *huh´-ree-buk´-tee-shoo-doh´-dah-yuh*
Ishvara: *eesh´-vuh-ruh*
Kesha: *kay´-shuh*
Lalita: *luh-lee-tah´*
Mimamsaka: *mee-mahm´-suh-kuh*
mukti: *muhk´-tee*
Mukunda: *moo-koon´-duh*
Nandagrama: *nun´-duh-grah´-muh*
Narada: *nah´-ruh-duh*
Narada Pancharatra: *nah´-ruh-duh pun´-chuh-rah´-truh*
Padma Purana: *pud´-muh poo-rah´-nuh*
Pali: *puh´-lee*
prema: *pray´-muh*
Radha: *rah´-duh*
Radhakunda: *rah´-duh-koon´-duh*
rasa: *ruh´-suh*
Rupa Goswamin: *roo´-puh goh´-swah´-min*
sadhana: *sah´-duh-nuh*
Sanatana: *suh-nah´-tuh-nuh*
Sankhya: *sahn´-kyuh*
Shesha: *shay´-shuh*
Shri Narada Pancharatra: *shree nah´-ruh-duh pun´-chuh-rah´-truh*
Shyama: *shyah´-mah*
Soma: *soh´-muh*
Tantra: *tun´-truh*
Taraka: *tah´-ruh-kah´*
Uddhava: *ood´-duh-vuh*
Vasudeva: *vuh´-soo-day´-vuh*
Vraja: *vruh´-juh*
Vrinda: *vrin´-duh*
Yadu: *yuh´-doo*
Yamuna: *yuh´-moo-nah´*
Yashoda: *yuh-shoh´-dah´*
Yudishthira: *yoo-dish´-tee-ruh*

THE GENERAL CHARACTERISTICS OF DEVOTION

In the Sanskrit *Bhaktirasamritasindhu* ("The Ocean of the Elixir of the Emotion of Devotion"), Rupa Goswamin defines the religious life of *bhakti* in terms of the aesthetic theory of classical drama. *Rasa* here comes to mean "dramatic sentiment" or "aesthetic enjoyment," and, finally, the supreme bliss of loving god. In this opening chapter of the work, he defines the general characteristics of *bhakti*, quoting a number of Sanskrit texts, including the well-known tenth-century *Bhagavata Purana* ("Krishna," p. 247), the *Padma Purana* (a later, also popular Purana), the *Narada Pancharatra* and *Haribhaktisudhodaya* (more obscure Vaishnava texts), and the *Bhavarthadipika*, Shridhara Swamin's commentary on the *Bhagavata Purana*.

Glory be to the Moon (Krishna), whose form is the essence of all *rasas*, who subdued Taraka and Pali with his radiant beauty, excited Shyama and Lalita,[1] and is the beloved of Radha. Even though I am unworthy I praise the lotus-feet of Hari,[2] compelled in my heart by the command of Chaitanya. May this Ocean[3] of Nectar of Devotional Rasa always delight the Lord of Delight whose form is eternal, and be a temple for his rest. And . . . May this Ocean of Nectar of Devotional Rasa ever satisfy my spiritual master, Sanatana, and be a temple for his rest. I pay homage to the porpoise-like devotees swimming in the Ocean of Nectar of Devotional Rasa, who have overcome the fear of the fishnets of time, and have left behind the rivers of liberation.[4] O Sanatana, may your Ocean of Nectar of Devotional Rasa outshine even the Mimamsaka[5] fire, dulling its cruel tongue for all time. Though I am ignorant, I undertake this praise of Devotional Rasa which makes all worlds joyful, for the delight of sensitive people.

Four divisions of the Lord's Ocean of Nectar of Devotional Rasa will now be described in order, beginning with the Eastern. Within this Eastern Division, which explains the distinctions of devotion, four waves will be discussed in due order. The first wave involves the general characteristics of devotion, the second relates to the means of realization (*sadhana*), the third concerns the foundational emotions (*bhava*), and the fourth considers supreme love (*prema*). The distinguishing characteristic of the highest devotion, fully known by the sages, is clearly explained in this First Wave.

The highest devotion is defined as devoted service to Krishna which is agreeably rendered, is devoid of desire for another, and is not dependent on intellectual knowledge or sacrificial action.[6] As the *Shri Narada Pancharatra* says:

> Service with the senses to the Lord of Senses,[7] a service which is pure, and being devoted to Him and free from all restrictions, is called devotion.

TRANSLATED BY David Haberman.

1. These are all names of the cowherd women who are in love with Krishna.
2. Hari (Vishnu) is here equated with Chaitanya.
3. The author imagines that his text, "The Ocean of the Elixir . . . ," might be the cosmic ocean on which Vishnu sleeps when the universe is at rest between periods of creation. Rupa's "Ocean" is divided into four sections (called the four directions) and numerous subsections (called waves).
4. This verse asserts that *bhakti* is superior to liberation (*mukti* or *moksha*).
5. Rupa regards the Mimsamsakas, or theorists of the Veda, as dry ritualists.
6. Knowledge (*jnana*) and sacrificial action (*karma*) are here regarded as inferior to *bhakti*, as they are in the *Gita* (p. 166).
7. Krishna.

And the third canto of the *Bhagavata Purana* says:

> Devotion to the Supreme Lord is motiveless and ceaseless. Even if the five kinds of liberation are offered, namely, residence in the same world, equality in power, proximity, similarity in form, and even oneness, my people do not accept them unless they can serve me. This yoga of devotion is the highest goal.

The explanation of the superiority of the devotee mentioned in the previous verses illustrates that quality of devotion which is a manifestation of supreme purity. Devotion: (a) destroys suffering, (b) bestows auspiciousness, (c) easily accomplishes liberation, (d) is very difficult to obtain, (e) consists of a special concentrated joy, and (f) attracts Shri Krishna.

(a) The destruction of suffering

This suffering is of three kinds: sin, the seeds of sin, and ignorance. Sin is of two kinds: that which has not yet begun to yield effects, and that which has already begun to yield effects. Concerning the destruction of sin which has not yet begun to yield effects, the eleventh canto of the *Bhagavata Purana* says:

> Just as a blazing fire turns all fuel into ashes, O Uddhava, so devotion focused on me completely consumes all sins.

Concerning the destruction of sin which has already begun to yield effects, the third canto of the *Bhagavata Purana* says:

> Even a lowly dog-eater is immediately made fit for the Soma sacrifice by singing, hearing, and meditating on your name, and also by bowing to you and remembering you. How much more so is this true of a direct vision of you, O Lord.

A bad birth is known to be the reason for one's ineligibility for the Soma sacrifice, and that sin which has already begun to yield effects is the cause of a bad birth. The *Padma Purana* says:

> Sins which have not yet begun to yield effects, the highest sins, the seeds of sins, and sins which are about to yield effects are gradually dissolved for those intent upon devotion to Vishnu.

Concerning the destruction of the seed of sin, the sixth canto of the *Bhagavata Purana* says:

> Such practices as asceticism, charity, vows, etc. cleanse these sins, but not the heart of one born wicked. Yet even such a heart is purified by means of service to the feet of the Lord.

Concerning the destruction of ignorance, the fourth canto of the *Bhagavata Purana* says:

> The wise loosen the knots of accumulated karma by means of devotion which delights in the lotus-blossom feet of Vasudeva;[8] while the ascetics who have emptied their minds (i.e. do not bear Vasudeva in mind) and have suppressed the senses are not able to accomplish this. Therefore, take refuge in Vasudeva.

8. The personal god, Krishna, in contrast with the impersonal *brahman*.

The *Padma Purana* says:

> The highest devotion for Hari, which is attended by knowledge, quickly burns up ignorance as a forest fire burns up serpents.

(b) The bestowal of auspiciousness

The wise speak of such auspicious things as these: the pleasing of the whole world, the endearing of the whole world, good qualities, and happiness. Concerning the two-fold pleasing and endearing of the world, the *Padma Purana* says:

> The whole world is pleased by him who worships Hari; all animate and even inanimate creatures become enamored of him.

Concerning the bestowal of good qualities, the fifth canto of the *Bhagavata Purana* says:

> The gods who are accompanied by all good qualities abide in him in whom there exists a pure devotion for the Lord; but where are these great qualities for the one who lacks devotion for Hari and whose mind is rushing outward toward the unreal?

Happiness is of three kinds: ordinary, that relating to ultimate reality, and that relating to Ishvara. As the Tantra says:

> The most marvelous powers, ordinary enjoyment, eternal liberation (i.e. the enjoyment of ultimate reality), and the never-ending highest joy (i.e. the enjoyment of Ishvara) are all obtained from devotion to Govinda.

The *Haribhaktisudhodaya* says:

> O God of gods, I pray again and again that firm devotion to you be mine, a devotion which like a creeper bears happiness and the fruit of the four goals[9] which end in liberation.

(c) Easily accomplishes liberation

When the heart is filled with even a little love for the Lord, the four goals of life (which culminate in liberation) become completely like straw.

The *Narada Pancharatra* says:

> All powers, liberation, and so forth, and all marvelous enjoyments, accompany the Great Goddess of Devotion to Hari like her servants.

(d) Difficult to obtain

It is difficult to obtain for two reasons: it is not obtainable through even long periods of much practice which is devoid of attachment, and is not given immediately by Hari. Concerning the former, the Tantra says:

> Freedom is easily obtained from knowledge, and ordinary enjoyment is easily obtained from the merit of sacrifices, but devotion to Hari is very difficult to obtain even by means of a thousand practices.

9. Dharma, *artha*, *kama*, and *moksha* ("Shastras," p. 200).

Concerning the latter, the fifth canto of the *Bhagavata Purana* says:

> O King, the Lord is the protector, the teacher, the deity, the dear friend, the family guardian, and sometimes even the servant of you Yadus. So be it! The Lord Mukunda grants liberation to his worshippers any time, but he certainly does not always grant the yoga of devotion.

(e) Consists of a special concentrated joy

The joy of ultimate reality, which is accomplished over millions of years, does not approach even a drop of the ocean of the happiness of devotion.

The *Haribhaktisudhodaya* says:

> Even the happiness of ultimate reality is like the water contained in the hoof-print of a cow for one situated in the ocean of pure bliss which comes from the direct perception of you, O Lord of the Universe.

And the *Bhavarthadipika* says:

> Skillful people, who are extremely joyful, wander about in the ocean of the nectar of your stories and easily accomplish the four goals, the highest of which seems like straw.

(f) The attraction of Shri Krishna

Having made Hari, who is surrounded by dear friends, the receptacle of its love, devotion subdues Him. For this reason, devotion is known as the attractor of Shri Krishna. The eleventh canto of the *Bhagavata Purana* says:

> Neither yoga, nor Sankhya philosophy, nor righteous duty, nor study of the Vedas, nor asceticism, nor renunciation accomplish me, O Uddhava, as does powerful devotion to me.

And in the seventh canto of the *Bhagavata Purana* Narada says (to King Yudhishthira):

> Ah! You are the most fortunate in the world of humans; sages who sanctify the world visit your houses because the highest, ultimate reality disguised in the form of a man clearly dwells there.

The three types of devotion (*sadhana-*, *bhava-*, and *prema-bhakti*) have first been described in due order, as the magnanimity of devotion has been proclaimed by means of six phrases arranged in corresponding hierarchical pairs. Even a tiny taste of devotion involves an understanding of the essence of devotion, while mere argumentative reasoning does not, since it lacks a solid basis for such understanding. Thus it has been said by the ancient teachers: A position which is asserted with even meticulous effort by clever logicians is proven to be otherwise by those who are even more clever.

THE EIGHTFOLD ACTIVITIES OF RADHA AND KRISHNA

This passage is taken from a Sanskrit poem by Rupa Goswamin entitled "Auspicious Praise of the Remembrance of the Divine Play, Divided into Eight Time Periods" (*Ashta-kaliya-lila-smarana-mangala-stotram*). The text provides a skeletal script for a meditation known as "remembering the divine play," which involves withdrawing the mind from the illusory, everyday world and visualizing the ultimate world of Krishna and Radha. The eight periods of the meditative cycle begin with night's end, two and a half hours before sunrise, regarded as the most auspicious time of the day. This is the moment when serious practitioners get up and begin their meditations. The poem simultaneously sketches the daily schedule of services for the images of Krishna in the temples of Vrindavan.

I praise Krishna's eternal activities in Vraja in order now to explain the mental worship to be performed by those traveling on the path of passion.[1] This mental worship achieves the service of love at the lotus-feet of the dear friend of Shri Radha (i.e. Krishna), a service which is attained by those absorbed in the activities of Vraja with eager desire, but is inaccessible to Kesha, Shesha, and Adi (Brahma, Shiva, and Ananta-Shesha,[2] i.e. those following the path of 'liberation' [*mukti*]).

May we be protected by Krishna, who at night's end leaves the bower and returns to the cowherd village, in the morning and at sunset milks the cows and enjoys his meals, at midday roams about playing with his friends and tending cattle, in the afternoon returns to the cowherd village, in the late evening amuses his dear ones, and at night makes love in the forest with Radha.

At night's end, I remember Radha and Krishna who are awakened by the songs of parrots and cuckoo birds, both pleasing and displeasing, and by many other noises sent by a concerned Vrinda (goddess of the forest). Arising from their bed of joy, these two are looked upon and pleased by their female friends (*sakhis*), and though filled with desire and trembling from the passion that occurs at that time, they return to the beds of their own homes, fearful of the crowing cock.

In the morning, I take refuge with Radha who, bathed and decorated, is summoned with her friends by Yashoda[3] to his house (Krishna's house at Nandagrama) where she cooks the prescribed food and enjoys Krishna's remnants. And I take refuge with Krishna who awakens and goes to the cowshed to milk the cows; he is then well bathed and fed in the company of his friends.

TRANSLATED BY David Haberman.

1. The *raganuga bhakti*, in which the worshipper imagines himself or herself as one of the various people who love Krishna in different ways.
2. The great serpent, who is infinite (*ananta*) and left over (*shesha*) when the rest of the universe is destroyed, forming a bed in the cosmic ocean upon which Vishnu sleeps until the universe is re-created.
3. Krishna's mother in the cowherd village.

In the forenoon, I remember Krishna who goes to the forest accompanied by his friends and cows and is followed by the cowherds. Desiring to possess Radha, he goes to the bank of her pond (Radhakunda) at the time of their secret rendezvous. And I remember Radha, who having observed Krishna leaves the house for the purpose of performing the sun-worship as instructed by an ascetic. She keeps her eye on the path for her own girl friend who had been sent to make arrangements with Krishna.

At midday, I remember Radha and Krishna who are full of desire and are decorated and made lovely by the various changes brought about by their mutual union. They are served by a host of attendants, are delighted by the jokes of their girl friends such as Lalita, which arouse the god of Love, are trembling with passion and coyness, and are engaged in such playful activities as swinging, playing in the forest, splashing in the water, stealing the flute, making love, drinking honey wine, worshipping the sun, and so forth.

In the afternoon, I remember Radha who returns home, prepares various gifts for her lover, is bathed and beautifully dressed, and is then filled with pleasure at the sight of the lotus-face of her lover. And I remember Krishna who is accompanied back to Vraja by his friends and the herd of cattle, is pleased by the sight of Shri Radha, is greeted by the face of his father, and is bathed and dressed by his mother.

At sunset, I remember Radha who by means of a girl friend sends many kinds of foods which she prepared for her lover, and whose heart is delighted upon eating the remnants brought back by her friend. And I remember the Moon of Vraja (Krishna) who is well bathed, beautifully dressed, and caressed by his mother. He goes to the cowshed and milks the cows, then returns to his house and enjoys his meal.

In the late evening, I remember Radha, who is dressed appropriately for either a light or dark night and accompanied by her group of girl friends, and who by means of a female messenger makes plans, according to Vrinda's instructions, to rendezvous at a bower consisting of trees of desire located on the bank of the Yamuna. And I remember Krishna who, after watching the performance of skilful arts with the assembly of cowherds, is carefully taken home and put to bed by his affectionate mother. Later, he secretly arrives at the bower.

At night, I remember Radha and Krishna who, being full of desire, have possessed one another. They are worshipped by Vrinda and the many attendants, and they play with their dear friends with songs, jokes, riddles, and sweet speech, which are all associated with the circle dance and the love dance. The minds of these two are on love and they drink prepared honey wine. Masters of love, their hearts expand by the acts performed in the bower, and they experience the various *rasas* of love.

These two are delighted by the company of their girl friends and are lovingly served with betel nut, fragrant garlands, fans, cold water, foot massages, and so forth. After their girl friends have fallen asleep, they too drift off to sleep on their bed of flowers, murmuring the utterances of lovers full of the *rasa* of a secret love.

NAROTTAMA DAS

Narottama Das Thakur was a Gaudiya Vaishnava poet who lived in the seventeenth century. He wrote, in Bangla, about the religious practice called Manjari Sadhana, in which the worshipper visualizes the divine love-play of Krishna and Radha and assumes the identity of one of the female servants (*manjaris*) mentioned in Rupa Goswamin's Sanskrit poem "Auspicious Praise" ("The Eightfold Activities"). But unlike the Goswamins, who generally wrote in Sanskrit prose, Narottama Das wrote in the genre of Bangla *pada-vali*, in the poetic tradition of Vidyapati and Chandidas.

PRONOUNCING GLOSSARY

Goswamin: *goh´-swah´-min*
Hari: *huh´-ree*
Narottama Das: *nuh-roh´-tuh-muh dahs´*
Rupa: *roo´-puh*
Sanatana: *suh-nah´-tuh-nuh*
Vraja: *vruh´-juh*
Vrindavana: *vrin-dah´-vuh-nuh*
Yamuna: *yuh´-moo-nah´*

POEMS TO KRISHNA AND RADHA

These three poems, which address Krishna as "Hari" (Vishnu), express three desires: to give up everything in the ordinary world, to join the world of Vrindavan or Vraj, and to serve Krishna and Radha in the body of a servant girl, a *manjari*.

Hari! O Hari! When shall I be transformed into such a state that having become indifferent to everything I will go to the land of Vrindavana? This is the desire I hold in my heart.

Renouncing family, wealth, sons, and wife, and becoming all alone, when shall I go? Casting off all sorrows, I will dwell in the town of Vraja. Begging from door to door, I will eat what is offered.

When shall I fill my stomach with the water of the Yamuna River, the immortal nectar? When shall I fall into and bathe in the waters of Radha's pond, delightfully known also as Krishna's pond?

I will roam through and play love games in the twelve forests, all of which cause one to welter in supreme love. Having touched their feet, I will humbly petition the residents of Vraja dwelling in those places.

When shall I set eyes on the feasting place? And how much longer until I see the secret bower? The desire of Narottama Das's heart is the feet of the divine couple in the middle of this bower of Vrindavana.

TRANSLATED BY David Haberman.

Hari! O Hari! When shall I attain such a state in which I will serve the feet of the divine couple?

Becoming a bumblebee, I will forever reside at your feet and ceaselessly drink the blessed nectar from these feet.

Fulfil this hope of all the female friends. All that is desired is fulfilled by your grace.

Day after day I wish for this fulfilment. After all have assembled, be merciful and show your grace.

Day and night Narottama weeps for the hope of your service. By your kindness, makes me a faithful female servant.

Hari! O Hari! When shall I attain such a state? When shall I, abandoning this male body, assume the body of a female and apply sandalwood paste to the bodies of the divine couple?

Having drawn up your topknot of hair, when shall I bind and encircle it with fresh *gunja*[1] seeds, string various flowers and offer them to you as a necklace, assist your female friends in dressing your body with yellow cloth, and place betel nut[2] in your mouth?

When shall my eyes be filled with the sight of the two forms which steal away the mind? This is my heart's desire. Glory be to Rupa and Sanatana (Goswamin). This female body is my treasure. Humbly, Narottama Das.

1. Cannabis seeds, used here just as decorations.
2. Spices wrapped in a betel leaf ("As the Mirror to My Hand," p. 485).

KETAKA DAS

Mangal ("Auspiciousness") poetry, which took shape in the fifteenth century, with the *Manasa-Vijay* of Vipradasa, is probably based on much earlier individual poems to goddesses. It is a distinctly Bengali, and Bangla, genre of village poetry that is concerned primarily with the theme of the emergence of new deities, especially female deities, and the establishment of their worship on earth. In particular, it tells of what is to be gained from worshipping the deity and the dangers that result from failing to worship him or her. Manasa, Bengali goddess of snakes, whose worship usually involves the use of a sacred pot, is invoked for many purposes, such as granting fertility, curing diseases, and obtaining wealth (for snakes are thought to be the guardians of treasure).

The *Manasa-mangal (Epic Poem of Manasa)* of Ketaka Das (also called Kshemananda), which probably dates from the seventeenth century, tells how Manasa won over the worshippers of other deities by releasing her powers of destruction in the form of snakes.

PRONOUNCING GLOSSARY

arati: *uh´-ruh-tee*
Baliraja: *bah´-lee-rah´-jah*
Banya: *bun-yah´*
Behula: *bay´-hoo-lah´*
Bholanatha: *boh´-luh-nah´-tuh*
Birata: *bi´-ruh-tuh*
Bishahari: *bih´-shuh-huh´-ree*
Champakanagara: *chum´-puh-kuh-nuh´-guh-ruh*
Chandi: *chun´-dee*
Chandika: *chun´-dee-kah´*
Chando: *chahn´-doh*
Chandraketu: *chun´-druh-kay´-too*
chengamuri: *chen´-guh-moo´-ree*
Chengamuri Kani: *chen´-guh-moo´-ree kah´-nee*
Cheri: *chay´-ree*
Dharmaketu: *dar´-muh-kay´-too*
Digambara: *dih-gum´-buh-ruh*
Durga: *door´-gah*
Ganapati: *guh´-nuh-puh´-tee*
Gandheshvari: *gun-daysh´-vuh-ree´*
Gauri: *gow´-ree*
Gosai: *goh-sai´*
Hanuman: *huh´-noo-mahn*
Hara: *huh´-ruh*
hental: *hen´-tuhl*
Ishana: *ee-shah´-nuh*
Jagannatha: *juh-guh-nah´-thuh*
Jagati: *juh´-guh-tee*
Janaki: *juh´-nuh-kee*
Jaratkaru: *juh´-rut-kah´-roo*
Jaya Bishahari: *jah´-yuh bih´-shuh-huh´-ree*
kahan: *kah´-hun*
Kalidaha: *kah´-lee-duh´-huh*
Kamala: *kuh-muh-lah´*
Karttika: *kar´-tee-kuh*
Ketaka Das: *kay´-tuh-kuh dahs´*
ketaki: *kay´-tuh-kee´*
Kshemananda: *kuh-shay´-mah-nun´-duh*
Kurma: *koor´-muh*
lakh: *lahk*
Lakhai: *luh-kai´*
Lakhindar: *luh´-kin´-dar*
Mahamaya: *muh-hah´-mah´-yah´*
Mahesha: *muh-hay´-shuh*
Manasa: *muh-nuh-shah´*
Manasa-mangal: *muh-nuh-shah´–mun´-gul*
Ojha: *oh´-jah*
Paduma: *puh´-doo-muh*
pan: *pahn*
Pandava: *pahn´-duh-vuh*
Pashupati: *puh´-shoo-puh´-tee*
phota: *foh´-tah*

pranam: *pruh-nahm´*
puja: *poo´-jah*
pushpajhara: *poosh´-puh-jah´-ruh*
Rakshasa: *rahk´-shuh-suh*
Ramakesha: *rah´-muh-kay´-shuh*
Ramayana: *rah-mah´-yuh-nuh*
Ravana: *rah´-vuh-nuh*
sadhu: *sah´-doo*
Sanaka: *suh-nuh-kah´*
Savitri: *sah´-vih-tree´*
Shankara: *shun´-kuh-ruh*
Shulapani: *shoo´-luh-pah´-nee*
shraddha: *shrah´-duh*
Shrivatsa: *shree-vut´-suh*
Sugriva: *soo-gree´-vuh*
Trilochana: *tree-loh´-chuh-nuh*
Vasuki: *vah´-soo-kee´*
Vishvakarma: *vish´-vuh-kar´-muh*

THE BIRTH OF MANASA

Shiva in this tradition is not the terrifying or ascetic god of the Sanskrit tradition but a lusty, philandering husband. Stories in which his wife disguises herself in order to seduce him in the form of another woman are common in the folk traditions of Shaivism, and they sometimes result in the birth of a child, as in this tale.

Lord Shiva, Ruler of the Animals (Pashupati), arose one morning and said lovingly to Durga: 'Dear, I am going out to fetch flowers to use in worship. Take (our sons) Karttika and Ganesha inside the house and play dice.' The Destroyer (Hara) then took a basket and knife in his hand, sounded his drum and horn, and mounted his bull. Telling the lords Karttika and Ganesha to remain in the house, the Lord with Beautiful Hair (Ramakesha) went away. The Destroyer set out for the peak of the mountain to gather flowers.

About this time Gauri (Durga) had an idea: 'I will play a trick on Shiva by turning myself into a passionate ferrywoman, and I will see how the Bearer of the Trident (Shulapani) picks flowers.' Durga remained in the house and said to her two sons: 'This morning I will go out to bathe, and then I will come back and cook our meal.' Having said this, with much affection in her heart she gave her two sons sweet candies to eat. After securing her two sons in the house, the Destroyer's wife transformed herself into a very attractive young ferrywoman.

Her beautiful body was a cannon of sex loaded with the god of Love, and her eyes and mouth were armed with ten arrows of passion. Her nose was lovely as a flower, and oh, how beautiful her lips; her bright teeth were as brilliant as a flash of lightning. And oh, how gorgeous were her two breasts, like two sumptuously soft fruits, and how graceful her hair, which hung all the way down to her waist. The vermilion beauty mark on her forehead was like the rays of the sun, and so enchanting was the glance of her eyes that it snatched away one's breath.

Chandika (Durga), Daughter of the Mountain, arrived at the top of the mountain before Shiva and caused a great river of grand illusion to flow. Then she fashioned a boat out of a palm tree, took an oar, and sat waiting near the edge of that river. In the meantime, Shiva came to that place, and

TRANSLATED BY David Haberman.

when he saw the beauty of the ferrywoman, he was overcome by an arrow of passion. Ketaka Das composed this at the feet of the Goddess. Mother will skillfully protect the best of her devotees.

The Goddess rowed the enchanting boat on the water; seeing her beauty, the Destroyer fell completely into delusion. The sensuous ferrywoman heard him say, moved by her beauty: 'Take your boat and ferry me to the other side of the river.' To this married woman who sat all alone on the water (Shiva said): 'You are like a doll made out of fine cream; your body is so soft and tender. Seeing your complexion, even the moon becomes humbled. Again and again the arrows from your eyes strike me. When I see your beauty, my heart is ruptured. Why don't you just row us about anywhere you like?'

The sensuous ferrywoman replied to the Great God (Mahesha): 'Come, I will take you to the other shore. This is an opportune moment.' With these words, the ferrywoman placed the boat near him. Shiva then took the hand of the ferrywoman into his own. The sensuous ferrywoman chided him: 'Oh, how disgraceful! How can there be such lust in an ascetic? My husband's name is Shiva and he is at home, but if he were suddenly to come what would he say to me? My intention was simply to take you to the other shore! You old man, why did you take hold of my hand?' The Destroyer said: 'It is useless to depend on your husband. How can he protect your heart after sending you here?' The ferrywoman replied: 'If my husband catches sight of this he will grab hold of your torn rags and kill you. You keep your dignity! I will take you to the other shore, old man, and will not even charge you any money.' Shiva pressed on: 'Hey woman, I am your slave; hug me and give me bliss.' But when she heard this, the ferrywoman said: 'We should never do such a thing.'

About that time, a male and a female heron came together to make love, and a bee was drinking honey from a clump of lotuses. There was much drinking of honey and much love-making. The Destroyer spoke: 'Dear ferrywoman, lift up your eyes and look at this love-play. I am unable to speak any more; my body is shaking. (If you don't submit) my rage will be upon you.' The ferrywoman said: 'This boat is my dharma. If it is violated, my boat will sink. If it becomes heavy with sin it will sink into the water. A wave will then come into my boat and wash me completely away.' Shiva assured her: 'I will do no such thing to your boat, O Lotus-Woman; I will hold you on my lap and just play with you a bit.' Having placed her on his lap, the old man's mind went wild, and Shiva remarked: 'Promise me more, O Moon-Faced Lady.' The beautiful lady replied boastfully: 'I will take you out and dump this confident old man in the water.' The Destroyer declared: 'You will not shove me in the water, for I am the God of Gods; satisfy me!'

The ferrywoman said: 'Listen, O Three-Eyed (Trilochana) God, a group of sages sits and meditates at this place. If anyone sees this, a scandal will spread across the country. I will take your tigerskin and spread it out to make a bed.' Shiva declared: 'By means of a mantra I can make it dark. Even if I die, I will not leave this tigerskin.' The ferrywoman said: 'You don't want this love-play; come to my home and I will embrace you completely.' When he heard this, God, the Ruler of the Universe (Jagannatha), turned day into night and spread out his tigerskin. With a voice choked by passion Shiva muttered: 'Come, sit close to my heart and satisfy me, O Moon-Faced Lady.' Trembling, the old man waited with his arms outstretched. Alone, he got ready and finally began to express himself.

Having released his powerful sperm, Shiva laid back and said: 'I have made love with a beautiful lady.' After making love Shiva turned around to find that the Lady of Grand Illusion (Mahamaya) had suddenly vanished from that place. Chandi (Durga) was thinking: 'What have I done? The sperm will now pass into my body, and if this sperm passes into my body I will carry a baby in my womb. And if I give birth to a child at this old age, the gods will ridicule me. I would then be very miserable in the presence of the gods.' Thinking this she placed the sperm on a lotus leaf.

The blood and sperm had come together and were united, and the resulting egg fell near Vasuki, king of the snakes. The Imperishable Vasuki saw it, and by means of his meditative insight determined that it was very powerful. 'This sperm of the Great God has tumbled down to the underworld.' Carefully he placed it in a copper shell. The Imperishable Vasuki placed it in a copper shell; so writes Ketaka Das, who has become very happy.

Paduma (Manasa) was born on a lotus leaf in the underworld and was unequaled in beauty. Seeing her beauty, Vasuki evaluated her in his own mind: 'You will be famous throughout the world and will be regarded as auspicious for the world. This child of Shiva's desire will be successful throughout the three worlds and the whole world will worship her. This will result from the churning of the ocean. The Three-Eyed God will churn the ocean and will drink the poison; he will then whirl around and fall to the surface of the earth. You will rescue that lifeless corpse and bring it back to life, giving honor to my name. He will travel by waterways and will float on the ocean, and then you will revive him.' At this thought, Vasuki felt very happy and gave instructions to many snakes to adorn her body with various ornaments. They made her body very graceful by providing her with a snake throne, snake ornaments, snake poison, a snake's conch for her hand, and a bodice for her breasts. It was as if hundreds of moons were drinking from the circle of her lips, and oh, how beautiful was her curly hair arranged in the chignon of a young girl. It was wonderful. She had pearls in her ears, a bright diamond in her nose, a necklace between her breasts, bracelets of snakes on her arms, and special ornaments on her clothing. There was no one to equal her. Dressed in this manner and riding on a snake, she bid them a joyful farewell. The Princess Manasa bowed to them and happily mounted the lotus throne. In this way she sat on the lotus throne revealing her smiling face. Kshemanada says: It was at this time that Shiva stopped by to pick flowers.

When he saw the fine and beautiful girl in his path, the Destroyer became enchanted with her physical charm. 'Whose nymphet is this and why is she on a lotus leaf?' The girl bowed to the Forgetful Lord (Bholanatha). Shiva said: 'Tell me quickly: who are you?' Overcome with desire he took her by the hand. Greatly surprised, the Goddess replied, turning aside: 'What are you doing? You are my father! I am your daughter! This is disgraceful! As my father, how can you disgrace your daughter? There will be a scandal in the world of the gods!' When he heard this, the Destroyer was amazed:

'How can you be my daughter?' The daughter of the Lord (Ishana) answered: 'Listen to the reason. You made love with a certain woman. The sperm was not absorbed into her womb. She took the blood and sperm and placed it on a lotus leaf. This blood and sperm was so heavy that it broke the lotus leaf and tumbled to the house of Vasuki. Vasuki nurtured this sperm, and that is how, O Father, I was born.' When the Princess of the Underworld provided this information, the Destroyer of course realized that this was his daughter.

CHANDO DEFIES MANASA

The centerpiece of the *Manasa-mangal* is the story of the merchant Chando, who defies Manasa, worshipping only Shiva (Shankara), but is ultimately forced to acknowledge her and worship her. Manasa takes many forms and has many names. In addition to her snakes, she is represented by lotuses: in East Bengal she is called Padma ("Lotus"), and in Bengal, Kamala ("Lotus"); she is born from a lotus; and she sends a lotus to Chando when he is drowning. She is also called Chengamuri (a term of uncertain meaning, perhaps "repulsive as a dirty shrine"), Bisahari ("The One Who Removes Poison"), and Kani ("One-eyed"). She calls upon the services of Ganesha or Ganapati, the elephant-headed god, son of Shiva's wife Parvati, whose vehicle is a bandicoot or a rat, and upon Hanuman, the monkey son of the wind god, who serves Manasa throughout the *Manasa-mangal*. Hanuman had served Rama in the *Ramayana* (p. 186), particularly by helping Rama and Sugriva, king of the monkeys, build a bridge to the island of Lanka and make war on the Rakshasa Ravana, who had stolen Sita. The text also refers to the other Sanskrit epic, the *Mahabharata* (p. 130), whose heroes, the five Pandava brothers, together with their wife Draupadi, live in disguise at the court of Birata (Sanskrit Virata).

This and the following two selections are translated by Edward C. Dimock.

I

In Champakanagara lived Chando the Merchant, who carried on an endless feud with Manasa. That goddess, in her wrath, had killed his six sons, but even then he did not worship her or call her goddess. Though his pain and misery were very great, he did not bow his head to her, but said:

—That *chengamuri* wench—of what is she the goddess? And with staff in hand he watched both day and night, prowling from house to house, searching for Manasa, saying:

—If I could catch sight of her, I would break her head and kill her. If I could rid myself of her, my misery would disappear. No more would she afflict my house. I should be released, and live in joy in all my lands.

Thus thinking he spent his days. But finally he had to go for trade to a southern city. He took the name of Shiva and set out upon his journey. He boarded his ship in gladness, and shouted:

—Cast off! Take care, and head her for the open water.

When they heard the command of Chando, the helmsmen steered the seven ships toward Kalidaha.[1] But with Chando the Merchant went the curse of Manasa. She knew, by the power of her meditation, when he had reached Kalidaha; she went to Neto, her companion:

—Chando is against me; he constantly calls me Chengamuri Kani. Today I shall get even—I shall sink his ships. As he drowns, I know that he will worship me.

So quickly she summoned the rain-holding clouds:

—Go forth, together with the winds, O heroes great as Hanuman.

And so to Kalidaha the fierce winds went. The goddess gave them flowers and pan,[2] and said to the clouds:

—You will sink the seven ships of Chando in the sea.

And at the command of the goddess, the clouds went forth.

Kshemananda prays: Forgive our sins, O goddess.

II

At the order of the goddess, the rain-holders rushed forth; fierce hail-clouds went swiftly to Kalidaha to sink the *sadhu's*[3] ship. The great hero Hanuman was with them; the winds blew fiercely; earth and sky grew dark in the roaring and tumult of the winds. The oarsmen and sailors were afraid; they saw no deliverance from the storm. From darkened shapes like elephants with trunks the rain poured down; all around the ships the thunder crashed and rumbled. Fear seized Chando's heart; he cried:

—I shall never reach the land again.

Flashing and crackling lightning struck and pellets of hail were driven with awful force before the wind. The helmsman said:

—We shall not escape—if our skulls are not broken, we shall surely drown.

And the merchant cried:

—I should not have set out on this voyage.

The lightning was awesome to behold, and the sun hid in the heavens. Hanuman then leapt aboard the seven ships, which whirled about like wheels. The storm blew, and the cabin roofs were carried away; the howling of the wind was like the sound of Desolation. The crocodiles and sharks and all the awful creatures of the water swam round and round the ships; the serpents of the sea swam to the whirling ships, in lust for food. The waters of Kalidaha swelled up, full of danger. The helmsman was frozen by the icy winds; he could not move his hands or feet, and he lay senseless in a corner of the deck. A shark seized the anchor in his jaws, and others the lines. Then Hanuman himself boarded and crushed the ships, rocking and swinging; the lightning fell, breaking, and the drums of cargo were washed away and floated on the black-waved sea. His ships were sinking, but Chando did not utter the name of Manasa. He said:

—He who worships Shiva's trident will surely reach the shore. And when I do, I shall wrench the breath from Manasa!

1. Literally, "place of the deep black waters," the name of a place sacred to Manasa.
2. Spices wrapped in a betel leaf.
3. *Sadhu* is usually a term for a holy man, though throughout this text it designates a merchant.

So said the Merchant. And when he heard these harsh and bitter words, Hanuman began to burn with rage. The storm raged with awful violence, and Hanuman, grown in strength, suiting his deeds to the desires of Manasa, sank the seven ships with blows of his feet. The Bangali[4] sailors all cried out:
—We are lost.

The cargo of the ships, the jars of poppy-seeds, went floating on the water. And at the last moment, on the very brink of death, the Merchant leaped from the deck of his ship. The seven ships sank, and Chando, drowning, choked and coughed up water. Manasa was smiling to herself.

Swift Manasa, my hope lies at your feet. So writes Ketaka Das.

III

So while the Bangali sailors wept in despair, Hanuman leapt aboard the ships and smashed them. The ships shuddered and spun in circles, and the despairing Chando, terror-stricken, fell into the sea. His ships were sunk by the wrath of Manasa; his crewmen, clutching their heads with their hands, wept; and the cargo, jars of poppy-seed covered with cloth, floated on the water. The bales of cloth were also washed away. The sailors cried:
—Our clothes and goods are lost! We no longer have even a cloth with which to hide our nakedness!
—We are dying, brothers! Not even by piracy, but only because of Chando's foolishness we are to lose our lives in this strange place, far from our homes.

And the sailors looked in vain in all the four directions. By the wrath of Manasa, Chando was choked with water; his eyes were red, his belly swollen; he was drowning, choking on the water, and he cried:
—The One-eyed Chengamuri has brought this misery upon me!

In her chariot, hearing this, Manasa laughed aloud, victorious. But as she watched him drown, her heart softened. She dropped a lotus on the water. Chando, choking, close to death, drew thickened breath. And then the lotus floated close to him. He thought:
—Manasa's birth was in a lotus. He who touches one commits great sin.

So thinking thus, Chando did not touch the flower, though he was close to death. Nor could he reach the shore. Then Mother Kamala, seeing his danger, cut a banana-tree and sent it to him as a raft. To save himself, Chando swam quickly to the tree. Saying:
—Shiva, Shiva!

Seven times he made obeisance to that God. But because he was naked he did not pull himself out of the water.

Then Neto the washerwoman went and said to Manasa:
—Chando the Merchant still does not recognize your name. But though he is still opposed to you, O Devi, do not kill him. Let him live; for then only will your worship spread. Save his life.

When she heard the words of her friend, the Mother of the World took the disguise of a virtuous wife.

4. People from East Bengal.

IV

So Manasa took the form of a beautiful woman; I cannot begin to describe her beauty. With several other women she went, the wife of Jaratkaru, Jaya Bishahari, to bring water. She took a water-jar on her hip and went to where Chando the Merchant was, cast up naked on the beach. When he saw the women, Chando was ashamed, and hid his nakedness in the water. The women said to him:

—O mad Digambara,[5] why do you sit there like that? Put this winding-sheet around your nakedness.

And so the Merchant, in shame, put on the sheet taken from a corpse, and began to make his way from place to place, begging for food to eat. In his left hand he held a staff, and on his body he wore the ragged winding-cloth. Because of the wrath of Manasa, the *sadhu* had to beg for food.

So Kshemananda sings, such is the great power of Manasa. Be merciful, O thou full of compassion.

V

Staff in hand, the once-great merchant went from house to house to beg his food. Thinking him a madman, boys pelted him with sticks and clods of earth. Chando said:

—Why do you strike me? I am Chando the Merchant.

But no one knew him; people laughed at him. His lips were red, his body strong and healthy; but he wore a ragged winding-sheet. He wandered from place to place, a broken begging-bowl in his hand. Some, who were pious, gave to him. He begged, and got a little food and money. And finally he came to a ruined and deserted hut, and in a corner of it he made his home.

Manasa knew this. She went to the place of Ganesha and said to him:

—O brother, lend me your rat a little while. This favor I ask of you.

Ganapati replied:

—Of course, O Jagati, I shall give you the rat. But tell me this: to whom will you now do injury?

Jagati said:

—Ganapati, even if I tell you, remember that you have promised to give the rat to me. Chando the Merchant always calls me Chengamuri Kani. What more need I say? I shall take my revenge. Now give me the rat, you glutton.

She took the rat and showed to it the grain which Chando had gathered by begging. The rat entered the earth; wily, it quickly chewed a tunnel through the earth. It stole the grain and came again before Ganesha.

Ketaka Das prays for the feet of Manasa.

VI

So the rat stole Chando's grain, and when the Merchant saw that this had happened, he was much disturbed.

—I got that grain by begging alms, and now the One-eyed Chengamuri has stolen it from me.

5. "Sky-clad," i.e., naked. It is also the term for a naked Jain monk.

And so, cursing Manasa, he set forth again, wandering from forest to forest. And at the angry hands of Manasa, he suffered even greater misery.

Once Manasa took the form of a white fly, and settled near a group of hunters who were hunting birds in that same forest. For twelve years they had hunted and had not caught their prey, but on this day again were setting out on the chase. They took their nets and ropes and lures and went forth to hunt in the forest. Surrounding the forest and dropping the bait on the ground, silently and carefully they lured the birds down. The birds fed there, contented.

In this same forest Chando was wandering in misery, crying out in his distress. When they heard his weeping, the birds rose up in fright and flew away. Then in anger the bird-hunters surrounded the *sadhu,* and seizing him by the hair they beat him fiercely. Chando cried:

—Do not beat me! Why do you beat me, brothers? I am not a thief!

But they replied:

—Why did you frighten off our birds? O son of a sheep, where have you come from?

And finally they let him go. At last Chando, weeping, arrived at the house of a friend. The friend's name was Chandraketu, son of Dharmaketu. In hope of safety and comfort, Chando ran toward his house, calling:

—Friend, O friend!

So goes the song of Manasa, composed by Kshemananda.

VII

Then Chando the Merchant said to his friend:

—O friend, how can I tell you the story of my grief? An evil fate is written on my forehead. The Chengamuri One-eyed One has devoured my six sons and sunk my seven ships. By great good fortune and the grace of Shiva my own life was saved, and now, at last, we two friends have met. Help me now, in this time of my great danger and despair—be my friend. For friends are those who do each other service. It says in the *Ramayana* that Rama, giving up his kingdom, took Lakshmana and the daughter of Janaki and went into the forest; then Ravana stole Sita, daughter of Janaki, and put her in the golden city. But the friend of Rama, Sugriva, king of monkeys, did service for his friend, at that time of his great anguish in the forest. Killing Baliraja, Rama gave Sugriva the power of a kingdom when with a single arrow he split the seven trees. So did Sugriva, king of monkeys, do his friend a service, and built the bridge to Lanka over the waters of the sea. The two, then, being friends, were of service to each other to the ends of their lives. Because of the glory of Rama and Sugriva, the rocks and trees floated on the water, and now all the people of the world sing their praises. So it was too with the five Pandava brothers, great heroes in battle. They lost the game of dice and went to live in the forest. The five remained unknown, as friends, in the house of Birata the king. So also with the king Shrivatsa, who, performing *puja*[6] to Shiva, kept that god in his mind both day and night. But evil and ill fortune tormented him, and he was forced to leave his throne and kingdom and live twelve years in the forest. Like him, I have fallen on evil days; with fear and sorrow in my heart I have come to you.

6. Worshipping a deity, usually with offerings of fruit, flowers, and prayers.

But the Merchant did not know that his friend was a worshipper of Manasa, that he did daily *puja* to her sacred pots.
—It is good that you have come to my house. It is many days since last we met.
And he led him in, and offered him water and a seat. But in the room was the altar of Manasa: two pots were on a throne, garlanded with flowers, and on the pots vermilion and *ketaki* leaves. Then Chando said:
—O Chengamuri, you have sunk my ships and all my cargo, and now you come here secretly. To the house of my own friend you come to cause me grief. O stupid One-eyed One, you shall not make me bow to you. I do not know what makes my friend worship you, but I shall not!
And then, in rage, Chando went to break the pots of Manasa with his staff. But knowing well the danger, his friend restrained him:
—My good friend, you have lost your reason. Do do not antagonize the goddess more. Had I not restrained your staff in time, you would now be in mortal peril.
But Chando would not be restrained. Seeing him mad, some held him, others struck him on the head; Chandraketu said:
—He has come to my house to break the sacred pots. Beat him and throw him out.
So, scorned and insulted, in grief and anger, Chando continued his wandering from forest to forest.
Such is the song of Manasa Devi, composed by Kshemananda, who says: Pardon us our sins, Daughter of Ishana.

VIII

The *sadhu* then, receiving only scorn at his friend's house, went once more to wander in the forest. Alone he wandered, and in his time of peril he found no companion. But then he saw a group of woodsmen on the path. He said to them:
—Brothers, tell me, to what work do you go now, so loudly and so happily?
They answered him:
—We are going to the forest to cut wood. By selling it in the city, we shall get money. This is the work of our caste, for we are woodcutters.
Chando replied:
—I am stronger than most of you. I shall go with you, and if I take a double load on my head, perhaps I shall get a *kahan*[7] for it. Why do I wander thus in sadness in the forest? Take me with you, brothers, to cut wood. By your kindness I also shall cut wood and eat.
And they all said:
—Why are you so sad? Come with us. Cut wood and sell it, and live.
So the unfortunate *sadhu* went with them to cut wood. And when they had cut much wood, the woodsmen tied it into bundles. Chando the Ojha[8] knew good sandalwood; he tied up great bundles of this wood, and seven or eight men hoisted them to his shoulders. Taking his great load of wood, the *sadhu* walked ahead. His body, which had matured in happiness, was racked with pain; but he was going to sell his wood and eat.
Bishahari saw this from her swan chariot, and said:

7. A unit of money worth 1,280 cowries.
8. A person who has magic powers, especially over snakes and snakebites.

—Tell me now, O Neto, what I should do. Chando the Merchant is cutting wood, and goes to sell it. If he earns money by this and returns to his own country, he can curse me to his heart's content.

Neto replied:

—O Bishahari, do not be disturbed by this. Remember the Son of the Wind—let Hanuman mount the load of wood, and Chando will not be able to carry it.

When she heard the words of her friend, Manasa summoned the Son of the Wind. Immediately the hero Hanuman appeared and made *pranam*[9] at the feet of the Devi.

—Order me, O Bishahari, and I shall bring you the sun or moon from the sky. I can bring you Vasuki[1] from hell, or the Kurma,[2] or the Mountain itself.

So saying, the great hero stood respectfully with folded hands. The Devi gave him *pan* and flowers, and said to him:

—O Hanuman, Son of the Wind, you are my cousin. For Rama's sake, because of Sita, you made war with the Rakshasa. Now, look there—Chando the Merchant is going with a load of wood. Go, mount that load and press him down. But do not put such weight on him that his back is broken and he dies; for if he dies my worship will never be established in the world.

At the Devi's command, Hanuman went and climbed up on the load of wood. Under his tremendous weight, the Merchant fell, crying out in pain. He could not lift the load again. Tears streamed down his cheeks, as in agony of mind and body he cried:

—The Chengamuri Kani has sent this misery to me.

The greater was his pain, the more he cursed the Devi. And in her swan chariot, the Devi said to Neto:

—Hear—his curses increase as does his pain. He is ready to die for his pride, but not to abandon his belief.

And so again, despondent, he went from forest to forest. He walked until he could walk no more, weak, with only the fruits of the forest to eat. Luckily, a worthy Brahmin had in the forest performed a *shraddha*[3] ceremony for his father; when he had left the forest for his home, he had left banana skins and joints of sugar-cane behind. When he saw this, Chando stood erect. Delighted, he took a bath in a nearby pond and worshipped Shankara. As he ate the banana skins and cane, his strength returned to him. Meditating on Shiva, he drank some water. He who would not have touched the best bananas now ate their skins with pleasure.

So says Ketaka Das, serving the Mother of the World. Grant your blessings to your devotee, O gracious one.

IX

Despairing, the *sadhu* came to a Brahmin's house. He made *pranam* and said:

—Hear my words, Gosai.[4] My name is Chando; Champakanagara is my home. I was once a rich man, but have fallen into the condition in which

9. Bowing with the head on the ground, a gesture of respect.
1. King of the Nagas, or cobra people, who live in the watery underworld.
2. The tortoise avatar of Vishnu, with which he supports the mountain, Mount Meru, at the center of the earth.
3. The memorial service for dead ancestors ("How to Perform a Funeral," p. 213).
4. An honorific title for Vaishnavas of high status, probably derived from "Goswamin."

you see me now. Let me stay with you for some few days. I shall carry water-jugs for you—you need only give me food and water. Whatever work you ask of me, I shall do. I am Chando, once the greatest of merchants and ruler of Champakanagara.

Hearing this, the Brahmin said to him:

—Attend then to the work of my household. If you do so, I shall increase your wealth and honor as I would that of my own eldest son. Today, go and weed my paddy-fields.

When he had said this, the Brahmin took him out and sat him down in the paddy-fields to weed the paddy. But Bishahari, with her dark magic, prevented Chando from telling rice from weed. He weeded out all the stalks of paddy, and let the weeds remain. When he saw what Chando had done, the Brahmin cursed him and slapped him with his hand. Bewildered, the *sadhu* hugged the Brahmin's feet. And seeing his misery and grief, the Brahmin refrained from beating him.

So from that place too he went away, tears streaming from his eyes, saying over and over again:

—The Chengamuri Kani has sent this grief to me. What can I do? What work can I find?

He wandered aimlessly. Indeed, what could he do?

CHANDO COMES HOME

Chando and his wife Sanaka have a son, Lakhindar (also called Lakhai), who will eventually marry a woman named Behula; their ill-starred love story, which here interrupts the narrative of Chando, is one of the best-loved parts of the *Manasa-mangal*. We rejoin the story when Chando returns home.

XIII

Many miseries Chando endured, but finally his endless journey brought him to his own house. Under the curse of Manasa, subject to her power, his ships all sunk, the Merchant returned home. Manasa had put upon him clothes of indescribable foulness, and, having sunk his ships, had brought him home again.

To torment him more, Bishahari became a fortune teller, with the manuscript of an almanac in her hand. She drew a *phota*[1] on her forehead, and having placed the manuscript on the ground, sat down before the *sadhu's* house. When the people of the house saw the soothsayer, they brought her a mat to sit upon. Then she drew chalk lines upon the ground and began to read the divination.—Here, O Sanaka, lovely woman. A thief will come to your house today. There will be no hair upon his head, and he will be dressed in rags. You must remain alert, for surely such a man will come. Seize him and beat him, to the point of death.

When she had said this, the goddess went away, and once more resumed her own form. As she was doing so, Chando came. He came slowly through

1. A decorative mark.

the forest—for in the daylight he was ashamed to leave the forest. He hid in the banana grove; peeping out, he watched his son Lakhai at play in the courtyard of his house.

As evening came, the servant Cheri went to the banana grove. She saw hiding there a man all dressed in rags, who had the appearance of a thief. She ran at once to Sanaka; and when she heard, Sanaka ran to the banana grove. Inside the grove she heard a rustling sound, as Chando paced slowly through the leaves. Sanaka leapt up and ran to the house:

—A thief! There is a thief! Bring sticks and beat him!

And as the night was dark, Chando was not recognized. His mind was numbed, but he cried out:

—Do not beat me any more! I am Chando the Merchant!

When they heard this they stopped beating him, and lowered a lamp to see his face. His wife knew him then, and her heart was greatly anguished.

Kshemananda sings the story of the goddess Manasa.

XIV

Chando had come home, without his ships, without his goods. Tears streaming from her eyes, the lovely Sanaka said to him:

—The lord of my life is safe! But tell me, good and holy man, my lover, I entreat you—tell me where you have been . . . what has happened . . . where is your ship Madhukara . . .

Then the *sadhu* said to Sanaka:

—My ships are sunk in Kalidaha. I know not how. The Chengamuri Kani has twisted me and greyed my hair in sorrow . . . my ships were sinking, and I jumped into the water, and water came in my nose and mouth . . .

And Sanaka, in sorrow and in pity, burst into tears, and said:

—How can I go on? Our six sons dead, and now the ships all sunk and their cargo lost because of the wrath of Manasa. You have cursed her. It is the failure of your wisdom which has caused all this—ah, my fate is one of misery.

When he heard these words from Sanaka, Chando burned in anger:

—Do not speak of her! She has killed our sons. She has taken our ships and wealth. What more can she do to me now?

Falling at his feet, Sanaka tried to make him understand:

—Hear me, my lord, O righteous man. While you were in another country, from my womb was born another son, Lakhindar. You anger and revile the goddess—do you not see what can come of this? Put my mind at ease, my husband. Do not deny your duty any longer. There is no point in anger any more.

But when he saw the face of his son, the Merchant was joyful, and he forgot his former woe. He took his little son into his lap and kissed his face.

MANASA RELENTS

Lakhindar, like Chando's other son, dies, this time from the bite of a snake sent by Manasa, but Behula revives him, as the paradigmatic good wife, Savitri, revives her husband in the *Mahabharata*. After many more disasters, Chando still stubbornly resists Manasa. She finally decides to try to win him over with blessings rather than curses.

XLIX

Manasa knew that to be accepted in the world of men, Chando must worship her. So with special joy she gave this order:
—Listen, powerful snakes, Chando, that most wicked-hearted man, still does not praise or meditate upon me. Hear me. Go and carry the fourteen ships.

So Jagati[1] spoke, and gave *arati*.[2] And four hundred serpents went and took the ships upon their backs and carried them to the house of the *sadhu*. Seeing this, with joyful heart, Sanaka took her sons from the ships and with her daughters-in-law, went into the house. Incense was lit, the conch-shells sounded as the ships were worshipped. The Devi had been gracious to them, and all the people said:
—The merit of Behula must be very great. Never has anything like this been seen. But even though all has been restored to him the *sadhu* does not worship the Devi's feet.

Sanaka herself then said to Chando:
—Hear, O Merchant. Now worship Bishahari, toward whom you have had such hostility. It is by her blessing that our sons have been brought back to life, and that our ships have been restored. O you who are chief of merchants, I beg you, let your anger pass away, and ask her blessing; worship her sacred pots. There is nothing to be gained by further anger and bitterness. Give me peace of mind. Now worship her; do not ignore my prayer.

Thus, falling at his feet, Sanaka implored him and disturbed his mind.
So writes Ketaka Das.

L

But the *sadhu* paid no heed to Sanaka's words; though he had regained all that he had lost, he still refused to worship Manasa. Instead, he turned over in his mind the insult and disgrace which she had brought upon him.
—How shall I force my mind to meditate on Manasa? Shall I now worship her whom I have always fought? Shall I now fall at her feet? This is madness! I have cursed her, and called her Chengamuri Kani. Shall I now in repentance and shame bow my head and clasp my hands before her? To shave my head for her would be worse than death for me. I cannot find it in my heart to worship her. Shall I make offerings to Bishahari with this hand, with which I have worshipped my golden Gandheshvari?[3] Yet, my son's wife is a new Savitri. I have my sons and fourteen ships. If I do not worship her, I shall surely lose all that I have regained.

The *sadhu* remained sunk in thought:
—Should I now abandon my quarrel and worship Jagati?

Meanwhile, Vishvakarma[4] made a pot of gold and decorated it with vermilion, and fashioned a *pushpajhara*.[5] On it was placed an unbroken *sij*

1. Another name of Manasa, goddess of all that moves.
2. A form of offering that consists of waving lamps in front of an image.
3. A great river in Bengal, and the goddess of that river.
4. The blacksmith, architect, and craftsman of the gods.
5. A kind of colander from which a stream of water flows over a sacred object during rituals.

branch, with bananas and unboiled rice and other things, and all within the house began *puja* to Manasa. In Champakanagara were nine lakhs of Banyas;[6] they all came to the *puja* for Manasa. Faith in their hearts, they meditated on her.

—Appear to us, O Devi Bishahari!

To receive the *puja*, Bishahari with nine crores[7] of snakes descended to the earth. The Devi knew in her heart of Chando's hesitation and was wary.

—I do not understand his actions; at any time he may strike me with his *hental* staff.

And so she said aloud:

—Hear me, Merchant. I have been against you for a long time. But now I would show you my mercy. Cast your staff away, O Merchant.

When he heard this, Chando smiled to himself.

—Do not fear my staff any more. It is by your blessing that I have gained what was lost to me. I shall worship your feet as should be done.

The Devi said:

—Throw away your staff.

Chando replied:

—Then I shall throw my staff away.

And Manasa granted him the highest blessing, and, descending to receive the *puja*, forgave all sins. In all the *sadhu*'s lands a glad outcry arose, and Chando worshipped her with many offerings.

So writes Kshemananda, the servant of the goddess.

6. People of the merchant castes.

7. A crore is ten million.

RAMPRASAD SEN

The poetry of Ramprasad Sen (ca. 1720–1781) bristles with references to real life: to poverty, farmers, debts, absentee landlords, lawyers, leaking boats, merchants, and traders. His celebration of poverty served both as solace for people truly in need and as a metaphor for spiritual poverty, though the upper castes supported Ramprasad and he did not oppose caste. Strong Tantric influences are evident both in his celebration of Kali's union with Shiva and in the wine and drunkenness that pervade his poetry and (as the stories go) pervaded his life.

But most of the poems in this selection take a different tack. Here he scolds the divine Mother, the unpredictable other, often in the petulant voice of one of her children. His devotion to the fierce, often naked goddess Kali produced a powerful and unique form of *bhakti* poetry in Bangla.

The poems in this section are translated by Leonard Nathan and Clinton B. Seely.

PRONOUNCING GLOSSARY

Durga: *door´-gah*
Gaya: *guh-yah´*
Hari: *huh´-ree*
Kali: *kah´-lee*
Kashi: *kah´-shee*
Prasad: *pruh-sahd´*
Ramprasad Sen: *rahm´-pruh-sahd´ sen´*

I SPENT MY DAYS IN FUN

A poem about poverty and death, firmly rooted in the renunciant tradition as well as in the self-mocking line of poets that we can trace back to Kabir (p. 399), but here in an entirely original voice.

I spent my days in fun,
Now, Time's up and I'm out of a job.
I used to go here and there making money,
Had brothers, friends, wife, and children
Who listened when I spoke. Now they scream at me
Just because I'm poor. Death's
Field man is going to sit by my pillow
Waiting to grab my hair, and my friends
And relations will stack up the bier,
Fill the pitcher,[1] ready my shroud and say
So long to the old boy

1. The water poured as libation for the dead, beside the cremation bier, "the pile."

In his holy man's get-up.
They'll shout Hari a few times,
Dump me on the pile and walk off.
That's it for old Ramprasad.
They'll wipe off the tears
And dig in to their supper.

TELL ME, BROTHER, WHAT HAPPENS AFTER DEATH?

Here Ramprasad acknowledges the variety of views about death in the Hindu tradition, though he does not mention the one that is probably most prevalent, namely, reincarnation. The image of merging in water in the final stanza resonates with the idea of the soul merging with the universal *brahman*, a process that the Upanishads sometimes analogize to rivers flowing into an ocean, or salt melting in water.

Tell me, brother, what happens after death?
The whole world is arguing about it—
Some say you become a ghost,
Others that you go to heaven,
And some that you get close to God,
And the Vedas insist you're a bit of sky
Reflected in a jar fated to shatter.

When you look for sin and virtue in nothing,
You end up with nothing.
The elements live in the body together
But go their own ways at death.

Prasad says: you end, brother,
Where you began, a reflection
Rising in water, mixing with water,
Finally one with water.

WHAT DID I DO WRONG?

Ramprasad here invokes the law of karma, the belief that present sufferings are payment for past misdeeds ("Transmigration," p. 114), a belief also alluded to in the image of Death spinning the great wheel, the circle of rebirths. The poet blames his inability to cut loose—to renounce the things of this world, to devote himself only to Kali—on Kali herself. This is another sort of circle.

What did I do wrong?
Every day it gets harder.
I sit here blubbering all the time,
Telling myself I'm going to get out
Of this place, I've had it with this life.
The Lord of Death, a good servant,
Came in and spun the great wheel.
So I say to myself that I'm getting out of here
To spend what's left of my life reciting
Your name, but Kali, You've got me so hooked
To the things of this world, I can't cut loose.

Ramprasad cries at Kali's feet:
O my dark Devi, I move through the shadows
Of Your world in a black mood.

HOW MANY TIMES, MOTHER

The wheel of rebirth takes on newly vivid details in this poem, written in the genre of blaming the god, which we know from early South Indian poets (*Tevaram*, p. 315). Here Ramprasad blames the goddess, whom he calls Durga ("Hard to Reach"), for being a bad mother on two accounts—for giving birth to him over and over, and for failing to comfort him in his present life.

How many times, Mother, are you going
To trundle me on this wheel like a blind-
Folded ox grinding out oil? You've got me
Tied to this old trunk of a world, flogging me
On and on. What have I done to be forced to serve
These Six Oily Dealers, the Passions?
All these births—eighty times 100,000—
As beast and bird and still the door
Of the womb is not shut on me
And I come out hurting once more!
When a child cries out, calling the precious name
Of mother, then a mother takes it in her arms.
Everywhere I look I see that's the rule,
Except for me. All some sinners need to do
Is shout "Durga" and—pouf!—they're saved.

Take this blindfold off so I can see
The feet that give comfort. There are many
Bad children, but who ever heard
Of a bad mother?

There's only one hope
For Ramprasad, Mother—that in the end
He will be safe at Your feet.

YOU THINK MOTHERHOOD IS CHILD'S PLAY?

As in so many of Ramprasad's poems, the poet criticizes Kali for her lack of compassion; here, the poet attributes her coldness to the influence of her father, stony-hearted Death.

You think motherhood is child's play?
One child doesn't make a mother if she's cruel.
Mine carried me ten months and ten days
But doesn't notice where I've gone when it's time to eat.

When a child is bad, his parents correct him,
But You can watch Death come at me
With murder in His heart
And turn away yawning.

Ramprasad asks: Who taught You to be so cold?
If You want to be like Your father—
Stone—don't call Yourself
The Mother.

MIND, YOU GAMBLED

The poet laments that he, more precisely his mind, is a loser, in a double-tiered metaphor that moves back and forth between images of the chessboard (bishops, pawns, horses as knights, and elephants as castles—chess having come from India) and real life (horses, elephants, and becalmed ships), ending with the metaphorical image of death as checkmate—a term that is derived from the Persian for "the king is paralyzed" (*shah-mat*).

Mind, you gambled
And lost everything
So how do I move now?

My five best chessmen
Have led me on
And now there's my minister trembling,
Exposed on that pawn's square
And my horses hang back

And my elephant—why?
And my ships, laden with salt,
Sails set, lie idle at the dock
Though the wind is fair.

Ramprasad says: so that's that.
And, look—it's check-mate
In my back row.

I'M NOT CALLING YOU ANYMORE

The poet now blames Kali for spoiling him, her son, with the goods of this world—which did not last, of course.

I'm not calling You
Anymore, crazy Kali.

You, only a girl, waving a big sword,
Went into battle and without a stitch.

And there's that pittance You gave me
Only to snatch it right back.

As for this half-wit son,
You spoiled him all right, Mother.

Poor Ramprasad cries:
Look what You've done Mother—
Piled this old tub
Full of goods, then sunk it.

WHY SHOULD I GO TO KASHI?

The poet mocks both the famous shrines of conventional Hinduism, starting with Kashi (Varanasi, Benares), and the goal of *moksha*, merging back into god, which he likens to merging with sugar; he prefers to eat sugar.

Why should I go to Kashi?
At Her feet you'll find it all—
Gaya, the Ganges, Kashi.
Meditating in my lotus heart

I float on blissful waters.
Her feet are red lotuses
Crammed with shrines
And Her name spoken
Consumes evil like a fire
In a pile of dry cotton.
If there is no head to worry,
You can't have a headache.

Everytime I hear about Gaya,
The offerings there, the good deeds
Recited, I laugh. I know Shiva
Has said that dying at Kashi saves.
But I know too that salvation
Always follows worship around
Like a slave, and what's this salvation
If it swallows the saved like water
In water? Sugar I love
But haven't the slightest desire
To merge with sugar.

Ramprasad says with amazement:
Grace and mercy in Her wild hair—
Think of that
And all good things are yours.

MOTHER, INCOMPARABLY ARRAYED

The poet celebrates the Tantric image of Kali dancing on top of Shiva.

Mother, incomparably arrayed,
Hair flying, stripped down,
You battle-dance on Shiva's heart,
A garland of heads that bounce off
Your heavy hips, chopped-off hands
For a belt, the bodies of infants
For earrings, and the lips,
The teeth like jasmine, the face
A lotus blossomed, the laugh,
And the dark body boiling up and out
Like a storm cloud, and those feet
Whose beauty is only deepened by blood.

So Prasad cries: My mind is dancing!
Can I take much more? Can I bear
An impossible beauty?

FAKIR LALON SHAH

Fakir Lalon Shah lived in the eighteenth century and was a member of one of the bands of Bauls ("Crazies") who wandered in Bengal villages, singing songs heavily influenced by the Sahajiya tradition (p. 478). Like Kabir (p. 399), Fakir Lalon Shah drew upon both Muslim and Hindu sources, and his songs are sung both in the Hindu communities of West Bengal and among Muslims in Bangladesh.

PRONOUNCING GLOSSARY

Fakir Lalon Shah: *fuh-keer´ lah´-lun shah´*

THE BIRD AND THE CAGE, AND THE FLOWER

In these two short poems, the bird in the cage stands for the soul in the body (cf. "Two Birds," p. 120), and the flower stands for the ultimate divinity that the Bauls seek so passionately to reach.

This bird may fly away any time now; a bad wind has struck its cage.

The resting post suspended in the cage has fallen down; how then will the bird remain? Now I sit and worry, and endure a feverish terror in my body.

Whose cage is this? And who is this bird? Which do I consider my own; and which as stranger? Which is my eye most eager for? This bird wants to charm me.

If I had only known earlier that this wild thing could never be tamed, I wouldn't have fallen in love with it, but now I see no way out.

On the day my beloved bird flies away, the cage will suddenly be empty. On that day there will be no companion to console me. So mourns the wanderer Lalon.

A certain flower contains four colors; and oh, what beauty exists in the city of love within this flower!

The flower floats in the middle of the primordial waters, drifting from shore to shore. An anxious white bumblebee buzzes around in hopeful expectation of the flower's nectar.

Translated by David Haberman.

The flower's creeper is without roots and its leaves without branches. All this is quite true, but who can I talk to about the existence of this flower?

Dive deep into the waters and explore with an open heart, O mind. A saint is born in that flower, and that flower is certainly no ordinary flower. Lalon says: It has no roots in this world.

JAMES BATTRAY AND W. H. MACNAGHTEN

It may seem strange to include in an anthology of Hinduism documents created by two British bureaucrats, Mr. James Battray, a magistrate, and W. H. (later Sir William Hay) Macnaghten. But it would not surprise the many scholars who have argued that the British "imagined," i.e., virtually created, modern Hinduism. Without going quite so far, it would be safe to suggest that one significant part of modern Hinduism, so-called Reformed Hinduism, particularly in Bengal, underwent major changes both by absorbing aspects of the British critique of Hinduism and by reacting against it.

Nowhere was this ambivalent influence felt more strongly than in the argument about the practice that Anglo-Indian English called "suttee": the burning alive of certain Indian women on the funeral pyres of their dead husbands. (Sanskrit and Hindi texts call the woman who commits the act a *sati*, literally, a "good woman.") This practice had been around for quite a while before the British Raj. Several queens commit suttee in the *Mahabharata*, and the first-century-B.C.E. Greek author Diodorus Siculus mentions suttee in his account of the Punjab. Through the ages, many Hindus protested suttee. But it first became a public issue under the Raj, and then both Europeans and Indians expressed widely differing opinions about it.

Every British schoolchild was once taught the following story: "In 1829 the British government in India put an end to the Hindu practice of suttee, their moral outrage at this barbaric violation of human rights outweighing their characteristic liberal tolerance of the religious practices of people under their benign rule." But almost every element in this credo is false. True, a law was passed in India in 1829 making it illegal for widows to be burned with their husbands, but moral outrage was not the predominant factor in the British decision to outlaw suttee, nor did the British actually end it. On the contrary, the fear of offending high-caste Hindus serving in the British army and civil service, and concern about the political costs of legal interdiction, led the British for many years to sanction suttee under some circumstances (as long as the woman had no children and persuaded the magistrate that she was acting of her own free will), thus effectively encouraging it by giving it a legal support it had never had before, making it a colonially enhanced atavism.

In 1680, the governor of Madras prevented the burning of a Hindu widow, and ten years later, an Englishman in Calcutta was said to have rescued a Brahmin widow from the flames of her husband's funeral pyre and taken her as his common-law wife. After that, the British generally looked the other way where suttee was concerned, or argued that they should not hinder but help the Hindus do as (the British thought) their scriptures dictated. But most of the dharma texts do not mention suttee, concentrating instead on ascetic widowhood; several condemn it in no uncertain terms; and a few late commentaries argue for it. (One commentary—Aparakra on Yajnavalkya, probably around 1100 C.E.—says that a widow may burn herself on her husband's pyre if she is impelled by her own deep grief, but she must not be forced.)

And so, on April 20, 1813 (the same year that the British government first allowed Christian missionaries into India), a British circular proclaimed that suttee was meant to be voluntary, and that it would be permitted in cases where it was countenanced by the Hindu religion and prevented when the religious authorities prohibited it, as when the woman was less than sixteen years old, pregnant, intoxicated, or coerced. In fact, there was a dramatic *increase* in the number of suttees from 1815 to 1818, the first three years of data collection: the toll went from 378 to 839 cases per year. After that, the numbers declined and then fluctuated between five hundred and six hundred. The 1817–18 cholera epidemic may have increased the numbers, with more men dead and more widows to die with them, or the clerks may have refined their methods of data collection. But there was also a suspicion that the numbers grew *because of* government intervention: the government had authorized suttee (their work made it seem as if a legal suttee was better than an illegal one) and given it interest and celebrity (so that there were copycat suttees).

Finally, in 1829, several years after prominent Brahmins had spoken up against suttee, and at a time when there were many Indians in the legislature and William Bentinck, an evangelical sympathizer, was governor general (1828–35), the desire to justify their continuing paternalistic rule over Indians, whom they characterized as savage children, led the British to ban suttee altogether, as well as child marriage, with much self-aggrandizing fanfare.

The main effect of the British law of 1829 was to stigmatize Hinduism as an abomination in Christian eyes. But the Raj had it both ways, boasting both that they did not interfere with other peoples' religions and that they defended human rights. The debate, in both India and Britain, turned what had been an exceptional practice into a symbol of the oppression of all Indian women and the moral bankruptcy of Hinduism. Nor did the 1829 law, or, for that matter, the legislation enacted by India after its Independence, end suttee; at least forty widows have burned since 1947, most of them largely ignored until the suttee of a woman named Rup Kanwar in 1987 became a cause célèbre (and inspired other suttees) and some even now attested only in obscure local archives.

PRONOUNCING GLOSSARY

Many words in these selections are idiosyncratically spelled to approximate Indian words in English.

sahamarana: *suh´-huh-muh´-ruh-nuh*
Yama: *yuh´-muh*
Tricanda: *tree´-cun´-duh*

HINDOO WIDOWS, &C

This passage and the one that follows are excerpts from "Papers Relating to East Indian Affairs, viz. Hindoo Widows, and Voluntary Immolations," a detailed catalogue of the suttees performed in India between 1797 and 1830, published in London by the House of Commons. These papers, the source of controversy in both Britain and India, include statistics, debates, and detailed accounts of particular cases, noting the name, age, and caste of the woman, as well as the date of her suttee, the number of her children, the name of her dead husband, and the place where the suttee took place. This first passage, by James Battray, describes a suttee from in 1797.

Hindoo Widows, &c.

Extract Bengal Judicial Consultations, the 19th May 1797

N° 1.—(Criminal.)—Acting Magistrate of Midnapore, to the Honourable Sir John Shore, bart. Governor General in Council, Fort William.

Honourable Sir,—On receiving information this morning from the cutwal,[1] that a child, by name Kumly, intended sacrificing herself with her husband, I thought it my duty to endeavour to prevent its taking place. She is scarcely nine years of age, and I am convinced can give no good reason whatever for so doing. Her aunt, who accompanied her, used her endeavours to dissuade her from such an act, but the superstition of the higher order of Hindoos has filled her head with such notions of its propriety, that I fear the business may yet sooner or later be accomplished. I may have erred in interfering with their religion, of which they say this is a part, but as the information was brought to me, I thought it my duty as magistrate to prevent it, as also from motives of humanity, and hope my conduct will meet with your approbation.

I have, &c. (signed)
James Battray, act[g] mag[ts].
Zillah Midnapore, 17th May 1797.

Ordered, That the acting magistrate be informed, that the Governor General in Council desires he will use every means of persuasion in his power, to induce Kumly to relinquish her intention of sacrificing herself; and that he will also endeavour to persuade her family to exert their influence in discouraging her from the execution of such an intention.

1. A *cutwal* (from the Hindi *kotwal*) was a chief officer of police for a city or town in northeastern India; a native town magistrate.

QUESTIONS TO THE PUNDITS OF THE COURT OF SUDDER DEWANNY ADAWLAT

This document, published by W. H. Macnaghten in 1817, consists of a series of questions posed to several pandits (scholars of Sanskrit, whom the British called "pundits") about the authenticity and legitimacy of suttee in Hinduism. The judicial process involved citations from the sacred texts, here called Shasters ("Shastras," p. 200), often invoking Sanskrit terms and texts, too numerous here to gloss any but those essential to the argument.

(F.)—Questions to the Pundits of the Court of Sudder Dewanny Adawlut; 21st March 1817.

1. In a case of sahamarana,[1] or a widow's burning herself with the corpse of her deceased husband, are any and what rules prescribed by the Shaster for the manner in which the rite is to be performed; particularly as to the widow's ascending the funeral pile previously to its being lighted, or subsequently casting herself into the flame? And are the same rules applicable to persons of every cast? or if not, what are the distinctions prescribed for different casts? Give a full answer to this question, with authorities from the Shaster current in Bengal and the Western Provinces respectively.

2. Is it authorized by the Shaster to bind or restrain in any manner a woman who has ascended the funeral pile of her husband, by tying her down with cords or placing bamboos over her, or using any other means to prevent her escape from the pile? If there be any authorities for such measures state them at length.

3. Are any and what persons expressly authorized by the Shaster to assist a widow in burning herself with the body of her deceased husband, in a case of sahamarana? or on a separate pile in a case of annoomaruna?[2] If so, state the authorities; or, if not, what aid is indispensably requisite to enable a woman to become a suttee, whether by ignition or by interment.

4. State at the same time whether any persons are expressly authorized by the Shaster to assist lepers, and others afflicted with incurable diseases, in putting themselves to death, as declared in a former bewasta[3] (recorded the 7th August 1810), to be sanctioned in the Brahma Purawna, with respect to the suicide of the deceased persons themselves.

(Copy.)

(signed) *M. H. Turnbull*, register.

(G.)—Translation of certain Questions proposed to the Hindoo Law Officers of the Sudder Dewanny Adawlut, regarding the burning of Widows, &c. and their Replies in conformity with the authorities current in Bengal and Benares.

Question 1.—In a case of sahamarana, or a widow's burning herself with the corpse of her deceased husband, are any and what rules prescribed by the Shasters for the manner in which the rite is to be performed; particularly as to the widow's ascending the funeral pile, previously to its being lighted, or subsequently casting herself into the flames? And are the same rules applicable to persons of every cast: or if not, what are the distinctions prescribed for different casts? Give a full answer to this question with authorities from the Shasters current in Bengal and the Western Provinces respectively.

Answer.—There are certain rules, prescribed both by the practice and Shasters of Bengal, to be attended to in a case of sahamarana. Whatever

1. Literally, "dying with," the usual Sanskrit term for what the British called "suttee" and Rammohun Roy (p. 538) called "Concremation."
2. Sanskrit *anumarana*, "dying after" (what Roy translated as "Postcremation"), when a woman did not join her husband on his pyre but built a separate fire afterward and was burned on it.
3. Anglo-Indian term for a type of native deposition.

rules exist relative to ascending the funeral pile previously or subsequently to its being lighted, extend equally to all classes. There are no distinct rules for the different classes. In certain villages of Burdwan, a district in Bengal, the following ceremonies are observed:—When women are desirous of dying with their husbands, in the mode termed sahamarana, they signified their intention of so doing, either previously or subsequently to the death of their husbands, by placing five couries under a mangoe tree, and (having walked three times round the tree, and having broken off a branch) by sitting down at the feet of their dying or deceased lords, at the same time continuing to hold the branch in their hands.

The following rules are universally observed in Bengal:—The woman about to perform the act of sahamarana, previously to ascending the funeral pile, must clothe herself in new apparel, and rub lac on her feet; she must also apply cotton dyed with lac to her hands, tying it on with red thread; on her forehead she must apply minium plentifully. She must separate her hair in front, and place two combs between the partitions. After having placed couries rubbed over with turmeric, and fried wheat, in a sieve, let her ascend the funeral pile, and scatter them on all sides.

The following ceremonies are prescribed by the Shasters current in Bengal:—Ablution, achumurrun or sipping water from the palm of the hand; the repetition of the sunkulph (or declaration);[4] the invocation of the guardians of the eight regions of the world, the sun, moon, air, ether, earth and water, soul, day, night and twilight; the ceremony of walking three times round the funeral pile; the expression by a brahmin of the texts extracted from the Rig Vida and Poorawnas; the utterance of the salutation; and lastly, the ascending the funeral pile.

The authority which enjoins the above ceremonies is the Anlyeshlee Puthulee, "Fire being applied by the sons to the funeral pile of their father, let the woman who wishes to accompany her deceased husband, having bathed, sipped water from the palm of her hand, and turning towards the east, pronounce the sunkulph or declaration. Then having made the following invocation, 'I call on you, ye guardians of the eight regions of the world, sun, moon, &c. &c.' Having walked three times round the funeral pile, having made use of the prescribed salutation, let her ascend the funeral pile; the brahmins having first repeated this text, 'Om, let these women, not to be widowed, devoted to their lords, virtuous and beautifully adorned, enter the fire with the bodies of their deceased husbands.'" The authority of the Shoodhee Futwa also confirms the above, "The fire being applied by the sons, according to the girhya, or peculiar ritual of the deceased's family, having first bathed, the widow dressed in two clean garments, holding some cusa grass in her hand, sips water from the palm of her hand, bearing fruit, flowers, tila water, and three blades of cusa grass in her hand, the brahmin utters the mystic words 'Om Tatsut;' she then bows to Narayana with the usual salutation, and utters the sunkulph (or declaration.) She then invokes the guardians of the eight regions of the earth, the sun, moon, &c. to bear witness that she follows her husband's corpse on the funeral pile. She then walks three times round the funeral pile, and makes the customary saluta-

4. Sanskrit *samkalpa,* "intention," a statement made at the beginning of every ritual, stating the intention to do it.

tion; and the brahmins having recited the text of the Rig Vida and Poorawnas, she ascends the flaming funeral pile."

The following rules are to be universally observed throughout Benares by women who are anxious to depart with their deceased husbands. On the demise of her husband, a woman must abstain from lamentation. Should she lament, she must refrain from the act of sahamarana. The following practical rules are observed by some dravida women. Having ascertained that her husband is dead, or on the point of death, the widow anoints herself with oil, bathes, clothes herself in red or yellow garments, applies an additional quantity of turmeric, &c. to her forehead, rubs her arms with sandal, applies collyrium to her eyes, eats curds and rice, and if this latter be not procurable sweetmeats and curds, chews betel nut, adorns her hair with red garlands, places a red necklace round her neck, ties a cloth filled with turmeric, sooparee and betel nut on her navel; at the time of quitting the house she looks with circumspection into the chambers of all her relations for the sake of prosperity; she scatters grains of rice over the house, and ultimately leaves it, carrying a cocoa nut in her hand. She then proceeds to the place of sacrifice, accompanied by various sorts of music, having previously worshipped the peculiar deities of the city or village. Such are the ceremonies generally observed.

The Rules prescribed by the Vedas are as follow:—

The widows of ahitagnees, or such as preserve the sacrificial fires, are enjoined to proceed to the burning place in close conjunction with the corpse and the three fires. The widows of anahitagnees are merely enjoined to remain on the road in close company with the corpses of their husbands. In the place where the corpse is deposited, the formula attendant on the ceremony must be expressed in the dual number; and the widow must be made to sit down at the same time. All the ceremonies that occur on the road are to be observed in the same manner. Having arrived at the place of burning, the widow must be laid on the funeral pile at the side of her deceased husband. If she be then destitute of the wish to perform the act of sahagumun, she must be lifted off. The widow being desirous of burning with the corpse of her deceased husband (provided he was an ahitagnee) is to be laid on the pile with its face upwards, and the sacrificial vessels having been applied to his members, the widow is to be laid upon him with her face downwards. At the time of applying the fire, the pile is to be lighted for both at once; and the formula on this occasion is to be recited in the dual number. The texts, propitiatory of Yama, are also to be recited in the same manner by him who officiates at the sacrifice, standing near the funeral pile. In the case of a widow of an anahitagnee, the sacrificial vessels termed smarta being applied, the widow is to be laid beside the corpse. The remaining ceremonies are similar in both cases.

The authorities for the above opinion are the text of the Tricanda Munduree, "In crossing a river, in passing over a boundary, and in the interval between two boundaries, the fires should always accompany their owners." This passage is declared in the commentary to affect both husband and wife, as the ownership of the sacrificial fires extends to them both. The text of Apustumba, "Dying together, the pitrimedha is to be performed for them both at once; and the texts must be recited in the dual number."

The Nernuya Sindhoo quotes the text of Apustumba, which declares, that as the term Pitrimedha comprehends all ceremonies, including the act of cremation, all those ceremonies are to be performed for both at once.

The same rule applies to a case of sahagamana, as to the case of both parties dying at the same moment. This appears from the text of Kupurdee, "Whenever a woman follows her deceased husband by ascending the flaming pile, the act of cremation will be simultaneous. The asthee kya, or ceremony of collecting the ashes, will be performed separately." The text of Apustumba ordains, that "the widow shall be placed on the right side of her deceased husband." If having arrived at the place of burning, she determine to burn, the ceremonies of depositing the widow, &c. must again be gone through. If she afterwards express a wish to rise, she must be lifted off; the two texts commencing with the word Oodursheree, having been previously recited. The commentary of Kupurdee on the above passage is as follows:—"In this interval, the officiating priest shall deposit;" that is to say, shall cause to be laid down the widow by the right side of her deceased husband, having recited the text commencing with the words "this woman." If the widow wishes to get off afterwards, the brother of the deceased husband, or some other brahmin, repeating the text commencing with the words Oodurshwee naree, shall lift her up. But if she subsequently refuses to rise, the fire is to be applied to both at once. The text of Apustumba, "An ahitagnee must be consumed with his three fires and sacrificial vessels." The text of Ashwalagama, "The widow of a man of the military tribe must be placed on the north side of him, together with his weapons; if she wishes to rise, the younger brother, or some other representative of her husband, or his pupil, or an old servant of the family, shall lift her up, pronouncing the text commencing with the words Oodurshwee naree." The following is the commentary of Purawna on the above passages:—"The body of the deceased being brought to the north of the fire, the head is to be turned to the south; the widow is to be made to sit to the northward of the corpse, and she, (thus lying to the north of the deceased, being devoid of courage), the younger brother of the husband, the disciple or old servant, shall salute and take hold of by the hand, repeating the texts Oodurshwee." The Nirnuya Sindhoo, "The younger brother of the deceased husband, or his disciple, shall raise up the terrified widow, laying to the northward of the deceased; the texts Oodurshwee, &c. having been repeated." In some villages situated in Benares, the following practices obtain among the widows of merchants and other traders:—The husband being laid on the funeral pile, she ascends it, placing the head of the corpse on her lap, when the fire is communicated.

Some observe the following practice:—The deceased husband being laid on the funeral pile, and the widow being about to ascend it, she takes in the palm of her hands a lamp inserted in a vessel filled with ghee; and the skirt of her garments having taken fire from the flame of that lamp, she immediately ascends the pile. The lamp so used is termed the Mainkeen Deepa. The ceremonies practically observed, differ as to the various tribes and districts.

The rules to be observed in Benares, in conformity to the Purawnas current there, are as follow:—

The sunkulph or declaration, is to be made, in which the time and place is to be noticed, being decked with minium and collyrium, &c. The widow is to bestow presents on the by-standers; then, having approached the fire, she adorns her wrist with five jewels, and applies a pearl ornament to her nose; she then invokes the fire, sacrifices to fire, Vishnu, Yumu, the earth, water, the wind, ether, Kalapa, Brahma, Roadree, by offering an oblation of clarified butter; she then walks three times round the fire, worships her household utensils; then, holding flowers in her hand, she invokes the fire and enters it. The authorities enjoining these practices are as follow:—The Nurnuya Sindhoo, adverting to the time and place, "Let the widow first make the sunkulph or declaration, intimating her desire that she may be equal to Arundhatt; and then distribute presents, accompanying that act with the text, 'May Luchesmee and Narrayuna, the depositories of constancy and truth, being pleased with these offerings, grant me undeviating constancy. I, anxious to obtain the favour of Luchesmee and Narrayuna, and desirous of constancy, present these offerings.' Let her then, having approached the fire, fold up five jewels in the skirt of her garment, anointing herself with collyrium, and apply a pearl ornament to her nose; then let her invoke the fire with this text, 'O fire! ever to be mentioned with the term Sueehu, all pervading and universal, conduct me to my husband by the path of constancy.' Let her, having offered an oblation of clarified butter, make a salutation to fire, as the lord of energy; to Vishnu, the lord of truth; to Yumu, the lord of justice; to Prethira, as presiding over the world; to the waters, as presiding over tastes; to the wind, as the lord of strength; to ether, as presiding over all; to Yumu, as presiding over justice; to the waters, as universal witnesses; to Brahma, as the lord of the Vedas; and to Roadree, as the lord of smushanus, or receptacles of the dead. Then let her, having thrice circumambulated the fire, worshipped her household utensils, and taken flowers into her hand, invoke the fire thus: 'O fire! thou secretly pervadest all beings; thou, O deity! knowest what mortals are ignorant of. Being afflicted with the dread of widowhood, I follow my lord; conduct me to my husband by the path of constancy.' Having uttered this text let her deliberately enter the fire."

Another extract from the Nernuyu Sindhoo.

Question 2.—Is it authorized by the Shasters to bind, or restrain in any manner, a woman who has ascended the funeral pile of her husband, by tying her down with cords, or placing bamboos over her, or using any other means to prevent her escape from the pile? If there be any authorities for such measures state them at length.

Answer.—No authority permits any restraint to be used. An expiation is ordained for the widow who has slipped off the pile, both in the Shoodhee Futwa and Nunuyu Sindhoo. The same is to be met with in the text of Apustumba, Keepurdie and Ashwulagunu. In the text of Narayumu, its commentary, and in the Nunuya Sindoo, mention is there also made of taking a woman off the funeral pile in the event of her being terrified, and of the persons by whom this is to be done.

The authority for the above opinion is the text of Apustumba, quoted in the Shoodhu Futwa and Nunuyu Sindhoo: "Whatever woman may have left the funeral pile, or slipped from it, through want of firmness, that woman will be purified from sin by undergoing the penance of praja putya."

The other authorities, in confirmation of the illegality of restraint, have been cited in the answer to the first question, treating of the manner in which the widow should be laid on the pile.

Question 3.—Are any, and what persons expressly authorized by the Shaster to assist a widow in burning herself with the body of her deceased husband, in a case of sahamarana? or on a separate pile, in a case of anoomarana? If so, state the authorities; or if not, what aid is indispensably requisite to enable a woman to become a suttee, whether by ignition or by interment.

Answer.—The sons or next heirs of a widow are expressly enjoined to assist her in the acts of sahamarana or anoomarana. This opinion is in conformity with the authorities current in Bengal and Benares. The text of the Vishnu Poorawna, cited in the Shoodhee Futwa and Nunuyu Sindhoo, is confirmatory of the above: "The son, grandson, great grandson, brother's offspring, or descendant of Sapinda, are competent to the performance of obsequies, O prince." The text of Yajnia Vulkia, cited in the same authorities, "He who performs the obsequies of her deceased husband shall perform also those of her, who ascending the same funeral pile, accompanies him."

Question 4.—State, at the same time, whether any persons are expressly authorized by the Shasters to assist lepers, and others afflicted with incurable diseases, in putting themselves to death, as declared in a former bewasta (recorded 7th of August 1810) to be sanctioned in the Brahma Poorawna, with respect to the suicide of the deceased persons themselves?

Answer.—The sons or nearest heirs are enjoined to assist at such suicides, as appears from the text of the Chandog Purisheshta, quoted in the Shoodhu Futwa: "Then let the sons or others, having collected a large heap of sticks, place them in the shape of a funeral pile, in an even and clean piece of ground."

(A true translation.)

(signed) *W. H. Macnaghten,*
acting deputy reg'.

RAMMOHUN ROY

The Hindus were divided in complex ways on the issue of suttee, and the grounds shifted in the arguments that they made for and against it in response to colonial discourse. On one side were those who supported a strict enforcement of the caste system, held onto their old ways, and opposed any change in caste customs, including suttee. On the other side were the radicals, who included in their ranks both militant Hindus and college-educated students who renounced Hinduism, imitated the British, became Anglophile Christians, ate beef, and drank beer. Somewhere in between the extremes of Indians and Europeans were Rammohun Roy and the Indian Liberal movement, who opposed child marriages and suttee, preached nonviolence, and tried to build a world that would combine the best of Hindu and Christian/British values.

Raja Rammohun (or Ram Mohun, or Rammohan) Roy (1774–1833), a Bengali Brahmin who knew Arabic, Persian, Hebrew, Greek, Latin, and Sanskrit, in addition to his native Bangla, read the scriptures of many religions, only to find, he said, that there was not much difference between them. In 1814 he settled in Calcutta, where he was prominent in the movement that advocated Western-style education, urging Hindus to learn mathematics, natural philosophy, chemistry, anatomy, and "other useful sciences."

Roy always wore the sacred thread that marked him as a Brahmin, and he kept most of the customs of a Brahmin, but his theology was surprisingly eclectic. He was one of the first prominent Hindus to visit Europe, where he was a great success among the intelligentsia of Britain and France. In 1828 he founded the Brahmo Sabha ("Assembly of God"), based on the doctrines of the Upanishads, several of which he had translated into Bangla in 1825. In 1843, Debendranath Tagore revived the organization, which had largely died away after Roy's death, and formed the Brahmo Samaj ("Society of God"). This movement, which began what is sometimes called the Hindu Renaissance or the Bengal Renaissance, was developed and augmented by a number of important Hindu reformers, each of whom made significant changes in the doctrines: Shri Ramakrishna Paramahamsa (1836–1886), Swami Vivekananda (1863–1902) (p. 550), Rabindranath Tagore (1861–1941) (p. 623), and Shri Aurobindo Ghose (1872–1950). The ideas of the Brahmo Samaj form an important part of the belief systems of many Hindus to this day.

THE PRACTICE OF BURNING WIDOWS ALIVE

Rammohun Roy was a major voice raised in opposition to suttee. Though he was unwilling to endorse government interference in matters of religion, his writings were one of the factors that influenced the British to take action against suttee in 1829. He wrote two tracts against suttee, publishing each first in Bangla and then in his own English translation. The earlier tract, published in two parts, in 1818 and 1820 (of which the first part, from 1818, is here reproduced), vehemently defended the rights of women and offered a passionate plea for the prohibition of suttee; it is written as a dialogue between an advocate of suttee and an opponent. Roy argues that there is no basis for suttee in the legal texts of Hinduism, and that the practice is to be opposed even when it is voluntary and, as such, faithful to "the scriptures"; he advocates ascetic widowhood instead. In the course of his argument, he cites a number of Sanskrit authorities, spelling their names with the usual British distortions ("Shastrus" for Shastras, etc.) to approximate Indian words in English. His second tract, published in 1830, was entitled "Abstract of the Arguments Regarding the Burning of Widows Considered As a Religious Rite." He also published, in 1822, "Brief Remarks Regarding Modern Encroachments on the Ancient Rights of Females," a tract on women's rights to property.

Translation of a Conference between an Advocate for, and an Opponent of, the Practice of Burning Widows Alive

Advertisement

The little tract, of which the following is a literal translation, originally written in Bungla, has been for several weeks past in extensive circulation in those parts of the country where the practice of Widows burning themselves on the pile of their Husbands is most prevalent. An idea that the arguments it contains might tend to alter the notions that some European Gentleman entertain on this subject, has induced the Writer to lay it before the British Public also in its present dress.

Nov. 30, 1818.

Conference between an Advocate for, and an Opponent of, the Practice of Burning Widows Alive

Advocate.—I am surprised that you endeavour to oppose the practice of Concremation and Postcremation of Widows, as long observed in this country.

Opponent.—Those who have no reliance on the Shastru, and those who take delight in the self-destruction of women, may well wonder that we should oppose that suicide which is forbidden by all the Shastrus, and by every race of men.

Advocate.—You have made an improper assertion, in alleging that Concremation and Postcremation are forbidden by the Shastrus. Hear what Unggira and other saints have said on this subject:

'That woman who, on the death of her husband, ascends the burning pile with him, is exalted to heaven, as equal to Uroondhooti.[1]

'She who follows her husband to another world, shall dwell in a region of joy for so many years as there are hairs in the human body, or thirty-five millions.

'As a serpent-catcher forcibly draws a snake from his hole, thus raising her husband by her power, she enjoys delight along with him.

1. Sanskrit Arundhati, a mythological woman who appears in Sanskrit texts as the paradigm of the faithful wife.

'The woman who follows her husband expiates the sins of three races; her father's line, her mother's line, and the family of him to whom she was given a virgin.

'There possessing her husband as her chiefest good, herself the best of women, enjoying the highest delights, she partakes of bliss with her husband as long as fourteen Indrus reign.

'Even though the man had slain a Brahmun, or returned evil for good, or killed an intimate friend, the woman expiates those crimes.

'There is no other way known for a virtuous woman except ascending the pile of her husband. It should be understood that there is no other duty whatever after the death of her husband.'

Hear also what Vyas has written in the parable of the pigeon:

'A pigeon devoted to her husband, after his death entered the flames, and ascending to heaven, she there found her husband.'

And hear Hareet's words:

'As long as a woman shall not burn herself after her husband's death, she shall be subject to transmigration in a female form.'

Hear too what Vishnoo the saint says:

'After the death of her husband a wife must live as an ascetic, or ascend his pile.'

Now hear the words of the *Bruhmu Pooran* on the subject of Postcremation:

'If her lord die in another country, let the faithful wife place his sandals on her breast, and pure enter the fire.'

The faithful widow is declared no suicide by this text of the *Rig Ved*: 'When three days of impurity are gone she obtains obsequies.'

Gotum says:

'To a Brahmunee[2] after the death of her husband, Postcremation is not permitted. But to women of the other classes it is esteemed a chief duty.'

'Living let her benefit her husband; dying she commits suicide.'

'The woman of the Brahmun tribe that follows her dead husband cannot, on account of her self-destruction, convey either herself or her husband to heaven.'

Concremation and Postcremation being thus established by the words of many sacred lawgivers, how can you say they are forbidden by the Shastrus, and desire to prevent their practice?

Opponent.—All those passages you have quoted are indeed sacred law; and it is clear from those authorities, that if women perform Concremation or Postcremation, they will enjoy heaven for a considerable time. But attend to what Munoo[3] and others say respecting the duty of widows: 'Let her emaciate her body, by living voluntarily on pure flowers, roots, and fruits, but let her not, when her lord is deceased, even pronounce the name of another man.'

'Let her continue till death forgiving all injuries, performing harsh duties, avoiding every sensual pleasure, and cheerfully practising the incomparable rules of virtue which have been followed by such women as were devoted to one only husband.'

Here Munoo directs, that after the death of her husband, the widow should pass her whole life as an ascetic. Therefore, the laws given by Unggira

2. Sanskrit Brahmani, a Brahmin woman.
3. Sanskrit Manu, author of a dharma text (p. 202).

and the others whom you have quoted, being contrary to the law of Munoo, cannot be accepted; because the *Ved* declares, 'whatever Munoo has said is wholesome;' and Virhusputi, 'whatever law is contrary to the law of Munoo is not commendable.' The Ved especially declares, 'by living in the practice of regular and occasional duties the mind may be purified. Thereafter by hearing, reflecting, and constantly meditating on the Supreme Being, absorption in Bruhmu[4] may be attained. Therefore from a desire during life of future fruition, life ought not to be destroyed.' Munoo, Yagnyuvulkyu, and others, have then, in their respective codes of laws, prescribed to widows the duties of ascetics only. By this passage of the *Ved*, therefore, and the authority of Munoo and others, the words you have quoted from Unggira and the rest are set aside; for by the express declaration of the former, widows after the death of their husbands may, by living as ascetics, obtain absorption.

Advocate.—What you have said respecting the laws of Unggira and others, that recommended the practice of Concremation and Postcremation, we do not admit: because, though a practice has not been recommended by Munoo, yet, if directed by other lawgivers, it should not on that account be considered as contrary to the law of Munoo. For instance, Munoo directs the performance of Sundhya,[5] but says nothing of calling aloud on the name of Huri; yet Vyas prescribes calling on the name of Huri. The words of Vyas do not contradict those of Munoo. The same should be understood in the present instance. Munoo has commended widows to live as ascetics; Vishnoo and other saints direct that they should either live as ascetics or follow their husbands. Therefore the law of Munoo may be considered to be applicable as an alternative.

Opponent.—The analogy you have drawn betwixt the practice of Sundhya and invoking Huri, and that of Concremation and Postcremation, does not hold. For, in the course of the day the performance of Sundhya, at the prescribed time, does not prevent one from invoking Huri at another period; and, on the other hand, the invocation of Huri need not interfere with the performance of Sundhya. In this case, the direction of one practice is not inconsistent with that of the other. But in the case of living as an ascetic or undergoing Concremation, the performance of the one is incompatible with the observance of the other. Spending one's whole life as an ascetic after the death of a husband, is incompatible with immediate Concremation as directed by Unggira and others; and, vice versa, Concremation, as directed by Unggira and others, is inconsistent with living as an ascetic, in order to attain absorption. Therefore those two authorities are obviously contradictory of each other. More especially as Unggira, by declaring that 'there is no other way known for a virtuous woman except ascending the pile of her husband,' has made Concremation an indispensable duty. And Hareet also, in his code, by denouncing evil consequences, in his declaration, that 'as long as a woman shall not burn herself after the death of her husband, she shall be subject to transmigration in a female form,' has made this duty absolute. Therefore all those passages are in every respect contradictory to the law of Munoo and others.

4. Sanskrit *brahman*, the divine substratum of the universe ("Upanishads," p. 105). "Absorption" translates *moksha*, "Release."

5. Sanskrit Sandhya, twilight, a Vedic ritual performed at sunrise and sunset.

Advocate.—When Unggira says that there is no other way for a widow except Concremation, and when Hareet says that the omission of it is a fault, we reconcile their words with those of Munoo, by considering them as used merely for the purpose of exalting the merit of Concremation, but not as prescribing this as an indispensable duty. All these expressions, moreover, convey a promise of reward for Concremation, and thence it appears that Concremation is only optional.

Opponent.—If, in order to reconcile them with the text of Munoo, you set down the words of Unggira and Hareet, that make the duty incumbent, as meant only to convey an exaggerated praise of Concremation, why do you not also reconcile the rest of the words of Unggira, Hareet, and others, with those in which Munoo prescribes to the widow the practice of living as an ascetic as her absolute duty? And why do you not keep aloof from witnessing the destruction of females, instead of tempting them with the inducement of future fruition? Moreover, in the text already quoted, self-destruction with the view of reward is expressly prohibited.

Advocate.—What you have quoted from Munoo and Yagnyavulkyu and the text of the *Ved* is admitted. But how can you set aside the following text of the *Rig Ved* on the subject of Concremation? 'O fire! let these women, with bodies anointed with clarified butter, eyes coloured with collyrium, and void of tears, enter thee, the parent of water, that they may not be separated from their husbands, but may be, in unison with excellent husbands, themselves sinless and jewels amongst women.'

Opponent.—This text of the *Ved*, and the former passages from Hareet and the rest whom you have quoted, all praise the practice of Concremation as leading to fruition, and are addressed to those who are occupied by sensual desires; and you cannot but admit that to follow these practices is only optional. In repeating the Sunkulpyu of Concremation, the desire of future fruition is declared as the object. The text therefore of the *Ved* which we have quoted, offering no gratifications, supersedes, in every respect, that which you have adduced, as well as all the words of Unggira and the rest. In proof we quote the text of the *Kuthopunishut*: 'Faith in God which leads to absorption is one thing; and rites which have future fruition for their object, another. Each of these, producing different consequences, holds out to man inducements to follow it. The man, who of these two chooses faith, is blessed; and he, who for the sake of reward practises rites, is dashed away from the enjoyment of eternal beatitude.' Also the *Moonduk Opunishut*: 'Rites, of which there are eighteen members, are all perishable: he who considers them as the source of blessing shall undergo repeated transmigrations; and all those fools who, immersed in the foolish practice of rites, consider themselves to be wise and learned, are repeatedly subjected to birth, disease, death, and other pains. When one blind man is guided by another, both subject themselves on their way to all kinds of distress.'

It is asserted in the *Bhugvut Geeta*, the essence of all the Smritis, Poorans, and Itihases, that, 'all those ignorant persons who attach themselves to the words of the *Veds* that convey promises of fruition, consider those falsely alluring passages as leading to real happiness; and say, that besides them there is no other reality. Agitated in their minds by these desires, they believe the abodes of the celestial gods to be the chief object; and they devote themselves to those texts which treat of ceremonies and their fruits, and entice by promises of enjoyment. Such people can have no real confidence in the Supreme Being.' Thus also do the *Moonduk Opunishut* and the *Geeta* state that, 'the science by which a knowledge of God is attained is superior to all other knowledge.' Therefore it is clear, from those passages of the *Ved* and of the *Geeta*, that the words of the *Ved* which promise fruition, are set aside by the texts of a contrary import. Moreover, the ancient saints and holy teachers, and their commentators, and yourselves, as well as we and all others, agree that Munoo is better acquainted than any other lawgiver with the spirit of the *Veds*. And he, understanding the meaning of those different texts, admitting the inferiority of that which promised fruition, and following that which conveyed no promise of gratification, has directed widows to spend their lives as ascetics. He has also defined in his 12th chapter, what acts are observed merely for the sake of gratifications, and what are not. 'Whatever act is performed for the sake of gratifications in this world or the next is called Pruburttuk, and those which are performed according to the knowledge respecting God, are called Niburttuk. All those who perform acts to procure gratifications, may enjoy heaven like the gods; and he who performs acts free from desires, procures release from the five elements of this body; that is, obtains absorption.'

Advocate.—What you have said is indeed consistent with the *Veds*, with Munoo, and with the *Bhuguvut Geeta*. But from this I fear, that the passages of the *Veds* and other Shastrus, that prescribe Concremation and Postcremation as the means of attaining heavenly enjoyments, must be considered as only meant to deceive.

Opponent.—There is no deception. The object of those passages is declared. As men have various dispositions, those whose minds are enveloped in desire, passion, and cupidity, have no inclination for the disinterested worship of the Supreme Being. If they had no Shastrus of rewards, they would at once throw aside all Shastrus, and would follow their several inclinations, like elephants unguided by the hook. In order to restrain such persons from being led only by their inclinations, the Shastru prescribes various ceremonies; as Shuenjag, for one desirous of the destruction of the enemy; Pootreshti for one desiring a son; and Justishtom for one desiring gratifications in heaven, &c.; but again reprobates such as are actuated by those desires, and at the same moment expresses contempt for such gratifications. Had the Shastru not repeatedly reprobated both those actuated by desire and the fruits desired by them, all those texts might be considered as deceitful. In proof of what I have advanced I cite the following text of the *Opunishut*: 'Knowledge and rites together offer themselves to every man. The wise man considers which of these two is the better and which the worse. By reflection, he becomes convinced of the superiority of the former, despises rites, and takes refuge in knowledge. And the unlearned, for the sake of bodily gratification, has recourse to the performance of rites.' The *Bhuguvut Geeta*: 'The Veds that treat of rites are for the sake of those who are possessed of desire; therefore, O Urjoon! do thou abstain from desires.'

Hear also the text of the *Ved* reprobating the fruits of rites: 'As in this world the fruits obtained from cultivation and labour perish, so in the next world fruits derived from rites are perishable.' Also the *Bhuguvut Geeta*: 'All those who observe the rites prescribed by the three Veds, and through those ceremonies worship me and seek for heaven, having become sinless from eating the remains of offerings, ascending to heaven, and enjoying the pleasures of the gods, after the completion of their rewards, again return to earth. Therefore, the observers of rites for the sake of rewards, repeatedly ascend to heaven, and return to the world, and cannot obtain absorption.'

Advocate.—Though what you have advanced from the *Ved* and sacred codes against the practice of Concremation and Postcremation, is not to be set aside, yet we have had the practice prescribed by Hareet and others handed down to us.

Opponent.—Such an argument is highly inconsistent with justice. It is every way improper to persuade to self-destruction, by citing passages of inadmissible authority. In the second place, it is evident from your own authorities, and the Sunkulpu recited in conformity with them, that the widow should voluntarily quit life, ascending the flaming pile of her husband. But, on the contrary, you first bind down the widow along with the corpse of her husband, and then heap over her such a quantity of wood that she cannot rise. At the time too of setting fire to the pile, you press her down with large bamboos. In what passage of Hareet or the rest do you find authority for thus binding the woman according to your practice? This then is, in fact, deliberate female murder.

Advocate.—Though Hareet and the rest do not indeed authorize this practice of binding, &c., yet were a woman after having recited the Sunkulpu not to perform Concremation, it would be sinful, and considered disgraceful by others. It is on this account that we have adopted the custom.

Opponent.—Respecting the sinfulness of such an act, that is mere talk: for in the same codes it is laid down, that the performance of a penance will obliterate the sin of quitting the pile. Or in case of inability to undergo the regular penance, absolution may be obtained by bestowing the value of a cow, or three kahuns of kowries. Therefore the sin is no cause of alarm. The disgrace in the opinion of others is also nothing: for good men regard not the blame or reproach of persons who can reprobate those who abstain from the sinful murder of women. And do you not consider how great is the sin to kill a woman; therein forsaking the fear of God, the fear of conscience, and the fear of the Shastrus, merely from a dread of the reproach of those who delight in female murder?

Advocate.—Though tying down in this manner be not authorized by the Shastrus, yet we practise it as being a custom that has been observed throughout Hindoosthan.

Opponent.—It never was the case that the practice of fastening down widows on the pile was prevalent throughout Hindoosthan: for it is but of late years that this mode has been followed, and that only in Bengal, which is but a small part of Hindoosthan. No one besides who has the fear of God and man before him, will assert that male or female murder, theft, &c., from having been long practiced, cease to be vices. If, according to your argument, custom ought to set aside the precepts of the Shastrus, the inhabitants of the forests and mountains who have been in the habits of plunder, must be considered as guiltless of sin, and it would be improper to endeavour to restrain their habits. The Shastrus, and the reasonings connected with them, enable us to discriminate right and wrong. In those Shastrus such female murder is altogether forbidden. And reason also declares, that to bind down a woman for her destruction, holding out to her the inducement of heavenly rewards, is a most sinful act.

Advocate.—This practice may be sinful or any thing else, but we will not refrain from observing it. Should it cease, people would generally apprehend that if women did not perform Concremation on the death of their husbands, they might go astray; but if they burn themselves this fear is done away. Their family and relations are freed from apprehension. And if the husband could be assured during his life that his wife would follow him on the pile, his mind would be at ease from apprehensions of her misconduct.

Opponent.—What can be done, if, merely to avoid the possible danger of disgrace, you are unmercifully resolved to commit the sin of female murder. But is there not also a danger of a woman's going astray during the life-time of her husband, particularly when he resides for a long time in a distant country? What remedy then have you got against this cause of alarm?

Advocate.—There is a great difference betwixt the case of the husband's being alive, and of his death; for while a husband is alive, whether he resides near her or at a distance, a wife is under his control; she must stand in awe of him. But after his death that authority ceases, and she of course is divested of fear.

Opponent.—The Shastrus which command that a wife should live under the control of her husband during his life, direct that on his death she shall live under the authority of her husband's family, or else under that of her parental relations; and the Shastrus have authorized the ruler of the country to maintain the observance of this law. Therefore, the possibility of a woman's going astray cannot be more guarded against during the husband's life than it is after his death. For you daily see, that even while the husband is alive, he gives up his authority, and the wife separates from him. Control alone cannot restrain from evil thoughts, words, and actions; but the suggestions of wisdom and the fear of God may cause both man and woman to abstain from sin. Both the Shastrus and experience show this.

Advocate.—You have repeatedly asserted, that from want of feeling we promote female destruction. This is incorrect, for it is declared in our *Ved* and codes of law, that mercy is the root of virtue, and from our practice of hospitality, &c. our compassionate dispositions are well known.

Opponent.—That in other cases you shew charitable dispositions is acknowledged. But by witnessing from your youth the voluntary burning of women amongst your elder relatives, your neighbours, and the inhabitants of the surrounding villages, and by observing the indifference manifested at the time when the women are writhing under the torture of the flames, habits of insensibility are produced. For the same reason, when men or women are suffering the pains of death, you feel for them no sense of compassion. Like the worshippers of the female deities, who, witnessing from their infancy the slaughter of kids and buffaloes, feel no compassion for them in the time of their suffering death; while followers of Vishnoo are touched with strong feelings of pity.

Advocate.—What you have said I shall carefully consider.

Opponent.—It is to me a source of great satisfaction, that you are now ready to take this matter into your consideration. By forsaking prejudice and reflecting on the Shastru, what is really conformable to its precepts may be perceived, and the evils and disgrace brought on this country by the crime of female murder will cease.

MICHAEL MADHUSUDAN DATTA

Michael Madhusudan Datta (1824–1873) lived in Kolkata (then Calcutta) at a time when Calcutta was, after London, the Second City of the British Empire. This was the period when reforms were taking place in Hinduism, a period often referred to as the Bengal Renaissance, though in retrospect it may also be seen as a time in which parts of Hinduism were dimmed rather than illuminated in the effort to accommodate European values. Datta's name is already an indication of this fusion, one part European, two parts Bengali Hindu ("Madhusudan," from the Sanskrit Madhusudana, being an epithet of Krishna, "Slayer of the Demon Madhu," and "Datta," "given" or "gift," often paired with the name of a god, as in the common name of Devadatta, "God-Given"). His father, a well-known lawyer, knew Persian and probably taught it to his son; Datta grew up speaking English, his primary language, and Bangla, which he spoke with his mother. In 1843, at the age of nineteen, he converted to Christianity, in part to avoid an arranged Hindu marriage, in part in the hope (which proved vain at that time) of getting to England. As a result of his conversion, he had to leave Calcutta's famous Hindoo College, where he had been educated until then. In 1847, estranged from his father, he moved to Madras, took the name of Michael, and, in 1848, married an Englishwoman. He finally set off in 1862, the year after he wrote *The Slaying of Meghanada*, to study law at Gray's Inn in London. He returned to Calcutta in 1867 and died there in 1873.

PRONOUNCING GLOSSARY

Abhaya: *uh-buh-yah´*
Agni: *ug´-nee*
Daitya: *dait´-yuh*
Danava: *dah´-nuh-vuh*
Durga Puja: *door´-gah poo´-jah*
Jahnavi: *jah´-nuh-vee´*
Kailasa: *kai-lah´-suh*
Karburas: *kar-boo´-rus*
Lakshmi: *luk´-shmee*
lila: *lee´-lah*
Madhusudan Datta: *muh´-doo-soo´-dun dut´-tuh*
Mandakini: *mun-dah´-kee-nee´*
Mandodari: *mun-doh´-duh-ree´*
mantra: *mun´-truh*
Meghanada: *may´-guh-nah´-duh*
Nagendra: *nah-gen´-druh*
Naikasheya: *nai´-kuh-shay´-yuh*
purohit: *poo´-roh-heet´*
Pramila: *pruh-mee´-lah´*
Raghu: *ruh´-goo*
Rahu: *rah´-hoo*
Rakshasa: *rahk´-shuh-suh*
Sati: *suh´-tee*
Shakta: *shahk´-tuh*
Shakti: *shuh´-tee*
Shuli: *shoo´-lee*
Tripathaga: *tree-puh´-tuh-gah´*
Trishuli: *tree´-shoo-lee´*
Vasanti: *vah-sun´-tee´*
Vasava: *vah´-suh-vuh*

THE FUNERAL RITES OF MEGHANADA

Michael Madhusudan Datta's *The Slaying of Meghanada* (1861) is a retelling of a part of the *Ramayana*: it tells how Meghanada, Ravana's eldest son, fought to defend his father's people, died, and was buried. It is regarded as a landmark in the history of Indian literature, the beginning of a new period, often called the modern period, in which new literary forms were created to express a revolutionary view of the Indian classics. To begin with, Ravana, not Rama, is the hero, and the relationship between Ravana and his son Meghanada is colored by the poet's personal feelings about his troubled relationship with his own father. The poem fuses Datta's personal knowledge of the Indian *Ramayana*, which he surely learned from his mother, with his knowledge of the European epics—Homer, Milton, Dante—which he learned from the English-medium schools that his father sent him to.

The characters of Ravana and Meghanada and Rama are much the same as they are in the Sanskrit source, but the brilliance of the poem lies in the way that they are made to occupy the opposite moral positions from those that they held in the earlier work. And there are also other changes, such as the introduction of Pramila, Meghanada's only wife, and her friend Vasanti, neither of whom appears in the Valmiki *Ramayana*.

The passage here is the very end of the poem, after the death of Meghanada; it describes his funeral, carried out by the Rakshasas, Daityas, Danavas, and Karburas (ogres and demons), his people. Ravana is called Naikesheyi (a matronymic from his mother Nikasha) and vanquisher of Vasava (Indra, king of the gods, whom Ravana bested in battle). Significantly, Meghanada's wife commits suttee on his pyre and goes to heaven with him. Shiva (also called Shuli ["Trident-bearer"], Dhurjati ["Burdened with Matted Hair"], and Mahesha ["Great Lord"]), Ravana's god in the Valmiki text, too, suffers for Ravana; the god watches him from his home on Mount Kailasa, along with his wife Sati (also called Abhaya ["Fearless"], Mother, Nagendra's daughter [because she is the daughter of the Lord of Mountains or Nagas, Himalaya], and Kshemankari ["Giver of Rest"]). Sati defends Rama ("the Raghu warrior").

They reached the seashore whereat Rakshasas quickly built a proper pyre. Bearers brought sweet scented sandalwood and ghee[1] in quantities. With sacred Mandakini[2] water, those Rakshasas washed carefully the corpse, then dressed it in fine silken garments, and placed it on the pyre. Solemnly, their *purohit*[3] recited *mantras*.[4] Having bathed her body in that sacred place of pilgrimage, the ocean, the most chaste of faithful wives, that pretty Pramila, divested herself of ornaments and jewels, bestowing them on all those present. With obeisance to her revered elders, that one of honeyed speech addressed the group of Daitya maids saying sweetly, "O companions, after all this time my life today comes to an end in this arena of the living. Return, all of you, to our Daitya homeland. Speak politely at my father's feet, Vasanti, all the news. And to my mother." Alas, the tears began to stream. That chaste wife kept silent—the Danava women sobbed out loud.

TRANSLATED BY Clinton B. Seely.

1. Purified butter, used in worship.
2. A name of the Ganges River, also called Jahnavi (named after the sage Jahnu) and Tripathaga ("Going on Three Paths," through the sky [as the Milky Way], the atmosphere, and earth).
3. The family priest.
4. Verses, in this case probably Vedic verses.

Then a moment later, holding back her grief, that pretty one spoke up, "Tell my mother, that which Fortune wrote upon the forehead of this humble servant finally today has come to pass. To whose hands my parents gave this humble slave, it is with him, my dear, I go this day—within our world what refuge is there for a wife without her husband? What more shall I say, my friend? Do not forget her, dearest ones—this is Pramila's most earnest plea to all of you."

That purest wife then mounted the pyre (as though onto a floral throne) and sat with peace of mind at her husband's feet, a garland of full-blown blossoms wrapped around her chignon. The Rakshasa musicians played, and aloud those versed in texts recited from the Vedas. The women Rakshasa gave out auspicious calls of *ululu* which, when joined with ululations, rose into the skies. Flowers showered all around. The Rakshasa maidens, as was proper, proffered sundry ornaments and articles of clothing, sandal paste, musk, saffron, vermilion and so forth. The Rakshasas carefully arranged on all four sides sharp arrows smeared with ghee, arrows used for killing beasts, just as is done the ninth day during Durga Puja[5] in households of the Shakta[6] devotees, O Shakti, before your altar's pedestal.

The monarch of the Rakshasas stepped forward, then spoke with anguish, "It was my hope, Meghanada, that I would close these eyes of mine for the final time with you before me—transferring to you, son, the responsibility for this kingdom, I would set out on my greatest journey. But Fate—how shall I ever comprehend His *lila*?[7] That joy eluded me. It was my hope to soothe my eyes, dear lad, by seeing you upon the Rakshasas' regal throne, on your left my daughter-in-law, the Lakshmi[8] of this clan of Rakshasas, as consort. Futile were those hopes. For due to fruits of a previous birth I observe you both today upon the throne of Time. That sun, the pride of Karburas, is forever swallowed up by Rahu.[9] Did I serve with care Shiva just to gain but these ends? How shall I ever turn back now—ah, who can tell me how I might return to Lanka and our empty home? By what feigned consolation shall I console your mother—who can tell me that? 'Where are my son and daughter-in-law?'—Queen Mandodari,[1] when she asks me, 'For what pleasures did you leave them at the seashore, sovereign of the Rakshasas?'—what shall I say to make her understand? Alas, what can I say? Son. Preeminent of warriors. Victorious in battle always. Little mother, Lakshmi of the Rakshasas. For what transgression did Fate write this cruel pain upon the monarch's forehead?"

At his Kailasa home, Shuli was beside himself. His matted hair tilted to one side upon his head; with a vicious roar his serpents hissed; from his forehead flames leapt forth; the Tripathaga poured down her frightful crashing waves, like swiftly flowing streams through mountain caverns. Mount Kailasa shook violently. In panic the universe quaked. Fearful, faithful Abhaya, hands cupped humbly, addressed Mahesha,

"For what reason are you angry, lord? Tell me, your servant, please. He died in war, that Rakshasa, by Fate's decree. Do not blame the Raghu war-

5. The worship of Durga, especially in Bengal during a special period in autumn.
6. The Shaktas are worshippers of the Shakti, the "energy" of the Goddess ("Sects and Sex in the Tantras," p. 275).
7. The "play" or "sport" of the god, in creating the world ("The Paradox of Religious Complaint and Dissent," p. 392).
8. Goddess of good fortune.
9. Demon of eclipse.
1. Ravana's wife.

rior. If you wrongly harm him, lord, first burn me to ashes." And at that, Mother hugged his feet.

With feeling, raising Sati, Dhurjati replied, "My heart breaks, Nagendra's daughter, from the Rakshasas' woe. You know how I love the champion Naikasheya. But, for your sake, Kshemankari, I forgive that Rama and his brother."

To Agni, god of fire, Trishuli commanded sadly, "Sanctify them by your touch, you who are most pure, and bring at once to this auspicious home that Rakshasa and wife."

In the form of lightning streaks, Agni ran to earth. Then at once the pyre burst ablaze. All, startled, looked upon that fiery chariot. There on a seat of gold within the chariot sat the warrior, vanquisher of Vasava, in celestial form. On his left, pretty Pramila whose splendor of unending youth shone from her graceful figure and on whose honeyed lips, a smile of everlasting joy.

With great speed that best of chariots climbed its skyward path as the god clan in concert rained down flowers, and the universe filled with blissful sounds. The Rakshasas put out those brilliant flames in streams of pure milk. With utmost care they gathered up the ashes and immersed them in the ocean. Having washed that cremation site using water from the Jahnavi, Rakshasa craftsmen by the thousands built with golden bricks a temple on the spot where stood the pyre—that temple's lofty spire, cleaving clouds, rose to the sky.

After bathing in waters of the sea, those Rakshasas now headed back toward Lanka, wet still with water of their grief—it was as if they had immersed the image of the goddess on the lunar tenth day of the Durga Puja. The Lanka wept in sorrow seven days and seven nights.

Thus ends canto number nine,
called "Funeral Rites," in the poem
The Slaying of Meghanada

SWAMI VIVEKANANDA

Swami Vivekananda was born Narendranath Datta into an upper-middle-class Kayastha family in Calcutta in 1863. He was educated at an English-style university, where he was exposed to European philosophy, Christianity, and science. He joined the Brahmo Samaj (Rammohun Roy, p. 538), attracted by its social programs dedicated to eliminating child marriage and illiteracy and educating women and the lower castes. He maintained his dedication to Indian spirituality but combined it with an interest in Western material progress, maintaining that the two supplemented and complemented one another.

Later he became a disciple of Ramakrishna Paramahamsa (1836–1886) ("If God Is Everywhere," p. 574), and was the first in a long line of proselytizing gurus who exported the ideals of reformed Hinduism to foreign soil and, in turn, brought back American ideas that he infused into Indian Vedanta ("Theology and/or Philosophy in the Vedanta," p. 285). Influenced by progressive Western political ideas, Vivekananda set himself firmly against all forms of caste distinction and openly ate beef. He made a powerful impression at the World's Parliament of Religions in Chicago in 1893 and toured America, making many converts to the Vedanta movement. In 1897 he Vedanticized the Theosophical Society that the Russian psychic Helena Blavatsky (1831–1891) had founded in New York City in 1875, and that continued to prosper under the leadership of the women's rights activist and Indian Nationalist Annie Besant (1847–1933).

Vivekananda returned to India in 1897 with a small band of Western disciples. There, at a monastery on the Ganges in Calcutta, he founded the Ramakrishna Mission, whose branches proclaimed its version of Hinduism in many parts of the world. He died in 1902 in Calcutta.

PRONOUNCING GLOSSARY

Swami: *swah´-mee*

Vivekananda: *vih-vay´-kuh-nun´-duh*

SPEECHES TO THE WORLD'S PARLIAMENT OF RELIGIONS, CHICAGO 1893

In 1893, from September 11 to 27, the World's Parliament of Religions brought representatives of many religions to Chicago. Though B. B. Nagarkar represented the Brahmo Samaj at the Parliament, it was Vivekananda who made such a stunning impression on the crowd of over seven thousand that a newspaper account described him as "an orator by divine right and undoubtedly the greatest figure at the Parliament." His three short speeches there, two of which we reproduce here, awakened Americans, for the first time, to the possibility that Hinduism was a religion that might have meaning for them.

RESPONSE TO WELCOME

At the World's Parliament of Religions, Chicago, 11th September, 1893

Portrait of Swami Vivekananda, September 1893, Chicago. On the right Vivekananda has signed his name, and on the left he has written: "One infinite pure & holy–beyond thought beyond qualities–I bow down to thee."

Sisters and Brothers of America,

It fills my heart with joy unspeakable to rise in response to the warm and cordial welcome which you have given us. I thank you in the name of the most ancient order of monks in the world; I thank you in the name of the mother of religions; and I thank you in the name of the millions and millions of Hindu people of all classes and sects.

My thanks, also, to some of the speakers on this platform who referring to the delegates from the Orient have told you that these men from far-off nations may well claim the honour of bearing to different lands the idea of toleration. I am proud to belong to a religion which has taught the world both tolerance and universal acceptance. We believe not only in universal toleration, but we accept all religions as true. I am proud to belong to a nation which has sheltered the persecuted and the refugees of all religions and all nations of the earth. I am proud to tell you that we have gathered in our bosom the purest remnant of the Israelites, who came to Southern India and took refuge with us in the very year in which their holy temple was shattered to pieces by Roman tyranny. I am proud to belong to the religion which has sheltered and is still fostering the remnant of the grand Zoroastrian nation. I will quote to you, brethren, a few lines from a hymn which I remember to have repeated from my earliest boyhood, which is every day repeated by millions of human beings: *"As the different streams having their sources in different places all mingle their water in the sea, so, O Lord, the different paths which men take through different tendencies, various though they appear, crooked or straight, all lead to Thee."*

The present convention, which is one of the most august assemblies ever held, is in itself a vindication, a declaration to the world of the wonderful doctrine preached in the Gita: *"Whosoever comes to Me, through whatsoever form, I reach him; all men are struggling through paths which in the end lead to Me."* Sectarianism, bigotry, and its horrible descendant, fanaticism, have long possessed this beautiful earth. They have filled the earth with violence, drenched it often and often with human blood, destroyed civilisation and sent whole nations to despair. Had it not been for these horrible demons, human society would be far more advanced than it is now. But their time is come; and I fervently hope that the bell that tolled this morning in honour of this convention may be the death knell of all fanaticism, of all persecutions with the sword or with the pen and of all uncharitable feelings between persons wending their way to the same goal.

ADDRESS AT THE FINAL SESSION

27th September, 1893

The World's Parliament of Religions has become an accomplished fact, and the merciful Father has helped those who laboured to bring it into existence, and crowned with success their most unselfish labour.

My thanks to those noble souls whose large hearts and love of truth first dreamed this wonderful dream and then realised it. My thanks to the shower of liberal sentiments that has overflowed this platform. My thanks to this enlightened audience for their uniform kindness to me and for their appreciation of every thought that tends to smooth the friction of religions. A few jarring notes were heard from time to time in this harmony. My special thanks to them, for they have, by their striking contrast, made general harmony the sweeter.

Much has been said of the common ground of religious unity. I am not going just now to venture my own theory. But if any one here hopes that this unity will come by the triumph of any one of the religions and the destruction of the others, to him I say: "Brother, yours is an impossible hope." Do I wish that the Christian would become Hindu? God forbid. Do I wish that the Hindu or Buddhist would become Christian? God forbid.

The seed is put in the ground, and earth and air and water are placed around it. Does the seed become the earth, or the air, or the water? No. It becomes a plant, it develops after the law of its own growth, assimilates the air, the earth and the water, converts them into plant substance, and grows into a plant.

Similar is the case with religion. The Christian is not to become a Hindu or a Buddhist, nor a Hindu or a Buddhist to become a Christian. But each must assimilate the spirit of the others and yet preserve his individuality and grow according to his own law of growth.

If the Parliament of Religions has shown anything to the world it is this: It has proved to the world that holiness, purity and charity are not the exclusive possessions of any church in the world and that every system has produced men and women of the most exalted character. In the face of this evidence, if anybody dreams of the exclusive survival of his own religion and the destruction of the others, I pity him from the bottom of my heart, and point out to him that upon the banner of every religion will soon be written, in spite of their resistance: "Help and not Fight," "Assimilation and not Destruction," "Harmony and Peace and not Dissension."

THE HINDU AUTHORS OF MODERNITY 1900 AND AFTER

HINDUISM ON THE MARGINS

"Modernity" in Europe is often said to begin in the seventeenth century, sometimes in the nineteenth. For Hinduism, "modernity" might be located at the turn of the twentieth century, as the Indian nation was emerging from colonial subjugation. This was also a time when more palpable, though disputed, boundaries began to be drawn between groups that were distinguished by their language, caste, regional or national base, and/or religion. The newly defined, or recognized, margins now often took center stage with the inclusion in the conversation of voices that the Brahmins scarcely regarded as Hindu at all. This dynamic, religiously potent change affected language, literature, politics, law, art, and, above all, social customs all across India.

The various vernacular traditions had begun to publish more and more widely, simultaneously incorporating more oral traditions and, even while English rule in India was being challenged, reflecting increasing knowledge of the English language and English literary traditions. English and Indian words had crossfertilized one another for centuries. On the one hand, traveling from India to England, many Indian words entered the English dictionary in the eighteenth and nineteenth centuries; an alphabetical list would include *bungalow, calico, cash, candy, catamaran, cheroot, curry, gymkhana, jodhpur, juggernaut, loot, madras, mango, mogul, moola, mosquito, mulligatawny, pajama, pariah, pukka, punch, pundit, thug, tourmaline*, and *veranda*. More recently, words about religion rather than loot and moola entered English through American rather than British sources, words such as *dharma* from Jack Kerouac's 1958 novel *The Dharma Bums* (more Buddhist than Hindu) as well as *yoga* and *tantra*, *guru* and *ashram*, *Kali* and *karma*.

On the other hand, traveling from England to India, English words in Indian languages spawned what is now called Hinglish, a colloquial form of Hindi heavily flavored with English words and constructions, as well as new forms of Anglo-Indian literature. "Anglo-Indian" was a highly ambiguous term from the start, in the period of the British Raj, when it confusingly denoted two opposite sorts of people (according to the *Oxford English Dictionary*): "a. A person of British birth resident, or once resident, in India," which is to say a culturally multiple person, a privileged Englishman ruling India; and "b. A Eurasian of India," that is, a mixed breed, an underprivileged person that the British regarded as the lowest of all castes. In the modern period, "Anglo-Indian" took on a third meaning, designating a new form of English used by bilingual (or, more often, tri- or quadrilingual) Indians who enrich English with the vocabulary and structures of Indian languages.

The flowers sold at this market in Varanasi are primarily used for religious offerings at the many Hindu temples in this sacred city.

Language was a dichotomizing political issue, too, under the British Raj. On the one hand, Indians high up in the service of the Raj spoke English better than they spoke any Indian language (better, indeed, than most Englishmen and -women spoke English); on the other, by the twentieth century, the growing resistance against the Raj (and against the imposition of English in government and schools) in revolutionary and nationalist groups inspired a new wave of literature in the vernacular Indian languages. These vernaculars competed with one another, Hindi-speakers insisting that theirs, the most widely spoken of all the North Indian languages derived from Sanskrit, was in effect the lingua franca of India alongside English and should be the national language, Tamil-speakers reacting with threats to secede from the nation of India, and so forth.

Diaspora Hinduism spread throughout the British Empire, carried by the British and their Indian colleagues and by the reform movements that arose in reaction to the Raj, movements such as the Brahmo Samaj and Arya Samaj ("Rammohun Roy," p. 538). These diasporas continued to feed back into the home country, sometimes bringing fresh breezes of liberalism and democracy but sometimes transmitting a more conservative, even reactionary influence.

In addition to the diasporas outside of India, Hinduism was transformed by what might be called internal diasporas, a parallel to the more obvious diaspora groups in Southeast Asia, the United Kingdom, and the United States. The internal diasporas are communities that live within India but are wholly or in part marginal to Hinduism, such as the Muslims, tribals (Adivasis), and Dalits. An internal critique of Hinduism was offered by village tales ("Folk Hinduism," p. 561) that were often irreverent, sometimes to the point of blasphemy. The Muslim influence on Hinduism that began even before the Delhi Sultanate in the thirteenth century continues to the present day, with writers like Salman Rushdie (*Midnight's Children*, p. 688) fusing Hindu and Muslim themes even as they infuse Hindi and Bangla and Tamil words into English. The emerging literatures of Adivasis (p. 579) and Dalits (p. 596) are also a passionate fusion, a bricolage of Hinduism, colonialism (including Christianity), and concepts unique to particular castes and tribes.

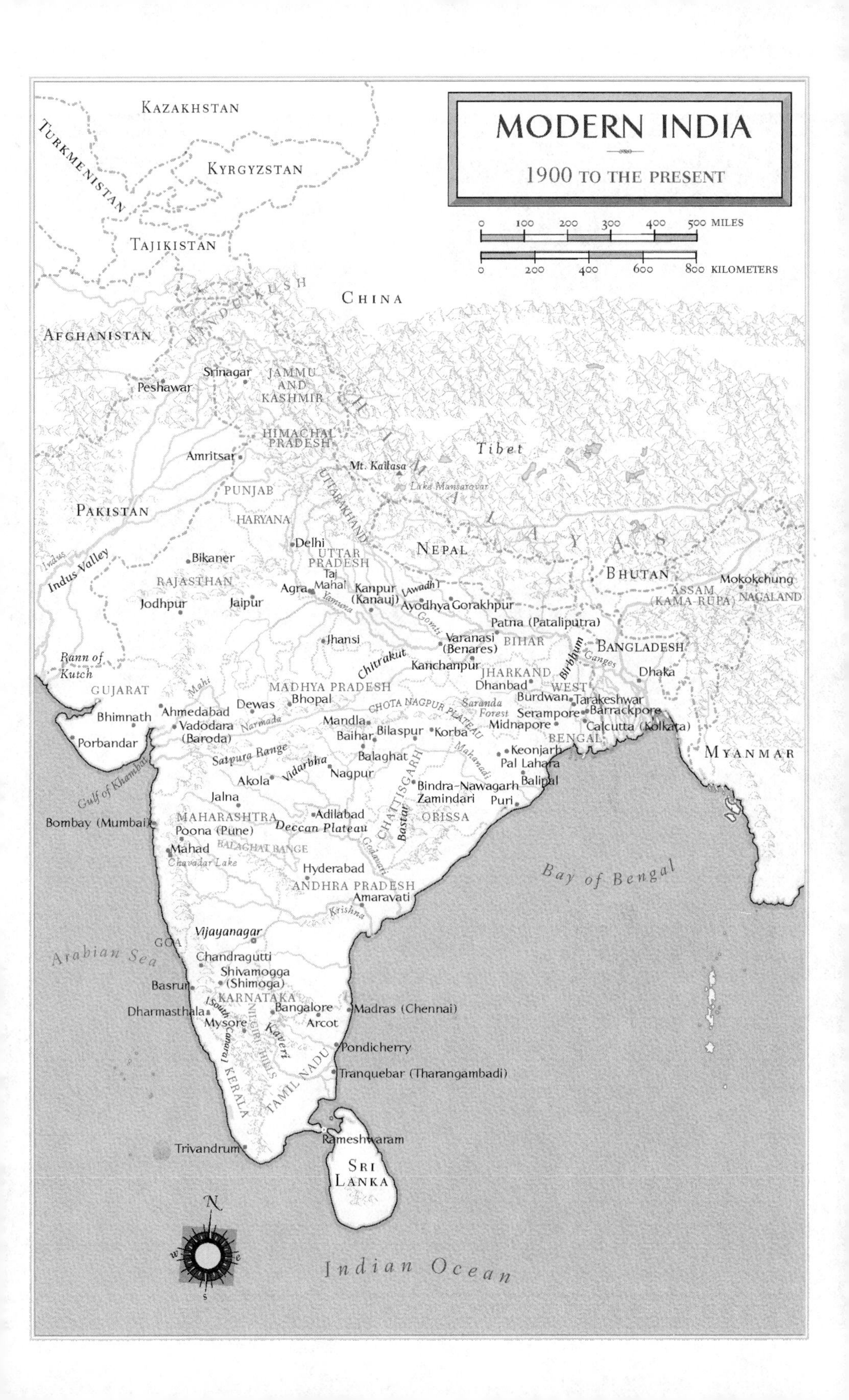
MODERN INDIA
1900 TO THE PRESENT
0 100 200 300 400 500 MILES
0 200 400 600 800 KILOMETERS
Kazakhstan
Turkmenistan
Kyrgyzstan
Tajikistan
Hindu Kush
China
Afghanistan
Srinagar
Jammu and Kashmir
Peshawar
Himachal Pradesh
Himalayas
Tibet
Amritsar
Mt. Kailasa
Lake Mansarovar
Punjab
Uttarakhand
Pakistan
Haryana
Delhi
Nepal
Bhutan
Uttar Pradesh
Indus
Indus Valley
Bikaner
Rajasthan
Taj Mahal
Agra
Kanpur (Kanauj)
Awadh
Mokokchung
Assam (Kama-Rupa)
Nagaland
Jodhpur
Jaipur
Yamuna
Ayodhya
Gorakhpur
Gomti
Patna (Pataliputra)
Jhansi
Varanasi (Benares)
Bihar
Birbhum
Bangladesh
Ganges
Rann of Kutch
Chitrakut
Kanchanpur
Jharkand
Dhaka
Gujarat
Mahi
Madhya Pradesh
Dhanbad
West Bengal
Bhopal
Dewas
Saranda Forest
Burdwan
Tarakeshwar
Ahmedabad
Chota Nagpur Plateau
Serampore
Barrackpore
Bhimnath
Vadodara (Baroda)
Narmada
Mandla
Bilaspur
Korba
Midnapore
Calcutta (Kolkata)
Porbandar
Baihar
Satpura Range
Mahanadi
Keonjarh
Pal Lahara
Myanmar
Balaghat
Gulf of Khambat
Akola
Vidarbha
Nagpur
Chattisgarh
Balipal
Bindra-Nawagarh Zamindari
Jalna
Puri
Adilabad
Bombay (Mumbai)
Maharashtra
Orissa
Bastar
Poona (Pune)
Deccan Plateau
Godavari
Mahad
Balaghat Range
Chavadar Lake
Hyderabad
Bay of Bengal
Andhra Pradesh
Amaravati
Krishna
Vijayanagar
Goa
Arabian Sea
Chandragutti
Shivamogga (Shimoga)
Basrur
Karnataka
Dharmasthala
South Canara
Nilgiri Hills
Bangalore
Madras (Chennai)
Mysore
Kaveri
Arcot
Pondicherry
Kerala
Tamil Nadu
Tranquebar (Tharangambadi)
Rameshwaram
Trivandrum
Sri Lanka
Indian Ocean
N
W
E
S

Folk, Tribal, and Dalit Hinduism

Village religion has always been one of the main wellsprings of Hinduism; village tales found their way into Sanskrit texts from the earliest Vedas to the most recent Puranas. Folklore became both a major nineteenth-century academic hobby and one of the mainstays of nationalist literature. European folklorists, including colonial administrators (and their wives, the intrepid memsahibs with their sensible shoes), and Indian folklorists began to collect village stories in various vernaculars and translate them into European languages. Rudyard Kipling's *Kim* (1900) immortalized both the Indian folklorist (in the Bengali Babu who sends his reports to the Asiatic Society in London) and the European (in the British master spy whose front is that of an anthropologist collecting local customs).

In the twentieth century, the narratives of groups on the fringes of Hinduism, in particular the Adivasis (tribal peoples), found their way into print through English translations by anthropologists such as Verrier Elwin (1902–1964). The Indian government still calls the Adivasis "Scheduled Tribes" and groups them with the "Scheduled Castes" (Dalits, or Untouchables) in the Fifth Schedule of the Constitution of India, in a category called "Scheduled Castes and Tribes."

This painting by Dr. Govind Gare, a member of the Warlis, a tribal group of foragers and slash-and-burn cultivators in coastal northern Maharashtra, depicts a village in which bands of men and women are dancing to the rhythm of drums.

The late twentieth century also witnessed the emergence of a literature by Dalits, who finally achieved enough political clout, and education, to publish their own stories. Some of the Dalit and Adivasi texts go further than the village folktales in expressing attitudes that are highly antagonistic to conventional Hinduism, Sanskrit, caste, the lawbook of Manu (p. 202), and all that goes with them; these writings are therefore likely to offend some Hindus today.

Though some of these internal diasporas regard themselves as non-Hindus, and many are totally ostracized by (other) Hindus, Hindu concepts and even Hindu gods pervade their stories, even as many of their ideas have, over the centuries, enriched Hindu texts. They are an essential part of the Hindu tradition. Many of these authors, both in the center of Hinduism and on the margins, beginning with Tuka (p. 449) and continuing through the modern period, protest the abuses of the caste system. The number and passion of these native voices testify to an ongoing social criticism entirely independent of the more intellectual reforms that took place under the British raj, and both better informed and more deeply understanding than the European critique.

FOLK HINDUISM

The local village traditions, which the American anthropologist Robert Redfield (1897–1958) labeled "little," in fact constitute most of Hinduism and are a significant source of the so-called pan-Indian traditions (such as the Puranas), which Redfield called the "great" tradition. "Little" has pejorative as well as geographical connotations: not just small individual villages but a minor, cruder, less civilized tradition beneath scholarly contempt. Yet in terms of both the area that the villages cover in India *as a whole* and their populations (72 percent of the national total, according to the 2001 census), not to mention the size of their creative contributions, the terms should be reversed: the pan-Indian tradition is little, while the village cultures are a (the) great tradition. Many of the authors are anonymous, especially for stories collected before the twentieth century, but most collectors identify the geographic location and the language of the narrator, and some of the later collectors actually recorded the narrators' names.

We have arranged the folktales according to the regions in which they were collected: three tales from Gujarat (in the west, bordering on the Arabian Sea), one from Nagaland (a state in the far northeast of India, bordering on Assam), six from Bengal, and two from Andhra Pradesh (a Telugu-speaking state on the southeast coast).

THE GODDESS OF THE MAHI RIVER

This tale portrays the great Mahi River of Gujarat as a bold, young, dark-skinned girl of the forest, fierce as the goddess Durga ("The Birth of the Goddess," p. 253). She leaves her home in the mountains to flow to the ocean, her true love, as most Hindu wives leave their parents to go to the homes of their husbands. Mahi challenges the ocean, as Durga challenges her enemy and suitor Mahisha, but, unlike Mahisha, the ocean surrenders, and they wed.

This and the following five tales are translated by Brenda E. F. Beck, Peter J. Claus, Prapulladatta Goswami, and Jawaharlal Handoo.

PRONOUNCING GLOSSARY

Baraiya: *buh-rai´-yuh*
Bhil: *beel*
Cambay: *kum´-bay*
Dharala: *duh´-ruh-luh*
Gujarat: *goo´-juh-raht´*
Madhya Pradesh: *mud´-yuh pruh-desh´*
Mahi: *muh´-hee*
Patanwadi: *puh-tahn´-wah´-dee*
Satpura: *sut´-poo-ruh*

Told by Sendabhai Sendha, a watchman, in Gujarat, in 1962

The eastern part of Gujarat contains a lovely area known as the Satpura hills. The Mahi river flows out of these hills and is said to be their daughter. This watercourse flows down toward the central area of the state. The hills themselves are often spoken of as a kind of parental house for the river. The Mahi is wide and strong. It is also somewhat blackish in color. The hills, too, are dark colored, and they serve as a home for the Dharala, Bhil, Baraiya, and Patanwadi tribes. These people are known for their dark complexion. So too, the Mahi river is seen to be a dark-skinned girl.

People say that when the Mahi river first matured she wanted to marry the sea. Because this river is a woman of Herculean strength and strong will, she left no path untried in her efforts to fulfil her cherished desire. However, Mahi's father, the Satpura hills, never favored such a wedding for his daughter. Unsympathetic, he did not even try to understand the reasoning of his willful daughter. Still, Mahi was an independent woman. So she ultimately left her father's house to fulfil her heart's desire on her own. First she traveled to the West in her attempt to embrace the sea. The way was strewn with thorns and stones, and she had to pass through many jungles. She met ferocious tigers and leopards. Still, Mahi longed for the sea. Along the way she met the Gulf of Cambay. Dissatisfied and still eager to meet her true lover, she began to dream about him. Then she continued her search, crossing the rocky lands of eastern Gujarat and showing the energy and spirit of a true jungle maiden. Mahi was confident that she would finally be warmly welcomed by her lover and embraced by the arms of the sea.

By the time the river finally found the sea, however, she was exhausted. Her face was covered with dust and she had a strange, dark look. Beads of perspiration dropped from her forehead. Seeing this dark-complexioned maiden, the sea turned his face away. He rejected the offer of marriage. So the Mahi river, being a woman who valued self-respect, left the house of her lover in anger. She recrossed the dusty, thorny, and stony regions of Gujarat with great speed. Daring this wild and hazardous course once again, she returned to her father's house as quickly as she could. Now she entered her home with a sad look on her face. Seeing this her father tried to comfort her saying, "Oh pupil, the center of my eye, do not look so dejected! Turn your face toward me and tell me what you have experienced. Do not hold back any details." Hearing the soft words of her father, tears began to roll from the eyes of the Mahi river. These droplets looked like dew on the cotton leaves in the hills on a sunny morning. But the river concealed her mind. She asked her father only for an army to wage war against her lover. Her father tried his best to calm his daughter's wrath but he did not succeed. When he questioned her, she simply replied, "Father! If you love me, if you at least feel sympathy for me in your heart, then lend me your army."

Finally the hill-father made up his mind to assist his daughter, and he put his army at her disposal. The Mahi river was extremely pleased. She now led her warriors and marched back through the jungles like the commander of an invading force. First she crossed Madhya Pradesh, a state in central India, and then she entered the Gujarat hills. Next she passed through a large area of rocky land and approached the sea. Finally she called out, "Oh, Lord of the sea waters, be ready with your army! Open your arms and accept my challenge of war." The stones of the Mahi river were now in an excited mood. Their din and the sound of their movements terrified the sea. The Mahi river, on the other hand, had confidence in her army. She looked forward to the battle. But she had a surprise. The sea soon surrendered unconditionally. He married her, and her army of stones was laid to rest in the bed of the river, forever.

LORD SHIVA AND THE SATWARAS

This tale from Saurashtra, in Gujarat, justifies the dominance over agriculture there by a landowning community called the Satwaras. It gives the caste a divine lineage as sons-in-law of Shiva, who grants them land only to be tricked by them with a tried-and-true folk device of keeping the best part of something and fooling your victim into choosing the worst part. The local agricultural concerns are linked to the wider and more classical Hindu tradition by the participation of both Shiva and Parashurama, "Rama with an Axe," an incarnation of Vishnu (p. 481), famed for exterminating the entire class of Kshatriyas. The Satyuga is a name of one of the four ages (p. 228), the first age, usually called the Krita Yuga or Winning Age or the Satya Yuga (Age of Truth), here called the "Good" (*sat*) age, perhaps to explain the name of the *Sat*-waras.

PRONOUNCING GLOSSARY

Kailasa: *kai-lah´-suh*
Kshatriya: *kuh-shah´-tree-yuh*
Parashuram: *puh-rah´-soo-rahm´*
Satwara: *sut-wah´-ruh*
Satyuga: *sut´-yoo´-guh*
Saurashtra: *sow-rahsh´-truh*

Told by Shri Karsanbhai Jiwabhai Natum, a farmer, in Saurashtra, Gujarat, in 1968

Once long ago, in a period called the Satyuga, Parashuram wanted to exterminate the Kshatriyas, a class of warriors. Parashuram wandered all over the earth carrying an axe in the hopes of killing these fearsome men. Once he pursued sixteen young Kshatriyas who were frightened and who sought refuge in a temple dedicated to Lord Shiva. The Kshatriyas began to pray saying, "Oh Shiva, ocean of compassion and mercy, save us from the sharpened edge of Parashuram's axe." Lord Shiva, in his mercy, heeded these prayers and created sixteen maidens out of the perspiration and dust of his own body. Shiva then asked the warriors to marry these maidens and they agreed.

When Parashuram saw the sixteen warriors he raised his axe to kill them. But Lord Shiva intervened at once and told him not to kill the men as they were all farmers and his sons-in-law. As a result Parashuram did not kill the Kshatriyas, and they lived on to claim their status as farmers. But this created a problem for Lord Shiva. The Kshatriyas were sitting around with nothing to do. So they asked Shiva to give them land. Shiva agreed but only on certain specific terms. The great Lord insisted that each farmer give back to him half the produce on all lands that he would grant to them. The farmers agreed to comply with this request. Then the men asked, "Lord, what part of the crop would you like to share, the upper or the lower?" Shiva answered, "The lower!" The farmers agreed, saying, "Well and good, Lord!"

Soon afterwards Lord Shiva left for the Himalayas, and the sixteen farmers began to cultivate the land they had been given. These sons-in-law planted millet. After some months Lord Shiva returned for another visit, at the farmers' request. But when he arrived he saw that all the grain had already been harvested and that only stalks remained behind in the fields to be shared. Lord Shiva now realized that he had been cheated. But he did not utter a word. Instead he resolved not to be cheated again the following year. So he devised a plan to this effect. Next Shiva returned to his home in the Himalayas.

When the rainy season arrived all sixteen Satwara farmers called on Lord Shiva again. They prayed to him and turned to his mountain abode saying, "Oh, Lord Shiva, you are the greatest amongst all the gods." On hearing these prayers, Lord Shiva opened his eyes and interrupted his meditations. He asked the farmers the reason for their visitation. The Satwaras replied, "Oh Lord Shiva, we wanted to ask what part of the new crop you would prefer, the upper or the lower?" Lord Shiva replied at once, "Only the upper part!" So the farmers agreed. They all bowed at the feet of the Lord and requested his blessings. Shiva wished them well and they returned to their farms. The men plowed the fields with care and worked very hard. When it was time to sow they now planted sweet potatoes.

The farms were properly tilled, manured and watered, and the crop of sweet potatoes was abundant. The men were all delighted and they were in a jovial mood. They had never imagined that they would harvest such a prosperous crop. They were also gloomy, however, at the thought that half of this harvest would have to go to Lord Shiva. Then one of the men realized that, "We will have to leave only the leaves of sweet potatoes for Shiva. That is the upper part of the crop!" A second answered, "Yes, yes! You are correct. Shiva demanded only the upper half." Then all the men agreed and they began to dance around in happiness. Later one of them traveled to Lord Shiva's abode in the Himalayas. When he reached Mount Kailasa he asked Shiva to descend to the farm to collect his share of the harvest. As in the agreement, Lord Shiva's portion had been kept to one side. But it was obviously nothing but leaves and creepers. Lord Shiva saw this but could say nothing as this was the bargain that had been struck beforehand. Henceforth, Shiva agreed to give the entire harvest to his sons-in-law, saying, "You are the best and the most industrious agriculturalists in the world."

It is how the Kshatriyas became Satwara agriculturists, and how they became famous for their prosperity throughout Saurashtra and Gujarat.

THE ORIGIN OF THE SHIVA-*LINGA* AT BHIMNATH

This story is one of a large genre of folktales that spin new episodes out of the well-known stories of the *Mahabharata* or *Ramayana*. Many of these tales take place during the time of limbo when the Pandavas wandered through India in exile, the third book of the *Mahabharata* (p. 130), which is already filled with so many incidental tales that several more, like this one, could easily be inserted. Yudhishthira, here identified as (the son of the god) Dharma ("The Pandavas Go to Heaven," p. 145), plays only a minor role. But Bhima's colossal appetite, already noted in the Sanskrit text, is the excuse for this story, which soon develops in an entirely different direction and becomes one of a widespread genre of devotional stories about the accidental creation of a Shiva-*linga* ("The Origin of *Linga* Worship," p. 235). Here, an overturned earthenware pot becomes a "small shrine" into which the god Shiva actually enters. The flowing of milk is a miraculous sign of the presence of the god in the *linga* ("The Origin of the Temple at Tarakeshvar," p. 570).

PRONOUNCING GLOSSARY

Arjuna: *ar´-joo-nuh*
Bhima: *bee´-muh*
Bhimnath: *bim´-naht*
bili: *bee´-lee*
Dharma: *dar´-muh*
Draupadi: *drow´-puh-dee´*
linga: *ling´-guh*
Nilaka: *nee´-luh-kah*
Pandava: *pahn´-duh-vuh*
piludi: *pih-loo´-dee*

Told by Mrs. Champaben U. Dave, of Bhimnath, Gujarat, in 1948

During the time when the great Pandava heroes were in exile for twelve years, they once stopped to rest on the banks of the river Nilaka. The whole area was heavily forested at that time. Lovely neem trees, *piludi* trees, Indian fig trees, and many others all grew nearby. As soon as Arjuna, the famous young Pandava, saw this beautiful site he became enthralled. Arjuna was tired and fatigued by the great distance they had all walked. So he asked his elder brother, Dharma, if the group could rest there for a while. Dharma agreed and said, "This is a beautiful spot. The river water is crystal clear, and there are small fishes darting about here and there. We can also watch the cranes, the storks, and admire the greenery." But the middle brother, in the group, Bhima, was uncomfortable. He was extremely hungry, befitting his reputation for having an enormous appetite. Bhima thus started to murmur, "What is so beautiful about nature? Things look the same all over this country. The trees are the same, and the water never changes its color." The eldest brother then spoke out, "You are right, Bhima, but we are all exhausted. We want to stop here to rest." "All right, we will rest. But shall we at least begin cooking?" asked Bhima. "Indeed, let us begin cooking," replied Dharma. Draupadi, the wife of the brothers, was then asked by the brothers to begin preparations for a meal.

Then Bhima began thinking to himself and suddenly remembered that his younger brother, Arjuna, would never eat unless he first worshipped Lord Shiva. But there was no temple dedicated to Lord Shiva anywhere in sight. Bhima began to worry that the meal might be delayed. So he set out in search of a Shiva temple. Dharma and Arjuna remained on the riverbank to bathe, and Bhima went alone into the jungle. The latter carried with him a small earthen pot filled with river water. After he entered the forest he wandered here and there, but he was unable to find a Shiva temple anywhere. Meanwhile, Bhima had become very, very hungry. He was also angry with his brother Arjuna for always insisting on so many ritual procedures. He was trying to think of some way he could arrange for Arjuna to worship Lord Shiva before taking his food. He knew that as long as Arjuna did not worship Shiva, his elder brother Dharma would refuse to eat. And he knew that as long as his elder brother refused food, he could not eat either. Being so hungry, Bhima had a real problem. Then Bhima found a large *piludi* tree where he decided to sit down to think.

At last Bhima got an idea. He now stood up quickly and overturned the earthen pot he had been carrying. He then fixed it firmly to the ground by surrounding it with earth. Next, he found a small spring and poured some water from that over the pot. He then adorned it with leaves of the bili, or woodapple tree, and with wild flowers. He thus created something that looked like a small shrine dedicated to Lord Shiva. It even looked as if it had been freshly worshipped by some devotees who had recently passed that way. Now Bhima was happy. He had found a clever way to solve his problem. So he returned to the riverbank and called to his brother saying, "Oh Arjuna. Come out of the water! I have brought good news." "What news do you bring?" asked Arjuna. "Did you not want to worship Lord Shiva, my brother?" "Of course, I must worship Lord Shiva," replied Arjuna. "Come out of the water then. I shall accompany you and show you the place where I have found a shrine. It lies on open ground, under a *piludi* tree."

Then Arjuna came out of the water and joined his brother Bhima. His clothes were still wet as he proceeded to fill a small pot with water. He also collected a few flowers and leaves. These were to be used in the worship of Lord Shiva. Bhima was smiling, and he kept thinking all the while of how he was managing to fool his brother Arjuna. After a time, the two brothers arrived at the spot where the shrine had been built. Arjuna now worshipped it with great respect and decorated it freshly with the leaves and flowers he had brought. He also sprinkled water over it from his little pot. When the ceremonies were finished, Bhima turned to his brother and asked, "Arjuna, have you finished your worship?" "Can there be any doubt about that?" replied Arjuna. "No, I have no doubt about it," replied Bhima. "Then why do you bother to ask me such a silly question?" said Arjuna. Bhima then said, "My question actually concerns whether you worshipped Lord Shiva at all." "Yes, of course I have worshipped Lord Shiva," said Arjuna. "Your Lord Shiva?" said Bhima and he burst into laughter. "Why do you laugh?" asked Arjuna.

Bhima then raised a wooden stick over his head and gave a great blow to the earthen pot which he had so carefully arranged under the tree. But to his great surprise, milk now started to flow from the broken pot. "What a mystery!" cried Bhima. He was amazed to see milk flowing from this makeshift shrine. He then removed all the leaves and flowers that were on top of the pot and found a *linga*, the very image of Lord Shiva hidden underneath. But this *linga* had been broken into pieces because of the force of his blow. Then Bhima also decided to worship Lord Shiva.

Henceforth this small shrine became known as the Bhimnath shrine. It is the place where Bhima discovered Lord Shiva. The temple can be seen today on the banks of the river Nilaka. It is overshadowed by an old *piludi* tree, a very special sight in this dry area of Gujarat.

THE GIRL WHO WAS LOVED BY A TREE SPIRIT

This story comes from Nagaland, a state in far northeast India, bordering on Assam. It is a variant of the widespread tale of a human man or woman who is visited at night by a lover who appears to be human but is in fact from another world—a deity (as in the Cupid and Psyche myth, which appears in India as the story of Pururavas and Urvashi) or an animal (such as a swan maiden or mermaid) and here, unusually, a tree. The particular cultural inflection includes such details as a *dao,* a belt that a woman tied around a suitor whom she accepted, like the garland that a woman in the Sanskrit tradition placed around the neck of her chosen husband in the "self-choice" (*svayamvara*) ceremony. The end of the story here is, as usual in stories of this genre, tragic.

PRONOUNCING GLOSSARY

Chungliyimit: *choong´-lee-yee-meet´*
dao: *dow*
morung: *moh´-roong*

Collected by Dulal Chaudhuri and J. T. P. A. from the Makong Chung area of Nagaland, between 1975 and 1977

In Chungliyimit village there once lived a beautiful girl, the daughter of a rich family. Many young men came to her dormitory *(morung)* at night to court her. But she gave all her attention to one particular young man, the most handsome of them all. He came to her every night and went away before dawn. But he could never be found during the daytime. The girl looked for him among the village bachelors in the fields, in people's private houses, and in many other places. But her search was always in vain. At last she reported her experiences to her father and mother. On the advice of her parents, she tied a new *dao* belt around her lover's waist one night. He departed with it at the usual time. To the girl's surprise, when she went out for a walk the next morning, she found the *dao* belt tied around a tree that was standing below her house near the bank of a stream. The family now began to suspect that the young man was not a human being at all but the spirit of that tree.

To confirm their suspicions, the girl put an indigo-dyed shawl on the man's shoulders the following night in the same manner as she had tied the *dao* on him during his previous visit. He departed as usual. In the morning they found that same shawl hanging from a forked branch of the special tree. It stood near the edge of a well where the girl often went for water. Then the daughter remembered that she had gone to that well often during the period of courtship with her lover. She had washed her hands, and legs, and face daily and had liked to sing as she bathed. She now remembered that the branches of the tree above her used to move up and down, as if blown by the wind, whenever she came to that spot and realized that the spirit of this particular tree had come to court her in the form of a handsome bachelor.

The girl's father soon decided to see these mysterious happenings for himself and so kept a watch one night outside the girl's dormitory. When the stranger left before dawn, he secretly followed him. Instead of going to the young men's dormitory, as all the other youths did, this man went straight to the stream. There he stood at the side of the well and quickly transformed himself into an ordinary tree. His body turned into the trunk, his arms into branches, and his hair into leaves. And behold, there stood a big tree in place of the youth!

The father then decided to cut this mysterious tree down. He called the villagers together and asked their help in felling it, after telling the whole story to explain his concern. He also asked his daughter to remain inside the house, just in case anything dangerous happened. The men cut and cut, but the tree would not fall. And as they chopped, a small chip of wood flew toward the girl's house. At that very moment the girl was watching the cutters by peeping through a small hole in the wall. The flying wood chip entered the hole and struck her in the eye. It moved with such speed that it damaged her brain and the girl died instantly.

At the same moment that the girl fell to the floor, the tree also fell with a huge crash. The father was now happy. He came home rejoicing, relieved at the thought that the tree spirit would no longer chase and haunt his lovely daughter. To his utter shock and horror, he found his daughter dead. The two lovers had died together.

THE BIRTH AND MARRIAGE OF SHIVA

This creation myth combines motifs from the Puranic corpus, Bangla literature, and village traditions. The basic creation themes of incest and sexual reproduction, and the basic creative substances of spittle and poison, are, however, connected in new ways, and the god Dharma, generally associated with the moral law ("The Karma of Dharma," p. 156; "The Pandavas Go to Heaven," p. 145), here violates that law by causing his daughter to become pregnant, albeit indirectly and unintentionally. More in character, he subjects the three gods of the so-called trinity ("The Origin of *Linga* Worship," p. 235) to a test, as he often tests mortals, and Shiva (who here, as often, has three eyes) alone passes the test. (In another popular myth, a sage tests the three gods, and Shiva alone fails and is cursed to be worshipped as the *linga*.) The goddess Shakti or Adi-Shakti ("Primeval Shakti"), the female power, is the primary force here, and among the male gods her consort Shiva is supreme.

PRONOUNCING GLOSSARY

Adi-Shakti: *ah´-dee–shuk´-tee*

uluk: *oo´-look*

Told by Mr. Pratap Chandra Misra, a Brahmin priest, in 1947

Long ago, the primeval goddess Adi-Shakti was born from the sweat of Lord Dharma. But soon after creating this daughter, Dharma went to the riverbank to practice his meditation exercises. He remained absorbed in his own thoughts for fourteen long years. Finally, he was disturbed by his airborne vehicle, the owl [*uluk*]. This owl reminded him of his daughter and persuaded him to abandon his meditations and return home to check on her. But in fourteen years this daughter had become a young woman. When Dharma saw this he went in search of a groom for her. He left behind one pot of honey and one pot of poison. During his absence the daughter became more and more desirous. Finally, when she could not bear the feeling any longer, she drank the poison. This made her pregnant. In due course she gave birth to the three great gods: Brahma, Vishnu, and Shiva. All three of these sons were born blind. They were also very religious. They soon went to the bank of a river to give themselves up to divine contemplation.

Seeing these three men absorbed thus in meditation, Dharma now determined to test them. So he floated down the river in the form of a putrid-smelling corpse. As Dharma's transformed body approached Brahma, he began to notice a terrible smell. So the sage took three palmfuls of water and ceremoniously sent the corpse on down the river. Next, the great Lord Dharma floated in front of Vishnu. The mighty Vishnu also noticed a foul smell and soon did the same, sending the corpse on down the river using three palmfuls of water. Finally, the corpse arrived in front of Shiva. When Shiva noticed the bad smell, however, he thought to himself, "How could there already be a smell of death when there has been no birth?" Shiva, being a famous master of mysteries, thus came to realize that this smell could be nothing more than an illusion created by the great Lord himself. So instead of sending the body on down the river, Shiva grabbed a hold of it with his two hands and began to dance. He also realized that he had been the only one of the brothers to have recognized Lord Dharma in his concealed form. Dharma was very pleased with Shiva and responded by bestowing him with the gift of eyesight. Dharma's words were, "You were blind in both eyes. In recompense I now grant sight in those, plus one additional eye that can also see." Shiva was very pleased. He bowed down at the Lord's feet and began to sing his praise. He then prayed to Dharma, asking him to bless his two brothers with eyesight as well. Dharma then explained to Shiva that his spittle would be enough to bring sight to both his brothers. Shiva then used his spittle and blessed both his brothers with divine vision.

The three brothers next went together to visit Adi-Shakti. Dharma then commanded Brahma to create the world. He charged Vishnu with protecting it and asked the three-eyed Shiva to assume the task of destroying it. Then Dharma turned to Adi-Shakti and asked her to take on the work of giving birth to all creatures. But Shakti responded in puzzlement asking, "How am I to bring forth creatures in this world? I was born without parents and I do not possess the power of conception. O master, what shall I do to carry out your orders?" Lord Dharma then asked her to follow his advice. She was to marry Lord Shiva once in each of her many births to come. Adi-Shakti agreed. The fruit of her union with Shiva was the birth of the many creatures in this world.

THE ORIGIN OF THE TEMPLE AT TARAKESHVAR

Most temples in India have stories narrating their origins and extolling their healing powers. Sometimes these stories are written down and published, either in Sanskrit or in the vernaculars, as "Puranas of the Place" (*sthala-puranas*). Often they also circulate in the oral tradition as tales such as this one. No reason is given here for the villagers' hostility toward the *sannyasi*, a renouncer and ascetic, but such hostility, not uncommon in India, may be caused by any or all of several factors: fear of his powers, resentment of his failure to contribute to the village's food supply, distrust of his motives, disapproval of his smoking of *ganja* (usually marijuana rather than opium), and, perhaps, guilt on the part of the villagers, since theoretically they, too, ought to renounce. The *sannyasi*'s miraculous ability to ride a three-legged horse is an unusual village twist on the many stories of miraculous horses and miraculous riders from the vernacular Kshatriya epic traditions of Rajasthan and Andhra Pradesh. The stone on which the cow pours its milk is never identified as a *linga*, but it is the stone of Shiva, who here describes it in terms often applied to the Shiva-*linga* ("The Origin of *Linga* Worship," p. 235), and there are many stories, particularly but not only in South India, of cows watering the *linga* with their milk.

PRONOUNCING GLOSSARY

Amdanga Mattha: *ahm-dahn´-guh mut´-tuh*
copila: *kuh´-pee-lah´*
Dhumropan Giri: *doom´-roh-pahn´ gee´-ree*
ganja: *gahn´-juh*
Joshi Mattha: *joh´-shee mut´-tuh*
Mohanto: *moh-hahn´-toh*
Mukundu Gowalla: *moo-koon´-doo goh´-wah-luh*
pashan: *pah´-shahn*
puja: *poo´-jah*
purani kahini: *poo-rah´-nee kuh-hee´-nee*
sannyasi: *sun-yah´-see*
shishya: *shish´-yuh*
Tarakeshvar: *tah´-ruh-kay´-shvar*

Told by Poromananda Chattopadhyay, a Brahmin priest, in 1977

I cannot speak with certainty about the history of the Tarakeshvar temple, but what I do know has come from '*purani kahini*' [ancient stories]. In the beginning, this place was covered by a dense forest. In the forest lived a *sannyasi* by the name of Dhumropan Giri. He belonged to the Joshi Mattha.[1] This man lived in the forest and worshipped Baba [Shiva]. The house of the king of the area was only three miles from where this *sannyasi* stayed, and the king often heard about the holy man living in his vicinity. Sometimes local villagers reported to the king that certain bad incidents in the village had been caused by this *sannyasi*. So the king finally sent his men to fetch the *sannyasi* and had him imprisoned. But soon afterwards, it was noticed that the cell of the *sannyasi* was empty during the day despite his having been locked up. He was only to be found there at night when he returned to rest. This man came and went at will, as if unbarred. This was reported to the king, who now became anxious. He soon went to meet the *sannyasi* and asked him how this was possible. The *sannyasi* then explained that he was a devoted man whose only occupation was performing a daily *puja* [worship]

1. The Joshi Mattha (Sanskrit Jyotir-Matha, "Northern Monastery") is a school of philosophers and renouncers who trace their lineage back to Shankara ("Shankara Dreams," p. 286).

for Baba. What the villagers had said was untrue. The king believed him and immediately ordered his release. The *sannyasi* returned to his place in the forest. The king then became a frequent visitor there, often requesting some needed advice.

The *sannyasi* had a horse with three legs. He looked after this horse like his own child. Now the villagers again started rumors that something was unusual about a *sannyasi* taking such good care of a useless beast. This horse excited their suspicion. When the king asked the *sannyasi* about these reports of his behavior, a hot argument ensued. The *sannyasi* maintained that, even though three-legged, this horse was not a useless animal. He rode him frequently, far and wide. The king then offered the man a deal. If the *sannyasi* could ride this horse, the king would give him all the land which the beast could cover. The *sannyasi* then mounted his horse and began to ride. He rode from Burdwan to Midnapore and from there to Hooghly, to Amdanga Mattha, and to Gorbeta [Midnapore]. From there he returned to Tarakeshvar again. The king verified the *sannyasi*'s journey, found that he had visited the entire area, and then, as he had promised, he gave the *sannyasi* all of the land which he had covered with his horse. Hence the *sannyasi* became the first Mohanto[2] of this place, the owner of the land. The people called him Dhumropan Giri because he was fond of *ganja* [opium]. This name means "He who is always smoking."

In this jungle there was a stone or, rather, a solid stone mound (*pashan*). It happened that the same king had a herd of cattle. In that herd there was a cow of the variety called *copila*,[3] which used to visit that *pashan* every day and stand just over it. It would then pour its milk onto the stone. The chief cowherd, whose name was Mukundu Gowalla, noticed this one day. He then told the king, who thought that there must be something supernatural about such behavior. So he decided to take the stone to his own place. When his workers began digging it up, however, they could find no base to it. During the night, several days after the digging had begun, the sleeping king had a vision of Lord Shiva. Shiva spoke to him and said, I have no limits, and so you will not find the end of me [in that stone]. You must build a temple on that spot.

The stone had a slight depression on the top because it had frequently been used by local cowherd boys for beating paddy husks. This use of the stone was also known to the king.

Soon the king had a temple built. It came to stand in the area which he had given to the Mohanto, so he handed the temple over to that man. The king then gave up his throne, came to Dhumropan Giri, became the Mohanto's disciple [*shishya*], and took the vows of a *sannyasi*. His queen tried to convince him to give up these vows and return to the palace. Failing at this, she committed suicide.

The temple was built about two hundred and fifty years ago, according to the history and facts which we know. We cannot be certain. These events could have taken place earlier, but we are sure of its existence for at least the last two and a half centuries.

2. A rural landowner.
3. *Copila* (Sanskrit *kapila*) is a brown cow, particularly prized.

THE BRAHMIN WHO SWALLOWED A GOD

This story takes delight in imagining the sort of revenge that an ordinary man, troubled with perennial bad luck, might take on the powers that be if he got lucky one day. The Brahmin (addressed as *Thakur* ["Lord"]) in this story manages to bring the universe to the brink of collapse by putting Fate (Bidatha: Sanskrit *Vidhatri*, the "apportioner") out of commission. The form of the story is that of a widespread Sanskrit genre in which a universal disaster is threatened because a human being or anti-god amasses such power that he is able to put Death or Fate or Indra (king of heaven) out of commission. The solution in those stories, as in this one, is to introduce a god of the devotional, *bhakti*, world—in this case, Shiva—who takes the unusual human to heaven, effectively putting *him* out of commission so that the world can revert to its usual pattern, in the grip of death and fate.

This and the following five tales are translated by A. K. Ramanujan.

PRONOUNCING GLOSSARY

bel: *bel*
Bidatha: *bee-dah´-tuh*
Maharaj: *muh´-huh-rahj´*
puja: *poo´-jah*
raja: *rah´-jah*
Saraswati: *suh´-ruh-swuh´-tee*
Shaiva: *shai´-vuh*
Thakur/thakur: *tuh´-koor*

Retold from Rev. William McCulloch, Bengal Household Tales *(1912)*

Bidatha, the god who writes his or her future on everyone's forehead at birth, had doomed a poor Brahmin to a peculiar fate. This Brahmin was fated never to eat to his heart's content. When he had eaten half his rice, something or other always occurred to interrupt him, so that he could eat no more.

One day he received an invitation to the raja's house. He was delighted and said to his wife, "Half my rice is all I can ever eat. Never once in my whole life has my hunger been satisfied. Today I've by some good luck received this invitation to the raja's house. But how am I to go? My clothes are torn and dirty, and if I go like this, most likely the gatekeeper will turn me away." His wife said, "I'll repair and clean your clothes. Then you can go." And when she had provided him with decent clothes, he set out for the raja's house.

There, though he was late and it was evening, he was royally received. As he viewed the dishes spread out before him, the old Brahmin was delighted. He thought, "Whatever happens, today I'll eat my fill." He then sat down and began eating. Now, it happened that a little earthen pot was hanging from a beam of the roof. Just as the Brahmin had half finished his dinner, the pot broke and the pieces fell into his food. He immediately stopped eating, took his ritual sip of water to close the meal, got up, washed his hands and mouth, and went to the raja. The raja welcomed him respectfully and asked, "Thakur, are you fully satisfied?" The Brahmin answered, "Maharaj, your servants were very good to me and served me all I wanted. My own fate is to blame that I couldn't eat my fill." "Why?" said the raja. "What happened?" "Maharaj, while I was eating, a little earthen pot fell from the ceiling and spoiled my rice," said the Brahmin. The raja was very angry when he heard this and gave his servants a scolding. Then he said to the Brahmin, "Sir, you stay with me tonight. Tomorrow, I'll have fresh food made and serve it to you with my own hands." So the Brahmin stayed in the raja's house that night.

Next day, the raja supervised the cooking himself, even prepared some of the dishes with his own hands, and served the Brahmin. In the great room where he was served, there was nothing that could spoil the meal. The Brahmin looked around, rejoiced at the raja's hospitality, and sat down to eat. But when he was halfway through his dinner, Bidatha saw that he must be stopped, and yet he could not see any way of doing it. So he himself took the form of a golden frog, came to the edge of the Brahmin's plantain leaf, and tumbled into his food.

The Brahmin was too busy to notice anything. He ate up his rice, frog and all. Dinner over, the raja asked him, "How is it now, *thakur?* Were you satisfied today?" The Brahmin answered, "Maharaj, I've never dined so well in all my life." Saying this, he took his leave, received gifts and money from the good raja, and set off for home.

That evening on his way home, while he was walking through a jungle, he suddenly heard a voice: "Brahmin, let me go! Brahmin, let me go!" The Brahmin looked all around him, but he could see nobody. Again he heard the voice: "Brahmin, let me go!" Then he said, "Who are you?" The answer came: "I'm Bidatha, I'm Bidatha!" The Brahmin asked again, "Where are you?" Bidatha answered, "Inside your stomach. You've swallowed me." "Impossible!" said the Brahmin. "Yes," said Bidatha, "in the form of a frog, I tumbled into your food, and you ate me up." "Ah, nothing could be better," replied the Brahmin. "You've bothered me all my life, you rascal. I won't let you go! I'll rather close up my throat." Bidatha, in great fear, said again, "Brahmin, let me go! I'm stifled in here!" But the Brahmin hurried home quickly, and when he arrived, said to his wife, "Give me a hookah, and you hold a stick ready in your hand." His wife did so at once, and the Brahmin sat down and smoked the hookah for a long time contentedly, taking great care not to set Bidatha free. The god was further stifled by the smoke, but the Brahmin quite ignored all his cries for help.

Meanwhile, there was a terrible commotion in the three worlds. Without Bidatha to regulate matters, the universe was on the verge of a collapse. Then the gods assembled in council decided that one of them must be sent to the Brahmin. But who? They all agreed that the goddess Lakshmi would be the right one to go. She said, "If I go to that Brahmin, I shall never come back." But they all prayed and begged, so she agreed and went to the Brahmin's house. When the Brahmin learned that it was Lakshmi, the goddess of wealth and fortune, at his door, he put his upper cloth around his neck as a mark of respect, gave her a seat, and asked her what, in the name of wonder, had brought her to a poor man's house. "*Thakur*," said the goddess, "you've taken Bidatha a prisoner. Let him go, or the universe will be ruined." "Give me the stick," said the Brahmin to his wife, "and I'll show you what I think of this goddess of good fortune. From the day I was born, she has shunned me, I've had nothing but bad luck, and here she comes to my house, this Lakshmi!" When she heard this, the goddess vanished, trembling with fear. No one had ever talked to her like that before in all the ages. She told the gods what had happened, and, after another huddle, the gods sent Saraswati, the goddess of learning.

When Saraswati reached his house and called out, "Brahmin, are you in? Brahmin, are you in?" the Brahmin saluted her with great respect and said, "Mother, great goddess, what do you want in a poor man's house?" "*Thakur*, the universe is fast coming apart. Let Bidatha go." The Brahmin burst into a great rage and cried, "Wife, give me the stick! I'll teach this goddess of learning. She didn't give me even the first letters of the alphabet. Saraswati comes to my house now, does she?" Hearing this, the goddess got up in a hurry and fled, stumbling.

Finally, the great god Shiva himself undertook the mission. Now the Brahmin was a Shaiva, a devout worshipper of Shiva, so devout that he would not even touch water without doing *puja* to Shiva. Therefore, as soon as the god came, he and his wife gave him water to wash his feet, offered him *bel* leaves, holy grass, flowers, rice, and sandalwood, and did *puja* to him. Shiva then sat down and said to the Brahmin, "Brahmin, let Bidatha go." The Brahmin said, "As you have come personally, O great Shiva, of course I must let him go. But what am I to do? I've suffered hardships from the day I was born, thanks to this Bidatha. He is the cause of it all." Then the great god said, "Do not trouble yourself. I'll take you, body and soul, to heaven." When he heard that, the Brahmin relaxed his throat and opened his mouth, and Bidatha jumped out. Then Shiva took the Brahmin and his wife with him to his special heaven.

IF GOD IS EVERYWHERE

A satire on the Upanishadic doctrine of pantheism (Upanishads, p. 105), the belief that the universe is entirely pervaded by the world-soul (*brahman*). This tale and the two that follow are from the oral tradition attributed to the great nineteenth-century Vedantic sage Shri Ramakrishna (Swami Vivekananda, p. 550), who told many parables that became part of the oral tradition. These versions have been adopted from *The Gospel of Ramakrishna* (New York: The Vedanta Society, 1907).

A sage had a number of disciples. He taught them his deepest belief: "God is everywhere and dwells in everything. So you should treat all things as God and bow before them."

One day when a disciple was out on errands, a mad elephant was rushing through the marketplace, and the elephant driver was shouting, "Get out of the way! Get out of the way! This is a mad elephant!" The disciple remembered his guru's teachings and refused to run. "God is in this elephant as He is in me. How can God hurt God?" he thought, and just stood there full of love and devotion. The driver was frantic and shouted at him, "Get out of the way! You'll be hurt!" But the disciple did not move an inch. The mad elephant picked him up with its trunk, swung him around, and threw him in the gutter. The poor fellow lay there, bruised, bleeding, but more than all, disillusioned that God should do this to him. When his guru and the other disciples came to help him and take him home, he said, "You said God is in everything! Look what the elephant did to me!"

The guru said, "It's true that God is in everything. The elephant is certainly God. But so was the elephant driver, telling you to get out of the way. Why didn't you listen to him?"

NONVIOLENCE

A satire on the concept of nonviolence (*ahimsa*) ("Killing the Sacrificial Horse," p. 96; "King Shibi," p. 160), as well as on stories in which animals change their natures ("The Dog Who Would Be Lion," p. 158) or, by implication, low-caste people change their way of life.

A particularly wicked snake infested a road and bit passers-by. A holy man happened to pass that way, and the snake rushed at him to bite him. He calmly looked at it and said, "You want to bite me, don't you? Go ahead."

The snake was subdued by this unusual response and was overpowered by the gentleness of the holy man. The holy man said, "Listen, dear friend, how about promising me that you won't bite anyone from now on?" The snake bowed and nodded assent. The holy man went his way, and the snake began its life of innocence and nonviolence.

Very soon, the neighborhood discovered that the snake was harmless and the boys began to tease it mercilessly. They pelted it with stones and dragged it around by its tail. Still it kept its promise to the holy man and suffered.

Fortunately, the holy man happened to come by to see his latest disciple and was touched by the bruised and battered condition of the snake. When he asked it what had happened, the snake said feebly, "O swami, you said I should not bite anyone. But people are so merciless!"

The holy man said, "I asked you not to bite anyone. But I didn't ask you not to hiss!"

WALKING ON WATER

A satire on magical yogic powers ("The Discipline of Mind and Body," p. 122).

A holy man was once meditating on the bank of a river, when another holy man wanted to impress him with the extraordinary powers he had achieved through his ascetic practices. So he came towards him, walking on the water.

When he reached the place where the first holy man was quietly sitting, he said, "Did you see what I just did?"

"Oh yes, I saw you come across the river, walking on the water. Where did you learn that?"

"I practiced yoga and penances for twelve years in the foothills of the Himalayas, standing on one leg, fasting six days of the week. And so I acquired this power."

"Really?" said the first holy man. "Why did you go to all that trouble to do this? Our ferryman here will ferry you across any day for two pennies."

HOW TENALI RAMA BECAME A JESTER and TENALI RAMA'S *RAMAYANA*

Tenali Rama, a jester and trickster, is a very popular figure in Telugu country (primarily Andhra Pradesh and Karnataka). His character is said to be based upon the court poet of Krishnadeva Raya, who ruled a great empire from the now ruined capital city of Vijayanagara, in Karnataka, in the sixteenth century. The first story is a satire on the Vedic concept of a god with a thousand heads or faces ("The Hymn of the Primeval Man," p. 82). The second story satirizes the adventures of the monkey Hanuman in the *Ramayana* ("Lost Loves . . . in the *Ramayana*," p. 186) and the Hindu storytelling tradition that often blurs the frame that separates a story from real life.

PRONOUNCING GLOSSARY

Hanuman: *huh´-noo-mahn*
Kali: *kah´-lee*
Lanka: *lahn´-kah*
Ramayana: *ruh-mah´-yuh-nuh*
sannyasi: *sun-yah´-see*
Tenali: *tay-nah´-lee*
Tenali Rama: *tay-nah´-lee rah´-muh*
Vijayanagara: *vih´-jah´-yuh-nuh´-guh-ruh*
vikatakavi: *vih´-kuh-tuh-kuh´-vee*

Heard by A. K. Ramanujan in childhood

In a South Indian village called Tenali there lived a clever Brahmin boy. His name was Rama. Once, a wandering *sannyasi* was impressed with the boy's looks and clever ways. So he taught him a chant and told him, "If you go to the goddess Kali's temple one night and recite these words three million times, she will appear before you with all her thousand faces and give you what you ask for—if you don't let her scare you."

Rama waited for an auspicious day, went to the Kali temple outside his village, and did as he was told. As he finished his three-millionth chant, the goddess did appear before him with her thousand faces and two hands. When the boy looked at her horrific appearance, he wasn't frightened. He fell into a fit of laughter. No one had ever dared to laugh in the presence of this fearsome goddess. Offended, she asked him, "You little scalawag, why are you laughing at me?"

He answered, "O Mother, we mortals have enough trouble wiping our noses when we catch a cold, though we have two hands and only one nose. If you, with your thousand faces, should catch a cold, how would you manage with just two hands for all those thousand runny noses?"

The goddess was furious. She said, "Because you laughed at me, you'll make a living only by laughter. You'll be a *vikatakavi*, a jester."

"Oh, a *vi-ka-ta-ka-vi*! That's terrific! It's a palindrome. It reads *vi-ka-ta-ka-vi* whether you read it from right to left or from left to right," replied Rama.

The goddess was pleased by Rama's cleverness that saw a joke even in a curse. She at once relented and said, "You'll be a *vikatakavi*, but you will be jester to a king." And she vanished.

Soon after that, Tenali Rama began to make a living as jester to the king of Vijayanagara.

A courtesan once invited Tenali Rama to recite the story of the *Ramayana*. He began the story by saying, "Rama and Sita went to the forest," and stopped there. He said nothing more. The courtesan waited and waited and finally asked, "Then what happened?" "Don't be impatient," said Tenali Rama. "They're still walking in the forest."

At another time, he was angered by a similar request from another arrogant courtesan. "I'll really make you experience the *Ramayana*, just as it happened," he said, and continued: "In the *Ramayana*, Hanuman the monkey set fire to the city of Lanka, just like this!" And he set fire to the courtesan's house.

THE GURU AND THE IDIOT

This story satirizes rich gurus and reveres the powers of holy fools.

From A. K. Ramanujan's field notes.

A rich guru had hundreds of disciples all over the country. He lived like a lord and traveled in a palanquin from town to town, visiting his followers and receiving gifts and donations. It took him twelve years to visit all of them even once.

While he was on one of these rounds, he was stopped on the road outside a certain town by a man who looked and acted like an idiot. He stood right in the middle of the road and would not let the palanquin pass till the guru had talked to him. The guru was impatient but agreed to talk to him for a minute. "What do you want?" he asked testily.

The man said, "I want to go to heaven. People tell me that you are a guru and know the way."

The guru laughed and said, "You want to go to heaven? That's easy. Just stand there with your hands lifted to the sky. You'll go to heaven." The man said, "That's all?" and before he could ask any more, the guru had ordered his palanquin bearers to move on and was gone.

Twelve years later, the guru had occasion to come that way again. As he reached the outskirts of the town, he saw a man standing there, looking at the sky, his hands lifted towards heaven. His hair and beard had turned grey, his nails had grown long and dirty, his clothes were in tatters. He didn't seem to mind. His eyes were riveted to the sky.

As the guru approached him, he saw an astonishing thing happen. He saw the man, the idiot, slowly rise towards heaven. The guru had a flash of understanding and knew what he should do. He at once got down from his palanquin, held on to the feet of the idiot, and rose with him to heaven. That was the only way he could have gone to heaven, and he knew it now.

ADIVASI (TRIBAL) HINDUISM

Generally speaking, Adivasis ("first-dwellers," or ab-originals, indigenous), as they are usually called now, or tribal Hindus, as they used to be called, ignore, and are ignored by, the Hindu caste system. The various groups differ greatly, but most do not acknowledge the superiority of Brahmins or have any compunctions about killing cows. Their oral traditions, however, largely unique to these tribes, include a number of recognizable Hindu names and themes, as well as variants of Hindu myths, often combined with concepts that have no Hindu parallel. Like many Dalits, the Adivasis form a kind of internal diaspora Hinduism. They are a real presence in India, comparable to though arguably more influential than Native Americans in the United States.

A great many tribal stories were collected by Verrier Elwin (1902–1964), who first came to India as a missionary but was caught up in the freedom movement (he made contact with Nehru and Gandhi), incurring the displeasure of the British government. He then worked with Shamrao Hivale, an associate of Gandhi, to study the Gonds of (present-day) Madhya Pradesh, and, with Hivale, began to agitate for their rights and to argue that their culture was in many ways morally superior to Christianity. Not surprisingly, this angered his Christian church, and Elwin resigned his missionary post in 1931, converted to Hinduism, and married a Gond woman (Kosi), eventually taking a second wife (Leela), in the tribal tradition. After Independence (1947), he became the chief of the Anthropological Survey of India and continued to dedicate his life and his money to make the citizens of the forests citizens of free India.

The texts in this section were collected and translated by Verrier Elwin.

Gonds

The Gonds are a group of Adivasis, or aboriginal peoples, several million in number, who live in central India, in Madhya Pradesh, Maharashtra, Andhra Pradesh, Bihar, and Orissa. The southern part of Madhya Pradesh and several neighboring states is popularly called "Gondwana," or "Land of the Gonds." Most Gonds speak Gondi, an unwritten language of the Dravidian family, which has many dialects, some of which are mutually unintelligible; many Gonds, however, do not speak Gondi but rather the dominant language of the place where they live, be it Hindi, Marathi, or Telugu. The stories here were all recorded from Hindi-speaking Gonds.

PRONOUNCING GLOSSARY

Ahir: *uh-heer´*
Bara Deo: *buh-rah´ day´-oh*
Bara Pen: *buh-rah´ pen*
Bhagavan: *buh-guh-vahn´*
Binjpahar: *binj´-puh-har*
Chamar: *chuh-mar´*
Chamarin: *chuh-mah´-rin*
chaprasi: *chuh-prah´-see*
Dano: *dah´-no*
Dhimar: *dih´-mar*
Gond: *gohnd*
Jam Raja: *jum´ rah´-jah*
Jogini: *joh´-gee-nee´*
Kutlisingh Mata: *koot´-lee-sing mah´-tah*
Mahadeo: *muh-hah´-day´-oh*
Panka: *pun´-kuh*

Parvati: *par´-vuh-tee´*
Raja: *rah´-jah*
Rani: *rah´-nee*
sadhu: *sah´-doo*
tamasha: *tuh-mah´-shuh*

MAHADEO AND PARVATI WERE LIVING IN THE BINJPAHAR HILLS

In this story Shiva (called Mahadeo, from the Sanskrit Mahadeva) and Parvati descend from the sublime to the ridiculous and provide humankind with a banal but useful skill: tickling.

From Baratola, Mandla District

Mahadeo and Parvati were living in the Binjpahar hills. Mahadeo took a gourd and went to beg food from a village. When he returned Parvati cooked what he had got and they ate it. After this Mahadeo went away somewhere and Parvati thinking that he would not return, went to the house of a Dano[1] and stayed there. But Mahadeo returned suddenly and found his house shut up and a lock on the door. He lost his temper and kicked the door open, went in, spread his bed and lay down to sleep.

Presently Parvati returned. When she saw Mahadeo sleeping there she woke him up, but he was so angry that he would not speak to her. Six months passed and Mahadeo neither ate nor spoke. In despair Parvati went from house to house seeking advice as to what she should do. Somewhere in the village lived an old Panka[2] woman. When this woman heard what had happened, she gave Parvati an oil extracted from the body of a caterpillar and obtained a blessing for her from Kutlisingh Mata.[3] She said, "Put this oil *kut-kut-kut-kut* on his body beginning from the legs upwards." Parvati took the oil and went home.

Parvati put the oil on Mahadeo's legs and gradually rubbed it up his body. He felt more and more ticklish and began to laugh. Soon he was talking again to Parvati and had a good meal. He gave mankind this blessing, "Whenever anyone is in a bad temper his wife should tickle him and all will be well."

1. A Baiga tribesman.
2. A Central Indian tribe.
3. A local goddess.

IN THE UNDER WORLD

The sixty-four Joginis (Sanskrit Yoginis) are important figures in Tantric mythology ("Tantric Points in the Body," p. 276); they are often associated with menstrual blood that is ingested during some Tantric ceremonies. According to one model of Hindu embryology, a drop of menstrual blood combines with a drop of semen to make an embryo; here the mere shadow of a hawk provides the male element. The idea of nectar (or fire) stored in, and then stolen from, a hollow bamboo is even older than the Vedas in India; the idea of becoming immortal by being excreted is a new twist added by this Gond story.

From Jubbulpore District

In the Under World the sixty-four Jogini were all menstruating. They went down to the sea to bathe. They had with them a carpet made of cowhide. Standing upon it they removed their clothes. As they did so some blood dripped on the cowhide and the shadow of a hawk flying overhead fell on the blood and from it a girl was born. The girl flew up into the air like a hawk and flying flying saw the whole world. She came down and in the form of a girl sat on the shoulder of the eldest Jogini. The Jogini said, "You were born on cowhide. Therefore, your name is Chamarin."[1]

The girl asked the Jogini for food and they said, "There are plenty of men in the world; go and eat them." The girl took the form of a hawk again and flew to the world where she pecked off men's heads and ate their bodies. But the men went through her body and passed out in her excreta and so returned to life, for in those days men had the Water of Immortality in a hollow bamboo.

Soon the girl found out that she could never get enough to eat and she went back to the Jogini and said, "No sooner do I eat than they get out and then I am hungry again." The sixty-four Jogini went to Mahadeo and asked him what they had better do. Mahadeo went to the Middle World and stole the Water of Immortality and now when the girl ate men they did not come back to life afterwards. She used to eat the bodies and take their souls to Jam Raja.[2] He used to stuff them into a gourd. Many days passed in this manner and at last the hawk-girl said to Jam Raja, "I am tired of going to and fro carrying the souls of men. After this you must send your own chaprasis[3] for them." Since then there has been death in the world and Jam Raja has sent his servants to fetch the souls of men.

1. The Chamars (or Chamarins) are a Dalit caste who work with leather, called *charman* in Sanskrit.

2. Sanskrit Yama Raja, the king of the dead ("Bhrigu's Journey in the Other World," p. 101).

3. Messenger boys.

AN OLD GOND AND HIS WIFE

A story mocking belief in ghosts.

From Bhendi, Dondi-Lahara Zamindari

An old Gond and his wife had a violent quarrel about their food. There were seven chapatis[1] for supper, and the old woman said, "I have cooked them, so I should have more." The man said, "I have paid for them, so I should have more." They quarreled till they were exhausted and lay down to sleep, their supper still uneaten. At midnight the old man sat up and said, "Whoever speaks first will have three of the chapatis; whoever keeps silence longest will have four."

Then they both lay down and kept silent. Not a word did they speak all night and when dawn came they remained quiet. They stayed lying down all that day and the next and then the neighbors said, "What has happened?" and went to see. They opened the door of the house and saw the man and wife lying silent on the ground. They called to them, but they said not a word, and the people decided that they were dead and should be taken out to burial.

Seven men came to carry them to the burial-ground, but when they were about to lower them into their graves the old woman said to her husband, "I will eat three; you can have four." When the seven men heard the corpse speak, they thought it was referring to them, and ran for their lives. The old man and woman, wondering what was the matter, ran after them. The seven men reached the village crying that ghosts were coming to devour them and the people ran for their lives. They went to the Police Station and reported the matter, but the Sub-Inspector looked out and saw the old man and woman coming and he and his constables too ran for their lives. They went on to the Raja and the Rani, and soon the palace was deserted.

The old man and woman occupied the palace and lived there in great comfort. But after this fear came to the world, and men have been afraid of ghosts.

1. Wheat pancakes, the basic bread of North India.

FORMERLY THE WHOLE COUNTRY BELONGED TO THE GOND

This story about the British hostility to the Gond people and their religion blames their loss of land not on British military superiority but on British theft of Gond religion: the sacrifice of pigs and fowl (animals that poor people can afford) is trumped by the sacrifice of cows (Vedic sacrificial animals ["Humans, Animals, and Gods in the *Rig Veda*," p. 73]) and human beings (often imagined as Vedic sacrificial animals ["Hymn of the Primeval Man," p. 82]).

From Bamhni, Bindra-Nawargarh Zamindari

Formerly the whole country belonged to the Gond and they were strong because of the help they had from Bara Pen,[1] whom they pleased with many offerings of pig and fowl. The English invaders came but found the Gond too strong for them. But the English have great wisdom; they thought and thought how to win the kingdom and discovered that the obstacle was Bara Pen. They decided to sacrifice a cow and a human being to Bara Pen. They found a Panka[2] boy and a cow and sacrificed them. Bara Pen was pleased and went over to their side. The English made the god a fine bungalow with seven doors. These were always kept shut and four-and-twenty watchmen, twelve for the day, twelve for the night, guarded them. And the land came under their control.

The Gond wondered how to get the land back. A Gond dressed as an Ahir.[3] He bought a bottle of liquor for Bara Pen; he cut open his thigh, hid the bottle inside and sewed it up. He went to Bara Pen and said, "I am an Ahir: I will clean the house and worship." They let him go in and, as he approached, the doors opened of their own accord. The watchmen thus knew he was a Gond, and they killed him. In Bara Pen's hand were two swords: if the Gond had got them he could have saved the land. Now Bara Pen is only a name. We worship him, but he has no power, for he is in the hands of the English.

1. Another name of Bara Deo, the Great God.
2. A Central Indian tribe.
3. Another Central Indian tribe.

A CHAMAR'S SONS

This story about the origin of dreams depicts the virtue of a Dalit man and the sins of a Raja, rewarding the Dalit and punishing the Raja—a reversal of normal expectations that is itself a tribal dream.

From Baihar, Balaghat District

A Chamar's[1] son and a Raja's son were friends. The Chamar were very generous, but the Raja and his son were mean. In time the Raja died, and the Death Chaprasis[2] came to arrest him. They carried him off beating and kicking him.

The Raja's daughter-in-law had a mirror which was dream. She saw in this mirror-dream what was happening, and said to her husband, the friend of the Chamar's son, "Your father was very mean and now I have seen his punishment in a dream."

But when the Chamar died, the Death Chaprasis carried him to Bhagavan[3] in their arms.

1. A Dalit caste of leatherworkers.
2. Messenger boys.
3. God.

Now as the Chaprasis were taking the Raja through the air, and he was struggling and screaming and they were beating and abusing him, they passed over a river where a rich Dhimar[4] was catching fish. He looked up and saw them. "Why are you beating him?" he called. They said, "He was very mean." This Dhimar also was a very mean man, and so was his wife. He ran home and called his wife. "Come and see the tamasha[5] down by the river." She too called to them, "Why are you beating him?" They answered, "Because he was so mean."

When she heard that, the wife was frightened and ran home as fast as she could. There she gave a great feast and opened her store to give presents to children and widows and any sadhu[6] that came to beg.

Since the Raja's daughter-in-law looked in her mirror, there have been dreams in the world.

4. A member of a large caste of fishermen.
5. A celebration or entertainment.
6. A wandering holy man.

Rajnengi Pardhan

The Pardhan, a subgroup among the Gonds, traditionally served as bardic priests. The Rajnengi Pardhan, a subgroup among the Pardhan, live mainly in the Mandla District of Madhya Pradesh, in the basin of the Narmada River. Much of the district is forested and is now home to Kanha National Park, which has more tigers than any other district in India.

PRONOUNCING GLOSSARY

Baiga: *bai´-guh*
Bijloki: *beej´-loh-kee*
Dano: *dah´-noh*
dewar: *day´-war*
Gond: *gohnd*
Jhalsura: *jul´-soo-ruh*
Kalpadi Deo: *kahl´-puh-dee day´-oh*
Kapila: *kuh´-pee-luh*
kos: *kohs*
Lakshman: *luk´-shmun*
Lakshmanjati: *luk´-shmun-jah´-tee*
Lamsena: *lahm´-say´-nuh*
Mahadeo: *muh-hah´-day´-oh*
Nag: *nahg*
Phulmandi: *fool´-mahn-dee*
Raimandi: *rai´-mahn-dee*
Rajnengi Pardhan: *rahj-nen´-gee par-dahn´*
Shesh Nag: *saysh´ nahg*
thil puris: *teel poo´-rees*

THE SUN AND THE MOON

A brief episode in the story of Rama, his wife Sita, and his brother Lakshmana ("Lost Loves . . . in the *Ramayana*," p. 186), which departs dramatically from the extant *Ramayanas* in the classical written languages of India (Sanskrit, Hindi, Tamil, Bangla, etc.). The Sun and Moon are central to many Gond and Rajnengi Pardhan myths.

From Sanhwachhapar, Mandla District

The Sun and Moon are the eyes of Rama. After Lakshmanjati's death, Rama went in anger to the jungle and tore out his eyes. These became the Sun and Moon.

ONE NIGHT WHILE SITA AND RAMA WERE LYING TOGETHER

Another very different version of the *Ramayana*, playing upon the relationship between a brother-in-law (*dewar*) and sister-in-law (*bhauji*), a highly charged connection in village Hinduism. This story replaces the classical episode of Sita's fire ordeal ("Lost Loves . . . in the *Ramayana*," p. 196) with a fire ordeal that Lakshman insists upon. Here, Sita pursues Lakshman in a series of intimate encounters, and it is Lakshman, not Sita, who goes down into the earth. But in this case the world under the surface of the earth is the land of Nagas, cobra people, snake from the waist down and anthropomorphic from the waist up. The Naga world is a familiar setting for adventures such as the one that Lakshman has here, which ends by explaining the origin of snakes in our world.

From Patahgarh, Mandla District

One night while Sita and Rama were lying together, Sita discussed Lakshman very affectionately. She said, "There he is sleeping alone. What is it that keeps him away from woman? Why doesn't he want to marry?" This roused suspicion in Rama's mind. Sita slept soundly, but Rama kept awake the whole night imagining things. Early next morning he sent for Lakshman from his lonely palace and asked him suddenly, "Do you love Sita?" Lakshman was taken aback and could hardly look at his brother. He stared at the ground for a long time and was full of shame.

Without saying anything Lakshman went to the mountains with his axe and cut down a forest of twelve hills and brought the wood to a place near the palace. Seeing the great heap of wood the people of the town came to discover what was the matter. Among them was a little child who was screaming. Lakshman took him in his arms and climbed on the heap of wood. Then he shouted, "Set fire to this wood and if I am pure and innocent I will not be burnt." The people set fire to the wood and it began to blaze, but Lakshman stood there with the crying child; to keep him quiet he began to play on his fiddle. When the fire burnt down, the villagers, and Rama and Sita too, were standing anxiously to see if Lakshman and the baby had been burnt or no. But there they were standing free and not even singed.

After this test, Lakshman left his brother and said he would never visit his palace again. Rama tried his best to persuade him, but Lakshman would not listen to any persuasion. Sita, however, considered how she might win him round. As her *dewar* was going rapidly through the jungle he saw a vixen leave a little newly-born cub on the road and run away. The poor cub was blind and could not get any milk and Lakshman chased the vixen with the cub in his hand. At last he was able to catch the vixen and with one hand he caught one of its udders and put it in the cub's mouth. Suddenly there was Sita, instead of the vixen, with Sita's breast in Lakshman's hand. Lakshman was very embarrassed and immediately removed his hand, but Sita said, "For truth and purity, you ran away from your brother only to touch my breast. Now I know how virtuous you are." Lakshman was very annoyed by this taunt and ran away again, but Sita went forward and now became a fig tree.

Lakshman was hungry and when he saw a beautiful fig tree in the way, he caught a ripe fig in his hand—and there was Sita standing there instead of the fig tree and he was holding her breast in his hands.

Then Lakshman ran away again but Sita could not leave him. She turned her pubic cloth into a tobacco plant growing by the path. Lakshman was very tired and seeing the beautiful tobacco desired to have it, but as he caught it in his hand he found he was holding his *bhauji's* cloth. Sita again appeared saying, "Why are you trying to pull off my cloth?"

But Lakshman now was weary of the world and stamped so violently that he made a hole in the ground and he walked down and reached the Under World. There he found Shesh Nag[1] sitting in his palace with the Sun and Moon as two lamps. With him were his three unmarried daughters. When the three girls, Raimandi, Phulmandi and Bijloki, saw the young man they begged their father to keep him as a Lamsena[2] in their house. Lakshman was very sad and he agreed. The Nag was not very pleased with the boy and tested him harshly.

The first trial given to Lakshman was to plough twelve *kos*[3] of land which had never been ploughed before, with a share made of brittle cotton wood. But by his merit Lakshman was able to plough it.

Then twelve measures of sesamum[4] were given to sow in it, but when he had sown the seed the Nag sent for Lakshman and said, "I don't want sesamum to be sown, so remove all the grains, for I am going to sow rice instead." Lakshman went to the field and sat weeping. A wood pigeon heard him and was very sorry. She went and brought her friends and they soon picked up all the seeds and Lakshman was able to take all the twelve measures back to the Nag. That is why the wild pigeon always sings "*Thil puris, thil puris?*" (Is the sesamum enough to fill all the measures?)

There were many other tests and Lakshman could hardly ever eat his food. For misery and anxiety he used to throw his food away and it turned into great mountains.

After three years of labor, however, Lakshman was married to the three girls, but he insisted that they should be married not to him but to his sword. The Nag put the three girls in three baskets and took them round the sacred pole with the sword. At the time of giving the girls his offering all the three demanded that the Moon and Sun should be given as their wedding present. The Nag gave them these two gifts on one condition, that the Sun

1. Shesa Naga (Sanskrit), the great serpent that supports the earth ("The River Yamuna," p. 259).
2. A bridegroom.
3. A measurement of land, between 1 and 5 kilometers, varying among different parts of India.
4. A plant whose seeds are used in cooking and in religious rituals.

and Moon would only remain half the time in the Upper World and half the time in the Under World.

When the party started back to the World, as they were going along Lakshman wanted to open the baskets and look at the girls. The youngest girl Bijloki suddenly turned into the lightning, and even today Lakshman is madly trying to hit her with his arrow but has never been able to possess her.

The two other girls were stolen by a Dano.[5] They appear in the world every ninth year as the mohati and amhera flowers. When these flowers blossom, the world has all the honey that it desires, because the bees love them. The Nag had put food for the girls in the baskets, and when Lakshman in his rage and disappointment saw it, he kicked it away and it turned into snakes and all the poisonous creatures that are in the world today.

5. The name of people of the Baiga caste who live in Amadob, Bilaspur District.

WHEN COWS WERE FIRST BORN

This story about the origin of the taboo against eating beef differs from the Sanskritic Hindu myths on the subject ("How Men Changed Skins with Animals," p. 100; "To Eat or Not to Eat Meat," p. 203) and includes clearly tribal terms such as the reference to a Dano, a member of the Baiga tribe. But the use of several Sanskrit terms, such as *Kapila* (traditionally a brown cow, though here she is white), *Kalpadi* (the beginning of an eon), and *Deo* (from Deva, god), indicates a familiarity with Hindu thinking, including, surely, the taboo against eating beef. The storyteller may well have known the relevant Hindu mythology and rejected it in favor of a different story.

From Kanchanpur, Mandla District

When cows were first born in the world there was a great forest all over the land and many wild men lived there and ate much meat. If on any day they were not able to get deer or wild goats or hares they used to catch the cows and eat them. So eating eating the cows they grew very fat and presently turned into Dano.

But the race of cows began to disappear. When this happened the Kapila cow was born out of the ground. She was white as an egg, everything about her was white, her ears, horns, feet, tail all were white. She went to the jungle called Jhalsura and there prayed to Kalpadi Deo, "I have been born to give milk to the world and to care for men." Kalpadi Deo said, "Go without fear and I will protect you. Anyone who now eats a cow and swallows the liver will find fire in his belly and he will die." This happened and many Dano died. Presently they gave up eating beef.

BEFORE MAHADEO SENT MEN TO LIVE

This tale about Mahadeo (Shiva) explicitly compares a Hindu with two tribals and mocks Hindu food taboos.

From Patangarh, Mandla District

Before Mahadeo sent men to live in the world he wanted to test them. He called a Hindu, a Gond and a Baiga and put before them food made by mixing everything in the world—liquor, the blood of living creatures, the sap of bitter trees, bits of meat, the legs of frogs and red ants. When the Hindu ate the mixture he vomited and was very ill, but the Gond and Baiga swallowed it without difficulty and enjoyed it. Since then the Hindu has been very careful of what he eats but the Gond and Baiga eat anything in the world.

Muria

The Muria live in the highlands of Bastar in Madhya Pradesh. They are known for their youth dormitories, or *ghotul*, where unmarried young people of both sexes lead a highly organized social life and receive training in civic duties and sexual practices.

PRONOUNCING GLOSSARY

Bhimul: *bee-mool´*
Darbar: *dur´-bahr*
Gara-surial-pite: *gah´-ruh–soo´-ree-yul–pee´-tay*
Huppe Piyer: *hoop´-pay pee´-yer*
Kosa Kana: *koh´-suh kah´-nuh*
Lagir: *lah´-geer*
Lingo: *ling´-goh*
Mahapurub: *muh-hah´-poo-roob´*
Muria: *moo´-ree-yuh*
Raja: *rah´-jah*

WHEN THIS WORLD WAS FIRST MADE

This creation story includes the sacrifice of a great man (Mahapurusha) that echoes the Vedic "Hymn of the Primeval Man [Purusha]" (p. 82).

From Ulera, Bastar State

When this world was first made there was neither Sun nor Moon and the clouds and the earth were like husband and wife, they lay so close together. Men were very small and had to move between them. They ploughed with rats and to pick brinjals[1] they had to reach up as though they were getting mangoes from a tree. As they walked to and fro they used to knock their heads against the clouds.

1. Eggplants.

Then Lingo and his brothers raised the clouds into the sky and there was room for men on earth, but there was no Sun or Moon and everything was dark. There was a tree called Huppe Piyer. When this tree blossomed it was day, when it dried up it was night. The twelve Lingo brothers and the thirteen Bhimul brothers thought and thought how they could bring more light to the world. "Where can we find something which will make light and darkness?" So thinking they came to the tree Huppe Piyer. "This is what we want," they said and began to cut it down. It was so big that the twelve Lingo brothers and the thirteen Bhimul brothers could cook their food and sleep in the space cut by their axes. When it was nearly cut through, it still did not fall, for on the top of the tree sat the bird called Gara-surial-pite holding it up. Said Lingo to his brother, "We must kill this bird," and Kosa Kana took his axe and killed it. Then the tree fell to the ground.

When the tree came down it fell on the thirteen Bhimul brothers and they shouted with fear. Lingo picked it up with one hand and threw it aside. Now this tree stood in the kingdom of twelve Rajas, and when these heard the noise they sent their police to see if the tree was safe. The police reported that someone or other had cut it down and the Rajas sent their soldiers to arrest the culprits. Lingo said to the soldiers, "We have come to make two lanterns so that there may be light by day and light by night. We have done no evil." So said Lingo. But the soldiers took no heed of what he said and attacked the brothers with their spears and swords. Lingo took the blows in his own body and saved his brothers. Then he himself took his sword and fought and killed all the soldiers. With their blood the tree became red, for its roots drank it. Then the brothers stripped off the bark and cut the wood into two great rings.

They made the lower ring into the Sun and the upper ring into the Moon. The Sun was as big as the kingdoms of the twelve Rajas, but the Moon was smaller. When they were ready, the brothers wondered how to put into them a living soul. Mahapurub[2] had a son. "Only by killing Mahapurub's son and giving his blood to the Sun and Moon to drink will they become alive and be man and woman." So said Lingo. The brothers thought and thought how to catch Mahapurub's son, but at last Lingo said, "I will catch him," and went to the Upper World.

Mahapurub was working in his fields. His wife put the child in a swing and went for water. Lingo stole the child and brought him down to earth. There he sacrificed him and offered his blood to the Sun and Moon. The Sun, who is a man, drank a lot of the blood and that is why he is always red. The Moon, who is a woman, only drank a little and is always pale.

When Mahapurub's wife returned and could not find her son, she ran to tell her husband and they were full of sorrow. But next morning when the Sun rose red into the sky, Mahapurub cried to his wife, "Look, there's your baby in the sky; don't weep, for you will always be able to look at him."

2. Mahapurub is, like Lingo (unrelated to the linga), a tribal culture hero and creator god.

LONG AGO MEN COULD READ THE FUTURE

This story challenges the Upanishadic view that dreams reflect a deeper reality than waking reality (“Dreaming,” p. 111). It also explores the relationship between dreaming and dying, explains why human beings die, and proclaims that the gods' disapproval of interspecies (i.e, intercaste) marriage made them curse humans and dreams. All in a brief paragraph.

From Berma, Bastar State

Long ago men could read the future in their dreams. An owl heard of it and said, “If men can see the future in dreams, they will never die.” The owl waited till the gods were holding a Darbar[1] and then fell with a bang into the midst of them. The gods said, “What is the matter?” The owl replied, “I have had a dream, and in that dream I was marrying a Raja's daughter. We had done eleven rounds of the Lagir;[2] had it been twelve she would have been mine; but I awoke and fell to the ground. Now I must marry this girl. What am I to do?” The gods were concerned and said to one another, “How can a red-eyed bird marry a Raja's daughter?” The owl replied, “But all the world gets what it sees in dreams; how can it be that only my dreams are false?” At that the gods cursed men saying, “From now on, let all dreams be false.”

1. A large court assembly or ceremonial occasion.
2. Perhaps a Gond ritual that is part of a wedding ceremony; more likely, a form of *lagur,* the stick, staff, club, iron bar, or pole that the couple circumambulate in the marriage ritual.

Other Tribal Groups

The following is a small sample of stories from other tribal communities on the porous borders of Hinduism.

BHAGAVAN WANTED TO PISS

This story is peopled by gods with Sanskrit names, including several characters from the *Ramayana* (“Lost Loves . . . in the *Ramayana*,” p. 186). The hollow bamboo filled with piss is a tribal variation on the Sanskrit theme of the hollow reed filled with the elixir of immortality (“In the Under World”). And the idea of the creative eliminations of the deity can be traced back to the Puranas, in which the Creator (Prajapati) eats rice and emits the human race, and emits the anti-gods by breaking wind (*Bhagavata Purana* 2.6.8; *Linga Purana* 1.70.190). The king who cuts off his own limbs is reminiscent of King Shibi (“King Shibi Saves the Dove,” p. 160). But the Gogia Pardhan story is far earthier in its concerns and its language than any of the Puranic or Epic myths; and Sun and Moon have the prominence that they have in many Gond myths but not in Puranic myths.

PRONOUNCING GLOSSARY

Agindeo: *uh´-gin-day´-oh*
Amarpur: *uh´-mar-poor*
Bhagavan: *buh-guh-vahn´*
Gogia Pardhan: *goh´-gee-yuh par-dahn´*

Jagat Raja: *juh´-gut rah´-jah*
Kalipatpar: *kah´-lee-put´-par*
Madodri: *mah´-doh-dree´*
Mahadeo: *muh-hah´-day´-oh*
Maharawan: *muh-hah´-rah´-wun*
Raja: *rah´-jah*
Raja Vishesha: *rah´-jah vih-shay´-shuh*
Rawan: *rah´-wun*

From the Gogia Pardhan, in Jhanki, Mandla District, in the Central Provinces

Bhagavan[1] wanted to piss. There was nowhere for him to do it, for there was danger that he would drown the earth. But when he could wait no longer, he got a great bamboo, cut the top and bottom, hollowed it out and pissed into it. In the Under World there was a lake called Kalipatpar: Bhagavan closed the bamboo and put it there.

In that place, where the bamboo full of Bhagavan's urine was put, Rawan,[2] Maharawan and Madodri were born.

The spangle from Bhagavan's forehead fell into that urine and turned into the Sun and Moon. Before that the only light in the world was that from the sandal[3] on Bhagavan's forehead.

Raja Vishesha lived in Amarpur. In that kingdom nothing ever died. Bhagavan thought, "This man is greater than me." So he sent Agindeo[4] and Mahadeo[5] there to take away the souls. When they reached the place the Raja asked, "What will you eat?" Mahadeo replied, "A measure of raw meat." The Raja thought in his mind, "How can I sin in killing one of my own subjects?" So he cut off his own foot and went to weigh it. It did not come to a full measure, so he cut off his leg and an arm, and gradually his whole body. Mahadeo said, "You are a true Raja: is there any greater than you?" "Yes, Jagat[6] Raja."

Guru Mahadeo returned to Bhagavan and told him what he had seen. Bhagavan set out to visit Jagat Raja, but on the way he met Rawan, Maharawan and Madodri, and Bhagavan, who is Rama, killed them. Then he caught the Sun and Moon and took them into his control.

From that time people in Amarpur[7] began to die and their souls went to Bhagavan. Then Bhagavan married Sun and Moon and blessed them: "Sun, you are master of the day: Moon, you are mistress of the night." Sometimes Sun and Moon have intercourse in the east, sometimes in the west.

1. God.
2. Sanskrit Ravana, the enemy of Rama in the *Ramayana*; Maharawan would be the Great Ravana, and Madodri would be Mandodari, the wife of Ravana.
3. Sandalwood paste, bright and aromatic.
4. Agnideva, the god of fire.
5. Mahadeva, Shiva.
6. The universe.
7. Amarapura, the city of the immortal gods.

WHY MEN AND ANIMALS NO LONGER TALK TOGETHER

The Ahir are a caste of cowherds and milkmen, also known as Guala and Rawat. This story is an example of an idea found throughout the world, the imagination of a happier time when there was peace and conversation between humans and animals as well as between various species of animals; we have seen a Sanskrit version of that myth ("How Men Changed Skins with Animals," p. 100). As usual, human beings destroy that peace. A footnote by Verrier Elwin remarks that rats are still said to understand human speech, which is why, when people in the Punjab used to make rat poison, they said that they were cooking food for the neighbors, because rats knew the word for poison.

PRONOUNCING GLOSSARY

Ahir: *ah-heer´*
Dumketi Kachhar: *doom´-kay-tee kah´-char*
Kawar Rawat: *kah´-war rah´-wut*
Rawat: *rah´-wut*

An Ahir story from Panderwa, Bilaspur District

In the old days all the animals, cows, tigers, dogs, bears, goats, jackals used to graze together and talk with the Rawat who took them to the forest. For at that time men and animals could talk together freely.

On the Dumketi Kachhar hills, Kawar Rawat used to graze his herd of animals and daily he talked and laughed with them. One day when his wife was pregnant he wanted to go home early. He asked the cow, "Is your belly full yet? If it is, we will go home; if not, we will go further in the jungle." The cow said, "No, my belly is not full; I still am hungry." At home the Rawat's wife began to feel her pains and she sent a boy to call her husband.

"Come, your wife is in pain; there will be a child." The Rawat said to the herd, "Come, brothers, let us go home. There will be a child." But they said, "Our bellies are not full. We won't go yet." Kawar Rawat took his stick and beat the cow so hard that still on one side of her body there is a hollow place and only one side is full. To the tigers and bears he said, "Go away into the jungle; I will graze you no more." To all the animals he said, "From today you will be dumb. I don't want to hear you talk again." He drove the bears and tigers into the jungle and took the cows home quickly, and that day there was a child in the house.

THERE WAS NO DEATH

These stories about death were collected from various villages belonging to the Juang tribe, whose women, until the mid-twentieth century, wore clothes made of leaves.

PRONOUNCING GLOSSARY

Jamudeota: *jah´-moo-day´-oh-tuh*
Juang: *joo-ahng´*
Mahapurub: *muh-hah´-poo-roob´*
mahua: *mah´-hoo-uh*
Rawatin: *rah´-wuh-teen´*
Rusain: *roo-sain´*
Rusi: *roo´-see*

From Gonasika, Keonjhar State

There was no death at first. Dharam Deota[1] sent Kalpar Rakas[2] to give death to the world. But after men had died and their bodies were thrown out, they used to get up and walk home. So Kalpar Rakas used to catch the bodies and cut off their feet. They could not walk home and they remained dead.

From Balipal, Keonjhar State

At first men did not die. In those days Rusi and Rusain had many children. Mahapurub[3] thought, "Soon there will be no room in the world. How can so many people live in such a small place?" So he sent Jamudeota[4] to Rusi and Rusain and said, "I am great, I am great, I am great, I am great"—that was all he said; he said nothing more. When Rusi heard it he was angry and said, "No, I am great, for it is I who give birth." Jamudeota said, "Well, if you are great, if you give birth, prove you are greater still by eating your children." Rusi devoured all his children. "Now bring them out again," said Jamudeota. But they were dead, and that is how death came into the world.

From Kirtanpur, Dhenkanal State

In the days before men began to die, there was a Brahmin who lived by begging. One day he got a little rice and mahua[5] and was very pleased. When he got home he thought, "How hungry I am! What shall I cook first?" As he was cooking the mahua, a poisonous centipede came by and asked the Brahmin, "What are you doing?" The Brahmin said, "Why are you wasting my time by talking when you can see that I am dying of hunger?" The centipede said, "What, do you know what dying is?" "No, I have never heard of it. What is it? Teach me, brother, and I will then know how to die." In front of the Brahmin the centipede fell into pieces. The Brahmin stood up and tried to do the same. While he was trying hard to break into little bits, the centipede came alive and bit him so that he died. Since then all men have died.

From Kirtanpur, Dhenkanal State

At first no one died. An old man was counting grains of oil-seed during the night. There was no sleep in those days. The old man used to spend all night counting oil-seeds. He spent all day counting oil-seeds. He even forgot to eat. Then Mahapurub sent a Rawatin[6] to sell curds. The curds had sleep-medicine in them. The old man bought the curds and mixed them with rice. After he had eaten sleep came to him and he died.

From Tambur, Pal Lahara State

An old man and woman had seven sons and one grandson. In those days no one ever died. Mahapurub thought in his mind, "None die, what shall I do?" Now everyone in that family loved the little grandson. "If he was not

1. *Dharma Deva* in Sanskrit, the god of Dharma: Yama, the god of the dead.
2. An ogre (Sanskrit *rakshasa*) named Kalpa, the Eon.
3. Perhaps a form of the Sanskrit *mahapurusha*, meaning "Great Man." A tribal culture hero and creator god.
4. The divinity (*deota*, Sanskrit *devata*) named Jamu (Sanskrit *Yama*), king of the dead.
5. An edible seed.
6. A man of the Ahir caste.

with us, how wretched we would be." But Mahapurub called the mother of his mother and said to her, "The old man and woman have a grandson. Bring him here; I want to play with him." She said, "How can a little child come such a long way?" But she dressed in tattered clothes and leaning on a stick hobbled along to the house and said to one of the sons, "Where has your mother gone? You must certainly give me something." When she saw the grandson, she felt pity on him for his beauty and because they all loved him. "I won't take him," she said, "or they'll die of weeping." She returned and told Mahapurub, "They look on him as their very life; how could I bring him?"

But Mahapurub was angry and drove her away. "You must bring him," he said. This time the grandmother took the form of a black cow and she caught the boy as he was playing and killed him with her horns. They wept and threw the body away. Then the grandmother took her own form again and carried the child to Mahapurub who restored him to life. But on earth the family wept and wept and found no comfort. "I have done a great wrong," thought the old grandmother. She carried the child back to the place where they had thrown him away. In her own form she went to beg at the house. When she saw them weeping, she asked, "What is the matter?" When they told her she said, "Take me to the place and let me see him." They took her to the place and she made the child alive again.

But the boy had been very happy with Mahapurub. He had as much food as he could eat and there were always games to play. He had no desire to stay on earth. Every day he would say, "I must go back to Mahapurub." In the end they had to keep him tied up to stop him going. Then he refused to eat or drink; he only thought of Mahapurub. At last he died and from that day there has been death in the world.

From Korba, Keonjhar State

In the old days men used to die, but they came back to life again. When the people took a man's corpse to bury it, the man would get out of the grave and sit beside it. An old man and woman had no children. When the old man died, the widow could not dig the grave, so she dragged the body to the jungle and threw it away. Mahapurub thought, "It is those who have relatives who bury their dead; others are only thrown away." He came to the Middle World[7] and said to the people, "If you bury the dead they return to life; if you throw them away they become dangerous ghosts and devour you. If you find such a one returning, burn him and he will trouble you no more." The people were very frightened and collected a great deal of wood. When the old man came back in the usual way, they thought he was a ghost. They caught him and took him to the pyre and burnt him. That is why we burn the corpses of the dead for fear they may return to life and trouble us.

7. Our world, below the Upper World where the gods live.

THERE WAS ONCE A GOD CALLED AMRIT

The Kol are a very large tribe, said to be over two million strong; they live mainly in Chota Nagpur, but are widely dispersed throughout Middle India. Amrit ("Immortal") here is a god, also called Amrit Deo, who is sometimes referred to as "she" and who keeps the revivifying elixir in her belly, as a woman would keep a child in her womb. This story justifies subjecting cows to the hard work of plowing, perhaps in response to criticism of this practice by Hindus who advocated more respect for cows.

PRONOUNCING GLOSSARY

Amrit: *ahm´-rit*
Amrit Deo: *ahm´-rit day´-oh*
Bhachka Dano: *bahch´-kuh dah´-noh*
Dano: *dah´-noh*
Kol: *kohl*

From the Kol tribe of Sanhrwachhapar, Mandla District

There was once a god called Amrit in whose belly was the Water of Immortality. Whenever any human child was born, she used to take a little of this water from her belly and give it to drink, whereupon the child would become immortal.

Bhachka Dano had a child born in his house and went to Amrit Deo to get some of the water for it, but the god refused and there was a quarrel. The Dano turned himself into an old cow and fell into a ditch near the house. Presently Amrit Deo came by. "Whose poor old cow is this?" He tried to get it out of the ditch but when he had got it on its feet the cow suddenly turned on him and pierced his belly with its sharp horn. The Water of Immortality poured out and fell to the ground. Another god heard Amrit's cries and came running to help him. When he saw what had happened he said, "Take your belly to a stream and wash it there." He did so and the other god pushed the entrails back inside him and tied up the wound.

Before this people did not eat because of the Water of Immortality in the belly, nor did they excrete, nor did cattle do any work. But now they had to eat and excrete and they began to die. For its share in bringing death to the world the cow was put to the plough and made to work.

DALIT HINDUISM

Contemporary Dalit texts, like Adivasi (tribal) texts, form a kind of internal diaspora. As Kancha Ilaiah remarks ("Hindu Gods and Us," p. 698), Hinduism uses "various images of Gods and Goddesses, some of whom have been co-opted from the social base that it wanted to exploit." Dalit castes exist throughout India, but Maharashtra has always taken the lead in the Dalit movement; the great Marathi poet Tuka was not a Dalit, but he was a Shudra, a man of very low caste (Tukaram, p. 449), and the word "Dalit" comes from Marathi into Hindi. Our selections are from several well-known Dalit writers, whose work is increasingly accessible, in translations from Marathi.

PRONOUNCING GLOSSARY

Angulimal: *ahn-goo´-lih-mahl´*
Arun Kamble: *ah´-roon kahm´-blay*
Atishudra: *uh´-tee-shoo´-druh*
Atman: *aht´-mun*
Baburao Bagul: *bah´-boo-row´ bah´-gool*
Bheema: *bee´-muh*
Bhide Kanya Shala: *bee´-day kun-yah´ shah´-luh*
Bhimrao Ramji Ambedkar: *bim´-row rahm´-jee ahm-bayd´-kar*
Bhonsale: *bohn´-sah´-lay*
Chavadar: *chah´-vuh-dar*
Dakshina: *duk´-shee-nuh*
dhoti: *doh´-tee*
Duryodhana: *door-yoh´-duh-nuh*
Eklavya: *ek´-luv´-yuh*
Eknath: *ek´-naht*
Gayatri: *gah´-yuh-tree´*
Gokhale: *goh-kah´-lay*
Gokhale Guruji: *goh-kah´-lay goo´-roo-jee*
Hatekar: *hah´-tay-kar*
hinsa: *hin´-suh*
Jagjivan Ram: *jug´-jee´-vun rom´*
Jyotiba Phule: *jyoh´-tee-buh foo´-lay*
Kaliyug: *kah´-lee-yoog´*
Kamla Bhasin: *kahm´-lah bah´-sin*
kartumakartumanyathakartum: *kar´-toom-uh´-kur´-toom-un´-yuh-tah´-kar´-toom*
kirtan: *keer´-tan*
Kolte: *kohl´-tay*
Kumud Pawde: *koo´-mood pow´-day*
Kumud Somkuwar: *koo´-mood sohm´-koo-war*
ladoo: *luh´-doo*
Mahad: *muh´-hud*
Mahal: *muh-hahl´*
Mahar: *muh-har´*
Maharashtra: *muh-hah´-rahsh´-truh*
Mahatma Jyotiba Phule: *muh-haht´-muh jyoh´-tee-buh foo´-lay*
Nagpur: *nahg´-poor*
Narayan Surve: *nuh-rah´-yun soor´-vay*
pallav: *puh´-luv*
pandal: *pahn´-dul*
pandit: *pun´-dit*
poha: *poh´-hah*
Pune Brahmin: *poo´-nay brah´-min*
rangoli: *rahn´-goh-lee´*
Sahastrabuddhe: *suh-hus´-truh-boo´-day*
sanyasi: *sun-yah´-see*
Satyagraha: *sut´-yah-gruh´-huh*
Satyakam Jabali: *sut´-yah-kahm´ jah´-buh-lee*
Savitribai Phule: *suh-vih´-tree´-bai´ foo´-lay*
shikakai: *shih´-kuh-kai´*
shirish: *shee´-rish*
Shri Madhukarrao Chaudhary: *shree muh´-doo-kuh-row´ chow´-duh-ree*
Shudra: *shoo´-druh*
Svaha: *suh-vah´-hah´*
Tryambak Sapkale: *tri-yum´-buk sahp´-kah´-lay*

tulsi vrindavan: *tool´-see vrin´-dah´-vun*
Vijaya Dashami: *vih´-jah-yuh dah´-shah-mee*
Yeshwantrao Chavan: *yesh-wahn´-trow chah´-vun*

DR. AMBEDKAR'S SPEECH AT MAHAD

Bhimrao Ramji Ambedkar (1891–1956) was born of a Dalit Mahar family and was educated on scholarships in Baroda, the United States, Britain, and Germany. He agitated for human rights for Dalits and contested Gandhi's right to speak for them. In 1947 he became the law minister of the new government of India. He played a crucial role in the framing of the Indian constitution, outlawing discrimination against Untouchables, as Dalits were then called. Eventually despairing of reforming Hinduism from within, in 1956 he became a Buddhist, together with about 200,000 fellow Dalits, at a ceremony in Nagpur.

On December 25, 1927, a landmark day in the history of the Dalit movement, Dr. Ambedkar led an agitation by the Dalits to draw water from the Chavadar Lake at Mahad, in Maharashtra; for the first time, Dalits drank the water, which higher caste Hindus henceforth avoided. The crowd burned the *Laws of Manu* (p. 202) in protest against Untouchability. The following is the speech that Dr. Ambedkar made on that occasion.

Gentlemen, you have gathered here today in response to the invitation of the Satyagraha[1] Committee. As the Chairman of that Committee, I gratefully welcome you all.

Many of you will remember that on the 19th of last March all of us came to the Chavadar Lake here. The caste Hindus of Mahad had laid no prohibition on us; but they showed they had objections to our going there by the attack they made. The fight brought results that one might have expected. The aggressive caste Hindus were sentenced to four months' rigorous imprisonment, and are now in jail. If we had not been hindered on 19th March, it would have been proved that the caste Hindus acknowledge our right to draw water from the lake, and we should have had no need to begin our present undertaking.

Unfortunately we were thus hindered, and we have been obliged to call this meeting today. This lake at Mahad is public property. The caste Hindus of Mahad are so reasonable that they not only draw water from the lake themselves but freely permit people of any religion to draw water from it, and accordingly people of other religions such as the Islamic do make use of this permission. Nor do the caste Hindus prevent members of species considered lower than the human, such as birds and beasts, from drinking at the lake. Moreover, they freely permit beasts kept by untouchables to drink at the lake.

TRANSLATED BY Rameshchandra Sirkar.

1. "Holding Fast onto Truth" (Sanskrit); nonviolent resistance. The Satyagraha Committee was the committee that Gandhi organized in South Africa to protest discrimination against Indians; it was later taken up by other movements such as Ambedkar's.

Caste Hindus are the very founts of compassion. They practise no *hinsa*[2] and harass no one. They are not of the class of miserly and selfish folk who would grudge even a crow some grains of the food they are eating. The proliferation of *sanyasis*[3] and mendicants is a living testimony to their charitable temperament. They regard altruism as religious merit and injury to another as a sin.

Even further, they have imbibed the principle that injury done by another must not be repaid but patiently endured, and so, they not only treat the harmless cow with kindness, but spare harmful creatures such as snakes. That one *Atman* or Spiritual Self dwells in all creatures has become a settled principle of their conduct. Such are the caste Hindus who forbid some human beings of their own religion to draw water from the same Chavadar Lake! One cannot help asking the question, why do they forbid us alone?

It is essential that all should understand thoroughly the answer to this question. Unless you do, I feel, you will not grasp completely the importance of today's meeting. The Hindus are divided, according to sacred tradition, into four castes; but according to custom, into five: Brahmins, Kshatriyas, Vaishyas, Shudras and Atishudras.[4] The caste system is the first of the governing rules of the Hindu religion. The second is that the castes are of unequal rank. They are ordered in a descending series of each meaner than the one before.

Not only are their ranks permanently fixed by the rule, but each is assigned boundaries it must not transgress, so that each one may at once be recognized as belonging to its particular rank. There is a general belief that the prohibitions in the Hindu religion against intermarriage, interdining, interdrinking and social intercourse are bounds set to degrees of association with one another. But this is an incomplete idea. These prohibitions are indeed limits to degrees of association; but they have been set to show people of unequal rank what the rank of each is. That is, these bounds are symbols of inequality.

Just as the crown on a man's head shows he is a king, and the bow in his hand shows him to be a Kshatriya, the class to which none of the prohibitions applies is considered the highest of all and the one to which they all apply is reckoned the lowest in rank. The strenuous efforts made to maintain the prohibitions are for the reason that, if they are relaxed, the inequality settled by religion will break down and equality will take its place.

The caste Hindus of Mahad prevent the untouchables from drinking the water of the Chavadar Lake not because they suppose that the touch of the untouchables will pollute the water or that it will evaporate and vanish. Their reason for preventing the untouchables from drinking it is that they do not wish to acknowledge by such a permission that castes declared inferior by sacred tradition are in fact their equals.

Gentlemen! you will understand from this the significance of the struggle we have begun. Do not let yourselves suppose that the Satyagraha Committee has invited you to Mahad merely to drink the water of the Chavadar Lake of Mahad.

It is not as if drinking the water of the Chavadar Lake will make us immortal. We have survived well enough all these days without drinking it. We are not going to the Chavadar Lake merely to drink its water. We are going to the

2. Injury or violence, the opposite of *ahimsa*, noninjury or nonviolence.
3. Renouncers.
4. Castes below the Shudras, the lowest of the four classes ("Hymn of the Primeval Man," p. 82).

Lake to assert that we too are human beings like others. It must be clear that this meeting has been called to set up the norm of equality.

I am certain that no one who thinks of this meeting in this light will doubt that it is unprecedented. I feel that no parallel to it can be found in the history of India. If we seek for another meeting in the past to equal this, we shall have to go to the history of France on the continent of Europe. A hundred and thirty-eight years ago, on 24 January 1789, King Louis XVI had convened, by royal command, an assembly of deputies to represent the people of the kingdom. This French National Assembly has been much vilified by historians. The Assembly sent the King and the Queen of France to the guillotine; persecuted and massacred the aristocrats; and drove their survivors into exile. It confiscated the estates of the rich and plunged Europe into war for fifteen years. Such are the accusations levelled against the Assembly by the historians. In my view, the criticism is misplaced; further, the historians of this school have not understood the gist of the achievement of the French National Assembly. That achievement served the welfare not only of France but of the entire European continent. If European nations enjoy peace and prosperity today, it is for one reason: the revolutionary French National Assembly convened in 1789 set new principles for the organization of society before the disorganized and decadent French nation of its time, and the same principles have been accepted and followed by Europe.

To appreciate the importance of the French National Assembly and the greatness of its principles, we must keep in mind the state of French society at the time. You are all aware that our Hindu society is based on the system of castes. A rather similar system of classes existed in the France of 1789: the difference was that it was a society of three castes. Like the Hindu society, the French had a class of Brahmins and another of Kshatriyas. But instead of three different castes of Vaishya, Shudra and Atishudra, there was one class that comprehended these. This is a minor difference. The important thing is that the caste or class system was similar. The similarity to be noted is not only in the differentiation between classes: the inequality of our caste system was also to be found in the French social system. The nature of the inequality in the French society was different: it was economic in nature. It was, however, equally intense. The thing to bear in mind is there is a great similarity between the French National Assembly that met on 5 May 1789 at Versailles and our meeting today. The similarity is not only in the circumstances in which the two meetings took place but also in their ideals.

That Assembly of the French people was convened to reorganize French society. Our meeting today too has been convened to reorganize Hindu society. Hence, before discussing on what principles our society should be reorganized, we should all pay heed to the principles on which the French Assembly relied and the policy it adopted. The scope of the French Assembly was far wider than that of our present meeting. It had to carry out the threefold organization of the French political, social and religious systems. We must confine ourselves to how social and religious reorganization can be brought about. Since we are not, for the present, concerned with political reorganization, let us see what the French Assembly did in the matter of the religious and social reorganization of their nation. The policy adopted by the French National Assembly in this area can be seen plainly by anyone from three important proclamations issued by that Assembly. The first was issued on 17 June 1789. This was a proclamation about the class systems in France.

As said before, French society was divided into three classes. The proclamation abolished the three classes and blended them into one. Further, it abolished the seats reserved separately for the three classes (or estates) in the political assembly. The second proclamation was about the priests. By ancient custom, to appoint or remove these priests was outside the power of the nation, that being the monopoly of a foreign religious potentate, the Pope. Anyone appointed by the Pope was a priest, whether or not he was fit to be one in the eyes of those to whom he was to preach. The proclamation abolished the autonomy of the religious orders and assigned to the French nation the authority to decide who might follow this vocation, who was fit for it and who was not, whether he was to be paid for preaching or not, and so on. The third proclamation was not about the political, economic or religious systems. It was of a general nature and laid down the principles on which all social arrangements ought to rest. From that point of view, the third proclamation is the most important of the three; it might be called the king of these proclamations. It is renowned the world over as the declaration of human birthrights. It is not only unprecedented in the history of France; more than that, it is unique in the history of civilized nations. For every European nation has followed the French Assembly in giving it a place in its own constitution. So one may say that it brought about a revolution not only in France but the whole world. This proclamation has seventeen clauses, of which the following are important:

1) All human beings are equal by birth; and they shall remain equal till death. They may be distinguished in status only in the public interest. Otherwise, their equal status must be maintained.

2) The ultimate object of politics is to maintain these human birthrights.

3) The entire nation is the mother-source of sovereignty. The rights of any individual, group or special class, unless they are given by the nation, cannot be acknowledged as valid on any other ground, be it political or religious.

4) Any person is free to act according to his birthright. Any limit placed upon this freedom must be only to the extent necessary to permit other persons to enjoy their birthrights. Such limits must be laid down by law: they cannot be set on the grounds of the religion or on any other basis than the law of the land.

5) The law will forbid only such actions as are injurious to society. All must be free to do what has not been forbidden by law. Nor can anyone be compelled to do what the law has not laid down as a duty.

6) The law is not in the nature of bounds set by any particular class. The right to decide what the law shall be rests with the people or their representatives. Whether such a law is protective or punitive, it must be the same for all. Since justice requires that all social arrangements be based on the equality of all, all individuals are equally eligible for any kind of honor, power and profession. Any distinction in such matters must be owing to differences of individual merit; it must not be based on birth.

I feel our meeting today should keep the image of this French National Assembly before the mind. The road it marked out for the development of the French nation, the road that all progressed nations have followed, ought to be the road adopted for the development of Hindu society by this meeting. We need to pull away the nails which hold the framework of caste-bound Hindu society together, such as those of the prohibition of intermarriage down to the prohibition of social intercourse so that Hindu society becomes all of one caste. Otherwise untouchability cannot be removed nor can equality be established.

Some of you may feel that since we are untouchables, it is enough if we are set free from the prohibitions of interdrinking and social intercourse. That we need not concern ourselves with the caste system; how does it matter if it remains? In my opinion this is a total error. If we leave the caste system alone and adopt only the removal of untouchability as our policy, people will say that we have chosen a low aim. To raise men, aspiration is needed as much as outward efforts. Indeed it is to be doubted whether efforts are possible without aspiration. Hence, if a great effort is to be made, a great aspiration must be nursed. In adopting an aspiration one need not be abashed or deterred by doubts about one's power to satisfy it. One should be ashamed only of mean aspirations; not of failure that may result because one's aspiration is high. If untouchability alone is removed, we may change from Atishudras to Shudras; but can we say that this radically removes untouchability? If such puny reforms as the removal of restrictions on social intercourse etc., were enough for the eradication of untouchability, I would not have suggested that the caste system itself must go. Gentlemen! you all know that if a snake is to be killed it is not enough to strike at its tail—its head must be crushed. If any harm is to be removed, one must seek out its root and strike at it. An attack must be based on the knowledge of the enemy's vital weakness. Duryodhana was killed because Bheema[5] struck at his thigh with his mace. If the mace had hit Duryodhana's head he would not have died; for his thigh was his vulnerable spot. One finds many instances of a physician's efforts to remove a malady proving fruitless because he has not perceived fully what will get rid of the disease; similar instances of failure to root out a social disease because it is not fully diagnosed are rarely recorded in history; and so one does not often become aware of them. But let me acquaint you with one such instance that I have come across in my reading. In the ancient European nation of Rome, the patricians were considered upper class, and the plebians, lower class. All power was in the hands of the patricians, and they used it to ill-treat the plebians. To free themselves from this harassment, the plebians, on the strength of their unity, insisted that laws should be written down for the facilitation of justice and for the information of all. Their patrician opponents agreed to this; and a charter of twelve laws was written down. But this did not rid the oppressed plebians of their woes. For the officers who enforced the laws were all of the patrician class; moreover the chief officer, called the tribune, was also a patrician. Hence, though the laws were uniform, there was partiality in their enforcement. The plebians then demanded that instead of the administration being in the hands of one tribune there should be two tribunes, of whom one should be elected by the plebians and the other by the patricians. The patricians yielded to this too, and the plebians rejoiced, supposing they would now be free of their miseries. But their rejoicing was short-lived. The Roman people had a tradition that nothing was to be done without the favourable verdict of the oracle at Delphi. Accordingly, even the election of a duly elected tribune—if the oracle did not approve of him—had to be treated as annulled, and another had to be elected, of whom the oracle

5. Bhima, one of the Pandava brothers (*Mahabharata*, p. 130), brought down his enemy Duryodhana by striking him with a mace on his thigh, a clear violation of the ancient Indian code of war, what we would call hitting below the belt.

approved. The priest who put the question to the oracle was required, by sacred religious custom, to be one born of parents married in the mode the Romans called *conferatio*; and this mode of marriage prevailed only among the patricians; so that the priest of Delphi was always a patrician.

The wily priest always saw to it that if the plebians elected a man really devoted to their cause, the oracle went against him. Only if the man elected by the plebians to the position of tribune was amenable to the patricians, would the oracle favour him and give him the opportunity of actually assuming office. What did the plebians gain by their right to elect a tribune? The answer must be, nothing in reality. Their efforts proved meaningless because they did not trace the malady to its source. If they had, they would, at the same time that they demanded a tribune of their election, have also settled the question of who should be the priest at Delphi. The disease could not be eradicated by demanding a tribune; it needed control of the priestly office; which the plebians failed to perceive. We too, while we seek a way to remove untouchability, must inquire closely into what will eradicate the disease; otherwise we too may miss our aim. Do not be foolish enough to believe that removal of the restrictions on social intercourse or interdrinking will remove untouchability.

Remember that if the prohibitions on social intercourse and interdrinking go, the roots of untouchability are not removed. Release from these two restrictions will, at the most, remove untouchability as it appears outside the home; but it will leave untouchability in the home untouched. If we want to remove untouchability in the home as well as outside, we must break down the prohibition against intermarriage. Nothing else will serve. From another point of view, we see that breaking down the bar against intermarriage is the way to establish real equality. Anyone must confess that when the root division is dissolved, incidental points of separateness will disappear by themselves. The interdictions on interdining, interdrinking and social intercourse have all sprung from the one interdiction against intermarriage. Remove the last and no special efforts are needed to remove the rest. They will disappear of their own accord. In my view the removal of untouchability consists in breaking down the ban on intermarriage and doing so will establish real equality. If we wish to root out untouchability, we must recognize that the root of untouchability is in the ban on intermarriage. Even if our attack today is on the ban against interdrinking, we must press it home against the ban on intermarriage; otherwise untouchability cannot be removed by the roots. Who can accomplish this task? It is no secret that the Brahmin class cannot do it.

While the caste system lasts, the Brahmin caste has its supremacy. No one, of his own will, surrenders power which is in his hands. The Brahmins have exercised their sovereignty over all other castes for centuries. It is not likely that they will be willing to give it up and treat the rest as equals. The Brahmins do not have the patriotism of the Samurais of Japan. It is useless to hope that they will sacrifice their privileges as the Samurai class did, for the sake of national unity based on a new equality. Nor does it appear likely that the task will be carried out by other caste Hindus. These others, such as the class comprising the Marathas and other similar castes, are a class between the privileged and those without any rights.

A privileged class, at the cost of a little self-sacrifice, can show some generosity. A class without any privileges has ideals and aspirations; for, at least as a matter of self-interest, it wishes to bring about a social reform. As a result it develops an attachment to principles rather than to self-interest. The class of caste Hindus other than Brahmins lies in between: it cannot practise the generosity possible to the class above and it does not develop the attachment to principles that develops in the class below. This is why this class is seen to be concerned not so much about attaining equality with the Brahmins as about maintaining its status above the untouchables.

For the purposes of the social reform required, the class of caste Hindus other than Brahmins is feeble. If we are to await its help, we should fall into the difficulties that the farmer faced, who depended on his neighbour's help for his harvesting, as in the story of the mother lark and her chicks found in many textbooks.

The task of removing untouchability and establishing equality that we have undertaken, we must carry out ourselves. Others will not do it. Our life will gain its true meaning if we consider that we are born to carry out this task and set to work in earnest. Let us receive this merit which is awaiting us.

This is a struggle in order to raise ourselves; hence we are bound to undertake it, so as to remove the obstacles to our progress. We all know how at every turn, untouchability muddies and soils our whole existence. We know that at one time our people were recruited in large numbers into the troops. It was a kind of occupation socially assigned to us and few of us needed to be anxious about earning our bread. Other classes of our level have found their way into the troops, the police, the courts and the offices, to earn their bread. But in the same areas of employment you will no longer find the untouchables.

It is not that the law debars us from these jobs. Everything is permissible as far the law is concerned. But the Government finds itself powerless because other Hindus consider us untouchables and look down upon us, and it acquiesces in our being kept out of Government jobs. Nor can we take up any decent trade. It is true, partly, that we lack money to start business, but the real difficulty is that people regard us as untouchables and no one will accept goods from our hands.

To sum up, untouchability is not a simple matter; it is the mother of all our poverty and lowliness and it has brought us to the abject state we are in today. If we want to raise ourselves out of it, we must undertake this task. We cannot be saved in any other way. It is a task not for our benefit alone; it is also for the benefit of the nation.

Hindu society must sink unless the untouchability that has become a part of the four-castes system is eradicated. Among the resources that any society needs in the struggle for life, a great resource is the moral order of that society. And everyone must admit that a society in which the existing moral order upholds things that disrupt the society and condemns those that would unite the members of the society, must find itself defeated in any struggle for life with other societies. A society which has the opposite moral order, one in which things that unite are considered laudable and things that divide are condemned, is sure to succeed in any such struggle.

This principle must be applied to Hindu society. Is it any wonder that it meets defeat at every turn when it upholds a social order that fragments its members, though it is plain to anyone who sees it that the four-castes system is such a divisive force and that a single caste for all, would unite society? If we wish to escape these disastrous conditions, we must break down the framework of the four-castes system and replace it by a single caste system.

Even this will not be enough. The inequality inherent in the four-castes system must be rooted out. Many people mock at the principles of equality. Naturally, no man is another's equal. One has an impressive physique; another is slow-witted. The mockers think that, in view of these inequalities that men are born with, the egalitarians are absurd in telling us to regard them as equals. One is forced to say that these mockers have not understood fully the principle of equality.

If the principle of equality means that privilege should depend, not on birth, wealth, or anything else, but solely on the merits of each man, then how can it be demanded that a man without merit, and who is dirty and vicious, should be treated on a level with a man who has merit and is clean and virtuous? Such is a counter-question sometimes posed. It is essential to define equality as giving equal privileges to men of equal merit.

But before people have had an opportunity to develop their inherent qualities and to merit privileges, it is just to treat them all equally. In sociology, the social order is itself the most important factor in the full development of qualities that any person may possess at birth. If slaves are constantly treated unequally, they will develop no qualities other than those appropriate to slaves, and they will never become fit for any higher status. If the clean man always repulses the unclean man and refuses to have anything to do with him, the unclean man will never develop the aspiration to become clean. If the criminal or immoral castes are given no refuge by the virtuous castes, the criminal castes will never learn virtue.

The examples given above show that, although an equal treatment may not create good qualities in one who does not have them at all, even such qualities where they exist need equal treatment for their development; also, developed good qualities are wasted and frustrated without equal treatment.

On the one hand, the inequality in Hindu society stunts the progress of individuals and in consequence stunts society. On the other hand, the same inequality prevents society from bringing into use powers stored in individuals. In both ways, this inequality is weakening Hindu society, which is in disarray because of the four-castes system.

Hence, if Hindu society is to be strengthened, we must uproot the four-castes system and untouchability, and set the society on the foundations of the two principles of one caste only and of equality. The way to abolish untouchability is not any other than the way to invigorate Hindu society. Therefore I say that our work is beyond doubt as much for the benefit of the nation as it is in our own interest.

Our work has been begun to bring about a real social revolution. Let no one deceive himself by supposing that it is a diversion to quieten minds entranced with sweet words. The work is sustained by strong feeling, which is the power that drives the movement. No one can now arrest it. I pray to God that the social revolution which begins here today may fulfil itself by peaceful means.

None can doubt that the responsibility of letting the revolution take place peacefully rests more heavily on our opponents than on us. Whether this social revolution will work peacefully or violently will depend wholly on the conduct of the caste Hindus. People who blame the French National Assembly of 1789 for atrocities forget one thing. That is, if the rulers of France had not been treacherous to the Assembly, if the upper classes had not resisted it, had not committed the crime of trying to suppress it with foreign help, it would have had no need to use violence in the work of the revolution and the whole social transformation would have been accomplished peacefully.

We say to our opponents too: please do not oppose us. Put away the orthodox scriptures. Follow justice. And we assure you that we shall carry out our program peacefully.

WHICH LANGUAGE SHOULD I SPEAK?

Arun Kamble (1953–2009) was a Dalit activist, one of the founders of the revolutionary Dalit Panther movement. He wrote this poem about the tension between Sanskrit and the vernaculars, a tension symbolic of the whole spectrum of contrasts between people who ate trotters (pigs' feet, forbidden to both Hindus and Muslims) and those who ate ghee (clarified butter, essential to both Vedic ritual and high-caste Hindu cooking).

Chewing trotters in the badlands
my grandpa,
the permanent resident of my body,
the household of tradition heaped on his back,
hollers at me,
'You whore-son, talk like we do.
Talk, I tell you!'

Picking through the Vedas
his top-knot well-oiled with ghee,
my Brahmin teacher tells me,
'You idiot, use the language correctly!'
Now I ask you,
Which language should I speak?

TRANSLATED BY Priya Adarkar.

YOU WHO HAVE MADE THE MISTAKE

A poem by Baburao Bagul (1930–2008), a pioneer of Dalit literature in Marathi, calling on his fellow Dalits to take violent action or to leave India.

Those who leave for foreign lands,
embrace other tongues, dress in alien garb
and forget this country

TRANSLATED BY Vilas Sarang.

—them I salute.
And those who don't forget,
and don't change even after being beaten up for centuries
—such hypocrites I ask:
What will you say if someone asked you—
What is untouchability?
Is it eternal like God?
What's an untouchable like? What does he look like?
Does he look like the very image of leprosy?
Or like the prophet's enemy?
Does he look like a heretic, a sinner, a profligate, or an atheist?
Tell me,
What will your answer be?
Will you reply without hesitation:
'Untouchable—that's me?'
That's why I say—
You who have made the mistake of being born in this country
must now rectify it: either leave the country,
or make war!

THE STORY OF 'MY SANSKRIT'

Kumud Pawde was born in 1938 and became an activist in the Dalit movement in Vidarbha as well as a revered university professor. Her essay takes up the issue of language that is also addressed by Arun Kamble's poem "Which Language Should I Speak?" As a woman and a Dalit, Pawde addresses both prejudices at once.

A lot of things are often said about me to my face. I've grown used to listening to them quietly; it's become a habit. What I have to listen to is praise. Actually, I don't at all like listening to praise. You may say that this itself is a form of self-indulgence. But that isn't so. I mean it sincerely. When I hear myself praised, it's like being stung by a lot of gadflies. As a result, I look askance at the person praising me. This expression must look like annoyance at being praised, for many misunderstandings have arisen about me in this connection. But it can't be helped. My acquaintances get angry with me because I am unable to accept compliments gracefully. I appear ill-mannered to them, because there isn't in me the courtesy they are expecting.

Now if you want to know why I am praised—well, it's for my knowledge of Sanskrit, my ability to learn it and to teach it. Doesn't anyone ever learn Sanskrit? That's not the point. The point is that Sanskrit and the social group I come from, don't go together in the Indian mind. Against the background of my caste, the Sanskrit I have learned appears shockingly strange.

TRANSLATED BY Priya Adarkar.

That a woman from a caste that is the lowest of the low should learn Sanskrit, and not only that, also teach it—is a dreadful anomaly to a traditional mind. And an individual in whose personality these anomalies are accumulated becomes an object of attraction—an attraction blended of mixed acceptance and rejection. The attraction based on acceptance comes from my caste-fellows, in the admiration of whose glance is pride in an impossible achievement. That which for so many centuries was not to be touched by us, is now within our grasp. That which remained encased in the shell of difficulty, is now accessible. Seeing this knowledge hidden in the esoteric inner sanctum come within the embrace, not just of any person, but one whom religion has considered to be vermin—that is their victory.

The other attraction—based on rejection—is devastating. It pricks holes in one's mind—turning a sensitive heart into a sieve. Words of praise of this kind, for someone who is aware, are like hot spears. It is fulsome praise. Words that come out from lips' edge as filthy as betel-stained spit. Each word gleaming smooth as cream. Made up of the fragility of a honey-filled *shirish*-blossom. Polished as marble. The sensation is that of walking on a soft velvety carpet—but being burnt by the hot embers hidden in someone's breast, and feeling the scorching pain in one's soul. The one who's speaking thinks the listener can't understand—for surely a low-caste person hasn't the ability to comprehend. But some people intend to be understood, so that I'll be crushed by the words. 'Well, isn't that amazing! So you're teaching Sanskrit at the Government College, are you? That's very gratifying, I must say.' The words are quite ordinary; their literal meaning is straight-forward. But the meaning conveyed by the tone in which they are said torments me in many different ways! 'In what former life have I committed a sin that I should have to learn Sanskrit even from you?' 'All our sacred scriptures have been polluted.' Some despair is also conveyed by their facial expressions. 'It's all over! *Kaliyug*[1] has dawned. After all, they're the government's favourite sons-in-law![2] We have to accept it all.'

There are some other people I know, who have a genuine regard for me. They are honestly amazed by how I talk, by my clean, clear pronunciation. They speak with affectionate admiration about my mode of living. The food I cook is equated with ambrosia. They detect a Brahminical standard of culture in my every thought and action—enough to surprise them. They constantly try to reconcile the contradiction. It's my good luck that I'm not always being asked to account for my antecedents, like Satyakam Jabali.[3] The main point is that they are trying to understand my evident good breeding in the context of my caste, and that is what makes everything so novel for them.

The result is that although I try to forget my caste, it is impossible to forget. And then I remember an expression I heard somewhere: 'What comes by birth, but can't be cast off by dying—that is caste.'

Beyond the accepters and the rejecters lies yet another group. In wholeheartedly welcoming the admiration of this group, every corner of my

1. The last of the four ages, the present age of degeneration ("The Four Ages," p. 228).
2. The Mandal Commission reserved places for Dalits in government and state schools ("Hindu Gods and Us," p. 698).
3. The *Chandogya Upanishad* (4.4) tells the story of Satyakama, whose mother, Jabala, did not know which of the several men she had slept with was Satyakama's father; and so he called himself Jabali after his mother, and still the Brahmins accepted him as a student.

being is filled with pleasure. This group consists of my students. Far removed from hostile feelings. Without even an iota of caste consciousness. Away from the prejudices of their elders. Pure, innocent admiration, prompted by the boundless respect they feel, fills their eyes. Actually these girls have reached the age of understanding. The opinions they hear around them should by rights have made an impression on their mind. But these precious girls are full to the brim with the ability to discriminate impartially. And they keep their admiration within the limits of their gaze; they do not allow it to reach their lips. And that's why I yearn for that admiration. The occasional forward girl who has suppressed her timidity makes bold to express her feelings. 'Madam, I wish your lesson would never end!' And I answer her woodenly: 'But the college doesn't feel that way.' She feels snubbed, but I don't wish to encourage her admiration, in case it becomes a habit.

If the admiration had stayed limited to this individual level, I would tolerate it, but it goes beyond the prescribed boundaries. In other words, it starts to be blazoned even at the official level. As usual they start beating the drum of my caste, and tunes of praise of my knowledge of Sanskrit begin to mingle with the drumbeat. On the Vijaya Dashami[4] day of 1971, the Maharashtra State Government arranged, at Nagpur, a felicitation meeting to honor scholars of the Vedas. According to the wishes of the Honorable ex-Minister of Education, Shri Madhukarrao Chaudhary, I was to introduce these honored scholars. Of course the inspiration was that of Dr Kolte. The introduction was to be made in Sanskrit. 'In the times of the Aryans it was noted down, and moreover impressed on the minds of the common Indian people, from the Himalayas to the tip of the peninsula, that my ancestors should consider themselves guilty of a crime if they even heard the sound of this language. And that is the language in which I have to speak.' My God! How I was I going to manage? My heart began to beat rapidly. My mind was dark with anxiety, and I was drowned in feelings of inferiority. A conflict of emotions—and once again a confrontation with public praise. 'Whereas our traditional books have forbidden the study of Sanskrit by women and Shudras, a woman from those very Shudras, from the lowest caste among them, will today, in Sanskrit, introduce these scholars. This is the beginning of a progressive way of thinking in independent India.' A thunder of applause. I look towards the sound of the applause. Most of the people here are from the government offices. Looking at them through an artist's eyes, I see what looks like a wild disco-dance of different emotions. The frustration of the defeated, the fury of the traditionalists, the respect of some acquaintances, the hostility and disgust of others, are obvious to my experienced eye. Some gazes ask me, 'Why did you need to make the introductions in this manner? To humiliate us?'

In response to these hissings of wounded pride, I experience a mixture of emotions. Seeing this hostility and disgust, I slip into the past. This disgust is extremely familiar to me. In fact, that is what I have grown accustomed to, ever since I was old enough to understand. Actually, I shouldn't have any feelings about this disgust, and if I do have any feelings at all, they should be of gratitude. For it was this disgust that inclined me towards Sanskrit. It so

4. "The Victory of the Tenth Day," also called Dasara, a festival for the goddess Durga celebrated throughout India on the tenth day of the waxing fortnight in September or October.

happened that the ghetto in which there stood my place of birth, the house where I was welcome, was encircled on all sides by the houses of caste Hindus. The people in our ghetto referred to them as the Splendid People. A small girl like me, seven or eight years old, could not understand why they called them 'Splendid.' And even as today's mature female with learning from innumerable books, I still cannot understand it. That is, I have understood the literal meaning of the word 'splendid.' But not why it should be applied to them, or whether they deserve to have it applied. The girls who studied along with me were Brahmins or from other higher castes. I had to pass their houses. I paused, waiting casually for their company. Right in front of me, the mothers would warn their daughters, 'Be careful! Don't touch her. Stay away from her. And don't play with her. Or I won't let you into the house again.' Those so-called educated, civilized mothers were probably unconscious of the effect of this on my young mind. It wasn't as if I could not understand them.

Every day, I bathed myself clean with Pears soap. My mother rubbed Kaminia oil on my hair, and plaited it neatly. My clothes were well-washed and sparkling clean. The girls of my own caste liked to play with me because it enabled them to smell some fragrance. For my father himself was fond of toiletries. So there was always a variety of oils, soaps and perfumes in the house. The other girls in my class (except for those who lived near my ghetto) also liked to sit next to me. So why should these women have talked like that?

What's more, if one were to compare houses, our house was cleaner than theirs. My mother daily smeared the floor with fresh cowdung. The white-powder borders were delicately drawn. The courtyard was well-sprinkled, and decorated with *rangoli*[5] designs. Almost every fortnight, on the occasion of a festival, the house was whitewashed from top to bottom. Every scrap of cloth was boiled in a solution of soda bicarb before it was washed. The metal vessels were scrubbed to gleaming. On the other hand, one could see water stains and a greasy film on even the drinking-vessels those girls had. In fact, it was I who didn't like to sit next to those girls. For, from my childhood, my sense-organs had been sharp and vigorous. My sense of smell, in particular, had sharpened beyond limit. Though, of course, the nose that conveyed it was broad and misshapen. The sour smell, like buttermilk, that rose from the bodies of those girls! I couldn't bear the smell of *shikakai*[6] mixed with the smell of their hair. Their bad breath, too, was unbearable. And, in spite of all this, *they* found *me* disgusting? So, even at that young age, this emotion of disgust taught me to think. It inspired me to be introspective. At an age which was meant for playing and skipping around, these thoughts would rouse me to fury.

One event outraged my self-respect. There was to be a thread-ceremony[7] for the brother of one of my classmates. I had not actually been invited but my restless curiosity would not let me sit quiet. I stood outside the *pandal*[8] looking in at the ceremony going on inside. The sacrificial fire was lit; the air all around was filled with the smoke and fragrance of incense and the

5. A form of sand-painting on the ground.
6. A fragrant oil used on the hair.
7. A ceremony of confirmation, like a Bar Mitzvah.
8. A temporary platform and enclosure put up to worship the goddess Durga.

grain burnt-offering. The reverberations of the Vedic chants threatened to burst through the cloth walls of the *pandal*. I was lost in watching the head-movements that accompanied the chant of 'Svaha!'[9] each time a libation was poured. All this was extremely new, unknown, never seen before. I was totally engrossed, at one with the chants and the incense.

My concentration was suddenly broken. One voice: 'Hey, girl! What are you staring at? Can you make head or tail of it? Here, take a *ladoo*[1]—and be off!' A decked-up woman past her prime, dripping with gold and pearls, stood in front of me, adjusting the *pallav*[2] of her heavily-brocaded sari. Her nose was wrinkled in disgust, like a shrivelled fig. 'What do you take me for—a beggar? Giving me a *ladoo!* Can you see injuries on anyone just because I watched them?' I retorted, and briskly walked away.

Words followed me: 'These Mahars[3] have really got above themselves.' The intonation was the typical superior nasal tone of the Pune Brahmin.[4]

My young mind thought, 'Why was I so wrapped up in watching? What had that ceremony to do with me? And why should that woman behave so bitchily with me?' There was definitely some intimate connection between me and those Vedic mantras.[5] Otherwise why should that woman have noticed my innocent absorption? Why should she have taunted me disgustedly? She must have been unwilling to let those chants enter my ears. I used to ask my father, 'What language are the Vedic mantras composed in?' He used to say, 'They're in Sanskrit, my girl.' 'Is Sanskrit very difficult? Can't we learn it?' My father used to answer, 'Why shouldn't we? After all, we're independent now. Those days are gone. Learn Sanskrit. Don't I too know the Gayatri mantra?'[6] And he used to say 'Om' and begin to recite the Gayatri mantra. In simple delight, I used to tell my neighbors, 'I'm going to learn Sanskrit.' The educated people next door used to poke fun at me. 'Is Sanskrit such an easy language? It's very difficult. Did our forefathers ever learn it?' Hearing this, I would be discouraged. Seeing my crestfallen face, my father would start cursing those people, sometimes obscenely, sometimes more elegantly. He used to encourage me, and the encouragement would make me glow with confidence once again.

After I entered High School, I took Sanskrit as an elective subject in class nine. The school where I went supported Brahminical prejudices. All sorts of indirect efforts were systematically made to prevent me from learning Sanskrit. 'You won't be able to manage. There will be no one at home to help you. Sanskrit is very difficult,' etc., etc. But I was as firm as a rock. Seeing that no form of persuasion had any effect on me, the persuaders stopped persuading. But how to remove the prejudice in their minds? I did not want to pay heed to every single opinion. I just wanted to keep my teacher, Hatekar, happy. He had been full of praise of me since I was in class six. 'How can this little slip of a girl give answers so fast in every subject?' I asked him, 'Sir, I should take Sanskrit, shouldn't I?' 'Do take it. But you've taken all the Arts subjects, though you're good at maths. Take science and maths, along with Sanskrit.' 'But sir, I don't enjoy maths.' 'But you can become a

9. The word spoken by the Vedic priest as he throws the butter into the fire and it blazes up ("Prajapati Creates Fire," p. 94).
1. A sweet made of flour, sugar, and other ingredients, formed into balls (also spelled "laddu").
2. The loose end of a woman's sari.
3. A large Dalit caste in Maharashtra who are said to have been warriors and to have given *Maharashtra* its name.
4. Pune is a famous center for Sanskrit learning.
5. Vedic prayers.
6. The most frequently recited Vedic prayer (*Rig Veda*, p. 79).

doctor, can't you?' 'I don't want to be a doctor. I can't bear suffering.' He laughed and said, 'On the contrary, it is precisely those who can't bear suffering, who are fit to become doctors. Won't you be able to help the afflicted? That's what's needed among your people. But it's your decision.'

With great eagerness and interest, I began my study of Sanskrit. As I learnt the first-declension masculine form of the word 'deva',[7] I picked up the rhythm of the chant. I must make special mention of the person who helped me to learn by rote the first lesson about aspirates—my teacher Gokhale. If I omit to do so, I shall feel a twinge of disloyalty in every drop of my blood. Gokhale Guruji. Dhoti, long-sleeved shirt, black cap, a sandalwood-paste mark on his forehead. The typical robust and clear pronunciation of the Vedic school. And an incredible concern for getting his students to learn Sanskrit. At first I was afraid. But this proved groundless. What actually happened was the very opposite of what I had expected.

I had been sent by the Bhide Kanya Shala[8] to take part in some essay competition or the other. The center for the competition was the Bhonsale Vedic School. No part of the Mahal area was familiar to me. I timidly explained my difficulty to Gokhale Guruji. He said, 'Why don't you come to my house? [He never addressed us in the second person singular; it was always a respectful plural.] I'll take you along.' And he gave me his address. I reached the address asking for directions repeatedly in the lanes and alleys of the Mahal area. My teacher's house was in fact a sprawling mansion. A huge, well-swept courtyard with a *tulsi vrindavan*[9] and a well, and a small Shiva temple within it. All looked as antique as a well-preserved old Benares brocade. I hesitantly entered. 'Welcome,' he greeted me in friendly tones. Two boys, aged about ten or eleven years old, came out to see who had arrived. From their general appearance—the dhoti, shirt, top-knot and sandalwood mark, as well as their features—they appeared to be Guruji's children. After a while, on being called by Guruji, his wife came outside. She was dressed in silk for ritual purity. Her face brimmed with godliness. Every movement of her body was eloquent with hospitality. The formalities of introduction were completed. She hurried inside, and after a while, the older boy came out bearing plates full of cooked *poha*.[1] I became nervous, fear crept over my mind. Suppose this lady were to find out my caste? Along with sips of water, I swallowed the lump in my throat as well as mouthfuls of *poha*. I couldn't concentrate on what anyone was saying. My only worry was when and how I could escape from there. Suppose someone from the Buldy area were to come there?

'God deliver me from this ordeal!' I kept praying to the Almighty. But nothing terrible happened. For those people were indeed very kind. Open and relaxed in their conversation. My teacher, for one, definitely knew my caste. But I was not made to experience any feeling of inferiority. And I felt a profound respect for him. The broadmindedness of this Brahmin incarnate, with his old-fashioned upbringing, remained constant even towards a student of the very lowest caste. Needless to say, it was evidence of his high thinking and his generous heart. It became my aim to study faithfully as my teacher instructed me and never to anger him by inattention to studies. You can never tell who will become a shining light to whose life. Guruji was

7. A god (Sanskrit).
8. A school for girls.
9. A structure for a tulsi plant (the basil sacred to Vishnu) representing Vrindavan, the village home of Krishna ("Sati Takes the Form of Sita," p. 432).
1. A dish made from flattened rice.

probably unaware that he had the power to add a touch of glory to the life of an insignificant being. After I matriculated, I did not meet him again. Perhaps he won't even recognize me. But I wish to lighten my load of respect by paying back a fraction of my sacred debt with the fee of words. For if Guruji had not shown me that warmth, but had instead shown the base feelings appropriate to his orthodox nature, would I have learnt Sanskrit?

Against all obstacles, I at last matriculated. On seeing the marks I got for Sanskrit, I announced, 'I shall do an M.A. in Sanskrit.' Our enlightened neighbors laughed as they had before. Some college lecturers and lawyers also joined in the joke. 'How can that be possible? You may have got good marks at Matric.[2] But it isn't so easy to do an M.A. in Sanskrit. You shouldn't make meaningless boasts; you should know your limitations.' The discouragers said what they usually do. The point was that the people who discouraged me were all of my caste. But their words could not turn me from my purpose. I didn't reply—I wanted to answer them by action. For that, I needed to study very hard. In order to take an M.A. in Sanskrit, I would have to go to the famous Morris College.[3] I had heard so many things about the college from my friend's sister. About the learned professors with their cultivated tastes, about the mischievous male students, the beautiful girls, and the huge library. My interest was limited to the professors who would teach me, and to the library. And I joined the college.

The Hindus from the high-caste areas used to taunt me. 'Even these wretched outcastes are giving themselves airs these days—studying in colleges.' I pretended to be deaf. I had begun to have some idea of what Savitribai Phule[4] must have had to endure on account of her husband Mahatma Jyotiba Phule's zeal for women's education.

I went through some mixed experiences while I studied. I would call my lecturers' even-handed fairness a very remarkable thing. I was never scared by the prejudice of which repute and rumor had told me. What is more, praise and encouragement were given according to merit. Some people may have felt dislike in their heart of hearts, but they never displayed it. One thing alone irked me—the ironical comments about the scholarship I got. 'She's having fun and games at the expense of a scholarship. Just bloated with government money!' From the peons themselves to the senior officials, there was the same attitude. I couldn't understand. Was it charity they were dispensing from their personal coffers? They were giving me government money and if that money was going from them to the government in the form of taxes, then equally, a tax was being levied on the public to pay their salaries. And that tax was collected in indirect forms even from the parents of the scholarship holders. So who paid whom? When the Dakshina Prize Committee[5] used to give stipends, there was no complaint of any kind from any level of society. Then why now? Oh, well.

I passed my B.A. The figures in my B.A. mark-sheet were worthy of high praise. I had got good marks without falling behind in any way. Not only did I have respect for my teachers' fairness, but it made me happy too. But in

2. Matriculation, entrance examinations.
3. One of the oldest colleges in India, founded in Nagpur in 1885.
4. Jyotiba Phule (1827–1890) and his wife, Savitribai Phule, were activists and social reformers from Maharashtra, working especially on behalf of women and Dalits.
5. A charitable grant, originally made by officials of the Maratha empire, distributed chiefly to learned Brahmins.

human life, no joy is unmixed. It can't be attained fully without some little blemish. So now, the story of my M.A.

In the second year of our M.A. we went to the Postgraduate Department in the University. Very well-known scholars taught us there. The Head of the Department was a scholar of all-India repute. He didn't like my learning Sanskrit, and would make it clear that he didn't. And he took a malicious delight in doing so. The sharp claws of his taunts left my mind wounded and bleeding. In a way, I had developed a terror of this great pandit. His manner of speaking was honeyed and reasonable, but filled with venom. I would unconsciously compare him with Gokhale Guruji. I couldn't understand why this great man with a doctorate, so renowned all over India, this man in his modern dress, who did not wear the traditional cap, who could so eloquently delineate the philosophy of the Universal Being, and with such ease explain difficult concepts in simple terms, could not practice in real life the philosophy in the books he taught. This man had been exposed to modernity; Gokhale Guruji was orthodox. Yet one had been shrivelled by tradition, the other enriched by it, like a tree weighed down with fruit. Days go by; you survive calamities; but the memory of them sets up its permanent abode in you. In the inmost recesses of your inner being. I survived even through such a difficult ordeal. I got my M.A. with distinction.

A congratulatory bouquet of colorful, fragrant flowers came from Professor (Dr.) Kolte, the former Vice-Chancellor of Nagpur University. I stared at it unblinkingly. In those flowers, I could see Dr. Kolte's heart blossoming, petal by petal, with pride. And smell the sweet fragrance of unalloyed joy, thrilling my senses and arousing my self-confidence.

And now I would be a lecturer in Sanskrit! My dreams were tinted with turquoise and edged in gold. The images I nursed about myself were taking strange shapes in my mind.

A high-paid job would come to me on a platter from the government. For I must have been the first woman from a scheduled caste to pass with distinction in Sanskrit. Every nook and cranny of my mind was filled with such hopes and expectations. But those ideas were shattered. My illusions proved as worthless as chaff. I became despondent about the efficiency of the government. I started attending interviews in private colleges. And that was a complete farce. Some said, 'But how will you stay on with us, when you've passed so well?' (In other words, they must have wanted to say, 'How will you work for less pay?') In other places, the moment I had been interviewed and stepped out of the room, there would be a burst of derisive laughter. I would hear words like sharp needles: 'So now even these people are to teach Sanskrit! Government Brahmins, aren't they?' And the ones who said this weren't even Brahmins, but so-called reformers from the lower castes, who considered themselves anti-Brahmin, and talked of the heritage of Jyotiba Phule, and flogged the mass of the lower castes for their narrow caste consciousness. And yet they found it distasteful that a girl from the Mahar caste, which was one of the lower castes, should teach Sanskrit. When people like these, wearing hypocritical masks, are in responsible positions in society, it does not take even a minute for that society to fall.

Two years after my M.A., I was still unemployed. There must be many whose position is the same as mine. In my frustration I took a bold step to get out of the trap. I presented my case in writing to the Honorable Shri Jagjivan Ram, the noted Minister in the Central Cabinet. I condemned the flimsy pretense of the state government and the administration that flouted the Constitution. My words had all the power of a sharp sword. For they were a cry from the heart of a person being crushed to death under the wheels of circumstance—like the screeching of the eagle Jatayu[6] in his last struggles.

The Honorable Minister Jagjivan Ram placed the letter before Pandit Nehru, who was astonished by it, and sent me an award of Rs.250/-, telling me to meet the Chief Minister of Maharashtra. Accordingly the Chief Minister of that time, Yeshwantrao Chavan, sent me a telegram asking me to meet him. Within a day or two, one wire after another had electrified me into wondering who I'd suddenly become. Getting past the ranks of spearmen and macebearers at the government office was quite an ordeal. But finally I got to see the 'Saheb.' Now, I thought, I would get a job at once—as a clerk in the government office, at least. A naive expectation. The Chief Minister made me fulsome promises in his own style. 'We'll definitely make efforts for you—but you won't get a job in minutes; it'll take us some time. We'll have to give thought to it; have to hunt out something.'

And with this assurance came a fine speech that qualified as an example of literature. 'A student of Sanskrit is intoxicated with idealism. It is a deeply felt personal desire. You shouldn't run after a job. Involve yourself in research. Pursue your studies.' Now the controls of endurance that restrained me started to break rapidly, and the words that had been bound within me broke out. 'Saheb, if you can't give me a job, tell me so, clearly. I don't want promises. Promises keep false hopes alive. Research is the fruit of mental peace. How do you expect me to have mental peace, when I am starving? And I'm tired of speeches.' I was fed up with life. Otherwise in A.D. 1960 it would have been impossible for a wretch like me even to stand before a dignitary like this, with all the power of *kartumakartumanyathakartum*, 'to do, omit to do, or do in another way,' let alone speak out to him.

Waiting for a job, I passed the first year of an M.A. in English Literature. It was just an excuse to keep myself occupied. That year I got married—an intercaste marriage. That is a story by itself—a different glimpse of the nature of Indian society. Let that be the subject of another story. The surprising thing is that two months after my marriage, I got an Assistant Lecturership in a government college. Deputy Director Sahastrabuddhe, who was on the interview board, was amazed. 'How did this girl remain unemployed for two years?' Dr. Kolte's good will remained a constant support here, too. Today, I am a professor in the famous college where I studied, whose very walls are imbued with the respect I felt for that institution. But one thought still pricks me: the credit for Kumud Somkuwar's job is not hers, but that of the name Kumud Pawde. I hear that a woman's surname changes to match her husband's—and so does her caste. That's why I say that the credit of being a professor of Sanskrit is that of the presumed higher caste status of Mrs. Kumud Pawde. The caste of her maiden status remains deprived.

6. A noble bird in the *Ramayana*, who dies trying to save Sita.

ANGULIMAL

Tryambak Sapkale, born in 1930, was a ticket-taker on a railway until his retirement. This poem, first published in 1978, begins by paying homage to his mother, which turns into homage to Eknath, a sixteenth-century Marathi poet-saint who was noted for his compassion toward Dalits. Angulimal ("Garlanded with Fingers") was a robber and murderer in Buddhist legends, named for his garland made of the little fingers of the people he had killed before the Buddha converted him. *Kirtan,* "praising," is a ceremony in which the group sings the songs of the poet-saint, the central ritual of the *bhakti* movement to which Eknath belonged.

When I came into this world
I was crying,
the world was laughing.
Two hands caressed me,
on my back, on my stomach.

When I was crawling
I used to fall,
then get up,
supported by the little fingers
of those hands.

When understanding came,
I cried.
The world only laughed.
Two hands raised the whip
to my back, to my stomach.

As I ran through this
bounteous, plentiful land
my feet burned,
my mind wept.
I ran yelling for my life
Hoping to meet someone like Eknath.

I met quite a few
who revered Eknath.

They were engrossed
In their *kirtan.*
My cry did not
enter their hearts.

Even the Sahara
has an oasis.
I ran in search of

Translated by Jayant Karve and Eleanor Zelliot.

something like an oasis.

I tried to catch hold of
this turning earth.
My hands were brushed off.
I fell.
The world laughed,
pointing its fingers at me.

Tears dried.
Feet froze.
Gathering all my strength,
I laughed at this world.
Ha . . . Ha . . . Ha . . . Ha . . .
There was a tremor in the earth
when I laughed.

Hey—how come you
rabbit spawn aren't laughing anymore?
Those fingers that point at me
will become fingers dangling
from the garland around my neck.

Angulimal
I am Angulimal . . .
I am Angulimal—

EKLAVYA

This poem by Tryambak Sapkale imagines an active response in place of the passive resignation of Eklavya in the well-known story from the *Mahabharata* ("Ekalavya Cuts Off His Thumb," p. 143).

The round earth.
A steel lever
in my hand.
But no leverage?
O Eklavya
you ideal disciple!
Give me
the finger you cut off;
that will be my fulcrum.

TRANSLATED BY Jayant Karve and Eleanor Zelliot, with A. K. Ramanujan.

FOR I AM BRAHMA

Narayan Surve, born in 1926 in Bombay, orphaned and casteless, became a staunch Communist. This poem takes the Upanishadic formulation that each person is *brahman* and turns it into a fantasy of divine power.

I will protect all that belongs to Brahma,
all that is Brahma
I'll undo the knot of time.

I'll bring the world to my door
where it will frolic like a child.
I'll play lagori[1] with the sun.

I'll tie up big clouds like cows outside my house.
I'll milk them to fill pots with ambrosia.

I'll hold the wind in my yard
where it will spin like a top.
I'll raise the rooftops of heaven.

I'll straighten out the bending sky,
single-handed
and punish whoever bent it in the first place!

The mole's mountain, the mountain's mole—
they're both inside of me.

TRANSLATED BY Jayant Karve and Eleanor Zelliot, with Pam Espeland.

1. A ball game, played by teams, originating in Karnataka.

EVERY WOMAN IN THIS COUNTRY

Kamla Bhasin, born in 1946, has held many positions of authority in major NGOs and organizations on behalf of women and the poor in India. She is one of a number of feminist poets in India who write about the role that goddesses (such as Kali Mata, Mother Kali, the fierce goddess) play in Indian tradition, striving to find ways in which that role might be transformed and used by human women.

Every woman in this country is dishonored, degraded,
With your hand on your heart, say, how can such a country be free

TRANSLATED BY Gail Omvedt.

In this country, they say, there are goddesses without number,
Tell me, have they loosened even a link of our chains?
Have we gained anything of honor from the veil?
Beneath the veil we have remained smothered, beneath the veil we
 burned . . .
Make the veil into a flag, unfurl it everywhere,
We will bring humanity's rule to this land.
You will not be able to challenge the power of women now
We are resolved to take on even the form of Kali Mata.

Hinduism and the Twentieth-Century Writer

As we noted from the start, the lived, experienced aspects of Hinduism always elude the printed page; for the modern period, these aspects might be accessed by film documentaries, newspaper articles, YouTube postings, or even blogs. What we can do in an anthology, however, is to include the insights into Hinduism expressed not only by current religious leaders but also by outstanding thinkers from the literary and political worlds of contemporary India, the widely read writers and the most influential political minds. These authors often draw on the well-known classical texts but twist or turn them to new ends.

The great themes of Hinduism live on, always in transformation, in authors writing in contemporary Indian languages in the twentieth and twenty-first centuries. There is no way to do justice to this vast field, but the present moment, however important it may seem to us, must take its place within the long, long history of Hinduism. The texts that follow were chosen for the light that each sheds on that history as well as on contemporary Hinduism.

In the North Indian languages, Rabindranath Tagore (1861–1941) was in many ways the father of modern Indian literature; his poetry, both in his native Bangla and in English, made him famous throughout the world. Two of the most famous writers in Hindi and in Urdu (a closely related, Persian-influenced language) are Prem Chand (1880–1936) and Nirala (1899–1961). Prem Chand

Rabindranath Tagore, reading with some of his students, in 1939.

writes about two men from the Dalit caste of leatherworkers; Nirala mocks Brahmins, memorializes the students who died in political action against the British in 1946, and retells the *Ramayana* story of Shurpanakha. Mohandas K. Gandhi (1869–1948) is best known as a political leader, but he was also a religious leader and a prodigious writer of religious texts, in both English and Gujarati; his essay on the *Bhagavad Gita* attempts to reconcile the *Gita* with his own crucial principle of nonviolence. The Bangla writer Mahasveta Devi (b. 1926) uses the story of the stripping of Draupadi, in the *Mahabharata*, to speak out against police brutality toward tribal women in the present.

In the South Indian languages, the novel *Samskara*, by the Kannada writer Anantha Murthy (b. 1932) raises still-pressing issues of caste. Contemporary Kannada literature models its forms on those of European literature, particularly the novel and the short story. On the other hand, a number of Indian writers have produced original Hindu texts in English. Anglo-Indian writers have a strong presence in English literature, carrying off some of the most coveted prizes, such as the Man Booker prize, which was won by V. S. Naipaul in 1971, Salman Rushdie in 1981, Arundhati Roy in 1997, and Aravind Adiga in 2008. Hinduism played a crucial role in the novels of each of these authors, as it does in all the selections from modern Indian writers in this anthology. Vilas Sarang (b. 1942) writes both in English and in Marathi, playing bizarre tricks upon Vedic themes. And although Salman Rushdie (b. 1947) is not a Hindu, his novel *Midnight's Children* presents, among many other things, the view of a Muslim who, like Kabir centuries before him, understood Hinduism from the vantage point of a brilliant outsider who was also very much an insider. Purushottam Nagesh Oak (1917–2007) provides a typical Hindutva attempt to rewrite Indian history in support of an anti-Muslim agenda. Coming at Hinduism from a different angle, Kancha Ilaiah (b. 1952), who announces officially that he is not a Hindu, writes brilliantly as the outsider within, the Dalit who simultaneously illuminates the Hinduism that he rejects, and that rejects him, and his own Dalit strain of a religion that strangely resembles Hinduism. And finally, A. K. Ramanujan (1929–1993) translates ancient myths that he learned during his boyhood in Tamilnadu into modern English poems full of meaning for a Hindu who lived, worked, and died in America.

RABINDRANATH TAGORE

Rabindranath Tagore (1861–1941) was the youngest son of Debendranath Tagore, a leader of the Brahmo Samaj (Rammohun Roy, p. 538). Educated at home, and then sent to England for schooling, Tagore eventually started an experimental school that was largely based on the teachings of the Upanishads, at Shantiniketan, near Birbhum in Bengal. His poetry in Bangla, beginning with *Manasi* (The Ideal One) (1890), made him world-famous, though his own translations into English failed to capture the beauty of the original Bangla. *Gitanjali: Song Offerings* (1912), his most famous book in English, contains poems published in Bangla in 1910. Tagore also wrote musical dramas, novels, short stories, dance dramas, essays, travel diaries, and two autobiographies, the second shortly before his death in 1941. In 1913 he was awarded the Nobel Prize for Literature.

Tagore was a close friend of Gandhi and participated in the Indian nationalist movement, though in a detached and idealistic way. He was knighted by the British government in 1915, but a few years later he resigned the honor in protest against British policies in India.

PRONOUNCING GLOSSARY

Gitanjali: *gee-tahn´-juh-lee*
Maya: *mah-yah´*
Rabindranath Tagore: *ruh-bin´-druh-nahth´ tuh-gor´*

TEN POEMS FROM *GITANJALI*

The following poems come from *Gitanjali: Song Offerings* (1912), an anthology that Tagore himself chose and translated with an English-speaking audience in mind. It was reissued by BookSurge Classics in 2003.

"Mind Without Fear" is on one level a description of the purification of the mind that is the goal of yoga ("Quieting the Mind," p. 122). But on another level it is a political poem ("let my / country awake"), a lament for the factionalism that was rampant among competing strains of Indian nationalists and the British (an India "broken up / into fragments by narrow domestic walls") and a hope for the prevailing of truth and reason.

"Fool" and "Leave This" echo the riddles ("carry thyself upon thy own shoulders!" and "beg at thy own door!") and the scorn for false worship ("telling of beads") that were the hallmarks of Kabir (p. 399) and Tukaram (p. 449). Both poems urge the extinction of desire and the surrender to the love of god.

"Seashore" visualizes the "death-dealing waves" of the ocean, seen from the shore where children meet and play in innocent ignorance. "Sail Away" expresses a longing for a voyage over the now "shoreless ocean" of death to final freedom.

"Maya" depicts the illusion (Vedanta, p. 285) that god creates to form a "self-separation," the "hiding and seeking of thee and me" that echoes the Upanishadic mantra of "thou art that" (*tat tvam asi*) (Upanishads, p. 105). "Song Unsung" is in the tradition of *viraha*, "love in separation," the lament of so many of the South Indian saints (*Tiruvaymoli*, p. 303; *Tevaram*, p. 315).

Three poems about time speak of the accidental grace ("The Fruits of Hearing a Purana," p. 225) gained through seemingly wasted time ("Lost Time"); of the approaching time of joyous union with god ("Distant Time"); and of the infinitely expandable gift of god's time ("Endless Time").

Mind Without Fear

Where the mind is without fear and the head is held
high;

Where knowledge is free;

Where the world has not been broken up
into fragments by narrow domestic walls;

Where words come out from the depth of truth;

Where tireless striving stretches its arms towards
perfection;

Where the clear stream of reason
has not lost its way into the dreary desert sand of dead
habit;

Where the mind is led forward by thee into ever-
widening thought and action—

Into that heaven of freedom, my Father, let my
country awake.

Fool

O Fool, try to carry thyself upon thy own shoulders!
O beggar, to come beg at thy own door!

Leave all thy burdens on his hands who can bear all,
and never look behind in regret.

Thy desire at once puts out the light from the lamp it
touches with its breath.

It is unholy—take not thy gifts through its unclean
hands.
Accept only what is offered by sacred love.

Leave This

Leave this chanting and singing and telling of beads!
Whom dost thou worship in this lonely dark corner of
a temple with doors all shut?
Open thine eyes and see thy God is not before thee!

He is there where the tiller is tilling the hard ground
and where the pathmaker is breaking stones.
He is with them in sun and in shower,
and his garment is covered with dust.
Put off thy holy mantle and even like him come down
on the dusty soil!

Deliverance?
Where is this deliverance to be found?
Our master himself has joyfully taken upon him the
bonds of creation;
he is bound with us all forever.

Come out of thy meditations and leave aside thy
flowers and incense!
What harm is there if thy clothes become tattered and stained?
Meet him and stand by him in toil and in sweat of thy brow.

Seashore

On the seashore of endless worlds children meet.
The infinite sky is motionless overhead
and the restless water is boisterous.
On the seashore of endless worlds
the children meet with shouts and dances.

They build their houses with sand
and they play with empty shells.
With withered leaves they weave their boats
and smilingly float them on the vast deep.
Children have their play on the seashore of worlds.

They know not how to swim, they know not how to
cast nets.
Pearl fishers dive for pearls, merchants sail in their
ships,
while children gather pebbles and scatter them again.

They seek not for hidden treasures, they know not
how to cast nets.

The sea surges up with laughter
and pale gleams the smile of the sea beach.
Death-dealing waves sing meaningless ballads to the
children,
even like a mother while rocking her baby's cradle.
The sea plays with children,
and pale gleams the smile of the sea beach.

On the seashore of endless worlds children meet.
Tempest roams in the pathless sky,
ships get wrecked in the trackless water,
death is abroad and children play.
On the seashore of endless worlds is the
great meeting of children.

Sail Away

Early in the day it was whispered that we should sail in
a boat,
only thou and I, and never a soul in the world would
know of this our
pilgrimage to no country and to no end.

In that shoreless ocean,
at thy silently listening smile my songs would swell in
melodies,
free as waves, free from all bondage of words.

Is the time not come yet?
Are there works still to do?
Lo, the evening has come down upon the shore
and in the fading light the seabirds come flying to their
nests.

Who knows when the chains will be off,
and the boat, like the last glimmer of sunset,
vanish into the night?

Maya

That I should make much of myself and turn it on all
sides,
thus casting colored shadows on thy radiance
—such is thy Maya.

Thou settest a barrier in thine own being
and then callest thy severed self in myriad notes.
This thy self-separation has taken body in me.

The poignant song is echoed through all the sky in many-colored tears
and smiles, alarms and hopes; waves rise up and sink again,
dreams break and form.
In me is thy own defeat of self.

This screen that thou hast raised is painted with innumerable figures
with the brush of the night and the day.
Behind it thy seat is woven in wondrous mysteries of curves,
casting away all barren lines of straightness.

The great pageant of thee and me has overspread the sky.
With the tune of thee and me all the air is vibrant,
and all ages pass with the hiding and seeking of thee and me.

Song Unsung

The song that I came to sing remains unsung to this day.

I have spent my days in stringing and in unstringing my instrument.

The time has not come true, the words have not been rightly set;
only there is the agony of wishing in my heart.

The blossom has not opened; only the wind is sighing by.

I have not seen his face, nor have I listened to his voice;
only I have heard his gentle footsteps from the road before my house.

The livelong day has passed in spreading his seat on the floor;
but the lamp has not been lit and I cannot ask him into my house.

I live in the hope of meeting with him; but this meeting is not yet.

Lost Time

On many an idle day have I grieved over lost time.
But it is never lost, my lord.
Thou hast taken every moment of my life in thine own hands.

Hidden in the heart of things thou art nourishing seeds into sprouts,
buds into blossoms, and ripening flowers into fruitfulness.

I was tired and sleeping on my idle bed
and imagined all work had ceased.
In the morning I woke up
and found my garden full with wonders of flowers.

Distant Time

I know not from what distant time
thou art ever coming nearer to meet me.
Thy sun and stars can never keep thee hidden from me for aye.

In many a morning and eve thy footsteps have been heard
and thy messenger has come within my heart and called me in secret.

I know not only why today my life is all astir,
and a feeling of tremulous joy is passing through my heart.

It is as if the time were come to wind up my work,
and I feel in the air a faint smell of thy sweet presence.

Endless Time

Time is endless in thy hands, my lord.
There is none to count thy minutes.

Days and nights pass and ages bloom and fade like flowers.
Thou knowest how to wait.

Thy centuries follow each other perfecting a small wild flower.

We have no time to lose,
and having no time we must scramble for a chance.
We are too poor to be late.

And thus it is that time goes by
while I give it to every querulous man who claims it,
and thine altar is empty of all offerings to the last.

At the end of the day I hasten in fear lest thy gate be shut;
but I find that yet there is time.

MOHANDAS KARAMCHAND GANDHI

Born on October 2, 1869, in Porbandar, in Gujarat, and assassinated on January 30, 1948, in Delhi, M. K. Gandhi, called Mahatma ("Great-Soul"), was the leader of the Indian nationalist movement against British rule, internationally esteemed for his doctrine of nonviolent protest or noncooperation, in the name of political and social progress, which others (but not Gandhi) sometimes called passive resistance. He read and admired Tolstoy's Christian texts and the Qu'ran in translation, but he regarded the *Bhagavad Gita* (p. 166) as his "spiritual dictionary."

PRONOUNCING GLOSSARY

ahimsa: *uh-him´-suh*
Almora: *uhl-moh´-rah*
bhakti: *buk´-tee*
Gita: *gee´-tah*
Gujarat: *goo´-juh-raht´*
himsa: *him´-suh*
Janaka: *juh´-nuh-kah*
Kosani: *koh´-suh-nee´*
Lokamanya: *lohk´-uh-mahn-yah´*
lota: *loh´-tah*
Mahatma: *muh-haht´-mah*
Marathi: *muh-rah´-tee*
Mohandas Karamchand Gandhi: *moh-hun´-dahs kuh´-rum-chund gahn´-dee*
pandit: *pun´-dit*
sannyasa: *sun-yah´-suh*
Shudra: *shoo´-druh*
Swami Anand: *swah´-mee ah´-nund*
Yeravda: *yeh-rahv´-duh*

THE GOSPEL OF SELFLESS ACTION

In the twentieth century, some Hindu nationalist leaders and members of the Congress Party took up the *Bhagavad Gita* as a call to action. They viewed Krishna as a highly ethical person who was asking his friend and devotee, Arjuna, whom they saw as a Hindu nationalist warrior, to overcome his hesitation and to fight against injustice. They also viewed Krishna's exhortation to Arjuna as a clear antecedent of their own call to other Indians to rise up against the British Raj. To them, the *Gita* advocated justifiable violence. Gandhi argued against extreme nationalists and against their interpretation of the *Gita*. Following is the first part of the essay on the *Gita* that he wrote, in Gujarati, in 1929, in prison, arrested by the British because of his work in the Independence movement.

[It was at Kosani in Almora on 24th June, 1929, i. e. after two years' waiting, that I finished the introduction in Gujarati to my translation of the *Gita*. The whole was then published in due course. It has been translated in Hindi,

TRANSLATED BY Mahadev Desai.

Mahatma Gandhi marching to the shore at Dandi in 1930 to collect salt in violation of the law he was protesting. On the right is Mrs. Sarojini Naidu, a leader of the Indian National Congress, who was jailed with Gandhi.

Bengali and Marathi. There has been an insistent demand for an English translation. I finished the translation of the introduction at the Yeravda prison. Since my discharge it has lain with friends, and now I give it to the reader. Those, who take no interest in the Book of Life, will forgive the trespass on these columns. To those who are interested in the poem and treat it as their guide in life, my humble attempt might prove of some help.

—M. K. G.]

I

Just as, acted upon by the affection of co-workers like Swami Anand and others, I wrote *My Experiments with Truth*, so has it been regarding my rendering of the *Gita*. "We shall be able to appreciate your meaning of the message of the *Gita*, only when we are able to study a translation of the whole text by yourself, with the addition of such notes as you may deem necessary. I do not think it is just on your part to deduce *ahimsa*[1] etc. from stray verses," thus spoke Swami Anand to me during the non-co-operation days. I felt the force of his remarks. I, therefore, told him that I would adopt his suggestion when I got the time. Shortly afterwards I was imprisoned. During my incarceration I was able to study the *Gita* more fully. I went reverently through the Gujarati translation of the Lokamanya's[2] great work. He had kindly presented me with the Marathi original and the translations in Gujarati and Hindi, and had asked me, if I could not tackle the original, at least to go through the Gujarati translation. I had not been able to follow the advice outside the prison walls. But when I was imprisoned I read the Gujarati translation. This reading whetted my appetite for more and I glanced through several works on the *Gita*.

2. My first acquaintance with the *Gita* began in 1888–89 with the verse translation by Sir Edwin Arnold known as the *Song Celestial*. On reading it I felt a keen desire to read a Gujarati translation. And I read as many translations as I could lay hold of. But all such reading can give me no passport for presenting my own translation. Then again my knowledge of Sanskrit is limited; my knowledge of Gujarati too is in no way scholarly. How could I then dare present the public with my translation?

3. It has been my endeavor, as also that of some companions, to reduce to practice the teaching of the *Gita* as I have understood it. The *Gita* has become for us a spiritual reference book. I am aware that we ever fail to act in perfect accord with the teaching. The failure is not due to want of effort, but is in spite of it. Even through the failures we seem to see rays of hope. The accompanying rendering contains the meaning of the *Gita* message which this little band is trying to enforce in its daily conduct.

4. Again this rendering is designed for women, the commercial class, the so-called Shudras and the like, who have little or no literary equipment, who have neither the time nor the desire to read the *Gita* in the original, and yet who stand in need of its support. In spite of my Gujarati being unscholarly, I must own to having the desire to leave to the Gujaratis, through the mother-tongue, whatever knowledge I may possess. I do indeed wish, that at a time when literary output of a questionable character is pouring in upon the Gujaratis, they should have before them a rendering the majority can understand of a book that is regarded as unrivalled for its spiritual merit and so withstand the overwhelming flood of unclean literature.

5. This desire does not mean any disrespect to the other renderings. They have their own place. But I am not aware of the claim made by the translators of enforcing their meaning of the *Gita* in their own lives. At the back of my reading there is the claim of an endeavor to enforce the meaning in my own conduct for an unbroken period of forty years. For this reason I do indeed harbor the wish that all Gujarati men or women, wishing to shape their conduct according to their faith, should digest and derive strength from the translation here presented.

6. My co-workers, too, have worked at this translation. My knowledge of Sanskrit being very limited, I should not have full confidence in my literal

1. Noninjury or nonviolence (*Mahabharata*, p. 130).
2. An honorific title ("Honored by the People") for Bal Gangadhar Tilak (1856–1920), an Indian nationalist leader, author of *The Arctic Home in the Vedas* (1903) and of an analysis of *karma-yoga* in the *Gita*, the book to which Gandhi here refers.

translation. To that extent, therefore, the translation has passed before the eyes of Vinoba, Kaka Kalelkar, Mahadev Desai and Kishorlal Mashruwala.

II

7. Now about the message of the *Gita*.

8. Even in 1888–89, when I first became acquainted with the *Gita*, I felt that it was not a historical work, but that, under the guise of physical warfare, it described the duel that perpetually went on in the hearts of mankind, and that physical warfare was brought in merely to make the description of the internal duel more alluring. This preliminary intuition became more confirmed on a closer study of religion and the *Gita*. A study of the *Mahabharata* gave it added confirmation. I do not regard the *Mahabharata* as a historical work in the accepted sense. The *Adiparva*[3] contains powerful evidence in support of my opinion. By ascribing to the chief actors superhuman or subhuman origins, the great Vyasa[4] made short work of the history of kings and their peoples. The persons therein described may be historical, but the author of the *Mahabharata* has used them merely to drive home his religious theme.

9. The author of the *Mahabharata* has not established the necessity of physical warfare; on the contrary he has proved its futility. He has made the victors shed tears of sorrow and repentance, and has left them nothing but a legacy of miseries.

10. In this great work the *Gita* is the crown. Its second chapter, instead of teaching the rules of physical warfare, tells us how a perfected man is to be known. In the characteristics of the perfected man of the *Gita*, I do not see any to correspond to physical warfare. Its whole design is inconsistent with the rules of conduct governing the relations between warring parties.

11. Krishna of the *Gita* is perfection and right knowledge personified; but the picture is imaginary. That does not mean that Krishna, the adored of his people, never lived. But perfection is imagined. The idea of a perfect incarnation is an aftergrowth.

12. In Hinduism, incarnation is ascribed to one who has performed some extraordinary service of mankind. All embodied life is in reality an incarnation of God, but it is not usual to consider every living being an incarnation. Future generations pay this homage to one who, in his own generation, has been extraordinarily religious in his conduct. I can see nothing wrong in this procedure; it takes nothing from God's greatness, and there is no violence done to Truth. There is an Urdu saying which means, "Adam is not God but he is a spark of the Divine." And therefore he who is the most religiously behaved has most of the divine spark in him. It is in accordance with this train of thought, that Krishna enjoys, in Hinduism, the status of the most perfect incarnation.

13. This belief in incarnation is a testimony of man's lofty spiritual ambition. Man is not at peace with himself till he has become like unto God. The endeavor to reach this state is the supreme, the only ambition worth having. And this is self-realization. This self-realization is the subject of the *Gita*, as it is of all scriptures. But its author surely did not write it to establish that doctrine. The object of the *Gita* appears to me to be that of showing the

3. The first book of the *Mahabharata*, narrating the births of the heroes fathered by gods.

4. The mythical author of the *Mahabharata*.

most excellent way to attain self-realization. That which is to be found, more or less clearly, spread out here and there in Hindu religious books, has been brought out in the clearest possible language in the *Gita* even at the risk of repetition.

14. *That matchless remedy is renunciation of fruits of action.*

15. This is the center round which the *Gita* is woven. This renunciation is the central sun, round which devotion, knowledge and the rest revolve like planets. The body has been likened to a prison. There must be action where there is body. Not one embodied being is exempted from labor. And yet all religions proclaim that it is possible for man, by treating the body as the temple of God, to attain freedom. Every action is tainted, be it ever so trivial. How can the body be made the temple of God? In other words how can one be free from action, i.e. from the taint of sin? The *Gita* has answered the question in decisive language: "By desireless action; by renouncing fruits of action; by dedicating all activities to God, i.e., by surrendering oneself to Him body and soul."

16. But desirelessness or renunciation does not come for the mere talking about it. It is not attained by an intellectual feat. It is attainable only by a constant heart-churn. Right knowledge is necessary for attaining renunciation. Learned men possess a knowledge of a kind. They may recite the *Vedas* from memory, yet they may be steeped in self-indulgence. In order that knowledge may not run riot, the author of the *Gita* has insisted on devotion accompanying it and has given it the first place. Knowledge without devotion will be like a misfire. Therefore, says the *Gita*, "Have devotion, and knowledge will follow." This devotion is not mere lip worship, it is a wrestling with death. Hence the *Gita's* assessment of the devotee's qualities is similar to that of the sage's.

17. Thus the devotion required by the *Gita* is no soft-hearted effusiveness. It certainly is not blind faith. The devotion of the *Gita* has the least to do with externals. A devotee may use, if he likes, rosaries, forehead marks, make offerings, but these things are no test of his devotion. He is the devotee who is jealous of none, who is a fount of mercy, who is without egotism, who is selfless, who treats alike cold and heat, happiness and misery, who is ever forgiving, who is always contented, whose resolutions are firm, who has dedicated mind and soul to God, who causes no dread, who is not afraid of others, who is free from exultation, sorrow and fear, who is pure, who is versed in action and yet remains unaffected by it, who renounces all fruit, good or bad, who treats friend and foe alike, who is untouched by respect or disrespect, who is not puffed up by praise, who does not go under when people speak ill of him, who loves silence and solitude, who has a disciplined reason. Such devotion is inconsistent with the existence at the same time of strong attachments.

18. We thus see, that to be a real devotee is to realize oneself. Self-realization is not something apart. One rupee can purchase for us poison or nectar, but knowledge or devotion cannot buy us either salvation or bondage. These are not media of exchange. They are themselves the thing we want. In other words, if the means and the end are not identical, they are almost so. The extreme of means is salvation. Salvation of the *Gita* is perfect peace.

19. But such knowledge and devotion, to be true, have to stand the test of renunciation of fruits of action. Mere knowledge of right and wrong will not

make one fit for salvation. According to common notions, a mere learned man will pass as a *pandit*.[5] He need not perform any service. He will regard it as bondage even to lift a little *lota*.[6] Where one test of knowledge is non-liability for service, there is no room for such mundane work as the lifting of a *lota*.

20. Or take *bhakti*.[7] The popular notion of *bhakti* is soft-heartedness, telling beads and the like, and disdaining to do even a loving service, lest the telling of beads etc. might be interrupted. This *bhakti*, therefore, leaves the rosary only for eating, drinking and the like, never for grinding corn or nursing patients.

21. But the *Gita* says: "No one has attained his goal without action. Even men like Janaka[8] attained salvation through action. If even I were lazily to cease working, the world would perish. How much more necessary then for the people at large to engage in action?"

22. While on the one hand it is beyond dispute that all action binds, on the other hand it is equally true that all living beings have to do some work, whether they will or no. Here all activity, whether mental or physical, is to be included in the term of action. Then how is one to be free from the bondage of action, even though he may be acting? The manner in which the *Gita* has solved the problem is to my knowledge unique. The *Gita* says: "Do your allotted work but renounce its fruit—be detached and work—have no desire for reward and work."

This is the unmistakable teaching of the *Gita*. He who gives up action falls. He who gives up only the reward rises. But renunciation of fruit in no way means indifference to the result. In regard to every action one must know the result that is expected to follow, the means thereto, and the capacity for it. He, who, being thus equipped, is without desire for the result and is yet wholly engrossed in the due fulfilment of the task before him is said to have renounced the fruits of his action.

23. Again let no one consider renunciation to mean want of fruit for the renouncer. The *Gita* reading does not warrant such a meaning. Renunciation means absence of hankering after fruit. As a matter of fact, he who renounces reaps a thousandfold. The renunciation of the *Gita* is the acid test of faith. He who is ever brooding over result often loses nerve in the performance of his duty. He becomes impatient and then gives vent to anger and begins to do unworthy things; he jumps from action to action never remaining faithful to any. He who broods over results is like a man given to objects of senses; he is ever distracted, he says goodbye to all scruples, everything is right in his estimation and he therefore resorts to means fair and foul to attain his end.

24. From the bitter experiences of desire for fruit the author of the *Gita* discovered the path of renunciation of fruit and put it before the world in a most convincing manner. The common belief is that religion is always opposed to material good. "One cannot act religiously in mercantile and such other matters. There is no place for religion in such pursuits: religion is only for attainment of salvation," we hear many worldly-wise people say. In

5. A learned man, particularly one who knows Sanskrit.

6. A small brass water-pot.

7. Devotion to a god (*Bhagavad Gita*, p. 166), involving acts of worship such as "telling" prayers for each bead of the rosary.

8. A king, father of Sita, in the *Ramayana* ("The Birth of Sita," p. 189).

my opinion the author of the *Gita* has dispelled this delusion. He has drawn no line of demarcation between salvation and worldly pursuits. On the contrary he has shown that religion must rule even our worldly pursuits. I have felt that the *Gita* teaches us that what cannot be followed out in day-to-day practice cannot be called religion. Thus, according to the *Gita*, all acts that are incapable of being performed without attachment are taboo. This golden rule saves mankind from many a pitfall. According to this interpretation murder, lying, dissoluteness and the like must be regarded as sinful and therefore taboo. Man's life then becomes simple, and from that simpleness springs peace.

25. Thinking along these lines, I have felt that in trying to enforce in one's life the central teaching of the *Gita*, one is bound to follow Truth and *ahimsa*. When there is no desire for fruit, there is no temptation for untruth or *himsa*. Take any instance of untruth or violence, and it will be found that at its back was the desire to attain the cherished end. But it may be freely admitted that the *Gita* was not written to establish *ahimsa*. It was an accepted and primary duty even before the *Gita* age. The *Gita* had to deliver the message of renunciation of fruit. This is clearly brought out as early as the second chapter.

26. But if the *Gita* believed in *ahimsa* or it was included in desirelessness, why did the author take a warlike illustration? When the *Gita* was written, although people believed in *ahimsa*, wars were not only not taboo, but nobody observed the contradiction between them and *ahimsa*.

27. In assessing the implications of renunciation of fruit, we are not required to probe the mind of the author of the *Gita* as to his limitations of *ahimsa* and the like. Because a poet puts a particular truth before the world, it does not necessarily follow that he has known or worked out all its great consequences, or that having done so, he is able always to express them fully. In this perhaps lies the greatness of the poem and the poet. A poet's meaning is limitless. Like man, the meaning of great writings suffers evolution. On examining the history of languages, we notice that the meaning of important words has changed or expanded. This is true of the *Gita*. The author has himself extended the meanings of some of the current words. We are able to discover this even on a superficial examination. It is possible that, in the age prior to that of the *Gita*, offering of animals as sacrifice was permissible. But there is not a trace of it in the sacrifice in the *Gita* sense. In the *Gita* continuous concentration on God is the king of sacrifices. The third chapter seems to show that sacrifice chiefly means body-labor for service. The third and the fourth chapters read together will give us other meanings for sacrifice, but never animal-sacrifice. Similarly has the meaning of the word *sannyasa*[9] undergone, in the *Gita*, a transformation. The *sannyasa* of the *Gita* will not tolerate complete cessation of all activity. The *sannyasa* of the *Gita* is all work and yet no work. Thus the author of the *Gita*, by extending meanings of words, has taught us to imitate him. Let it be granted, that according to the letter of the *Gita* it is possible to say that warfare is consistent with renunciation of fruit. But after forty years' unremitting endeavor fully to enforce the teaching of the *Gita* in my own life, I have, in all humility, felt that perfect renunciation is impossible without perfect observance of *ahimsa* in every shape and form.

9. Renunciation (Upanishads, p. 105).

28. The *Gita* is not an aphoristic work; it is a great religious poem. The deeper you dive into it, the richer the meanings you get. It being meant for the people at large, there is pleasing repetition. With every age the important words will carry new and expanding meanings. But its central teaching will never vary. The seeker is at liberty to extract from this treasure any meaning he likes so as to enable him to enforce in his life the central teaching.

29. Nor is the *Gita* a collection of Do's and Don'ts. What is lawful for one may be unlawful for another. What may be permissible at one time, or in one place, may not be so at another time, and in another place. Desire for fruit is the only universal prohibition. Desirelessness is obligatory.

30. The *Gita* has sung the praises of Knowledge, but it is beyond the mere intellect; it is essentially addressed to the heart and capable of being understood by the heart. Therefore the *Gita* is not for those who have no faith. The author makes Krishna say:

"Do not entrust this treasure to him who is without sacrifice, without devotion, without the desire for this teaching and who denies Me. On the other hand, those who will give this precious treasure to My devotees will, by the fact of this service, assuredly reach Me. And those who, being free from malice, will with faith absorb this teaching, shall, having attained freedom, live where people of true merit go after death."

PREM CHAND

Prem Chand was the pseudonym of Dhanpat Rai Srivastava, who was born, on July 31, 1880, into the Kayastha caste (often said to have the dual status of both Brahmins and Kshatriyas) in a village near Varanasi. He was educated in Urdu in a Muslim school (a *madrassa*) by a Muslim teacher, and he wrote at first in Urdu but then switched to a straightforward dialect of Hindi with much less Sanskrit vocabulary than was generally used in "literary" Hindi. Prem Chand was the first to popularize the short-story form in Hindi and among the first to adapt Indian themes to Western literary styles. He both lived and wrote against what he regarded as the injustices perpetrated by Hinduism. He married a Hindu child widow, despite much opposition from conservative Hindus, and joined Gandhi's Noncooperation Movement. His many novels and stories depict village India in evocative detail; they provide a critique of arranged marriages, a protest against the abuses perpetrated by the British in India, and an exposé of the exploitation of poor farmers by officials and moneylenders. He died in 1936.

PRONOUNCING GLOSSARY

anna: *un´-nuh*
Budhiya: *boo´-dee-yah´*
Dada: *dah´-dah*
dhoti: *doh´-tee*
ghee: *gee*
Ghisu: *gee´-soo*
Madhav: *mah´-duv*
paan: *pahn*
Prem Chand: *prem´ chund*
puri: *poo´-ree*
Sahuji: *suh´-hoo-jee´*
zamindar: *zuh´-min-dahr´*

THE SHROUD

In this story from 1936, a man from the Dalit caste of Chamars, leatherworkers, whom higher-caste Hindus regard as polluted because they deal with the carcasses of cows, loses his wife in childbirth. He and his father collect money for her funeral rites but spend it on food and drink. Their drunken philosophizing parodies central Hindu beliefs about human suffering.

Father and son sat in silence at the door of their hut before a burnt-out fire and inside Budhiya, the son's young wife, lay fainting in the throes of child-birth. From time to time such an agonizing cry came out of her that their hearts skipped a beat. It was a winter night, all was silent, and the whole village was obliterated in the darkness.

TRANSLATED BY David Rubin.

Ghisu said, 'It looks as though she won't make it. You spent the whole day running around—just go in and have a look.'

Annoyed, Madhav said, 'If she's going to die why doesn't she get it over with? What can I do by looking?'

'You're pretty hard-hearted, aren't you? You live at your ease with somebody all year and then you don't give a damn about her.'

'But I couldn't stand looking at her writhing and thrashing.'

They were a family of Untouchable leather-workers and had a bad name throughout the whole village. If Ghisu worked one day he'd take three off. Madhav was such a loafer that whenever he worked for a half hour he'd stop and smoke his pipe for an hour. So they couldn't get work anywhere. If there was even a handful of grain in the house then the two of them swore off work. After a couple of days fasting Ghisu would climb up a tree and break off branches for firewood and Madhav would bring it to the market to sell. And so long as they had any of the money they got for it they'd both wander around in idleness. There was no shortage of heavy work in the village. It was a village of farmers and there were any number of chores for a hard-working man. But whenever you called these two you had to be satisfied with paying them both for doing one man's work between them. If the two of them had been wandering ascetics there would have been absolutely no need for them to practice. This was their nature. A strange life theirs was! They owned nothing except for some clay pots; a few torn rags was all that covered their nakedness. They were free of worldly cares! They were loaded with debts, people abused them, beat them, but they didn't suffer. People would loan them a little something even though they were so poor there was no hope of getting it back. At the time of the potato and pea harvest they would go into other people's fields and dig up potatoes and gather peas and roast them or they'd pick sugarcane to suck at night. Ghisu had reached the age of sixty living this hand-to-mouth existence, and like a good son Madhav was following in his father's footsteps in every way, and if anything he was adding luster to his father's fame. The two of them were sitting before the fire now roasting potatoes they'd dug up in some field. Ghisu's wife had died a long time ago. Madhav had been married last year. Since his wife had come she'd established order in the family and kept those two good-for-nothings' bellies filled. And since her arrival they'd become more sluggish than ever. In fact, they'd begun to let it go to their heads. If someone sent for them to do a job, they'd bare-facedly ask for twice the wages. This same woman was dying today in child-birth and it was as though they were only waiting for her to die so they could go to sleep in peace and quiet.

Ghisu took a potato and while he peeled it said, 'Go and look, see how she is. She must be possessed by some ghost, what else? But the village exorcist wants a rupee for a visit.'

Madhav was afraid that if he went into the hut Ghisu would do away with most of the potatoes. He said, 'I'm scared to go in there.'

'What are you afraid of? I'll be right here.'

'Then why don't you go and look?'

'When my woman died I didn't stir from her side for three days. And then she'd be ashamed if I saw her bare like that when I've never even seen her face before. Won't she be worried about her modesty? If she sees me she won't feel free to thrash around.'

'I've been thinking, if there's a baby what's going to happen? There's nothing we're supposed to have in the house—ginger, sugar, oil.'

'Everything's going to be all right, God will provide. The very people who wouldn't even give us a pice before will send for us tomorrow and give us rupees. I had nine kids and there was never a thing in the house but somehow or other the Lord got us through.'

In a society where the condition of people who toiled day and night was not much better than theirs and where, on the other hand, those who knew how to profit from the weaknesses of the peasants were infinitely richer, it's no wonder they felt like this. We could even say that Ghisu was much smarter than the peasants and instead of being one of the horde of empty-headed toilers he'd found a place for himself in the disreputable society of idle gossipmongers. Only he didn't have the ability to stick to the rules and code of such idlers. So while others of his crowd had made themselves chiefs and bosses of the village, the whole community pointed at him in contempt. Nevertheless, there was the consolation that although he was miserably poor at least he didn't have to do the back-breaking labor the farmers did, and other people weren't able to take unfair advantage of his simplicity and lack of ambition.

They ate the potatoes piping hot. Since yesterday they'd eaten nothing and they didn't have the patience to let them cool. Several times they burned their tongues. When they were peeled the outside of the potatoes didn't seem very hot but as soon as they bit into them the inside burned their palates, tongues and throats. Rather than keep these burning coals in their mouths it was a lot safer to drop them down into their bellies, where there was plenty of equipment to cool them. So they swallowed them quickly, even though the attempt brought tears to their eyes.

At this moment Ghisu recalled the Thakur's[1] wedding, which he'd attended twenty years before. The way the feast had gratified him was something to remember all his life, and the memory was still vivid today. He said, 'I won't forget that feast. Since then I've never seen food like it or filled my belly so well. The bride's people crammed everybody with *puris*,[2] everybody! Bigshots and nobodies all ate *puris* fried in real *ghee*.[3] Relishes and curds with spices, three kinds of dried vegetables, a tasty curry, sweets—how can I describe how delicious that food was? There was nothing to hold you back, you just asked for anything you wanted and as much as you wanted. We ate so much that nobody had any room left for water. The people serving just kept on handing out hot, round, mouth-watering savouries on leaves. And we'd say, 'Stop, you mustn't,' and put our hands over the plates to stop them but they kept right on handing it out. And when everybody had rinsed his mouth we got *paan*[4] and cardamom too. But how could I take any *paan*? I couldn't even stand up. I just went and lay down in my blanket right away. That's how generous that Thakur was!'

Relishing the banquet in his imagination Madhav said, 'Nobody feeds us like that now.'

'Who'd feed us like that today? That was another age. Now everybody thinks about saving his money. Don't spend for weddings, don't spend for

1. A lord, a rich man.
2. A puffed-up fried bread.
3. Clarified butter.
4. Betel, spices wrapped in a leaf ("As the Mirror to My Hand," p. 485).

funerals! I ask you, if they keep on hoarding the wealth they've squeezed out of the poor, where are they going to put it? But they keep on hoarding. When it comes to spending any money they say they have to economize.'

'You must have eaten a good twenty *puris*?'

'I ate more than twenty.'

'I would have eaten fifty!'

'I couldn't have eaten any less than fifty. I was a husky lad in those days. You're not half so big.'

After finishing the potatoes they drank some water and right there in front of the fire they wrapped themselves up in their *dhotis*[5] and pulling up their knees they fell asleep—just like two enormous coiled pythons.

And Budhiya was still moaning.

In the morning Madhav went inside the hut and saw that his wife had turned cold. Flies were buzzing around her mouth. Her stony eyes stared upwards. Her whole body was covered with dust. The child had died in her womb.

Madhav ran to get Ghisu. Then they both began to moan wildly and beat their chests. When they heard the wailing the neighbors came running and according to the old tradition began to console the bereaved.

But there was not much time for moaning and chest-beating. There was the worry about a shroud and wood for the pyre. The money in the house had disappeared like carrion in a kite's nest.

Father and son went weeping to the village *zamindar.*[6] He hated the sight of the two of them and several times he'd thrashed them with his own hands for stealing or for not coming to do the work they'd promised to do. He asked, 'What is it, little Ghisu, what are you crying about? You don't show yourself much these days. It seems as though you don't want to live in this village.'

Ghisu bowed his head all the way to the ground, his eyes full of tears, and said, 'Excellency, an awful thing's happened to me. Madhav's woman passed away last night. She was in agony the whole time. The two of us never once left her side. We did whatever we could, gave her medicine—but to make a long story short, she gave us the slip. And now there's nobody left even to give us a piece of bread, master. We're ruined! My house has been destroyed! I'm your slave—except for you now who is there to see that she's given a decent funeral? Whatever we had we spent on medicine. If your excellency is merciful, then she'll have a good funeral. Whose door can we go to except yours?'

The *zamindar* was soft-hearted. But to be kind to Ghisu was like trying to dye a black blanket. He was tempted to say, 'Get out and don't come back! When we send for you, you don't show up but today when you're in a jam you come and flatter me. You're a sponging bastard!' But this was not the occasion for anger or scolding. Exasperated, he took out a couple of rupees and threw them on the ground. But he didn't utter a word of consolation. He didn't even look at Ghisu. It was as though he'd shoved a load off his head.

When the *zamindar* had given two rupees how could the shopkeepers and moneylenders of the village refuse? Ghisu knew how to trumpet the

5. A garment worn by many Indian men, made of a rectangular piece of cloth, usually white, wrapped about the waist and legs in a complex manner.

6. A landlord, an official in precolonial India assigned to collect the land taxes of his district.

zamindar's name around. Somebody gave him a couple of *annas*,[7] somebody else four. Within an hour Ghisu had harvested a tidy sum of five rupees. He got grain at one place, wood from somewhere else. And at noon Ghisu and Madhav went to the market to get a shroud. There were people already cutting the bamboo to make a litter for the corpse.

The tender-hearted women of the village came and looked at the dead woman, shed a few tears over her forlorn state and went away.

When they reached the market Ghisu said, 'We have enough wood to burn her up completely, haven't we, Madhav?'

'Yes, there's plenty of wood, now we need the shroud.'

'That's right, come along and we'll pick up a cheap one.'

'Of course, what else? By the time we move the corpse it will be night—who can see a shroud at night?'

'What a rotten custom it is that somebody who didn't even have rags to cover herself while she was alive has to have a new shroud when she dies!'

'The shroud just burns right up with the body.'

'And what's left? If we'd had these five rupees before then we could have got some medicine.'

Each of them guessed what was in the other's mind. They went on wandering through the market, stopping at one cloth-merchant's shop after another. They looked at different kinds of cloth, silk and cotton, but nothing met with their approval. This went on until evening. Then the two of them, by some divine inspiration or other, found themselves in front of a liquor shop, and as though according to a previous agreement they went inside. For a little while they stood there, hesitant. Then Ghisu went up to where the tavernkeeper sat and said, 'Sahuji, give us a bottle too.'

Then some snacks arrived, fried fish was brought and they sat on the verandah and tranquilly began to drink.

After drinking several cups in a row they began to feel tipsy. Ghisu said, 'What's the point of throwing a shroud over her? In the end it just burns up. She can't take anything with her.'

Madhav looked toward heaven and said, as though calling on the gods to witness his innocence, 'It's the way things are done in the world, otherwise why would people throw thousands of rupees away on Brahmins? Who can tell if anybody gets it in the next world or not?'

'The bigshots have lots of money to squander so let them squander it, but what have we got to squander?'

'But how will you explain it to people? Won't they ask, "Where's the shroud?"'

Ghisu laughed. 'So what? We'll say the money fell out of the knot in our *dhotis* and we looked and looked but couldn't find it. They won't believe it but they'll give the money again.'

Madhav laughed too over this unexpected stroke of luck. He said, 'She was good to us, that poor girl—even dying she got us fine things to eat and drink.'

They'd gone through more than half a bottle. Ghisu ordered four pounds of *puris*. Then relish, pickle, livers. There was a shop right across from the

7. Pennies.

tavern. Madhav brought everything back in a trice on a couple of leaf-platters. He'd spent one and a half rupees; only a few pice were left.

The two of them sat eating their *puris* in the lordly manner of tigers enjoying their kill in the jungle. They felt neither fear of being called to account nor concern for a bad reputation. They had overcome those sensibilities long before.

Ghisu said philosophically, 'If our souls are content won't it be credited to her in heaven as a good deed?'

Respectfully Madhav bowed his head and confirmed, 'Absolutely will! Lord, you know all secrets. Bring her to paradise—we bless her from our hearts . . . the way we've eaten today we've never eaten before in our whole lives.'

A moment later a doubt rose in his mind. He said, 'What about us, are we going to get there some day too?'

Ghisu gave no answer to this artless question. He didn't want to dampen his pleasure by thinking about the other world.

'But if she asks us there, "Why didn't you people give me a shroud?" What will you say?'

'That's a stupid question!'

'But surely she'll ask!'

'How do you know she won't get a shroud? Do you think I'm such a jackass? Have I been wasting my time in this world for sixty years? She'll have a shroud and a good one too.'

Madhav was not convinced. He said, 'Who'll give it? You've eaten up all the money. But she'll ask me. I was the one who put the cinnabar in her hair at the wedding.'

Getting angry, Ghisu said, 'I tell you she'll have a shroud, aren't you listening?'

'But why don't you tell me who's going to give it?'

'The same people who gave before will give the money again—well, not the money this time but the stuff we need.'

As the darkness spread and the stars began to glitter the gaiety of the tavern also increased steadily. People sang, bragged, embraced their companions, lifted the jug to the lips of friends. All was intoxication, the very air was tipsy. Anybody who came in got drunk in an instant from just a few drops, the air of the place turned their heads more than the liquor. The sufferings of their lives drew them all there and after a little while they were no longer aware if they were alive or dead, not alive or not dead.

And father and son went on slopping it up with zest. Everyone was staring at them. How lucky the two of them were, they had a whole bottle between themselves.

When he was crammed full Madhav handed the leftover *puris* on a leaf to a beggar who was standing watching them with famished eyes. And for the first time in his life he experienced the pride, the happiness and the pleasure of giving.

Ghisu said, 'Take it, eat it and say a blessing—the one who earned it is—well, she's dead. But surely your blessing will reach her. Bless her from your heart, that food's the wages for very hard labor.'

Madhav looked heavenward again and said, 'She'll go to heaven, *Dada*, she'll be a queen in heaven.'

Ghisu stood up and as though bathing in waves of bliss he said, 'Yes, son, she'll go to heaven. She didn't torment anybody, she didn't oppress anybody. At the moment she died she fulfilled the deepest wish of all our lives. If she doesn't go to heaven then will those big fat people go who rob the poor with both hands and swim in the Ganges and offer holy water in the temples to wash away their sins?'

Their mood of credulity suddenly changed. Volatility is the special characteristic of drunkenness. Now was the turn for grief and despair.

'But *Dada*,' Madhav said, 'the poor girl suffered so much in this life! How much pain she had when she died.'

He put his hands over his eyes and began to cry, he burst into sobs.

Ghisu consoled him. 'Why weep, son? Be glad she's slipped out of this maze of illusion and left the whole mess behind her. She was very lucky to escape the bonds of the world's illusion so quickly.'

And the two of them stood up and began to sing.

'Deceitful world, why do you dazzle us with your eyes?
Deceitful world!'

The eyes of all the drunkards were glued on them and the two of them became inebriated in their hearts. Then they started to dance, they jumped and sprang, fell back, twisted, they gesticulated, they mimed their feelings, and finally they collapsed dead drunk right there.

NIRALA

The writer known as Nirala was born in Bengal around 1899 and died in 1961. The details of his life are disputed. He was born Suraj Kumar Tevari, and was later known as Suryakant Tripathi and, finally, Nirala. He spoke Bangla and Baiswari (a dialect of Hindi) and was educated in Hindi. He failed his high school matriculation examinations, married, and had two children.

He wrote poetry, novels, stories, and essays. There were many attacks on him and on his work, which often set out to shock the Brahmins, praising meat-eating and attacking Nehru and Gandhi. His later years were marked by ill health, financial problems, and mental instability.

The selections are translated by David Rubin.

PRONOUNCING GLOSSARY

Anasuya: *uh´-nuh-soo´-yah*
Bharat: *bhuh´-rut*
chakora: *chuh´-koh-ruh*
Chitrakut: *chih´-truh-koot´*
Gandharva: *gun-dahr´-vuh*
Godavari: *goh-dah´-vuh-ree*
Gomti: *gohm´-tee*
Holi: *hoh´-lee*
Koshala: *koh´-shuh-luh*
Lakhanlal: *lah´-kun-lahl´*
Lal: *lahl*
madhumadhavi: *muh´-doo-mah´-duh-vee*
mallika: *muh´-lee-kah´*
Mansarovar: *mahn´-suh-roh-var*
Narayana: *nuh-rah´-yuh´-nuh*
Nirala: *nih-rah´-lah*
Parashurama: *puh-rah´-shoo-rah´-muh*
Ramaa: *ruh-mah´*
Ramayana: *ruh-mah´-yuh-nuh*
Rambhaa: *rum-bah´*
Shurpanakha: *shoor´-puh-nuh-kah´*
Sumitra: *soo´-mee-trah´*

A LOOK AT DEATH

Nirala's mother died when he was two; his father in 1917, when he was eighteen; and in the influenza epidemic of 1918 he lost his wife, brother, and sister-in-law, and was left to raise their children and his alone. His daughter died at the age of nineteen, in 1935, three years before he wrote this poem. Nirala imagined Death as a woman, as she is often imagined in Hindu texts, beginning in the *Mahabharata* (12.249–50).

What I've not said, say now,
you ever-youthful goddess,
create and yet again create your songs.

In a world too vast
you locked me in
and humbled me with grief.
And what you say is:
    "Through sorrow's workings
    I've granted you new riches.
    Transform those bird's wings now,
    in the water become a fish;
    the free sky's gone, so let
    existence in the sea
    suffice."
Clear, everything you said to me,
and still I didn't understand,
and that caused all my suffering.
That loving kiss you gave to me
today's a cup, brimming with poison.
And you laugh and tell me, "Drink, my lover,
my desperate lover, drink. Freedom am I!
In death I come.
Fear not."

GIVING

A strong condemnation of Brahmins.

The early-risen sun
revels in the young bosom of the spring,
kissed, laughing, pliant, tender,
the rays like flickering girls, the lips
of the sprouting leaves red with the honey
of youth, the obliging bees in flight
from one opened bud to another
thrilling with new hope, new feeling,
the swarms in woods and gardens
sweetly buzzing in their bliss.
The cassias gold-garlanded,
the red-clad mirthful flame-of-the-forest,
the jasmine petals strewn as for
a ritual offering, and *mallika*
bursting into blossom;
the clustering *madhumadhavi*
lets droop its blooms as though in shame;
the lotus, opened for the first time, pure,
to stare upon the glorious mystery.
The breezes float their fragrance
along with echoed tales of lovers.

Capricious, slender as a dancer's waist,
twisting in her desire: the Gomti's[1] stream.

Returning from a stroll this morning
I lingered on the bridge, thinking:
unalterable law of the world—
as you do so shall you be rewarded
by bountiful Nature herself—
there's nothing new to be said about this.
Beauty, song, the colors, scent,
speech and all the range of feelings,
and whatever higher joys may be:
these are the gifts of nature. Unsought
or labored-for they fall
to everybody's lot. And the best
of all (thanks be to God) is man's
high place as chief of all creation.

Then on the bridge I saw monkeys
beyond the counting crowded together.
And on the other side a man,
black-bodied, skeletal, half-dead—
misery given a human form—
staring unwaveringly in hope of alms,
throat shrunk, breath hoarse
merely to live a painful burden.
What curse had he brought on himself?
what sin committed to incur such grief?—
such questions come up often
in these streets and never get an answer.
The highest mercy—and all one could do—
was to give him a pice.[2]

Leaning over I saw below
one of our glorious Brahmins
at his bath, pouring water
in the ritual offering to Shiva.
Taking his bag crammed with rice,
sesame and herbs he came back up.
The monkeys in a flash trooped around him.

This twice-born Brahmin, devotee of Rama,
also worshipped Shiva with high hopes
the twelve months of the year. He was
my neighbor: always deep in the Ramayana
and muttering the holy name Narayana[3]
and faithful in his daily ritual bath.
When suffering some minor grief
he'd join his hands

1. The Gomati River, a tributary of the Ganges.
2. A fraction of a penny, a farthing.
3. A name of Vishnu.

and tell it to the monkeys.[4]
From his capacious bag he took
some little cakes and flung them toward
the monkeys' outstretched hands.

He didn't so much as glance
where that other beggar sat
but screeched, "Out of the way,
you devil!" I said, "Well done,
you best of all creation."

4. So that the monkeys would report it to Hanuman, the monkey general, who would then intercede for him with Rama ("Lost Loves . . . in the *Ramayana*," p. 186).

BLOOD HOLI

Holi is a carnivalesque spring festival, celebrated with bonfires, dancing, singing, and especially by throwing colored powders and squirting colored water, particularly red powders and water. Nirala wrote this poem to honor the students who took part in the violent agitations of 1946.

Boys and girls made life the game.
  They played Holi with their blood.
Among the people winning fame,
  they played Holi with their blood.

Bright as blossoms of the flame
  of the forest tree, bewitching as
crimson: lotus come to life—
  they played Holi with their blood.

How the red sprouts have started up,
  how the bonfires hurl their flames!
Singing the difficult songs of spring
  they played Holi with their blood.

Again the nights of song, again
  the brightening of the morning ray,
and flowers offered by every hand—
  they played Holi with their blood.

Enter a gaudy spring, clustered
  mango and lichi bloom.
the scent of jackfruit in the air—
  they played Holi with their blood.

The ebony trees put out their flags
  the cassias are hung with garlands;

scarlet flowers and red lips smiling—
they played Holi with their blood.

SHURPANAKHA

In Valmiki's *Ramayana*, Shurpanakha, an ogress and the sister of the great ogre Ravana, never meets Sita and never changes her hideous form. She meets Rama and his brother Lakshmana in the forest, is smitten with love for Rama, and propositions him, in response to which Rama and Lakshmana tease her and then Lakshmana cuts off her nose and ears ("The Mutilation of Shurpanakha," p. 438). In Kampan's Tamil version of the *Ramayana*, composed in the twelfth century C.E., Shurpanakha impersonates Sita and confronts her, but Rama immediately knows which is the real Sita. Nirala's poem, composed ca. 1922, introduces several preludes: Sita and Rama express their mutual love, Sita rehearses the virtues of a faithful wife, Lakshmana professes that he loves Sita only as a mother, and Lakshmana and Rama engage in a philosophical discussion. But then Shurpanakha, who describes herself as beautiful rather than hideous, propositions Rama in Sita's presence. The result is the same as in the Sanskrit and Tamil versions: the two brothers tease her and mutilate her.

I

SITA

The memory of that day comes to me now,
beloved!
the day when in our flower-garden,
king of flowers!
beneath the rays of the young sun
the blue lotus, newly opened, laughed,
and you, bewitching-eyed, with Lakshmana
strolled contentedly.
But is not this scene, Lord, still lovelier than that?
That bower of vines was charming there,
but still more beautiful the cool roof
of jasmine spread atop that tree.
For now it seems to me, there I was a slave,
while here I play the game of freedom,
and you are with me.
Where else could I find greater ease?
Where else could I sit and watch
the quick-dancing feet of heavenly nymphs
on the flashing waves of the restless stream?
Where else could I hear
such birds trilling in the mild breeze
or the sweet singing of the Gandharvas[1]

1. Celestial musicians, husbands of the celestial nymphs named Apsarases.

within the rustling leaves?
Where else could I drink the sweet words from my beloved's mouth?
Or where else find
the clean radiance of insight, knowledge and devotion
except in a forest hermitage?

RAMA

Within the little limits of a mean house
vile feelings are locked in—
this is the truth, beloved—
while the ocean of love spills over,
inexhaustible, on the earth.
The beating of love's mighty waves
shatters the mean frame,
scattering like straws
all the trivial desires of the worldly.
The ocean of love resounds with laughter
when it sees the entreaty
in the eyes of the terrified coward
standing silent on the shore,
hands joined, but steeped in illusions,
fearing to drown in that deep sea,
troubled by the hope of surviving,
which makes his whole body shrivel
as he remembers the fearful submarine blaze of passion—
and he turns his back on it.
Only one, beloved, with a body celestial
dares leap in—and he finds the nectar of love,
drinking which he becomes immortal.
And truly I find it too in sages,
a matchless love such as until today
I've never found before.
And more than any passion-blighted
palace pleasure garden
is this forest
pleasing to me.

SITA

Not for a moment was Lady Anasuya[2] wrong:
when just before setting out
I touched her feet with my forehead
she raised me up affectionately—
oh that gentle touch!—
and said, "Thou knowest, Sita,
the virtues of a faithful wife—
still let me speak to thee of them."
And all those qualities of wifeliness
respectfully she explained to me,

2. The virtuous wife of the virtuous sage Atri; she gives Sita a long lecture on the proper behavior of a woman ("The Crow and Anasuya," p. 435).

embracing me—how loving, oh,
how guileless and how selfless—
not for an instant do I forget it.

(Enter Lakshmana)

LAKSHMANA

Sir, some time ago, I brought
fragrant garlands of wood-apple
to our hut for the ceremony.

RAMA

Yes, Lal,[3] we come.

SITA

And bring me Malti blossoms, Lal,
I myself will string them together
and offer them
at the dear and lovely feet
of my beloved husband.

(Exit Lakshmana)

How understanding he is!
Except to serve he's capable of nothing.
When he approaches he bows his head,
looks only at your feet,
and says, so like a child,
"Mother, what's your command?"

RAMA

He has assumed all the virtues of his mother, Sumitra[4]—
like her he's eager to serve, self-sacrificing,
like her simple, clean-hearted and luminous.
As Mother Sumitra pounced like lightning on any imperfection,
just so Lakhanlal springs like lightning on the foe.
Did you not see his wrath in the fray with Parashurama?[5]
or at the time we set out for the forest?
Or when Bharat came up the mountain of Chitrakut?[6]
But you alone know how great
is his devotion to me.

3. *Lal* is a term of affection, *Lakhan* a dialect form of Lakshmana.
4. Dasharatha had several wives; Sumitra was the mother of Lakshmana, Kausalya was Rama's mother, and Kaikeyi was Bharata's mother.
5. Rama with an Axe, an avatar of Vishnu ("The Ten Avatars of Vishnu," p. 480).
6. Rama, Sita, and Lakshmana had stopped in Chitrakut, where they met Atri and Anasuya. At that time, Rama's brother Bharata, who had been given the throne that should have come to Rama (*Ramayana*, p. 186), came to visit his brothers in exile, and Lakshmana mistakenly thought that Bharata had come to attack them.

II

LAKSHMANA

Service is the one recourse of life
and indeed the very precept of Mother Sita,
for whose love alone I garner flowers and leaves.
Apart from that I know nothing
nor have I even the desire to know.
My greatest strength is the very dust of her feet,
and her satisfaction, for me, equals the eight perfections,
and her affectionate words my highest joy.
Fortunate I am—
she for whose glance myriads of Shivas and Vishnus and Brahmas,
millions of suns, moons, stars and constellations,
of Indras,[7] gods and demons,
universes of sentient and nonsentient beings
are born and bred and finally destroyed,
she who shines radiant in the very roots of all the Universes
as the primal shaping power,
by whose strength existence itself is in the strong—
she is my mother.
She, singing whose virtues men cross the ocean of being,
of whose reality alone is seen the firm impress
even in the "Om" of every charm and spell—
she is my mother.
She who has no equal
for her woman's greatness, her wife's devotion so profound,
she is my mother.
As a tangle of weeds afloat on the watery current,
homeless, aimless, without a will,
but—with the Lord's loving impulse in it—
finds at the end a sheltering heart vaster than the sea,
and so is freed,
so I too, renouncing the desire for pleasures,
home, riches and family,
I flow in the honeyed sea-wake of my Mother's feet.
I know not liberation, but devotion alone,
and it is enough.
If I but be the merest atom on her sweet lip,
that is the supreme bliss;
or if I could become a chakora[8] and go on drinking
the lily's night perfume rained in nectar from such a Moon—
for me what more contentment could there be?
No doubt of this:
it's an ill to be made happy,
to find one's happiness is far better.
When the pure drops of Mansarovar[9]
gathered by the sun's rays
take on their subtlest form, a form unmanifest,
they disappear for a time in the blue sphere of the sky,

7. Indra is the king of the gods.
8. A bird believed to live by drinking moonbeams.
9. "Lake of the Heart," a lake in the Himalayas, said to be the source of the Ganges.

singing an unheard melody—
they only know how great the bliss they find!
But meantime it is plain,
when they take on their cloudy shape,
signaling their advance,
then begins their youthful stage;
they change—how playfully! the colors
on the mountain peak, in the pathways of the welkin,
they dance, they mime, they shout and carol—
when the soft south wind kisses the cloud's tender cheek,
the heart fills with happiness,
and the bosom of Mansarovar is sprinkled with the drops,
breathing up watery sighs, remembering the past,
and when they see this wonder the multitude of blooming lotus,
tenderly smiling,
fling out a necklace of pearls.
For all of which I always hearken to the Supreme God:
"Oh Lord, folk call you the Wishing Tree
that grants the wish of every heart.
If you are content with me, oh Lord,
then this one boon I crave—
let me be sacrificed, utterly,
spirit and body,
for the satisfaction of the Mother;
let me know how to cut myself apart
from all trivial longings;
if any desire remain,
let it be for devotion."
It's late, I'll go now
and gather flowers.

III

SHURPANAKHA

When gods and Titans together
churned up the sea they took from it the fourteen jewels;
and I have heard,
two women, Rambhaa and Ramaa,[1] came from that churning too,
said by all to be most beautiful.
And yet it seems to me
the Creator, squeezing out
the full portion of all the beauty in the Universe,
has filled this body with it—
with love—
else with his trembling fingers
the architect of this old scheme of things
had reduced all his artist's skill to dust.
And this is true as well:
no woman fairer has ever been conceived;
I'm a queen,

1. Two Apsarases, born from the churning of the ocean ("The Churning of the Ocean," p. 149).

Nature my handmaiden:
when it sees my form
all the garnered loveliness of Nature humbly bows its head;
the woodland vines, wind-jostled,
all incline, lower their eyes,
as though hiding their faces at the sight
of this unparalleled beauty of mine.
Could even the Godavari stream,[2]
reflecting the blue sky, the lightning and the stars,
and rushing swift as a girl to her lover,
be compared to these woven tresses,
laced with flowers, yet unbound?
Never!
Startled as a little girl would be
the imagination of poets
confronting my brows
whence shoot the bewitching arrows of primal sex,
in turn spell-casting, subjugating, mind-ravishing.
Overcome are all eyes that see those eyes,
for into them the Creator has poured
intoxication enough to make the whole world drunk.
The wondrous nose, fish-hook shaped to catch the god of love,[3]
these round cheeks, pink and soft as flowers,
the charming chin, flashing its laugh like lightning,
the mouth's sphere, with its far-reaching flower-fragrance,
that delights all the quarters with its scattered pollen
and entices the darling bees.
Regard this dove's throat,
the arms like lianas, the lotus hands,
the breasts swelling and erect, the narrow waist,
the capacious buttocks and the delicate feet,
the gait so graceful—
destroying the serenity of sages and ascetics:
truly a wondrous matter for gods and voluptuaries.
The greatest heroes fall at my feet,
like beggars craving my favors,
and folding their hands they say, "Fair one, be merciful now!"
But I, superb in triumph,
casting a scornful glance
on the vanquished heroes at my feet,
turn away my radiant world-conquering face.
What wonder in that?
Not long ago this glorious brightness was not here,
Nature cruel and violent stifled the very breath of life,
all places like a desert waste
threw up dust and scorched the body,
and helped by the fierce sun
cruelly tormented every wayfarer.
But today, what a transformation!
The hands of Nature, guilty no doubt of countless killings,
now serve, opening the portals of the heart,

2. A great river in South India, second only to the Ganges.

3. Kama, who has a fish or a crocodile on his banner.

eagerly bearing sweet fruit and cool water.
Hey dey! new animation finds its way into brute matter.
I feel an urge,
intoxicated now with love,
to sing strange songs with my attendant buds,
to play games with the flowers,
festooning myself with blossoms
and twining them in garlands around my throat.

(Decks herself with flowers.)

But what cottage is that?
Has some holy sage come?
I'll draw closer and find out
who's come to waste his life so stupidly here.

IV

LAKSHMANA

What do they mean by the end of the world?

RAMA

The dissolution of mind, wisdom and ego is the end of the world.

LAKSHAMANA

Tell me, Lord, how is that the end of the world?

RAMA

Between the individual and the all there's no distinction—
distinctions are begotten by error,
which we call illusion.[4]

Not one man, brother, is ever deceived
by that light, through whose power
you see, resplendent, this solar universe entire.

The one form penetrates the individual and the All,
and is the source of bliss and understanding.
When curiosity stirs in the brain of the curious man,
when there's a longing to escape from error,
when consciousness gives warning: leave off your playing!
then a man's soul awakens
and he goes to dwell with sages and learn a discipline.[5]
No longer coarse, he becomes subtle and more than subtle;
when he begins to struggle with mind, wisdom and ego
in the battle every day his strength increases two-fold.

Gradually he discerns
inside his very self

4. *Maya* (Vedanta, p. 285).

5. Yoga.

sun moon planets stars
and countless whirling universes.

Then he sees clearly
the World-soul within the ego,
and knows with certainty
that the individual is not to be distinguished from the All;
he sees, there is one cause and working
of creation, existence and dissolution,
and his desire is for skill in the fashioning,
the fostering and the dissolution.

So brother these all are qualities of Nature.
And true it is, then Nature gives him all its power—
and with the eight perfections
he becomes all-powerful,
and when he gives it up,
when he crosses the frontier of subject-and-object,
he mounts up to the seventh heaven—
even then is the world come to its end
and he takes on the ultimate form
of truth, spirit and bliss.

LAKSHMANA

Then how is the world created anew?

RAMA

Those who through desire take body in this world,
their souls depart and come again
and their desire creates ever new creations.

For them, see, Lal,
all's useless here.
He who has become free
returns no more.

The endless series of myriad creations,
with them Nature sports for all eternity.

Well, these are other matters—
you asked about the dissolution of the solar universe.
Hear, brother,
just as the individual assumes one minute form,
just so the All
has its subtle state.
So all the seeds of Nature
are contained in the ether.
And it is also true that then
Nature's three basic strands[6] become identical.

6. The three elements of Nature or matter, in Sankhya philosophy: lucidity, passion, and darkness ("The Two Paths," p. 178).

SITA

These concepts are most perplexing, Lord—
tell us of the path of devotion!

RAMA

The paths of devotion, action and knowledge are all the same
even though they appear different to the great authorities.

There's only One, no second's there at all.
The sense of Two is the only error.
And all the same, beloved,
from the very heart of error
we must rise and pass beyond it.

The sages first considered
the restlessness of men's minds.
Therefore they filled with devotion
those who had held to dualism.
To those thirsting for love
they taught the loving service of the people,
than which there is naught purer.
Through service the spirit is purified.
In the cleansed soul the seed of love springs up.

If the mind be not immaculate
then love is wasted
and draws men into bestiality.

SITA

Behold, Lord, a woman comes.

RAMA

Sit now and let her approach.

V

SHURPANAKHA (ASIDE)

There are three of them here,
one more beautiful than the other.
The woman with them too
is fair and graceful—
but surely not more than myself.

(Smiles a little, observing the garland on her breast.)

These handsome men, it's clear,
have never been ascetics;
those supple limbs have never endured austerities;
they must be princes
or else celestial heroes taking the forms of men
to wander in the forest.

The luster of the dark-blue lotus[7]
ravishes with ease
the love garnered in the heart—
the hidden riches of women.
I should like to spend this day in dalliance
on the lake's blue water,
drinking love's lotus nectar,
blooming, laughing, like the fortunate lily,
and sipping honey from the lips of the dark God.

(Approaching Rama)

Oh beautiful!
your unequaled comeliness
has quite bewitched me.
As I am beautiful,
so you alone are worthy of me.
This will of mine insists
that you fulfill my wish.
Do not leave unanswered, man,
the urgent desire of a woman aroused!
Come you with me
to my forest, lover,
and I'll set you on a heavenly throne!
There's nothing will be denied you,
you'll taste divine delights, you best of men!
You shall be king over all in heaven
and I your queen.
Seated beneath the tree of Paradise you'll hearken to
the sweet-voiced Sirens'[8] ambrosial morning song.
And when this jasmine bends quivering from its weight of bees—

RAMA

Fair one, I'm married,
behold my wife.
But go to him,
a youth unmarried and handsome too.

LAKSHMANA

Fair one, I am his slave
and he the king of Koshala.[9]
One wife? why, he can marry many times if he wishes,
but I'm his servant,
and hope of my pleasuring you
is wishing for flowers from the sky.

SHURPANAKHA (TO RAMA)

You alone are worthy of me.

7. Like Krishna, Rama is usually portrayed as dark blue, and the lotus is the symbol of beauty.
8. The Apsarases, celestial courtesans, nymphs, and dancers.
9. The kingdom on the Ganges where Rama was born and eventually ruled.

RAMA

But just look and see
how fair he is, bright as gold!

SHURPANAKHA (TO LAKSHMANA)

In the mirror of my heart
love's reflection—
how glorious, how radiant—
behold it!

LAKSHMANA

Be off, vile woman!

SHURPANAKHA (TO RAMA)

Shame, thou wretch!
Imposter! Cheat!
You've scorned one who came to you
with passion
ready to offer you her living youth.
Seeing you guileless, charming, fair as the god of love,
I thought,
he surely is some amorist,
skilled in the sensual arts.
How could I know,
this was the dark hue not of love
but of poison?—
and spread a fearful venom?
What I took for a rose
turned out, alas, a scentless jungle blossom.
My error—a mirage,
like the thirsting roe's in the parched desert.
As you have cheated me
so will you enjoy the fruit of it forthwith.
So long as breath is in me
I'll lie in wait for you like the black she-cobra.
I'll make you weep too
as you have made me weep.

RAMA

I've not yet made you weep,
but if that is your wish—

(Signaling Lakshmana.)

LAKSHMANA

Now weep to your heart's content.

(Cuts off her nose and ears.)

MAHASVETA DEVI

Mahasveta Devi was born in 1926 to Brahmin parents, both writers, in Dhaka, in what is now Bangladesh; after Partition she moved to West Bengal. She has a master's degree in English from Shantiniketan, the experimental university that Rabindranath Tagore founded in the Bengal countryside (p. 623). She is an activist who has devoted herself to women, Dalits, and the tribal communities of West Bengal, whose oppression she depicts in her fiction.

PRONOUNCING GLOSSARY

Arijit: *ah´-ree-jeet´*
Arjan Singh: *ar´-jun sing´*
Bakuli: *buh-koo´-lee´*
Bankrajarh: *bahn´-kruh-jahr´*
Bankura: *bahn´-koo-ruh*
Bhagunal: *buh´-goo-nahl´*
Bhupati: *boo´-puh-tee*
Bibidha Bharti: *bee´-bee-duh bar´-tee*
Biddibabu: *bih´-dee-bah´-boo*
Birbhum: *beer´-boom*
Budhna: *bood´-nuh*
Burdwan: *boord´-wahn*
Chamru: *chahm´-roo*
Champabhumi: *chahm´-puh-boo´-mee*
Cherakhan: *chay´-ruh-kahn´*
Dipak: *dee´-puk*
Dopdi Mejhen: *dohp´-dee may´-jen*
Draupadi: *drau´-puh-dee*
Dukhiram Ghavari: *doo´-kee-rahm guh-rah´-ree*
Dulna Majhi: *dool´-nuh mah´-jee*
ghat: *gaht*
Golok: *goh´-lohk*
Jharkhani: *jar-kah´-nee*
Jugal: *joo´-guhl*
Kali: *kah´-lee*
Lakkhi Bera: *lah´-kee bay´-ruh*
Mahasveta Devi: *muh-hah´-svay´-tah day´-vee*
Maldah: *mahl´-duh*
Malini: *mah´-lee-nee´*
Mantu: *mahn´-too*
Munda: *moon´-duh*
Mundari: *moon-dah´-ree*
Murshidabad: *moor-shee´-duh-bahd´*
Mushai Tudu: *moo´-shai too´-doo*
Naran Bera: *nah´-run bay´-ruh*
Paltakuri: *pahl´-tuh-koo´-ree*
Panchayat: *pun´-chah-yaht*
Prabir: *pruh-beer´*
Radhabhumi: *rah´-duh-boo´-mee*
Rana: *rah´-nuh*
Rotoni Sahu: *roh´-toh-nee´ sah´-hoo*
Sankhya: *sahn´-kyuh*
Sahib: *suh-heeb´*
Sanjeev Kumar: *sahn´-jeev koo´-mar*
Santal: *sun-tahl*
Satish: *suh-teesh´*
Senanayak: *say´-nuh-nah´-yuk*
Shamu: *shah´-moo*
Shomai: *shoh´-mai*
Shomra: *shohm´-ruh*
Surja Sahu: *soor´-juh suh´-hoo*
Upi Mejhen: *oo´-pee may´-jen*

DOPDI (DRAUPADI)

Draupadi, the heroine of the *Mahabharata* ("The Stripping of Draupadi," p. 134), lives on in contemporary India in many forms; she has become a goddess, worshipped in rituals performed in Tamil Nadu, and she is the subject of a famous Tamil poem ("Panchali Sapatam," or "Draupadi's Vow") by Subramanya Bharathi (1882–1921), in which Draupadi's public humiliation represents simultaneously the plight of all women in a male society and the British oppression of "Mother India." Mahasveta Devi transposes the story of Draupadi to a time in 1971 when Indian government troops destroyed the rebellious sections of the rural population, particularly Naxalites (militant Indian Communists) and tribals (Santals), in East Bengal (now Bangladesh) and West Bengal. The theme of the Sanskrit of tribals and Dalits ("Which Language Should I Speak?," p. 605; "The Story of 'My Sanskrit,'" p. 606) opens this story, published in 1981, where the protagonist is caught between two versions of her name, Dopdi and Draupadi; it appears that, as a tribal, she cannot pronounce the Sanskrit, but it is also possible that the tribalized form, Dopdi, is the proper name of the ancient Draupadi. The literary scholar Gayatri Spivak, who translated this story, suggests that tribal people "have no right to heroic Sanskrit names. . . . This pious, domesticated Hindu name was given Dopdi at birth by her mistress, in the usual mood of benevolence felt by the oppressor's wife toward the tribal bond servant. It is the killing of this mistress's husband that sets going the events of the story."

Spivak goes on to spell out the relationship between Dopdi and the Draupadi of the Sanskrit *Mahabharata*:

> It is Draupadi who provides the only example of polyandry, not a common system of marriage in India. . . . Within a patriarchal and patronymic context, she is exceptional, indeed "singular" in the sense of odd, unpaired, uncoupled. . . . Mahasveta's story questions this "singularity" by placing Dopdi first in a comradely, activist, monogamous marriage and then in a situation of multiple rape. . . . Dopdi is (as heroic as) Draupadi. She is also what Draupadi—written into the patriarchal and authoritative sacred text as proof of male power—could not be. Dopdi is at once a palimpsest and a contradiction.

It is at the moment when she is stripped and raped that the woman known, until then, as Dopdi suddenly begins to be called Draupadi. By refusing to cover her nakedness, Dopdi rejects the womanly modesty that implicitly protects Draupadi in the earliest *Mahabharata* version, or the intervention of a protective male like the god Krishna that protects Draupadi in later versions. By rewriting Hindu history she has, paradoxically, earned her Sanskrit name.

Name Dopdi Mejhen, age twenty-seven, husband Dulna Majhi (deceased), domicile Cherakhan, Bankrahjarh, information whether dead or alive and/or assistance in arrest, one hundred rupees . . .

An exchange between two liveried uniforms.

First Livery: What's this, a tribal called Dopdi? The list of names I brought has nothing like it! How can anyone have an unlisted name?

Second: Draupadi Mejhen. Born the year her mother threshed rice at Surja Sahu (killed)'s at Bakuli. Surja Sahu's wife gave her the name.

Translated by Gayatri Chakravorty Spivak.

FIRST: These officers like nothing better than to write as much as they can in English. What's all this stuff about her?

SECOND: Most notorious female. Long wanted in many . . .

Dossier: Dulna and Dopdi worked at harvests, rotating between Birbhum, Burdwan, Murshidabad, and Bankura. In 1971, in the famous Operation Bakuli, when three villages were cordoned off and machine gunned, they too lay on the ground, faking dead. In fact, they were the main culprits. Murdering Surja Sahu and his son, occupying upper-caste wells and tubewells during the drought, not surrendering those three young men to the police. In all this they were the chief instigators. In the morning, at the time of the body count, the couple could not be found. The blood-sugar level of Captain Arjan Singh, the architect of Bakuli, rose at once and proved yet again that diabetes can be a result of anxiety and depression. Diabetes has twelve husbands—among them anxiety.

Dulna and Dopdi went underground for a long time in a Neanderthal darkness. The Special Forces, attempting to pierce that dark by an armed search, compelled quite a few Santals in the various districts of West Bengal to meet their Maker against their will. By the Indian Constitution, all human beings, regardless of caste or creed, are sacred. Still, accidents like this do happen. Two sorts of reasons: (1), the underground couple's skill in self-concealment; (2), not merely the Santals but all tribals of the Austro-Asiatic Munda tribes appear the same to the Special Forces.

In fact, all around the ill-famed forest of Jharkhani, which is under the jurisdiction of the police station at Bankrajharh (in this India of ours, even a worm is under a certain police station), even in the southeast and southwest corners, one comes across hair-raising details in the eyewitness records put together on the people who are suspected of attacking police stations, stealing guns (since the snatchers are not invariably well educated, they sometimes say "give up your chambers" rather than give up your gun), killing grain brokers, landlords, moneylenders, law officers, and bureaucrats. A black-skinned couple ululated like police sirens before the episode. They sang jubilantly in a savage tongue, incomprehensible even to the Santals. Such as:

Samaray hijulenako mar goekope

and,

Hende rambra keche keche
Pundi rambra keche keche

This proves conclusively that they are the cause of Captain Arjan Singh's diabetes.

Government procedure being as incomprehensible as the Male Principle in Sankhya[1] philosophy or Antonioni's early films, it was Arjan Singh who was sent once again on Operation Forest Jharkhani. Learning from Intelligence that the above-mentioned ululating and dancing couple was the escaped corpses, Arjan Singh fell for a bit into a zombie-like state and

1. In Sankhya ("Quieting the Mind," p. 122; "The Two Paths," p. 178), the Male Principle (Purusha) or Primeval Man ("The Hymn of the Primeval Man," p. 82) is balanced by the force of Nature (Prakriti). Michaelangelo Antonioni (1912–2007) was an Italian modernist filmmaker.

finally acquired so irrational a dread of black-skinned people that whenever he saw a black person in a ball-bag, he swooned, saying "They're killing me," and drank and passed a lot of water. Neither uniform nor Scriptures could relieve that depression. At long last, under the shadow of a premature and forced retirement, it was possible to present him at the desk of Mr. Senanayak,[2] the elderly Bengali specialist in combat and extreme-Left politics.

Senanayak knows the activities and capacities of the opposition better than they themselves do. First, therefore, he presents an encomium on the military genius of the Sikhs. Then he explains further: Is it only the opposition that should find power at the end of the barrel of a gun? Arjan Singh's power also explodes out of the male organ of a gun. Without a gun even the "five Ks"[3] come to nothing in this day and age. These speeches he delivers to all and sundry. As a result, the fighting forces regain their confidence in the *Army Handbook*. It is not a book for everyone. It says that the most despicable and repulsive style of fighting is guerrilla warfare with primitive weapons. Annihilation at sight of any and all practitioners of such warfare is the sacred duty of every soldier. Dopdi and Dulna belong to the category of such fighters, for they too kill by means of hatchet and scythe, bow and arrow, etc. In fact, their fighting power is greater than the gentlemen's. Not all gentlemen become experts in the explosion of "chambers"; they think the power will come out on its own if the gun is held. But since Dulna and Dopdi are illiterate, their kind have practiced the use of weapons generation after generation.

I should mention here that, although the other side make little of him, Senanayak is not to be trifled with. Whatever his practice, in theory he respects the opposition. Respects them because they could be neither understood nor demolished if they were treated with the attitude, "It's nothing but a bit of impertinent game-playing with guns." In order to destroy the enemy, become one. Thus he understood them by (theoretically) becoming one of them. He hopes to write on all this in the future. He has also decided that in his written work he will demolish the gentlemen and highlight the message of the harvest workers. These mental processes might seem complicated, but actually he is a simple man and is as pleased as his third great-uncle after a meal of turtle meat. In fact, he knows that, as in the old popular song, turn by turn the world will change. And in every world he must have the credentials to survive with honor. If necessary he will show the future to what extent he alone understands the matter in its proper perspective. He knows very well that what he is doing today the future will forget, but he also knows that if he can change color from world to world, he can represent the particular world in question. Today he is getting rid of the young by means of "apprehension and elimination," but he knows people will soon forget the memory and lesson of blood. And at the same time, he, like Shakespeare, believes in delivering the world's legacy into youth's hands. He is Prospero as well.

At any rate, information is received that many young men and women, batch by batch and on jeeps, have attacked police station after police station,

2. Sanskrit, "Leader of the Army."

3. The five marks of identity for a Sikh: *kes* (uncut hair), *kachh* (pants that extend down to the knee), *karha* (iron bangle), *kipran* (dagger), and *kanga* (comb).

terrified and elated the region, and disappeared into the forest of Jharkhani. Since after escaping from Bakuli, Dopdi and Dulna have worked at the house of virtually every landowner, they can efficiently inform the killers about their targets and announce proudly that they too are soldiers, rank and file. Finally the impenetrable forest of Jharkhani is surrounded by real soldiers, the army enters and splits the battlefield. Soldiers in hiding guard the falls and springs that are the only source of drinking water; they are still guarding, still looking. On one such search, army informant Dukhiram Gharari saw a young Santal man lying on his stomach on a flat stone, dipping his face to drink water. The soldiers shot him as he lay. As the .303 threw him off spread-eagled and brought a bloody foam to his mouth, he roared "Ma—ho" and then went limp. They realized later that it was the redoubtable Dulna Majhi.

What does "Ma—ho" mean? Is this a violent slogan in the tribal language? Even after much thought, the Department of Defense could not be sure. Two tribal-specialist types are flown in from Calcutta, and they sweat over the dictionaries put together by worthies such as Hoffmann-Jeffer and Golden-Palmer. Finally the omniscient Senanayak summons Chamru, the water carrier of the camp. He giggles when he sees the two specialists, scratches his ear with his "bidi," and says, the Santals of Maldah did say that when they began fighting at the time of King Gandhi! It's a battle cry. Who said "Ma—ho" here? Did someone come from Maldah?

The problem is thus solved. Then, leaving Dulna's body on the stone, the soldiers climb the trees in green camouflage. They embrace the leafy boughs like so many great god Pans and wait as the large red ants bite their private parts. To see if anyone comes to take away the body. This is the hunter's way, not the soldier's. But Senanayak knows that these brutes cannot be dispatched by the approved method. So he asks his men to draw the prey with a corpse as bait. All will come clear, he says. I have almost deciphered Dopdi's song.

The soldiers get going at his command. But no one comes to claim Dulna's corpse. At night the soldiers shoot at a scuffle and, descending, discover that they have killed two hedgehogs copulating on dry leaves. Improvidently enough, the soldiers' jungle scout Dukhiram gets a knife in the neck before he can claim the reward for Dulna's capture. Bearing Dulna's corpse, the soldiers suffer shooting pains as the ants, interrupted in their feast, begin to bite them. When Senanayak hears that no one has come to take the corpse, he slaps his anti-Fascist paperback copy of *The Deputy* and shouts, "What?" Immediately one of the tribal specialists runs in with a joy as naked and transparent as Archimedes' and says, "Get up, sir! I have discovered the meaning of that 'hende rambra' stuff. It's Mundari language."

Thus the search for Dopdi continues. In the forest belt of Jharkhani, the Operation continues—will continue. It is a carbuncle on the government's backside. Not to be cured by the tested ointment, not to burst with the appropriate herb. In the first phase, the fugitives, ignorant of the forest's topography, are caught easily, and by the law of confrontation they are shot at the taxpayer's expense. By the law of confrontation, their eyeballs, intestines, stomachs, hearts, genitals, and so on become the food of fox, vulture, hyena, wildcat, ant, and worm, and the untouchables go off happily to sell their bare skeletons.

They do not allow themselves to be captured in open combat in the next phase. Now it seems that they have found a trustworthy courier. Ten to one it's Dopdi. Dopdi loved Dulna more than her blood. No doubt it is she who is saving the fugitives now.

"They" is also a hypothesis.

Why?

How many went originally?

The answer is silence. About that there are many tales, many books in press. Best not to believe everything.

How many killed in six years' confrontation?

The answer is silence.

Why after confrontations are the skeletons discovered with arms broken or severed? Could armless men have fought? Why do the collarbones shake, why are legs and ribs crushed?

Two kinds of answer. Silence. Hurt rebuke in the eyes. Shame on you! Why bring this up? What will be will be. . . .

How many left in the forest? The answer is silence.

A legion? Is it justifiable to maintain a large battalion in that wild area at the taxpayer's expense?

Answer: Objection. "Wild area" is incorrect. The battalion is provided with supervised nutrition, arrangements to worship according to religion, opportunity to listen to "Bibidha Bharti"[4] and to see Sanjeev Kumar[5] and the Lord Krishna face-to-face in the movie *This Is Life*. No. The area is not wild.

How many are left?

The answer is silence.

How many are left? Is there anyone *at all*?

The answer is long.

Item: *Well,* action still goes on. Moneylenders, landlords, grain brokers, anonymous brothel keepers, ex-informants are still terrified. The hungry and naked are still defiant and irrepressible. In some pockets the harvest workers are getting a better wage. Villages sympathetic to the fugitives are still silent and hostile. These events cause one to think. . . .

Where in this picture does Dopdi Mejhen fit?

She must have connections with the fugitives. The cause for fear is elsewhere. The ones who remain have lived a long time in the primitive world of the forest. They keep company with the poor harvest workers and the tribals. They must have forgotten book learning. Perhaps they are orienting their book learning to the soil they live on and learning new combat and survival techniques. One can shoot and get rid of the ones whose only recourse is extrinsic book learning and sincere intrinsic enthusiasm. Those who are working practically will not be exterminated so easily.

Therefore Operation Jharkhani Forest cannot stop. Reason: the words of warning in the *Army Handbook*.

4. A popular radio program.

5. A popular film star, who encounters Krishna in the film mentioned in the story; perhaps a reference to Krishna's role in rescuing Draupadi, in the *Mahabharata*.

2

Catch Dopdi Mejhen. She will lead us to the others.

Dopdi was proceeding slowly, with some rice knotted into her belt. Mushai Tudu's wife had cooked her some. She does so occasionally. When the rice is cold, Dopdi knots it into her waistcloth and walks slowly. As she walked, she picked out and killed the lice in her hair. If she had some kerosene, she'd rub it into her scalp and get rid of the lice. Then she could wash her hair with baking soda. But the bastards put traps at every bend of the falls. If they smell kerosene in the water, they will follow the scent.

Dopdi!

She doesn't respond. She never responds when she hears her own name. She has seen in the Panchayat[6] office just today the notice for the reward in her name. Mushai Tudu's wife had said, "What are you looking at? Who is Dopdi Mejhen! Money if you give her up!"

"How much?"

"Two—hundred!"

Oh God!

Mushai's wife said outside the office: "A lot of preparation this time. A—ll new policemen."

Hm.

Don't come again.

Why?

Mushai's wife looked down. Tudu says that Sahib has come again. If they catch you, the village, our huts . . .

They'll burn again.

Yes. And about Dukhiram . . .

The Sahib knows?

Shomai and Budhna betrayed us.

Where are they?

Ran away by train.

Dopdi thought of something. Then said, Go home. I don't know what will happen, if they catch me don't know me.

Can't you run away?

No. Tell me, how many times can I run away? What will they do if they catch me? They will counter me. Let them.

Mushai's wife said, We have nowhere else to go.

Dopdi said softly, I won't tell anyone's name.

Dopdi knows, has learned by hearing so often and so long, how one can come to terms with torture. If mind and body give way under torture, Dopdi will bite off her tongue. That boy did it. They countered him. When they counter you, your hands are tied behind you. All your bones are crushed, your sex is a terrible wound. Killed by police in an encounter . . . unknown male . . . age twenty-two . . .

As she walked thinking these thoughts, Dopdi heard someone calling, Dopdi!

She didn't respond. She doesn't respond if called by her own name. Here her name is Upi Mejhen. But who calls?

6. An elected body of village self-government.

Spines of suspicion are always furled in her mind. Hearing "Dopdi" they stiffen like a hedgehog's. Walking, she unrolls the film of known faces in her mind. Who? No Shomra, Shomra is on the run. Shomai and Budhna are also on the run, for other reasons. Not Golok, he is in Bakuli. Is it someone from Bakuli? After Bakuli, her and Dulna's names were Upi Mejhen, Matang Majhi. Here no one but Mushai and his wife knows their real names. Among the young gentlemen, not all of the previous batches knew.

That was a troubled time. Dopdi is confused when she thinks about it. Operation Bakuli in Bakuli. Surja Sahu arranged with Biddibabu to dig two tubewells and three wells within the compound of his two houses. No water anywhere, drought in Birbhum. Unlimited water at Surja Sahu's house, as clear as a crow's eye.

Get your water with canal tax, everything is burning.

What's my profit in increasing cultivation with tax money?

Everything's on fire.

Get out of here. I don't accept your Panchayat nonsense. Increase cultivation with water. You want half the paddy for sharecropping. Everyone is happy with free paddy. Then give me paddy at home, give me money, I've learned my lesson trying to do you good.

What good did you do?

Have I not given water to the village?

You've given it to your kin Bhagunal.

Don't you get water?

No. The untouchables don't get water.

The quarrel began there. In the drought, human patience catches easily. Satish and Jugal from the village and that young gentleman, was Rana his name?, said a landowning moneylender won't give a thing, put him down.

Surja Sahu's house was surrounded at night. Surja Sahu had brought out his gun. Surja was tied up with cow rope. His whitish eyeballs turned and turned, he was incontinent again and again. Dulna had said, I'll have the first blow, brothers. My greatgrandfather took a bit of paddy from him, and I still give him free labor to repay that debt.

Dopdi had said, His mouth watered when he looked at me. I'll put out his eyes.

Surja Sahu. Then a telegraphic message from Shiuri. Special train. Army. The jeep didn't come up to Bakuli. March-march-march. The crunch-crunch-crunch of gravel under hobnailed boots. Cordon up. Commands on the mike. Jugal Mandal, Satish Mandal, Rana alias Prabir alias Dipak, Dulna Majhi-Dopdi Mejhen surrender surrender surrender. No surrender surrender. Mow-mow-mow down the village. Putt-putt putt-putt—cordite in the air—putt-putt—round the clock—putt-putt. Flame thrower. Bakuli is burning. More men and women, children . . . fire—fire. Close canal approach. Over-over-over by nightfall. Dopdi and Dulna had crawled on their stomachs to safety.

They could not have reached Paltakuri after Bakuli. Bhupati and Tapa took them. Then it was decided that Dopdi and Dulna would work around the Jharkhani belt. Dulna had explained to Dopdi, Dear, this is best! We won't get family and children this way. But who knows? Landowner and moneylender and policemen might one day be wiped out!

Who called her from the back today?

Dopdi kept walking. Villages and fields, bush and rock—Public Works Department markers—sound of running steps in back. Only one person running. Jharkhani Forest still about two miles away. Now she thinks of nothing but entering the forest. She must let them know that the police have set up notices for her again. Must tell them that that bastard Sahib has appeared again. Must change hideouts. Also, the plan to do to Lakkhi Bera and Naran Bera what they did to Surja Sahu on account of the trouble over paying the field hands in Sandara must be canceled. Shomai and Budhna knew everything. There was the urgency of great danger under Dopdi's ribs. Now she thought there was no shame as a Santal in Shomai and Budhna's treachery. Dopdi's blood was the pure unadulterated black blood of Champabhumi.[7] From Champa to Bakuli the rise and set of a million moons. Their blood could have been contaminated; Dopdi felt proud of her forefathers. They stood guard over their women's blood in black armor. Shomai and Budhna are half-breeds. The fruits of the war. Contributions to Radhabhumi by the American soldiers stationed at Shiandanga. Otherwise, crow would eat crow's flesh before Santal would betray Santal.

Footsteps at her back. The steps keep a distance. Rice in her belt, tobacco leaves tucked at her waist. Arijit, Malini, Shamu, Mantu—none of them smokes or even drinks tea. Tobacco leaves and limestone powder. Best medicine for scorpion bite. Nothing must be given away.

Dopdi turned left. This way is the camp. Two miles. This is not the way to the forest. But Dopdi will not enter the forest with a cop at her back.

I swear by my life. By my life Dulna, by my life. Nothing must be told.

The footsteps turn left. Dopdi touches her waist. In her palm the comfort of a half-moon. A baby scythe. The smiths at Jharkhani are fine artisans. Such an edge we'll put on it Upi, a hundred Dukhirams—Thank God Dopdi is not a gentleman. Actually, perhaps they have understood scythe, hatchet, and knife best. They do their work in silence. The lights of the camp at a distance. Why is Dopdi going this way? Stop a bit, it turns again. Huh! I can tell where I am if I wander all night with my eyes shut. I won't go in the forest, I won't lose him that way. I won't outrun him. You fucking jackal[8] of a cop, deadly afraid of death, you can't run around in the forest. I'd run you out of breath, throw you in a ditch, and finish you off.

Not a word must be said. Dopdi has seen the new camp, she has sat in the bus station, passed the time of day, smoked a "bidi" and found out how many police convoys had arrived, how many radio vans. Squash four, onions seven, peppers fifty, a straightforward account. This information cannot now be passed on. They will understand Dopdi Mejhen has been countered. Then they'll run. Arijit's voice. If anyone is caught, the others must catch the timing and change their hideout. If Comrade Dopdi arrives late, we will not remain. There will be a sign of where we've gone. No comrade will let the others be destroyed for her own sake.

Arijit's voice. The gurgle of water. The direction of the next hideout will be indicated by the tip of the wooden arrowhead under the stone.

Dopdi likes and understands this. Dulna died, but, let me tell you, he didn't lose anyone else's life. Because this was not in our heads to begin

7. Archaic names for areas of Bengal.
8. The jackal that follows the tiger, living off the braver animal's scraps, is an ancient Indian fable and metaphor ("The Foxes That Became Horses," p. 356; "Beast-Meat and Man-Meat," p. 407).

with, one was countered for the other's trouble. Now a much harsher rule, easy and clear. Dopdi returns—good; doesn't return—bad. Change hideout. The clue will be such that the opposition won't see it, won't understand even if they do.

Footsteps at her back. Dopdi turns again. These three and a half miles of land and rocky ground are the best way to enter the forest. Dopdi has left that way behind. A little level ground ahead. Then rocks again. The army could not have struck camp on such rocky terrain. This area is quiet enough. It's like a maze, every hump looks like every other. That's fine. Dopdi will lead the cop to the burning "ghat."[9] Patitpaban of Saranda had been sacrificed in the name of Kali of the Burning Ghats.

Apprehend!

A lump of rock stands up. Another. Yet another. The elderly Senanayak was at once triumphant and despondent. If you want to destroy the enemy, become one. He had done so. As long as six years ago he could anticipate their every move. He still can. Therefore he is elated. Since he has kept up with the literature, he has read *First Blood*[1] and seen approval of his thought and work.

Dopdi couldn't trick him, he is unhappy about that. Two sorts of reasons. Six years ago he published an article about information storage in brain cells. He demonstrated in that piece that he supported this struggle from the point of view of the field hands. Dopdi is a field hand. Veteran fighter. Search and destroy. Dopdi Mejhen is about to be apprehended. Will be destroyed. Regret.

Halt!

Dopdi stops short. The steps behind come around to the front. Under Dopdi's ribs the canal dam breaks. No hope. Surja Sahu's brother Rotoni Sahu. The two lumps of rock come forward. Shomai and Budhna. They had not escaped by train.

Arijit's voice. Just as you must know when you've won, you must also acknowledge defeat and start the activities of the next stage.

Now Dopdi spreads her arms, raises her face to the sky, turns toward the forest, and ululates with the force of her entire being. Once, twice, three times. At the third burst the birds in the trees at the outskirts of the forest awake and flap their wings. The echo of the call travels far.

3

Draupadi Mejhen was apprehended at 6:53 P.M. It took an hour to get her to camp. Questioning took another hour exactly. No one touched her, and she was allowed to sit on a canvas camp stool. At 8:57 Senanayak's dinner hour approached, and saying, "Make her. Do the needful," he disappeared.

Then a billion moons pass. A billion lunar years. Opening her eyes after a million light years, Draupadi, strangely enough, sees sky and moon. Slowly the bloodied nailheads shift from her brain. Trying to move, she feels her arms and legs still tied to four posts. Something sticky under her ass and waist. Her own blood. Only the gag has been removed. Incredible thirst. In case she says "water" she catches her lower lip in her teeth. She senses that her vagina is bleeding. How many came to make her?

9. Corpses are burned on the steps (ghats) leading down to rivers. The goddess Kali presides over the ghats in the temple to Kali in Calcutta/Kolkata (Kali-ghata).

1. *First Blood* is a 1972 novel by David Morrell, about a Vietnam War veteran named Rambo.

Shaming her, a tear trickles out of the corner of her eye. In the muddy moonlight she lowers her lightless eye, sees her breasts, and understands that, indeed, she's been made up right. Her breasts are bitten raw, the nipples torn. How many? Four-five-six-seven—then Draupadi had passed out.

She turns her eyes and sees something white. Her own cloth. Nothing else. Suddenly she hopes against hope. Perhaps they have abandoned her. For the foxes to devour. But she hears the scrape of feet. She turns her head, the guard leans on his bayonet and leers at her. Draupadi closes her eyes. She doesn't have to wait long. Again the process of making her begins. Goes on. The moon vomits a bit of light and goes to sleep. Only the dark remains. A compelled spread-eagled still body. Active pistons of flesh rise and fall, rise and fall over it.

Then morning comes.

Then Draupadi Mejhen is brought to the tent and thrown on the straw. Her piece of cloth is thrown over her body.

Then, after breakfast, after reading the newspaper and sending the radio message "Draupadi Mejhen apprehended," etc., Draupadi Mejhen is ordered brought in.

Suddenly there is trouble.

Draupadi sits up as soon as she hears "Move!" and asks, Where do you want me to go?

To the Burra Sahib's tent.

Where is the tent?

Over there.

Draupadi fixes her red eyes on the tent. Says, Come, I'll go.

The guard pushes the water pot forward.

Draupadi stands up. She pours the water down on the ground. Tears her piece of cloth with her teeth. Seeing such strange behavior, the guard says, She's gone crazy, and runs for orders. He can lead the prisoner out but doesn't know what to do if the prisoner behaves incomprehensibly. So he goes to ask his superior.

The commotion is as if the alarm had sounded in a prison. Senanayak walks out surprised and sees Draupadi, naked, walking toward him in the bright sunlight with her head high. The nervous guards trail behind.

What is this? He is about to cry, but stops.

Draupadi stands before him, naked. Thigh and pubic hair matted with dry blood. Two breasts, two wounds.

What is this? He is about to bark.

Draupadi comes closer. Stands with her hand on her hip, laughs and says, The object of your search, Dopdi Mejhen. You asked them to make me up, don't you want to see how they made me?

Where are her clothes?

Won't put them on, sir. Tearing them.

Draupadi's black body comes even closer. Draupadi shakes with an indomitable laughter that Senanayak simply cannot understand. Her ravaged lips bleed as she begins laughing. Draupadi wipes the blood on her palm and says in a voice that is as terrifying, sky splitting, and sharp as her ululation, What's the use of clothes? You can strip me, but how can you clothe me again? Are you a man?

She looks around and chooses the front of Senanayak's white bush shirt to spit a bloody gob at and says, There isn't a man here that I should be ashamed. I will not let you put my cloth on me. What more can you do? Come on, counter me—come on, counter me—?

Draupadi pushes Senanayak with her two mangled breasts, and for the first time Senanayak is afraid to stand before an unarmed target, terribly afraid.

ANANTHA MURTHY

Udupi Rajagopalacharya Anantha Murthy, born in 1932 in Karnataka, is a contemporary Kannada writer and critic. After earning a master's degree from the University of Mysore, he went to England to do his Ph.D. at the University of Birmingham. Since returning to India, he has taught English in Mysore, Bangalore, and Kerala. His short stories and novels have won many prizes.

PRONOUNCING GLOSSARY

Acharya: *ah-char´-yuh*
agrahara: *uh´-gruh-hah´-ruh*
Anantha Murthy: *uh-nun´-tuh moor´-tee*
Bhagirathi: *buh´-gee-ruh´-tee*
Chandri: *chun´-dree*
Dharmasthala: *dar´-muh-stah´-luh*
Durgabhatta: *door´-guh-buh´-tuh*
Garuda: *guh-roo´-duh*
Garudacharya: *guh-roo´-dah-char´-yuh*
Gowri: *gow´-ree*
Kashi: *kah´-shee*
Lakshmanacharya: *luhk´-shmuh-nuh-char´-yuh*
Lakshmidevamma: *luhk´-shmee-day-vah´-mah*
Madhva: *mahd´-vuh*
Maruti: *muh-roo´-tee*
Naranappa: *nuh´-ruh-nup´-puh*
Narayana: *nuh-rah´-yuh-nuh*
Praneshacharya: *pruh-naysh´-ah-char´-yuh*
Samskara: *sum-skah´-ruh*
Saru: *suh´-roo*
Shivamogge: *shih´-vuh-moh´-gay*
Sitadevi: *see´-tuh-day´-vee*
Smarta: *smar-tuh*
Udupi: *oo´-doo-pee´*

SAMSKARA: A RITE FOR A DEAD MAN

Samskara, Anantha Murthy's most famous work, created a furor when it was first published, in Kannada, in 1965, largely because the author, a Brahmin, portrayed a Brahmin village, called an *agrahara*, in such an uncompromising light. But it quickly became a great critical and popular success, and was made into a film in 1970. The novel deals with issues of religion and caste arising out of the funeral of Naranappa, a Brahmin who violated many Brahmin rules: he lived openly with a low-caste prostitute, drank alcohol, and ate meat with his Muslim friends, with whom he also caught and ate fish from the temple tank. His death is even more problematic than his life: the Brahmins in his *agrahara* cannot eat until the body is cremated, but any Brahmin who performs the cremation ceremony for a Brahmin so polluted will be polluted, nor can anyone but a Brahmin cremate a Brahmin. Our selection is the very opening of the novel.

He bathed Bhagirathi's body, a dried-up wasted pea-pod, and wrapped a fresh sari around it; then he offered food and flowers to the gods as he did every day, put the flowers in her hair, and gave her holy water. She touched his feet, he blessed her. Then he brought her a bowlful of cracked wheat porridge from the kitchen.

Bhagirathi said in a low voice, 'You finish your meal first.'

'No, no. Finish your porridge. That first.'

The words were part of a twenty-year routine between them. A routine that began with the bath at dawn, twilight prayers, cooking, medicines for his wife. And crossing the stream again to the Maruti[1] temple for worship. That was the unfailing daily routine. After their meals, the brahmins of the *agrahara* would come to the front of his house, one by one, and gather there to listen to his recitation of sacred legends, always new and always dear to them and to him. In the evening he would take another bath, say more twilight prayers, make porridge for his wife, cook, eat dinner. Then there would be more recitations for the brahmins who collected again on the verandah.

Now and then Bhagirathi would say: 'Being married to me is no joy. A house needs a child. Why don't you just get married again?' Praneshacharya would laugh aloud. 'A wedding for an old man . . .'

'Come now, what kind of an old man are you? You haven't touched forty yet. Any father would love to give you his girl and bless her with wedding water. You studied Sanskrit in Kashi. . . . A house needs a child to make it home. You've had no joy in this marriage.'

Praneshacharya wouldn't answer. He would smile and pat his wife who was trying to get up, and ask her to try and go to sleep. Didn't the Lord Krishna say: Do what's to be done with no thought of fruit? The Lord definitely means to test him on his way to salvation; that's why He's given him a brahmin birth this time and set him up in this kind of family. The Acharya[2] is filled with pleasure and a sense of worth as sweet as the five-fold nectar[3] of holy days; he is filled with compassion for his ailing wife. He proudly swells a little at his lot, thinking, 'By marrying an invalid, I get ripe and ready.'

Before he sat down to his meal, he picked up the fodder for Gowri, the cow, on a banana leaf and placed it in front of Gowri who was grazing in the backyard. Worshipfully he caressed the cow's body, till the hair on her hide rose in pleasure. In a gesture of respect, he touched his own eyes with the hand that had touched the holy animal. As he came in, he heard a woman's voice calling out, 'Acharya, Acharya.'

It sounded like Chandri's voice; Chandri, Naranappa's concubine. If the Acharya talked to her, he would be polluted; he'd have to bathe again before his meal. But how can a morsel go down the gullet with a female waiting in the yard?

He came out; Chandri quickly pulled the end of her sari over her head, blanched, and stood there, afraid.

TRANSLATED BY A. K. Ramanujan.

1. Hanuman, the monkey god, son of the wind (Marut) (*Ramayana*, p. 186).
2. Teacher.
3. A mixture of milk, curd, ghee, honey, and sugar offered to gods on holy days.

'What's the matter?'

'He . . . He . . .'

Chandri shivered, words stuck in her mouth. She held on to the pillar.

'What? Naranappa? What happened?'

'Gone . . .'

She covered her face with her hands.

'Narayana, Narayana[4]—when was that?'

'Just now.'

Between sobs Chandri answered:

'He came back from Shivamogge and took to bed in a fever. Four days of fever, that's all. He had a painful lump on his side, the kind they get with fever.'

'Narayana.'

Praneshacharya ran out, still wrapped in the ritual raw silk, ran to Garudacharya's house and went straight to the kitchen, calling out, 'Garuda, Garuda!'

The dead Naranappa had been related to Garuda for five generations. Naranappa's great grandfather's grandmother and Garuda's great grandfather's grandmother were sisters.

Garudacharya was in the act of raising a handful of rice mixed with *Saru*[5] to his mouth, when Praneshacharya entered and said, 'Narayana. Don't, Garuda, don't eat. I hear Naranappa is dead,' and wiped the sweat of midday from his face. Dumbstruck, Garuda took a gulp of consecrated water[6] and threw down the mixed rice in his hand on the leaf before him, rising from his seat. He couldn't eat, even though he had quarrelled with Naranappa, severed all relations with him, and shed his kinship long ago. His wife, Sitadevi, stood there motionless, ladle in hand. He said to her, 'It's all right for the children. They can eat. Only we adults shouldn't, till the funeral rites are done.' He came out with Praneshacharya. They feared that the kinsmen next door might eat before they got the news, so they ran from house to house—Praneshacharya to Udupi Lakshmanacharya, Garudacharya to Lakshmidevamma the half-wit and to Durgabhatta down the street. The news of death spread like a fire to the other ten houses of the *agrahara*. Doors and windows were shut, with children inside. By god's grace, no brahmin had yet eaten. Not a human soul there felt a pang at Naranappa's death, not even women and children. Still in everyone's heart an obscure fear, an unclean anxiety. Alive, Naranappa was an enemy; dead, a preventer of meals; as a corpse, a problem, a nuisance. Soon the males moved towards the Acharya's house-front. The wives blew words of warning into their husbands' ears:

'Don't be in a hurry. Wait till Praneshacharya gives you a decision. Don't agree too quickly to perform the rites. You may do the wrong thing and the guru will excommunicate you.'

The brahmins gathered again, just as they did for the daily reading of the holy legends, and crowded one against the other. But today an obscure anxiety brooded among them. Fingering the basil-bead rosary round his neck, Praneshacharya said to them, almost as if to himself:

4. A name of Vishnu, uttered as an exclamation.

5. A spicy sauce eaten with rice.

6. A ritual of sipping water before and after a meal.

'Naranappa's death rites have to be done: that's problem one. He has no children. Someone should do it: that's problem two.'

Chandri, standing against the pillar in the yard, waited anxiously for the brahmins' verdict. The brahmin wives had come in through the backdoor into the middle hall, unable to contain their curiosity, afraid their husbands might do something rash.

Fondling his fat black naked arms, Garudacharya said as usual:

'Yes. Ye . . . es. Ye . . . es.'

'No one can eat anything until the body's cremated,' said Dasacharya, one of the poorer brahmins, thin, bony as a sick cow.

'True . . . true . . . Quite true,' said Lakshmanacharya, rubbing his belly—jerking his face forwards and backwards, batting his eyelids rapidly. The only well-fed part of his body was his belly, swollen with malarial bubo.[7] Sunken cheeks, yellow eyes deep in sockets, ribs protruding, a leg twisted—altogether an unbalanced body. The rival brahmins of Parijatapura mocked at him for walking with his buttocks out.

No one had a direct suggestion. Praneshacharya said:

'So the problem before us is—who should perform the rites? The Books say, any relative can. Failing that, any brahmin can offer to do them.'

When relatives were mentioned, everyone looked at Garuda and Lakshmana. Lakshmana closed his eyes, as if to say it's not for him. But Garuda was familiar with law courts, having walked up and down many; he felt it was his turn to speak up. So he raised a pinch of snuff to his nose and cleared his throat:

'It's but right we should go by the ancient Law-Books. Acharya, you are our greatest scholar, your word is Vedic gospel to us. Give us the word, we'll do it. Between Naranappa and me, it's true, there's a bond of kinship going back several generations. But as you know, his father and I fought over that orchard and went to court. After his father's death, I appealed to the guru at the Dharmasthala monastery. He decreed in my favor. Yet Naranappa defied it, even god's word—What do you say?—So we swore we'd have nothing between us for generations to come, nothing, no exchange of words, no wedding nor rite, no meal nor hospitality. That's what we swore—what do you say . . .'

Garudacharya's nasal sentences punctuated by his what-do-you-says suddenly halted, but were spurred on again by two more pinches of snuff. He gathered courage, looked around, saw Chandri's face and said boldly:

'The guru will also agree to what you say. What do you say? Let's set aside the question of whether I should do the rites. The real question is: is he a brahmin at all? What do you say?—he slept regularly with a lowcaste woman . . .'

There was only one man from the *Smarta*[8] sect, Durgabhatta, in this colony of *Madhva*[9] brahmins. He was always checking and measuring the rival sect's orthodoxy with a questioning eye. He looked sideways at Chandri and cackled:

'Chi Chi Chi, don't be too rash, Acharya. O no, a brahmin isn't lost because he takes a lowborn prostitute. Our ancestors after all came from

7. The swellings produced by the disease.
8. A high Brahmin Non-dualist caste.
9. A great Vedantic philosopher of the Dualist school (Vedanta, p. 285).

the North—you can ask Praneshacharya if you wish—history says they cohabited with Dravidian women. Don't think I am being facetious. Think of all the people who go to the brothels of Basrur in South Canara . . .'

Garudacharya got angry. This fellow was mischievous.

* * *

ANUMANDLA BHUMAYYA

A leading Telugu poet, Anumandla Bhumayya was formerly vice-chancellor of Potti Sri Ramulu Telugu University. This selection is abridged from his long Telugu poem, *Jvalita Kausalaya* (1999).

KAUSALYA IN FURY

According to the Sanskrit text of Valmiki, when Rama, the eldest son of Dasharatha (the reigning king in Ayodhya) and the son of the oldest queen, Kausalya, was about to ascend the throne, a younger queen, Kaikeyi, forced Dasharatha to put her son, Bharata, on the throne instead and send Rama into exile ("Dasharatha Kills a Boy," p. 192). She achieved her purpose in part by reminding him of a promise he had made to her years ago and in part by playing upon his desire for her. Rama and his brother Lakshmana acquiesced in obedience to their father, though Lakshmana occasionally expressed his anger against him for this bad decision. When the *Ramayana* is retold, however, the anger is often expressed more forcefully and more widely.

In this excerpt from *Jvalita Kausalaya*, Rama's father (Dasharatha) sends word for Rama to come to him at the home of Rama's "other mother" (Kaikeyi, here called Kaika), where Rama learns of his command. Rama then goes to his own mother, Kausalya, and tells her of the "two wishes" (the earlier promise), which mean his exile. And in this version, unlike Valmiki's, we hear Kausalya lament her unhappiness with Dasharatha. This poem poses a serious challenge to the dominant *bhakti* reading of the *Ramayana*, but one that is also far more elegant and gentle than the harsh critiques provided by some of the village and tribal tellings, and by other modern pieces such as Nirala's version of the Shurpanakha story (p. 649) or Kumaran Asan's version of Sita's final thoughts ("Sita Lost in Thought," p. 372). These very different bold readings testify to the ongoing vitality of the tradition.

Father sends word.
Rama goes to his other mother's palace
and tastes her bitter command.
Now he is at his mother's place,
to tell her he has to go (5)
to the forest.

He bows to her feet.
She embraces him
and kisses his forehead.

TRANSLATED BY Velcheru Narayana Rao.

Rama says:
Sometime ago in the past
father gave to Kaika
two wishes and she asks them now.
She remembers.

Bharata should be the young king.
And I, Rama, should go to the forest
for fourteen years.

Bless me mother, I have to go.
This is father's command,

2.

Kausalya says:
Rama, my son,
Why does the sun rise today?
They are daggers—not his rays.
His heart is made of stone.
In all my life I have not known
or seen a day like this.
This is the end; I won't see you again.
They put poison in my life
sweetened only by your birth.

Whatever joy I had when I was young
in my parent's house, that was all.
I never knew a happy day
since I set foot in your father's house.
You were born and washed the tears off my eyes.
I was hoping to see good days
when you are king, but now this word
comes like a snake that bites you
when you reach up the tree
to pluck the fruit.

I have a range of jewels to wear
seven days of the week.
And servants ready to serve.
But my husband does not love me.
What good are all these to me!

People think I am the queen.
Chief Queen of all his wives.
But what can I say about those wives!
Words do not come out of my mouth.

They are all younger than me, true.
No one equal to me, but they say
words that kill me. And now you want to
go to the forest.

I am the queen but I am not
even worth a servant of his beloved wife;
that's how your father treats me.
Take me to the forest too.

I can't live in the city without you.
My Ayodhya is wherever you are.

3.

Lakshmana says:
This king is given to lust,
and is now a slave to his pleasures.
He doesn't know what he is doing, or saying.
It's wrong to treat his words as law.
Rama should refuse to go
to the forest; it is not right.

Rama, take my word,
I will put Bharata in prison
If Kaika should instigate
the king to turn against me,
I'll put away my love for my father
and imprison him as well.

Kausalya says:
Rama, have you heard what Lakshmana says?
Don't go to the forest.
Your other mother doesn't care for dharma.
Don't go to the forest.

Rama says:
Whatever has happened happened.
I don't want to find fault with father.
Whatever might happen in the future,
Sita will be my only wife.

* * *

Kausalya's grief has gone
as if a fragrant flower has bloomed.
Kausalya looks at her son.
The sun shines in Rama's eyes,
The river from the sky has come down.
The earth has become a jasmine garden.

VILAS SARANG

Vilas Sarang was born in 1942 in the sea-going Kshatriya Bhandari caste on the west coast of India, south of Maharashtra. He was educated in Marathi and eventually obtained a doctorate in English literature from Bombay University and a second doctorate in comparative literature from Indiana University in Bloomington. He writes short stories, poems, novels, and criticism in Marathi and English.

PRONOUNCING GLOSSARY

Agni: *uh´-nee*
Angiras: *un-gee´-ruhs*
Bhava: *bhah´-vuh*
Bhutapati: *boo´-tuh-puh´-tee*
drona: *droh´-nuh*
Marut: *muh´-root*
maya: *mah-yah´*
Mruga: *mroo´-guh*
Mrugashiras: *mroo-gah´-see-ruhs*
Pashupati: *puh´-shoo-puh´-tee*
pat: *puht*
pati: *puh´-tee*
patni: *puht´-nee*
Prajapati: *pruh-jah´-puh-tee´*
Rohini: *roh´-hee-nee´*
Rudra: *roo´-druh*
sura: *soo´-ruh*
Vaishvanara: *vaish-vah´-nuh-ruh*
Vilas Sarang: *vee´-lahs sah-rahng´*
yagna: *yug´-nuh*
yuga: *yoo´-guh*

RUDRA THE UNTOUCHABLE GOD

In this excerpt from the first chapters of his novel, published in 2006, Vilas Sarang retells the Vedic story of the origins of Rudra ("Have Mercy on Us, Rudra," p. 90), the Vedic god who was later incorporated in the Hindu god Shiva, violently forcing himself (according to the myth) upon the other gods ("Daksha's Sacrifice," p. 162). Sarang begins with paraphrases of Vedic texts—the creation of the Cosmic Man or Primeval Man (p. 82), the *Brihadaranyaka Upanishad* story of creation ("Creation," p. 110) and several Brahmana texts about the creation of Rudra—and moves on to his own modern interpretation.

Chapter 1. The Burning of the Semen

Man alone was afraid. Of what was he afraid? He thought, if there is no one else on Earth why or of whom should I be afraid?

A very long time—or many yugas[1]—he searched for an answer. Then he thought: To be alone may be called a kind of fear. For, when one is alone, one does not experience joy. Before whom will one express joy? One may laugh to one's heart's content, but one knows, that it rings hollow. It seems absurd: Absurd it is.

1. Ages ("The Four Ages," p. 228).

He created the other in his own image. That was the easy way. Creators don't take chances with on-hand creatures. The two of them got on reasonably well. The other was amicable, and harmless.

But soon the one realized that one was still afraid. With a little thought, one understands. One was afraid of the Other. No matter how nice and accommodating the other was, one was afraid of the Other's presence. This was new knowledge. The fear of Man-Alone did not disappear with the appearance of the Other. This was disquieting. This did not augur well for man's existence on earth.

But a greater anxiety was in stock for One. One had made the Other sort of casually, almost carelessly. One realized now that creating the other as a kind of a doll would not do. For the survival and increase of mankind, something much more complicated was required. Nature would seem to dictate the division between the sexes. Only in that manner, could increase by procreation be assured.

Then, with much effort and not a little brainwork and speculative thought, the One caused himself to fall into two pieces; 'cause to fall' is in Sanskrit *pat*. The one caused himself to fall into two pieces, a husband and a wife, which, in Sanskrit, is *pati* and *patni*. A husband and a wife were born. Thus, this part of creation involved, literally, a Fall. Interestingly, there is another world view that speaks of creation as Fall. That view is different. But it is meaningful that both views—may be there are others?—boil down to the Fall. Was there no way, in the beginning or beginnings, except for the agency of the Fall? Which suggests that human existence began with separation, tearing and rending apart, cleavage, mutilation, and severance. The roots of human existence are in a sundering. Even if it is a little tinkering with the ribs, the memory of the sense of hurt and pain are perhaps enduring and all-pervading.

But what was to follow is far more abominable. *Pati* and *patni*: man and wife. They were destined to unite.

But whose union was it? Woman was fashioned out of man's body. They were both of the same blood, the same genes.

So, the union of man and woman was not a union, truly, of disparates. It was not quite moral, as one might view it. It was a coupling which could only be called incestuous.

As might be expected, woman did not take kindly to the matter. She reasoned: I was created out of man's body. And now am I to have carnal relations with him? The very idea is repugnant. This is incest, my Lord! What will people say?

To be precise, there was not a soul in the world to observe and to tattle about upon the matter. But ways of thought are deeply embedded, and will not be dislodged even if time travels backwards.

Many yugas had elapsed by this time. Man-Alone was no more Alone. He was irremediably stuck with a polarity. Also, he had attained the status of a kind of god. Many other gods had also been appended to the company. This band of newly added gods named the father figure Prajapati, 'lord of creatures'; or 'lord of the people.'

Prajapati was unhappy with the state of things. He recalled the words of his *patni*: 'This is incest, my lord!'. He said to himself: 'I did what had to be done. Where am I at fault? Why am I accused of a grievous sin? This is unjust.'

Prajapati was in a rebellious, defiant mood. He said to himself: 'I am called incestuous, as it is. So why not indulge in some hard-boiled, glamorous piece of incest?'

Prajapati created a youthful, lissome woman, not what one generally thinks of as *patni*. Of course, she was his daughter, to call a spade a spade.

The daughter of Prajapati took the form of a doe.[2] She was the blue sky. Then she was the rose-colored dawn. She was the elements.

The father matched the *maya*[3] with the vision of a stag in the prime of youth, with shining antlers and a sleek, muscular body. Under the clear, blue sky, the sheen of the two burnished bodies was breathtaking.

The father pursued the daughter lustily, and they were united against the background of the wide heavens.

The gods were watching. They could not but admire the splendor of the sight. But the gods were mindful more of the morality than the beauty of the sight. They shook their heads collectively and said: "Prajapati is now doing what is not done."

All the gods agreed that the Grandfather must be punished for his deed. But who is going to do it? That was the big question. None of the gods had the guts to act against the father of the gods.

Then the gods thought up a way to overcome the impasse. They put together all the malignant and horrible forms in the world, and fused them into a being. Thus was created a being (a god? A demon?) of fearsome powers. This is the being that came to be known as Rudra, which has a long primal history weaving down the centuries. He is known also as Bhutapati, 'lord of the ghosts.'

The gods said to Bhutapati: 'Prajapati is now doing what is not done. Snip off the appendage that is culpable.'

'I will do as you wish,' said Bhutapati. 'But what boon will you give me?'

'Choose yourself, Lord of the Ghosts.'

'Make me the overlord of the bovine kingdom.'

'Granted.'

From that time, Rudra is also known as Pashupati, 'lord of the cattle.'

Rudra took aim and shot an arrow. In a moment, the coupling of father and daughter was severed. The fusion of the doe and the stag, covering much of the primeval sky, with the antlers of the mighty stag reaching up to the zenith of the heavens, collapsed tragically, though majestically. It was like a cosmic sundering. Even today the descendants of the human race can observe in the heavens the stag, or the Mruga,[4] in the constellation of Capricorn, also called Deer's Head, Mrugashiras. The doe, or the female gazelle, is identified as Rohini. In the clear Indian sky, you may be able to trace the stellar form of the stag, and the awesome, distant pattern may look back at you with an enigmatic gaze that radiates a defiant taintedness, and which yet possesses the fixity of the heavenly bodies; depending on your mood, you may read the lineaments as those of infinite sadness, or of the survival of the protagonists equally as cosmic bodies and the human race.

Mirrored before your eyes in the wide heavens is a permanent reminder of man's primal sin, without which nothing would have begun. Is it despicable?

2. In the Upanishads, she begins as a mare; in the Brahmanas, she becomes a doe.

3. Illusion ("The Two Birds," p. 120).

4. Sanskrit *mriga*, a deer or any other animal that is hunted (from the verb *mrig*, which also yields the word for "path," *marga*).

Or is it to be condoned, forgiven? Since that time gods as sinners, or gods as demons, have tried a well-worn path. You are perplexed and stare long at the horizon, but then, if you crane your neck and look afresh at the heavens, you re-trace the figures which have been etched in man's conscious memory for a few thousand years, and there would be no appeal against that sort of authority. If you are keen to revive the cinders of the ancient memory, you may carry it around in your consciousness as a molten seal, barely tolerated by a mind with strange compulsions.

The sexual act interrupted, Prajapati's semen spilt over onto the earth. That great and continuous torrent of the thick liquid occupied a great stretch of land. Finally, it became a lake. The strong, acid odor of the potent, mighty semen filled the atmosphere of the earth.

Now the gods faced a fresh problem: What is to be done with the lake of semen? If it remained for long as a standing body, it might fester, give off greater stench, and be the cause of pestilence. So the thing had got to be done.

The gods summoned Agni, the god of fire, for help. Perhaps it was the first—and the last—instance of the use of Fire Brigade for such an emergency in the history of the earth.

Agni took the help of 'Maruts,' minor gods of strong winds. The winds blew at cyclone speed. But, despite the great efforts by Agni and his cohorts, they had no success in breaking up the lake of semen.

Then a form of Agni called Vaishvanara[5]—a superior power—was put to the test. With the formless head of Vaishvanara, the lake of the semen at last was breached. Rivulets of semen began to flow in all directions. The fires that the Vaishvanara had ignited continued to burn for a long while. The large, boulder-sized coals burned for a long time. Little by little, the coals went out. The completely charred coals became the black cattle. The reddish coals became the tawny cattle. As the fires died down, quantities of ash spread all over. The gobs of ash took on various forms; the buffalo, the antelope, the camel, the ass and so on.

So many animals materializing out of the forms of ash enchanted Rudra, who watched the process of their creation enthralled and entranced. Rudra said to himself, 'Not all creation took place out of dust, or out of clay. Creation took place also out of fire, out of the waning fire, out of extinguished coals, out of ash. Ash is a large part of creation, and some of the best. Some of the best and the most useful animals have risen out of ash. And some of most beautiful—the bullocks and cows with their elegantly curved horns, horns of various shapes and shades of color, the cattle with their beautiful, comforting and friendly sounds, especially the call of the mother cow to her young, and also the variety of the kinds, the ass, the mule, the camel, and much later, the zebra, and the variety of the shapes of these other species, like the amazingly long limbs of the camel, and the absolutely charming stripes of the zebra.

All creation is delightful, but the creation of the bovine kingdom is especially delightful and gladdening.

Like a great big furnace the lake of semen was bubbling at the edges with the fires tapering down. When the entire lake was set on fire by the power

5. "In all men," the fire in the human belly, which "cooks" (i.e., digests) food.

of Angiras,[6] it looked like a volcano flaming, spewing, and bubbling. Then the fires slowly dried out the lake. But it was a lake of semen, and, when it dried out, much sticky stuff remained at the bottom. Quantities of sticky semen, still hot, sent out vapors over the primeval landscape. The semen was so potent that, even if it had burned and was still burning, its ability for generation was still vigorous, and that is why, just when the fires were going out, the life force had thrown out these assorted, minor forms of animal life, almost casually, like the auxiliary forces when the main army is routed.

These bovine animals were born fully formed, and struggled to get out of the lake. The lake was not a fiery cauldron any more; but parts of it still had liquid edges, and the animals, clambering up with their back to the drained lake could still feel the glow of the heat on their backs, which prompted them to gain the edge of the lake as quickly as possible, and to disappear and disperse amidst pleasanter surroundings. The typical bovine mode of hooking the forelegs over the obstacle and using the hooves as leverage was much in evidence.

Such clambering up is still evident on the Serengeti plain, where, at critical points, a ford has to be crossed, and thousands of animals assemble, with one purpose in mind, which is to get up the edge of the bank at the other side. They made it, most of them anyway.

Rudra arranged a shelter for the cattle. With his strong arm, he broke off large branches of the trees. He made sure that there was plenty to chew on for his animals. Pashupati, the Lord of the Cattle, ensured that his animals were taken good care of. The cattle got busy chewing the cud.

Rudra watched with satisfaction. An inner peace enveloped his mind. There is something reassuring, soul-satisfying about cattle chewing their cud. The strong but slow movement of their jaws, the rhythmical grinding, the sense of peace that it creates, all these were immeasurably comforting. Rudra watched. As they chewed the cud, from time to time, the cattle waved their tails to ward off flies. The wagging of the tails as they ingested their food was fascinating. The movement of the tails, with a bunch of hair at the end, was a delightful sight, as though the cattle were, from time to time, waving their flag of peace. They were stationary and still, except for the movement of their jaws, but waving their tails proclaimed that they were free and capable of taking good care of themselves.

As Rudra watched with fascination, he wondered which other animals ate this way. The lion, the tiger, the wild boar, or the horse? the dog, the cat? None of the other animals ate in that particular way. (And the hyena was the picture of crudeness, of selfish, belligerent, blood-thirsty brutalization.)

And Man? There were infinite ways of crudeness and revolting action in his act of eating. Cattle were perhaps the only animals that ate in this civilized, amiable way.

Rudra watched. Then he thought there was time to go for the party that was arranged in celebration of the success with the lake of semen.

Rudra walked with confident steps. He conjectured that the party would have begun some time ago. Huge pots of the *sura*[7]—alcoholic drinks of many types, to satisfy the taste-buds of the distinguished guests—would

6. A powerful Vedic sage and priest.

7. Wine.

have been brought; huge chunks of prime beef, which Rudra himself had provided, must be getting nicely roasted. A sacrificial fire must be burning in one corner, the priests must be chanting their hymns. The *yagna*,[8] the oblation, was only an excuse to give the feast a modicum of observing the dharma.

Rudra wondered if he might be the chief guest at the gathering. He had accomplished the main task in the day's events. He deserved the honor.

As he walked through the jungle and the grassy places, he could see the glare of lights at the gathering. The lights came near. The strong and mouth-watering scent of beef roasting over the fire was over-powering.

Rudra reached the place, where many gods had gathered. Each had wine in the *drona*—a cup made of leaves—in their hands. The cups were frequently refilled.

Rudra walked to the bench where the wine was dispensed. He asked for a cup. The god who was doing the chore of distributing and refilling the cups looked at Rudra, and hesitated.

But after a few moments, he gave a cup to Rudra.

Rudra walked around the gathering. Strangely, nobody talked to him. He noticed that they avoided him. He stood alone in the party crowd.

Some of the senior gods huddled together to discuss some urgent matter. Then the chief of the gathering approached Rudra.

"Hail, Rudra."

Rudra returned the greeting.

"Rudra, I am afraid, I cannot admit you to this *yagna* and its ceremonies."

"Ceremonies! You were getting drunk on the *sura*, and generally having a great time." Rudra laughed loudly. Then he asked. "What may be the reason that I am excluded from this party cum *yagna*?"

"Because, Rudra, you are not a god. A god is made by birth. You have no father or mother."

"Is that the reason? I performed the most difficult task today, all the gods were pleased. And yet I am excluded from the party at sacrifice?"

"Rudra, the rules of Heaven permit us not to do otherwise. We are thankful for your help but we cannot go beyond that."

"Heaven is an unjust place."

The chief god remained silent.

Then, turning towards the congregation, Rudra said loudly:

"Listen, all of you! You have done a grievous insult to me, have behaved unjustly. When I am needed, you treat me nicely; but if injustice and evil are done to me, I shall hit back with vengeance. Remember that."

With these words, Rudra walked away. He returned to his cattle shed. Petting the cattle somewhat relieved his anger. Then he stood up on high ground and with his hands cupped, let out a ferocious roar. At that moment, clouds had suddenly gathered and thunder broke out. It was not possible to distinguish which was the howl of Rudra and which was the noise of thunder in the sky. Together, they made a terrifying noise. Rudra howled again. This time, all the cattle bellowed in unison, as if in support of their lord and master.

The sounds were heard in the ground where the gods had gathered. They were gods, but they were frightened.

8. Sacrifice.

All the joy and merriment left the crowd of gods. They decided to leave. But most of the gods were so inebriated, they were hardly able to walk. They rolled upon the ground and slept.

Rudra roared for a third time. His howl went over the hills and valleys, and reverberated a long time.

Chapter 2. Existence

Rudra the outsider thought long and deep into the night. He had been shown his place—the Untouchable.

In the morning, he rounded up all the cattle on earth as if he were a general. The cattle greeted him with joyful bellows. Rudra then amalgamated all cattle into a single being. It was a being with a thousand eyes and a thousand faces. This being began to walk towards the place where the grand sacrifice was conducted the night before.

It was early morning, but the host of gods was still sleeping in the open.

Dawn, the daughter of Prajapati, appeared before them. She had taken the form of a celestial nymph. The great light of her beauty caused the gods to wake up. Enchanted by the vision of her beauty, they did not move. The gods had been lying flat on the grass, and watching the celestial nymph enraptured. The lascivious gestures of the maid caused their penises to become erect beneath their flimsy loin clothes. Finally the gods ejaculated their semen one by one. The sight was like a field full of fresh flowers opening up in the morning hour.

Dawn, the daughter of Prajapati, had got bolder after her majestic coupling with her father. Now she had got bold enough to tempt the sons of Prajapati. This was incest again, but she did not seem to care.

While the fountains of semen were gushing forth, the unexpected happened. A giant creature with a thousand feet walked in the pleasure-field and silently began to trample the puny bodies of the puny gods underneath. Those who survived exclaimed in alarm:

"Who are you, O terrible man, or creature? How many are you?"

"I am one, I take the world for my province. I am the Cosmic Man."

"Spare us, O, Cosmic Man. We accept your sovereignty."

"I am not in your sovereignty. I am the sovereign of the animal kingdom. A far more decent place than being the sovereign of man or gods or devils. I leave you to your fate. Roll as much as you can in incest, in your piggish sacrifices and the cutting up of human bodies. I have no interest in that type of life."

And the Cosmic Man walked away into the sunrise. But after a while, he began to experience a strange dissatisfaction, a kind of deprivation. He was the Cosmic Man, but he had no name. The terrible condition of being without a name grieved his soul. The thousand feet and the thousand eyes seemed to turn in vain. Finally, he went to his father, Prajapati. a father who shamelessly enjoyed incest, and who encouraged his own sons to indulge in incest.

The rebellious son approached his father, and straightaway caught him by the throat. Prajapati was terrified.

"Why do you grasp me? What do you want?"

"Father, give me a name; no father fathered me, nor no mother. I have lived without a father and without a mother. I feel abandoned. Give me a name, father, for, without a name, I will not eat food."

"Okay, son, have your name."

Prajapati swallowed some air after his unsettling experience of almost getting strangled.

"*Bhava* or Existence, that is your name."

"Ah, Existence. That's a wide, inclusive name."

"You like the name?"

"Existence—untouchability. It is universal."

Prajapati remained silent.

"Father, I am Existence. And you and your daughter and sons live in ignorance, illusion."

Existence walked out. In the long future, Existence conducted his life with the bitterness and contempt fresh in his eyes, bitterness, compassion and tolerance. This strange combination of qualities made him generally despised.

Fate displayed a strange kind of irony in making Existence an untouchable man, or god, or demon. It is as if Existence, or all existence, at the source, were branded by untouchability. From the beginning, Being is defiled by untouchability. The Cosmic Man as Existence is the icon of the world's untouchability. Untouchability exists at some point, looked at from some angle, somewhere. Even gods such as Indra have been untouchable at some point or other. The spectre of untouchability looms over everything, over everyone.

Existence walked the long and hard road over the centuries to claim godhood. Though he also remained in the shadow of the doubt that he was a demon, a god, or animal. Existence quickly gathered the experience of the deviousness of the world of gods and men. And yet rose above it.

SALMAN RUSHDIE

Salman Rushdie was born in Bombay in 1947, the son of a prosperous Muslim businessman. He was educated at the Rugby School and received a Master's degree in history at the University of Cambridge. His first novel, *Grimus*, was published in 1975 and his second, *Midnight's Children*, in 1980, bringing him international critical and popular success. He won the Man Booker Prize for *Midnight's Children* and subsequently won the Booker of Bookers (1993) and the Best of the Booker (2008), special prizes voted on by the public in honor of the Booker's twenty-fifth and fortieth anniversaries.

PRONOUNCING GLOSSARY

Arjuna: *ar´-joo-nuh*
Bhima: *bee´-muh*
Jalna: *jahl´-nah*
Kali Yuga: *kah´-lee yoo´-guh*
Kerala: *keh-ruh-luh*
Kuru: *koo´-roo*
Markandaya: *mar´-kahn-dayh´-yuh*
Narada: *nah´-ruh-duh*
Nilgiri: *nil-gee´-ree*
Oudh: *ood*
Padma: *pud´-muh*
Pandava: *pahn´-duh-vuh*
Parvati: *par´-vuh-tee*
Vindhya: *vin´-dyuh*

MIDNIGHT'S CHILDREN

In this excerpt from the middle of his novel, Rushdie imagines that the children born on the stroke of midnight, August 15, 1947, the moment when India became independent from the British Empire, had various miraculous powers, in addition to the ability to communicate with one another mentally through what we might now call an internal Internet. It is a brilliant interpretation of a pivotal moment in modern Indian history in terms of the classical Hindu philosophy of the essential connections between all people through the medium of the godhead, *brahman*.

Because none of the children suspected that their time of birth had anything to do with what they were, it took me a while to find it out. At first, after the bicycle accident (and particularly once language marchers had purged me of Evie Burns), I contented myself with discovering, one by one, the secrets of the fabulous beings who had suddenly arrived in my mental field of vision, collecting them ravenously, the way some boys collect insects, and others spot railways trains; losing interest in autograph books and all other manifestations of the gathering instinct, I plunged whenever possible into the separate, and altogether brighter reality of the five hundred and eighty-one. (Two hundred and sixty-six of us were boys; and we were outnumbered by our female counterparts—three hundred and fifteen of them, including Parvati. Parvati-the-witch.)[1]

Midnight's children! . . . From Kerala, a boy who had the ability of stepping into mirrors and re-emerging through any reflective surface in the land—through lakes and (with greater difficulty) the polished metal bodies of automobiles . . . and a Goanese girl with the gift of multiplying fish . . . and children with powers of transformation: a werewolf from the Nilgiri Hills, and from the great watershed of the Vindhyas, a boy who could increase or reduce his size at will, and had already (mischievously) been the cause of wild panic and rumors of the return of Giants . . . from Kashmir, there was a blue-eyed child of whose original sex I was never certain, since by immersing herself in water he (or she) could alter it as she (or he) pleased. Some of us called this child Narada, others Markandaya,[2] depending on which old fairy story of sexual change we had heard . . . near Jalna in the heart of the parched Deccan I found a water-divining youth, and at Budge-Budge outside Calcutta a sharp-tongued girl whose words already had the power of inflicting physical wounds, so that after a few adults had found themselves bleeding freely as a result of some barb flung casually from her lips, they had decided to lock her in a bamboo cage and float her off down the Ganges to the Sundarbans jungles[3] (which are the rightful home of monsters and phantasms); but nobody dared approach her, and she moved through the town surrounded by a vacuum of fear; nobody had the courage to deny her food. There was a boy who could eat metal and a girl whose fingers were so green that she could grow prize aubergines in the Thar desert; and more and more and more . . . overwhelmed by their numbers, and by the exotic multiplicity of their gifts, I paid little attention, in those early days, to their ordinary selves; but inevitably our problems, when they arose, were the everyday, human problems which arise from character-and-environment; in our quarrels, we were just a bunch of kids.

One remarkable fact: the closer to midnight our birth-times were, the greater were our gifts. Those children born in the last seconds of the hour were (to be frank) little more than circus freaks: bearded girls, a boy with the full-operative gills of a freshwater mahaseer trout, Siamese twins with two bodies dangling off a single head and neck—the head could speak in two voices, one male, one female, and every language and dialect spoken in the subcontinent; but for all their marvellousness, these were the unfortunates, the living casualties of that numinous hour. Towards the half-hour came more interesting and useful faculties—in the Gir Forest lived a witch-girl with the power of healing by the laying-on of hands, and there was a wealthy tea-planter's son in Shillong who had the blessing (or possibly the curse) of being incapable of forgetting anything he ever saw or heard. But the children born in the first minute of all—for these children the hour had reserved the highest talents of which men had ever dreamed. If you, Padma, happened to possess a register of births in which times were noted down to the exact second, you, too, would know what scion of a great Lucknow family (born at twenty-one seconds past midnight) had completely mastered, by the age of ten, the lost arts of alchemy, with which he regenerated the fortunes

1. Here, a witch; in Hindu mythology, the wife of the god Shiva.
2. Two sages whom the god Vishnu cursed to become women for a period, before changing back into men; their stories are told in the Puranas.
3. In Bengal, where tigers live.

of his ancient but dissipated house; and which dhobi's daughter from Madras (seventeen seconds past) could fly higher than any bird simply by closing her eyes; and to which Benarsi silversmith's son (twelve seconds after midnight) was given the gift of traveling in time and thus prophesying the future as well as clarifying the past . . . a gift which, children that we were, we trusted implicitly when it dealt with things gone and forgotten, but derided when he warned us of our own ends . . . fortunately, no such records exist; and, for my part, I shall not reveal—or else, in appearing to reveal, shall falsify—their names and even their locations; because, although such evidence would provide absolute proof of my claims, still the children of midnight deserve, now, after everything, to be left alone; perhaps to forget; but I hope (against hope) to remember . . .

Parvati-the-witch was born in Old Delhi in a slum which clustered around the steps of the Friday mosque. No ordinary slum, this, although the huts built out of old packing cases and pieces of corrugated tin and shreds of jute sacking which stood higgledy-piggledy in the shadow of the mosque looked no different from any other shanty-town . . . because this was the ghetto of the magicians, yes, the very same place which had once spawned a Hummingbird whom knives had pierced and pie-dogs had failed to save . . . the conjurers' slum, to which the greatest fakirs and prestidigitators and illusionists in the land continually flocked, to seek their fortune in the capital city. They found tin huts, and police harassment, and rats . . . Parvati's father had once been the greatest conjurer in Oudh; she had grown up amid ventriloquists who could make stones tell jokes and contortionists who could swallow their own legs and fire-eaters who exhaled flames from their arse-holes and tragic clowns who could extract glass tears from the corners of their eyes; she had stood mildly amid gasping crowds while her father drove spikes through her neck; and all the time she had guarded her own secret, which was greater than any of the illusionist flummeries surrounding her; because to Parvati-the-witch, born a mere seven seconds after midnight on August 15th, had been given the powers of the true adept, the illuminatus, the genuine gifts of conjuration and sorcery, the art which required no artifice.

So among the midnight children were infants with powers of transmutation, flight, prophecy and wizardry . . . but two of us were born on the stroke of midnight. Saleem[4] and Shiva, Shiva and Saleem, nose and knees and knees and nose . . . to Shiva, the hour had given the gifts of war (of Rama, who could draw the undrawable bow;[5] of Arjuna and Bhima; the ancient prowess of Kurus and Pandavas[6] united, unstoppably, in him!) . . . and to me, the greatest talent of all—the ability to look into the hearts and minds of men.

But it is Kali-Yuga;[7] the children of the hour of darkness were born, I'm afraid, in the midst of the age of darkness; so that although we found it easy to be brilliant, we were always confused about being good.

4. A Muslim name.
5. "The Birth of Sita and the Bending of the Bow," p. 189.
6. Characters in the *Mahabharata* (p. 130).
7. The last of the four ages, the present, wicked age ("The Four Ages," p. 228).

PURUSHOTTAM NAGESH OAK

We've sampled the Hindu past in hundreds of documents; but how are we to anthologize the future? From present signs, the Hinduism of the future appears to be heavily politicized, and so it is appropriate that one of our final texts should be driven by an extreme political agenda. A steadily growing faction of Hinduism in the twenty-first century is the nationalist movement known as Hindutva ("Hindu-ness"), a word coined by the nationalist Vinayak Damodar Savarkar (1888–1966) in his 1923 pamphlet *Hindutva: Who Is a Hindu?* Hindutva is the doctrine of a number of political organizations, including the Rashtriya Swayamsevak Sangh (RSS, "National Volunteer Organization"), the Bharatiya Janata Party (BJP, "Indian Peoples' Party"), and the Vishwa Hindu Parishad (VHP, "World Hindu Council"). Hindutvavadis (as its adherents are called), like Christian and Muslim fundamentalists, seek to purify their own tradition of what they regard as foreign and impure elements. They want to claim India for Hindus, at the expense of other religions in India, such as Islam and Christianity. Since they ground their claims to ownership in claims of ancient origins, Hindutvavadis present a revisionist history of India, ignoring the many moments of mutual enrichment between Muslims and Hindus that we have noted throughout this anthology and capitalizing instead on the inter-religious tensions that have always smoldered in India and that erupted into volcanic communal violence after the Partition of India and Pakistan in August 1947, when hundreds of thousands died.

One of the spokespersons for this movement was Purushottam Nagesh Oak (1917–2007), who once worked and acted as an assistant to the Indian nationalist leader Subhas Chandra Bose and went on to found, in 1964, an "Institute for Rewriting Indian History." Oak was fond of deriving non-Sanskrit religious terms from Sanskrit, such as "Vatican" from the Sanskrit *vatika,* "hermitage," and "Christianity" from *Krishna-niti* ("ethics of Krishna"). He also argued that both the Kaaba in Mecca and Westminster Abbey were originally shrines to the Hindu god Shiva.

THE TAJ MAHAL IS A HINDU PALACE

For centuries some Hindus have claimed that the great mosque built in Ayodhya in 1572 by the first Mughal emperor, Babur, was erected over a Hindu temple commemorating the birth of Rama there. In December 1992, Hindutva factions, backed by the police, demolished the mosque, triggering violence throughout India that left more than a thousand dead, both Hindu and Muslim. A similar claim—not merely that a great Muslim monument was built on sacred Hindu grounds, but that this one was actually a Hindu monument—was made by P. N. Oak for the Taj Mahal.

In a series of four books, Oak argued that the Taj Mahal, in Agra, is not a Muslim mausoleum but an ancient temple to the Hindu god Shiva that King Paramardi Dev built in 1155, and that it eventually became a palace that the Mughal emperor Shah Jahan commandeered from Jai Singh, the Maharaja of Jaipur. Though Oak's arguments have led neither to widespread violence nor (as he himself lamented) to general acceptance, and there is much indignant mockery of his agenda by more liberal Hindus, his theories are widely cited by Hindutvavadis—both in India and in the

American diaspora—as part of a broader political agenda. The Hindutva movement co-opted certain Enlightenment discourses of the scientific study of history as part of a postcolonial discourse meant to "Europeanize" Indian thought, proving that Hindus have always been just as "scientific" as Europeans. At the same time, however, Hindutvavadis attempt both to challenge European archaeological findings and to assert the historical reality of religious texts, as when they succeeded, in September 2007, in ending a major government project to build a canal through the area that was where, they said, Rama, in the *Ramayana*, built a bridge to what is now Sri Lanka. (The debate continues.) Moreover, matters of "history" and "religion" in India, including Hindu-Muslim infighting, occur largely through the medium of lawyers, and legalistic nit-picking. All of this is reflected in Oak's argument.

Oak cites a crucial passage from the court records of Shah Jahan describing what Shah Jahan got from Jai Singh: "[T]here was a tract of land (*zamini*) of great eminence and pleasantness toward the south of that large city, on which there was before this the mansion (*manzil*) of Raja Man Singh, and which now belonged to his grandson Raja Jai Singh." Oak alone reads this passage to mean that Shah Jahan commandeered not merely the land but also the building that had previously been situated on it, and that that building was not a "mansion" but the Taj Mahal. This flies in the face of massive evidence, which is summarized as follows by the 2010 *Encyclopedia Britannica* entry on the Taj Mahal:

> Building commenced about 1632. More than 20,000 workers were employed from India, Persia, the Ottoman Empire, and Europe to complete the mausoleum itself by about 1638–39; the adjunct buildings were finished by 1643, and decoration work continued until at least 1647. In total, construction of the 42-acre (17-hectare) complex spanned 22 years.

Oak further argued that "Taj Mahal" is not a Persian (from Arabic) phrase meaning "crown of palaces," as linguists would assert, but a corrupt form of the Sanskrit term "Tejo Mahalaya," which signifies a Shiva temple. Oak maintained that persons connected with the repair and the maintenance of the Taj Mahal have seen the Shiva *linga* and "other idols" that were sealed in the thick walls and in chambers in a secret red stone level below the marble basement. In 2000 India's Supreme Court dismissed Oak's petition to declare that a Hindu king had built the Taj Mahal and reprimanded him for bringing the action. The following excerpt from the introduction to his second book about the Taj Mahal spells out the further implications of his theories.

PRONOUNCING GLOSSARY

Ajmer: *ahj´-mayr*
Anangpal: *uh-nang´-pahl*
Babur: *bah´-boor*
Badshahnama: *bahd´-shah´-nah´-muh*
Fatehpur Sikri: *fah´-teh-poor sih´-kree*
Gwalior: *gwah´-lee-yor*
Jaipur: *jai´-poor*
kabar: *kah´-bar*
makabra: *muh-kah´-bruh*
Mansingh: *mahn´-sing´*
Mohammad Ghaus: *moh-hah´-mud gows´*
Moinuddin Chisti: *moh´-ih-noo-din´ chis´-tee*
Mulla Abdul Hamid Lahori: *moo´-luh ahb-dool´ hah-mid´ lah-hoh´-ree*
Mumtaz: *moom´-tahz*
Nizamuddin: *nih-zah´-moo-din´*
Purushottam Nagesh Oak: *poo-roo-shoh´-tum nah´-gaysh´ ohk*
Rajasthan: *rah´-jah-stahn´*
Rajput: *rahj´-poot*
Shahjahan: *shah´-juh-hahn´*
Shilpashastra: *shil´-puh-shahs´-truh*

Introduction

Unlike this book and its forerunner, titled *Taj Mahal Was a Rajput Palace*,[1] which are research works, all other books and accounts of the Taj Mahal written during the last 300 years are based on pure fantasy. We were surprised to learn after meticulous inquiry that despite the plethora of printed hocus-pocus[2] churned out on the Taj Mahal all the world over there is not a single book containing a well-documented, comprehensive account of the origin of the Taj Mahal quoting exhaustively only contemporary authorities. Subsequent hearsay accounts are hardly worth any notice for historical research, since one writer's opinion is as good as any other's.[3]

Since the Taj Mahal is a building-complex of world renown the absence of a single coherent and unquestionably authentic account is indeed surprising. How and why have universities and research institutions the world over bypassed such a stupendous and attractive subject like the Taj Mahal? Why do all accounts of the Taj Mahal content themselves with merely lisping the self-same, confused, irreconcilable and slipshod, imaginary details about its origin, the period of construction, the expense incurred, the source of the money spent, the designers and workmen, the date of Mumtaz's burial in it, and every other facet?

Perhaps it is just as well that no scholarly body ever succeeded in producing a coherent and authoritative account of the building of the Taj Mahal. Whosoever attempted to do any research on the subject got lost in such a maze of inconsistent and contradictory accounts that he found himself helplessly repeating the same old abracadabra. He had to be content with placing before the reader loose bits of inconsistent, anomalous and contradictory versions on every point. All aspects of the Shahjahan legend regarding the Taj Mahal being suspect, it was but natural that attempts at compiling an authoritative account of the origin of the Taj Mahal should miserably fail. Nobody ever succeeded in or hoped to say the last convincing word on the origin of the Taj Mahal. All previous attempts were bound to fail since they were all based on a wrong notion. Starting with wrong premises, they could not arrive at the right conclusion.

We are going to prove in the following pages that the Taj Mahal—meaning "the Very Crown Among Residences"—is an ancient Hindu palace and not a Muslim tomb. We shall also show how all the loose bits of information—whether factual or concocted—dished out on the platter of the Shahjahan legend, fall in place and fully support our research. Just as the solution to a mathematical problem may be tested for its accuracy by various methods, similarly, sound historical research provides a consistent and coherent story reconciling all apparent inconsistencies.

1. A series of four books: first, *Taj Mahal Was a Rajput Palace* (New Delhi: P. N. Oak, 1965); second, *The Taj Mahal Is a Hindu Palace* (Bombay: Pearl Publications, 1968) [from which the present selection was taken]; third, *Taj Mahal Is a Temple Palace* (New Delhi: P. N. Oak, 1974); fourth, *Tajmahal—The True Story; The Tale of a Temple Vandalized* (Houston, TX: A. Ghosh, 1989).
2. See Srinivas Aravamudan, *Guru English: South Asian Religion in a Cosmopolitan Language* (Princeton, NJ: Princeton University Press, 2005).
3. For Hindutva revisionism, see Jyotirmaya Sharma, *Hindutva: Exploring the Idea of Hindu Nationalism* (Penguin Global, 2004); Kumkum Roy, Kunal Chakrabarti, and Tanika Sarkar, *The Vedas, Hinduism, Hindutva* (Kolkata: Alpha, 2005).

In this book we have reproduced in photostat a passage from Shahjahan's court chronicle, the Badshahnama,[4] which disarmingly admits that the Taj Mahal is a commandeered Hindu palace. We have also quoted the French merchant Tavernier,[5] who visited India during Shahjahan's reign, to say that the cost of the scaffolding exceeded that of the entire work done regarding the mausoleum. This proves that all that Shahjahan had to do was engrave Koranic texts on the walls of a Hindu palace; that is why the cost of the scaffolding was much more than the value of the entire work done. We have cited the *Encyclopaedia Britannica*[6] as stating that the Taj Mahal building-complex comprises stables and guest and guard rooms. We have quoted Mr. Nurul Hasan Siddiqui's book[7] admitting, as the *Badshahnama* does, that a Hindu palace was commandeered to bury Mumtaz in. We have cited Shahjahan's fifth-generation ancestor Babur to prove that he lived in what we call the "Taj Mahal," 100 years before the death of the lady for whom the Taj is believed to have been built as a mausoleum. We have also quoted Vincent Smith[8] to show that Babur died in the Taj Mahal. In addition to these proofs we have scotched the Shahjahan legend in every detail and cited other voluminous evidence proving conclusively that the Taj Mahal is an ancient Hindu palace.

The overwhelming proof that we have produced in this book should once for all silence all doubters of the correctness of our finding and convince them that the whole world can go wrong where one man proves right. This has happened time and again in human history. Galileo and Einstein, for example, shocked contemporary humanity out of their rusted dogma-shells.

It was by sheer luck that we happened to find corroboration for our earlier finding on the Taj Mahal, in the *Badshahnama*, Mr. Siddiqui's book, Tavernier's travel account and Babur's *Memoirs*.[9] But we wish to take this opportunity to alert posterity and our contemporaries interested in research and tell them that the proofs set out in our earlier book (*Taj Mahal Was a Rajput Palace*) were more than enough to convince all those well versed in judicial procedure, and logic, that the Taj Mahal existed much before Mumtaz's death whose tomb it is supposed to be.

Even if Mulla Abdul Hamid Lahori (the author of the *Badshahnamah*) and others had prevaricated, the evidence we marshalled in our earlier book was enough to question their veracity and impel us to seek their motives. This is

4. The *Padshah Nama*, the corpus of court records of the reign of Shah Jahan, in Persian. The portions written by Mulla Abdul Hamid Lahori and by Amin-e-Qazwini contain the crucial passages; Oak cites Lahori but not Qazwini, though Qazwini is regarded as the definitive source of information on Shah Jahan's early years. See W. E. Begley and Z. A. Desai, *Taj Mahal: The Illumined Tomb* (Seattle: University of Washington Press, 1989), pp. 42–43.

5. Jean Baptiste Tavernier visited the court of Shah Jahan in the seventeenth century and left a detailed, but not always accurate, travel narrative.

6. But this passage from the 2010 *Encyclopedia Britannica* narrative contradicts Oak's assertions:

> It was built by the Mughal, emperor Shah Jahān (reigned 1628–58) to immortalize his wife Mumtaz Mahal ("Chosen One of the Palace"). The name Taj Mahal is a derivation of her name. She died in childbirth in 1631, after having been the emperor's inseparable companion since their marriage in 1612. The plans for the complex have been attributed to various architects of the period, though the chief architect was probably Ustad Ahmad Lahawri, an Indian of Persian descent. The five principal elements of the complex—main gateway, garden, mosque, *jawab* (literally "answer"; a building mirroring the mosque), and mausoleum (including its four minarets)—were conceived and designed as a unified entity according to the tenets of Mughal building practice, which allowed no subsequent addition or alteration.

7. Nurul Hasan Siddiqui, *The City of Taj*, with a foreword by Tara Chand (Allahabad, 1940).

8. Vincent Arthur Smith (1843–1920) was a leading historian of India.

9. The emperor Babur (whose mosque was torn down in 1992) wrote an unusually candid memoir, the *Baburnama*. See *Memoirs of Babur, Prince and Emperor*, trans. Wheeler M. Thackston, intro. Salman Rushdie (New York: Modern Library, 2002; also trans. A. S. Beveridge [London: Luzac, 1921]).

a lesson worth imbibing by the lay public, and by researchers who have to wade through a mire of falsified and distorted accounts.

We confess that we have not been able to find out which ancient Hindu king built the Taj Mahal as his palace though we have hazarded a hypothesis that it could be Anangpal[1] around 372 A.D.—but that was never the object of our quest. That is a subsequent task. It was first and foremost necessary to open the eyes of everybody to the fact that the Taj Mahal is a Hindu palace.

We have in this book proved to the hilt that the Taj Mahal has been built to its minutest detail according to the ancient Hindu science of architecture[2] of the Hindus, for the Hindus and by the Hindus. Now that we have firmly established it in this and in the earlier book, the topic should encourage further research to trace the history of the Taj Mahal prior to Mansingh's[3] and Babur's possession of it until we get to the original Hindu builder. Jaipur royal records in the Rajasthan Archives at Bikaner or in the possession of the Jaipur ruling house might possess valuable clues.

We had to face a veritable barrage of scoffs and sneers and other worse reactions when we first published our findings. But we are unshaken in our conviction. Those jeers and sneers came from all quarters. Particularly painful were those emanating from eminent students of history. Most expressed nothing but vehement contempt either audibly or through various acts of commission and omission. The lay public looked on dazed in disbelief, and looked up to history teachers and professors, as if they are oracles, for cues whether to laud or condemn us.

It is painful to note that scholars who felt themselves committed to the Shahjahan legend of the Taj Mahal, either by having authored books on the topic or guided post-graduate students along the beaten track, or by virtue of their bureaucratic and academic standing, showed a marked tendency to remain strait-jacketed in their beliefs. Obstructionist and obscurantist objections were flung at us. Many angrily asserted that we had not proved our case. But that was a most unscholarly attitude. A true devotion to academic research should have urged them to give a second thought to the matter. If they were right, the revision would have worked to their own advantage, because it would have bolstered up their own earlier belief by giving them an opportunity to fill up the holes which we had pointed out. If they were in the wrong their holding on to their earlier dogmas was unwarranted. They thus failed to be guided by the maxim that, "If you are in the right you can afford to keep your temper; if in the wrong you cannot afford to lose it."

There is another maxim for the genuine researcher, that any loopholes pointed out in an existing belief should lead to immediate intensified research rather than anger and hate against one who questions traditional beliefs. Trying to find fault with one who questions hackneyed beliefs is neither good ethics nor good scholarship. Finding fault with the method by which the discovery has been arrived at is worse. For all we know the method employed may be unorthodox or even occult. But what others should worry about is the end product or the result. They may later ask to be enlightened on the meth-

1. Anangpal Tomar was a king of Delhi in the eighth century C.E.

2. Refutations for nearly everything Oak asserts in this regard can be found in Ebba Koch, *The Complete Taj Mahal and Riverfront Gardens of Agra* (London: Thames & Hudson, 2006).

3. Man Singh (1550–1614) was a Hindu king of Jaipur and close friend of the Mughal emperor Akbar (whose name means "Great"). See also P. N. Oak, *Who Says Akbar Was Great?* (New Delhi: P. N. Oak, 1968).

ods used, but refusing to examine the conclusion by caviling at the method is missing the wood for the trees.

Luckily for us much water has flown down all the rivers since we first mooted our finding, and today our discovery is not looked upon—at least by some—as fantastic, quixotic, eccentric or just chauvinistic. The matter does not end with merely admitting the Taj Mahal to be a Hindu palace. That finding has a very far-reaching bearing on both Indian and world history.

The Taj Mahal has all along been wrongly believed to be the very flower of the mythical Indo-Saracenic architecture. Now that we have proved it to be an ancient Hindu palace it should not be difficult for readers to regard with a little more respect and attention our finding explained in the book *Some Blunders of Indian Historical Research*[4] that all mediaeval mosques and tombs in India are conquered and misused Hindu palaces and temples. Thus Mohammad Ghaus's tomb in Gwalior, Salim Chisti's mausoleum in Fatehpur Sikri, Nizamuddin's *kabar* in Delhi, Moinuddin Chisti's *makabra* in Ajmer,[5] are all erstwhile Hindu buildings lost to Muslim conquest and use.

The other corollary to our finding on the Taj Mahal is that the Indo-Saracenic theory of architecture is a figment of the imagination. It should be deleted forthwith from history books and text books of civil engineering and architecture.

A third corollary is that the dome is a Hindu form of architecture.

A fourth corollary is that buildings in India and West Asia which have a resemblance to the Taj Mahal are products of Hindu architecture (*Shilpa-shastra*), just as in our own times we find Western architecture to be in vogue all over the world.

During our discussions with university teachers and book-reviewers we came across some curious objections to our thesis. Having read the earlier book they objected to our methodology as being argumentative, deductive and lawyer-like.

This raises a very interesting point. Do they mean to say that deductive logic and lawyer-like arguments, having no place in or being detrimental to arriving at correct conclusions in historical research, should be altogether avoided? Their objection amounts to asserting that the conclusions arrived at by deductive logic or by the adjudicative process are all wrong.

We then ask whether Man did not arrive at his present state of knowledge in every branch of human inquiry with the help of his logical faculty? How else did he progress? Take the case of geography. Thousands of years before Man could send up spacecraft to photograph the earth did he not correctly conclude that the earth was round, by sheer logic? This should thoroughly expose the hollowness of the objection. Logic is justly called the science of sciences because it treats of reasoning which is the basis of all knowledge, from which history can claim no exemption.

4. P. N. Oak, *Some Blunders of Indian Historical Research* (New Delhi: P. N. Oak, 1966).

5. These are all Muslim holy places in India.

KANCHA ILAIAH

Kancha Ilaiah was born in 1952 to a family of the Kuruma Golla caste, an Other Backward Caste, in a small South Indian village. He earned his Ph.D. in political science from Osmania University in Hyderabad, where he is now professor and chair of the Department of Political Science. Ilaiah is an activist on behalf of what he calls the Dalitbahujan, "the Dalit Majority"—that is, the Dalits who constitute what he regards as the majority population of India, including all the so-called Scheduled Castes, also called Backward Castes.

PRONOUNCING GLOSSARY

Adi-Dravidian: *ah´-dee–druh-vih´-dee-yun*
Ambedkar: *ahm-bed´-kar*
Anjaneya: *un-juh-nay´-yuh*
avatara: *uh´-vuh-tah´-ruh*
bahujan: *buh´-hoo-jun´*
Bali: *buh´-lee*
Bali Chakravarthi: *buh´-lee chuk-ruh-var´-tee*
Baniya: *bah´-nee-yuh*
Bhagavad Gita: *buh´-guh-vud gee´-tah*
Bhasmasura: *bus-mah´-soo-ruh*
chakram: *chuk´-rum*
Dalitbahujan: *dah´-lit-buh´-hoo-jun´*
Deevatideeva: *deev´-uh´-tee-dee´-vuh*
Draupadi: *drow´-puh-dee´*
Gauri: *gow´-ree*
gopika: *goh´-pih-kah´*
hamsa: *hum´-sah*
Hindutva: *hin´-doo-tvuh*
Kaamaabhimaani: *kah´-mah´-bee-mah´-nee*
Kancha Ilaiah: *kahn´-chuh ih-lai´-yuh*
Karna: *kar´-nuh*
Kaurava: *kow´-ruh-vuh*
Kautilya: *kow´-til´-yuh*
Kautilyan: *kow-til´-yun*
Kishkinda: *kish-kin´-duh*
kula: *koo´-luh*
Kunti: *koon´-tee*
Mahabharatha: *muh-hah´-bah´-ruh-tuh*
Maheshwara: *muh-haysh´-wuh-ruh*
Mandal: *mahn´-dul*
Manu: *muh´-noo*
murthies: *moor´-tees*
Pandava: *pahn´-duh-vuh*
Parvathi: *par´-vuh-tee´*
Phule: *foo´-lay*
raayabhaaram: *rah´-yuh-bah´-rum*
Radha: *rah´-dah*
Ramayana: *rah-mah´-yuh-nuh*
Ramba: *rum´-bah*
Ravana: *rah´-vuh-nuh*
rishi: *ree´-shee*
Saraswathi: *suh-ruh´-swuh-tee´*
Shambuka: *shahm´-boo-kuh´*
Shukracharya: *shoo´-kruh-char´-yuh*
Shurpanaka: *shoor´-puh-nuh-kah´*
Sugreeva: *soo-gree´-vuh*
Tataki: *tah´-tuh-kee*
Tilothama: *tee-loh´-tuh-muh*
trimurthies: *tree´-moor´-tees*
trishula: *tree´-shoo-luh*
Urvashi: *oor-vah´-shee*
Vali: *vuh´-lee*
Vamana: *vah´-muh-nuh*
vara: *vuh´-ruh*
varnadharma: *var´-nuh-dar´-muh*
Vasishta: *vuh-sish´-tuh*
Vedavyasa: *vay´-duh-vyah´-suh*
vishnu-chakram: *vish´-noo–chuk´-rum*
Vishwamitra: *vish´-wuh-mih´-truh*
Yadava: *yah´-duh-vuh*
yuddha radhasarathi: *yoo´-duh rah´-duh-suh-rah´-tee*
yuga: *yoo´-guh*

HINDU GODS AND US

Kancha Ilaiah here offers his own version of some of the major themes of Hinduism and subjects them to a social critique from the standpoint of the Dalitbahujan ("the Dalit Majority"). This long selection reviews the main texts of Hindu history, many of them included in this anthology, and calls for a radically new reading of them.

What is the relationship between the Hindu Gods and ourselves? Did the Hindu brahminical Gods treat us as part of their people, or even as legitimate devotees? Why did Hinduism create the images of many Gods as against the universal ethic of monotheism? Did brahminical polytheism work in the interest of Dalitbahujan masses or did it work in the interest of brahminical forces who are a small minority? Further, what is the relationship between the Dailtbahujan Goddesses and Gods and the Hindus? Did the Hindus respect these deities or worship them? What are the socioeconomic and cultural forms of the Dalitbahujan Goddesses and Gods? Since the majority of the people relate to the Dalitbahujan Goddesses and Gods, isn't there a need to present their narratives? I shall discuss all these aspects in this chapter.

Hinduism has a socioeconomic and cultural design that manipulates the consciousness of the Dalitbahujans systematically. It has created several institutions to sustain the hegemony of the brahminical forces. Through the ages it has done this by two methods: (*i*) creating a consent system which it maintains through various images of Gods and Goddesses, some of whom have been co-opted from the social base that it wanted to exploit; and (*ii*) when such a consent failed or lost its grip on the masses, it took recourse to violence. In fact, violence has been Hinduism's principal mechanism of control. That is the reason why many of the Hindu Gods were weapon-wielders in distinct contrast to the Gods of all other religions. No religion in the world has created such a variety of Gods who use both consent and violence to force the masses into submission. Thus, the relationship between the Hindu Gods and the Dalitbahujans has been that of the oppressor and oppressed, the manipulator and the manipulated. Of course, one of the 'merits' of Hinduism has been that it addressed both the mind and the body of the oppressed.

Brahminical theoreticians have constructed their own theory of consciousness with a specific notion that the majority (bahujan) consciousness is confined to one specific activity and that that consciousness has to be constantly monitored in order to arrest its further growth. If a consciousness is manipulated to become and remain the slave of another consciousness, some day or the other it will rebel. These revolts are mostly suppressed. All religions have worked out strategies to manipulate and contain such revolts by teaching the slaves a so-called divine morality. But no religion has succeeded in suppressing the slaves for ever.

Other religions admitted slaves into their fold, although they suppressed them in the political and economic domains. But the Dalitbahujans never became part of Hinduism.

Hinduism differs from other religions even in terms of the way it has structured its Gods and Goddesses. All the Gods and Goddesses are institutionalized, modified and contextualized in a most brazen anti-Dalitbahujan mode. Hinduism has been claiming that the Dalitbahujans are Hindus, but at the same time their very Gods are openly against them. As a result, this religion, from its very inception, has a fascist nature, which can be experienced and understood only by the Dalitbahujans, not by Brahmins who regard the manipulation and exploitation as systemic and not as part of their own individual consciousness. But the reality is that every 'upper' caste person takes part in that exploitation and manipulation and contributes towards the creation and perpetuation of such cultures in the Indian context. The creation and perpetuation of Hindu Gods is a major achievement of this culture.

In the face of the Dalitbahujan revolts, the brahminical forces of India invoked their Gods to suppress the consciousness of the revolt. The most obvious and immediate example in the all-India context, is that of the Hindu response to the implementation of the Mandal report,[1] in 1990. The 'upper' castes opposed the reservations to OBCs with all the strength at their command, and the Hindutva[2] movement was organized mainly to oppose the proreservation movement. Hence, unless one examines in detail how all the main Hindu Gods are only killers and oppressors of the Dalitbahujans, and how the Dalitbahujan castes have built a cultural tradition of their own, and Gods and Goddesses of their own (who have never been respected by the brahminical castes), one cannot open up the minds of the Dalitbahujans to reality.

THE BRAHMINICAL GODS AND GODDESSES

The head of the brahminical Gods, Indra,[3] is known as the *Deevatideeva.*[4] He is the original Aryan leader who led the mass extermination of the Indus valley based Adi-Dravidians,[5] who were also Adi-Dalitbahujans. Brahmins consider him a hero because he killed hundreds and thousands of Dalitbahujans at that time. After conquering the Dalitbahujans, he established a pastoral Aryan kingdom. In this kingdom, he did not organize people into production, he merely established a big harem. Enjoying the pleasures of that harem and dancing and drinking were his main tasks. Ramba, Urvashi, Tilothama[6] who are again and again symbolized as representing Hindu beauty and Hindu ideals of service were part of his harem. He might have also been a seducer of many Dalitbahujan women which is

1. The Mandal Commission issued a report in 1980 upholding Indian laws for affirmative action for members of the Other Backward Classes (OBCs) and Scheduled Castes and Tribes. It reserved a certain portion of government jobs and positions in public universities for these groups, measures that met with strong resistance from caste Hindus. Not until 1993 were some of the recommendations for government positions implemented, and in 2008 some of those for higher education.
2. "Hinduness," a nationalist and conservative movement, anti-Muslim, anti-Dalit ("The Taj Mahal Is a Hindu Palace," p. 691).
3. King of the Vedic gods (*Rig Veda*, p. 73).
4. "The god beyond the gods."
5. A great civilization thrived in the Indus Valley, now mostly in Pakistan, well before 2000 B.C.E.; it left massive physical remains but no decipherable texts. Theories that its inhabitants spoke an early form of Dravidian (the language group of Tamil, Telugu, and Kannada), and that they were destroyed by invading people who spoke an early form of Sanskrit, have been popular for many years, but there is insufficient evidence either to substantiate or to refute them.
6. Celestial nymphs and courtesans (Apsarases) who danced in heaven for Indra and whom he often dispatched to earth to seduce overambitious ascetics.

probably why brahminical literature constructs him as a powerful *Kaamaabhimaani* (one who enjoys sex) hero. But the most important aspect is that he was the main political leader of the Aryans. It was he who led them to political victory. This leader was first and foremost a killer and an exploiter of Dalitbahujans.

BRAHMA AND SARASWATHI

The most important Hindu God—the first of the three murthies[7]—is Brahma. Physically Brahma is represented as a light brown-skinned Aryan. He bears the name of Brahma, which means wisdom. Sometimes he is shown as a person who has four hands, sometimes as one who has only two hands. This God of wisdom is armed with weapons to attack his enemies—the Dalitbahujans. He was the one who worked out the entire strategy of war designed to defeat the Adi-Dalitbahujans. It was he who was responsible for the reconstruction of brahminical society. The Brahmins have worked out the social divisions of caste by claiming that they were born from his head,[8] Kshatriyas from his chest, Vaishyas from his thighs and Shudras from his feet. Such an explanation gave a divine justification for the four classes—which have come to be known as the four *varnas.* Subsequently these classes—particularly the Shudra-slave class—were divided into further castes so that class revolt could be curbed once and for all. Brahminical theoreticians—Kautilya,[9] Manu,[1] Vedavyasa[2] and Valmiki[3]—all worked out mechanisms that structured these castes/classes basically in the interest of the brahminical forces. As we have seen in earlier chapters, it is because of this ideological hegemony that the brahminical order—in philosophy, economy and politics—could be maintained from ancient times to the present age of post-colonial capitalism.

Brahma's wife is known as Saraswathi,[4] which also means learning. The construction of the Brahma-Saraswathi relationship takes place strictly within the philosophical bounds of patriarchy. Brahma himself is shown as the source of wisdom in the Vedas, the early Brahmin writings, which were designed to subordinate the native masses of India. The Vedas themselves express the mixed feelings of crude Brahminism. But since they were written by the Brahmins (i.e. by the early literate Aryans), the texts go against Dalitbahujans. In fact, they are anti-Dalitbahujan texts. The absurdity of Brahmin patriarchy is clear in these texts. The source of education, Saraswathi, did not write any book as the Brahmins never allowed women to write their texts. Nowhere does she speak even about the need to give education to women. How is it that the source of education is herself an illiterate woman? This is diabolism of the highest order. Brahminism never allowed women to be educated. * * *

7. The Trimurti is the trinity formed by Brahma, Vishnu, and Shiva ("The Origin of *Linga* Worship," p. 235).
8. The myth of the four classes ("The Hymn of the Primeval Man," p. 82).
9. Author of the *Arthashastra*, the ancient Indian textbook of political science; a notoriously amoral author, whose nickname, Kautilya, actually means "Crookedness." He was also called Chanakya and Vishnugupta, and was said to have been prime minister to the emperor Chandragupta Maurya, in the third century B.C.E.
1. Author of the *Laws of Manu* (p. 202).
2. "Divider of the Vedas," also called Vyasa. The author of the *Mahabharata* (p. 130).
3. Author of the *Ramayana* (p. 186).
4. Goddess of literature and music.

Leave alone the ancient and medieval periods, even in the twentieth century, Hindutva attempts to seduce us into accepting this first enemy of Dalitbahujans as our prime deity. The manipulator of knowledge is being projected as knowledge itself. But there are two kinds of knowledge: (*i*) the oppressor's knowledge and (*ii*) the knowledge of the oppressed. Brahma's knowledge is the oppressor's knowledge. The Dalitbahujans have their own knowledge, reflected in several of the ideas of the Charvakas[5] (Dalitbahujan materialists) of the ancient period. The ancient Brahmins hegemonized their knowledge and marginalized the knowledge of the Dalitbahujan Charvakas, using the image of Brahma. Brahma thus represented the Brahmin patriarchs, and Saraswathi represented the Brahmin women who had been turned into sexual objects.

Saraswathi is also a contradictory figure. Though she was said to be the source of education, she never represented the case of Brahmin women who had themselves been denied education, and of course she never thought of the Dalitbahujan women. She herself remains a tool in the hands of Brahma. She becomes delicate because Brahma wants her to be delicate. She is portrayed as an expert in the strictly defined female activities of serving Brahma or playing the veena—always to amuse Brahma. Brahma is never said to have looked after cattle, or driven a plough; similarly, Saraswathi never tends the crops, plants the seed or weeds the fields. She is said to have become so delicate that she could stand on a lotus flower. She could travel on a *hamsa* (a swan, a delicate bird). This kind of delicateness is a negative delicateness. It only shows that her alienation from nature is total. In order to live this alienated but luxurious life, the Brahmins have built up an oppressive culture. That oppressive culture was sought to be made universally acceptable.

VISHNU AND LAKSHMI

The second God who is said to have played a predominant brahminical role, yuga after yuga,[6] is Vishnu. Why is Vishnu said to have been a blue-skinned God? The reason is quite obvious. He is the projection of an association between the Brahmins and the Kshatriyas. This godhead might have been created at a time when the Kshatriyas (a hybrid caste that might perhaps have emerged in cross-breeding between white-skinned Aryans and dark-skinned Dravidian Dalitbahujans) were in revolt against the Brahmins. Jainism and Buddhism were perhaps the last of such revolts. Vishnu is said to be the upholder and preserver of all the principles that Brahma evolved. He is assigned the task of preserving and expanding Brahmin dharma. He wields the *vishnu-chakram*,[7] an extremely dangerous weapon, designed to injure all those who rebel against the Brahmins. He is supposed to be merciless in suppressing revolts. Interestingly, he is shown sleeping on a snake which suggests his wickedness more than it does his humanism. For an average Dalitbahujan the snake symbolizes evil, not virtue. He is monogamous as he is married to Lakshmi.[8] The relationship between Lakshmi and Vishnu is no different from that between Brahma and Saraswathi. Lakshmi is

5. Ancient materialists, named after their founder Charvaka; also called Lokayatas ("worldly") ("Salvation and Damnation," p. 183).
6. "The Four Ages" (p. 228).
7. The discus.
8. Goddess of wealth and good fortune ("Churning of the Ocean," p. 149).

supposed to aid Vishnu in his anti-Dalitbahujan designs. Her role is very clear: she must keep pressing the feet of Vishnu as he lies cogitating about the prosperity of Brahmins and the destruction of the Dalitbahujans. She is supposed to procure wealth and victory for the Brahmins, the Kshatriyas and the Vaishyas. But she must also keep a watch on Dalitbahujans. If she comes to know that a Dalitbahujan man or woman has acquired wealth or is revolting against the caste system, she is required to bring that to the notice of Vishnu who will go and exterminate such persons.

Brahminism is so diabolical that even Brahmin and Kshatriya women are assigned significant roles that keep the Dalitbahujans suppressed. Saraswathi must see to it that the Dalitbahujans do not become literate and ensure that they can never understand the brahminical methods of manipulation. Lakshmi is assigned the role of alienating Dalitbahujans from private property: land, gold and other metals. In other words, the Brahmin woman is supposed to see that the Dalitbahujans are denied the right to education and the Kshatriya woman is assigned the duty of denying the right to property to Dalitbahujans. These kinds of roles for 'upper' caste women have played an important part in assimilating them into Brahminism—but as unequal partners. In fact, as Phule[9] repeatedly said, Brahmins were so cunning that they have assigned to Lakshmi the role of being the source of wealth and property while all Brahmin women are denied the right to property. As in the case of Saraswathi, Lakshmi, the source of wealth, is herself a poor dependent.

Assigning these roles to women has had a double-edged function. Within the caste, gender roles are strictly defined but even the oppressed gender is assimilated into the opposition against the other caste/class. Brahmin and Kshatriya men play the role of producing knowledge that lies outside the domain of production, and through which the enemies of brahminical consciousness are controlled. As a result, Dalitbanujan consciousness itself is made to consent to its oppression. If the consent system is broken, the Kshatriya God—Vishnu—is always vigilant to suppress the offenders by using violence. By creating such images of the Gods and Goddesses—Indra, Brahma, Saraswathi, Vishnu, Lakshmi—the possibility of breaking the brahminical system was arrested from several aspects: knowledge, wealth and war being predominant.

It is not very clear why Vishnu and not Brahma was chosen to be reincarnated in different forms at different times to suppress Dalitbahujan assertion. Perhaps it was because the Kshatriyas already wielded political power, but it was important to make the Kshatriya kings acquiesce in their subordination to the Brahmins. If such a message emerges from the Kshatriya Gods and Goddesses themselves, building up consent from the Kshatriyas becomes easier. To a large extent that purpose was also served because through the message of Vishnu and Lakshmi the Brahmins ensured their philosophical and ideological hegemony even over the Kshatriyas, and through the message of Lakshmi even while being out of responsible positions of running the state or conducting wars, the Brahmins could acquire wealth for the mere asking. More important, the Dalitbahujans were suppressed year after year, century after century and yuga after yuga.

9. Jotiba Phule (1827–1890) and his wife, Savitribai Phule, were activists and social reformers from Maharashtra, working especially on behalf of women and Dalits.

W. W. Norton & Company has been independent since its founding in 1923, when William Warder Norton and Mary D. Herter Norton first published lectures delivered at the People's Institute, the adult education division of New York City's Cooper Union. The firm soon expanded its program beyond the Institute, publishing books by celebrated academics from America and abroad. By midcentury, the two major pillars of Norton's publishing program—trade books and college texts—were firmly established. In the 1950s, the Norton family transferred control of the company to its employees, and today—with a staff of four hundred and a comparable number of trade, college, and professional titles published each year—W. W. Norton & Company stands as the largest and oldest publishing house owned wholly by its employees.

Printed in the United States of America
First Edition

Manufacturing by LSC Communications Crawfordsville
Composition by Westchester Book
Book design by Jo Anne Metsch
Production Manager: Sean Mintus

LIBRARY OF CONGRESS CATALOGING-IN-PUBLICATION DATA

The Norton anthology of world religions / Jack Miles, General Editor, Distinguished Professor of English and Religious Studies, University of California, Irvine; Wendy Doniger, Hinduism; Donald S. Lopez, Jr., Buddhism; James Robson, Daoism. — First Edition.
volumes cm
Includes bibliographical references and index.
ISBN 978-0-393-91257-9 (hardcover)
1. Religions. 2. Religions—History—Sources. I. Miles, Jack, 1942– editor. II. Doniger, Wendy, editor. III. Lopez, Donald S., 1952– editor. IV. Robson, James, 1965 December 1– editor.
BL74.N67 2014
208—dc23

2014030756

Hinduism (978-0-393-35501-7): Jack Miles, General Editor; Wendy Doniger, Editor

W. W. Norton & Company, Inc.
500 Fifth Avenue
New York NY 10110
wwnorton.com

W. W. Norton & Company Ltd.
15 Carlisle Street, London W1D 3BS

1 2 3 4 5 6 7 8 9 0

THE NORTON ANTHOLOGY OF

WORLD RELIGIONS

HINDUISM

Wendy Doniger

JACK MILES, *General Editor*
DISTINGUISHED PROFESSOR OF ENGLISH AND RELIGIOUS STUDIES
UNIVERSITY OF CALIFORNIA, IRVINE

W · W · NORTON & COMPANY
NEW YORK · LONDON

THE NORTON ANTHOLOGY OF

WORLD RELIGIONS

HINDUISM

The influence of the figures of brahminized women like Saraswathi and Lakshmi is enormous on 'upper' caste women in India. The image of Lakshmi gets reinforced day in and day out since she is said to be the source of wealth. During the 1990 Mandal debate many well-known women writers began to feel insecure and opposed the anti-caste movements without even realizing that these were in essence anti-caste movements. Internalization of personalities like Lakshmi and Sita by 'upper' caste women has several implications for Dalitbahujan movements and also for women's movements. In a casteized patriarchal system Dalitbahujan movements and women's movements should extend helping hands to each other. Such coordination becomes possible only when 'upper' caste women overcome the influence of Brahminism, which restrict their worldview. It is unfortunate that no women writers, not even feminists, have deconstructed the socio-political influences of these Goddesses on women—particularly on brahminical women.

SHIVA AND PARVATHI

The third among the *trimurthies*, the one who is least powerful, and who is easily fooled, is Shiva or Maheshwara. In terms of color and costume he neither resembles Brahma and the Brahmins nor does he resemble Vishnu and the Kshatriyas. He is dark-skinned and dressed like a tribal. Though this God is associated with Brahma and Vishnu, he is assigned a third position and he does not have as defined a role as Brahma and Vishnu do. Though he is also powerful and wields the *trishula*[1] as his weapon, basically he plays the subordinate role to Brahma and Vishnu. His behavior is a little different from that of the Brahmin and the Kshatriya Gods. He loves dancing and gets himself into all sorts of difficulties from which he needs to be rescued by Brahma or Vishnu. The story of Bhasmasura[2] is a good example of Shiva's dependence on Vishnu.

His wife, Parvathi, or Gauri as she is also called, also does not have as specific a role as Saraswathi or Lakshmi. She joins her husband in many of his activities. They dance and roam around. But Parvathi, unlike Saraswathi and Lakshmi, questions many of the activities of her husband. She also plays certain roles which do not, strictly speaking, fall within the domain of ritual Hinduism. Perhaps this couple comes from a tribal origin. On the whole, however, Parvathi supports Saraswathi and Lakshmi in their anti-Dalitbahujan activities. The question is, then, for what purpose was the image of Shankara and Parvathi constructed? To my mind there is a definite purpose in these images. The images of Brahma, Vishnu, Saraswathi and Lakshmi were enough to control the minds of those Dalitbahujans, Vaishyas and Kshatriyas who have already come into the grip of brahminical civil society. These four figures were adequate for ensuring Dalitbahujan consent or, when necessary, suppression. This was because, by and large, the theory of karma[3] had already been universalized among them, although, as I said in earlier chapters, these Gods were not at all known to the Dalitbahujans.

1. The trident.
2. "Demon of Ashes." He won from Shiva a boon that he could burn anyone to ashes by putting his hand over his victim's head. He was defeated when another deity—usually said to be Durga but here, apparently, Vishnu—tricked him into putting his hand over his own head.
3. The theory that past actions determine the course of future lives (Upanishads, p. 105).

To the extent that they were known, the concept of karma has created an ideological preserve of consent, and worked to ensure that the Dalitbahujans did nothing to challenge their hegemony.

* * *

THE AVATARA GODS

Though the trimurthies and their wives had achieved the main objective of the Brahmins, Dalitbahujan revolts continued to take place. As a result, Brahmins went on creating more and more God and Goddess images through the technique of *avataras.* From among the later *avatara* Gods and Goddesses, Vamana, Krishna, Rama and Sita are important. Though Phule and Ambedkar[4] did build up a 'Shudra' critique of some of these *avataras*, it is important to extend this analysis in the light of post-colonial Hindutva. Of the ten so-called *avataras* of Vishnu, the Buddha[5] is an obvious cooptation. Even an average, urban-educated Indian knows this and therefore, I do not need to analyse the question of the Buddha.

VAMANA

Of the remaining avataras, three are important for our purpose—Vamana, Krishna and Rama. Like many historians, I am also of the opinion that the *Ramayana* was written after the *Mahabharatha.* After Brahma, Vamana is the only God who was said to have been born as a Brahmin. In setting up the story of the origin of this God the Brahmins have not been so intelligent. The narrative depicts Vamana as being incarnated to kill the Dalitbahujan king, Bali Chakravarthi,[6] who did not believe in Hindu Brahminism and worked to establish a casteless society. Upset by Bali's moves, the Brahmins of the area projected a dwarf Brahmin boy as the incarnation of Vishnu. A great deal of propaganda was done about the capacities of Vamana around that area to enthuse confidence among Brahmins and intimidate the Dalitbahujans. They also announced that on a particular day Vamana would visit Bali. They terrified the Dalitbahujan masses and also Bali with this very propaganda. One fine morning all the Brahmins of the area went to Bali's place along with Vamana. Though Bali was told by his teacher Shukracharya[7] that this dwarf was only a disguised Brahmin, Bali was tempted to believe that he was God. The Brahmins managed to pour acid in Shukracharya's eyes and Bali was rendered supportless.

Vamana asks Bali for three *varas* (gifts). Bali agrees. Vamana asks for three footspans of land. Without realizing its implications, Bali agrees. Then Vamana uses his brahminical trick. He goes up to the top of the building and points one foot towards the sky and declares that the whole of the sky is covered by that foot. Then he points another foot towards the earth and says it covered the whole earth. The protests of Bali that such claims are lies are shouted down by the Brahmins around. Vamana then descends from the building and asks for a place for the third foot. Before Bali recovers from the shock of godly lies, Vamana claims that since there was no land to put his

4. Activist on behalf of Dalits ("Dr. Ambedkar's Speech at Mahad," p. 597).
5. See "Vishnu as the Buddha," p. 242. See also Kancha Ilaiah, *God as Political Philosopher: Buddha's Challenge to Brahminism* (2000).
6. The world-ruler (or Chakravartin) named Bali, an anti-god defeated by Vishnu in the form of a dwarf (*vamana*) ("The Three Strides of Vishnu," p. 91; "The Ten Avatars of Vishnu," p. 480).
7. Guru of the anti-gods.

third foot he will put it on Bali's head. He breaks Bali's head by stamping on him with his iron-studded footwear. Thus, the Dalitbahujan kingdom was conquered by Hindu treachery and the most humanitarian Baliraja was murdered. Phule in all his writings speaks of the injustice done to Bali by the Brahmins and asks the Dalitbahujans to establish an egalitarian society such as the one in which Bali was the leader. Phule also exposes the Brahmins' inhuman treachery.

KRISHNA

Who is Krishna?[8] Why did the Brahmins create such a God? Why is it that he was said to have been brought up by a Yadava[9] family, though he was born a Kshatriya? Suddenly, and only with regard to Krishna (all other Gods and Goddesses are Brahmins and Kshatriyas), why is such a compromise made? Even Karna who was said to have been brought up in a Dalitbahujan family, though he was born a Kshatriya, is condemned, but not Krishna whose life-story has a similar caste narrative. The accounts of his childhood mischief in cowherd houses, the stories of his promiscuous relationships, and his other nefarious activities—with Radha and other Yadava women—are all projected as divine. Krishna is represented as the guru, leader and war strategist for minority (Pandava) dharma against the majority (Kaurava) dharma. Finally it is the same Krishna who is said to have authored the most brahminical text—the Bhagavad Gita[1]—which became the sacred text of the Hindus, just as the Bible is the sacred text of the Christians, and the Koran of the Muslims. At a time when the Shudras had no right to education, how did a Yadava write the Gita? How did a Yadava writer not provide any social space for Yadavas themselves, leave alone the other Dalitbahujans? There is a need for deliberation on all these questions.

* * *

Even in the period of the *Mahabharatha*, the Brahmins needed to project a person who could rebuild a consent system to contain the Yadava revolts. The Brahmins created an image of one who was said to have been born and brought up among the Yadavas themselves, but they had to ensure that it would not result in having to include the entire Yadava community as had happened in the case of the Kshatriyas. If this happened, it would result in expanding the number and scope of brahminical castes. That itself would endanger the hegemony of the Brahmin-Kshatriyas. In order to overcome this problem they worked out the strategy of creating a Krishna (dark blue in color) who was said to have been born in a Kshatriya family and brought up in a Yadava family. But the narrative is cleverly manipulated. The young Krishna grows up in Yadava culture, but the political Krishna never identifies himself with Yadava culture. His political role is that of a Kshatriya, defending brahminical dharma.

In no single incident did he stand by the Dalitbahujans. It did not matter whether his beloved was a Yadava-Radha or whether the other gopikas were

8. An incarnation of Vishnu; one of the heroes of the *Mahabharata* ("Krishna," p. 247).

9. Descendants of King Yadu, an ancestor of Krishna. The *Mahabharata*, in which the story is first told, clearly regards the Yadavas as Kshatriyas, of the warrior class, though Ilaiah regards them as Dalitbahujans. Krishna was adopted and brought up among cowherds and their women (*gopikas*), presumably of low (but not necessarily Dalit) caste, but his Yadava ancestry was in his birth family, who were not cowherds but kings.

1. See the *Bhagavad Gita*, p. 166.

Yadavas. All his legal wives were Kshatriya women. That fitted very well into the brahminical patriarchal culture of having sexual relations with Dalitbahujan women but marrying only women of their own caste. Krishna is the only *avatara* who is presented as a believer in polygamy. He had eight wives and all of them were Kshatriya women. He is represented as having assimilated some aspects of Dalitbahujan (Yadava) culture—and that part of his character is attributed to his 'Dalitness.' All his brahminical characteristics are attributed to his 'Kshatriyaness.' With Krishna's *avatara* the Brahmins played their politics extremely well.

* * *

In this war Karna[2] and Krishna represent two different values. Karna, though born to a Kshatriya woman, Kunti, owns up to Dalitbahujan culture and tradition as he was brought up in a Dalitbahujan family, whereas Krishna, who was brought up by Yadavas, consciously owns up to the Kshatriya cultural tradition. Even in the war Karna represents the majority whereas Krishna represents the minority. Krishna was also a weapon-wielding God: he wields a *chakram*, he is also the *yuddha radhasarathi* (chariot driver) of the minority. All the skills of Kautilyan statecraft were exhibited by Krishna in the battlefield. For him the end justifies the means and war resolves all contradictions. In defence of minority dharma he justifies violence, brutality and treachery. Karna was killed only through treachery.

In the story of his *raayabhaaram* (ambassadorship) it was very clear that he failed to win the majority through the brahminical mechanism of consent creation. The majority were not willing to give up the land they had acquired through sweat and blood. Finally Krishna resorts to violence. Some of the members of his camp (like Arjuna) were not willing to indulge in such bloody violence but Krishna forces them to kill anyone—guilty or otherwise—from the majority camp, as they had rebelled against brahminical dharma. It was in defence of brahminical ideology that he taught, as is evident in the Gita, the theory of violence, varnadharma and karma. This is the reason why Krishna was so acceptable to brahminical forces. After the defeat of the majority in the struggle for land the Gita was used to create a much stronger consent system to ensure that no serious revolts emerged from the Dalitbahujan social base. Whenever such attempts were made, either by Yadavas or by other Dalit forces, Krishna's Gita was effectively used to manipulate them into submission. During the freedom struggle the Hindu brahminical forces, particularly Gandhi, propagated the Gita message to build a modern consent system for the continued maintenance of brahminical hegemony in the era of capitalism and democracy.

* * *

RAMA AND SITA

The Brahmins did not mince words when they created the last and the most powerful epic images of the powerful monogamous male and female. Both Rama and Sita were said to have been born in Kshatriya families. Rama is

2. In the *Mahabharata*, Karna was born illegitimately to Kunti, who abandoned him; he was raised by a low-caste family of Sutas (charioteers and bards), and learned of his noble birth only when he was grown and had suffered the indignities of a low-caste person ("The Stripping of Draupadi," p. 134).

a blue-skinned Kshatriya *avatara* of Vishnu, and Sita is a pale-complexioned *avatara* of Lakshmi. Why did the Brahmins create these images by writing the *Ramayana* and what did they expect to achieve through this epic narrative?

In North India, after the Dalitbahujan revolts were suppressed, both through consent and through war, the Dalitbahujans of that area were completely subdued. Varnadharma theory and practice became part of mass consciousness. Even the Jain and Buddhist schools that were antagonistic to Brahmin ideology were completely suppressed. Through the establishment of the Kautilyan state (economic and political) Manu's laws were implemented systematically. Brahmins ruled the roost in the system and even Kshatriya assertion no longer continued with the creation of the image of Krishna and after the writing of the Gita. The consent system was so total that no one could raise a finger against the Brahmins. All sections of the population in North India had been subjugated to such an extent that they had lost confidence in themselves and had given up all hope of change.

The Brahmins thought that this was the right time to expand their hegemony to South India, where the Dalitbahujans were ruling. The kingdoms of Tataki, Shambuka, Vali and Ravana[3] were all Dalitbahujan kingdoms. Some Brahmins claim that Ravana was also a Brahmin. This is nonsense. Ravana was a powerful Dravida Dalitbahujan ruler. He was also a militant Shaivaite. Ravana tried to separate Shaivism from Brahminism and to create an autonomous space for Dalitbahujan Shaivism, which is what Basava[4] finally managed to some extent. He established a powerful kingdom with its capital in Sri Lanka so that he could withstand brahminical aggression. The North Indian Brahmins decided that at a time when their dominance was total in the North, the South Indian Dalitbahujan kingdoms must be defeated and the hold of Brahminism extended. Therefore, they planned an aggression on the Dalitbahujan South. The rishis played a very crucial role in deciding on what steps Rama should take. Vishwamitra and Vasishta were the driving forces in the *Ramayana* narrative. They are known as Rama's *kula gurus*,[5] people whose words must be respected under any circumstance.

Apart from extending the hold of Brahminism to the South, the *Ramayana* narrative is also a means of subordinating women by establishing role models for them. It asserts that a wife must be subordinate to her husband, irrespective of the caste/class nature of the man; that no woman ought to be a ruler since such exercise of political power by women within the subcontinent (even among Dalitbahujans) might influence the brahminical Aryans, who had by then established a strong patriarchal system. Northern Brahminism decided to place gender roles hierarchically into brahminical patriarchy even in South India. The later Brahmins were not at all pleased about the 'unbrahminical' relationships that were made respectable by Draupadi and Radha.[6] Draupadi became a public figure though she had five husbands and Radha was said to have had relations with Krishna, though she was not married to him. It is surprising that Hindus give the name Radha

3. Enemies of Rama, killed by Rama in the *Ramayana*. Tataki is an ogress; Shambuka a Shudra; Vali a monkey, ruler in the kingdom of Kishkindha (where Rama befriended Vali's brother, Sugriva, who had usurped the monkey throne); and Ravana an ogre (Rakshasa).

4. The founder of the low-caste Virashaiva movement ("The Basava Purana," p. 354).

5. Family teachers.

6. The heroine of the *Mahabharata* ("The Stripping of Draupadi," p. 134) and the beloved of Krishna (Jayadeva, p. 480; "The Eightfold Activities," p. 502).

to their female children but not of Draupadi. That is because Draupadi had five husbands. Hindus have no disrespect for a man like Krishna who had eight wives but have no respect for Draupadi who had five husbands. Hinduism respects polygamy but not polyandry. In the period of the *Ramayana*, Hinduism was settling down in patriarchal monogamy. So they decided to institutionalize patriarchal monogamy even among the Dravida Dalitbahujans, because the Dravida region still retained elements of a strong matriarchal tradition. The autonomy of men and women was systemic among South Indian masses. This is clear from the Goddess-centered rituals that are universally in vogue in South India even today.

The *Ramayana* is an ancient account of the aggression aimed at brahminizing the Dalitbahujan society of South India, turning it into a brahminizing patriarchy. With this objective the Brahmin rishies came along with Rama, Sita and Lakshmana, attacked the tribal oligarchies and destabilized several independent Dalitbahujan states. Tataki, the famous Dalitbahujan woman, was killed and her state was brought under Brahminism. Then the famous Shambuka was killed, and his kingdom usurped. The major opposition to Rama's aggression came from the ruler of Kishkinda, a tribal king called Vali. The Brahmins befriended Vali's brother Sugreeva and his nephew Anjaneya and, aided by their treachery, killed the powerful Vali. When a beautiful Dalitbahujan woman, Shurpanaka,[7] wanted to marry Rama, the latter said she should ask Lakshmana.[8] But Lakshmana in response cut off her nose and her earlobes. This incident enraged her brother Ravana. He kidnapped Sita to teach Rama a lesson. Of course Rama uses this incident to mobilize the same tribal Dalitbahujans to attack Sri Lanka. Somehow he reaches Sri Lanka and kills Ravana. With the killing of Ravana the Dalitbahujans of South India were conquered by the brahminical Aryans. In fact, what was worse, was after the defeat of Ravana many Brahmin rishies migrated from the North to the whole of South India, which had basically been a casteless society. It was turned into a caste-based society and the Brahmins established their ideological hegemony over the whole of South India.

* * *

In addition to the anti-Brahmin micromovements there were also several cultural traditions in civil society which were antithetical to the brahminical tradition, cultural ethos and economic system. As a result, the brahminical tradition remained only a surface system in the South. In fact, if in North India, brahminical Hinduism kept Muslim culture confined to the converts and to the state institutions, not allowing it into civil society, in South India the Dalitbahujan masses did the same to Brahminism. At one level the Brahmin priest kept himself in touch with the Dalitbahujan masses on certain occasions like marriages and deaths and extracted money, food materials, cows and land in the form of dakshina.[9] But at another level, Dalitbahujans retained their cultural ethos, their economic notions of life, and their political and scientific tempers which were distinct.

* * *

7. Ravana's sister ("The Mutilation of Shurpanakha," p. 438; "Shurpanakha," p. 649).

8. Rama's brother.

9. The fee paid to the priest.

It is important that scholars from the Dalitbahujan tradition enter into a debate with brahminical scholars in a big way. These brahminical scholars and leaders who talk about Hindutva being the religion of all castes must realize that the Scheduled Castes, Other Backward Classes, and Scheduled Tribes of this country have nothing in common with the Hindus. For centuries, even when Dalitbahujans tried to unite all castes, the Brahmins, the Baniyas[1] and the Kshatriyas opposed the effort. Even today, no Brahmin adopts the names of our Goddesses/Gods; even today, they do not understand that the Dalitbahujans have a much more humane and egalitarian tradition and culture than the Hindu tradition and culture. Even today, our cultural tradition is being treated as meritless. If the Brahmins, the Baniyas, the Kshatriyas and the neo-Kshatriyas of this country want unity among diversity, they should join us and look to Dalitization, not Hinduization.

1. Baniyas or Banias (from the Sanskrit *vanijya*, "trade") are traditionally merchants and moneylenders.

A. K. RAMANUJAN

A(ttipat) K(rishnaswami) Ramanujan (1929–1993) was a scholar of Indian literature, religion, and culture who was fluent in English, Kannada, Tamil, Telugu, and Sanskrit. A scholar, philologist, folklorist, translator, poet, and playwright, he was largely responsible for the inclusion of Tamil in programs of South Asian Studies, a discipline that he helped to create and shape in the 1960s at the University of Chicago. In 1976, the government of India awarded him the honorific title Padma Sri, and in 1983 he was awarded a MacArthur Fellowship.

Ramanujan's 1991 essay "Three Hundred Ramayanas: Five Examples and Three Thoughts on Translations" was about some of the many versions of the *Ramayana* that contradict Valmiki and Tulsidas. ("One Night While Sita and Rama Were Lying Together," p. 585, "Sita Lost in Thought," p. 372, and "Kausalya in Fury," p. 677, are such versions, though not among those that Ramanujan cited.) In 2006 this essay was included in the B.A., History syllabus of Delhi University. A student wing of the Bharatiya Janata Party (BJP) opposed its inclusion in the syllabus, and in Oxford University Press's in-print catalog, on the grounds that it hurt Hindu sentiments. In October 2011 the academic council of Delhi University voted to remove the essay from its syllabus. Nothing could bring into more vivid focus the threat to freedom of speech in contemporary India than this incident; and nothing gives more hope for the survival of democracy in India than the extent and (qualified) success of the international protest against the attempt to silence Ramanujan's powerful voice.

Ramanujan's poems, in both English and Kannada, have been widely praised; Dom Moraes, writing in the *Times of India*, called his volume of collected poems the best "of not only an Indian poet but any poet for the last tenth of a century." The three poems included here were written, in English, shortly before Ramanujan's unexpected death in 1993. They express his passionate devotion to the Hinduism that he absorbed from his parents, Iyengar Brahmins, in Mysore, and that grew deeper and stronger as he divided his life between India and America. The ancient themes remain fully alive in these modern poems, a testament to the enduring power of the Hindu vision of the world.

MYTHOLOGIES 1: PUTANA

The ogress Putana's attempt to kill the infant Krishna, "the Child" ("Krishna Kills the Ogress Putana," p. 247), results in her death rather than his, but also in her salvation through accidental grace ("The Fruits of Hearing a Purana: Devaraja the Sinner," p. 225): Putana's passionate feeling for Krishna, however negative, transfigures her—and will, the poet prays, transfigure him.

The breast she offered was full
of poison and milk.
Flashing eyes suddenly dull,
her voice was silk.

The Child took her breast
in his mouth and sucked it right out of her chest.
Her carcass stretched from north to south.

She changed, undone by grace,
from deadly mother to happy demon,
found life in death.

O Terror with a baby face,
suck me dry. Drink my venom.
Renew my breath.

MYTHOLOGIES 2: NARA-SIMHA

This poem views the myth of Vishnu's avatar as the Man-Lion (Nara-Simha) ("The Ten Avatars of Vishnu," p. 480) from the standpoint of Prahlada, the devotee whom Vishnu saves from his demonic father by becoming a loophole in the contract that the cunning demon had forced the gods to make with him. The poet prays to the god to give him a vision that will transcend the categories of doubles (day/night, outside/inside, etc.), the dualities that Hindu philosophy challenges.

When the clever man asks the perfect boon:
not to be slain by demon, god, or by
beast, not by day nor by night,
by no manufactured weapon, not out
of doors nor inside, not in the sky
nor on earth,

come now come soon,
Vishnu, man, lion, neither and both, to hold
him in our lap to disembowel his pride
with the steel glint of bare claws at twilight.

O midnight sun, eclipse at noon,
net of loopholes, a house all threshold,
connoisseur of negatives and assassin
of certitudes, slay now my faith in doubt.
End my commerce with bat and night-
owl. Adjust my single eye, rainbow bubble,
so I too may see all things double.

MYTHOLOGIES 3: MAHADEVIYAKKA

Ramanujan had translated the poems of Mahadeviyakka (p. 348). Here he imagines the vision of the god Shiva that she might have had when she left her husband.

"Keep off when I worship Shiva.
Touch me three times, and you'll never
see me again," said Akka to her new groom
who couldn't believe his ears.

Om, Om!
she seemed to intone in bed with every breath
and all he could think of was her round breast, her musk,
her darling navel and the rest.
So he hovered and touched her, her body death-

ly cold to mortal touch but hot for God's
first move, a caress like nothing on earth.
She fled his hand as she would a spider,

threw away her modesty, as the rods
and cones of her eyes gave the world a new birth:
She saw Him then, unborn, form of forms, the Rider,

His white Bull chewing cud in her backyard.

APPENDICES

Glossary

Words in SMALL CAPS are defined in their own entries.

Acharya (Sanskrit, "knowing or teaching the rules"). A title given to highly learned men or scholars, especially BRAHMIN religious teachers; it is sometimes combined with their names.

Adivasis (Sanskrit, "first dwellers"). A collective adjective for the various TRIBAL, ethnic, and aboriginal peoples of India.

Agni. The god of fire, or fire personified. Agni's prime task is to receive sacrifices in ritual fires and to transmit those sacrifices to the rest of the gods; by extension, he receives the dead on cremation pyres. Agni appears first in the *RIG VEDA*.

ahimsa (Sanskrit, "non-injuring"). The principle of nonviolence, particularly construed to mean not killing or eating animals.

antinomian. In defiance of or beyond rules or convention. In Hindu and Buddhist contexts, antinomian practices flout purity, caste, or monastic rules; they are central to much of the teaching and practice of TANTRA.

Apsaras (pl., Apsarases). Beautiful female water-spirits, dancers, and courtesans who live in the sky. Known for their elegance and dancing, they are the consorts of the GANDHARVAS.

Arjuna. The middle PANDAVA brother. Son of the god INDRA, Arjuna, the chief protagonist of the *MAHABHARATA*, particularly the *BHAGAVAD GITA*, is famous for his heroism and his archery skills.

ashramas (Sanskrit, pl.). The four stages of life, according to the SHASTRAS, through which an individual progresses to fulfill different religious goals: religious learning (the student, or *BRAHMACHARIN*, phase), worldly and social life (HOUSEHOLDER), contemplation (forest dweller, retirement, or partial withdrawal), and Release (full renunciation of social and worldly life).

Ashvins. Twin horse-headed gods. First mentioned in the VEDAS, the Ashvins are associated both with the rising and setting sun and with medicine.

Asura (Sanskrit, "spirit"). A power-seeking spirit or demonic anti-god. Asuras are the opposites or opponents of the gods (*devas*), and over time they became increasingly negative figures in Hindu literature.

atman (Sanskrit, "breath," "self"). The enduring essence of a human being, the soul. The atman is that which migrates between bodies in successive lives on the WHEEL OF REBIRTH (*SAMSARA*), in accordance with KARMA. Individual souls are all a part of the universal divine soul, the Atman.

avatar (Sanskrit, "descent," "crossing down"). The manifestation of a divine being, generally VISHNU, in a corporeal form on earth. Vishnu's two most important human avatars are KRISHNA and RAMA.

Bali. An ASURA king defeated by VISHNU in his AVATAR of the dwarf, Vamana.

Bangla / Bengali. The dominant language of the easternmost coastal areas of India around Calcutta (now Kolkata).

Baul (Bangla, "possessed," "crazy"). A traveling musician or poet in Bengal who engages in ecstatic devotional performances. Bauls may represent a variety of religious traditions, but most are either VAISHNAVA Hindus or Sufi Muslims, and many incorporate aspects of TANTRA in their worship and practice.

Bhagavad Gita (Sanskrit, "song of the lord"). A portion of the *MAHABHARATA* epic often read and circulated as an independent text. A dialogue between ARJUNA and KRISHNA, it explores the complexity of ethical action; the *Bhagavad Gita* is one of the first SANSKRIT texts to posit *BHAKTI* as a path to salvation.

Bhagavan (Sanskrit, "fortunate," "holy," "divine"). Supreme god, a title sometimes used generically and sometimes as an epithet, especially for VISHNU or SHIVA.

bhakta (Sanskrit, "one who is attached or devoted"). A devotee, one possessed of *BHAKTI* for a god or goddess.

bhakti (Sanskrit, "devotion"). The commitment an individual feels and demonstrates toward a deity, who returns the devotee's love. Sometimes ecstatic or even erotic, the *bhakti* movement has given rise to India's traditions of devotional poetry.

Bhima. The second-born of the five PANDAVA brothers in the *MAHABHARATA*, son of the god of the wind, known for his great strength.

Brahma. The god typically credited with creating the universe. Though often presented in a trinity with VISHNU and SHIVA, Brahma is not the object of a devotional tradition.

brahmacharin (Sanskrit). A chaste student who studies the VEDAS and SHASTRAS under the tutelage of a GURU in the first of the four *ASHRAMAS*.

brahman (Sanskrit). The abstract, nonpersonal spirit or essence pervading the universe, according to the philosophy developed in the UPANISHADS.

Brahmanas. The canonical commentaries on the VEDAS, likely composed between about 900 and 600 B.C.E. Notably, they offer authoritative instructions on the proper performance of rituals.

Brahmin. A member of the class of hereditary priests. Of the four classes or *VARNAS*, Brahmins are the most ritually pure. For most of Indic history, they maintained exclusive or near-exclusive access to many sacred texts, rituals, and spaces, as well as to the SANSKRIT language.

caste (from the Portuguese *casta*, "breed" or "race"). The social category or status group into which a Hindu is born. Castes are hierarchically ranked in prestige and purity: they overlap with but are far more complex than the four *VARNAS* (headed by BRAHMINS).

Chandala. An exceptionally low-status DALIT caste of people traditionally charged with disposal of corpses.

Dalit (Marathi, "broken"). The preferred term for people belonging to CASTES formerly known as UNTOUCHABLES. Dalits make up 15 to 20 percent of the Indian population; despite legal reforms, they continue to be marginalized by deep-rooted prejudice as well as by poverty and other disadvantages.

darshan (Sanskrit, "seeing"). The reciprocal experience of seeing and being seen by a superior being—most often a god (e.g., via an image in a temple), but also a king or a holy person.

dharma (Sanskrit). The notion (often glossed as "duty," "law," "righteousness," or "religion") that people are enjoined to particular social conduct, ritual obligations, and ethical actions. Some of these are shared by all human beings, but many are tailored to an individual's specific social status or role.

dharma-shastra (Sanskrit, "textbooks of duty"). The body of literature systematically outlining morally correct behavior; the most famous is attributed to Manu.

Draupadi. The wife of all five PANDAVA brothers in the *MAHABHARATA*—a strong, intelligent, and highly resourceful character.

Ganapati (Sanskrit, "lord of the group/troops"). Another name of GANESHA.

Gandharva. A demigod associated with music and fertility; Gandharvas are husbands of APSARASES.

Ganesha (Sanskrit, "lord of the group/troops"). The elephant-headed god who clears away obstacles. One of the most popular deities in India, he is the son of PARVATI/UMA but also regarded as the son of SHIVA.

Ganges. The sacred river that runs west to east through northern India. Water from the Ganges is widely thought to have mystical, magical, and medicinal powers.

Garuda. The celestial eagle (sometimes quite birdlike, sometimes more anthropomorphic) upon which VISHNU rides.

ghee (Hindi and Urdu). Clarified (heated and filtered) butter, which is slow to spoil even without refrigeration. Clarified butter is considered an exceptionally pure substance and features prominently in religious ritual.

gopi (Sanskrit). A female cowherd. According to tradition, KRISHNA engaged in erotic play with the *gopis* in the forests of Vrindavana. The *gopis* were his lovers and his *BHAKTAS*, and human devotees of Krishna are encouraged to relate to him with the ecstatic passion of the *gopis*.

Gujarati. A language spoken in the state of Gujarat, on India's northwestern coast. It is the native language of Mohandas Gandhi.

guru (Sanskrit, "venerable"). A teacher who guides a student through the process of developing intellectually, morally, and religiously. He is often but not always a BRAHMIN with an education in SANSKRIT language and literature.

Hanuman. A supernatural monkey who appears in the *RAMAYANA*. He is noted for his physical strength and his devotion to RAMA.

Hari. An epithet for a god, usually VISHNU or his AVATAR, KRISHNA.

Hindi. One of the most widely spoken languages in modern India, used throughout most of northern India and by much of Indian media. Related to SANSKRIT but influenced by Persian, Hindi is mutually intelligible with spoken URDU; however, Hindi is written in the *nagari* script used for Sanskrit, while URDU is written in Arabic script.

householder. The second stage in the system of *ASHRAMAS*, when Hindus are expected to start families, run households, and uphold conventional society.

Indra. The king of the gods, and the god of rain. Indra is first attested in the VEDAS, but in Hindu narrative he often appears as a vulnerable, helpless, or even buffoonish figure.

Ishvara (Sanskrit, "the Lord"). A name used to designate a great or transcendent god. The term is often used alone or with the prefix "great" (*maha-*, thus "Maheshvara") as a title specific to SHIVA.

Jainism. A tradition that arose alongside Buddhism and Hinduism, stressing a radical commitment to *AHIMSA* (nonviolence).

jati (Sanskrit, "birth"). The "natural class" into which each human is believed to be born (best translated as "CASTE"). There are dozens of major *jatis* and hundreds of subcategories hierarchically ranked around purity practices.

Kailasa. The Himalayan mountain where SHIVA lives and meditates.

Kali (Sanskrit, "black"). The foremost fierce and chaotic goddess, a violent and unpredictable manifestation of feminine energy, *SHAKTI*. Kali is typically depicted wearing a necklace of skulls, exposing her tongue, brandishing a bloody sword, and dancing on a corpse.

Kali Age. The fourth and final phase in the development (or devolution) of the universe, a chaotic, violent, disordered time. For all of recorded history, Hindus have considered themselves to be living in the Kali Age.

Kali Yuga. See KALI AGE.

Kama. The god of erotic love and desire.

Kannada. A language of the Dravidian family, spoken primarily in the southwestern state of Karnataka.

karma (Sanskrit, "action"). The ongoing ramifications and consequences of actions (particularly ethical or ritual actions); specifically, the rewards or punishments that actions can trigger in future times or births.

Krishna. An AVATAR of VISHNU, and the center of a vibrant *BHAKTI* movement. Krishna is depicted as handsome and blue-skinned, and may be shown as a chubby baby, an endearingly mischievous child, a flute-playing youth, or a handsome young man. He appears as ARJUNA's interlocutor in the *BHAGAVAD GITA*.

Kshatriya. A member of the warrior class, the second of the four *VARNAS*.

Lakshmana. The younger brother and closest companion of RAMA. A formidable and fiercely loyal warrior, Lakshmana is sometimes considered Rama's assistant, sometimes his devotee. In some traditions emphasizing Rama's AVATAR status, Lakshmana himself is held to be an avatar of VISHNU's servant, the cobra SHESHA.

Lakshmi. The goddess of wealth, prosperity, and beauty, depicted as a calm figure holding a lotus. Though identified as the consort of VISHNU, she is often worshipped on her own.

lila (Sanskrit, "play"). The playful or whimsical action of gods in the world, creating the illusion (*MAYA*) in which we all play our parts.

linga (from Sanskrit *lingam*, "characteristic" or "sign"). A physical representation of the creative power of SHIVA. *Lingas* range in shape from abstract stones and domes to sometimes overtly phallic columns or pillars.

lotus. An aquatic plant featuring flowers with large white or pink petals, which rise on long stems directly up from mud beds. The lotus is a common symbol of purity and divinity across Asia.

***Mahabharata*.** A massive SANSKRIT epic poem. Though it ostensibly chronicles a great war between the PANDAVAS and Kauravas, it incorporates much material peripheral to the central plot, including myths and philosophical discourses on the nature of action. Its most famous section, the *BHAGAVAD GITA*, is often read as an independent text.

Mahadeo. A vernacular rendering of the SANSKRIT MAHADEVA.

Mahadeva (Sanskrit, "great god"). An epithet for SHIVA.

Maharaja (Sanskrit, "great king"). An epithet for a king.

Malayalam. A language in the Dravidian language family, primarily spoken in the state of Kerala on the southwestern coast of India.

Mandara. A mythological mountain, described in the *MAHABHARATA* and the PURANAS, uprooted and used by the gods to churn an ocean of milk.

mantra (Sanskrit, "instrument of thought"). A sacred sound or phrase, understood to have the power to affect the world or deities. *Mantras* may include real words or may lack conventional syntax or meaning. Many Hindu *mantras* are verses from the VEDAS.

Marathi. The language dominant in the southwestern Indian state of Maharashtra.

maya (Sanskrit, "illusion"). Illusion—sometimes the specific magic that a god casts over a particular human but often the more pervasive illusion of the reality of the material world.

Meru. A mythical mountain at the center of the universe. Also often called Sumeru ("Good Meru").

moksha (Sanskrit, "release"). Escape, release, or liberation from the WHEEL OF REBIRTH. This is the ultimate soteriological goal of some Hindu movements.

Naga. A serpent deity, imagined sometimes in a fully cobralike body and sometimes in a form mixing features of human and cobra.

Narayana. A name of VISHNU, occasionally extended to KRISHNA, his AVATAR.

Om. The mystical syllable used as an invocation at the beginning of most *MANTRAS* and sacred texts.

Pandavas (Sanskrit, "[sons] of Pandu"). The five brothers who are the protagonists of the *MAHABHARATA*. The Pandavas fight the *Mahabharata* war against their cousins, the Kauravas, and are all married to DRAUPADI.

pandit (from the Sanskrit *pandita*, "learned" or "skilled") A learned man, a teacher: in particular, a BRAHMIN who is an expert in SANSKRIT language and literature.

Pariah (from the Tamil *Paraiyar*, the name of the caste of drummers in South India). An outcast, a low-caste person, a DALIT.

Parvati (Sanskrit, "daughter of the mountain"). The consort of SHIVA and mother of GANESHA. Parvati is also known as UMA.

Prajapati (Sanskrit, "lord of the creatures"). A single creator god in the VEDAS and later; in the plural, a collection of minor deities presiding over classes of creatures.

Prakrit. A set of spoken languages related to SANSKRIT; later, this vernacular was incorporated into written literature as well as spoken. Many early Buddhist inscriptions and texts were written in Prakrit.

puja (Sanskrit, from the Dravidian *pu*, "flower"). The ritual veneration of a deity or special being. *Pujas*, which may be grand or modest in scale, can be performed at home, in temples, or anywhere a special power is recognized.

Purana. A key genre of texts, devoted primarily to mythological narratives (though often also including ritual, historical, ethical, and genealogical discussions). The prominent Puranas are in SANSKRIT, but Puranic materials circulate in all Indic vernaculars, whether as translations of Sanskrit versions or as original narratives.

Radha. The consort of KRISHNA, and his paradigmatic *BHAKTA*. Unlike other goddesses who are paired to major gods, Radha is not described as Krishna's spouse; rather, they are lovers whose relationship is passionate and potentially transgressive.

Rahu. An ASURA, whose immortal dismembered head chases the moon and periodically swallows either it or the sun, causing eclipses.

raja (Sanskrit and Hindi). King.

Rakshasa (from Sanskrit *rakshas*, "injury"). An earthly ogre—a fierce warrior or magician who creates chaos in the world. The Rakshasas are the villains of many narratives, including the *RAMAYANA*, where the Rakshasa king RAVANA captures SITA.

Rama. One of the most important AVATARS of VISHNU and the hero of the *RAMAYANA*. Rama is famed for his skill as an archer, and his marriage to SITA is often held up as the model of a stable marriage for Hindu HOUSEHOLDERS.

Ramayana. An epic tradition relating the adventures of RAMA and his wife SITA. The oldest *Ramayana* is the SANSKRIT poem attributed to Valmiki, but there are hundreds of *Ramayanas* in Sanskrit and vernacular languages, as well as vibrant oral and performative traditions.

rasa (Sanskrit, "nectar," "juice"). In Indian aesthetic theory, the "flavor" of a poem, play, etc. that the audience appreciates and savors. In canonical theories of drama and dance, there are eight *rasas*: romantic love, humor, wrath, compassion, disgust, fright, wonder, and heroism.

Ravana. The king of the RAKSHASAS and the villain of the *RAMAYANA*. Ravana kidnaps RAMA's wife SITA and holds her hostage on the island of Sri Lanka.

renunciation. The act of giving up all property and social ties in order to live as an ascetic or mendicant. As a heroic religious act, it is widely admired in India and often regarded as a precondition for achieving *MOKSHA*.

Rig Veda (Sanskrit, "Knowledge of Verses"). A collection of SANSKRIT hymns. One of the world's oldest texts still in use, and the oldest of the four VEDAS, the *Rig Veda* was likely composed in the second millennium B.C.E.

Rudra. A god in the VEDAS associated with storms and hunting. Rudra is one of several deities who combined to become the god SHIVA, who himself is often called Rudra.

Sahaja / Sahajiya (Sanskrit, "Spontaneous" or "Naturalist"). A *BHAKTI* movement of Bengal and northeastern India, inspired by TANTRA and devoted to the ascetic and ecstatic worship of KRISHNA.

samsara (Sanskrit, "wandering through"). The cycle of death and rebirth, which can be escaped through *MOKSHA*. See WHEEL OF REBIRTH.

Sankhya (Sanskrit, "based on calculation"). A system of philosophy that explains the universe in terms of the complex interplay between masculine "spirit" (*purusha*) and feminine "matter" (*prakriti*).

Sanskrit. An Indo-European language, for many centuries confined to literature and ritual and largely controlled by BRAHMIN men. Sanskrit is the high-prestige language of Hinduism: the language in which the most authoritative texts are written and the most orthodox rituals are conducted.

Sanskritization. The process by which a marginal, peripheral, or low-status group adopts the values and practices of high-status Hinduism as practiced and described by BRAHMINS and SANSKRIT texts.

Sant (Hindi, from Sanskrit *sat*, "pious"). A term from the fifteenth century onward for North Indian devotees occupied with praising god; in particular, it is applied to the *BHAKTI* poets who wrote in HINDI and MARATHI.

Sarasvati / Saraswati. The goddess of learning. Often identified as the consort of BRAHMA, Sarasvati is frequently worshipped on her own.

***sati* / suttee** (Sanskrit, "true" [fem. adj.]). A woman who commits suicide by burning herself on her husband's funeral pyre, or the practice of such suicide. Suttee became a particularly contentious issue during the British colonial period.

Shaiva. Of or devoted to SHIVA.

shakti (Sanskrit). A dynamic creative energy in the world. Grammatically feminine, *shakti* is often personified as a goddess who embodies the power of her male consort; it can also name the abstract principle or force embodied by all the various goddesses.

shastra (Sanskrit, "instruction"). A text, teaching, or tradition of learning characterized by systematic inquiry; a science.

Shesha. The king of the NAGAS, Shesha is typically represented as a cobra with five, seven, or thousands of heads. Shesha is the supporter of VISHNU (who is frequently depicted lying on a bed made of Shesha's body, or with Shesha's heads framing his own).

Shiva. One of the most powerful and widely revered gods of Hinduism. Shiva is a wild deity, known for his destructive capabilities, ascetic practices, and sexual powers, but he is also the patron of BRAHMINS.

shraddha (Sanskrit, "faithful"). A ritual performed in commemoration of the death anniversaries of male ancestors or relatives.

shruti (Sanskrit, "what is heard"). Sacred knowledge that is transmitted orally, particularly the VEDAS. *Shruti* is generally understood to be "heard" as spoken by the gods, and therefore fundamentally, unquestionably true.

Shudras. The lowest of the four *VARNAS*, designated as servants, and the only one of the four *varna* categories whose men are not TWICE-BORN. Shudras are not the same as DALITS or UNTOUCHABLES, however, as some can be ritually pure or neutral (rather than actively impure).

Siddha (Sanskrit, "accomplished," "fulfilled"). An adept who has achieved a high level of religious practice, particularly in tantric traditions.

Sita. Wife of RAMA and heroine of the *RAMAYANA*. Sita is worshipped as a goddess in her own right.

smriti (Sanskrit, "that which is remembered"). The category of Hindu texts that are acknowledged to be human-authored. They are thus less authoritative than the VEDAS (which are eternal *SHRUTI*).

Soma. A substance described in the VEDAS as a plant (unidentified) and its extracted juice, often anthropomorphized as a deity. It was said to have ritual uses and psychotropic effects, capable of making human beings immortal.

Surya. The sun, anthropomorphized as a deity.

Tamil. The most widely spoken language of the Dravidian language family, and the only Indic language to rival SANSKRIT in age, prestige, and richness of literature. Tamil is the official language of India's southernmost state, Tamil Nadu, and is one of the national languages of Sri Lanka.

tantra (Sanskrit, "loom"). Esoteric learning or practice, often but not necessarily transgressive or ANTINOMIAN. In order to acquire tantric knowledge or engage in tantric practices, a person must be initiated and trained.

tapas (Sanskrit, "heat" or "ardor"). Inner heat generated by asceticism or otherwise physically demanding religious practice.

Telugu. A language in the Dravidian family. Telugu is the third most commonly spoken language in India (after HINDI and BANGLA); like SANSKRIT and TAMIL, it is also a classical literary language. Spoken throughout southern India, Telugu is the official language of the state of Andhra Pradesh.

Thakur (Hindi). Lord (sometimes "landlord"), a title of respect.

tirtha (Sanskrit, "crossing"). A shrine: especially, a sacred ford believed close to divine realms or realities, often located at the junction of two rivers. Such *tirthas* became major points of pilgrimage (one in Benares/Varanasi, on the banks of the GANGES, is considered by Hindus an unusually auspicious location in which to die).

tribal. Of or relating to the many ethnic groups of India that live in forests and hills, on the fringes of villages. Tribal people who are Hindu do not practice Brahminical Hinduism, observe purity regulations, or participate fully in the CASTE system, though they often worship pan-Indic as well as local gods.

Tulsi. A type of basil plant sacred to VISHNU, often anthropomorphized and worshipped as Vishnu's consort.

twice-born. A term for high-caste Hindu males (BRAHMINS, KSHATRIYAS, and VAISHYAS), who undergo an initiation ceremony (a second birth) when they come of age. They thereby gain access to rituals and responsibilities denied to women and lower-status men.

Uma. Another name for SHIVA's consort, PARVATI.

Untouchables. The former name of people now called DALITS, born into a very low-status CASTE or *JATI* grouping, which confers a permanent state of ritual impurity. To preserve their own higher status, other Hindus will often avoid not only social interactions but even mundane physical contact with such individuals.

Upanishads (Sanskrit, "Connections"). A corpus of philosophical texts. While ostensibly explaining and commenting on the VEDAS, they often advance novel ideas and positions and may be tied only loosely to the older texts. Of the more than two hundred Upanishads, about a dozen are considered ancient and foundational.

Urdu. The dominant language of northwestern India and Pakistan. Spoken Urdu is mutually intelligible with HINDI, but Urdu is more heavily influenced by Persian and is written in Arabic rather than Sanskritic script.

Vaishnava. Relating or devoted to VISHNU.

Vaishya. The class of merchants, the third category of the *VARNA* system.

varna (Sanskrit, "character, quality"). A four-tier social system described by classical SANSKRIT texts: BRAHMINS at the top, then KSHATRIYAS, VAISHYAS, and SHUDRAS. Though also hereditary, this system is not identical to CASTE or *JATI*, since it has only four categories and no excluded group equivalent to DALITS.

Vedanta (Sanskrit, "end/seal of the Vedas"). A system of philosophy, based on the teachings of the UPANISHADS, emphasizing the profound interconnectedness of the universe. Dvaita (dual) Vedanta articulates a view of gods and humans differentiated

but connected through devotion; Advaita (nondual) Vedanta argues for the ultimate oneness of gods and humans, indeed of all things, connected in *BRAHMAN*.

Vedas (sing., Veda). A body of texts, composed in SANSKRIT, considered to be *SHRUTI*, or eternal, revealed truth. The Vedas are made up of four collections: the *RIG VEDA*, the *Yajur Veda*, the *Sama Veda*, and the *Atharva Veda*.

vermillion. A bright red powder used as a cosmetic (especially on a woman's forehead or in the part of her hair) and for *PUJA* (smeared or sprinkled on a divine image).

Vishnu. One of the most powerful and widely revered gods of Hinduism. Vishnu is best known for taking on ten AVATARS to intervene in the world, most famously as KRISHNA and as RAMA.

wheel of rebirth. The cycle in which living beings are repeatedly reincarnated after death. The quality of subsequent births is determined by the actions of this or previous lifetimes. The wheel of rebirth ensures that all actions have consequences and all experiences (good and bad) have antecedents (see KARMA).

Yama. The god of the dead. Yama, who presides over the Hindu underworld or hell, is also sometimes identified as a god of justice. He appears first in the *RIG VEDA* and continues to be a key figure in the UPANISHADS and the PURANAS.

Yashoda. The human mother of Krishna; generally depicted as unaware of her son's divinity.

yoga (Sanskrit, "yoking" or "union"). The practice of self-cultivation, potentially involving the control or manipulation of the body, breath, and consciousness. In the *Yoga Sutras*, yoga is described in both physical and philosophical terms; in the *BHAGAVAD GITA*, it is almost synonymous with "discipline."

yogi (from Sanskrit, "yogin," m. / "yogini," f.). An expert practitioner of yoga.

Yudhishthira. The eldest of the PANDAVA brothers, son of the god DHARMA personified.

Selected Bibliography

Reference Works and General Introductions

The reader seeking further information on a specific text is urged to go to the source of the translation of each text (provided in the Permissions Acknowledgments at the end of the volume). In addition, useful discussions as well as further bibliography may be found in the relevant chapters in general sources such as Wendy Doniger, *The Hindus: An Alternative History*, 2009; Gavin Flood, *An Introduction to Hinduism*, 1996; Gavin Flood, ed., *The Blackwell Companion to Hinduism*, 2003; Alex Michaels, *Hinduism: Past and Present*, 2004; and Sushil Mittal and Gene Thursby, eds., *The Hindu World*, 2004. A fine anthology complementary to this one is *Sources of Indian Tradition*, first compiled by William Theodore de Bary et al., 1958–64 (2 vols.), and updated by Ainslee T. Embree and Stephen Hay, 1988 (2 vols.); a third edition is in preparation by Rachel McDermott. Information on individual topics may always be found in Maureen L. P. Patterson's mammoth *South Asian Civilizations: A Bibliographic Synthesis*, 1981.

A basic structure is provided by J. N. Farquhar, *An Outline of the Religious Literature of India*, 1920; more detailed summaries of the principal literary components of Hinduism can be found in Moriz Winternitz's three-volume *A History of Indian Literature*, trans. Silavati Ketkar and Helen Kohn, 1959–67, and in the ten-volume series edited by Jan Gonda, *A History of Indian Literature*, 1973–88. Still the best introduction to all aspects of India, including Hinduism, is Arthur L. Basham, *The Wonder That Was India: A Survey of the History and Culture of the Sub-Continent before the Coming of the Muslims*, 3rd rev. ed., 1967.

The textual approach inevitable in an anthology should ideally be supplemented by studies of the anthropology, archaeology, and art of Hinduism. The more anthropological, lived aspects of Hinduism are well presented in Vasudha Narayanan, *Understanding Hinduism: Origins, Beliefs, Practices, Holy Texts, Sacred Places*, 2004, and John Stratton Hawley and Vasudha Narayanan, eds., *The Life of Hinduism*, 2006. The historical and archaeological context are discussed in Ariel Glucklich, *The Strides of Vishnu: Hindu Culture in Historical Perspective*, 2008. Among the best studies of Indian art are T. A. Gopinatha Rao's old and massive *Elements of Hindu Iconography*, 1914–16 (2 vols.; 2nd ed., 1968); Stella Kramrisch, *The Hindu Temple*, 1946 (2 vols.); Jitendra Nath Banerjea, *The Development of Hindu Iconography*, 2nd ed., 1956; George Michell, *The Hindu Temple: An Introduction to Its Meaning and Forms*, 1977; George Michell, *Hindu Art and Architecture*, 2000; Richard Davis, *Lives of Indian Images*, 1997; and Partha Mitter, *Indian Art*, 2001.

Sanskrit Texts

A magisterial survey, as well as a penetrating analysis, of the role of Sanskrit in India, including (but only indirectly) its place in Hinduism, is Sheldon Pollock's *The Language of the Gods in the World of Men: Sanskrit, Culture, and Power in Premodern India*, 2006.

The *Rig Veda*

There are good, complete translations of the *Rig Veda* into French, German, and Russian, and now at last there is a translation into English by Stephanie W. Jamison and Joel P. Brereton, 2014 (3 vols.). There are also several useful partial translations, including those in Franklin Edgerton, *The Beginnings of Indian Philosophy: Selections from the Rig Veda, Atharva Veda, Upanisads, and Mahabharata,*

1965, and Wendy Doniger O'Flaherty, *The Rig Veda: An Anthology: One Hundred and Eight Hymns*, 1981. And there are many excellent studies of particular aspects of the *Rig Veda*: Louis Renou, ed., *The Destiny of the Veda in India*, 1965; Charles Malamoud, *Cuire le monde: Rite et pensée dans l'Inde ancienne*, 1989, translated by David Gordon White as *Cooking the World: Ritual and Thought in Ancient India*, 1996; Stephanie W. Jamison, *Sacrificed Wife/Sacrificer's Wife: Women, Ritual, and Hospitality in Ancient India*, 1996; and Michael Witzel, ed., *Inside the Texts, Beyond the Texts: New Approaches to the Study of the Vedas*, 1997.

The Brahmanas

Several Brahmanas have been well translated into English, including the *Aitareya* and *Kaushitaki*, by Arthur Berriedale Keith, in *Rigveda Brahmanas: The Aitreya and Kausītaki Brahmanas of the Rigveda*, 1920, and the *Shatapatha*, by Julius Eggeling, in *The Satapatha-Brahmana: According to the Text of the Madhyandina School*, 1882–1900 (5 vols.). Jan C. Heesterman offers brilliant insights into the Brahmanas in *The Inner Conflict of Tradition: Essays in Indian Ritual, Kingship, and Society*, 1985, and *The Broken World of Sacrifice: An Essay in Ancient Indian Ritual*, 1994. Very different, but equally stimulating, ideas about the Brahmanas appear in Brian K. Smith's *Reflections on Resemblance, Ritual, and Religion*, 1989.

The Upanishads and Patanjali

The Upanishads have been translated into English more often than any other Hindu text but the *Bhagavad Gita*. Robert Hume's translation—*Thirteen Principal Upanishads*, 2nd ed., rev., 1931—is elegant and readable and quite accurate; Patrick Olivelle's rendition—*Early Upanishads: Annotated Text and Translation*, 1998—is more precise and has more extensive notes. The translation by the Irish poet William Butler Yeats, with Shree Purohit Swami, *The Ten Principal Upanishads*, 1937, is charming, and not as inaccurate as one might have feared. (Books about particular philosophical aspects of the Upanishads and Patanjali are discussed below under the heading "Vedanta and Other Indian Philosophies.")

The *Mahabharata* of Vyasa

Complete English translations of the *Mahabharata* were published by Kisari Mohan Ganguli and Pratapachandra Raya, 1884–96 (18 vols.), most recently reprinted in 2000 (4 vols.), and by Manmatha Nath Dutt, 1895–1905 (18 vols.), most recently reprinted in 2003 (7 vols.). For more accurate, but only incomplete or partial, translations, see Johannes Adrianus Bernardus van Buitenen, 1973–78 (3 vols.); James L. Fitzgerald, 2004; John D. Smith, 2009; and the authors of fifteen volumes in the now discontinued Clay Sanskrit Library: Paul Wilmot (book 2, 2006), William J. Johnson (3, 2005), Kathleen Garbutt (4–5, 2007–08), Alex Cherniak (6, 2009), Vaughan Pilikian (7, 2006–09 [partial]), Adam Bowles (8, 2007–08), Justin Meiland (9, 2005–07), Kate Crosby (10–11, 2007), and Alex Wynne (12, 2009 [partial]). Various aspects of the text are discussed by V. S. Sukthankar, *On the Meaning of the Mahabharata*, 1957; Iravati Karve, *Yuganta: The End of an Epoch*, 1969; Alf Hiltebeitel, *The Ritual of Battle: Krishna in the Mahabharata*, 1976; Alf Hiltebeitel, *Rethinking India's Oral and Classical Epics: Draupadī among Rajputs, Muslims, and Dalits*, 1999; Alf Hiltebeitel, *Rethinking the Mahabharata: A Reader's Guide to the Education of the Dharma King*, 2001; Arvind Sharma, ed., *Essays on the Mahabharata*, 1991; John Brockington, *The Sanskrit Epics*, 1998; and Luis González-Riemann, *The Mahabharata and the Yugas: India's Great Epic Poem and the Hindu System of World Ages*, 2002.

The *Bhagavad Gita*

Almost every major Hindu thinker expressed his ideas in the form of a commentary on the *Gita*, and it sometimes seems as if every major (or minor) Anglophone scholar of Hinduism, beginning with Charles Wilkins in 1785, has tried to earn a badge of honor by translating the *Gita* into English, writing about it, or both. Among all of these *Gita* translations, the most readable are Franklin Edgerton, *The Bhagavad Gita*, 1944 (2 vols.); Barbara Stoler Miller, *The Bhagavad-Gita: Krishna's Counsel in Time of War*, 1986; and Laurie Patton, *The Bhagavad Gita*, 2008; Robert Charles Zaehner's *The Bhagavad-Gita*, 1969, has the most interesting notes.

The *Ramayana* of Valmiki

Hari Prasad Shastri's complete English translation, *The Ramayana*, 3rd ed., 1957–62 (3 vols.), is readable, but the still incomplete

translation edited by Robert P. Goldman, *The Ramayana of Valmiki: An Epic of Ancient India*, 1984– (6 vols. to date), is far more accurate and has a superb critical apparatus, including a fine bibliography. Three volumes edited by Paula Richman—*Many Ramayanas: The Diversity of a Narrative Traditions in South Asia*, 1991; *Questioning Ramayanas: A South Asian Tradition*, 2001; and *Ramayana Stories in Modern South India: An Anthology*, 2008—and one by Mandakranta Bose, ed., *The Ramayana Revisited*, 2004, contain a wide range of essays tracing the history of the many Ramayanas.

The Shastras

Pandurang Vaman Kane's five-volume *History of Dharmasastra (Ancient and Mediæval Religious and Civil Law in India)*, rev. and enl. ed., 1968–77, is still the place to go for information about the Shastras. For the ancient Hindu social system, the best studies are Patrick Olivelle, *The Asrama System: The History and Hermeneutics of a Religious Institution*, 1993, and Brian K. Smith, *Classifying the Universe: The Ancient Indian Varna System and the Origins of Caste*, 1994.

The Puranas

R. C. Hazra, *Studies in the Puranic Records on Hindu Rites and Customs*, 2nd ed., 1975, remains the classic study, now well supplemented and updated by Ludo Rocher, *The Puranas*, 1986. Studies of particular aspects of the Puranas include Hans T. Bakker, ed., *Origin and Growth of the Puranic Text Corpus: With Special Reference to the Skandapurana*, 2004; Sures Chandra Banerji, *Studies in the Mahapuranas*, 1991; Wendy Doniger, ed., *Purana Perennis: Reciprocity and Transformation in Hindu and Jaina Texts*, 1993; and Vijay Nath, *Puranas and Acculturation: A Historico-Anthropological Perspective*, 2001.

The Tantras

A basic source for Tantra is Sanjukta Gupta, Dirk Jan Hoens, and Teun Goudriaan, *Hindu Tantrism*, 1979. Sir John Woodroffe published a number of Tantric texts, many with his own translations and interpretations: a few—such as *Shakti and Shakta: Essays and Addresses on the Shakta Tantrashastra*, 3rd ed., 1929—appeared under his own name, but most were published under a pseudonym, Arthur Avalon. Aghehananda Bharati (Leopold Fischer), *The Tantric Tradition*, 1965, is a fascinating scholarly study infused with questionable autobiographical insights. Scattered among the many wrongheaded or simply inaccurate books about Tantra are a number of studies based on a genuine knowledge of the texts and practices, including Stephan Beyer, *The Cult of Tara: Magic and Ritual in Tibet*, 1973; David Gordon White, *The Alchemical Body: Siddha Traditions in Medieval India*, 1996; David Gordon White, *Kiss of the Yogini: "Tantric Sex" in Its South Asian Contexts*, 2003; Douglas Renfrew Brooks, *The Secret of the Three Cities: An Introduction to Hindu Sakta Tantrism*, 1990; Douglas Renfrew Brooks, *Auspicious Wisdom: The Texts and Traditions of Srividya Sakta Tantrism in South India*, 1992; Hugh B. Urban, *Tantra: Sex, Secrecy, Politics, and Power in the Study of Religion*, 2003; and Hugh B. Urban, *The Economics of Ecstasy: Tantra, Secrecy, and Power in Colonial Bengal*, 2001.

Vedanta and Other Indian Philosophies

For all Indian philosophical texts, including the Upanishads, the standard works are Surendranath Dasgupta's five-volume *A History of Indian Philosophy*, 1922–55, and Karl H. Potter's series in progress, *Encyclopedia of Indian Philosophies*, 1970– (13 vols. to date, and 15 more projected). *A Source Book in Indian Philosophy*, ed. Sarvepalli Radhakrishnan and Charles A. Moore, 1957, is dated but still reliable. For the philosophy of *maya* and dreams, see Wendy Doniger O'Flaherty, *Dreams, Illusion, and Other Realities*, 1984. For the materialistic counterarguments to Indian idealism, see Debiprasad Chattopadhyaya, *Lokayata: A Study in Ancient Indian Materialism*, 1959, and Debiprasad Chattopadhyaya, ed., *Carvaka/Lokayata: An Anthology of Source Materials and Some Recent Studies*, 1990.

The Vernaculars

The essays in *The Literatures of India: An Introduction*, by Edward Cameron Dimock et al., 1974, provide a fine survey of the literatures of Bangla, Urdu, Hindi, Tamil, and Sanskrit. The essays in Sheldon Pollock, ed., *Literary Cultures in History: Reconstructions from South Asia*, 2003, provide cutting-edge studies of the Hindi, Indian-English, Persian, Tibetan, Urdu, and Sanskrit traditions. Other vernacular literatures are illuminated by Stuart H. Blackburn et al., eds., *Oral Epics in India*, 1989, and Ron Inden, Jon Walters, and Daud Ali, *Querying the*

Medieval: Texts and the History of Practices in South Asia, 2000.

Tamil

Attipat Krishnaswami Ramanujan sparked the Tamil renaissance in European scholarship with his many amazing translations and studies, beginning with *The Interior Landscape: Poems from a Classical Tamil Anthology*, 1967. His essays, published posthumously in *The Collected Essays of A. K. Ramanujan* (ed. Vinay Dharwadkar), 1999, touch on the most central aspects of Tamil literature, Hinduism, and Indian culture in general. Another great trailblazer for Tamil was the Czech scholar Kamil Vaclav Zvelebil, in *The Smile of Murugan: On Tami Literature of South India*, 1973, and *Tamil Literature*, 1974. The third in this illustrious trio is David Shulman, whose many books—starting with *Tamil Temple Myths: Sacrifice and Divine Marriage in the South Indian Śaiva Tradition*, 1980, and *The King and the Clown in South Asian Myth and Poetry*, 1985, and continuing through (most recently as of this writing) *Spring, Heat, Rains: A South Indian Diary*, 2009—revolutionized the field.

Tamil attracted some of the most innovative Indologists of the second half of the twentieth century: Friedhelm Hardy, *Viraha-Bhakti: The Early History of Krsna Devotion in South India*, 1983; E. Valentine Daniel, *Fluid Signs: Being a Person the Tamil Way*, 1984; Norman Cutler, *Songs of Experience: The Poetics of Tamil Devotion*, 1987; and Margaret Trawick, *Notes on Love in a Tamil Family*, 1990.

Telugu

Velcheru Narayana Rao almost single-handedly (with the help of David Shulman) carved out the field of Telugu studies in American and European Indology. Their co-edited book, *Classical Telugu Poetry: An Anthology*, 2002, is one of many in an ongoing project.

Hindi and Marathi

For North Indian Sants, basic books are Daniel Gold, *The Lord as Guru: Hindi Sants in North Indian Tradition*, 1987, and John Stratton Hawley and Mark Juergensmeyer, *Songs of the Saints of India*, rev. ed., 2004. For Kabir, translations and interpretations are provided by Linda Hess and Shukdev Singh, in *The Bijak of Kabir*, 1983, and *A Touch of Grace: Songs of Kabir*, 1994; by Charlotte Vaudeville, in *Kabir*, 1974, and *A Weaver Named Kabir: Selected Verses with a Detailed Biographical and Historical Introduction*, 1993; and by Vinay Dharwadkar, in *The Weaver's Songs*, 2003. For Krishna-*bhakti* in Hindi, the starting point is John Stratton Hawley, *Krishna, the Butter Thief*, 1983; useful insights also appear in David Kinsley, *The Sword and the Flute: Kali and Krsna, Dark Visions of the Terrible and the Sublime in Hindu Mythology*, 1975. For Hinduism in both Hindi-speaking and Marathi-speaking North India, valuable essays by Charlotte Vaudeville are collected (and edited by Vasudha Dalmia) in *Myths, Saints, and Legends in Medieval India*, 1996. For essential reading on Maharashtra, see the works of Gunther-Dietz Sontheimer, such as *Pastoral Deities in Western India*, trans. Anne Feldhaus, 1989, and *King of Warriors, Hunters, and Shepherds: Essays on Khandoba* (ed. Anne Feldhaus, Aditya Malik, and Heidrun Brückner), 1997, and of Anne Feldhaus, including her translation of *The Deeds of God in Rddhipur*, 1984, and *Connected Places: Region, Pilgrimage, and Geographical Imagination in India*, 2003.

Bangla

The fundamental work on Bengal Hinduism is Sushil Kumar De, *The Early History of the Vaisnava Faith and Movement in Bengal: From Sanskrit and Bengali Sources*, 2nd ed., 1961. The field of Bengal studies in America was largely founded by Edward Cameron Dimock, in books such as *The Place of the Hidden Moon: Erotic Mysticism in the Vaisnavasahajiya Cult of Bengal*, 1966. Dimock's pupil David L. Haberman carried the field forward in *Acting as a Way of Salvation: A Study of Raganuga Bhakti Sadhana*, 1988, and *Journey through the Twelve Forests: An Encounter with Krishna*, 1994. Other aspects of the religion of Bengal are well treated by Malcolm McLean, *Devoted to the Goddess: The Life and Work of Ramprasad*, 1998, and by Rachel Fell McDermott, *Singing to the Goddess: Poems to Kali and Uma from Bengal*, 2001.

Hinduism under the British

This has naturally been a growth industry for Anglophone scholars, leading to a number of excellent books on the subject. Three of the best are two by Peter van der Veer—

Gods on Earth: The Management of Religious Experience and Identity in a North Indian Pilgrimage Centre, 1988, and *Imperial Encounters: Religion and Modernity in India and Britain*, 2001—and Brian A. Hatcher's *Bourgeois Hinduism, or Faith of the Modern Vedantists: Rare Discourses from Early Colonial Bengal*, 2007. For the particular topic on which the selections in this volume focus, suttee/*sati*, there are useful discussions in Arvind Sharma, with Ajit Ray, Alaka Hejib, and Katherine K. Young, *Sati: Historical and Phenomenological Essays*, 1988; John Stratton Hawley, ed., *Sati, the Blessing and the Curse: The Burning of Wives in India*, 1994; and Lata Mani, *Contentious Traditions: The Debate on Sati in Colonial India*, 1998.

Folk, Village, and Tribal Hinduism

The old British collections are worth reading both for insights into the British attitudes toward, and influence on, Hinduism during the period of the Raj and for information about village Hinduism in that period: the best known are James Tod's much-reprinted *Annals and Antiquities of Rajasthan, or the Central and Western Rajpoot States of India*, 1829–32 (2 vols.); Sir Richard Carnac Temple, *The Legends of the Panjab*, 1883–90 (3 vols.); and William Crooke, *The Popular Religion and Folk-lore of Northern India*, 2nd ed., 1896. More recently, the many fine ethnographies of Hindu village life by anthropologists on the ground provide the context of lived experience, among them Mysore Narasimhachar Srinivas, *Religion and Society among the Coorgs of South India*, 1952; E. Valentine Daniel, *Fluid Signs: Being a Person the Tamil Way*, 1984; Ann Grodzins Gold, *Fruitful Journeys: The Ways of Rajasthani Pilgrims*, 1988; William S. Sax, *Mountain Goddess: Gender and Politics in a Himalayan Pilgrimage*, 1991; Margaret Trawick, *Notes on Love in a Tamil Family*, 1990; Kirin Narayan and Urmila Devi Sood, *Mondays on the Dark Night of the Moon: Himalayan Foothill Folktales*, 1997; and Alf Hiltebeitel, *The Cult of Draupadi*, 1988–91 (2 vols.). In addition, there are wonderful books about village art: Stella Kramrisch, *Unknown India: Ritual Art in Tribe and Village*, 1968; Stephen P. Huyler, *Village India*, 1985; Stephen P. Huyler, *Painted Prayers: Village Art in Village India*, 1994; and David L. Szanton and Malini Bakshil, *Mithila Painting: The Evolution of an Art Form*, 2007.

Verrier Elwin was the most prolific chronicler of tribal religion in India; his many books include *Maria Murder and Suicide*, 2nd ed., 1950, and *The Religion of an Indian Tribe*, 1955. Elwin was succeeded, and bitterly attacked, by the anthropologist, historian, and Sanskritist Govind Sadashiv Ghurye, author of *The Aborigines—"So-Called"—and Their Future*, 1943, republished as *The Scheduled Tribes*, 3rd ed., 1963. A more historical approach to tribal religion was taken by David Hardiman (one of the founders of subaltern studies) in *The Coming of the Devi: Adivasi Assertion in Western India*, 1987.

Dalit Hinduism

The literature of Dalits in the modern period essentially begins with the writings of Bhimrao Ramji Ambedkar: *What Congress and Gandhi Have Done to the Untouchables*, 1945; *Who Were the Shudras? How They Came to Be the Fourth Varna in the Indo-Aryan Society*, 1946; and *The Untouchables: Who Were They? And Why They Became Untouchables*, 1948. Since then, a number of excellent books about Dalits have appeared: Harold R. Isaacs, *India's Ex-Untouchables*, 1964; Marc Galanter, *Competing Equalities: Law and the Backward Classes in India*, 1984; Gail Omvedt, *Dalit Visions: The Anti-caste Movement and the Construction of an Indian Identity*, 1995; Saurabh Dube, *Untouchable Pasts: Religion, Identity, and Power among a Central Indian Community, 1780–1950*, 1998; Robert Deliège, *The Untouchables of India*, trans. Nora Scott, 1999; Vasant Moon, *Growing Up Untouchable in India: A Dalit Autobiography*, trans. Gail Omvedt, intro. Eleanor Zelliot, 2001; and Eleanor Zelliot, *From Untouchable to Dalit: Essays on the Ambedkar Movement*, 1992.

Twentieth-Century Hindu Writers

A good place at which to enter this vast field is Amit Chaudhuri, ed., *The Picador Book of Modern Indian Literature*, 2001, an eclectic collection of writings—fiction as well as essays and autobiography—from the 1850s to the present, by eighteen writers who work mainly in English and (translations of) twenty writers in Hindi, Bangla, Urdu, Tamil, and other Indian languages. Karimpumannil Mathai George, ed., *Modern Indian Literature: An Anthology*, 1992–94 (3 vols.), collects

"surveys and poems," "fiction," and "plays and prose" from the literatures of twenty-two Indian languages, from Sanskrit to Konkani. Nalini Natarajan, ed., *Handbook of Twentieth-Century Literatures of India*, 1996, surveys the major regional literatures of contemporary India. Many but not all of the writers in these collections are Hindus; and although not all of them write about Hinduism, many do.

Mohandas K. Gandhi occupies a unique place in modern Hindu writings, and a good starting point to begin to understand him is his *An Autobiography: or, The Story of My Experiments with Truth*, trans. Mahadev Desai, 2nd ed., 1940; the next step is *The Collected Works of Mahatma Gandhi*, 1958–2001 (100 vols.). The other giant in this period is Rabindranath Tagore, whose life and writings are the subject of Mary M. Lago, *Rabindranath Tagore*, 1976; Krishna Kripalani, *Rabindranath Tagore: A Biography*, 2nd rev. ed., 1980; Krishna Dutta and Andrew Robinson, *Rabindranath Tagore: The Myriad-Minded Man*, 1995; and Krishna Dutta and Andrew Robinson, eds., *Rabindranath Tagore: An Anthology*, 1997.

Permissions Acknowledgments

GENERAL INTRODUCTION

Kay Ryan: "On the Nature of Understanding," from *The New Yorker,* July 25, 2011. Copyright © 2011 by Kay Ryan. Reprinted by permission of the author.

TEXT

The *Rig Veda*: "I Pray to Agni," "Creation Hymn," "Aditi and the Birth of the Gods," "The Hymn of the Primeval Man," "The Funeral Fire," "Burial Hymn," "Varuna Provoked to Anger," "Agastya and Lopamudra," "Have Mercy on Us, Rudra," "The Three Strides of Vishnu": From THE RIG VEDA: AN ANTHOLOGY OF ONE HUNDRED AND EIGHT HYMNS, selected, translated, and annotated by Wendy Doniger O'Flaherty (Penguin Classics, 1981). Copyright © 1981 by Wendy Doniger O'Flaherty. Reprinted by permission of Penguin Group (UK).

The Brahmanas: "Prajapati Creates Fire," "The Fish Saves Manu from the Flood": From HINDU MYTHS, translated and with an introduction by Wendy Doniger O'Flaherty (Penguin Classics, 1975). Copyright © 1975 by Wendy Doniger O'Flaherty. Reprinted by permission of Penguin Group (UK). "Killing the Sacrificial Horse," "Restoring the Horse": From TEXTUAL SOURCES FOR THE STUDY OF HINDUISM, edited by Wendy Doniger O'Flaherty. Copyright © 1988 by Wendy Doniger O'Flaherty. Reprinted by permission of Wendy Doniger O'Flaherty. "How Men Changed Skins with Animals," "Bhrigu's Journey in the Other World," "The Gods Make Men Evil": From TALES OF SEX AND VIOLENCE: FOLKLORE, SACRIFICE, AND DANGER IN THE JAIMINIYA BRAHMANA, translated by Wendy Doniger O'Flaherty. Reprinted by permission of Wendy Doniger O'Flaherty.

The Upanishads: "The Creator Creates Death," "Dreaming," "The Origins of the Self," "Transmigration," "The Two Birds": From TEXTUAL SOURCES FOR THE STUDY OF HINDUISM, edited by Wendy Doniger O'Flaherty. Copyright © 1988 by Wendy Doniger O'Flaherty. Reprinted by permission of Wendy Doniger O'Flaherty. "Creation," "The Self," "Janashruti and Raikva": From UPANISHADS, translated by Patrick Olivelle. Copyright © 1996 by Patrick Olivelle

The *Yoga-sutra* of Patanjali: "Quieting the Mind": From YOGA: DISCIPLINE OF FREEDOM: THE YOGA SUTRA ATTRIBUTED TO PATANJALI, translated by Barbara Stoler Miller. Copyright © 1996 by the Regents of the University of California. Published by the University of California Press. Reprinted by permission of the University of California.

The Mahabharata: "The Stripping of Draupadi": From THE MAHABHARATA, translated by John C. Smith. Copyright © 2009. Reprinted by permission of Penguin Books Ltd. "Ekalavya Cuts Off His Thumb" and "The End of Female Promiscuity": From THE MAHABHARATA, BOOK 1: THE BOOK OF THE BEGINNING, translated by J. A. B. van Buitenen. Copyright © 1973 by University of Chicago Press. Reprinted by permission of University of Chicago Press. "The Pandavas Go to Heaven, with a Dog" and "The Karma of Dharma": From TEXTUAL SOURCES FOR THE STUDY OF HINDUISM, edited by Wendy Doniger O'Flaherty. Copyright © 1988 by Wendy Doniger O'Flaherty. Reprinted by permission of Wendy Doniger O'Flaherty. "The Churning of the Ocean": From HINDU MYTHS, translated and with an introduction by Wendy Doniger O'Flaherty (Penguin Classics, 1975). Copyright © 1975 by Wendy Doniger O'Flaherty. Reprinted by permission of Penguin Group (UK). "The Dog Who Would Be Lion": From THE MAHABHARATA, VOLUME 7: BOOK 11: THE BOOK OF THE WOMEN AND BOOK 12: THE BOOK OF PEACE, PART 1, translated by James L. Fitzgerald. Copyright © 2004 by University of Chicago Press. Reprinted by permission of University of Chicago Press. "King Shibi Saves the Dove from the Hawk": From THE MAHABHARATA, BOOK 3: THE BOOK OF THE FOREST, translated by J. A. B. van Buitenen. Copyright © 1973 by University of Chicago Press. Reprinted by permission of University of Chicago Press. "Daksha's Sacrifice": From THE SAUPTIKAPARVAN OF THE MAHABHARATA: THE MASSACRE AT NIGHT, translated by W. J. Johnson. Copyright © 1998 by W. J. Johnson. Reprinted by permission of Oxford University Press.

The *Bhagavad Gita*: "Arjuna Questions Krishna," "The Soul Does Not Die," "The Two Paths," "The True Nature of Action," "The Path of Devotion": From THE BHAGAVAD GITA, translated by Laurie L. Patton (Penguin Classics, 2008). Translation and editorial material copyright © 2008 by Laurie L. Patton. Reprinted with permission of Penguin Books Ltd. "Salvation and Damnation": From TEXTUAL SOURCES FOR THE STUDY OF HINDUISM, edited by Wendy Doniger O'Flaherty. Copyright © 1988 by Wendy Doniger O'Flaherty. Reprinted by permission of Wendy Doniger O'Flaherty.

The *Ramayana*: "The Birth of Sita and the Bending of the Bow": From TEXTUAL SOURCES FOR THE STUDY OF HINDUISM, edited by Wendy Doniger O'Flaherty. Copyright © 1988 by Wendy Doniger O'Flaherty. Reprinted by permission of Wendy Doniger O'Flaherty. "Dasharatha Kills a Boy He Mistakes for an Elephant": From THE

RAMAYANA OF VALMIKI: AN EPIC OF ANCIENT INDIA. VOLUME II: AYHODHYAKANDA, translated by Sheldon Pollock. Copyright © 1984 by Princeton University Press. Reprinted by permission of Princeton University Press. "The Gods Interrupt Shiva and Parvati": From THE RAMAYANA OF VALMIKI: AN EPIC OF ANCIENT INDIA. VOLUME I: BALAKANDA. Translated by Robert Goldman. Copyright ©1984 by Princeton University Press. Reprinted by permission of Princeton University Press.

The Shastras: "To Eat or Not to Eat Meat," "The Dependence of Women," "Retribution in Rebirth": From THE LAWS OF MANU, translated with an introduction and notes by Wendy Doniger O'Flaherty with Brian K. Smith (Penguin Classics, 1991). Copyright © 1991 by Wendy Doniger O'Flaherty and Brian K. Smith. Reprinted by permission of Penguin Group (UK). "The Etiology of Diseases," "How to Perform a Funeral": From TEXTUAL SOURCES FOR THE STUDY OF HINDUISM, edited by Wendy Doniger O'Flaherty. Copyright © 1988 by Wendy Doniger O'Flaherty. Reprinted by permission of Wendy Doniger O'Flaherty. "How to Read the Stars": From THE PANCASIDDHANTIKA OF VARAHAMIHIRA, translated by Otto Edward Neugebauer and David Pingree. Reprinted by permission of Gerry Neugebauer.

The Puranas: "The Fruits of Hearing a Purana: Devaraja the Sinner," "The Four Ages," "The Transfer of Karma in Hell," "The Origin of *Linga* Worship," "How Rudra Destroys the Universe," "Embryology," "Suffering," "Hell": From TEXTUAL SOURCES FOR THE STUDY OF HINDUISM, edited by Wendy Doniger O'Flaherty. Copyright © 1988 by Wendy Doniger O'Flaherty. Reprinted by permission of Wendy Doniger O'Flaherty. "Mankanaka Dances for Shiva," "Vishnu as the Buddha," "Vishnu as Kalki," "Krishna Kills the Ogress Putana," "Krishna's Mother Looks Inside His Mouth," "The Birth of the Goddess," "The Death of the Buffalo Demon": From HINDU MYTHS, translated with an introduction by Wendy Doniger O'Flaherty O'Flaherty (Penguin Classics, 1975). Copyright © 1975 by Wendy Doniger O'Flaherty O'Flaherty. Reprinted by permission of Penguin Group (UK). "The Descent of the Ganges," "The River Yamuna," "The Virtues of Varanasi," "The Pilgrimage of Shiva to Varanasi," "Yudhishthira at Prayaga": From CLASSICAL HINDU MYTHOLOGY: A READER IN THE SANSKRIT PURANAS, edited by Cornelia Dimmitt and J. A. B. van Buitenen. Used by permission of Temple University Press. Copyright © 1978 by Temple University Press. All rights reserved.

The Tantras: "Tantric Points in the Body," "The Tantric Gander," "Terrifying Tantric Visions": From KISS OF THE YOGINI, edited by David Gordon White. Copyright © 2003 by University of Chicago Press. Reprinted by permission of University of Chicago Press. "The Five Elements of Tantric Ritual," "Tantric Sins of Excess": From TEXTUAL SOURCES FOR THE STUDY OF HINDUISM, edited by Wendy Doniger O'Flaherty. Copyright © 1988 by Wendy Doniger O'Flaherty. Reprinted by permission of Wendy Doniger O'Flaherty.

The Vedanta: "Shankara Dreams," "Ramanuja Dreams," "The Man Who Built a House of Air": From TEXTUAL SOURCES FOR THE STUDY OF HINDUISM, edited by Wendy Doniger O'Flaherty. Copyright © 1988 by Wendy Doniger O'Flaherty. Reprinted by permission of Wendy Doniger O'Flaherty.

Nammalvar: "He Is Both the Crooked and the Straight," "Worker of Miracles," "You Do Stunts," "Look Here," "It's True," "Talking of Monism," "Kings Who Rule the Earth All Alone," "Our Masters": From *Hymns for the Drowning: Poems for Visnu by Nammalvar,* translated by A. K. Ramanujan. Copyright © 1981 by Princeton University Press. Reprinted by permission of Molly Daniels Ramanujan and Krishna Ramanujan. "Who Is He Possessing the Highest Good?," "Beyond the Range," "If You Say He Exists," "He Is Diffused in Every Drop," "People of This world," "Lord of Shiva," "He Became and Exists," The Whirling Age of Kali Ends," "Monarch of Lions," "Perhaps You Will Destroy My Sorrow," "You Do Not Come," "I Shall Die If You Go to Graze the Cows," "You Were Gone the Whole Day": From THE TAMIL VEDA: PILLAN'S INTERPRETATION OF THE TIRUVAYMOLI, translated by John Carman and Vasudha Narayanan. Copyright © 1989 by University of Chicago Press. Reprinted by permission of University of Chicago Press.

Cuntarar: "A Dog Am I," "You Won't Remove the Fierce Karma," "You Slew a Murderous Elephant," "What Is the Use of Release?," "You Kill Time Telling Lies," "When I Hear Death Has Come," "Can't You See How False They Are," "I Placed Before Him," "I Don't Call to Him as My Mother": From SONGS OF THE HARSH DEVOTEE, translated by David Dean Shulman. Copyright © 1990 Department of South Asian Regional Studies, University of Pennsylvania. Reprinted with permission of the Department of South Asian Regional Studies, University of Pennsylvania and David Dean Shulman.

Cekkilar: "Maran Feeds a Guest" and "Kannappar Gives His Eye to Shiva": From THE HISTORY OF THE HOLY SERVANTS OF THE LORD SIVA: A TRANSLATION OF THE PERIYA PURANAM OF CEKKILAR, translated by Alastair McGlashan. Copyright © 2006 by Alastair McGlashan. Reprinted by permission of Alastair McGlashan.

Atikal: "Pattini Is Worshipped": From THE CILAPPATIKARAM OF ILANKO ATIKAL: AN EPIC OF SOUTH INDIA, translated by R. Parthasarathy. Copyright © 1993 by Columbia University Press. Reprinted by permission of the publisher.

Basava: "Shiva, You Have No Mercy," "As a Mother Runs," "The Master of the House," "Does It Matter How Long," "When a Whore with a Child," "I Went to Fornicate," "Don't You Take On," "The Pot Is a God," "The Rich Will Make Temples": From SPEAKING OF SIVA, translated and with an introduction by A. K. Ramanujan (Penguin Classics, 1973). Copyright © 1973 by A. K. Ramanujan. Reprinted by permission of Penguin Group (UK).

Mahadeviyakka: "My Body Is Dirt," "Husband Inside," "Who Cares," "If One Could," "People, Male and Female": From SPEAKING OF SIVA, translated and with an introduction by A. K. Ramanujan (Penguin Classics, 1973). Copyright © 1973 by A. K. Ramanujan. Reprinted by permission of Penguin Group (UK).

Somanatha: "The Story of the Eggplants That Became *Lingas*," "The Herdswoman's Buttermilk Pot," "The Foxes That Became Horses": From SIVA'S WARRIORS: THE BASAVA PURANA OF PALKURIKI SOMANATHA, translated by Velcheru Narayana Rao; assisted by Gene H. Roghair. Reprinted by permission of Princeton University Press.

Annamayya: "Why Cross the Boundary," "Seeing Is One Thing," "I'll Serve You as Best I Can," "Lord, I Give Up," "You Think I'm Someone Special," "It's No Small Thing," "I Was Better Off Then": From GOD ON THE HILL: TEMPLE POEMS FROM TIRUPATI by Tallapaka Annamacharya, translated by Velcheru Narayana Rao and David Shulman. Copyright © 2005 by Oxford University Press. Reprinted by permission of Oxford University Press.

Kshetrayya: "A Courtesan to a Young Customer," "A Courtesan to Her Lover," "A Courtesan to Her Friend," "A Married Woman to Her Lover": From WHEN GOD IS A CUSTOMER: TELUGU COURTESAN SONGS BY KSETRAYYA AND OTHERS, translated by A. K. Ramanujan, Velcheru Narayana Rao, David Shulman. Copyright © 1994 by the Regents of the University of California. Published by the University of California Press. Reproduced by permission of Oxford University Press, India, New Delhi, and the University of California Press.

Asan: "Feet Like Lotus Powder": By Kumaran Asan, translated by George Pati. Reprinted by permission of the translator. "Sita Lost in Thought": From SELECTED POEMS OF KUMARAN ASAN, translated by Kainikkara M. Kumara Pillai.

Diaspora Interlude:"The Sdok Kak Thom Inscription": From STORIES IN STONE: THE SDOK KAK THOM INSCRIPTION & THE ENIGMA OF KHMER HISTORY, translated by Chhany Sak-Humphrey and Philip N. Jenner. Reprinted by permission of the translators. "The Perfect Knowledge": From JNANASIDDHANTA, translated by Haryati Soebadio. "The Romance of Arjuna and Ulupi": From PARTHAYANA: THE JOURNEYING OF PARTHA: AN EIGHTEENTH-CENTURY BALINESE KAKAWIN, translated by Helen Creese. Reprinted by permission of Koninklijk Instituut voor Taal-, Land-en Volkenkunde.

Kabir: "Saints, I've Seen Both Ways," "Brother, Where Did Your Two Gods Come From?," "That Con Man Hari," "Here's How the World Fights against God," "The Pandits' Pedantries Are Lies," "Pandit, Look in Your Heart for Knowledge," "Think, Pandit, Figure It Out," "Hey Pandits, Who Didn't Die?," "Pandit, Think Before You Drink," "She Went with Her Husband," "Beast-meat and Man-meat," "It's a Heavy Confusion," "The Self Forgets Itself," "Qazi, What Book Are You Lecturing On?": From THE BIJAK OF KABIR, translated by Linda Hess and Shukdeo Singh. Copyright © 2002 by Linda Hess. Reprinted by permission of Oxford University Press.

Surdas: "If You Drink the Milk," "Far Off and Furtive," "Look, My Friend," "She's Found Him," "Radha Is Lost," "With Love There's Never a Thought," "Black Storm Clouds," "Gopal Has slipped In," "Thoughts of Him Stalk Me," "Ever Since Your Name Has Entered," "Having Seen Hari's Face," "Madhav, Please, Control That Cow": From SONGS OF THE SAINTS OF INDIA, texts and notes by John Stratton Hawley, translation by J. S. Hawley and Mark Juergensmeyer. Copyright © 1988 by Oxford University Press. Reprinted by permission of Oxford University Press.

Mirabai: "I'm Colored with the Color of Dusk," "Life without Hari," "The Bhil Woman Tasted Them," "Sister, I Had a Dream," "Oh, the Yogi," "Let Us Go to a Realm Beyond Going": From SONGS OF THE SAINTS OF INDIA, texts and notes by John Stratton Hawley, translation by J. S. Hawley and Mark Juergensmeyer. Copyright © 1988 by Oxford University Press. Reprinted by permission of Oxford University Press.

Tulsi Das: "The Fire of My Stomach," "It Is Said in Ancient Writings," "A Blind, Mean-minded," "Say Ram, Say Ram, Say Ram," "The Name of King Ram," "O Shiva, Great Giver," "This Darkest of Ages": From SONGS OF THE SAINTS OF INDIA, texts and notes by John Stratton Hawley, translation by J. S. Hawley and Mark Juergensmeyer. Copyright © 1988 by Oxford University Press. Reprinted by permission of Oxford University Press. "Sati Takes the Form of Sita" (*Ramcharitmanas*): From TEXTUAL SOURCES FOR THE STUDY OF HINDUISM, edited by Wendy Doniger O'Flaherty. Copyright © 1988 by Wendy Doniger O'Flaherty. Reprinted by permission of Wendy Doniger O'Flaherty and Daniel Gold. "The Crow and Anasuya," "The Mutilation of Shurpanakha," "The Abduction of Sita": From TULASIDASA'S SHRIRAMACHARITAMANASA, translated and edited by R. C. Prasad. Copyright © 1990 by Motilal Banarsidass Publishers Private Limited. Reprinted by permission of Motilal Banarsidass Publishers Private Limited.

Tukaram: "I Was Only Dreaming," "Insects in a Fig," "When My Father Died," "I Was Held Captive," "The Thug Has Arrived," "God's Own Dog," "Lord You Could Become," "With a Bizarrely Painted Face," "The Great Mother of the Shakta," "The Ascetic," "Once There Was a Celibate Man," "The Real Reason Why You Created," "We Are Lucky! We Are Lucky!": From SAYS TUKA: SELECTED POETRY OF TUKARAM, translated by Dilip Chitre. Copyright © 1991 by Dilip Chitre. Published by Penguin Books Indian. Reprinted by permission of Viju Chitre. "I Pretend to Laugh" "By Caste and Lineage a Shudra," "I've Not a Single Fraud," "Good You Made Me a Kunbi" "I Feel Shame When People Honor Me," "Born of Shudra Family," "What Will I Gain by Remaining Deferent?," "Oh Listen Now to Me," "He's Not a Brahmin Who Abhors," "He Sells His Daughter, Cows, and Stories," "The Cunning Grab for Coins," "If You Don't Keep the *Ashramas*," "*Brahmachari* Dharma Is Reciting the Vedas," "Call Him Pandit, He's in Bliss," "It Is for This I Wander Wild," "A God Without a Devotee," "Hari, You Are Cruel and Without Qualities," "I Gave Birth to Myself," "We've Treated *Moksha* with Scorn Because," "Silence in Speech, Life in Death," "Brahma Is Illusion, Say the Crooks of Religion," "Accumulating Wealth by a Noble Business," "Avatar of Buddha, O My Invisible One," "I've Built a House in Boundless Space": From THE SONGS OF TUKOBA, translated by Gail Omvedt and Bharat Patankar. Reprinted by permission of Gail Omvedt.

Jayadeva: "The Ten Avatars of Vishnu": From LOVE SONG OF THE DARK LORD: JAYADEVA'S GITAGOVINDA, translated by Barbara Stoler Miller. Copyright © 1977 by Columbia University Press. Reprinted by permission of Columbia University Press and Motilal Banarsidass Publishers Private Limited.

Vidyapati: "The Necklace-Snake," "Counterfeit," "Let No One Be a Girl," "My Body Hid My Body": From LOVE SONGS OF VIDYAPATI, translated by Deben Bhattacharya. "As the Mirror to My Hand" and "Children, Wife, Friend": From IN PRAISE OF KRISHNA by Edward C. Dimock and Denise Levertov. Copyright © 1967 by The Asia Society, Inc. Used by permission of the Asia Society, Inc. and Doubleday, a division of Random House, Inc.

Chandidas: "What God Is That," "He Was Black," "It's No Use Telling Me," "Mastering *Sahaja* Love," "My Body Corrodes": From LOVE SONGS OF CHANDIDAS: THE REBEL POET-PRIEST OF BENGAL, translated by Deben Bhattacharya. "Beloved, What More Shall I Say?": From IN PRAISE OF KRISHNA by Edward C. Dimock and Denise Levertov. Copyright © 1967 by The Asia Society, Inc. Used by permission of the Asia Society, Inc. and Doubleday, a division of Random House, Inc.

Govinda-das: "O Madhava" and "The Marks of Fingernails": From IN PRAISE OF KRISHNA by Edward C. Dimock and Denise Levertov. Copyright © 1967 by The Asia Society, Inc. Used by permission of the Asia Society, Inc. and Doubleday, a division of Random House, Inc.

Balarama-das: "A Wicked Woman": From IN PRAISE OF KRISHNA by Edward C. Dimock and Denise Levertov. Copyright © 1967 by The Asia Society, Inc. Used by permission of the Asia Society, Inc. and Doubleday, a division of Random House, Inc.

Chaitanya: "An Encounter with the Dual Form": From TEXTUAL SOURCES FOR THE STUDY OF HINDUISM, edited by Wendy Doniger O'Flaherty. Copyright © 1988 by Wendy Doniger O'Flaherty. Reprinted by permission of Wendy Doniger O'Flaherty and David Haberman.

Rupa Goswamin: "The General Characteristics of Devotion" and "The Eightfold Activities of Radha and Krishna": From TEXTUAL SOURCES FOR THE STUDY OF HINDUISM, edited by Wendy Doniger O'Flaherty. Copyright © 1988 by Wendy Doniger O'Flaherty. Reprinted by permission of Wendy Doniger O'Flaherty and David Haberman.

Narottama Das: "Poems to Krishna and Radha": From TEXTUAL SOURCES FOR THE STUDY OF HINDUISM, edited by Wendy Doniger O'Flaherty. Copyright © 1988 by Wendy Doniger O'Flaherty. Reprinted by permission of Wendy Doniger O'Flaherty and David Haberman.

Ketaka Das: "The Birth of Manasa": From TEXTUAL SOURCES FOR THE STUDY OF HINDUISM, edited by Wendy Doniger O'Flaherty. Copyright © 1988 by Wendy Doniger O'Flaherty. Reprinted by permission of Wendy Doniger O'Flaherty and David Haberman. "Chando Defies Manasa," "Chando Comes Home," "Manasa Relents": From THE THIEF OF LOVE: BENGALI TALES FROM COURT AND VILLAGE, translated by Edward C. Dimock. Copyright © 1963 by University of Chicago Press. Reprinted by permission of University of Chicago Press.

Ramprasad Sen: "I Spent My Days in Fun," "Tell Me, Brother, What Happens after Death?," "What Did I Do Wrong?," "How Many Times, Mother," "You Think Motherhood Is Child's Play?," "Mind, You Gambled," "I'm Not Calling You Anymore," "Why Should I Go to Kashi?," "Mother, Incomparably Arrayed": From GRACE AND MERCY IN HER WILD HAIR, translated by Leonard Nathan and Clinton Seely. Copyright © 1999 by Leonard Nathan and Clinton Seely. Reprinted by permission of Hohm Press.

Fakir Lalon Shah: "The Bird and the Cage, and the Flower": From TEXTUAL SOURCES FOR THE STUDY OF HINDUISM, edited by Wendy Doniger O'Flaherty. Copyright © 1988 by Wendy Doniger O'Flaherty. Reprinted by permission of Wendy Doniger O'Flaherty and David Haberman.

James Battray and W. H. Macnaghten: "Hindoo Widows &c" and "Questions to the Pundits of the Court of Sudder Dewanny Adawlat": From HINDUISM: A READER, edited by Deepak Sarma. Copyright © 2008 by Blackwell Publishing Ltd. Reproduced with permission of Blackwell Publishing Ltd.

Rammohun Roy: "The Practice of Burning Widows Alive": From HINDUISM: A READER, edited by Deepak Sarma. Copyright © 2008 by Blackwell Publishing Ltd. Reproduced with permission of Blackwell Publishing Ltd.

Michael Madhusudan Datta: "The Funeral Rites of Meghanada": From THE SLAYING OF THE MEGHANADA: A RAMAYANA FROM COLONIAL BENGAL, translated by Clinton B. Seely. Copyright © 2004 by Oxford University Press. Reprinted by permission of Oxford University Press.

Folk Hinduism: "The Goddess of Mahi River," "Lord Shiva and the Satwaras," "The Origin of the Shiva-*linga* at Bhimnath," "The Girl Who Was Loved by a Tree Spirit," "The Birth and Marriage of Shiva," "The Origin of the Temple at Tarakeshvar": From FOLKTALES OF INDIA, translated by Brenda E. F. Beck, Peter Claus, Prapulladatta Goswami, and Jawaharlal Handoo. Copyright © 1987 by University of Chicago Press. Reprinted by permission of University of Chicago Press. "The Brahmin Who Swallowed a God," "If God Is Everywhere," "Nonviolence," "Walking on Water," "How Tenali Rama Became a Jester," "Tenali Rama's *Ramayana*," "The Guru and the Idiot": From FOLKTALES FROM INDIA: A SELECTION OF ORAL TALES FROM TWENTY-TWO LANGUAGES, edited by A. K. Ramanujan. Copyright © A. K. Ramanujan. Reprinted by permission of Molly Daniels Ramanujan and Krishna Ramanujan.

Adivasi (Tribal) Hinduism: "Mahadeo and Parvati Were Living in the Binjpahar Hills," "In the Under World," "An Old Gond and His Wife," "Formerly the Whole Country Belonged to the Gond," "A Chamar's sons," "The Sun and the Moon," "One Night While Sita and Rama Were Lying Together," "When Cows Were First Born," "Before Mahadeo Sent Men to Live," "When This World Was First Made," "Long Ago Men Could Read the Future," "Bhagavan Wanted to Piss," "Why Men and Animals No Longer Talk Together," "There Was No Death," "There Was Once a God Called Amrit": From MYTHS OF MIDDLE INDIA, translated by Verrier Elwin. Reproduced by permission of Oxford University Press India, New Delhi.

Dalit Hinduism: "Dr. Ambedkar's Speech at Mahad" (translated by Rameshchandra Sirkar); "Which Language Should I Speak?" (by Arun Kamble; translated by Priya Adarkar), "You Who Have Made the Mistake" (by Baburao Bagul; translated by Vilas Sarang), "The Story of 'My Sanskrit'" (by Kumud Pawde; translated by Priya Adarkar): From POISONED BREAD: TRANSLATIONS FROM MODERN MARATHI DALIT LITERATURE, edited by Arjun Dangle. Published by Orient Blackswan Pvt Ltd. Copyright © 1992 by Orient Blackswan Pvt Ltd. Reprinted by permission of the publisher. "Angulimal"and "Eklavya" (by Tryambak Sapkale), "For I am Brahma" (by Narayan Surve): From AN ANTHOLOGY OF DALIT LITERATURE, translated by Jayant Karve and Eleanor Zelliot. Copyright © 1992 by Eleanor Zelliot. Reprinted by permission of Eleanor Zelliot. "Every Woman in This Country" (by Kamla Bhasin): From DALIT VISIONS: THE ANTI-CASTE MOVEMENT AND THE CONSTRUCTION OF AN INDIAN IDENTITY, translated by Gail Omvedt. Published by Orient Blackswan Pvt. Ltd. Copyright © 1995 by Orient Blackswan Pvt. Ltd, India. Reprinted by permission of the publisher.

Mohandas K. Gandhi: "The Gospel of Selfless Action": From THE GOSPEL OF SELFLESS ACTION, OR THE GITA ACCORDING TO GANDHI, translated by Mahadev Desai. Reprinted by permission of the Navajivan Trust.

Prem Chand: "The Shroud": From THE WORLD OF PREMCHAND: SELECTED SHORT STORIES, translated by David Rubin. Copyright © 2001 by Oxford University Press. Reproduced by permission of Oxford University Press India, New Delhi.

Nirala: "A Look at Death," "Giving," "Blood Holi," "Shurpanakha": From *A Season on the Earth: Selected Poems of Nirala*, translated by David Rubin. Copyright © 1977 by Columbia University Press. Reprinted with permission of the Estate of David Rubin.

Mahasveta Devi: "Dopdi (Draupadi)": From IN OTHER WORDS: ESSAYS IN CULTURAL POLITICS, by Gayatri Chakravorty Spivak. Copyright © 1987 by Methuen Inc. Reproduced with permission of Taylor & Francis Books UK.

Anantha Murthy: From SAMSKARA: A RITE FOR A DEAD MAN. A TRANSLATION OF U. R. ANANTHA MURTHY'S KANNADA NOVEL, translated by A. K. Ramanujan. Copyright © 1976 by Oxford University Press. Reproduced by permission of Oxford University Press India, New Delhi.

Anumandla Bhumayya: From "Kausalya in Fury." Translated by Velcheru Narayana Rao.

Vilas Sarang: From RUDRA: THE UNTOUCHABLE GOD. Reprinted with permission from a representative on the author's behalf.

Salman Rushdie: From MIDNIGHT'S CHILDREN. Copyright © 1980 by Salman Rushdie. Published by Jonathan Cape. Reprinted by permission of The Random House Group Ltd. and The Wylie Agency.

P. N. Oak: From THE TAJ MAHAL IS A HINDU PALACE.

Kancha Ilaiah: "Hindu Gods and Us": From WHY I AM NOT A HINDU: A SUDRA CRITIQUE OF HINDUTVA CULTURE, PHILOSOPHY AND POLITICAL ECONOMY. Copyright © 2012 by Kancha Ilaiah, Samya, Calcutta. By permission.

A. K. Ramanujan: "Mythologies 1: Putana," "Mythologies 2: Nara-Simha," "Mythologies 3: Mahadeviyakka": From THE OXFORD INDIA RAMANUJAN, edited by Molly Daniels Ramanujan. Copyright © 2004 by Molly Daniels Ramanujan. Reproduced by permission of Oxford University Press India, New Delhi, and Molly Daniels Ramanujan.

ILLUSTRATIONS

Mohenjo-Daro, Pakistan: © Diego Lezama Orezzoli/CORBIS
Seals from the Indus Valley Civilization: © The Metropolitan Museum of Art. Image source: Art Resource, NY
Dancing girl: National Museum of India, New Delhi/The Bridgeman Art Library International
Vedic fire sacrifice: V&A Images, London/Art Resource, NY
Teacher with students: Forster-ullstein bild/The Granger Collection.
Agni, god of fire: Ancient Art & Architecture/DanitaDelimont.com
Older sage instructing a younger sage: The San Diego Museum of Art, www.TheSanDiegoMuseumofArt.org
Bas-relief of a battle scene from the *Mahabharata*: © Michael Freeman/CORBIS
Shiva-linga: American Institute of Indian Studies, Center for Art & Archaeology, Gurgaon, India
Rama breaks the bow of Shiva: V&A Images, London/Art Resource, NY
Bronze statue of Rama: The Philadelphia Museum of Art/Art Resource, NY
Temple at Ellora: Pratheepps/Wikimedia Commons
Chariot festival: © Charles & Josette Lenars/CORBIS
Stone carving of celestial courtesan: © Lindsay Hebberd/CORBIS
Wood carving of Krishna killing Putana: Photography © The Art Institute of Chicago
Durga killing Mahisha (relief): © Atlantide Phototravel/Corbis
Story of Karna (comic): © 1972 Amar Chitra Katha Private Limited, All Rights Reserved
Kali dancing on the corpse of Shiva (lithograph): Private Collection/Archives Charmet/The Bridgeman Art Library
Tamil inscription on stone: © Ocean/Corbis
Frieze at Mamallapuram: © Tibor Bognar/Corbis
Shiva grabs Kannappar: V&A Images, London/Art Resource, NY
Dancers in Bangalore: © JAGADEESH NV/epa/Corbis
Granite statue of Shiva's bull: © BOTTLE BRUSH/Balan Madhavan / Alamy
Mural of Shiva and Parvati: © Frederic Soltan/Corbis
Kabir at his loom (painting): The Art Archive at Art Resource, NY
Hindu temple, Northern Rajasthan: © David South/Alamy
Kavad (mobile temple): © Aroon Thaewchatturat/Alamy
People reading *Ramcharitmanas*: Philip A. Lutgendorf
Radha-Krishna (chromolithograph): The Art Archive/Ashmolean Museum
Varanasi flower market: © Jeremy Horner/Corbis
Warli painting (by Dr. Govind Gare): Dinodia Photo/AGE FOTOSTOCK
Tagore reading with students: © E. O. Hoppe/Corbis
Gandhi in 1930: Dinodia Photo/AGE FOTOSTOCK

Index

Proy

for

NAIIA

Not

Pray

for

Allah

Not

This